A SELECT LIBRARY

OF

NICENE AND POST-NICENE FATHERS

OF

THE CHRISTIAN CHURCH.

Second Series.

TRANSLATED INTO ENGLISH WITH PROLEGOMENA AND EXPLANATORY NOTES

UNDER THE EDITORIAL SUPERVISION OF

PHILIP SCHAFF, D.D., LL.D., AND HENRY WACE, D.D.,

Professor of Church History in the Union Theological Seminary,
New York.

Principal of King's College,
London.

IN CONNECTION WITH A NUMBER OF PATRISTIC SCHOLARS OF EUROPE AND AMERICA.

VOLUME II.

SOCRATES, SOZOMENUS:

CHURCH HISTORIES.

T&T CLARK
EDINBURGH

WM. B. EERDMANS PUBLISHING COMPANY
GRAND RAPIDS, MICHIGAN

British Library Cataloguing in Publication Data

Nicene & Post-Nicene Fathers. — 2nd series
1. Fathers of the church
I. Schaff, Philip   II. Mace, Henry
230′.11   BR60.A62

T&T Clark ISBN 0 567 09411 1

Eerdmans ISBN 0-8028-8116-5

Reprinted 1997

PHOTOLITHOPRINTED BY EERDMANS PRINTING COMPANY
GRAND RAPIDS, MICHIGAN, UNITED STATES OF AMERICA

CONTENTS OF VOLUME II.

THE

ECCLESIASTICAL HISTORY

OF

SOCRATES SCHOLASTICUS.

———◆◆◆———

Revised, with Notes, by

THE REV. A. C. ZENOS, D.D.,

PROFESSOR OF NEW TESTAMENT EXEGESIS IN THE THEOLOGICAL
SEMINARY AT HARTFORD, CONN.

PREFATORY NOTE.

THE basis of the present edition of Socrates' *Ecclesiastical History* is the translation in Bagster's series mentioned in the Introduction, Part IV. The changes introduced, however, are numerous. The translation was found unnecessarily free; so far as the needs of the English idiom require freedom no fault could, of course, have been found with the translation; but the divergences from the original in multitudes of cases were not warranted by any such need; they were more probably induced by the prevailing style of rhetoric common in the days when the translation was made. The change which has gradually come about in this respect called for modifications in the present edition. Many more might have been introduced without damage to the work. But it was felt that the scope and purpose of the edition only called for the most necessary of these changes.

In the preparation of the notes the editions of Hussey and Reading, containing Valesius' and Reading's annotations, were freely used. Whenever a note was taken bodily from these, it has been quoted and duly credited. It was thought best, however, usually to condense and reduce the number and bulk of these notes and introduce sparingly such new notes as were suggested by more recent study in ecclesiastical history.

The Introduction is almost altogether dependent on the literature quoted in Part I. The writer claims no original discovery respecting Socrates or his work. The facts had been diligently collected by his predecessors; he has simply rearranged them and put them into expression such as, to his mind, suits the requirements of the plan of the series.

A. C. ZENOS.

INTRODUCTION.

I. Sources and Literature.[1]

U. Chevalier in his *Repertoire des sources historiques du Moyen Age* gives the following list of authorities on Socrates Scholasticus.

Baronius:* *Ann.* [1593] 439, 39.   Cf. Pagi, Crit. [1689] 9, 11, 427, 15–6.
Bellarmin Labbé: S. E. [1728] 164.
Brunet:* *Manuel* [1864] V. 425.
Cave:* S. E. [1741] I. 427.
Ceillier:* *Hist. Aut. Eccl.* [1747] XIII. p. 669–88.   (2 *a* VIII. 514–25.)
Darling:* *Cyclopædia Bibliographica ; Authors.*
Du Pin:* *Bibl. Aut. Eccl.* [1702] III. ii. 183.
Ebed-Jesu: *Cat. Scr. Eccl.* 29.   (Assemani: *Bibl. Orient.* III. 141.)
Fabricius:* *Bibl. Græc.* [1714] VI. 117–21.   (2 *a* VII. 423–7.)
Graesse:* *Trésor* [1865] VI. 1, 429.
Hoffmann: *Lex. Bibl. Gr.* [1836] III. 625–6.
Holzhausen: *Commentatio de fontibus quibus Socrates, Sozomenus ac Theodoretus usi sunt,* &c.   Götting. 1825.
Jöcher.
Nouvelle Biog. Gen.* [1868] XLIV. 127–8.
Nolte:[2] *Tübing. Quartalschrift* [1860] 518; [1861] 417–51.
Patrologia Græca * (Migné) LXVII. 9–26.
Sigebert: *Gembl.* S. E. 10.
Tillemont[1]: *Hist. des Emp.* [1738] VI. 119–22.
Trithemius: *Scr. Eccl.* 137.
Vossius: *Hist. Græca* [1651] 259.
Walford:[3] in *Bohn's Eccl. Libr.* VI. 1853.

To these there should be added important notices of Socrates or his Ecclesiastical History as follows :

F. C. Baur: *Die Epochen der Kirchlichen Geschichtschreibung.*   Tübing. 1852, p. 7–32.
J. G. Dowling: *An Introduction to the Critical Study of Ecclesiastical History.*
Ad. Harnack: In Herzog-Plitt's *Real Enkyclop.* vol. 14, *Sokrates und Sozomenos* and in *Encyclop. Britannica, Socrates.*
K. O. Müller: *History of Greek Literature :* English translation and continuation by Donaldson, Vol. III.
Rössler: *Bibliothek der Kirchenväter.*
Jeep: *Quellenuntersuchungen zu der griech. Kirchenhistorikern.*   Leipsic, 1884.
Sarrazin: *De Theodoro Lectore, Theophanis Fonte præcipuo,* 1881.
Stäudlin: *Gesch. und Literatur der Kirchen-geschichte,* 1827.
Overbeck: *Theol. Liter.-Zeitung,* 1879.   No. 20.

Also articles on Socrates in Smith's *Dictionary of Greek and Roman Biography and Mythology* (by John Calrow Means) and Smith & Wace: *Dictionary of Christian Biography* (William Milligan), as well as passing notices in standard ecclesiastical histories such as Neander, Hase, Killen, Schaff, &c., and Introductory notices of Valesius (Hussey), Parker, Bright, &c.

---

[1] All works marked with a star in Chevalier's list were used in the present edition, and all but two or three of those added to the list of Chevalier.

[2] Nolte's article is on the textual emendations needed in the edition of Socrates.   The text of our historian has not been as thoroughly and completely examined and corrected as other writings. Valesius' edition (Hussey) gives an account of a few MSS. examined by himself; nothing further has been done of any importance. It is to be hoped that Gebhardt and Harnack may find it convenient to incorporate a new collation and revision in their *Texte und Untersuchungen.*

[3] E. Walford, A.M., appears as the translator of Sozomen, not of Socrates.   See IV. of Introduction, note 6.

II. Life of Socrates.

We cannot but regret the fact that the age in which Socrates lived cared little, if at all, about recording the lives of its literary men. The only sources of information in this respect are the writings themselves of these literary men and the public records, in case they held the double character of literary men and political or ecclesiastical officials. As Socrates did not participate in the public affairs of his day, our information respecting him is confined to the scanty and incidental items we may gather from his history. As he was not very fond of speaking of himself, these data are few and often of doubtful significance. In fact, the reconstruction of his biography from these scattered items is a matter of difficult critical investigation.

All that these inadequate materials yield of his biography may be summed up as follows :

He was born in Constantinople.[1] He nowhere mentions his parents or ancestry, and no information has reached us on this point from any other source. The year of his birth is inferred from what he says of his education at the hands of the grammarians Helladius and Ammonius.[2] These grammarians were originally Egyptian priests living in Alexandria — the former of Jupiter, and the latter of Pithecus (Simius) ; they fled from their native city in consequence of the disturbances which followed the cleansing of the Mithreum and destruction of the Serapeum by the bishop Theophilus. It appears that at that time an open conflict took place between the pagans and Christians, and many of the pagans having taken part in the tumult, laid themselves open to criminal prosecution, and to avoid this, took refuge in other cities, — a large number of them naturally in Constantinople. The *Chronicon* of Marcellinus puts this event in the consulship of Timasius and Promotus, i.e. 389 A.D. Now, as Socrates was very young[3] when he came to these grammarians, and it was the custom to send children to the schools at the age of ten, Valesius has reasoned that Socrates must have been born in 379 ; others have named 380[4] as a more probable date for this event. Other data for ascertaining the exact date of Socrates' birth are of very doubtful significance. He speaks, for instance, of Auxanon,[5] a Novatian presbyter, from whom he had received certain information ; but as Auxanon lived till after the accession of Theodosius the Younger in 408 A.D., it is impossible to draw any conclusion from this fact. So again Socrates mentions the patriarchate of Chrysostom in Constantinople (398–403) as if he had received his information at second hand,[6] and thus implies that he was perhaps too young to be an interested eye-witness of the events of that period. But how young he was we cannot infer from this fact ; and so cannot take the patriarchate of Chrysostom as a starting-point for our chronology of Socrates' life. Still another item that might have served as a datum in the case, had it been definitely associated with a known event in Socrates' career, is his mention of a dispute between the Eunomians and Macedonians which took place in Constantinople in 394.[7] If he were an eye-witness of this quarrel, he must have been old enough to take an interest in it, hence about fourteen or fifteen years of age. But this conclusion, even though it coincides exactly with the date found previously (379), is not at all certain, as he does not state that he was an eye-witness ; and if the reasoning is correct, then he was not too young to be interested in the events of Chrysostom's patriarchate which occurred a little later. Thus, on the whole, while it is extremely probable that Valesius is right in setting the date of Socrates' birth in 379, this event may have taken place several years later.

Nothing further is known of Socrates' early life and education except that he studied under Ammonius and Helladius, as already noted. Valesius has conjectured from the mention of Troi-

---

[1] So he says in V. 24.

[2] V. 16. On the destruction of the Serapeum, see Sozom. VII. 15; Theodoret, *H.E.* V. 22; Nicephor. XII. 25; Eunap. *Ædes.* par. 77; Suidas, Σάραπις. Helladius, according to Suidas, wrote a Dictionary, besides other works. Cf. s.v. Ἑλλάδιος.

[3] κομιδῆ νέος ὤν.

[4] Valesius' reasoning is based on the assumption that Socrates

was sent to the grammarians as soon as they arrived at Constantinople. If, however, an interval of several years elapsed before his going to them, the date of his birth must be put correspondingly later. The only certainty reached through this datum is that he was born not earlier than 379.

[5] I. 13 and II. 38.

[6] VI. 3, and ὡς φασι.   [7] V. 24.

lus, the famous rhetorician,[8] that Socrates must have received instruction from this teacher also, but with no sufficient foundation.[9]

Socrates always remained a resident of Constantinople, and was evidently proud of his native city, and fond of alluding to its history as well as its actual condition. He relates how the Emperor Constantine enlarged it and gave it its present name in place of the former heathen name it bore (Byzantium).[10] He speaks of its populousness, and at the same time of its ability to support its many inhabitants from its abundant resources.[11] He looks on its public structures very much as the ancient Israelite did on the 'towers and battlements' of Jerusalem. He mentions especially the walls built by Theodosius the Younger, the Forums of Constantine and Theodosius, the Amphitheatre, the Hippodrome with its Delphic tripods, the baths, especially that called Zeuxippus,[12] the churches of which he names at different times as many as five; viz.: the church of the *Apostles*, erected by Constantine especially for the burying of the emperors and priests;[13] the church of *St. Sophia*, which he calls 'the great church'; the church of *St. Irene*,[14] located in the same enclosure as that of St. Sophia; the church of *St. Acacius*, together with its appendages;[15] and the chapel of *St. John*, built seven miles outside the city.[16] Besides these he also mentions circumstantially the porch and shambles and porphyry column near which Arius was attacked with his sudden and fatal illness,[17] the region called Sycæ, and the tomb of Alexander the Paphlagonian, who was tortured and died in prison during the temporary supremacy of the Arians.[18]

Although there is no distinct mention of his ever having left the great city,[19] it is improbable that, like his great Athenian namesake, he was averse to traveling. In fact, his frequent mention of the customs of Paphlagonians, Thessalians, Cyprians, and others with minuteness of detail, rather gives the impression that he had visited these places.

According to the preponderance of evidence Socrates was trained as a pleader or advocate, and practiced this profession for a time. Hence his cognomen of *Scholasticus*.[20] At the instance of a certain Theodorus he undertook to write a continuation of the Ecclesiastical History of Eusebius, bringing it down to the seventeenth consulate of the Emperor Theodosius the Younger (439 A.D.).[21]

This year is the last definitely mentioned in his work. He must have lived, however, until some time after that date, as he speaks of a revision of the first two books of the History.[22] How much later it is impossible to tell: it was not certainly till after the end of Theodosius' reign; for then he would have brought down his history to that event, and thus completed his seventh book according to the plan, which is evident in his whole work, of assigning one complete book to each one of the emperors comprised in his period.

Of the character of Socrates as a man we know as little as of the events of his life. Evidently he was a lover of peace, as he constantly speaks with abhorrence of the atrocities of war, and deprecates even differences in theological standpoint on account of the strife and ill-feeling which they engender.

---

[8] VII. 1 and 2. See note on VII. 1. Socrates speaks of Troilus as a native of Side in Pamphilia, and mentions Eusebius and Silvanus and Alabius (both the latter bishops) as distinguished pupils of Troilus, and finally adds that Anthemius, who during the minority of Theodosius acted as regent, was dependent on the influence of Troilus; in which connection he further adds that Troilus was not inferior to Anthemius in political sagacity.

[9] Professor Milligan, in Smith & Wace's *Dictionary of Biography*, even says that Socrates assisted Troilus, but adduces no proof for the statement.

[10] I. 16.

[11] IV. 16, end; VII. 37.

[12] II. 16.

[13] I. 40.

[14] II. 16; I. 37.

[15] II. 38 and VI. 23.

[16] VI. 6.

[17] I. 38.

[18] II. 38.

[19] V. 8.

[20] The various meanings of this word may be found in Du Cange's *Glossarium Mediæ et Infimæ Græcitates* and in Sophocles' *Greek Lexicon of the Roman and Byzantine Periods*. From its primary meaning of 'student' it came to be applied to any one who had passed through study to the professions, of which the advocate's was one. From the absence of the cognomen in Photius' account of Socrates, *Bibliotheca Cod.* 28, as well as in that of Nicephorus Callisti, *H. E.* I. 1, Hamburger, as quoted by Fabricius, *Bibl. Græc.* VII. p. 423, note *g*, and Ceillier, *Auteurs Sacrés*, XIII. p. 669, doubt whether the title was rightly applied to him. Valesius argues from internal grounds that Socrates was a layman and a lawyer. Harnack, on the other hand, denies that there is any evidence of juristic knowledge in Socrates' *History*, even in such passages as I. 30, 31, and V. 18.

[21] VII. 48.

[22] II. 1.

Socrates' knowledge of Latin has been inferred from his use of Rufinus,[23] but Dodwell[24] conjectures that Socrates read Rufinus in a Greek translation, and that such translation had been made by Gelasius.

Inasmuch as he lived in, and wrote of, an age of controversies, and his testimony must be weighed according to his theological standpoint, this standpoint has been made the subject of careful study. There is no doubt left by his explicit declarations about his agreement in the main with the position of the orthodox or catholic church of his age, as far as these are distinguished from those of Arians, Macedonians, Eunomians, and other heretics. But as to his attitude towards Novatianism there has been considerable difference of opinion. That he was a member of the Novatian sect has been held after Nicephorus Callisti[25] by Baronius, Labbæus, and others, and argued from various considerations drawn from his work. Some of these are : that he gives the succession of the Novatian bishops of Constantinople ;[26] that he knows and mentions Novatian bishops of other places, e.g. of Rome,[27] of Scythia,[28] of Nicæa ;[29] that he mentions Novatian churches as existing in Phrygia and Paphlagonia,[30] in Lydia,[31] in Cyzicum,[32] in Nicæa,[33] in Nicomedia and Cotyæum,[34] and in Alexandria ;[35] that he knows and describes their church edifices ;[36] that he knows their internal troubles and trials,[37] especially their position on the Paschal controversy ;[38] that he gives vent to expressions of a sympathetic nature with the rigor practiced by the Novatian church ;[39] that he records the criticisms of Novatians on Chrysostom and the opinion that his deposition was a just retribution for his persecution of the Novatians ;[40] that he attributes miracles to Paul, Novatian bishop of Constantinople,[41] takes the testimony of Novatian witnesses,[42] rejects current charges against them,[43] and finally speaks of the death of Novatian as a martyrdom.[44]

On the other hand, Valesius, followed by most of the more recent writers on Socrates, claims that all these facts are due to the extreme impartiality of the historian, his sense of the justice due to a sect whose good he appreciated, together with his lack of interest in the differences between their standpoint and that of the Catholics. Socrates treats other heretical sects with the same generous consideration, e.g. the Arian Goths, whose death he records as a martyrdom ;[45] and yet he has never been suspected of inclining towards Arianism. At the same time he mentions the Novatians as distinct from the Catholic Church,[46] and everywhere implies that the *Church* for him is the latter.

To account for the apparently different conclusions to which these two series of considerations point, some have assumed that Socrates had been a Novatian, but before the writing of his history had either gradually drifted into the Catholic Church, or for reasons of prudence had severed his connection with the lesser body and entered the state church, retaining, however, throughout his whole course a strong sympathy for the communion of his earlier days.[47] Others attribute his favorable attitude towards Novatianism to his general indifference for theological refinements, others to mere intellectual sympathy for their tenets. In the absence of any definite utterance of his own on the subject, a combination of the last two motives comes nearest to sufficiently explaining the position of Socrates, although his rather unappreciative estimate of Chrysostom[48] and his severe censure of Cyril of Alexandria[49] are both more easily accounted for on the ground of a more intimate relation between the historian and the Novatians, as both of the above-named eminent men were declared enemies of Novatianism.

In other respects it cannot be doubted that the creed of Socrates was very simple and primi-

---

[23] I. 12, 19; III. 19; IV. 24, 26.
[24] *De jure sacerdotali*, p. 278. Cf. on translation by Gelasius, Smith & Wace, *Dictionary of Christian Biography*, II. p. 621.
[25] Niceph. *H. E.* I. 1.
[26] Cf. V. 21; VII. 6, 12, 17.
[27] V. 14; VII. 9, 11.
[28] VII. 46.
[29] VII. 25.
[30] IV. 28.
[31] VI. 19.
[32] II. 38; III. 11.
[33] VII. 12.
[34] IV. 28.
[35] VII. 7.
[36] II. 38; VII. 39.
[37] V. 21.
[38] V. 22.
[39] IV. 28; V. 19; VI. 21, 22; VII. 25.
[40] VI. 19 and 21.
[41] VII. 17, 39.
[42] I. 10, 13; II. 38; IV. 28.
[43] V. 10.
[44] IV. 28.
[45] IV. 33.
[46] VI. 20, 23; IV. 28; V. 19; VII. 3.
[47] So Harnack in Herzog-Plitt, *Real-Encykl.* and *Encyclop. Britan.*
[48] VI. 3, 4, 5, 15, 18, 19, 21.
[49] VII. 15.

tive. The one essential article in it was the doctrine of the Trinity; all others were subordinate. Even as to the Trinity, he would have accepted a much less rigid definition than the one propounded at Nicæa. As, however, the latter had been generally adopted by the church, he finds himself defending it against Arianism as well as against all sorts of compromise. He believed in the inspiration of the great synods as well as in that of the Scriptures, and was satisfied to receive without questioning the decisions of the former as he did the teachings of the latter. He was not, however, particular about the logical consequences of his theological positions, but ready to break off upon sufficient extra-theological reasons. His warm defense of Origen and arraignment of Methodius, Eustathius, Apollinaris, and Theophilus,[50] for attempting to belittle the great Alexandrian, shows how his admiration of a genius came into and modified his estimates. He considered all disputes on dogmatic statements as unnecessary and injurious, due to misunderstanding; and this chiefly because the parties in the dispute did not take pains to understand one another, and perhaps did not desire to do so because of personal jealousies or previous and private hatreds.[51] He is willing to refer such lawful questions on doctrinal points as may come before him to the clergy for decision, and is never backward about confessing his ignorance and incompetency to deal with theological refinements.

He makes a cogent defense of the use of pagan writings by Christians,[52] alleging that some of the pagan writers were not far from the knowledge of the true God; that Paul himself had read and used their works; that the neglect or refusal to use them could only lead to ignorance and inability to meet pagans in debate; that St. Paul's 'prove all things, hold fast that which is good,'[53] and Jesus Christ's 'be ye approved bankers'[54] gave distinct support to the study of the whole field of knowledge; and that whatever is worth studying in non-Christian literature is capable of being separated from the rest and known as the truth. Socrates himself was acquainted more or less extensively with the works of Sophocles, Euripides, Plato, Xenophon, from among the classic writers, besides those of Porphyry, Libanius, Julian, and Themistius of a later period, and perhaps with those of many others.

One more characteristic of Socrates must be mentioned; viz., his respect for the church and its institutions. He had a high regard for clergymen in virtue of their ordination. And although, as already shown, he took occasion to express himself critically of the highest dignitaries, such as Chrysostom and Cyril of Alexandria, yet the person of a bishop or presbyter is in a certain sense surrounded by sacredness to him. Monks are models of piety. In his eulogy of Theodosius the Younger,[55] he compares the emperor's devoutness to that of the monks, making the latter, of course, the high-water mark in that respect. But even as respects the ordinances of the church, his regard for them was not slavish or superstitious. He advocates extremely broad views in regard to the observance of Easter, considering a very precise determination of it too formalistic to be consistent with the liberty of the New Dispensation. So, likewise, in regard to many other of the ceremonies of the church, he takes pains to show by a description of the various ways in which they were performed in different quarters that they were not essential, but of subordinate importance.[56]

III. SOCRATES' ECCLESIASTICAL HISTORY.

UNTIL the beginning of the fourth century historiography remained a pagan science. With the exception of the Acts of the Apostles and its apocryphal imitations, no sort of attempt had

---

[50] VI. 13, 17; VII. 45.

[51] I. 23; cf. also II. 40, end: ἀλλ' ὅπως μὴν ταῦτα ἔχει, &c.

[52] III. 16.

[53] 1 Thess. v. 21, with which he combines Col. ii. 8. The latter passage can only be acted upon, according to Socrates, as the ground of a knowledge of that philosophy which is to be guarded against as vain.

[54] Γίνεσθε δόκιμοι τραπεζῖται. This saying is sometimes attributed to Paul, but more usually to Jesus. It occurs in Clem. Hom. II. 51; III. 50; XVIII. 20; Ap. Const. 36, 37; Epiph. Hær. 44. 2; Orig. (in Joan.) IV. 283; Clem. Alex. Strom. I. 28; Eus. H. E. VII. 7, 3.

[55] VII. 22.

[56] V. 22.

been made to record even the annals of the Christian Church. At the opening of the fourth century Eusebius conceived the idea of writing a history which should include a complete account of the Church's life to his own days. Hence he has correctly been called the Father of Church History. His work was done so satisfactorily to his contemporaries and immediate successors that none of them undertook to go over the same field again.[1] They estimated the thoroughness and accuracy of his work much higher than later ages have done. But this respect, which enhanced the magnitude of his work in their eyes, at the same time inspired many of them with a desire to imitate him.

Thus a school of church historians arose, and a number of continuations of Eusebius' *History* were undertaken. Of these, six are known to have seen the light: three of these again are either in part or wholly lost; viz., those of *Philippus Sidetes*, of *Philastorgius*, and of *Hesychius*. The first because of internal characteristics which made it difficult to use; the second because its author was a heretic (an Arian), and with the wane of the sect to which he belonged, his work lost favor and was gradually ostracized by the orthodox, and thus was lost, with the exception of an abstract preserved by Photius; and the third, for reasons unknown and undiscoverable, met with the same fate, not leaving even as much as an abstract behind. The remaining three are the histories of *Socrates, Sozomen*, and *Theodoret*. That of Theodoret begins with the rise of Arianism, and ends with Theodore of Mopsuestia (429 A.D.). That of Sozomen was begun with the purpose of including the history of the years between 323 (date of the overthrow of Licinius by Constantine) and 439 (the seventeenth consulship of Theodosius the Younger), but for some reason was closed with the death of the Emperor Honorius (423), and so covers just one hundred years. The work of Socrates, being evidently older than either of the other two, is more directly a continuation of the *Ecclesiastical History* of Eusebius. The motives which actuated him to continue the narratives of Eusebius may be gathered from the work to be his love for history,[2] especially that of his own times,[3] his respect for Eusebius, and the exhortation of Theodorus, to whom the work is dedicated.[4] The author opens with a statement of his purpose to take up the account where Eusebius had left it off, and to review such matters as, according to his judgment, had not been adequately treated by his predecessor. Accordingly he begins with the accession of Constantine (306 A.D.), when the persecution begun by Diocletian came to an end, and stops with the year 439. He mentions the number of years included in his work as 140. As a matter of fact, only 133 years are recorded; but the number given by the author is doubtless not meant to be rather a round than a precise number. The close of his history is the seventeenth consulship of Theodosius the Younger — the same as the proposed end of Sozomen's work. Why Socrates did not continue his history later is not known, except perhaps because, as he alleges, peace and prosperity seemed to be assured to the church, and history is made not in time of peace, but in the turmoils and disturbances of war and debate. The period covered by the work is very eventful. It is during this period that three of the most important councils of the church were held: those of Nicæa (325), of Constantinople (381), and the first council of Ephesus (431), besides the second of Ephesus, called the "*Robbers*' Council" (ληστρική), and that of Chalcedon, which were held not much later. It is this period which saw the church coming to the ascendant. Instead of its being persecuted, or even merely tolerated, it then becomes dominant. With its day of peace from without comes the day of its internal strife, and so

---

[1] That this was not due to a general conviction that one history of a period rendered another of the same period unnecessary is evident from the fact that the period immediately succeeding is treated of by three successive historians, and that the second of these, at least, knows and uses the work of his predecessor.

[2] Harnack, however, successfully proves that Socrates' ideal of history, in spite of his love for it, was far from being the scientific idea which existed among pagan writers even of the age preceding his own. Cf. Herzog-Plitt, *Real-Encyk.* Vol. 14, p. 413 sq.

[3] VI. 1.

[4] Cf. II. 1; VI. Int.; VII. 47. This Theodorus is simply addressed as ἱερὲ τοῦ θεοῦ ἄνθρωπε, from which it has been rightly inferred that he was an ordained presbyter. The view that Theodore of Mopsuestia is the person addressed has been proved to be erroneous from the date of his death, 429 A.D. The *Ecclesiastical History* was no doubt completed after that event, and could not have contained an address to the eminent Theodore.

various sects and heresies spring up and claim attention in church history. Socrates appreciated the importance which these contentions gave to his work.[5]

Geographically Socrates' work is limited to the East. The western branch of the church is mentioned in it only as it enters into relations with the eastern. The division of the history into seven books is made on the basis of the succession in the eastern branch of the Roman Empire. The seven books cover the reigns of eight eastern emperors. Two of these reigns — that of Julian (361–363) and that of Jovian (363–364) — were so brief that they are combined and put into one book, but otherwise the books are each devoted to the reign of one emperor. The first book treats of the church under Constantine the Great (306–337) ; the second, of the period under Constantius II. (337–360) ; the third, of that under Julian and Jovian taken together (360–364) ; the fourth, of the church under Valens (364–378) ; the fifth, of Theodosius the Great (379–395) ; the sixth, of Arcadius (395–408) ; and the seventh, to those years of Theodosius the Younger (408–439) which came within the period of Socrates' work.

As the title of the work (Ἐκκλησιαστικὴ Ἱστορία) indicates, the subject is chiefly the vicissitudes and experiences of the Christian Church ; but the author finds various reasons for interweaving with the account of ecclesiastical affairs some record also of the affairs of the state. His statement[6] of these reasons puts first among them the relief his readers would experience by passing from the accounts of the perpetual wranglings of bishops to something of a different character ; second, the information which all ought to have on secular as well as ecclesiastical matters ; and third, the interlacing of these two lines, on account of which the understanding of the one cannot be full without some knowledge of the other. ' By a sort of sympathy,' says he, ' the church takes part in the disturbances of the state,' and ' since the emperors became Christians, the affairs of the church have become dependent on them, and the greatest synods have been held and are held at their bidding.' It cannot be said, however, that Socrates either thoroughly realized or attempted any systematic treatment of his subject from the point of view of the true relations of church and state ; he simply had the consciousness that the two spheres were not as much dissociated as one might assume.

On the general character of Socrates' *History* it may be said that, compared with those produced by his contemporaries, it is a work of real merit, surpassing in some respects even that of his great predecessor, Eusebius. The latter has confused his account by adopting, under the influence of his latest informant, differing versions of facts already narrated, without erasing the previous versions or attempting to harmonize or unify them. Compare with this feature Socrates' careful and complete revision of his first two books on obtaining new and more trustworthy information.[7]

In the collection of his facts Socrates everywhere tried to reach primary sources. A great portion of his work is drawn from oral tradition, the accounts given by friends and countrymen, the common, but not wild, rumors of the capital, and the transient literature of the day. Whenever he depends on such information, Socrates attempts to reach as far as possible the accounts of eye-witnesses,[8] and appends any doubts he may have as to the truth of the statements they make. Of written works he has used for the period where his work and that of Eusebius overlap the latter's *Ecclesiastical History* and *Life of Constantine ;*[9] for other events he follows Rufinus,[10] abandoning him, however, in his second edition, whenever he conflicts with more trustworthy authorities. He has also made use of Archelaus' *Acts*,[11] of Sabinus' *Collection of the Acts of the Synods*, which he criticises for unfairness,[12] Epiphanius' *Ancoratus*,[13] George of Laodicea,[14] Athanasius' *Apolog.*,[15] *de Syn.*,[16] and *de Decr. Nic.*,[17] Evagrius,[18] Palladius,[19] Nestorius,[20] and Origen.[21]

---

[5] VII. 47.   [6] V. Int.

[7] II. 1. The new information here referred to is drawn from the works of Athanasius, which had come into the hands of the author. Cf. II. 17.

[8] I. Int.; V. 19; VI. Int.

[9] I. 8.

[10] I. 12, 19; II. 1; III. 19; IV. 24, 26.

[11] I. 22.

[12] I. 8; II. 15, 17, 20; III. 10, 25; IV. 12, 22.

[13] V. 24.   [16] II. 37.   [19] IV. 23.

[14] I. 24.   [17] VI. 13.   [20] VII. 19–24.

[15] II. 28; III. 8.   [18] III. 7.   [21] III. 7.

Christian writers before Origen are known to him and mentioned by him, such as Irenæus, Clement of Alexandria, Apollinaris the Elder, Serapion, and others; but he does not seem to have used their works as sources, probably because they threw no light on the subject at hand, his period being entirely different from that in which they flourished. Besides these writers, Socrates has also used public documents, pastoral and episcopal letters, decrees, acts, and other documents not previously incorporated in written works. Some of these the author has used, but does not quote *in extenso*, on account of their length.[22] Of the sources that he might have used, but has not, may be mentioned Dexippus, Eunapius (χρονικὴ ἱστορία), Olympiodorus (λόγοι ἱστορικοί), and especially Zosimus, his contemporary (ἱστορία νέα). Whether these were unknown to him, or whether he deemed it unnecessary to make use of the information given by them, or considered them untrustworthy, it cannot be ascertained. It is sufficient to say that for the period he covers, and the geographical limitation he has put on his work, his array of facts is sufficiently large and to the purpose. The use he makes of these facts also shows sufficiently the historian as thorough as he could be considering the time and environment in which he flourished. There is an evident attempt throughout his work at precision. He marks the succession of bishops, the years in which each event took place by the consulships and Olympiads of Roman and Greek history. He has made painstaking investigations on various topics, such as the different usages in various localities, respecting the observance of Easter, the performance of the rites of baptism and marriage, the manner of fasting, of church assemblies, and other ecclesiastical usages.[23] His accuracy has been questioned from the time of Photius [24] to our own days. It cannot be denied that there are a number of errors in the *History*. He confused Maximian and Maximin.[25] He ascribes three 'Creeds' to the first Council of Sirmium, whereas these belonged to other councils. In general he is confused on the individuals to whom he ascribes the authorship of the Sirmian creeds.[26] Similar confusion and lack of trustworthiness is noticed in his version of the sufferings of Paul of Constantinople and the vicissitudes of the life of Athanasius. He has wrongly given the number of those who dissented from the decision of the Council of Nicæa as five. The letter of the Council only mentions two, — Theonas and Secundus. The exile of Eusebius and Theognis is ascribed to a later period and a different cause by Jerome and Philostorgius, and it is generally conceded that Socrates' information was erroneous on this subject also. He is incorrect on several particulars in the lives of Basil and Gregory of Nazianzus, as also in assigning the attack at night on the church of St. Theonas to the usurpation of Gregory, the Arian bishop of Alexandria.[27]

The chronology of Socrates is generally accurate to about the beginning of the sixth book, or the year 398. A number of errors are found in it after that. But even before the date named, the dates of the Council of Sardica (347) and of the death of Athanasius (373, for which Socrates gives 371) are given wrong. St. Polycarp's martyrdom is also put out of its proper place by about one hundred years.[28] Valens' stay at Antioch and persecution of the orthodox is put too early.[29] The Olympiads are given wrong.[30]

Socrates is generally ignorant of the affairs of the Western Church. He gives a cursory account of Ambrose, but says nothing of the great Augustine, or even of the Donatist controversy, in spite of all its significance and also of the extreme probability that he knew of it; as Pelagius and Celestius, who traveled in the East about this time, could not but have made the Eastern Church acquainted with its details. In speaking of the Arian council of Antioch in 341, he seems to think that the Roman bishop had a sort of veto-power over the decisions of Occidental councils. The only legitimate inference, however, from the language of the bishop's claim is that he thought he had a right to be invited to attend in common with the other bishops of Italy.[31] So,

[22] II. 17.
[23] V. 22.
[24] Phot. *Biblioth. Cod.* 28. ἀλλὰ.καὶ ἐν τοῖς δόγμασι.οὐ λίαν ἀκριβής. Whether in this phrase he meant to accuse Socrates with inaccuracy in the narration of facts or indifference to theological dogma is not very clear. Probably the former.
[25] I. 2.
[26] II. 30.
[29] IV. 17.
[30] On the chronology of Socrates, see Harnack and Jeep.
[31] II. 8 and 17.
[27] II. 11.
[28] V. 22.

again, on the duration of the fast preceding Easter among the western churches, he makes the mistaken statement that it was three weeks, and that Saturdays and Sundays were excepted.

Finally, the credence which Socrates gives to stories of miracles and portents must be noted as a blemish in his history. On the other hand, he was certainly not more credulous than his contemporaries in this respect; many of them, if we are to judge from Sozomen as an illustration, were much more so. The age was not accustomed to sifting accounts critically with a view to the elimination of the untrue. Socrates shows in this respect the historical instinct in the matter of distinguishing between various degrees of probability and credibility, but does not seem to exercise this instinct in dealing with accounts of the prodigious.

To offset these faults we must take account, on the other hand, of the persistent and successful attempt of our historian at impartiality. Of all the Christian writers of his day he is the fairest towards those who differed from the creed of his church. No one else has done justice to Julian,[32] or to the various heretical sects of the day, as Socrates has. To avoid even the appearance of partiality, he makes a rule for himself not to speak in terms of praise of any living person;[33] and it must be said that he faithfully observes this rule, making but one exception in favor of the emperor Theodosius the Younger.[34] Of this prince he gives a eulogistic picture, altogether different from the representations universally found in the other historians of the age.[35] His independence of judgment is more signally manifested in his estimates of ecclesiastics, especially the more prominent ones,[36] bordering at times on unjust severity. ' In short,' says Harnack, summing up his estimate of Socrates, ' the rule to be applied to Socrates is that his learning and knowledge can be trusted only a little, but his good will and straightforwardness a great deal. Considering the circumstances under which he wrote and the miseries of the times, it can only be matter for congratulation that such a man should have been our informant and that his work has been preserved to us.'[37]

Socrates' style is characterized by simplicity and perspicuity. From the very start he informs us that he is about to make a new departure in this respect.[38] Eusebius' language was not entirely satisfactory to him, nor that of older writers.[39] Hence his own attempt everywhere at plain, unadorned expression. The criticism of Photius,[40] that Socrates' style ' had nothing remarkable about it,' although made in the spirit of censure, is true, and according to Socrates' standard (which is also that of modern times) amounts to a commendation. Socrates, however, was not lacking in good humor and satire,[41] as well as in appreciation of short and pithy utterances; he often quotes proverbs and epigrammatic sayings,[42] and knows the influence of the anecdote and reminiscence in interesting the reader.

The value of Socrates' History cannot be overestimated. It will always remain a source of primary importance. Though, as already noted, its ideal as a history is below that set up by Thucydides, Tacitus, and others of an earlier age, — below even that of Eusebius, — yet as a collection of facts and documents in regard to some of the most important events of the church's life it is invaluable. Its account of the great Arian controversy, its details of the Councils of Nicæa, Chalcedon, Constantinople, and Ephesus, besides those of the lesser, local conventions, its biographical items relative to the lives of the emperors, the bishops, and monks — some of whom are of pivotal importance in the movements of the times, its sketches of Ulphilas and Hypatia, its record of the manner and time of the conversion of the Saracens, the Goths, the Burgundians, the Iberians, and the Persians, as well as of the persecution of the Jews, the paschal controversy,

---

[32] III. 1, 12, 14, 21, 23.

[33] VI. Int.   [34] VII. 22.

[35] Cf. Sozomen, IX. 1, and Gibbon, IV. 163.

[36] Cf. attitude towards Chrysostom and Cyril of Alexandria, above alluded to; also his censure of pride and contention among members of the clergy. See V. Int. 15, 23; VI. 6; VII. 11, 29.

[37] In *Encycl. Britan.*

[38] I. 1, οὐ φράσεως ὄγκου φροντίζοντες; so in III. 1, μηδεὶς ἐπι-

ζητείτω κόμπον φράσεως; and VI. Int., ʼΙσθι δὲ ἡμᾶς μὴ ἐσπουδα-κέναι περὶ τὴν φράσιν, where he adds that if he had attempted a different style, he might have failed of his purpose of writing a popular history.

[39] VI. 22; VII. 27.

[40] *Biblioth. Cod.* 28.

[41] III. 16; IV. 22; VI. 13; VII. 21, 34.

[42] II. 8; III. 21; V. 15; VII. 29, 31.

not to mention a vast number of other details of minor importance, will always be read and used with the deepest interest by lovers of ecclesiastical history.

IV. HISTORY OF SOCRATES' WORK.

A. *Uses made before the First Printed Edition of the Greek Text.*

SOCRATES' *Ecclesiastical History* was used, according to the best authorities, by Sozomen in the composition of his parallel history.[1] It was certainly used by Liberatus, the Carthaginian deacon, in his *Breviarium caussæ Nestorianorum et Eutychianorum*, and by Theodorus Anagnostes (Lector) in his *Ecclesiastical History*.[2] It was also quoted in the second Council of Nicæa, under the name of Rufinus, and also under its author's name.[3]

Epiphanius, surnamed Scholasticus, translated the history of Socrates, together with those of Sozomen and Theodoret, under the auspices of Cassiodorus, about the beginning of the sixth century. This translation, under the name of *Historiæ Ecclesiasticæ Tripartitæ*, consists of twelve books, and was printed at Paris, without date, by Regnault in 8vo; afterwards also at Bâle in 1523, 1528, 1533, 1539, and 1568. It was revised by BEATUS RHENANUS, and published in Frankfort on the Main in 1588, together with the history of Eusebius, which was translated and continued by Rufinus. It is also found in the new edition of Cassiodorus printed at Rouen by Jo. GARETIUS in 1679 and in Venice, 1729. It served as a basis for a French translation by ÆGIDIUS GOURLINUS (Gille Gourlin), published in Paris in 1538 (cited by CYANEUS), and of a German translation by CASPAR HEDIO at Strasburg, 1545.

B. *Editions.*

There are two independent editions of Socrates' *Ecclesiastical History*, each of which has served as a basis for reprints, secondary editions, and translations. These are:

1. EUSEBII PAMPHILI: *Hist. Eccl.* LL. X.; ejd. *de Vita Constantini* LL. V.; SOCRATIS *Hist. Eccl.* LL. VII.; THEODORETI Episc. Cyrensis *Hist. Eccl.* LL. V.; *Collectaneum ex hist. eccl.* THEODORI LECTORIS LL. II.; HERMIÆ SOZOMENI *Hist. Eccl.* LL. IX.; EVAGRII *Hist. Eccl.* LL. VI. Lut. Paris, ex off. Rob. Stephani 1544 pridie Cal. Jul.

a. Upon this edition is based a Latin translation by WOLFGANG MUSCULUS, Bâle 1544, 1549, 1557, 1594, and one by J. J. CHRISTOPHORSON, bishop of Chichester, Paris 1571, Cologne 1581, Bâle 1570; with notes by GRYNÆUS and by HENRICUS PETRI 1611; incorporated into the *Bibliotheca Patrum*, ed. Cologne 1618 as Vol. V. and ed. Lyons 1677 as Vol. VII.

b. The Greek text of Stephens and the Latin translation of Christophorson were published together in Geneva, 1612.

c. An English translation of Socrates' Ecclesiastical History was made by MEREDITH HANMER,[4] and is contained in his *Ancient Ecclesiastical Histories of the first six hundred years after Christ, written in the Greek tongue by three learned Historiographers, Eusebius, Socrates and Evagrius.* London 1577. [This work also contains Dorotheus' *Lives of the Prophets, Apostles, and Seventy Disciples*, reprinted in 1585 and 1650.]

2. The second independent edition of Socrates is that which has been received as standard and served as a basis for all subsequent uses, viz.:

Historia Ecclesiastica Socratis, Scholastici, Hermiæ, Sozomeni, &c., ed. HENRICUS VALESIUS. Paris 1668. Valesius ostensibly revised the text of Stephens, but as a matter of fact he made a new collation of the MS. used by Stephens, and compared this with MSS. in the Vatican, so that

---

[1] So Harnack and Jeep. Cf. also Hartranft in the present vol., p. oo.

[2] Theodorus' works were two: (1) An epitome of the histories written previous to his time, and (2) an original history continuing the narrative to the days of Justinian I.

[3] Cf. Mansi, *Concil.* XII. Coll. 1035 and 1042.

[4] Cf. Woods, *Athenæ Oxonienses*, Vol. I. p. 326.

his edition amounts to an entirely new work. He also made a new Latin translation and appended numerous notes. This edition was reprinted in Mayence in 1677. Its Latin portion was reprinted in Paris also in 1677. The reprint of Mayence was reproduced under a new title, as if in Amsterdam, in 1675.

a. GUL. READING appended additional notes, and together with the Latin translation of Valesius, published the work in Cambridge in three vols. 1720. Reading's edition was reprinted at Turin in 1746. Valesius' original edition was again reprinted in Oxford by PARKER in 1844 and *Cura* BUCKLEY in London, also in 1844. It was revised and published in Oxford in 3 vols. by R. HUSSEY in 1853, and again in 1860 and in 1879. Again it was incorporated into MIGNE'S *Patrologia Græca* as Vol. LXVII. (Petit Montrouge) in 1859, and finally the Greek text alone was revised and published in a single volume by WILLIAM BRIGHT in Oxford 1878.

b. The translations based on Valesius' edition exclusive of those in Latin mentioned above are as follows :

In *French* by L. COUSIN : *Histoire de l'Eglise écrite par Eusèbe, Socrate, Sozomène, Theodoret,* &c. 4 vols. Paris 1675, and 6 vols. Amsterdam 1686. [Containing also Photius' abstract of Philostorgius.]

In *English* by SHORTING[5] : *The History of the Church as written in Greek by Eusebius, Socrates, and Evagrius* [contains also the four books of the Life of Constantine, Constantine's Oration to the Convention of the Saints, and Eusebius' speech in praise of Constantine], translated from the edition of Valesius, with a translation also of Valesius' notes and his account of the lives and writings of those historians. Cambridge 1683, 1692, 1709.

By S. PARKER : *The Ecclesiastical Histories of Eusebius, Socrates, Sozomen, and Theodoret . . . . abridged from the originals.* London 1707, 3d ed. 1729.

And ANONYMOUSLY [E. Walford][6] *The Greek Ecclesiastical Historians of the first six centuries of the Christian Era* in 6 vols. [Socrates Scholasticus' History forms Vol. III. of this series]. London, Samuel Bagster and Sons, 1843–46. This translation was reprinted in Bohn's Ecclesiastical Library, 4 vols., 1851 and 1888, and by Bagster in 1868.

---

[5] So Crusè.

[6] The volume containing Sozomen in this series bears the name of Walford. The translation of Socrates is anonymous, but generally ascribed to Walford also. This cannot be a matter of inference from the appearance of the two historians in the same series, as Eusebius, also in the same series, is translated by Crusè. Those who attribute the translation to Walford give no reason for doing so.

THE TABLE OF CONTENTS.

BOOK I.

BOOK II.

BOOK III.

BOOK VI.

BOOK VII.

THE

ECCLESIASTICAL HISTORY,

BY

SOCRATES SCHOLASTICUS.

—◦◦◦—

BOOK I.

CHAPTER I.

Introduction to the Work.

EUSEBIUS, surnamed Pamphilus,[1] writing the History of the Church[2] in ten books, closed it with that period of the emperor Constantine, when the persecution which Diocletian had begun against the Christians came to an end. Also in writing the life of Constantine, this same author has but slightly treated of matters regarding Arius, being more intent on the rhetorical finish of his composition and the praises of the emperor, than on an accurate statement of facts. Now, as we propose to write the details of what has taken place in the churches since his time to our own day, we begin with the narration of the particulars which he has left out, and we shall not be solicitous to display a parade of words, but to lay before the reader what we have been able to collect from documents, and what we have heard from those who were familiar with the facts as they told them. And since it has an important bearing on the matter in hand, it will be proper to enter into a brief account of Constantine's conversion to Christianity, making a beginning with this event.

CHAPTER II.

By what Means the Emperor Constantine became a Christian.

WHEN Diocletian and Maximian,[1] surnamed Herculius, had by mutual consent laid aside the imperial dignity, and retired into private life, Maximian, surnamed Galerius, who had been a sharer with them in the government, came into Italy and appointed two Cæsars, Maximin in the eastern division of the empire, and Severus in the Italian. In Britain, however, Constantine was proclaimed emperor, instead of his father Constantius, who died in the first year of the two hundred and seventy-first[2] Olympiad, on the 25th of July. And at Rome Maxentius, the son of Maximian Herculius, was raised by the prætorian soldiers to be a tyrant rather than an emperor. In this state of things Herculius, impelled by a desire to regain the sovereignty, attempted to destroy his son Maxentius; but this he was prevented by the soldiery from effecting, and he soon afterwards died at Tarsus in Cilicia. At the same time Severus Cæsar being sent to Rome by Galerius Maximian, in order to seize Maxentius, was slain, his own soldiers having betrayed him. At length Galerius Maximian, who had exercised the chief authority,[3] also died, having previously appointed as his successor, his old friend and companion in arms, Licinius, a Dacian by birth. Meanwhile Maxentius sorely oppressed the Roman people, treating them as a tyrant rather than as a king, shamelessly violating the wives of the nobles, putting many innocent persons to death, and perpetrating other similar atrocities. The emperor Constantine being informed of this, exerted himself to free the Romans from the slavery under him (i.e. Maxentius), and began immediately to consider by what means he might overthrow the tyrant. Now while his mind was occupied with

[1] Eusebius seems to have adopted this name as a token of friendship and respect for Pamphilus, bishop of Cæsarea. See McGiffert, *Prolegomena* in Vol. I., Second Series of Post-Nicene Fathers.
[2] Eusebius' *Ecclesiastical History* ends with the death of Licinius in 323. His *Life of Constantine* is in a sense a continuation of the History, and yet as it is very well characterized by Socrates, it is a eulogy, and therefore its style and selection of facts are affected by its purpose, rendering it too inadequate as a continuation of the *Ecclesiastical History;* hence Socrates' constraint to review some of the events which naturally fall in Eusebius' period.
[1] 'Socrates is here in error; for Maximianus Herculius, who was

otherwise called Maximian the Elder, was, by Constantine's command, slain in Gallia in 310 A.D. But Maximius Cæsar, two years after, being conquered by Licinius, died at Tarsus.' (Valesius.) On the confusion of Maximian and Maximin, see Introd. III.
[2] 305 or 306 A.D.
[3] πάντα περιέπων, not to be taken literally, inasmuch as there were two other Augusti — Constantine and Maxentius; and hence though senior Augustus, he was not sole ruler. On the appointment of the Augusti under Diocletian, and meaning of the title, see Gibbon, *Decline and Fall*, chap. xiii.

this great subject, he debated as to what divinity's aid he should invoke in the conduct of the war. He began to realize that Diocletian's party had not profited at all by the pagan deities, whom they had sought to propitiate; but that his own father Constantius, who had renounced the various religions of the Greeks, had passed through life far more prosperously. In this state of uncertainty, as he was marching at the head of his troops, a preternatural vision, which transcends all description, appeared to him. In fact, about that part of the day when the sun after passing the meridian begins to decline towards the west, he saw a pillar of light in the heavens, in the form of a cross, on which were inscribed these words, BY THIS CONQUER.[4] The appearance of this sign struck the emperor with amazement, and scarcely believing his own eyes, he asked those around him if they beheld the same spectacle; and as they unanimously declared that they did, the emperor's mind was strengthened by this divine and marvelous apparition. On the following night in his slumbers he saw Christ, who directed him to prepare a standard according to the pattern of that which had been seen; and to use it against his enemies as an assured trophy of victory. In obedience to this divine oracle, he caused a standard in the form of a cross to be prepared, which is preserved in the palace even to the present time: and proceeding in his measures with greater earnestness, he attacked the enemy and vanquished him before the gates of Rome, near the Mulvian bridge, Maxentius himself being drowned in the river. This victory was achieved in the seventh year of the conqueror's reign.[5] After this, while Licinius, who shared the government with him, and was his brother-in-law, having married his sister Constantia, was residing in the East, the emperor Constantine, in view of the great blessing he had received, offered grateful thanksgivings to God as his benefactor; these consisted in his relieving the Christians from persecution, recalling those who were in exile, liberating such as were imprisoned, and causing the confiscated property of the proscribed to be restored to them; he moreover rebuilt the churches, and performed all these things with the greatest ardor. About this time Diocletian, who had abdicated the imperial authority, died at Salona in Dalmatia.[6]

---

[4] Ἐν τούτῳ νίκα. For an extensive and satisfactory treatment of this famous passage in the life of Constantine, see Richardson, *Prolegomena to the Life of Const.*, Vol. I., Second Series, Post-Nicene Fathers.

[5] 312 A.D.

[6] Cf. an account of these events in Sozomen, I. 3. See also on the persecution instituted by Diocletian Neander, *Hist. of the Christ. Ch.* Vol. I. pp. 143-156; Schaff, *Hist. of the Christ. Ch.* Vol. I. pp. 174-177; Euseb. *H. E.*, Books VIII.-X. Lactantius, *de Mortibus persec.* c. 7 seq. Diocletian abdicated in 305 A.D.

CHAPTER III.

While Constantine favors the Christians, Licinius, his Colleague, persecutes them.

Now Constantine, the emperor, having thus embraced Christianity, conducted himself as a Christian of his profession, rebuilding the churches, and enriching them with splendid offerings: he also either closed or destroyed the temples of the pagans,[1] and exposed the images which were in them to popular contempt. But his colleague Licinius, holding his pagan tenets, hated Christians; and although from fear of the emperor Constantine he avoided exciting open persecution, yet he managed to plot against them covertly, and at length proceeded to harass them without disguise. This persecution, however, was local, extending only to those districts where Licinius himself was: but as these and other public outrages did not long remain concealed from Constantine, finding out that the latter was indignant at his conduct, Licinius had recourse to an apology. Having thus propitiated him, he entered into a feigned league of friendship, pledging himself by many oaths not to act again tyrannically. But no sooner did he pledge himself than he committed perjury; for he neither changed his tyrannical mood nor ceased persecuting Christians. Indeed, he even prohibited the bishops by law from visiting the unconverted pagans, lest it should be made a pretext for proselyting them to the Christian faith. And the persecution was thus at the same time well known and secret. It was concealed in name but manifest in fact; for those who were exposed to his persecution suffered most severely both in their persons and property.

CHAPTER IV.

War arises between Constantine and Licinius on Account of the Christians.

By this course he drew upon himself the emperor Constantine's heaviest displeasure; and they became enemies, the pretended treaty of friendship between them having been violated. Not long afterwards they took up arms against each other as declared enemies. And after several engagements both by sea and land, Licinius was at last utterly defeated near Chrysopolis in Bithynia, a port of the Chalcedonians, and surrendered himself to Constantine. Accordingly he having taken him alive, treated him with the utmost humanity, and would by no means put him to death, but ordered him to

---

[1] Ἑλλήνων: the word is used without the sense of nationality. So also in the New Testament often: Mark vii. 26; Gal. ii. 3 and iii. 28, where the Syriac (Peschitto) version renders, more according to sense than according to the letter, 'an Aramæan.'

take up his abode and live in tranquillity at Thessalonica. He having, however, remained quiet a short time, managed afterwards to collect some barbarian mercenaries and made an effort to repair his late disaster by a fresh appeal to arms. The emperor being made acquainted with his proceedings, directed that he should be slain, which was carried into effect. Constantine thus became possessed of the sole dominion, and was accordingly proclaimed sovereign Autocrat,[1] and again sought to promote the welfare of Christians. This he did in a variety of ways, and Christianity enjoyed unbroken peace by reason of his efforts. But an internal dissension soon succeeded this state of repose, the nature and origin of which I shall now endeavor to describe.

CHAPTER V.

The Dispute of Arius with Alexander, his Bishop.

AFTER Peter, bishop of Alexandria, had suffered martyrdom under Diocletian, Achillas was installed in the episcopal office, whom Alexander succeeded, during the period of peace above referred to. He, in the fearless exercise of his functions for the instruction and government of the Church, attempted one day in the presence of the presbytery and the rest of his clergy, to explain, with perhaps too philosophical minuteness, that great theological mystery — *the* UNITY *of the Holy Trinity.* A certain one of the presbyters under his jurisdiction, whose name was Arius, possessed of no inconsiderable logical acumen, imagining that the bishop was subtly teaching the same view of this subject as Sabellius the Libyan,[1] from love of controversy took the opposite opinion to that of the Libyan, and as he thought vigorously responded to what was said by the bishop. ' If,' said he, ' the Father begat the Son, he that was begotten had a beginning of existence : and from this it is evident, that there was a time when the Son was not. It therefore necessarily follows, that he had his subsistence[2] from nothing.'

---

[1] After a victory the soldiers greeted their prince with acclamations of ' Emperor!' ' Augustus!' So also did the citizens on his triumphal entry into the city. So it appears Constantine was formally greeted on assuming the sole control of affairs.

[1] Though Sabellius was the originator of one of the earliest and most plausible attempts at explanation of the mystery of the Trinity (for which see life of Sabellius in Smith and Wace, *Dict. of Christian Biog.*, and Hodge, *System. Theol.* Vol. I. p. 452, 459), nothing is known of him, not even why he is called a Libyan here (also by other ancient writers, e.g. Philastrius, *de Hæres.* 26, and Asterius, quoted by Phot. *Biblioth. Cod.* 27). Some say that he was a native and resident of Libya, others that he was an ecclesiastic appointed to some position there; nor is it known whether the Libya meant is the Libyan Pentapolis or the Pentapolitan Ptolemais.

[2] ὑπόστασιν. Through the Arian controversy this word is used in its metaphysical sense of ' real nature of a thing as underlying and supporting its outward form and properties'; hence it is equivalent to the Latin *substantia,* Eng. *essence* and Greek οὐσία. Cf. below III. 7. Later it was applied to the ' special or characteristic nature of a thing,' and so became the very opposite of οὐσία (the general nature); hence equivalent to *person.*

CHAPTER VI.

Division begins in the Church from this Controversy; and Alexander Bishop of Alexandria excommunicates Arius and his Adherents.

HAVING drawn this inference from his novel train of reasoning, he excited many to a consideration of the question ; and thus from a little spark a large fire was kindled : for the evil which began in the Church at Alexandria, ran throughout all Egypt, Libya, and the upper Thebes, and at length diffused itself over the rest of the provinces and cities. Many others also adopted the opinion of Arius ; but Eusebius in particular was a zealous defender of it: not he of Cæsarea, but the one who had before been bishop of the church at Berytus, and was then somehow in possession of the bishopric of Nicomedia in Bithynia. When Alexander became conscious of these things, both from his own observation and from report, being exasperated to the highest degree, he convened a council of many prelates ; and excommunicated Arius and the abettors of his heresy ; at the same time he wrote as follows to the bishops constituted in the several cities : —

The Epistle of Alexander Bishop of Alexandria.

To our beloved and most honored fellow-Ministers of the Catholic Church everywhere, Alexander sends greeting in the Lord.

Inasmuch as the Catholic Church is one body, and we are commanded in the holy Scriptures to maintain ' the bond of unity and peace,'[1] it becomes us to write, and mutually acquaint one another with the condition of things among each of us, in order that ' if one member suffers or rejoices, we may either sympathize with each other, or rejoice together.'[2] Know therefore that there have recently arisen in our diocese lawless and anti-christian men, teaching apostasy such as one may justly consider and denominate the forerunner of Antichrist. I wished indeed to consign this disorder to silence, that if possible the evil might be confined to the apostates alone, and not go forth into other districts and contaminate the ears of some of the simple. But since Eusebius, now in Nicomedia, thinks that the affairs of the Church are under his control because, forsooth, he deserted his charge at Berytus and assumed authority over the church at Nicomedia with impunity, and has put himself at the head of these apostates, daring even to send commendatory letters in all directions concerning them, if by any means he might inveigle some of the ignorant into this most impious and anti-christian heresy, I felt imperatively called

---

[1] Eph. iv. 3.   [2] 1 Cor. xii. 26.

on to be silent no longer, knowing what is written in the law, but to inform you of all of these things, that ye might understand both who the apostates are, and also the contemptible character of their heresy, and pay no attention to anything that Eusebius should write to you. For now wishing to renew his former malevolence, which seemed to have been buried in oblivion by time, he affects to write in their behalf; while the fact itself plainly shows that he does this for the promotion of his own purposes. These then are those who have become apostates: Arius, Achillas, Aithales, and Carpones, another Arius, Sarmates, Euzoïus, Lucius, Julian, Menas, Helladius, and Gaius; with these also must be reckoned Secundus and Theonas, who once were called bishops. The dogmas they have invented and assert, contrary to the Scriptures, are these: That God was not always the Father, but that there was a period when he was not the Father; that the Word of God was not from eternity, but was made out of nothing;[3] for that the ever-existing God ('the I AM'— the eternal One) made him who did not previously exist, out of nothing; wherefore there was a time when he did not exist, inasmuch as the Son is a creature and a work. That he is neither like the Father as it regards his essence, nor is by nature either the Father's true Word, or true Wisdom, but indeed one of his works and creatures, being erroneously called Word and Wisdom, since he was himself made by God's own Word and the Wisdom which is in God, whereby God both made all things and him also. Wherefore he is as to his nature mutable and susceptible of change, as all other rational creatures are: hence the Word is alien to and other than the essence of God; and the Father is inexplicable by the Son, and invisible to him, for neither does the Word perfectly and accurately know the Father, neither can he distinctly see him. The Son knows not the nature of his own essence: for he was made on our account, in order that God might create us by him, as by an instrument; nor would he ever have existed, unless God had wished to create us.

Some one accordingly asked them whether the Word of God could be changed, as the devil has been? and they feared not to say, 'Yes, he could; for being begotten, he is susceptible of change.' We then, with the bishops of Egypt and Libya, being assembled together to the number of nearly a hundred, have anathematized Arius for his shameless avowal of these heresies, together with all such as have countenanced them. Yet the partisans of Eusebius have received them; endeavoring to blend falsehood with truth, and that which is impious with what

is sacred. But they shall not prevail, for the truth must triumph; and 'light has no fellowship with darkness, nor has Christ any concord with Belial.'[4] Who ever heard such blasphemies? or what man of any piety is there now hearing them that is not horror-struck, and stops his ears, lest the filth of these expressions should pollute his sense of hearing? Who that hears John saying, 'In the beginning was the Word,'[5] does not condemn those that say, 'There was a period when the Word was not'? or who, hearing in the Gospel of 'the only-begotten Son,' and that 'all things were made by him,' will not abhor those that pronounce the Son to be one of the things made? How can he be one of the things which were made by himself? Or how can he be the only-begotten, if he is reckoned among created things? And how could he have had his existence from nonentities, since the Father has said, 'My heart has indited a good matter';[6] and 'I begat thee out of my bosom before the dawn'?[7] Or how is he unlike the Father's essence, who is 'his perfect image,'[8] and 'the brightness of his glory'[9] and says: 'He that hath seen me, hath seen the Father'? Again, how if the Son is the Word and Wisdom of God, was there a period when he did not exist? for that is equivalent to their saying that God was once destitute both of Word and Wisdom. How can he be mutable and susceptible of change, who says of himself, 'I am in the Father, and the Father in me';[10] and 'I and the Father are one';[11] and again by the Prophet,[12] 'Behold me because I am, and have not changed'? But if any one may also apply the expression to the Father himself, yet would it now be even more fitly said of the Word; because he was not changed by having become man, but as the Apostle says,[13] 'Jesus Christ, the same yesterday, to-day, and forever.' But what could persuade them to say that he was made on our account, when Paul has expressly declared[14] that 'all things are for him, and by him'? One need not wonder indeed at their blasphemous assertion that the Son does not perfectly know the Father; for having once determined to fight against Christ, they reject even the words of the Lord himself, when he says,[15] 'As the Father knows me, even so know I the Father.' If therefore the Father but partially knows the Son, it is manifest that the Son also knows the Father but in part. But if it would be improper to affirm this, and it be admitted that the Father perfectly knows the

---

3 ἐξ οὐκ ὄντων γέγονεν, lit. 'came into existence from nothing.'

4 2 Cor. vi. 14.   5 John i. 1–3, 18.
6 Ps. xliv. 1, according to the LXX.
7 'Ἑωσφόρον, the morning-star; taken from Ps. cix. 3. Cf. the LXX, quoted from Ps. lxxii.
8 Col. i. 15.   12 Mal. iii. 6.
9 Heb. i. 3.   13 Heb. xiii. 8.
10 John xiv. 10.   14 Heb. ii. 10.
11 John x. 30.   15 John x. 15.

Son, it is evident that as the Father knows his own Word, so also does the Word know his own Father, whose Word he is. And we, by stating these things, and unfolding the divine Scriptures, have often confuted them: but again as chameleons they were changed, striving to apply to themselves that which is written, 'When the ungodly has reached the depths of iniquity, he becomes contemptuous.'[16] Many heresies have arisen before these, which exceeding all bounds in daring, have lapsed into complete infatuation: but these persons, by attempting in all their discourses to subvert the Divinity of THE WORD, as having made a nearer approach to Antichrist, have comparatively lessened the odium of former ones. Wherefore they have been publicly repudiated by the Church, and anathematized. We are indeed grieved on account of the perdition of these persons, and especially so because, after having been previously instructed in the doctrines of the Church, they have now apostatized from them. Nevertheless we are not greatly surprised at this, for Hymenæus and Philetus[17] fell in like manner; and before them Judas, who had been a follower of the Saviour, but afterwards deserted him and became his betrayer. Nor were we without forewarning respecting these very persons: for the Lord himself said: 'Take heed that no man deceive you: for many shall come in my name, saying, I am Christ: and shall deceive many';[18] and 'the time is at hand; Go ye not therefore after them.'[19] And Paul, having learned these things from the Saviour, wrote, 'That in the latter times some should apostatize from the faith, giving heed to deceiving spirits, and doctrines of devils,'[20] who pervert the truth. Seeing then that our Lord and Saviour Jesus Christ has himself enjoined this, and has also by the apostle given us intimation respecting such men, we having ourselves heard their impiety, have in consequence anathematized them, as we before said, and declared them to be alienated from the Catholic Church and faith. Moreover we have intimated this to your piety, beloved and most honored fellow-ministers, in order that ye might neither receive any of them, if they should presume to come to you, nor be induced to put confidence in Eusebius, or any other who may write to you about them. For it is incumbent on us who are Christians, to turn away from all those who speak or entertain a thought against Christ, as from those who are resisting God, and are destroyers of the souls of men: neither does it become us even 'to salute such men,'[21] as the blessed John has prohibited, 'lest we should at

any time be made partakers of their sins.' Greet the brethren which are with you; those who are with me salute you.

Upon Alexander's thus addressing the bishops in every city, the evil only became worse, inasmuch as those to whom he made this communication were thereby excited to contention. And some indeed fully concurred in and subscribed to the sentiments expressed in this letter, while others did the reverse. But Eusebius, bishop of Nicomedia, was beyond all others moved to controversy, inasmuch as Alexander in his letter had made a personal and censorious allusion to him. Now at this juncture Eusebius possessed great influence, because the emperor resided at Nicomedia. For in fact Diocletian had a short time previously built a palace there. On this account therefore many of the bishops paid their court to Eusebius. And he repeatedly wrote both to Alexander, that he might set aside the discussion which had been excited, and again receive Arius and his adherents into communion; and also to the bishops in each city, that they might not concur in the proceedings of Alexander. By these means confusion everywhere prevailed: for one saw not only the prelates of the churches engaged in disputing, but the people also divided, some siding with one party, and some with the other. To so disgraceful an extent was this affair carried, that Christianity became a subject of popular ridicule, even in the very theatres. Those who were at Alexandria sharply disputed about the highest points of doctrine, and sent deputations to the bishops of the several dioceses; while those who were of the opposite faction created a similar disturbance.

With the Arians the Melitians mingled themselves, who a little while before had been separated from the Church: but who these [Melitians] are must now be stated.

By Peter, bishop of Alexandria, who in the reign of Diocletian suffered martyrdom, a certain Melitius, bishop of one of the cities in Egypt, in consequence of many other charges, and more especially because during the persecution he had denied the faith and sacrificed, was deposed. This person, being stripped of his dignity, and having nevertheless many followers, became the leader of the heresy of those who are to this day called from him Melitians throughout Egypt. And as he had no rational excuse for his separation from the Church, he pretended that he had simply been wronged and loaded Peter with calumnious reproaches. Now Peter died the death of a martyr during the persecution, and so Melitius transferred his abuse first to Achillas, who succeeded Peter in the bishopric, and afterwards again to Alexan-

[16] Prov. xviii. 3, according to the LXX.
[17] 2 Tim. ii. 17, 18.
[18] Matt. xxiv. 4.
[19] Luke xxi. 8.
[20] 1 Tim. iv. 1; Tit. i. 14.
[21] 2 John 10, 11.

der, the successor of Achillas. In this state of things among them, the discussion in relation to Arius arose; and Melitius with his adherents took part with Arius,[22] entering into a conspiracy with him against the bishop. But as many as regarded the opinion of Arius as untenable, justified Alexander's decision against him, and thought that those who favored his views were justly condemned. Meanwhile Eusebius of Nicomedia and his partisans, with such as favored the sentiments of Arius, demanded by letter that the sentence of excommunication which had been pronounced against him should be rescinded; and that those who had been excluded should be readmitted into the Church, as they held no unsound doctrine. Thus letters from the opposite parties were sent to the bishop of Alexandria; and Arius made a collection of those which were favorable to himself, while Alexander did the same with those which were adverse. This therefore afforded a plausible opportunity of defense to the sects, which are now prevalent, of the Arians, Eunomians, and such as receive their name from Macedonius; for these severally make use of these epistles in vindication of their heresies.

CHAPTER VII.

The Emperor Constantine being grieved at the Disturbance of the Churches, sends Hosius the Spaniard to Alexandria, exhorting the Bishop and Arius to Reconciliation and Unity.

WHEN the emperor was made acquainted with these disorders, he was very deeply grieved; and regarding the matter as a personal misfortune, immediately exerted himself to extinguish the conflagration which had been kindled, and sent a letter to Alexander and Arius by a trustworthy person named Hosius, who was bishop of Cordova, in Spain. The emperor greatly loved this man and held him in the highest estimation. It will not be out of place to introduce here a portion of this letter, the whole of which is given in the life of Constantine by Eusebius.[1]

Victor Constantine Maximus Augustus to Alexander and Arius.

I am informed that your present controversy originated thus. When you, Alexander, inquired of your presbyters what each thought on a cer-

tain inexplicable passage of the written Word, rather on a subject improper for discussion; and you, Arius, rashly gave expression to a view of the matter such as ought either never to have been conceived, or when suggested to your mind, it became you to bury it in silence. This dispute having thus been excited among you, communion[2] has been denied; and the most holy people being rent into two factions, have departed from the harmony of the common body. Wherefore let each one of you, showing consideration for the other, listen to the impartial exhortation of your fellow-servant. And what counsel does he offer? It was neither prudent at first to agitate such a question, nor to reply to such a question when proposed: for the claim of no law demands the investigation of such subjects, but the idle useless talk of leisure occasions them. And even if they should exist for the sake of exercising our natural faculties, yet we ought to confine them to our own consideration, and not incautiously bring them forth in public assemblies, nor thoughtlessly confide them to the ears of everybody. Indeed how few are capable either of adequately expounding, or even accurately understanding the import of matters so vast and profound!

And even if any one should be considered able to satisfactorily accomplish this, how large a portion of the people would he succeed in convincing? Or who can grapple with the subtilties of such investigations without danger of lapsing into error? It becomes us therefore on such topics to check loquacity, lest either on account of the weakness of our nature we should be incompetent to explain the subject proposed; or the dull understanding of the audience should make them unable to apprehend clearly what is attempted to be taught: and in the case of one or the other of these failures, the people must be necessarily involved either in blasphemy or schism. Wherefore let an unguarded question, and an inconsiderate answer, on the part of each of you, procure equal forgiveness from one another. No cause of difference has been started by you bearing on any important precept contained in the Law; nor has any new heresy been introduced by you in connection with the worship of God; but ye both hold one and the same judgment on these points, which is the Creed.[3] Moreover, while you thus pertinaciously contend with one another about matters of small or scarcely the least importance, it is unsuitable for you to have charge of so many people of God, because you are divided in opinion:[4] and not only is it unbe-

---

[22] Valesius makes the assertion that Socrates is mistaken here, that the Melitians joined themselves to the Arians after the council of Nicæa, and were induced by Eusebius, bishop of Nicomedia, to cast slanderous aspersion upon Athanasius, as he himself testifies in his second apology against the Arians. It appears unlikely that the Fathers of the Nicene Council would have treated the Melitians as leniently as they did had they sided with Arius before the council.

[1] Euseb. *Life of Const.* II. 64–72.

[2] σύνοδος; lit., ' coming together.'

[3] κοινωνίας σύνθημα = σύμβολον τῆς πίστεως. Cf. Eus. *Life of Const* II 70.

[4] For the textual variation at this place, see Valesius, note.

coming, but it is also believed to be altogether unlawful.

In order to remind you of your duty by an example of an inferior kind, I may say: you are well aware that even the philosophers themselves are united under one sect. Yet they often differ from each other on some parts of their theories: but although they may differ on the very highest branches of science, in order to maintain the unity of their body, they still agree to coalesce. Now, if this is done amongst them, how much more equitable will it be for you, who have been constituted ministers of the Most High God, to become unanimous with one another in such a religious profession. But let us examine with closer consideration, and deeper attention, what has been already stated. Is it right on account of insignificant and vain contentions between you about words, that brethren should be set in opposition against brethren; and that the honorable communion should be distracted by unhallowed dissension, through our striving with one another respecting things so unimportant, and by no means essential? These quarrels are vulgar and rather consistent with puerile thoughtlessness, than suitable to the intelligence of priests and prudent men. We should spontaneously turn aside from the temptations of the devil. The great God and Saviour of us all has extended to all the common light. Under his providence, allow me, his servant, to bring this effort of mine to a successful issue; that by my exhortation, ministry, and earnest admonition, I may lead you, his people, back to unity of communion.[5] For since, as I have said, there is but one faith among you, and one sentiment respecting religion,[6] and since the precept of the law,[7] in all its parts, combines all in one purpose of soul, let not this diversity of opinion, which has excited dissension among you, by any means cause discord and schism, inasmuch as it does not affect the force of the law as a whole. Now, I say these things, not as compelling you all to see exactly alike on this very insignificant subject of controversy, whatever it may be; since the dignity[8] of the communion may be preserved unaffected, and the same fellowship with all be retained, even though there should exist among you some dissimilarity of sentiment on unimportant matters. For, of course, we do not all desire the same thing in every respect; nor is there one unvarying nature, or standard of judgment in us. There-

fore, in regard to divine providence, let there be one faith, one sentiment, and one covenant of the Godhead:[9] but those minute investigations which ye enter into among yourselves with so much nicety, even if ye should not concur in one judgment in regard to them, should remain within the sphere of your own reflection, kept in the secret recesses of the mind. Let then an ineffable and select bond of general friendship, with faith in the truth, reverence for God, and a devout observance of his law, remain unshaken among you. Resume mutual friendship and grace; restore to the whole people their accustomed familiar embraces; and do ye yourselves, on the strength of having purified your own souls, again recognize one another. For friendship often becomes sweeter after the removal of animosity. Thus restore to me tranquil days, and nights free from care; that to me also some pleasure in the pure light may be preserved, and a cheerful serenity during the rest of my life: otherwise, I must necessarily groan, and be wholly suffused with tears; neither will the remaining period of my earthly existence be peacefully sustained. For while the people of God (I speak of my fellow-servants) are severed from one another by so unworthy and injurious a contest, how is it possible for me to maintain my usual equanimity? But in order that you may have some idea of my excessive grief on account of this unhappy difference, listen to what I am about to state. On my recent arrival at the city of Nicomedia, it was my intention immediately after to proceed into the East: but while I was hastening toward you, and had advanced a considerable distance on my way, intelligence of this affair altogether reversed my purpose, lest I should be obliged to see with my own eyes a condition of things such as I could scarcely bear the report of. Open to me therefore by your reconciliation henceforth, the way into the East, which ye have obstructed by your contentions against one another: and permit me speedily to behold both you and all the rest of the people rejoicing together; and to express my due thanks to the Divine Being, because of the general harmony and liberty of all parties, accompanied by the cordial utterance of your praise.[10]

---

[5] συνόδου κοινωνίαν.
[6] αἱρέσεως σύνεσις: lit. 'understanding of heresy.' On the various uses of the word αἱρεσις, see Sophocles, *Greek Lex. of the Rom. and Byz. Periods.* Here it evidently means the common creed of the whole Church looked at as a sect.
[7] νόμος, used in analogy to the law of the Old Testament. The law here is the ethical system of Christianity.
[8] τίμιον, 'honor.'

[9] τοῦ κρείττονος: for this use of the word, see Eus. *Life of Const.* II. 24 *et al.;* Greg. Naz. III. 1101 B; Jul. 398 A; Clem. *Hom.* V. 5.
[10] Socrates' lack of theological training can be inferred from his admiration for this rather superficial letter of Constantine's; so also the rudimentary character of Constantine's views of Gospel truth and his want of appreciation for the vital nature of the question in the Arian controversy. It may be noted, however, that the statesmanship shown in the tone and recommendations of the letter is just as far-sighted as the theology of it is superficial. Constantine had sought to unite the empire through the church, and now that very church threatened to disrupt the empire; and this, at the very time, when by his final victory over Licinius and the foundation of his new capital, he seemed to have realized the ideal of a reunited empire.

CHAPTER VIII.

Of the Synod which was held at Nicæa in Bithynia, and the Creed there [1] put forth.

SUCH admirable and wise counsel did the emperor's letter contain. But the evil had become too strong both for the exhortations of the emperor, and the authority of him who was the bearer of his letter: for neither was Alexander nor Arius softened by this appeal; and moreover there was incessant strife and tumult among the people. Moreover another local source of disquietude had pre-existed there, which served to trouble the churches, — the dispute namely in regard to the Passover, which was carried on in the regions of the East only.[2] This arose from some desiring to keep the Feast more in accordance with the custom of the Jews; while others preferred its mode of celebration by Christians in general throughout the world. This difference, however, did not interfere with their communion, although their mutual joy was necessarily hindered. When, therefore, the emperor beheld the Church agitated on account of both of these causes, he convoked a General Council,[3] summoning all the bishops by letter to meet him at Nicæa in Bithynia. Accordingly the bishops assembled out of the various provinces and cities; respecting whom Eusebius Pamphilus thus writes, word for word, in his third book of the life of Constantine: [4]

'Wherefore the most eminent of the ministers of God in all the churches which have filled Europe, Africa, and Asia, were convened. And one sacred edifice, dilated as it were by God, contained within it on the same occasion both Syrians and Cilicians, Phœnicians, Arabs and Palestinians, and in addition to these, Egyptians, Thebans, Libyans, and those who came from Mesopotamia. At this synod a Persian bishop was also present, neither was the Scythian absent from this assemblage. Pontus also and Galatia, Pamphylia, Cappadocia, Asia and Phrygia, supplied those who were most distinguished among them. Besides, there met there Thracians and Macedonians, Achaians and Epirots, and even those who dwelt still further away than these, and the most celebrated of the Spaniards himself [5] took his seat among the rest. The prelate [6] of the imperial city was absent on account of age; but some of his presbyters were present and filled his place. Such a crown, composed as a bond of peace, the emperor Constantine alone has ever dedicated to Christ his Saviour, as a thank-offering worthy of God for victory over his enemies, having appointed this convocation among us in imitation of the Apostolic Assembly.[7] For among them it is said were convened " devout men of every nation under heaven; Parthians, Medes and Elamites, and those who dwelt in Mesopotamia, Judæa and Cappadocia, Pontus and Asia, Phrygia and Pamphylia, Egypt and the part of Libya which is toward Cyrene, strangers from Rome also, both Jews and proselytes, with Cretans and Arabs." That congregation, however, was inferior in this respect, that all present were not ministers of God: whereas in this assembly the number of bishops exceeded three hundred; [8] while the number of the presbyters, deacons, and acolyths [9] and others who attended them was almost incalculable. Some of these ministers of God were eminent for their wisdom, some for the strictness of their life, and patient endurance [of persecution], and others united in themselves all these distinguished characteristics: some were venerable from their advanced age, others were conspicuous for their youth and vigor of mind, and others had but recently entered on their ministerial career.[10] For all these the emperor appointed an abundant supply of daily food to be provided.'

Such is Eusebius' account of those who met on this occasion. The emperor having completed the festal solemnization of his triumph over Licinius, came also in person to Nice.

There were among the bishops two of extraordinary celebrity, Paphnutius, bishop of Upper Thebes, and Spyridon, bishop of Cyprus: why I have so particularly referred to these two individuals, I shall state hereafter. Many of the laity were also present, who were practiced in the art of reasoning,[11] and each eager to advocate the cause of his own party. Eusebius, bishop of Nicomedia, as was before said, sup-

---

meant was the bishop of Rome. The reason alleged is that at the time of the meeting of the council, Constantinople had not yet been made the 'imperial city.' But considering the general indifference of Socrates to the affairs of the Western Church, and the fact that when he wrote, the imperial city was actually Constantinople, it is very probable that it is the bishop of that city he means to name here, and not the bishop of Rome.

[7] Acts ii. 5-11.

[8] The exact number is variously given as 250 by Eusebius (*Life of Const.* III. 8); 270 by Eustathius; 318 by Evagrius (*H. E.* III. 31); Athanasius (*Ep.* to the African bishops); Hilarius (*Contra Constantium*); Jerome (*Chronicon*), and Rufinus.

[9] Young priests; lit. 'followers,' from ἀκόλουθος.

[10] τῷ μέσῳ τρόπῳ: besides the meaning given to these words here they may be taken (1) as describing the temperate and genial character of the men so characterized, on the assumption that μέσος = μέτριος as often elsewhere, or (2) as applicable to those who occupied the middle ground in the controversy; of these, (2) is not admissible, as nothing has been said in the immediate context about the controversy, and as age is the main basis of classification in the passage; (1) also is less probable than the rendering given above.

[11] Dialectics.

---

[1] Cf. the parallel account in Sozom. I. 17.

[2] In a single sentence this controversy was as to whether the Easter should be observed on a fixed day in every year or on the 14th of the lunar month Nisan of the Jews, on whatever day of the week that might happen to fall. For a fuller discussion of the controversy, see Smith's *Dict. of the Bible*, and the literature there referred to.

[3] οἰκουμενικήν: hence this is called the first Ecumenical Council.

[4] Euseb. *Life of Const.* III. 7–9.

[5] Hosius mentioned before in chap. 7.

[6] According to Valesius, who follows Musculus, the prelate here

ported the opinion of Arius, together with Theognis and Maris ; of these the former was bishop of Nicæa, and Maris of Chalcedon in Bithynia. These were powerfully opposed by Athanasius, a deacon of the Alexandrian church, who was highly esteemed by Alexander, his bishop, and on that account was much envied, as will be seen hereafter. Now a short time previous to the general assembling of the bishops, the disputants engaged in preparatory logical contests before the multitudes ; and when many were attracted by the interest of their discourse, one of the laity, *a confessor*,[12] who was a man of unsophisticated understanding, reproved these reasoners, telling them that Christ and his apostles did not teach us dialectics, art, nor vain subtilties, but simple-mindedness, which is preserved by faith and good works. As he said this, all present admired the speaker, and assented to the justice of his remarks ; and the disputants themselves, after hearing his plain statement of the truth, exercised a greater degree of moderation : thus then was the disturbance caused by these logical debates suppressed at this time.

On the following day all the bishops were assembled together in one place ; the emperor arrived soon after, and on his entrance stood in their midst, and would not take his place, until the bishops by bowing intimated their desire that he should be seated : such was the respect and reverence which the emperor entertained for these men. When a silence suitable to the occasion had been observed, the emperor from his seat began to address them words of exhortation to harmony and unity, and entreated each to lay aside all private pique. For several of them had brought accusations against one another, and many had even presented petitions to the emperor the day before. But he, directing their attention to the matter before them, and on account of which they were assembled, ordered these petitions to be burnt ; merely observing that 'Christ enjoins him who is anxious to obtain forgiveness, to forgive his brother.' When therefore he had strongly insisted on the maintenance of harmony and peace, he sanctioned again their purpose of more closely investigating the questions at issue. But it may be well to hear what Eusebius says on this subject, in his third book of the Life of Constantine.[13] His words are these :

'A variety of topics having been introduced by each party, and much controversy being excited from the very commencement, the emperor listened to all with patient attention, deliberately

and impartially considering whatever was advanced. He in part supported the statements which were made on either side, and gradually softened the asperity of those who contentiously opposed each other, conciliating each by his mildness and affability. And as he addressed them in the Greek language, for he was not unacquainted with it, he was at once interesting and persuasive, and wrought conviction on the minds of some, and prevailed on others by entreaty, those who spoke well he applauded. And inciting all to unanimity at length he succeeded in bringing them into similarity of judgment, and conformity of opinion on all the controverted points : so that there was not only unity in the confession of faith, but also a general agreement as to the time for the celebration of the feast of Salvation.[14] Moreover the doctrines which had thus the common consent, were confirmed by the signature of each individual.'

Such in his own words is the testimony respecting these things which Eusebius has left us in writing ; and we not unfitly have used it, but treating what he has said as an authority, have introduced it here for the fidelity of this history. With this end also in view, that if any one should condemn as erroneous the faith professed at this council of Nicæa, we might be unaffected by it, and put no confidence in Sabinus the Macedonian,[15] who calls all those who were convened there ignoramuses and simpletons. For this Sabinus, who was bishop of the Macedonians at Heraclea in Thrace, having made a collection of the decrees published by various Synods of bishops, has treated those who composed the Nicene Council in particular with contempt and derision ; not perceiving that he thereby charges Eusebius himself with ignorance, who made a like confession after the closest scrutiny. And in fact some things he has willfully passed over, others he has perverted, and on all he has put a construction favorable to his own views. Yet he commends Eusebius Pamphilus as a trustworthy witness, and praises the emperor as capable in stating Christian doctrines : but he still brands the faith which was declared at Nicæa, as having been set forth by ignorant persons, and such as had no intelligence in the matter. And thus he voluntarily contemns the words of a man whom he himself pronounces a wise and true witness : for Eusebius declares, that of the ministers of God who were present at the Nicene Synod, some were eminent for the word of wisdom, others for the strictness of their life ; and that the emperor himself being

---

[12] εἰς τῶν ὁμολογητῶν: the term ὁμολογητής was applied to those who during the persecutions had refused to sacrifice to idols, persisting in his profession of Christianity in spite of suffering. Cf. Clem. *Strom.* IV. 12; Petr. Alex. *Epist. Can.* 14.
[13] Euseb. *Life of Const.* III. 13.

[14] The Passover, or Easter.
[15] Macedonian = follower of Macedonius, not a native resident of Macedonia. Sabinus was the author of a collection of the acts of the Synod used by Socrates quite freely (cf. I. 15, 17 *et al.*). Socrates, however, criticises him for prejudice against the orthodox. Sabinus was bishop of the church of the Macedonians in Heraclea, a city in Thrace.

present, leading all into unanimity, established unity of judgment, and agreement of opinion among them. Of Sabinus, however, we shall make further mention as occasion may require. But the agreement of faith, assented to with loud acclamation at the great council of Nicæa is this :

'We believe in one God, the Father Almighty, Maker of all things visible and invisible : — and in one.[16] Lord Jesus Christ, the Son of God, the only-begotten of the Father, that is of the substance of the Father ; God of God and Light of light ; true God of true God ; begotten, not made, consubstantial[17] with the Father : by whom all things were made, both which are in heaven and on earth : who for the sake of us men, and on account of our salvation, descended, became incarnate, and was made man ; suffered, arose again the third day, and ascended into the heavens, and will come again to judge the living and the dead. [We] also [believe] in the Holy Spirit. But the holy Catholic and Apostolic church anathematizes those who say " There was a time when he was not," and " He was not before he was begotten," and " He was made from that which did not exist," and those who assert that he is of other substance or essence than the Father, or that he was created, or is susceptible of change.'[18]

This creed was recognized and acquiesced in by three hundred and eighteen [bishops] ; and being, as Eusebius says, unanimous in expression and sentiment, they subscribed it. Five only would not receive it, objecting to the term *homoousios,* ' of the same essence,' or *consubstantial :* these were Eusebius bishop of Nicomedia, Theognis of Nice, Maris of Chalcedon, Theonas of Marmarica, and Secundus of Ptolemaïs. ' For,' said they, ' since that is *consubstantial* which is from another either by partition, derivation or germination ; by germination, as a shoot from the roots ; by derivation, as children from their parents ; by division, as two or three vessels of gold from a mass, and the Son is from the Father by none of these modes : therefore they declared themselves unable to assent to this creed.' Thus having scoffed at the word *consubstantial,* they would not subscribe to the deposition of Arius. Upon this the Synod anathematized Arius, and all who adhered to his opin-

ions, prohibiting him at the same time from entering into Alexandria. At the same time an edict of the emperor sent Arius himself into exile, together with Eusebius and Theognis and their followers ; Eusebius and Theognis, however, a short time after their banishment, tendered a written declaration of their change of sentiment, and concurrence in the faith of the *consubstantiality* of the Son with the Father, as we shall show as we proceed.

At this time during the session of the Synod, Eusebius, surnamed Pamphilus, bishop of Cæsarea in Palestine, who had held aloof for a short time, after mature consideration whether he ought to receive this definition of the faith, at length acquiesced in it, and subscribed it with all the rest : he also sent to the people under his charge a copy of the Creed, with an explanation of the word *homoousios,* that no one might impugn his motives on account of his previous hesitation. Now what was written by Eusebius was as follows in his own words :

'You have probably had some intimation, beloved, of the transactions of the great council convened at Nicæa, in relation to the faith of the Church, inasmuch as rumor generally outruns true account of that which has really taken place. But lest from such report alone you might form an incorrect estimate of the matter, we have deemed it necessary to submit to you, in the first place, an exposition of the faith proposed by us in written form ; and then a second which has been promulgated, consisting of ours with certain additions to its expression. The declaration of faith set forth by us, which when read in the presence of our most pious emperor, seemed to meet with universal approbation, was thus expressed :

' " According as we received from the bishops who preceded us, both in our instruction[19] [in the knowledge of the truth], and when we were baptized ; as also we have ourselves learned from the sacred Scriptures : and in accordance with what we have both believed and taught while discharging the duties of presbyter and the episcopal office itself, so now we believe and present to you the distinct avowal of our faith. It is this :

' " We believe in one God, the Father Almighty, Maker of all things visible and invisible : — and in one Lord, Jesus Christ, the Word of God, God of God, Light of light, Life of life, the only-begotten Son, born before all creation,[20] begotten of God the Father, before all ages, by whom also all things were made ; who on account of our salvation became incarnate, and lived

---

[16] This is according to the reading of Valesius, Hussey, and Bright. The reading, ' *our* Lord,' &c., of the English translations in Bagster and Bohn's series is probably a typographical error, though strangely perpetuated down to the reprint of 1888.

[17] ὁμοούσιον, ' of the same essence '; the word has become a historic landmark in theological debate, and one of the stock words of theological terminology.

[18] This creed is found twelve times in eleven ancient sources, two versions being given in the Acts of the Council of Chalcedon. The second version of the Council of Chalcedon contains certain additions from the creed of Constantinople; all the rest substantially agree. Cf. Schaff, *Creeds of Christendom,* Vol. I. p. 24, and Vol. II. p. 50, 91; Walch, *Antiquitates Symbolicæ* (1772), p. 87 seq.; Hahn, *Bibliothek der Symbole,* p. 40-107, and other literature referred to in Schaff's *Creeds,* &c.

[19] κατηχήσει; the word is used of the steps preliminary to baptism, chief among which was instruction in the truth. Cf. VII. 17, and Smith's *Dict. of the Bible.*

[20] πρωτότοκον πάσης κτίσεως, taken from Col. i. 15. For the uses of πρῶτος instead of πρότερος, see John i. 15.

among men; and who suffered and rose again on the third day, and ascended to the Father, and shall come again in glory to judge the living and the dead. We believe also in one Holy Spirit. We believe in the existence and subsistence of each of these [persons] : that the Father is truly Father, the Son truly Son, and the Holy Spirit truly Holy Spirit; even as our Lord also, when he sent forth his disciples to preach the Gospel, said,[21] 'Go and teach all nations, baptizing them in the name of the Father, and of the Son, and of the Holy Spirit.' Concerning these doctrines we steadfastly maintain their truth, and avow our full confidence in them; such also have been our sentiments hitherto, and such we shall continue to hold until death : and in an unshaken adherence to this faith, we anathematize every impious heresy. In the presence of God Almighty, and of our Lord Jesus Christ we testify, that thus we have believed and thought from our heart and soul, since we have possessed a right estimate of ourselves; and that we now think and speak what is perfectly in accordance with the truth. We are moreover prepared to prove to you by undeniable evidences, and to convince you that in time past we have thus believed, and so preached."

'When these articles of faith were proposed, there seemed to be no ground of opposition : nay, our most pious emperor himself was the first to admit that they were perfectly correct, and that he himself had entertained the sentiments contained in them; exhorting all present to give them their assent, and subscribe to these very articles, thus agreeing in a unanimous profession of them, with the insertion, however, of that single word "*homoousios*" (consubstantial), an expression which the emperor himself explained, as not indicating corporeal affections or properties; and consequently that the Son did not subsist from the Father either by division or abscission : for, said he, a nature which is immaterial and incorporeal cannot possibly be subject to any corporeal affection; hence our conception of such things can only be in divine and mysterious terms. Such was the philosophical view of the subject taken by our most wise and pious sovereign; and the bishops on account of the word *homoousios*, drew up this formula of faith.

The Creed.[22]

' " We believe in one God, the Father Almighty, Maker of all things visible and invisible : —and in one Lord Jesus Christ, the Son of God, the only-begotten of the Father, that is of the substance of the Father; God of God,

Light of light, true God of true God; begotten not made, consubstantial with the Father; by[23] whom all things were made both which are in heaven and on earth; who for the sake of us men, and on account of our salvation, descended, became incarnate, was made man, suffered and rose again on the third day; he ascended into the heavens, and will come to judge the living and the dead. [We believe] also in the Holy Spirit. But those who say 'There was a time when he was not,' or 'He did not exist before he was begotten,' or 'He was made of nothing,' or assert that 'He is of other substance or essence than the Father,' or that the Son of God is created, or mutable, or susceptible of change, the Catholic and apostolic Church of God anathematizes."

'Now this declaration of faith being propounded by them, we did not neglect to investigate the distinct sense of the expressions " of the substance of the Father, and consubstantial with the Father." Whereupon questions were put forth and answers, and the meaning of these terms was clearly defined; when it was generally admitted that *ousias* (of the essence or substance) simply implied that the Son is of the Father indeed, but does not subsist as a part of the Father. To this interpretation of the sacred doctrine which declares that the Son is of the Father, but is not a part of his substance, it seemed right to us to assent. We ourselves therefore concurred in this exposition; nor do we cavil at the word " *homoousios* " having regard to peace, and fearing to lose a right understanding of the matter. On the same grounds we admitted also the expression " begotten, not made " : " for *made*," said they, " is a term applicable in common to all the creatures which were made by the Son, to whom the Son has no resemblance. Consequently he is no creature like those which were made by him, but is of a substance far excelling any creature; which substance the Divine Oracles teach was begotten of the Father by such a mode of generation as cannot be explained nor even conceived by any creature." Thus also the declaration that " the Son is consubstantial with the Father " having been discussed, it was agreed that this must not be understood in a corporeal sense, or in any way analogous to mortal creatures; inasmuch as it is neither by division of substance, nor by abscission, nor by any change of the Father's substance and power, since the underived nature of the Father is inconsistent with all these things. That he is consubstantial with the Father then simply implies, that the Son of God has no resemblance to created things, but is in every respect like the Father only who begat him; and that he is of

---

[21] μαθητεύσατε, from Matt. xxviii. 19.
[22] τὸ μάθημα: lit. 'lesson.'

[23] Through.

no other substance or essence but of the Father. To which doctrine, explained in this way, it appeared right to assent, especially since we knew that some eminent bishops and learned writers among the ancients have used the term *"homoousios"* in their theological discourses concerning the nature of the Father and the Son. Such is what I have to state to you in reference to the articles of faith which have been promulgated ; and in which we have all concurred, not without due examination, but according to the senses assigned, which were investigated in the presence of our most highly favored emperor, and for the reasons mentioned approved. We have also considered the anathema pronounced by them after the declaration of faith inoffensive ; because it prohibits the use of illegitimate [24] terms, from which almost all the distraction and commotion of the churches have arisen. Accordingly, since no divinely inspired Scripture contains the expressions, " of things which do not exist," and " there was a time when he was not," and such other phrases as are therein subjoined, it seemed unwarrantable to utter and teach them : and moreover this decision received our sanction the rather from the consideration that we have never heretofore been accustomed to employ these terms. We deemed it incumbent on us, beloved, to acquaint you with the caution which has characterized both our examination of and concurrence in these things : and that on justifiable grounds we resisted to the last moment the introduction of certain objectionable expressions as long as these were not acceptable ; and received them without dispute, when on mature deliberation as we examined the sense of the words, they appeared to agree with what we had originally proposed as a sound confession of faith.'

Such was the letter addressed by Eusebius Pamphilus to the Christians at Cæsarea in Palestine. At the same time the Synod itself also, with one accord, wrote the following epistle to the church of the Alexandrians, and to believers in Egypt, Libya, and Pentapolis.

CHAPTER IX.

The Letter of the Synod, relative to its Decisions : and the Condemnation of Arius and those who agreed with him.

To the holy, by the grace of God, and great church of the Alexandrians, and to our beloved brethren throughout Egypt, Libya, and Pentapolis, the bishops assembled at Nicæa, constituting

the great and holy Synod, send greeting in the Lord.

Since, by the grace of God, a great and holy Synod has been convened at Nicæa, our most pious sovereign Constantine having summoned us out of various cities and provinces for that purpose, it appeared to us indispensably necessary that a letter should be written to you on the part of the sacred Synod ; in order that ye may know what subjects were brought under consideration and examined, and what was eventually determined on and decreed.

In the first place, then, the impiety and guilt of Arius and his adherents were examined into, in the presence of our most religious emperor Constantine : and it was unanimously decided that his impious opinion should be anathematized, with all the blasphemous expressions he has uttered, in affirming that ' the Son of God sprang from nothing,' and that ' there was a time when he was not' ; saying moreover that ' the Son of God, because possessed of free will, was capable either of vice or virtue ; and calling him a creature and a work. All these sentiments the holy Synod has anathematized, having scarcely patience to endure the hearing of such an impious opinion, or, rather, madness, and such blasphemous words. But the conclusion of our proceedings against him you must either have been informed of already or will soon learn ; for we would not seem to trample on a man who has received the chastisement which his crime deserved. Yet so contagious has his pestilential error proved, as to drag into perdition Theonas, bishop of Marmarica, and Secundus of Ptolemaïs ; for they have suffered the same condemnation as himself. But when the grace of God delivered us from those execrable dogmas, with all their impiety and blasphemy, and from those persons, who had dared to cause discord and division among a people previously at peace, there still remained the contumacy of Melitius [to be dealt with] and those who had been ordained by him ; and we now state to you, beloved brethren, what resolution the Synod came to on this point. It was decreed, the Synod being moved to great clemency towards Melitius, although strictly speaking he was wholly undeserving of favor, that he remain in his own city, but exercise no authority either to ordain or nominate for ordination ; and that he appear in no other district or city on this pretense, but simply retain a nominal dignity. That those who had received appointments from him, after having been confirmed by a more legitimate ordination, should be admitted to communion on these conditions : that they should continue to hold their rank and ministry, but regard themselves as inferior in every respect to all those who have been ordained and established in each place and church by our most-honored fellow-minister, Alexander, so that they shall have no authority to propose or nominate whom they please, or to do anything at all without the concurrence of some bishop of the Catholic Church who is one of Alexander's suffragans. On the other hand, such as by the grace of God and your prayers have been found in no schism, but have continued in the Catholic Church blameless, shall have authority to nominate and ordain those who are worthy of the sacred office,[1] and to act in all things according to ecclesiastical law and usage. When it may happen that any of those holding preferments in the church die, then let these who have been thus recently admitted be advanced to the dignity of the deceased, provided that they should appear worthy, and that the people should elect them, the bishop of Alexandria also ratifying their choice. This privilege is conceded to all the others indeed, but to Melitius personally we by no means grant the same license, on account of his former disorderly conduct, and because of the rashness and levity of his character, in order that no authority or jurisdiction should be given him as a man liable again to create similar disturbances. These are the things which specially affect Egypt, and the most holy church of the Alexandrians: and if any other canon or ordinance has been established, our Lord and most-honored fellow-minister and brother Alexander being present with us, will on his return to you enter into more minute details, inasmuch as he has been a participator in whatever is transacted, and has had the principal direction of it. We have also gratifying intelligence to communicate to you relative to unity of judgment on the subject of the most holy feast of Easter: for this point also has been happily settled through your prayers; so that all the brethren in the East who have heretofore kept this festival when the Jews did, will henceforth conform to the Romans and to us, and to all who from the earliest time have observed our period of celebrating Easter. Rejoicing therefore in these conclusions and in the general unanimity and peace, as well as in the extirpation of all heresy, receive with the greater honor and more abundant love our fellow-minister and your bishop Alexander, who has greatly delighted us by his presence, and even at his advanced age has undergone extraordinary exertions in order that peace might be re-established among you. Pray on behalf of us all, that the things decided as just may be inviolably maintained through Almighty God, and our Lord Jesus Christ, together with the Holy Spirit; to whom be glory for ever. Amen.

This epistle of the Synod makes it plain that they not only anathematized Arius and his ad-

herents, but the very expressions of his tenets; and that having agreed among themselves respecting the celebration of Easter, they readmitted the heresiarch Melitius into communion, suffering him to retain his episcopal rank, but divesting him of all authority to act as a bishop. It is for this reason I suppose that even at the present time the Melitians in Egypt are separated from the church, because the Synod deprived Melitius of all power. It should be observed moreover that Arius had written a treatise on his own opinion which he entitled *Thalia;* but the character of the book is loose and dissolute, similar in its style and metres to the songs of Sotades.[2] This production also the Synod condemned at the same time. Nor was it the Synod alone that took the trouble to write letters to the churches announcing the restoration of peace, but the emperor Constantine himself also wrote personally and sent the following address to the church of the Alexandrians.

The Emperor's Letter.

Constantine Augustus, to the Catholic church of the Alexandrians. Beloved brethren, hail! We have received from Divine Providence the inestimable blessing of being relieved from all error, and united in the acknowledgment of one and the same faith. The devil will no longer have any power against us, since all that which he had malignantly devised for our destruction has been entirely overthrown from the foundations. The splendor of truth has dissipated at the command of God those dissensions, schisms, tumults, and so to speak, deadly poisons of discord. Wherefore we all worship one true God, and believe that he is. But in order that this might be done, by divine admonition I assembled at the city of Nicæa most of the bishops; with whom I myself also, who am but one of you, and who rejoice exceedingly in being your fellow-servant, undertook the investigation of the truth. Accordingly, all points which seemed in consequence of ambiguity to furnish any pretext for dissension, have been discussed and accurately examined. And may the Divine Majesty pardon the fearful enormity of the blasphemies which some were shamelessly uttering concerning the mighty Saviour, our life and hope; declaring and confessing that they believe things contrary to the divinely inspired Scriptures. While more than three hundred bishops remarkable for their moderation and intellectual keenness, were unanimous in their confirmation of one and the same faith, which according to the truth and legitimate construction of the law

---

[1] κλήρου: cf. Bingham, *Eccl. Antiq.* I. 5.
[2] Sotades, a Maronite, characterized as obscene. On the doctrines of the Maronites, cf. Gibbon's *Decline and Fall,* Ch. XLVII. sect. 3.

of God can only be *the* faith; Arius alone beguiled by the subtlety of the devil, was discovered to be the sole disseminator of this mischief, first among you, and afterwards with unhallowed purposes among others also. Let us therefore embrace that doctrine which the Almighty has presented to us: let us return to our beloved brethren from whom an irreverent servant of the devil has separated us: let us go with all speed to the common body and our own natural members. For this is becoming your penetration, faith and sanctity; that since the error has been proved to be due to him who is an enemy to the truth, ye should return to the divine favor. For that which has commended itself to the judgment of three hundred bishops cannot be other than the doctrine of God; seeing that the Holy Spirit dwelling in the minds of so many dignified persons has effectually enlightened them respecting the Divine will. Wherefore let no one vacillate or linger, but let all with alacrity return to the undoubted path of duty; that when I shall arrive among you, which will be as soon as possible, I may with you return due thanks to God, the inspector of all things, for having revealed the pure faith, and restored to you that love for which ye have prayed. May God protect you, beloved brethren.

Thus wrote the emperor to the Christians of Alexandria, assuring them that the exposition of the faith was neither made rashly nor at random, but that it was dictated with much research, and after strict investigation: and not that some things were spoken of, while others were suppressed in silence; but that whatever could be fittingly advanced in support of any opinion was fully stated. That nothing indeed was precipitately determined, but all was previously discussed with minute accuracy; so that every point which seemed to furnish a pretext for ambiguity of meaning, or difference of opinion, was thoroughly sifted, and its difficulties removed. In short he terms the thought of all those who were assembled there the thought of God, and does not doubt that the unanimity of so many eminent bishops was effected by the Holy Spirit. Sabinus, however, the chief of the heresy of the Macedonians, willfully rejects these authorities, and calls those who were convened there ignorant and illiterate persons; nay, he almost accuses Eusebius of Cæsarea himself of ignorance: nor does he reflect, that even if those who constituted that synod had been laymen, yet as being illuminated by God, and the grace of the Holy Spirit, they were utterly unable to err from the truth.[3] Nevertheless, hear farther

what the emperor decreed in another circular both against Arius and those who held his opinions, sending it in all directions to the bishops and people.

Another Epistle of Constantine.

Victor Constantine Maximus Augustus, to the bishops and people. — Since Arius has imitated wicked and impious persons, it is just that he should undergo the like ignominy. Wherefore as Porphyry,[4] that enemy of piety, for having composed licentious treatises against religion, found a suitable recompense, and such as thenceforth branded him with infamy, overwhelming him with deserved reproach, his impious writings also having been destroyed; so now it seems fit both that Arius and such as hold his sentiments should be denominated Porphyrians, that they may take their appellation from those whose conduct they have imitated. And in addition to this, if any treatise composed by Arius should be discovered, let it be consigned to the flames, in order that not only his depraved doctrine may be suppressed, but also that no memorial of him may be by any means left. This therefore I decree, that if any one shall be detected in concealing a book compiled by Arius, and shall not instantly bring it forward and burn it, the penalty for this offense shall be death; for immediately after conviction the criminal shall suffer capital punishment. May God preserve you!

Another Epistle.[5]

Constantine Augustus, to the Churches.

Having experienced from the flourishing condition of public affairs, how great has been the grace of divine power, I judged this to be an object above all things claiming my care, that one faith, with sincere love, and uniform piety toward Almighty God should be maintained amongst the most blessed assemblies of the Catholic Church. But inasmuch as I perceived that this could not be firmly and permanently established, unless all, or at least the greatest part of the bishops could be convened in the same place, and every point of our most holy religion should be discussed by them in council; therefore as many as possible were assembled, and I myself also as one of you was present; for I will not deny what I especially rejoice in, that I am your fellow-servant. All points were then minutely investigated, until a decision acceptable to Him who is the inspector of all things, was published for the promotion of uni-

---

[3] It has always been the common belief of the Eastern Church that the ecumenical councils were inspired in the same sense as the writers of the Sacred Scriptures. Socrates in this respect simply reflects the opinion of the age and region.

[4] Cf. III. 23, where the author makes further mention of Porphyry and his writings; see also Smith, *Dict. of Greek and Roman Biog.*
[5] Euseb. *Life of Const.* III. 17-19.

formity of judgment and practice ; so that nothing might be henceforth left for dissension or controversy in matters of faith.   There also the question having been considered relative to the most holy day of Easter, it was determined by common consent that it should be proper that all should celebrate it on one and the same day everywhere.   For what can be more appropriate, or what more solemn, than that this feast from which we have received the hope of immortality, should be invariably kept in one order, and for an obvious reason among all?   And in the first place, it seemed very unworthy of this most sacred feast, that we should keep it following the custom of the Jews ; a people who having imbrued their hands in a most heinous outrage, have thus polluted their souls, and are deservedly blind.   Having then cast aside their usage, we are free to see to it that the celebration of this observance should occur in future in the more correct order which we have kept from the first day of the Passion until the present time. Therefore have nothing in common with that most hostile people the Jews.   We have received from the Saviour another way ; for there is set before us both a legitimate and accurate course in our holy religion : unanimously pursuing this, let us, most honored brethren, withdraw ourselves from that detestable association.   For it is truly absurd for them to boast that we are incapable of rightly observing these things without their instruction.   For on what subject will they be competent to form a correct judgment, who after that murder of their Lord, having been bereft of their senses, are led not by any rational motive, but by an ungovernable impulse, wherever their innate fury may drive them?   Thence it is therefore, that even in this particular they do not perceive the truth, so that they constantly erring in the utmost degree, instead of making a suitable correction, celebrate the Feast of Passover a second time in the same year.[6]   Why then should we follow the example of those who are acknowledged to be infected with grievous error?   Surely we should never suffer Easter to be kept twice in one and the same year !   But even if these considerations were not laid before you, it became your prudence at all times to take heed, both by diligence and prayer, that the purity of your soul should in nothing have communion, or seem to do so with the customs of men so utterly depraved.   Moreover this should also be considered, that in a matter so important and of such religious significance, the slightest disagreement is most irreverent.   For our Sa-

viour left us but one day to be observed in commemoration of our deliverance, that is the day of his most holy Passion : he also wished his Catholic Church to be one ; the members of which, however much they may be scattered in various places, are notwithstanding cherished by one Spirit, that is by the will of God.   Let the prudence consistent with your sacred character consider how grievous and indecorous it is, that on the same days some should be observing fasts, while others are celebrating feasts ; and after the days of Easter some should indulge in festivities and enjoyments, and others submit to appointed fastings.   On this account therefore Divine Providence directed that an appropriate correction should be effected, and uniformity of practice established, as I suppose you are all aware.

Since then it was desirable that this should be so amended that we should have nothing in common with that nation of parricides, and of those who slew their Lord ; and since the order is a becoming one which is observed by all the churches of the western, southern, and northern parts, and by some also in the eastern ; from these considerations for the present all thought it to be proper, and I pledged myself that it would be satisfactory to your prudent penetration, that what is observed with such general unanimity of sentiment in the city of Rome, throughout Italy, Africa, all Egypt, Spain, France, Britain, Libya, the whole of Greece, and the dioceses of Asia, Pontus, and Cilicia, your intelligence also would cheerfully accept ; reflecting too that not only is there a greater number of churches in the places before mentioned, but also that this in particular is a most sacred obligation, that all should in common desire whatever strict reason seems to demand, and what has no communion with the perjury of the Jews. But to sum up matters briefly, it was determined by common consent that the most holy festival of Easter should be solemnized on one and the same day ; for it is not even seemly that there should be in such a hallowed solemnity any difference : and it is more commendable to adopt that opinion in which there will be no intermixture of strange error, or deviation from what is right.   These things therefore being thus consistent, do you gladly receive this heavenly and truly divine command : for whatever is done in the sacred assemblies of the bishops is referable to the Divine will.   Wherefore, when ye have indicated the things which have been prescribed to all our beloved brethren, it behooves you to publish the above written statements and to accept the reasoning which has been adduced, and to establish this observance of the most holy day : that when I arrive at the long and earnestly desired view of your order, I may be able to

---

[6] As the Jewish Passover month was a lunar month and began on the fifth day of March and ended on the third of April, it happened sometimes that their Passover began before the equinox (the beginning of the solar year), so that they celebrated two Passovers during the same solar year.   Their own year being lunar, of course they never celebrated the Passover twice in a year according to their point of view.

celebrate the sacred festival with you on one and the same day ; and may rejoice with you for all things, in seeing Satanic cruelty frustrated by divine power through our efforts, while your faith, peace and concord are everywhere flourishing. May God preserve you, beloved brethren.

Another Epistle to Eusebius.[7]

Victor Constantine Maximus Augustus, to Eusebius.

Since an impious purpose and tyranny have even to the present time persecuted the servants of God our Saviour, I have been credibly informed and am fully persuaded, most beloved brother, that all our sacred edifices have either by neglect gone to decay, or from dread of impending danger have not been adorned with becoming dignity. But now that liberty has been restored, and that persecuting dragon Licinius has by the providence of the Most High God, and our instrumentality, been removed from the administration of public affairs, I imagine that the divine power has been made manifest to all, and at the same time that those who either through fear or unbelief fell into any sins, having acknowledged the living God, will come to the true and right course of life. Wherefore enjoin the churches over which you yourself preside, as well as the other bishops presiding in various places, together with the presbyters and deacons whom you know, to be diligent about the sacred edifices, either by repairing those which remain standing, or enlarging them, or by erecting new ones wherever it may be requisite. And do you yourself ask, and the rest through you, the necessary supplies both from the governors of the provinces, and the officers of the prætorian prefecture : for directions have been given to them to execute with all diligence the orders of your holiness. May God preserve you, beloved brother.

These instructions, concerning the building of churches were sent by the emperor to the bishops in every province : but what he wrote to Eusebius of Palestine respecting the preparation of some copies of the Scriptures, we may ascertain from the letters themselves : [8]

Victor Constantine Maximus Augustus, to Eusebius of Cæsarea.

In the city which derives its name from us, a very great multitude of persons, through the assisting providence of our Saviour God, have united themselves to the most holy Church, so that it has received much increase there. It is therefore requisite that more churches should be furnished in that place : wherefore do you most cordially enter into the purpose which I have conceived. I have thought fit to intimate this to your prudence, that you should order to be transcribed on well-prepared parchment, by competent writers accurately acquainted with their art, fifty copies of the Sacred Scriptures, both legibly described, and of a portable size, the provision and use of which you know to be needful for the instruction of the Church. Letters have also been despatched from our clemency, to the financial agent[9] of the diocese that he be careful to provide all things necessary for the preparation of them. That these copies may be got ready as quickly as possible, let it be a task for your diligence : and you are authorized, on the warrant of this our letter, to use two of the public carriages for their conveyance ; for thus the copies which are most satisfactorily transcribed, may be easily conveyed for our inspection, one of the deacons of your church fulfilling this commission ; who when he has reached us shall experience our bounty. May God preserve you, beloved brother.

Another Epistle to Macarius.[10]

Victor Constantine Maximus Augustus, to Macarius of Jerusalem. — Such is the grace of our Saviour, that no supply of words seems to be adequate to the expression of its present manifestation. For that the monument[11] of his most holy passion, long since hidden under the earth, should have lain concealed for a period of so many years, until, through the destruction of the common enemy of all,[12] it should shine forth to his own servants after their having regained their freedom, exceeds all admiration. For if all those who throughout the whole habitable earth are accounted wise, should be convened in one and the same place, desiring to say something worthy of the event, they would fall infinitely short of the least part of it ; for the apprehension of this wonder as far transcends every nature capable of human reasoning, as heavenly things are mightier than human. Hence therefore this is always my especial aim, that as the credibility of the truth daily demonstrates itself by fresh miracles, so the souls of us all should become more diligent respecting the holy

---

[7] Valesius thinks this letter is misplaced; as it alludes to the death of Licinius as a recent event, he thinks it must have been written about 315-316 A.D., hence ten years before the Council of Nicæa. Cf. Euseb. *Life of Const.* II. 46.
[8] Euseb. *Life of Const.* IV. 36.

[9] διοικήσεως καθολικόν: this office was peculiar to the Eastern Church. The nearest equivalent to it in the terminology of the Western Church is that of vicar-general; but as the non-technical expression 'financial agent' describes the official to the modern reader, it has been adopted in the present translation. Concerning the office, cf. Euseb. *H. E.* VII. 10. It may be also noted that the very common ecclesiastical term diocese (διοίκησις) originated during the reign of Constantine, as becomes evident from his letters. See Euseb. *Life of Const.* III. 36.
[10] Euseb. *Life of Const.* III. 30.
[11] γνώρισμα: the sepulchre near Calvary commonly known as the Saviour's is meant.
[12] Licinius.

law, with modesty and unanimous eagerness. But I desire that you should be fully aware of what I conceive is pretty generally known, that it is now my chief care, that we should adorn with magnificent structures that hallowed spot, which by God's appointment I have disencumbered of a most disgraceful addition [13] of an idol, as of some grievous burden; which was consecrated indeed from the beginning in the purpose of God, but has been more manifestly sanctified since he has brought to light the evidence of the Saviour's passion. Wherefore it is becoming your prudence to make such arrangements, and provision of everything necessary, that not only a church [14] should be built in itself superior to any elsewhere, but that the rest of its parts also may be such that all the most splendid edifices in every city may be excelled by this. With regard to the workmanship and chaste execution of the walls, know that we have entrusted the care of these things to our friend Dracilian, deputy to the most illustrious prefects of the prætorium, and to the governor of the province : for my piety has ordered that artificers and workmen, and whatever other things they may be informed from your sagacity to be necessary for the structure, shall through their care be immediately sent. Respecting the columns or the marbles, whatever you may judge to be more precious and useful, do you yourself after having inspected the plan take care to write to us ; that when we shall understand from your letter how many things and of what kind there may be need of, these may be conveyed to you from all quarters : for it is but just that the most wonderful place in the world, should be adorned in accordance with its dignity. But I wish to know from you, whether you consider that the vault of the basilica should be fretted, or constructed on some other plan : for if it is to be fretted, it can also be decorated with gold. It remains that your holiness should inform the officers before mentioned as soon as possible, how many workmen and artificers, and what money for expenses you will want. Be careful at the same time to report to me speedily, not only concerning the marbles and columns, but also concerning the fretted vault, if indeed you should decide this to be the more beautiful. May God preserve you, beloved brother

The emperor having also written other letters of a more oratorical character against Arius and his adherents, caused them to be everywhere published throughout the cities, exposing him to ridicule, and taunting him with irony. More-

over, writing to the Nicomedians against Eusebius and Theognis, he censures the misconduct of Eusebius, not only on account of his Arianism, but because also having formerly been well-affected to the ruler, he had traitorously conspired against his affairs. He then exhorts them to elect another bishop instead of him. But I thought it would be superfluous to insert here the letters respecting these things, because of their length : those who wish to do so may find them elsewhere and give them a perusal. This is sufficient notice of these transactions.

CHAPTER X.

The Emperor also summons to the Synod Acesius, Bishop of the Novatians.

THE emperor's diligence induces me to mention another circumstance expressive of his mind, and serving to show how much he desired peace. For aiming at ecclesiastical harmony, he summoned to the council Acesius also, a bishop of the sect of Novatians. Now, when the declaration of faith had been written out and subscribed by the Synod, the emperor asked Acesius whether he would also agree to this creed to the settlement of the day on which Easter should be observed. He replied, 'The Synod has determined nothing new, my prince : for thus heretofore, even from the beginning, from the times of the apostles, I traditionally received the definition of the faith, and the time of the celebration of Easter.' When, therefore, the emperor further asked him, ' For what reason then do you separate yourself from communion with the rest of the Church?' he related what had taken place during the persecution under Decius ; and referred to the rigidness of that austere canon which declares, that it is not right persons who after baptism have committed a sin, which the sacred Scriptures denominate 'a sin unto death' [1] to be considered worthy of participation in the sacraments : [2] that they should indeed be exhorted to repentance, but were not to expect remission from the priests, but from God, who is able and has authority to forgive sins.[3] When Acesius had thus spoken, the emperor said to him, ' Place a ladder, Acesius, and climb alone into heaven.' [4] Neither Eusebius Pamphilus nor any other has ever mentioned these things : but I heard them from a man by no means prone to falsehood, who was very old, and simply stated what had taken place in the council in the course of a narrative. From which I conjecture that those who have passed by this occur-

---

[13] A temple of Venus built by Adrian, the emperor, on Mount Calvary.
[14] βασιλικήν, ' basilica '; the ancient Roman basilicas were often turned into churches. The term has become familiar in ecclesiastical architecture.

[1] John v. 16.
[2] θείων μυστηρίων.
[3] Cf. IV. 28.
[4] Sozom. I. 22.

rence in silence, were actuated by motives which have influenced many other historians: for they frequently suppress important facts, either from prejudice against some, or partiality towards others.

CHAPTER XI.

Of the Bishop Paphnutius.

As we have promised above [1] to make some mention of Paphnutius and Spyridon, it is time to speak of them here. Paphnutius then was bishop of one of the cities in Upper Thebes: he was a man so favored divinely that extraordinary miracles were done by him. In the time of the persecution he had been deprived of one of his eyes. The emperor honored this man exceedingly, and often sent for him to the palace, and kissed the part where the eye had been torn out. So great devoutness characterized the emperor Constantine. Let this single fact respecting Paphnutius suffice: I shall now explain another thing which came to pass in consequence of his advice, both for the good of the Church and the honor of the clergy. It seemed fit to the bishops to introduce a new law into the Church, that those who were in holy orders, I speak of bishops, presbyters, and deacons, should have no conjugal intercourse with the wives whom they had married while still laymen.[2] Now when discussion on this matter was impending, Paphnutius having arisen in the midst of the assembly of bishops, earnestly entreated them not to impose so heavy a yoke on the ministers of religion: asserting that 'marriage itself is honorable, and the bed undefiled';[3] urging before God that they ought not to injure the Church by too stringent restrictions. 'For all men,' said he, 'cannot bear the practice of rigid continence; neither perhaps would the chastity of the wife of each be preserved': and he termed the intercourse of a man with his lawful wife chastity. It would be sufficient, he thought, that such as had previously entered on their sacred calling should abjure matrimony, according to the ancient tradition of the Church: but that none should be separated from her to whom, while yet unordained, he had been united. And these sentiments he expressed, although himself without experience of marriage, and, to speak plainly, without ever having known a woman: for from a boy he had been brought up in a monastery,[4] and was specially renowned above

all men for his chastity. The whole assembly of the clergy assented to the reasoning of Paphnutius: wherefore they silenced all further debate on this point, leaving it to the discretion of those who were husbands to exercise abstinence if they so wished in reference to their wives. Thus much concerning Paphnutius.

CHAPTER XII.

Of Spyridon, Bishop of the Cypriots.

WITH respect to Spyridon, so great was his sanctity while a shepherd, that he was thought worthy of being made a Pastor of men: and having been assigned the bishopric of one of the cities in Cyprus named Trimithus, on account of his extreme humility he continued to feed his sheep during his incumbency of the bishopric. Many extraordinary things are related of him: I shall however record but one or two, lest I should seem to wander from my subject. Once about midnight, thieves having clandestinely entered his sheepfold attempted to carry off some of the sheep. But God who protected the shepherd preserved his sheep also; for the thieves were by an invisible power bound to the folds. At daybreak, when he came to the sheep and found the men with their hands tied behind them, he understood what was done: and after having prayed he liberated the thieves, earnestly admonishing and exhorting them to support themselves by honest labor, and not to take anything unjustly. He then gave them a ram, and sent them away, humorously adding, 'that ye may not appear to have watched all night in vain.' This is one of the miracles in connection with Spyridon. Another was of this kind. He had a virgin daughter named Irene, who was a partaker of her father's piety. An acquaintance entrusted to her keeping an ornament of considerable value: she, to guard it more securely, hid what had been deposited with her in the ground, and not long afterwards died. Subsequently the owner of the property came to claim it; and not finding the virgin, he began an excited conversation with the father, at times accusing him of an attempt to defraud him, and then again beseeching him to restore the deposit. The old man, regarding this person's loss as his own misfortune, went to the tomb of his daughter, and called upon God to show him before its proper season the promised resurrection. Nor was he disappointed in his hope: for the virgin again reviving appeared to her father, and having pointed out to him the spot where she had hidden the ornament, she once more departed. Such characters as these adorned the churches in the

---

[1] Above, chap. 8.
[2] Cf. *Apost. Cann.* 5, 17, 26, 51. In general, voluntary celibacy of the clergy was encouraged in the ancient Church.
[3] Heb. xiii. 4.
[4] ἀσκητηρίῳ: lit. 'place for the exercise' *of virtue.*

time of the emperor Constantine. These details I obtained from many inhabitants of Cyprus. I have also found a treatise composed in Latin by the presbyter Rufinus, from which I have collected these and some other things which will be hereafter adduced.[1]

CHAPTER XIII.

Of Eutychian the Monk.

I HAVE heard moreover concerning Eutychian, a devout person who flourished about the same time ; who also belonged to the Novatian church, yet was venerated for the performance of similar miracles. I shall unequivocally state my authority for this narrative, nor will I attempt to conceal it, even though I give offense to some parties. It was Auxanon, a very aged presbyter of the Novatian church ; who when quite a youth accompanied Acesius to the Synod at Nicæa, and related to me what I have said concerning him. His life extended from that period to the reign of Theodosius the Younger ; and when I was a mere youth he recounted to me the acts of Eutychian, enlarging much on the divine grace which was manifested in him : but one circumstance he alluded to, which occurred in the reign of Constantine, peculiarly worthy of mention. One of those military attendants, whom the emperor calls his domestic [or body] guards having been suspected of treasonable practices, sought his safety in flight. The indignant monarch ordered that he should be put to death, wherever he might be found : who, having been arrested on the Bithynian Olympus, was bound with heavy and painful chains and kept imprisoned near those parts of Olympus where Eutychian was leading a solitary life, and healing both the bodies and souls of many. The aged Auxanon being then very young was with him, and was being trained by him in the discipline of the monastic life. Many persons came to this Eutychian, entreating him to procure the release of the prisoner by interceding for him with the emperor. For the fame of the miracles done by Eutychian had reached the ears of the emperor. He readily promised to go to the sovereign ; but as the chains inflicted intolerable suffering, those who interested themselves on his behalf declared that death caused by the effect of his chains would anticipate both the emperor's vengeance and any intercession that might be made for the prisoner. Accordingly Eutychian sent to the jailers requesting them to relieve the man ; but they having answered that they should bring themselves into danger by relieving a criminal, he went himself to the prison, attended by Auxanon ; and as they refused to open the jail, the grace which rested on Eutychian was rendered more conspicuous : for the gates of the prison opened of their own accord, while the jailers had the keys in their custody. As soon as Eutychian, together with Auxanon, had entered the prison, to the great astonishment of all then present the fetters spontaneously fell from the prisoner's limbs. He then proceeded with Auxanon to the city which was anciently called Byzantium but afterwards Constantinople, where having been admitted into the imperial palace, he saved the man from death ; for the emperor, entertaining great veneration for Eutychian, readily granted his request. This indeed occurred some time after [the period to which this part of our history refers].

The bishops who were convened at the council of Nicæa, after having drawn up and enrolled certain other ecclesiastical regulations which they are accustomed to term canons, again departed to their respective cities : and as I conceive it will be appreciated by lovers of learning, I shall here subjoin the names of such as were present, as far as I have been able to ascertain them, with the province and city over which they severally presided, and likewise the date at which this assembly took place. Hosius, who was I believe bishop of Cordova in Spain, as I have before stated. Vito and Vicentius, presbyters of Rome, Alexander, bishop of Egypt, Eustathius of Antiochia Magna, Macarius of Jerusalem, and Harpocration of Cynopolis : the names of the rest are fully reported in *The Synodicon*[1] of Athanasius, bishop of Alexandria. This Synod was convened (as we have discovered from the notation of the date prefixed to the record of the Synod) in the consulate of Paulinus and Julian, on the 20th day of May, and in the 636th year from the reign of Alexander the Macedonian.[2] Accordingly the work of the council was accomplished. It should be noted that after the council the emperor went into the western parts of the empire.

CHAPTER XIV.

Eusebius Bishop of Nicomedia, and Theognis Bishop of Nicæa, who had been banished for agreeing in Opinion with Arius, having published their Recantation, and assented to the Creed, are reinstated in their Sees.

EUSEBIUS[1] and Theognis having sent a penitential confession to the principal bishops, were

---

[1] On the use Socrates made of Rufinus, and the question of his knowledge of Latin therein involved, see Introd. p. x.

[1] This work of Athanasius is not now extant.
[2] May 20, 325 A.D.
[1] This is not in its place according to chronological order, inasmuch as it occurred in 328 A.D. It appears also from the accounts

by an imperial edict recalled from exile and restored to their own churches, displacing those who had been ordained in their places; Eusebius [displacing] Amphion, and Theognis Chrestus. This is a copy of their written retraction:

'We having been sometime since condemned by your piety, without a formal trial, ought to bear in silence the decisions of your sacred adjudication. But since it is unreasonable that we by silence should countenance calumniators against ourselves, we on this account declare that we entirely concur with you in the faith; and also that, after having closely considered the import of the term *consubstantial*, we have been wholly studious of peace, having never followed the heresy. After suggesting whatever entered our thought for the security of the churches, and fully assuring those under our influence, we subscribed the declaration of faith; we did not subscribe the anathematizing; not as objecting to the creed, but as disbelieving the party accused to be such as was represented, having been satisfied on this point, both from his own letters to us, and from personal conversations. But if your holy council was convinced, we not opposing but concurring in your decisions, by this statement give them our full assent and confirmation: and this we do not as wearied with our exile, but to shake off the suspicion of heresy. If therefore ye should now think fit to restore us to your presence, ye will have us on all points conformable, and acquiescent in your decrees: especially since it has seemed good to your piety to deal tenderly with and recall even him who was primarily accused. It would be absurd for us to be silent, and thus give presumptive evidence against ourselves, when the one who seemed responsible has been permitted to clear himself from the charges brought against him. Vouchsafe then, as is consistent with that Christ-loving piety of yours, to remind our most religious emperor, to present our petitions, and to determine speedily concerning us in a way becoming yourselves.'

Such was the language of the recantation of Eusebius and Theognis; from which I infer that they had subscribed the articles of faith which had been set forth, but would not become parties to the condemnation of Arius. It appears also that Arius was recalled before them; but, although this may be true, yet he had been forbidden to enter Alexandria. This is evident from the fact that he afterwards devised a way of return for himself, both into the church and into Alexandria, by having made a fictitious repentance, as we shall show in its proper place.

CHAPTER XV.

After the Synod, on the Death of Alexander, Athanasius is constituted Bishop of Alexandria.

A LITTLE after this, Alexander bishop of Alexandria having died,[1] Athanasius was set over that church. Rufinus relates, that this [Athanasius] when quite a boy, played with others of his own age at a sacred game: this was an imitation of the priesthood and the order of consecrated persons. In this game therefore Athanasius was allotted the episcopal chair, and each of the other lads personated either a presbyter or a deacon. The children engaged in this sport on the day in which the memory of the martyr and bishop Peter was celebrated. Now at that time Alexander bishop of Alexandria happening to pass by, observed the play in which they were engaged, and having sent for the children, enquired from them the part each had been assigned in the game, conceiving that something might be portended by that which had been done. He then gave directions that the children should be taken to the church, and instructed in learning, but especially Athanasius; and having afterwards ordained him deacon on his becoming of adult age, he brought him to Nicæa to assist him in the disputations there when the Synod was convened. This account of Athanasius Rufinus has given in his own writings; nor is it improbable that it took place, for many transactions of this kind have often occurred. Concerning this matter it will suffice to have said the above.[2]

CHAPTER XVI.

The Emperor Constantine having enlarged the Ancient Byzantium, calls it Constantinople.

AFTER the Synod the emperor spent some time in recreation, and after the public celebration of his twentieth anniversary of his accession,[1] he immediately devoted himself to the reparation of the churches. This he carried into effect in other cities as well as in the city named after him, which being previously called Byzantium, he enlarged, surrounded with massive walls,[2] and adorned with various edifices;

---

of the other historians of this period that Socrates does not give the correct reason for the banishment of Eusebius and Theognis. Cf. Theodoret, *H. E.* I. 20; also Sozom. I. 21.

---

[1] Socrates and Sozomen are both mistaken in putting the death of Alexander and ordination of Athanasius after the return of Eusebius and Theognis from exile. According to Theodoret (*H. E.* I. 26), Alexander died a few months after the Council of Nicæa, hence in 325 A.D., and Athanasius succeeded him at the end of the same year, or at the beginning of the next.
[2] See, for additional features of the story not reproduced by Socrates, Rufinus, *H. E.* I. 14.
[1] The Vicennalia.
[2] These walls were superseded by the great walls built under Theodosius the Younger; see VII. 31.

and having rendered it equal to imperial Rome, he named it *Constantinople*, establishing by law that it should be designated *New Rome*. This law was engraven on a pillar of stone erected in public view in the Strategium,[3] near the emperor's equestrian statue.[4] He built also in the same city two churches, one of which he named *Irene*, and the other *The Apostles*.[5] Nor did he only improve the affairs of the Christians, as I have said, but he also destroyed the superstition of the heathens; for he brought forth their images into public view to ornament the city of Constantinople, and set up the Delphic tripods publicly in the Hippodrome. It may indeed seem now superfluous to mention these things, since they are seen before they are heard of. But at that time the Christian cause received its greatest augmentation; for Divine Providence preserved very many other things during the times of the emperor Constantine.[6] Eusebius Pamphilus has in magnificent terms recorded the praises of the emperor;[7] and I considered it would not be ill-timed to advert thus to them as concisely as possible.

CHAPTER XVII.

The Emperor's Mother Helena having come to Jerusalem, searches for and finds the Cross of Christ, and builds a Church.

HELENA, the emperor's mother (from whose name having made Drepanum, once a village, a city, the emperor called it Helenopolis), being divinely directed by dreams went to Jerusalem. Finding that which was once Jerusalem, desolate 'as a Preserve for autumnal fruits,'[1] according to the prophet, she sought carefully the sepulchre of Christ, from which he arose after his burial; and after much difficulty, by God's help she discovered it. What the cause of the difficulty was I will explain in a few words. Those who embraced the Christian faith, after the period of his passion, greatly venerated this tomb; but those who hated Christianity, having covered the spot with a mound of earth, erected on it a temple to Venus, and set up her image there, not caring for the memory of the place.[2] This succeeded for a long time; and it became known to the emperor's mother. Accordingly

she having caused the statue[3] to be thrown down, the earth to be removed, and the ground entirely cleared, found three crosses in the sepulchre: one of these was that blessed cross on which Christ had hung, the other two were those on which the two thieves that were crucified with him had died. With these was also found the tablet[4] of Pilate, on which he had inscribed in various characters, that the Christ who was crucified was king of the Jews. Since, however, it was doubtful which was the cross they were in search of, the emperor's mother was not a little distressed; but from this trouble the bishop of Jerusalem, Macarius, shortly relieved her. And he solved the doubt by faith, for he sought a sign from God and obtained it. The sign was this: a certain woman of the neighborhood, who had been long afflicted with disease, was now just at the point of death; the bishop therefore arranged it so that each of the crosses should be brought to the dying woman, believing that she would be healed on touching the precious cross. Nor was he disappointed in his expectation: for the two crosses having been applied which were not the Lord's, the woman still continued in a dying state; but when the third, which was the true cross, touched her, she was immediately healed, and recovered her former strength. In this manner then was the genuine cross discovered. The emperor's mother erected over the place of the sepulchre a magnificent church,[5] and named it *New Jerusalem*, having built it facing that old and deserted city. There she left a portion of the cross, enclosed in a silver case, as a memorial to those who might wish to see it: the other part she sent to the emperor, who being persuaded that the city would be perfectly secure where that relic should be preserved, privately enclosed it in his own statue, which stands on a large column of porphyry in the forum called Constantine's at Constantinople. I have written this from report indeed; but almost all the inhabitants of Constantinople affirm that it is true. Moreover the nails with which Christ's hands were fastened to the cross (for his mother having found these also in the sepulchre had sent them) Constantine took and had made into bridle-bits and a helmet, which he used in his military expeditions. The emperor supplied all materials for the construction of the churches, and wrote to Macarius the bishop to expedite these edifices. When the emperor's mother had completed the *New Jerusalem*, she reared another church not at all inferior, over the cave at Bethlehem where Christ was born according to the flesh: nor did she stop here, but built a third on the

---

[3] 'Mansion house,' the building in which the two chief magistrates had their headquarters.
[4] The city was formally dedicated as the capital of the empire in 330 A.D.
[5] Cf. II. 16, and I. 40.
[6] The text seems somewhat doubtful here. Valesius conjectures τά τε ἄλλα πλείστα καὶ τοῦτο μάλιστα, idiomatically, 'this among many other things'; but the MSS. read more obscurely, καὶ ἄλλα πλείστα.
[7] Euseb. *Life of Const.* III. 33; cf. also 52–55.
[1] Isa. i. 8. ὀπωροφυλάκιον, 'a lodge in a garden of cucumbers,' according to the English versions (both authorized and revised), which follows the Hebrew; in the LXX the words ἐν σικυηράτῳ are added.
[2] See the Ep. of Constantine to Macarius, in chap. 9 above.

[3] ξόανον, as distinguished from ἄγαλμα, or ἀνδριάς, used with less reverence; the word is derived from ξέω, 'to polish.'
[4] σανίς, 'board.'
[5] οἶκον εὐκτήριον, 'house of prayer.'

mount of his Ascension. So devoutly was she affected in these matters, that she would pray in the company of women; and inviting the virgins enrolled in the register[6] of the churches to a repast, serving them herself, she brought the dishes to table. She was also very munificent to the churches and to the poor; and having lived a life of piety, she died when about eighty years old. Her remains were conveyed to New Rome, the capital, and deposited in the imperial sepulchres.

CHAPTER XVIII.

The Emperor Constantine abolishes Paganism and erects many Churches in Different Places.

AFTER this the emperor became increasingly attentive to the interests of the Christians, and abandoned the heathen superstitions. He abolished the combats of the gladiators, and set up his own statues in the temples. And as the heathens affirmed that it was Serapis who brought up the Nile for the purpose of irrigating Egypt, because a cubit was usually carried into his temple, he directed Alexander to transfer the cubit to the church. And although they predicted that the Nile would not overflow because of the displeasure of Serapis, nevertheless there was an inundation in the following year and afterwards, taking place regularly: thus it was proved by fact that the rising of the Nile was not in consequence of their superstition, but by reason of the decrees of Providence. About the same time those barbarians the Sarmatians and Goths made incursions on the Roman territory; yet the emperor's earnestness respecting the churches was by no means abated, but he made suitable provision for both these matters. Placing his confidence in the Christian banner,[1] he completely vanquished his enemies, so as even to cast off the tribute of gold which preceding emperors were accustomed to pay the barbarians: while they themselves, being terror-struck at the unexpectedness of their defeat, then for the first time embraced the Christian religion, by means of which Constantine had been protected. Again he built other churches, one of which was erected near the Oak of Mamre, under which the Sacred Oracles declare that Abraham entertained angels. For the emperor having been informed that altars had been reared under that oak, and that pagan sacrifices were offered upon them, censured by letter Eusebius bishop of Cæsarea, and ordered that the altars should be demolished, and a house of

prayer erected beside the oak. He also directed that another church should be constructed in Heliopolis in Phœnicia, for this reason. Who originally legislated for the inhabitants of Heliopolis I am unable to state, but his character and morals may be judged of from the [practice of that] city; for the laws of the country ordered the women among them to be common, and therefore the children born there were of doubtful descent, so that there was no distinction of fathers and their offspring. Their virgins also were presented for prostitution to the strangers who resorted thither. The emperor hastened to correct this evil which had long prevailed among them. And passing a solemn law of chastity, he removed the shameful evil and provided for the mutual recognition of families. And having built churches there, he took care that a bishop and sacred clergy should be ordained. Thus he reformed the corrupt manners of the people of Heliopolis. He likewise demolished the temple of Venus at Aphaca on Mount Libanus, and abolished the infamous deeds which were there celebrated. Why need I describe his expulsion of the Pythonic demon from Cilicia, by commanding the mansion in which he was lurking to be razed from its foundations? So great indeed was the emperor's devotion to Christianity, that when he was about to enter on a war with Persia, he prepared a tabernacle formed of embroidered linen on the model of a church, just as Moses had done in the wilderness;[2] and this so constructed as to be adapted to conveyance from place to place, in order that he might have a house of prayer even in the most desert regions. But the war was not at that time carried on, being prevented through dread of the emperor. It would, I conceive, be out of place here to describe the emperor's diligence in rebuilding cities and converting many villages into cities; as for example Drepanum, to which he gave his mother's name, and Constantia in Palestine, so called from his sister. For my task is not to enumerate of the emperor's actions, but simply such as are connected with Christianity, and especially those which relate to the churches. Wherefore I leave to others more competent to detail such matters, the emperor's glorious achievements, inasmuch as they belong to a different subject, and require a distinct treatise. But I myself should have been silent, if the Church had remained undisturbed by divisions: for where the subject does not supply matter for relation, there is no necessity for a narrator. Since however subtle and vain disputation has confused and at the same time scattered the apostolic faith of Christianity, I thought it desirable to record these things, in order that the

---

[6] κανόνι: a word of many meanings; see Sophocles' Lex. and a dissertation on the word in Westcott *On the Canon* Appendix A, p. 499.
[1] τροπαίῳ: see above, chap. 2.

[2] Ex. xxxv.–xl.

transactions of the churches might not be lost in obscurity. For accurate information on these points procures celebrity among the many, and at the same time renders him who is acquainted with them more secure from error, and instructs him not to be carried away by any empty sound of sophistical argumentation which he may chance to hear.

CHAPTER XIX.[1]

In what Manner the Nations in the Interior of India were Christianized in the Times of Constantine.

WE must now mention in what manner Christianity was spread in this emperor's reign: for it was in his time that the nations both of the Indians in the interior, and of the Iberians first embraced the Christian faith. But I shall briefly explain why I have used the appended expression *in the interior*. When the apostles went forth by lot among the nations, Thomas received the apostleship of the Parthians; Matthew was allotted Ethiopia; and Bartholomew the part of India contiguous to that country: but the interior India, in which many barbarous nations using different languages lived, was not enlightened by Christian doctrine before the times of Constantine. I now come to speak of the cause which led them to become converts to Christianity. A certain philosopher, Meropius, a Tyrian by race, determined to acquaint himself with the country of the Indians, being stimulated to this by the example of the philosopher Metrodorus, who had previously traveled through the region of India. Having taken with him therefore two youths to whom he was related, who were by no means ignorant of the Greek language, Meropius reached the country by ship; and when he had inspected whatever he wished, he touched at a certain place which had a safe harbor, for the purpose of procuring some necessaries. It so happened that a little before that time the treaty between the Romans and Indians had been violated. The Indians, therefore, having seized the philosopher and those who sailed with him, killed them all except his two youthful kinsmen; but sparing them from compassion for their tender age, they sent them as a gift to the king of the Indians. He being pleased with the personal appearance of the youths, constituted one of them, whose name was Edesius, cup-bearer at his table; the other, named Frumentius, he entrusted with the care of the royal records. The king dying soon after, left them free, the government devolving on his wife and infant son. Now the queen seeing her son thus left in his minority, begged the young men to undertake the charge of him, until he should become of adult age. Accordingly, the youths accepted the task, and entered on the administration of the kingdom. Thus Frumentius controlled all things and made it a task to enquire whether among the Roman merchants trafficking with that country, there were any Christians to be found: and having discovered some, he informed them who he was, and exhorted them to select and occupy some appropriate places for the celebration of Christian worship. In the course of a little while he built a house of prayer; and having instructed some of the Indians in the principles of Christianity, they fitted them for participation in the worship. On the young king's reaching maturity, Frumentius and his associates resigned to him the administration of public affairs, in the management of which they had honorably acquitted themselves, and besought permission to return to their own country. Both the king and his mother entreated them to remain; but being desirous of revisiting their native place, they could not be prevailed on, and consequently departed. Edesius for his part hastened to Tyre to see his parents and kindred; but Frumentius arriving at Alexandria, reported the affair to Athanasius the bishop, who had but recently been invested with that dignity; and acquainting him both with the particulars of his wanderings and the hopes Indians had of receiving Christianity.[2] He also begged him to send a bishop and clergy there, and by no means to neglect those who might thus be brought to salvation. Athanasius having considered how this could be most profitably effected, requested Frumentius himself to accept the bishopric, declaring that he could appoint no one more suitable than he was. Accordingly this was done; Frumentius invested with episcopal authority, returned to India and became there a preacher of the Gospel, and built several churches, being aided also by divine grace, he performed various miracles, healing with the souls also the bodily diseases of many. Rufinus assures us that he heard these facts from Edesius, who was afterwards ordained to the priesthood at Tyre.[3]

---

[1] 'In this chapter Socrates has translated Rufinus (*H. E.* I. 9) almost word for word; and calls those τόπους ἰδιάζοντας, which Rufinus has termed *conventicula*. Now *conventicula* are properly private places wherein collects or short prayers are made; and from these places churches are distinguished, which belong to the right of the public, and are not in the power of any private person. It is to be observed that there are reasons for thinking that this conversion of the Indians by Frumentius happened in the reign of Constantius and not of Constantine' (Valesius). See also Euseb. *H. E.* V. 10, attributing an earlier work to the apostles Matthew and Bartholomew;

and Cave, *Lives of the Apostles*. The Indians mentioned in this chapter are no other than the Abyssinians. The name India is used as an equivalent of Ethiopia. The christianization of Ethiopia is attributed by the Ethiopians in their own records to Fremonatos and Sydracos. See Ludolf *Hist. Eth.* III. 2.

[2] Christianity here must mean Christian instruction.

[3] εὐκτήρια: see note 5, chap. 17 above.

CHAPTER XX.

In what Manner the Iberians were converted to Christianity.

It is now proper to relate how the Iberians[1] about the same time became proselytes to the faith. A certain woman leading a devout and chaste life, was, in the providential ordering of God, taken captive by the Iberians. Now these Iberians dwelt near the Euxine Sea, and are a colony of the Iberians of Spain. Accordingly the woman in her captivity exercised[2] herself among the barbarians in the practice of virtue: for she not only maintained the most rigid continence, but spent much time in fastings and prayers. The barbarians observing this were astonished at the strangeness of her conduct. It happened then that the king's son, then a mere babe, was attacked with disease; the queen, according to the custom of the country, sent the child to other women to be cured, in the hope that their experience would supply a remedy. After the infant had been carried around by its nurse without obtaining relief from any of the women, he was at length brought to this captive. She had no knowledge of the medical art, and applied no material remedy; but taking the child and laying it on her bed which was made of horsecloth, in the presence of other females, she simply said, 'Christ, who healed many, will heal this child also'; then having prayed in addition to this expression of faith, and called upon God, the boy was immediately restored, and continued well from that period. The report of this miracle spread itself far and wide among the barbarian women, and soon reached the queen, so that the captive became very celebrated. Not long afterwards the queen herself having fallen sick sent for the captive woman. Inasmuch as she being a person of modest and retiring manners excused herself from going, the queen was conveyed to her. The captive did the same to her as she had done to her son before; and immediately the disease was removed. And the queen thanked the stranger; but she replied, 'this work is not mine, but Christ's, who is the Son of God that made the world'; she therefore exhorted her to call upon him, and acknowledge the true God. Amazed at his wife's sudden restoration to health, the king of the Iberians wished to requite with gifts her whom he had understood to be the means of effecting these cures; she however said that she needed not riches, inasmuch as she possessed as riches the consolations of religion; but that she would regard as the greatest present he could offer her, his recognition of the God whom she worshiped and declared. With this she sent back the gifts. This answer the king treasured up in his mind, and going forth to the chase the next day, the following circumstance occurred: a mist and thick darkness covered the mountain tops and forests where he was hunting, so that their sport was embarrassed, and their path became inextricable. In this perplexity the prince earnestly invoked the gods whom he worshiped; and as it availed nothing, he at last determined to implore the assistance of the captive's God; when scarcely had he begun to pray, ere the darkness arising from the mist was completely dissipated. Wondering at that which was done, he returned to his palace rejoicing, and related to his wife what had happened; he also immediately sent for the captive stranger, and begged her to inform him who that God was whom she adored. The woman on her arrival caused the king of the Iberians to become a preacher of Christ: for having believed in Christ through this devoted woman, he convened all the Iberians who were under his authority; and when he had declared to them what had taken place in reference to the cure of his wife and child not only, but also the circumstances connected with the chase, he exhorted them to worship the God of the captive. Thus, therefore, both the king and the queen were made preachers of Christ, the one addressing their male, and the other their female subjects. Moreover, the king having ascertained from his prisoner the plan on which churches were constructed among the Romans, ordered a church to be built, and immediately provided all things necessary for its erection; and the edifice was accordingly commenced. But when they came to set up the pillars, Divine Providence interposed for the confirmation of the inhabitants in the faith; for one of the columns remained immovable, and no means were found capable of moving it; but their ropes broke and their machinery fell to pieces; at length the workmen gave up all further effort and departed. Then was proved the reality of the captive's faith in the following manner: going to the place at night without the knowledge of any one, she spent the whole time in prayer; and by the power of God the pillar was raised, and stood erect in the air above its base, yet so as not to touch it. At daybreak the king, who was an intelligent person, came himself to inspect the work, and seeing the pillar suspended in this position

---

[1] These Iberians dwelt on the east shore of the Black Sea in the present region of Georgia. What their relation to the Spanish Iberians was, or why both the peoples had the same name it is not possible to know at present. It was probably not the one suggested by Socrates. For a similar identity of name in peoples living widely apart, compare the Gauls of Europe and the Galatæ of Asia.

[2] ἐφιλοσόφει: the ethical sense here attached to the word became very common after the time of the Stoics and their attempt to make ethics the basis and starting-point of philosophy.

without support, both he and his attendants were amazed. Shortly after, in fact before their very eyes, the pillar descended on its own pedestal, and there remained fixed. Upon this the people shouted, attesting the truth of the king's faith, and hymning the praise of the God of the captive. They believed thenceforth, and with eagerness raised the rest of the columns, and the whole building was soon completed. An embassy was afterwards sent to the Emperor Constantine, requesting that henceforth they might be in alliance with the Romans, and receive from them a bishop and consecrated clergy, since they sincerely believed in Christ. Rufinus says that he learned these facts from Bacurius,[3] who was formerly one of the petty princes[4] of the Iberians, but subsequently went over to the Romans, and was made a captain of the military force in Palestine; being at length entrusted with the supreme command in the war against the tyrant Maximus, he assisted the Emperor Theodosius. In this way then, during the days of Constantine, were the Iberians also converted to Christianity.

CHAPTER XXI.

Of Anthony the Monk.

WHAT sort of a man the monk Anthony was, who lived in the same age, in the Egyptian desert, and how he openly contended with devils, clearly detecting their devices and wily modes of warfare, and how he performed many miracles, it would be superfluous for us to say; for Athanasius, bishop of Alexandria, has anticipated us, having devoted an entire book to his biography.[1] Of such good men there was a large number at one time during the years of the Emperor Constantine.

CHAPTER XXII.

Of Manes, the Founder of the Manichæan Heresy, and on his Origin.

BUT amidst the good wheat, tares are accustomed to spring up; for envy loves to plot insidiously against the good. Hence it was that a little while before the time of Constantine, a species of heathenish Christianity made its appearance together with that which was real; just as false prophets sprang up among the true,

and false apostles among the true apostles. For at that time a dogma of Empedocles, the heathen philosopher, by means of Manichæus, assumed the form of Christian doctrine. Eusebius Pamphilus has indeed mentioned this person in the seventh book of his Ecclesiastical History,[1] but has not entered into minute details concerning him. Wherefore, I deem it incumbent on me to supply some particulars which he has left unnoticed: thus it will be known who this Manichæus was, whence he came, and what was the nature of his presumptuous daring.

A Saracen named Scythian married a captive from the Upper Thebes. On her account he dwelt in Egypt, and having versed himself in the learning of the Egyptians, he subtly introduced the theory of Empedocles and Pythagoras among the doctrines of the Christian faith. Asserting that there were two natures, a good and an evil one, he termed, as Empedocles had done, the latter Discord, and the former Friendship. Of this Scythian, Buddas, who had been previously called Terebinthus, became a disciple; and he having proceeded to Babylon, which the Persians inhabit, made many extravagant statements respecting himself, declaring that he was born of a virgin, and brought up in the mountains. The same man afterwards composed four books, one he entitled *The Mysteries*, another *The Gospel*, a third *The Treasure*, and the fourth *Heads* [*Summaries*]; but pretending to perform some mystic rites, he was hurled down a precipice by a spirit,[2] and so perished. A certain woman at whose house he had lodged buried him, and taking possession of his property, bought a boy about seven years old whose name was Cubricus: this lad she enfranchised, and having given him a liberal education, she soon after died, leaving him all that belonged to Terebinthus, including the books he had written on the principles inculcated by Scythian. Cubricus, the freedman, taking these things with him and having withdrawn into the regions of Persia, changed his name, calling himself Manes; and disseminated the books of Buddas or Terebinthus among his deluded followers as his own. Now the contents of these treatises apparently agree with Christianity in expression, but are pagan in sentiment: for Manichæus being an atheist, incited his disciples to acknowledge a plurality of gods, and taught them to worship the sun. He also introduced the doctrine of Fate, denying human free-will; and affirmed a transmutation[3] of bodies, clearly following the opinions of Empedocles, Pythagoras, and the Egyptians. He

---

[3] Rufinus, *H. E.* I. 10, gives their story and adds that Bacurius was a faithful and religious person and rendered service to Theodosius in his war with Eugenius.

[4] βασιλίσκος: lit. ' little king.'

[1] Athanasius' *Life of Anthony* is included in the editions of his works, such as the Benedictine (1698), that of Padua (1777). On Anthony, see also Soz. I. 3; II. 31, 34.

[1] Cf. Eus. *H. E.* VII. 31. The literature of Manichæism is voluminous and will be found in Smith, *Dict. of the Bible*, as well as encyclopædias like Herzog, McClintock and Strong, &c.

[2] πνεύματος: possibly ' wind.'

[3] μετενσωμάτωσιν, the converse of metempsychosis.

denied that Christ existed in the flesh, asserting that he was an apparition; and rejected moreover the law and the prophets, calling himself the 'Comforter,'—all of which dogmas are totally at variance with the orthodox faith of the church. In his epistles he even dared to call himself an apostle; but for a pretension so unfounded he brought upon himself merited retribution in the following manner. The son of the Persian monarch having been attacked with disease, his father became anxious for his recovery, and left no means untried in order to effect it; and as he had heard of the wonder-working of Manichæus, and thinking that these miracles were real, he sent for him as an apostle, trusting that through him his son might be restored. He accordingly presented himself at court, and with his assumed manner undertook the treatment of the young prince. But the king seeing that the child died in his hands shut up the deceiver in prison, with the intention of putting him to death. However, he contrived to escape, and fled into Mesopotamia; but the king of Persia having discovered that he was dwelling there, caused him to be brought thence by force, and after having flayed him alive, he stuffed his skin with chaff, and suspended it in front of the gate of the city. These things we state not having manufactured them ourselves, but collected from a book entitled *The disputation of Archelaus bishop of Caschara* (one of the cities of Mesopotamia).[4] For Archelaus himself states that he disputed with Manichæus face to face, and mentions the circumstances connected with his life to which we have now alluded. Envy thus delights, as we before remarked, to be insidiously at work in the midst of a prosperous condition of affairs. But for what reason the goodness of God permits this to be done, whether he wishes thereby to bring into activity the excellence of the principles of the church, and to utterly break down the self-importance which is wont to unite itself with faith; or for what other cause, is, at the same time, a difficult question, and not relevant to the present discussion. For our object is neither to examine the soundness of doctrinal views, nor to analyze the mysterious reasons for the providences and judgments of God; but to detail as faithfully as possible the history of transactions which have taken place in the churches. The way in which the superstition of the Manichæans sprang up a little before the time of Constantine has been thus described; now let us return to the times and events which are the proper subjects of this history.

CHAPTER XXIII.

Eusebius Bishop of Nicomedia, and Theognis Bishop of Nicæa, having recovered Confidence, endeavor to subvert the Nicene Creed, by plotting against Athanasius.

THE partisans of Eusebius and Theognis having returned from their exile, these latter were reinstated in their churches, having expelled, as we observed, those who had been ordained in their stead. Moreover, they came into great consideration with the emperor, who honored them exceedingly, as those who had returned from error to the orthodox faith. They, however, abused the license thus afforded them, by exciting greater commotions in the world than they had done before; being instigated to this by two causes—on the one hand the Arian heresy with which they had been previously infected, and bitter animosity against Athanasius on the other, because he had so vigorously withstood them in the Synod while the articles of faith were under discussion. And in the first place they objected to the ordination of Athanasius partly as a person unworthy of the prelacy, and partly because he had been elected by disqualified persons. But when Athanasius had shown himself superior to this calumny (for having assumed control of the church of Alexandria, he ardently contended for the Nicene creed), then Eusebius exerted himself to the utmost insidiously to cause the removal of Athanasius and to bring Arius back to Alexandria; for he thought that thus only he should be able to expunge the doctrine of consubstantiality, and introduce Arianism. Eusebius therefore wrote to Athanasius, desiring him to re-admit Arius and his adherents into the church. Now the tone of his letter indeed was that of entreaty, but openly he menaced him. And as Athanasius would by no means accede to this, he endeavored to induce the emperor to give Arius an audience, and then permit him to return to Alexandria: and by what means he attained his object, I shall mention in its proper place. Meanwhile before this another commotion was raised in the church. In fact, her own children again disturbed her peace. Eusebius Pamphilus says,[1] that immediately after the Synod, Egypt became agitated by intestine divisions: not assigning, however, the reason for this, so that hence he has won the reputation of disingenuousness, and of avoiding to specify the causes of

---

[4] The more commonly known name of the town is 'Carrha,' and the exact title of Archelaus' work as it appears in Valesius' *Annotationes* [ed. of 1677, see Introd. p. xvi.] is *Disputatio adversus* *Manichæum*. It constitutes p. 197–203 of the *Annotationes*, and is in Latin. It has been published also in Latin by L. A. Zacagui in his *collectanea monumentorum veterum Ecclesiæ Græcæ ac Latinæ*, 1698.

[1] Euseb. *Life of Const.* III. 23.

these dissensions, from a determination on his part not to give his sanction to the proceedings at Nicæa. Yet as we ourselves have discovered from various letters which the bishops wrote to one another after the Synod, the term *homoousios* troubled some of them. So that while they occupied themselves in a too minute investigation of its import, they roused the strife against each other; it seemed not unlike a contest in the dark; for neither party appeared to understand distinctly the grounds on which they calumniated one another. Those who objected to the word *homoousios*, conceived that those who approved it favored the opinion of Sabellius[2] and Montanus;[3] they therefore called them blasphemers, as subverting the existence of the Son of God. And again the advocates of this term, charging their opponents with polytheism, inveighed against them as introducers of heathen superstitions. Eustathius, bishop of Antioch, accuses Eusebius Pamphilus of perverting the Nicene Creed; Eusebius again denies that he violates that exposition of the faith, and recriminates, saying that Eustathius was a defender of the opinion of Sabellius. In consequence of these misunderstandings, each of them wrote as if contending against adversaries: and although it was admitted on both sides that the Son of God has a distinct person and existence, and all acknowledged that there is one God in three Persons, yet from what cause I am unable to divine, they could not agree among themselves, and therefore could in no way endure to be at peace.

CHAPTER XXIV.

Of the Synod held at Antioch, which deposed Eustathius, Bishop of Antioch, on whose account a Sedition broke out and almost ruined the City.

HAVING therefore convened a Synod at Antioch, they deposed Eustathius, as a supporter of the Sabellian heresy, rather than of the tenets which the council at Nicæa had formulated. As some affirm [this measure was taken] for other and unsatisfactory reasons, though none other have been openly assigned: this is a matter of common occurrence; the bishops are accustomed to do this in all cases, accusing and pronouncing impious those whom they depose, but not explaining their warrant for so doing. George, bishop of Laodicea in Syria, one of the

number of those who abominated the term *homoousios*, assures us in his *Encomium of Eusebius Emisenus*, that they deposed Eustathius as favoring Sabellianism, on the impeachment of Cyrus, bishop of Berœa. Of Eusebius Emisenus we shall speak elsewhere in due order.[1] George has written of Eustathius [somewhat inconsistently]; for after asserting that he was accused by Cyrus of maintaining the heresy of Sabellius, he tells us again that Cyrus himself was convicted of the same error, and degraded for it. Now how was it possible that Cyrus should accuse Eustathius as a Sabellian, when he inclined to Sabellianism himself? It appears likely therefore that Eustathius must have been condemned on other grounds. At that time, however, there arose a dangerous sedition at Antioch on account of his deposition: for when they proceeded to the election of a successor, so fierce a dissension was kindled, as to threaten the whole city with destruction. The populace was divided into two factions, one of which vehemently contended for the translation of Eusebius Pamphilus from Cæsarea in Palestine to Antioch; the other equally insisted on the reinstatement of Eustathius. And the populace of the city were infected with the spirit of partisanship in this quarrel among the Christians, a military force was arrayed on both sides with hostile intent, so that a bloody collision would have taken place, had not God and the dread of the emperor repressed the violence of the multitude. For the emperor through letters, and Eusebius by refusing to accept the bishopric, served to allay the ferment: on which account that prelate was exceedingly admired by the emperor, who wrote to him commending his prudent determination, and congratulating him as one who was considered worthy of being bishop not of one, city merely, but of almost the whole world. Consequently it is said that the episcopal chair of the church at Antioch was vacant for eight consecutive years after this period;[2] but at length by the exertions of those who aimed at the subversion of the Nicene creed, Euphronius was duly installed. This is the amount of my information respecting the Synod held at Antioch on account of Eustathius. Immediately after these events Eusebius, who had long before left Berytus, and was at that time presiding over the church at Nicomedia, strenuously exerted himself in connection to those of his party, to bring back Arius to Alexandria. But how they managed to effect this, and by what means the emperor was pre-

---

[2] Cf. ch. 5, and note.
[3] It is not clear why Socrates joins the name of Montanus to that of Sabellius; the former was undoubtedly in accord with the common doctrine of the church as to the Trinity. Cf. Epiphan. *Hær.* XLVIII. and Tertullian *ad. Praxeam.* It was, however, frequently alleged by various writers of the age that Montanus and the Montanists held erroneous views concerning the Godhead. See Eus. *H. E.* V. 16.

[1] See II. 9.
[2] Socrates is in error here, as according to Eusebius (*H. E.* X. 1), immediately after the deposition of Eustathius and his own refusal of the bishopric of Antioch, Paulinus was transferred there from the see of Tyre. This was in 329 A.D., so that no vacancy of eight years intervened.

vailed on to admit both Arius and with him Euzoïus into his presence must now be related.

CHAPTER XXV.

Of the Presbyter who exerted himself for the Recall of Arius.[1]

THE Emperor Constantine had a sister named Constantia, the widow of Licinius, who had for some time shared the imperial dignity with Constantine, but had assumed tyrannical powers and had been put to death in consequence. This princess maintained in her household establishment a certain confidential presbyter, tinctured with the dogmas of Arianism; Eusebius and others having prompted him, he took occasion in his familiar conversations with Constantia, to insinuate that the Synod had done Arius injustice, and that the common report concerning him was not true. Constantia gave full credence to the presbyter's assertions, but durst not report them to the emperor. Now it happened that she became dangerously ill, and her brother visited her daily. As the disease became aggravated and she expected to die, she commended this presbyter to the emperor, testifying to his diligence and piety, as well as his devoted loyalty to his sovereign. She died soon after, whereupon the presbyter became one of the most confidential persons about the emperor; and having gradually increased in freedom of speech, he repeated to the emperor what he had before stated to his sister, affirming that Arius had no other views than the sentiments avowed by the Synod; and that if he were admitted to the imperial presence, he would give his full assent to what the Synod had decreed: he added, moreover, that he had been unreasonably slandered. The presbyter's words appeared strange to the emperor, and he said, 'If Arius subscribes with the Synod and holds its views, I will both give him an audience, and send him back to Alexandria with honor.' Having thus said, he immediately wrote to him in these words:

Victor Constantine Maximus Augustus, to Arius.

It was intimated to your reverence some time since, that you might come to my court, in order to obtain an interview with us. We are not a little surprised that you did not do this immediately. Wherefore having at once mounted a public vehicle, hasten to arrive at our court; that when you have experienced our clemency and regard for you, you may return to your own country. May God protect you, beloved. Dated the twenty-fifth of November.

This was the letter of the emperor to Arius. And I cannot but admire the ardent zeal which the prince manifested for religion : for it appears from this document that he had often before exhorted Arius to change his views, inasmuch as he censures his delaying to return to the truth, although he had himself written frequently to him. Now on the receipt of this letter, Arius came to Constantinople accompanied by Euzoïus, whom Alexander had divested of his deaconship when he excommunicated Arius and his partisans. The emperor accordingly admitted them to his presence, and asked them whether they would agree to the creed. And when they readily gave their assent, he ordered them to deliver to him a written statement of their faith.

CHAPTER XXVI.

Arius, on being recalled, presents a Recantation to the Emperor, and pretends to accept the Nicene Creed.

THEY having drawn up a declaration to the following effect, presented it to the emperor.

'Arius and Euzoïus, to our Most Religious and Pious Lord, the Emperor Constantine.

'In accordance with the command of your devout piety, sovereign lord, we declare our faith, and before God profess in writing, that we and our adherents believe as follows :

'We believe in one God the Father Almighty : and in the Lord Jesus Christ his Son, who was begotten[1] of him before all ages, God the Word through whom all things were made, both those which are in the heavens and those upon the earth; who descended, and became incarnate, and suffered, and rose again, ascended into the heavens, and will again come to judge the living and the dead. [We believe] also in the Holy Spirit, and in the resurrection of the flesh, and in the life of the coming age, and in the kingdom of the heavens, and in one Catholic Church of God, extending from one end of the earth to the other.

'This faith we have received from the holy gospels, the Lord therein saying to his disciples :[2] "Go and teach all nations, baptizing them in the name of the Father, and of the Son, and of the Holy Spirit." If we do not so believe and truly receive the Father, the Son, and the Holy Spirit, as the whole Catholic Church and the holy

---

[1] Cf. Rufinus, *H. E.* I. 11. The fact that the name of this presbyter is not mentioned, and Athanasius' apparent ignorance of the story, together with the untrustworthiness of Rufinus, throw suspicion on the authenticity of this account. Cf. also ch. 39, note 2.

[1] The old English translation rendered 'made' on the assumption that the Greek was γεγενημένον, not γεγεννημένον. So also Valesius read and translated '*factum*'; but Bright without mentioning any variant reading, gives γεγεννημένον, and we have ventured to translate accordingly.

[2] Matt. xxviii. 9.

Scriptures teach (in which we believe in every respect), God is our judge both now, and in the coming judgment. Wherefore we beseech your piety, most devout emperor, that we who are persons consecrated to the ministry, and holding the faith and sentiments of the church and of the holy Scriptures, may by your pacific and devoted piety be reunited to our mother, the Church, all superfluous questions and disputings being avoided : that so both we and the whole church being at peace, may in common offer our accustomed prayers for your tranquil reign, and on behalf of your whole family.'

CHAPTER XXVII.

Arius having returned to Alexandria with the Emperor's Consent, and not being received by Athanasius, the Partisans of Eusebius bring Many Charges against Athanasius before the Emperor.

ARIUS having thus satisfied the emperor, returned to Alexandria. But his artifice for suppressing the truth did not succeed ; for on his arrival at Alexandria, as Athanasius would not receive him, but turned away from him as a pest, he attempted to excite a fresh commotion in that city by disseminating his heresy. Then indeed both Eusebius' himself wrote, and prevailed on the emperor also to write, in order that Arius and his partisans might be readmitted into the church. Athanasius nevertheless wholly refused to receive them, and wrote to inform the emperor in reply, that it was impossible for those who had once rejected the faith, and had been anathematized, to be again received into communion on their return. But the emperor, provoked at this answer, menaced Athanasius in these terms :

' Since you have been apprised of my will, afford unhindered access into the church to all those who are desirous of entering it. For if it shall be intimated to me that you have prohibited any of those claiming to be reunited to the church, or have hindered their admission, I will forthwith send some one who at my command shall depose you, and drive you into exile.'

The emperor wrote thus from a desire of promoting the public good, and because he did not wish to see the church ruptured ; for he labored earnestly to bring them all into harmony. Then indeed the partisans of Eusebius, ill-disposed towards Athanasius, imagining they had found a seasonable opportunity, welcomed the emperor's displeasure as an auxiliary to their own purpose : and on this account they raised a great disturbance, endeavoring to eject him from his bishopric ; for they entertained the hope

that the Arian doctrine would prevail only upon the removal of Athanasius. The chief conspirators against him were Eusebius bishop of Nicomedia, Theognis of Nicæa, Maris of Chalcedon, Ursacius of Singidnum in Upper Mœsia, and Valens of Mursa in Upper Pannonia. These persons suborn by bribes certain of the Melitian heresy to fabricate various charges against Athanasius ; and first they accuse him through the Melitians Ision, Eudæmon and Callinicus, of having ordered the Egyptians to pay a linen garment as tribute to the church at Alexandria. But this calumny was immediately disproved by Alypius and Macarius, presbyters of the Alexandrian church, who then happened to be at Nicomedia ; they having convinced the emperor that these statements to the prejudice of Athanasius were false. Wherefore the emperor by letter severely censured his accusers, but urged Athanasius to come to him. But before he came the Eusebian faction anticipating his arrival, added to their former accusation the charge of another crime of a still more serious nature than the former ; charging Athanasius with plotting against his sovereign, and with having sent for treasonable purposes a chest full of gold to one Philumenus. When, however, the emperor had himself investigated this matter at Psamathia, which is in the suburbs of Nicomedia, and had found Athanasius innocent, he dismissed him with honor ; and wrote with his own hand to the church at Alexandria to assure them that their bishop had been falsely accused. It would indeed have been both proper and desirable to have passed over in silence the subsequent attacks which the Eusebians made upon Athanasius, lest from these circumstances the Church of Christ should be judged unfavorably of by those who are adverse to its interests.[1] But since having been already committed to writing, they have become known to everybody, I have on that account deemed it necessary to make as cursory allusion to these things as possible, the particulars of which would require a special treatise. Whence the slanderous accusation originated, and the character of those who devised it, I shall now therefore state in brief. Mareotes[2] is a district of Alexandria ; there are contained in it very many villages, and an abundant population, with numerous splendid churches ; these churches are all under the jurisdiction of the bishop of Alexandria, and are

---

[1] From the sentiments expressed here may be inferred the respect of the author for the church. His view on the suppression of facts which did not redound to the honor of the church does not show a very high ideal of history, but it bespeaks a laudable regard for the good name of Christianity.

[2] This description is probably dependent on Athanasius, who says in his *Apologia contra Arianos*, 85, 'Mareotes is a region of Alexandria. In that region there never was a bishop or a deputy bishop; but the churches of the whole region are subject to the bishop of Alexandria. Each of the presbyters has separate villages, which are numerous, — sometimes ten or more.' Ischyras was probably a resident of one of the obscurest of these villages;

subject to his city as parishes.[3] There was in this region a person named Ischyras, who had been guilty of an act deserving of many deaths;[4] for although he had never been admitted to holy orders, he had the audacity to assume the title of presbyter, and to exercise sacred functions belonging to the priesthood. But having been detected in his sacrilegious career, he made his escape thence and sought refuge in Nicomedia, where he implored the protection of the party of Eusebius; who from their hatred to Athanasius, not only received him as a presbyter, but even promised to confer upon him the dignity of the episcopacy, if he would frame an accusation against Athanasius, listening as a pretext for this to whatever stories Ischyras had invented. For he spread a report that he had suffered dreadfully in consequence of an assault; and that Macarius had rushed furiously toward the altar, had overturned the table, and broken a mystical cup: he added also that he had burnt the sacred books. As a reward for this accusation, the Eusebian faction, as I have said, promised him a bishopric; foreseeing that the charges against Macarius would involve, along with the accused party, Athanasius, under whose orders he would seem to have acted. But this charge they formulated later; before it they devised another full of the bitterest malignity, to which I shall now advert. Having by some means, I know not what, obtained a man's hand; whether they themselves had murdered any one, and cut off his hand, or had severed it from some dead body, God knows and the authors of the deed: but be that as it may, they publicly exposed it as the hand of Arsenius, a Melitian bishop, while they kept the alleged owner of it concealed. This hand, they asserted, had been made use of by Athanasius in the performance of certain magic arts; and therefore it was made the gravest ground of accusation which these calumniators had concerted against him: but as it generally happens, all those who entertained any pique against Athanasius came forward at the same time with a variety of other charges. When the emperor was informed of these proceedings, he wrote to his nephew Dalmatius the censor, who then had his residence at Antioch in Syria, directing him to order the accused parties to be brought before him, and after due investigation, to inflict punishment on such as might be convicted. He also sent thither Eusebius and Theognis, that the case might be tried in their presence. When Athanasius knew that he was to be summoned before the censor, he sent into Egypt to make a strict search after

Arsenius; and he ascertained indeed that he was secreted there, but was unable to apprehend him, because he often changed his place of concealment. Meanwhile the emperor suppressed the trial which was to have been held before the censor, on the following account.

CHAPTER XXVIII.

On Account of the Charges against Athanasius, the Emperor convokes a Synod of Bishops at Tyre.

THE emperor had ordered a Synod of bishops to be present at the consecration of the church which he had erected at Jerusalem. He therefore directed that, as a secondary matter, they should on their way first assemble at Tyre, to examine into the charges against Athanasius; in order that all cause of contention being removed there, they might the more peacefully perform the inaugural ceremonies[1] in the dedication of the church of God. This was the thirtieth year of Constantine's reign, and sixty bishops were thus convened at Tyre from various places, on the summons of Dionysius the consul. As to Macarius the presbyter, he was conducted from Alexandria in chains, under a military escort; while Athanasius was unwilling to go thither, not so much from dread, because he was innocent of the charges made, as because he feared lest any innovations should be made on the decisions of the council at Nicæa; he was, however, constrained to be present by the menacing letters of the emperor. For it had been written him that if he did not come voluntarily, he should be brought by force.

CHAPTER XXIX.

Of Arsenius, and his Hand which was said to have been cut off.

THE special providence of God drove Arsenius also to Tyre; for, disregarding the injunctions he had received from the accusers who had bribed him, he went thither disguised to see what would be done. It by some means happened that the servants of Archelaus, the governor of the province, heard some persons at an inn affirm that Arsenius, who was reported to have been murdered, was concealed in the house of one of the citizens. Having heard this and marked the individuals by whom this statement was made, they communicated the information to their master, who causing strict search to be made for the man immediately,

---

and it can be seen that what is said of his doings here could easily come to pass.

[3] παροικία = later '. parochia'; hence the derivatives.

[4] Another evidence of the author's reverence for the institutions of religion. For subsequent history of Ischyras, see II. 20.

[1] ἐπιβατηρια: lit. 'ceremonies performed at embarkation.'

discovered and properly secured him; after which he gave notice to Athanasius that he need not be under any alarm, inasmuch as Arsenius was alive and there present. Arsenius on being apprehended, at first denied that he was the person; but Paul, bishop of Tyre, who had formerly known him, established his identity. Divine providence having thus disposed matters, Athanasius was shortly after summoned by the Synod; and as soon as he presented himself, his traducers exhibited the hand, and pressed their charge. He managed the affair with great prudence, for he enquired of those present, as well as of his accusers, who were the persons who knew Arsenius? and several having answered that they knew him, he caused Arsenius to be introduced, having his hands covered by his cloak. Then he again asked them, 'Is this the person who has lost a hand?' All were astonished at the unexpectedness of this procedure, except those who knew whence the hand had been cut off; for the rest thought that Arsenius was really deficient of a hand, and expected that the accused would make his defense in some other way. But Athanasius turning back the cloak of Arsenius on one side showed one of the man's hands; again, while some were supposing that the other hand was wanting, permitting them to remain a short time in doubt, afterward he turned back the cloak on the other side and exposed the other hand. Then, addressing himself to those present, he said, 'Arsenius, as you see, is found to have two hands: let my accusers show the place whence the third was cut off.'[1]

CHAPTER XXX.

Athanasius is found Innocent of what he was accused; his Accusers take to Flight.

MATTERS having been brought to this issue with regard to Arsenius, the contrivers of this imposture were reduced to perplexity; and Achab,[1] who was also called John, one of the principal accusers, having slipped out of court in the tumult, effected his escape. Thus Athanasius cleared himself from this charge, without having recourse to any pleading;[2] for he was confident that the sight only of Arsenius alive would confound his calumniators.

---

[1] A full account of the circumstances narrated in this and the following chapters is given by Athanasius in his *Apol. contra Arianos*, 65, 71 and 72. Parallel accounts may also be found in Sozom. II. 25; Theodoret, *H. E.* I. 28; Rufinus, *H. E.* X. 17; Philostorgius, II. 11.

[1] In Athanasius' account (*Apol. c. Arian.* 65) this man's name is given as Ἀρχαφ (Archaph), which is an Egyptian name; its assonance with the biblical Ἀχαάβ may have made the latter a current appellation. John was no doubt his monastic name.

[2] παραγραφή, legal term; γραφή = 'indictment,' παραγραφή = 'demurrer,' so used by Isocrates, Demosthenes, &c., of the classical authors.

CHAPTER XXXI.

When the Bishops will not listen to Athanasius' Defense on the Second Charge, he betakes himself to the Emperor.

BUT in refuting the false allegations against Macarius, he made use of legal forms; taking exception in the first place to Eusebius and his party, as his enemies, protesting against the injustice of any man's being tried by his adversaries. He next insisted on its being proved that his accuser Ischyras had really obtained the dignity of presbyter; for so he had been designated in the indictment. But as the judges would not allow any of these objections, the case of Macarius was entered into, and the informers being found deficient of proofs, the hearing of the matter was postponed, until some persons should have gone into Mareotis, in order that all doubtful points might be examined on the spot. Athanasius seeing that those very individuals were to be sent to whom he had taken exception (for the persons sent were Theognis, Maris, Theodorus, Macedonius, Valens, and Ursacius), exclaimed that 'their procedure was both treacherous and fraudulent; for that it was unjust that the presbyter Macarius should be detained in bonds, while the accuser together with the judges who were his adversaries, were permitted to go, in order that an *ex parte* collection of the facts in evidence might be made.' Having made this protest before the whole Synod and Dionysius the governor of the province, and finding that no one paid any attention to his appeal, he privately withdrew. Those, therefore, who were sent to Mareotis, having made an *ex parte* investigation, held that what the accuser said was true.

CHAPTER XXXII.

On the Departure of Athanasius, those who composed the Synod vote his Deposition.

THUS Athanasius departed, hastening to the emperor, and the Synod in the first place condemned him in his absence; and when the result of the enquiry which had been instituted at Mareotis was presented, they voted to depose him; loading him with opprobrious epithets in their sentence of deposition, but being wholly silent respecting the disgraceful defeat of the charge of murder brought by his calumniators. They moreover received into communion Arse-

---

[1] ἐκ μονομεροῦς, Lat. *ex parte;* the term, however, is not restricted to this technical sense, but may be used of any form of partiality. Cf. Sophocles' *Greek Lex. of Rom. and Byz.* As already noted in the Intro. p. ix, Harnack denies that there is any special juristic knowledge shown here; it must be conceded that the language used is such as might have been at the command of any intelligent and educated non-professional man.

nius, who was reported to have been murdered; and he who had formerly been a bishop of the Melitian heresy subscribed to the deposition of Athanasius as bishop of the city of Hypselopolis. Thus by an extraordinary course of circumstances, the alleged victim of assassination by Athanasius, was found alive to assist in deposing him.

CHAPTER XXXIII.

The Members of the Synod proceed from Tyre to Jerusalem, and having celebrated the Dedication of the ' New Jerusalem,' receive Arius and his Followers into Communion.

LETTERS in the meantime were brought from the emperor directing those who composed the Synod to hasten to the *New Jerusalem:* [1] having therefore immediately left Tyre, they set forward with all despatch to Jerusalem, where, after celebrating a festival in connection with the consecration of the place, they readmitted Arius [2] and his adherents into communion, in obedience, as they said, to the wishes of the emperor, who had signified in his communication to them, that he was fully satisfied respecting the faith of Arius and Euzoïus. They moreover wrote to the church at Alexandria,[3] stating that all envy being now banished, the affairs of the church were established in peace : and that since Arius had by his recantation acknowledged the truth, it was but just that, being thenceforth a member of the church, he should also be henceforth received by them, alluding to the banishment of Athanasius [in their statement that ' all envy was now banished']. At the same time they sent information of what had been done to the emperor, in terms nearly to the same effect. But whilst the bishops were engaged in these transactions, other letters came unexpectedly from the emperor, intimating that Athanasius had fled to him for protection; and that it was necessary for them on his account to come to Constantinople. This unanticipated communication from the emperor was as follows.

CHAPTER XXXIV.

The Emperor summons the Synod to himself by Letter, in order that the Charges against Athanasius might be carefully examined before him.

VICTOR CONSTANTINE MAXIMUS AUGUSTUS, to the bishops convened at Tyre.

I am indeed ignorant of the decisions which have been made by your Council with so much turbulence and storm : but the truth seems to have been perverted by some tumultuous and disorderly proceedings : because, that is to say, in your mutual love of contention, which you seem desirous of perpetuating, you disregard the consideration of those things which are acceptable to God. It will, however, I trust, be the work of Divine Providence to dissipate the mischiefs resulting from this jealous rivalry, as soon as they shall have been detected ; and to make it apparent to us, whether ye who have been convened have had regard to truth, and whether your decisions on the subjects which have been submitted to your judgment have been made apart from partiality or prejudice. Wherefore it is indispensable that you should all without delay attend upon my piety, that you may yourselves give a strict account of your transactions. For what reason I have deemed it proper to write thus, and to summon you before me, you will learn from what follows. As I was making my entry into the city which bears our name, in this our most flourishing home, Constantinople, — and it happened that I was riding on horseback at the time, — suddenly the Bishop Athanasius, with certain ecclesiastics whom he had around him, presented himself so unexpectedly in our path, as to produce an occasion of consternation. For the Omniscient God is my witness that at first sight I did not recognize him until some of my attendants, in answer to my enquiry, informed me, as was very natural, both who he was, and what injustice he had suffered. At that time indeed I neither conversed, nor held any communication with him. But as he repeatedly entreated an audience, and I had not only refused it, but almost ordered that he should be removed from my presence, he said with greater boldness, that he petitioned for nothing more than that you might be summoned hither, in order that in our presence, he, driven by necessity to such a course, might have a fair opportunity afforded him of complaining of his wrongs. Wherefore as this seems reasonable, and consistent with the equity of my government, I willingly gave instructions that these things should be written to you. My command therefore is, that all, as many as composed the Synod convened at Tyre, should forthwith hasten to the court of our clemency, in order that from the facts themselves you may make clear the purity and integrity of your decision in my presence, whom you cannot but own to be a true servant of God. It is in consequence of the acts of my religious service towards God that peace is everywhere reigning ; and that the name of God is sincerely had in reverence even among the bar-

---

[1] See above, ch. 17.

[2] Arius, the originator of the Arian heresy, died before the council at Jerusalem; hence Valesius infers that this Arius must be another man of the same name mentioned in the encyclical of Alexander of Alexandria as a partisan of the arch-heretic. Cf. ch. 6.

[3] This letter is contained in Athanasius' *de Synod,* 21, and a portion of it in *Apol. contra Arian,* 84.

barians themselves, who until now were ignorant of the truth. Now it is evident that he who knows not the truth, does not have a true knowledge of God also: yet, as I before said, even the barbarians on my account, who am a genuine servant of God, have acknowledged and learned to worship him, whom they have perceived in very deed protecting and caring for me everywhere. So that from dread of us chiefly, they have been thus brought to the knowledge of the true God whom they now worship. Nevertheless we who pretend to have a religious veneration for (I will not say who guard) the holy mysteries of his church, we, I say, do nothing but what tends to discord and animosity, and to speak plainly, to the destruction of the human race. But hasten, as I have already said, all of you to us as speedily as possible: and be assured that I shall endeavor with all my power to cause that what is contained in the Divine Law may be preserved inviolate, on which neither stigma nor reproach shall be able to fasten itself; and this will come to pass when its enemies, who under covert of the sacred profession introduce numerous and diversified blasphemies, are dispersed, broken to pieces, and altogether annihilated.

CHAPTER XXXV.

The Synod not having come to the Emperor, the Partisans of Eusebius accuse Athanasius of having threatened to divert the Corn supplied to Constantinople from Alexandria: the Emperor being exasperated at this banishes Athanasius into Gaul.[1]

THIS letter rendered those who constituted the Synod very fearful, wherefore most of them returned to their respective cities. But Eusebius, Theognis, Maris, Patrophilus, Ursacius, and Valens, having gone to Constantinople, would not permit any further enquiry to be instituted concerning the broken cup, the overturned communion table, and the murder of Arsenius; but they had recourse to another calumny, informing the emperor that Athanasius had threatened to prohibit the sending of corn which was usually conveyed from Alexandria to Constantinople. They affirmed also that these menaces were heard from the lips of Athanasius by the bishops Adamantius, Anubion, Arbathion and Peter, for slander is most prevalent when the assertor of it appears to be a person worthy of credit. Hence the emperor being deceived, and excited to indignation against Athanasius

by this charge, at once condemned him to exile, ordering him to reside in the Gauls. Now some affirm that the emperor came to this decision with a view to the establishment of unity in the church, since Athanasius was inexorable in his refusal to hold any communion with Arius and his adherents. He accordingly took up his abode at Treves, a city of Gaul.

CHAPTER XXXVI.

Of Marcellus Bishop of Ancyra, and Asterius the Sophist.

THE bishops assembled at Constantinople deposed also Marcellus bishop of Ancyra, a city of Galatia Minor, on this account. A certain rhetorician of Cappadocia named Asterius having abandoned his art, and professed himself a convert to Christianity, undertook the composition of some treatises, which are still extant, in which he commended the dogmas of Arius; asserting that Christ is the power of God, in the same sense as the locust and the palmer-worm are said by Moses to be the power of God,[1] with other similar utterances. Now Asterius was in constant association with the bishops, and especially with those of their number who did not discountenance the Arian doctrine: he also attended their Synods, in the hope of insinuating himself into the bishopric of some city: but he failed to obtain ordination, in consequence of having sacrificed during the persecution.[2] Going therefore throughout the cities of Syria, he read in public the books which he had composed. Marcellus being informed of this, and wishing to counteract his influence, in his over-anxiety to confute him, fell into the diametrically opposite error; for he dared to say, as the Samosatene[3] had done, that Christ was a mere man. When the bishops then convened at Jerusalem had intelligence of these things, they took no notice of Asterius, because he was not enrolled even in the catalogue of ordained priests; but they insisted that Marcellus, as a priest, should give an account of the book which he had written. Finding that he entertained Paul of Samosata's sentiments, they required him to retract his

---

[1] Cf. Theodoret, *H. E.* I. 31. The ancient Gallia or Gaul included the modern France, Belgium, Lombardy, and Sardinia.

[1] Joel ii. 25.
[2] In the persecution under Decius (249 A.D.), those who yielded so far as to perform the heathen rites were branded with the title of 'the lapsed'; and a controversy arose later on the manner in which they should be treated. One of the consequences of lapsing was disqualification for high office in the church. See Neander, *Hist. of Christ. Ch.* Vol. I. p. 226 seq.
[3] Paul of Samosata, who has been surnamed in modern times the Socinus of the third century, was deposed in 269 A.D. by a council held at Antioch for unchristian character and unsound views. His peculiarity in the latter respect was his denial of the divinity of Jesus Christ. For fuller information, see Eus. *H. E.* VII. 30; Epiphan. *Hær.* LXVII.; Neander, *Hist. of the Christ. Ch.* Vol. I. 602 seq.; Gieselee, *Hist. of the Ch.* Vol. I. 201; Smith and Wace *Dict. of Christ. Biog.*

opinion; and he being thoroughly ashamed of himself, promised to burn his book. But the convention of bishops being hastily dissolved by the emperor's summoning them to Constantinople, the Eusebians on their arrival at that city, again took the case of Marcellus into consideration; and as Marcellus refused to fulfil his promise of burning his untimely book, those present deposed him, and sent Basil into Ancyra in his stead. Moreover Eusebius wrote a refutation of this work in three books, in which he exposed its erroneous doctrine. Marcellus however was afterwards reinstated[4] in his bishopric by the Synod at Sardica, on his assurance that his book had been misunderstood, and that on that account he was supposed to favor the Samosatene's views. But of this we shall speak more fully in its proper place.

CHAPTER XXXVII.

After the Banishment of Athanasius, Arius having been sent for by the Emperor, raises a Disturbance against Alexander Bishop of Constantinople.

WHILE these things were taking place, the thirtieth year of Constantine's reign was completed. But Arius with his adherents having returned to Alexandria, again disturbed the whole city; for the people of Alexandria were exceedingly indignant both at the restoration of this incorrigible heretic with his partisans, and also because their bishop Athanasius had been sent to exile. When the emperor was apprised of the perverse disposition of Arius, he once more ordered him to repair to Constantinople, to give an account of the commotions he had afresh endeavored to excite. It happened at that time that Alexander, who had some time before succeeded Metrophanes, presided over the church at Constantinople. That this prelate was a man of devoted piety was distinctly manifested by the conflict he entered into with Arius; for when Arius arrived and the people were divided into two factions and the whole city was thrown into confusion: some insisting that the Nicene Creed should be by no means infringed on, while others contended that the opinion of Arius was consonant to reason. In this state of affairs, Alexander was driven to straits: more especially since Eusebius of Nicomedia had violently threatened that he would cause him to be immediately deposed, unless he admitted Arius and his followers to communion. Alexander, however, was far less troubled at the thought of his own deposition as fearful of the subversion of the principles of the faith, which

they were so anxious to effect: and regarding himself as the constituted guardian of the doctrines recognized, and the decisions made by the council at Nicæa, he exerted himself to the utmost to prevent their being violated or depraved. Reduced to this extremity, he bade farewell to all logical resources, and made God his refuge, devoting himself to continued fasting and never ceased from praying. Communicating his purpose to no one, he shut himself up alone in the church called *Irene:* there going up to the altar, and prostrating himself on the ground beneath the holy communion table, he poured forth his fervent prayers weeping; and this he ceased not to do for many successive nights and days. What he thus earnestly asked from God, he received: for his petition was such a one: 'If the opinion of Arius were correct, he might not be permitted to see the day appointed for its discussion; but that if he himself held the true faith, Arius, as the author of all these evils, might suffer the punishment due to his impiety.'

CHAPTER XXXVIII.

The Death of Arius.[1]

SUCH was the supplication of Alexander. Meanwhile the emperor, being desirous of personally examining Arius, sent for him to the palace, and asked him whether he would assent to the determinations of the Synod at Nicæa. He without hesitation replied in the affirmative, and subscribed the declaration of the faith in the emperor's presence, acting with duplicity. The emperor, surprised at his ready compliance, obliged him to confirm his signature by an oath. This also he did with equal dissimulation. The way he evaded, as I have heard, was this: he wrote his own opinion on paper, and carried it under his arm, so that he then swore truly that he really held the sentiments he had written. That this is so, however, I have written from hearsay, but that he added an oath to his subscription, I have myself ascertained, from an examination of the emperor's own letters. The emperor being thus convinced, ordered that he should be received into communion by Alexander, bishop of Constantinople. It was then Saturday, and Arius was expecting to assemble with the church on the day following: but divine retribution overtook his daring criminalities. For going out of the imperial palace, attended by a crowd of Eusebian partisans like guards, he paraded proudly through the midst of the city, attracting the notice of all the people. As he

---

[4] See II. 20.

[1] For a reproduction of the circumstances related in this chapter, together with a historical estimate of them based on additional evidence, see Neander, *Hist. of the Christ. Ch.* Vol. II. p. 384–388.

approached the place called Constantine's Forum, where the column of porphyry is erected, a terror arising from the remorse of conscience seized Arius, and with the terror a violent relaxation of the bowels: he therefore enquired whether there was a convenient place near, and being directed to the back of Constantine's Forum, he hastened thither. Soon after a faintness came over him, and together with the evacuations his bowels protruded, followed by a copious hemorrhage, and the descent of the smaller intestines: moreover portions of his spleen and liver were brought off in the effusion of blood, so that he almost immediately died. The scene of this catastrophe still is shown at Constantinople, as I have said, behind the shambles in the colonnade: and by persons going by pointing the finger at the place, there is a perpetual remembrance preserved of this extraordinary kind of death. So disastrous an occurrence filled with dread and alarm the party of Eusebius, bishop of Nicomedia; and the report of it quickly spread itself over the city and throughout the whole world. As the king grew more earnest in Christianity and confessed that the confession at Nicæa was attested by God, he rejoiced at the occurrences. He was also glad because of his three sons whom he had already proclaimed Cæsars; one of each of them having been created at every successive decennial anniversary of his reign. To the eldest, whom he called Constantine, after his own name, he assigned the government of the western parts of the empire, on the completion of his first decade. His second son Constantius, who bore his grandfather's name, he constituted Cæsar in the eastern division, when the second decade had been completed. And Constans, the youngest, he invested with a similar dignity, in the thirtieth year of his own reign.

CHAPTER XXXIX.

The Emperor falls sick and dies.

A YEAR having passed, the Emperor Constantine having just entered the sixty-fifth year of his age, was taken with a sickness; he therefore left Constantinople, and made a voyage to Helenopolis, that he might try the effect of the medicinal hot springs which are found in the vicinity of that city. Perceiving, however, that his illness increased, he deferred the use of the baths; and removing from Helenopolis to Nicomedia, he took up his residence in the suburbs,

and there received Christian baptism.[1] After this he became cheerful; and making his will, appointed his three sons heirs to the empire, allotting to each one of them his portion, in accordance with the arrangements he had made while living. He also granted many privileges to the cities of Rome and Constantinople; and entrusting the custody of his will[2] to that presbyter by whose means Arius had been recalled, and of whom we have already made mention, he charged him to deliver it into no one's hand, except that of his son Constantius, to whom he had given the sovereignty of the East. After the making of his will, he survived a few days and died. Of his sons none were present at his death. A courier was therefore immediately despatched into the East, to inform Constantius of his father's decease.

CHAPTER XL.

The Funeral of the Emperor Constantine.

THE body of the emperor was placed in a coffin of gold by the proper persons, and then conveyed to Constantinople, where it was laid out on an elevated bed of state in the palace, surrounded by a guard, and treated with the same respect as when he was alive, and this was done until the arrival of one of his sons. When Constantius was come out of the eastern parts of the empire, it was honored with an imperial sepulture, and deposited in the church called *The Apostles:* which he had caused to be constructed for this very purpose, that the emperors and prelates might receive a degree of veneration but little inferior to that which was paid to the relics of the apostles. The Emperor Constantine lived sixty-five years, and reigned thirty-one. He died in the consulate of Felician and Tatian, on the twenty-second of May, in the second year of the 278th Olympiad.[3] This book, therefore, embraces a period of thirty-one years.

---

[1] It was the belief of many in the earlier ages of the church that baptism had a certain magical power purging away the sins previous to it, but having no force as regards those that might follow; this led many to postpone their baptism until disease or age warned them of the nearness of death; such delayed baptism was called 'clinic baptism,' and was discouraged by the more judicious and spiritual-minded Fathers, some of whom doubted its validity and rebuked those who delayed as actuated by selfishness and desire to indulge in sin. The church, however, encouraged it in the cases of gross offenders. Cf. Bingham, *Eccl. Antiq.* IV. 3, and XI. 11, and Bennett, *Christian Archæology*, pp. 407 and 409.

[2] Cf. Euseb. *Life of Const.* IV. 63, and Rufinus, *H. E.* I. 11. The story is, however, doubtful, as Valesius observes. It is more likely that some one of the lay officials of the government, or, as Philostorgius says, Eusebius of Nicomedia, was entrusted with this will, and not a mere presbyter. That it was probably Eusebius of Nicomedia becomes the more probable when we consider that that bishop also probably baptized Constantine.

[3] 337 A.D. The 22d of May that year was the day of Pentecost.

BOOK II.

CHAPTER I.

Introduction containing the Reason for the Author's Revision of his First and Second Books.

RUFINUS, who wrote an Ecclesiastical History in Latin,[1] has erred in respect to chronology. For he supposes that what was done against Athanasius occurred after the death of the Emperor Constantine : he was also ignorant of his exile to the Gauls and of various other circumstances. Now we in the first place wrote the first two books of our history following Rufinus ; but in writing our history from the third to the seventh, some facts we collected from Rufinus, others from different authors, and some from the narration of individuals still living. Afterward, however, we perused the writings of Athanasius, wherein he depicts his own sufferings and how through the calumnies of the Eusebian faction he was banished, and judged that more credit was due to him who had suffered, and to those who were witnesses of the things they describe, than to such as have been dependent on conjecture, and had therefore erred. Moreover, having obtained several letters of persons eminent at that period, we have availed ourselves of their assistance also in tracing out the truth as far as possible. On this account we were compelled to revise the first and second books of this history, using, however, the testimony of Rufinus where it is evident that he could not be mistaken. It should also be observed, that in our former edition, neither the sentence of deposition which was passed upon Arius, nor the emperor's letters were inserted, but simply the narration or facts in order that the history might not become bulky and weary the readers with tedious matters of detail. But in the present edition, such alterations and additions have been made for your sake, O sacred man of God, Theodore,[2] in order that you might not be ignorant what the princes wrote in their own words, as well as the decisions of the bishops in their various Synods,

wherein they continually altered the confession of faith. Wherefore, whatever we have deemed necessary we have inserted in this later edition. Having adopted this course in the first book, we shall endeavor to do the same in the consecutive portion of our history, I mean the second. On this let us now enter.

CHAPTER II.

Eusebius, Bishop of Nicomedia, and his Party, by again endeavoring to introduce the Arian Heresy, create Disturbances in the Churches.

AFTER the death of the Emperor Constantine, Eusebius, bishop of Nicomedia, and Theognis of Nicæa, imagining that a favorable opportunity had arisen, used their utmost efforts to expunge the doctrine of *homoousion*, and to introduce Arianism in its place. They, nevertheless, despaired of effecting this, if Athanasius should return to Alexandria : in order therefore to accomplish their designs, they sought the assistance of that presbyter by whose means Arius had been recalled from exile a little before. How this was done shall now be described. The presbyter in question presented the will and the request of the deceased king to his son Constantius ; who finding those dispositions in it which he was most desirous of, for the empire of the East was by his father's will apportioned to him, treated the presbyter with great consideration, loaded him with favors, and ordered that free access should be given him both to the palace and to himself. This license soon obtained for him familiar intercourse with the empress, as well as with her eunuchs. There was at that time a chief eunuch of the imperial bed-chamber named Eusebius ; him the presbyter persuaded to adopt Arian's views, after which the rest of the eunuchs were also prevailed on to adopt the same sentiments. Not only this but the empress also, under the influence of the eunuchs and the presbyters, became favorable to the tenets of Arius ; and not long after the subject was introduced to the emperor himself. Thus it became gradually diffused throughout the court, and among the officers of the imperial household and guards, until at length it spread itself over the whole population of the city. The chamberlains in

---

[1] Rufinus' *Historia Ecclesiastica*, in two books, begins with Arius and ends with Theodosius the Great. It is not very accurate, but written largely from memory. It is dedicated to Chromatius, bishop of Aquileja, and translated into Greek by Gelasius and Cyril of Jerusalem. On the edition used by Socrates, see Introd. and I. 12, note 1. Cf. also on his knowledge of Latin, II. 23, 30, and 37.
[2] ὦ ἱερὲ τοῦ Θεοῦ ἄνθρωπε Θεόδωρε; cf. Introd. p. x, also VI. Introd. and VII. 48.

the palace discussed this doctrine with the women ; and in the family of every citizen there was a logical contest. Moreover, the mischief quickly extended to other provinces and cities, the controversy, like a spark, insignificant at first, exciting in the auditors a spirit of contention : for every one who inquired the cause of the tumult, found immediately occasion for disputing, and determined to take part in the strife at the moment of making the inquiry. By general altercation of this kind all order was subverted ; the agitation, however, was confined to the cities of the East, those of Illyricum and the western parts of the empire meanwhile were perfectly tranquil, because they would not annul the decisions of the Council of Nicæa. As this affair increased, going from bad to worse, Eusebius of Nicomedia and his party looked upon popular ferment as a piece of good fortune. For only thus they thought they would be enabled to constitute some one who held their own sentiments bishop of Alexandria. But the return of Athanasius at that time defeated their purpose ; for he came thither fortified by a letter from one of the Augusti, which the younger Constantine, who bore his father's name, addressed to the people of Alexandria, from Treves, a city in Gaul.[1] A copy of this epistle is here subjoined.

CHAPTER III.

Athanasius, encouraged by the Letter of Constantine the Younger, returns to Alexandria.

Constantine Cæsar to the members of the Catholic Church of the Alexandrians.

It cannot, I conceive, have escaped the knowledge of your devout minds, that Athanasius, the expositor of the venerated law, was sent for a while unto the Gauls, lest he should sustain some irreparable injury from the perverseness of his blood-thirsty adversaries, whose ferocity continually endangered his sacred life. To evade this [perverseness], therefore, he was taken from the jaws of the men who threatened him into a city under my jurisdiction, where, as long as it was his appointed residence, he has been abundantly supplied with every necessity : although his distinguished virtue trusting in divine aid would have made light of the pressure of a more rigorous fortune. And since our sovereign, my father, Constantine Augustus of

blessed memory, was prevented by death from accomplishing his purpose of restoring this bishop to his see, and to your most sanctified piety, I have deemed it proper to carry his wishes into effect, having inherited the task from him. With how great veneration he has been regarded by us, ye will learn on his arrival among you ; nor need any one be surprised at the honor I have put upon him, since I have been alike influenced by a sense of what was due to so excellent a personage, and the knowledge of your affectionate solicitude respecting him. May Divine Providence preserve you, beloved brethren.

Relying on this letter, Athanasius came to Alexandria, and was most joyfully received by the people of the city. Nevertheless as many in it as had embraced Arianism, combining together, entered into conspiracies against him, by which frequent seditions were excited, affording a pretext to the Eusebians for accusing him to the emperor of having taken possession of the Alexandrian church on his own responsibility, in spite of the adverse judgment of a general council of bishops. So far indeed did they succeed in pressing their charges, that the emperor became exasperated, and banished him from Alexandria. How indeed this came about I shall hereafter explain.

CHAPTER IV.

On the Death of Eusebius Pamphilus, Acacius succeeds to the Bishopric of Cæsarea.

At this time Eusebius, who was bishop of Cæsarea in Palestine, and had the surname of Pamphilus, having died, Acacius, his disciple, succeeded him in the bishopric. This individual published several books, and among others a biographical sketch of his master.

CHAPTER V.

The Death of Constantine the Younger.

Not long after this the brother of the Emperor Constantius, Constantine the younger, who bore his father's name, having invaded those parts of the empire which were under the government of his younger brother Constans, engaging in a conflict with his brother's soldiery, was slain by them. This took place under the consulship of Acindynus and Proclus.[1]

---

[1] There is some difference of opinion as to the exact year of the recall of Athanasius. Baronius and others allege that this took place in 338 A.D., the year after the death of Constantine; but Valesius maintains that Athanasius was recalled the year preceding. This he infers from the words of Athanasius (*Apol. c. Arian,* 61), and the title of the letter which Constantine the younger addressed to the church in Alexandria.

[1] 340 A.D.

CHAPTER VI.

Alexander, Bishop of Constantinople, when at the Point of Death proposes the Election either of Paul or of Macedonius as his Successor.

ABOUT the same time another disturbance in addition to those we have recorded, was raised at Constantinople on the following account. Alexander, who had presided over the churches in that city, and had strenuously opposed Arius, departed this life,[1] having occupied the bishopric for twenty-three years and lived ninety-eight years in all, without having ordained any one to succeed him. But he had enjoined the proper persons to choose one of the two whom he named ; that is to say, if they desired one who was competent to teach, and of eminent piety, they should elect Paul, whom he had himself ordained presbyter, a man young indeed in years, but of advanced intelligence and prudence ; but if they wished a man of venerable aspect, and external show only of sanctity, they might appoint Macedonius, who had long been a deacon among them and was aged. Hence there arose a great contest respecting the choice of a bishop which troubled the church exceedingly ; for ever since the people were divided into two parties, one of which favored the tenets of Arius, while the other held what the Nicene Synod had defined, those who held the doctrine of consubstantiality always had the advantage during the life of Alexander, the Arians disagreeing among themselves and perpetually conflicting in opinion. But after the death of that prelate, the issue of the struggle became doubtful, the defenders of the orthodox faith insisting on the ordination of Paul, and all the Arian party espousing the cause of Macedonius. Paul therefore was ordained bishop in the church called *Irene*,[2] which is situated near the great church of *Sophia;* whose election appeared to be more in accordance with the suffrage of the deceased.

CHAPTER VII.

The Emperor Constantius ejects Paul after his Election to the Bishopric, and sending for Eusebius of Nicomedia, invests him with the Bishopric of Constantinople.

NOT long afterwards the emperor having arrived at Constantinople was highly incensed

at the consecration [of Paul] ; and having convened an assembly of bishops of Arian sentiments, he divested Paul of his dignity, and translating Eusebius from the see of Nicomedia, he appointed him bishop of Constantinople. Having done this the emperor proceeded to Antioch.

CHAPTER VIII.

Eusebius having convened Another Synod at Antioch in Syria, causes a New Creed to be promulgated.

EUSEBIUS, however, could by no means remain quiet, but as the saying is, left no stone unturned, in order to effect the purpose he had in view. He therefore causes a Synod to be convened at Antioch in Syria, under pretense of dedicating the church which the father of the Augusti had commenced, and which his son Constantius had finished in the tenth year after its foundations were laid, but with the real intention of subverting and abolishing the doctrine of the *homoousion*. There were present at this Synod ninety bishops from various cities. Maximus, however, bishop of Jerusalem, who had succeeded Macarius, did not attend, recollecting that he had been deceived and induced to subscribe the deposition of Athanasius. Neither was Julius, bishop of the great Rome,[1] there, nor had he sent a substitute, although an ecclesiastical canon[2] commands that the churches shall not make any ordinances against the opinion of the bishop of Rome. This Synod assembled at Antioch in presence of the emperor Constantius in the consulate of Marcellus and Probinus,[3] which was the fifth year after the death of Constantine, father of the Augusti. Placitus, otherwise called Flaccillus, successor to Euphronius, at that time presided over the church at Antioch. The confederates of Eusebius had previously designed to calumniate Athanasius ; accusing him in the first place of having acted contrary to a canon which they then constituted, in resuming his episcopal authority without the license of a general council of bishops, inasmuch as on his return from exile he had on his own responsibility taken possession of the church ; and then because a tumult had been excited on his entrance and many were killed in the riot ;

---

[1] Socrates is undoubtedly mistaken in setting the date of Alexander's death as late as 340 A.D. The council convened to examine and confute the charges against Athanasius met in 339 A.D., and the record at that date has it (see chap. 7) that Eusebius had taken possession of the see of Constantinople. Alexander must therefore have died before 339.
[2] So called, not because there was a saint or eminent person of that name, but on the same principle as the church called Sophia.

For the history of the latter church, see Dehio and Bezold, *Die Kirchliche Baukuns des Abendlandes*, I. p. 21.
[1] So called in distinction from the "New Rome," or Constantinople. Cf. *Canons of Council of Chalcedon*, XXVIII.
[2] The word ' canon ' here is evidently used in its general sense. There is no record of any enactment requiring the consent of the bishop of Rome to the decisions of the councils before they could be considered valid. There may have been a general understanding to that effect, having the force of an unwritten law. In any case the use of the word by Socrates is quite singular, unless we assume that he supposed there was such an enactment somewhere, as is implied by its use ordinarily.
[3] 341 A.D.

moreover that some had been scourged by him, and others brought before the tribunals. Besides they brought forward what had been determined against Athanasius at Tyre.

CHAPTER IX.

Of Eusebius of Emisa.

ON the ground of such charges as these, they proposed another bishop for the Alexandrian church, and first indeed Eusebius surnamed Emisenus. Who this person was, George, bishop of Laodicea, who was present on this occasion, informs us. For he says in the book which he has composed on his life, that Eusebius was descended from the nobility of Edessa in Mesopotamia, and that from a child he had studied the holy Scriptures;[1] that he was afterwards instructed in Greek literature by a master resident at Edessa; and finally that the sacred books were expounded to him by Patrophilus and Eusebius, of whom the latter presided over the church at Cæsarea, and the former over that at Scythopolis. Afterwards when he dwelt in Antioch, it happened that Eustathius was deposed on the accusation of Cyrus of Berœa for holding the tenets of Sabellius. Then again he associated with Euphronius, successor of Eustathius, and avoiding a bishopric, he retired to Alexandria, and there devoted himself to the study of philosophy. On his return to Antioch, he formed an intimate acquaintance with Placitus [or Flaccillus], the successor of Euphronius. At length he was ordained bishop of Alexandria, by Eusebius, bishop of Constantinople; but did not go thither in consequence of the attachment of the people of that city to Athanasius, and was therefore sent to Emisa. As the inhabitants of Emisa excited a sedition on account of his appointment, — for he was commonly charged with the study and practice of judicial astrology,[2] — he fled and came to Laodicea, to George, who has given so many historical details of him. George having taken him to Antioch, procured his being again brought back to Emisa by Placitus and Narcissus; but he was afterwards charged with holding the Sabellian views. George more elaborately describes the circumstances of his ordination and adds at the close that the emperor took him with him in his expedition against the barbarians, and that miracles were

wrought by his hand. The information given by George concerning Eusebius of Emisa may be considered reproduced at sufficient length by me here.

CHAPTER X.

The Bishops assembled at Antioch, on the Refusal of Eusebius of Emisa to accept the Bishopric of Alexandria, ordain Gregory, and change the Language of the Nicene Creed.

Now at that time Eusebius having been proposed and fearing to go to Alexandria, the Synod at Antioch designated Gregory as bishop of that church. This being done, they altered the creed; not as condemning anything in that which was set forth at Nicæa, but in fact with a determination to subvert and nullify the doctrine of consubstantiality by means of frequent councils, and the publication of various expositions of the faith, so as gradually to establish the Arian views. How these things issued we will set forth in the course of our narrative; but the epistle then promulgated respecting the faith was as follows:[1]

'We have neither become followers of Arius, — for how should we who are bishops be guided by a presbyter? — nor have we embraced any other faith than that which was set forth from the beginning. But being constituted examiners and judges of his sentiments, we admit their soundness, rather than adopt them from him: and you will recognize this from what we are about to state. We have learned from the beginning to believe in one God of the Universe, the Creator and Preserver of all things both those thought of and those perceived by the senses: and in one only-begotten Son of God, subsisting before all ages, and co-existing with the Father who begat him, through whom also all things visible and invisible were made; who in the last days according to the Father's good pleasure, descended, and assumed flesh from the holy virgin, and having fully accomplished his Father's will, that he should suffer, and rise again, and ascend into the heavens, and sit at the right hand of the Father; and is coming to judge the living and the dead, continuing King and God for ever. We believe also in the Holy Spirit. And if it is necessary to add this, we believe in the resurrection of the flesh, and the life everlasting.'

Having thus written in their first epistle, they sent it to the bishops of every city. But after remaining some time at Antioch, as if to condemn the former, they published another letter in these words:

---

[1] Sozom. *H. E.* III. 6. From the passage in Sozomen it appears that it was customary in Edessa to teach the Scriptures to boys, and that many of them thus became quite familiar with the Bible, knowing many passages by heart.

[2] μαθηματικήν. From its use in astronomy the science of mathematics soon came to be identified with that counterfeit of astronomy, — astrology. It is so used by Sextus Empiricus (616. 20; 728. 20) and by Iamblichus, *Myrt.* 277. 2.

[1] Athanas. *de Synodd.* 22, 23.

Another Exposition of the Faith.

In conformity with evangelic and apostolic tradition, we believe in one God the Father Almighty, the Creator and Framer of the universe. And in one Lord Jesus Christ, his Son, God the only-begotten, through whom all things were made: begotten of the Father before all ages, God of God, Whole of Whole, Only of Only, Perfect of Perfect, King of King, Lord of Lord; the living Word, the Wisdom, the Life, the True Light, the Way of Truth, the Resurrection, the Shepherd, the Gate; immutable and inconvertible; the unaltering image of the Divinity, Substance and Power, and Counsel and Glory of the Father; born 'before all creation'; who was in the beginning with God, God the Word, according as it is declared in the Gospel,[2] and the Word was God, by whom all things were made, and in whom all things subsist: who in the last days came down from above, and was born of the virgin according to the Scriptures; and was made man, the Mediator between God and men, the Apostle of our Faith, and the Prince of Life, as he says,[3] 'I came down from heaven, not to do mine own will, but the will of him that sent me.' Who suffered on our behalf, and rose again for us on the third day, and ascended into the heavens, and is seated at the right hand of the Father; and will come again with glory and power to judge the living and the dead. [We believe] also in the Holy Spirit, who is given to believers for their consolation, sanctification, and perfection; even as our Lord Jesus Christ commanded his disciples, saying,[4] 'Go and teach all nations, baptizing them in the name of the Father, and of the Son, and of the Holy Spirit'; that is to say of the Father who is truly the Father, of the Son who is truly the Son, and of the Holy Spirit who is truly the Holy Spirit, these words not being simply or insignificantly applied, but accurately expressing the proper subsistence, glory, and order, of each of these who are named: so that there are three in person, but one in concordance. Holding therefore this faith in the presence of God and of Christ, we anathematize all heretical and false doctrine. And if any one shall teach contrary to the sound and right faith of the Scriptures, affirming that there is or was a period or an age before the Son of God existed, let him be accursed. And if any one shall say that the Son is a creature as one of the creatures, or that he is offspring as one of the offsprings, and shall not hold each of the aforesaid doctrines as the Divine Scriptures have delivered them to us: or if any one shall teach or preach any other doctrine contrary to that which we have received, let him be accursed.

For we truly and unreservedly believe and follow all things handed down to us from the sacred Scriptures by the prophets and apostles.

Such was the exposition of the faith published by those then assembled at Antioch, to which Gregory also subscribed as bishop of Alexandria, although he had not yet entered that city. The Synod having done these things, and legislated some other canons, was dissolved. At this time it happened that public affairs also were disturbed. The nation called Franks made incursions into the Roman territories in Gaul, and at the same time there occurred violent earthquakes in the East, and especially at Antioch, which continued to suffer concussions during a whole year.

CHAPTER XI.

On the Arrival of Gregory at Alexandria, attended by a Military Escort, Athanasius flees.

AFTER these things, Syrian, the military commander, and the corps of heavy armed soldiers, five thousand in number, conducted Gregory to Alexandria; and such of the citizens as were of Arian sentiments combined with them. But it will be proper here to relate by what means Athanasius escaped the hands of those who wished to apprehend him, after his expulsion from the church. It was evening, and the people were attending the vigil there, a service[1] being expected. The commander arrived, and posted his forces in order of battle on every side of the church. Athanasius having observed what was done, considered within himself how he might prevent the people's suffering in any degree on his account: accordingly having directed the deacon to give notice of prayer, after that he ordered the recitation of a psalm; and when the melodious chant of the psalm arose, all went out through one of the church doors. While this was doing, the troops remained inactive spectators, and Athanasius thus escaped unhurt in the midst of those who were chanting the psalm, and immediately hastened to Rome. Gregory then prevailed in the church: but the people of Alexandria, being indignant at this procedure, set the church called that of Dionysius on fire. Let this be sufficient on this subject. Now Eusebius, having thus far obtained his object, sent a deputation to Julius, bishop of Rome,[2] begging that he would himself take cog-

---

[2] John i. 1.   [3] John vi. 38.   [4] Matt. xxviii. 19.

[1] συνάξεως: literally 'congregation,' from συνάγω; but later applied to any service held in the church. In mod. Συναξάριον, 'Prayer-book.'
[2] So also Sozom. III. 7. But according to Valesius, both Socrates and Sozomen are here mistaken, and Eusebius sent the deputation before the council at Antioch, as is shown by the words of Athanasius in his *Apol. contra Arian.*, 21.

nizance of the charges against Athanasius, and order a judicial investigation to be made in his presence.[3]

CHAPTER XII.

The People of Constantinople restore Paul to his See after the Death of Eusebius, while the Arians elect Macedonius.

BUT Eusebius did not live to learn the decision of Julius concerning Athanasius, for he died a short time after that Synod was held. Whereupon the people introduced Paul again into the church of Constantinople: the Arians, however, ordained Macedonius at the same time, in the church dedicated to Paul. This those who had formerly co-operated with Eusebius (that disturber of the public peace) brought about, assuming all his authority. These were Theognis, bishop of Nicæa, Maris of Chalcedon, Theodore of Heraclea in Thrace, Ursacius of Singidunum in Upper Mysia, and Valens of Mursa in Upper Pannonia. Ursacius and Valens indeed afterward altered their opinions, and presented a written recantation of them to bishop Julius, so that on subscribing the doctrine of consubstantiality they were again admitted to communion; but at that time they warmly supported the Arian error, and were instigators of the most violent conflicts in the churches, one of which was connected with Macedonius at Constantinople. By this intestine war among the Christians, continuous seditions arose in that city, and many lives were sacrificed in consequence of these occurrences.

CHAPTER XIII.

Paul is again ejected from the Church by Constantius, in consequence of the Slaughter of Hermogenes, his General.

INTELLIGENCE of these proceedings reached the ears of the Emperor Constantius, whose residence was then at Antioch. Accordingly he ordered his general Hermogenes, who had been despatched to Thrace, to pass through Constantinople on his way, and expel Paul from the church. He, on arriving at Constantinople, threw the whole city into confusion, attempting to cast out the bishops; for sedition immediately arose from the people in their eagerness to defend the bishop. And when Hermogenes persisted in his efforts to drive out Paul by means of his military force, the people became exasperated

as is usual in such cases; and making a desperate attack upon him, they set his house on fire, and after dragging through the city, they at last put him to death. This took place in the consulate[1] of the two Augusti, — that is to say, the third consulship, — Constantius, and the second of Constans: at which time Constans, having subdued the Franks, compelled them to enter into a treaty of peace with the Romans. The Emperor Constantius, on being informed of the assassination of Hermogenes, set off on horseback from Antioch, and arriving at Constantinople immediately expelled Paul, and then punished the inhabitants by withdrawing from them more than 40,000 measures of the daily allowance of wheat which had been granted by his father for gratuitous distribution among them: for prior to this catastrophe, nearly 80,000 measures of wheat brought from Alexandria had been bestowed on the citizens.[2] He hesitated, however, to ratify[3] the appointment of Macedonius to the bishopric of that city, being irritated against him not only because he had been ordained without his own consent; but also because on account of the contests in which he had been engaged with Paul, Hermogenes, his general, and many other persons had been slain. But having given him permission to minister in the church in which he had been consecrated, he returned to Antioch.

CHAPTER XIV.

The Arians remove Gregory from the See of Alexandria, and appoint George in his Place.[1]

ABOUT the same time the Arians ejected Gregory from the see of Alexandria, on the ground that he was unpopular and at the same time because he had set a church[2] on fire, and did not manifest sufficient zeal in promoting the interests of their party.[3] They therefore inducted George into his see, who was a native of Cappadocia, and had acquired the reputation of being an able advocate of their tenets.

---

[1] 342 A.D. This assassination of Hermogenes was evidently recorded in that portion of Am. Marcellinus' work which has been lost; at least a record of it is referred to in that author's *Rerum Gestarum*, XIV. x. 2 (ed. Eyssenhart).
[2] On the gratuitous distribution of grain or bread practised under Constantine and later under Theodosius, see *Cod. Theod.* XIV. tit. XVI., and cf. Eunap. *Aedes.* par. 22.
[3] Cf. Bingham, *Christ. Antiq.* IV. xi. 19, on the control over the appointment of bishops by the emperor at this time.
[1] There is an error here, repeated also by Sozomen (III. 7), but corrected by Theodoret, *H. E.* II. 4 and 12, without the mention of the names of his predecessors. The error consists in the statement that Gregory was ejected at this time. It appears that he remained in his position until the Council of Sardica, by which he was deposed and excommunicated. He survived this council by six months.
[2] That of Dionysius.
[3] This is the same Gregory that is mentioned in ch. 10 as violently put into possession of the sea of Alexandria by the Arians. It is evident that they were disappointed in him.

[3] See Hammond, *Canons of the Church* (notes on the Canons of Nicæa), for the prerogatives of the see of Rome recognized at this time.

CHAPTER XV.

Athanasius and Paul[1] going to Rome, and having obtained Letters from Bishop Julius, recover their respective Dioceses.

ATHANASIUS, meanwhile, after a lengthened journey, at last reached Italy. The western division of the empire was then under the sole power of Constans, the youngest of Constantine's sons, his brother Constantine having been slain by the soldiers, as was before stated. At the same time also Paul, bishop of Constantinople, Asclepas of Gaza, Marcellus of Ancyra, a city of the Lesser Galatia, and Lucius of Adrianople, having been accused on various charges, and expelled from their several churches, arrived at the imperial city. There each laid his case before Julius, bishop of Rome. He on his part, by virtue of the Church of Rome's peculiar privilege, sent them back again into the East, fortifying them with commendatory letters ; and at the same time restored to each his own place, and sharply rebuked those by whom they had been deposed. Relying on the signature of the bishop Julius, the bishops departed from Rome, and again took possession of their own churches, forwarding the letters to the parties to whom they were addressed. These persons considering themselves treated with indignity by the reproaches of Julius, called a council at Antioch, assembled themselves and dictated a reply to his letters as the expression of the unanimous feeling of the whole Synod.[2] It was not his province, they said, to take cognizance of their decisions in reference to any whom they might wish to expel from their churches ; seeing that they had not opposed themselves to him, when Novatus was ejected from the church. These things the bishops of the Eastern church communicated to Julius, bishop of Rome. But, as on the entry of Athanasius into Alexandria, a tumult was raised by the partisans of George the Arian, in consequence of which, it is affirmed, many persons were killed ; and since the Arians endeavor to throw the whole odium of this transaction on Athanasius as the author of it, it behooves us to make a few remarks on the subject. God the Judge of all only knows the true causes of these disorders ; but no one of any experience can be ignorant of the fact, that such fatal accidents are for the most part concomitants of the factious movements of the populace. It is vain, therefore, for the calumniators of Athanasius to attribute the blame to him ; and especially Sabinus,[3] bishop of the Macedonian heresy. For had the latter reflected on the number and magnitude of the wrongs which Athanasius, in conjunction with the rest who hold the doctrine of consubstantiality, had suffered from the Arians, or on the many complaints made of these things by the Synods convened on account of Athanasius, or in short on what that arch-heretic Macedonius himself has done throughout all the churches, he would either have been wholly silent, or if constrained to speak, would have spoken more plausible words, instead of these reproaches. But as it is intentionally overlooking all these things, he willfully misrepresents the facts. He makes, however, no mention whatever of the heresiarch, desiring by all means to conceal the daring enormities of which he knew him to be guilty. And what is still more extraordinary, he has not said one word to the disadvantage of the Arians, although he was far from entertaining their sentiments. The ordination of Macedonius, whose heretical views he had adopted, he has also passed over in silence ; for had he mentioned it, he must necessarily have recorded his impieties also, which were most distinctly manifested on that occasion. Let this suffice on this subject.

CHAPTER XVI.

The Emperor Constantius, through an Order to Philip the Prætorian Prefect, secures the Exile of Paul, and the Installation of Macedonius in his See.

WHEN the Emperor Constantius, who then held his court at Antioch, heard that Paul had again obtained possession of the episcopal throne, he was excessively enraged at his presumption. He therefore despatched a written order to Philip, the Prætorian Prefect, whose power exceeded that of the other governors of provinces, and who was styled the second person from the emperor,[1] to drive Paul out of the church again, and introduce Macedonius into it in his place. Now the prefect Philip, dreading an insurrectionary movement among the people, used artifice to entrap the bishop : keeping, therefore, the emperor's mandate secret, he went to the

---

[1] Julius, in his letter to the Eastern bishops (*Ep. I. adv. Eusebianos,* 4 and 5), mentions Athanasius and Marcellus, ex-bishop of Ancyra, as with him at this time, but does not allude to Paul; from which it has been inferred that Socrates is in error here in setting the date of Paul's visit to Rome at this time, as otherwise Julius would have named him also with Athanasius and Marcellus. Sozomen, as usual, copies the mistake of Socrates; cf. Sozom. III. 15.

[2] It appears from this that there was no recognition of any special prerogative or right belonging to the bishop of Rome as yet. The position of that bishop during these agitations in the Eastern church, when the Western church was in comparative peace, seems to be that of an arbitrator voluntarily invoked, rather than of an official judge. Cf. Neander, *Hist. of the Christ. Church,* Vol. II. p. 171, 172.

[3] i.e. in his *Collection of Synodical Transactions,* mentioned in chap. 17.

[1] δεύτερος μετὰ βασιλέα; not only second in rank, but first after him in power, ' his right-hand man.' · Cf. Vergil's *alter ab illo, Ecl.* V. 49, and VIII. 39.

public bath called Zeuxippus, and on pretense of attending to some public affairs, sent to Paul with every demonstration of respect, requesting his attendance there, on the ground that his presence was indispensable. The bishop came; and as he came in obedience to this summons, the prefect immediately showed him the emperor's order; the bishop patiently submitted condemnation without a hearing. But as Philip was afraid of the violence of the multitude — for great numbers had gathered around the building to see what would take place, for their suspicions had been aroused by current reports — he commanded one of the bath doors to be opened which communicated with the imperial palace, and through that Paul was carried off, put on board a vessel provided for the purpose, and so sent into exile immediately. The prefect directed him to go to Thessalonica, the metropolis of Macedonia, whence he had derived his origin from his ancestors; commanding him to reside in that city, but granting him permission to visit other cities of Illyricum, while he strictly forbade his passing into any portion of the Eastern empire. Thus was Paul, contrary to his expectation, at once expelled from the church, and from the city, and again hurried off into exile. Philip, the imperial prefect, leaving the bath, immediately proceeded to the church. Together with him, as if thrown there by an engine, Macedonius rode seated in the same seat with the prefect in the chariot seen by everybody, and a military guard with drawn swords was about them. The multitude was completely overawed by this spectacle, and both Arians and Homoousians hastened to the church, every one endeavoring to secure an entrance there. As the prefect with Macedonius came near the church, an irrational panic seized the multitude and even the soldiers themselves; for as the assemblage was so numerous and no room to admit the passage of the prefect and Macedonius was found, the soldiers attempted to thrust aside the people by force. But the confined space into which they were crowded together rendering it impossible to recede, the soldiers imagined that resistance was offered, and that the populace intentionally stopped the passage; they accordingly began to use their naked swords, and to cut down those that stood in their way. It is affirmed that about 3150 persons were massacred on this occasion; of whom the greater part fell under the weapons of the soldiers, and the rest were crushed to death by the desperate efforts of the multitude to escape their violence. After such distinguished achievements, Macedonius, as if he had not been the author of any calamity, but was altogether guiltless of what had been perpetrated, was seated in the episcopal chair by the prefect,

rather than by the ecclesiastical canon. Thus, then, by means of so many murders in the church, Macedonius and the Arians grasped the supremacy in the churches. About this period the emperor built the great church called *Sophia*, adjoining to that named *Irene*, which being originally of small dimensions, the emperor's father had considerably enlarged and adorned. In the present day both are seen within one enclosure, and have but one appellation.

CHAPTER XVII.

Athanasius, intimidated by the Emperor's Threats, returns to Rome again.

AT this time another accusation was concocted against Athanasius by the Arians, who invented this pretext for it. The father of the Augusti had long before granted an allowance of corn to the church of the Alexandrians for the relief of the indigent. This, they asserted, had usually been sold by Athanasius, and the proceeds converted to his own advantage. The emperor, giving credence to this slanderous report, threatened Athanasius with death, as a penalty; who, becoming alarmed at the intimation of this threat, took to flight, and kept himself concealed. When Julius, bishop of Rome, was apprised of these fresh machinations of the Arians against Athanasius, and had also received the letter of the then deceased Eusebius, he invited the persecuted Athanasius to come to him, having ascertained where he was secreted. The epistle also of the bishops who had been some time before assembled at Antioch, just then reached him; and at the same time others from the bishops in Egypt, assuring him that the entire charge against Athanasius was a fabrication. On the receipt of these contradictory communications, Julius first replied to the bishops who had written to him from Antioch, complaining of the acrimonious feeling they had evinced in their letter, and charging them with a violation of the canons, because they had not requested his attendance at the council,[1] seeing that the ecclesiastical law required that the churches should pass no decisions contrary to the views of the bishop of Rome: he then censured them with great severity for clandestinely attempting to pervert the faith; in addition, that their former proceedings at Tyre were fraudulent, because the investigation of what had taken place at Mareotes was on one side of the question only; not only this, but that the charge respect-

---

[1] Sozom. X. 3 follows Socrates. The contents of the letter written by Julius to the Eusebians, found in Athanasius' *Apologia contra Arianos*, c. 20, are different from those here given by Socrates. Julius there complains of their ignoring his invitation to the synod at Rome, but says nothing of any canon such as is mentioned here. Cf. ch. 8, note 2.

ing Arsenius had plainly been proved a false charge. Such and similar sentiments did Julius write in his answer to the bishops convened at Antioch; we should have inserted here at length, these as well as those letters which were addressed to Julius, did not their prolixity interfere with our purpose. But Sabinus, the advocate of the Macedonian heresy, of whom we have before spoken, has not incorporated the letters of Julius in his Collection of Synodical Transactions;[2] although he has not omitted that which the bishops of Antioch sent to Julius. This, however, is usual with him; he carefully introduces such letters as make no reference to, or wholly repudiate the term *homoousion;* while he purposely passes over in silence those of a contrary tendency. This is sufficient on this subject. Not long after this, Paul, pretending to make a journey from Thessalonica to Corinth, arrived in Italy: upon which both the bishops[3] made an appeal to the emperor of those parts, laying their respective cases before him.

CHAPTER XVIII.

The Emperor of the West requests his Brother to send him Three Persons who could give an Account of the Deposition of Athanasius and Paul. Those who are sent publish Another Form of the Creed.

WHEN the Western emperor[1] was informed of their affairs, he sympathized with their sufferings; and wrote to his brother [Constantius], begging him to send three bishops who should explain to him the reason for the deposition of Athanasius and Paul. In compliance with this request, Narcissus the Cilician, Theodore the Thracian, Maris of Chalcedon, and Mark the Syrian, were deputed to execute this commission; who on their arrival refused to hold any communication with Athanasius or his friends, but suppressing the creed which had been promulgated at Antioch, presented to the Emperor Constans another declaration of faith composed by themselves, in the following terms:

Another Exposition of the Faith.

We believe in one God the Father Almighty, the Creator and Maker of all things, of whom the whole family in heaven and upon earth is named;[2] and in his only-begotten Son, our Lord Jesus Christ, who was begotten of the Father before all ages; God of God; Light of Light; through whom all things in the heavens and upon the earth, both visible and invisible, were made: who is the Word, and Wisdom, and Power, and Life, and true Light: who in the last days for our sake was made man, and was born of the holy virgin; was crucified, and died; was buried, arose again from the dead on the third day, ascended into the heavens, is seated at the right hand of the Father, and shall come at the consummation of the ages, to judge the living and the dead, and to render to every one according to his works: whose kingdom being perpetual, shall continue to infinite ages; for he shall sit at the right hand of the Father, not only in this age, but also in that which is to come. [We believe] in the Holy Spirit, that is, in the Comforter, whom the Lord, according to his promise, sent to his apostles after his ascension into the heavens, to teach them, and bring all things to their remembrance: by whom also the souls of those who have sincerely believed on him shall be sanctified; and those who assert that the Son was made of things which are not, or of another substance, and not of God, or that there was a time when he did not exist, the Catholic Church accounts as aliens.

Having delivered this creed to the emperor, and exhibited it to many others also, they departed without attending to anything besides. But while there was yet an inseparable communion between the Western and Eastern churches, there sprang up another heresy at Sirmium, a city of Illyricum; for Photinus, who presided over the churches in that district, a native of the Lesser Galatia, and a disciple of that Marcellus who had been deposed, adopting his master's sentiments, asserted that the Son of God was a mere man. We shall, however, enter into this matter more fully in its proper place.[3]

CHAPTER XIX.

Of the Creed sent by the Eastern Bishops to those in Italy, called the Lengthy Creed.[1]

AFTER the lapse of about three years from the events above recorded, the Eastern bishops again assembled a Synod, and having composed another form of faith, they transmitted it to those in Italy by the hands of Eudoxius, at that time bishop of Germanicia, and Martyrius, and Macedonius, who was bishop of Mopsuestia[2] in Cilicia. This expression of the Creed, being written in more lengthy form, contained many additions to

---

2 See above, ch. 15.   3 Athanasius and Paul.
1 Constantine the Younger. See I. 38, end.
2 Eph. iii. 15.

3 See below, ch. 29.
1 This creed was called μακρόστιχος from its length, and the date of its promulgation must be put after the Council of Sardica, according to Hefele. See Hefele, *History of the Church Councils,* Vol. II. p. 85, 89, and 180 (ed. T. & T. Clark).
2 Μόψου ἑστία, lit. 'the hearth of Mopsus,' son of Apollo and Manto, daughter of Tiresias, according to the Greek mythology. Mopsuestia has become famous in the history of the church through its great citizen, Theodore. Cf. Smith and Wace, *Dict. of Christ. Biog.*

those which had preceded it, and was set forth in these words :

' We believe in one God, the Father Almighty, the Creator and Maker of all things, of whom the whole family in heaven and upon earth is named ; and in his only-begotten Son Jesus Christ our Lord, who was begotten of the Father before all ages ; God of God ; Light of Light ; through whom all things in the heavens and upon the earth, both visible and invisible, were made : who is the Word, and Wisdom, and Power, and Life, and true Light : who in the last days for our sake was made man, and was born of the holy virgin ; who was crucified, and died, and was buried, and rose again from the dead on the third day, and ascended into heaven, and is seated at the right hand of the Father, and shall come at the consummation of the ages, to judge the living and the dead, and to render to every one according to his works : whose kingdom being perpetual shall continue to infinite ages ; for he sits at the right hand of the Father, not only in this age, but also in that which is to come. We believe also in the Holy Spirit, that is, in the Comforter, whom the Lord according to his promise sent to his apostles after his ascension into heaven, to teach them and bring all things to their remembrance, through whom also the souls of those who sincerely believe on him are sanctified. But those who assert that the Son was made of things not in being, or of another substance, and not of God, or that there was a time or age when he did not exist,[3] the holy catholic Church accounts as aliens. The holy and catholic Church likewise anathematizes those also who say that there are three Gods, or that Christ is not God before all ages, or that he is neither Christ, nor the Son of God, or that the same person is Father, Son, and Holy Spirit, or that the Son was not begotten, or that the Father begat not the Son by his own will or desire. Neither is it safe to affirm that the Son had his existence from things that were not, since this is nowhere declared concerning him in the divinely inspired Scriptures. Nor are we taught that he had his being from any other pre-existing substance besides the Father, but that he was truly begotten of God alone ; for the Divine word teaches that there is one unbegotten principle without beginning, the Father of Christ. But those who unauthorized by Scripture rashly assert that there was a time when he was not, ought not to preconceive any antecedent interval of time, but God only who without time begat him ; for both times and ages were made through him. Yet it must not be thought that

the Son is co-inoriginate,[4] or co-unbegotten[5] with the Father : for there is properly no father of the co-inoriginate or co-unbegotten. But we know that the Father alone being inoriginate and incomprehensible,[6] has ineffably and incomprehensibly to all begotten, and that the Son was begotten before the ages, but is not unbegotten like the Father, but has a beginning, viz. the Father who begat him, for " the head of Christ is God."[7]   Now although according to the Scriptures we acknowledge three things or persons, viz. that of the ·Father, and of the Son, and of the Holy Spirit, we do not on that account make three Gods : since we know that that there is but one God perfect in himself, unbegotten, inoriginate, and invisible, the God and Father of the only-begotten, who alone has existence from himself, and alone affords existence abundantly to all other things.   But neither while we assert that there is one God, the Father of our Lord Jesus Christ, the only-begotten, do we therefore deny that Christ is God before the ages, as the followers of Paul of Samosata do, who affirm that after his incarnation he was by exaltation deified, in that he was by nature a mere man. We know indeed that he was subject to his God and Father : nevertheless he was begotten of God, and is by nature true and perfect God, and was not afterwards made God out of man ; but was for our sake made man out of God, and has never ceased to be God.   Moreover we execrate and anathematize those who falsely style him the mere unsubstantial word of God, having existence only in another, either as the word to which utterance is given, or as the word conceived in the mind : and who pretend that before the ages he was neither the Christ, the Son of God, the Mediator, nor the Image of God ; but that he became the Christ, and the Son of God, from the time he took our flesh from the virgin, about four hundred years ago.[8] For they assert that Christ had the beginning of his kingdom from that time, and that it shall have an end after the consummation of all things and the judgment. Such persons as these are the followers of Marcellus and Photinus, the Ancyro-Galatians, who under pretext of establishing his sovereignty, like the Jews set aside

---

[3] This is the end of the first creed adopted at Antioch, as given in the preceding chapter; it is couched in almost identical terms in both these versions.   The rest of the version here given is the addition that constitutes the characteristic of the ' Lengthy Creed.'

[4] συνάναρχον.   It has been thought advisable to retain the above uncouth rendering of this word, as also of one or two others immediately following, on the ground that the etymological precision at which they aim compensates for their non-classical ring.
[5] συναγέννητον.   [6] ἀνέφικτον.   [7] 1 Cor. xi. 3.
[8] ' There has arisen in our days a certain Marcellus of Galatia, the most execrable of all heretics, who with a sacrilegious mind and impious mouth and wicked argument will needs set bounds to the perpetual, eternal, and timeless kingdom of our Lord Christ, saying that he began to reign four hundred years since, and shall end at the dissolution of the present world.'   This is the description given of the heresy here hinted at by the synodical letter of the Oriental bishops at Sardica.   On Marcellus and the various opinions concerning him, see Zahn, *Marcellus von Ancyra*, Gotha, 1867; also monographs on Marcellus by Rettberg (1794) and by Klose (1837 and 1859).   Cf. Neander, *Hist. of Chr. Ch.* Vol. II. p. 394.

the eternal existence and deity of Christ, and the perpetuity of his kingdom. But we know him to be not simply the word of God by utterance or mental conception, but God the living Word subsisting of himself; and Son of God and Christ; and who did, not by presence only, co-exist and was conversant with his Father before the ages, and ministered to him at the creation of all things, whether visible or invisible, but was the substantial Word of the Father, and God of God: for this is he to whom the Father said, "Let us make man in our image, and according to our likeness:" who in his own person appeared to the fathers, gave the law, and spake by the prophets; and being at last made man, he manifested his Father to all men, and reigns to endless ages. Christ has not attained any new dignity; but we believe that he was perfect from the beginning, and like his Father in all things; and those who say that the Father, Son, and Holy Spirit, are the same person, impiously supposing the three names to refer to one and the same thing and person, we deservedly expel from the church because by the incarnation they render the Father, who is incomprehensible and insusceptible of suffering, subject to comprehension and suffering. Such are those denominated Patropassians[9] among the Romans, and by us Sabellians. For we know that the Father who sent, remained in the proper nature of his own immutable deity; but that Christ who was sent, has fulfilled the economy of the incarnation. In like manner those who irreverently affirm that Christ was begotten not by the will and pleasure of his Father; thus attributing to God an involuntary necessity not springing from choice, as if he begat the Son by constraint, we consider most impious and strangers to the truth because they have dared to determine such things respecting him as are inconsistent with our common notions of God, and are contrary indeed to the sense of the divinely-inspired Scripture. For knowing that God is self-dependent and Lord of himself we devoutly maintain that of his own volition and pleasure he begat the Son. And while we reverentially believe what is spoken concerning him;[10] "The Lord created me the beginning of his ways on account of his works": yet we do not suppose that he was made similarly to the creatures or works made by him. For it is impious and repugnant to the church's faith to compare the Creator with the works created by him; or to imagine that he had the same manner of generation as things of a nature totally different from himself: for the sacred Scriptures

teach us that the alone only-begotten Son was really and truly begotten. Nor when we say that the Son is of himself, and lives and subsists in like manner to the Father, do we therefore separate him from the Father, as if we supposed them dissociated by the intervention of space and distance in a material sense. For we believe that they are united without medium or interval, and that they are incapable of separation from each other: the whole Father embosoming the Son; and the whole Son attached to and eternally reposing in the Father's bosom. Believing, therefore, in the altogether perfect and most holy Trinity, and asserting that the Father is God, and that the Son also is God, we do not acknowledge two Gods, but one only, on account of the majesty of the Deity, and the perfect blending and union of the kingdoms: the Father ruling over all things universally, and even over the Son himself; the Son being subject to the Father, but except him, ruling over all things which were made after him and by him; and by the Father's will bestowing abundantly on the saints the grace of the Holy Spirit. For the Sacred Oracles inform us that in this consists the character of the sovereignty which Christ exercises.

'We have been compelled, since the publication of our former epitome, to give this more ample exposition of the creed; not in order to gratify a vain ambition, but to clear ourselves from all strange suspicion respecting our faith which may exist among those who are ignorant of our real sentiments. And that the inhabitants of the West may both be aware of the shameless misrepresentations of the heterodox party; and also know the ecclesiastical opinion of the Eastern bishops concerning Christ, confirmed by the unwrested testimony of the divinely-inspired Scriptures, among all those of unperverted minds.'

CHAPTER XX.

Of the Council at Sardica.

THE Western prelates on account of their being of another language, and not understanding this exposition, would not admit of it; saying that the Nicene Creed was sufficient, and that they would not waste time on anything beyond it. But when the emperor had again written to insist on the restoration to Paul and Athanasius of their respective sees, but without effect in consequence of the continual agitation of the people — these two bishops demanded that another Synod should be convened, so that

---

9 Cf. Tertull. *Adv. Prax.* i. and ii.; Epiph. *Hær.* LVII.
10 Prov. viii. 22. The ancient bishops quote the LXX *verbatim*. The English versions (Authorized and Revised) follow the Hebrew, 'The LORD possessed me in the beginning of his way, before his works of old.'

1 Cf. Sozom. III. 11; Theodoret, *H. E.* II. 7; also Hefele, *Hist. of the Church Councils*, Vol. II. p. 87-176.

their case, as well as other questions in relation to the faith might be settled by an ecumenical council, for they made it obvious that their deposition arose from no other cause than that the faith might be the more easily perverted. Another general council was therefore summoned to meet at Sardica, — a city of Illyricum, — by the joint authority of the two emperors; the one requesting by letter that it might be so, and the other, of the East, readily acquiescing in it. It was the eleventh year after the death of the father of the two Augusti, during the consulship of Rufinus and Eusebius,[2] that the Synod of Sardica met. According to the statement of Athanasius[3] about 300 bishops from the western parts of the empire were present; but Sabinus says there came only seventy from the eastern parts, among whom was Ischyras of Mareotes,[4] who had been ordained bishop of that country by those who deposed Athanasius. Of the rest, some pretended infirmity of body; others complained of the shortness of the notice given, casting the blame of it on Julius, bishop of Rome, although a year and a half had elapsed from the time of its having been summoned: in which interval Athanasius remained at Rome awaiting the assembling of the Synod. When at last they were convened at Sardica, the Eastern prelates refused either to meet or to enter into any conference with those of the West, unless they first excluded Athanasius and Paul from the convention. But as Protogenes, bishop of Sardica, and Hosius, bishop of Cordova, a city in Spain, would by no means permit them to be absent, the Eastern bishops immediately withdrew, and returning to Philippopolis in Thrace, held a separate council, wherein they openly anathematized the term *homoousios;* and having introduced the Anomoian[5] opinion into their epistles, they sent them in all directions. On the other hand, those who remained at Sardica, condemning in the first place their departure, afterwards divested the accusers of Athanasius of their dignity; then confirming the Nicene Creed, and rejecting the term *anomoion,* they more distinctly recognized the doctrine of consubstantiality, which they also inserted in epistles addressed to all the churches. Both parties believed they had acted rightly: those of the East, because the Western bishops had countenanced those whom they had deposed; and these again, in consequence not only of the retirement of those who

had deposed them before the matter had been examined into, but also because they themselves were the defenders of the Nicene faith, which the other party had dared to adulterate. They therefore restored to Paul and Athanasius their sees, and also Marcellus of Ancyra in Lesser Galatia, who had been deposed long before, as we have stated in the former book.[6] At that time indeed he exerted himself to the utmost to procure the revocation of the sentence pronounced against him, declaring that his being suspected of entertaining the error of Paul of Samosata arose from a misunderstanding of some expressions in his book. It must, however, be noticed that Eusebius Pamphilus wrote three entire books against Marcellus,[7] in which he quotes that author's own words to prove that he asserts with Sabellius the Libyan, and Paul of Samosata, that the Lord [Jesus] was a mere man.

CHAPTER XXI.

Defense of Eusebius Pamphilus.

BUT since some have attempted to stigmatize even Eusebius Pamphilus himself as having favored the Arian views in his works, it may not be irrelevant here to make a few remarks respecting him. In the first place then he was both present at the council of Nicæa, which defined the doctrine of the *homoousion* and gave his assent to what was there determined. And in the third book of the Life of Constantine, he expressed himself in these words:[1] 'The emperor incited all to unanimity, until he had rendered them united in judgment on those points on which they were previously at variance; so that they were quite agreed at Nicæa in matters of faith.' Since therefore Eusebius, in mentioning the Nicene Synod, says that all differences were removed, and that all came to unity of sentiment, what ground is there for assuming that he was himself an Arian? The Arians are also certainly deceived in supposing him to be a favorer of their tenets. But some one will perhaps say that in his discourses he seems to have adopted the opinions of Arius, because of his frequently saying through Christ,[2] to whom we should answer that ecclesiastical writers often use this mode of expression and others of a similar kind denoting the economy of our Saviour's humanity: and that before

---

[2] 347 A. D.
[3] Athanasius' statement is that those who were present at the Council of Sardica, together with those who afterwards subscribed the Synodical Epistle sent to them and those who before the council had written in his behalf out of Phrygia, Asia, and Isauria, were in all about three hundred and forty. So in his *Apol. contra Arianos,* c. 50. In his *Ep. ad Solitar.* c. 15, he gives the number of those who met at Sardica as about one hundred and seventy, — no more.
[4] Cf. I. 27.   [5] ἀνομοίου, 'different,' 'unlike.'

[6] I. 36.
[7] There are two works of Eusebius extant against Marcellus. The one described here is *de Ecclesiastica Theologia adversus Marcellum,* in three books; the other is entitled *contra Marcellum,* and consists of two books. As there is no mention of the latter, it is doubtful whether Socrates had ever seen them. At the end of the second book, Eusebius asserts that he had written at the request of the bishops who had excommunicated Marcellus.
[1] *Life of Const.* III. 13.
[2] Eusebius was accustomed to end his sermons with the formula 'Glory be to the unborn God through his only-begotten Son,' &c. So also at the end of his *contra Sabell.* I.

all these the apostle[3] made use of such expressions, and never has been accounted a teacher of false doctrine. Moreover, inasmuch as Arius has dared to say that the Son is a creature, as one of the others, observe what Eusebius says on this subject, in his first book against Marcellus :[4]

'He alone, and no other, has been declared to be, and is the only-begotten Son of God; whence any one could justly censure those who have presumed to affirm that he is a Creature made of nothing, like the rest of the creatures; for how then would he be a Son? and how could he be God's only-begotten, were he assigned the same nature as the other creatures . . . and were he one of the many created things, seeing that he, like them, would in that case be partaker of a creation from nothing? But the Sacred Scriptures do not thus instruct us.' He again adds a little afterwards : 'Whoever then defines the Son as made of things that are not, and as a creature produced from nothing pre-existing, forgets that while he concedes the name of Son, he denies him to be a Son in reality. For he that is made of nothing, cannot truly be the Son of God, any more than the other things which have been made; but the true Son of God, forasmuch as he is begotten of the Father, is properly denominated the only-begotten and beloved of the Father. For this reason also, he himself is God; for what can the offspring of God be, but the perfect resemblance of him who begat him? A sovereign indeed builds a city, but does not beget it; and is said to beget a son, not to build one. An artificer, also, may be called the framer, but not the father of his work; while he could by no means be styled the framer of him whom he had begotten. So also the God of the Universe is the Father of the Son; but might be fitly termed the Framer and Maker of the world. And although it is once said in Scripture,[5] "The Lord created me the beginning of his ways on account of his works," yet it becomes us to consider the import of this phrase, which I shall hereafter explain; and not, as Marcellus has done, from a single passage to jeopardize the most important doctrine of the church.'

These and many other such expressions Eusebius Pamphilus has given utterance to in the first book against Marcellus; and in his third book,[6] declaring in what sense the term *creature* is to be taken, he says:

'Accordingly, these things being thus established, it follows that in the same sense as that which preceded, the words, "The Lord created me the beginning of his ways, on account of

his works," must have been spoken. For although he says that he was created, it is not as if he should say that he had arrived at existence from what was not, nor that he himself also was made of nothing like the rest of the creatures, which some have erroneously supposed; but as subsisting, living, pre-existing, and being before the constitution of the whole world; and having been appointed to rule the universe by his Lord and Father : the word created being here used instead of ordained or constituted. Certainly the apostle[7] expressly called the rulers and governors among men creature, when he said, "Submit yourselves to every human creature for the Lord's sake; whether to the king as supreme, or to governors as those sent by him." The prophet also[8] when he says, "Prepare, Israel, to invoke thy God. For behold he who confirms the thunder, creates the Spirit, and announces his Christ unto men" : . . . has not used the word "he who creates" in the sense of makes out of nothing. For God did not then create the Spirit, when he declared his Christ to all men, since[9] "There is nothing new under the sun"; but the Spirit existed, and had being previously : but he was sent at what time the apostles were gathered together, when like thunder "There came a sound from heaven as of a rushing mighty wind; and they were filled with the Holy Spirit."[10] And thus they declared unto all men the Christ of God, in accordance with that prophecy which says,[11] "Behold he who confirms the thunder, creates the Spirit, and announces his Christ unto men" : the word "creates" being used instead of "sends down," or appoints; and thunder in another figure implying the preaching of the Gospel. Again in that says, "Create in me a clean heart, O God,"[12] said not this as if he had no heart; but prayed that his mind might be purified. Thus also it is said,[13] "That he might create the two into one new man," instead of unite. Consider also whether this passage is not of the same kind,[14] "Clothe yourselves with the new man, which is created according to God"; and this,[15] "If, therefore, any one be in Christ, he is a new creature"; and whatever other expressions of a similar nature any one may find who shall carefully search the divinely inspired Scripture. Wherefore, one should not be surprised if in this passage, "The Lord created me the beginning of his ways," the term "created" is used metaphorically, instead of "appointed" or constituted.'

Such words Eusebius uses in his work against

---

[3] 1 Cor. i.; Eph. iii. 9.
[4] *De Eccl. Theol.* I. 8, 9, and 10.
[5] Prov. viii. 22.   [6] *De Eccl. Theol.* III. 2.

[7] 1 Pet. ii. 13.
[8] Amos iv. 12, 13 (LXX).
[9] Eccl. i. 9.
[10] Acts ii. 2, 4.
[11] Amos iv. 13.
[12] Psalms li. 10 (LXX).
[13] Eph. ii. 15.
[14] Eph. iv. 24.
[15] 2 Cor. v. 17.

Marcellus; we have quoted them on account of those who have slanderously attempted to traduce and criminate him. Neither can they prove that Eusebius attributes a beginning of subsistence to the Son of God, although they may find him often using the expressions by accomodation; and especially so, because he was an emulator and admirer of the works of Origen, in which those who are able to comprehend the depth of Origen's writings, will perceive it to be everywhere stated that the Son was begotten of the Father. These remarks have been made in passing, in order to refute those who have misrepresented Eusebius.

CHAPTER XXII.

The Council of Sardica restores Paul and Athanasius to their Sees; and on the Eastern Emperor's Refusal to admit them, the Emperor of the West threatens him with War.

THOSE convened at Sardica, as well as those who had formed a separate council at Philippopolis in Thrace, having severally performed what they deemed requisite, returned to their respective cities. From that time, therefore, the Western church was severed from the Eastern;[1] and the boundary of communion between them was the mountain called Soucis,[2] which divides the Illyrians from the Thracians. As far as this mountain there was indiscriminate communion, although there was a difference of faith; but beyond it they did not commune with one another. Such was the perturbed condition of the churches at that period. Soon after these transactions, the emperor of the Western parts informed his brother Constantius of what had taken place at Sardica, and begged him to restore Paul and Athanasius to their sees. But as Constantius delayed to carry this matter into effect, the emperor of the West again wrote to him, giving him the choice either of re-establishing Paul and Athanasius in their former dignity, and restoring their churches to them; or, on his failing to do this, of regarding him as his enemy, and immediately expecting war. The letter which he addressed to his brother was as follows:

'Athanasius and Paul are here with me; and I am quite satisfied after investigation, that they are persecuted for the sake of piety. If, therefore, you will pledge yourself to reinstate them in their sees, and to punish those who have so unjustly injured them, I will send them to you; but should you refuse to do this, be assured, that I will myself come thither, and restore them to their own sees, in spite of your opposition.'

CHAPTER XXIII.

Constantius, being Afraid of his Brother's Threats, recalls Athanasius by Letter, and sends him to Alexandria.

ON receiving this communication the emperor of the East fell into perplexity; and immediately sending for the greater part of the Eastern bishops, he acquainted them with the choice his brother had submitted to him, and asked what ought to be done. They replied, it was better to concede the churches to Athanasius, than to undertake a civil war. Accordingly the emperor, urged by necessity, summoned Athanasius and his friends to his presence. Meanwhile the emperor of the West sent Paul to Constantinople, with two bishops and other honorable attendance, having fortified him with his own letters, together with those of the Synod. But while Athanasius was still apprehensive, and hesitated to go to him, — for he dreaded the treachery of his calumniators, — the emperor of the East not once only, but even a second and a third time, invited him to come to him; this is evident from his letters, which, translated from the Latin tongue, are as follows:

Epistle of Constantius to Athanasius.[1]

Constantius Victor Augustus to Athanasius the bishop.

Our compassionate clemency cannot permit you to be any longer tossed and disquieted as it were by the boisterous waves of the sea. Our unwearied piety has not been unmindful of you driven from your native home, despoiled of your property, and wandering in pathless solitudes. And although I have too long deferred acquainting you by letter with the purpose of my mind, expecting your coming to us of your own accord to seek a remedy for your troubles; yet since fear perhaps has hindered the execution of your wishes, we therefore have sent to your reverence letters full of indulgence, in order that you may fearlessly hasten to appear in our presence, whereby after experiencing our benevolence, you may attain your desire, and be re-established in your proper position. For this reason I have requested my Lord and brother Constans Victor Augustus to grant you permission to come, to the end that by the consent of us both you may be restored to your country, having this assurance of our favor.

---

[1] This separation was only temporary and must be distinguished from the great schism, which grew slowly and culminated with the adoption of the expression '*filioque*' into the Apostles' Creed by the Western church in the eleventh century. On the various degrees of unity and communion recognized in the ancient church, see Bingham, *Eccl. Antiq.* Bk. XVI. 1.

[2] Τισοῦκις.

[1] Athan. *Apol. c. Arian.* 51.

Another Epistle to Athanasius.

Constantius Victor Augustus to the bishop Athanasius.

Although we have abundantly intimated in a former letter that you might confidently come to our court,[2] as we are extremely anxious to reinstate you in your proper place, yet we have again addressed this letter to your reverence. We therefore urge you, without any distrust or apprehension, to take a public vehicle and hasten to us, in order that you may be able to obtain what you desire.

Another Epistle to Athanasius.

Constantius Victor Augustus to the bishop Athanasius.

While we were residing at Edessa, where your presbyters were present, it pleased us to send one of them to you, for the purpose of hastening your arrival at our court, in order that after having been introduced to our presence, you might forthwith proceed to Alexandria. But inasmuch as a considerable time has elapsed since you received our letter, and yet have not come, we now therefore hasten to remind you to speedily present yourself before us, that you may be able to return to your country, and obtain your desire. For the more ample assurance of our intention, we have despatched to you Achetas the deacon, from whom you will learn both our mind in regard to you, and that you will be able to secure what you wish; viz., our readiness to facilitate the objects you have in view.

When Athanasius had received these letters at Aquileia, — for there he abode after his departure from Sardica, — he immediately hastened to Rome; and having shown these communications to Julius the bishop, he caused the greatest joy in the Roman Church. For it seemed as if the emperor of the East also had recognized their faith, since he had recalled Athanasius. Julius then wrote to the clergy and laity of Alexandria on behalf of Athanasius as follows:

Epistle of Julius, Bishop of Rome, to those at Alexandria.[3]

Julius, the bishop, to the presbyters, deacons, and people inhabiting Alexandria, brethren beloved, salutations in the Lord.

I also rejoice with you, beloved brethren, because you at length see before your eyes the fruit of your faith. For that this is really so, any one may perceive in reference to my brother and fellow-prelate Athanasius, whom God has restored to you, both on account of his purity of life, and in answer to your prayers. From this it is evident that your supplications to God have unceasingly been offered pure and abounding with love; for mindful of the divine promises and of the charity connected with them, which ye learned from the instruction of my brother, ye knew assuredly, and according to the sound faith which is in you clearly foresaw that your bishop would not be separated from you for ever, whom ye had in your devout hearts as though he were ever present. Wherefore it is unnecessary for me to use many words in addressing you, for your faith has already anticipated whatever I could have said; and the common prayer of you all has been fulfilled according to the grace of Christ. I therefore rejoice with you, and repeat that ye have preserved your souls invincible in the faith. And with my brother Athanasius I rejoice equally; because, while suffering many afflictions, he has never been unmindful of your love and desire; for although he seemed to be withdrawn from you in person for a season, yet was he always present with you in spirit. Moreover, I am convinced, beloved, that every trial which he has endured has not been inglorious; since both your faith and his has thus been tested and made manifest to all. But had not so many troubles happened to him, who would have believed, either that you had so great esteem and love for this eminent prelate, or that he was endowed with such distinguished virtues, on account of which also he will by no means be defrauded of his hope in the heavens? He has accordingly obtained a testimony of confession in every way glorious both in the present age and in that which is to come. For having suffered so many and diversified trials both by land and by sea, he has trampled on every machination of the Arian heresy; and though often exposed to danger in consequence of envy, he despised death, being protected by Almighty God, and our Lord Jesus Christ, ever trusting that he should not only escape the plots [of his adversaries], but also be restored for your consolation, and bring back to you at the same time greater trophies from your own conscience. By which means he has been made known even to the ends of the whole earth as glorious, his worth having been approved by the purity of his life, the firmness of his purpose, and his steadfastness in the heavenly doctrine, all being attested by your unchanging esteem and love. He therefore returns to you, more illustrious now than when he departed from you. For if the fire tries the precious metals (I speak of gold and silver) for purification, what can be said of so excellent a man

---

[2] κομιτάτον = Lat. *comitatus;* by analogy of the New Test. words κῆνσος κουστωδία, σπεκουλάτωρ, &c., and frequently in Byzantine Greek κομβίνευμα σουφράγιον, &c.

[3] Athan. *Apol. c. Arian.* 52.

proportionate to his worth, who after having overcome the fire of so many calamities and dangers, is now restored to you, being declared innocent not only by us, but also by the whole Synod? Receive therefore with godly honor and joy, beloved brethren, your bishop Athanasius, together with those who have been his companions in tribulation. And rejoice in having attained the object of your prayers, you who have supplied with meat and drink, by your supporting letters, your pastor hungering and thirsting, so to speak, for your spiritual welfare. And in fact ye were a comfort to him while he was sojourning in a strange land; and ye cherished him in your most faithful affections when he was plotted against and persecuted. As for me, it makes me happy even to picture to myself in imagination the delight of each one of you at his return, the pious greetings of the populace, the glorious festivity of those assembled to meet him, and indeed what the entire aspect of that day will be when my brother shall be brought back to you again; when past troubles will be at an end, and his prized and longed-for return will unite all hearts in the warmest expression of joy. This feeling will in a very high degree extend to us, who regard it as a token of divine favor that we should have been privileged to become acquainted with so eminent a person. It becomes us therefore to close this epistle with prayer. May God Almighty and his Son our Lord and Saviour Jesus Christ afford you this grace continually, thus rewarding the admirable faith which ye have manifested in reference to your bishop by an illustrious testimony: that the things most excellent which 'Eye has not seen, nor ear heard, neither have entered into the heart of man; even the things which God has prepared for them that love him,'[4] may await you and yours in the world to come, through our Lord Jesus Christ, through whom be glory to God Almighty for ever and ever, Amen. I pray that ye may be strengthened, beloved brethren.

Athanasius, relying on these letters, arrived at the East. The Emperor Constantius did not at that time receive him with hostility of feeling; nevertheless at the instigation of the Arians he endeavored to circumvent him, and addressed him in these words: 'You have been reinstated in your see in accordance with the decree of the Synod, and with our consent. But inasmuch as some of the people of Alexandria refuse to hold communion with you, permit them to have one church in the city.' To this demand Athanasius promptly replied: 'You have the power, my sovereign, both to order, and to carry into effect,

whatever you may please. I also, therefore, would beg you to grant me a favor.' The emperor having readily promised to acquiesce, Athanasius immediately added, that he desired the same thing might be conceded to him, which the emperor had sought from him, viz.: that in every city one church should be assigned to those who might refuse to hold communion with the Arians. The Arians perceiving the purpose of Athanasius to be inimical to their interests, said that this affair might be postponed to another time: but they suffered the emperor to act as he pleased. He therefore restored to Athanasius, Paul, and Marcellus their respective sees; as also to Asclepas, bishop of Gaza, and Lucius of Adrianople. For these, too, had been received by the Council of Sardica: Asclepas, because he showed records from which it appeared that Eusebius Pamphilus, in conjunction with several others, after having investigated his case, had restored him to his former rank; and Lucius, because his accusers had fled. Hereupon the emperor's edicts were despatched to their respective cities, enjoining the inhabitants to receive them readily. At Ancyra indeed, when Basil was ejected, and Marcellus was introduced in his stead, there was a considerable tumult made, which afforded his enemies an occasion of calumniating him: but the people of Gaza willingly received Asclepas. Macedonius at Constantinople, for a short time gave place to Paul, convening assemblies by himself separately, in a separate church in that city. Moreover the emperor wrote on behalf of Athanasius to the bishops, clergy, and laity, in regard to receiving him cheerfully: and at the same time he ordered by other letters, that whatever had been enacted against him in the judicial courts should be abrogated. The communications respecting both these matters were as follows:

The Epistle of Constantius in Behalf of Athanasius.[5]

Victor Constantius Maximus Augustus, to the bishops and presbyters of the Catholic Church.

The most reverend bishop Athanasius has not been forsaken by the grace of God. But although he was for a short time subjected to trial according to men, yet has he obtained from an omniscient Providence the exoneration which was due to him; having been restored by the will of God, and our decision, both to his country and to the church over which by divine permission he presided. It was therefore suitable that what is in accordance with this should be duly attended to by our clemency: so that all things which have been heretofore determined against those who held communion with

---

[4] 1 Cor. ii. 9.

[5] Athan. *Apol. c. Arian.* 54.

him should now be rescinded ; that all suspicion against him should henceforward cease ; and that the immunity which those clergymen who are with him formerly enjoyed, should be, as it is meet, confirmed to them.   Moreover, as we thought it just to add this to our grace toward him, that the whole ecclesiastical body should understand that protection is extended to all who have adhered to him, whether bishops or other clergymen : and union with him shall be a sufficient evidence of each person's right intention. Wherefore we have ordered, according to the similitude of the previous providence, that as many as have the wisdom to enroll themselves with the sounder judgment and party and to choose his communion, shall enjoy that indulgence which we have now granted in accordance with the will of God.

Another Epistle sent to the Alexandrians.[6]

Victor Constantius Maximus Augustus, to the people of the Catholic Church at Alexandria.

Setting before us as an aim your good order in all respects, and knowing that you have long since been bereft of episcopal oversight, we thought it just to send back to you again Athanasius your bishop, a man known to all by the rectitude and sanctity of his life and manners. Having received him with your usual and becoming courtesy, and constituted him the assistant of your prayers to God, exert yourselves to maintain at all times, according to the ecclesiastical canon, harmony and peace, which will be alike honorable to yourselves, and grateful to us.   For it is unreasonable that any dissension or faction should be excited among you, hostile to the prosperity of our times ; and we trust that such a misfortune will be wholly removed from you.   We exhort you, therefore, to assiduously persevere in your accustomed devotions, by his assistance, as we before said : so that when this resolution of yours shall become generally known, entering into the prayers of all, even the pagans, who are still enslaved in the ignorance of idolatrous worship, may hasten to seek the knowledge of our sacred religion, most beloved Alexandrians.   Again, therefore, we exhort you to give heed to these things : heartily welcome your bishop, as one appointed you by the will of God and our decree ; and esteem him worthy of being embraced with all the affections of your souls.   For this becomes you, and is consistent with our clemency.   But in order to check all tendency to seditions and tumult in persons of a factious disposition, orders have been issued to our judges to give up to the severity of the laws all whom they may discover to be seditious.   Having regard,

therefore, to our determination and God's,[7] as well as to the anxiety we feel to secure harmony among you, and remembering also the punishment that will be inflicted on the disorderly, make it your especial care to act agreeably to the sanctions of our sacred religion, with all reverence honoring your bishop ; that so in conjunction with him you may present your supplications to the God and Father of the universe, both for yourselves, and for the orderly government of the whole human race.

An Epistle respecting the Rescinding of the Enactments against Athanasius.

Victor Constantius Augustus to Nestorius, and in the same terms to the governors of Augustamnica, Thebaïs, and Libya.

If it be found that at any time previously any enactment has been passed prejudicial and derogatory to those who hold communion with Athanasius the bishop, our pleasure is that it should now be wholly abrogated ; and that his clergy should again enjoy the same immunity which was granted to them formerly.   We enjoin strict obedience to this command, to the intent that since the bishop Athanasius has been restored to his church, all who hold communion with him may possess the same privileges as they had before, and such as other ecclesiastics now enjoy : that so their affairs being happily arranged, they also may share in the general prosperity.

CHAPTER XXIV.

Athanasius, passing through Jerusalem on his Return to Alexandria, is received into Communion by Maximus: and a Synod of Bishops, convened in that City, confirms the Nicene Creed.

ATHANASIUS the bishop being fortified with such letters as these, passed through Syria, and came into Palestine.   On arriving at Jerusalem he acquainted Maximus the bishop both with what had been done in the Council of Sardica, and also that the Emperor Constantius had confirmed its decision : he then proposed that a Synod of the bishops there should be held. Maximus,[1] therefore, without delay sent for certain of the bishops of Syria and Palestine, and having assembled a council, he restored Athanasius to communion, and to his former dignity. After which the Synod communicated by letter[2]

---

[6] Athan. *Apol. c. Arian.* 55.

[7] τοῦ κρείτονος; cf. I. 7, and note.
[1] The bishop of Jerusalem was under the jurisdiction of the metropolitan bishop of Cæsarea, and according to later usage and canon, had no right to call a synod without the permission of the metropolitan.   Evidently usage had not yet become fixed into uniformity in this respect.
[2] Cf. Athan. *Apol. c. Arian.* 57.

to the Alexandrians, and to all the bishops of Egypt and Libya, what had been determined respecting Athanasius. Whereupon the adversaries of Athanasius exceedingly derided Maximus, because having before assisted in his deposition, he had suddenly changed his mind, and as if nothing had previously taken place, had voted for his restoration to communion and rank. When Ursacius and Valens, who had been fiery partisans of Arianism, ascertained these things, condemning their former zeal, they proceeded to Rome, where they presented their recantation to Julius the bishop, and gave their assent to the doctrine of consubstantiality: they also wrote to Athanasius, and expressed their readiness to hold communion with him in future. Thus Ursacius and Valens were at that time subdued by the good fortune of Athanasius and induced to recognize the orthodox faith. Athanasius passed through Pelusium on his way to Alexandria, and admonished the inhabitants of every city to beware of the Arians, and to receive those only that professed the Homoousian faith. In some of the churches also he performed ordination; which afforded another ground of accusation against him, because of his undertaking to ordain in the dioceses of others.[3] Such was the progress of affairs at that period in reference to Athanasius.

CHAPTER XXV.

Of the Usurpers Magnentius and Vetranio.

ABOUT this time an extraordinary commotion shook the whole state, of the principal heads, of which we shall give a brief account, deeming it necessary not to pass over them altogether. We mentioned in our first book,[1] that after the death of the founder of Constantinople, his three sons succeeded him in the empire: it must now be also stated, that a kinsman of theirs, Dalmatius, so named from his father, shared with them the imperial authority. This person after being associated with them in the sovereignty for a very little while, the soldiers put to death,[2] Constantius having neither commanded his destruction, nor forbidden it. The manner in which Constantine the younger was also killed by the soldiers, on his invading that division of the empire which belonged to his brother, has already been recorded[3] more than once. After

his death, the Persian war was raised against the Romans, in which Constantius did nothing prosperously: for in a battle fought by night on the frontiers of both parties, the Persians had to some slight extent the advantage. And this at a time when the affairs of the Christians became no less unsettled, there being great disturbance throughout the churches on account of Athanasius, and the term *homoousion*. Affairs having reached this pass, there sprang up a tyrant in the western parts called Magnentius,[4] who by treachery slew Constans, the emperor of the western division of the empire, at that time residing in the Gauls. This being done, a furious civil war arose, and Magnentius made himself master of all Italy, reduced Africa and Libya under his power, and even obtained possession of the Gauls. But at the city of Sirmium in Illyricum, the military set up another tyrant whose name was Vetranio;[5] while a fresh trouble threw Rome itself into commotion. For there was a nephew of Constantine's, Nepotian by name, who, supported by a body of gladiators, there assumed the sovereignty. He was, however, slain by some of the officers of Magnentius, who himself invaded the western provinces, and spread desolation in every direction.

CHAPTER XXVI.

After the Death of Constans, the Western Emperor, Paul and Athanasius are again ejected from their Sees: the Former on his Way into Exile is slain; but the Latter escapes by Flight.

THE conflux of these disastrous events occurred during a short space of time; for they happened in the fourth year after the council at Sardica, during the consulate of Sergius and Nigrinian.[1] When these circumstances were published, the entire sovereignty of the empire seemed to devolve on Constantius alone, who, being accordingly proclaimed in the East sole Autocrat, made the most vigorous preparations against the usurpers. Hereupon the adversaries of Athanasius, thinking a favorable crisis had arisen, again framed the most calumnious charges against him, before his arrival at Alexandria; assuring the Emperor Constantius that he was subverting all Egypt and Libya. And his having undertaken to ordain out of the limits of his own diocese, tended not a little to accredit the accusations against him. Meanwhile in this conjuncture, Athanasius entered Alexandria; and having convened a council of the bishops in Egypt, they

---

[3] Cf. *Apost. Cann.* XXXV. 'Let not a bishop dare to ordain beyond his limits, in cities and places not subject to him.' It follows, therefore, that the whole of Egypt was not under the bishop of Alexandria; otherwise no such charge as is here mentioned could have been made against Athanasius. That these ordinations were made in Egypt is evident from the mention of Pelusium, which Athanasius had already passed through.
[1] I. 38.
[2] The same account is given by Eunap. X. 9, and by Zosimus, II. 40.
[3] Ch. 5, above.

[4] Magnentius was governor of the provinces of Rhœtia, and assassinated Constans, as above. Cf. Zosimus, II. 43.
[5] This whole affair is treated extensively in Zosimus, II. 43-48.
[1] 350 A.D.

confirmed by their unanimous vote, what had been determined in the Synod at Sardica, and that assembled at Jerusalem by Maximus. But the emperor, who had been long since imbued with Arian doctrine, reversed all the indulgent proceedings he had so recently resolved on. And first of all he ordered that Paul, bishop of Constantinople, should be sent into exile ; whom those who conducted strangled, at Cucusus in Cappadocia. Marcellus was also ejected, and Basil again made ruler of the church at Ancyra. Lucius of Adrianople, being loaded with chains, died in prison. The reports which were made concerning Athanasius so wrought on the emperor's mind, that in an ungovernable fury he commanded him to be put to death wherever he might be found : he moreover included Theodulus and Olympius, who presided over churches in Thrace, in the same proscription. Athanasius, however, was not ignorant of the intentions of the emperor ; but learning of them he once more had recourse to flight, and so escaped the emperor's menaces. The Arians denounced this retreat as criminal, particularly Narcissus, bishop of Neronias in Cilicia, George of Laodicæa, and Leontius who then had the oversight of the church at Antioch. This last person, when a presbyter, had been divested of his rank,[2] because in order to remove all suspicion of illicit intercourse with a woman named Eustolium, with whom he spent a considerable portion of his time, he had castrated himself, and thenceforward lived more unreservedly with her, on the ground that there could be no longer any ground for evil surmises. Afterwards however, at the earnest desire of the Emperor Constantius, he was created bishop of the church at Antioch, after Stephen, the successor of Placitus. So much respecting this.

CHAPTER XXVII.

Macedonius having possessed himself of the See of Constantinople inflicts much Injury on those who differ from him.

AT that time Paul having been removed in the manner described, Macedonius became ruler of the churches in Constantinople ; who, acquir-

ing very great ascendancy over the emperor, stirred up a war among Christians, of a no less grievous kind than that which the usurpers themselves were waging. For having prevailed on his sovereign to co-operate with him in devastating the churches, he procured that whatever pernicious measures he determined to pursue should be ratified by law. And on this account throughout the several cities an edict was proclaimed, and a military force appointed to carry the imperial decrees into effect. Accordingly those who acknowledged the doctrine of consubstantiality were expelled not only from the churches, but also from the cities. Now at first they were satisfied with expulsion ; but as the evil grew they resorted to the worse extremity of inducing compulsory communion with them, caring but little for such a desecration of the churches. Their violence indeed was scarcely less than that of those who had formerly obliged the Christians to worship idols ; for they applied all kinds of scourgings, a variety of tortures, and confiscation of property. Many were punished with exile ; some died under the torture ; and others were put to death while they were being led into exile. These atrocities were exercised throughout all the eastern cities, but especially at Constantinople ; the internal strife which was but slight before was thus savagely increased by Macedonius, as soon as he obtained the bishopric. The cities of Greece, however, and Illyricum, with those of the western parts, still enjoyed tranquillity ; inasmuch as they preserved harmony among themselves, and continued to adhere to the rule of faith promulgated by the council of Nicæa.

CHAPTER XXVIII.

Athanasius' Account of the Deeds of Violence committed at Alexandria by George the Arian.

WHAT cruelties George perpetrated at Alexandria at the same time may be learned from the narration of Athanasius, who both suffered in and witnessed the occurrences. In his ' Apology for his flight,'[1] speaking of these transactions, he thus expresses himself :

' Moreover, they came to Alexandria, again seeking to destroy me : and on this occasion their proceedings were worse than before ; for the soldiery having suddenly surrounded the church, there arose the din of war, instead of the voice of prayer. Afterwards, on his arrival during Lent,[2] George, sent from Cappadocia, added to the evil which he was instructed to

---

[2] Cf. *Apost. Cann.* XXII. and XXIII.; according to these any cleric was to be deposed if found guilty of such a crime. The Council of Nicæa also passed a canon on the subject which is as follows: ' If a man has been mutilated by physicians during sickness, or by barbarians, he may remain among the clergy; but if a man in good health has mutilated himself, he must resign his post after the matter has been proved among the clergy, and in future no one who has thus acted should be ordained. But as it is evident that what has just been said only concerns those who have thus acted with intention, and have dared to mutilate themselves, those who have been made eunuchs by barbarians or by their masters will be allowed, conformably to the canon, to remain among the clergy, if in other respects they are worthy.' *Canon* I. See Hefele, *Hist. of the Councils*, Vol. I. p. 375, 376.

---

[1] Athan. *Apol. de Fuga*, 6.
[2] Τεσσαρακοστή, lit. = ' forty days' fast,' formed by mistaken analogy to πεντηκοστή.

work. When Easter-week[3] was passed, the virgins were cast into prison, the bishops were led in chains by the military, and the dwellings even of orphans and widows were forcibly entered and their provisions pillaged. Christians were assassinated by night; houses were sealed;[4] and the relatives of the clergy were endangered on their account. Even these outrages were dreadful; but those that followed were still more so. For in the week after the holy Pentecost, the people, having fasted, went forth to the cemetery to pray, because all were averse to communion with George: that wickedest of men being informed of this, instigated against them Sebastian, an officer who was a Manichæan. He, accordingly, at the head of a body of troops armed with drawn swords, bows, and darts, marched out to attack the people, although it was the Lord's day: finding but few at prayers, — as the most part had retired because of the lateness of the hour, — he performed such exploits as might be expected from them. Having kindled a fire, he set the virgins near it, in order to compel them to say that they were of the Arian faith: but seeing they stood their ground and despised the fire, he then stripped them, and so beat them on the face, that for a long time afterwards they could scarcely be recognized. Seizing also about forty men, he flogged them in an extraordinary manner: for he so lacerated their backs with rods fresh cut from the palm-tree, which still had their thorns on, that some were obliged to resort repeatedly to surgical aid in order to have the thorns extracted from their flesh, and others, unable to bear the agony, died under its infliction. All the survivors with one virgin they banished to the Great Oasis.[5] The bodies of the dead they did not so much as give up to their relatives, but denying them the rites of sepulture they concealed them as they thought fit, that the evidences of their cruelty might not appear. They did this acting as madmen. For while the friends of the deceased rejoiced on account of their confession, but mourned because their bodies were uninterred, the impious inhumanity of these acts was sounded abroad the more conspicuously. For soon after this they sent into exile out of Egypt and the two Libyas the following bishops: Ammonius,

Thmuïs, Caïus, Philo, Hermes, Pliny, Psenosiris, Nilammon, Agatho, Anagamphus, Mark, Ammonius, another Mark, Dracontius, Adelphius, and Athenodorus; and the presbyters Hierax and Discorus. And so harshly did they treat them in conducting them, that some expired while on their journey, and others in the place of banishment. In this way they got rid of more than thirty bishops, for the anxious desire of the Arians, like Ahab's, was to exterminate the truth if possible.'

Such are the words of Athanasius in regard to the atrocities perpetrated by George at Alexandria. The emperor meanwhile led his army into Illyricum. For there the urgency of public affairs demanded his presence; and especially the proclamation of Vetranio[6] as emperor by the military. On arriving at Sirmium, he came to a conference with Vetranio during a truce; and so managed, that the soldiers who had previously declared for him changed sides, and saluted Constantius alone as Augustus and sovereign autocrat. In the acclamations, therefore, no notice was taken of Vetranio. Vetranio, perceiving himself to be abandoned, immediately threw himself at the feet of the emperor; Constantius, taking from him his imperial crown and purple, treated him with great clemency, and recommended him to pass the rest of his days tranquilly in the condition of a private citizen: observing that a life of repose at his advanced age was far more suitable than a dignity which entailed anxieties and care. Vetranio's affairs came to this issue; and the emperor ordered that a liberal provision out of the public revenue should be given him. Often afterwards writing to the emperor during his residence at Prusa in Bithynia, Vetranio assured him that he had conferred the greatest blessing on him, by liberating him from the disquietudes which are the inseparable concomitants of sovereign power. Adding that he himself did not act wisely in depriving himself of that happiness in retirement, which he had bestowed upon him. Let this suffice on this point. After these things, the Emperor Constantius having created Gallus his kinsman Cæsar, and given him his own name,[7] sent him to Antioch in Syria, providing thus for the guarding of the eastern parts. When Gallus was entering this city, the Saviour's sign appeared in the East:[8] for a pillar in the form of a cross seen in the heavens gave occasion of great amazement to the spectators. His other generals the emperor

---

[3] Suspending, i.e., all violence during the period of festivity attending the observance of Easter.

[4] Houses are often sealed by state and municipal officials in the East, even at the present time, when their contents are to be confiscated, or for any other reason an inventory is to be made by the authorities. The sealing consists in fastening and securing the locks and bolts and attaching the impression of the official seal to some sealing-wax which is put over them. In this case the object of the sealing was apparently the confiscation of the contents.

[5] The modern *El-Onah* or *El-Kharjeh*, situated west of the Nile, seven days' journey from Thebes, contains several small streams, and abounds in vegetation, including palm-trees, orange and citron groves, olive orchards, &c. See Smith, *Dict. of Geogr.*

[6] Sozomen (IV. 4) calls him Οὐετερανίων; cf. also Zosimus, II. 44, on the way in which he was elevated and soon afterwards reduced.

[7] See I. 1, and note on the name of Eusebius Pamphilus; cf. Smith and Cheetham, *Dict. of Christ. Ant. Names.*

[8] Similar to the appearance mentioned in I. 2. See note on that passage.

despatched against Magnentius with considerable forces, and he himself remained at Sirmium, awaiting the course of events.

CHAPTER XXIX.

Of the Heresiarch Photinus.

DURING this time Photinus,[1] who then presided over the church in that city, more openly avowed the creed he had devised ; wherefore a tumult being made in consequence, the emperor ordered a Synod of bishops to be held at Sirmium. There were accordingly convened there of the Oriental bishops,[2] Mark of Arethusa, George of Alexandria, whom the Arians sent, as I have before said, having placed him over that see on the removal of Gregory, Basil who presided over the church at Ancyra after Marcellus was ejected, Pancratius of Pelusium, and Hypatian of Heraclea. Of the Western bishops there were present Valens of Mursa, and the then celebrated Hosius of Cordova in Spain, who attended much against his will. These met at Sirmium, after the consulate of Sergius and Nigrinian,[3] in which year no consul celebrated the customary inaugural[4] solemnities, in consequence of the tumults of war ; and having met and found that Photinus held the heresy of Sabellius the Libyan, and Paul of Samosata, they immediately deposed him. This decision was both at that time and afterwards universally commended as honorable and just ; but those who continued there, subsequently acted in a way which was by no means so generally approved.

CHAPTER XXX.

Creeds published at Sirmium in Presence of the Emperor Constantius.

As if they would rescind their former determinations respecting the faith, they published anew other expositions of the creed, viz.: one which Mark of Arethusa composed in Greek ; and others in Latin, which harmonized neither in expression nor in sentiment with one another, nor with that dictated by the bishop of Arethusa. I shall here subjoin one of those drawn up in Latin, to that prepared in Greek by Mark : the

other, which was afterwards recited at Sirmium,[1] will be given when we describe what was done at Ariminum. It must be understood, however, that both the Latin forms were translated into Greek. The declaration of faith set forth by Mark, was as follows :[2]

'We believe in one God the Father Almighty, the Creator and Maker of all things, of whom the whole family in heaven and on earth is named,[3] and in his only begotten Son, our Lord Jesus Christ, who was begotten of the Father before all ages, God of God, Light of Light, by whom all things visible and invisible, which are in the heavens and upon the earth, were made : who is the Word, and the Wisdom, and the true Light, and the Life ; who in the last days for our sake was made man and born of the holy virgin, and was crucified and died, and was buried, and rose again from the dead on the third day, and was received up into heaven, and sat at the right hand of the Father, and is coming at the completion of the age to judge the living and the dead, and to requite every one according to his works : whose kingdom being everlasting, endures into infinite ages ; for he will be seated at the Father's right hand, not only in the present age, but also in that which is to come. [We believe] also in the Holy Spirit, that is to say the Comforter, whom, having promised to his apostles after his ascension into the heavens, to teach them, and bring all things to their remembrance, he sent ; by whom also the souls of those who have sincerely believed in him are sanctified. But those who affirm that the Son is of things which are not, or of another substance, and not of God, and that there was a time or an age when he was not, the holy and catholic Church recognizes to be aliens. We therefore again say, if any one affirms that the Father and Son are two Gods, let him be anathema. And if any one admits that Christ is God and the Son of God before the ages, but does not confess that he ministered to the Father in the formation of all things, let him be anathema. If any one shall dare to assert that the Unbegotten, or a part of him, was born of Mary, let him be anathema. If any one should say that the Son was of Mary according to foreknowledge, and not that he was with God, begotten of the Father before the ages, and that all things were not made by him, let him be anathema. If any one affirms the essence of God to be dilated or contracted, let him be anathema. If any one says that the dilated essence of God makes the Son, or shall

---

[1] A disciple of Marcellus (see ch. 18). See Hilar. de Synod. 61, Cave on Photinus.
[2] The bishops here mentioned, according to Valesius, took part not in this council, but in another held at the same place nine years later, under the consuls Eusebius and Hypatius.
[3] 351 A.D. So also Sozomen, IV. 6.
[4] The Ludi circenses, consisting of five games, leaping, wrestling, boxing, racing, and hurling, — called in Greek πένταθλον, — with scenic representations and spectacles of wild beasts at the amphitheatre; with these the consuls entertained the people at their entrance on the consulate. Alluded to by Tacitus (Ann. I. 2) and Juvenal (Sat. X. 1). Cf. Smith, Dict. of Greek and Rom. Antiq.

---

[1] There were three councils held at Sirmium: one in 351, as already indicated in note 3, ch. 29; another in 357, in which Hosius and Potamius composed their blasphemy; and one in 359. It was in this last council that that creed was drawn up which was recited in Ariminum. The confusion of Socrates on this point has been alluded to in the Introd.
[2] Athan. de Synod. 27.   [3] Eph. iii. 15.

term the Son the dilatation of his essence, let him be anathema. If any one calls the Son of God the internal or uttered word, let him be anathema. If any one declares that the Son that was born of Mary was man only, let him be anathema. If any man affirming him that was born of Mary to be God and man, shall imply the unbegotten God himself, let him be anathema. If any one shall understand the text, " I am the first, and I am the last, and besides me there is no God,"[4] which was spoken for the destruction of idols and false gods, in the sense the Jews do, as if it were said for the subversion of the only-begotten of God before the ages, let him be anathema. If any one hearing " the Word was made flesh,"[5] should imagine that the Word was changed into flesh, or that he underwent any change in assuming flesh, let him be anathema. If any one hearing that the only-begotten Son of God was crucified, should say that his divinity underwent any corruption, or suffering, or change, or diminution, or destruction, let him be anathema.. If any one should affirm that the Father said not to the Son, " Let us make man,"[6] but that God spoke to himself, let him be anathema. If any one says that it was not the Son that was seen by Abraham, but the unbegotten God, or a part of him, let him be anathema. If any one says that it was not the Son that as man wrestled with Jacob, but the unbegotten God, or a part of him, let him be anathema. If any one shall understand the words, " The Lord rained from the Lord,"[7] not in relation to the Father and the Son, but shall say that he rained from himself, let him be anathema : for the Lord the Son rained from the Lord the Father. If any one hearing " the Lord the Father, and the Lord the Son," shall term both the Father and the Son Lord, and saying " the Lord from the Lord " shall assert that there are two Gods, let him be anathema. For we do not co-ordinate the Son with the Father, but [conceive him to be] subordinate to the Father. For he neither came down to the body[8] without his Father's will ; nor did he rain from himself, but from *the Lord* (i.e. the Father) who exercises supreme authority : nor does he sit at the Father's right hand of himself, but in obedience to the Father saying, " Sit thou at my right hand "[9] [let him be anathema]. If any one should say that the Father, Son, and Holy Spirit are one person, let him be anathema. If any one, speaking of the Holy Spirit the Comforter, shall call him the unbegotten God, let him be anathema. If any

one, as he hath taught us, shall not say that the Comforter is other than the Son, when he has himself said, " the Father, whom I will ask, shall send you another Comforter,"[10] let him be anathema. If any one affirm that the Spirit is part of the Father and of the Son, let him be anathema. If any one say that the Father, Son, and Holy Spirit are three Gods, let him be anathema. If any one say that the Son of God was made as one of the creatures by the will of God, let him be anathema. If any one shall say that the Son was begotten without the Father's will, let him be anathema : for the Father did not, as compelled by any natural necessity, beget the Son at a time when he was unwilling ; but as soon as it pleased him, he has declared that of himself without time and without passion, he begat him. If any one should say that the Son is unbegotten, and without beginning, intimating that there are two without beginning, and unbegotten, so making two Gods, let him be anathema : for the Son is the head and beginning of all things ; but " the head of Christ is God."[11] Thus do we devoutly trace up all things by the Son to one source of all things who is without beginning. Moreover, to give an accurate conception of Christian doctrine, we again say, that if any one shall not declare Christ Jesus to have been the Son of God before all ages, and to have ministered to the Father in the creation of all things ; but shall affirm that from the time only when he was born of Mary, was he called the Son and Christ, and that he then received the commencement of his divinity, let him be anathema, as the Samosatan.'[12]

Another Exposition of the Faith set forth at Sirmium in Latin, and afterwards translated into Greek.[13]

Since it appeared good that some deliberation respecting the faith should be undertaken, all points have been carefully investigated and discussed at Sirmium, in presence of Valens, Ursacius, Germinius, and others. It is evident that there is one God, the Father Almighty, according as it is declared over the whole world ; and his only-begotten Son Jesus Christ, our Lord, God, and Saviour, begotten of him before the ages. But we ought not to say that there are two Gods, since the Lord himself has said ' I go unto my Father and your Father, and unto my God and your God.'[14] Therefore he is God even of all, as the apostle also taught, ' Is he the God of the Jews only ? Is he not

---

[4] Isa. xliv. 6.　　[5] John i. 14.　　[6] Gen. i. 26.
[7] Gen. xix. 24: ' Then the LORD . . . rained brimstone and fire from the LORD out of heaven.'
[8] Athanasius reads ἐπὶ Σόδομα, not εἰς σῶμα. If this be the true reading, we should translate ' came down to Sodom,' &c.
[9] Ps. cix. 1 (LXX).

[10] John xiv. 16, 26.　　[11] 1 Cor. xi. 3.
[12] Paul of Samosata, see I. 36, note 3.
[13] Athan. *de Synod.* 28, and Hilar. *de Synod.* calls this creed ' The blasphemy composed at Sirmium by Hosius and Potamius.'
[14] John xx. 17.

also of the Gentiles? Yea of the Gentiles also ;
seeing that it is one God who shall justify the
circumcision by faith.'[15]   And in all other matters there is agreement, nor is there any ambiguity.   But since it troubles very many to
understand about that which is termed *substantia* in Latin, and *ousia* in Greek ; that is to
say, in order to mark the sense more accurately,
the word *homoousion*[16] or *homoiousion*,[17] it is altogether desirable that none of these terms should
be mentioned : nor should they be preached on
in the church, for this reason, that nothing is
recorded concerning them in the holy Scriptures ;
and because these things are above the knowledge of mankind and human capacity, and that
no one can explain the Son's generation, of
which it is written, 'And who shall declare his
generation?'[18]   It is manifest that the Father
only knows in what way he begat the Son ; and
again the Son, how he was begotten by the
Father.   But no one can doubt that the Father
is greater in honor, dignity, and divinity, and
in the very name of Father ; the Son himself
testifying 'My Father who hath sent me is greater
than I.'[19]   And no one is ignorant that this is
also catholic doctrine,[20] that there are two persons of the Father and Son, and that the Father
is the greater : but that the Son is subject, together with all things which the Father has
subjected to him.   That the Father had no
beginning, and is invisible, immortal, and im-
passible : but that the Son was begotten of the
Father, God of God, Light of Light ; and that
no one comprehends his generation, as was
before said, but the Father alone.   That the
Son himself, our Lord and God, took flesh or
a body, that is to say human nature, according
as the angel brought glad tidings : and as the
whole Scriptures teaches, and especially the apostle who was the great teacher of the Gentiles,
Christ assumed the human nature through which
he suffered, from the Virgin Mary.   But the summary and confirmation of the entire faith is,
that [the doctrine of] the Trinity should be
always maintained, according as we have read
in the gospel, 'Go ye and disciple all nations,
baptizing them in the name of the Father, and
of the Son, and of the Holy Spirit.'[21]   Thus the
number of the Trinity is complete and perfect.
Now the Comforter, the Holy Spirit, sent by
the Son, came according to his promise, in
order to sanctify and instruct the apostles and
all believers.

They endeavored to induce Photinus, even
after his deposition, to assent to and subscribe
these things, promising to restore him his bish-

opric, if by recantation he would anathematize
the dogma he had invented, and adopt their
opinion.   But he did not accept their proposal,
and on the other hand he challenged them to a
disputation :[22] and a day being appointed by
the emperor's arrangement, the bishops who
were there present assembled, and not a few of
the senators, whom the emperor had directed
to attend to the discussion.   In their presence,
Basil, who at that time presided over the church
at Ancyra, was appointed to oppose Photinus,
and short-hand writers took down their respective speeches.   The conflict of arguments on
both sides was extremely severe ; but Photinus
having been worsted, was condemned, and spent
the rest of his life in exile, during which time
he composed treatises in both languages — for
he was not unskilled in Latin — against all heresies, and in favor of his own views.   Concerning
Photinus let this suffice.

Now the bishops who were convened at Sirmium, were afterwards dissatisfied with that
form of the creed which had been promulgated by them in Latin ; for after its publication, it appeared to them to contain many
contradictions.   They therefore endeavored to
get it back again from the transcribers ; but
inasmuch as many secreted it, the emperor by
his edicts commanded that the version should
be sought for, threatening punishment to any
one who should be detected concealing it.
These menaces, however, were incapable of suppressing what had already fallen into the hands
of many.   Let this suffice in regard to these
affairs.

CHAPTER XXXI.

Of Hosius, Bishop of Cordova.

SINCE we have observed that Hosius the Spaniard was present [at the council of Sirmium]
against his will, it is necessary to give some
brief account of him.   A short time before he
had been sent into exile by the intrigues of the
Arians : but at the earnest solicitation of those
convened at Sirmium, the emperor summoned
him thither, wishing that by persuasion, or by
compulsion he should give his sanction to their
proceedings ; for if this could be effected, they
considered it would give great authority to their
sentiments.   On this ground, therefore, as I
have said, he was most unwillingly obliged to
be present : and when he refused to concur with
them, stripes and tortures were inflicted on the
old man.   Wherefore he was constrained by

---

[15] Rom. iii. 29, 30.
[16] Of the same substance.
[17] Of similar substance.
[18] Isa. liii. 5.

[19] John xiv. 28.
[20] καθολικόν, 'universally accepted.'
[21] Matt. xxviii. 19.

[22] 'Epiphanius relates that Photinus, after he had been condemned
and deposed in the synod of Sirmium, went to Constantius, and requested he might dispute concerning the faith before judges
nominated by him ; and that Constantius enjoined Basilius, bishop
of Ancyra, to undertake a disputation with Photinus, and gave leave
that Thalassiuss, Datianus, Cerealis, and Taurus should be arbiters'
(Valesius).

force to acquiesce in and subscribe to their exposition of the faith. Such was the issue of affairs at that time transacted at Sirmium. But the emperor Constantius after these things still continued to reside at that place, awaiting there the result of the war against Magnentius.

CHAPTER XXXII.

Overthrow of the Usurper Magnentius.

MAGNENTIUS in the meanwhile having made himself master of the imperial city Rome, put to death many members of the senatorial council, as well as many of the populace. But as soon as the commanders under Constantius had collected an army of Romans, and commenced their march against him, he left Rome, and retired into the Gauls. There several battles were fought, sometimes to the advantage of one party, and sometimes to that of the other: but at last Magnentius having been defeated near Mursa — a fortress of Gaul — was there closely besieged. In this place the following remarkable incident is said to have occurred. Magnentius desiring to reassure the courage of his soldiers who were disheartened by their late overthrow, ascended a lofty tribunal for this purpose. They, wishing to give utterance to the usual acclamation with which they greet emperors, contrary to their intention simultaneously all shouted the name, not of Magnentius, but of Constantius Augustus. Regarding this as an omen unfavorable to himself, Magnentius immediately withdrew from the fortress, and retreated to the remotest parts of Gaul. Thither the generals of Constantius hastened in pursuit. An engagement having again taken place near Mount Seleucus,[1] Magnentius was totally routed, and fled alone to Lyons, a city of Gaul, which is distant three days' journey from the fortress at Mursa. Magnentius, having reached this city, first slew his own mother; then having killed his brother also, whom he had created Cæsar, he at last committed suicide by falling on his own sword. This happened in the sixth consulate of Constantius, and the second of Constantius Gallus, on the fifteenth[2] day of August. Not long after, the other brother of Magnentius, named Decentius, put an end to his own life by hanging himself. Such was the end of the enterprises of Magnentius. The affairs of the empire were not altogether quieted; for soon after this another usurper arose whose name was Silvanus: but the generals of Constantius speedily put him also out of the way, whilst raising disturbances in Gaul.

CHAPTER XXXIII.

Of the Jews inhabiting Dio-Cæsarea in Palestine.

ABOUT the same time there arose another intestine commotion in the East: for the Jews who inhabited Dio-Cæsarea in Palestine took up arms against the Romans, and began to ravage the adjacent places. But Gallus who was also called Constantius, whom the emperor, after creating Cæsar, had sent into the East, despatched an army against them, and completely vanquished them: after which he ordered that their city Dio-Cæsarea should be razed to the foundations.

CHAPTER XXXIV.

Of Gallus Cæsar.

GALLUS, having accomplished these things, was unable to bear his success with moderation; but forthwith attempted innovations against the authority of him who had constituted him Cæsar, himself aspiring to the sovereign power. His purpose was, however, soon detected by Constantius: for he had dared to put to death, on his own responsibility, Domitian, at that time Prætorian prefect of the East, and Magnus the quæstor, not having disclosed his designs to the emperor. Constantius, extremely incensed at this conduct, summoned Gallus to his presence, who being in great terror went very reluctantly; and when he arrived in the western parts, and had reached the island of Flanona, Constantius ordered him to be slain. But not long after he created Julian, the brother of Gallus, Cæsar, and sent him against the barbarians in Gaul. It was in the seventh consulate[1] of the emperor Constantius that Gallus, who was surnamed Constantius, was slain, when he himself was a third time consul: and Julian was created Cæsar on the 6th of November in the following year, when Arbetion[2] and Lollian were consuls; of him we shall make farther mention in the next book.[3] When Constantius was thus relieved from the disquietudes which had occupied him, his attention was again directed to ecclesiastical contentions. Going therefore from Sirmium to the imperial city Rome, he again appointed a synod of bishops, summoning some of the eastern prelates to hasten into Italy,[4] and arranging for those of the west to meet them there. While preparations were making in the east for this purpose, Julius bishop of Rome died, after having presided over the church in that place fifteen years, and was succeeded in the episcopal dignity by Liberius.

---

[1] So in the Allat. MS., with the variant reading in other MSS. Μιλτοσέλευκοϛ.
[2] 353 A.D.; but the date is given differently in Idatius' Fasti.

[1] 354 A.D.   [2] 355 A.D.   [3] See III. 1.
[4] So rightly in the Allat. MS.; the variant Γαλλίαν is inconsistent with the context.

CHAPTER XXXV.

Of Aëtius the Syrian, Teacher of Eunomius.

AT Antioch in Syria another heresiarch sprang up, Aëtius, surnamed Atheus. He agreed in doctrine with Arius, and maintained the same opinions : but separated himself from the Arian party because they had admitted Arius into communion. For Arius, as I have before related,[1] entertaining one opinion in his heart, professed another with his lips ; having hypocritically assented to and subscribed the form of faith set forth at the council of Nicæa, in order to deceive the reigning emperor. On this account, therefore, Aëtius separated himself from the Arians. He had, however, previously been a heretic, and a zealous advocate of Arian views. After receiving some very scanty instruction at Alexandria, he departed thence, and arrived at Antioch in Syria, which was his native place, was ordained deacon by Leontius, who was then bishop of that city. Upon this he began to astonish those who conversed with him by the singularity of his discourses. And this he did in dependence on the precepts of Aristotle's *Categories;* there is a book of that name, the scope of which he neither himself perceived, nor had been enlightened on by intercourse with learned persons : so that he was little aware that he was framing fallacious arguments to perplex and deceive himself. For Aristotle had composed this work to exercise the ingenuity of his young disciples, and to confound by subtle arguments the sophists who affected to deride philosophy. Wherefore the Ephectic academicians,[2] who expound the writings of Plato and Plotinus, censure the vain subtlety which Aristotle has displayed in that book: but Aëtius, who never had the advantage of an academical preceptor, adhered to the sophisms of the *Categories.* For this reason he was unable to comprehend how there could be generation without a beginning, and how that which was begotten can be co-eternal with him who begat. In fact, Aëtius was a man of so superficial attainments, and so little acquainted with the sacred Scriptures, and so extremely fond of caviling, a thing which any clown might do, that he had never carefully studied those ancient writers who have interpreted the Christian oracles ; wholly rejecting Clemens and Africa-

nus and Origen, men eminent for their information in every department of literature and science. But he composed epistles both to the emperor Constantius, and to some other persons, wherein he interwove tedious disputes for the purpose of displaying his sophisms. He has therefore been surnamed Atheus. But although his doctrinal statements were similar to those of the Arians, yet from the abstruse nature of his syllogisms, which they were unable to comprehend, his associates in Arianism pronounced him a heretic. Being for that reason expelled from their church, he pretended to have separated himself from their communion. Even in the present day there are to be found some who from him were formerly named Aëtians, but now Eunomians. For some time later Eunomius, who had been his amanuensis, having been instructed by his master in this heretical mode of reasoning, afterwards became the head of that sect. But of Eunomius we shall speak more fully in the proper place.[3]

CHAPTER XXXVI.

Of the Synod at Milan.

Now at that time the bishops met in Italy, very few indeed from the East, most of them being hindered from coming either by the infirmities of age or by the distance ; but of the West there were more than three hundred.[1] It was a command of the emperor that they should be assembled at Milan. On meeting, the Eastern prelates opened the Synod by calling upon those convened to pass a unanimous sentence of condemnation against Athanasius ; with this object in view, that he might thenceforward be utterly shut out from Alexandria. But Paulinus, bishop of Treves in Gaul, and Dionysius, of whom the former was bishop of Alba,[2] the metropolis of Italy, and Eusebius of Vercellæ, a city of Liguria in Italy, perceiving that the Eastern bishops, by demanding a ratification of the sentence against Athanasius, were intent on subverting the faith, arose and loudly exclaimed that 'this proposition indicated a covert plot against the principles of Christian truth. For they insisted that the charges against Athanasius were unfounded, and merely invented by his accusers as a means of corrupting the faith.'

---

[1] I. 26.

[2] Diogenes Laertius, *Proem.* XI (16), says: 'Philosophers were generally divided into two classes, — the dogmatics, who spoke of things as they might be comprehended ; and the ephectics, who refused to define anything, and disputed so as to make the understanding of them impossible.' The word 'ephectic' is derived from the verb ἐπέχω, 'to hold back,' and was used by the philosophers to whom it is applied as a title because they claimed to hold back their judgment, being unable to reach a conclusion. Cf. also the name 'skeptic,' from σκέπτομαι. See Zeller, *Stoics, Epicureans, and Skeptics,* p. 525.

[3] IV. 7.

[1] So also Sozomen, IV. 9; but the number appears exorbitant. Valesius conjectures that the texts of Socrates and Sozomen are corrupted, and that we must read thirty instead of three hundred. The smaller number agrees exactly with the list given in the epistle of this council to Eusebius of Vercellæ; in this list thirty bishops are named as agreeing to the condemnation of Athanasius, Marcellus, and Photinus. Cf. Baronius, *Annal.* year 355.

[2] Sozomen (IV. 9) agrees here also with Socrates; but Athanasius, in *Epist. ad Solitar.,* and after him Baronius and Valesius, make Milan and not Alba, the metropolis of Italy, and Dionysius bishop of Milan, and not of Alba.

Having made this protest with much vehemence of manner, the congress of bishops was then dissolved.

CHAPTER XXXVII.

Of the Synod at Ariminum, and the Creed there published.[1]

THE emperor on being apprised of what had taken place, sent these three bishops into exile ; and determined to convene an ecumenical council, that by drawing all the Eastern bishops into the West, he might if possible bring them all to agree. But when, on consideration, the length of the journey seemed to present serious obstacles, he directed that the Synod should consist of two divisions ; permitting those present at Milan to meet at Ariminum in Italy : but the Eastern bishops he instructed by letters to assemble at Nicomedia in Bithynia. The emperor's object in these arrangements was to effect a general unity of opinion ; but the issue was contrary to his expectation. For neither of the Synods was in harmony with itself, but each was divided into opposing factions : for those convened at Ariminum could not agree with one another ; and the Eastern bishops assembled at Seleucia in Isauria made another schism. The details of what took place in both we will give in the course of our history,[2] but we shall first make a few observations on Eudoxius. About that time Leontius having died, who had ordained the heretic Aëtius[3] as deacon, Eudoxius bishop of Germanicia — this city is in Syria — who was then at Rome, thinking no time was to be lost, speciously represented to the emperor that the city over which he presided was in need of his counsel and care, and requested permission to return there immediately. This the emperor readily acceded to, having no suspicion of a clandestine purpose : Eudoxius having some of the principal officers of the emperor's bedchamber as coadjutors, deserted his own diocese, and fraudulently installed himself in the see of Antioch. His first desire was to restore Aëtius ; accordingly he convened a council of bishops for the purpose of reinvesting Aëtius with the dignity of the diaconate. But this could in no way be brought about, for the odium with which Aëtius was regarded was more prevalent than the exertions of Eudoxius in his favor. When the bishops were assembled

at Ariminum, those from the East declared that they were willing to pass in silence the case of Athanasius : a resolution that was zealously supported by Ursacius and Valens, who had formerly maintained the tenets of Arius ; but, as I have already stated, had afterwards presented a recantation of their opinion to the bishop of Rome, and publicly avowed their assent to the doctrine of consubstantiality. For these men always inclined to side with the dominant party. Germinius, Auxentius, Demophilus and Gaïus made the same declaration in reference to Athanasius. When therefore some endeavored to propose one thing in the convocation of bishops, and some another, Ursacius and Valens said that all former draughts of the creed ought to be considered as set aside, and the last alone, which had been prepared at their late convention at Sirmium, regarded as authorized. They then caused to be read a paper which they held in their hands, containing another form of the creed : this had indeed been drawn up at Sirmium, but had been kept concealed, as we have before observed, until their present publication of it at Ariminum. It has been translated from the Latin into Greek, and is as follows :[4]

'The catholic faith was expounded at Sirmium in presence of our lord Constantius,[5] in the consulate[6] of the most illustrious Flavius Eusebius, and Hypatius, on the twenty-third of May.

'We believe in one only and true God, the Father Almighty, the Creator and Framer of all things : and in one only-begotten Son of God, before all ages, before all beginning, before all conceivable time, and before all comprehensible thought, begotten without passion : by whom the ages were framed, and all things made : who was begotten as the only-begotten of the Father, only of only, God of God, like to the Father who begat him, according to the Scriptures : whose generation no one knows, but the Father only who begat him. We know that this his only-begotten Son came down from the heavens by his Father's consent for the putting away of sin, was born of the Virgin Mary, conversed with his disciples, and fulfilled every dispensation according to the Father's will : was crucified and died, and descended into the lower parts of the earth, and disposed matters there ; at the sight of whom the (door-keepers of Hades

---

[1] Cf. Sozomen, III. 19; IV. 15-19; Theodoret, *H. E.* II. 18-21; Rufin. II. 21; Philostorgius, IV. 10. Also Hefele, *Hist. of the Ch. Councils*, Vol. II. p. 246-271.
[2] Ch. 39.
[3] According to Theodoret (*H. E.* II. 19) Aëtius was promoted to the diaconate under Leontius at Antioch; but Leontius, on being censured by Flavian and Diodorus for ordaining one who was notorious for his blasphemous utterances, divested him of his diaconate. Hence, later, Eudoxius attempted to restore him, as is here said.

[4] Athan. *de Synod.* 8; but Athanasius does not say that this creed was translated from Latin, as he does whenever he produces any document put into Greek; whence it appears, according to Valesius, that this is the form drawn up in Greek by Marcus of Arethusa, and submitted to the third Sirmium council in 359, but read at Ariminum as here said (cf. ch. 30, and note). The argument is not considered conclusive by Reading as far as it regards the original language of the creed; that it was written by Marcus of Arethusa, however, seems to be proved.
[5] The title of the emperor in Athanasius' version is 'The most pious and victorious emperor Constantius Augustus, eternal Augustus,' &c., which agrees with the representations of the ancients on the vainglory of Constantius. Cf. Amm. Marcellin. *Rerum Gestarum*, XVI. 10. 2, 3 (ed. Eyssenhardt).
[6] 359 A.D.

trembled [7]) : having arisen on the third day, he again conversed with his disciples, and after forty days were completed he ascended into the heavens, and is seated at the Father's right hand ; and at the last day he will come in his Father's glory to render to every one according to his works. [We believe] also in the Holy Spirit, whom the only-begotten Son of God Jesus Christ himself promised to send to the human race according to that which is written : [8] "I go away to my Father, and will ask him, and he will send you another Comforter, the Spirit of truth. He shall receive of mine, and shall teach you, and bring all things to your remembrance." As for the term "substance," which was used by our fathers for the sake of greater simplicity, but not being understood by the people has caused offense on account of the fact that the Scriptures do not contain it, it seemed desirable that it should be wholly abolished, and that in future no mention should be made of substance in reference to God, since the divine Scriptures have nowhere spoken concerning the substance of the Father and the Son. But we say that the Son is in all things *like* the Father, as the Holy Scriptures affirm and teach.'

These statements having been read, those who were dissatisfied with them rose and said : 'We came not hither because we were in want of a creed ; for we preserve inviolate that which we received from the beginning ; but we are here met to repress any innovation upon it which may have been made. If therefore what has been recited introduces no novelties, now openly anathematize the Arian heresy, in the same manner as the ancient canon of the church has rejected all heresies as blasphemous : for it is evident to the whole world that the impious dogma of Arius has excited the disturbances of the church, and the troubles which exist until now.' This proposition, which was not accepted by Ursacius, Valens, Germinius, Auxentius, Demophilus, and Gaïus, rent the church asunder completely : for these prelates adhered to what had then been recited in the Synod of Ariminum ; while the others again confirmed the Nicene Creed. They also ridiculed the superscription of the creed that had been read ; and especially Athanasius, in a letter which he sent to his friends, wherein he thus expresses himself : [9]

'What point of doctrine was wanting to the piety of the catholic church, that they should now make an investigation respecting the faith, and prefix moreover the consulate of the present times to their published exposition of it ? For

Ursacius, Valens, and Germinius have done what was neither done, nor even heard of, at any time before among Christians : having composed a creed such as they themselves are willing to believe, they prefaced it with the consulate, month, and day of the present time, in order to prove to all discerning persons that theirs is not the ancient faith, but such as was originated under the reign of the present emperor Constantius.[10] Moreover they have written all things with a view to their own heresy : and besides this, pretending to write respecting the Lord, they name another " Lord " as theirs, even Constantius, who has countenanced their impiety, so that those who deny the Son to be eternal, have styled him eternal emperor. Thus are they proved to be the enemies of Christ by their profanity. But perhaps the holy prophets' record of time afforded them a precedent for [noticing] the consulate ! Now even if they should presume to make this pretext, they would most glaringly expose their own ignorance. The prophecies of these holy men do indeed mark the times. Isaiah and Hosea lived in the days of Uzziah, Joatham, Ahaz, and Hezekiah ; [11] Jeremiah in the time of Josiah ; [12] Ezekiel and Daniel in the reign of Cyrus and Darius ; and others uttered their predictions in other times. Yet they did not then lay the foundations of religion. That was in existence before them, and always was, even before the creation of the world, God having prepared it for us in Christ. Nor did they designate the commencement of their own faith ; for they were themselves men of faith previously : but they signified the times of the promises given through them. Now the promises primarily referred to our Saviour's advent ; and all that was foretold respecting the course of future events in relation to Israel and the Gentiles was collateral and subordinate. Hence the periods mentioned indicated not the beginning of their faith, as I before observed, but the times in which these prophets lived and foretold such things. But these sages of our day, who neither compile histories, nor predict future events, after writing, " The Catholic Faith was published," immediately add the consulate, with the month and the day : and as the holy prophets wrote the date of their records and of their own ministration, so these men intimate the era of their own faith. And would that they had written concerning *their own* faith only — since they have now begun to believe — and had not undertaken to write respecting the Catholic faith. For they have not written, "Thus we believe"; but,

---

7 Job xxxviii. 17 (LXX).   8 John xiv. 16; xvi. 14.
9 Athan. *de Synod*. 8.

10 This appeal to antiquity, as the test of truth, is very common with the earlier Fathers; cf. Eusebius' treatment of the Scriptures of the New Testament, *H. E.* III. 3, 24, 25, *et al.*
11 Isa. i. 2; Hos. i. 1.   12 Jer. i. 2.

"The Catholic Faith was published." The temerity of purpose herein manifested argues their ignorance ; while the novelty of expression found in the document they have concocted shows it to be the same as the Arian heresy. By writing in this manner, they have declared when they themselves began to believe, and from what time they wish it to be understood their faith was first preached. And just as when the evangelist Luke says,[13] "A decree of enrolment was published," he speaks of an edict which was not in existence before, but came into operation at that time, and was published by him who had written it ; so these men by writing "The faith has now been published," have declared that the tenets of their heresy are of modern invention, and did not exist previously. But since they apply the term "Catholic" to it, they seem to have unconsciously fallen into the extravagant assumption of the Cataphrygians, asserting even as they did, that "the Christian faith was first revealed to us, and commenced with us." And as those termed Maximilla and Montanus, so these style Constantius their Lord, instead of Christ. But if according to them the faith had its beginning from the present consulate, what will the fathers and the blessed martyrs do? Moreover what will they themselves do with those who were instructed in religious principles by them, and died before this consulate? By what means will they recall them to life, in order to obliterate from their minds what they seemed to have taught them, and to implant in its stead those new discoveries which they have published? So stupid are they as to be only capable of framing pretenses, and these such as are unbecoming and unreasonable, and carry with them their own refutation.'

Athanasius wrote thus to his friends : and the interested who may read through his whole epistle will perceive how powerfully he treats the subject ; but for brevity's sake we have here inserted a part of it only. The Synod deposed Valens, Ursacius, Auxentius, Germinius, Gaïus, and Demophilus for refusing to anathematize the Arian doctrine ; who being very indignant at their deposition, hastened directly to the emperor, carrying with them the exposition of faith which had been read in the Synod. The council also acquainted the emperor with their determinations in a communication which translated from the Latin into Greek, was to the following effect :[14]

Epistle of the Synod of Ariminum to the Emperor Constantius.

We believe that it was by the appointment of God, as well as at the command of your piety, that the decrees formerly published have been executed. Accordingly we Western bishops came out of various districts to Ariminum, in order that the faith of the catholic church might be made manifest, and that those who held contrary views might be detected. For on a considerate review by us of all points, our decision has been to adhere to the ancient faith which the prophets, the gospels, and the apostles have revealed through our Lord Jesus Christ, the guardian of your empire, and the protector of your person, which faith also we have always maintained. We conceived that it would be unwarrantable and impious to mutilate any of those things which have been justly and rightly ratified, by those who sat in the Nicene council with Constantine of glorious memory, the father of your piety. Their doctrine and views have been infused into the minds and preached in the hearing of the people, and found to be powerfully opposed, even fatal, to the Arian heresy. And not only this heresy, but also all others have been put down by it. Should therefore anything be added to or taken away from what was at that time established, it would prove perilous ; for if either of these things should happen, the enemy will have boldness to do as they please.[15]

Wherefore Ursacius and Valens being heretofore suspected of entertaining Arian sentiments, were suspended from communion : but in order to be restored to it they made an apology, and claimed that they had repented of their shortcoming, as their written recantation attests : they therefore obtained pardon and complete absolution.

The time when these things occurred was when the council was in session at Milan, when the presbyters of the church of Rome were also present.

At[16] the same time, having known that Constantine, who even after his death is worthy of honorable mention, exposed the faith with due precision, but being born of men was baptized and departed to the peace due to him as his reward, we have deemed it improper to innovate after him disregarding so many holy

---

[13] Luke ii. 1.
[14] Athan. *de Synod.* 10. The Latin original which is given in Hilar. *Fragm.* 8, was adopted by Valesius in this place, and subsequently also by the English translators. We have followed the Greek of Socrates, giving the most important differences in the following four notes ; viz. 15, 16, 17, and 18. How these variations originated it is impossible to tell with assurance ; but it is not improbable that they may represent two drafts, of which one was originally tentative.

[15] The Latin original here contains the following paragraph not reproduced by Socrates: 'These matters having been strictly investigated and the creed drawn up in the presence of Constantine, who after being baptized, departed to God's rest in the faith of it, we regard as an abomination any infringement thereon, or any attempt to invalidate the authority of so many saints, confessors, and successors of the martyrs, who assisted at that council, and themselves preserved inviolate all the determinations of the ancient writers of the catholic church: whose faith has remained unto these times in which your piety has received from God the Father, through Jesus Christ our God and Lord, the power of ruling the world.'
[16] The Latin original omits the following paragraph, ending with the words 'over our portion of the world.'

confessors and martyrs, who also were authors of this confession, and persevered in their faith in the ancient system of the catholic church. Their faith God has perpetuated down to the years of your own reign through our Lord Jesus Christ, through whose grace it also became possible for you to so strengthen your dominion as to rule over one portion of the world.

Yet have these infatuated and wretched persons, endued with an unhappy disposition, again had the temerity to declare themselves the propagators of false doctrine, and even endeavor to subvert the constitution of the Church. For when the letters of your piety had ordered us to assemble for the examination of the faith, they laid bare their intention, stripped of its deceitful garb. For they attempted with certain craft and confusion to propose innovations, having in this as allies Germinius, Auxentius,[17] and Gaius, who continually cause strife and dissension, and their single teaching has surpassed the whole body of blasphemies. But when they perceived that we had not the same disposition or mind as they in regard to their false views, they changed their minds during our council, and said another expression of belief should be put forth. And short indeed was the time which convinced them of the falsity of their views.

In order, therefore, that the affairs of the Church may not be continually brought into the same condition, and in order that trouble and tumult may not continually arise and confuse all things, it appeared safe to preserve the previously determined views firm and unalterable, and to separate from our communion the persons above named; for which reason we have despatched to your clemency delegates who will communicate the opinion of the council to you. And to our delegates we have given this commission above all, that they should accredit the truth taking their motive from the ancient and right decisions. They will inform your holiness that peace will not be established as Ursacius and Valens say when some point of the right be overturned. For how can those be at peace who destroy peace? Rather will strife and tumult be occasioned by these things in the church of Rome also, as in the other cities. Wherefore, now, we beseech your clemency that you should look upon our delegation with a calm eye and listen to it with favor, and not allow that anything should be changed, thus bringing insult to the deceased, but permit us to continue in those things which have been defined and legislated by our ancestors; who, we should say, acted with shrewdness and wisdom and with the Holy Spirit. For the innovations they introduce at present fill the believing with

distrust and the unbelieving with cruelty.[18] We further implore you to instruct that the bishops who dwell in foreign parts, whom both the infirmity of age and the ills of poverty harass should be assisted to return easily and speedily to their own homes, so that the churches may not remain bereft of their bishops. Still further we beg of you this also, that nothing be stricken off, nor anything be added, to the articles [of faith] remaining over from the times of your pious father even until now; but that these may continue inviolate. Permit us not to toil and suffer longer, nor to be separated from our dioceses, but that together with our own peoples we may in peace have time to offer prayers and thanksgiving, supplicating for your safety and continuance in the dominion, which may the divinity grant unto you perpetually. Our delegates bear the signatures and greetings of the bishops. These [delegates] will from the Divine Scriptures themselves instruct your piety.

The Synod then thus wrote and sent their communications to the emperor by the bishops [selected for that purpose]. But the partisans of Ursacius and Valens having arrived before them, did their utmost to calumniate the council, exhibiting the exposition of the faith which they had brought with them. The emperor, prejudiced beforehand towards Arianism, became extremely exasperated against the Synod, but conferred great honor on Valens and Ursacius and their friends. Those deputed by the council were consequently detained a considerable time, without being able to obtain an answer: at length, however, the emperor replied through those who had come to him, in the manner following:

'Constantius Victor and Triumphator Augustus to all the bishops convened at Ariminum.

'That our especial care is ever exercised respecting the divine and venerated law even your sanctity is not ignorant. Nevertheless we have hitherto been unable to give an audience to the twenty bishops sent as deputation from you, for an expedition against the barbarians has become necessary. And since, as you will admit, matters relative to the divine law ought to be entered on with a mind free from all anxiety; I have therefore ordered these bishops to await our return to Adrianople; that when all public business shall have been duly attended to, we may be able then to hear and consider what they shall propose. In the meanwhile let it not seem troublesome to your gravity to wait for their return; since when they shall convey to

---

[17] The Latin original in Hilar. omits the name of Auxentius.

[18] Instead of the Greek words here translated, 'fill the believing with distrust and the unbelieving with cruelty,' the Latin original reads '*verum etiam infideles ad credulitatem vetantur accedere.*'

you our resolution, you will be prepared to carry into effect such measures as may be most advantageous to the welfare of the catholic church.'

The bishops on receipt of this letter wrote thus in reply : [19]

'We have received your clemency's letter, sovereign lord, most beloved of God, in which you inform us that the exigencies of state affairs have hitherto prevented your admitting our delegates to your presence : and you bid us await their return, until your piety shall have learnt from them what has been determined on by us in conformity with the tradition of our ancestors. But we again protest by this letter that we can by no means depart from our primary resolution ; and this also we have commissioned our deputies to state. We beseech you therefore, both with serene countenance to order this present epistle of our modesty to be read ; and also to listen favorably to the representations with which our delegates have been charged. Your mildness doubtless perceives, as well as we, to how great an extent grief and sadness prevail, because of so many churches being bereft of their bishops in these most blessed times of yours. Again therefore we entreat your clemency, sovereign lord most dear to God, to command us to return to our churches, if it please your piety, before the rigor of winter ; in order that we may be enabled, in conjunction with the people, to offer up our accustomed prayers to Almighty God, and to our Lord and Saviour Jesus Christ, his only-begotten Son, for the prosperity of your reign, as we have always done, and even now do in our prayers.'

The bishops having waited together some time after this letter had been despatched, inasmuch as the emperor deigned no reply, they departed to their respective cities. Now the emperor had long before intended to disseminate Arian doctrine throughout the churches ; and was anxious to give it the pre-eminence ; hence he pretended that their departure was an act of contumely, declaring that they had treated him with contempt by dissolving the council in opposition to his wishes. He therefore gave the partisans of Ursacius unbounded license to act as they pleased in regard to the churches : and directed that the revised form of creed which had been read at Ariminum should be sent to the churches throughout Italy ; ordering that whoever would not subscribe it should be ejected from their sees, and that others should be substituted in their place.[20] And first Liberius, bishop of Rome, having refused his assent to that creed, was sent into

exile ; the adherents of Ursacius appointing Felix to succeed him, who had been a deacon in that church, but on embracing the Arian heresy was elevated to the episcopate. Some however assert that he was not favorable to that opinion, but was constrained by force to receive the ordination of bishop. After this all parts of the West were filled with agitation and tumult, some being ejected and banished, and others established in their stead. These things were effected by violence, on the authority of the imperial edicts, which were also sent into eastern parts. Not long after indeed Liberius was recalled, and reinstated in his see ; for the people of Rome having raised a sedition, and expelled Felix from their church, the emperor even though against his wish consented. The partisans of Ursacius, quitting Italy, passed through the eastern parts ; and arriving at Nice, a city of Thrace, they dwelt there a short time and held another Synod, and after translating the form of faith which was read at Ariminum into Greek, they confirmed and published it afresh in the form quoted above, giving it the name of the general council, in this way attempting to deceive the more simple by the similarity of names, and to impose upon them as the creed promulgated at Nicæa in Bithynia, that which they had prepared at Nice in Thrace.[21] But this artifice was of little advantage to them ; for it was soon detected, they became the object of derision. Enough now has been said of the transactions which took place in the West : we must now proceed to the narrative of what was done in the East at the same time.

CHAPTER XXXVIII.

Cruelty of Macedonius, and Tumults raised by him.

The bishops of the Arian party began to assume greater assurance from the imperial edicts. In what manner they undertook to convene a Synod, we will explain somewhat later. Let us now briefly mention a few of their previous acts. Acacius and Patrophilus having ejected Maximus, bishop of Jerusalem, installed Cyril in his see. Macedonius subverted the order of things in the cities and provinces adjacent to Constantinople, promoting to ecclesiastical honors his assistants in his intrigues against the churches.[1]

---

[19] Cf. Theodoret, *H. E.* II. 20.
[20] Cf. Theodoret, *H. E.* II. 16.

[21] Hilar. *Fragm.* 8; Hefele, *Hist. of Ch. Councils*, Vol. II. p. 257.
[1] From this place it plainly appears, as Valesius remarks, that the authority of the see of Constantinople was acknowledged, even before the council of Constantinople, throughout the region of the Hellespont and Bithynia, which conclusion is also confirmed by the acts of Eudoxius, bishop of Constantinople, who made Eunomius bishop of Cyzicus. Two causes co-operated to secure this authority, viz. (1) the official establishment of the city as the capital of the empire by Constantine, and (2) the transference to it of Eusebius

He ordained Eleusius bishop of Cyzicus, and Marathonius, bishop of Nicomedia: the latter had before been a deacon under Macedonius himself, and proved very active in founding monasteries both of men and women. But we must now mention in what way Macedonius desolated the churches in the cities and provinces around Constantinople. This man, as I have already said,[2] having seized the bishopric, inflicted innumerable calamities on such as were unwilling to adopt his views. His persecutions were not confined to those who were recognized as members of the catholic church, but extended to the Novatians also, inasmuch as he knew that they maintained the doctrine of the *homoousion;* they therefore with the others underwent the most intolerable sufferings, but their bishop, Angelius by name, effected his escape by flight. Many persons eminent for their piety were seized and tortured, because they refused to communicate with him: and after the torture, they forcibly constrained the men to be partakers of the holy mysteries, their mouths being forced open with a piece of wood, and then the consecrated elements thrust into them. Those who were so treated regarded this as a punishment far more grievous than all others. Moreover they laid hold of women and children, and compelled them to be initiated [by baptism]; and if any one resisted or otherwise spoke against it, stripes immediately followed, and after the stripes, bonds and imprisonment, and other violent measures. I shall here relate an instance or two whereby the reader may form some idea of the extent of the harshness and cruelty exercised by Macedonius and those who were then in power. They first pressed in a box, and then sawed off, the breasts of such women as were unwilling to communicate with them. The same parts of the persons of other women they burnt partly with iron, and partly with eggs intensely heated in the fire. This mode of torture which was unknown even among the heathen, was invented by those who professed to be Christians. These facts were related to me by the aged Auxanon, the presbyter in the Novatian church of whom I spoke in the first book.[3] He said also that he had himself endured not a few severities from the Arians, prior to his reaching the dignity of presbyter; having been thrown into prison and beaten with many stripes, together with Alexander the Paphlagonian, his companion in the monastic life. He added that he had himself been able to sustain these tortures, but that Alexander died in prison from the effects of their infliction. He is now buried on the right of those sailing into the bay of

Constantinople which is called Ceras, close by the rivers, where there is a church of the Novatians named after Alexander. Moreover the Arians, at the instigation of Macedonius, demolished with many other churches in various cities, that of the Novatians at Constantinople near Pelargus. Why I particularly mention this church, will be seen from the extraordinary circumstances connected with it, as testified by the same aged Auxanon. The emperor's edict and the violence of Macedonius had doomed to destruction the churches of those who maintained the doctrine of consubstantiality; the decree and violence reached this church, and those also who were charged with the execution of the mandate were at hand to carry it into effect. I cannot but admire the zeal displayed by the Novatians on this occasion, as well as the sympathy they experienced from those whom the Arians at that time ejected, but who are now in peaceful possession of their churches. For when the emissaries of their enemies were urgent to accomplish its destruction, an immense multitude of Novatians, aided by numbers of others who held similar sentiments, having assembled around this devoted church, pulled it down, and conveyed the materials of it to another place: this place stands opposite the city, and is called Sycæ, and forms the thirteenth ward of the town of Constantinople. This removal was effected in a very short time, from the extraordinary ardor of the numerous persons engaged in it: one carried tiles, another stones, a third timber; some loading themselves with one thing, and some with another. Even women and children assisted in the work, regarding it as the realization of their best wishes, and esteeming it the greatest honor to be accounted the faithful guardians of things consecrated to God. In this way at that time was the church of the Novatians transported to Sycæ. Long afterwards when Constantius was dead, the emperor Julian ordered its former site to be restored, and permitted them to rebuild it there. The people therefore, as before, having carried back the materials, reared the church in its former position; and from this circumstance, and its great improvement in structure and ornament, they not inappropriately called it *Anastasia.* The church as we before said was restored afterwards in the reign of Julian. But at that time both the Catholics and the Novatians were alike subjected to persecution: for the former abominated offering their devotions in those churches in which the Arians assembled, but frequented the other three[4] — for this is the number of the

---

of Nicomedia, a most vigorous and aggressive bishop, who missed no opportunity for enlarging and consolidating the power of his see.
　[2] See above, ch. 16.　　　　[3] I. 13.

　[4] According to Valesius it appears incredible that the Catholics should have done what Socrates says they did. ‘For there is nothing more contrary to ecclesiastical discipline than to communicate with heretics either in the sacraments or in prayer.’ Hence ‘Socrates was probably imposed upon by the aged Auxano, who

churches which the Novatians have in the city — and engaged in divine service with them. Indeed they would have been wholly united, had not the Novatians refused from regard to their ancient precepts. In other respects however, they mutually maintained such a degree of cordiality and affection, as to be ready to lay down their lives for one another: both parties were therefore persecuted indiscriminately, not only at Constantinople, but also in other provinces and cities. At Cyzicus, Eleusius, the bishop of that place, perpetrated the same kind of enormities against the Christians there, as Macedonius had done elsewhere, harassing and putting them to flight in all directions; and [among other things] he completely demolished the church of the Novatians at Cyzicus. But Macedonius consummated his wickedness in the following manner. Hearing that there was a great number of the Novatian sect in the province of Paphlagonia, and especially at Mantinium, and perceiving that such a numerous body could not be driven from their homes by ecclesiastics alone, he caused, by the emperor's permission, four companies of soldiers to be sent into Paphlagonia, that through dread of the military they might receive the Arian opinion. But those who inhabited Mantinium, animated to desperation by zeal for their religion, armed themselves with long reap-hooks, hatchets, and whatever weapon came to hand, and went forth to meet the troops; on which a conflict ensuing, many indeed of the Paphlagonians were slain, but nearly all the soldiers were destroyed. I learnt these things from a Paphlagonian peasant who said that he was present at the engagement; and many others of that province corroborate this account. Such were the exploits of Macedonius on behalf of Christianity, consisting of murders, battles, incarcerations, and civil wars: proceedings which rendered him odious not only to the objects of his persecution, but even to his own party. He became obnoxious also to the emperor on these accounts, and particularly so from the circumstance I am about to relate. The church where the coffin lay that contained the relics of the emperor Constantine threatened to fall. On this account those that entered, as well as those who were accustomed to remain there for devotional purposes, were in much fear. Macedonius, therefore, wished to remove the emperor's remains, lest the coffin should be injured by the ruins. The populace getting intelligence of this, endeavored to prevent it, insisting 'that the emperor's bones should not be disturbed, as such a disinterment would be equivalent, to their being dug up': many however affirmed that its removal could not possibly injure the dead body, and thus two parties were formed on this question; such as held the doctrine of consubstantiality joining with those who opposed it on the ground of its impiety. Macedonius, in total disregard of these prejudices, caused the emperor's remains to be transported to the church where those of the martyr Acacius lay. Whereupon a vast multitude rushed toward that edifice in two hostile divisions, which attacked one another with great fury, and great loss of life was occasioned, so that the churchyard was covered with gore, and the well also which was in it overflowed with blood, which ran into the adjacent portico, and thence even into the very street. When the emperor was informed of this unfortunate occurrence, he was highly incensed against Macedonius, both on account of the slaughter which he had occasioned, and because he had dared to move his father's body without consulting him. Having therefore left the Cæsar Julian to take care of the western parts, he himself set out for the east. How Macedonius was a short time afterwards deposed, and thus suffered a most inadequate punishment for his infamous crimes, I shall hereafter relate.[5]

CHAPTER XXXIX.

Of the Synod at Seleucia, in Isauria.

BUT I must now give an account of the other Synod, which the emperor's edict had convoked in the east, as a rival to that of Ariminum. It was at first determined that the bishops should assemble at Nicomedia in Bithynia; but a great earthquake having nearly destroyed that city, prevented their being convened there. This happened in the consulate[1] of Tatian and Cerealis, on the 28th day of August.[2] They were therefore planning to transfer the council to the neighboring city of Nicæa: but this plan was again altered, as it seemed more convenient to meet at Tarsus in Cilicia. Being dissatisfied with this arrangement also, they at last assembled themselves at Seleucia, surnamed Aspera,[3] a city of Isauria. This took place in the same year [in which the council of Ariminum was held],

---

fixed upon all the Catholics what was perhaps done by some few Christians who were less cautious.' But Socrates' own attitude towards the Novatians (cf. Introd. p. x.) shows that the difference between them and the Catholics (οἱ τῆς ἐκκλησίας) was not universally regarded as an absolute schism forbidding communication even during such times of trial as these described here, which might certainly have drawn together parties already as near to one another as the Novatians and Catholics.

[5] See below, ch. 42.
[1] 358 A.D.
[2] In this calamity Cecropius, the bishop of Nicomedia, perished, and the splendid cathedral of the city was ruined; both of which misfortunes were attributed by the heathen to the wrath of their gods. See Sozom. IV. 16ι
[3] Τραχεία, on account of the neighboring steep mountains. This Seleucia was the capital of Isauria.

under the consulate of Eusebius and Hypatius,[4] the number of those convened being about 160. There was present on this occasion Leonas, an officer of distinction attached to the imperial household, before whom the emperor's edict had enjoined that the discussion respecting the faith should be entered into. Lauricius also, the commander-in-chief of the troops in Isauria, was ordered to be there, to serve the bishops in such things as they might require. In the presence of these personages therefore, the bishops were there convened on the 27th of the month of September, and immediately began a discussion on the basis of the public records, shorthand writers being present to write down what each might say. Those who desire to learn the particulars of the several speeches, will find copious details of them in the collection of Sabinus; but we shall only notice the more important heads. On the first day of their being convened, Leonas ordered each one to propose what he thought fit: but those present said that no question ought to be agitated in the absence of those prelates who had not yet arrived; for Macedonius, bishop of Constantinople, Basil of Ancyra, and some others who were apprehensive of an impeachment for their misconduct, had not made their appearance. Macedonius pleaded indisposition, and failed to attend; Patrophilus said he had some trouble with his eyes, and that on this account it was needful for him to remain in the suburbs of Seleucia; and the rest offered various pretexts to account for their absence. When, however, Leonas declared that the subjects which they had met to consider must be entered on, notwithstanding the absence of these persons, the bishops replied that they could not proceed to the discussion of any question, until the·life and conduct of the parties accused had been investigated: for Cyril of Jerusalem, Eustathius of Sebastia in Armenia, and some others, had been charged with misconduct on various grounds long before. A sharp contest arose in consequence of this demur; some affirming that cognizance ought first to be taken of all such accusations, and others denying that anything whatever should have precedence of matters of faith. The emperor's orders contributed not a little to augment this dispute, inasmuch as letters of his were produced urging now this and now that as necessary to be considered first. The dispute having arisen on this subject, a schism was thus made, and the Seleucian council was divided into two factions, one of which was headed by Acacius of Cæsarea in Palestine, George of Alexandria, Uranius of Tyre, and Eudoxius of Antioch, who were supported by only about thirty-two other bishops. Of the opposite party, which was by far the more numerous, the principal were George of Laodicea in Syria, Sophronius of Pompeiopolis in Paphlagonia, and Eleusius of Cyzicus. It being determined by the majority to examine doctrinal matters first, the party of Acacius openly opposed the Nicene Creed, and wished to introduce another instead of it. The other faction,[5] which was considerably more numerous, concurred in all the decisions of the council of Nicæa, but criticised its adoption of the term *homoousion*. Accordingly they debated on this point, much being said on each side, until late in the evening, when Silvanus, who presided over the church at Tarsus, insisted with much vehemence of manner, 'that there was no need of a new exposition of the faith; but that it was their duty rather to confirm that which was published at Antioch,[6] at the consecration of the church in that place.' On this declaration, Acacius and his partisans privately withdrew from the council; while the others, producing the creed composed at Antioch, read it, and then separated for that day. Assembling in the church of Seleucia on the day following, after having closed the doors, they again read the same creed, and ratified it by their signatures. At this time the readers and deacons present signed on behalf of certain absent bishops, who had intimated their acquiescence in its form..

CHAPTER XL.

Acacius, Bishop of Cæsarea, dictates a new Form of Creed in the Synod at Seleucia.

ACACIUS and his adherents criticised what was done: because, that is to say, they closed the church doors and thus affixed their signatures; declaring that 'all such secret transactions were justly to be suspected, and had no validity whatever.' These objections he made because he was anxious to bring forward another exposition of the faith drawn up by himself, which he had already submitted to the governors Leonas and Lauricius, and was now intent on getting it alone confirmed and established, instead of that which had been subscribed. The second day was thus occupied with nothing else but exertions on his part to effect this object. On the third day Leonas endeavored to produce an amicable meeting of both parties; Macedonius of Constantinople, and also Basil of Ancyra, having arrived during its course. But when the Acacians found that both the parties had come to the same position, they refused to meet; saying

---

[4] 359 A.D. See, on this double council of Ariminum and Seleucia, Hefele, *Hist. of the Ch. Councils*, Vol. II. p. 346-371.

[5] Cf. Athan. *de Synodd.* 12.
[6] See chaps. 8 and 10.

that not only those who had before been deposed, but also such as were at present under any accusation, ought to be excluded from the assembly.' And as after much cavilling on both sides, this opinion prevailed; those who lay under any charge went out of the council, and the party of Acacius entered in their places. Leonas then said that a document had been put into his hand by Acacius, to which he desired to call their attention: but he did not state that it was the draught of a creed, which in some particulars covertly, and in others unequivocally contradicted the former. When those present became silent, thinking that the document contained something else besides an exposition of a creed, the following creed composed by Acacius, together with its preamble, was read.

'We having yesterday assembled by the emperor's command at Seleucia, a city of Isauria, on the 27th day of September, exerted ourselves to the utmost, with all moderation, to preserve the peace of the church, and to determine doctrinal questions on prophetic and evangelical authority, so as to sanction nothing in the ecclesiastic confession of faith at variance with the sacred Scriptures, as our Emperor Constantius most beloved of God has ordered. But inasmuch as certain individuals in the Synod have acted injuriously toward several of us, preventing some from expressing their sentiments, and excluding others from the council against their wills; and at the same time have introduced such as have been deposed, and persons who were ordained contrary to the ecclesiastical canon, so that the Synod has presented a scene of tumult and disorder, of which the most illustrious Leonas, the Comes, and the most eminent Lauricius, governor of the province, have been eye-witnesses, we are therefore under the necessity of making this declaration. That we do not repudiate the faith which was ratified at the consecration of the church at Antioch;[1] for we give it our decided preference, because it received the concurrence of our fathers who were assembled there to consider some controverted points. Since, however, the terms *homoousion* and *homoiousion* have in time past troubled the minds of many, and still continue to disquiet them; and moreover that a new term has recently been coined by some who assert the *anomoion* of the Son to the Father: we reject the first two, as expressions which are not found in the Scriptures; but we utterly anathematize the last, and regard such as countenance its use, as alienated from the church. We distinctly acknowledge the *homoion* of the Son to the Father, in accordance with what the

apostle has declared concerning him,[2] "Who is the image of the invisible God."

'We confess then, and believe in one God the Father Almighty, the Maker of heaven and earth, and of things visible and invisible. We believe also in his Son our Lord Jesus Christ, who was begotten of him without passion before all ages, God the Word, the only-begotten of God, the Light, the Life, the Truth, the Wisdom: through whom all things were made which are in the heavens and upon the earth, whether visible or invisible. We believe that he took flesh of the holy Virgin Mary, at the end of the ages, in order to abolish sin; that he was made man, suffered for our sin, and rose again, and was taken up into the heavens, to sit at the right hand of the Father, whence he will come again in glory to judge the living and the dead. We believe also in the Holy Spirit, whom our Lord and Saviour has denominated the Comforter, and whom he sent to his disciples after his departure, according to his promise: by whom also he sanctifies all believers in the church, who are baptized in the name of the Father, and of the Son, and of the Holy Ghost. Those who preach anything contrary to this creed, we regard as aliens from the catholic church.'

This was the declaration of faith proposed by Acacius, and subscribed by himself and as many as adhered to his opinion, the number of whom we have already given. When this had been read, Sophronius bishop of Pompeiopolis in Paphlagonia, thus expressed himself: 'If to express a separate opinion day after day be received as the exposition of the faith, we shall never arrive at any accurate understanding of the truth.' These were the words of Sophronius. And I firmly believe, that if the predecessors of these prelates, as well as their successors, had entertained similar sentiments in reference to the Nicene creed, all polemical debates would have been avoided; nor would the churches have been agitated by such violent and irrational disturbances. However let those judge who are capable of understanding how these things are. At that time after many remarks on all sides had been made both in reference to this doctrinal statement, and in relation to the parties accused, the assembly was dissolved. On the fourth day they all again met in the same place, and resumed their proceedings in the same contentious spirit as before. On this occasion Acacius expressed himself in these words: 'Since the Nicene creed has been altered not once only, but frequently, there is no hindrance to our publishing another at this time.' To which Eleusius bishop of Cyzicus,

---

[1] Athanas. (*de Synod.* 29) gives the following portion of this creed apparently as the only declaration made by the council.

[2] Col. i. 15.

replied : 'The Synod is at present convened not to learn what it had no previous knowledge of, nor to receive a creed which it had not assented to before, but to confirm the faith of the fathers, from which it should. never recede, either in life or death.' Thus Eleusius opposing Acacius spoke meaning by 'the faith of the fathers,' that creed which had been promulgated at Antioch. But surely he too might have been fairly answered in this way : 'How is it, O Eleusius, that you call those convened at Antioch "the fathers," seeing that you do not recognize those who were their fathers? The framers of the Nicene creed, by whom the *homoousian* faith was acknowledged, have a far higher claim to the title of "the fathers"; both as having the priority in point of time, and also because those assembled at Antioch were by them invested with the sacerdotal office. Now if those at Antioch have disowned their own fathers, those who follow them are unconsciously following parricides. Besides how can they have received a legitimate ordination from those whose faith they pronounce unsound and impious? If those, however, who constituted the Nicene Synod had not the Holy Spirit which is imparted by the imposition of hands,[3] those at Antioch have not duly received the priesthood : for how could they have received it from those who had not the power of conferring it?' Such considerations as these might have been submitted to Eleusius in reply to his objections. But they then proceeded to another question, connected with the assertion made by Acacius in his exposition of the faith, 'that the Son was like the Father'; enquiring of one another in what this resemblance consisted. The Acacian party affirmed that the Son was like the Father as it respected his will only, and not his 'substance' or 'essence'; but the rest maintained that the likeness extended to both essence and will. In altercations on this point, the whole day was consumed; and Acacius, being confuted by his own published works, in which he had asserted that 'the Son is in all things like the Father,' his opponents asked him 'how do you now deny the likeness of the Son to the Father as to his "essence"?' Acacius in reply said, that 'no author, ancient or modern, was ever condemned out of his own writings.' As they kept on their discussion on this matter to a most tedious extent, with much acrimonious feeling and subtlety of argument, but without any approach to unity of judgment, Leonas arose and dissolved the council : and this was the conclusion of the Synod at Seleucia. For on the following day [Leonas] being urged

to do so would not again meet with them. 'I have been deputed by the emperor,' said he, 'to attend a council where unanimity was expected to prevail : but since you can by no means come to a mutual understanding, I can no longer be present : go therefore to the church, if you please, and indulge in vain babbling there.' The Acacian faction conceiving this decision to be advantageous to themselves, also refused to meet with the others. The adverse party left alone met in the church and requested the attendance of those who followed Acacius, that cognizance might be taken of the case of Cyril, bishop of Jerusalem : for that prelate had been accused long before, on what grounds however I am unable to state. He had even been deposed, because owing to fear, he had not made his appearance during two whole years, after having been repeatedly summoned in order that the charges against him might be investigated. Nevertheless, when he was deposed, he sent a written notification to those who had condemned him, that he should appeal to a higher jurisdiction : and to this appeal the emperor Constantius gave his sanction. Cyril was thus the first and indeed only clergyman who ventured to break through ecclesiastical usage, by becoming an appellant, in the way commonly done in the secular courts of judicature :[4] and he was now present at Seleucia, ready to be put upon his trial; on this account the other bishops invited the Acacian party to take their places in the assembly, that in a general council a definite judgment might be pronounced on the case of those who were arraigned : for they cited others also charged with various misdemeanors to appear before them at the same time, who to protect themselves had sought refuge among the partisans of Acacius. When therefore that faction persisted in their refusal to meet, after being repeatedly summoned, the bishops deposed Acacius himself, together with George of Alexandria, Uranius of Tyre, Theodulus of Chæretapi in Fhrygia, Theodosius of Philadelphia in Lydia, Evagrius of the island of Mytilene, Leontius of Tripolis in Lydia, and Eudoxius who had formerly been bishop of Germanica, but had afterwards insinuated himself into the bishopric of Antioch in Syria. They also deposed Patrophilus for contumacy, in not having presented himself to answer a charge preferred against him by a presbyter named Dorotheus. These they deposed : they also excommunicated Asterius, Eusebius, Algarus, Basilicus, Phœbus, Fidelis, Eutychius, Magnus, and Eustathius ; determining that they should

---

[3] See Chrysostom, *Homilies* 9 and 27, *on Acts*, and *Hom.* 1, *on 2 Tim.*, for the belief of the ancient Church in the descent of the Holy Spirit on the ordained in and through ordination.

[4] He was the only one, inasmuch as the General Synod of Constantinople (381 A.D.) expressly forbade all appeals from the ecclesiastical to the civil courts, attaching severe penalties to the violation of its canon on this subject. Cf. Canon 6 of Council of Constantinople. Hefele, *Hist. of the Ch. Councils*, Vol. II. p. 364.

not be restored to communion, until they made such a defense as would clear them from the imputations under which they lay. This being done, they addressed explanatory letters to each of the churches whose bishops had been deposed. Anianus was then constituted bishop of Antioch instead of Eudoxius : but the Acacians having soon after apprehended him, he was delivered into the hands of Leonas and Lauricius, by whom he was sent into exile. The bishops who had ordained him being incensed on this account, lodged protests against the Acacian party with Leonas and Lauricius, in which they openly charged them with having violated the decisions of the Synod. Finding that no redress could be obtained by this means, they went to Constantinople to lay the whole matter before the emperor.

CHAPTER XLI.

On the Emperor's Return from the West, the Acacians assemble at Constantinople, and confirm the Creed of Ariminum, after making Some Additions to it.

AND now the emperor returned from the West and appointed a prefect over Constantinople, Honoratus by name, having abolished the office of proconsul.[1] But the Acacians being beforehand with the bishops, calumniated them to the emperor, persuading him not to admit the creed which they had proposed. This so annoyed the emperor that he resolved to disperse them ; he therefore published an edict, commanding that such of them as were subject to fill certain public offices should be no longer exempted from the performance of the duties attached to them. For several of them were liable to be called on to occupy various official departments,[2] connected both with the city magistracy, and in subordination to the presidents and governors of provinces.[3] While these were thus harassed the partisans of Acacius remained for a considerable time at Constantinople and held another Synod. Sending for the bishops at Bithynia, about fifty assembled on this occasion, among whom was Maris, bishop of Chalcedon : these confirmed the creed read at Ariminum to which the names of the consuls had been prefixed.[4] It would have been un-

necessary to repeat it here, had there not been some additions made to it ; but since that was done, it may be desirable to transcribe it in its new form.[5]

'We believe in one God the Father Almighty, of whom are all things. And in the only-begotten Son of God, begotten of God before all ages, and before every beginning ; through whom all things visible and invisible were made : who is the only-begotten born of the Father, the only of the only, God of God, like to the Father who begat him, according to the Scriptures, and whose generation no one knows but the Father only that begat him. We know that this only-begotten Son of God, as sent of the Father, came down from the heavens, as it is written, for the destruction of sin and death : and that he was born of the Holy Spirit, and of the Virgin Mary according to the flesh, as it is written, and conversed with his disciples ; and that after every dispensation had been fulfilled according to his Father's will, he was crucified and died, and was buried and descended into the lower parts of the earth, at whose presence hades itself trembled : who also arose from the dead on the third day, again conversed with his disciples, and after the completion of forty days was taken up into the heavens, and sits at the right hand of the Father, whence he will come in the last day, the day of the resurrection, in his Father's glory, to requite every one according to his works. [We believe] also in the Holy Spirit, whom he himself the only-begotten of God, Christ our Lord and God, promised to send to mankind as the Comforter, according as it is written,[6] "the Spirit of truth" ; whom he sent to them after he was received into the heavens. But since the term *ousia* [*substance or essence*], which was used by the fathers in a very simple and intelligible sense, but not being understood by the people, has been a cause of offense, we have thought proper to reject it, as it is not contained even in the sacred writings ; and that no mention of it should be made in future, inasmuch as the holy Scriptures have nowhere mentioned the substance of the Father and of the Son. Nor ought the "subsistence" of the Father, and of the Son, and of the Holy Spirit to be even named. But we affirm that the Son is like the Father, in such a manner as the sacred Scriptures declare and teach. Let therefore all heresies which have been already condemned, or may have arisen of late, which are opposed to this exposition of the faith, be anathema.'

These things were recognized at that time at Constantinople. And now as we have at length

---

[1] On the distinction between the prefect and proconsul and the different functions of each, see Smith, *Diction. of Greek and Roman Ant.* The statement of Socrates here that Constantius first put Constantinople under a prefect is borne out by Athanasius' mention of Donatus as proconsul of Europe, with Constantinople as chief city.

[2] The General Synod of Chalcedon, 451 A.D., in its seventh canon forbade, under pain of anathema, the mixing of the clerical office with political and worldly matters.

[3] The τάξεις here mentioned were classes of officials appointed under a sort of military law, to serve for a given length of time as agents of the presidents and governors of provinces. Cf. Justin. *Cod.* 12, *tit.* 52–59.

[4] Cf. chap. 37.

[5] Athanas. *de Synodd.* 30.   [6] John xv. 26.

wound our way through the labyrinth of all the various forms of faith, let us reckon the number of them. After that which was promulgated at Nicæa, two others were proposed at Antioch at the dedication of the church there.[7] A third was presented to the Emperor Constans in Gaul by Narcissus and those who accompanied him.[8] The fourth was sent by Eudoxius into Italy.[9] There were three forms of the creed published at Sirmium, one of which having the consuls' names prefixed was read at Ariminum.[10] The Acacian party produced an eighth at Seleucia.[11] The last was that of Constantinople, containing the prohibitory clause respecting the mention of 'substance' or 'subsistence' in relation to God. To this creed Ulfilas bishop of the Goths gave his assent, although he had previously adhered to that of Nicæa; for he was a disciple of Theophilus bishop of the Goths, who was present at the Nicene council, and subscribed what was there determined. Let this suffice on these subjects.

CHAPTER XLII.

On the Deposition of Macedonius, Eudoxius obtains the Bishopric of Constantinople.

ACACIUS, Eudoxius, and those at Constantinople who took part with them, became exceedingly anxious that they also on their side might depose some of the opposite party. Now it should be observed that neither of the factions were influenced by religious considerations in making depositions, but by other motives: for although they did not agree respecting the faith, yet the ground of their reciprocal depositions was not error in doctrine. The Acacian party therefore availing themselves of the emperor's indignation against others, and especially against Macedonius, which he was cherishing and anxious to vent, in the first place deposed Macedonius, both on account of his having occasioned so much slaughter, and also because he had admitted to communion a deacon who had been found guilty of fornication.[1] They then depose Eleusius bishop of Cyzicus, for having baptized, and afterwards invested with the diaconate, a priest of Hercules at Tyre named Heraclius, who was known to have practiced magic arts.[2] A like sentence was pronounced against Basil, or Basilas, — as he was also called, — who had been constituted bishop of Ancyra instead of Marcellus: the causes assigned for this condemnation were, that he had unjustly imprisoned a

certain individual, loaded him with chains, and put him to the torture; that he had traduced some persons; and that he had disturbed the churches of Africa by his epistles. Dracontius was also deposed, because he had left the Galatian church for that of Pergamos. Moreover they deposed, on various pretenses, Neonas bishop of Seleucia, the city in which the Synod had been convened, Sophronius of Pompeiopolis in Paphlagonia, Elpidius of Satala, in Macedonia, and Cyril of Jerusalem, and others for various reasons.

CHAPTER XLIII.

Of Eustathius Bishop of Sebastia.

BUT Eustathius bishop of Sebastia in Armenia was not even permitted to make his defense; because he had been long before deposed by Eulalius, his own father, who was bishop of Cæsarea in Cappadocia, for dressing in a style unbecoming the sacerdotal office.[1] Let it be noted that Meletius was appointed his successor, of whom we shall hereafter speak. Eustathius indeed was subsequently condemned by a Synod convened on his account at Gangra in Paphlagonia; he having, after his deposition by the council at Cæsarea, done many things repugnant to the ecclesiastical canons. For he had 'forbidden marriage,'[2] and maintained that meats were to be abstained from: he even separated many from their wives, and persuaded those who disliked to assemble in the churches to commune at home. Under the pretext of piety, he also seduced servants from their masters. He himself wore the habit of a philosopher, and induced his followers to adopt a new and extraordinary garb, directing that the hair of women should be cropped. He permitted the prescribed fasts to be neglected, but recommended fasting on Sundays. In short, he forbade prayers to be offered in the houses of married persons: and declared that both the benediction and the communion of a presbyter who continued to live with a wife whom he might have lawfully married, while still a layman, ought to be shunned as an abomination. For doing and teaching these things and many others of a similar nature, a Synod convened, as we have said, at Gangra[3] in Paphlagonia de-

---

[7] Chap. 10.
[8] Chap. 18.
[9] Chap. 19.
[2] Cf. Tertull. de Idol. IX.: Post evangelium nusquam invenies aut sophistas, aut Chaldæos, aut Incantatores, aut Conjectores, aut magos, nisi plane punitos. See also Bingham, Eccl. Antiq. XVI. 5.

[10] Chaps. 30, 37.
[11] Chap. 41.
[1] Cf. Apost. Canon. XXV.

[1] On the prescribed dress of the clergy, and the puhishment of those who did not constantly adopt it, see Bingham, Eccl. Antiq. VI. 4. 15.
[2] 1 Tim. iv. 3. Cf. Euseb. H. E. IV. 29, on the earliest forms of expression against marriage in the Christian Church; also Apost. Canon. LI. and Augustine, Hærr. XXV., XL., XLVI. See Bingham, Eccl. Antiq. XXII. 1.
[3] On Synod of Gangra, see Hefele, Hist. of the Ch. Councils, Vol. II. p. 325–339. Almost all the canons of the synod seem to be addressed against the teachings of Eustathius. The fourth canon is expressly on the celibacy of the clergy, as follows: 'If any one maintains that, when a married priest offer the sacrifice, no one should take part in the service, let him be anathema.'

posed him, and anathematized his opinions. This, however, was done afterwards. But on Macedonius being ejected from the see of Constantinople, Eudoxius, who now looked upon the see of Antioch as secondary in importance, was promoted to the vacant bishopric; being consecrated by the Acacians, who in this instance cared not to consider that it was inconsistent with their former proceedings. For they who had deposed Dracontius because of his translation from Galatia to Pergamos, were clearly acting in contrariety to their own principles and decisions, in ordaining Eudoxius, who then made a second change. After this they sent their own exposition of the faith, in its corrected and supplementary form, to Arminium, ordering that all those who refused to sign it should be exiled, on the authority of the emperor's edict. They also informed such other prelates in the East as coincided with them in opinion of what they had done; and more especially Patrophilus bishop of Scythopolis, who on leaving Seleucia had proceeded directly to his own city. Eudoxius having been constituted bishop of the imperial city, the great church named *Sophia* was at that time consecrated,[4] in the tenth consulate[5] of Constantius, and the third of Julian Cæsar, on the 15th day of February. It was while Eudoxius occupied this see, that he first uttered that sentence which is still everywhere current, 'The Father is impious, the Son is pious.' When the people seemed startled by this expression, and a disturbance began to be made, 'Be not troubled,' said he, 'on account of what I have just said: for the Father is impious, because he worships no person; but the Son is pious because he worships the Father.' Eudoxius having said this, the tumult was appeased, and great laughter was excited in the church: and this saying of his continues to be a jest, even in the present day. The heresiarchs indeed frequently devised such subtle phrases as these, and by them rent the church asunder. Thus was the Synod at Constantinople terminated.

CHAPTER XLIV.

Of Meletius[1] *Bishop of Antioch.*

It becomes us now to speak of Meletius, who, as we have recently observed, was created bishop of Sebastia in Armenia, after the deposition of Eustathius; from Sebastia he was transferred to Berœa, a city of Syria. Being present at the Synod of Seleucia, he subscribed the creed set forth there by Acacius, and immediately returned thence to Berœa. When the convention of the Synod at Constantinople was held, the people of Antioch finding that Eudoxius, captivated by the magnificence of the see of Constantinople, had contemned their church, they sent for Meletius, and invested him with the bishopric of the church at Antioch. Now he at first avoided all doctrinal questions, confining his discourses to moral subjects; but subsequently he expounded to his auditors the Nicene creed, and asserted the doctrine of the *homoousion*. The emperor being informed of this, ordered that he should be sent into exile; and caused Euzoïus, who had before been deposed together with Arius, to be installed bishop of Antioch in his stead. Such, however, as were attached to Meletius, separated themselves from the Arian congregation, and held their assemblies apart: nevertheless, those who originally embraced the *homoousian* opinion would not communicate with them, because Meletius had been ordained by the Arians, and his adherents had been baptized by them. Thus was the Antiochian church divided, even in regard to those whose views on matters of faith exactly corresponded. Meanwhile the emperor getting intelligence that the Persians were preparing to undertake another war against the Romans, repaired in great haste to Antioch.

CHAPTER XLV.

The Heresy of Macedonius.

Macedonius on being ejected from Constantinople, bore his condemnation ill and became restless; he therefore associated himself with the other faction that had deposed Acacius and his party at Seleucia, and sent a deputation to Sophronius and Eleusius, to encourage them to adhere to that creed which was first promulgated at Antioch, and afterwards confirmed at Seleucia, proposing to give it the counterfeit[1] name of the 'homoiousian' creed.[2] By this means he drew around him a great number of adherents, who from him are still denominated 'Macedonians.' And although such as dissented from the Acacians at the Seleucian Synod had not previously used the term *homoiousios*, yet from that period they distinctly asserted it. There was, however, a popular report that this

---

[4] This was evidently the second consecration of the earlier church of St. Sophia (cf. I. 16, II. 6); the first consecration was celebrated in 326 A.D. Later, the structure was destroyed in a fire, in connection with a popular uprising; and the great church of St. Sophia, at present a Mohammedan mosque, was erected by Justinian, with Isidore of Miletus and Anthimius of Tralles as architects.

[5] 360 A.D.

[1] The name has been written 'Melitius' thus far, but is found as 'Meletius' from this point, and through Bk. III. Cf. Euseb. *H. E.* VII. 32.

[1] παράσημος; just as a counterfeit coin has the appearance of the genuine, and is meant to deceive those who do not investigate its genuineness, so the term 'homoioousios' (ὁμοιοούσιος), the author implies, was meant to deceive the popular ear by its likeness to the genuine 'homoousios.'

[2] See Theodoret, *H. E.* II. 6.

term did not originate with Macedonius, but was the invention rather of Marathonius, who a little before had been set over the church at Nicomedia; on which account the maintainers of this doctrine were also called 'Marathonians.' To this party Eustathius joined himself, who for the reasons before stated had been ejected from the church at Sebastia. But when Macedonius began to deny the Divinity of the Holy Spirit in the Trinity, Eustathius said: 'I can neither admit that the Holy Spirit is God, nor can I dare affirm him to be a creature.' For this reason those who hold the *homoousion* of the Son call these heretics '*Pneumatomachi*.'[3] By what means these Macedonians became so numerous in the Hellespont, I shall state in its proper place.[4] The Acacians meanwhile became extremely anxious that another Synod should be convened at Antioch, in consequence of having changed their mind respecting their former assertion of the likeness 'in all things' of the Son to the Father. A small number of them therefore assembled in the following consulate[5] which was that of Taurus and Florentius, at Antioch in Syria, where the emperor was at that time residing, Euzoïus being bishop. A discussion was then renewed on some of those points which they had previously determined, in the course of which they declared that the term '*homoios*' ought to be erased from the form of faith which had been published both at Ariminum and Constantinople; and they no longer concealed but openly declared that the Son was altogether unlike the Father, not merely in relation to his essence, but even as it respected his will; asserting boldly also, as Arius had already done, that he was made of nothing. Those in that city who favored the heresy of Aëtius, gave their assent to this opinion; from which circumstance in addition to the general appellation of Arians, they were also termed 'Anomœans,'[6] and 'Exucontians,'[7] by those at Antioch who embraced the homoousian, who nevertheless were at that time divided among themselves on account of Meletius, as I have before observed. Being therefore questioned by them, how they dared to affirm that the Son is unlike the Father, and has his existence from nothing, after having acknowledged him 'God of God' in their former creed? they endeavored to elude this objection by such fallacious subterfuges as these. 'The expression, "*God of God*," ' said they, ' is to be understood in the same sense as the words of the apostle,[8] " *but all things of God.*" Where-

fore the Son is *of God*, as being one of these *all things :* and it is for this reason the words "according to the Scriptures" are added in the draught of the creed.' The author of this sophism was George bishop of Laodicea, who being unskilled in such phrases, was ignorant of the manner in which Origen had formerly explained these peculiar expressions of the apostle, having thoroughly investigated the matter. But notwithstanding these evasive cavilings, they were unable to bear the reproach and contumely they had drawn upon themselves, and fell back upon the creed which they had before put forth at Constantinople; and so each one retired to his own district. George returning to Alexandria, resumed his authority over the churches there, Athanasius still not having made his appearance. Those in that city who were opposed to his sentiments he persecuted; and conducting himself with great severity and cruelty, he rendered himself extremely odious to the people. At Jerusalem Arrenius[9] was placed over the church instead of Cyril: we may also remark that Heraclius was ordained bishop there after him, and after him Hilary. At length, however, Cyril returned to Jerusalem, and was again invested with the presidency over the church there. About the same time another heresy sprang up, which arose from the following circumstance.

CHAPTER XLVI.

Of the Apollinarians, and their Heresy.[1]

THERE were two men of the same name at Laodicea in Syria, a father and son: their name was Apollinaris; the former of them was a presbyter, and the latter a reader in that church. Both taught Greek literature, the father grammar, and the son rhetoric. The father was a native of Alexandria, and at first taught at Berytus, but afterwards removed to Laodicea, where he married, and the younger Apollinaris was born. They were contemporaries of Epiphanius the sophist, and being true friends they became intimate with him; but Theodotus bishop of Laodicea, fearing that such communication should pervert their principles, and lead them into paganism, forbade their associating with him: they, however, paid but little attention to this prohibition, their familiarity with Epiphanius being still continued. George, the successor of Theodotus, also endeavored to prevent their conversing with Epiphanius; but not being able in any way to persuade them on this point, he excommunicated them. The younger Apolli-

---

[3] Πνευματομάχοι, lit. 'active enemies of the Spirit.'
[4] I. 4.   [5] 361 A.D.
[6] 'Ανόμοιοι, because they held that the essence of the Son was 'dissimilar,' ἀνόμοιος, to that of the Father.
[7] 'Εξουκόντιοι, from the phrase ἐξ οὐκ ὄντων = 'from [things] not existing,' because they asserted that the Son was made *ex nihilo*. The term might be put roughly in some such form as 'Fromnothingians.'   [8] 1 Cor. xi. 12.

[9] Written 'Errenius' in the Allat. MS.
[1] Cf. Sozom. VI. 25; Schaff, *Hist. of the Christ. Ch.*, Vol. III. p. 708 seq.; Walch, *Ketzerhistorie*, III. p. 119-229.

naris regarding this severe procedure as an act of injustice, and relying on the resources of his rhetorical sophistry, originated a new heresy, which was named after its inventor, and still has many supporters. Nevertheless some affirm that it was not for the reason above assigned that they dissented from George, but because they saw the unsettledness and inconsistency of his profession of faith; since he sometimes maintained that the Son is like the Father, in accordance with what had been determined in the Synod at Seleucia, and at other times countenanced the Arian view. They therefore made this a pretext for separation from him: but as no one followed their example, they introduced a new form of doctrine, and at first they asserted that in the economy of the incarnation, God the Word assumed a human body without a soul. Afterwards, as if changing mind, they retracted, admitting that he took a soul indeed, but that it was an irrational one, God the Word himself being in the place of a mind. Those who followed them and bear their name at this day affirm that this is their only point of distinction [from the Catholics]; for they recognize the consubstantiality of the persons in the Trinity. But we will make further mention of the two Apollinares in the proper place.[2]

CHAPTER XLVII.

Successes of Julian; Death of the Emperor Constantius.

WHILE the Emperor Constantius continued his residence at Antioch, Julian Cæsar engaged with an immense army of barbarians in the Gauls, and obtaining the victory over them, he became extremely popular among the soldiery and was proclaimed emperor by them. When this was made known, the Emperor Constantius was affected most painfully; he was therefore baptized by Euzoïus, and immediately prepared to undertake an expedition against Julian. On arriving at the frontiers of Cappadocia and Cilicia, his excessive agitation of mind produced apoplexy, which terminated his life at Mopsucrene, in the consulate of Taurus and Florentius,[1] on the 3d of November. This was in the first year of the 285th Olympiad. Constantius had lived forty-five years, having reigned thirty-eight years; thirteen of which he was his father's colleague in the empire, and after his father's death for twenty-five years [sole emperor], the history of which latter period is contained in this book.

---

[2] III. 16.

[1] 361 A.D.

END OF THE SECOND BOOK.

BOOK III.

CHAPTER I.

Of Julian; his Lineage and Education; his Elevation to the Throne; his Apostasy to Paganism.

THE Emperor Constantius died on the frontiers of Cilicia on the 3d of November, during the consulate of Taurus and Florentius; Julian leaving the western parts of the empire about the 11th of December following, under the same consulate, came to Constantinople, where he was proclaimed emperor.[1] And as I must needs speak of the character of this prince who was eminently distinguished for his learning, let not his admirers expect that I should attempt a pompous rhetorical style, as if it were necessary to make the delineation correspond with the dignity of the subject: for my object being to compile a history of the Christian religion, it is both proper in order to the being better understood, and consistent with my original purpose, to maintain a humble and unaffected style.[2] However, it is proper to describe his person, birth, education, and the manner in which he became possessed of the sovereignty; and in order to do this it will be needful to enter into some antecedent details. Constantine who gave Byzantium his own name, had two brothers named Dalmatius and Constantius, the offspring of the same father, but by a different mother. The former of these had a son who bore his own name: the latter had two sons, Gallus and Julian. Now as on the death of Constantine who founded Constantinople, the soldiery had put the younger brother Dalmatius to death, the lives of his two orphan children were also endangered: but a disease which threatened to be fatal preserved Gallus from the violence of his father's murderers; while the tenderness of Julian's age — for he was only eight years old at the time — protected him. The emperor's jealousy toward them having been gradually subdued, Gallus attended the schools at Ephesus in Ionia, in which country considerable hereditary possessions had been left them. And Julian, when he was grown up, pursued his studies at Constantinople, going constantly to the palace, where the schools then were, in plain clothes, under the superintendence of the eunuch Mardonius. In grammar Nicocles the Lacædemonian was his instructor; and Ecebolius the Sophist, who was at that time a Christian, taught him rhetoric: for the emperor had made provision that he should have no pagan masters, lest he should be seduced to the pagan superstitions. For Julian was a Christian at the beginning. His proficiency in literature soon became so remarkable, that it began to be said that he was capable of governing the Roman empire; and this popular rumor becoming generally diffused, greatly disquieted the emperor's mind, so that he had him removed from the Great City to Nicomedia, forbidding him at the same time to frequent the school of Libanius the Syrian Sophist. For Libanius having been driven at that time from Constantinople, by a combination of the educators there, had retired to Nicomedia, where he opened a school. Here he gave vent to his indignation against the educators in the treatise he composed regarding them. Julian was, however, interdicted from being his auditor, because Libanius was a pagan in religion: nevertheless he privately procured his orations, which he not only greatly admired, but also frequently and with close study perused. As he was becoming very expert in the rhetorical art, Maximus the philosopher arrived at Nicomedia (not the Byzantine, Euclid's father) but the Ephesian, whom the emperor Valentinian afterwards caused to be executed as a practicer of magic. This took place later; at that time the only thing that attracted him to Nicomedia was the fame of Julian. From him [Julian] received, in addition to the principles of philosophy, his own religious sentiments, and a desire to possess the empire. When these things reached the ears of the emperor, Julian, between hope and fear, became very anxious to lull the suspicions which had been awakened, and therefore began to assume the external semblance of what he once was in reality. He was shaved to the very skin,[3] and pretended to live a monastic life: and while in private he pursued his philosophical studies, in public he read the sacred writings of the Christians, and moreover

---

[1] December, 361 A.D. This proclamation must be distinguished from the one in Gaul (II. 47); the latter was the proclamation by the army, and occurred during the lifetime of Constantius.

[2] Cf. I. 1.

[3] See Bingham, *Eccl. Antiq.* VI. 4, end.

was constituted a reader[4] in the church of Nicomedia. Thus by these specious pretexts he succeeded in averting the emperor's displeasure. Now he did all this from fear, but he by no means abandoned his hope; telling his friends that happier times were not far distant, when he should possess the imperial sway. In this condition of things his brother Gallus having been created Cæsar, on his way to the East came to Nicomedia to see him. But when not long after this Gallus was slain, Julian was suspected by the emperor; wherefore he directed that a guard should be set over him: he soon, however, found means of escaping from them, and fleeing from place to place he managed to be in safety. At last the Empress Eusebia having discovered his retreat, persuaded the emperor to leave him uninjured, and permit him to go to Athens to pursue his philosophical studies. From thence — to be brief — the emperor recalled him, and after created him Cæsar; in addition to this, uniting him in marriage to his own sister Helen, he sent him against the barbarians. For the barbarians whom the Emperor Constantius had engaged as auxiliary forces against the tyrant Magnentius, having proved of no use against the usurper, were beginning to pillage the Roman cities. And inasmuch as he was young he ordered him to undertake nothing without consulting the other military chiefs.

Now these generals having obtained such authority, became lax in their duties, and the barbarians in consequence strengthened themselves. Julian perceiving this allowed the commanders to give themselves up to luxury and revelling, but exerted himself to infuse courage into the soldiery, offering a stipulated reward to any one who should kill a barbarian. This measure effectually weakened the enemy and at the same time conciliated to himself the affections of the army. It is reported that as he was entering a town a civic crown which was suspended between two pillars fell upon his head, which it exactly fitted: upon which all present gave a shout of admiration, regarding it as a presage of his one day becoming emperor. Some have affirmed that Constantius sent him against the barbarians, in the hope that he would perish in an engagement with them. I know not whether those who say this speak the truth; but it certainly is improbable that he should have first contracted so near an alliance with him, and then have sought his destruction to the prejudice of his own interests. Let each form his own judgment of the matter. Julian's complaint to the emperor of the inertness of his military officers procured for him a coadjutor in the command more in sympathy with his own ardor; and by their combined efforts such an assault was made upon the barbarians, that they sent him an embassy, assuring him that they had been ordered by the emperor's letters, which were produced, to march into the Roman territories. But he cast the ambassador into prison, and vigorously attacking the forces of the enemy, totally defeated them; and having taken their king prisoner, he sent him alive to Constantius. Immediately after this brilliant success he was proclaimed emperor by the soldiers; and inasmuch as there was no imperial crown at hand, one of his guards took the chain which he wore about his own neck, and bound it around Julian's head. Thus Julian became emperor: but whether he subsequently conducted himself as became a philosopher, let my readers determine. For he neither entered into communication with Constantius by an embassy, nor paid him the least homage in acknowledgment of past favors; but constituting other governors over the provinces, he conducted everything just as it pleased him. Moreover, he sought to bring Constantius into contempt, by reciting publicly in every city the letters which he had written to the barbarians; and thus having rendered the inhabitants of these places disaffected, they were easily induced to revolt from Constantius to himself. After this he no longer wore the mask of Christianity, but everywhere opened the pagan temples, offering sacrifice to the idols; and designating himself 'Pontifex Maximus,'[5] gave permission to such as would to celebrate their superstitious festivals. In this manner he managed to excite a civil war against Constantius; and thus, as far as he was concerned, he would have involved the empire in all the disastrous consequences of a war. For this philosopher's aim could not have been attained without much bloodshed: but God, in the sovereignty of his own councils, checked the fury of these antagonists without detriment to the state, by the removal of one of them. For when Julian arrived among the Thracians, intelligence was brought him that Constantius was dead; and thus was the Roman empire at that time preserved from the intestine strife that threatened it. Julian forthwith made his public entry into Constantinople; and considered with himself how he might best conciliate the masses and secure popular favor. Accordingly he had recourse to the following measures: he knew that Constantius had rendered himself odious to the defenders of the homoousian faith by having driven them from the churches, and proscribed their bishops.[6] He was also aware that the pagans

---

[4] The 'reader,' ἀναγνώστης, lector, was commonly a young man possessed of a good voice, who read the Scriptures from the pulpit or reading-desk (not the altar). Bennett, *Christ. Archæol.* P. 374.

[5] See Smith, *Dict. of Greek and Rom. Antiq.* See also, on sacrificing to idols as a sign of apostasy, Bingham, *Eccl. Antiq.* XVI. iv. 5.   [6] See II. 7, 13, 16, &c.

were extremely discontented because of the prohibitions which prevented their sacrificing to their gods, and were very anxious to get their temples opened, with liberty to exercise their idolatrous rites. In fact, he was sensible that while both these classes secretly entertained rancorous feelings against his predecessor, the people in general were exceedingly exasperated by the violence of the eunuchs, and especially by the rapacity of Eusebius the chief officer of the imperial bed-chamber. Under these circumstances he treated all parties with subtlety: with some he dissimulated; others he attached to himself by conferring obligations upon them, for he was fond of affecting beneficence; but to all in common he manifested his own predilection for the idolatry of the heathens. And first in order to brand the memory of Constantius by making him appear to have been cruel toward his subjects, he recalled the exiled bishops, and restored to them their confiscated estates. He next commanded the suitable agents to see that the pagan temples should be opened without delay. Then he directed that such individuals as had been victims of the extortionate conduct of the eunuchs, should receive back the property of which they had been plundered. Eusebius, the chief of the imperial bed-chamber, he punished with death, not only on account of the injuries he had inflicted on others, but because he was assured that it was through his machinations that his brother Gallus had been killed. The body of Constantius he honored with an imperial funeral, but expelled the eunuchs, barbers, and cooks from the palace. The eunuchs he dispensed with, because they were unnecessary in consequence of his wife's decease, as he had resolved not to marry again; the cooks, because he maintained a very simple table; and the barbers, because he said one was sufficient for a great many persons. These he dismissed for the reasons given; he also reduced the majority of the secretaries to their former condition, and appointed for those who were retained a salary befitting their office. The mode of public traveling[7] and conveyance of necessaries he also reformed, abolishing the use of mules, oxen, and asses for this purpose, and permitting horses only to be so employed. These various retrenchments were highly lauded by some few, but strongly reprobated by all others, as tending to bring the imperial dignity into contempt, by stripping it of those appendages of pomp and magnificence which exercise so powerful an influence over the minds of the vulgar. Not only so, but at night he was accustomed to sit up composing orations which he

afterwards delivered in the senate: though in fact he was the first and only emperor since the time of Julius Cæsar who made speeches in that assembly. To those who were eminent for literary attainments, he extended the most flattering patronage, and especially to those who were professional philosophers; in consequence of which, abundance of pretenders to learning of this sort resorted to the palace from all quarters, wearing their palliums, being more conspicuous for their costume than their erudition. These impostors, who invariably adopted the religious sentiments of their prince, were all inimical to the welfare of the Christians; and Julian himself, whose excessive vanity prompted him to deride all his predecessors in a book which he wrote entitled *The Cæsars*, was led by the same haughty disposition to compose treatises against the Christians also.[8] The expulsion of the cooks and barbers is in a manner becoming a philosopher indeed, but not an emperor; but ridiculing and caricaturing of others is neither the part of the philosopher nor that of the emperor: for such personages ought to be superior to the influence of jealousy and detraction. An emperor may be a philosopher in all that regards moderation and self-control; but should a philosopher attempt to imitate what might become an emperor, he would frequently depart from his own principles. We have thus briefly spoken of the Emperor Julian, tracing his extraction, education, temper of mind, and the way in which he became invested with the imperial power.

CHAPTER II.

Of the Sedition excited at Alexandria, and how George was slain.

IT is now proper to mention what took place in the churches under the same [emperor]. A great disturbance occurred at Alexandria in consequence of the following circumstance. There was a place in that city which had long been abandoned to neglect and filth, wherein the pagans had formerly celebrated their mysteries, and sacrificed human beings to Mithra.[1] This being empty and otherwise useless, Constantius had granted to the church of the Alexandrians; and George wishing to erect a church on the site of it, gave directions that the place should be cleansed. In the process of clearing it, an adytum[2] of vast depth was discovered which unveiled the nature of their heathenish rites:

---

[7] It is difficult to determine in what particulars the improvements mentioned here were made. Gregory Nazianzen, *Contra Julianum*, I. lxxv., confesses that Julian had made reforms in the matter.

[8] See chap. 23.
[1] The friendly or propitious divinity of the Persian theology; hence identified with the light and life-giving sun.
[2] The secret or innermost sanctuary of the temple, where none but priests were permitted to enter; afterwards applied to any secret place.

for there were found there the skulls of many persons of all ages, who were said to have been immolated for the purpose of divination by the inspection of entrails, when the pagans performed these and such like magic arts whereby they enchanted the souls of men. The Christians on discovering these abominations in the adytum of the Mithreum, went forth eagerly to expose them to the view and execration of all; and therefore carried the skulls throughout the city, in a kind of triumphal procession, for the inspection of the people. When the pagans of Alexandria beheld this, unable to bear the insulting character of the act, they became so exasperated, that they assailed the Christians with whatever weapon chanced to come to hand, in their fury destroying numbers of them in a variety of ways: some they killed with the sword, others with clubs and stones; some they strangled with ropes, others they crucified, purposely inflicting this last kind of death in contempt of the cross of Christ: most of them they wounded; and as it generally happens in such a case, neither friends nor relatives were spared, but friends, brothers, parents, and children imbrued their hands in each other's blood. Wherefore the Christians ceased from cleansing the Mithreum: the pagans meanwhile having dragged George out of the church, fastened him to a camel, and when they had torn him to pieces, they burnt him together with the camel.[3]

CHAPTER III.

The Emperor Indignant at the Murder of George, rebukes the Alexandrians by Letter.

THE emperor being highly indignant at the assassination of George, wrote to the citizens of Alexandria, rebuking their violence in the strongest terms. A report was circulated that those who detested him because of Athanasius, perpetrated this outrage upon George: but as for me I think it is undoubtedly true that such as cherish hostile feelings against particular individuals are often found identified with popular commotions; yet the emperor's letter evidently attaches the blame to the populace, rather than to any among the Christians. George, however, was at that time, and had for some time previously been, exceedingly obnoxious to all classes, which is sufficient to account for the burning indignation of the multitude against him. That the emperor charges the people with the crime may be seen from his letter which was expressed in the following terms.

Emperor Cæsar Julian Maximus Augustus to the Citizens of Alexandria.[1]

Even if you have neither respect for Alexander the founder of your city, nor, what is more, for that great and most holy god Serapis; yet how is it you have made no account not only of the universal claims of humanity and social order, but also of what is due to us, to whom all the gods, and especially the mighty Serapis, have assigned the empire of the world, for whose cognizance therefore it became you to reserve all matters of public wrong? But perhaps the impulse of rage and indignation, which taking possession of the mind, too often stimulate it to the most atrocious acts, has led you astray. It seems, however, that when your fury had in some degree moderated, you aggravated your culpability by adding a most heinous offense to that which had been committed under the excitement of the moment: nor were you, although but the common people, ashamed to perpetrate those very acts on account of which you justly detested them. By Serapis I conjure you tell me, for what unjust deed were ye so indignant at George? You will perhaps answer, it was because he exasperated Constantius of blessed memory against you: because he introduced an army into the sacred city: because in consequence the governor[2] of Egypt despoiled the god's most holy temple of its images, votive offerings, and such other consecrated apparatus as it contained; who, when ye could not endure the sight of such a foul desecration, but attempted to defend the god from sacrilegious hands, or rather to hinder the pillage of what had been consecrated to his service, in contravention of all justice, law, and piety, dared to send armed bands against you. This he probably did from his dreading George more than Constantius: but he would have consulted better for his own safety had he not been guilty of this tyrannical conduct, but persevered in his former moderation toward you. Being on all these accounts enraged against George as the adversary of the gods, you have again polluted your sacred city; whereas you ought to have impeached him before the judges. For had you thus acted, neither murder, nor any other unlawful deed would have been committed; but justice being equitably dispensed, would have preserved you innocent of these disgraceful excesses, while it brought on him the punishment due to his impious crimes. Thus too, in short, the insolence of those would have been curbed who contemn the gods, and respect neither cities of such magnitude, nor so flourishing a

---

[3] This George is, according to some authorities, the St. George of the legend. In its Arian form the legend represents St. George as warring against the wizard Athanasius; later, the wizard was transformed to a dragon, and George to an armed knight slaying the dragon. On other forms and features of the legend, see Smith & Wace, *Dict. of Christ. Biog.*, GEORGIUS (43).

[1] Julian, *Ep.* 10.
[2] Artemius, whom the Emperor Julian afterwards beheaded for desecrating the pagan temple.

population ; but make the barbarities they practice against them the prelude, as it were, of
their exercise of power. Compare therefore
this my present letter, with that which I wrote
you some time since. With what high commendation did I then greet you ! But now, by the
immortal gods, with an equal disposition to
praise you I am unable to do so on account of
your heinous misdoings. The people have had
the audacity to tear a man in pieces, like dogs ;
nor have they been subsequently ashamed of
this inhuman procedure, nor desirous of purifying their hands from such pollution, that they
may stretch them forth in the presence of the
gods undefiled by blood. You will no doubt be
ready to say that George justly merited this
chastisement ; and we might be disposed perhaps to admit that he deserved still more acute
tortures. Should you farther affirm that on your
account he was worthy of these sufferings, even
this might also be granted. But should you add
that it became you to inflict the vengeance due
to his offenses, that I could by no means acquiesce
in ; for you have laws to which it is the duty of
every one of you to be subject, and to evince
your respect for both publicly, as well as in private. If any individual should transgress those
wise and salutary regulations which were originally constituted for the well-being of the community, does that absolve the rest from obedience
to them ? It is fortunate for you, ye Alexandrians, that such an atrocity has been perpetrated
in our reign, who, by reason of our reverence
for the gods, and on account of our grandfather
and uncle [3] whose name we bear, and who governed Egypt and your city, still retain a fraternal
affection for you. Assuredly that power which
will not suffer itself to be disrespected, and such
a government as is possessed of a vigorous and
healthy constitution, could not connive at such
unbridled licentiousness in its subjects, without
unsparingly purging out the dangerous distemper
by the application of remedies sufficiently potent.
We shall however in your case, for the reasons
already assigned, restrict ourselves to the more
mild and gentle medicine of remonstrance and
exhortation ; to the which mode of treatment
we are persuaded ye will the more readily submit, inasmuch as we understand ye are Greeks
by original descent, and also still preserve in
your memory and character the traces of the
glory of your ancestors. Let this be published
to our citizens of Alexandria.

Such was the emperor's letter.

CHAPTER IV.

*On the Death of George, Athanasius returns to
Alexandria, and takes Possession of his
See.*

Not long after this, Athanasius returning from
his exile, was received with great joy by the
people of Alexandria. They expelled at that
time the Arians from the churches, and restored
Athanasius to the possession of them. The
Arians meanwhile assembling themselves in low
and obscure buildings, ordained Lucius to supply
the place of George. Such was the state of
things at that time at Alexandria.

CHAPTER V.

Of Lucifer and Eusebius.

About the same time Lucifer and Eusebius [1]
were by an imperial order, recalled from banishment out of the Upper Thebaïs ; the former
being bishop of Carala, a city of Sardinia, the
latter of Vercellæ, a city of the Ligurians in Italy,
as I have said [2] previously. These two prelates
therefore consulted together on the most effectual
means of preventing the neglected canons [3] and
discipline of the church from being in future
violated and despised.

CHAPTER VI.

*Lucifer goes to Antioch and consecrates Pau-
linus.*

It was decided therefore that Lucifer should
go to Antioch in Syria, and Eusebius to Alexandria, that by assembling a Synod in conjunction
with Athanasius, they might confirm the doctrines of the church. Lucifer sent a deacon
as his representative, by whom he pledged himself to assent to whatever the Synod might
decree ; but he himself went to Antioch, where
he found the church in great disorder, the people
not being agreed among themselves. For not
only did the Arian heresy, which had been introduced by Euzoïus, divide the church, but, as we
before said,[1] the followers of Meletius also, from
attachment to their teacher, separated themselves from those with whom they agreed in
sentiment. When therefore Lucifer had constituted Paulinus their bishop, he again departed.

[3] Philostorgius (VII. 10) calls this Julian ' the governor of the
East, who was the uncle on the maternal side of Julian the Apostate.' Sozomen also (V. 7 and 8) and Theodoret (*H. E.* III.
12, 13) furnish information regarding him, as well as Ammianus
Marcellius XXIII. i. Cf. also Julian, *Epist.* XIII. (Spanheim, p.
382).

[1] Theodoret, *H. E.* III. 4, mentions Hilarius, Astenius, and
some other bishops who were at this time recalled from exile by
Julian's edict, and joined Lucifer and Eusebius in these deliberations about restoring the authority of the canons and correcting
abuses in the church.
[2] Cf. II. 36.
[3] More especially the canons of the Council of Nicæa.
[1] II. 44.

CHAPTER VII.

*By the Co-operation of Eusebius and Athanasius
a Synod is held at Alexandria, wherein the
Trinity is declared to be Consubstantial.*

As soon as Eusebius reached Alexandria, he
in concert with Athanasius immediately convoked
a Synod. The bishops assembled on this occasion out of various cities, took into consideration
many subjects of the utmost importance. They
asserted the divinity of the Holy Spirit[1] and
comprehended him in the consubstantial Trinity:
they also declared that the Word in being made
man, assumed not only flesh, but also a soul, in
accordance with the views of the early ecclesiastics. For they did not introduce any new doctrine of their own devising into the church,
but contented themselves with recording their
sanction of those points which ecclesiastical tradition has insisted on from the beginning, and
wise Christians have demonstratively taught.
Such sentiments the ancient fathers have uniformly maintained in all their controversial writings. Irenæus, Clemens, Apollinaris of Hierapolis,
and Serapion who presided over the church at
Antioch, assure us in their several works, that it
was the generally received opinion that Christ
in his incarnation was endowed with a soul.
Moreover, the Synod convened on account of
Beryllus[2] bishop of Philadelphia in Arabia,
recognized the same doctrine in their letter to
that prelate. Origen also everywhere in his
extant works accepts that the Incarnate God
took on himself a human soul. But he more
particularly explains this mystery in the ninth
volume of his *Comments upon Genesis*, where
he shows that Adam and Eve were types of
Christ and the church. That holy man Pamphilus, and Eusebius who was surnamed after
him, are trustworthy witnesses on this subject:
both these witnesses in their joint life of Origen,
and admirable defense of him in answer to such
as were prejudiced against him, prove that he
was not the first who made this declaration, but
that in doing so he was the mere expositor of
the mystical tradition of the church. Those
who assisted at the Alexandrian Council examined also with great minuteness the question
concerning 'Essence' or 'Substance,' and
'Existence,' 'Subsistence,' or 'Personality.' For
Hosius, bishop of Cordova in Spain, who has
been before referred to as having been sent by

the Emperor Constantine to allay the excitement
which Arius had caused, originated the controversy about these terms in his earnestness to
overthrow the dogma of Sabellius the Libyan.
In the council of Nicæa, however, which was
held soon after, this dispute was not agitated;
but in consequence of the contention about it
which subsequently arose, the matter was freely
discussed at Alexandria.[3] It was there determined that such expressions as *ousia* and *hypostasis* ought not to be used in reference to God:
for they argued that the word *ousia* is nowhere
employed in the sacred Scriptures; and that
the apostle has misapplied the term *hypostasis*[4]
owing to an inevitable necessity arising from the
nature of the doctrine. They nevertheless
decided that in refutation of the Sabellian error
these terms were admissible, in default of more
appropriate language, lest it should be supposed that one thing was indicated by a threefold designation; whereas we ought rather to
believe that each of those named in the Trinity
is God in his own proper person. Such were
the decisions of this Synod. If we may express
our own judgment concerning substance and
personality, it appears to us that the Greek
philosophers have given us various definitions
of *ousia*, but have not taken the slightest notice
of *hypostasis*. Irenæus[5] the grammarian indeed, in his Alphabetical [Lexicon entitled]
Atticistes, even declares it to be a barbarous
term; for it is not to be found in any of the
ancients, except occasionally in a sense quite
different from that which is attached to it in the
present day. Thus Sophocles, in his tragedy
entitled *Phœnix*, uses it to signify 'treachery':
in Menander it implies 'sauces'; as if one should
call the 'sediment' at the bottom of a hogshead
of wine *hypostasis*. But although the ancient
philosophical writers scarcely noticed this word,
the more modern ones have frequently used it
instead of *ousia*. This term, as we before observed,
has been variously defined: but can that which
is capable of being circumscribed by a definition
be applicable to God who is incomprehensible?
Evagrius in his *Monachicus*,[6] cautions us against
rash and inconsiderate language in reference to
God; forbidding all attempt to define the divinity, inasmuch as it is wholly simple in its nature:
'for,' says he, 'definition belongs only to things
which are compound.' The same author further
adds, 'Every proposition has either a "genus"

---

[1] The bishops composing the Council of Nicæa simply declared
their faith in the Holy Spirit, without adding any definition; they
were not met with any denial of the divinity of the Holy Spirit.
This denial was first made by Macedonius, in the fourth century.
[2] Euseb. *H. E.* VI. 33, says that this Beryllus denied that Christ
was God before the Incarnation. He, however, gives the see of
Beryllus as Bostra in Arabia, instead of Philadelphia. So also Epiphanius Scholasticus; though Nicephorus, X. 2, calls him Cyrillus,
instead of Beryllus.

[3] Valesius conjectures that Socrates is wrong here in attributing
such an action to the Synod of Alexandria, as the term *ousia*
does not occur in the Nicene Creed, and such action would therefore
be in manifest contradiction to the action at Nicæa. This, however,
is not probable, in view of the dominating influence of Athanasius
in both. But, as the acts of the Alexandrian synod are not extant,
it is impossible to verify this conjecture.
[4] Heb. i. 3.
[5] See Suidas, *Lexicon*.
[6] The only work of Evagrius preserved to our days is his *Ecclesiastical History*.

which is predicted, or a "species," or a "differentia," or a "proprium," or an "accidens," or that which is compounded of these : but none of these can be supposed to exist in the sacred Trinity. Let then what is inexplicable be adored in silence.' Such is the reasoning of Evagrius, of whom we shall again speak hereafter.[7] We have indeed made a digression here, but such as will tend to illustrate the subject under consideration.

CHAPTER VIII.

Quotations from Athanasius' 'Defense of his Flight.'

ON this occasion Athanasius read to those present the *Defense* which he had composed some time before in justification of his flight ; a few passages from which it may be of service to introduce here, leaving the entire production, which is too long to be transcribed, to be sought out and perused by the studious.[1]

See the daring enormities of the impious persons ! Such are their proceedings : and yet instead of blushing at their former clumsy intrigues against us, they even now abuse us for having effected our escape out of their murderous hands ; nay, are grievously vexed that they were unable to put us out of the way altogether. In short, they overlook the fact that while they pretend to upbraid us with 'cowardice,' they are really criminating themselves : for if it be disgraceful to flee, it is still more so to pursue, since the one is only endeavoring to avoid being murdered, while the other is seeking to commit the deed. But Scripture itself directs us to flee :[2] and those who persecute unto death, in attempting to violate the law, constrain us to have recourse to flight. They should rather, therefore, be ashamed of their persecution, than reproach us for having sought to escape from it : let them cease to harass, and those who flee will also cease. Nevertheless they set no bounds to their malevolence, using every art to entrap us, in the consciousness that the flight of the persecuted is the strongest condemnation of the persecutor : for no one runs away from a mild and beneficent person, but from one who is of a barbarous and cruel disposition. Hence it was that ' Every one that was discontented and in debt ' fled from Saul to David.[3] Wherefore these [foes of ours] in like manner desire to kill such as conceal themselves, that no evidence may exist to convict them of their wickedness. But in this also these misguided men most egregiously deceive themselves : for the more obvious the effort to elude them, the more manifestly will their deliberate slaughters and exiles be exposed. If

they act the part of assassins, the voice of the blood which is shed will cry against them the louder : and if they condemn to banishment, they will raise so everywhere living monuments of their own injustice and oppression. Surely unless their intellects were unsound they would perceive the dilemma in which their own counsels entangle them. But since they have lost sound judgment, their folly is exposed when they vanish, and when they seek to stay they do not see their wickedness.[4] But if they reproach those who succeed in secreting themselves from the malice of their blood-thirsty adversaries, and revile such as flee from their persecutors, what will they say to Jacob's retreat from the rage of his brother Esau,[5] and to Moses[6] retiring into the land of Midian for fear of Pharaoh ? And what apology will these babblers make for David's[7] flight from Saul, when he sent messengers from his own house to dispatch him ; and for his concealment in a cave, after contriving to extricate himself from the treacherous designs of Abimelech,[8] by feigning madness ? What will these reckless asserters of whatever suits their purpose answer, when they are reminded of the great prophet Elijah,[9] who by calling upon God had recalled the dead to life, hiding himself from dread of Ahab, and fleeing on account of Jezebel's menaces ? At which time the sons of the prophets also, being sought for in order to be slain, withdrew, and were concealed in caves by Obadiah ;[10] or are they unacquainted with these instances because of their antiquity ? Have they forgotten also what is recorded in the Gospel, that the disciples retreated and hid themselves for fear of the Jews ?[11] Paul,[12] when sought for by the governor [of Damascus] 'was let down from the wall in a basket, and thus escaped the hands of him that sought him.' Since then Scripture relates these circumstances concerning the saints, what excuse can they fabricate for their temerity ? If they charge us with ' cowardice,' it is in utter insensibility to the condemnation it pronounces on themselves. If they asperse these holy men by asserting that they acted contrary to the will of God, they demonstrate their ignorance of Scripture. For it was commanded in the Law that ' cities of refuge ' should be constituted,[13] by which provision was made that such as were pursued in order to be put to death might have means afforded of preserving themselves. Again in the consummation of the ages, when the Word of the Father, who had before spoken by Moses, came himself to the earth, he gave this express injunction, ' When

---

[7] IV. 23.
[1] Athan. *de Fuga*. 7.
[2] Matt. x. 23.
[3] 2 Kings xxii. 2 (LXX).

[4] Athanas. *de Fuga*. 10.
[5] Gen. xxviii.
[6] Ex. ii. 15.
[7] 1 Sam. xix. 12.
[8] Rather Achisch, king of Gath, 1 Sam. xxi. 10.
[9] 1 Kings xix. 3.
[10] 1 Kings xviii. 4.
[11] Matt. xxvi. 56.
[12] 2 Cor. xi. 32, 33.
[13] Num. xxxv. 11.

they persecute you in one city, flee unto another:'[14] and shortly after, 'When therefore ye shall see the abomination of desolation, spoken of by Daniel the prophet, stand in the holy place (let whosoever reads, understand), then let those in Judea flee unto the mountains: let him that is on the house-top not come down to take anything out of his house; nor him that is in the fields return to take his clothes.'[15] The saints therefore knowing these precepts, had such a sort of training for their action: for what the Lord then commanded, he had before his coming in the flesh already spoken of by his servants. And this is a universal rule for man, leading to perfection, 'to practice whatever God has enjoined.' On this account the Word himself, becoming incarnate for our sake, deigned to conceal himself when he was sought for;[16] and being again persecuted, condescended to withdraw to avoid the conspiracy against him. For thus it became him, by hungering and thirsting and suffering other afflictions, to demonstrate that he was indeed made man.[17] For at the very commencement, as soon as he was born, he gave this direction by an angel to Joseph: 'Arise and take the young child and his mother, and flee into Egypt, for Herod will seek the infant's life.'[18] And after Herod's death, it appears that for fear of his son Archelaüs he retired to Nazareth. Subsequently; when he gave unquestionable evidence of his Divine character by healing the withered hand, 'when the Pharisees took council how they might destroy him,[19] Jesus knowing their wickedness withdrew himself thence.' Moreover, when he had raised Lazarus from the dead, and they had become still more intent on destroying him, [we are told that] 'Jesus walked no more openly among the Jews,[20] but retired into a region on the borders of the desert.' Again when the Saviour said, 'Before Abraham was, I am;'[21] and the Jews took up stones to cast at him; Jesus concealed himself, and going through the midst of them out of the Temple, went away thence, and so escaped. Since then they see these things, or rather understand them,[22] (for they will not see,) are they not deserving of being burnt with fire, according to what is written, for acting and speaking so plainly contrary to all that the Lord did and taught? Finally, when John had suffered martyrdom, and his disciples had buried his body, Jesus having heard what was done, departed thence by ship into a desert place apart.[23] Now the Lord did these things and so taught. But would that these men of whom I speak, had the modesty

to confine their rashness to men only, without daring to be guilty of such madness as to accuse the Saviour himself of 'cowardice'; especially after having already uttered blasphemies against him. But even if they be insane they will not be tolerated and their ignorance of the gospels be detected by every one. The cause for retreat and flight under such circumstances as these is reasonable and valid, of which the evangelists have afforded us precedents in the conduct of our Saviour himself: from which it may be inferred that the saints have always been justly influenced by the same principle, since whatever is recorded of him as man, is applicable to mankind in general. For he took on himself our nature, and exhibited in himself the affections of our infirmity, which John has thus indicated: 'Then they sought to take him; but no man laid hands on him, because his hour was not yet come.'[24] Moreover, before that hour came, he himself said to his mother, 'Mine hour is not yet come;'[25] and to those who were denominated his brethren, 'My time is not yet come.' Again when the time had arrived, he said to his disciples, 'Sleep on now, and take your rest: for behold the hour is at hand, and the Son of man shall be betrayed into the hands of sinners.'[26] ... So[27] that he neither permitted himself to be apprehended before the time came; nor when the time was come did he conceal himself, but voluntarily gave himself up to those who had conspired against him.[28] ... Thus also the blessed martyrs have guarded themselves in times of persecution: being persecuted they fled, and kept themselves concealed; but being discovered they suffered martyrdom.

Such is the reasoning of Athanasius in his apology for his own flight.

CHAPTER IX.

After the Synod of Alexandria, Eusebius proceeding to Antioch finds the Catholics at Variance on Account of Paulinus' Consecration; and having exerted himself in vain to reconcile them, he departs; Indignation of Lucifer and Origin of a Sect called after him.

As soon as the council of Alexandria was dissolved, Eusebius bishop of Vercellæ went from Alexandria to Antioch; there finding that Paulinus had been ordained by Lucifer, and that the people were disagreeing among themselves,— for the partisans of Meletius held their assemblies apart,— he was exceedingly grieved at the want of harmony concerning this election, and in his own mind disapproved of what had taken

[14] Matt. x. 23.
[15] Matt. xxiv. 15–18.
[16] John viii. 59.
[17] Abbreviated from Athanasius.
[18] Matt. ii. 13, 22.
[19] Matt. xii. 14, 15.
[20] John xi. 53, 54.
[21] John viii. 58.
[22] Matt. xiii. 13; Isa. ix. 5.
[23] Matt. xiv. 12, 13.
[24] John vii. 30.
[25] John ii. 4; iii. 6.
[26] Matt. xxvi. 45.
[27] Athan. de Fuga. 15.
[28] Athan. de Fuga. 22.

place. His respect for Lucifer however induced him to be silent about it, and on his departure he engaged that all things should be set right by a council of bishops. Subsequently he labored with great earnestness to unite the dissentients, but did not succeed. Meanwhile Meletius returned from exile; and finding his followers holding their assemblies apart from the others, he set himself at their head. But Euzoïus, the chief of the Arian heresy, had possession of the churches: Paulinus[1] only retained a small church within the city, from which Euzoïus had not ejected him, on account of his personal respect for him. But Meletius assembled his adherents without the gates of the city. It was under these circumstances that Eusebius left Antioch at that time. When Lucifer understood that his ordination of Paul was not approved of by Eusebius, regarding it as an insult, he became highly incensed; and not only separated himself from communion with him, but also began, in a contentious spirit, to condemn what had been determined by the Synod. These things occurring at a season of grievous disorder, alienated many from the church; for many attached themselves to Lucifer, and thus a distinct sect arose under the name of 'Luciferians.'[2] Nevertheless Lucifer was unable to give full expression to his anger, inasmuch as he had pledged himself by his deacon to assent to whatever should be decided on by the Synod. Wherefore he adhered to the tenets of the church, and returned to Sardinia to his own see: but such as at first identified themselves with his quarrel, still continue separate from the church. Eusebius, on the other hand, traveling throughout the Eastern provinces like a good physician, completely restored those who were weak in the faith, instructing and establishing them in ecclesiastical principles. After this he passed over to Illyricum, and thence to Italy, where he pursued a similar course.

CHAPTER X.

Of Hilary Bishop of Poictiers.

THERE, however, Hilary bishop of Poictiers (a city of Aquitania Secunda) had anticipated him, having previously confirmed the bishops of Italy and Gaul in the doctrines of the orthodox faith; for he first had returned from exile to these countries. Both therefore nobly combined their energies in defense of the faith: and Hilary being a very eloquent man, maintained with great power the doctrine of the *homoousion* in books which he wrote in Latin. In these he gave sufficient support [to the doc-

trine] and unanswerably confuted the Arian tenets. These things took place shortly after the recall of those who had been banished. But it must be observed, that at the same time Macedonius, Eleusius, Eustathius, and Sophronius, with all their partisans, who had but the one common designation Macedonians, held frequent Synods in various places.[1] Having called together those of Seleucia who embraced their views, they anathematized the bishops of the other party, that is the Acacian: and rejecting the creed of Ariminum, they confirmed that which had been read at Seleucia. This, as I have stated in the preceding book,[2] was the same as had been before promulgated at Antioch. When they were asked by some one, 'Why have ye, who are called Macedonians hitherto, retained communion with the Acacians, as though ye agreed in opinion, if ye really hold different sentiments?' they replied thus, through Sophronius, bishop of Pompeiopolis, a city of Paphlagonia: 'Those in the West,' said he, 'were infected with the homoousian error as with a disease: Aëtius in the East adulterated the purity of the faith by introducing the assertion of a dissimilitude of substance. Now both of these dogmas are illegitimate; for the former rashly blended into one the distinct persons of the Father and the Son, binding them together by that cord of iniquity the term *homoousion;* while Aëtius wholly separated that affinity of nature of the Son to the Father, by the expression *anomoion,* unlike as to substance or essence. Since then both these opinions run into the very opposite extremes, the middle course between them appeared to us to be more consistent with truth and piety: we accordingly assert that the Son is "like the Father as to subsistence."'

Such was the answer the Macedonians made by Sophronius to that question, as Sabinus assures us in his *Collection of the Synodical Acts.* But in decrying Aëtius as the author of the Anomoion doctrine, and not Acacius, they flagrantly disguise the truth, in order to seem as far removed from the Arians on the one side, as from the Homoousians on the other: for their own words convict them of having separated from them both, merely from the love of innovation. With these remarks we close our notice of these persons.

CHAPTER XI.

The Emperor Julian extracts Money from the Christians.

ALTHOUGH at the beginning of his reign the Emperor Julian conducted himself mildly toward

---

[1] V. 5.   [2] Cf. Sozom. III. 15, and V. 12.

[1] Sozom. V. 14; Theodoret, *Hæret. Fabul.* IV.
[2] II. 10. 39.

all men ; but as he went on he did not continue to show the same equanimity. He most readily indeed acceded to the requests of the Christians, when they tended in any way to cast odium on the memory of Constantius ; but when this inducement did not exist, he made no effort to conceal the rancorous feelings which he entertained towards Christians in general. Accordingly he soon ordered that the church of the Novatians at Cyzicus, which Euzoïus had totally demolished, should be rebuilt, imposing a very heavy penalty upon Eleusius bishop of that city, if he failed to complete that structure at his own expense within the space of two months. Moreover, he favored the pagan superstitions with the whole weight of his authority : and the temples of the heathen were opened, as we have before stated ;[1] but he himself also publicly offered sacrifices to Fortune, goddess of Constantinople, in the cathedral,[2] where her image was erected.

CHAPTER XII.

Of Maris Bishop of Chalcedon ; Julian forbids Christians from entering Literary Pursuits.

ABOUT this time, Maris bishop of Chalcedon in Bithynia being led by the hand into the emperor's presence, — for on account of extreme old age he had a disease in his eyes termed 'cataract,' — severely rebuked his impiety, apostasy, and atheism. Julian answered his reproaches by loading him with contumelious epithets : and he defended himself by words calling him 'blind.' 'You blind old fool,' said he, 'this Galilæan God of yours will never cure you.' For he was accustomed to term Christ 'the Galilæan,'[1] and Christians Galilæans. Maris with still greater boldness replied, 'I thank God for bereaving me of my sight, that I might not behold the face of one who has fallen into such awful impiety.' The emperor suffered this to pass without farther notice at that time ; but he afterwards had his revenge. Observing that those who suffered martyrdom under the reign of Diocletian were greatly honored by the Christians, and knowing that many among them were eagerly desirous of becoming martyrs, he determined to wreak his vengeance upon them in some other way. Abstaining therefore from the excessive cruelties which had been practiced under Diocletian ; he did not however altogether abstain from persecution (for any measures adopted to disquiet and molest I regard as persecution). This then

was the plan he pursued : he enacted a law[2] by which Christians were excluded from the cultivation of literature ; ''lest,' said he, ' when they have sharpened their tongue, they should be able the more readily to meet the arguments of the heathen.'

CHAPTER XIII.

Of the Outrages committed by the Pagans against the Christians.

HE moreover interdicted such as would not abjure Christianity, and offer sacrifice to idols, from holding any office at court : nor would he allow Christians to be governors of provinces ; 'for,' said he, 'their law forbids them to use the sword against offenders worthy of capital punishment.'[1] He also induced many to sacrifice, partly by flatteries, and partly by gifts. Immediately, as if tried in a furnace, it at once became evident to all, who were the real Christians, and who were merely nominal ones. Such as were Christians in integrity of heart, very readily resigned their commission,[2] choosing to endure anything rather than deny Christ. Of this number were Jovian, Valentinian, and Valens, each of whom afterwards became emperor. But others of unsound principles, who preferred the riches and honor of this world to the true felicity, sacrificed without hesitation. Of these was Ecebolius, a sophist[3] of Constantinople who, accommodating himself to the dispositions of the emperors, pretended in the reign of Constantius to be an ardent Christian ; while in Julian's time he appeared an equally vigorous pagan : and after Julian's death, he again made a profession of Christianity. For he prostrated himself before the church doors, and called out, 'Trample on me, for I am as salt that has lost its savor.' Of so fickle and inconstant a character was this person, throughout the whole period of his history. About this time the emperor wishing to make reprisals on the Persians, for the frequent incursions they had made on the Roman territories in the reign of Constantius, marched with great expedition through Asia into the East. But as he well knew what a train of calamities attend a war, and what immense resources are needful to carry it on successfully and that without it cannot be carried on, he craftily devised a plan for collecting money by extorting it from the Christians. On all those who refused to sacrifice he imposed

---

[1] Chap. 1.
[2] Βασιλικῆ. On the origin and history of the term, see Bennett, *Christian Archæology*, pp. 157–163. The special basilica meant here was situated, according to Valesius, in the fourth precinct, and alone called βασιλικῆ, or 'cathedral' without qualification. The 'Theodosian cathedral' was situated in the seventh ward.
[1] Cf. John i. 46, and Acts ii. 7. Later the word was used by the heathen also, contemptuously, as a term of reproach.

[2] Chap. 16.
[1] Based, probably, on Matt. xxvi. 52, and John xviii. 11.
[2] ζώνην ἀπετίθεντο; literally, ' put off their girdle,' as the badge of office.
[3] The term was used first by traveling teachers of rhetoric at the time of the philosopher Socrates as descriptive of their profession; and although it later acquired an unfavorable significance, it continued to be used also as a professional name given to teachers of rhetoric, as here.

a heavy fine, which was exacted with great rigor from such as were true Christians, every one being compelled to pay in proportion to what he possessed. By these unjust means the emperor soon amassed immense wealth; for this law was put in execution, both where Julian was personally present, and where he was not. The pagans at the same time assailed the Christians; and there was a great concourse of those who styled themselves 'philosophers.' They then proceeded to institute certain abominable mysteries;[4] and sacrificing pure children both male and female, they inspected their entrails, and even tasted their flesh. These infamous rites were practiced in other cities, but more particularly at Athens and Alexandria; in which latter place, a calumnious accusation was made against Athanasius the bishop, the emperor being assured that he was intent on desolating not that city only, but all Egypt, and that nothing but his expulsion out of the country could save it. The governor of Alexandria was therefore instructed by an imperial edict to apprehend him.

CHAPTER XIV.

Flight of Athanasius.

BUT he fled again, saying to his intimates, 'Let us retire for a little while, friends; it is but a small cloud which will soon pass away.' He then immediately embarked, and crossing the Nile, hastened with all speed into Egypt, closely pursued by those who sought to take him. When he understood that his pursuers were not far distant, his attendants were urging him to retreat once more into the desert, but he had recourse to an artifice and thus effected his escape. He persuaded those who accompanied him to turn back and meet his adversaries, which they did immediately; and on approaching them they were simply asked 'where they had seen Athanasius': to which they replied that 'he was not a great way off,' and, that 'if they hastened they would soon overtake him.' Being thus deluded, they started afresh in pursuit with quickened speed, but to no purpose; and Athanasius making good his retreat, returned secretly to Alexandria; and there he remained concealed until the persecution was at an end. Such were the perils which succeeded one another in the career of the bishop of Alexandria, these last from the heathen coming after that to which he was before subjected from Christians. In addition to these things, the governors of the provinces taking advantage of the emperor's superstition to feed

their own cupidity, committed more grievous outrages on the Christians than their sovereign had given them a warrant for; sometimes exacting larger sums of money than they ought to have done, and at others inflicting on them corporal punishments. The emperor learning of these excesses, connived at them; and when the sufferers appealed to him against their oppressors, he tauntingly said, 'It is your duty to bear these afflictions patiently; for this is the command of your God.'

CHAPTER XV.

Martyrs at Merum in Phrygia, under Julian.

AMACHIUS governor of Phrygia ordered that the temple at Merum, a city of that province, should be opened, and cleared of the filth which had accumulated there by lapse of time: also that the statues it contained should be polished fresh. This in being put into operation grieved the Christians very much. Now a certain Macedonius and Theodulus and Tatïan, unable to endure the indignity thus put upon their religion, and impelled by a fervent zeal for virtue, rushed by night into the temple, and broke the images in pieces. The governor infuriated at what had been done, would have put to death many in that city who were altogether innocent, when the authors of the deed voluntarily surrendered themselves, choosing rather to die themselves in defense of the truth, than to see others put to death in their stead. The governor seized and ordered them to expiate the crime they had committed by sacrificing: on their refusal to do this, their judge menaced them with tortures; but they despising his threats, being endowed with great courage, declared their readiness to undergo any sufferings, rather than pollute themselves by sacrificing. After subjecting them to all possible tortures he at last laid them on gridirons under which a fire was placed, and thus slew them. But even in this last extremity they gave the most heroic proofs of fortitude, addressing the ruthless governor thus: 'If you wish to eat broiled flesh, Amachius, turn us on the other side also, lest we should appear but half cooked to your taste.' Thus these martyrs ended their life.

CHAPTER XVI.

Of the Literary Labors of the Two Apollinares and the Emperor's Prohibition of Christians being instructed in Greek Literature.

THE imperial law[1] which forbade Christians to study Greek literature, rendered the two Apolli-

---

[4] Cf. Tertull. *Apol.* IX. 'In the bosom of Africa infants were publicly sacrificed to Saturn, even to the days of a proconsul under Tiberius,' &c.

[1] Cf. Sozom. V. 18; also above, II. 46.

nares of whom we have above spoken, much more distinguished than before. For both being skilled in polite learning, the father as a grammarian, and the son as a rhetorician, they made themselves serviceable to the Christians at this crisis. For the former, as a grammarian, composed a grammar consistent with the Christian faith: he also translated the Books of Moses into heroic verse; and paraphrased all the historical books of the Old Testament, putting them partly into dactylic measure, and partly reducing them to the form of dramatic tragedy. He purposely employed all kinds of verse, that no form of expression peculiar to the Greek language might be unknown or unheard of amongst Christians. The younger Apollinaris, who was well trained in eloquence, expounded the gospels and apostolic doctrines in the way of dialogue, as Plato among the Greeks had done. Thus showing themselves useful to the Christian cause they overcame the subtlety of the emperor through their own labors. But Divine Providence was more potent than either their labors, or the craft of the emperor: for not long afterwards, in the manner we shall hereafter explain,[2] the law became wholly inoperative; and the works of these men are now of no greater importance, than if they had never been written. But perhaps some one will vigorously reply saying: 'On what grounds do you affirm that both these things were effected by the providence of God? That the emperor's sudden death was very advantageous to Christianity is indeed evident: but surely the rejection of the Christian compositions of the two Apollinares, and the Christians beginning afresh to imbue their minds with the philosophy of the heathens, this works out no benefit to Christianity, for pagan philosophy teaches Polytheism, and is injurious to the promotion of true religion.' This objection I shall meet with such considerations as at present occur to me. Greek literature certainly was never recognized either by Christ or his Apostles as divinely inspired, nor on the other hand was it wholly rejected as pernicious. And this they did, I conceive, not inconsiderately. For there were many philosophers among the Greeks who were not far from the knowledge of God; and in fact these being disciplined by logical science, strenuously opposed the Epicureans and other contentious Sophists who denied Divine Providence, confuting their ignorance. And for these reasons they have become useful to all lovers of real piety: nevertheless they themselves were not acquainted with the Head of true religion, being ignorant of the mystery of Christ which 'had been hidden from genera-

tions and ages.'[3] And that this was so, the Apostle in his epistle to the Romans thus declares:[4] 'For the wrath of God is revealed from heaven against all ungodliness and unrighteousness of men, who hold the truth in unrighteousness. Because that which may be known of God is manifest in them; for God has shown it unto them. For the invisible things of him from the creation of the world are clearly seen, being understood by the things that are made, even his eternal power and Godhead, that they may be without excuse; because that when they knew God, they glorified him not as God.' From these words it appears that they had the knowledge of truth, which God had manifested to them; but were guilty on this account, that when they knew God, they glorified him not as God. Wherefore by not forbidding the study of the learned works of the Greeks, they left it to the discretion of those who wished to do so. This is our first argument in defense of the position we took: another may be thus put: The divinely inspired Scriptures undoubtedly inculcate doctrines that are both admirable in themselves, and heavenly in their character: they also eminently tend to produce piety and integrity of life in those who are guided by their precepts, pointing out a walk of faith which is highly approved of God. But they do not instruct us in the art of reasoning, by means of which we may be enabled successfully to resist those who oppose the truth. Besides adversaries are most easily foiled, when we can use their own weapons against them. But this power was not supplied to Christians by the writings of the Apollinares. Julian had this in mind when he by law prohibited Christians from being educated in Greek literature, for he knew very well that the fables it contains would expose the whole pagan system, of which he had become the champion to ridicule and contempt. Even Socrates, the most celebrated of their philosophers, despised these absurdities, and was condemned on account of it, as if he had attempted to violate the sanctity of their deities. Moreover, both Christ and his Apostle enjoin us 'to become discriminating money-changers,'[5] so that we might 'prove all things, and hold fast that which is good':[6] directing us also to 'beware lest any one should spoil us through philosophy and vain deceit.'[7] But this we cannot do, unless we possess ourselves of the weapons of our adversaries: taking care that in making this acquisition we do not adopt their sentiments, but testing them, reject the evil, but retain all that is good and true: for good wher-

---

[2] Chap. 21.

[3] Col. i. 26.   [4] Rom. i. 18-21.
[5] On this extra-Scriptural saying attributed to Jesus Christ, see n. 54, Introd. p. xi.
[6] 1 Thess. v. 21.   [7] Col. ii. 8.

ever it is found, is a property of truth. Should any one imagine that in making these assertions we wrest the Scriptures from their legitimate construction, let it be remembered that the Apostle not only does not forbid our being instructed in Greek learning, but that he himself seems by no means to have neglected it, inasmuch as he knows many of the sayings of the Greeks. Whence did he get the saying, 'The Cretans are always liars, evil beasts, slow-bellies,'[8] but from a perusal of *The Oracles* of Epimenides,[9] the Cretan Initiator? Or how would he have known this, 'For we are also his offspring,'[10] had he not been acquainted with *The Phenomena* of Aratus[11] the astronomer? Again this sentence, 'Evil communications corrupt good manners,'[12] is a sufficient proof that he was conversant with the tragedies of Euripides.[13] But what need is there of enlarging on this point? It is well known that in ancient times the doctors of the church by unhindered usage were accustomed to exercise themselves in the learning of the Greeks, until they had reached an advanced age : this they did with a view to improve themselves in eloquence and to strengthen and polish their mind, and at the same time to enable them to refute the errors of the heathen. Let these remarks be sufficient in the subject suggested by the two Apollinares.

CHAPTER XVII.

The Emperor preparing an Expedition against the Persians, arrives at Antioch, and being ridiculed by the Inhabitants, he retorts on them by a Satirical Publication entitled 'Misopōgon, or the Beard-Hater.'

THE emperor having extorted immense sums of money from the Christians, hastening his expedition against the Persians, arrived at Antioch in Syria. There, desiring to show the citizens how much he affected glory, he unduly depressed the prices of commodities; neither taking into account the circumstances of that time, nor reflecting how much the presence of an army inconveniences the population of the provinces,

and of necessity lessens the supply of provisions to the cities. The merchants and retailers[1] therefore left off trading, being unable to sustain the losses which the imperial edict entailed upon them ; consequently the necessaries failed. The Antiochians not bearing the insult, — for they are a people naturally impatient with insult, — instantly broke forth into invectives against Julian ; caricaturing his beard also, which was a very long one, and saying that it ought to be cut off and manufactured into ropes. They added that the bull which was impressed upon his coin, was a symbol of his having desolated the world. For the emperor, being excessively superstitious, was continually sacrificing bulls[2] on the altars of his idols ; and had ordered the impression of a bull and altar to be made on his coin. Irritated by these scoffs, he threatened to punish the city of Antioch, and returned to Tarsus in Cilicia, giving orders that preparations should be made for his speedy departure thence. Whence Libanius the sophist took occasion to compose two orations, one addressed to the emperor in behalf of the Antiochians, the other to the inhabitants of Antioch on the emperor's displeasure. It is however affirmed that these compositions were merely written, and never recited in public. Julian abandoning his former purpose of revenging himself on his satirists by injurious deeds, expended his wrath in reciprocating their abusive taunts ; for he wrote a pamphlet against them which he entitled *Antiochicus, or Misopōgon*, thus leaving an indelible stigma upon that city and its inhabitants. But we must now speak of the evils which he brought upon the Christians at Antioch.

CHAPTER XVIII.

The Emperor consulting an Oracle, the Demon gives no Response, being awed by the Nearness of Babylas the Martyr.

HAVING ordered that the pagan temples at Antioch should be opened, he was very eager to obtain an oracle from *Apollo of Daphne*. But the demon that inhabited the temple remained silent through fear of his neighbor, Babylas[1] the martyr ; for the coffin which contained the body of that saint was close by. When the emperor was informed of this circumstance, he commanded that the coffin should be immediately

---

[8] Tit. i. 12.
[9] Cf. Theophrastus, VII. x. and Diogenes Laertius, I. x. The latter gives a list of Epimenides' works, but makes no mention of any 'Oracles.' Socrates must have used this term in a more general sense therefore, and meant some collection of obscure and mystical writings. He also calls Epimenides an 'Initiator,' because, according to the testimony of Theophrastus, he was versed particularly in lustration and coruscation.
[10] Acts xvii. 28.
[11] Fabricius, *Bibl. Græc.* II. p. 451 seq.
[12] 1 Cor. xv. 33.
[13] Menander, and not Euripides, is the only author to whom this line can be traced (see Tertull. *ad Uxor*. 1. 8, and Meineke, *Fragm. Comic. Græc.* Vol. IV. p. 132), but it may have been a popular proverb, or even originally a composition of Euripides, which Menander simply used.

[1] μεταβολεῖς. Cf. μεταβολή, used to designate all merchandising, Julius Pollux, III. 25; hence μεταβολευς, a 'retailer,' 'small merchant.'
[2] Hence Gregory of Nazianus calls him κανσίταυρος, 'a burner of bulls.'
[1] See Euseb. *H. E.* VI. 20 and 39: also Chrysostom, *de S. Babyl.* According to these authorities Babylas was bishop of Antioch, succeeding Sabrinus, and was beheaded in prison during the reign of Decius. His remains were transferred to a church built over against the temple of Apollo of Daphne (Sozom. V. 19) by Gallus, Julian's brother.

removed : upon which the Christians of Antioch, including women and children, transported the coffin from Daphne to the city, with solemn rejoicings and chanting of psalms. The psalms[2] were such as cast reproach on the gods of the heathen, and those who put confidence in them and their images.

CHAPTER XIX.

Wrath of the Emperor, and Firmness of Theodore the Confessor.

THEN indeed the emperor's real temper and disposition, which he had hitherto kept as much as possible from observation, became fully manifested : for he who had boasted so much of his philosophy, was no longer able to restrain himself; but being goaded almost to madness by these reproachful hymns, he was ready to inflict the same cruelties on the Christians, with which Diocletian's agents had formerly visited them. Since, however, his solicitude about the Persian expedition afforded him no leisure for personally executing his wishes, he commanded Sallust the Prætorian Prefect to seize those who had been most conspicuous for their zeal in psalm-singing, in order to make examples of them. The prefect, though a pagan, was far from being pleased with his commission; but since he durst not contravene it, he caused several of the Christians to be apprehended, and some of them to be imprisoned. One young man named Theodore, whom the heathens brought before him, he subjected to a variety of tortures, causing his person to be so lacerated and only released him from further punishment when he thought that he could not possibly outlive the torments : yet God preserved this sufferer, so that he long survived that confession. Rufinus, the author of the *Ecclesiastical History* written in Latin, states that he himself conversed with the same Theodore a considerable time afterwards : and enquired of him whether in the process of scourging and racking he had not felt the most intense pains ; his answer was, that he felt the pain of the tortures to which he was subjected for a very short time ; and that a young man stood by him who both wiped off the sweat which was produced by the acuteness of the ordeal through which he was passing, and at the same time strengthened his mind, so that he rendered this time of trial a season of rapture rather than of suffering. Let this suffice concerning the most wonderful Theodore. About this time Persian ambassadors came to the emperor, requesting him to terminate the war on certain express conditions. But Julian abruptly dismissed them, saying, 'You shall very shortly see me in person, so that there will be no need of an embassy.'

CHAPTER XX.

The Jews instigated by the Emperor attempt to rebuild their Temple, and are frustrated in their Attempt by Miraculous Interposition.

THE emperor in another attempt to molest the Christians exposed his superstition. Being fond of sacrificing, he not only himself delighted in the blood of victims, but considered it an indignity offered to him, if others did not do likewise. And as he found but few persons of this stamp, he sent for the Jews and enquired of them why they abstained from sacrificing, since the law of Moses enjoined it? On their replying that it was not permitted them to do this in any other place than Jerusalem, he immediately ordered them to rebuild Solomon's temple. Meanwhile he himself proceeded on his expedition against the Persians. The Jews who had been long desirous of obtaining a favorable opportunity for rearing their temple afresh in order that they might therein offer sacrifice, applied themselves very vigorously to the work. Moreover, they conducted themselves with great insolence toward the Christians, and threatened to do them as much mischief, as they had themselves suffered from the Romans. The emperor having ordered that the expenses of this structure should be defrayed out of the public treasury, all things were soon provided, such as timber and stone, burnt brick, clay, lime, and all other materials necessary for building. On this occasion Cyril bishop of Jerusalem, called to mind the prophecy of Daniel, which Christ also in the holy gospels has confirmed, and predicted in the presence of many persons, that the time had indeed come 'in which one stone should not be left upon another in that temple,' but that the Saviour's prophetic declaration[1] should have its full accomplishment. Such were the bishop's words : and on the night following, a mighty earthquake tore up the stones of the old foundations of the temple and dispersed them all together with the adjacent edifices. Terror consequently possessed the Jews on account of the event; and the report of it brought many to the spot who resided at a great distance : when therefore a vast multitude was assembled, another prodigy took place. Fire came down from heaven and consumed all the builders' tools : so that the flames were seen preying upon mallets, irons to smooth and polish stones, saws, hatchets, adzes, in short all the various implements which the workmen had procured as necessary for the undertaking ;

---

[2] Ps. xcvi. 7 (LXX).

[1] Matt. xxiv. 2, 15.

and the fire continued burning among these for a whole day. The Jews indeed were in the greatest possible alarm, and unwillingly confessed Christ, calling him God : yet they did not do his will ; but influenced by inveterate prepossessions they still clung to Judaism. Even a third miracle which afterwards happened failed to lead them to a belief of the truth. For the next night luminous impressions of a cross appeared imprinted on their garments, which at daybreak they in vain attempted to rub or wash out. They were therefore 'blinded' as the apostle says,[2] and cast away the good which they had in their hands : and thus was the temple, instead of being rebuilt, at that time wholly overthrown.

CHAPTER XXI.

The Emperor's Invasion of Persia, and Death.

THE emperor meanwhile invaded the country of the Persians a little before spring, having learnt that the races of Persia were greatly enfeebled and totally spiritless in winter. For from their inability to endure cold, they abstain from military service at that season, and it has become a proverb that 'a Mede will not then draw his hand from underneath his cloak.' And well knowing that the Romans were inured to brave all the rigors of the atmosphere he let them loose on the country. After devastating a considerable tract of country, including numerous villages and fortresses, they next assailed the cities ; and having invested the great city Ctesiphon, he reduced the king of the Persians to such straits that the latter sent repeated embassies to the emperor, offering to surrender a portion of his dominions, on condition of his quitting the country, and putting an end to the war. But Julian was unaffected by these submissions, and showed no compassion to a suppliant foe : nor did he think of the adage, 'To conquer is honorable, but to be more than conqueror gives occasion for envy.' Giving credit to the divinations of the philosopher Maximus, with whom he was in continual intercourse, he was deluded into the belief that his exploits would not only equal, but exceed those of Alexander of Macedon ; so that he spurned with contempt the entreaties of the Persian monarch. He even supposed in accordance with the teachings of Pythagoras and Plato on 'the transmigration of souls,'[1] that he was possessed of Alexander's soul, or rather that he himself was Alexander in another body. This ridiculous fancy deluded and caused him to reject the negotiations for peace proposed by the king of

the Persians. Wherefore the latter convinced of the uselessness of them was constrained to prepare for conflict, and therefore on the next day after the rejection of his embassy, he drew out in order of battle all the forces he had. The Romans indeed censured their prince, for not avoiding an engagement when he might have done so with advantage : nevertheless they attacked those who opposed them, and again put the enemy to flight. The emperor was present on horseback, and encouraged his soldiers in battle ; but confiding simply in his hope of success, he wore no armor. In this defenceless state, a dart cast by some one unknown, pierced through his arm and entered his side, making a wound. In consequence of this wound he died. Some say that a certain Persian hurled the javelin, and then fled ; others assert that one of his own men was the author of the deed, which indeed is the best corroborated and most current report. But Callistus, one of his body-guards, who celebrated this emperor's deeds in heroic verse, says in narrating the particulars of this war, that the wound of which he died was inflicted by a demon. This is possibly a mere poetical fiction, or perhaps it was really the fact ; for vengeful furies have undoubtedly destroyed many persons. Be the case however as it may, this is certain, that the ardor of his natural temperament rendered him incautious, his learning made him vain, and his affectation of clemency exposed him to contempt. Thus Julian ended his life in Persia,[2] as we have said, in his fourth consulate,[3] which he bore with Sallust his colleague. This event occurred on the 26th of June, in the third year of his reign, and the seventh from his having been created Cæsar by Constantius, he being at that time in the thirty-first year of his age.

CHAPTER XXII.

Jovian is proclaimed Emperor.

THE soldiery being thrown into extreme perplexity by an event so unexpected, and without delay, on the following day proclaimed Jovian emperor, a person alike distinguished for his courage and birth. He was a military tribune when Julian put forth an edict giving his officers the option of either sacrificing or resigning their rank in the army, and chose rather to lay down his commission,[1] than to obey the mandate of an impious prince. Julian, however, being pressed by the urgency of the war which was

---

[2] Rom. xi. 25; 2 Cor. iii. 14.
[1] μετενσωματώσεως, lit. 'exchange of bodies,' formed in analogy with μετεμψύχωσις and logically inseparable from that doctrine.

[2] Theodoret, *H. E.* III. 25, gives the familiar version of the death of Julian, according to which, on perceiving the character of his wound, the dying emperor filled his hand with blood and threw it up into the air, crying, 'Galilean, thou hast overcome!'
[3] 363 A.D.   [1] See above, chap. 13.

before him, retained him among his generals. On being saluted emperor, he positively declined to accept the sovereign power: and when the soldiers brought him forward by force, he declared that 'being a Christian, he did not wish to reign over a people who chose to adopt paganism as their religion.' They all then with one voice answered that they also were Christians: upon which he accepted the imperial dignity. Perceiving himself suddenly left in very difficult circumstances, in the midst of the Persian territory, where his army was in danger of perishing for want of necessaries, he agreed to terminate the war, even on terms by no means honorable to the glory of the Roman name, but rendered necessary by the exigencies of the crisis. Submitting therefore to the loss of the government of Syria,[2] and giving up also Nisibis, a city of Mesopotamia, he withdrew from their territories. The announcement of these things gave fresh hope to the Christians; while the pagans vehemently bewailed Julian's death. Nevertheless the whole army reprobated his intemperate heat, and ascribed to his rashness in listening to the wily reports of a Persian deserter, the humiliation of ceding the territories lost: for being imposed upon by the statements of this fugitive, he was induced to burn the ships which supplied them with provisions by water, by which means they were exposed to all the horrors of famine. Then also Libanius composed a funeral oration on him, which he designated *Julianus, or Epitaph,* wherein he celebrates with lofty encomiums almost all his actions; but in referring to the books which Julian wrote against the Christians, he says that he has therein clearly demonstrated the ridiculous and trifling character of their sacred books. Had this sophist contented himself with extolling the emperor's other acts, I should have quietly proceeded with the course of my history; but since this famous rhetorician has thought proper to take occasion to inveigh against the Scriptures of the Christian faith, we also propose to pause a little and in a brief review consider his words.

CHAPTER XXIII.

Refutation of what Libanius the Sophist said concerning Julian.

'WHEN the winter,' says he,[1] 'had lengthened the nights, the emperor made an attack on those books which made the man of Palestine both God, and the Son of God: and by a long series of arguments having proved that these writings, which are so much revered by Christians, are ridiculous and unfounded, he has evinced himself wiser and more skillful than the Tyrian[2] old man. But may this Tyrian sage be propitious to me, and mildly bear with what has been affirmed, seeing that he has been excelled by his son!' Such is the language of Libanius the Sophist. But I confess, indeed, that he was an excellent rhetorician, but am persuaded that had he not coincided with the emperor in religious sentiment, he would not only have given expression to all that has been said against him by Christians, but would have magnified every ground of censure as naturally becomes a rhetorician. For while Constantius was alive he wrote encomiums upon him; but after his death he brought the most insulting and reproachful charges against him. So that if Porphyry had been emperor, Libanius would certainly have preferred his books to Julian's: and had Julian been a mere sophist, he would have termed him a very indifferent one, as he does Ecebolius in his *Epitaph upon Julian.* Since then he has spoken in the spirit of a pagan, a sophist, and the friend of him whom he lauded, we shall endeavor to meet what he has advanced, as far as we are able. In the first place he says that the emperor undertook to 'attack' these books during the long winter nights. Now to 'attack' means to make the writing of a confutation of them a task, as the sophists commonly do in teaching the rudiments of their art; for he had perused these books long before, but attacked them at this time. But throughout the long contest into which he entered, instead of attempting to disprove anything by sound reasoning, as Libanius asserts, in the absence of truth he had recourse to sneers and contemptuous jests, of which he was excessively fond; and thus he sought to hold up to derision what is too firmly established to be overthrown. For every one who enters into controversy with another, sometimes trying to pervert the truth, and at others to conceal it, falsifies by every possible means the position of his antagonist. And an adversary is not satisfied with doing malignant acts against one with whom he is at variance, but will speak against him also, and charge upon the object of his dislike the very faults he is conscious of in himself. That both Julian and Porphyry, whom Libanius calls the 'Tyrian old man,' took great delight in scoffing, is evident from their own works. For Porphyry in his *History of the Philosophers* has treated with ridicule the life of Socrates, the most eminent of

---

[2] So the MSS. and Bright. The same reading was also before Epiphanius Scholasticus and Nicephorus; but Valesius conjecturally amends the reading τοὺς Σύρους τῆς ἀρχῆς into τοὺς ὅρους τῆς ἀρχῆς, alleging that Socrates himself later mentions the loss as ζημίαν τῶν ὅρων. If the reading of Valesius be considered correct, then we must translate 'submitting to the loss of the borders,' supplying 'of the empire.' This would include the districts beyond the Tigris.　　[1] Liban. *Orat.* xviii. (*Opera,* i. Reiske).

[2] Porphyry. See above, I. 9.

all the philosophers, making such remarks on him as neither Melitus, nor Anytus, his accusers, would have dared to utter; of Socrates, I say, who was admired by all the Greeks for his modesty, justice, and other virtues; whom Plato,[3] the most admirable among them, Xenophon, and the rest of the philosophic band, not only honor as one beloved of God, but also are accustomed to think of as having been endowed with superhuman intelligence. And Julian, imitating his 'father,' displayed a like morbidness of mind in his book, entitled *The Cæsars*, wherein he traduces all his imperial predecessors, not sparing even Mark the philosopher.[4] Their own writings therefore show that they both took pleasure in taunts and reviling; and I have no need of profuse and clever expressions to do this; but what has been said is enough concerning their mood in this respect. Now I write these things, using the oration of each as witnesses respecting their dispositions, but of Julian in particular, what Gregory of Nazianzus[5] says in his *Second Oration against the Pagans* is in the following terms:

'These things were made evident to others by experience, after the possession of imperial authority had left him free to follow the bent of his inclinations: but I had foreseen it all, from the time I became acquainted with him at Athens. Thither he came, by permission of the emperor, soon after the change in his brother's fortune. His motive for this visit was twofold: one reason was honorable to him, viz. to see Greece, and attend the schools there; the other was a more secret one, which few knew anything about, for his impiety had not yet presumed to openly avow itself, viz. to have opportunity of consulting the sacrificers and other impostors respecting his own destiny. I well remember that even then I was no bad diviner concerning this person, although I by no means pretend to be one of those skilled in the art of divination: but the fickleness of his disposition, and the incredible extravagancy of his mind, rendered me prophetic; if indeed he is the "best prophet who conjectures correctly"[6] events. For it seemed to me that no good was portended by a neck seldom steady, the frequent shrugging of shoulders, an eye scowling and always in motion, together with a frenzied aspect; a gait irregular and tottering, a nose breathing only contempt and insult, with ridiculous contortions of countenance expressive of the same thing; immoderate and very loud laughter, nods as it were of assent, and drawings back of the head as if in denial, without any visible cause; speech with

hesitancy and interrupted by his breathing; disorderly and senseless questions, answers no better, all jumbled together without the least consistency or method. Why need I enter into minute particulars? Such I foresaw he would be beforehand as I found him afterwards from experience. And if any of those who were then present and heard me, were now here, they would readily testify that when I observed these prognostics I exclaimed, "Ah! how great a mischief to itself is the Roman empire fostering!" And that when I had uttered these words I prayed God that I might be a false prophet. For it would have been far better [that I should have been convicted of having formed an erroneous judgment], than that the world should be filled with so many calamities, and that such a monster should have appeared as never before had been seen: although many deluges and conflagrations are recorded, many earthquakes and chasms, and descriptions are given of many ferocious and inhuman men, as well as prodigies of the brute creation, compounded of different races, of which nature produced unusual forms. His end has indeed been such as corresponds with the madness of his career.'

This is the sketch which Gregory has given us of Julian. Moreover, that in their various compilations they have endeavored to do violence to the truth, sometimes by the corruption of passages of sacred Scripture, at others by either adding to the express words, and putting such a construction upon them as suited their own purpose, many have demonstrated, by confuting their cavils, and exposing their fallacies. Origen in particular, who lived long before Julian's time, by himself raising objections to such passages of Holy Scripture[7] as seemed to disturb some readers, and then fully meeting them, has shut out the invidious clamors of the thoughtless. And had Julian and Porphyry given his writings a candid and serious perusal, they would have discoursed on other topics, and not have turned to the framing of blasphemous sophisms. It is also very obvious that the emperor in his discourses was intent on beguiling the ignorant, and did not address himself to those who possess the 'form' of the truth as it is presented in the sacred Scriptures. For having grouped together various expressions in which God is spoken of dispensationally, and more according to the manner of men, he thus comments on them.[8] 'Every one of these expressions is full of blasphemy against

---

[3] In his *Crito, Phædo, Phædrus*, and *Apology of Socrates*. See also Xenophon's *Memorabilia of Socrates* and *Symposium*.
[4] Marcus Aurelius. [5] Gregor. Nazianz. *Orat.* V. 23.
[6] Euripid. *Fragm.*

[7] Probably Socrates means Origen's lost work, known as *Stromata*, which Jerome (in his *Ep. ad Magnum*) says was written to show the harmony of the Christian doctrines and the teachings of the philosophers. The description here given does not tally more precisely with any other work of Origen now extant.
[8] Cyril, *Contra Julian*. III. (p. 93, ed. Spanheim).

God, unless the phrase contains some occult and mysterious sense, which indeed I can suppose.' This is the exact language he uses in his third book against the Christians. But in his treatise *On the Cynic Philosophy*, where he shows to what extent fables may be invented on religious subjects, he says that in such matters the truth must be veiled: ' For,' to quote his very words,[9] ' Nature loves concealment; and the hidden substance of the gods cannot endure being cast into polluted ears in naked words.' From which it is manifest that the emperor entertained this notion concerning the divine Scriptures, that they are mystical discourses, containing in them some abstruse meaning. He is also very indignant because all men do not form the same opinion of them; and inveighs against those Christians who understand the sacred oracles in a more literal sense. But it ill became him to rail so vehemently against the simplicity of the vulgar, and on their account to behave so arrogantly towards the sacred Scriptures: nor was he warranted in turning with aversion from those things which others rightly apprehended, because forsooth they understood them otherwise than he desired they should. But now as it seems a similar cause of disgust seems to have operated upon him to that which affected Porphyry, who having been beaten by some Christians at Cæsarea in Palestine and not being able to endure [such treatment], from the working of unrestrained rage renounced the Christian religion: and from hatred of those who had beaten him he took to write blasphemous works against Christians, as Eusebius Pamphilus has proved who at the same time refuted his writings. So the emperor having uttered disdainful expressions against the Christians in the presence of an unthinking multitude, through the same morbid condition of mind fell into Porphyry's blasphemies. Since therefore they both willfully broke forth into impiety, they are punished by the consciousness of their guilt. But when Libanius the Sophist says [10] in derision, that the Christians make ' a man of Palestine both God and the Son of God,' he appears to have forgotten that he himself has deified Julian at the close of his oration. ' For they almost killed,' says he, ' the first messenger of his death, as if he had lied against a god.' And a little afterwards he adds, ' O thou cherished one of the gods! thou disciple of the gods! thou associate [11] with the gods!' Now although Libanius may have meant otherwise, yet inasmuch as he did not avoid the ambiguity of a word which is sometimes taken in a bad sense, he seems to

have said the same things as the Christians had done reproachfully. If then it was his intention to praise him, he ought to have avoided equivocal terms; as he did on another occasion, when being criticised he avoided a certain word, cutting it out of his works. Moreover, that man in Christ was united to the Godhead, so that while he was apparently but man, he was the invisible God, and that both these things are most true, the divine books of Christians distinctly teach. But the heathen before they believe, cannot understand: for it is a divine oracle that declares [12] ' Unless ye believe, assuredly ye shall not understand.' Wherefore they are not ashamed to place many men among the number of their gods: and would that they had done this, at least to the good, just, and sober, instead of the impure, unjust, and those addicted to drunkenness, like the Hercules, the Bacchus, and the Æsculapius, by whom Libanius does not blush to swear frequently in his orations. And were I to attempt to enumerate the unnatural debaucheries and infamous adulteries of these, the digression would be lengthened beyond measure: but for those who desire to be informed on the subject, *Aristotle's Peplum, Dionysius' Corona, Rheginus' Polymnemon*, and the whole host of poets will be enough to show that the pagan theology is a tissue of extravagant absurdities. We might indeed show by a variety of instances that the practice of deifying human beings was far from uncommon among the heathen, nay, that they did so without the slightest hesitation: let a few examples suffice. The Rhodians having consulted an oracle on some public calamity, a response was given directing them to pay their adoration to Atys, a pagan priest who instituted frantic rites in Phrygia. The oracle was thus expressed:

' Atys propitiate, the great god, the chaste Adonis, the blessed fair-haired Dionysius rich in gifts.'

Here Atys, who from an amatory mania had castrated himself, is by the oracle designated as Adonis and Bacchus.

Again, when Alexander, king of the Macedonians, passed over into Asia, the Amphictyons courted his favor, and the Pythoness uttered this oracle:

' To Zeus supreme among the gods, and Athene Tritogenia pay homage, and to the king divine concealed in mortal form, him Zeus begat in honor to be the protector and dispenser of justice among mortals, Alexander the king.'

These are the words of the demon at Delphi, who when he wished to flatter potentates, did not scruple to assign them a place among the gods. The motive here was perhaps to concili-

---

[9] Julian, *Orat.* VII.
[10] Liban. *Orat.* XVIII. (*Oper.* I. 625, Reiske).
[11] παρεδρευτά, term applied to associates on the bench in judicatories.

[12] Isa. vii. 9 (LXX, καὶ ἐὰν μὴ πιστεύσητε, οὐδὲ μὴ συνῆτε).

ate by adulation : but what could one say of the case of Cleomedes the pugilist, whom they ranked among the gods in this oracle ?

'The last of the heroes is Cleomedes, the Astypalian. Him honor with sacrifices ; for he is no longer a mortal.'

Because of this oracle Diogenes the cynic, and Oënomaus the philosopher, strongly condemned Apollo. The inhabitants of Cyzicus declared Hadrian to be the thirteenth god ; and Adrian himself deified his own catamite Antinoüs.[13] Libanius does not term these 'ridiculous and contemptible absurdities,' although he was familiar with these oracles, as well as with the work of Adrias on the life of Alexander[14] (the pseudo-prophet of Paphlagonia) : nor does he himself hesitate to dignify Porphyry in a similar manner, when after having preferred Julian's books to his, he says, 'May the Syrian be propitious to me.' This digression will suffice to repel the scoffs of the sophist, without following him farther in what he has advanced ; for to enter into a complete refutation would require an express work. We shall therefore proceed with our history.

CHAPTER XXIV.

The Bishops flock around Jovian, each attempting to draw him to his own Creed.

JOVIAN having returned from Persia, ecclesiastical commotions were again renewed : for those who presided over the churches endeavored to anticipate each other, in the hope that the emperor would attach himself to their own tenets. He however had from the beginning adhered to the homoousian faith, and openly declared that he preferred this to all others. Moreover, he wrote letters to and encouraged Athanasius bishop of Alexandria, who immediately after Julian's death had recovered the Alexandrian church, and at that time gaining confidence from the letters [spoken of] put away all fear. The emperor further recalled from exile all those prelates whom Constantius had banished, and who had not been re-established by Julian. Moreover, the pagan temples were again shut up, and they secreted themselves wherever they were able. The philosophers also laid aside their palliums, and clothed themselves in ordinary attire. That public pollution by the blood of victims, which had been profusely lavished even to disgust in the reign of Julian, was now likewise taken away.

CHAPTER XXV.

The Macedonians and Acacians meet at Antioch, and proclaim their Assent to the Nicene Creed.

MEANWHILE the state of the church was by no means tranquil ; for the heads of the sects assiduously paid their court to the emperor their king that protection for themselves meant also power against their acknowledged opponents. And first the Macedonians presented a petition to him, in which they begged that all those who asserted the Son to be unlike the Father, might be expelled from the churches, and themselves allowed to take their place. This supplication was presented by Basil bishop of Ancyra, Silvanus of Tarsus, Sophronius of Pompeiopolis, Pasinicus of Zelæ,[1] Leontius of Comana, Callicrates of Claudiopolis, and Theophilus of Castabala. The emperor having perused it, dismissed them without any other answer than this : 'I abominate contentiousness; but I love and honor those who exert themselves to promote unanimity.' When this remark became generally known, it subdued the violence of those who were desirous of altercation and thus was realized in the design of the emperor. At this time the real spirit of the Acacian sect, and their readiness to accommodate their opinions to those invested with supreme authority, became more conspicuous than ever. For assembling themselves at Antioch in Syria, they entered into a conference with Melitius, who had separated from them a little before, and embraced the 'homoousian' opinion. This they did because they saw Melitius was in high estimation with the emperor, who then resided at Antioch ; and assenting therefore by common consent, they drew up a declaration of their sentiments acknowledging the *homoousion* and ratifying the Nicene Creed and presented it to the emperor. It was expressed in the following terms.

'The Synod of bishops convened at Antioch out of various provinces, to the most pious and beloved of God, our lord Jovian Victor Augustus.

'That your piety has above all things aimed at establishing the peace and harmony of the church, we ourselves, most devout emperor, are fully aware. Nor are we insensible that you have wisely judged an acknowledgment of the

---

[13] For a full account of Antinoüs and his relations to Hadrian, see Smith, *Dict. of Greek and Roman Biogr. and Mythol.*, article ANTINOÜS. The story has been put into literary fiction in the historical novels *Antinoüs*, by George Taylor (A. Hausrath), and *The Emperor*, by Georg Ebers.
[14] It is uncertain what the true reading should be here. In one of the MSS. it is Ἀδρίας, in another Ἀνδρίας; according to others Ἀδριανός, or Ἀρριανός. Valesius suggests the substitution of

Λουκιανός. If this be adopted, then the Alexander suggested is Lucian's Alexander of Abonoteichus. For a lucid and suggestive reproduction of this story, see Froude, *Short Studies on Great Subjects*, essay on *Lucian*.
[1] The MSS. and all the Greek texts read Ζήνων, making the name 'Pasinicus Zenon, or Zeno.' The translation here given assumes the alteration in the process of transcription of a single letter, making the original Ζηλῶν, which probably means the city of Zeleia, on the southeastern coast of the Euxine, famous for a victory of Mithridates over Triarius, the lieutenant of Lucullus, in 67 B.C.

orthodox faith to be the sum and substance of this unity. Wherefore lest we should be included in the number of those who adulterate the doctrine of the truth, we hereby declare to your piety that we embrace and steadfastly hold the faith of the holy Synod formerly convened at Nicæa. Especially since the term *homoousios*, which to some seems novel[2] and inappropriate, has been judiciously explained by the fathers to denote that the Son was begotten of the Father's substance, and that he is like the Father as to substance. Not indeed that any passion is to be understood in relation to that ineffable generation. Nor is the term *ousia*, "substance," taken by the fathers in any usual signification of it among the Greeks; but it has been employed for the subversion of what Arius impiously dared to assert concerning Christ, viz. —that he was made of things "not existing." Which heresy the Anomœans, who have lately sprung up, still more audaciously maintain, to the utter destruction of ecclesiastical unity. We have therefore annexed to this our declaration, a copy of the faith set forth by the bishops assembled at Nicæa, with which also we are fully satisfied. It is this: "We believe in one God the Father Almighty," and all the rest of the Creed in full. We, the undersigned, in presenting this statement, most cordially assent to its contents. Melitius bishop of Antioch, Eusebius of Samosata, Evagrius of Sicily, Uranius of Apamæa, Zoilus of Larissa, Acacius of Cæsarea, Antipater of Rhosus, Abramius of Urimi,[3] Aristonicus of Seleucia-upon-Belus, Barlamenus of Pergamus, Uranius of Melitina, Magnus of Chalcedon, Eutychius of Eleutheropolis, Isacocis of Armenia Major, Titus of Bostra, Peter of Sippi,[4] Pelagius of Laodicæa, Arabian of Antros, Piso of Adana through Lamydrion a presbyter, Sabinian bishop of Zeugma, Athanasius of Ancyra through Orphitus and Aëtius presbyters, Irenion bishop of Gaza, Piso of Augusta, Patricius of Paltus through Lamyrion a presbyter, Anatolius bishop of Berœa, Theotimus of the Arabs, and Lucian of Arca.'[5]

This declaration we found recorded in that work of Sabinus, entitled *A Collection of the Acts of Synods*. Now the emperor had resolved to allay if possible the contentious spirit of the parties at variance, by bland manners and persuasive language toward them all; declaring that he 'would not molest any one on account of his religious sentiments, and that he should love and highly esteem such as would zealously promote the unity of the church.' The philosopher Themistius attests that such was his conduct, in the oration he composed on his 'consulate.' For he extols the emperor for his overcoming the wiles of flatterers by freely permitting every one to worship God according to the dictates of his conscience. And in allusion to the check which the sycophants received, he facetiously observes[6] that experience has made it evident that such persons 'worship the purple and not God; and resemble the changeful Euripus,[7] which sometimes rolls its waves in one direction, and·at others the very opposite way.'

CHAPTER XXVI.

Death of the Emperor Jovian.

THUS did the emperor repress at that time the impetuosity of those who were disposed to cavil: and immediately departing from Antioch, he went to Tarsus in Cilicia, where he duly performed the funeral obsequies of Julian, after which he was declared consul. Proceeding thence directly to Constantinople, he arrived at a place named Dadastana, situated on the frontiers of Galatia and Bithynia. There Themistius the philosopher, with others of the senatorial order, met him, and pronounced the consular oration before him, which he afterwards recited before the people at Constantinople. And indeed the Roman empire, blest with so excellent a sovereign, would doubtless have flourished exceedingly, as it is likely that both the civil and ecclesiastical departments would have been happily administered, had not his sudden death bereft the state of so eminent a personage. For disease caused by some obstruction, having attacked him at the place above mentioned during the winter season, he died there on the 17th day of February, in his own and his son Varronian's consulate,[1] in the thirty-third year of his age, after having reigned seven months.

This book contains an account of the events which took place in the space of two years and five months.

---

[2] This word, whose original is ξένον, is inserted by Valesius. If it were omitted, the translation would be, 'which to some seems *acceptable.*'
[3] On the present borders of Turkey and Persia.
[4] According to Valesius Hippi.
[5] The name of this city is variously given as Archis, Arca, Arcæ, Arcas, Arcæa, Arcena. It lies at the foot of Mount Lebanon. See Joseph. *Antiq.* V. 1 and *de Bello*, XII. 13.

[6] Themist. *Orat.* V. (p. 80, ed. Harduin).
[7] Straits between Eubœa and the mainland.
[1] 364 A.D.

END OF THE THIRD BOOK.

BOOK IV.

CHAPTER I.

After Jovian's Death, Valentinian is proclaimed Emperor, and takes his Brother Valens as Colleague in the Empire; Valentinian holds the Orthodox Faith, but Valens is an Arian.

THE Emperor Jovian having died, as we have said, at Dadastana, in his own consulate and that of Varronian his son on the 17th of February, the army leaving Galatia arrived at Nicæa in Bithynia in seven days' march, and there unanimously proclaimed Valentinian emperor, on the 25th of February, in the same consulate. He was a Pannonian by race, a native of the city of Cibalis, and being entrusted with a military command, had displayed great skill in tactics. He was moreover endowed with such greatness of mind, that he always appeared superior to any degree of honor he might have attained. As soon as they had created him emperor, he proceeded forthwith to Constantinople; and thirty days after his own possession of the imperial dignity, he made his brother Valens his colleague in the empire. They both professed Christianity, but did not hold the same Christian creed: for Valentinian respected the Nicene Creed; but Valens was prepossessed in favor of the Arian opinions. And this prejudice was caused by his having been baptized by Eudoxius bishop of Constantinople. Each of them was zealous for the views of his own party; but when they had attained sovereign power, they manifested very different dispositions. For previously in the reign of Julian, when Valentinian was a military tribune, and Valens held a command in the emperor's guards, they both proved their zeal for the faith; for being constrained to sacrifice, they chose rather to give up their military rank than to do so and renounce Christianity.[1] Julian, however, knowing the necessity of the men to the state, retained them in their respective places, as did also Jovian, his successor in the empire. Later on, being invested with imperial authority, they were in accord in the management of public affairs, but as regards Christianity, as I have said, they behaved themselves very differently: for Valentinian while he favored those who agreed with him in sentiment, offered no violence to the Arians; but Valens, in his anxiety to promote the Arian cause, grievously disturbed those who differed from them, as the course of our history will show. Now at that time Liberius presided over the Roman church; and at Alexandria Athanasius was bishop of the Homoousians, while Lucius had been constituted George's successor by the Arians. At Antioch Euzoïus was at the head of the Arians: but the Homoousians were divided into two parties, of one of which Paulinus was chief, and Melitius of the other. Cyril was again constituted over the church at Jerusalem. The churches at Constantinople were under the government of Eudoxius, who openly taught the dogmas of Arianism, but the Homoousians had but one small edifice in the city wherein to hold their assemblies. Those of the Macedonian heresy who had dissented from the Acacians at Seleucia, then retained their churches in every city. Such was the state of ecclesiastical affairs at that time.[2]

CHAPTER II.

Valentinian goes into the West; Valens remains at Constantinople, and grants the Request of the Macedonians to hold a Synod, but persecutes the Adherents of the 'Homoousion.'

OF the emperors one, i.e. Valentinian, speedily went to the western parts of the empire; for the exigencies of affairs required his presence thither: meanwhile Valens, residing at Constantinople, was addressed by most of the prelates of the Macedonian heresy, requesting that another Synod might be convened for the correction of the creed. The emperor supposing they agreed in sentiment with Eudoxius and Acacius, gave them permission to do so: they therefore made preparations for assembling in the city of Lampsacus. But Valens proceeded with the utmost despatch toward Antioch in Syria, fearing lest the Persians should violate the treaty into which they had entered for thirty years in the reign of Jovian, and invade the Roman territories. They however remained quiet; and Valens employed this season of external tranquillity to prosecute a

---

[1] Cf. III. 13.

[2] Cf. V. 3.

war of extermination against all who acknowl-edged the *homoousion*. Paulinus their bishop, because of his eminent piety, he left unmolested. Melitius he punished with exile : and all the rest, as many as refused to communicate with Euzoïus, he drove out from the churches in Antioch, and subjected to various losses and punishments. It is even affirmed that he caused many to be drowned in the river Orontes, which flows by that city.

CHAPTER III.

While Valens persecutes the Orthodox Chris-tians in the East, a Usurper arises at Con-stantinople named Procopius : and at the Same Time an Earthquake and Inundation take Place and injure Several Cities.

WHILE Valens was thus occupied in Syria, there arose a usurper at Constantinople named Procopius ; who having collected a large body of troops in a very short time, meditated an ex-pedition against the emperor. This intelligence created extreme solicitude in the emperor's mind and checked for a while the persecution he had commenced against all who dared to differ from him in opinion. And while the commotions of a civil war were painfully anticipated, an earthquake occurred which did much damage to many cities. The sea also changed its accus-tomed boundaries, and overflowed to such an extent in some places, that vessels might sail where roads had previously existed ; and it retired so much from other places, that the ground became dry. These events happened in the first consulate of the two emperors.[1]

CHAPTER IV.

The Macedonians hold a Synod at Lampsacus, during a Period of Both Secular and Eccle-siastical Agitation ; and after confirming the Antiochian Creed, and anathematizing that promulgated at Ariminum, they again rat-ify the Deposition of Acacius and Eudoxius.

WHILE these events were taking place there could be no peace either in the church or in the state. Now those who had been empowered by the emperor to hold a council assembled at Lampsacus in the consulate just mentioned : this was seven years after the council of Seleu-cia. There, after confirming the Antiochian Creed, to which they had subscribed at Seleu-cia,[1] they anathematized that which had been set forth at Ariminum[2] by their former associates

in opinion. They moreover again condemned the party of Acacius and Eudoxius, and declared their deposition to have been just.[3] The civil war which was then impending prevented Eu-doxius bishop of Constantinople from either gainsaying or revenging these determinations. Wherefore Eleusius bishop of Cyzicus and his adherents became for a little while the stronger party ; inasmuch as they supported the views of Macedonius, which although before but ob-scurely known, acquired great publicity through the Synod at Lampsacus. This Synod, I think, was the cause of the increase of the Macedoni-ans in the Hellespont ; for Lampsacus is situated in one of the narrow bays of the Hellespont. Such was the issue of this council.

CHAPTER V.

Engagement between Valens and Procopius near Nacolia in Phrygia ; after which the Usurper is betrayed by his Chief Officers, and with them put to Death.

UNDER the consulate[1] of Gratian and Daga-laïfus in the following year, the war was begun. For as soon as the usurper Procopius, leaving Constantinople, began his march at the head of his army toward the emperor, Valens hastened from Antioch, and came to an engagement with him near a city of Phrygia, called Nacolia. In the first encounter he was defeated ; but soon after he took Procopius alive, through the treach-ery of Agilo and Gomarius, two of his generals, whom he subjected to the most extraordinary punishments.[2] The traitors he caused to be ex-ecuted by being sawn asunder, disregarding the oaths he had sworn to them. Two trees standing near each other being forcibly bowed down, one of the usurper's legs was fastened to each of them, after which the trees being suddenly per-mitted to recover their erect position, by their rise rent the tyrant into two parts ; and thus torn apart the usurper perished.

CHAPTER VI.

After the Death of Procopius Valens constrains those who composed the Synod, and All Chris-tians, to profess Arianism.

THE emperor having thus successfully termi-nated the conflict, immediately began to move

---

[3] Cf. II. 40, end.   [1] 366 A.D.
[2] Ammianus Marcellinus, *Rerum Gestarum*, XXVI. ix. 8–10, says that Florentius and Barchalba, after the fight at Nacolia, deliv-ered Procopius bound to Valens, and that Procopius was immedi-ately beheaded, and Florentius and Barchalba soon underwent the same punishment. Philostorgius also (IX.) relates that Procopius was beheaded, and that Florentius, who delivered him to Valens, was burnt.

---

[1] 365 A.D.   [1] Cf. II. 40.
[2] Cf. II. 37. Six years previous to the point of time reached by the historian thus far ; i.e. 359 A.D.

against the Christians, with the design of converting every sect to Arianism. But he was especially incensed against those who had composed the Synod at Lampsacus, not only on account of their deposition of the Arian bishops, but because they had anathematized the creed published at Ariminum. On arriving therefore at Nicomedia in Bithynia, he sent for Eleusius bishop of Cyzicus, who, as I have before said,[1] closely adhered to the opinions of Macedonius. Therefore the emperor having convened a council of Arian bishops, commanded Eleusius to give his assent to their faith. At first he refused to do so, but on being terrified with threats of banishment and confiscation of property, he was intimidated and assented to the Arian belief. Immediately afterwards, however, he repented; and returning to Cyzicus, bitterly complained in presence of all the people, asserting that his acquiescence was due to violence, and not of his own choice. He then exhorted them to seek another bishop for themselves, since he had been compelled to renounce his own opinion. But the inhabitants of Cyzicus loved and venerated him too much to think of losing him; they therefore refused to be subject to any other bishop, nor would they permit him to retire from his own church: and thus continuing under his oversight, they remained steadfast in their own heresy.

CHAPTER VII.

Eunomius supersedes Eleusius the Macedonian in the See of Cyzicus. His Origin and Imitation of Aëtius, whose Amanuensis he had been.

THE bishop of Constantinople being informed of these circumstances, constituted Eunomius bishop of Cyzicus, inasmuch as he was a person able by his eloquence to win over the minds of the multitude to his own way of thinking. On his arrival at Cyzicus an imperial edict was published in which it was ordered that Eleusius should be ejected, and Eunomius installed in his place. This being carried into effect, those who attached themselves to Eleusius, after erecting a sacred edifice without the city, assembled there with him. But enough has been said of Eleusius: let us now give some account of Eunomius. He had been secretary to Aëtius, surnamed Atheus, of whom we have before spoken,[1] and had learnt from conversing with him, to imitate his sophistical mode of reasoning; being little aware that while exercising himself in framing fallacious arguments, and in the use of certain insignificant terms, he was really deceiving himself. This habit however inflated him with pride, and he fell into blasphemous heresies, and so became an advocate of the dogmas of Arius, and in various ways an adversary to the doctrines of truth. And as he had but a very slender knowledge of the letter of Scripture, he was wholly unable to enter into the spirit of it. Yet he abounded in words, and was accustomed to repeat the same thoughts in different terms, without ever arriving at a clear explanation of what he had proposed to himself. Of this his seven books *On the Apostle's Epistle to the Romans*, on which he bestowed a quantity of vain labor, is a remarkable proof: for although he has employed an immense number of words in the attempt to expound it, he has by no means succeeded in apprehending the scope and object of that epistle. All other works of his extant are of a similar character, in which he that would take the trouble to examine them, would find a great scarcity of sense, amidst a profusion of verbiage. This Eunomius Eudoxius promoted to the see of Cyzicus;[2] who being come thither, astonished his auditors by the extraordinary display of his 'dialectic' art, and thus a great sensation was produced at Cyzicus. At length the people unable to endure any longer the empty and assumptious parade of his language, drove him out of their city. He therefore withdrew to Constantinople, and taking up his abode with Eudoxius, was regarded as a titular[3] bishop. But lest we should seem to have said these things for the sake of detraction, let us hear what Eunomius himself has the hardihood to utter in his sophistical discourses concerning the Deity himself, for he uses the following language: 'God knows no more of his own substance than we do; nor is this more known to him, and less to us: but whatever we know about the Divine substance, that precisely is known to God; and on the other hand, whatever he knows, the same also you will find without any difference in us.' This and many other similar tedious and absurd fallacies Eunomius was accustomed to draw up in utter insensibility to his own folly. On what account he afterwards separated from the Arians, we shall state in its proper place.[4]

---

[1] Cf. II. 38.   [1] II. 35, end.

[2] Sozom. VI. 8, gives the same account; but Philostorgius (V. 3) and Theodoret (*H. E.* II. 37 and 39) say that Eunomius was made bishop of Cyzicus under the Emperor Constantius immediately after the Synod of Seleucia. He was banished by Valens because he favored the usurper Procopius.

[3] σχολαῖος, defined by Sophocles (*Greek Lexicon of the Rom. and Byzantine Periods*) as *suspended*. It appears, however, that among the civil and military officers in the Roman system there were some who bore the title without being concerned in the management of their offices, and that these were termed *vacantes* and therefore that Socrates is using the Greek equivalent of a Latin term and applying it in ecclesiastical matters as its original was applied in civil and military affairs. Cf., on the position of bishops without churches Bingham, *Christ. Antiq.* IV. ii. 14. This system of clerics without charges was abused so much that the Council of Chalcedon (Canon 6) forbade further ordination *sine titulo*.

[4] See chap. 3, and on the Eunomians with their subsequent fortunes, V. 24.

CHAPTER VIII.

Of the Oracle found inscribed on a Stone, when the Walls of Chalcedon were demolished by Order of the Emperor Valens.

AN order was issued by the emperor that the walls of Chalcedon, a city opposite to Byzantium, should be demolished : for he had sworn to do this, after he should have conquered the usurper, because the Chalcedonians had sided with the usurper, and had used insulting language toward Valens,[1] and shut their gates against him as he passed by their city. In consequence of the imperial decree, therefore, the walls were razed and the stones were conveyed to Constantinople to serve for the formation of the public baths which are called Constantianæ.[2] On one of these stones an oracle was found engraven, which had lain concealed for a long time, in which it was predicted that when the city should be supplied with abundance of water, then should the wall serve for a bath ; and that innumerable hordes of barbarous nations having overrun the provinces of the Roman empire, and done a great deal of mischief, should themselves at length be destroyed. We shall here insert this oracle for the gratification of the studious :[3]

' When nymphs their mystic dance with wat'ry feet
  Shall tread through proud Byzantium's stately street;
  When rage the city wall shall overthrow,
  Whose stones to fence a bathing-place shall go :
  Then savage lands shall send forth myriad swarms,
  Adorned with golden locks aud burnished arms,
  That having Ister's silver streams o'erpast,
  Shall Scythian fields and Mœsia's meadows waste.
  But when with conquest flushed they enter Thrace,
  Fate shall assign them there a burial-place.'

Such was the prophecy. And indeed it afterwards happened, that when Valens by building an aqueduct supplied Constantinople with abundance of water, the barbarous nations made various irruptions, as we shall hereafter see. But it happened that some explained the prediction otherwise. For when that aqueduct was completed, Clearchus the prefect of the city built a stately bath, to which the name of ' the Plentiful Water '[4] was given, in that which is now called the Forum of Theodosius : on which account the people celebrated a festival with great re-joicings, whereby there was, say they, an accomplishment of those words of the oracle,

  ' their mystic dance with wat'ry feet
  Shall tread through proud Byzantium's stately street.'

But the completion of the prophecy took place afterwards. While the demolition was in progress the Constantinopolitans besought the emperor to suspend the destruction of the walls ; and the inhabitants of Nicomedia and Nicæa sending from Bithynia to Constantinople, made the same request. But the emperor being exceedingly exasperated against the Chalcedonians, was with difficulty prevailed upon to listen to these petitions in their favor : but that he might perform his oath, he commanded that the walls should be pulled down, while at the same time the breaches should be repaired by being filled up with other small stones. Whence it is that in the present day one may see in certain parts of the wall very inferior materials laid upon prodigiously large stones, forming those unsightly patches which were made on that occasion. So much will be sufficient on the walls of Chalcedon.

CHAPTER IX.

Valens persecutes the Novatians, because they accepted the Orthodox Faith.

THE emperor however did not cease his persecution of those who embraced the doctrine of the *homoousion,* but drove them away from Constantinople : and as the Novatians acknowledged the same faith, they also were subjected to similar treatment. He commanded that their churches should be shut up, also their bishop they sent into exile. His name was Agelius, a person that had presided over their churches from the time of Constantine, and had led an apostolic life : for he always walked barefoot, and used but one coat, observing the injunction of the gospel.[1] But the emperor's displeasure against this sect was moderated by the efforts of a pious and eloquent man named Marcian, who had formerly been in military service at the imperial palace, but was at that time a presbyter in the Novatian church, and taught Anastasia and Carosa, the emperor's daughters, grammar ; from the former of whom the public baths yet standing, which Valens erected at Constantinople, were named.[2] From respect for this person therefore the Novatian churches which had been

---

[1] Ammianus Marcellinus (*Rerum Gestarum* XXVI. viii. 2 *seq.*) says, ' From the walls of Chalcedon they uttered reproaches to him and insultingly reviled him as Sabaiarius. For, sabaia is a poor drink made of wheat or barley in Illyricum (whence Valens came).' On the Pannonian or Illyrian origin of Valens, see IV. 1. It appears also that the Pannonians were accustomed to live on poor diet in general.

[2] Sozom. VIII. 21, mentions these baths. Am. Marcellinus (*Rerum. Gestarum*, XXXI. 1. 4) relates that Valens built a bath out of the stones of the walls of Chalcedon. So also Themist. *Orat. Decen. ad Valentem,* and Gregory Nazianzen, *Orat.* 25; the latter calls it a ' subterraneous and aerial river.' Zonaras and Cedrenus, however, affirm that the structure built was not a bath, but an aqueduct. Cf. Cedrenus, I. 543 (p. 310, B).

[3] Cedrenus, I. 543 (p. 310, B).   [4] Δαψιλὲς ὕδωρ.

---

[1] Matt. x. 10.

[2] Am. Marcellinus (*Rerum Gestarum*, XXVI. 4. 14), in speaking of Procopius, the usurper, says: ' Procopius . . . resorted to the Anastasian baths, named from the sister of Constantine ' ; from which it appears that either (1) there were two baths of the same name, or (2) the baths here alluded to were named after Constantine's sister and renamed on the occasion of their being repaired or altered, or (3) that Socrates is in error. From the improbabilities connected with (1) and (2) we may infer that (3) is the right view.

for some time closed, were again opened. The Arians however would not suffer this people to remain undisturbed, for they disliked them on account of the sympathy and love the Novatians manifested toward the Homoousians, with whom they agreed in sentiment. Such was the state of affairs at that time. We may here remark that the war against the usurper Procopius was terminated about the end of May, in the consulate[3] of Gratian and Dagalaïfus.

CHAPTER X.

Birth of Valentinian the Younger.

SOON after the conclusion of this war, and under the same consulate,[1] a son was born to Valentinian, the emperor in the Western parts, to whom the same name as his father's was given. For Gratian had been born previously to his becoming emperor.

CHAPTER XI.

Hail of Extraordinary Size; and Earthquakes in Bithynia and the Hellespont.

ON the 2d of June of the following year, in the consulate[1] of Lupicin and Jovian, there fell at Constantinople hail of such a size as would fill a man's hand. Many affirmed that this hail had fallen as a consequence of the Divine displeasure, because of the emperor's having banished several persons engaged in the sacred ministry, those, that is to say, who refused to communicate with Eudoxius.[2] During the same consulate, on the 24th of August, the emperor Valentinian proclaimed his son Gratian Augustus. In the next year,[3] when Valentinian and Valens were a second time consuls, there happened on the 11th of October, an earthquake in Bithynia which destroyed the city of Nicæa on the eleventh day of October. This was about twelve years after Nicomedia had been visited by a similar catastrophe. Soon afterwards the largest portion of Germa in the Hellespont was reduced to ruins by another earthquake. Nevertheless no impression was made on the mind of either Eudoxius the Arian bishop, or the emperor Valens, by these occurrences; for they did not desist from their relentless persecution of those who dissented from them in matters of faith. Meanwhile these convulsions of the earth were

regarded as typical of the disturbances which agitated the churches: for many of the clerical body were sent into exile, as we have stated; Basil and Gregory alone, by a special dispensation of Divine Providence, being on account of their eminent piety exempted from this punishment. The former of these individuals was bishop of Cæsarea in Cappadocia; while Gregory presided over Nazianzus,[4] a little city in the vicinity of Cæsarea. But we shall have occasion to mention both Basil and Gregory again in the course of our history.[5]

CHAPTER XII.

The Macedonians, pressed by the Emperor's Violence toward them, send a Deputation to Liberius Bishop of Rome, and subscribe the Nicene Creed.

WHEN the maintainers of the 'homoousian' doctrine had been thus severely dealt with, and put to flight, the persecutors began afresh to harass the Macedonians; who impelled by fear rather than violence, send deputations to one another from city to city, declaring the necessity of appealing to the emperor's brother, and also to Liberius bishop of Rome: and that it was far better for them to embrace their faith, than to communicate with the party of Eudoxius. They sent for this purpose Eustathius bishop of Sebastia, who had been several times deposed, Silvanus of Tarsus in Cilicia, and Theophilus of Castabala in the same province; charging them to dissent in nothing from Liberius concerning the faith, but to enter into communion with the Roman church, and confirm the doctrine of the *homoousion*. These persons therefore proceeded to Old Rome, carrying with them the letters of those who had separated themselves from Acacius at Seleucia. To the emperor they could not have access, he being occupied in the Gauls with a war against the Sarmatæ; but they presented their letters to Liberius. He at first refused to admit them; saying they were of the Arian faction, and could not possibly be received into communion by the church, inasmuch as they had rejected the Nicene Creed. To this they replied that by change of sentiment they had acknowledged the truth, having long since renounced the Anomœan[1] Creed, and avowed the Son to be in every way 'like the Father': moreover that they considered the terms 'like'

---

[3] 366 A.D.
[1] Sozemen (VI. 10) says the same. There were two Valentinians in the second generation; one a son of Valens, and another the son of Valentinian the Elder. According to Idatius' *Fasti*, it was the former that was born during the consulate of Gratian and Dagalaïfus; so that Socrates was in error here, confusing perhaps the two younger Valentinians. Valesius adduces other reasons proving the same, which it is unnecessary to repeat here.
[1] 367 A.D.   [2] See II. 43.   [3] 368 A.D.

[4] If Socrates means to speak with precision here of the offices occupied by these men during the year which his narrative has reached he is mistaken, for Basil became bishop of Cæsarea in Cappadocia the year following, and Gregory was made bishop, not of Nazianzus at this time, but of Sisima. He did not, however, enter on the duties of this bishopric as he says in his letters.
[5] Chap. 26.
[1] See II. 35, and Hefele, *Hist. of the Ch. Councils*, Vol. II. p. 218 *seq.*

(*homoios*) and *homoousios* to have precisely the same import. When they had made this statement, Liberius demanded of them a written confession of their faith; and they accordingly presented him a document in which the substance of the Nicene Creed was inserted. I have not introduced here, because of their length, the letters from Smyrna, Asia, and from Pisidia, Isauria, Pamphylia, and Lycia, in all which places they had held Synods. The written profession which the deputies sent with Eustathius, delivered to Liberius, is as follows:

'To our Lord, Brother, and fellow-Minister Liberius: Eustathius, Theophilus, and Silvanus, salutations in the Lord.

'On account of the insane opinion of heretics, who cease not to introduce occasions of offense into the catholic churches, we being desirous of checking their career, come forward to express our approbation of the doctrines recognized by the Synod of orthodox bishops which has been convened at Lampsacus, Smyrna, and various other places: from which Synod we being constituted a deputation, bring a letter to your benignity and to all the Italian and Western bishops, by which we declare that we hold and maintain the catholic faith which was established in the holy council at Nicæa under the reign of Constantine of blessed memory, by three hundred and eighteen bishops, and has hitherto continued entire and unshaken; in which creed the term *homoousios* is holily and devoutly employed in opposition to the pernicious doctrine of Arius. We therefore, together with the aforesaid persons whom we represent, profess under our own hand, that we have held, do hold, and will maintain the same faith even unto the end. We condemn Arius, and his impious doctrine, with his disciples, and those who agree with his sentiments; as also the same heresy of Sabellius,[2] the Patripassians,[3] the Marcionites,[4] the Photinians,[5] the Marcellians,[6] that of Paul of Samosata,[7] and those who countenance such tenets; in short all the heresies which are opposed to the aforesaid sacred creed, which was piously and in a catholic spirit set forth by the holy fathers at Nicæa. But we especially anathematize that form of the creed which was recited at the Synod of Ariminum,[8] as altogether contrary to the before-mentioned creed of the

holy Synod of Nicæa, to which the bishops at Constantinople affixed their signatures, being deceived by artifice and perjury, by reason of its having been brought from Nice,[9] a town of Thrace. Our own creed, and that of those whose delegates we are, is this:

' "We believe in one God the Father Almighty, the Maker of all things visible and invisible: and in one only-begotten God, the Lord Jesus Christ, the Son of God; begotten of the Father; that is of the substance of the Father; God of God, Light of Light, very God of very God; begotten not made, of the same substance with the Father, through whom all things were made which are in heaven, and which are upon the earth: who for us men, and for our salvation, descended, became incarnate, and was made man; suffered, and rose again the third day; ascended into the heavens, and will come to judge the living and the dead. [We believe] also in the Holy Spirit. But the Catholic and Apostolic Church of God anathematizes those who assert that 'there was a time when he was not,' and 'that he was not before he was begotten,' and that 'he was made of things which are not'; or those that say 'the Son of God is of another hypostasis' or 'substance than the Father,' or that 'he is mutable, or susceptible of change.'

' "I, Eustathius, bishop of the city of Sebastia, with Theophilus and Silvanus, delegates of the Synod of Lampsacus, Smyrna, and other places, have voluntarily subscribed this confession of faith with our own hands. And if, after the publication of this creed, any one shall presume to calumniate either us, or those who sent us, let him come with the letters of your holiness before such orthodox bishops as your sanctity shall approve of, and bring the matter to an issue with us before them; and if any charge shall be substantiated, let the guilty be punished." '

Liberius having securely pledged the delegates by this document, received them into communion, and afterwards dismissed them with this letter:

The Letter of Liberius Bishop of Rome, to the Bishops of the Macedonians.

To our beloved brethren and fellow-ministers, Evethius, Cyril, Hyperechius, Uranius, Heron, Elpidius, Maximus, Eusebius, Eucarpius, Heortasius, Neon, Eumathius, Faustinus, Proclinus, Pasinicus, Arsenius, Severus, Didymion, Brittanius, Callicrates, Dalmatius, Ædesius, Eustochius, Ambrose, Gelonius, Pardalius, Macedonius, Paul, Marcellus, Heraclius, Alexander, Adolius, Marcian, Sthenelus, John, Macer, Charisius,

---

[2] See I. 5, and note.
[3] The Patripassians were a sect of the early Church (end of second century), who asserted the identity of the Son with the Father. And, as on being confronted with the question whether it was the Father that suffered on the cross they answered in the affirmative, they were called Patri-passians. Their leader was Praxeas. See Tertull. *Adv. Praxeam* (the whole treatise is meant to be a refutation of this heresy).
[4] Followers of the well-known Gnostic leader of the second century. For his peculiar views, see Tertull. *Adv. Marcionem*; Epiphan. *Hæres.* XLII.; also Smith and Wace, *Dict. of Christ. Biog.*, under MARCION, and ecclesiastical histories.
[5] Cf. II. 18 and 29.   [7] See note, I. 36.
[6] Cf. I. 36; II. 20.   [8] See II. 37.

[9] See II. 37. As it appears from V. 4, Liberius was actually deceived by the artifice.

Silvanus, Photinus, Anthony, Aythus, Celsus, Euphranon, Milesius, Patricius, Severian, Eusebius, Eumolpius, Athanasius, Diophantus, Menodorus, Diocles, Chrysampelus, Neon, Eugenius, Eustathius, Callicrates, Arsenius, Eugenius, Martyrius, Hieracius, Leontius, Philagrius, Lucius, and to all the orthodox bishops in the East, Liberius bishop of Italy, and the bishops throughout the West, salutations always in the Lord.

Your letters, beloved brethren, resplendent with the light of faith, delivered to us by our highly esteemed brethren, the bishops Eustathius, Silvanus, and Theophilus, brought to us the much longed-for joy of peace and concord: and this chiefly because they have demonstrated and assured us that your opinion and sentiments are in perfect harmony with those both of our insignificance, and also with those of all the bishops in Italy and the Western parts. We acknowledge this to be the Catholic and Apostolic faith, which until the time of the Synod at Nicæa had continued unadulterated and unshaken. This creed your legates have professed that they themselves hold, and to our great joy have obliterated every vestige and impression of an injurious suspicion, by attesting it not only in word, but also in writing. We have deemed it proper to subjoin to these letters a copy of this their declaration, lest we should leave any pretext to the heretics for entering into a fresh conspiracy, by which they might stir up the smouldering embers of their own malice, and according to their custom, rekindle the flames of discord. Moreover our most esteemed brethren, Eustathius, Silvanus, and Theophilus, have professed this also, both that they themselves, and also your love, have always held, and will maintain unto the last, the creed approved of at Nicæa by 318 Orthodox Bishops; which contains the perfect truth, and both confutes and overthrows the whole swarm of heretics. For it was not of their own will, but by Divine appointment that so great a number of bishops was collected against the madness of Arius, as equaled that of those by whose assistance blessed Abraham through faith destroyed so many thousand of his enemies.[10] This faith being comprehended in the terms *hypostasis* and *homoousios*, like a strong and impregnable fortress checks and repels all the assaults and vain machinations of Arian perverseness. Wherefore when all the Western bishops were assembled at Ariminum, whither the craft of the Arians had drawn them, in order that either by deceptive persuasions, or to speak more truly, by the coercion of the secular power, they might erase, or indirectly revoke what had been introduced into the creed with so much prudence, their subtlety was not

of the least avail. For almost all those who at Ariminum were either allured into error, or at that time deceived, have since taken a right view of the matter; and after anathematizing the exposition of faith set forth by those who were convened at Ariminum, have subscribed the Catholic and Apostolic Creed which was promulgated at Nicæa. They have entered into communion with us, and regard the dogma of Arius and his disciples with increased aversion, and are even indignant against it. Of which fact when the legates of your love saw the indubitable evidences, they annexed yourselves to their own subscription; anathematizing Arius, and what was transacted at Ariminum against the creed ratified at Nicæa, to which even you yourselves, beguiled by perjury, were induced to subscribe. Whence it appeared suitable to us to write to your love, and to accede to your just request, especially since we are assured by the profession of your legates that the Eastern bishops have recovered their senses, and now concur in opinion with the orthodox of the West. We further give you to understand, lest ye should be ignorant of it, that the blasphemies of the Synod of Ariminum have been anathematized by those who seem to have been at that time deceived by fraud, and that all have acknowledged the Nicene Creed. It is fit therefore that it should be made generally known by you that such as have had their faith vitiated by violence or guile, may now emerge from heretical darkness into the Divine light of catholic liberty. Moreover whosoever of them, after this council, shall not disgorge the poison of corrupt doctrine, by abjuring all the blasphemies of Arius, and anathematizing them, let them know that they are themselves, together with Arius and his disciples and the rest of the serpents, whether Sabellians, Patripassians, or the followers of any other heresy, dissevered and excommunicated from the assemblies of the Church, which does not admit of illegitimate children. May God preserve you steadfast, beloved brethren.

When the adherents of Eustathius had received this letter, they proceeded to Sicily, where they caused a Synod of Sicilian bishops to be convened, and in their presence avowed the homoousian faith, and professed their adherence to the Nicene Creed: then having received from them also a letter to the same effect as the preceding, they returned to those who had sent them. They on their part, on the receipt of the letters of Liberius, sent delegates from city to city to the prominent supporters of the doctrine of the *homoousion*, exhorting them to assemble simultaneously at Tarsus in Cilicia, in order to confirm the Nicene Creed, and ter-

---

[10] Gen. xiv. 14.

minate all the contentions which had subsequently arisen. And indeed this would probably have been accomplished had not the Arian bishop, Eudoxius, who at that time possessed great influence with the emperor, thwarted their purpose; for on learning of the Synod that had been summoned to meet [at Tarsus], he became so exasperated that he redoubled his persecution against them. That the Macedonians by sending legates to Liberius were admitted to communion with him, and professed the Nicene Creed, is attested by Sabinus himself, in his *Collection of Synodical Transactions.*

CHAPTER XIII.

Eunomius separates from Eudoxius; a Disturbance is raised at Alexandria by Eudoxius, and Athanasius flees into Voluntary Exile again, but in Consequence of the Clamors of the People the Emperor recalls and re-establishes him in his See.

ABOUT the same time Eunomius[1] separated himself from Eudoxius, and held assemblies apart, because after he had repeatedly entreated that his preceptor Aëtius might be received into communion, Eudoxius continued to oppose it. Now Eudoxius did this against his preference, for he did not reject the opinion with Aëtius since it was the same as his own;[2] but he yielded to the prevailing sentiment of his own party, who objected to Aetius as heterodox. This was the cause of the division between Eunomius and Eudoxius, and such was the state of things at Constantinople. But the church at Alexandria was disturbed by an edict of the prætorian prefects, sent hither by means of Eudoxius. Whereupon Athanasius, dreading the irrational impetuosity of the multitude, and fearing lest he should be regarded as the author of the excesses that might be committed, concealed himself for four entire months in an ancestral tomb. Inasmuch however as the people, on account of their affection for him, became seditious in impatience of his absence, the emperor, on ascertaining that on this account agitation prevailed at Alexandria, ordered by his letters that Athanasius should be suffered to preside over the churches without molestation; and this was the reason why the Alexandrian church enjoyed tranquillity until the death of Athanasius. How the Arian faction became possessed of the churches after his decease, we shall unfold in the course of our history.[3]

CHAPTER XIV.

The Arians ordain Demophilus after the Death of Eudoxius at Constantinople; but the Orthodox Party constitute Evagrius his Successor.

THE Emperor Valens leaving Constantinople again set out towards Antioch; but on his arrival at Nicomedia, a city of Bithynia, his progress was arrested by the following circumstances. Eudoxius the bishop of the Arian church who has been in possession of the seat of the Constantinopolitan church for nineteen[1] years, died soon after the emperor's departure from that city, in the third consulate[2] of Valentinian and Valens. The Arians therefore appointed Demophilus to succeed him; but the Homoousians considering that an opportunity was afforded them, elected a certain Evagrius, a person who maintained their own principles; and Eustathius, who had been bishop of Antioch, formally ordained him. He had been recalled from exile by Jovian, and had at this time privately come to Constantinople, for the purpose of confirming the adherents to the doctrine of the *homoousion.*

CHAPTER XV.

The Emperor banishes Evagrius and Eustathius. The Arians persecute the Orthodox.

WHEN this had been accomplished the Arians renewed their persecution of the Homoousians: and the emperor was very soon informed of what had taken place, and apprehending the subversion of the city in consequence of some popular tumult, immediately sent troops from Nicomedia to Constantinople; ordering that both he who had been ordained, and the one who had ordained him, should be apprehended and sent into exile in different regions. Eustathius therefore was banished to Bizya a city of Thrace; and Evagrius was conveyed to another place. After this the Arians, becoming bolder, grievously harassed the orthodox party, frequently beating them, reviling them, causing them to be imprisoned, and fined; in short they practiced distressing and intolerable annoyances against them. The sufferers were induced to appeal to the emperor for protection against their adversaries if haply they might obtain some relief from this oppression. But whatever hope of redress they might have cherished from this quarter, was altogether frustrated, inasmuch as they thus merely spread their grievances before him who was the very author of them.

---

[1] Eunomius adopted the standpoint and also the views of Aëtius and gave them his own name. Briefly his fundamental principle was that the Son is absolutely unlike the Father in substance, and hence a creature among other creatures, a mere man.
[2] See II. 35.   [3] Cf. chap. 21.

[1] Epiphanius Scholasticus reads δεκαέυα for δεκαευυέα; if he be followed, the incumbency of the bishopric of Constantinople by Eudoxius lasted seven years.
[2] 370 A.D.

CHAPTER XVI.

*Certain Presbyters burnt in a Ship by Order of
Valens. Famine in Phrygia.*

CERTAIN pious men of the clerical order, eighty
in number, among whom Urbanus, Theodore,
and Menedemus were the leaders, proceeded to
Nicomedia, and there presented to the emperor
a supplicatory petition, informing him and complaining of the ill-usage to which they had been
subjected. The emperor was filled with wrath ;
but dissembled his displeasure in their presence,
and gave Modestus the prefect a secret order
to apprehend these persons, and put them to
death. The manner in which they were destroyed being unusual, deserves to be recorded.
The prefect fearing that he should excite the
populace to a seditious movement against himself, if he attempted the public execution of so
many, pretended to send the men away into
exile. Accordingly as they received the intelligence of their destiny with great firmness of mind,
the prefect ordered that they should be embarked
as if to be conveyed to their several places of
banishment, having meanwhile enjoined on the
sailors to set the vessel on fire, as soon as they
reached the mid sea, that their victims being so
destroyed, might even be deprived of burial.
This injunction was obeyed ; for when they
arrived at the middle of the Astacian Gulf, the
crew set fire to the ship, and then took refuge
in a small barque which followed them, and so
escaped. Meanwhile it came to pass that a
strong easterly wind blew, and the burning ship
was roughly driven but moved faster and was
preserved until it reached a port named Dacidi-
zus, where it was utterly consumed together with
the men who were shut up in it. Many have
asserted that this impious deed was not suffered
to go unpunished : for there immediately after
arose so great a famine throughout all Phrygia,
that a large proportion of the inhabitants were
obliged to abandon their country for a time, and
betake themselves some to Constantinople and
some to other provinces. For Constantinople,
notwithstanding the vast population it supplies,
yet always abounds with the necessaries of life,
all manner of provisions being imported into it
by sea from various regions ; and the Euxine
which lies near it, furnishes it with wheat to any
extent it may require.[1]

CHAPTER XVII.

*The Emperor Valens, while at Antioch, again
persecutes the Adherents of the 'Homoousion.'*

THE Emperor Valens, little affected by the
calamities resulting from the famine, went to

[1] Cf. Herodot. VII. 147.

Antioch in Syria, and during his residence there
cruelly persecuted such as would not embrace
Arianism. For not content with ejecting out
of almost all the churches of the East those
who maintained the 'homoousian' opinion, he
inflicted on them various punishments besides.
He destroyed a greater number even than before, delivering them up to many different kinds
of death, but especially drowning in the river.

CHAPTER XVIII.

*Events at Edessa: Constancy of the Devout
Citizens, and Courage of a Pious Woman.*

BUT we must here mention certain circumstances that occurred at Edessa in Mesopotamia.
There is in that city a magnificent church[1] dedicated to St. Thomas the Apostle, wherein, on
account of the sanctity of the place, religious
assemblies are incessantly held. The Emperor
Valens wishing to inspect this edifice, and having learnt that all who usually congregated there
were opposed to the heresy which he favored,
he is said to have struck the prefect with his
own hand, because he had neglected to expel
them thence also. As the prefect after submitting to this ignominy, was most unwillingly constrained to subserve the emperor's indignation
against them, — for he did not desire to effect
the slaughter of so great a number of persons,
— he privately suggested that no one should be
found there. But no one gave heed either to
his admonitions or to his menaces ; for on the
following day they all crowded to the church.[2]
And when the prefect was going towards it
with a large military force in order to satisfy
the emperor's rage, a poor woman leading her
own little child by the hand hurried hastily by,
on her way to the church, breaking through the
ranks of the prefect's company of soldiers.
The prefect irritated at this, ordered her to
be brought to him, and thus addressed her :
'Wretched woman ! whither are you running in
so disorderly a manner?' She replied, 'To
the same place that others are hastening.'
'Have you not heard,' said he, ' that the prefect
is about to put to death all that shall be found
there ?' 'Yes,' said the woman, ' and therefore
I hasten that I may be found there.' 'And
whither are you dragging that little child?' said
the prefect : the woman answered, 'That he
also may be made worthy of martyrdom.'[3] The

[1] The kind of church here meant was a memorial structure for
a martyr, erected where his relics were deposited, and was called
Μαρτύριον. See Bingham, *Christ. Antiq.* VIII. 1.
[2] The same church which above was called a μαρτύριον from
its origin, is here called εὐκτήριος τόπος, from its use ('a place of
prayer').
[3] Gibbon, in his *Decline and Fall*, chap. 16, quotes a number
of extracts from Sulpicius Severus and Ignatius, showing the honor
in which martyrdom was held in the early church, and the eagerness

prefect on hearing these things, conjecturing that a similar resolution actuated the others who were assembled there, immediately went back to the emperor, and informed him that all were ready to die in behalf of their own faith. He added that it would be preposterous to destroy so many persons at one time, and thus persuaded the emperor to control his wrath. In this way were the Edessenes preserved from being massacred by order of their sovereign.

CHAPTER XIX.

Slaughter of Many Persons by Valens on Account of their Names, in Consequence of a Heathen Prediction.[1]

THE cruel disposition of the emperor was at this time abused by an execrable demon, who induced certain curious persons to institute an inquiry by means of necromancy as to who should succeed Valens on the throne. To their magical incantations the demon gave responses not distinct and unequivocal, but as the general practice is, full of ambiguity; for displaying the four letters θ, ϵ, o, and δ, he declared that the name of the successor of Valens began with these; and that it was a compound name. When the emperor was apprised of this oracle, instead of committing to God, who alone can penetrate futurity, the decision of this matter, in contravention of those Christian principles to which he pretended the most zealous adherence, he put to death very many persons of whom he had the suspicion that they aimed at the sovereign power: thus such as were named 'Theodore,' 'Theodotus,' 'Theodosius,' 'Theodulus,' and the like, were sacrificed to the emperor's fears; and among the rest was Theodosiolus, a very brave man, descended from a noble family in Spain. Many persons therefore, to avoid the danger to which they were exposed, changed their names, giving up those which they had received from their parents in infancy as dangerous. This will be enough on that subject.

CHAPTER XX.

Death of Athanasius, and Elevation of Peter to His See.[1]

IT must be said that as long as Athanasius, bishop of Alexandria, was alive, the emperor,

restrained by the Providence of God, abstained from molesting Alexandria and Egypt: indeed he knew very well that the multitude of those who were attached to Athanasius was very great; and on that account he was careful lest the public affairs should be hazarded, by the Alexandrians, who are an irritable race, being excited to sedition. But Athanasius, after being engaged in so many and such severe conflicts on behalf of the church, departed this life in the second consulate[2] of Gratian and Probus, having governed that church amidst the greatest perils forty-six years. He left as his successor Peter, a devout and eloquent man.

CHAPTER XXI.

The Arians are allowed by the Emperor to imprison Peter and to set Lucius over the See of Alexandria.

UPON this the Arians, emboldened by their knowledge of the emperor's religious sentiments, again took courage, and without delay informed him of the circumstance. He was then residing at Antioch. Then indeed Euzoïus who presided over the Arians of that city, eagerly embracing the favorable opportunity thus presented, begged permission to go to Alexandria, for the purpose of putting Lucius the Arian in possession of the churches there. The emperor acceded to this request, and as speedily as possible Euzoïus proceeded forthwith to Alexandria, attended by the imperial troops. Magnus, also, the emperor's treasurer, went with him. Moreover an imperial mandate had been issued to Palladius, the governor of Egypt, enjoining him to aid them with a military force. Wherefore having apprehended Peter, they cast him into prison; and after dispersing the rest of the clergy, they placed Lucius in the episcopal chair.

CHAPTER XXII.

Silence of Sabinus on the Misdeeds of the Arians; Flight of Peter to Rome; Massacre of the Solitaries at the Instigation of the Arians.

OF the outrages perpetrated upon the installation of Lucius, and the treatment of those who were ejected, both in the courts and outside of the courts, and how some were subjected to a variety of tortures, and others sent into exile even after this excruciating process, Sabinus takes not the slightest notice. In fact, being half disposed

---

with which it was sought. To check the excess of zeal which was thus manifested, the Council of Elvira, in 306 A.D., passed a canon (its sixtieth) to the following intent: 'that if any one should overthrow idols, and should therefore be put to death, inasmuch as this is not written in the Gospel nor found done among the apostles at any time, such a one should not be received among the martyrs.'
[1] Amm. Marcellinus, *Rerum Gertarum*, XXIX. 1. 29 *seq.*
[1] Sozomen, VI. 19; Theodoret, *H. E.* IV. 20.

[2] 371 A.D. But Jerome, *Chronic.* II. (ninth year of Valens), makes the consecration of Athanasius' successor in 373 A.D., and hence also the death of Athanasius himself in the same year. The later date is now universally accepted.

to Arianism himself, he purposely veils the atrocities of his friends. Peter, however, has exposed them, in the letters he addressed to all the churches, when he had escaped from prison. For this [bishop] having managed to escape from prison, fled to Damasus, bishop of Rome. The Arians though not very numerous, becoming thus possessed of the Alexandrian churches, soon after obtained an imperial edict directing the governor of Egypt to expel not only from Alexandria but even out of the country, the favorers of the 'homoousian' doctrine, and all such as were obnoxious to Lucius. After this they assailed and disturbed and terribly harassed the monastic institutions in the desert; armed men rushed in the most ferocious manner upon those who were utterly defenceless, and who would not lift an arm to repel their violence : so that numbers of unresisting victims were in this manner slaughtered with a degree of wanton cruelty beyond description.

CHAPTER XXIII.

The Deeds of Some Holy Persons who devoted themselves to a Solitary Life.[1]

SINCE I have referred to the monasteries of Egypt, it may be proper here to give a brief account of them. They were founded probably at a very early period, but were greatly enlarged and augmented by a devout man whose name was Ammoun. In his youth this person had an aversion to matrimony; but when some of his relatives urged him not to contemn marriage, but to take a wife to himself, he was prevailed upon and was married. On leading the bride with the customary ceremonies from the banquet-room to the nuptial couch, after their mutual friends had withdrawn, he took a book[2] containing the epistles of the apostles and read to his wife Paul's Epistle to the Corinthians, explaining to her the apostle's admonitions to married persons.[3] Adducing many external considerations besides, he descanted on the inconveniences and discomforts attending matrimonial intercourse, the pangs of child-bearing, and the trouble and anxiety connected with rearing a family. He contrasted with all this the advantages of chastity; described the liberty, and immaculate purity of a life of continence; and affirmed that virginity places persons in the

nearest relation to the Deity. By these and other arguments of a similar kind, he persuaded his virgin bride to renounce with him a secular life, prior to their having any conjugal knowledge of each other. Having taken this resolution, they retired together to the mountain of Nitria, and in a hut there inhabited for a short time one common ascetic apartment, without regarding their difference of sex, being according to the apostles, 'one in Christ.'[4] But not long after, the recent and unpolluted bride thus addressed Ammoun : 'It is unsuitable,' said she, 'for you who practice chastity, to look upon a woman in so confined a dwelling; let us therefore, if it is agreeable to you, perform our exercise apart.' This agreement again was satisfactory to both, and so they separated, and spent the rest of their lives in abstinence from wine and oil, eating dry bread alone, sometimes passing over one day, at others fasting two, and sometimes more. Athanasius, bishop of Alexandria, asserts in his *Life of Anthony*,[5] that the subject of his memoir who was contemporary with this Ammoun, saw his soul taken up by angels after his decease. Accordingly, a great number of persons emulated Ammoun's manner of life, so that by degrees the mountains of Nitria and Scitis were filled with monks, an account of whose lives would require an express work. As, however, there were among them persons of eminent piety, distinguished for their strict discipline and apostolic lives, who said and did many things worthy of being recorded, I deem it useful to interweave with my history a few particulars selected out of the great number for the information of my readers. It is said that Ammoun never saw himself naked, being accustomed to say that 'it became not a monk to see even his own person exposed.' And when once he wanted to pass a river, but was unwilling to undress, he besought God to enable him to cross without his being obliged to break his resolution; and immediately an angel transported him to the other side of the river. Another monk named Didymus[6] lived entirely alone to the day of his death, although he had reached the age of ninety years. Arsenius, another of them, would not separate young delinquents from communion, but only those that were advanced in age : 'for,' said he, 'when a young person is excommunicated he becomes hardened; but an elderly one is soon sensible of the misery of excommunication.' Pior was accustomed to take his food as he walked along. As a certain one asked him, 'Why do you eat thus?' 'That I may not

---

[1] On the growth of the monastic system, see Bingham, *Eccl. Antiq.* VII.; on its philosophy, briefly, Bennett, *Christian Archæol.* p. 468. Socrates uses Palladius' *Historia Lausiaca* copiously in this chapter.

[2] βιβλίον ἀποστολικόν. The books of the New Testament came to be divided into the two classes of 'gospels' and 'apostolic epistles,' the first being called εὐαγγέλιον or εὐαγγέλια, and the second, ἀπόστολος, ἀπόστολοι or βιβλίον ἀποστολικόν. Cf. Epiph. *Hær.* XLII. 10. Euthal. Diacon. (Ed. Migné, Vol. LXXXV. col. 720, C.   [3] 1 Cor. vii. 10 *seq.*

[4] Gal. iii. 28. What Socrates here says of Ammoun is attributed by Theodoret (*H. E.* IV. 12) to Pelagius, who afterwards became bishop of Laodicea.

[5] Athanas. *Vit. Anton.* 60.   [6] Cf. chap. 25.

seem,' said he, 'to make eating serious business, but rather a thing done by the way.' To another putting the same question he replied, 'Lest even in eating my mind should be sensible of corporeal enjoyment.' Isidore affirmed that he had not been conscious of sin even in thought for forty years; and that he had never consented either to lust or anger. Pambos being an illiterate man went to some one for the purpose of being taught a psalm; and having heard the first verse of the thirty-eighth psalm, 'I said I will take heed to my ways, that I offend not with my tongue,'[7] he departed without staying to hear the second verse, saying, 'this one will suffice, if I can practically acquire it.' And when the person who had given him the verse reproved him because he had not seen him for the space of six months, he answered that he had not yet learnt to practice the verse of the psalm. After a considerable lapse of time, being asked by one of his friends whether he had made himself master of the verse, his answer was, 'I have scarcely succeeded in accomplishing it during nineteen years.' A certain individual having placed gold in his hands for distribution to the poor, requested him to reckon what he had given him. 'There is no need of counting,' said he, 'but of integrity of mind.' This same Pambos, at the desire of Athanasius the bishop, came out of the desert to Alexandria; and on beholding an actress there, he wept. When those present asked him why he wept, he replied, 'Two causes have affected me: one is the destruction of this woman; the other is that I exert myself less to please my God than she does to please obscene characters.' Another said that 'a monk who did not work ought to be regarded as on a level with the covetous man.' Piterus was well-informed in many branches of natural philosophy, and was accustomed frequently to enter into expositions of the principles sometimes of one and sometimes of another department of science, but he always commenced his expositions with prayer. There were also among the monks of that period, two of the same name, of great sanctity, each being called Macarius; one of whom was from Upper Egypt, the other from the city of Alexandria. Both were celebrated for their ascetic discipline, the purity of their life and conversation, and the miracles which were wrought by their hands. The Egyptian Macarius performed so many cures, and cast out so many devils, that it would require a distinct treatise to record all that the grace of God enabled him to do. His manner toward those who resorted to him was austere, yet at the same time calculated to inspire veneration. The Alexandrian Macarius, while in all

respects resembling his Egyptian namesake, differed from him in this, that he was always cheerful to his visitors; and by the affability of his manners led many young men to asceticism. Evagrius[8] became a disciple of these men, acquired from them the philosophy of deeds, whereas he had previously known that which consisted in words only. He was ordained deacon at Constantinople by Gregory of Nazianzus, and afterwards went with him into Egypt, where he became acquainted with these eminent persons, and emulated their course of conduct, and miracles were done by his hands as numerous and important as those of his preceptors. Books were also composed by him of very valuable nature, one of which is entitled *The Monk*, or, *On Active Virtue;* another *The Gnostic,*[9] or, *To him who is deemed worthy of Knowledge:* this book is divided into fifty chapters. A third is designated *Antirrheticus*, and contains selections from the Holy Scriptures against tempting spirits, distributed into eight parts, according to the number of the arguments. He wrote moreover *Six Hundred Prognostic Problems*, and also two compositions in verse, one addressed *To the Monks living in Communities*, and the other *To the Virgin*. Whoever shall read these productions will be convinced of their excellence. It will not be out of place here, I conceive, to subjoin to what has been before stated, a few things mentioned by him respecting the monks. These are his words:[10]

It becomes us to enquire into the habits of the pious monks who have preceded us, in order that we may correct ourselves by their example: for undoubtedly very many excellent things have been said and done by them. One of them was accustomed to say, that 'a drier and not irregular diet combined with love, would quickly conduct a monk into the haven of tranquillity.' The same individual freed one of his brethren from being troubled by apparitions at night, by enjoining him to minister while fasting to the sick. And being asked why he prescribed this: 'Such affections,' said he, 'are by nothing so effectually dissipated as by the exercise of compassion.' A certain philosopher of those times coming to Anthony the Just, said to him, 'How can you endure, father, being deprived of the comfort of books?' 'My book, O philosopher,' replied Anthony, 'is the nature of things that are made, and it is present whenever I wish to read the words of God.' That 'chosen vessel,'[11] the aged Egyptian Macarius, asked me, why the

[7] According to the LXX.

[8] Cf. Palladius, *Hist. Lausiaca*, chap. 86. But Palladius says that Evagrius was ordained by Gregory of Nyssa, not of Nazianzus. Cf. Sozomen, VI. 30.
[9] Palladius calls this work Ἱερά 'Sacred [matter].' *Hist. Lausiaca*, 86.
[10] Cf. Coteler. *Eccl. Gr. Mon.* 3. 59, containing also other fragments of Evagrius.
[11] Acts ix. 15.

strength of the faculty of memory is impaired by cherishing the remembrance of injury received from men; while by remembering those done us by devils it remains uninjured? And when I hesitated, scarcely knowing what answer to make, and begged him to account for it: 'Because,' said he, 'the former is an affection contrary to nature, and the latter is conformable to the nature of the mind.' Going on one occasion to the holy father Macarius about mid-day, and being overcome with the heat and thirst, I begged for some water to drink: 'Content yourself with the shade,' was his reply, 'for many who are now journeying by land, or sailing on the deep, are deprived even of this.' Discussing with him afterwards the subject of abstinence, 'Take courage, my son,' said he: 'for twenty years I have neither eaten, drunk, nor slept to satiety; my bread has always been weighed, my water measured, and what little sleep I have had has been stolen by reclining myself against a wall.'[12] The death of his father was announced to one of the monks: 'Cease your blasphemy,' said he to the person that told him; 'my father is immortal.' One of the brethren who possessed nothing but a copy of the Gospels, sold it, and distributed the price in food to the hungry, uttering this memorable saying — 'I have sold the book which says, "Sell that thou hast and give to the poor."'[13] There is an island about the northern part of the city of Alexandria, beyond the lake called Maria, where a monk from Parembole[14] dwells, in high repute among the Gnostics. This person was accustomed to say, that all the deeds of the monks were done for one of these five reasons; — on account of God, nature, custom, necessity, or manual labor. The same also said that there was only one virtue in nature, but that it assumes various characteristics according to the dispositions of the soul: just as the light of the sun is itself without form, but accommodates itself to the figure of that which receives it. Another of the monks said, 'I withdraw myself from pleasures, in order to cut off the occasions of anger: for I know that it always contends for pleasures, disturbing my tranquillity of mind, and unfitting me for the attainment of knowledge.' One of the aged monks said that 'Love knows not how to keep a deposit either of provisions or money.' He added, 'I never remember to have been twice deceived by the devil in the same thing.' Thus wrote Evagrius in his book entitled *Practice*.[15] And in that which he called *The Gnostic* he says, 'We have learned from

Gregory the Just, that there are four virtues, having distinct characteristics: — prudence and fortitude, temperance and justice. That it is the province of prudence to contemplate the sacred and intelligent powers apart from expression, because these are unfolded by wisdom: of fortitude to adhere to truth against all opposition, and never to turn aside to that which is unreal: of temperance to receive seed from the chief husbandman,[16] but to repel him who would sow over it seed of another kind: and finally, of justice to adapt discourse to every one, according to their condition and capacity; stating some things obscurely, others in a figurative manner, and explaining others clearly for the instruction of the less intelligent.' That pillar of truth, Basil of Cappadocia, used to say that 'the knowledge which men teach is perfected by constant study and exercise; but that which proceeds from the grace of God, by the practice of justice, patience, and mercy.' That the former indeed is often developed in persons who are still subject to the passions; whereas the latter is the portion of those only who are superior to their influence, and who during the season of devotion, contemplate that peculiar light of the mind which illumines them. That luminary of the Egyptians, holy Athanasius, assures us 'that Moses was commanded to place the table on the north[17] side. Let the Gnostics therefore understand what wind is contrary to them, and so nobly endure every temptation, and minister nourishment with a willing mind to those who apply to them.' Serapion, the angel of the church of the Thmuïtæ, declared that 'the mind is completely purified by drinking in spiritual knowledge': that 'charity cures the inflammatory tendencies of the soul'; and that 'the depraved lusts which spring up in it are restrained by abstinence.' 'Exercise thyself continually,' said the great and enlightened teacher Didymus, 'in reflecting on providence and judgment; and endeavor to bear in memory the material of whatever discourses thou mayst have heard on these topics, for almost all fail in this respect. Thou wilt find reasonings concerning judgment in the difference of created forms, and the constitution of the universe: sermons on providence comprehended in those means by which we are led from vice and ignorance to virtue and knowledge.'

These few extracts from Evagrius we thought it would be appropriate to insert here. There was another excellent man among the monks, named Ammonius, who had so little interest in secular matters, that when he went to Rome with Athanasius, he chose to investigate none

12 Cf. Ezra iv. 10, 11.   13 Matt. xix. 21.
14 Parembole is a village near Alexandria, mentioned by Athanasius in his second Apol. against the Arians, who names Macarius as its presbyter.
15 See above, III. 7.

16 Matt. xiii. 24.   17 Ex. xxvi. 35.

of the magnificent works of that city, contenting himself with examining the Cathedral of Peter and Paul only. This same Ammonius on being urged to enter upon the episcopal office, cut off his own right ear, that by mutilation of his person he might disqualify himself for ordination. But when long afterwards Evagrius, whom Theophilus, bishop of Alexandria, wished to make a bishop, having effected his escape without maiming himself in any way, afterwards happened to meet Ammonius, and told him jocosely, that he had done wrong in cutting off his own ear, as he had by that means rendered himself criminal in the sight of God. To which Ammonius replied, 'And do you think, Evagrius, that you will not be punished, who from self-love have cut out your own tongue, to avoid the exercise of that gift of utterance which has been committed to you?' There were at the same time in the monasteries very many other admirable and devout characters whom it would be too tedious to enumerate in this place, and besides if we should attempt to describe the life of each, and the miracles they did by means of that sanctity with which they were endowed, we should necessarily digress too far from the object we have in view. Should any one desire to become acquainted with their history, in reference both to their deeds and experiences and discourses for the edification of their auditors, as well as how wild beasts became subject to their authority, there is a specific treatise [18] on the subject, composed by the monk Palladius, who was a disciple of Evagrius, and gives all these particulars in minute detail. In that work he also mentions several women, who practiced the same kind of austerities as the men that have been referred to. Both Evagrius and Palladius flourished a short time after the death of Valens. We must now return to the point whence we diverged.

CHAPTER XXIV.

Assault upon the Monks, and Banishment of their Superiors, who exhibit Miraculous Power.

THE emperor Valens having issued an edict commanding that the orthodox should be persecuted both in Alexandria and in the rest of Egypt, depopulation and ruin to an immense extent immediately followed : some were dragged before the tribunals, others cast into prison, and many tortured in various ways, and in fact all sorts of punishments were inflicted upon persons who aimed only at peace and quiet. When these outrages had been perpetrated at Alexan-

dria just as Lucius thought proper, Euzoïus returned to Antioch, and Lucian the Arian, attended by the commander-in-chief of the army with a considerable body of troops, immediately proceeded to the monasteries of Egypt, where the general in person assailed the assemblage of holy men with greater fury even than the ruthless soldiery. On reaching these solitudes they found the monks engaged in their customary exercises, praying, healing diseases, and casting out devils. Yet they, regardless of these extraordinary evidences of Divine power, suffered them not to continue their solemn devotions, but drove them out of the oratories by force. Rufinus declares that he was not only a witness of these cruelties, but also one of the sufferers. Thus in them were renewed those things which are spoken of by the apostle : [1] 'for they were mocked, and had trial of scourgings, were stripped naked, put in bonds, stoned, slain with the sword, went about in the wilderness clad in sheep-skins and goat-skins, being destitute, afflicted, tormented, of whom the world was not worthy, wandering in deserts, in mountains, in dens and caves of the earth.' In all these things 'they obtained a good report' for their faith and their works, and the cures which the grace of Christ wrought by their hands. But as it appears Divine Providence permitted them to endure these evils, 'having for them provided something better,' [2] that through their sufferings others might obtain the salvation of God, and this subsequent events seem to prove. When therefore these wonderful men proved superior to all the violence which was exercised toward them, Lucius in despair advised the military chief to send the fathers of the monks into exile : these were the Egyptian Macarius, and his namesake of Alexandria, both of whom were accordingly banished to an island where there was no Christian inhabitant, and in this island there was an idolatrous temple, and a priest whom the inhabitants worshiped as a god. On the arrival of these holy men at the island, the demons of that place were filled with fear and trepidation. Now it happened at the same time that the priest's daughter became suddenly possessed by a demon, and began to act with great fury, and to overturn everything that came in her way ; nor was any force sufficient to restrain her, but she cried with a loud voice to these saints of God, saying : — 'Why are ye come here to cast us out from hence also?' [3] Then did the men there also display the peculiar power which they had received through Divine grace : for having cast out the demon from the maid, and presented her cured to her father, they led the priest himself, and also all the in-

[18] *Hist. Lausiaca* (Vol. XXXIV. in Migné's *Patrologia Græca*).

[1] Heb. xi. 36–38.   [2] Heb. xi. 40.   [3] Matt. viii. 29.

habitants of the island to the Christian faith. Whereupon they immediately brake their images in pieces, and changed the form of their temple into that of a church ; and having been baptized, they joyfully received instruction in the doctrines of Christianity.   Thus these marvelous individuals, after enduring persecution on account of the 'homoousian' faith, were themselves more approved, became the means of salvation to others, and confirmed the truth.

CHAPTER XXV.

Of Didymus the Blind Man.[1]

ABOUT the same period God brought into observation another faithful person, deeming it worthy that through him faith might be witnessed unto : this was Didymus, a most admirable and eloquent man, instructed in all the learning of the age in which he flourished.   At a very early age, when he had scarcely acquired the first elements of learning, he was attacked by disease in the eyes which deprived him of sight.   But God compensated to him the loss of corporeal vision, by bestowing increased intellectual acumen.   For what he could not learn by seeing, he was enabled to acquire through the sense of hearing ; so that being from his childhood endowed with excellent abilities, he soon far surpassed his youthful companions who possessed the keenest sight.   He made himself master of the principles of grammar and rhetoric with astonishing facility ; and proceeded thence to philosophical studies, dialectics, arithmetic, music, and the various other departments of knowledge to which his attention was directed ; and he so treasured up in his mind these branches of science, that he was prepared with the utmost readiness to enter into a discussion of these subjects with those who had become conversant therewith by reading books.   Not only this, but he was so well acquainted with the Divine oracles contained in the Old and New Testament that he composed several treatises in exposition of them, besides three books on the *Trinity*.   He published also commentaries[2] on Origen's book *Of Principles*, in which he commends these writings, saying that they are excellent, and that those who calumniate their author, and speak slightingly of his works, are mere cavilers.   'For,' says he, 'they are destitute of sufficient penetration to comprehend the profound wisdom of that extraordinary man.' Those who may desire to form a just idea of the extensive erudition of Didymus, and the

intense ardor of his mind, must peruse with attention his diversified and elaborate works. It is said that after Anthony had conversed for some time with this Didymus, long before the reign of Valens, when he came from the desert to Alexandria on account of the Arians, perceiving the learning and intelligence of the man, he said to him, 'Didymus, let not the loss of your bodily eyes distress you : for you are deprived of such eyes merely as are the common possession of gnats and flies ; rather rejoice that you have eyes such as angels see with, by which the Deity himself is discerned, and his light comprehended.'   This address of the pious Anthony to Didymus was made long before the times we are describing : in fact Didymus was then regarded as the great bulwark of the true faith, answering the Arians, whose sophistic cavilings he fully exposed, triumphantly refuting all their vain subtleties and deceptive reasonings.

CHAPTER XXVI.

Of Basil of Cæsarea, and Gregory of Nazianzus.[1]

Now Providence opposed Didymus to the Arians at Alexandria.   But for the purpose of confuting them in other cities, it raised up Basil of Cæsarea and Gregory of Nazianzus ; concerning these it will be reasonable to give a brief account in this place.   Indeed the universally prevalent memory of the men would be enough as a token of their fame ; and the extent of their knowledge is sufficiently perceptible in their writings.   Since, however, the exercise of their talents was of great service to the Church, tending in a high degree to the maintenance of the catholic faith, the nature of my history obliges me to take particular notice of these two persons.   If any one should compare Basil and Gregory with one another, and consider the life, morals, and virtues of each, he would find it difficult to decide to which of them he ought to assign the pre-eminence : so equally did they both appear to excel, whether you regard the rectitude of their conduct, or their deep acquaintance with Greek literature and the sacred Scriptures.   In their youth they were pupils at Athens of Himerius[2] and Prohæresius,[3] the most celebrated sophists of that age : subsequently they frequented the

---

[1] Sozom. III. 15; Theodoret, IV. 26; Pallad. *Hist. Lausiac.* 4; Jerom. *de Script. Eccl.* 109.
[2] Mentioned by Jerome, *adv. Rufinum*, 1.

[1] For full accounts of the lives of these eminent men, see Smith and Wace, *Dict. of Christ. Biog.*, and the sources and literature therein referred to.
[2] Himerius, a native of Prusias (mod. Broussa) in Bithynia, flourished about 360 A.D. as a sophist under Julian the Apostate. He published various discourses, which, according to Photius, contained insidious attacks on Christianity.   Cf. Eunapius, p. 153, under title *Prohæresius;* Photius, *Bibl. Cod.* 165.
[3] Prohæresius was a native of Cæsarea in Cappadocia, and taught in Athens a short time before Libanius. Cf. Eunapius, *Prohæresius*, par. 129–162.

school of Libanius[4] at Antioch in Syria, where they cultivated rhetoric to the utmost. Having been deemed worthy of the profession of sophistry, they were urged by many of their friends to enter the profession of teaching eloquence; others would have persuaded them to practice law: but despising both these pursuits, they abandoned their former studies, and embraced the monastic life. Having had some slight taste of philosophical science from him who then taught it at Antioch, they procured Origen's works, and drew from them the right interpretation of the sacred Scriptures; for the fame of Origen was very great and widespread throughout the whole world at that time; after a careful perusal of the writings of that great man, they contended against the Arians with manifest advantage. And when the defenders of Arianism quoted the same author in confirmation, as they imagined, of their own views, these two confuted them, and clearly proved that their opponents did not at all understand the reasoning of Origen. Indeed, although Eunomius,[5] who was then their champion, and many others on the side of the Arians were considered men of great eloquence, yet whenever they attempted to enter into controversy with Gregory and Basil, they appeared in comparison with them ignorant and illiterate. Basil being ordained to the office of deacon, was by Meletius, bishop of Antioch, from that rank elevated to the bishopric of Cæsarea in Cappadocia, which was his native country. Thither he therefore hastened, fearing lest these Arian dogmas should have infected the provinces of Pontus; and in order to counteract them, he founded several monasteries, diligently instructed the people in his own doctrines, and confirmed the faith of those whose minds were wavering. Gregory being constituted bishop of Nazianzus,[6] a small city of Cappadocia over which his own father had before presided, pursued a course similar to that which Basil took; for he went through the various cities, and strengthened the weak in faith. To Constantinople in particular he made frequent visits, and by his ministrations there, comforted and assured the orthodox believers, wherefore a short time after, by the suffrage of many bishops, he was made bishop of the church at Constantinople. When intelligence of the proceedings

of these two zealous and devoted men reached the ears of the emperor Valens, he immediately ordered Basil to be brought from Cæsarea to Antioch;[7] where being arraigned before the tribunal of the prefect, that functionary asked him 'why he would not embrace the emperor's faith?' Basil with much boldness condemned the errors of that creed which his sovereign countenanced, and vindicated the doctrine of the *homoousion:* and when the prefect threatened him with death, 'Would,' said Basil, 'that I might be released from the bonds of the body for the truth's sake.' The prefect having exhorted him to reconsider the matter more seriously, Basil is reported to have said, 'I am the same to-day that I shall be to-morrow: but I wish that you had not changed yourself.' At that time, therefore, Basil remained in custody throughout the day. It happened, however, not long afterwards that Galates, the emperor's infant son, was attacked with a dangerous malady, so that the physicians despaired of his recovery; when the empress Dominica, his mother, assured the emperor that she had been greatly disquieted in her dreams by fearful visions, which led her to believe that the child's illness was a chastisement on account of the ill treatment of the bishop. The emperor after a little reflection sent for Basil, and in order to prove his faith said to him, 'If the doctrine you maintain is the truth, pray that my son may not die.' 'If your majesty should believe as I do,' replied Basil, 'and the church should be unified, the child shall live.' To these conditions the emperor would not agree: 'God's will concerning the child will be done then,' said Basil; as Basil said this the emperor ordered him to be dismissed; the child, however, died shortly after. Such is an epitome of the history of these distinguished ecclesiastics, both of whom have left us many admirable works, some of which Rufinus says he has translated into Latin. Basil had two brothers, Peter and Gregory; the former of whom adopted Basil's monastic mode of life; while the latter emulated his eloquence in teaching, and completed after his death Basil's treatise on the *Six Days' Work,* which had been left unfinished. He also pronounced at Constantinople the funeral oration of Meletius, bishop of Antioch; and many other orations of his are still extant.

CHAPTER XXVII.

Of Gregory Thaumaturgus (the Wonder-Worker).

BUT since from the likeness of the name, and the title of the books attributed to Gregory,

---

[4] This is doubted by Valesius on the ground that Gregory in his autobiography (in verse) says that he was thirty years of age when he left Athens, where his friends wished him to stay and teach rhetoric; but if he stayed at Athens until the thirtieth year of his age, it is not likely that he could have studied with Libanius after that time. So also Rufinus, *H. E.* II. 9.

[5] Cf. chap. 7 of the present book.

[6] Rufinus (*H. E.* II. 9) says this. But from Gregory's own works (*Orat.* VIII.) it appears that he was not made bishop of Nazianzus but assistant to his father, and on the express condition that he should not succeed his father. He was first consecrated bishop of Sasimi by Basil the Great, from thence transferred to Constantinople, but resigned that bishopric (V. 7) and retired to Nazianzus, where he remained bishop until he chose his successor there.

[7] Sozomen (VI. 16) says that Valens came from Antioch to Cæsarea and ordered Basil to be brought before the prefect of the prætorium. This account agrees better with what both Gregory of Nazianzus and Gregory of Nyssa say of this experience of Basil.

persons are liable to confound very different parties, it is important to notice that Gregory of Pontus is a different person. He was a native of Neocæsarea in Pontus, of greater antiquity than the one above referred to, inasmuch as he was a disciple of Origen.[1] This Gregory's fame was celebrated at Athens, at Berytus, throughout the entire diocese of Pontus, and I might almost add in the whole world. When he had finished his education in the schools of Athens, he went to Berytus to study civil law, where hearing that Origen expounded the Holy Scriptures at Cæsarea, he quickly proceeded thither; and after his understanding had been opened to perceive the grandeur of these Divine books, bidding adieu to all further cultivation of the Roman laws, he became thenceforth inseparable from Origen, from whom having acquired a knowledge of the true philosophy, he was recalled soon after by his parents and returned to his own country; and there, while still a layman, he performed many miracles, healing the sick, and casting out devils even by his letters, insomuch that the pagans were no less attracted to the faith by his acts, than by his discourses. Pamphilus Martyr mentions this person in the books which he wrote in defence of Origen; to which there is added a commendatory oration of Gregory's, composed in praise of Origen, when he was under the necessity of leaving him. There were then, to be brief, several Gregories: the first and most ancient was the disciple of Origen; the second was the bishop of Nazianzus; the third was Basil's brother; and there was another Gregory[2] whom the Arians constituted bishop during the exile of Athanasius. But enough has been said respecting them.

CHAPTER XXVIII.

Of Novatus and his Followers. The Novatians of Phrygia alter the Time of keeping Easter, following Jewish Usage.

ABOUT this time the Novatians[1] inhabiting Phrygia changed the day for celebrating the Feast of Easter. How this happened I shall state, after first explaining the reason of the strict discipline which is maintained in their church, even to the present day, in the provinces of Phrygia and Paphlagonia. Novatus,[2] a presbyter of the Roman Church, separated from it,

because Cornelius the bishop received into communion believers who had sacrificed during the persecution which the Emperor Decius[3] had raised against the Church. Having seceded on this account, on being afterwards elevated to the episcopacy by such bishops as entertained similar sentiments, he wrote to all the churches[4] that 'they should not admit to the sacred mysteries those who had sacrificed; but exhorting them to repentance, leave the pardoning of their offense to God, who has the power to forgive all sin.' Receiving such letters, the parties in the various provinces, to whom they were addressed, acted according to their several dispositions and judgments. As he asked that they should not receive to the sacraments those who after baptism had committed any deadly sin[5] this appeared to some a cruel and merciless course: but others received the rule as just and conducive to the maintenance of discipline, and the promotion of greater devotedness of life. In the midst of the agitation of this question, letters arrived from Cornelius the bishop, promising indulgence to delinquents after baptism. Thus as these two persons wrote contrary to one another, and each confirmed his own procedure by the testimony of the Divine word, as it usually happens, every one identified himself with that view which favored his previous habits and inclinations. Those who had pleasure in sin, encouraged by the license then granted them, took occasion from it to revel in every species of criminality. Now the Phrygians appear to be more temperate than other nations, and are seldom guilty of swearing. The Scythians, on the other hand, and the Thracians, are naturally of a very irritable disposition: while the inhabitants of the East are addicted to sensual pleasures. But the Paphlagonians and Phrygians are prone to neither of these vices; nor are the sports of the circus and theatrical exhibitions in much estimation among them even to the present day. And for this reason, it seems to me, these people, as well as others of the same character, so readily assented to the letters then written by Novatus. Fornication and adultery are regarded among them as the grossest enormities: and it is well known that there is no race of men on the face of the earth who more rigidly govern their passions in this respect than the Phrygians and Paphlagonians. The same reason I think had force with those who dwelt in the West and followed Novatus. Yet although for the sake of stricter discipline Novatus became a separatist,

---

[1] On Gregory Thaumaturgus in general, see Euseb. *H. E.* VI. 30.
[2] Cf. II. 11.
[1] On the Novatians and their schism, see Schaff, *Hist. of the Christ. Ch.* Vol. I. p. 450, 451; Neander, *Hist. of Christ. Ch.* Vol. I. p. 237-248. On Socrates' attitude toward Novatianism, see Introd. p. ix. Cf. also Euseb. *H. E.* VI. 43.
[2] His right name was Novatian, although the Greek writers call him uniformly Navatus, ignoring or confusing him with another person whose name is strictly Novatus. Cf. Jerome, *Scriptor. Eccles.* LXX.; also Smith and Wace, *Dict. of Christ. Biog.*

[3] This was the great *Seventh Persecution*, and the first which historians agree in calling strictly 'general.' It took place in 249-251 A.D., and consisted in a systematic effort to uproot Christianity throughout the empire. Many eminent Christians were put to death during its course, and others, among whom was Origen, were tortured. Cf. Origen, *Contra Celsum*, III.; Gregory of Nyssa, *Vita Gregori Thaumaturg.* III.; Euseb. *H. E.* VI. 40-42.
[4] Cf. I. 10.   [5] 1 John v. 16, 17.

he made no change in the time of keeping Easter,[6] but invariably observed the practice that obtained in the Western churches. For they celebrate this feast after the equinox, according to the usage which had of old been delivered to them when first they embraced Christianity. He himself indeed afterwards suffered martyrdom in the reign of Valerian,[7] during the persecution which was then raised against the Christians. But those in Phrygia[8] who are named after him Novatians, about this period changed the day of celebrating Easter, being averse to communion with other Christians even on this occasion. This was effected by means of a few obscure bishops of that sect convening a Synod at the village of Pazum, which is situated near the sources of the river Sangarius; for there they framed a canon appointing its observance on the same day as that on which the Jews annually keep the feast of Unleavened Bread. An aged man, who was the son of a presbyter, and had been present with his father at this Synod, gave us our information on this matter. But both Agelius, bishop of the Novatians at Constantinople, and Maximus of Nicæa, as also the bishops of Nicomedia and Cotyæum, were absent, although the ecclesiastical affairs of the Novatians were for the most part under the control of these bishops. How the church of the Novatians soon after was divided into two parties in consequence of this Synod, shall be related in its proper course :[9] but we must now notice what took place about the same time in the Western parts.

CHAPTER XXIX.

Damasus ordained Bishop of Rome. Sedition and Loss of Life caused by the Rivalry of Ursinus.

WHILE the emperor Valentinian governed in peace, and interfered with no sect, Damasus after Liberius undertook the administration of the bishopric at Rome ;[1] whereupon a great disturbance was caused on the following account.[2] A certain Ursinus, a deacon of that church, had been nominated among others when the election of a bishop took place ; as Damasus[3] was preferred, this Ursinus, unable to bear the disappointment of his hopes, held schismatic assemblies apart from the church, and even induced certain bishops of little distinction to ordain him in secret. This ordination was made, not in a church,[4] but in a retired place called the Palace of Sicine, whereupon dissension arose among the people ; their disagreement being not about any article of faith or heresy, but simply as to who should be bishop. Hence frequent conflicts arose, insomuch that many lives were sacrificed in this contention ; and many of the clergy as well as laity were punished on that account by Maximin, the prefect of the city. Thus was Ursinus obliged to desist from his pretensions at that time, and those who were minded to follow him were reduced to order.

CHAPTER XXX.

Dissension about a Successor to Auxentius, Bishop of Milan. Ambrose, Governor of the Province, going to appease the Tumult, is by General Consent and with the Approval of the Emperor Valentinian elected to the Bishopric of that Church.

ABOUT the same time it happened that[1] another event took place at Milan well worthy of being recorded. On the death of Auxentius, who had been ordained bishop of that church by the Arians, the people again were disturbed respecting the election of a successor ; for as some proposed one person, and others favored another, the city was full of contention and uproar. In this state of things the governor of the province, Ambrose by name,[2] who was also of consular dignity, dreading some catastrophe from the popular excitement, ran into the church in order to quell the disturbance. As he arrived there and the people became quiet, he repressed the irrational fury of the multitude by a long and appropriate address, by urging such motives as they felt to be right, and all present suddenly came to an unanimous agreement, crying out 'that Ambrose was worthy of the bishopric,' and demanding his ordination : 'for by that means only,' it was alleged, 'would the peace of the

---

[6] Cf. I. 8 and note.
[7] The accuracy of this statement is disputed by Valesius, who asserts that the Novatians wrote a book entitled *The Martyrdom of Novatian*, but that this book was full of false statements and fables, and had been disproved by Eulogius, bishop of Alexandria, in the sixth book of his treatise *Against the Novatians*. Besides, in this *Martyrdom of Novatian* the founder of the sect was not represented as suffering martyrdom, but simply as being a ' confessor.' Cf. I. 8, note 12.
[8] Let it be noted that Novatian was a native of Phrygia and naturally had many followers in that province.
[9] V. 21.
[1] Socrates follows Rufinus here (cf. Rufin. *H. E.* II. 10); but Jerome, *Chronicon*, puts the consecration of Damasus as bishop of Rome in the third year of Valentinian's reign, i.e. in 367. Cf. also Clinton, *Fasti Rom. Ann.* 367.
[2] Am. Marcellinus (*Rerum Gestarum*, XXVII. 3. 12, 13) says that during the disturbance one hundred and thirty-seven citizens were killed in the course of a single day.

[3] Damasus was a Spaniard by race, native of Mantua, patron of Jerome in his biblical researches. Cf. Jerome, *ad Damas.* Smith & Wace, *Dict. of Christ. Biog.*
[4] On the illegality of ordination without a church, see Bingham, *Christ. Antiq.* IV. 6. 8. Cf. Gregory Nazianz. *Carm. de Vita.*
[1] Synchronization of the events attending the accession of Damasus and Ambrose, the former in Rome, the latter at Milan, is dependent on Rufinus. Cf. *H. E.* II. 11. The events of this chapter more properly fall within the time reached by Socrates, i.e. 374 A.D. (see chap. 29, note 1). Hence rightly seven years later than the events of the preceding chapter.
[2] A Roman by race, born in 333 A.D., turned to ecclesiastical and literary pursuits in the manner described in this chapter. Cf. Sozom. VI. 24; Theodoret, *H. E.* IV. 6; Rufinus, *H. E.* II. 11.

church be secured, and all be reunited in the same faith and judgment.' And inasmuch as such unanimity among the people appeared to the bishops then present to proceed from some Divine appointment, immediately they laid hands on Ambrose; and having baptized him — for he was then but a catechumen — they were about to invest him with the episcopal office. But although Ambrose willingly received baptism, he with great earnestness refused to be ordained: upon which the bishops referred the matter to the Emperor Valentinian. This prince regarding the universal consent of the people as the work of God, sent word to the bishops to do the will of God by ordaining him; declaring that 'his choice was by the voice of God rather than by the votes of men.' Ambrose was therefore ordained; and thus the inhabitants of Milan, who were divided among themselves, were once more restored to unity.

CHAPTER XXXI.

Death of Valentinian.

THE Sarmatæ after this having made incursions into the Roman territories, the emperor marched against them with a numerous army: but when the barbarians understood the formidable nature of this expedition, they sent an embassy to him to sue for peace on certain conditions. As the ambassadors were introduced to the emperor's presence, and appeared to him to be not very dignified fellows, he enquired whether all the Sarmatæ were such as these? As they replied that the noblest personages of their whole nation had come to him, Valentinian became excessively enraged, and exclaimed with great vehemence, that 'the Roman empire was indeed most wretched in devolving upon him at a time when a nation of such despicable barbarians, not content with being permitted to exist in safety within their own limits, dared to take up arms, invade the Roman territories, and break forth into open war.' The violence of his manner and utterance of these words was so great, that all his veins were opened by the effort, and all the arteries ruptured; and from the quantity of blood which thereupon gushed forth he died. This occurred at Bergition Castle, after Gratian's third consulate[1] in conjunction with Equitius, on the seventeenth day of November, Valentinian having lived fifty-four years and reigned thirteen. Upon the decease of Valentinian, six days after his death the army in Italy proclaimed his son Valentinian, then a young child, emperor, at Acincum, a city of Italy.[2] When this was announced to the other

two emperors, they were displeased, not because the brother of the one and the nephew of the other had been declared emperor, but because the military presumed to proclaim him without consulting them, whom they themselves wished to have proclaimed. They both, however, ratified the transaction, and thus was Valentinian the younger seated on his father's throne. Now this Valentinian was born of Justina, whom Valentinian the elder married while Severa his former wife was alive, under the following circumstances. Justus the father of Justina, who had been governor of Picenum under the reign of Constantius, had a dream in which he seemed to himself to bring forth the imperial purple out of his right side. When this dream had been told to many persons, it at length came to the knowledge of Constantius, who conjecturing it to be a presage that a descendant of Justus would become emperor, caused him to be assassinated. Justina being thus bereft of her father, still continued a virgin. Some time after she became known to Severa, wife of the emperor Valentinian, and had frequent intercourse with the empress, until their intimacy at length grew to such an extent that they were accustomed to bathe together. When Severa saw Justina in the bath she was greatly struck with the beauty of the virgin, and spoke of her to the emperor; saying that the daughter of Justus was so lovely a creature, and possessed of such symmetry of form, that she herself, though a woman, was altogether charmed with her. The emperor, treasuring this description by his wife in his own mind, considered with himself how he could espouse Justina, without repudiating Severa, as she had borne him Gratian, whom he had created Augustus a little while before. He accordingly framed a law, and caused it to be published throughout all the cities, by which any man was permitted to have two lawful wives.[3] The law was promulgated and he married Justina, by whom he had Valentinian the younger, and three daughters, Justa, Grata, and Galla; the two former of these remained virgins: but Galla was afterwards married to the emperor Theodosius the Great, who had by her a daughter named Placidia. For that prince had Arcadius and Honorius by Flaccilla his former wife: we shall however enter into particulars respecting Theodosius and his sons in the proper place.[4]

---

[3] Baronius (*Am.* IV. 272) and Valesius in this passage agree in looking upon this whole story as a groundless fiction which some pretended eyewitness palmed off on Socrates. The law mentioned here is never mentioned by any other historian; no vestige of it is found in any of the codes; on the contrary, according to Bingham (*Christ. Antiq.* XVI. 11), bigamy and polygamy were treated with the utmost severity in the ancient Church, and the Roman law was very much against them; furthermore, Am. Marcellinus (XXX.) says that Valentinian was remarkable for his chastity, both at home and abroad, and Zosimus (IV. 19) that his second wife had been married to Magnentius previously [and hence was not a virgin as here stated] and that he married her after the death of his first wife; all of which considerations taken together render it historically certain that the story is not true.

[4] Cf. V. 2; VI. 1.

---

[1] 375 A.D.   [2] Rather Pannonia.

CHAPTER XXXII.

The Emperor Valens, appeased by the Oration of Themistius the Philosopher, abates his Persecution of the Christians.

IN the meanwhile Valens, making his residence at Antioch, was wholly undisturbed by foreign wars; for the barbarians on every side restrained themselves within their own boundaries. Nevertheless, he himself waged a most cruel war against those who maintained the 'homoousian' doctrine, inflicting on them more grievous punishments every day; until the philosopher Themistius by his *Appealing Oration*[1] somewhat moderated his severity. In this speech he tells the emperor, 'That he ought not to be surprised at the difference of judgment on religious questions existing among Christians; inasmuch as that discrepancy was trifling when compared with the multitude of conflicting opinions current among the heathen; for these amount to above three hundred; that dissension indeed was an inevitable consequence of this disagreement; but that God would be the more glorified by a diversity of sentiment, and the greatness of his majesty be more venerated, from the fact of its not being easy to have a knowledge of Him.' The philosopher having said these and similar things, the emperor became milder, but did not completely give up his wrath; for although he ceased to put ecclesiastics to death, he continued to send them into exile, until this fury of his also was repressed by the following event.

CHAPTER XXXIII.

The Goths, under the Reign of Valens, embrace Christianity.

THE barbarians, dwelling beyond the Danube, called the Goths,[1] having engaged in a civil war among themselves, were divided into two parties, one of which was headed by Fritigernes, the other by Athanaric. When the latter had obtained an evident advantage over his rival, Fritigernes had recourse to the Romans, and implored their assistance against his adversary. This was reported to the Emperor Valens, and he ordered the troops which were garrisoned in Thrace to assist those barbarians who had appealed to him against their more powerful countrymen; and by means of this subsidy they won a complete victory over Athanaric beyond the Danube, totally routing the enemy. This became the occasion for the conversion of many of the barbarians to the Christian religion:[2] for Fritigernes, to express his sense of the obligation the emperor had conferred upon him, embraced the religion of his benefactor, and urged those who were under his authority to do the same. Therefore it is that so many of the Goths are even to the present time infected with the errors of Arianism, they having on the occasion preferred to become adherents to that heresy on the emperor's account. Ulfilas, their bishop at that time, invented the Gothic letters,[3] and translating the Sacred Scriptures into their own language, undertook to instruct these barbarians in the Divine oracles. And as Ulfilas did not restrict his labors to the subjects of Fritigernes, but extended them to those who acknowledged the sway of Athanaric also, Athanaric regarding this as a violation of the privileges of the religion of his ancestors, subjected those who professed Christianity to severe punishments; so that many of the Arian Goths of that period became martyrs. Arius indeed, failing in his attempt to refute the opinion of Sabellius the Libyan, fell from the true faith, and asserted the Son of God to be 'a new God':[4] but the barbarians embracing Christianity with greater simplicity of mind despised the present life for the faith of Christ. With these remarks we shall close our notice of the Christianized Goths.

CHAPTER XXXIV.

Admission of the Fugitive Goths into the Roman Territories, which caused the Emperor's Overthrow, and eventually the Ruin of the Roman Empire.

NOT long after the barbarians had entered into a friendly alliance with one another, they were again vanquished by other barbarians, their neighbors, called the Huns; and being driven out of their own country, they fled into the

---

[1] This oration of Themistius is extant in a Latin translation by Dudithius appended to G. Remo's *Themistii Phil. orationes sex augustales*, and entitled, *ad Valentem, pro Libertate relligionis.* The passage alluded to by Socrates is found in Dudithius as follows: 'Wherefore, in regard God has removed himself at the greatest distance from our knowledge, and does not humble to the capacity of our understanding; it is a sufficient argument that he does not require one and the same law and rule of religion from all persons, but leaves every man a license and faculty concerning himself, according to his own, not another man's, liberty and choice. Whence it also happens that a greater admiration of the Deity, and a more religious veneration of his eternal majesty, is engendered in the minds of men. For it usually comes to pass that we loathe and disregard those things which are readily apparent and prostrated to every understanding.'
[1] The fullest and best ancient authors on the origin and history of the Goths are Procopius of Cæsarea (*Historia*, IV.–VIII., *de Bello Italico adversus Gothos gesto*), Jornandes (*de Getarum* [*Gothorum*] *origine et rebus gestis*), and Isidore Hispalensis (*Historia Gothorum*). On the conversion of the Goths to Christianity, see Neander, *Hist. of the Christ. Ch.* Vol. II. p. 125–129, and Schaff, *Hist. of the Christ. Ch.* Vol. III. p. 640, 641.

[2] For a slightly differing account of the conversion of the Goths and the labors of Ulfilas, see Philostorgius, II. 5.
[3] By selecting from the Greek and Latin alphabets such characters as appeared to him to best suit the sounds of his native language. For a similar invention of an alphabet as a consequence of the introduction of Christianity, compare the Slavonic invented by Cyril and Methodius and a great number of instances in the history of modern missions.
[4] Cf. Deut. xxxii. 7.

territory of the Romans, offering to be subject to the emperor, and to execute whatever he should command them. When Valens was made acquainted with this, not having the least presentiment of the consequences, he ordered that the suppliants should be received with kindness; in this one instance alone showing himself compassionate. He therefore assigned them certain parts of Thrace for their habitation, deeming himself peculiarly fortunate in this matter: for he calculated that in future he should possess a ready and well-equipped army against all assailants; and hoped that the barbarians would be a more formidable guard to the frontiers of the empire even than the Romans themselves. For this reason he in the future neglected to recruit his army by Roman levies; and despising those veterans who had bravely struggled and subdued his enemies in former wars, he put a pecuniary value on the militia which the inhabitants of the provinces, village by village, had been accustomed to furnish, ordering the collectors of his tribute to demand eighty pieces of gold for every soldier, although he had never before lightened the public burdens. This change was the origin of many disasters to the Roman empire subsequently.

CHAPTER XXXV.

Abatement of Persecution against the Christians because of the War with the Goths.

THE barbarians having been put into possession of Thrace, and securely enjoying that Roman province, were unable to bear their good fortune with moderation; but committing hostile aggressions upon their benefactors, devastated all Thrace and the adjacent countries. When these proceedings came to the knowledge of Valens, he desisted from sending the adherents of the *homoousion* into banishment; and in great alarm left Antioch, and came to Constantinople, where also the persecution of the orthodox Christians was for the same reason come to an end. At the same time Euzoïus, bishop of the Arians at Antioch, departed this life, in the fifth consulate [1] of Valens, and the first of Valentinian the younger; and Dorotheus was appointed in his place.

CHAPTER XXXVI.

The Saracens, under Mavia their Queen, embrace Christianity; and Moses, a Pious Monk, is consecrated their Bishop.

No sooner had the emperor departed from

Antioch, than the Saracens,[1] who had before been in alliance with the Romans, revolted from them, being led by Mavia their queen, whose husband was then dead. All the regions of the East therefore were at that time ravaged by the Saracens: but a certain divine Providence repressed their fury in the manner I am about to describe. A person named Moses, a Saracen by birth, who led a monastic life in the desert, became exceedingly eminent for his piety, faith, and miracles. Mavia the queen of the Saracens was therefore desirous that this person should be constituted bishop over her nation, and promised on this condition to terminate the war. The Roman generals considering that a peace founded on such terms would be extremely advantageous, gave immediate directions for its ratification. Moses was accordingly seized, and brought from the desert to Alexandria, in order that he might there be invested with the bishopric: but on his presentation for that purpose to Lucius, who at that time presided over the churches in that city, he refused to be ordained by him, protesting against it in these words: 'I account myself indeed unworthy of the sacred office; but if the exigences of the state require my bearing it, it shall not be by Lucius laying his hand on me, for it has been filled with blood.' When Lucius told him that it was his duty to learn from him the principles of religion, and not to utter reproachful language, Moses replied, 'Matters of faith are not now in question: but your infamous practices against the brethren sufficiently prove that your doctrines are not Christian. For a Christian is "no striker, reviles not, does not fight"; for "it becomes not a servant of the Lord to fight."[2] But your deeds cry out against you by those who have been sent into exile, who have been exposed to the wild beasts, and who had been delivered up to the flames. Those things which our own eyes have beheld are far more convincing than what we receive from the report of another.' As Moses expressed these and other similar sentiments his friends took him to the mountains, that he might receive ordination from those bishops who lived in exile there. Moses having thus been consecrated, the Saracen war was terminated; and so scrupulously did Mavia observe the peace thus entered into with the Romans that she gave her daughter in marriage to Victor the commander-in-chief of the Roman army. Such were the transactions in relation to the Saracens.

---

[1] The name Saracen (Σαρακηνός, perhaps from the Arabic *Sharkeen* 'Orientals') was used vaguely at first; the Greek writers of the first centuries gave it to the Bedouin Arabs of Eastern Arabia, while others used it to designate the Arab races of Syria and Palestine, and others the Berber of North Eastern Africa, who later conquered Spain and Sicily and invaded France. The name became very familiar in Europe during the period of the Crusades. On Saracens, consult the interesting fiftieth chapter. of Gibbon's *Decline and Fall of the Roman Empire.*
[2] 2 Tim. ii. 24.

CHAPTER XXXVII.

After the Departure of Valens from Antioch, the Alexandrians expel Lucius, and restore Peter, who had come with Letters from Damasus Bishop of Rome.

ABOUT the same time, as soon as the Emperor Valens left Antioch, all those who had anywhere been suffering persecution began again to take courage, and especially those of Alexandria. Peter returned to that city from Rome, with letters from Damasus the Roman bishop, in which he confirmed the 'homoousian' faith, and sanctioned Peter's ordination. The people therefore resuming confidence, expelled Lucius, who immediately embarked for Constantinople : but Peter survived his re-establishment a very short time, and at his death appointed his brother Timothy to succeed him.

CHAPTER XXXVIII.

The Emperor Valens is ridiculed by the People on Account of the Goths; undertakes an Expedition against them and is slain in an Engagement near Adrianople.

THE Emperor Valens arrived at Constantinople on the 30th of May, in the sixth year of his own consulate,[1] and the second of Valentinian the Younger, and found the people in a very dejected state of mind : for the barbarians, who had already desolated Thrace, were now laying waste the very suburbs of Constantinople, there being no adequate force at hand to resist them. But when they undertook to make near approaches, even to the walls of the city, the peo-

[1] 378 A.D.

ple became exceedingly troubled, and began to murmur against the emperor ; accusing him of having brought on the enemy thither, and then indolently prolonging the struggle there, instead of at once marching out against the barbarians. Moreover at the exhibition of the sports of the Hippodrome, all with one voice clamored against the emperor's negligence of the public affairs, crying out with great earnestness, 'Give us arms, and we ourselves will fight.' The emperor provoked at these seditious clamors, marched out of the city, on the 11th of June ; threatening that if he returned, he would punish the citizens not only for their insolent reproaches, but for having previously favored the pretensions of the usurper Procopius ; declaring also that he would utterly demolish their city, and cause the plough to pass over its ruins, he advanced against the barbarians, whom he routed with great slaughter, and pursued as far as Adrianople, a city of Thrace, situated on the frontiers of Macedonia. Having at that place again engaged the enemy, who had by this time rallied, he lost his life on the 9th of August, under the consulate just mentioned, and in the fourth year of the 289th Olympiad. Some have asserted that he was burnt to death in a village whither he had retired, which the barbarians assaulted and set on fire. But others affirm that having put off his imperial robe he ran into the midst of the main body of infantry ; and that when the cavalry revolted and refused to engage, the infantry were surrounded by the barbarians, and completely destroyed in a body. Among these it is said the emperor fell, but could not be distinguished, in consequence of his not having on his imperial habit. He died in the fiftieth year of his age, having reigned in conjunction with his brother thirteen years, and three years after the death of the brother. This book therefore contains [the course of events during] the space of sixteen years.

END OF THE FOURTH BOOK.

BOOK V.

INTRODUCTION.

BEFORE we begin the fifth book of our history, we must beg those who may peruse this treatise, not to censure us too hastily because having set out to write a church history we still intermingle with ecclesiastical matters, such an account of the wars which took place during the period under consideration, as could be duly authenticated. For this we have done for several reasons: first, in order to lay before our readers an exact statement of facts; but secondly, in order that the minds of the readers might not become satiated with the repetition of the contentious disputes of bishops, and their insidious designs against one another; but more especially that it might be made apparent, that whenever the affairs of the state were disturbed, those of the Church, as if by some vital sympathy, became disordered also.[1] Indeed whoever shall attentively examine the subject will find, that the mischiefs of the state, and the troubles of the church have been inseparably connected; for he will perceive that they have either arisen together, or immediately succeeded one another. Sometimes the affairs of the Church come first in order; then commotions in the state follow, and sometimes the reverse, so that I cannot believe this invariable interchange is merely fortuitous, but am persuaded that it proceeds from our iniquities; and that these evils are inflicted upon us as merited chastisements, if indeed as the apostle truly says, 'Some men's sins are open beforehand, going before to judgment; and some men they follow after.'[2] For this reason we have interwoven many affairs of the state with our ecclesiastical history. Of the wars carried on during the reign of Constantine we have made no mention, having found no account of them that could be depended upon because of their iniquity: but of subsequent events, as much information as we could gather from those still living[3] in the order of their occurrence, we have passed in rapid review. We have continually included the emperors in these historical details; because from the time

they began to profess the Christian religion, the affairs of the Church have depended on them, so that even the greatest Synods have been, and still are convened by their appointment. Finally, we have particularly noticed the Arian heresy, because it has so greatly disquieted the churches. Let these remarks be considered sufficient in the way of preface: we shall now proceed with our history.

CHAPTER I.

After the Death of Valens the Goths again attack Constantinople, and are repulsed by the Citizens, aided by Some Saracen Auxiliaries.

AFTER the Emperor Valens had thus lost his life, in a manner which has never been satisfactorily ascertained,[1] the barbarians again approached the very walls of Constantinople, and laid waste the suburbs on every side of it. Whereat the people becoming indignant armed themselves with whatever weapons they could severally lay hands on, and sallied forth of their own accord against the enemy. The empress Dominica caused the same pay to be distributed out of the imperial treasury to such as volunteered to go out on this service, as was usually allowed to soldiers. A few Saracens also assisted the citizens, being confederates, who had been sent by Mavia their queen: the latter we have already mentioned.[2] In this way the people having fought at this time, the barbarians retired to a great distance from the city.

CHAPTER II.

The Emperor Gratian recalls the Orthodox Bishops, and expels the Heretics from the Churches. He takes Theodosius as his Colleague in the Empire.

GRATIAN being now in possession of the empire, together with Valentinian the younger, and condemning the cruel policy of his uncle Valens towards the [orthodox] Christians, recalled those whom he had sent into exile. He moreover enacted that persons of all sects, without distinction, might securely assemble together in their

---

[1] The views here expressed show a crude conception of the vital relation between church and state. The very tone of apology which tinges their expression is based on a misconception of the idea of history. But Socrates was not below his age in this respect. See Introd., p. xiii.   [2] 1 Tim. v. 24.
[3] For the risks of this method, see IV. 31 and note.

[1] See Gibbon, *Decline and Fall*, chap. 26.
[2] Cf. IV. 36.

churches; and that only the Eunomians,[1] Photinians,[2] and Manichæans[3] should be excluded from the churches. Being also sensible of the languishing condition of the Roman empire, and of the growing power of the barbarians and perceiving that the state was in need of a brave and prudent man, he took Theodosius as his colleague in the sovereign power. This [Theodosius] was descended from a noble family in Spain, and had acquired so distinguished a celebrity for his prowess in the wars, that he was universally considered worthy of imperial dignity, even before Gratian's election of him. Having therefore proclaimed him emperor at Sirmium a city of Illyricum in the consulate[4] of Ausonius and Olybrius, on the 16th of January, he divided with him the care of managing the war against the barbarians.

CHAPTER III.

The Principal Bishops who flourished at that Time.

Now at this time Damasus who had succeeded Liberius then presided over the church at Rome. Cyril was still in possession of that at Jerusalem. The Antiochian church, as we have stated, was divided into three parts: for the Arians had chosen Dorotheus as the successor of their bishop Euzoïus; while one portion of the rest was under the government of Paulinus, and the others ranged themselves with Melitius, who had been recalled from exile. Lucius, although absent, having been compelled to leave Alexandria, yet maintained the episcopal authority among the Arians of that city; the Homoousians there being headed by Timothy, who succeeded Peter. At Constantinople Demophilus the successor of Eudoxius presided over the Arian faction, and was in possession of the churches; but those who were averse to communion with him held their assemblies apart.[1]

CHAPTER IV.

The Macedonians, who had subscribed the 'Homoousian' Doctrine, return to their Former Error.

AFTER the deputation from the Macedonians to Liberius, that sect was admitted to entire communion with the churches in every city, intermixing themselves indiscriminately with those who from the beginning had embraced the form of faith published at Nicæa. But when the law of the Emperor Gratian permitted the several sects to reunite without restraint in the public services of religion, they again resolved to separate themselves; and having met at Antioch in Syria, they decided to avoid the word *homoousios* again, and in no way to hold communion with the supporters of the Nicene Creed. They however derived no advantage from this attempt; for the majority of their own party being disgusted at the fickleness with which they sometimes maintained one opinion, and then another, withdrew from them, and thenceforward became firm adherents of those who professed the doctrine of the *homoousion*.[1]

CHAPTER V.

Events at Antioch in Connection with Paulinus and Meletius.

ABOUT this time a serious contest was excited at Antioch in Syria, on account of Melitius. We have already observed[1] that Paulinus, bishop of that city, because of his eminent piety was not sent into exile: and that Melitius after being restored by Julian, was again banished by Valens, and at length recalled in Gratian's reign.[2] On his return to Antioch, he found Paulinus greatly enfeebled by old age; his partisans therefore immediately used their utmost endeavors to get him associated with that bishop in the episcopal office. And when Paulinus declared that 'it was contrary to the canons[3] to take as a coadjutor one who had been ordained by the Arians,' the people had recourse to violence, and caused him to be consecrated in one of the churches without the city. When this was done, a great disturbance arose; but afterwards the people were brought to unite on the following stipulations. Having assembled such of the clergy as might be considered worthy candidates for the bishopric, they found them six in number, of whom Flavian was one. All these they bound by an oath, not to use any effort to get themselves ordained, when either

---

[1] For an account of this deputation and their feigned subscription to the Nicene Creed, through which they prevailed upon Liberius to receive them into the communion of the church, see IV. 12.
[1] Cf. III. 9, and IV. 2.
[2] See above, chap. 3.
[3] In its eighth canon the Council of Nicæa, looking forward to the reconciliation of such Novatians or *Cathari* as might desire to return to the Catholic Church, enjoins that 'when in villages or in cities there are found only clergy of their own sect (*Cathari*), the oldest of these clerics shall remain among the clergy, and in their position; but if a Catholic priest or bishop be found among them, it is evident that the bishop of the Catholic Church should preserve the episcopal dignity, whilst any one who has received the title of bishop from the so-called *Cathari* would only have a right to the honors accorded to priests, unless the bishop thinks it right to let him enjoy the honor of the title. If he does not desire to do so, let him give him the place of rural bishop (*chorepiscopus*) or priest, in order that he may appear to be altogether a part of the clergy, and that there may not be two bishops in the same city.' Cf. Hefele, *Hist. of the Councils*, Vol. I. p. 410; Bingham, *Christ. Antiq.* II. 13. 1 and 2.

---

[1] Cf. IV. 7.   [4] 379 A.D.
[2] Cf. II. 18.   [1] Cf. IV. 1.
[3] Cf. I. 22.

of the two bishops should die, but to permit the survivor to retain undisturbed possession of the see of the deceased.[4] Thus pledges were given, and the people had peace and so no longer quarreled with one another. The Luciferians,[5] however, separated themselves from the rest, because Melitius who had been ordained by the Arians was admitted to the episcopate. In this state of the Antiochian church, Melitius was under the necessity of going to Constantinople.

CHAPTER VI.

Gregory of Nazianzus is transferred to the See of Constantinople. The Emperor Theodosius falling Sick at Thessalonica, after his Victory over the Barbarians, is there baptized by Ascholius the Bishop.

By the common suffrage of many bishops, Gregory was at this time translated from the see of Nazianzus to that of Constantinople,[1] and this happened in the manner before described. About the same time the emperors Gratian and Theodosius each obtained a victory over the barbarians.[2] And Gratian immediately set out for Gaul, because the Alemanni were ravaging those provinces: but Theodosius, after erecting a trophy, hastened towards Constantinople, and arrived at Thessalonica. There he was taken dangerously ill, and expressed a desire to receive Christian baptism.[3] Now he had been instructed in Christian principles by his ancestors, and professed the 'homoousian' faith. Becoming increasingly anxious to be baptized therefore, as his malady grew worse, he sent for the bishop of Thessalonica, and first asked him what doctrinal views he held? The bishop having replied, 'that the opinion of Arius had not yet invaded the provinces of Illyricum, nor had the novelty to which that heretic had given birth begun to prey upon the churches in those countries; but they continued to preserve unshaken that faith which from the beginning was delivered by the apostles, and had been confirmed in the Nicene Synod,' the emperor was most gladly baptized by the bishop Ascholius; and having

recovered from his disease not many days after, he came to Constantinople on the twenty-fourth of November, in the fifth consulate of Gratian, and the first of his own.[4]

CHAPTER VII.

Gregory, finding Some Dissatisfaction about his Appointment, abdicates the Episcopate of Constantinople. The Emperor orders Demophilus the Arian Bishop either to assent to the 'Homoousion,' or leave the City. He chooses the Latter.

Now at that time Gregory of Nazianzus, after his translation to Constantinople, held his assemblies within the city in a small oratory, adjoining to which the emperors afterwards built a magnificent church, and named it *Anastasia*.[1] But Gregory, who far excelled in eloquence and piety all those of the age in which he lived, understanding that some murmured at his preferment because he was a stranger, after expressing his joy at the emperor's arrival, resigned the bishopric of Constantinople. When the emperor found the church in this state, he began to consider by what means he could make peace, effect a union, and enlarge the churches. Immediately, therefore, he intimated his desire to Demophilus,[2] who presided over the Arian party; and enquired whether he was willing to assent to the Nicene Creed, and thus reunite the people, and establish peace. Upon Demophilus' declining to accede to this proposal, the emperor said to him, 'Since you reject peace and harmony, I order you to quit the churches.' When Demophilus heard this, weighing with himself the difficulty of contending against superior power, he convoked his followers in the church, and standing in the midst of them, thus spoke: 'Brethren, it is written in the Gospel,[3] "If they persecute you in one city, flee ye into another." Since therefore the emperor needs the churches, take notice that we will henceforth hold our assemblies without the city.' Having said this he departed; not however as rightly apprehending the meaning of that expression in the Evangelist, for the real

---

[4] Theodoret (*H. E.* V. 3) gives a different account of the way in which the dispute between Melitius and Paulinus came to an end, giving the glory to Melitius for the eirenic overture above described, and representing Paulinus as constrained to accept it against his will by the political head of the community.
[5] Cf. III. 9; Sozom. III. 15, and V. 12.
[1] So also Gregory Nazianz. *Carmen de Vita Sua*, 595. 'The grace of the Spirit sent us, many shepherds and members of the flock inviting.' See, however, on Gregory's episcopate at Nazianzus, IV. 26 and note.
[2] Cf. Zosimus, IV.; Sozom. VII. 4; Am. Marcellinus, XXXI. 9 and 10.
[3] Cf. Zosimus, IV. 39, on the dangerous illness of Theodosius. On delayed baptism, called 'clinic,' see I. 39, note 2. Evidently baptism was not thought essential to one's title to be called a Christian. Theodosius and Constantine were both considered Christians and 'professed the homoousian faith, and yet they both postponed their baptism to what they believed to be the latest moments of their lives.'

[4] 380 A.D.
[1] It appears from several places in Gregory's writings (cf. *Somn. de Anastasia, Ad Popul. Anast.* and *Carmen de Vita Sua*, 1709) that he himself had used the name of Anastasia in speaking of the church, so that Socrates' statement that it was so called afterwards must be taken as inaccurate. It also appears that Gregory gave the name *Anastasia* to the house which he used as a church, and meant to signify by the name (Anastation = Resurrection) the resurrection of the orthodox community of Constantinople. It is possible, of course, that Socrates here means that the emperors later adopted the name given by Gregory on the occasion of building a large church in place of the original chapel. See also on Gregory's stay at Constantinople Sozom. VII. 5; Philostorgius, IX. 19; Theodoret, V. 8.
[2] Cf. Philostorgius, IX. 10 and 14, whence it appears that Demophilus was the Arian bishop who succeeded Eudoxius in Constantinople.
[3] Matt. x. 23.

import of the sacred oracle is that such as would avoid the course of this world must seek the heavenly Jerusalem.[4] He therefore went outside the city gates, and there in future held his assemblies. With him also Lucius went out, who being ejected from Alexandria, as we have before related,[5] had made his escape to Constantinople, and there abode. Thus the Arians, after having been in possession of the churches for forty years, were in consequence of their opposition to the peace proposed by the emperor Theodosius, driven out of the city, in Gratian's fifth consulate,[6] and the first of Theodosius Augustus, on the 26th of November. The adherents of the 'homoousian' faith in this manner regained possession of the churches.

CHAPTER VIII.

A Synod consisting of One Hundred and Fifty Bishops meets at Constantinople. The Decrees passed. Ordination of Nectarius.

THE emperor making no delay summoned a Synod[1] of the prelates of his own faith, in order that he might establish the Nicene Creed, and appoint a bishop of Constantinople: and inasmuch as he was not without hope that he might win the Macedonians over to his own views, he invited those who presided over that sect to be present also. There met therefore on this occasion of the Homoousian party, Timothy from Alexandria, Cyril from Jerusalem, who at that time recognized the doctrine of *homoousion*,[2] having retracted his former opinion; Melitius from Antioch, he having arrived there previously to assist at the installation of Gregory; Ascholius also from Thessalonica, and many others, amounting in all to one hundred and fifty. Of the Macedonians, the leaders were Eleusius of Cyzicus, and Marcian of Lampsacus; these with the rest, most of whom came from the cities of the Hellespont, were thirty-six in number. Accordingly they were assembled in the month of May, under the consulate[3] of Eucharius and Evagrius, and the emperor used his utmost exertions, in conjunction with the bishops who entertained similar sentiments to

his own, to bring over Eleusius and his adherents to his own side. They were reminded of the deputation they had sent by Eustathius to Liberius[4] then bishop of Rome; that they had of their own accord not long before entered into promiscuous communion with the orthodox; and the inconsistency and fickleness of their conduct was represented to them, in now attempting to subvert the faith which they once acknowledged, and professed agreement with the catholics in. But they paying little heed alike to admonitions and reproofs, chose rather to maintain the Arian dogma, than to assent to the 'homoousian' doctrine. Having made this declaration, they departed from Constantinople; moreover they wrote to their partisans in every city, and charged them by no means to harmonize with the creed of the Nicene Synod. The bishops of the other party remaining at Constantinople, entered into a consultation about the ordination of a bishop; for Gregory, as we have before said,[5] had resigned that see, and was preparing to return to Nazianzus. Now there was a person named Nectarius, of a senatorial family, mild and gentle in his manners, and admirable in his whole course of life, although he at that time bore the office of prætor. This man was seized upon by the people, and elected[6] to the episcopate, and was ordained accordingly by one hundred and fifty bishops then present. The same prelates moreover published a decree,[7] prescribing 'that the bishop of Constantinople should have the next prerogative of honor after the bishop of Rome, because that city was New Rome.' They also again confirmed the Nicene Creed. Then too patriarchs were constituted, and the provinces distributed, so that no bishop might exercise any jurisdiction over other churches[8] out of his own diocese: for this had been often indiscriminately done before, in consequence of the persecutions. To Nectarius therefore was allotted the great city and Thrace. Helladius, the successor of

4 Cf. IV. 12. 5 See above, chap. 7.
6 See Bingham, *Christ. Antiq.* IV. 2. 8 for other examples illustrating this method of electing bishops.
7 Canon 3 of the Synod; see Hefele, *History of the Councils*, Vol. II. p. 357. The canon is given by Socrates entire and in the original words. Valesius holds that the primacy conferred by this canon on the Constantinopolitan see was one of honor merely, and involved no prerogatives of patriarchal or metropolitan jurisdiction. For a full discussion of its significance, see Hefele, as above. The Council of Chalcedon in 451 confirmed the above action in the following words: 'We following in all things the decision of the Holy Fathers, and acknowledging the canon of the one hundred and fifty bishops ... do also determine and decree the same things respecting the privileges of the most holy city of Constantinople, New Rome. For the Fathers properly gave the primacy to the throne of the elder Rome.' Canon 28.
8 Canon 2. The words 'patriarch,' however, and 'patriarchate' are not used in the canon. According to Sophocles (*Greek Lexicon*) the modern sense of these words was introduced at the close of the fourth century. Valesius holds that the sixth canon of the Nicene Council had given sanction to the principle of patriarchal authority; but Beveridge is of opinion that patriarchs were first constituted by the second general council. Hefele takes substantially the same position as Valesius. See discussion of the subject in Hefele, *Hist. of the Councils*, Vol. I. p. 389 *seq.*

4 A specimen of allegorical interpretation due to the influence of Origen. See Farrar, *Hist. of Interpretation*, p. 183 *seq.* For similar cases of allegorizing, see Huet, *Origeniana passim*, and De la Rue, *Origenis Opera*, App. 240–244.
5 IV. 37.
6 The same consulate as at the end of chap. 6; i.e. 380 A.D.
1 Cf. parallel account in Sozom. VII. 7–9; Theodoret, *H. E.* V. 8. The Synod of Constantinople was the second great œcumenical or general council. Its title as an œcumenical council has not been disputed, although no Western bishop attended. Baronius, however (*Annal.* 381, notes 19, 20), attempts to prove, but unsuccessfully, that Pope Damasus summoned the council. For a full account of the council, see Hefele, *History of the Councils*, Vol. II. p. 340–374.
2 Sozomen adds that Cyril was previously a follower of Macedonius, and had changed his mind at this time. Cf. Sozom. VII. 7.
3 381 A.D.

Basil in the bishopric of Cæsarea in Cappadocia, obtained the patriarchate of the diocese of Pontus in conjunction with Gregory Basil's brother, bishop of Nyssa[9] in Cappadocia, and Otreïus bishop of Melitina in Armenia. To Amphilochius of Iconium and Optimus of Antioch in Pisidia, was the Asiatic diocese assigned. The superintendence of the churches throughout Egypt was committed to Timothy of Alexandria. On Pelagius of Laodicea, and Diodorus of Tarsus, devolved the administration of the churches of the East; without infringement however on the prerogatives of honor reserved to the Antiochian church, and conferred on Melitius then present. They further decreed that as necessity required it, the ecclesiastical affairs of each province should be managed by a Synod of the province. These arrangements were confirmed by the emperor's approbation. Such was the result of this Synod.

CHAPTER IX.

The Body of Paul, Bishop of Constantinople, is honorably transferred from his Place of Exile. Death of Meletius.

THE emperor at that time caused to be removed from the city of Ancyra, the body of the bishop Paul, whom Philip the prefect of the Prætorium[1] had banished at the instigation of Macedonius, and ordered to be strangled at Cucusus a town of Armenia, as I have already mentioned.[2] He therefore received the remains with great reverence and honor, and deposited in the church which now takes its name from him; which the Macedonian party were formerly in possession of while they remained separate from the Arians, but were expelled at that time by the emperor, because they refused to adopt his sentiments. About this period Melitius, bishop of Antioch, fell sick and died: in whose praise Gregory, the brother of Basil, pronounced a funeral oration. The body of the deceased

bishop was by his friends conveyed to Antioch; where those who had identified themselves with his interests again refused subjection to Paulinus, but caused Flavian to be substituted in the place of Melitius, and the people began to quarrel anew. Thus again the Antiochian church was divided into rival factions, not grounded on any difference of faith, but simply on a preference of bishops.

CHAPTER X.

The Emperor orders a Convention composed of All the Various Sects. Arcadius is proclaimed Augustus. The Novatians permitted to hold their Assemblies in the City of Constantinople: Other Heretics driven out.

GREAT disturbances occurred in other cities also, as the Arians were ejected from the churches. But I cannot sufficiently admire the emperor's prudence in this contingency. For he was unwilling to fill the cities with disturbance, as far as this was dependent on him, and so after a very short time[1] he called together a general conference of the sects, thinking that by a discussion among their bishops, their mutual differences might be adjusted, and unanimity established. And this purpose of the emperor's I am persuaded was the reason that his affairs were so prosperous at that time. In fact by a special dispensation of Divine Providence the barbarous nations were reduced to subjection under him: and among others, Athanaric king of the Goths made a voluntary surrender of himself to him,[2] with all his people, and died soon after at Constantinople. At this juncture the emperor proclaimed his son Arcadius Augustus, on the sixteenth of January, in the second consulate[3] of Merobaudes and Saturnilus. Not long afterwards in the month of June, under the same consulate, the bishops of every sect arrived from all places: the emperor, therefore, sent for Nectarius the bishop, and consulted with him on the best means of freeing the Christian religion from dissensions, and reducing the church to a state of unity. 'The subjects of controversy,' said he, 'ought to be fairly discussed, that by the detection and removal of the sources of discord, a universal agreement may be effected.' Hearing this proposition Nectarius fell into uneasiness, and communicated it to Agelius bishop of the Novatians, inasmuch as he entertained the same sentiments as himself in matters of

---

[9] Cf. IV. 27. On Gregory of Nyssa, one of the most prominent of the ancient Fathers, see Smith & Wace, *Dict. of Christ. Biog.;* Schaff, *Hist. of the Christ. Church,* Vol. III. p. 903 *et seq.,* and sources mentioned in the work.

[1] Constantine made an advance on his predecessors by dividing the management of the empire among four prefects of the prætorium, which they had committed to two officers of that name. These four were apportioned as follows: one to the East, a second to Illyricum, a third to Italy, and a fourth to Gaul. Each of these prefects had a number of dioceses under him, and each diocese was a combination of several provinces into one territory. In conformity with this model of civil government, the church abandoned gradually and naturally its metropolitan administration of the provinces and adopted the diocesan. The exact time of the change is, of course, uncertain, it having come about gradually. It is safe, however, to put it between the Nicene and Constantinopolitan councils. The Fathers in the latter of those councils seem to find it in practical operation and confirm it (Cf. Canon 2 of the councils), decreeing explicitly that it should be unlawful for clerics to perform any office or transact any business in their official character outside of the bounds of the diocese wherein they were placed, just as it was unlawful for the civil officer to intermeddle in any affair outside the limits of his civil diocese.   [2] II. 26.

[1] Socrates according to his custom omits all mention of events in the Western Church. Some of them are quite important; e.g. the council of Aquileia called by the Emperor Gratian. See Hefele, *Hist. of Church Councils,* Vol. II. p. 375 *seq.*
[2] This was in 382 A.D. as appears from the *Fasti* of Idatius. Cf. also Zosimus, IV. 34, and Jerome, *Chronicon.*
[3] 383 A.D.

faith. This man, though eminently pious, was by no means competent to maintain a dispute on doctrinal points; he therefore proposed to refer the subject to Sisinnius[4] his reader, as a fit person to manage a conference. Sisinnius, who was not only learned, but possessed of great experience, and was well informed both in the expositions of the sacred Scriptures and the principles of philosophy, being convinced that disputations, far from healing divisions, usually create heresies of a more inveterate character, gave the following advice to Nectarius, knowing well that the ancients have nowhere attributed a beginning of existence to the Son of God, conceiving him to be co-eternal with the Father, he advised that they should avoid dialectic warfare and bring forward as evidences of the truth the testimonies of the ancients. 'Let the emperor,' said he, 'demand of the heads of each sect, whether they would pay any deference to the ancients who flourished before schism distracted the church; or whether they would repudiate them, as alienated from the Christian faith? If they reject their authority, then let them also anathematize them: and should they presume to take such a step, they would themselves be instantly thrust out by the people, and so the truth will be manifestly victorious. But if, on the other hand, they are not willing to set aside the fathers, it will then be our business to produce their books, by which our views will be fully attested.' Nectarius having heard these words of Sisinnius, hastened to the palace, and acquainted the emperor with the plan which had been suggested to him; who at once perceiving its wisdom and propriety, carried it into execution with consummate prudence. For without discovering his object, he simply asked the chiefs of the heretics whether they had any respect for and would accept the teachings of those teachers who lived previous to the dissension in the church? As they did not repudiate them, but replied that they highly revered them as their masters; the emperor enquired of them again whether they would defer to them as accredited witnesses of Christian doctrine? At this question, the leaders of the several parties, with their logical champions, — for many had come prepared for sophistical debate, — found themselves extremely embarrassed. For a division was caused among them as some acquiesced in the reasonableness of the emperor's proposition while others shrunk from it, conscious that it was by no means favorable to their interests: so that all being variously affected towards the writings of the ancients, they could no longer agree among themselves, dissenting not only from other sects, but those of the same sect differing from one another. Accordant malice therefore, like the tongue of the giants of old, was confounded, and their tower of mischief overturned.[5] The emperor perceiving by their confusion that their sole confidence was in subtle arguments, and that they feared to appeal to the expositions of the fathers, had recourse to another method: he commanded every sect to set forth in writing their own peculiar tenets. Accordingly those who were accounted the most skillful among them, drew up a statement of their respective creeds, couched in terms the most circumspect they could devise; a day was appointed, and the bishops selected for this purpose presented themselves at the palace. Nectarius and Agelius appeared as the defenders of the 'homoousian' faith; Demophilus supported the Arian dogma; Eunomius himself undertook the cause of the Eunomians; and Eleusius, bishop of Cyzicus, represented the opinions of those who were denominated Macedonians. The emperor gave them all a courteous reception; and receiving from each their written avowal of faith, he shut himself up alone, and prayed very earnestly that God would assist him in his endeavors to ascertain the truth. Then perusing with great care the statement which each had submitted to him, he condemned all the rest, inasmuch as they introduced a separation of the Trinity, and approved of that only which contained the doctrine of the *homoousion*. This decision caused the Novatians to flourish again, and hold their meetings within the city: for the emperor delighted with the agreement of their profession with that which he embraced, promulgated a law securing to them the peaceful possession of their own church buildings, and assigned to their churches equal privileges with those to which he gave his more especial sanction. But the bishops of the other sects, on account of their disagreement among themselves, were despised and censured even by their own followers: so that overwhelmed with perplexity and vexation they departed, addressing consolatory letters to their adherents, whom they exhorted not to be troubled because many had deserted them and gone over to the homoousian party; for they said, 'Many are called, but few chosen'[6] — an expression which they never used when on account of force and terror the majority of the people was on their side. Nevertheless the orthodox believers were not wholly exempt from inquietude; for the affairs of the Antiochian church caused divisions among those who were present at the Synod. The bishops of Egypt, Arabia and Cyprus, combined against Flavian,

---

[4] For a further account of Sisinnius, see VI. 22.

[5] Referring no doubt to the Tower of Babel and the dispersion of its builders, Gen. xi. 8.
[6] Matt. xx. 16.

and insisted on his expulsion from Antioch : but those of Palestine, Phœnicia, and Syria, contended with equal zeal in his favor. What result issued from this contest I shall describe in its proper place.[7]

CHAPTER XI.

The Emperor Gratian is slain by the Treachery of the Usurper Maximus. From Fear of him Justina ceases persecuting Ambrose.

NEARLY at the same time with the holding of these Synods at Constantinople, the following events occurred in the Western parts. Maximus, from the island of Britain, rebelled against the Roman empire, and attacked Gratian, who was then wearied and exhausted in a war with the Alemanni.[1] In Italy, Valentinian being still a minor, Probus, a man of consular dignity, had the chief administration of affairs, and was at that time prefect of the Prætorium. Justina, the mother of the young prince, who entertained Arian sentiments, as long as her husband lived had been unable to molest the Homoousians ; but going to Milan while her son was still young, she manifested great hostility to Ambrose the bishop, and commanded that he should be banished.[2] While the people from their excessive attachment to Ambrose, were offering resistance to those who were charged with taking him into exile, intelligence was brought that Gratian had been assassinated by the treachery of the usurper Maximus. In fact Andragathius, a general under Maximus, having concealed himself in a litter resembling a couch, which was carried by mules, ordered his guards to spread a report before him that the litter contained the Emperor Gratian's wife. They met the emperor near the city of Lyons in France just as he had crossed the river : who believing it to be his wife, and not suspecting any treachery, fell into the hands of his enemy as a blind man into the ditch ; for Andragathius, suddenly springing forth from the litter, slew him.[3] Gratian thus perished in the consulate of Merogaudes and Saturninus,[4] in the twenty-fourth year of his age, and the fifteenth of his reign. When this happened the Empress Justina's indignation against Ambrose was repressed. Afterwards Valentinian most unwillingly, but constrained by the necessity of the time, admitted Maximus as his colleague in the empire. Probus alarmed at the power of Maximus, resolved to retreat into the regions of the

East : leaving Italy therefore, he proceeded to Illyricum, and fixed his residence at Thessalonica a city of Macedonia.

CHAPTER XII.

While the Emperor Theodosius is engaged in Military Preparations against Maximus, his Son Honorius is born. He then proceeds to Milan in Order to encounter the Usurper.

BUT the Emperor Theodosius was filled with great solicitude, and levied a powerful army against the usurper, fearing lest he should meditate the assassination of the young Valentinian also. While engaged in this preparation, an embassy arrived from the Persians, requesting peace from the emperor. Then also the empress Flaccilla bore him a son named Honorius, on the 9th of September, in the consulate of Richomelius and Clearchus.[1] Under the same consulate, and a little previously, Agelius bishop of the Novatians died.[2] In the year following, wherein Arcadius Augustus bore his first consulate in conjunction with Baudon,[3] Timothy bishop of Alexandria died, and was succeeded in the episcopate by Theophilus. About a year after this, Demophilus the Arian prelate having departed this life, the Arians sent for Marinus a leader of their own heresy out of Thrace, to whom they entrusted the bishopric : but Marinus did not long occupy that position, for under him that sect was divided into two parties, as we shall hereafter explain ;[4] for they invited Dorotheus[5] to come to them from Antioch in Syria, and constituted him their bishop. Meanwhile the emperor Theodosius proceeded to the war against Maximus, leaving his son Arcadius with imperial authority at Constantinople. Accordingly arriving at Thessalonica he found Valentinian and those about him in great anxiety, because through compulsion they had acknowledged the usurper as emperor. Theodosius, however, gave no expression to his sentiments in public ; he neither rejected nor admitted[6] the embassy of Maximus : but unable to endure tyrannical domination over the Roman empire, under the assumption of an imperial name, he hastily mustered his forces and advanced to Milan,[7] whither the usurper had already gone.

---

[7] Below, chap. 15.   [1] Cf. Zosimus, IV. 35 *seq.*
[2] Cf. IV. 30.
[3] The account of Gratian's death given by Zosimus, though not inconsistent with that of Socrates, does not contain the details given by Socrates. Andragathius is simply said to have pursued Gratian, and overtaking him near the bridge to have slain him. Cf. Zosimus, IV. 35 end.   [4] 383 A.D.

[1] 384 A.D. Honorius afterwards shared the empire with Arcadius, reigning in the West from 398 to 423 A.D. But although the whole of this period comes within the time of Socrates' history, he does not mention Honorius but once again before his death.
[2] Having been bishop of the Novatians for forty years; see chap. 21.
[3] 385 A.D.   [4] Chap. 23.
[5] Being in the ninety-eighth year of his age as appears from VII. 6.
[6] Zosimus, however, says (IV. 37) that the embassy of Maximus was received by Theodosius.
[7] Rather Aquileja as appears from Zosimus and other historians.

CHAPTER XIII.

The Arians excite a Tumult at Constantinople.

AT the time when the emperor was thus occupied on his military expedition, the Arians excited a great tumult at Constantinople by such devices as these. Men are fond of fabricating statements respecting matters about which they are in ignorance; and if at any time they are given occasion they swell to a prodigious extent rumors concerning what they wish, being ever fond of change. This was strongly exemplified at Constantinople on the present occasion: for each invented news concerning the war which was carrying on at a distance, according to his own caprice, always presuming upon the most disastrous results; and before the contest had yet commenced, they spoke of transactions in reference to it, of which they knew nothing, with as much assurance as if they had been spectators on the very scene of action. Thus it was confidently affirmed that 'the usurper had defeated the emperor's army,' even the number of men slain on both sides being specified; and that 'the emperor himself had nearly fallen into the usurper's hands.' Then the Arians, who had been excessively exasperated by those being put in possession of the churches within the city who had previously been the objects of their persecution, began to augment these rumors by additions of their own. But since the currency of such stories with increasing exaggeration, in time made even the farmers themselves believe them — for those who had circulated them from hearsay, affirmed to the authors of these falsehoods, that the accounts they had received from them had been fully corroborated elsewhere; then indeed the Arians were emboldened to commit acts of violence, and among other outrages, to set fire to the house of Nectarius the bishop. This was done in the second consulate[1] of Theodosius Augustus, which he bore with Cynegius.

CHAPTER XIV.

Overthrow and Death of the Usurper Maximus.

As the emperor marched against the usurper the intelligence of the formidable preparations made by him so alarmed the troops under Maximus, that instead of fighting for him, they delivered him bound to the emperor, who caused him to be put to death, on the twenty-seventh of August, under the same consulate.[1] Andra-

gathius, who with his own hand had slain Gratian, understanding the fate of Maximus, precipitated himself into the adjacent river, and was drowned. Then the victorious emperors made their public entry into Rome, accompanied by Honorius the son of Theodosius, still a mere boy, whom his father had sent for from Constantinople immediately after Maximus had been vanquished. They continued therefore at Rome celebrating their triumphal festivals: during which time the Emperor Theodosius exhibited a remarkable instance of clemency toward Symmachus, a man who had borne the consular office, and was at the head of the senate at Rome. For this Symmachus was distinguished for his eloquence, and many of his orations are still extant composed in the Latin tongue: but inasmuch as he had written a panegyric on Maximus, and pronounced it before him publicly, he was afterwards impeached for high treason; wherefore to escape capital punishment he took sanctuary in a church.[2] The emperor's veneration for religion led him not only to honor the bishops of his own communion, but to treat with consideration those of the Novatians also, who embraced the 'homoousian' creed: to gratify therefore Leontius the bishop of the Novatian church at Rome, who interceded in behalf of Symmachus, he graciously pardoned him for that crime. Symmachus, after he had obtained his pardon, wrote an apologetic address to the Emperor Theodosius. Thus the war, which at its commencement threatened so seriously, was brought to a speedy termination.

CHAPTER XV.

Of Flavian Bishop of Antioch.

ABOUT the same period, the following events took place at Antioch in Syria. After the death of Paulinus, the people who had been under his superintendence refused to submit to the authority of Flavian, but caused Evagrius to be ordained bishop of their own party.[1] As he did not survive his ordination long, no other was constituted in his place, Flavian having brought this about: nevertheless those who disliked Flavian on account of his having violated his oath, held their assemblies apart.[2] Meanwhile Flavian 'left no stone unturned,' as the phrase is, to bring these also under his control; and this he soon after effected, when he appeased the anger of Theophilus, then bishop of Alex-

---

1 388 A.D.
1 The same account is given in substance by Zosimus, IV. 46, who also confirms the statements of Socrates concerning the end of Andragathius. Valesius, however, relying on Idatius' *Fasti*, asserts that Maximus was put to death on the 28th of July, not on the 27th of August.

2 The churches were considered recognized places of asylum. Cf. Bingham, *Christ. Antiq.* VIII. 10 and 11.
1 Theodoret (*H. E.* V. 23) says that there was a double violation of order in the ordination of Evagrius; first in that he was ordained by his predecessor, and secondly in that he was ordained by one bishop, whereas the canon required that not less than three should take part in an episcopal ordination.
2 Cf. VI. 9; also chaps. 5 and 11 of this book.

andria, by whose mediation he conciliated Damasus bishop of Rome also. For both these had been greatly displeased with Flavian, as well for the perjury of which he had been guilty, as for the schism he had occasioned among the previously united people. Theophilus therefore being pacified, sent Isidore a presbyter to Rome, and thus reconciled Damasus, who was still offended; representing to him the propriety of overlooking Flavian's past misconduct, for the sake of producing concord among the people. Communion being in this way restored to Flavian, the people of Antioch were in the course of a little while induced to acquiesce in the union secured. Such was the conclusion of this affair at Antioch. But the Arians of that city being ejected from the churches, were accustomed to hold their meetings in the suburbs. Meanwhile Cyril bishop of Jerusalem having died about this time,[3] was succeeded by John.

CHAPTER XVI.

Demolition of the Idolatrous Temples at Alexandria, and the Consequent Conflict between the Pagans and Christians.

AT the solicitation of Theophilus bishop of Alexandria the emperor issued an order at this time for the demolition of the heathen temples in that city; commanding also that it should be put in execution under the direction of Theophilus. Seizing this opportunity, Theophilus exerted himself to the utmost to expose the pagan mysteries to contempt. And to begin with, he caused the Mithreum[1] to be cleaned out, and exhibited to public view the tokens of its bloody mysteries. Then he destroyed the Serapeum, and the bloody rights of the Mithreum he publicly caricatured; the Serapeum also he showed full of extravagant superstitions, and he had the phalli of Priapus carried through the midst of the forum. The pagans of Alexandria, and especially the professors of philosophy, were unable to repress their rage at this exposure, and exceeded in revengeful ferocity their outrages on a former occasion: for with one accord, at a preconcerted signal, they rushed impetuously upon the Christians, and murdered every one they could lay hands on. The Christians also made an attempt to resist the assailants, and so the mischief was the more augmented. This desperate affray was prolonged until satiety of bloodshed put an end to it. Then it was discovered that very few of the heathens had been killed, but a great number of Christians; while the number of wounded on each side was almost innumerable. Fear then possessed the pagans on account of what

was done, as they considered the emperor's displeasure. For having done what seemed good in their own eyes, and by their bloodshed having quenched their courage, some fled in one direction, some in another, and many quitting Alexandria, dispersed themselves in various cities. Among these were the two grammarians Helladius and Ammonius, whose pupil I was in my youth at Constantinople.[2] Helladius was said to be the priest of Jupiter, and Ammonius of Simius.[3] Thus this disturbance having been terminated, the governor of Alexandria, and the commander-in-chief of the troops in Egypt, assisted Theophilus in demolishing the heathen temples. These were therefore razed to the ground, and the images of their gods molten into pots and other convenient utensils for the use of the Alexandrian church; for the emperor had instructed Theophilus to distribute them for the relief of the poor. All the images were accordingly broken to pieces, except one statue of the god before mentioned, which Theophilus preserved and set up in a public place; 'Lest,' said he, 'at a future time the heathens should deny that they had ever worshiped such gods.' This action gave great umbrage to Ammonius the grammarian in particular, who to my knowledge was accustomed to say that 'the religion of the Gentiles was grossly abused in that that single statue was not also molten, but preserved, in order to render that religion ridiculous.' Helladius however boasted in the presence of some that he had slain in that desperate onset nine men with his own hand. Such were the doings at Alexandria at that time.

CHAPTER XVII.

Of the Hieroglyphics found in the Temple of Serapis.

WHEN the Temple of Serapis was torn down and laid bare, there were found in it, engraven on stones, certain characters which they call hieroglyphics, having the forms of crosses.[1] Both the Christians and pagans on seeing them, appropriated and applied them to their respective religions: for the Christians who affirm that the cross is the sign of Christ's saving passion,

---

[3] In 386 A.D.   [1] See III. 2.

[2] Cf. Introd. p. 8.   [3] πιθήκου, 'the ape-god.'
[1] There are several cruciform signs among the Egyptian hieroglyphics, as e.g. the simple determinative ✕, meaning 'to cross,' 'to multiply,' 'to mix' (see Birch, *Egyptian Texts*, p. 99); or the syllabic ✚, phonetically equivalent to *am* (see Birch, *ibid.* p. 101); or the cross with a ring at the head ♀; or the still more elaborate ⚥ (see Brugsh, *Thesaurus Inscript. Egyptiacarum*, p. 20; also Champollion, *Grammaire Egyptienne*, XII. p. 365, 440). To which of these Socrates refers it is impossible to say from their mere form. They occur commonly and we must infer that the discovery described in this passage is not the first bringing into light of the sign mentioned, but its occurrence in the Serapeum. The third of the above signs is usually interpreted as 'life' either 'happy' or 'immortal,' which agrees with the meaning given to the cruciform sign here mentioned.

claimed this character as peculiarly theirs; but the pagans alleged that it might appertain to Christ and Serapis in common; 'for,' said they, 'it symbolizes one thing to Christians and another to heathens.' Whilst this point was controverted amongst them, some of the heathen converts to Christianity, who were conversant with these heiroglyphic characters, interpreted the form of a cross and said that it signifies ' Life to come.' This the Christians exultingly laid hold of, as decidedly favorable to their religion. But after other hieroglyphics had been deciphered containing a prediction that ' When the cross should appear,' — for this was ' life to come,' — ' the Temple of Serapis would be destroyed,' a very great number of the pagans embraced Christianity, and confessing their sins, were baptized. Such are the reports I have heard respecting the discovery of this symbol in form of a cross. But I cannot imagine that the Egyptian priests foreknew the things concerning Christ, when they engraved the figure of a cross. For if ' the advent' of our Saviour into the world ' was a mystery hid from ages and from generations,'[2] as the apostle declares; and if the devil himself, the prince of wickedness, knew nothing of it, his ministers, the Egyptian priests, are likely to have been still more ignorant of the matter; but Providence doubtless purposed that in the enquiry concerning this character, there should something take place analogous to what happened heretofore at the preaching of Paul. For he, made wise by the Divine Spirit, employed a similar method in relation to the Athenians,[3] and brought over many of them to the faith, when on reading the inscription on one of their altars, he accommodated and applied it to his own discourse. Unless indeed any one should say, that the Word of God wrought in the Egyptian priests, as it did on Balaam[4] and Caïaphas;[5] for these men uttered prophecies of good things in spite of themselves. This will suffice on the subject.

CHAPTER XVIII.

Reformation of Abuses at Rome by the Emperor Theodosius.

THE emperor Theodosius during his short stay in Italy, conferred the greatest benefit on the city of Rome, by grants on the one hand, and abrogations on the other. His largesses were indeed very munificent; and he removed two most infamous abuses which existed in the city. One of them was the following: there were buildings of immense magnitude, erected in ancient Rome in former times, in which bread was made for distribution among the people.[1] Those who had the charge of these edifices, who Mancipes[2] were called in the Latin language, in process of time converted them into receptacles for thieves. Now as the bake-houses in these structures were placed underneath, they build taverns at the side of each, where they kept prostitutes; by which means they entrapped many of those who went thither either for the sake of refreshment, or to gratify their lusts, for by a certain mechanical contrivance they precipitated them from the tavern into the bake-house below. This was practiced chiefly upon strangers; and such as were in this way kidnapped were compelled to work in the bake-houses, where many of them were immured until old age, not being allowed to go out, and giving the impression to their friends that they were dead. It happened that one of the soldiers of the emperor Theodosius fell into this snare; who being shut up in the bake-house, and hindered from going out, drew a dagger which he wore and killed those who stood in his way: the rest being terrified, suffered him to escape. When the emperor was made acquainted with the circumstance he punished the Mancipes, and ordered these haunts of lawless and abandoned characters to be pulled down. This was one of the disgraceful nuisances of which the emperor purged the imperial city: the other was of this nature. When a woman was detected in adultery, they punished the delinquent not in the way of correction but rather of aggravation of her crime. For shutting her up in a narrow brothel, they obliged her to prostitute herself in a most disgusting manner; causing little bells to be rung at the time of the unclean deed that those who passed by might not be ignorant of what was doing within. This was doubtless intended to brand the crime with greater ignominy in public opinion. As soon as the emperor was apprised of this indecent usage, he would by no means tolerate it; but having ordered the *Sistra*[3] — for so these places of penal prostitution were denominated — to be pulled down, he appointed other laws for the punishment of adulteresses.[4]

---

[1] In the earlier periods of Roman history the government undertook to regulate the price of corn, so as to protect the poorer classes; in time of scarcity the government was to purchase the grain and sell it at a moderate price. This provision was gradually changed into a dispensation of public charity, at first by the sale of the grain below cost, and afterwards by the gratuitous distribution of the same. Some time before the reign of Aurelian, 270–275. A.D., the distribution of grain seems to have given place to the distribution of bread. Such distribution was made after the reign of Constantine at Constantinople as well as at Rome. See Smith, *Dict. of the Greek and Rom. Antiq.*, art. *Leges Frumentariæ.*

[2] Originally this name was applied to all farmers-general of the public revenues. See Smith, *Dict. of Greek and Rom. Antiq.*, art. MANCEPS.

[3] Lit. = ' bells.' Cf. Smith, *Dict. of Greek and Rom. Antiq.*, art. SISTRUM.

[4] From a law of Constantine's (*Cod.* 9. 30) whose genuineness is, however, disputed, the punishment of adultery was death. The

---

[2] 1 Cor. ii. 7, 8; Eph. iii. 5, 6; Col. i. 26.
[3] Acts xvii. 23.　　　[4] Num. xxiv.　　　[5] John xi. 51.

Thus did the emperor Theodosius free the city from two of its most discreditable abuses: and when he had arranged all other affairs to his satisfaction, he left the emperor Valentinian at Rome, and returned himself with his son Honorius to Constantinople, and entered that city of the 10th of November, in the consulate of Tatian and Symmachus.[5]

CHAPTER XIX.

Of the Office of Penitentiary Presbyters and its Abolition.

At this time it was deemed requisite to abolish the office of those presbyters in the churches who had charge of the penitences:[1] this was done on the following account. When the Novatians separated themselves from the Church because they would not communicate with those who had lapsed during the persecution under Decius, the bishops added to the ecclesiastical canon[2] a presbyter of penitence in order that those who had sinned after baptism might confess their sins in the presence of the presbyter thus appointed.[3] And this mode of discipline is still maintained among other heretical institutions by all the rest of the sects; the Homoousians only, together with the Novatians who hold the same doctrinal views, have abandoned it. The latter indeed would never admit of its establishment:[4] and the Homoousians who are now in possession of the churches, after retaining this function for a considerable period, abrogated it in the time of Nectarius, in consequence of an event which occurred in the Constantinopolitan church, which is as follows: A woman of noble family coming to the penitentiary, made a general confession of those sins she had committed since her baptism: and the presbyter enjoined fasting and prayer continually, that together with the acknowledgment of error, she might have to show works also meet for repentance. Some time after this, the same lady again presented herself, and confessed that she had been guilty of another crime, a deacon of the church having slept with her. When this was proved the deacon was ejected from the church:[5] but the

people were very indignant, being not only offended at what had taken place, but also because the deed had brought scandal and degradation upon the Church. When in consequence of this, ecclesiastics were subjected to taunting and reproach, Eudæmon a presbyter of the church, by birth an Alexandrian, persuaded Nectarius the bishop to abolish the office of penitentiary presbyter, and to leave every one to his own conscience with regard to the participation of the sacred mysteries:[6] for thus only, in his judgment, could the Church be preserved from obloquy. Having heard this explanation of the matter from Eudæmon I have ventured to put it in the present treatise: for as I have often remarked,[7] I have spared no pains to procure an authentic account of affairs from those who were best acquainted with them, and to scrutinize every report, lest I should advance what might be untrue. My observation to Eudæmon, when he first related the circumstance, was this: 'Whether, O presbyter, your counsel has been profitable for the Church or otherwise, God knows; but I see that it takes away the means of rebuking one another's faults, and prevents our acting upon that precept of the apostle,[8] "Have no fellowship with the unfruitful works of darkness, but rather reprove them."' Concerning this affair let this suffice.

CHAPTER XX.

Divisions among the Arians and Other Heretics.

I conceive it right moreover not to leave unnoticed the proceedings of the other religious bodies, viz. the Arians,[1] Novatians, and those who received their denominations from Macedonius and Eunomius. For the Church once being divided, rested not in that schism, but the separatists taking occasion from the slightest and most frivolous pretences, disagreed among themselves. The manner and time, as well as the causes for which they raised mutual dissensions, we will state as we proceed. But let it be observed here, that the emperor Theodosius persecuted none of them except Eunomius; but inasmuch as the latter, by holding meetings in private houses at Constantinople, where he read

---

same punishment appears to have been inflicted in specific cases mentioned by Am. Marcellinus. *Rerum Gestarum*, XXVII. 1. 28. Whence it appears that Socrates must have been misinformed concerning the facts mentioned here.

[5] 391 A.D.

[1] On account of which he was called the Penitentiary. Cf. Bingham, *Christ. Antiq.* XVIII. 3.

[2] 'The sacerdotal catalogue or order, clerical order, the clergy in general.' See Sophocles, *Greek Lex. of the Rom. and Byzant. Periods.*

[3] On the discipline of the ancient church, see Bennett, *Christ. Archæol.* p. 380 *seq.*

[4] See Euseb. *H. R.* VI. 43.

[5] The regulation of the earliest church was expressed as follows: 'If any bishop, presbyter, or deacon be found guilty of fornication . . . let him be deposed.' *Apostol. Can.* 25.

[6] Although the plural is used here, the reference is, no doubt, to the sacrament of the Lord's supper only. The mysteries recognized by Theodorus Studites, *Epist.* II. 165, are six; i.e. baptism, eucharist, unction, orders, monastic tonsure, and the mystery of death or funeral ceremonies. The Greek Church of modern times enumerates seven: baptism, unction, eucharist, orders, penitence, marriage, and extreme unction.

[7] Cf. I. 1; II. 1.

[8] Eph. v. 11. Valesius rightly infers from this answer of Socrates to Eudæmon that the former was not a Novatian. For he disapproves of the abolition of the penitentiary bishop's office, whereas as a Novatian he would have been against its institution before it was established, and in favor of its abolition afterwards. The Novatians never admitted either of penitence or of the penitentiary bishop.

[1] See chap. 23 of this book.

the works he had composed, corrupted many with his doctrines, he ordered him to be sent into exile. Of the other heretics he interfered with no one ; nor did he constrain them to hold communion with himself; but he allowed them all to assemble in their own conventicles, and to entertain their own opinions on points of Christian faith. Permission to build themselves churches without the cities was granted to the rest : but inasmuch as the Novatians held sentiments precisely identical with his own as to faith, he ordered that they should be suffered to continue unmolested in their churches within the cities, as I have before noticed.[2] Concerning these I think it opportune, however, to give in this place some farther account, and shall therefore retrace a few circumstances in their history.

CHAPTER XXI.

Peculiar Schism among the Novatians.[1]

Of the Novatian church at Constantinople Agelius was the bishop for the space of forty years,[2] viz. from the reign of Constantine until the sixth year of that of the emperor Theodosius, as I have stated somewhere previously.[3] He perceiving his end approaching, ordained Sisinnius to succeed him in the bishopric.[4] This person was a presbyter of the church over which Agelius presided, remarkably eloquent, and had been instructed in philosophy by Maximus, at the same time as the emperor Julian. Now as the Novatian laity were dissatisfied with this election, and wished rather that he had ordained Marcian, a man of eminent piety, on account of whose influence their sect had been left unmolested during the reign of Valens, Agelius therefore to allay his people's discontent, laid his hands on Marcian also. Having recovered a little from his illness, he went to the church and thus of his own accord addressed the congregation : 'After my decease let Marcian be your bishop ; and after Marcian, Sisinnius.' He survived these words but a short time ; Marcian accordingly having been constituted bishop of the Novatians, a division arose in their church also, from this cause. Marcian had promoted to the rank of presbyter a converted Jew named Sabbatius, who nevertheless continued to retain many of his Jewish prejudices ; and moreover he was very ambitious of being made a bishop. Having therefore confidentially attached to his interest two presbyters,

Theoctistus and Macarius, who were cognizant of his designs, he resolved to defend that innovation made by the Novatians in the time of Valens, at Pazum a village of Phrygia, concerning the festival of Easter, to which I have already adverted.[5] And in the first place, under pretext of more ascetic austerity, he privately withdrew from the church, saying that 'he was grieved on account of certain persons whom he suspected of being unworthy of participation in the sacrament.' It was however soon discovered that his object was to hold assemblies apart. When Marcian understood this, he bitterly censured his own error, in ordaining to the presbyterate persons so intent on vain-glory ; and frequently said, 'That it had been better for him to have laid his hands on thorns, than to have imposed them on Sabbatius.' To check his proceedings, he procured a Synod of Novatian bishops to be convened at Angarum,[6] a commercial town near Helenopolis in Bithynia. On assembling here they summoned Sabbatius, and desired him to explain the cause of his discontent. Upon his affirming that he was troubled about the disagreement that existed respecting the Feast of Easter, and that it ought to be kept according to the custom of the Jews, and agreeable to that sanction which those convened at Pazum had appointed, the bishops present at the Synod perceiving that this assertion was a mere subterfuge to disguise his desire after the episcopal chair, obliged him to pledge himself on oath that he would never accept a bishopric. When he had so sworn, they passed a canon respecting this feast, which they entitled 'indifferent,' declaring that 'a disagreement on such a point was not a sufficient reason for separation from the church ; and that the council of Pazum had done nothing prejudicial to the catholic canon. That although the ancients who lived nearest to the times of the apostles differed about the observance of this festival, it did not prevent their communion with one another, nor create any dissension. Besides that the Novatians at imperial Rome had never followed the Jewish usage, but always kept Easter after the equinox ; and yet they did not separate from those of their own faith, who celebrated it on a different day.' From these and many such considerations, they made the 'Indifferent' Canon, above-mentioned, concerning Easter, whereby every one was at liberty to keep the custom which he had by predilection in this matter, if he so pleased ; and that it should make no difference as regards communion, but even though celebrating differently they should be in accord in the church. After this rule had been thus

---

[2] See chap. 10, above.
[1] The main reason adduced for considering Socrates a Novatian is his peculiarly detailed account of the Novatian heresy, and the nearness in which he puts it to the orthodox faith. See Introd. p. ix and chap. 19 of this book, note 8; also II. 38 and VI. 21.
[2] See above, chap. 12, note 2. This was in 384 A.D.
[3] IV. 9 and 12 of this book.
[4] On he irregularity of this action, see chap. 15 above, note 1. Sisinnius is again mentioned in VI. 1. 31; VII. 6 and 12.

[5] Cf. IV. 28.
[6] Probably the modern Angora. Valesius, however, had conjecturally substituted the word Sangarum in this place, supposing that the place named was a town on the banks of the river Sangarius.

established, Sabbatius being bound by his oath, anticipated the fast by keeping it in private, whenever any discrepancy existed in the time of the Paschal solemnity, and having watched all night, he celebrated the sabbath of the passover; then on the next day he went to church, and with the rest of the congregation partook of the sacraments. He pursued this course for many years, so that it could not be concealed from the people; in imitation of which some of the more ignorant, and chiefly the Phrygians and Galatians, supposing they should be justified by this conduct imitated him, and kept the passover in secret after his manner. But Sabbatius afterwards disregarding the oath by which he had renounced the episcopal dignity, held schismatic meetings, and was constituted bishop of his followers, as we shall show hereafter.[7]

CHAPTER XXII.

The Author's Views respecting the Celebration of Easter, Baptism, Fasting, Marriage, the Eucharist, and Other Ecclesiastical Rites.

As we have touched the subject I deem it not unreasonable to say a few words concerning Easter. It appears to me that neither the ancients nor moderns who have affected to follow the Jews, have had any rational foundation for contending so obstinately about it. For they have not taken into consideration the fact that when Judaism was changed into Christianity, the obligation to observe the Mosaic law and the ceremonial types ceased. And the proof of the matter is plain; for no law of Christ permits Christians to imitate the Jews. On the contrary the apostle expressly forbids it; not only rejecting circumcision, but also deprecating contention about festival days. In his epistle to the Galatians[1] he writes, 'Tell me, ye that desire to be under the law, do ye not hear the law?' And continuing his train of argument, he demonstrates that the Jews were in bondage as servants, but that those who have come to Christ are 'called into the liberty of sons.'[2] Moreover he exhorts them in no way to regard 'days, and months, and years.'[3] Again in his epistle to the Colossians[4] he distinctly declares, that such observances are merely shadows: wherefore he says, 'Let no man judge you in meat, or in drink, or in respect of any holy-day, or of the new moon, or of the sabbath-days; which are a shadow of things to come.' The same truths are also confirmed by him in the epistle to the Hebrews[5] in these words: 'For the priesthood being changed,

there is made of necessity a change also of the law.' Neither the apostles, therefore, nor the Gospels,[6] have anywhere imposed the 'yoke of servitude'[7] on those who have embraced the truth; but have left Easter and every other feast to be honored by the gratitude of the recipients of grace. Wherefore, inasmuch as men love festivals, because they afford them cessation from labor: each individual in every place, according to his own pleasure, has by a prevalent custom celebrated the memory of the saving passion. The Saviour and his apostles have enjoined us by no law to keep this feast: nor do the Gospels and apostles threaten us with any penalty, punishment, or curse for the neglect of it, as the Mosaic law does the Jews. It is merely for the sake of historical accuracy, and for the reproach of the Jews, because they polluted themselves with blood on their very feasts, that it is recorded in the Gospels that our Saviour suffered in the days of 'unleavened bread.'[8] The aim of the apostles was not to appoint festival days, but to teach a righteous life and piety. And it seems to me that just as many other customs have been established in individual localities according to usage. So also the feast of Easter came to be observed in each place according to the individual peculiarities of the peoples inasmuch as none of the apostles legislated on the matter. And that the observance originated not by legislation, but as a custom the facts themselves indicate. In Asia Minor most people kept the fourteenth day of the moon, disregarding the sabbath: yet they never separated from those who did otherwise, until Victor, bishop of Rome, influenced by too ardent a zeal, fulminated a sentence of excommunication against the Quartodecimans[9] in Asia. Wherefore also Irenæus, bishop of Lyons in France, severely censured Victor by letter for his immoderate heat;[10] telling him that although the ancients differed in their celebration of Easter, they did not desist from intercommunion. Also that Polycarp, bishop of Smyrna, who afterwards suffered martyrdom under Gordian,[11] continued to communicate with Anicetus bishop of Rome, although he himself, accord-

6 ὁ ἀπόστολος . . . τὰ εὐαγγέλια, the two parts of the New Testament, speaking generally. See Sophocles' *Greek Lex. of the Rom. and Byzant. Periods* under ἀπόστολος and εὐαγγέλιον.
7 Gal. v. 1.
8 Matt. xxvi. 2; Mark xiv. 1; Luke xxii. 1.
9 τεσσαρεσκαιδεκατῖται, those who observed Easter on the fourteenth day of the lunar month (Nisan of the Jewish calendar). On the Quartodeciman controversy, see Schürer, *de Controversiis Paschalibus secundo post Christum natum Sæculo exortis*; also, Salmon, *Introduction to the New Testament*, 3 ed. p. 252–267.
10 Irenæus, *Hær.* III. 3, 4.
11 Polycarp suffered martyrdom in 156 A.D. (see Lightfoot, *Apostolic Fathers*, Part II. Vol. I. p. 629–702, containing conclusive proof of this, as well as a history of the question); whence it appears that it was under Antoninus Pius that he died. Valesius therefore infers that Socrates meant to speak of Irenæus as suffering martyrdom under Gordian, and not of Polycarp. If this be the case, we must assume a serious corruption of the text, or an unparalleled confusion in Socrates.

7 Cf. VII. 5 and 12.
1 Gal. iv. 21.
2 Gal. v. 13.
3 Gal. iv. 10.
4 Col. ii. 16, 17.
5 Heb. vii. 12.

ing to the usage of his native Smyrna, kept Easter on the fourteenth day of the moon, as Eusebius attests in the fifth book of his *Ecclesiastical History*.[12] While therefore some in Asia Minor observed the day above-mentioned, others in the East kept that feast on the sabbath indeed, but differed as regards the month. The former thought the Jews should be followed, though they were not exact: the latter kept Easter after the equinox, refusing to celebrate with the Jews ; 'for,' said they, 'it ought to be celebrated when the sun is in Aries, in the month called Xanthicus by the Antiochians, and April by the Romans.' In this practice, they averred, they conformed not to the modern Jews, who are mistaken in almost everything, but to the ancients, and to Josephus according to what he has written in the third book of his *Jewish Antiquities*.[13] Thus these people were at issue among themselves. But all other Christians in the Western parts, and as far as the ocean itself, are found to have celebrated Easter after the equinox, from a very ancient tradition. And in fact these acting in this manner have never disagreed on this subject. It is not true, as some have pretended, that the Synod under Constantine altered this festival :[14] for Constantine himself, writing to those who differed respecting it, recommended that as they were few in number, they could agree with the majority of their brethren. His letter will be found at length in the third book of the *Life of Constantine* by Eusebius ; but the passage in it relative to Easter runs thus :[15]

' It is a becoming order which all the churches in the Western, Southern, and Northern parts of the world observe, and some places in the East also. Wherefore all on the present occasion have judged it right, and I have pledged myself that it will have the acquiescence of your prudence, that what is unanimously observed in the city of Rome, throughout Italy, Africa, and the whole of Egypt, in Spain, France, Britain, Libya, and all Greece, the diocese of Asia and Pontus, and Cilicia, your wisdom also will readily embrace ; considering not only that the number of churches in the aforesaid places is greater, but also that while there should be a universal concurrence in what is most reasonable, it becomes us to have nothing in common with the perfidious Jews.'

Such is the tenor of the emperor's letter. Moreover the Quartodecimans affirm that the observance of the fourteenth day was delivered to them by the apostle John : while the Romans and those in the Western parts assure us that their usage originated with the apostles Peter and Paul. Neither of these parties however can produce any written testimony in confirmation of what they assert. But that the time of keeping Easter in various places is dependent on usage, I infer from this, that those who agree in faith, differ among themselves on questions of usage. And it will not perhaps be unseasonable to notice here the diversity of customs in the churches.[16] The fasts before Easter will be found to be differently observed among different people. Those at Rome fast three successive weeks before Easter, excepting Saturdays and Sundays.[17] Those in Illyrica and all over Greece and Alexandria observe a fast of six weeks, which they term 'The forty days' fast.'[18] Others commencing their fast from the seventh week before Easter, and fasting three five days only, and that at intervals, yet call that time 'The forty days' fast.' It is indeed surprising to me that thus differing in the number of days, they should both give it one common appellation ; but some assign one reason for it, and others another, according to their several fancies. One can see also a disagreement about the manner of abstinence from food, as well as about the number of days. Some wholly abstain from things that have life : others feed on fish only of all living creatures : many together with fish, eat fowl also, saying that according to Moses,[19] these were likewise made out of the waters. Some abstain from eggs, and all kinds of fruits : others partake of dry bread only ; still, others eat not even this : while others having fasted till the ninth hour,[20] afterwards take any sort of food without distinction. And among various nations there are other usages, for which innumerable reasons are assigned. Since however no one can produce a written command as an authority, it is evident that the apostles left each one to his own free will in the matter, to the end that each might

---

[12] Euseb. V. 24.
[13] Josephus, *Antiq.* III. 10. The passage is worth quoting entire, running as follows: 'In the month Xanthicus, which is called Nisan by us, and is the beginning of the year, on the fourteenth day of the moon, while the sun is in the sign of Aries (the Ram), for during this month we were freed from bondage under the Egyptians, he has also appointed that we should sacrifice each year the sacrifice which, as we went out of Egypt, they commanded us to offer, it being called the Passover.'
[14] The Audiani, who averred that the Synod of Nicæa first fixed the time of Easter.
[15] Euseb. *Life of Constant.* III. 19.

[16] Cf. Bingham, *Christ. Antiq.* XX. v.
[17] Baronius (*Ann.* 57 and 391 A.D.) finds two mistakes here: first, in the assertion that the Romans fasted three weeks only before Easter, and second, in the assertion that during those three weeks Saturdays were excepted. Cf. also Ceillier, *Hist. des Auteurs Sacrés et Ecclesiast.* Vol. VIII. p. 523, 524. Valesius, however, quotes Pope Leo (fourth sermon on the Lent Fast) and Venerable Beda to prove that Socrates' assertion concerning the exception of Saturday may be defended. See Quesnell, *de Jejunio Sabbati* ; Bingham, *Origin. Eccl.* XXI. 1. 14; also Beveridge, *de Jejunio Quadragesimali.*
[18] Τεσσαρακοστή = Lent; the Latin equivalent is, of course, *Quadragesima.* [19] Gen. i. 20.
[20] Valesius rightly conjectures that very few observed this mode of fasting during Lent, basing his opinion on the order of worship and various deprecatory expressions in ancient authors with respect to it. It may be noted that the Mohammedan Fast of Ramadan is observed on the same principle and in a similar manner. The fast begins with the dawn of the sun and continues until sunset, being complete for that space of time. With the setting of the sun, however, every person is at liberty to eat as he may please.

perform what is good not by constraint or necessity. Such is the difference in the churches on the subject of fasts. Nor is there less variation in regard to religious assemblies.[21] For although almost all churches throughout the world celebrate the sacred mysteries on the sabbath [22] of every week, yet the Christians of Alexandria and at Rome, on account of some ancient tradition, have ceased to do this. The Egyptians in the neighborhood of Alexandria, and the inhabitants of Thebaïs, hold their religious assemblies on the sabbath, but do not participate of the mysteries in the manner usual among Christians in general: for after having eaten and satisfied themselves with food of all kinds, in the evening making their offerings [23] they partake of the mysteries. At Alexandria again, on the Wednesday [24] in Passion week and on Good Friday, the scriptures are read, and the doctors expound them; and all the usual services are performed in their assemblies, except the celebration of the mysteries. This practice in Alexandria is of great antiquity, for it appears that Origen most commonly taught in the church on those days. He being a very learned teacher in the Sacred Books, and perceiving that the 'impotence of the law' [25] of Moses was weakened by literal explanation, gave it a spiritual interpretation; declaring that there has never been but one true Passover, which the Saviour celebrated when he hung upon the cross: for that he then vanquished the adverse powers, and erected this as a trophy against the devil. In the same city of Alexandria, readers and chanters [26] are chosen indifferently from the catechumens and the faithful; whereas in all other churches the faithful only are promoted to these offices. I myself, also, learned of another custom in Thessaly. If a clergyman in that country, after taking orders, should sleep with his wife, whom he had legally married before his ordination, he would be degraded.[27]

In the East, indeed, all clergymen, and even the bishops themselves, abstain from their wives: but this they do of their own accord, and not by the necessity of any law; for there have been among them many bishops, who have had children by their lawful wives, during their episcopate. It is said that the author of the usage which obtains in Thessaly was Heliodorus bishop of Tricca in that country; under whose name there are love books extant, entitled *Ethiopica*,[28] which he composed in his youth. The same custom prevails at Thessalonica, and in Macedonia, and in Greece. I have also known of another peculiarity in Thessaly, which is, that they baptize there on the days of Easter only; in consequence of which a very great number of them die without having received baptism. At Antioch in Syria the site of the church is inverted; so that the altar does not face toward the east, but toward the west.[29] In Greece, however, and at Jerusalem and in Thessaly they go to prayers as soon as the candles are lighted, in the same manner as the Novatians do at Constantinople. At Cæsarea likewise, and in Cappadocia, and in Cyprus, the presbyters and bishops expound the Scriptures in the evening, after the candles are lighted. The Novatians of the Hellespont do not perform their prayers altogether in the same manner as those of Constantinople; in most things, however, their usage is similar to that of the prevailing [30] church. In short, it is impossible to find anywhere, among all the sects, two churches which agree exactly in their ritual respecting prayers. At Alexandria no presbyter is allowed to address the public: a regulation which was made after Arius had raised a disturbance in that church. At Rome they fast every Saturday.[31] At Cæsarea of Cappadocia they exclude from communion those who have sinned after baptism as the Novatians do. The same discipline was practiced by the Macedonians in the Hellespont, and by the Quartodecimans in Asia. The Novatians in Phrygia do not admit such as have twice married;[32] but those of Constanti-

[21] συνάξεων. Sophocles (*Greek Lex. of the Rom. and Byzant. Period*) gives the following senses to the word: 1. 'Religious meeting'; 2. 'Religious service'; 3. 'Place of meeting'; 4. 'Congregation.' To these we may add on the authority of Casaubon (*Exercit.* XVI. ad Annal. Baronii, No. 42) 5. 'The celebration of the Eucharist.' It is in the second sense given by Sophocles that it is used here.

[22] i.e. Saturday. Sunday is never called 'the Sabbath' by the ancient Fathers and historians, but 'the Lord's day' (κυριακή). Sophocles (*Greek Lex. of the Rom. and Byzant. Period*) gives three senses to the word; viz., 1. 'The Sabbath' [of the Jews] (so in the LXX and Jewish writers). 2. 'The week.' 3. 'Saturday.' Many early Christians, however, continued to observe the Jewish Sabbath along with the first day of the week. Cf. Bingham, *Christ. Antiq.* XX. 3.

[23] προσφέροντες, freely = 'celebrating the Eucharist.' Irenæus, *Contra Hæres.* XVIII. 3; Euseb. *Demonstr. Evan.* X. 1; Athan. *Apol. Contr. Arian.* 28.

[24] 'If any bishop . . . does not fast on Wednesday or Friday let him be deposed.' So *Apost. Can.* 69. These two days are universally joined together by the Greek and Roman Catholic Churches.   [25] Cf. Rom. viii. 3.

[26] ὑποβολεῖς, lit. = 'prompters,' whose duty it was to read the Psalms which the people chanted.

[27] On the celibacy of the clergy and its gradual growth, see Bingham, *Christ. Antiq.* IV. 5; *Apost. Can.* 51, and Council of Gangra, Can. 1 (Hefele, *Hist. Ch. Councils*, Vol. II. p. 325 seq.).

[28] A novel on the adventures of Theagenes and Chariclea. The Heliodorus who wrote the *Ethiopica* was, according to Photius, *Biblioth.* chap. 94, a native of Phœnicia, hence not the same as the bishop of Tricca. Others ascribe the *Ethiopica* to Heliodorus the Sophist, who flourished under the Emperor Hadrian.

[29] According to the *Apost. Constit.* (II. 57) a church should be built so as to face the east. This regulation was generally followed, but there were exceptions. Cf. Bingham, *Christ. Antiq.* VIII. 3. 2.

[30] i.e. the catholic or orthodox church; used perhaps in the same way as the expression 'established church' in modern times.

[31] *Apost. Can.* 64, provides that no cleric or layman shall fast on the Sabbath day (Saturday, see note 22, above), the former on pain of being deposed, the latter of being excommunicated. It appears, however, that the Roman church observed the day as a fast, while the Greek church held it to be a feast. Socrates, however, seems to contradict the statement he had made above (see note 17) that at Rome Saturdays and Sundays were excepted from the list of fasting days in Lent. From Augustine's *Epistles*, 36. 31 et al., it appears that he fasted on Saturday and regarded this the regular and proper course to be pursued, and actually pursued by members of the church. Hence the present statement of Socrates must be taken as correct to the exclusion of the former.

[32] *Apost. Can.* 17. 'He who has been twice married after bap-

nople neither admit nor reject them openly, while in the Western parts they are openly received. This diversity was occasioned, as I imagine, by the bishops who in their respective eras governed the churches; and those who received these several rites and usages, transmitted them as laws to their posterity. However, to give a complete catalogue of all the various customs and ceremonial observances in use throughout every city and country would be difficult — rather impossible; but the instances we have adduced are sufficient to show that the Easter Festival was from some remote precedent differently celebrated in every particular province. They talk at random therefore who assert that the time of keeping Easter was altered in the Nicene Synod; for the bishops there convened earnestly labored to reduce the first dissenting minority to uniformity of practice with the rest of the people. Now that many differences existed even in the apostolic age of the church occasioned by such subjects, was not unknown even to the apostles themselves, as the book of *The Acts* testifies. For when they understood that a disturbance occurred among believers on account of a dissension of the Gentiles, having all met together, they promulgated a Divine law, giving it the form of a letter. By this sanction they liberated Christians from the bondage of formal observances, and all vain contention about these things; and they taught them the path of true piety, prescribing such things only as were conducive to its attainment. The epistle itself, which I shall here transcribe, is recorded in *The Acts of the Apostles.*[33]

' The apostles and elders and brethren send greeting unto the brethren which are of the Gentiles in Antioch and Syria and Cilicia. Forasmuch as we have heard, that certain which went out from us have troubled you with words, subverting your souls, saying, Ye must be circumcised, and keep the law; to whom we gave no such commandment: it seemed good unto us, being assembled with one accord, to send chosen men unto you, with our beloved Barnabas and Paul, men that have hazarded their lives for the name of our Lord Jesus Christ.

We have sent therefore Judas and Silas, who shall also tell you the same thing by mouth. For it seemed good to the Holy Ghost and to us, to lay upon you no greater burden than these necessary things: that ye abstain from meats offered to idols, and from blood, and from things strangled, and from fornication; from which if ye keep yourselves, ye shall do well. Fare ye well.'

These things indeed pleased God: for the letter expressly says, ' It seemed good to the Holy Ghost to lay upon you no greater burden than these necessary things.' There are nevertheless some persons who, disregarding these precepts, suppose all fornication to be an indifferent matter; but contend about holy-days as if their lives were at stake, thus contravening the commands of God, and legislating for themselves, and making of none effect the decree of the apostles: neither do they perceive that they are themselves practicing the contrary to those things which God approved. It is possible easily to extend our discourse respecting Easter, and demonstrate that the Jews observe no exact rule either in the time or manner of celebrating the paschal solemnity: and that the Samaritans, who are an offshoot from the Jews, always celebrate this festival after the equinox. But this subject would require a distinct and copious treatise: I shall therefore merely add, that those who affect so much to imitate the Jews, and are so very anxious about an accurate observance of types, ought to depart from them in no particular. For if they have chosen to be so correct, they must not only observe days and months, but all other things also, which Christ (who was 'made under the law')[34] did in the manner of the Jews; or which he unjustly suffered from them; or wrought typically for the good of all men. He entered into a ship and taught. He ordered the Passover to be made ready in an upper room. He commanded an ass that was tied to be loosed. He proposed a man bearing a pitcher of water as a sign to them for hastening their preparations for the Passover. [He did] an infinite number of other things of this nature which are recorded in the gospels. And yet those who suppose themselves to be justified by keeping this feast, would think it absurd to observe any of these things in a bodily manner. For no doctor ever dreams of going to preach from a ship — no person imagines it necessary to go up into an upper room to celebrate the Passover there — they never tie, and then loose an ass again — and finally no one enjoins another to carry a pitcher of water, in order that the symbols might be fulfilled. They have justly regarded such

---

tism . . . cannot become bishop, presbyter, or deacon, or any other [cleric] included in the sacerdotal list.'

[33] Acts xv. 23–39. The quotation is here from the Authorized Version. The Revised has it slightly altered. We subjoin it for comparison. ' The apostles and the elder brethren unto the brethren which are of the Gentiles in Antioch and Syria and Cilicia, greeting: Forasmuch as we have heard that certain which went out from us have troubled you with words, subverting your souls; to whom we gave no commandment; it seemed good unto us, having come to one accord, to choose out men and send them unto you with our beloved Barnabas and Paul, men that have hazarded their lives for the name of our Lord Jesus Christ. We have sent therefore Judas and Silas, who themselves also shall tell you the same things by word of mouth. For it seemed good to the Holy Ghost, and to us, to lay upon you no greater burden than these necessary things; that ye abstain from things sacrificed to idols, and from blood, and from things strangled, and from fornication; from which if ye keep yourselves, it shall be well with you. Fare ye well.'

[34] Gal. iv. 4.

things as savoring rather of Judaism : for the Jews are more solicitous about outward solemnities than the obedience of the heart ; and therefore are they under the curse, because they do not discern the spiritual bearing of the Mosaic law, but rest in its types and shadows. Those who favor the Jews admit the allegorical meaning of these things ; and yet they wage a deadly warfare against the observance of days and months, without applying to them a similar sense : thus do they necessarily involve themselves in a common condemnation with the Jews.

But enough I think has been said concerning these things. Let us now return to the subject we were previously treating of, the fact that the Church once divided did not stay with that division, but that those separated were again divided among themselves, taking occasion from the most trivial grounds. The Novatians, as I have stated, were divided among themselves on account of the feast of Easter, the controversy not being restricted to one point only. For in the different provinces some took one view of the question, and some another, disagreeing not only about the month, but the days of the week also, and other unimportant matters ; in some places they hold separate assemblies because of it, in others they unite in mutual communion.

CHAPTER XXIII.

Further Dissensions among the Arians at Constantinople. The Psathyrians.

BUT dissensions arose among the Arians [1] also on this account. The contentious questions which were daily agitated among them, led them to start the most absurd propositions. For whereas it has been always believed in the church that God is the Father of the Son, the Word, it was asked whether God could be called 'Father' before the Son had subsistence? Thus in asserting that the Word of God was not begotten of the Father, but was created out ' of nothing,' and thus falling into error on the chief and main point, they deservedly fell into absurd cavilings about a mere name. Dorotheus therefore being sent for by them from Antioch maintained that God neither was nor could be called Father before the Son existed. But Marinus whom they had summoned out of Thrace before Dorotheus, piqued at the superior deference which was paid to his rival, undertook to defend the contrary opinion. In consequence of these things there arose a schism among them, and being thus divided respecting this term, each party held separate meetings. Those under Dorotheus retained

their original places of assembly : but the followers of Marinus built distinct oratories for themselves, and asserted that the Father had always been Father, even when the Son was not. This section of the Arians was denominated *Psathyrians,*[2] because one of the most zealous defenders of this opinion was Theoctistus, a Syrian by birth, and a cake-seller [*Psathyropōla*][3] by trade. Selenas[4] bishop of the Goths adopted the views of this party, a man of mixed descent ; he was a Goth by his father's side, but by his mother's a Phrygian, by which means he taught in the church with great readiness in both these languages. This faction however soon quarreled among themselves, Marinus disagreeing with Agapius, whom he himself had preferred to the bishopric of Ephesus. They disputed, however, not about any point of religion, but in narrow-mindedness about precedence, in which the Goths sided with Agapius. Wherefore many of the ecclesiastics under their jurisdiction, abominating the vain-glorious contest between these two, abandoned them both, and became adherents to the 'homoousian' faith. The Arians having continued thus divided among themselves during the space of thirty-five years, were reunited in the reign of Theodosius the Younger, under the consulate[5] of Plintha the commander-in-chief of the army, he being a member of the sect of Psathyrians ; these were prevailed on to desist from contention. They afterwards passed a resolution, giving it all the cogency of law, that the question which had led to their separation, should never be mooted again. But this reconciliation extended no farther than Constantinople ; for in other cities where any of these two parties were found, they persisted in their former separation. So much respecting the division among the Arians.

CHAPTER XXIV.

The Eunomians divide into Several Factions.

BUT neither did the followers of Eunomius remain without dissensions : for Eunomius[1] himself had long before this separated from Eudoxius who ordained him bishop of Cyzicus, taking occasion from that bishop's refusal to restore to communion his master Aëtius who had been ejected. But those who derived their name from him were subsequently divided into several factions. For first Theophronius a Cappadocian, who had been instructed in the art of disputation by Eunomius, and had acquired a smat-

---

[1] See above, chap. 20.

[2] Cf. Theodoret, *Hæret. Fabal.* IV. 4; also Sozomen (probably dependent on Socrates), VII. 17.
[3] ψαθύριον, a species of cake; hence ψαθυροπώλης, 'cake-seller.'
[4] Sozomen (VII. 17) adds that Selenas was a secretary of Ulfilas and had been promoted to be his successor.
[5] 419 A.D.   [1] Cf. IV. 7 and 13.

tering of Aristotle's *Categories*, and his *Book of Interpretation*, composed some treatises which he entitled, *On the Exercise of the Mind*. Having, however, drawn down upon himself the reprobation of his own sect, he was ejected as an apostate. He afterwards held assemblies apart from them, and left behind him a heresy which bore his own name. Furthermore at Constantinople a certain Eutychius from some absurd dispute, withdrew from the Eunomians, and still continues to hold separate meetings. The followers of Theophronius are denominated 'Eunomiotheophronians'; and those of Eutychius have the appellation of 'Eunomieutychians.' What those nonsensical terms were about which they differed I consider unworthy of being recorded in this history, lest I should go into matters foreign to my purpose. I shall merely observe that they adulterated baptism : for they do not baptize in the name of the Trinity, but into the death of Christ.[2] Among the Macedonians also there was for some time a division, when Eutropius a presbyter held separate assemblies, and Carterius did not agree with him. There are possibly in other cities sects which have emanated from these : but living at Constantinople, where I was born and educated, I describe more particularly what has taken place in that city; both because I have myself witnessed some of these transactions, and also because the events which have there occurred are of pre-eminent importance, and are therefore more worthy of commemoration. Let it however be understood that what I have here related happened at different periods, and not at the same time. But if any one should be desirous of knowing the names of the various sects, he may easily satisfy himself, by reading a book entitled *Ancoratus*,[3] composed by Epiphanius, bishop of Cyprus : but I shall content myself with what I have already stated. The public affairs were again thrown into agitation from a cause I shall now refer to.

CHAPTER XXV.

The Usurper Eugenius compasses the Death of Valentinian the Younger. Theodosius obtains a Victory over him.

THERE was in the Western regions a gramma-

rian named Eugenius,[1] who after having for some time taught the Latin language, left his school, and was appointed to service at the palace, being constituted chief secretary to the emperor. Possessing a considerable degree of eloquence, and being on that account treated with greater distinction than others, he was unable to bear his good fortune with moderation. For associating with himself Arbogastes, a native of Galatia Minor, who then had the command of a division of the army, a man harsh in manner and very bloodthirsty, he determined to usurp the sovereignty. These two therefore agreed to murder the Emperor Valentinian, having corrupted the eunuchs of the imperial bed-chamber. These, on receiving tempting promises of promotion, strangled the emperor in his sleep. Eugenius immediately assuming the supreme authority in the Western parts of the empire, conducted himself in such a manner as might be expected from a usurper. When the Emperor Theodosius was made acquainted with these things, he was exceedingly distressed, because his defeat of Maximus had only prepared the way for fresh troubles. He accordingly assembled his military forces, and having proclaimed his son Honorius Augustus, on the 10th of January, in his own third consulate [2] which he bore with Abundantius, he again set out in great haste toward the Western parts, leaving both his sons invested with imperial authority at Constantinople. As he marched against Eugenius a very great number of the barbarians beyond the Danube volunteered their services, and followed him in this expedition. After a rapid march he arrived in the Gauls with a numerous army, where Eugenius awaited him, also at the head of an immense body of troops. Accordingly an engagement took place near the river Frigidus, which is [about thirty-six miles] distant [from Aquileia]. In that part of the battle where the Romans fought against their own countrymen, the conflict was doubtful : but where the barbarian auxiliaries of the Emperor Theodosius were engaged, the forces of Eugenius had greatly the advantage. When the emperor saw the barbarians perishing, he cast himself in great agony upon the ground, and invoked the help of God in this emergency : nor was his request unheeded ; for Bacurius [3] his principal officer, inspired with sudden and extraordinary ardor, rushed with his vanguard to the part where the barbarians were hardest pressed, broke through the ranks of the enemy, and put to flight those who a little before were themselves engaged in pursuit. Another marvelous circumstance

---

[2] *Apost. Can.* 50 reads: 'If any bishop or presbyter does not perform the one initiation with three immersions, but with one immersion only into the death of the Lord, let him be deposed.' Also the Second General Synod (that of Constantinople, 381) in its 7th Canon passed the following: 'But the Eunomians, *who only baptize with one immersion*, and the Montanists, who are here called Phrygians, and the Sabellians, who teach the doctrine of the Fatherhood of the Son . . . (if they wish to be joined to the Orthodox faith) we receive as heathen; on the first day we make them Christians, on the second, catechumens, &c.' See Hefele, *Hist. of the Church Councils*, Vol. II. p. 367, 368.
[3] Epiphan. *Ancoratus*, 13. Photius calls the *Ancoratus* a synopsis of the treatise of Epiphanius on *Heresies* (*Biblioth.* 123).

The subject here referred to was treated by Epiphanius in *Hær.* LXVI. and LXVIII.
[1] This account of Arbogastes and Eugenius is also given by Zosimus (IV. 53–58), who adds that Arbogastes was a Frank; and also by Philotorgius (XI. 1), who says that Eugenius was a pagan.
[2] 393 A.D.   [3] Cf. Zosimus, IV. 57.

also occurred. A violent wind suddenly arose, which retorted upon themselves the darts cast by the soldiers of Eugenius, and at the same time drove those hurled by the imperial forces with increased impetus against their adversaries.[4] So prevalent was the emperor's prayer. The success of the struggle being in this way turned, the usurper threw himself at the emperor's feet, and begged that his life might be spared : but as he lay a prostrate suppliant at the feet [of the emperor] he was beheaded by the soldiers, on the 6th of September, in the third consulate of Arcadius, and the second of Honorius.[5] Arbogastes, who had been the chief cause of so much mischief, having continued his flight for two days after the battle, and seeing no chance of escape, despatched himself with his own sword.

CHAPTER XXVI.

Illness and Death of Theodosius the Elder.

THE Emperor Theodosius was in consequence of the anxiety and fatigues connected with this war thrown into bodily illness; and believing the disease which had attacked him would be fatal, he became more concerned about the public affairs than his own life, considering how great calamities often overtook the people after the death of their sovereign. He therefore hastily summoned his son Honorius from Constantinople, being principally desirous of setting in order the state of things in the western parts of the empire. After his son's arrival at Milan, he seemed to recover a little, and gave directions for the celebration of the games of the hippodrome on account of his victory. Before dinner he was pretty well, and a spectator of the sports ; but after he had dined he became suddenly too ill to return to them, and sent his son to preside in his stead ; when the night came on he died, it being the seventeenth of January, during consulate of Olybrius and Probus.[1] This was in the first year of the two hundred and ninety-fourth Olympiad. The emperor Theodosius lived sixty years,[2] and reigned sixteen. This book therefore comprehends the transactions of sixteen years and eight months.

---

[1] 395 A.D.
[2] There is some doubt as to the length of Theodosius' life; most of the ancient historians (Sozomen, Theophanes, Cedrenus) agree with Socrates in giving it as sixty years. Am. Marcellinus, *Rerum Gestarum*, XXIX. 6. 15, and Victor, *Epit.* XLVII., leave the impression that he was fifty.

---

[4] Cf. Zosimus, IV. 58, who gives the additional item that the sun was eclipsed during this battle.
[5] 394 A.D.

END OF THE FIFTH BOOK.

BOOK VI.

INTRODUCTION.

THE commission with which you charged us, O holy man of God, Theodore, we have executed in the five foregoing books; in which to the best of our ability, we have comprised the history of the Church from the time of Constantine. Notice, however, that we have been by no means studious of style; for we considered that had we showed too great fastidiousness about elegance of expression we might have defeated the object in view.[1] But even supposing our purpose could still have been accomplished, we were wholly precluded from the exercise of that discretionary power of which ancient historians seem to have so largely availed themselves, whereby any one of them imagined himself quite at liberty to amplify or curtail matters of fact. Moreover, refined composition would by no means be edifying to the masses and illiterate men, who are intent merely on knowing the facts, and not on admiring beauty of diction. In order therefore not to render my production unprofitable to both classes of readers, — to the learned on the one hand, because no elaboration of language could satisfy them to rank it with the magniloquence of the writers of antiquity, and to the unlearned on the other, because they could not understand the facts, should they be clouded by a parade of words, — we have purposely adopted a style, divested indeed of all affectation of sublimity, but at the same time clear and perspicuous.

As we begin, however, our sixth book, we must premise this, that in undertaking to detail the events of our own age, we are apprehensive of advancing such things as may be unpalatable to many: either because, according to the proverb, 'Truth is bitter;' on account of our not mentioning with encomium the names of those whom some may love; or from our not magnifying their actions. The zealots of our churches will condemn us for not calling the bishops 'Most dear to God,' 'Most holy,' and such like. Others will be litigious because we do not bestow the appellations 'Most divine,' and 'Lords' on the emperors, nor apply to them such other epithets as they are commonly assigned. But since I could easily prove from the testimony of ancient authors,[2] that among them the servant was accustomed to address his master simply by name, without reference to his dignity or titles, on account of the pressure of business, I shall in like manner obey the laws of history, which demand a simple and faithful narration, unobscured by a veil of any kind. I shall proceed to record accurately what I have either myself seen, or have been able to ascertain from actual observers; having tested the truth by the unanimity of the witnesses that spoke of the same affairs, and by every means I could possibly command. The process of ascertaining the truth was indeed laborious, inasmuch as many and different persons gave different accounts and some claimed to be eyewitnesses, while others professed to be more intimately acquainted with these things than any others.

CHAPTER I.

On the Death of Theodosius his Two Sons divide the Empire. Rufinus is slain at the Feet of Arcadius.

AFTER the death of the Emperor Theodosius, in the consulate of Olybrius and Probinus or the seventeenth of January, his two sons undertook the administration of the Roman empire. Thus Arcadius assumed the government of the East, and Honorius of the West.[1] At that time Damasus was bishop of the church at Imperial Rome, and Theophilus of that of Alexandria, John of Jerusalem, and Flavian of Antioch; while the episcopal chair at Constantinople or New Rome was filled by Nectarius, as we mentioned in the foregoing book.[2] The body of the Emperor Theodosius was taken to Constantinople on the 8th of November in the same consulate, and was honorably interred by his son Arcadius with the usual funeral solemnities.[3] Not long afterwards on the 28th day of the same month the army also arrived, which had served under the Emperor Theodosius in the war against the usurper. When therefore

---

[1] Cf. V. Int.

[2] The comic poets, e.g. Menander, Plautus, Terence.
[1] Cf. Gibbon, *Decline and Fall of the Rom. Empire*, chap. 29.
[2] V 8.
[3] See Bennett, *Christian Archæology*, p. 210 *seq.*, and Bingham, *Christ. Antiq.* XXII. 1 and 2, for details on the burial of the dead in the early Church.

according to custom the Emperor Arcadius met the army without the gates, the soldiery slew Rufinus the Prætorian prefect. For he was suspected of aspiring to the sovereignty, and had the reputation of having invited into the Roman territories the Huns,[4] a barbarous nation, who had already ravaged Armenia, and were then making predatory incursions into other provinces of the East. On the very day on which Rufinus was killed, Marcian bishop of the Novatians died, and was succeeded in the episcopate by Sisinnius, of whom we have already made mention.[5]

CHAPTER II.

Death of Nectarius and Ordination of John.

A SHORT time after Nectarius[1] also, bishop of Constantinople died, during the consulate of Cæsarius and Atticus,[2] on the 27th of September. A contest thereupon immediately arose respecting the appointment of a successor, some proposing one person, and some another: at length however it was determined to send for John,[3] a presbyter of the church at Antioch, for there was a report that he was very instructive, and at the same time eloquent. By the general consent therefore of both the clergy and laity, he was summoned very soon afterwards to Constantinople by the Emperor Arcadius: and to render the ordination more authoritative and imposing, several prelates were requested to be present, among whom also was Theophilus bishop of Alexandria.[4] This person did everything he could to detract from John's reputation, being desirous of promoting to that see, Isidore[5] a presbyter of his own church, to whom he was greatly attached, on account of a very delicate and perilous affair which Isidore had undertaken to serve his interests. What this was I must now unfold. While the Emperor Theodosius was preparing to attack the usurper Maximus, Theodosius sent Isidore with gifts giving twofold letters, and enjoining him to present both the

gifts and the proper letters to him who should become the victor. In accordance with these injunctions Isidore on his arrival at Rome awaited there the event of the war. But this business did not long remain a secret: for a reader who accompanied him privately sequestered the letters; upon which Isidore in great alarm returned to Alexandria. This was the reason why Theophilus so warmly favored Isidore. The court however gave the preference to John: and inasmuch as many had revived the accusations against Theophilus, and prepared for presentation to the bishops then convened memorials of various charges, Eutropius[6] the chief officer of the imperial bed-chamber collected these documents, and showed them to Theophilus, bidding him 'choose between ordaining John, and undergoing a trial on the charges made against him.' Theophilus terrified at this alternative, consented to ordain John. Accordingly John was invested with the episcopal dignity on the 26th of February, under the following consulate,[7] which the Emperor Honorius celebrated with public games at Rome, and Eutychian, then Prætorian prefect, at Constantinople. But since the man is famous, both for the writings he has left, and the many troubles he fell into, it is proper that I should not pass over his affairs in silence, but to relate as compendiously as possible whence he was, and from what ancestry; also the particulars of his elevation to the episcopate, and the means by which he was subsequently degraded; and finally how he was more honored after his death, than he had been during his life.

CHAPTER III.

Birth and Education of John Bishop of Constantinople.

JOHN was a native of Antioch in Syria-Cœle, son of Secundus and Anthusa, and scion of a noble family in that country. He studied rhetoric under Libanius the sophist, and philosophy under Andragathius the philosopher.[1] Being on the point of entering the practice of civil law, and reflecting on the restless and unjust course of those who devote themselves to the practice of the forensic courts, he was turned to the more tranquil mode of life, which he adopted, following the example of Evagrius.[2] Evagrius

---

[4] Zosimus (V. 5) says Rufinus invited Alaric and the Goths to invade the Roman territories; Valesius reconciles Socrates' and Zosimus' statements by assuming that they are partial and supplementary to one another; Rufinus, according to him, invited both the Huns and the Goths.
[5] V. 10, 21, et al.   [1] Cf. V. 8.   [2] 397 A.D.
[3] The well-known bishop of Antioch and Constantinople, who on account of his extraordinary gift of eloquence was surnamed *Chrysostom*, 'the Golden-mouth.' See *The Nicene and Post-Nicene Fathers*, Vol. IX. Prolegomena on the life and writings of St. John Chrysostom by Dr. Schaff. Also cf. ancient authorities: Palladius, *Dialogus historicus de vita et conversatione beati Joannis Chrysostomi cum Theodoro Ecclesiæ Romanæ diacono*; Jerome, *de Viris Illustribus*, c. 129; Sozomen, VIII. 2–23; Theodoret, *H. E.* V. 27–36; and modern Smith & Wace, *Dict. of Christ. Biog.*; F. W. Farrar, *Lives of the Fathers*, Vol. II. p. 460–527, and many monograms and longer or briefer notices in the standard church histories.
[4] Cf. Theodoret, V. 22, under this Theophilus the pagan temples of Mithras and Serapis were attacked, as related above in V. 16 and 17. For a fuller notice of Theophilus, see Smith & Wace, *Dict. of Christ. Biog.*
[5] Cf. chap. 9 of this book.

[6] Cf. Zosimus, V. 3, 8, 10, 17, 18, and Eunapius, *Fragm.* 53, 56.
[7] 398 A.D.
[1] Sozomen (VIII. 2) also says that Chrysostom went from the school of Libanius to a private life instead of the legal profession as was expected of him, but from some utterances of Libanius, as well as from Chrysostom's own representation, *de Sacerdot.* I. 1. 4, it appears that he had spent some time in the practice of the law.
[2] It is not certain who this Evagrius was. Valesius thinks he was the presbyter of that name mentioned by Jerome, *de Scriptor. Eccl.*

himself had been educated under the same masters, and had some time before retired to a private mode of life. Accordingly he laid aside his legal habit, and applied his mind to the reading of the sacred scriptures, frequenting the church with great assiduity. He moreover induced Theodore and Maximus, who had been his fellow-students under Libanius the sophist, to forsake a profession whose primary object was gain, and embrace a life of greater simplicity. Of these two persons, Theodore afterwards became bishop of Mopsuestia[3] in Cilicia, and Maximus of Seleucia in Isauria. At that time being ardent aspirants after perfection, they entered upon the ascetic life, under the guidance of Diodorus[4] and Carterius, who then presided over a monastic institution. The former of these was subsequently elevated to the bishopric of Tarsus, and wrote many treatises, in which he limited his attention to the literal sense of scripture, avoiding that which was mystical.[5] But enough respecting these persons. Now John was then living on the most intimate terms with Basil,[6] at that time constituted a deacon by Meletius, but afterwards ordained bishop of Cæsarea in Cappadocia. Accordingly Zeno[7] the bishop on his return from Jerusalem, appointed him a reader in the church at Antioch. While he continued in the capacity of a reader he composed the book *Against the Jews.* Meletius having not long after conferred on him the rank of deacon, he produced his work *On the Priesthood,*[8] and those *Against Stagirius;* and moreover those also *On the Incomprehensibility of the Divine Nature,* and *On the Women*[9] *who lived with the Ecclesias-*

tics. Afterwards, upon the death of Meletius at Constantinople, — for there he had gone on account of Gregory Nazianzen's ordination, — John separated himself from the Meletians, without entering into communion with Paulinus, and spent three whole years in retirement. Later, when Paulinus was dead, he was ordained a presbyter by Evagrius the successor of Paulinus. Such is a brief outline of John's career previous to his call to the episcopal office. It is said that on account of his zeal for temperance he was stern and severe; and one of his early friends has said 'that in his youth he manifested a proneness to irritability, rather than to modesty.' Because of the rectitude of his life, he was free from anxiety about the future, and his simplicity of character rendered him open and ingenuous; nevertheless the liberty of speech he allowed himself was offensive to very many. In public teaching he was powerful in reforming the morals of his auditors; but in private conversation he was frequently thought haughty and assuming by those who did not know him.

CHAPTER IV.

Of Serapion the Deacon on whose Account John becomes Odious to his Clergy.

BEING such in disposition and manners, and promoted to the episcopacy, John was led to conduct himself toward his clergy with more than proper superciliousness, designing to correct the morals of the clergy under him. Having thus chafed the temper of the ecclesiastics, he was disliked by them; and so many of them stood aloof from him as a passionate man, and others became his bitter enemies. Serapion, a deacon of his retinue, led him to alienate their minds still more from him; and once in presence of the whole assembled clergy he cried out with a loud voice to the bishop — 'You will never be able to govern these men, my lord, unless you drive them all with a rod.' This speech of his excited a general feeling of animosity against the bishop; the bishop also not long after expelled many of them from the church, some for one cause, and some for another. And, as it usually happens when persons in office adopt such violent measures, those who were thus expelled by him formed combinations and inveighed against him to the people. What contributed greatly to gain credence for these complaints was the fact that the bishop was not willing to eat with any one else, and never accepted an invitation to a

[3] It has been supposed by some that this was the Theodore addressed in II. 1, VI. Int. and VII. 47; but not with good reason. Cf. note 4, p. xii. of Int. On Theodore of Mopsuestia, the great 'Exegete' and theologian, see Smith & Wace; also Sieffert, *Theodor. Mopsuestenus Vet. Test. Sobrie Interpret. Vindex* and H. B. Swete, *Theodori Episc. Mopsuestiæ* in *Epp. B. Pauli. Commentarii.*
[4] Sozomen also attests the simplicity of Diodorus' interpretations of the Old Testament. The principle which he adopted, of seeking for a literal and historical meaning in preference to the allegorical and mystical interpretations attached to the Old Testament by Origen and the Alexandrians, became the corner-stone of the Antiochian system of interpretation as elaborated by his pupils Theodore of Mopsuestia and Theodoret.
[5] θεωρίας, lit. 'speculations,' by which are evidently meant the allegorical and subjective or contemplative explanations of the Alexandrians.
[6] 'Socrates and Kurtz (in the tenth edition of his *Kirchengeschichte,* I. 223) confound this Basil with Basil the Great of Cappadocia, who was eighteen years older than Chrysostom, and died in 379. Chrysostom's friend was probably (as Baronius and Montfaucon conjecture) identical with Basil, bishop of Raphanea in Syria, near Antioch, who attended the Council of Constantinople in 381.' Comp. Venables in Smith and Wace; Schaff in Prolegomena to Vol. IX. of *The Nicene and Post-Nicene Fathers,* p. 6, note 2. The conjecture of Baronius is assented to also by Valesius.
[7] According to Baronius, this Zeno was bishop of Tyre, but Valesius makes an ingenious objection to this view, and asserts that some other city must have been the real see of Zeno.
[8] This treatise, commonly termed *de Sacerdotio,* and the *Homilies* are the most famous of Chrysostom's works; for a full account, as well as translation, of these works, see *Nicene and Post-Nicene Fathers,* Vol. IX.
[9] These were women who lived in the houses of the clergy as sisters, and exercised themselves in works of piety and charity. At a very early period, however, scandal seems to have arisen from this practice, and strong measures were repeatedly adopted by the Church

for their suppression. Paul of Samosata was, according to Eusebius (*H. E.* VII. 30), deposed ·partly for keeping these sisters in his house. They were called Syneisactæ (Συνείσακτοι). Cf. Bingham, *Christ. Antiq.* XVII. 5. 20, and Council of Nicæa, Can. 3. Hefele, *Hist. of Ch. Councils,* Vol. I. p. 379.

feast. On account of this the plot against him became widespread. His reasons for not eating with others no one knew with any certainty,[1] but some persons in justification of his conduct state that he had a very delicate stomach, and weak digestion, which obliged him to be careful in his diet, and therefore he ate alone; while others thought this was due to his rigid and habitual abstinence. Whatever the real motive may have been, the circumstance itself contributed not a little to the grounds of accusation by his calumniators. The people nevertheless continued to regard him with love and veneration, on account of his valuable discourses in the church, and therefore those who sought to traduce him, only brought themselves into contempt. How eloquent, convincing, and persuasive his sermons were, both those which were published by himself, and such as were noted down by short-hand writers as he delivered them, why should we stay to declare? Those who desire to form an adequate idea of them, must read for themselves, and will thereby derive both pleasure and profit.

CHAPTER V.

John draws down upon Himself the Displeasure of Many Persons of Rank and Power. Of the Eunuch Eutropius.

As long as John was in conflict with the clergy only, machinations against him were utterly powerless; but when he proceeded to rebuke many of those in public office also with immoderate vehemence, the tide of unpopularity began to set against him with far greater impetus. Hence many stories were told to his disparagement. And most of these found attentive and believing listeners. This growing prejudice was not a little increased by an oration which he pronounced at that time against Eutropius. For Eutropius was the chief eunuch of the imperial bed-chamber, and the first of all eunuchs that was admitted to the dignity of consul. He, desiring to inflict vengeance on certain persons who had taken refuge in the churches, induced the emperors to make a law[1] excluding delinquents from the privilege of sanctuary, and authorizing the seizure of those who had sought the shelter of the sacred edifices. But its author was punished for

this almost immediately; for scarcely had the law been promulgated, before Eutropius himself, having incurred the displeasure of the emperor, fled for protection to the church.[2] The bishop therefore, while Eutropius trembling with fear lay under the table of the altar, mounting the pulpit[3] from which he was accustomed to address the people in order to be the more distinctly heard, uttered an invective against him: wherefore he seemed to create greater displeasure in some, as he not only denied compassion to the unfortunate, but added insult to cruelty. By the emperor's order however, for certain offences committed by him, Eutropius, though bearing the consulate, was decapitated, and his name effaced from the list of consuls, that of Theodore his colleague being alone suffered to remain as in office for that year.[4] It is said that John afterwards used the same license towards Gaïnas also, who was then commander-in-chief of the army; treating him with characteristic rudeness, because he had presumed to request the emperor to assign the Arians, with whom he agreed in sentiment, one of the churches within the city. Many others also of the higher orders, for a variety of causes, he censured with the same unceremonious freedom, so that by these means he created many powerful adversaries. Wherefore Theophilus bishop of Alexandria, immediately after his ordination, was plotting his overthrow; and concerted measures for this purpose in secret, both with the friends who were around him, and by letter with such as were at a distance. For it was not so much the boldness with which John lashed whatever was obnoxious to him, that affected Theophilus, as his own failure to place his favorite presbyter Isidore in the episcopal chair of Constantinople. In such a state were the affairs of John the bishop at that time; mischief thus threatened him at the very commencement of his episcopate. But we shall enter into these things more at large as we proceed.

CHAPTER VI.

Gaïnas the Goth attempts to usurp the Sovereign Power; after filling Constantinople with Disorder, he is slain.

I SHALL now narrate some memorable circumstances that occurred at that period, in which it

---

[1] These reasons are given by Palladius as follows: 'He was accustomed to eat alone, as I partially know, for these reasons: first, he drank no wine . . secondly, his stomach was, on account of certain infirmities, irregular, so that often the food prepared for him was repugnant, and other food not put before him was desired. Again he at times neglected to eat, lengthening out his meal until evening, sometimes being absorbed in ecclesiastical cares and sometimes in contemplation; . . . but it is a custom with table companions if we do not relish the same articles of food which they do, or laugh at insignificant witticisms . . . to make this an occasion of ill-speech.' Palladius, *de Vita S. Joannis*, 12.

[1] Sozomen (VIII. 7) says that this law was rescinded very soon afterwards.

[2] See also Chrysostom, *Orat. in Eutropium*, I. 3 (*Nicene and Post-Nicene Fathers*, Vol. IX. p. 251). From these statements it appears that Zosimus is in error when he says (V. 18) that Eutropius was seized in violation of the law of sanctuary and taken out of the church. Chrysostom assigns his seizure to a time when he had left the church for some purpose or other.

[3] ἄμβων, high reading-desk from which the Scriptures were recited, situated toward the middle of the church and distinguished from the altar, where the main service of worship was chanted. Bishops were accustomed to preach from the steps of the altar (cf. Bingham, *Christ. Antiq.* VIII. 4. 5); but Chrysostom, on account of his little stature, as some say, used the 'ambón' as a pulpit.

[4] 399 A.D.

will be seen how Divine Providence interposed by extraordinary agencies for the preservation of the city and Roman empire from the utmost peril. Gaïnas was a barbarian by extraction, but after becoming a Roman subject, and having engaged in military service, and risen by degrees from one rank to another, he was at length appointed general-in-chief both of the Roman horse and foot. When he had obtained this lofty position, he forgot his position and relations, and was unable to restrain himself, and on the other hand according to the common saying 'left no stone unturned' in order to gain control of the Roman government. To accomplish this he sent for the Goths out of their own country, and gave the principal commissions in the army to his relations. Then when Tribigildus, one of his kinsmen who had the command of the forces in Phrygia, had at the instigation of Gaïnas broken out into open revolt, and was filling the people of Phrygia with confusion and dismay, he managed to have deputed to him the oversight of matters in the disturbed province. Now the Emperor Arcadius not suspecting [any harm] committed the charge of these affairs to him. Gaïnas therefore immediately set out at the head of an immense number of the barbarous Goths, apparently on an expedition against Tribigildus, but with the real intention of establishing his own unjust domination. On reaching Phrygia he began to subvert everything. Consequently the affairs of the Romans were immediately thrown into great consternation, not only on account of the vast barbarian force which Gaïnas had at his command, but also because the most fertile and opulent regions of the East were threatened with desolation. In this emergency the emperor, acting with much prudence, sought to arrest the course of the barbarian by address : he accordingly sent him an embassy with instructions to appease him for the present by every kind of concession. Gaïnas having demanded that Saturninus and Aurelian, two of the most distinguished of the senatorial order, and men of consular dignity, whom he knew to be unfavorable to his pretensions, should be delivered up to him, the emperor most unwillingly yielded to the exigency of the crisis ; and these two persons, prepared to die for the public good, nobly submitted themselves to the emperor's disposal. They therefore proceeded to meet the barbarian, at a place used for horse-racing some distance from Chalcedon, being resolved to endure whatever he might be disposed to inflict ; but however they suffered no harm. The usurper simulating dissatisfaction, advanced to Chalcedon, whither the emperor Arcadius also went to meet him. Both then entered the church where the body of the martyr Euphemia is deposited, and there entered into a mutual pledge on oath that neither would plot against the other. The emperor indeed kept his engagement, having a religious regard to an oath, and being on that account beloved of God. But Gaïnas soon violated it, and did not swerve from his original purpose ; on the contrary he was intent on carnage, plunder, and conflagration, not only against Constantinople, but also against the whole extent of the Roman empire, if he could by any means carry it into effect. The city was accordingly quite inundated by the barbarians, and its residents were reduced to a condition equivalent to that of captives. Moreover so great was the danger of the city that a comet of prodigious magnitude, reaching from heaven even to the earth, such as was never before seen, gave forewarning of it.[1] Gaïnas first most shamelessly attempted to make a seizure of the silver publicly exposed for sale in the shops : but when the proprietors, advised beforehand by report of his intention, abstained from exposing it on their counters, his thoughts were diverted to another object, which was to send an immense body of barbarians at night for the purpose of burning down the palace. Then indeed it appeared distinctly that God had providential care over the city : for a multitude of angels appeared to the rebels, in the form of armed men of gigantic stature, before whom the barbarians, imagining them to be a large army of brave troops, turned away with terror and departed. When this was reported to Gaïnas, it seemed to him quite incredible — for he knew that the greatest part of the Roman army was at a distance, dispersed as a garrison over the Eastern cities — and he sent others on the following night and repeatedly afterwards. Now as they constantly returned with the same statement — for the angels of God always presented themselves in the same form — he came with a great multitude, and at length became himself a spectator of the prodigy. Then supposing that what he saw was really a body of soldiers, and that they concealed themselves by day, and baffled his designs by night, he desisted from his attempt, and took another resolution which he conceived would be detrimental to the Romans ; but the event proved it to be greatly to their advantage. Pretending to be under demoniacal possession, he went forth as if for prayer to the church of *St. John the Apostle*, which is seven miles distant from the city. Together with him went barbarians who carried out arms, having concealed them in casks and other specious coverings. And when the soldiers who guarded the city gates detected these, and would not suffer them to pass, the barbarians drew their swords and put them to

---

[1] Cf. Vergil, *Georg.* I. 488, 'Nec diri toties arsere cometæ'; and *Am.* X. 272-274.

death. A fearful tumult thence arose in the city, and death seemed to threaten every one; nevertheless the city continued secure at that time, its gates being every where well defended. The emperor with timely wisdom proclaimed Gaïnas a public enemy, and ordered that all the barbarians who remained shut up in the city should be slain. Thus one day after the guards of the gates had been killed, the Romans attacked the barbarians within the walls near the church of the Goths — for thither such of them as had been left in the city had betaken themselves — and after destroying a great number of them, they set the church on fire, and burnt it to the ground. Gaïnas being informed of the slaughter of those of his party who did not manage to get out of the city, and perceiving the failure of all his artifices, left St. John's church, and advanced rapidly towards Thrace. On reaching the Chersonnese he endeavored to pass over from thence and take Lampsacus, in order that from that place he might make himself master of the Eastern parts. As the emperor had immediately dispatched forces in pursuit both by land and by sea, another wonderful interposition of Divine Providence occurred. For while the barbarians, destitute of ships, hastily put together rafts and were attempting to cross on them, suddenly the Roman fleet appeared, and the west wind began to blow hard. This afforded an easy passage to the Romans; but the barbarians with their horses, tossed up and down in their frail barks by the violence of the gale, were at length overwhelmed by the waves; many of them also were destroyed by the Romans. In this manner during the passage a vast number of the barbarians perished; but Gaïnas departing thence fled into Thrace, where he fell in with another body of the Roman forces and was slain by them together with the barbarians that attended him.[2] Let this cursory notice of Gaïnas suffice here.

Those who may desire more minute details of the circumstances of that war, should read *The Gaïnea* of Eusebius Scholasticus,[3] who was at that time a pupil of Troilus the sophist; and having been a spectator of the war, related the events of it in an heroic poem consisting of four books; and inasmuch as the events alluded to had but recently taken place, he acquired for himself great celebrity. The poet Ammonius has also very lately composed another description in verse of the same transactions, which he recited before the emperor in the sixteenth consulate[4] of Theodosius the younger, which he bore with Faustus.

This war was terminated under the consulate of Stilicho and Aurelian.[5] The year following,[6] the consulate was celebrated by Fravitus also a Goth by extraction, who was honored by the Romans, and showed great fidelity and attachment to them, rendering important services in this very war. For this reason he attained to the dignity of consul. In that year on the tenth of April there was born a son to the Emperor Arcadius, the good Theodosius.

But while the affairs of the state were thus troubled, the dignitaries of the Church refrained not in the least from their disgraceful cabals against each other, to the great reproach of the Christian religion; for during this time the ecclesiastics incited tumults against each other. The source of the mischief originated in Egypt in the following manner.

CHAPTER VII.

Dissension between Theophilus Bishop of Alexandria and the Monks of the Desert. Condemnation of Origen's Books.

THE question had been started a little before,[1] whether God is a corporeal existence, and has the form of man; or whether he is incorporeal, and without human or, generally speaking, any other bodily shape? From this question arose strifes and contentions among a very great number of persons, some favoring one opinion on the subject, and others patronizing the opposite. Very many of the more simple ascetics asserted that God is corporeal, and has a human figure: but most others condemn their judgment, and contended that God is incorporeal, and free of all form whatever. With these latter Theophilus bishop of Alexandria agreed so thoroughly that in the church before all the people he inveighed against those who attributed to God a human form, expressly teaching that the Divine Being is wholly incorporeal. When the Egyptian ascetics were apprised of this, they left their monasteries and came to Alexandria; where they excited a tumult against the bishop, accusing him of impiety, and threatening to put him to death. Theophilus becoming aware of his danger, after some consideration had recourse to this expedient to extricate himself from the threatened death. Going to the monks, he in a conciliatory tone thus addressed them: 'In seeing you, I behold the face of God.' The utterance of this saying moderated the fury of these men

---

[2] Cf. an account of Gaïnas and his rebellion in Zosimus, V. 18-22.
[3] On the surname of 'Scholasticus,' see Introd. p. ix. note 20, also Macar. *Homil.* 15, § 24. On Eusebius Scholasticus, see Smith and Wace, *Eusebius* (134) *Scholasticus*.
[4] 438 A.D.

[5] 400 A.D.   [6] 401 A.D.
[1] By Audius or Audæus, the founder of the Audian heresy. Cf. Epiphan. *Hær.* LXX.; Walch, *Histor. der Ketzereien*, Vol. III. p. 300; also Iselin, *Audios und die Audianer*, in *Jahrbücher für Protestant. Theologie*, April, 1890, p. 298 *seq.*

and they replied: 'If you really admit that God's countenance is such as ours, anathematize Origen's book;[2] for some drawing arguments from them oppose themselves to our opinion. If you will not do this, expect to be treated by us as an impious person, and the enemy of God.' 'But as far as I am concerned,' said Theophilus, 'I will readily do what you require: and be ye not angry with me, for I myself also disapprove of Origen's works, and consider those who countenance them deserving of censure.' Thus he succeeded in appeasing and sending away the monks at that time; and probably the whole dispute respecting this subject would have been set at rest, had it not been for another circumstance which happened immediately after. Over the monasteries in Egypt there were four devout persons as superintendents named Dioscorus, Ammonius, Eusebius, and Euthymius: these men were brothers, and had the appellation of 'the Tall Monks' given them on account of their stature. They were moreover distinguished both for the sanctity of their lives, and the extent of their erudition, and for these reasons their reputation was very high at Alexandria. Theophilus in particular, the prelate of that city, loved and honored them exceedingly: insomuch that he constituted one of them, Dioscorus, bishop of Hermopolis[3] against his will, having forcibly drawn him from his retreat. Two of the others he entreated to continue with him, and with difficulty prevailed upon them to do so; still by the exercise of his authority as bishop he accomplished his purpose: when therefore he had invested them with the clerical office, he committed to their charge the management of ecclesiastical affairs. They, constrained by necessity, performed the duties thus imposed on them successfully; nevertheless they were dissatisfied because they were unable to follow philosophical pursuits and ascetic exercises. And as in process of time, they thought they were being spiritually injured, observing the bishop to be devoted to gain, and greedily intent on the acquisition of wealth, and according to the common saying 'leaving no stone unturned' for the sake of gain, they refused to remain with him any longer, declaring that they loved solitude, and greatly preferred it to living in the city. As long as he was ignorant of the true motive for their departure, he earnestly begged them to abide with him; but when he perceived that they were dissatisfied with his conduct, he became excessively irritated, and threatened to do them all kinds of mischief. But they making little account of his menaces retired into the desert; upon which Theophilus, who was evidently of a hasty and malignant temperament, raised not a small clamor against them, and by every contrivance earnestly sought to do them injury. He also conceived a dislike against their brother Dioscorus, bishop of Hermopolis. He was moreover extremely annoyed at the esteem and veneration in which he was held by the ascetics. Being aware, however, that he would be able to do no harm to these persons unless he could stir up hostility in the minds of the monks against them, he used this artifice to effect it. He well knew that these men in their frequent theological discussions with him, had maintained that the Deity was incorporeal, and by no means had a human form; because [they argued] such a constitution would involve the necessary accompaniment of human passions. Now this has been demonstrated by the ancient writers and especially Origen. Theophilus, however, though entertaining the very same opinion respecting the Divine nature, yet to gratify his vindictive feelings, did not hesitate to pervert what he and they had rightly taught: but imposed upon the majority of the monks, men who were sincere but 'rude in speech,'[4] the greater part of whom were quite illiterate. Sending letters to the monasteries in the desert, he advised them not to give heed either to Dioscorus or to his brothers, inasmuch as they affirmed that God had not a body. 'Whereas,' said he, 'according to the sacred Scripture God has eyes, ears, hands, and feet, as men have; but the partisans of Dioscorus, being followers of Origen, introduce the blasphemous dogma that God has neither eyes, ears, feet, nor hands.' By this sophism he took advantage of the simplicity of these monks and thus a hot dissension was stirred up among them. Such as had a cultivated mind indeed were not beguiled by this plausibility, and therefore still adhere to Dioscorus and Origen; but the more ignorant who greatly exceeded the others in number, inflamed by an ardent zeal without knowledge, immediately raised an outcry against their brethren. A division being thus made, both parties branded each other as impious; and some listening to Theophilus called their brethren 'Origenists,' and 'impious' and the others termed those who were convinced by Theophilus 'Anthropomorphitæ.' On this account violent altercation arose, and an inextinguishable war between the monks. Theophilus on receiving intimation of the success of his device, went to Nitria where the monasteries are, accompanied by a multitude of persons, and armed the monks against Dioscorus and his brethren; who being

---

[2] On the dispute concerning Origen's views, see below, chap. 13.
[3] There were two cities named Hermopolis in Egypt; the most important of these in the Thebaid was known as Hermopolis proper, whereas the other (the one here alluded to) was situated in lower Egypt and designated Hermopolis *parva*.

[4] 2 Cor. xi. 6.

in danger of losing their lives, made their escape with great difficulty.

While these things were in progress in Egypt John bishop of Constantinople was ignorant of them, but flourished in eloquence and became increasingly celebrated for his discourses. Moreover he first enlarged the prayers contained in the nocturnal hymns, for the reason I am about to assign.

CHAPTER VIII.

The Arians and the Supporters of the 'Homoousion' hold Nocturnal Assemblies and sing Antiphonal Hymns, a Species of Composition ascribed to Ignatius, surnamed Theophorus.[1] Conflict between the Two Parties.

THE Arians, as we have said, held their meetings without the city. As often therefore as the festal days occurred — I mean Saturday[2] and Lord's day — in each week, on which assemblies are usually held in the churches, they congregated within the city gates about the public squares, and sang responsive verses adapted to the Arian heresy. This they did during the greater part of the night: and again in the morning, chanting the same songs which they called responsive, they paraded through the midst of the city, and so passed out of the gates to go to their places of assembly. But since they did not desist from making use of insulting expressions in relation to the Homoousians, often singing such words as these: 'Where are they that say three things are but one power?' — John fearing lest any of the more simple should be drawn away from the church by such kind of hymns, opposed to them some of his own people, that they also employing themselves in chanting nocturnal hymns, might obscure the effort of the Arians, and confirm his own party in the profession of their faith. John's design indeed seemed to be good, but it issued in tumult and dangers. For as the Homoousians performed their nocturnal hymns with greater display, — for there were invented by John silver crosses for them on which lighted wax-tapers were carried, provided at the expense of the empress Eudoxia, — the Arians who were very numerous, and fired with envy, resolved to revenge themselves by a desperate and riotous attack upon their rivals. For from the remembrance of their own recent domination, they were full of confidence in their ability to overcome, and of contempt for their adversaries. Without delay therefore, on one of these nights, they engaged in a conflict; and Briso, one of the eunuchs of the empress, who was at that time leading the chanters of these hymns, was wounded by a stone in the forehead, and also some of the people on both sides were killed. Whereupon the emperor being angered, forbade the Arians to chant their hymns any more in public. Such were the events of this occasion.

We must now however make some allusion to the origin of this custom in the church of responsive singing. Ignatius[3] third bishop of Antioch in Syria from the apostle Peter, who also had held intercourse with the apostles themselves, saw a vision of angels hymning in alternate chants the Holy Trinity. Accordingly he introduced the mode of singing he had observed in the vision into the Antiochian church; whence it was transmitted by tradition to all the other churches. Such is the account [we have received] in relation to these responsive hymns.

CHAPTER IX.

Dispute between Theophilus and Peter leading to an Attempt on the Part of the Former to depose John Bishop of Constantinople.

NOT long after this, the monks of the desert, together with Dioscorus and his brothers, came to Constantinople. There was also with them Isidore,[1] formerly the most intimate friend of the bishop Theophilus, but then become his bitterest enemy, on account of the following circumstance: A certain man named Peter was at that time the archpresbyter[2] of the Alexandrian church; Theophilus being irritated against this person, determined to eject him from the church; and as the ground of expulsion, he brought the charge against him of having admitted to a participation of the sacred mysteries, a woman of the Manichæan sect, without first compelling her to renounce her Manichæan heresy. As Peter in his defence declared, that not only had the errors of this woman been previously abjured, but that Theophilus himself had sanctioned her admission to the eucharist, Theophilus became indignant, as if he had been grievously calumniated; whereupon he affirmed that he was altogether

---

[1] Θεόφορος = 'borne by God,' used in the sense of being 'possessed by a god,' 'inspired,' by Æsch. *Agam.* 1150; but here 'borne in the arms of God' or 'carried by God,' and applied to Ignatius because tradition made him the very child whom the Saviour 'took up in his arms,' and 'set in the midst of his disciples.' Cf. Mark ix. 36; to be distinguished therefore from Θεοφόρος, 'bearing' or 'carrying a god.'

[2] The ancient Christians observed the Lord's day as the greatest day of the week, and also in the second place the Jewish Sabbath or Saturday. See Bingham, *Christ. Antiq.* XX. 2, on the Lord's day, and 3, on the Sabbath.

[3] There has been some difference of opinion as to whether Socrates is correct in here ascribing the institution of responsive chants to Ignatius. Valesius doubts Socrates' accuracy, but other authorities are inclined to the view that Ignatius did introduce these chants, and Flavian and Diodorus, during the reign of Constantine, to whom Valesius ascribes their origin, simply developed them. Cf. Bingham, *Christ. Antiq.* XIV. 1.

[1] For an account of Theophilus' outrageous treatment of Isidore, see Palladius, *Vita S. Joannis Chrysost.* chap. 6.

[2] See Bingham, *Christ. Antiq.* II. 19. 18, for a statement of the functions of this office.

unacquainted with the circumstance. Peter therefore summoned Isidore to bear witness to the bishop's knowledge of the facts concerning the woman. Now Isidore happened to be then at Rome, on a mission from Theophilus to Damasus the prelate of the imperial city, for the purpose of affecting a reconciliation between him and Flavian bishop of Antioch; for the adherents of Meletius had separated from Flavian in detestation of his perjury, as we have already observed.[3] When Isidore had returned from Rome, and was cited as a witness by Peter, he deposed that the woman was received by consent of the bishop; and that he himself had administered the sacrament to her. Upon this Theophilus became enraged and in anger ejected them both. This furnished the reason for Isidore's going to Constantinople with Dioscorus and his brethren, in order to submit to the cognizance of the emperor, and John the bishop, the injustice and violence with which Theophilus had treated them. John, on being informed of the facts, gave the men an honorable reception, and did not exclude them from communion at prayers, but postponed their communion of the sacred mysteries, until their affairs should be examined into. Whilst matters were in this posture, a false report was brought to Theophilus' ears, that John had both admitted them to a participation of the mysteries, and was also ready to give them assistance; wherefore he resolved not only to be revenged on Isidore and Dioscorus, but also if possible to cast John out of his episcopal chair. With this design he wrote to all the bishops of the various cities, and concealing his real motive, ostensibly condemned therein the books of Origen merely: which Athanasius,[4] his predecessor, had used in confirmation of his own faith, frequently appealing to the testimony and authority of Origen's writings, in his orations against the Arians.

CHAPTER X.

Epiphanius Bishop of Cyprus convenes a Synod to condemn the Books of Origen.

HE moreover renewed his friendship with Epiphanius[1] bishop of Constantia in Cyprus, with whom he had formerly been at variance. For Theophilus accused Epiphanius of entertaining low thoughts of God, by supposing him to have a human form.[2] Now although The-

ophilus was really unchanged in sentiment, and had denounced those who thought that the divinity was human in form, yet on account of his hatred of others, he openly denied his own convictions; and he now professed to be friendly with Epiphanius, as if he had altered his mind and agreed with him in his views of God. He then managed it so that Epiphanius by letter should convene a Synod of the bishops in Cyprus, in order to condemn the writings of Origen. Epiphanius being on account of his extraordinary piety a man of simple mind and manners was easily influenced by the letters of Theophilus: having therefore assembled a council of bishops in that island, he caused a prohibition to be therein made of the reading of Origen's works. He also wrote to John, exhorting him to abstain from the study of Origen's books, and to convoke a Synod for decreeing the same thing as he had done. Accordingly when Theophilus had in this way deluded Epiphanius, who was famous for his piety, seeing his design prosper according to his wish, he became more confident, and himself also assembled a great number of bishops. In that convention, pursuing the same course as Epiphanius, he caused a like sentence of condemnation to be pronounced on the writings of Origen, who had been dead nearly two hundred years: not having this as his first object, but rather his purpose of revenge on Dioscorus and his brethren. John paying but little attention to the communications of Epiphanius and Theophilus, was intent on instructing the churches; and he flourished more and more as a preacher, but made no account of the plots which were laid against him. As soon, however, as it became apparent to every body that Theophilus was endeavoring to divest John of his bishopric, then all those who had any ill-will against John, combined in calumniating him. And thus many of the clergy, and many of those in office, and of those who had great influence at the court, believing that they had found an opportunity now of avenging themselves upon John, exerted themselves to procure the convocation of a Grand Synod at Constantinople, partly by sending letters and partly by dispatching messengers in all directions for that purpose.

CHAPTER XI.

Of Severian and Antiochus: their Disagreement from John.

THE odium against John Chrysostom was considerably increased by another additional event as follows: two bishops flourished at that time,

---

[3] See above, V. 15.   [4] Cf. Athan. *de Decr. Nic.* 27.

[1] There were thirty-five bishops, besides several presbyters and laymen of some distinction in the ancient church, who bore the name of Epiphanius. The bishop here mentioned is the most illustrious of them all, being the author of the well-known treatise *de Hæres*. His see — that of Constantia in Cyprus — was the old 'Salamis' of Acts xiii. 5.

[2] It seems strange that Epiphanius should be classed with the Anthropomorphitæ as Epiphanius himself repudiates their views according to the testimony of Jerome. Cf. Jerome, *ad Pammachium*, 2 *et seq.* Socrates must have been imposed upon by some

Origenist, as the Origenists were accustomed to call all who condemned their views Anthropomorphitæ. Cf. above, chap. 7.

Syrians by birth, named Severian and Antiochus; Severian presided over the church at Gabala, a city of Syria, and Antiochus over that of Ptolemaïs in Phœnicia. They were both renowned for their eloquence; but although Severian was a very learned man, he did not succeed in using the Greek language perfectly; and so while speaking Greek he betrayed his Syrian origin. Antiochus came first to Constantinople, and having preached in the churches for some time with great zeal and ability, and having thus amassed a large sum of money,[1] he returned to his own church. Severian hearing that Antiochus had collected a fortune by his visit to Constantinople, determined to follow his example. He therefore exercised himself for the occasion, and having composed a number of sermons, set out for Constantinople. Being most kindly received by John, to a certain point, he soothed and flattered the man, and was himself no less beloved and honored by him: meanwhile his discourses gained him great celebrity, so that he attracted the notice of many persons of rank, and even of the emperor himself. And as it happened at that time that the bishop of Ephesus died, John was obliged to go to Ephesus for the purpose of ordaining a successor. On his arrival at that city, as the people were divided in their choice, some proposing one person, and some another, John perceiving that both parties were in a contentious mood, and that they did not wish to adopt his counsel, he resolved without much ado to end their dispute by preferring to the bishopric a certain Heraclides, a deacon of his own, and a Cypriot by descent. And thus both parties desisting from their strife with each other had peace.[2] Now as this detention [at Ephesus] was lengthened, Severian continued to preach at Constantinople, and daily grew in favor with his hearers. Of this John was not left ignorant, for he was promptly made acquainted with whatever occurred, Serapion, of whom we have before spoken,[3] communicating the news to him and asserting that the church was being troubled by Severian; thus the bishop was aroused to a feeling of jealousy. Having therefore among other matters deprived many of the Novatians and Quartodecimans of their churches, he returned to Constantinople.[4] Here he resumed

himself the care of the churches under his own especial jurisdiction. But Serapion's arrogance no one could bear; for thus having won John's unbounded confidence and regard, he was so puffed up by it that he treated every one with contempt. And on this account also animosity was inflamed the more against the bishop. On one occasion when Severian passed by him, Serapion neglected to pay him the homage due to a bishop, but continued seated [instead of rising], indicating plainly how little he cared for his presence. Severian, unable to endure patiently this [supposed] rudeness and contempt, said with a loud voice to those present, 'If Serapion should die a Christian, Christ has not become incarnate.' Serapion, taking occasion from this remark, publicly incited Chrysostom to enmity against Severian: for suppressing the conditional clause of the sentence, 'If Serapion die a Christian,' and saying that he had made the assertion that 'Christ has not become incarnate,' he brought several witnesses of his own party to sustain this charge. But on being informed of this the Empress Eudoxia severely reprimanded John, and ordered that Severian should be immediately recalled from Chalcedon in Bithynia. He returned forthwith; but John would hold no intercourse whatever with him, nor did he listen to any one urging

[1] The offerings of the congregations seem to have been divided usually among the officiating clergymen. Cf. Bingham, *Christ. Antiq.* V. 4. 1.

[2] In another version of this eleventh chapter of the sixth book, appended at the end of the sixth book in the Greek text of Bright, instead of the sentence beginning 'And thus both parties,' &c. is found the following more consistent statement: 'Inasmuch, however, as on this account a tumult arose at Ephesus, on the ground that Heraclides was not worthy of the bishopric, it became necessary for John to remain in Ephesus for a long time.'

[3] The alternative version inserts here the following sentence: 'And who was very much beloved by John and had been intrusted with the whole care of the episcopal administration, on account of his piety and faithfulness and watchfulness in respect to details of every sort, and diligence in matters pertaining to the interests of the bishop.'

[4] From this point to within one or two sentences of the end of the chapter the parallel version is so different at times that it will be well to insert it entire here for the purpose of comparison. It runs thus: 'Not long afterward John came to Constantinople and assumed himself the churches which belonged to his jurisdiction. But between Serapion, the deacon, and Severian there had arisen a certain coolness; Serapion was opposed to Severian because the latter seemed desirous of excelling John in public speaking, and Severian was jealous of Serapion because the bishop John favored him, and the care of the bishopric had been intrusted to him. They being thus disposed toward one another, it happened that the evil of hatred was increased from the following cause. As Severian was passing by on one occasion Serapion did not render him the homage due to a bishop, but he continued sitting; whether because he had not noticed him, as he afterwards affirmed upon oath before a council, or because he cared little for him, being himself the vicegerent of a bishop, as Severian asserted, I am unable to say; God only knows. At the time, however, Severian did not tolerate the contempt; but immediately, and in anticipation of a public investigation before a council, he condemned Serapion upon oath, and not only declared him deposed from the dignity of the diaconate, but also put him out of the church. John upon learning this was very much grieved. As the matter afterwards was investigated by a council and Serapion defended himself declaring that he had not perceived [the approach of the bishop], and summoned witnesses to the fact, the common verdict of the assembled bishops was in favor of acquitting him and urging Severian to accept the apology of Serapion. The Bishop John, for his part, suspended Serapion from the diaconate for a week; although he used him in all his affairs as his right hand, because he was very keen and diligent in ecclesiastical disputation. Severian however was not satisfied with these measures, but used all means to effect the permanent deposition of Serapion from the diaconate and his excommunication. John was extremely grieved at these words and arose from the council, leaving the adjudication of the case to the bishops present, saying to them, "Do you examine the matter in hand and render judgment according to your own conclusions; as for me I resign my part in the arbitration between them." These things having been said by John as he arose, the council likewise arose and left the case as it stood, blaming Severian the more for not yielding to the request of the Bishop John. After this John never received Severian into a private interview; but advised him to return to his own country, communicating to him the following message: "It is not expedient, Severian," said he, "that the parish intrusted to you should remain for so long without care and bereft of a bishop; wherefore hasten and take charge of your churches, and do not neglect the gift which is in you." As he now prepared for his journey and started, the Empress Eudoxia, on being informed of the facts,' &c. From this point the variations are few, verbal, and unimportant.

him to do so, until at length the Empress Eudoxia herself, in the church called *The Apostles*, placed her son Theodosius, who now so happily reigns, but was then quite an infant, before John's knees, and adjuring[5] him repeatedly by the young prince her son, with difficulty prevailed upon him to be reconciled to Severian. In this manner then these men were outwardly reconciled; but they nevertheless continued cherishing a rancorous feeling toward each other. Such was the origin of the animosity [of John] against Severian.

CHAPTER XII.

Epiphanius, in order to gratify Theophilus, performs Ordinations at Constantinople without John's Permission.

NOT long after this, at the suggestion of Theophilus, the bishop Epiphanius again came from Cyprus to Constantinople; he brought also with him a copy of the synodical decree in which they did not excommunicate Origen himself, but condemned his books. On reaching *St. John's* church, which is seven miles distant from the city, he disembarked, and there celebrated a service; then after having ordained a deacon,[1] he again entered the city. In complaisance to Theophilus he declined John's courtesy, and engaged apartments in a private house. He afterwards assembled those of the bishops who were then in the capital, and producing his copy of the synodical decree condemnatory of Origen's works, recited it before them; not being able to assign any reason for this judgment, than that it seemed fit to Theophilus and himself to reject them. Some indeed from a reverential respect for Epiphanius subscribed the decree; but many refused to do so; among whom was Theotimus bishop of Scythia, who thus addressed Epiphanius:— 'I neither choose, Epiphanius,' said he, 'to insult the memory of one who ended his life piously long ago; nor dare I be guilty of so impious an act, as that of condemning what our predecessors did not reject: and especially when I know of no evil doctrine contained in Origen's books.'

Having said this, he brought forward one of that author's works, and reading a few passages therefrom, showed that the sentiments propounded were in perfect accordance with the orthodox faith. He then added, 'Those who speak evil of these writings are unconsciously casting dishonor upon the sacred volume whence their principles are drawn.' Such was the reply which Theotimus, a bishop celebrated for his piety and rectitude of life, made to Epiphanius.

CHAPTER XIII.

The Author's Defence of Origen.[1]

BUT since carping detractors have imposed upon many persons and have succeeded in deterring them from reading Origen, as though he were a blasphemous writer, I deem it not unseasonable to make a few observations respecting him. Worthless characters, and such as are destitute of ability to attain eminence themselves, often seek to get into notice by decrying those who excel them. And first Methodius, bishop of a city in Lycia named Olympus, labored under this malady; next Eustathius, who for a short time presided over the church at Antioch; after him Apollinaris; and lastly Theophilus. This quaternion of revilers has traduced Origen, but not on the same grounds, one having found one cause of accusation against him, and another another; and thus each has demonstrated that what he has taken no objection to, he has fully accepted. For since one has attacked one opinion in particular, and another has found fault with another, it is evident that each has admitted as true what he has not assailed, giving a tacit approbation to what he has not attacked. Methodius indeed, when he had in various places railed against Origen, afterwards as if retracting all he had previously said, expresses his admiration of the man, in a dialogue which he entitled *Xenōn*.[2] But I affirm that from the censure of these men, greater commendation accrues to Origen. For those who have sought out whatever they deemed worthy of reprobation in him, and yet have never charged him with holding unsound views respecting the holy Trinity, are in this way most distinctly shown to bear witness to his orthodox piety: and by not reproaching him on this point, they commend him by their own testimony. But Athanasius the defender

---

[5] The ancients often swore by their children, especially when they wished to entreat others most earnestly. Cf. Vergil, *Æneid*, VI. 364, '*Per caput hoc juro, per spem surgentis Juli.*' The form of abjuration used by Eudoxia was probably this: 'By this little child of mine, and your spiritual son, whom I brought forth and whom you received out of the sacred font, be reconciled to Severian.' Valesius, however, doubts the reality of this affair.

[1] It was contrary to the canons of the church for a bishop to ordain a presbyter or a deacon in another's diocese. Cf. *Apostol. Can.* 35. 'Let not a bishop dare to ordain beyond his own limits, in cities and places not subject to him. But if he be convicted of doing so without the consent of those persons who have authority over such cities and places, let him be deposed, and those also whom he has ordained.' Also *Can.* 16 of the Council of Nicæa; 'If any one should dare to steal, as it were, a person who belongs to another [bishop], and to ordain him for his own church, without permission of the bishop from whom he was withdrawn, the ordination shall be void.'

[1] The views of Origen met with opposition from the very outset. During his own lifetime he was condemned at Alexandria, and after his death repeatedly until 541 A.D., and perhaps also by the fifth general council held at Constantinople in 553. For a full account of the Origenistic Controversy, see Smith and Wace, *Dict. of Christ. Biog. and Antiq.*, art. ORIGENISTIC CONTROVERSIES.

[2] 'The house of entertainment for strangers.' Methodius' works were in the literary form of the dialogue. Cf. his *Convivium decem Virginum* in Migné's *Patrologia Græca*, Vol. XVIII.

of the doctrine of consubstantiality, in his *Discourses against the Arians*,[3] continually cites this author as a witness of his own faith, interweaving his words with his own, and saying, 'The most admirable and assiduous Origen,' says he, 'by his own testimony confirms our doctrine concerning the Son of God, affirming him to be co-eternal with the Father.' Those therefore who load Origen with opprobrium, overlook the fact that their maledictions fall at the same time on Athanasius, the eulogist of Origen. So much will be enough for the vindication of Origen; we shall now return to the course of our history.

CHAPTER XIV.

Epiphanius is asked to meet John; on refusing he is admonished concerning his Anticanonical Proceedings; alarmed at this he leaves Constantinople.

JOHN was not offended because Epiphanius, contrary to the ecclesiastical canon, had made an ordination in his church;[1] but invited him to remain with him at the episcopal palace. He, however, replied that he would neither stay nor pray with him, unless he would expel Dioscorus and his brethren from the city, and with his own hand subscribe the condemnation of Origen's books. Now as John deferred the performance of these things, saying that nothing ought to be done rashly before investigation by a general council, John's adversaries led Epiphanius to adopt another course. For they contrived it so that as a meeting was in the church named *The Apostles*, Epiphanius came forth and before all the people condemned the books of Origen, excommunicated Dioscorus with his followers, and charged John with countenancing them. These things were reported to John; whereupon on the following day he sent the appended message to Epiphanius just as he entered the church: 'You do many things contrary to the canons, Epiphanius. In the first place you have made an ordination in the churches under my jurisdiction: then without my appointment, you have on your own authority officiated in them. Moreover, when heretofore I invited you hither, you refused to come, and now you take that liberty yourself. Beware therefore, lest a tumult being excited among the people, you yourself should also incur danger therefrom.' Epiphanius becoming alarmed on hearing these admonitions, left the church; and after accusing John of many things, he set out on his return to Cyprus. Some say that when he was about to depart, he said to John, 'I hope that

you will not die a bishop': to which John replied, 'Expect not to arrive at your own country.' I cannot be sure that those who reported these things to me spoke the truth; but nevertheless the event was in the case of both as prophesied above. For Epiphanius did not reach Cyprus, having died on board the ship during his voyage; and John a short time afterwards was driven from his see, as we shall show in proceeding.

CHAPTER XV.

John is expelled from his Church by a Synod held at Chalcedon on account of his Dispraise of Women.

WHEN Epiphanius was gone, John was informed by some person that the Empress Eudoxia had stimulated Epiphanius against him. And being of a fiery temperament, and of a ready utterance, he soon after pronounced a public invective against women in general. The people readily took this as uttered indirectly against the empress and so the speech was laid hold of by evil-disposed persons, and reported to those in authority. At length on being informed of it the empress immediately complained to her husband, telling him that the insult offered to herself was equally an insult against him. The emperor therefore authorized Theophilus to convoke a Synod without delay against John; Severian also co-operated in promoting this, for he still retained his grudge against Chrysostom. Not long time accordingly intervened before Theophilus arrived, having induced several bishops from different cities to accompany him; these however had been summoned by the emperor's orders also. Many of the bishops in Asia John had deposed when he went to Ephesus and ordained Heraclides. Accordingly they all by previous agreement assembled at Chalcedon in Bithynia. Cyrinus was at that time bishop of Chalcedon, an Egyptian by birth, who said many things to the bishops in disparagement of John, denouncing him as 'the impious,' 'the haughty,' 'the inexorable.' They indeed were very much satisfied at these denunciations. But Maruthas bishop of Mesopotamia having involuntarily trod on Cyrinus' foot, he was severely hurt by it and was unable to embark with the rest for Constantinople, but remained behind at Chalcedon. The rest crossed over. Now Theophilus had so openly avowed his hostility to John, that none of the clergy would go forth to meet him, or pay him the least honor; but some Alexandrian sailors happening to be on the spot — for at that time the grain transporting vessels were there — greeted him with joyful acclamations. He excused himself from entering the church, and

---

3 Athan. *de Decr. Nic.* 27.
1 See above, chap. 12 and note 1.

took up his abode at one of the imperial mansions called 'The Placidian.' Then on this account a torrent of accusations began to be poured forth against John; for no mention was now made of Origen, but all were intent on urging a variety of criminations, many of which were ridiculous. Preliminary matters being thus settled, the bishops were convened in one of the suburbs of Chalcedon, a place called 'The Oak,'[1] and immediately cited John to answer the charges which were brought against him. He also summoned Serapion the deacon; Tigris the eunuch presbyter, and Paul the reader, were likewise summoned to appear there with him, for these men were included in the impeachments, as participators in his guilt. And since John taking exception to those who had cited him, on the ground of their being his enemies, refused to attend,[2] and demanded a general council, without delay they repeated their citation four times in succession; and as he persisted in his refusal to meet them as his judges, always giving the same answer, they condemned him, and deposed him without assigning any other cause for his deposition but that he refused to obey the summons. This decision on being announced towards evening, incited the people to a most alarming sedition; insomuch that they kept watch all night, and would by no means suffer him to be removed from the church, but cried out that his cause ought to be determined in a larger assembly. A decree of the emperor, however, commanded that he should be immediately expelled, and sent into exile; which as soon as John was apprised of, he voluntarily surrendered himself about noon unknown to the populace, on the third day after his condemnation: for he dreaded any insurrectionary movement on his account, and was accordingly led away.

CHAPTER XVI.

Sedition on Account of John Chrysostom's Banishment. He is recalled.

THE people then became intolerably tumultuous; and as it frequently happens in such cases, many who before were adversely disposed against him, now changed their hostility into compassion, and said of him whom they had so recently desired to see deposed, that he had been traduced. By this means therefore they became very numerous who exclaimed against both the emperor and the Synod of bishops; but the origin of the intrigue they more particularly referred to Theophilus. For his fraudulent conduct could no longer be concealed, being exposed by many other indications, and especially by the fact of his having held communion with Dioscorus, and those termed 'the Tall Monks,'[1] immediately after John's deposition. But Severian preaching in the church, and thinking it a suitable occasion to declaim against John, said: 'If John had been condemned for nothing else, yet the haughtiness of his demeanor was a crime sufficient to justify his deposition. Men indeed are forgiven all other sins: but "God resisteth the proud,"[2] as the Divine Scriptures teach us.' These reproaches made the people still more inclined to opposition; so that the emperor gave orders for his immediate recall. Accordingly Briso a eunuch in the service of the empress[3] was sent after him, who finding him at Prænetum — a commercial town situated over against Nicomedia — brought him back toward Constantinople. And as he had been recalled, John refused to enter the city, declaring he would not do so until his innocence had been admitted by a higher tribunal. Thus he remained at a suburb called Marianæ. Now as he delayed at that place the commotion increased, and caused the people to break forth into very indignant and opprobrious language against their rulers, wherefore to check their fury John was constrained to proceed. On his way a vast multitude, with veneration and honor, conducted him immediately to the church; there they entreated him to seat himself in the episcopal chair, and give them his accustomed benediction. When he sought to excuse himself, saying that 'this ought to be brought about by an order from his judges, and that those who condemned him must first revoke their sentence,' they were only the more inflamed with the desire of seeing him reinstated, and of hearing him address them again. The people finally prevailed on him to resume his seat, and pray as usual for peace upon them; after which, acting under the same constraint, he preached to them. This compliance on John's part afforded his adversaries another ground of crimination; but respecting this they took no action at that time.

CHAPTER XVII.

Conflict between the Constantinopolitans and Alexandrians on Account of Heraclides; Flight of Theophilus and the Bishops of his Party.

IN the first place, then, Theophilus attempted to investigate the case of the ordination of Her-

---

[1] Hence this is called the Synod at 'the Oak' (*Synodus ad Quercum*). See Hefele, *History of the Church Councils*, Vol. II. p. 430.
[2] For a similar action of Athanasius based on the same reason, see I. 31.

[1] See above, chap. 7.   [2] 1 Pet. v. 5; James iv. 6.
[3] Chap. 8.

aclides,[1] that thereby he might if possible find occasion of again deposing John. Heraclides was not present at this scrutiny. He was nevertheless judged in his absence, on the charge of having unjustly beaten some persons, and afterwards dragged them in chains through the midst of the city of Ephesus. As John and his adherents remonstrated against the injustice of passing sentence upon an absent person, the Alexandrians contended that they ought to hear the accusers of Heraclides, although he was not present. A sharp contest therefore ensued between the Alexandrians and the Constantinopolitans, and a riot arose whereby many persons were wounded, and some were killed. Theophilus, seeing what was done, fled to Alexandria without ceremony; and the other bishops, except the few who supported John, followed his example, and returned to their respective sees. After these transactions, Theophilus was degraded in every one's estimation: ٬ but the odium attached to him was exceedingly increased by the shameless way in which he continued to read Origen's works. And when he was asked why he thus countenanced what he had publicly condemned, he replied, 'Origen's books are like a meadow enameled with flowers of every kind. If, therefore, I chance to find a beautiful one among them, I cull it: but whatever appears to me to be thorny, I step over, as that which would prick.' But Theophilus gave this answer without reflecting on the saying of the wise Solomon,[2] that 'the words of the wise are as goads'; and those who are pricked by the precepts they contain, ought not to kick against them. For these reasons then Theophilus was held in contempt by all men. Dioscorus bishop of Hermopolis, one of those termed 'the Tall Monks,' died a short time after the flight of Theophilus, and was honored with a magnificent funeral, being interred in the church at 'The Oak,' where the Synod was convened on John's account. John meanwhile was sedulously employed in preaching. He ordained Serapion bishop of Heraclea in Thrace, on whose account the odium against himself had been raised. Not long after the following events occurred.

CHAPTER XVIII.

Of Eudoxia's Silver Statue. On account of it John is exiled a Second Time.

At this time a silver statue of the Empress Eudoxia covered with a long robe was erected[1]

upon a column of porphyry supported by a lofty base. And this stood neither near nor far from the church named *Sophia*, but one-half the breadth of the street separated them. At this statue public games were accustomed to be performed; these John regarded as an insult offered to the church, and having regained his ordinary freedom and keenness of tongue, he employed his tongue against those who tolerated them. Now while it would have been proper to induce the authorities by a supplicatory petition to discontinue the games, he did not do this, but employing abusive language he ridiculed those who had enjoined such practices. The empress once more applied his expressions to herself as indicating marked contempt toward her own person: she therefore endeavored to procure the convocation of another council of bishops against him. When John became aware of this, he delivered in the church that celebrated oration commencing with these words:[2] 'Again Herodias raves; again she is troubled; she dances again; and again desires to receive John's head in a charger.' This, of course, exasperated the empress still more. Not long after the following bishops arrived: Leontius bishop of Ancyra in Asia, Ammonius of Laodicea in Pisidia, Briso of Philippi in Thrace, Acacius of Berœa in Syria, and some others. John presented himself fearlessly before them, and demanded an investigation of the charges which were made against him. But the anniversary of the birth of our Saviour having recurred, the emperor would not attend church as usual, but sent Chrysostom a message to the effect that he should not partake of the communion with him until he had cleared himself of the crimes with which he stood impeached. Now as John maintained a bold and ardent bearing, and his accusers seemed to grow faint-hearted, the bishops present, setting aside all other matters, said they would confine themselves to this sole consideration, that he had on his own responsibility, after his deposition, again seated himself in the episcopal chair, without being authorized by an ecclesiastical council. As he alleged that sixty-five bishops who had held communion with him had reinstated him, the partisans of Leontius objected, saying: 'A larger number voted against you, John, in the Synod.' But although John then contended that this was a canon of the Arians, and not of the catholic church, and therefore it was inoperative against him — for it had been framed in the council convened against Athanasius at Antioch, for the subversion of the doctrine of consubstantiality[3] —

---

[1] See above, chap. 11.   [2] Eccl. xii. 11.
[1] From Prosper Aquitamus and Marcellinus' *Chronicon*, we learn that this was done in 403 A.D., or rather the consulship of Theodosius the younger and Rumoridius.

[2] This discourse entitled '*In decollationem Præcursoris et baptistæ Joannis*' is to be found in Migné's *Patrologia Græcia*, Vol. LIV. p. 485, and in Savile's edition of Chrysostom's works, Vol. VII. 545. Savile, however, places it among the spurious pieces, and considers it unworthy of the genius of Chrysostom.
[3] Cf. II. 8.

the bishops would not listen to his defence, but immediately condemned him, without considering that by using this canon they were sanctioning the deposition of Athanasius himself. This sentence was pronounced a little before Easter; the emperor therefore sent to tell John that he could not go to the church, because two Synods had condemned him. Accordingly Chrysostom was silenced, and went no more to the church; but those who were of his party celebrated Easter in the public baths which are called Constantianæ, and thenceforth left the church. Among them were many bishops and presbyters, with others of the clerical order, who from that time held their assemblies apart in various places, and were from him denominated 'Johannites.' For the space of two months, John refrained from appearing in public; after which a decree of the emperor sent him into exile. Thus he was led into exile by force, and on the very day of his departure, some of the Johannites set fire to the church, which by means of a strong easterly wind, communicated with the senate-house. This conflagration happened on the 20th of June, under the sixth consulate of Honorius, which he bore in conjunction with Aristænetus.[4] The severities which Optatus, the prefect of Constantinople, a pagan in religion, and a hater of the Christians, inflicted on John's friends, and how he put many of them to death on account of this act of incendiarism, I ought, I believe, to pass by in silence.[5]

CHAPTER XIX.

Ordination of Arsacius as John's Successor. Indisposition of Cyrinus Bishop of Chalcedon.

AFTER the lapse of a few days, Arsacius was ordained bishop of Constantinople; he was a brother of Nectarius who so ably administered the see before John, although he was then very aged, being upwards of eighty years old. While he very mildly and peacefully administered the episcopate, Cyrinus bishop of Chalcedon, upon whose foot Maruthas bishop of Mesopotamia had inadvertently trodden, became so seriously affected by the accident, that mortification ensued, and it became necessary to amputate his foot. Nor was this amputation performed once only, but was required to be often repeated: for after the injured limb was cut off, the evil so permeated his whole system, that the other foot also having become affected by the disease had to submit to the same operation.[1] I have

alluded to this circumstance, because many have affirmed that what he suffered was a judgment upon him for his calumnious aspersions of John, whom he so often designated as arrogant and inexorable,[2] as I have already said.[3] Furthermore as on the 30th of September, in the last-mentioned consulate,[4] there was an extraordinary fall of hail of immense size at Constantinople and its suburbs, it also was declared to be an expression of Divine indignation on account of Chrysostom's unjust deposition: and the death of the empress tended to give increased credibility to these reports, for it took place four days after the hail-storm. Others, however, asserted that John had been deservedly deposed, because of the violence he had exercised in Asia and Lydia, in depriving the Novatians and Quartodecimans of many of their churches, when he went to Ephesus and ordained Heraclides. But whether John's deposition was just, as his enemies declare, or Cyrinus suffered in chastisement for his slanderous revilings; whether the hail fell, or the empress died on John's account, or whether these things happened for other reasons, or for these in connection with others, God only knows, who is the discerner of secrets, and the just judge of truth itself. I have simply recorded the reports which were current at that time.

CHAPTER XX.

Death of Arsacius, and Ordination of Atticus.

BUT Arsacius did not long survive his accession to the bishopric; for he died on the 11th of November under the following consulate, which was Stilicho's second, and the first of Anthemius.[1] In consequence of the fact that the bishopric became desirable and many aspired to the vacant see, much time elapsed before the election of a successor: but at length in the following consulate, which was the sixth of Arcadius, and the first of Probus,[2] a devout man named Atticus was promoted to the episcopate. He was a native of Sebastia in Armenia, and had followed an ascetic life from an early age: moreover in addition to a moderate share of learning, he possessed a large amount of natural prudence. But I shall speak of him more particularly a little later.[3]

CHAPTER XXI.

John dies in Exile.

JOHN taken into exile died in Comana on the Euxine, on the 14th of September, in the following

---

[4] 404 A.D.
[5] Some of these details presumably are given by Sozomen in VIII. 23 and 24.
[1] Palladius makes mention of this case without, however, naming Cyrinus. Cf. *Vit. S. Joan. Chrysostom*, chap. 17 (Vol. XIII. p. 63 A. of Benedictine ed. of Chrysostom).

[2] ἀγόνατον, lit. = 'kneeless.'
[3] Cf. chap. 15, above.
[4] 404 A.D.
[1] 405 A.D.
[2] 406 A.D.
[3] Cf. VII. 2.

consulate, which was the seventh of Honorius, and the second of Theodosius.[1] A man, as we have before observed,[2] who on account of zeal for temperance was inclined rather to anger than forbearance : and his personal sanctity of character led him to indulge in a latitude of speech which to others was intolerable. Indeed, it is most inexplicable to me, how with a zeal so ardent for the practice of self-control and blamelessness of life, he should in his sermons appear to teach a loose view of temperance. For whereas by the Synod of bishops repentance was accepted but once from those who had sinned after baptism ; he did not scruple to say, 'Approach, although you may have repented a thousand times.'[3] For this doctrine, many even of his friends censured him, but especially Sisinnius bishop of the Novatian ; who wrote a book condemnatory of the above quoted expression of Chrysostom's, and severely rebuked him for it. But this occurred long before.[4]

CHAPTER XXII.

Of Sisinnius Bishop of the Novatians. His Readiness at Repartee.

IT will not be out of place here, I conceive, to give some account of Sisinnius. He was, as I have often said,[1] a remarkably eloquent man, and well-instructed in philosophy. But he had particularly cultivated logic, and was profoundly skilled in the interpretation of the holy Scriptures ; insomuch that the heretic Eunomius often shrank from the acumen which his reasoning displayed. As regards his diet he was not simple ; for although he practised the strictest moderation, yet his table was always sumptuously furnished. He was also accustomed to indulge himself by wearing white garments, and bathing twice a day in the public baths. And when some one asked him 'why he, a bishop, bathed himself twice a day?' he replied, 'Because it is inconvenient to bathe thrice.' Going one day from courtesy to visit the bishop Arsacius, he was asked by one of the friends of that bishop, 'why he wore a garment so unsuitable for a bishop? and where it was written that an ecclesiastic should be clothed in white?' 'Do you tell me first,' said he, 'where it is written that a bishop should wear black?' When he that made the inquiry knew not what to reply

to this counter-question : 'You cannot show,' rejoined Sisinnius, 'that a priest should be clothed in black. But Solomon is my authority, whose exhortation is, "Let thy garments be white."[2] And our Saviour in the Gospels appears clothed in white raiment :[3] moreover he showed Moses and Elias to the apostles, clad in white garments.' His prompt reply to these and other questions called forth the admiration of those present. Again when Leontius bishop of Ancyra in Galatia Minor, who had taken away a church from the Novatians, was on a visit to Constantinople, Sisinnius went to him, and begged him to restore the church. But he received him rudely, saying, 'Ye Novatians ought not to have churches ; for ye take away repentance, and shut out Divine mercy.' As Leontius gave utterance to these and many other such revilings against the Novatians, Sisinnius replied : 'No one repents more heartily than I do.' And when Leontius asked him 'Why do you repent?' 'That I came to see you,' said he. On one occasion John the bishop having a contest with him, said, 'The city cannot have two bishops.'[4] 'Nor has it,' said Sisinnius. John being irritated at this response, said, 'You see you pretend that you alone are the bishop.' 'I do not say that,' rejoined Sisinnius ; 'but that I am not bishop in your estimation only, who am such to others.' John being still more chafed at this reply, said, 'I will stop your preaching ; for you are a heretic.' To which Sisinnius good-humoredly replied, 'I will give you a reward, if you will relieve me from so arduous a duty.' John being softened a little by this answer, said, 'I will not make you cease to preach, if you find speaking so troublesome.' So facetious was Sisinnius, and so ready at repartee : but it would be tedious to dwell further on his witticisms. Wherefore by means of a few specimens we have illustrated what sort of a person he was, deeming these as sufficient. I will merely add that he was celebrated for erudition, and on account of it all the bishops who succeeded him loved and honored him ; and not only they but all the leading members of the senate also esteemed and admired him. He is the author of many works : but they are characterized by too great an affectation of elegance of diction, and a lavish intermingling of poetic expressions. On which account he was more

---

[1] 407 A.D.   [2] Cf. above, chap. 3.
[3] These words are not found in any of Chrysostom's extant homilies. There is no reason, however, for thinking that they were not uttered by him in a sermon now not in existence. Socrates' remarks on Chrysostom's attitude made here are among the considerations which have led some to think that he was a Novatian. Cf. Introd. p. x.
[4] For further particulars on Chrysostom's life and the circumstances of his death, see authorities mentioned in chap. 2, note 3.
[1] Cf. V. 10 and 21.

[2] Eccl. ix. 8.
[3] Matt. xvii. 2; Mark ix. 3; Luke ix. 29. On the clothing of the clergy, see Bingham, *Christ. Antiq.* VI. 4. 18.
[4] The canons forbade the existence of two authoritative bishops in one city. Cf. V. 5, note 3. It was supposed to be an apostolic tradition that prescribed this practice, and the faithful always resisted and condemned any attempts to consecrate a second bishop in a city. Thus 'when Constantius proposed that Liberiu and Felix should sit as co-partners in the Roman see and govern the church in common, the people with one accord rejected the proposal, crying out "One God, one Christ, one bishop." The rule, however, did not apply to the case of coadjutors, where the bishop was too old or infirm to discharge his episcopal duties.' See Bingham, *Christ. Antiq.* II. 13.

admired as a speaker than as a writer ; for there was dignity in his countenance and voice, as well as in his form and aspect, and every movement of his person was graceful. On account of these features he was loved by all the sects, and he was in especial favor with Atticus the bishop. But I must conclude this brief notice of Sisinnius.

CHAPTER XXIII.

Death of the Emperor Arcadius.

Not long after the death of John, the Emperor Arcadius died also. This prince was of a mild and gentle disposition, and toward the close of his life was esteemed to be greatly beloved of God, from the following circumstance. There was at Constantinople an immense mansion called Carya; for in the court of it there is a walnut tree on which it is said Acacius suffered martyrdom by hanging ; on which account a chapel was built near it, which the Emperor Arcadius one day thought fit to visit, and after having prayed there, left again.   All who lived near this chapel ran in a crowd to see the emperor ; and some going out of the mansion referred to, endeavored to preoccupy the streets in order to get a better view of their sovereign and his suite, while others followed in his train, until all who inhabited it, including the women and children, had wholly gone out of it.   No sooner was this vast pile emptied of its occupants, the buildings of which completely environed the church, than the entire building fell.   On which there was a great outcry, followed by shouts of admiration, because it was believed the emperor's prayer had rescued so great a number of persons from destruction.   This event occurred in that manner.   On the 1st of May, Arcadius died, leaving his son Theodosius only eight years old, under the consulate of Bassus and Philip, in the second year of the 297th Olympiad.[1] He had reigned thirteen years with Theodosius his father, and fourteen years after his death, and had then attained the thirty-first year of his age.   This book includes the space of twelve years and six months.[2]

---

[1] 408 A.D.
[2] The Greek editions [of Stephens, Valesius, Hussey, Bright, &c.] add the alternate form of chap. 11 at this place. For purposes of convenience in comparing the two versions we have given the variants with chapter 11.

END OF THE SIXTH BOOK.

BOOK VII.

CHAPTER I.

Anthemius the Prætorian Prefect administers the Government of the East in Behalf of Young Theodosius.

AFTER the death of Arcadius on the first of May, during the consulate of Bassus and Philip,[1] his brother Honorius still governed the Western parts of the empire; but the administration of the East devolved on his son Theodosius the Younger, then only eight years old. The management of public affairs was therefore intrusted to Anthemius the Prætorian prefect, grandson of that Philip who in the reign of Constantius ejected Paul from the see of Constantinople, and established Macedonius in his place. By his directions Constantinople was surrounded with high walls.[2] He was esteemed and actually was the most prudent man of his time, and seldom did anything unadvisedly, but consulted with the most judicious of his friends respecting all practical matters, and especially with Troïlus[3] the sophist, who while excelling in philosophical attainments, was equal to Anthemius himself in political wisdom. Wherefore almost all things were done with the concurrence of Troïlus.

CHAPTER II.

Character and Conduct of Atticus Bishop of Constantinople.

WHEN Theodosius the emperor was in the eighth year of his age, Atticus was in the third year of his presidency over the church at Constantinople, a man as we have by anticipation said[1] distinguished alike for his learning, piety, and discretion, wherefore it came about that the churches under his episcopate attained a very flourishing condition. For he not only united those of 'the household of faith,'[2] but also by

his prudence called forth the admiration of the heretics, whom indeed he by no means desired to harass; but if he sometimes was obliged to impress them with the fear of himself, he soon afterward showed himself mild and clement toward them. But indeed he did not neglect his studies; for he assiduously labored in perusing the writings of the ancients, and often spent whole nights in the task; and thus he could not be confused by the reasonings of the philosophers, and the fallacious subtleties of the sophists. Besides this he was affable and entertaining in conversation, and ever ready to sympathize with the afflicted: and in a word, to sum up his excellences in the apostle's saying, 'He was made all things to all men.'[3] Formerly while a presbyter, he had been accustomed, after composing his sermons, to commit them to memory, and then recite them in the church: but by diligent application he acquired confidence and made his instruction extemporaneous and eloquent. His discourses however were not such as to be received with much applause by his auditors, nor to deserve to be committed to writing. Let these particulars respecting his talents, erudition, and manners suffice. We must now proceed to relate such things as are worthy of record, that happened in his time.

CHAPTER III.

Of Theodosius and Agapetus Bishops of Synada.

A CERTAIN Theodosius was bishop of Synada in Phrygia Pacata; he violently persecuted the heretics in that province — and there was a great number of them — and especially those of the Macedonian sect; he drove them out not only from the city, but also out of the country. This course he pursued not from any precedent in the orthodox church, nor from the desire of propagating the true faith; but being enslaved by the love of filthy lucre, he was impelled by the avaricious motive of amassing money, by extorting it from the heretics. To this end he made all sorts of attempts upon the Macedonians, putting arms into the hands of his clergy; and employing innumerable stratagems against them; nor did he refrain from de-

---

[1] 408 A.D. Cf. VI. 23. See Gibbon's *Decline and Fall of the Roman Empire*, chap. 32.

[2] This was done, according to Cedrenus, several years later by another prefect. For this reason and because of the grammatical construction in the original, Valesius rightly conjectures that the phrase is a gloss introduced from the margin, and should be expunged from the text.

[3] Troïlus was a sophist of distinction who taught at Constantinople under Arcadius and Honorius at the beginning of the fifth century A.D., a native of Side and author of a treatise entitled Λόγοι πολιτικοί. See Suidas s.v. Τρωΐλος.

[1] Cf. VI. 20.   [2] Gal. vi. 10.   [3] 1 Cor. ix. 22.

livering them up to the secular tribunals.[1] But he especially annoyed their bishop whose name was Agapetus : and finding the governors of the province were not invested with sufficient authority to punish heretics according to his wish, he went to Constantinople and petitioned for edicts of a more stringent nature from the Prætorian prefect. While Theodosius was absent on this business, Agapetus who, as I have said, presided over the Macedonian sect, came to a wise and prudent conclusion. Communicating with his clergy, he called all the people under his guidance together, and persuaded them to embrace the 'homoousian' faith. On their acquiescing in this proposition, he proceeded immediately to the church attended not merely by his own adherents, but by the whole body of the people. There having offered prayer, he took possession of the episcopal chair in which Theodosius was accustomed to seat himself; and preaching thenceforth the doctrine of consubstantiality, he reunited the people, and made himself master of the churches in the diocese of Synada. Soon after these transactions, Theodosius returned to Synada, bringing with him extended powers from the prefect, and knowing nothing of what had taken place, he proceeded to the church just as he was. Being forthwith unanimously expelled, he again betook himself to Constantinople ; upon his arrival at that place he complained to Atticus, the bishop, of the treatment he had met with, and the manner in which he had been deprived of his bishopric. Atticus perceiving that this movement had resulted advantageously to the church, consoled Theodosius as well as he could ; recommending him to embrace with a contented mind a retired life, and thus sacrifice his own private interests to the public good. He then wrote to Agapetus authorizing him to retain the episcopate, and bidding him be under no apprehension of being molested in consequence of Theodosius' grievance.

CHAPTER IV.

A Paralytic Jew healed by Atticus in Baptism.

THIS was one important improvement in the circumstances of the Church, which happened during the administration of Atticus. Nor were these times without the attestation of miracles and healings. For a certain Jew being a paralytic had been confined to his bed for many years ; and as every sort of medical skill, and the prayers of his Jewish brethren had been resorted to but had availed nothing, he had

recourse at length to Christian baptism, trusting in it as the only true remedy to be used.[1] When Atticus the bishop was informed of his wishes, he instructed him in the first principles of Christian truth, and having preached to him to hope in Christ, directed that he should be brought in his bed to the font. The paralytic Jew receiving baptism with a sincere faith, as soon as he was taken out of the baptismal font found himself perfectly cured of his disease, and continued to enjoy sound health afterwards. This miraculous power Christ vouchsafed to be manifested even in our times ; and the fame of it caused many heathens to believe and be baptized. But the Jews although zealously 'seeking after signs,'[2] not even the signs which actually took place induced to embrace the faith. Such blessings were thus conferred by Christ upon men.

CHAPTER V.

The Presbyter Sabbatius, formerly a Jew, separates from the Novatians.

MANY, however, making no account of these events yielded to their own depravity ; for not only did the Jews continue in unbelief after this miracle, but others also who love to follow them were shown to hold views similar to theirs. Among these was Sabbatius, of whom mention has before been made ;[1] who not being content with the dignity of presbyter to which he had attained, but aiming at a bishopric from the beginning, separated himself from the church of the Novatians, making a pretext of observing the Jewish Passover.[2] Holding therefore schismatic assemblies apart from his own bishop Sisinnius, in a place named Xerolophus, where the forum of Arcadius now is, he ventured on the performance of an act deserving the severest punishments. Reading one day at one of these meetings that passage in the Gospel where it is said,[3] 'Now it was the Feast of the Jews called the Passover,' he added what was never written nor heard of before : 'Cursed be he that celebrates the Passover out of the days of unleavened bread.' When these words were reported among the people, the more simple of the Novatian laity, deceived by this artifice, flocked to him. But his fraudulent fabrication was of no avail to him ; for his forgery issued in most disastrous consequences. For shortly afterwards he kept this feast in anticipation of the Christian Easter ; and many according to their custom

---

[1] On the limits of the secular power over ecclesiastical dignitaries, and the cases in which the clergy were amenable to the civil law as well as those in which they were not, see Bingham, *Christ. Antiq.* V. 2.

[1] On the supposed miraculous effects of baptism, see Tertullian, *de baptismo, passim.*   [2] 1 Cor. i. 22.
[1] V. 21.
[2] Cf. I. 8, note 2, and V. 22 and notes.
[3] Not an exact quotation. Luke xxii. 1, resembles it more than any other of the parallels.

flocked to him. While they were passing the night in the accustomed vigils, a panic as if caused by evil spirits fell upon them, as if Sisinnius their bishop were coming with a multitude of persons to attack them. From the perturbation that might be expected in such a case, and their being shut up at night in a confined place, they trod upon one another, insomuch that above seventy of them were crushed to death. On this account many deserted Sabbatius: some however, holding his ignorant prejudice, remained with him. In what way Sabbatius, by a violation of his oath, afterwards managed to get himself ordained a bishop, we shall relate hereafter.[4]

CHAPTER VI.

The Leaders of Arianism at this Time.

DOROTHEUS bishop of the Arians, who, as we have said,[1] was translated by that sect from Antioch to Constantinople, having attained the age of one hundred and nineteen years, died on the 6th of November, in the seventh consulate of Honorius, and the second of Theodosius Augustus.[2] After him Barbas presided over the Arian sect, in whose time the Arian faction was favored by possessing two very eloquent members, both having the rank of presbyter, one of whom was named Timothy, and the other George. Now George excelled in Grecian literature; Timothy, on the other hand, was proficient in the sacred Scriptures. George indeed constantly had the writings of Aristotle and Plato in his hands: Timothy found his inspiration in Origen; he also evinced in his public expositions of the holy Scriptures no inconsiderable acquaintance with the Hebrew language. Now Timothy had formerly identified himself with the sect of the Psathyrians;[3] but George had been ordained by Barbas. I have myself conversed with Timothy, and was exceedingly struck by the readiness with which he would answer the most difficult questions, and clear up the most obscure passages in the Divine oracles; he also invariably quoted Origen as an unquestionable authority in confirmation of his own utterances. But it is astonishing to me that these two men should continue to uphold the heresy of the Arians; the one being so conversant with Plato, and the other having Origen so frequently on his lips. For Plato does not say that the second and third cause, as he usually terms them, had a beginning of existence:[4] and Origen everywhere acknowledges the Son to be co-eternal[5] with the Father.

Nevertheless although they remained connected with their own church, still they unconsciously changed the Arian sect for the better, and displaced many of the blasphemies of Arius by their own teachings. But enough of these persons. Sisinnius bishop of the Novatians dying under the same consulate, Chrysanthus was ordained in his place, of whom we shall have to speak by and by.

CHAPTER VII.

Cyril succeeds Theophilus Bishop of Alexandria.

SHORTLY afterwards Theophilus bishop of Alexandria having fallen into a lethargic state, died on the 15th of October,[1] in the ninth consulate of Honorius, and the fifth of Theodosius. A great contest immediately arose about the appointment of a successor, some seeking to place Timothy the archdeacon in the episcopal chair; and others desiring Cyril, who was a nephew of Theophilus. A tumult having arisen on this account among the people, Abundantius, the commander of the troops in Egypt, took sides with Timothy. [Yet the partisans of Cyril triumphed.][2] Whereupon on the third day after the death of Theophilus, Cyril came into possession of the episcopate, with greater power than Theophilus had ever exercised. For from that time the bishopric of Alexandria went beyond the limits of its sacerdotal functions, and assumed the administration of secular matters.[3] Cyril immediately therefore shut up the churches of the Novatians at Alexandria, and took possession of all their consecrated vessels and ornaments; and then stripped their bishop Theopemptus of all that he had.

CHAPTER VIII.

Propagation of Christianity among the Persians by Maruthas Bishop of Mesopotamia.

ABOUT this same time it happened that Christianity was disseminated in Persia, by reason of the following causes. Frequent embassies were sent to and fro between the sovereigns of Persia and the Roman empire, for which there were continual occasions. Necessity brought it about at that time that the Roman emperor thought proper to send Maruthas bishop of Mesopotamia, who has been before mentioned,[1] on a mission to the king of the Persians. The king

---

[4] Cf. chap. 12 below.   [2] 407 A.D.
[1] Cf. V. 3, 12 and 23.   [3] Cf. V. 23, note 2.
[4] The special views of Plato which are here alluded to are probably those found in the *Timæus*. Cf. Jowett, *The Dialogues of Plato translated into English*, Vol. II. p. 451 *et seq.*
[5] Cf. VI. 13.

[1] 412 A.D. This chapter is out of chronological sequence, as appears from the fact that Alaric took Rome in 410 A.D. See chap. 10 below.
[2] The words included in brackets are not found in the Greek; they were probably inserted into the English translation as necessary to explain the context.
[3] Cf. chap. 11.   [1] Cf. VI. 15.

discovering great piety in the man treated him with great honor, and gave heed to him as one who was indeed beloved of God. This excited the jealousy of the magi,[2] whose influence is considerable over the Persian monarch, for they feared lest he should persuade the king to embrace Christianity. For Maruthas had by his prayers cured the king of a violent headache to which he had been long subject, and which the magi had been unable to relieve. The magicians therefore had recourse to this deception. As the Persians worship fire, and the king was accustomed to pay his adorations in a certain edifice to the fire which was kept perpetually burning, they concealed a man underneath the sacred hearth, ordering him to make this exclamation at the time of day when the king was accustomed to perform his devotion ! 'The king should be thrust out because he is guilty of impiety, in imagining a Christian priest to be loved by the Deity.' When Isdigerdes — for that was the king's name — heard these words, he determined to dismiss Maruthas, notwithstanding the reverence with which he regarded him. But Maruthas being truly a God-loving man, by the earnestness of his prayers, detected the imposition of the magi. Going to the king therefore, he addressed him thus : 'Be not deluded, O king,' said he, 'but when you again enter that edifice and hear the same voice, explore the ground below, and you will discover the fraud. For it is not the fire that speaks, but human contrivance does this.' The king received the suggestion of Maruthas and went as usual to the little house where the ever-burning fire was. When he again heard the same voice, he ordered the hearth to be dug up ; whereupon the impostor, who uttered the supposed words of the Deity, was discovered. Becoming indignant at the deception thus attempted the king commanded that the tribe of the magi should be decimated. When this was effected he permitted Maruthas to erect churches wherever he wished ; and from that time the Christian religion was diffused among the Persians. Then Maruthas being recalled went to Constantinople ; not long afterwards however, he was again sent as ambassador to the Persian court. Again the magi devised contrivances so as by all possible means to prevent the king from giving him audience. One of their devices was to cause a most disgusting smell where the king was accustomed to go, and then accuse the Christians of being the authors of it. The king however having already had occasion to suspect the magi, very diligently and closely scrutinized the matter ; and again the authors of the nuisance were detected.

Wherefore he punished several of them, and held Maruthas in still higher honor. For the Romans as a nation he had much regard, and prized good feeling on their part very highly. Nay, he almost embraced the Christian faith himself, as Maruthas in conjunction with Abdas bishop of Persia gave another experimental proof of its power : for these two by giving themselves to much fasting and prayer, had cast out a demon with which the king's son was possessed. But the death of Isdigerdes[3] prevented his making an open profession of Christianity. The kingdom then devolved on Vararanes his son, in whose time the treaty between the Romans and Persians was broken as we shall have occasion to narrate a little later.[4]

CHAPTER IX.

The Bishops of Antioch and Rome.

DURING this period upon the death of Flavian[1] Porphyry received the episcopate of Antioch, and after him Alexander[2] was set over that church. But at Rome, Damasus having held that bishopric eighteen years Siricius succeeded him ;[3] and Siricius having presided there fifteen years, Anastasius held sway over the church for three years ; after Anastasius Innocent [was promoted to the same see]. He was the first persecutor of the Novatians at Rome, and many of their churches he took away.

CHAPTER X.

Rome taken and sacked by Alaric.

ABOUT this same time[1] it happened that Rome was taken by the barbarians ; for a certain Alaric, a barbarian who had been an ally of the Romans, and had served as an ally with the emperor Theodosius in the war against the usurper Eugenius, having on that account been honored with Roman dignities, was unable to bear his good fortune. He did not choose to assume imperial authority, but retiring from Constantinople went into the Western parts, and arriving at Illyricum immediately laid waste the whole country. As he marched, however, the Thessalians opposed him at the mouths of the river Peneus, whence there is a pass over Mount Pindus to Nicopolis in Epirus ; and coming to an engagement, the Thessalians killed about three thousand of his men. After this

---

[2] A caste of priests who exercised great influence in Persia mentioned both in the Old and the New Testament. Cf. Smith, *Dict. of the Bible*, art. MAGI.

[3] 420 A.D.   [4] Chap. 18 below.
[1] 404 A.D.   [2] 414 A.D.   [3] 385 A.D.
[1] On Alaric's career, see Zosimus, V. 5, 6; 28–51 and V. 1–13. Cf. also parallel accounts in Sozomen, IX. 4, 6–9: and Philostorgius, XII. 2, 3; and Gibbon's *Decline and Fall*, chap. 31.

the barbarians that were with him destroying everything in their way, at last took Rome itself, which they pillaged, burning the greatest number of the magnificent structures and other admirable works of art it contained. The money and valuable articles they plundered and divided among themselves. Many of the principal senators they put to death on a variety of pretexts. Moreover, Alaric in mockery of the imperial dignity, proclaimed one Attalus[2] emperor, whom he ordered to be attended with all the insignia of sovereignty on one day, and to be exhibited in the habit of a slave on the next. After these achievements he made a precipitate retreat, a report having reached him that the emperor Theodosius had sent an army to fight him. Nor was this report a fictitious one; for the imperial forces were actually on their way; but Alaric, not waiting for the materialization of the rumor, decamped and escaped. It is said that as he was advancing towards Rome, a pious monk exhorted him not to delight in the perpetuation of such atrocities, and no longer to rejoice in slaughter and blood. To whom Alaric replied, 'I am not going on in this course of my own will; but there is a something that irresistibly impels me daily, saying, 'Proceed to Rome, and desolate that city.' Such was the career of this person.

CHAPTER XI.

The Bishops of Rome.

AFTER Innocent, Zosimus governed the Roman church for two years: and after him Boniface[1] presided over it for three years. He was succeeded by Celestinus. And this Celestinus took away the churches from the Novatians at Rome also, and obliged Rusticula their bishop to hold his meetings secretly in private houses. Until this time the Novatians had flourished exceedingly in Rome, possessing many churches there, which were attended by large congregations. But envy attacked them also, as soon as the Roman episcopate, like that of Alexandria, extended itself beyond the limits of ecclesiastical jurisdiction, and degenerated into its present state of secular domination. For thenceforth the bishops would not suffer even those who agreed with them in matters of faith to enjoy the privilege of assembling in peace, but stripped them of all they possessed, praising them merely for these agreements in faith. The bishops of Constantinople kept themselves free from this [sort of conduct]; inasmuch as in addition to tolerating them and permitting them to hold

their assemblies within the city, as I have already stated,[2] they treated them with every mark of Christian regard.

CHAPTER XII.

Of Chrysanthus Bishop of the Novatians at Constantinople.

AFTER the death of Sisinnius, Chrysanthus was constrained to take upon him the episcopal office. He was the son of Marcian the predecessor of Sisinnius, and having had a military appointment in the palace at an early age, he was subsequently under Theodosius the Great made governor[1] of Italy, and after that lord-lieutenant[2] of the British Isles, in both which capacities he elicited for himself the highest admiration. Returning to Constantinople at an advanced age, earnestly desiring to be constituted prefect of that city, he was made bishop of the Novatians against his will. For as Sisinnius, when at the point of death, had referred to him as a most suitable person to occupy the see, the people regarding this declaration as law, sought to have him ordained forthwith. Now as Chrysanthus attempted to avoid having this dignity forced upon him, Sabbatius imagining that a seasonable opportunity was now afforded him of making himself master of the churches, and making no account of the oath by which he had bound himself,[3] procured his own ordination at the hands of a few insignificant bishops.[4] Among these was Hermogenes, who had been excommunicated with curses by [Sabbatius] himself on account of his blasphemous writings. But this perjured procedure of Sabbatius was of no avail to him: for the people disgusted with his obstreperousness, used every effort to discover the retreat of Chrysanthus; and having found him secluded in Bithynia, they brought him back by force, and invested him with the bishopric. He was a man of unsurpassed modesty and prudence; and thus he established and enlarged the churches of the Novatians at Constantinople. Moreover he was the first to distribute gold among the poor out of his own private property. Futhermore he would receive nothing from the churches but two loaves of the consecrated bread[5] every

[2] This incident is also given by Procopius of Cæsarea in *Hist. Vandal.* I. p. 8.   [1] 418 A.D.

[2] Cf. V. 10.
[1] ὑπατικός = *consularis, consul honorarius;* the title was, during the period of the republic, given to ex-consuls, but later it became a common custom, especially under the emperors, for the governors of the imperial provinces to be called consuls, and the title *consularis* became the established designation of those intrusted with the administration of imperial provinces. See Smith, *Dict. of Greek and Rom. Antiq.*
[2] Βικάριος [οὐικάριος] transliterated from the Lat. *vicarius,* of which the Eng. 'lieutenant' is an exact equivalent.
[3] Cf. V. 21.   [4] Cf. Bingham, *Christ. Antiq.* II. 16.
[5] The loaves which were offered by the faithful as a sacrifice were called 'loaves of benediction,' and were used partly for the Eucharist and partly as food by the bishop and clergy.

Lord's day. So anxious was he to promote the advantage of his own church, that he drew Ablabius, the most eminent orator of that time, from the school of Troïlus, and ordained him a presbyter; whose sermons are in circulation, being remarkably elegant and full of point. But Ablabius was afterwards promoted to the bishopric of the church of the Novatians at Nicæa, where he also taught rhetoric at the same time.

CHAPTER XIII.

Conflict between the Christians and Jews at Alexandria : and breach between the Bishop Cyril and the Prefect Orestes.

ABOUT this same time it happened that the Jewish inhabitants were driven out of Alexandria by Cyril the bishop on the following account. The Alexandrian public is more delighted with tumult than any other people : and if at any time it should find a pretext, breaks forth into the most intolerable excesses; for it never ceases from its turbulence without bloodshed. It happened on the present occasion that a disturbance arose among the populace, not from a cause of any serious importance, but out of an evil that has become very popular in almost all cities, viz. a fondness for dancing exhibitions.[1] In consequence of the Jews being disengaged from business on the Sabbath, and spending their time, not in hearing the Law, but in theatrical amusements, dancers usually collect great crowds on that day, and disorder is almost invariably produced. And although this was in some degree controlled by the governor of Alexandria, nevertheless the Jews continued opposing these measures. And although they are always hostile toward the Christians they were roused to still greater opposition against them on account of the dancers. When therefore Orestes the prefect was publishing an edict — for so they are accustomed to call public notices — in the theatre for the regulation of the shows, some of the bishop Cyril's party were present to learn the nature of the orders about to be issued. There was among them a certain Hierax, a teacher of the rudimental branches of literature, and one who was a very enthusiastic listener of the bishop Cyril's sermons, and made himself conspicuous by his forwardness in applauding. When the Jews observed this person in the theatre, they immediately cried out that he had come there for no other purpose than to excite sedition among the people. Now Orestes had long regarded with jealousy the growing power of

the bishops, because they encroached on the jurisdiction of the authorities appointed by the emperor, especially as Cyril wished to set spies over his proceedings; he therefore ordered Hierax to be seized, and publicly subjected him to the torture in the theatre. Cyril, on being informed of this, sent for the principal Jews, and threatened them with the utmost severities unless they desisted from their molestation of the Christians. The Jewish populace on hearing these menaces, instead of suppressing their violence, only became more furious, and were led to form conspiracies for the destruction of the Christians; one of these was of so desperate a character as to cause their entire expulsion from Alexandria; this I shall now describe. Having agreed that each one of them should wear a ring on his finger made of the bark of a palm branch, for the sake of mutual recognition, they determined to make a nightly attack on the Christians. They therefore sent persons into the streets to raise an outcry that the church named after Alexander was on fire. Thus many Christians on hearing this ran out, some from one direction and some from another, in great anxiety to save their church. The Jews immediately fell upon and slew them; readily distinguishing each other by their rings. At daybreak the authors of this atrocity could not be concealed : and Cyril, accompanied by an immense crowd of people, going to their synagogues — for so they call their house of prayer — took them away from them, and drove the Jews out of the city, permitting the multitude to plunder their goods. Thus the Jews who had inhabited the city from the time of Alexander the Macedonian were expelled from it, stripped of all they possessed, and dispersed some in one direction and some in another. One of them, a physician[2] named Adamantius, fled to Atticus bishop of Constantinople, and professing Christianity, some time afterwards returned to Alexandria and fixed his residence there. But Orestes the governor of Alexandria was filled with great indignation at these transactions, and was excessively grieved that a city of such magnitude should have been suddenly bereft of so large a portion of its population; he therefore at once communicated the whole affair to the emperor. Cyril also wrote to him, describing the outrageous conduct of the Jews; and in the meanwhile sent persons to Orestes who should mediate concerning a reconciliation : for this the people had urged him to do. And when Orestes refused to listen to friendly advances, Cyril extended toward him the book of gospels,[3] believing that respect for religion would induce

---

[1] As to how the ancient Church looked upon theatrical shows, see Bingham, *Christ. Antiq.* XVI. 11. 15, and passages there referred to.

[2] ἰατρικῶν λόγων σοφιστής, also called by other writers of the period ἰατροσοφιστής; see Sophocles, *Greek Lex. of the Rom. and Byzant. Periods.*
[3] As a mode of abjuration, see VI. 11, note 5. In this case the sacred volume takes the place of the child.

him to lay aside his resentment. When, however, even this had no pacific effect on the prefect, but he persisted in implacable hostility against the bishop, the following event afterwards occurred.

CHAPTER XIV.

The Monks of Nitria come down and raise a Sedition against the Prefect of Alexandria.

SOME of the monks inhabiting the mountains of Nitria, of a very fiery disposition, whom Theophilus some time before had unjustly armed against Dioscorus and his brethren, being again transported with an ardent zeal, resolved to fight in behalf of Cyril. About five hundred of them therefore quitting their monasteries, came into the city ; and meeting the prefect in his chariot, they called him a pagan idolater, and applied to him many other abusive epithets. He supposing this to be a snare laid for him by Cyril, exclaimed that he was a Christian, and had been baptized by Atticus the bishop at Constantinople. As they gave but little heed to his protestations, and a certain one of them named Ammonius threw a stone at Orestes which struck him on the head, and covered him with the blood that flowed from the wound, all the guards with a few exceptions fled, plunging into the crowd, some in one direction and some in another, fearing to be stoned to death. Meanwhile the populace of Alexandria ran to the rescue of the governor, and put the rest of the monks to flight ; but having secured Ammonius they delivered him up to the prefect. He immediately put him publicly to the torture, which was inflicted with such severity that he died under the effects of it : and not long after he gave an account to the emperors of what had taken place. Cyril also on the other hand forwarded his statement of the matter to the emperor : and causing the body of Ammonius to be deposited in a certain church, he gave him the new appellation of Thaumasius,[1] ordering him to be enrolled among the martyrs, and eulogizing his magnanimity in church as that of one who had fallen in a conflict in defence of piety. But the more sober-minded, although Christians, did not accept Cyril's prejudiced estimate of him ; for they well knew that he had suffered the punishment due to his rashness, and that he had not lost his life under the torture because he would not deny Christ. And Cyril himself being conscious of this, suffered the recollection of the circumstance to be gradually obliterated by silence. But the animosity between Cyril and Orestes did not by any means subside at this point, but was kindled[2] afresh by an occurrence similar to the preceding.

CHAPTER XV.

Of Hypatia the Female Philosopher.

THERE was a woman at Alexandria named Hypatia,[1] daughter of the philosopher Theon, who made such attainments in literature and science, as to far surpass all the philosophers of her own time. Having succeeded to the school of Plato and Plotinus, she explained the principles of philosophy to her auditors, many of whom came from a distance to receive her instructions. On account of the self-possession and ease of manner, which she had acquired in consequence of the cultivation of her mind, she not unfrequently appeared in public in presence of the magistrates. Neither did she feel abashed in coming to an assembly of men. For all men on account of her extraordinary dignity and virtue admired her the more. Yet even she fell a victim to the political jealousy which at that time prevailed. For as she had frequent interviews with Orestes, it was calumniously reported among the Christian populace, that it was she who prevented Orestes from being reconciled to the bishop. Some of them therefore, hurried away by a fierce and bigoted zeal, whose ringleader was a reader named Peter, waylaid her returning home, and dragging her from her carriage, they took her to the church called *Cæsareum*, where they completely stripped her, and then murdered her with tiles.[2] After tearing her body in pieces, they took her mangled limbs to a place called Cinaron, and there burnt them. This affair brought not the least opprobrium, not only upon Cyril,[3] but also upon the whole Alexandrian church. And surely nothing can be farther from the spirit of Christianity than the allowance of massacres, fights, and transactions of that sort. This happened in the month of March during Lent, in the fourth year of Cyril's episcopate, under the tenth consulate of Honorius, and the sixth of Theodosius.[4]

but the context demands the very opposite meaning, unless indeed the outrage on Hypatia was considered the last in the series of occasions of quarrel between Orestes and Cyril, after which the difference gradually died out.

[1] The following incident has been popularized by Charles Kingsley in his well-known novel of *Hypatia*, which has, however, the accessory aim of antagonizing the over-estimation of early Christianity by Dr. Pusey and his followers. The original sources for the history of Hypatia, besides the present chapter, are the letters of her pupil Synesius, and Philostorgius, VIII. 9. Cf. also Wernsdorf, *de Hypatia, philosopha Alex.* diss. 4, Viteb. 1748.

[2] ὀστράκοις, lit. 'oystershells,' but the word was also applied to brick tiles used on the roofs of houses.

[3] The responsibility of Cyril in this affair has been variously estimated by different historians. ' Walch, Gibbon, and Milman incline to hold him guilty. J. C. Robertson ascribes him indirect responsibility, asserting that the perpetrators of the crime ' were mostly officers of his church, and had unquestionably drawn encouragement from his earlier proceedings.' *Hist. of the Christ. Ch.* Vol. I. p. 401. W. Bright says, ' Cyril was no party to this hideous deed, but it was the work of men whose passions he had originally called out. Had there been no onslaught on the synagogues, there would doubtless have been no murder of Hypatia.' *Hist. of the Church from 313 to 451,* pp. 274, 275. See also Schaff, *Hist. of the Christ. Ch.* Vol. III. p. 943.

[4] 415 A.D.

---

[1] Θαυμάσιος, 'wonderful,' 'admirable.'
[2] The original here has ἀπέσβεσε, 'quenched,' 'extinguished,'

CHAPTER XVI.

The Jews commit Another Outrage upon the Christians and are punished.

SOON afterwards the Jews renewed their malevolent and impious practices against the Christians, and drew down upon themselves deserved punishment. At a place named Inmestar, situated between Chalcis and Antioch in Syria, the Jews were amusing themselves in their usual way with a variety of sports. In this way they indulged in many absurdities, and at length impelled by drunkenness they were guilty of scoffing at Christians and even Christ himself; and in derision of the cross and those who put their trust in the Crucified One, they seized a Christian boy, and having bound him to a cross, began to laugh and sneer at him. But in a little while becoming so transported with fury, they scourged the child until he died under their hands. This conduct occasioned a sharp conflict between them and the Christians; and as soon as the emperors were informed of the circumstance, they issued orders to the governor of the province to find out and punish the delinquents. And thus the Jewish inhabitants of this place paid the penalty for the wickedness they had committed in their impious sport.

CHAPTER XVII.

Miracle performed by Paul Bishop of the Novatians at the Baptism of a Jewish Impostor.

ABOUT this time Chrysanthus bishop of the Novatians, after presiding over the churches of his own sect seven years, died on the 26th of August, under the consulate of Monaxius and Plintha.[1] He was succeeded in the bishopric by Paul, who had formerly been a teacher of the Latin language: but afterwards, setting aside the Latin language, had devoted himself to an ascetic course of life; and having founded a monastery of religious men, he adopted a mode of living not very different from that pursued by the monks in the desert. In fact I myself found him just such a person as Evagrius[2] says the monks dwelling in the deserts ought to be; imitating them in continued fastings, silence, abstinence from animal food, and for the most part abstaining also from the use of oil and wine. He was, moreover, solicitous about the wants of the poor to as great an extent as any other man; he untiringly visited those who were in prison, and in behalf of many criminals interceded with the judges, who readily attended to him on account of his eminent piety. But why should I lengthen my account of him? For I am about to mention a deed done by him which is well worthy of being recorded in writing. A certain Jewish impostor, pretending to be a convert to Christianity, was in the habit of being baptized often[3] and by that artifice he amassed a good deal of money. After having deceived many of the Christian sects by this fraud — for he received baptism from the Arians and Macedonians — as there remained no others to practise his hypocrisy upon, he at length came to Paul bishop of the Novatians, and declaring that he earnestly desired baptism, requested that he might obtain it at his hand. Paul commended the determination of the Jew, but told him he could not perform that rite for him, until he had been instructed in the fundamental principles of the faith, and given himself to fasting and prayer for many days.[4] The Jew compelled to fast against his will became the more importunate in his request for baptism; now as Paul did not wish to discourage him by longer delays, since he was so urgent, consented to grant his request, and made all the necessary preparations for the baptism. Having purchased a white vestment for him, he ordered the font to be filled with water, and then led the Jew to it in order to baptize him. But a certain invisible power of God caused the water suddenly to disappear. The bishop, of course, and those present, had not the least suspicion of the real cause, but imagined that the water had escaped by the channels underneath, by means of which they are accustomed to empty the font; these passages were therefore very carefully closed, and the font filled again. Again, however, as the Jew was taken there a second time, the water vanished as before. Then Paul addressing the Jew, said, 'Either you are an evil-doer, wretched man, or an ignorant person who has already been baptized.' The people having crowded together to witness this miracle, one among them recognized the Jew, and identified him as having been baptized by Atticus, the bishop, a little while before. Such was the portent wrought by the hands of Paul bishop of the Novatians.

CHAPTER XVIII.

Renewal of Hostilities between the Romans and Persians after the Death of Isdigerdes King of the Persians.

ISDIGERDES king of the Persians, who had in no way molested the Christians in his domin-

---

[3] The repetition of baptism, except in cases in which there was doubt as to the validity of a first baptism, was considered a sacrilege. See Smith and Cheetham, *Dict. of Christ. Antiq.* art. ITERATION BAPTISM.   [4] Cf. I. 8.

ions, having died,[1] his son Vararanes by name succeeded him in the kingdom. This prince yielding to the influence of the magi, persecuted the Christians there with rigor, by inflicting on them a variety of Persian punishments and tortures. They were therefore on account of the oppression obliged to desert their country and seek refuge among the Romans, entreating them not to suffer them to be completely extirpated. Atticus the bishop received these suppliants with great benignity, and did his utmost to help them in whatsoever way it was possible : accordingly he made the emperor Theodosius acquainted with the facts. It happened at the same time that another grievance of the Romans against Persians came to light. The Persians, that is to say, would not send back the laborers in the gold mines who had been hired from among the Romans; and they also plundered the Roman merchants. The bad feeling which these things produced was greatly increased by the flight of the Persian Christians into the Roman territories. For the Persian king immediately sent an embassy to demand the fugitives. But the Romans were by no means disposed to deliver them up ; not only as desirous of defending their suppliants, but also because they were ready to do anything for the sake of the Christian religion. For which reason they chose rather to renew the war with the Persians, than to suffer the Christians to be miserably destroyed. The league was accordingly broken, and a fierce war followed.[2] Of which war I deem it not unseasonable to give some brief account. The Roman emperor first sent a body of troops under the command of the general Ardaburius ;[3] who making an irruption through Armenia into Persia, ravaged one of its provinces called Azazene. Narsæus the Persian general marched against him with the Persian army ; but on coming to an engagement he was defeated, and obliged to retreat. Afterwards he judged it advantageous to make an unexpected irruption through Mesopotamia into the Roman territories there unguarded, thinking by this means to be revenged on the enemy. But this design of Narsæus did not escape the observation of the Roman general. Having therefore plundered Azazene, he then himself also hastily marched into Mesopotamia. Wherefore Narsæus, although furnished with a large army, was prevented from invading the Roman provinces ; but arriving at Nisibis — a city in the possession of the Persians situated on the frontiers of both empires — he sent to Ardaburius desiring that they might make mutual arrangements about carrying on the war, and

appoint a time and place for an engagement. But he said to the messengers, 'Tell Narsæus that the Roman emperors will not fight when it pleases him.' The emperor perceiving that the Persian was mustering his whole force, made additional levies to his army, and put his whole trust in God for the victory : and that the king was not without immediate benefit from this pious confidence the following circumstance proves. As the Constantinopolitans were in great consternation, and apprehensive respecting the issue of the war, angels from God appeared to some persons in Bithynia who were travelling to Constantinople on their own affairs, and bade them tell the people not to be alarmed, but pray to God and be assured that the Romans would be conquerors. For they said that they themselves were appointed by God to defend them. When this message was circulated it not only comforted the residents of the city, but rendered the soldiers more courageous. The seat of war being transferred, as we have said, from Armenia to Mesopotamia, the Romans shut up the Persians in the city of Nisibis, which they besieged ; and having constructed wooden towers which they advanced by means of machines to the walls, they slew great numbers of those who defended them, as well as of those who ran to their assistance. When Vararanes the Persian monarch learned that his province of Azazene on the one hand had been desolated, and that on the other his army was closely besieged in the city of Nisibis, he resolved to march in person with all his forces against the Romans : but dreading the Roman valor, he implored the aid of the Saracens, who were then governed by a warlike chief named Alamundarus. This prince accordingly brought with him a large reinforcement of Saracen auxiliaries, exhorted the king of the Persians to fear nothing, for that he would soon reduce the Romans under his power, and deliver Antioch in Syria into his hands. But the event did not realize these promises ; for God infused into the minds of the Saracens a terrible panic ; and imagining that the Roman army was falling upon them, and finding no other way of escape, they precipitated themselves, armed as they were, into the river Euphrates, wherein nearly one hundred thousand of them were drowned. Such was the nature of the panic.

The Romans besieging Nisibis, understanding that the king of Persia was bringing with him a great number of elephants, became alarmed in their turn, burnt all the machines they had used in carrying on the siege, and retired into their own country. What engagements afterwards took place, and how Areobindus another Roman general killed the bravest of the Persians in single combat, and by what means Ardaburius destroyed seven Persian com-

---

[1] Having reigned between 399 and 420 A.D. Cf. Clinton, *Fasti Romani*, year 420.
[2] There had been peace between the Persian and the Roman powers since 381. Cf. Pagi, *Ant.* 420, note 14.
[3] Mentioned in Theophanes' *Chronographia*, p. 74.

manders in an ambuscade, and in what manner Vitian another Roman general vanquished the remnant of the Saracen forces, I believe I ought to pass by, lest I should digress too far from my subject.

CHAPTER XIX.

Of Palladius the Courier.

How the Emperor Theodosius received intelligence of what was done in an incredibly short space of time, and how he was quickly informed of events taking place far away, I shall attempt to explain. For he had the good fortune to possess among his subjects a man endowed with extraordinary energy both of body and mind, named Palladius; who rode so vigorously that he would reach the frontiers of the Roman and Persian dominions in three days,[1] and again return to Constantinople in as many more. The same individual traversed other parts of the world on missions from the emperor with equal celerity: so that an eloquent man once said not unaptly, ' This man by his speed proves the vast expanse of the Roman Empire to be little.' The king of the Persians himself was astonished at the expeditious feats which were related to him of this courier: but we must be content with the above details concerning him.

CHAPTER XX.

A Second Overthrow of the Persians by the Romans.

Now the emperor of the Romans dwelling in Constantinople being fully aware that God had plainly given him the victory was so benevolent that although those under him had been successful in war nevertheless he desired to make peace; and to that end he dispatched Helion, a man in whom he placed the greatest confidence, with a commission to enter into a pacific treaty with the Persians. Helion having arrived in Mesopotamia, at the place where the Romans for their own security had formed a trench, sent before him as his deputy Maximin an eloquent man who was the associate of Ardaburius the commander-in-chief of the army, to make preliminary arrangements concerning the terms of peace. Maximin on coming into the presence of the Persian king, said he had been sent to him on this matter, not by the Roman emperor, but by his generals; for he said this war was not even known to the emperor, and if known would be considered insignificant by him. And as the sovereign of Persia had gladly decided to receive the embassy, — for his troops were suffering from want of provisions, — there came to him that corps among them which is distinguished by the name of ' the Immortals.' [1] This is a body of brave men numbering about ten thousand — and counselled the king not to listen to any overtures for peace, until they should have made an attack upon the Romans, who, they said, were now become extremely incautious. The king approving their advice, ordered the ambassador to be imprisoned and a guard set over him, and permitted the Immortals to put their design upon the Romans into execution. They therefore, on arriving at the place appointed, divided themselves into two bands, with a view to surround some portion of the Roman army. The Romans observing but one body of Persians approaching them, prepared themselves to receive it, not having seen the other division, in consequence of their suddenly rushing forth to battle. But just as the engagement was about to commence, Divine Providence so ordered it, that another division of the Roman army under Procopius a general emerged from behind a certain hill and perceiving their comrades in danger, attacked the Persians in the rear. Thus were they, who but a little before had surrounded the Romans, themselves encompassed. Having utterly destroyed these in a short time, the Romans turned upon those who broke forth from their ambuscade and in like manner slew every one of them with darts. In this way those who by the Persians were termed ' the Immortals ' were all of them shown to be mortal, Christ having executed this vengeance upon the Persians because they had shed the blood of so many of his pious worshippers. The king of the Persians on being informed of the disaster, pretended to be ignorant of what had taken place, and ordered the embassy to be admitted, he thus addressing the ambassador: ' I agree to the peace, not as yielding to the Romans, but to gratify you, whom I have found to be the most prudent of all the Romans.' Thus was that war concluded which had been undertaken on account of the suffering Christians in Persia, under the consulate of the two Augusti,[2] being the thirteenth of Honorius, and the tenth of Theodosius, in the fourth year of the 300th Olympiad: and with it terminated the persecution which had been excited in Persia against the Christians.

---

[1] Much, of course, depends, in estimating the rate of speed here recorded, on the exact distance between Constantinople and the rather indefinite limits of the Persian empire. But even if the minimum of 500 miles be taken as a basis, the speed seems almost incredible.

[1] A Persian body-guard called Ἀθάνατοι, ' Immortals,' existed during the period of the invasion of Greece by the Persians (cf. Herodotus, VII. 31). The organization and discipline of the later body must have been, of course, very different.
[2] 422 A.D.

CHAPTER XXI.

Kind Treatment of the Persian Captives by Acacius Bishop of Amida.

A NOBLE action of Acacius bishop of Amida, at that time greatly enhanced his reputation among all men. As the Roman soldiery would on no consideration restore to the Persian king the captives whom they had taken, these captives, about seven thousand in number, were being destroyed by famine in devastating Azazene, and this greatly distressed the king of the Persians. Then Acacius thought such a matter was by no means to be trifled with; having therefore assembled his clergy, he thus addressed them: 'Our God, my brethren, needs neither dishes nor cups; for he neither eats, nor drinks, nor is in want of anything. Since then, by the liberality of its faithful members, the church possesses many vessels both of gold and silver, it behooves us to sell them, that by the money thus raised we may be able to redeem the prisoners, and also supply them with food.' Having said these things and many others similar to these, he ordered the vessels to be melted down, and from the proceeds paid the soldiers a ransom for their captives, whom he supported for some time; and then furnishing them with what was needful for their journey, sent them back to their sovereign. This benevolence on the part of the excellent Acacius, astonished the king of the Persians, as if the Romans were accustomed to conquer their enemies as well by their beneficence in peace as their prowess in war. They say also that the Persian king wished that Acacius should come into his presence, that he might have the pleasure of beholding such a man; a wish which by the emperor Theodosius' order was soon gratified. So signal a victory having through Divine favor been achieved by the Romans, many who were illustrious for their eloquence, wrote panegyrics in honor of the emperor, and recited them in public. The empress herself also composed a poem in heroic verse: for she had excellent literary taste; being the daughter of Leontius the Athenian sophist, she had been instructed in every kind of learning by her father; Atticus the bishop had baptized her a little while previous to her marriage with the emperor, and had then given her the Christian name of Eudocia,[1] instead of her pagan one of Athenaïs.[2] Many, as I have said, produced eu-

logiums on this occasion. Some, indeed, were stimulated by the desire of being noticed by the emperor; while others were anxious to display their talents to the masses, being unwilling that the attainments they had made by dint of great exertion should lie buried in obscurity.

CHAPTER XXII.

Virtues of the Emperor Theodosius the Younger.

BUT although I am neither eager for the notice of the emperor, nor wish to make an exhibition of my oratorical powers, yet have I felt it my duty to record plainly the singular virtues with which the emperor is endowed: for I am persuaded that silence concerning them, as they are so excellent, would be injustice to those who should come after us. In the first place then, this prince though born and nurtured to empire, was neither stultified nor effeminated by the circumstances of his birth and education. He evinced so much prudence, that he appeared to those who conversed with him to have acquired wisdom from experience. Such was his fortitude in undergoing hardships, that he would courageously endure both heat and cold; fasting very frequently, especially on Wednesdays and Fridays;[1] and this he did from an earnest endeavor to observe with accuracy all the prescribed forms of the Christian religion. He rendered his palace little different from a monastery: for he, together with his sisters, rose early in the morning, and recited responsive hymns in praise of the Deity. By this training he learnt the holy Scriptures by heart; and he would often discourse with the bishops on scriptural subjects, as if he had been an ordained priest of long standing. He was a more indefatigable collector of the sacred books and of the expositions which had been written on them, than even Ptolemy Philadelphus[2] had formerly been. In clemency and humanity he far surpassed all others. For the emperor Julian although he professed to be a

---

[1] Εὐδοκία, 'Benevolence.'
[2] The *Chronicon Paschale* gives a different account of Eudocia. It says that her father's name was Heraclitus. When he died her brothers Gesius and Valerian refused to give her her share of the inheritance. She came to Constantinople to plead for her rights through Pulcheria, the sister of Theodosius, and impressed the latter so favorably that Pulcheria persuaded Theodosius to make her his wife (cf. *Chronic. Pasch.* year 420). Her brothers on

hearing of her elevation to the throne fled to Greece, but she sent for them and persuaded Theodosius to appoint them to high offices, on the ground that she was indebted to them for her good fortune (cf. *Chronic. Pasch.* year 421). Besides her ode commemorating the victory of the imperial forces over the Persians, several other works of hers are mentioned, viz. paraphrases of the Pentateuch, Joshua, and Judges into Greek hexameters, a version of the prophecies of Zachariah and Daniel, and a poem in three books on St. Cyprian and St. Justina; to these Zonaras adds that she completed the *Centones Homerici* of Patricius. Her later years were clouded by a misunderstanding between her husband and herself, which is variously given by the contemporaneous historians and altogether passed over by Socrates. Cf. Evagrius, *H. E.* I. 20, 22, and Zonaras, *Ann.* XIII.

[1] On the observance of these two days of the week as fast days in the early Church, see Bingham, *Christ. Antiq.* XXI. 3.
[2] Φιλάδελφος = 'lover of his brothers,' but applied to him by the rhetorical figure of antiphrasis because he killed his brothers. This Ptolemy Philadelphus reigned in Egypt from 285 to 247 B.C. and is famous for having the Old Testament translated from Hebrew into Greek, according to the common tradition, by seventy learned men, whence the translation has been known as the *Septuagint.*

philosopher, could not moderate his rage against the Antiochians who derided him, but inflicted upon Theodore the most agonizing tortures.[3] Theodosius on the contrary, bidding farewell to Aristotle's syllogisms, exercised philosophy in deeds, by getting the mastery over anger, grief, and pleasure. Never has he revenged himself on any one by whom he has been injured ; nor has any one ever even seen him irritated. And when some of his most intimate friends once asked him, why he never inflicted capital punishment upon offenders, his answer was, ' Would that it were even possible to restore to life those that have died.' To another making a similar inquiry he replied, ' It is neither a great nor a difficult thing for a mortal to be put to death : but it is God only that can resuscitate by repentance a person that has once died.' So habitually indeed did he practice mercy, that if any one were guilty and sentence of death was passed upon him, and he was conducted toward the place of execution, he was never suffered to reach the gates of the city before a pardon was issued, commanding his immediate return. Having once exhibited a show of hunting wild beasts in the Amphitheatre at Constantinople, the people cried out, ' Let one of the boldest bestiarii[4] encounter the enraged animal.' But he said to them, ' Do ye not know that we are wont to view these spectacles with feelings of humanity ? ' By this expression he instructed the people to be satisfied in future with shows of a less cruel description. His piety was such that he had a reverential regard for all who were consecrated to the service of God ; and honored in an especial manner those whom he ascertained to be eminent for their sanctity of life. It is said that the bishop of Chebron[5] having died at Constantinople, the emperor expressed a wish to have his cassock of sackcloth of hair ; which, although it was excessively filthy, he wore as a cloak, hoping that thus he should become a partaker in some degree of the sanctity of the deceased. In a certain year, during which the weather had been very tempestuous, he was obliged by the eagerness of the people to exhibit the usual sports in the Hippodrome ; and when the circus was filled with spectators, the violence of the storm increased, and there was a heavy fall of snow. Then the emperor made it very evident how his mind was affected towards God ; for he caused the herald to make a proclamation to the people to this effect : ' It is far better and fitter to desist from the show, and unite in common prayer to God, that we may be preserved unhurt from the impending storm.' Scarcely had the herald executed his commission, when all the people, with the greatest joy, began with one accord to offer supplication and sing praises to God, so that the whole city became one vast congregation ; and the emperor himself in unofficial garments, went into the midst of the multitude and commenced the hymns. Nor was he disappointed in his expectation, for the atmosphere began to resume its wonted serenity : and Divine benevolence bestowed on all an abundant harvest, instead of an expected deficiency of corn. If at any time war was raised, like David he had recourse to God, knowing that he is the arbiter of battles, and by prayer brought them to a prosperous issue. At this point therefore, I shall relate, how a little after the war against the Persians, by placing his confidence in God he vanquished the usurper John, after Honorius had died on the 15th of August, in the consulate of Asclepiodotus and Marian.[6] For I judge what then occurred worthy of mention, inasmuch as there happened to the emperor's generals who were dispatched against the tyrant, something analogous to what took place when the Israelites crossed the Red Sea under the guidance of Moses. These things however, I shall set forth very briefly, leaving to others the numerous details which would require a special treatise.

CHAPTER XXIII.

After the Death of the Emperor Honorius John usurps the Sovereignty at Rome. He is destroyed through the Prayers of Theodosius the Younger.

WHEN the Emperor Honorius died Theodosius — now sole ruler — having received the news concealed the truth as long as possible, misleading the people sometimes with one report, and then with another. But he privately dispatched a military force to Salonæ, a city of Dalmatia, that in the event of any revolutionary movement in the West there might be resources at hand to check it ; and after making these provisional arrangements, he at length openly announced his uncle's death. In the meantime John, the superintendent of the emperor's secretaries,[1] not content with the dignity to which he had already attained, seized upon the sovereign authority ; and sent an embassy to the emperor Theodosius, requesting that he might be recognized as his colleague in the empire. But that prince first caused the ambassadors to be arrested, then sent off Ardaburius, the commander-in-chief of the army, who had greatly distinguished himself in

---

[3] Cf. III. 19.
[4] Persons who fought with wild beasts in the games of the circus. They were of two classes : (1) professionals, those who fought for pay, and (2) criminals, allowed to use arms in defending themselves against the wild beasts to which they had been condemned. It is one of the first class that is here meant.
[5] An altogether unknown and doubtful diocese.

[6] 423 A.D.   [1] So also Zosimus, V. 40.

the Persian war.[2] He, on arriving at Salonæ, set sail from thence for Aquileia. And he was fortunate as was thought, but fortune was adverse to him as it afterwards appeared. For a contrary wind having arisen, he was driven into the usurper's hand. The latter having seized him became more sanguine in his hope that the emperor would be induced by the urgency of the case to elect and proclaim him emperor, in order to preserve the life of his general-in-chief. And the emperor was in fact greatly distressed when he heard of it, as was also the army which had been sent against the usurper, lest Ardaburius should be subjected to evil treatment by the usurper. Aspar the son of Ardaburius, having learnt that his father was in the usurper's power, and aware at the same time that the party of the rebels was strengthened by the accession of immense numbers of barbarians, knew not what course to pursue. Then again at this crisis the prayer of the pious emperor prevailed. For an angel of God, under the appearance of a shepherd, undertook the guidance of Aspar and the troops which were with him, and led him through the lake near Ravenna — for in that city the usurper was then residing — and there detained the military chief. Now, no one had ever been known to have forded that lake before; but God then rendered that passable, which had hitherto been impassable. Having therefore crossed the lake, as if going over dry ground, they found the gates of the city open, and overpowered the usurper. This event afforded that most devout emperor an opportunity of giving a fresh demonstration of his piety towards God. For the news of the usurper's being destroyed, having arrived while he was engaged at the exhibition of the sports of the Hippodrome, he immediately said to the people : ' Come now, if you please, let us leave these diversions, and proceed to the church to offer thanksgivings to God, whose hand has overthrown the usurper.' Thus did he address them; and the spectacles were immediately forsaken and neglected, the people all passing out of the circus singing praises together with him, as with one heart and one voice. And arriving at the church, the whole city again became one congregation ; and once in the church they passed the remainder of the day in these devotional exercises.

CHAPTER XXIV.

Valentinian a Son of Constantius and Placidia, Aunt of Theodosius, is proclaimed Emperor.

AFTER the usurper's death, the emperor Theodosius became very anxious as to whom he should proclaim emperor of the West. He had a cousin then very young named Valentinian ; the son of his aunt Placidia, daughter of Theodosius the Great, and sister of the two Augusti Arcadius and Honorius and of that Constantius who had been proclaimed emperor by Honorius,[1] and had died after a short reign with him. This cousin he created Cæsar, and sent into the Western parts, committing the administration of affairs to his mother Placidia. He himself also hastened towards Italy, that he might in person both proclaim his cousin emperor, and also being present among them, endeavor to influence the natives and residents by his counsels not to submit to usurpers readily. But when he reached Thessalonica he was prevented from proceeding further by sickness ; he therefore sent forward the imperial crown to his cousin by Helion the patrician, and he himself returned to Constantinople. But concerning these matters I deem the narrative here given sufficient.

CHAPTER XXV.

Christian Benevolence of Atticus Bishop of Constantinople. He registers John's Name in the Diptychs. His Fore-knowledge of his Own Death.

MEANWHILE Atticus the bishop caused the affairs of the church to flourish in an extraordinary manner ; administering all things with prudence, and inciting the people to virtue by his instruction. Perceiving that the church was on the point of being divided inasmuch as the Johannites[1] assembled themselves apart, he ordered that mention of John should be made in the prayers, as was customary to be done of the other deceased[2] bishops ; by which means he trusted that many would be induced to return to the Church. And he was so liberal that he not only provided for the poor of his own parishes, but transmitted contributions to supply the wants and promote the comfort of the indigent in the neighboring cities also. On one occasion as he sent to Calliopius a presbyter of the church at Nicæa, three hundred pieces[3] of gold he also dispatched the following letter.

' Atticus to Calliopius — salutations in the Lord.
' I have been informed that there are in your city ten thousand necessitous persons whose condition demands the compassion of the pious.

---

[1] Cf. I. 39, and II. 1.
[1] The adherents of Chrysostom. See VI. 3.
[2] He effected this restoration by having the name John enrolled in the diptychs or registers of those whose names should be included in the prayers of the liturgy.
[3] χρυσίνους, with στατῆρας probably to be supplied ; if so the value of these gold pieces was about $5.00, or £1 0s. 9d.

And I say ten thousand, designating their multitude rather than using the number precisely. As therefore I have received a sum of money from him, who with a bountiful hand is wont to supply faithful stewards; and since it happens that some are pressed by want, that those who have may be proved, who yet do not minister to the needy — take, my friend, these three hundred pieces of gold, and dispose of them as you may think fit. It will be your care, I doubt not, to distribute to such as are ashamed to beg, and not to those who through life have sought to feed themselves at others' expense. In bestowing these alms make no distinction on religious grounds; but feed the hungry whether they agree with us in sentiment, or not.'

Thus did Atticus consider even the poor who were at a distance from him. He labored also to abolish the superstitions of certain persons. For on being informed that those who had separated themselves from the Novatians, on account of the Jewish Passover, had transported the body of Sabbatius[4] from the island of Rhodes — for in that island he had died in exile — and having buried it, were accustomed to pray at his grave, he caused the body to be disinterred at night, and deposited in a private sepulchre; and those who had formerly paid their adorations at that place, on finding his tomb had been opened, ceased honoring that tomb thenceforth. Moreover he manifested a great deal of taste in the application of names to places. To a port in the mouth of the Euxine sea, anciently called Pharmaceus,[5] he gave the appellation of Therapeia;[6] because he would not have a place where religious assemblies were held, dishonored by an inauspicious name. Another place, a suburb of Constantinople, he termed Argyropolis,[7] for this reason. Chrysopolis[8] is an ancient port situated at the head of the Bosphorus, and is mentioned by several of the early writers, especially Strabo, Nicolaus Damascenus, and the illustrious Xenophon in the sixth book of his *Anabasis of Cyrus*;[9] and again in the first of his *Hellenica*[10] he says concerning it, 'that Alcibiades having walled it round, established a toll in it; for all who sailed out of Pontus were accustomed to pay tithes there.' Atticus seeing the former place to be directly opposite to Chrysopolis, and very delightfully situated, declared that it was most fitting it should be called Argyropolis; and as soon as this was said it firmly established the name. Some persons having said to him that the Novatians ought not to be permitted to hold their assemblies within the cities: 'Do you not know,' he replied, 'that they were fellow-sufferers with us in the persecution under Constantius and Valens?[11] Besides,' said he, 'they are witnesses to our creed: for although they separated from the church a long while ago, they have never introduced any innovations concerning the faith.' Being once at Nicæa on account of the ordination of a bishop, and seeing there Asclepiades bishop of the Novatians, then very aged, he asked him, 'How many years have you been a bishop?' When he was answered fifty years: 'You are a happy man,' said he, 'to have had charge of so "good a work"[12] for such a length of time.' To the same Asclepiades he observed: 'I commend Novatus; but can by no means approve of the Novatians.' And when Asclepiades, surprised at this strange remark, said, 'What is the meaning of your remark, bishop?' Atticus gave him this reason for the distinction. 'I approve of Novatus for refusing to commune with those who had sacrificed, for I myself would have done the same: but I cannot praise the Novatians, inasmuch as they exclude laymen from communion for very trivial offenses.' Asclepiades answered, 'There are many other "sins unto death,"[13] as the Scriptures term them, besides sacrificing to idols; on account of which even you excommunicate ecclesiastics only, but we laymen also, reserving to God alone the power of pardoning them.'[14] Atticus had moreover a presentiment of his own death; for at his departure from Nicæa, he said to Calliopius a presbyter of that place: 'Hasten to Constantinople before autumn if you wish to see me again alive; for if you delay beyond that time, you will not find me surviving.' Nor did he err in this prediction; for he died on the 10th of October, in the 21st year of his episcopate, under the eleventh consulate of Theodosius, and the first of Valentinian Cæsar.[15] The Emperor Theodosius indeed, being then on his way from Thessalonica, did not reach Constantinople in time for his funeral, for Atticus had been consigned to the grave one day before the emperor's arrival. Not long afterwards, on the 23d of the same month, October, the young Valentinian was proclaimed Augustus.[16]

---

[4] See above, chaps. 5 and 12.

[5] φαρμακέα = 'poisoner.'

[6] θεραπείας: the word occurs in three senses, viz. (1) healing, (2) service, (3) worship. Probably, and as the sentence following seems to indicate, the last of these was the one meant to be emphasized; this is also borne out by the plural number used. If the first sense were the one for which the word was chosen, it must have been because of its being in complete contrast to the previous name. The place retains the name thus given it to this day and constitutes one of the suburbs of Constantinople.

[7] Silver City.   [8] Golden City.

[9] Cf. Xenophon, *Anab.* VI. 6. 38.

[10] Cf. Xenophon, *Hellenica*, I. 1. 22.   The event mentioned took place in 411 B.C.

[11] Cf. IV. 1–6.   [12] 1 Tim. iii. 1.   [13] 1 John v. 17.

[14] The Catholic Church was more severe in its discipline regarding the clergy than the laity, but it does not appear that excommunication was in any case absolute and reinstatement impossible. See on this point the liberal views of Chrysostom, VI. 21. Cf. also Bennett, *Christ. Archæology*, p. 383.

[15] 425 A.D.

[16] This was Valentinian III. See chap. 24 above for his relationship to the reigning Theodosius.

CHAPTER XXVI.

Sisinnius is chosen to succeed Atticus.

AFTER the decease of Atticus, there arose a strong contest about the election of a successor, some proposing one person, and some another. One party, they say, was urgent in favor of a presbyter named Philip ; another wished to promote Proclus who was also a presbyter ; but the general desire of the people was that the bishopric should be conferred on Sisinnius. This person was also a presbyter but held no ecclesiastical office within the city, having been appointed to the sacred ministry in a church at Elæa, a village in the suburbs of Constantinople. This village is situated across the harbor from the city, and in it from an ancient custom the whole population annually assembled for the celebration of our Saviour's ascension. All of the laity were warmly attached to the man because he was famous for his piety, and especially because he was diligent in the care of the poor even 'beyond his power.'[1] The earnestness of the laity thus prevailed, and Sisinnius was ordained on the twenty-eighth day of February, under the following consulate, which was the twelfth of Theodosius, and the second of Valentinian.[2] The presbyter Philip was so chagrined at the preference of another to himself, that he even introduced the subject into his *Christian History*,[3] making some very censorious remarks, both about the person ordained and those who had ordained him, and much more severely on the laity. But he said such things as I cannot by any means commit to writing. Since I do not approve of his unadvised action in committing them to writing, I do not deem it unseasonable, however, to give some notice here of him and of his works.

CHAPTER XXVII.

Voluminous Productions of Philip, a Presbyter of Side.

PHILIP was a native of Side ; Side is a city of Pamphylia. From this place also Troïlus the sophist came, to whom Philip boasted himself to be nearly related. He was a deacon and thus admitted to the privilege of familiar intercourse with John Chrysostom, the bishop. He labored assiduously in literature, and besides making very considerable literary attainments, formed an extensive collection of books in every branch of knowledge. Affecting the Asiatic style,[1] he

became the author of many treatises, attempting among others a refutation of the Emperor Julian's treatises against the Christians, and compiled a *Christian History*, which he divided into thirty-six books ; each of these books occupied several volumes, so that they amounted altogether to nearly one thousand, and the mere argument[2] of each volume equalled in magnitude the volume itself. This composition he has entitled not an *Ecclesiastical*, but a *Christian History*, and has grouped together in it abundance of very heterogeneous materials, wishing to show that he is not ignorant of philosophical and scientific learning : for it contains a medley of geometrical theorems, astronomical speculations, arithmetical calculations, and musical principles, with geographical delineations of islands, mountains, forests, and various other matters of little moment. By forcing such irrelevant details into connection with his subject, he has rendered his work a very loose production, useless alike, in my opinion, to the ignorant and the learned ; for the illiterate are incapable of appreciating the loftiness of his diction, and such as are really competent to form a just estimate, condemn his wearisome tautology. But let every one exercise his own judgment concerning these books according to his taste. All I have to add is, that he has confounded the chronological order of the transactions he describes : for after having related what took place in the reign of the Emperor Theodosius, he immediately goes back to the times of the bishop Athanasius ; and this sort of thing he does frequently. But enough has been said of Philip : we must now mention what happened under the episcopate of Sisinnius.

CHAPTER XXVIII.

Proclus ordained Bishop of Cyzicus by Sisinnius, but rejected by the People.

THE bishop of Cyzicus having died, Sisinnius ordained Proclus to the bishopric of that city. But while he was preparing to depart thither, the inhabitants anticipated him, by electing an ascetic named Dalmatius. This they did in disregard of a law which forbade their ordination of a bishop without the sanction of the bishop of Constantinople ;[1] but they pretended that

---

rhetoricians of the better class from the time of Cicero onwards. Cf. Cicero, *Brut.* XIII. 51; Quinctilian, *Instit. Orat.* XII. 10, and Jerome, *ad Rustic.* (125. 6).

[2] ὑπόθεσις = lit. 'subject' or 'substance'; the contents, or as later, called the argument, or summary of contents.

[1] The Council in its 6th Canon declared that no one should be ordained bishop without the consent of his metropolitan; but that the bishop of Constantinople was the metropolitan of the Cyzicenes does not appear unless the decree of the (Canon 3d) Council of Constantinople making the latter a patriarchate is to be understood as rendering the see of Cyzicus subordinate to that of Constantinople, as an individual church is to the metropolitan. Cf. Bingham, *Christ. Antiq.* II. 16. 12.

---

[1] 2 Cor. viii. 3.   [2] 426 A.D.

[3] See Introd. p. 12. Photius, *Biblioth.* chap. 35, mentions Philip's attack on Sisinnius and assigns the reason for it as jealousy, because Philip and Sisinnius both being of the same rank in the clergy, the latter was made archbishop of Constantinople.

[1] This was a heavy, redundant, and turgid style deprecated by

this was a special privilege granted to Atticus personally. Proclus therefore continued destitute of the presidency over his own church, but acquired celebrity for his discourses in the churches of Constantinople. We shall however speak of him more particularly in an appropriate place. Sisinnius having survived his appointment to the bishopric by barely two entire years, was removed by death on the 24th of December, in the consulate of Hierius and Ardaburius.[2] For his temperance, integrity of life, and benignity to the poor, he was deservedly eminent; he was moreover singularly affable and guileless in disposition, and this rendered him rather averse to business, so that by men of active habits he was accounted indolent.

CHAPTER XXIX.

Nestorius of Antioch promoted to the See of Constantinople. His Persecution of the Heretics.

AFTER the death of Sisinnius, on account of the spirit of ambitious rivalry displayed by the ecclesiastics of Constantinople, the emperors resolved that none of that church should fill the vacant bishopric, notwithstanding the fact that many eagerly desired to have Philip ordained, and no less a number were in favor of the election of Proclus. They therefore sent for a stranger[1] from Antioch, whose name was Nestorius,[2] a native of Germanicia,[3] distinguished for his excellent voice and fluency of speech; qualifications which they judged important for the instruction of the people. After three months had elapsed therefore, Nestorius was brought from Antioch, being greatly lauded by some for his temperance: but what sort of a disposition he was of in other respects, those who possessed any discernment were able to perceive from his first sermon. Being ordained on the 10th of April, under the consulate of Felix and Taurus,[4] he immediately uttered those famous words, before all the people, in addressing the emperor, 'Give me, my prince, the earth purged of heretics, and I will give you heaven as a recompense.

Assist me in destroying heretics, and I will assist you in vanquishing the Persians.'[5] Now although these utterances were extremely gratifying to some of the multitude, who cherished a senseless antipathy to the very name of heretic; yet those, as I have said, who were skillful in predicating a man's character from his expressions, did not fail to detect his levity of mind, and violent and vainglorious temperament, inasmuch as he had burst forth into such vehemence without being able to contain himself for even the shortest space of time; and to use the proverbial phrase, 'before he had tasted the water of the city,' showed himself a furious persecutor. Accordingly on the fifth day after his ordination, having determined to demolish a chapel in which the Arians were accustomed to perform their devotions privately, he drove these people to desperation; for when they saw the work of destruction going forward in their chapel, they threw fire into it, and the fire spreading on all sides reduced many of the adjacent buildings also to ashes. A tumult accordingly arose on account of this throughout the city, and the Arians burning to revenge themselves, made preparations for that purpose: but God the Guardian of the city suffered not the mischief to gather to a climax. From that time, however, they branded Nestorius as an 'incendiary,' and it was not only the heretics who did this, but those also of his own faith. For he could not rest, but seeking every means of harassing those who embraced not his own sentiments, he continually disturbed the public tranquillity. He annoyed the Novatians also, being incited to jealousy because Paul their bishop was everywhere respected for his piety; but the emperor by his admonitions checked his fury. With what calamities he visited the Quartodecimans throughout Asia, Lydia, and Caria, and what multitudes perished in a popular tumult of which he was the cause at Miletus and Sardis, I think proper to pass by in silence. What punishment he suffered for all these enormities, and for that unbridled license of speech in which he indulged himself, I shall mention somewhat later.[6]

CHAPTER XXX.

The Burgundians embrace Christianity under Theodosius the Younger.

I MUST now relate an event well worthy of

---

2 427 A.D.
1 ἐπήλυδα, perhaps in a contemptuous sense = 'an imported fellow.'
2 Founder of Nestorianism (Nestorian church and heresy). For details on Nestorianism, see Assemani, *Bibliotheca Oriental.* tom. IV., said to be the most exhaustive work on the subject, ancient and modern alike, being a volume of 950 pp. and occupied with Nestorianism alone. 'It collects information from all quarters, especially from the Oriental writers, concerning the history, ritual, organization, schools, and missions.' (Stokes, in Smith and Wace.) The peculiar characteristic of the Nestorian Christology will appear in the sequel of Socrates' account. Other accessible sources of information on Nestorianism will be found in the standard ecclesiastical histories. Cf. Neander, *Hist. of the Christ. Church,* Vol. II. p. 446–524; Schaff, *Hist. of the Christ. Church,* Vol. III. p. 714–734; Kurtz, *Church Hist.* Vol. I. p. 334; also Gibbon, *Decline and Fall of the Rom. Empire,* chap. 47.
3 A city in Cilicia, on the western border of Syria.
4 428 A.D.

5 'What the bishops and especially the prelates of the greater churches said in their first sermon to the people was very carefully observed among the early Christians. For from that sermon a conjecture was made as to the faith, doctrine, and temper of every bishop. Hence the people were wont to take particular notice, and remember their sayings. A remark of this nature occurs above, Bk. II. chap. 43, concerning the first sermon of Eudoxius, bishop of Constantinople. And Theodoret and Epiphanius declare the same concerning the first sermon of Melitius to the people.'— VALESIUS.
6 Below, chap. 36.

being recorded, which happened about this time. There is a barbarous nation dwelling beyond the Rhine, denominated Burgundians; they lead a peaceful life; for being almost all artisans, they support themselves by the exercise of their trades. The Huns, by making continual irruptions on this people, devastated their country, and often destroyed great numbers of them. In this perplexity, therefore, the Burgundians resolved to have recourse not to any human being, but to commit themselves to the protection of some god: and having seriously considered that the God of the Romans mightily defended those that feared him, they all with common consent embraced the faith of Christ. Going therefore to one of the cities of Gaul, they requested the bishop to grant them Christian baptism: who ordering them to fast seven days, and having meanwhile instructed them in the elementary principles of the faith, on the eighth day baptized and dismissed them. Accordingly becoming confident thenceforth, they marched against their invaders; nor were they disappointed in their hope. For the king of the Huns, Uptar[1] by name, having died in the night from the effects of a surfeit, the Burgundians attacked that people then without a commander-in-chief; and although they were few in numbers and their opponents very many, they obtained a complete victory; for the Burgundians were altogether but three thousand men, and destroyed no less than ten thousand of the enemy. From that period this nation became zealously attached to the Christian religion. About the same time Barbas bishop of the Arians died, on the 24th of June, under the thirteenth consulate of Theodosius,[2] and the third of Valentinian, and Sabbatius was constituted his successor. Enough has been said of these matters.

CHAPTER XXXI.

Nestorius harasses the Macedonians.

NESTORIUS indeed acted contrary to the usage of the Church, and caused himself to be hated in other ways also,[1] as is evident from what happened during his episcopate. For Anthony bishop of Germa, a city of the Hellespont, actuated by the example of Nestorius in his intolerance of heretics, began to persecute the Macedonians, under the pretext of carrying out the

intentions of the patriarch. The Macedonians for some time endured his annoyance; but when Anthony proceeded to farther extremities, unable any longer to bear his harsh treatment, they were led to a sad desperation, and suborning two men, who put right in a secondary place and profit first, they assassinated their tormenter. When the Macedonians had perpetrated this crime, Nestorius took occasion from it to increase his violence of conduct against them, and prevailed on the emperor to take away their churches. They were therefore deprived of not only those which they possessed at Constantinople, before the old walls of the imperial city, but of those also which they had at Cyzicus, and many others that belonged to them in the rural districts of the Hellespont. Many of them therefore at that time came over to the Catholic church, and professed the 'homoousian' faith. But as the proverb says, 'drunkards never want wine, nor the contentious strife': and so it fell out with regard to Nestorius, who after having exerted himself to expel others from the church, was himself ejected on the following account.

CHAPTER XXXII.

Of the Presbyter Anastasius, by whom the Faith of Nestorius was perverted.

NESTORIUS had an associate whom he had brought from Antioch, a presbyter named Anastasius; for this man he had the highest esteem, and consulted him in the management of his most important affairs. This Anastasius preaching one day in the church said, 'Let no one call Mary Theotocos:[1] for Mary was but a woman;[2] and it is impossible that God should be born of a woman.' These words created a great sensation, and troubled many both of the clergy and laity; they having been heretofore taught to acknowledge Christ as God, and by no means to separate his humanity from his divinity on account of the economy of incarnation, heeding the voice of the apostle when he said, 'Yea, though we have known Christ after the flesh; yet now henceforth know we him no more.'[3] And again, 'Wherefore, leaving the word of the beginning of Christ, let us go on unto perfection.'[4] While great offense was taken in the church, as we have said, at what was thus propounded, Nestorius, eager to establish Anastasius' proposition — for he did not wish to have the man who was esteemed by himself found guilty of blasphemy — delivered several public dis-

---

[1] Octar, mentioned as an uncle (father's brother) of Attila by Jornandes, *Historia Getarum*, chap. 35.
[2] 430 A.D.
[1] By a slight change in the Greek text, Valesius renders this phrase 'but caused others also to imitate him,' alleging that the conduct of Anthony of Germa was in imitation of Nestorius; but the emendation seems unnecessary. Socrates means that Nestorius made himself odious in other ways, perhaps through other persons such as Anthony, &c.

---

[1] Θεοτόκον, i.e. 'Mother of God.' See Neander, *Hist. of Christ. Church*, Vol. II. p. 449.
[2] ἄνθρωπος, 'human being.'
[3] 2 Cor. v. 16.   [4] Heb. vi. 1.

courses on the subject, in which he assumed a controversial attitude, and totally rejected the epithet *Theotocos*. Wherefore the controversy on the subject being taken in one spirit by some and in another by others, the discussion which ensued divided the church, and resembled the struggle of combatants in the dark, all parties uttering the most confused and contradictory assertions. Nestorius thus acquired the reputation among the masses of asserting the blasphemous dogma that the Lord is a mere man, and attempting to foist on the Church the dogmas of Paul of Samosata and Photinus ; and so great a clamor was raised by the contention that it was deemed requisite to convene a general council to take cognizance of the matter in dispute. Having myself perused the writings of Nestorius, I have found him an unlearned man and shall candidly express the conviction of my own mind concerning him : and as in entire freedom from personal antipathies, I have already alluded to his faults, I shall in like manner be unbiassed by the criminations of his adversaries, to derogate from his merits. I cannot then concede that he was either a follower of Paul of Samosata or of Photinus, or that he denied the Divinity of Christ : but he seemed scared at the term *Theotocos*, as though it were some terrible phantom.[5] The fact is, the causeless alarm he manifested on this subject just exposed his extreme ignorance : for being a man of natural fluency as a speaker, he was considered well educated, but in reality he was disgracefully illiterate. In fact he contemned the drudgery of an accurate examination of the ancient expositors : and, puffed up with his readiness of expression, he did not give his attention to the ancients, but thought himself the greatest of all. Now he was evidently unacquainted with the fact that in the *First Catholic epistle of John* it was written in the ancient copies,[6] 'Every spirit that separates Jesus, is not of God.' The mutilation of this passage[7] is attributable to those who desired to separate the Divine nature from the human economy : or to use the very language of the early interpreters, some persons have corrupted this epistle, aiming at 'separating the manhood of Christ from his Deity.' But the humanity is united to the Divinity in the Saviour, so as to constitute not two persons but one only. Hence it was that the ancients, emboldened by this testimony, scrupled not to style Mary *Theotocos*. For thus Eusebius Pamphilus

in his third book of the Life of Constantine[8] writes in these terms :

'And in fact "God with us" submitted to be born for our sake ; and the place of his nativity is by the Hebrews called Bethlehem. Wherefore the devout empress Helena adorned the place of accouchement of the God-bearing virgin with the most splendid monuments, decorating that sacred spot with the richest ornaments.'

Origen also in the first volume of his *Commentaries* on the apostle's epistle to the Romans,[9] gives an ample exposition of the sense in which the term *Theotocos* is used. It is therefore obvious that Nestorius had very little acquaintance with the treatises of the ancients, and for that reason, as I observed, objected to the word only : for that he does not assert Christ to be a mere man, as Photinus did or Paul of Samosata, his own published homilies fully demonstrate. In these discourses he nowhere destroys the proper personality[10] of the Word of God ; but on the contrary invariably maintains that he has an essential and distinct personality and existence. Nor does he ever deny his subsistence as Photinus and the Samosatan did, and as the Manichæans and followers of Montanus have also dared to do. Such in fact I find Nestorius, both from having myself read his own works, and from the assurances of his admirers. But this idle contention of his has produced no slight ferment in the religious world.

CHAPTER XXXIII.

Desecration of the Altar of the Great Church by Runaway Slaves.

WHILE matters were in this state it happened that an outrage was perpetrated in the church. For the domestics of a man of quality who were foreigners, having experienced harsh treatment from their master, fled from him to the church ; and thus they ran up to the very altar with their swords drawn.[1] Nor could they be prevailed upon by any entreaties to withdraw ; so that they impeded the performance of the sacred services ; but inasmuch as they obstinately maintained their position for several days, brandishing their weapons in defiance of any one who dared to approach them — and in fact killed one of the ecclesiastics, and wounded another — they were finally compelled to slay themselves. A person who was present at this desecration of the sanctuary, remarked that such a profanation was an ominous presage, and in support of his view of the matter, quoted the two following iambics of an ancient poet : —

5 μορμολύκιον, 'hobgoblin,' 'bugbear.'
6 1 John iv. 2, 3. The findings of modern textual criticism are at variance with Socrates' opinion that the original in the Epistle of John was λύει (separates). Westcott and Hort admit λύει into their margin, but evidently in order to have it translated as the Revised Version has it (also in the margin) 'annulleth,' taking away all the force of the passage as used here.
7 Of what nature was this mutilation? Some authorities omitted it altogether (see Tischendorf, *Novum. Test.* ed. Octav. Maj., on the passage) ; others changed λύει into μὴ ὁμολογῇ.

8 Cf. Euseb. *Life of Const.* III. 43.
9 Cf. Origen, *Com. in Rom.* I. 1. 5.
10 ὑπόστασιν; see I. chap. 5, note 2.
1 Cf. Bingham, *Christ. Antiq.* VIII. 11.

"For such prognostics happen at a time
When temples are defiled by impious crime."

Nor was he who made the prediction disappointed in these inauspicious forebodings: for they signified as it seems a division among the people, and the deposition of the author of it.

CHAPTER XXXIV.

Synod at Ephesus against Nestorius.   His Deposition.

Not long time elapsed before a mandate from the emperor directed the bishops in all places to assemble at Ephesus.[1] Immediately after the festival of Easter therefore Nestorius, escorted by a great crowd of his adherents, repaired to Ephesus, and found many of the bishops already there. Cyril bishop of Alexandria making some delay, did not arrive till near Pentecost. Five days after Pentecost, Juvenal bishop of Jerusalem arrived. While John of Antioch was still absent, those who were now congregated entered into the consideration of the question; and Cyril of Alexandria began a sharp skirmish of words, with the design of terrifying Nestorius, for he had a strong dislike for him. When many had declared that Christ was God, Nestorius said: 'I cannot term him God who was two and three months old. I am therefore clear of your blood, and shall in future come no more among you.' Having uttered these words he left the assembly, and afterwards held meetings with the other bishops who entertained sentiments similar to his own. Accordingly those present were divided into two factions. That section which supported Cyril, having constituted themselves a council, summoned Nestorius: but he refused to meet them, and put them off until the arrival of John of Antioch. The partisans of Cyril therefore proceeded to the examination of the public discourses of Nestorius which he had preached on the subject in dispute; and after deciding from a repeated perusal of them that they contained distinct blasphemy against the Son of God, they deposed him. This being done, the partisans of Nestorius constituted themselves another council apart, and therein deposed Cyril himself, and together with him Memnon bishop of Ephesus. Not long after these events, John bishop of Antioch made his appearance; and being informed of what had taken place, he pronounced unqualified censure on Cyril as the author of all this confusion, in having so precipitately proceeded to the deposition of Nestorius. Upon

this Cyril combined with Juvenal to revenge themselves on John, and they deposed him also. When affairs reached this confused condition, Nestorius saw that the contention which had been raised was thus tending to the destruction of communion, in bitter regret he called Mary *Theotocos*, and cried out: 'Let Mary be called *Theotocos*, if you will, and let all disputing cease.' But although he made this recantation, no notice was taken of it; for his deposition was not revoked, and he was banished to the Oasis, where he still remains.[2] Such was the conclusion of this Synod. These things were done on the 28th of June, under the consulate of Bassus and Antiochus.[3] John when he had returned to his bishopric, having convened several bishops, deposed Cyril, who had also returned to his see: but soon afterwards, having set aside their enmity and accepting each other as friends, they mutually reinstated each other in their episcopal chairs. But after the deposition of Nestorius a mighty agitation prevailed through the churches of Constantinople. For the people was divided on account of what we have already called his unfortunate utterances; and the clergy unanimously anathematized him. For such is the sentence which we Christians are accustomed to pronounce on those who have advanced any blasphemous doctrines, when we set up their impiety that it may be publicly exposed, as it were, on a pillar, to universal execration.

CHAPTER XXXV.

Maximian elected to the Episcopate of Constantinople, though Some wished Proclus to take that Place.

After this there was another debate concerning the election of a bishop of Constantinople. Many were in favor of Philip, of whom we have already made mention; but a still greater number advocated the claims of Proclus. And the candidacy of Proclus would have succeeded, had not some of the most influential persons interfered, on the ground of its being forbidden by

---

[1] This was the third of the Ecumenical or General Synods; it was convened in 431 and dealt with the Nestorian controversy. Cf. Hefele, *Hist. of the Councils of the Ch.* Vol. III. p. 1; also Evagrius, *H. E.* I. 2, 3, 4.

[2] After his deposition Nestorius was banished to the Oasis, as above stated. This Oasis was 'a miserable place exposed to the wild nomad tribes; all around were shifting sands, forming a pathless solitude. He . . . employed himself in writing a defense of the opinions for which he had lost all. The Blemmyes at length invaded the Oasis, and took Nestorius, among others, captive; then, by what he calls a most unexpected act of compassion, released him, and bade him hurry away. He thought it best to proceed to Panopolis in the Thebaid, and voluntarily reported himself to the governor, who, unmoved by his pathetic entreaty that the imperial authorities would not be less merciful than the barbarians, ordered some soldiers to convey him to Elephantine. The journey under such circumstances exhausted the old man; a fall severely hurt his hand and side; and before he could reach Elephantine, a mandate came for his return to Panopolis. Two more compulsory changes of abode were added to sufferings which remind us perforce of the last days of S. John Chrysostom;' and then the unhappy Nestorius was no more. The exact year of his death cannot be ascertained.'— W. Bright, *Hist. of the Church* from A.D. 313 to 451, p. 371, 372.

[3] 431 A.D.

the ecclesiastical canon that a person nominated to one bishopric should be translated to that of another city.[1] The people believing this assertion, were thereby restrained ; and about four months after the deposition of Nestorius, a man named Maximian was promoted to the bishopric, who had lived an ascetic life, and was also ranked as a presbyter. He had acquired a high reputation for sanctity, on account of having at his own expense constructed sepulchral depositaries for the reception of the pious after their decease, but was 'rude in speech'[2] and inclined to live a quiet life.

CHAPTER XXXVI.

The Author's Opinion of the Validity of Translations from One See to Another.

BUT since some parties by appealing to a prohibition in the ecclesiastical canon, prevented the election of Proclus, because of his previous appointment to the see of Cyzicus, I wish to make a few remarks on this subject. Those who then presumed to interpose such a cause of exclusion do not appear to me to have stated the truth ; but they were either influenced by prejudice against Proclus, or at least have been themselves completely ignorant both of the canons, and of the frequent and often advantageous precedents that had been established in the churches. Eusebius Pamphilus relates in the sixth book of his *Ecclesiastical History*,[1] that Alexander bishop of a certain city in Cappadocia, coming to Jerusalem for devotional purposes, was detained by the inhabitants of that city, and constituted bishop, as the successor of Narcissus ; and that he continued to preside over the churches there during the remainder of his life. So indifferent a thing was it amongst our ancestors, to transfer a bishop from one city to another as often as it was deemed expedient. But if it is necessary to place beyond a doubt the falsehood of the statement of those who prevented the ordination of Proclus, I shall annex to this treatise the canon bearing on the subject. It runs thus :[2]
'If any one after having been ordained a bishop should not proceed to the church unto which he has been appointed, from no fault on his part,

but either because the people are unwilling to receive him, or for some other reason arising from necessity, let him be partaker of the honor and functions of the rank with which he has been invested, provided he intermeddles not with the affairs of the church wherein he may minister. It is his duty however to submit to whatever the Synod of the province may see fit to determine, after it shall have taken cognizance of the matter.'
Such is the language of the canon. That many bishops have been transferred from one city to another to meet the exigences of peculiar cases, I shall now prove by giving the names of those bishops who have been so translated.[3] Perigenes was ordained bishop of Patræ : but inasmuch as the inhabitants of that city refused to admit him, the bishop of Rome directed that he should be assigned to the metropolitan see of Corinth, which had become vacant by the decease of its former bishop ; here he presided during the rest of his days. Gregory was first made bishop of Sasima, one of the cities of Cappadocia, but was afterwards transferred to Nazianzus. Melitius after having presided over the church at Sebastia, subsequently governed that of Antioch. Alexander bishop of Antioch transferred Dositheus bishop of Seleucia, to Tarsus in Cilicia. Reverentius was removed from Arca in Phœnicia, and afterwards to Tyre. John was transferred from Gordum a city of Lydia, to Proconnesus, and presided over the church there. Palladius was transferred from Helenopolis to Aspuna ; and Alexander from the same city to Adriani. Theophilus was removed from Apamea in Asia, to Eudoxiopolis anciently called Salambria. Polycarp was transferred from Sexantaprista a city of Mysia, to Nicopolis in Thrace. Hierophilus from Trapezopolis in Phrygia to Plotinopolis in Thrace. Optimus from Agdamia in Phrygia to Antioch in Pisidia ; and Silvanus from Philippopolis in Thrace to Troas. This enumeration of bishops who have passed from one see to another is sufficient for the present ; concerning Silvanus who was removed from Philippopolis in Thrace to Troas I deem it desirable here to give a concise account.

CHAPTER XXXVII.

Miracle performed by Silvanus Bishop of Troas formerly of Philippopolis.

SILVANUS was formerly a rhetorician, and had been brought up in the school of Troïlus the sophist ; but aiming at perfection in his Chris-

---

[1] The canon referred to is probably the fifteenth of Nicæa, as follows: ' On account of the numerous troubles and divisions which have taken place, it has been thought good that . . . no bishop, priest, or deacon should remove from one city to another. If any one should venture, even after this ordinance of the holy and great Synod, to act contrary to this present rule, and should follow the old custom, the translation shall be null, and he shall return to the church to which he had been ordained bishop or priest.' Cf. also *Apostol. Can.* 14 and 15, and the twenty-first of the Council of Antioch given by Hefele, *Hist. of the Ch. Councils*, Vol. II. p. 72.
[2] 2 Cor. xi. 6.
[1] Cf. Euseb. *H. E.* VI. 11.
[2] The canon here quoted is the eighteenth of the Council of Antioch (see Hefele, *Hist. of the Ch. Councils*, Vol. II. p. 71) ; whereas the canon of that council bearing on that subject is the twenty-first, as noted in chap. 35, note 1.

[3] In what way these canons against the translation of bishops were understood and observed by the early church is discussed by Bingham, *Christ. Antiq.* VI. 4. 6.

tian course, he entered on the ascetic mode of life, and set aside the rhetorician's pallium. Atticus bishop of Constantinople having taken notice of him afterwards ordained him bishop of Philippopolis.[1] Thus he resided three years in Thrace; but being unable to endure the cold of that region — for his constitution was delicate and sickly — he begged Atticus to appoint some one else in his place, alleging that it was for no other reason but the cold that he resigned residence in Thrace. This having been done, Silvanus resided at Constantinople, where he practiced so great austerities that, despising the luxurious refinements of the age, he often appeared in the crowded streets of that populous city shod with sandals made of hay. Some time having elapsed, the bishop of Troas died; on which account the inhabitants of that city came to Atticus concerning the appointment of a successor. While he was deliberating whom he should ordain for them, Silvanus happened to pay him a visit, which at once relieved him from further anxiety; for addressing Silvanus, he said: 'You have now no longer any excuse for avoiding the pastoral administration of a church; for Troas is not a cold place: so that God has considered your infirmity of body, and provided you a suitable residence. Go thither then, my brother, without delay.' Silvanus therefore removed to that city.

Here a miracle was performed by his instrumentality, which I shall now relate. An immense ship for carrying burdens, such as they term 'float,'[2] intended for the conveyance of enormous pillars, had been recently constructed on the shore at Troas. This vessel it was necessary to launch. But although many strong ropes were attached to it, and the power of a vast number of persons was applied, the vessel was in no way moved. When these attempts had been repeated several days successively with the like result, the people began to think that a devil detained the ship; they therefore went to the bishop Silvanus, and entreated him to go and offer a prayer in that place. For thus only they thought it could be launched. He replied with his characteristic lowliness of mind that he was but a sinner, and that the work pertained to some one who was just and not to himself. Being at length prevailed on by their continued entreaties, he approached the shore, where after having prayed, he touched one of the ropes, and exhorting the rest to vigorous exertion, the ship

was by the first pull instantly set in motion, and ran swiftly into the sea. This miracle wrought by the hands of Silvanus, stirred up the whole population of the province to piety. But the uncommon worth of Silvanus was manifested in various other ways. Perceiving that the ecclesiastics made a merchandise of the contentions of those engaged in law-suits, he would never nominate any one of the clergy as judge: but causing the documents of the litigants to be delivered to himself, he summoned to him some pious layman in whose integrity he had confidence; and committing to him the adjudication of the case, he soon equitably settled all the differences of the litigants; and by this procedure Silvanus acquired for himself great reputation from all classes of persons.

We have indeed digressed pretty much from the course of our history in giving this account of Silvanus; but yet it will not, we imagine, be unprofitable. Let us now however return to the place from which we departed. Maximian, having been ordained on the 25th of October, under the consulate of Bassus and Antiochus,[3] the affairs of the church were reduced to a better ordered and more tranquil condition.

CHAPTER XXXVIII.

Many of the Jews in Crete embrace the Christian Faith.

ABOUT this period a great number of Jews who dwelt in Crete were converted to Christianity, through the following disastrous circumstance. A certain Jewish impostor pretended that he was Moses, and had been[1] sent from heaven to lead out the Jews inhabiting that island, and conduct them through the sea: for he said that he was the same person who formerly preserved the Israelites by leading them through the Red Sea. During a whole year therefore he perambulated the several cities of the island, and persuaded the Jews to believe such assurances. He moreover bid them renounce their money and other property, pledging himself to guide them through a dry sea into the land of promise. Deluded by such expectations, they neglected business of every kind, despising what they possessed, and permitting any one who chose to take it. When the day appointed by this deceiver for their departure had arrived, he himself took the lead, and all followed with their wives and children. He led them therefore until they reached a promontory that overhung the sea, from which he ordered them to fling themselves headlong

---

[1] Another indication that the patriarchal functions of the bishop of Constantinople were at this time exercised and recognized. The Council of Chalcedon somewhat later (in 451 A.D.) formally ordered in its twenty-eighth canon that the metropolitans of the Thracian, Pontic, and Asian dioceses should be ordained by the bishop of Constantinople, their election being first secured by the clergy and laity of the dioceses, and referred to the patriarch afterwards.

[2] πλατήν, a sort of raft; the word is incorrectly spelled πλατή according to Sophocles (*Greek Lexic.*, &c.), and should be πλωτή.

[3] 431 A.D.
[1] Nothing further is heard of this strange affair.

into it. Those who came first to the precipice did so, and were immediately destroyed, some of them being dashed in pieces against the rocks, and some drowned in the waters: and more would have· perished, had not the Providence of God led some fishermen and merchants who were Christians to be present. These persons drew out and saved some that were almost drowned, who then in their perilous situation became sensible of the madness of their conduct. The rest they hindered from casting themselves down, by telling them of the destruction of those who had taken the first leap. When at length the Jews perceived how fearfully they had been duped, they blamed first of all their own indiscreet credulity, and then sought to lay hold of the pseudo-Moses in order to put him to death. But they were unable to seize him, for he suddenly disappeared: which induced a general belief that it was some malignant fiend,[2] who had assumed a human form for the destruction of their nation in that place. In consequence of this experience many of the Jews in Crete at that time abandoning Judaism attached themselves to the Christian faith.

CHAPTER XXXIX.

Preservation of the Church of the Novatians from Fire.

A LITTLE while after this, Paul bishop of the Novatians acquired the reputation of a man truly beloved of God in a greater measure than he had before. For a terrible conflagration having broken out at Constantinople, such as had never happened before, — for the fire destroyed the greater part of the city, — as the largest of the public granaries, the Achillean bath,[1] and everything else in the way of the fire were being consumed, it at length approached the church of the Novatians situated near Pelargus. When the bishop Paul saw the church endangered, he ran upon the altar, where he commended to God the preservation of the church and all it contained; nor did he cease to pray not only for it, but also for the city. And God heard him, as the event clearly proved: for although the fire entered this oratory through all its doors and windows, it did no damage. And while many adjacent edifices fell a prey to the devouring element, the church itself was seen unscathed in the midst of the whole conflagration triumphing over its raging flames. This went on for two days and two nights, when

the fire was extinguished, after it had burnt down a great part of the city: but the church remained entire, and what is more marvelous still, there was not the slightest trace even of smoke to be observed either on its timbers or its walls. This occurred on the 17th of August, in the fourteenth consulate of Theodosius, which he bore together with Maximus.[2] Since that time the Novatians annually celebrate the preservation of their church, on the 17th of August, by special thanksgivings to God. And almost all men, Christians and most of the pagans from that time forth continue to regard that place with veneration as a peculiarly consecrated spot, because of the miracle which was wrought for its safeguard. So much concerning these affairs.

CHAPTER XL.

Proclus succeeds Maximian Bishop of Constantinople.

MAXIMIAN, having peacefully governed the church during two years and five months, died on the 12th of April, in the consulate of Areobindus and Aspar.[1] This happened to be on the fifth day of the week of fasts which immediately precedes Easter. The day of the week was Thursday. Then the Emperor Theodosius wishing to prevent the disturbances in the church which usually attend the election of a bishop, made a wise provision for this affair; for in order that there might be no dispute again about the choice of a bishop and tumult thus arise, without delaying, before the body of Maximian was interred, he directed the bishops who were then in the city to place Proclus in the episcopal chair. For he had received already letters from Cælestinus bishop of Rome approving of this election, which he had forwarded to Cyril of Alexandria, John of Antioch, and Rufus of Thessalonica; in which he assured them that there was no impediment to the translation to another see, of a person who had been nominated and really was the bishop of some one church. Proclus, being thus invested with the bishopric, performed the funeral obsequies of Maximian: but it is now time briefly to give some account of him also.

CHAPTER XLI.

Excellent Qualities of Proclus.

PROCLUS was a reader at a very early age, and assiduously frequenting the schools, became devoted to the study of rhetoric. On attaining

---

[2] ἀλάστωρ. Æschylus and Sophocles apply this word to the *Furies.*
[1] Rebuilt and rededicated, according to the *Chronicon* of Marcellinus, under the consuls Maximus and Paterius, i.e. 443 A.D. and ten years after the fire.

[2] 433 A.D.   [1] 434 A.D.

manhood he was in the habit of constant inter-course with Atticus the bishop, having been con-stituted his secretary. When he had made great progress, his patron promoted him to the rank of deacon; subsequently being elevated to the presbyterate, as we have before stated, he was ordained by Sisinnius to be bishop of Cyzicus.[1] But all these things were done long before. At this time he was allotted the episcopal chair of Constantinople. He was a man of moral excel-lence equal to any other; for having been trained by Atticus, he was a zealous imitator of all that bishop's virtues. Patience, however, he exercised to a greater degree than his master, who occa-sionally practiced severities upon the heretics; for Proclus was gentle towards everybody, being convinced that kindness is far more effective than violence in advancing the cause of truth. Re-solving therefore to vexatiously interfere with no heresy whatever, he restored in his own person to the church that mild and benign dignity of character, which had so often before been un-happily violated. In this respect he followed the example of the Emperor Theodosius; for as the latter had determined never to exercise his im-perial authority against criminals, so had Proclus likewise purposed not to disquiet those who en-tertained other sentiments on divine subjects than those which he cherished himself.

CHAPTER XLII.

Panegyric of the Emperor Theodosius the Younger.[1]

FOR these reasons the emperor had the highest esteem for Proclus. For in fact he himself was a pattern to all true clergymen, and never ap-proved of those who attempted to persecute others. Nay I may venture to affirm, that in meekness he surpassed all those who have ever faithfully borne the sacerdotal office. And what is recorded of Moses in the book of Numbers,[2] 'Now the man Moses was very meek, above all the men which were upon the face of the earth' — may most justly be applied at this day; for the Emperor Theodosius is 'meek above all the men which are upon the face of the earth.' It is because of this meekness that God subdued his enemies without martial conflicts, as the cap-ture of the usurper John,[3] and the subsequent discomfiture of the barbarians clearly demon-strate. For the God of the universe has afforded this most devout emperor in our times super-natural aid of a similar kind to what was vouch-safed to the righteous heretofore. I write not

these things from adulation, but truthfully narrate facts such as everybody can attest.

CHAPTER XLIII.

Calamities of the Barbarians who had been the Usurper John's Allies.

AFTER the death of the usurper, the barbarians whom he had called to his assistance against the Romans, made preparations for ravaging the Ro-man provinces. The emperor being informed of this, immediately, as his custom was, committed the management of the matter to God; and continuing in earnest prayer, he speedily ob-tained what he sought; for it is worth while to give attention to disasters which befell the barba-rians.[1] For their chief, whose name was Rougas, was struck dead with a thunderbolt. Then a plague followed which destroyed most of the men who were under him: and as if this was not sufficient, fire came down from heaven, and consumed many of the survivors. This filled the barbarians with the utmost terror; not so much because they had dared to take up arms against a nation of such valor as the Romans possessed, as that they perceived them to be assisted by a mighty God. On this occasion, Proclus the bishop preached a sermon in the church in which he applied a prophecy out of Ezekiel to the deliverance effected by God in the late emergency, and was in consequence much admired. This is the language of the prophecy:[2]

'And thou, son of man, prophesy against Gog the prince of Rhos, Mosoch, and Thobel. For I will judge him with death, and with blood, and with overflowing rain, and with hail-stones. I will also rain fire and brimstone upon him, and upon all his bands, and upon many nations that are with him. And I will be magnified, and glorified, and I will be known in the eyes of many nations: and they shall know that I am the Lord.'

This application of the prophecy was received with great applause, as I have said, and enhanced the estimation in which Proclus was held. More-over the providence of God rewarded the meek-ness of the emperor in various other ways, one of which was the following.

---

[1] See above, chap. 28. This was about the year 427 A.D.
[1] See chap. 22, above.
[2] Num. xii. 3.
[3] See above, chap. 23.

[1] Who these barbarians were it is impossible to find out pre-cisely, and that not because no mention is made of barbarian inroads on the imperial territories, but because so many are mentioned by the chronographers and the historians of the Goths (Jornandes, Prosper Aquitanus, Marcellinus, &c.) that it is impossible to iden-tify this with any of them to the exclusion of the rest. Rougas also appears in these historians as Rouas (in Priscus), Roas (in Jornandes), Rugilas (in Prosper Aquitanus), and is said to be related to Attila; but nothing certain can be drawn from the accounts.
[2] Ezek. xxxviii. 2, 22, 23. Ambrose has also used this prophecy, applying it to the Goths, and exhorted Gratian to make war against them. Cf. Ambrose, de Fide, 2. 16. The quotation here is from the LXX.

CHAPTER XLIV.

Marriage of the Emperor Valentinian with Eudoxia the Daughter of Theodosius.

HE had by the empress Eudocia, his wife, a daughter named Eudoxia. Her his cousin Valentinian, appointed by him emperor of the West, demanded for himself in marriage. When the emperor Theodosius had given his assent to this proposal, and they had consulted with each other as to the place on the frontiers of both empires, where it would be desirable that the marriage should be celebrated, it was decided that both parties should go to Thessalonica (which is about half-way) for this purpose. But Valentinian sent a message to the effect that he would not give him the trouble of coming, for that he himself would go to Constantinople. Accordingly, having secured the Western parts with a sufficient guard, he proceeded thither on account of his nuptials, which were celebrated in the consulate of Isidore and Sinator;[1] after which he returned with his wife into the West. This auspicious event took place at that time.

CHAPTER XLV.

The Body of John Chrysostom transferred to Constantinople, and placed in the Church of the Apostles by the Emperor at the Instigation of Proclus.

NOT long after this, Proclus the bishop brought back to the Church those who had separated themselves from it on account of Bishop John's deposition, he having soothed the irritation by a prudent expedient. What this was we must now recount. Having obtained the emperor's permission, he removed the body of John from Comana, where it was buried, to Constantinople, in the thirty-fifth year after his deposition. And when he had carried it in solemn procession through the city, he deposited it with much honor in the church termed *The Apostles*. By this means the admirers of that prelate were conciliated, and again associated in communion with the [catholic] Church. This happened on the 27th of January, in the sixteenth consulate of the Emperor Theodosius.[1] But it astonishes me that envy, which has been vented against Origen since his death, has spared John. For the former was excommunicated by Theophilus about two hundred years after his decease; while the latter was restored to communion by Proclus in the thirty-fifth year after his death! So different was Proclus from Theophilus. And men of observation and intelligence cannot be deceived in reference to how these things were done and are continually being done.

CHAPTER XLVI.

Death of Paul Bishop of the Novatians, and Election of Marcian as his Successor.

A LITTLE while after the removal of John's body, Paul bishop of the Novatians died, on the 21st of July, under the same consulate:[1] who at his own funeral united, in a certain sense, all the different sects into one church. For all parties attended his body to the tomb, chanting psalms together, inasmuch as even during his lifetime by his rectitude he was in universal esteem by all. But as Paul just before his death performed a memorable act, I deem it advantageous to insert it in this history as it may be interesting to the readers of this work to be acquainted with it. And lest the brilliancy of that important deed should be obscured by dwelling on circumstantial details of minor consequence, I shall not stay to expatiate on the strictness with which he maintained his ascetic discipline as to diet even throughout his illness, without the least departure from the course he had prescribed for himself, or the omission of any of the ordinary exercises of devotion with his accustomed fervor. But what was this deed? Conscious that his departure was at hand, he sent for all the presbyters of the churches under his care, and thus addressed them: 'Give your attention while I am alive to the election of a bishop to preside over you, lest the peace of your churches should hereafter be disturbed.' They having answered that this affair had better not be left to them: 'For inasmuch,' said they, 'as some of us have one judgment about the matter, and some another, we would by no means nominate the same individual. We wish therefore that you would yourself designate the person you would desire to succeed you.' 'Give me then,' said Paul, 'this declaration of yours in writing, that you will elect him whom I should appoint.' When they had written this pledge, and ratified it by their signatures, Paul, rising in his bed and sitting up, wrote the name of Marcian in the paper, without informing any of those present what he had inserted. This person had been promoted to the rank of presbyter, and instructed in the ascetic discipline by him, but was then gone abroad. Having folded this document and put his own seal on it, he caused the principal presbyters to seal it also; after which he delivered it into the hands of Marcus

---

a bishop of the Novatians in Scythia, who was at that time staying at Constantinople, to whom he thus spake, 'If it shall please God that I should continue much longer in this life, restore me this deposit, now entrusted to your safe keeping. But should it seem fit to him to remove me, you will herein discover whom I have chosen as my successor in the bishopric.' Soon after this he died; and on the third day after his death, the paper having been unfolded in the presence of a great number of persons, Marcian's name was found within it, when they all cried out that he was worthy of the honor. Messengers were therefore sent off without delay to bring him to Constantinople. These, by a pious fraud, finding him residing at Tiberiopolis in Phrygia, brought him back with them; whereupon he was ordained and placed in the episcopal chair on the 21st of the same month.[2]

CHAPTER XLVII.

The Empress Eudocia goes to Jerusalem; sent there by the Emperor Theodosius.

MOREOVER the Emperor Theodosius offered up thanksgivings to God for the blessings which had been conferred upon him; at the same time reverencing Christ with the most special honors. He also sent his wife Eudocia to Jerusalem,[1] she having bound herself by a vow to go thither, should she live to see the marriage of her daughter. The empress therefore, on her visit to the sacred city, adorned its churches with the most costly gifts; and both then, and after her return, decorated all the churches in the other cities of the East with a variety of ornaments.

---

[2] This seems hardly probable when compared with the opening sentence of the chapter, and so Valesius with Christophorson and others change it into August. The emendation suggested in the Greek is not a difficult one; it simply adds between αὐ- and τοῦ of the word αὐτοῦ (above translated 'the same'), the syllable γουσ- making it thus, αὐγουστου μηνός, 'month of August.' The emendation, or something equivalent to it, must be accepted, otherwise we are compelled to place the death of Paul and the ordination of Marcian together with the intervening events on the same day.

[1] On this visit of the empress to Jerusalem, see Evagrius, *H. E.* I. 20–23. During this visit for some reason or other — variously stated by the authors of the period — an alienation occurred between the emperor and Eudocia. See above, chap. 21, note 2.

CHAPTER XLVIII.

Thalassius is ordained Bishop of Cæsarea in Cappadocia.

ABOUT this same time, under the seventeenth consulate of Theodosius,[1] Proclus the bishop undertook the performance of an act, such as no one among the ancients had done. Firmus bishop of Cæsarea in Cappadocia being dead, the inhabitants of that place came to Constantinople to consult Proclus about the appointment of a bishop. While Proclus was considering whom he should prefer to that see, it so happened that all the senators came to the church to visit him on the sabbath day; among whom was Thalassius also, a man who had administered the government of the nations and cities of Illyricum. And as it was reported that the emperor was about to entrust the government of the Eastern parts to him, Proclus laid his hands on him, and ordained him bishop of Cæsarea, instead of Prætorian Prefect.

In such a flourishing condition were the affairs of the Church at this time. But we shall here close our history, praying that the churches everywhere, with the cities and nations, may live in peace; for as long as peace continues, those who desire to write histories will find no materials for their purpose. And we ourselves, O holy man of God, Theodore, should have been unable to accomplish in seven books the task we undertook at your request, had the lovers of seditions chosen to be quiet.

This last book contains an account of the transactions of thirty-two years: and the whole history which is comprised in seven books, comprehends a period of 140 years.[2] It commences from the first year of the 271st Olympiad, in which Constantine was proclaimed emperor; and ends at the second year of the 305th Olympiad, in which the Emperor Theodosius bore his seventeenth consulate.[3]

---

[1] 439 A.D.
[2] Evidently a round number, as he begun with the year 305 (cf. I. 1), and the exact number of years included in the history cannot be more than 135. [3] 439 A.D.

END OF THE HISTORY OF SOCRATES.

THE

ECCLESIASTICAL HISTORY

OF

SOZOMEN,

COMPRISING A

HISTORY OF THE CHURCH,

FROM A.D. 323 TO A.D. 425.

TRANSLATED FROM THE GREEK.

———◆◆◆———

REVISED BY

CHESTER D. HARTRANFT,

HARTFORD THEOLOGICAL SEMINARY.

THE TABLE OF CONTENTS.

INDEX OF CHAPTERS.

TABLE OF THE NINE BOOKS OF THE ECCLESIASTICAL HISTORY BY SALAMINIUS HERMIAS SOZOMEN, ARRANGED BY NICEPHORUS CALLISTUS.

BOOK I.

BOOK III.

BOOK IV.

BOOK VII.

BOOK VIII.

BOOK IX.

INTRODUCTION.

SALAMINIUS HERMIAS SOZOMEN.

PART I. — THE LIFE.

THE name is an unusual and difficult one. It seems desirable to give preference to the order which Photius adopts, but to preserve the spelling in Nicephorus Callistus, and in the captions of the chief manuscripts, and therefore to call him Salaminius Hermias Sozomen. What the term Salaminius indicates, cannot yet be accurately determined. There are no data to show any official connection of Sozomen with Salamis opposite Athens, or Salamis (Constantia) in Cyprus; certainly there is no record of any naval service. In vi. 32, where he speaks of the greater lights of monasticism in Palestine, Hilarion, Hesychas, and Epiphanius, he remarks, "At the same period in the monasteries, Salamines, Phuscon, Malachion, Crispion, four brethren, were highly distinguished." In the tart controversy between Epiphanius and the empress, the latter had said, "You have not power to revive the dead; otherwise your archdeacon would not have died." Sozomen explains, "She alluded to Crispion, the archdeacon, who had died a short time previously; he was brother to Phuscon and Salamanus, monks whom I had occasion to mention when detailing the history of events under the reign of Valens" (viii. 15). The readings in the first citation fluctuate between the forms Salamines and Salamanes. Since these monks were of the family of Alaphion, intimate friends and neighbors of the grandfather of Sozomen (v. 15), it might be conjectured that Salamines stood in some relationship with Sozomen, such as sponsor or teacher, and that the cognomen might have its origin from such a connection. It seems strange in such a case that he would not have dwelt upon the bond, or at least have emphasized the life of this particular brother by a special note; but he simply avers, "Some good men belonging to this family have flourished even in our own days; and in my youth I saw some of them, but they were then very aged." Nor in the other passages (vi. 32, viii. 15) is there any hint of intimacy. At the same time, this seems as yet the most warranted explanation of the epithet. Hermias was quite a common name even among Christians. It was originally connected with the household or local worship of Hermes, as the giver of an unexpected gift, or it may be as the utterance of a parental wish for the future success of the newcomer. Although it contained a heathen reminiscence, it was probably conferred in this case because it was ancestral. The name Sozomen itself is documentarily a very unusual one; and was probably bestowed upon the child by the father as a devout recognition of deliverance for himself and his boy, and in contrast with the family surname. A certain præfectus domestico, to whom Isidore of Pelusium addresses a letter (i. 300), was also so called; he must have been a cotemporary. It would be a pleasant surprise could he be identified with the historian; and it would not be at all impossible, for Evagrius, the advocate and historian, was so promoted (*H. E.* vi. 24). The biographical hints in Sozomen's surviving work are of the smallest; and outside tradition has preserved absolutely nothing. His ancestors were apparently from early times inhabitants of the village of Bethelia, in the territory of Gaza, and near to that important city.   By race, they were probably of Philistine rather than Jewish descent; for they were pagans (Hellenists) up to the time of Hilarion, in the second quarter of the fourth century, and our historian contrasts them with the Hebrews.   The family was one of distinction, belonging to a sort of village patricianate.   That of Alaphion was of still greater dignity. The village of Bethelia was populous with a mixture of Gentiles and Jews; the former, however, largely predominating.   Its name appears to have been derived from the Pantheon, erected on an artificial acropolis, and so overlooking the whole community, whose universalistic religious zeal was thus symbolized.   The term Bethel was first given to the temple, and then was transferred to the town as Bethelia; and the use of such a form indicates that the prevailing dialect was a variation of Syriac or Aramaic.   It is also spelled Bethelea (vi. 32).   Hilarion was born in Thabatha, another village near Gaza, to the south, on a wady of the same name.   He became a student in Alexandria, but adopted the monastic discipline, through the example of Antony; on returning to his home, he found his parents dead.   He distributed his share of the patrimony to his family and the poor, and then withdrew to a desert by the sea, twenty stadia from his native village, and began his career of monastic activity as the founder of that ethical system in Palestine.   Before his flight to other and distant seclusions, he came in contact with Alaphion, the head of a noble family in Bethelia, seemingly on very friendly footing with Sozomen's grandfather.   Alaphion was possessed of a demon; neither pagan formularies nor Jewish exorcists could relieve him; Hilarion had but to invoke the name of Christ, and the malignant agent was expelled.[1]   The healed man became at once a Christian; the grandfather of Sozomen was won to the same profession by the care of his friend.   The father, too, adopted the new faith; many other relatives joined the ranks of the believers, in this intensely pagan community and region; for Gaza, as the chief city, displayed a decided hostility to the Gospel.   The grandfather was a man of native intelligence, and had moderate cultivation in general studies, and was not without some knowledge of arithmetic.   His earlier social and intellectual position made him at once prominent among the converts, especially as an interpreter of the Scriptures.   He won the affections of the Christians in Ascalon and Gaza and their outlying regions.   In the estimation of his grandson, he was a necessary figure in the religious life of the Christian communities, and people carried doubtful points of holy writ to him for solution; yet it does not appear that he held any clerical function.

While the ancestor of Sozomen was conspicuous as the religious teacher of Southwestern Palestine, the old Philistine region, Alaphion and his family were distinguished for works of a practical quality: they founded churches and monasteries; they were active in the relief of strangers and the poor; some adopted the new philosophy; and out of their ranks came martyrs and bishops.   Sozomen says nothing of his father, excepting that he was originally a pagan, and therefore born before Hilarion's mission.   The edicts of Julian caused a sudden revival of the old state religion, and led to many local persecutions, where the pagans were the stronger party: Gaza and its dependencies were of this number, and some of the tragedies of that unhappy time are recorded by our historian.   The families of Alaphion and of Sozomen were compelled to flee, to what place is not told us; probably the southernmost monastic retreats: the exiles certainly returned (v. 15), not unlikely after the accession of Jovian.   We can only guess at the date of Sozomen's birth, and somewhat in this wise.   Hilarion's activity in Palestine was after the council of Nice, and before the accession of Julian; we may say about A.D. 345.   The grandfather at his conversion may have been about forty, since he had become a conspicuous local figure; the father, in all likelihood, was but a lad when this change came over the domestic worship.   The exile under Julian took place very nearly in 362, and the return in 364, when the patrician of Bethelia was verging on sixty, and the lad had become a young man.   We may place the date of Sozomen's birth somewhere between 370 and 380.   Hilarion passed away about 371: Ephraim Syrus, in 378; Gratian was emperor of the West; Theodosius the Great was just about to succeed

---

[1] v. 15, and *Hieron. de vita Hilarionis.*

Valens in the East. Ambrose was the most imposing ecclesiastic of the Occident; Gregory Nazianzen and Epiphanius were the leaders of orthodoxy in the Orient.

There are but few details concerning his education. That it was directed by the monks is sure; in fact, the only form of Christian life known in that region was of the ascetic type; the very bishops and clerical functionaries were selected from the ranks of the practical philosophers. There was a succession of pious men in the line of Alaphion, and with the elders of the second generation, Sozomen, as a youth, was more or less acquainted. The names of some of them have already been mentioned:[1] all had been pupils of Hilarion. The fourth of the brothers, Melachion by name, must have already passed away, and legends had speedily transfigured his memory. The influence of Epiphanius throughout Palestine, and particularly in its southern slopes and shepheloth, was dominant in shaping the quality of devotional thought and feeling: its force was scarcely spent when Sozomen was a boy.

This accounts for the exaggerated value he puts upon the monastic discipline as the true philosophy, and why he desires not to appear ungrateful to its cultivators, in the writing of his history; for he purposes to keep in mind that tremendous movement, and to commemorate its eminent leaders under different reigns; in fact, he decides to make it a feature of his treatment of church life and history. There is no warrant, however, for stating that he himself became a monk. With all his admiration for their spiritual superiority, he does not lay claim to any direct fellowship, but rather denies his right or competency to invade their domain. We may be sure that he received the ordinary education imparted in the monastic schools of the time, approximating that of similar institutions near Alexandria. In a degree it was narrow, and growingly hostile to pagan literature; moreover, it was apt to be provincial, if patriotic in its tone. This will account for his desire to elevate the importance of Palestine over against the supercilious tendency which centralized all culture in Constantinople. The main body of his studies was conducted in the Greek language, of which he is no slight master; indeed, he became one of the best imitative stylists of his time, according to so good a judge as Photius. His familiarity with the Syriac and Aramaic names, the exactness of their transliteration, and his larger acquaintance with the history of the Syrian church, point to a likely knowledge of at least a dialect of that widely diffused speech; indeed, he could hardly have escaped the patois, which seems to have predominated over the Greek in Bethelia. In iii. 16, he allows for the loss of force and original grace in every translation, but states that in Ephraim's works, the Greek rendition made in Ephraim's own day, suffered nothing by the change, and he institutes such a comparison between the original and its version, that one is inclined to think he could read both. So his effort to keep a balance in writing between the central and border lands of the empire, and indeed outside of it, would indicate a broader linguistic sympathy. In vi. 34, he speaks familiarly of Syrian monks, who had survived to his own period; the wider range of his knowledge may have been due also to the practice of his profession, or to Syrian cases brought to Constantinople, each of which would involve a comprehension of the language; nor less his use of the records written by the Christians of Persia, Syria, and particularly Edessa, to preserve the story of the Persian church and its many martyrs, whose material he used so copiously (ii. 9–14). It is difficult to be sure of his proficiency in Latin; on the one hand, as an advocate it would be absolutely necessary for him to understand that language of jurisprudence; for all edicts, laws, rescripts, were written therein: the Theodosian code itself was so compiled in his own day. On the other hand, where he quotes Latin documents, he invariably does it from translations into Greek made by other hands; thus in iii. 2, of Constantine's letter to the Alexandrians, he says, "I have met with a copy translated from the Latin into the Greek; I shall insert it precisely as I find it." So in iv. 18, the letter of the Synod of Ariminum to Constantius; and in viii. 26, the two epistles of Innocent. Probably his second-hand report about Hilary of Pictavium, v. 13,

---

[1] v. 15; vi. 32; viii. 15.

leans the same way. But on the whole we must allow his profession, which necessitated a knowledge of the law language, to outweigh the lack of original versions in his book.

It is difficult to judge from a solitary work what the degree of an author's general culture is.
Clemens Alexandrinus has multitudinous quotations ; it would be easy to conclude that he was a
scholar of universal reading, and a genuine polyhistor ; but their inaccuracy and frequent infelicity
make them rather appear as the excerpts from some florilegium or some rhetorical hand-book.
The classical allusions in Sozomen are not very many ; and he might well have considered it
out of place to indulge in overmuch reference in such a record as he presents ; the quality of
what appears would not compel a wide range of reading ; the dedication is most fertile in familiar
illustrations, poetical, historical, and mythological. In i. 6, because of his mentioning Aquilis,
he drags the Argonauts in by the ears, hardly from Pisander, but rather from Zosimus, who does
the same in mentioning the progress of Alaric.[1] When he describes Constantine's tentative
search for a favorable site on which to rear his new capital, the mention of the plain of Ilium
moves the historian to relate a little tradition about the Trojan town (ii. 3). He mentions
Aristotle, in whose philosophy Aetius was versed (iii. 15) ; and to whose dialectic work
Theophronius composed an introduction (vii. 17). When he dwells on the imitative literature
produced by Apolinarius, he alludes indirectly to the Homeric poems, and mentions outright his
writing " comedies in imitation of Menander, tragedies resembling those of Euripides, and odes
on the model of Pindar " (v. 18). In narrating the history of Daphne under Julian (v. 19), he
gives the myth of Apollo and Daphne. Such hints and others are no proof or disproof of any
extensive reading, and yet the way in which he alludes to some is more after a cyclopædic
fashion than any profound study of the authors themselves. In fact, his confession in the instance
of the Apollo and Daphne myth is naïve, " I leave this subject to those who are more accurately
acquainted with mythology." This acknowledgment is not born of any puritanic hesitancy, — for
he had ventured into the sensual bog a little way already, — but is rather a genuine declaration of
his ignorance, and that in the capital where Anthemius and Synesius were authorities. Probably
we have a little light in the limitations and illiberality of his early training, by recalling his attitude
toward the imitative writings of Apolinarius, which sprang up to countervail the Julian edict,
which the Christians interpreted as a prohibition to their enjoyment of the Hellenic culture.
While Socrates whole-souledly and forcibly advocates the humanizing effect of the ancient literature (iii. 16), Sozomen says, "Were it not for the extreme partiality with which the productions
of antiquity are regarded, I doubt not but that the writings of Apolinarius would be held in as
much estimation as those of the ancients," and he rather sides with the monks in their contempt
for classic studies (i. 12). He does not wholly commit himself; he is a bit hesitant, — a
characteristic of his make-up. This was an absorbing question in that and previous days, as it
has continued to agitate the church, more or less, until our own time. In his time the influence
of the monks and the clergy, who were pervaded with the ascetic spirit, was more and more
against the humanities ; the court fluctuated, while the training of the Valentinian and Theodosian
succession had been decidedly monastic, and its sympathies were mainly with the intolerant
tendency, the necessities of their position, and the splendid and overshadowing political abilities
of men like Libanius, Themistius, Anthemius, Troilus, could not be set aside. Some of them,
too, had proved themselves to be the saviours and uplifters of the state. The learning and
grace of Eudocia, the empress, the spirit of her early training as the daughter of an Athenian
philosopher, and her own poetic gifts, were persuasive agents in sustaining a classical survival
among the Christians at the court, before she fell under the blight of her husband's jealousy.
Cyrus, the restorer of Constantinople, filled his verses with the same antique flavor. The clergy,
whose preliminary training had been in the schools of the sophists, or at the Universities, could
not wholly bury their sympathy, although they went through casuistic struggles such as that of

---

[1] Zos. v. 29.

Jerome. The Arians, too, were frequently of a larger culture, and on the Germanic side, of signal military skill and political sagacity, whose services the state could not dispense with. The University which even the monastically drilled Theodosius the Younger organized in Constantinople, while seeking to give a Christian tone to the higher education, previously controlled by Athens, made very liberal provision for the languages, if not so much for philosophy. Sozomen, as we see, inclined to a less generous view, and thought Apolinarius had such a universal genius, that his numerous originals might be dispensed with ; Homer, Menander, Euripides, Pindar, but for an affectation, need not have been missed. This shows the thin quality of his reading, if not the restricted quantity of it, and lays bare the impotence of his critical faculty. These limitations were doubtless due in large measure to the shrunken ideals of his Palestinian education : it savored of Epiphanius' temper and impress.

His education on the religious side was in the Nicene faith as professed by the Catholic Church in the East, to which the monks remained, not always thoughtfully faithful, in all that stormy period. As Sozomen says, the people were unable to follow the refinements of theological discussion, and took their cue from those whose lives seemed better than that of the ordinary clergy. He had, however, no close drill in the arguments *pro* and *con*, judging from his own declarations of inability to follow the various aspects of Arian discussion. After citing the letter of Gregory Nazianzen to Nectarius, in which the distinctive features of the heresy of Apolinarius are given, he supplements : "What I have said, may, I think, suffice to show the nature of the sentiments maintained by Apolinarius and Eunomius. If any one desire more detailed information, I can only refer him to the works on the subject, written either by them or by others, concerning these men. I do not profess easily to understand or to expound these matters " (ἐπεὶ ἐμοὶ οὔτε συνιέναι τὰ τοιαῦτα, οὔτε μεταφράζειν εὐπετές, vi. 27). And when he enumerates the causes of rupture among the Eunomians, "I should be prolix were I to enter into further particulars ; and indeed the subject would be by no means an easy one to me, since I have no such dialectic skill " (ἐπεὶ μηδὲ ἐμπείρως ἔχω τῶν τοιούτων διαλέξεων, vii. 17). It would seem, then, that his logical training had not been of a very deep quality, and yet it must be said that such definitions and arguments as he does state in the history of controversy are orderly and lucid. Metaphysics also seems to have had no large place in his earlier studies ; but he certainly did become familiar with its later theological terms and distinctions, and he draws a clear line between the various contestants who warred for and against consubstantiality. His reading also covered some philosophical speculations, as one gathers from a sentence in v. 6, " For it is not true, as some assert, that as is the body, so is the soul." He probably also early learned to distinguish between ontology and ethics, by the practical lines drawn between the clerical disputant and the monastic philosopher. A sentence in his history of Meletius, bishop of Antioch (iv. 28), emphasizes this difference as we seldom find it in early Christian literature : " In his first discourse he confines himself to instructing the people in what we call ethics (τοὺς καλουμένους ἠθικοὺς λόγους), and then openly declared the Son to be of the same substance as the Father."

His spirit was taught to enslave itself with legalistic fetters, and where he does rise above them, it is with trembling misgivings ; he had a side for larger things, like Socrates, due probably to his profession, but he was afraid to venture quite so far, and yet he is magnanimous as compared with the better educated and clerical Theodoret.

To those early school years we must also attribute his statement, that he was a witness to the fidelity of Zeno, bishop of Majuma, the seaport of Gaza. " It is said, and I myself am witness of the truth of the assertion, that when he was bishop of the church in Majuma, he was never absent at morning or evening hymns, or any other worship of God, unless attacked by some malady ; and yet he was at this period an old man, being nearly a hundred years of age " (vii. 28). The patriarch's self-support and industry were in like manner the object of his youthful admiration. The struggle of the bishop of Gaza to assert his jurisdiction over Majuma, the seaport which had its own episcopate, and desired to retain its ecclesiastical autonomy, after it had lost its civil independence, Sozomen speaks of as happening in his day, and was one of the news of his youth; and one catches in his statement an inner satisfaction with the decision of the council which recognized the freedom of the Christian community by the sea (v. 3). In connection with public worship, he had very likely heard in those earlier days the reading of the Apocalypse of Peter. He says in vii. 19, "Thus the book entitled the Apocalypse of Peter, which was considered altogether spurious by the ancients, is still read in some of the churches of Palestine, on the day of preparation, when the people observe a fast in memory of the passion of the Saviour." And a favorite book he saw in the hands of the monks of his native land, was the Apocalypse of Paul, "although unrecognized by the ancients" (vii. 19). A familiarity with such books gives a key to his later attitude toward prophecy.

There is no evidence as to what persuaded him to study law, nor do we know when he was enrolled as a student. The fact that he mentions the school of Berytus as the place where Bishop Triphyllius had prosecuted jurisprudence for so long a while (i. 11) can hardly be taken as a suggestion of Sozomen's own residence there. It would have been more likely for him to have attended lectures at the University of Alexandria or Antioch, with which cities he shows a considerable acquaintance. His studies were probably based on the Codex Gregorianus, with its supplement, the Codex Hermogenianus; for it was in his own day, and during the writing of his history, that the Codex Theodosianus was begun, and one is sorry to miss his name from the list of its compilers; and it was not until A.D. 439, that it was proclaimed as the text-book of imperial law. That he was admitted to the practice of that profession, we have direct evidence, as in the case of Evagrius, (*H. E.* vi. 7) while as to Socrates, it is simply an uncertified tradition. Sozomen speaks of his afflicted friend Aquilinus (ii. 3), "who is even at the present time residing with us, and is an advocate in the same courts of justice as that to which we belong." From the tenor of the legal notices in his history it is likely that he practiced in the episcopal courts as well; for these had assumed form, and the function of an advocate is regulated in several synodical canons. He is more careful and systematic in stating the course of important legislation with regard to religion and the Church, than any other historian. Thus under Constantine, i. 3, 5, 8, 9, 21, 23, ii. 32; under Constantius, iii. 17, iv. 15; under Julian, v. 5, 15, 17; under Jovian, vi. 3; Valens, vi. 12, 19; Gratian, vii. 1; Gratian and Theodosius, vii. 4; under Theodosius, vii. 9, 12, 16, 20, 25, viii. 4; Valentinian, ii. (Justina), vii. 13; Arcadius, viii. 7, 24. There is no instance of his own practice such as Evagrius gives (*H. E.* vi. 7).

We can only guess at the time of his settlement in Constantinople. One would judge from his narrative, that he was not there during the riots excited by the deposition of Chrysostom, A.D. 404. He may have arrived a little after the elevation of Atticus to the see, as successor to Arsacius, who had followed John, somewhere about 406, a year before the death of the orator, and two years before the decease of the Emperor Arcadius. Under the sage Anthemius, he was finding his way in his profession. Under Pulcheria, one is inclined to suppose that he obtained some recognition. The capital thereafter remained the center of his practice, and he appears to be still in connection with the dikasteries while he is writing the second book of his history (ii. 3). There are a few personal points in his life at the imperial city which he hints at. Thirty-five stadia overland from the city, toward the Pontus, was Hestiæ; owing to an appearance of the Archangel Michael, a temple was built there, and, as a consequence, called Michaelium. It became noted for its curative properties, both for physical and mental disorders. Sozomen himself had been afflicted, how, he does not tell us,— whether by reverses, or dangers, or disease, or other suffering, — but he resorted thither and testifies to the benefit he received (ii. 3). There is another personal incident which he records in ix. 2. He was a spectator of the splendid ceremonials connected with the discovery and transfer of the remains of the Forty Martyrs: he saw the costly caskets, the festival, and the procession; he heard the music of the commemorative odes, and beheld the deposit of the relics by the body of St. Thyrsus. A number of other spectators whom he knew were there, the greater part of whom were living at the writing of his record.

This celebration took place much later, under the episcopate of Proclus; therefore after the year 434. A final personal hint is given in his statements of the overthrow of Uldis. Concerning the remnant of the Sciri, who as a result of that campaign were scattered as slaves over Asia Minor, he remarks, "I have seen many in Bithynia, near Mt. Olympus, living apart from one another, and cultivating the hills and valleys of that region" (ix. 15). As to the nature of this tour, we know nothing. He must have been active in many of the later ecclesiastical and secular matters which he narrates, for the first endeavor of his history is to mention the affairs in which he was concerned (μεμνήσομαι δὲ πραγμάτων οἷς παρέτυχον, i. 1). We can only deplore that he makes no sign, in the unfolding story, possibly some might have been indicated had he completed his ninth book.

The influential circles of the Eastern and Western capital were divided into parties on a variety of themes. One such, on the lines of culture, we have already considered. A second and very decisive one, was the question whether the foreigners, especially the Goths and the Persians, should be admitted into the service of the state. The stronger body believed in the use and incorporation of these new elements. What before was a variable matter, became a fixed policy under Theodosius the Great, and in all directions. His weak sons were controlled by both factions alternately. Anthemius, Pulcheria, and Theodosius II. adhered in the main to the liberal view. Yet the presence of a cry, Rome for the Romans, could overthrow such a man as Stilicho, and elevate such a weakling as Olympius. Sozomen, from his handling of the events, allied himself with the illiberal cabal; and while he sought room for a representation of foreign Christianity in his book, nevertheless opposed the intrusion of at least the northern element into the offices of the empire.

There was a third line of cleavage among the people and the court. A very strong and persistent faction set itself against the admission of pagans and Arians into political position. These two dying elements often combined to save themselves from extinction. The court itself fluctuated, because the Germanic politicians were mostly Arian, and the best scholars of political science were pagans. Exigencies compelled the recognition of masters like Anthemius and Troilus. Sozomen threw in his lot with the narrower clique. He does not condescend to mention the best statesman of his time, or the wisest political thinker. Socrates does, and with admiration. The portrayal of Alaric is from the estimate of him as a leader in whom the hopes of pagans and Arians revived. Gainas is traduced, because he was the rallying-point of expiring Arianism in the East.

Sozomen, as we have seen, sided also with the majority in honoring the monastic life, which was bitterly opposed by many politicians and ecclesiastics. Naturally, therefore, he regarded life from a more pietistic standpoint, than did the court under the leadership either of Eudoxia or Eudocia. He responded to the puritanism of Chrysostom and Pulcheria.

He is a defender of Chrysostom, and answers such criticisms as Socrates has made. We can scarcely doubt that his heart was with the Johnites, although he may not have entered their separatist communion.

We can gather from intimations in his history that Sozomen had traveled somewhat. He shows a better knowledge of Palestine, than even Epiphanius; he must have kept up his connection with his native land to have been so well informed as to its traditions, places, and customs. Naturally the greater part of this interest centers in Gaza and its neighborhood, as his old home. In ii. 1, 2, his story of the invention of the Cross and the holy buildings erected by Helena, improves on the original, by local detail and color. In ii. 4, he enlarges upon the Eusebian account of Constantine's purgation of Mamre or Terebinthus, as one familiar with the spot and with its fair. In ii. 5, he gives a bit of history of Gaza and Majuma under Constantine. In ii. 20, he narrates the election of Maximus as bishop of Jerusalem, from a source which no one else has used. In iii. 14, his biographical notices of Hilarion, Hesychas, and others, indicate an exact topographical knowledge. The Julian edict gives occasion to state the dissensions between Gaza and its seaport (vii. 3). Quite graphic is the martyrology of Gaza and its vicinity, given in v. 9. In discussing Julian's outrage on the image of Christ at Paneas (v. 27), and the miraculous well at Nicopolis, formerly Emmaus, we see signs of local acquaintanceship. In v. 22, Julian is said to write to the patriarchs, and rulers, and people, asking for their prayers for himself and his empire; here is a distinct reference to the then existing patriarchate; so all the details of the attempted restoration betray a well-informed hand, as well as state the fact of direct communication with the witnesses of the phenomena. The biographies in vi. 32 are bound up with Southern Palestine, and particularly with Bethelia and Gerar. Similar lives in vii. 28, of those more closely related to him, easily prove that he was near home. In viii. 13, Scythopolis is selected by the fugitive Egyptian monks, because its many palms afforded them their customary means of support, — a circumstance narrated by no one else. Nor are local hints wanting in the story of the finding of Zachariah's body (ix. 17), with its legends. There is in one sense a disproportionate mention of Palestine, and designedly, not only from patriotic motives, but from a desire to vindicate its historic position in the development of Church history, and to rebuke the prevailing tendency of churchmen and historians to press it into the background. It is a curious juxtaposition, that the councils of Chalcedon should so soon after have vindicated the primacy of Jerusalem. There is also a better acquaintance with the facts and purposes of Jewish history, the relation of Judaism to Christianity (i. 1); the genesis of the Saracens, and their association with the covenant people (vi. 38); the regulations of the paschal season, especially in vii. 18; as well as a greater accuracy in the transliteration of names of places.

It was no inconsiderable journey from Gaza to his school, and from his school to Constantinople. The hints concerning Palestine, already mentioned, indicate personal observation. Beyond these we have suggestions that may look to his having been in Arabia and Cyprus, as, when he speaks (vii. 19) of knowing the custom in both places, to have a chorepiscopus at the head of a local church. So, too, in Alexandria, he was struck with the strange position of the bishop in not rising when the Gospels were read, something he had never known or heard of in other communities, — words which point to familiarity with that city. One would be glad to think of his having visited Tarsus, since he was acquainted with Cilix, a presbyter of that city, whom he consulted about the origin of the Apocalypse of Paul (vii. 19). That he knew Bithynia from the sight of it, we have already seen (ix. 5). He describes or alludes to architectural or topographic features of Alexandria, Antioch, and possibly Edessa, in a way that scarcely leaves a doubt of his having seen those cities; we may suppose that his clientelage would compel journeys to and fro.

His work abounds with allusions to structures and regions of Constantinople, to say nothing of its vicinity. The general description of the building of the city by Constantine (ii. 3) already gives some of its principal features. Of the churches, he mentions the first of those dedicated to the Archangel St. Michael (ii. 3), at some remove from the city (Hestiæ, Michaelium), and to be distinguished from a later structure on the opposite shore, and one in the city, erected to the same patron angel;[1] — the church of the Apostles, which became the place of sepulture for emperors and even bishops (ii. 34, iv. 21, viii. 10); — the church of Acacius the martyr (iv. 21), to which Macedonius endeavored to remove the coffin of Constantine; — the church of Sophia (iv. 26), begun by Constantine, and dedicated under Constantius, with which was connected a baptistery (viii. 21); this great edifice was burned in the tumult which arose after the second exile of Chrysostom was announced (viii. 22); — the house of prayer begun by Chrysostom and completed by Sisinnius, containing the tomb of the martyred Notaries; this was outside the walls, in a spot previously devoted to the execution of criminals, and an object of dread, because of frequenting ghosts (iv. 3); — the church of the Novatians, situated in a part of the city called Pelargum; this was taken down by them and transferred to a suburb

---

[1] Procopius de Ædificis, i. 3, 8.

named Sycæ, hence the edifice was entitled Anastasia; it was restored to its original spot under Julian (iv. 20);—the little dwelling which was converted into a house of prayer for Gregory Nazianzen, and so became a church, also called Anastasia (vii. 5);—the church reared by Macedonius, which received the name of Paul, bishop of Constantinople, when Theodosius removed the confessor's body to that building; it is described as a spacious and distinguished temple (vii. 10); when Theodosius the Great conveyed the head of John the Baptist to Hebdomas, in the suburbs, where was the seventh milestone, he erected on that site a spacious and magnificent temple, which became a center of imperial devotion and miraculous cures (vii. 21, 24, viii. 4, 14);—the church reared in honor of St. Stephen, the proto-martyr (viii. 24); —the church dedicated to the memory of St. Mocus the Martyr, where Dioscorus was buried (viii. 17).;—the place where the body of Thyrsus the Martyr reposed, and whither the relics of the forty soldiers were transferred (ix. 2); this was a temple, according to Procopius.[1] In Chalcedon, he mentions the church of St. Euphemia, so glowingly described by Evagrius, and that of SS. Peter and Paul in the Oak (Ruffinum).

While he speaks of the number of monks and nuns, in and about Constantinople (iv. 2, viii. 9), and alludes in a general way to their dwellings (iv. 20), he mentions no particular establishment except that founded by Marathonius, which stood in Sozomen's time. He also refers to the Xenodochia, the Nosocomia, the Cherotrophia, and the Ptochotrophia (iv. 20, 27, viii. 9), but he does not specialize, not even concerning the group of institutions founded and endowed by Pulcheria (ix. 8). There were residences for the bishops and clergy, but these are only hinted at (vii. 14, viii. 14). The palaces and the forums are mentioned only in a general way, but the splendid council chamber (μέγιστος οἶκος τῆς συγκλήτου βουλῆς), which was burned with the Sophia, is described as south of that edifice. He refers to the Hippodrome in the third region, with a little description of its early form and place (vi. 39, viii. 21). Certain of the eight public baths are mentioned, the commodious thermæ called after Zeuxippus (iii. 9) is set forth as a conspicuous and large structure, and the palace as adjoining it near the sea-side. This was in the second region. He speaks correctly of baths bearing the names of Anastasia and Carosa, daughters of Valens, standing in his own time (vi. 9). The baths of Constantius are characterized as very spacious when he tells us how the followers of John resorted thither for the paschal feast (viii. 21).

We have some brief notices of a few friends outside the earlier circles in Bethelia and Gaza. By the advice of some pious acquaintants, who were versed in the mysteries, he decided not to publish the Nicene symbol (i. 20). Among those who experienced relief at the Michaelium, was a fellow-advocate, Aquilinus; the story of his cure is told us from Sozomen's own observation, and from the statements made by his colleague (ii. 3). He was on good terms with Cilix, the venerable presbyter of Tarsus (vii. 19). He had a friend or friends, who were cognizant of affairs under Theophilus (viii. 12); and similarly with some who had been intimate with Chrysostom (viii. 9). It is not unlikely that he knew Nicarete in her old age, a lady of Bithynia remarkable for her sacrificial life, whose memory is preserved by him alone (viii. 23). The facts which he brings to light concerning Pulcheria, and the submission of his work to the younger Theodosius, shows that he was received graciously by both.

PART II. — SOZOMEN AS AUTHOR.

WHEN seized with a desire to write history, Sozomen says: " I at first felt strongly inclined to trace the course of events from the very commencement, but on reflecting that similar records of the past, up to their own time, had been compiled by those wisest of men, Clemens and Hegesippus, successors of the Apostles, by Africanus, the historian, and by Eusebius, surnamed Pamphilus, a man intimately acquainted with Sacred Scriptures and the writings of the Greek

---

[1] de Ædificis, i. 4.

poets and historians, I merely drew up an epitome in two books, of all that is recorded to have happened to the churches, from the ascension of Christ to the deposition of Licinius." This work is unfortunately lost. It was not a simple chronicle, but an abbreviated account of these events; the abridgment was probably from the authors mentioned above. The habit of succinct narration is quite in his later vein. He doubtless commingled secular with the sacred detail. It may be suggestingly asked, whether his words in ix. 1 do not give a hint of another work: "But I willingly for awhile pass over the many separate manifestations of divine favor, that were granted to the sister of the emperor, as proofs that she was loved of God, lest anybody should blame me, for having set out to do other things, and yet had turned to the use of encomiums." This sudden arrest could not be owing to an intended resumption of such matters at a later portion of the history; for the method was already regarded as irrelevant, and the very reason for citing no more in that vein; is it not likely that he at least purposed an encomium of Pulcheria?

The attempt of Hieronymus, Wolf, Lambec, and Fenzel to ascribe Hermias' Διασυρμὸς τῶν ἔξω φιλοσόφων (*Irrisio gentilium philosophorum*) to Sozomen, because of identity of name, is now held by none.[1] The work by which we know him, is the Ecclesiastical History in nine Books. When did he write it? In trying to determine the time of its production, let us look at the data suggested in his work.

(1) In the dedication, the delineation of the emperor's culture and character discloses a man of fixity and repose; these qualities could not be ascribed to the time of his imperial majority, in his fifteenth year, nor to the time of his marriage (421); they are rather the features of settled experience; hence we would expect in general a period nearer the end of his reign, than one in the beginning or middle; certainly somewhere beyond his thirtieth year, and therefore beyond A.D. 438.

(2) Sozomen says that poets and authors, even those of prefectural dignity, as well as other subjects, celebrated the emperor. The usual literary incense was burned. Olympiodorus dedicated his history to him. Socrates was magniloquent; and more particularly did Cyrus, the friend of Eudocia, who attained the highest offices of the state from 439–441, write epigrams in praise of his monarch.[2] This would make a date after 441.[3]

(3) In illustration of the practiced self-control of his sovereign, he narrates an incident of the royal journey in the summer heat, through Bithynia, to the fallen city of Heraclea, in Pontus,[4] with the view of restoring it. This journey took place in June of A.D. 443.[5] This incident is introduced with πρώην, which would place the writing quite definitely as not very soon after June 443.

(4) The reign of Theodosius is described as above all others bloodless and pure from slaughter. This could only be moderately just, before the judicial murders connected with the jealous fits of Theodosius, from 442 on, and the united movement of outlying nations upon the East and West, as projected by the political sagacity of Attila.

(5) The professed terminus of his history is the seventeenth consulate of Theodosius: this was the year 439; hence the whole work was written after that time.

(6) The prayer at the conclusion of the proëmium may have in it a point of light; he hopes that through the favor of Christ, the imperium may be transmitted to Theodosius' sons and grandsons. The only child born to Eudocia was a daughter, Eudoxia, who was married to Valentinian III. It was because of the lack of succession, that Pulcheria married General Marcianus. Eudocia withdrew from the court somewhere between 441–443, but that would not have had to impede the succession, had Theodosius chosen to be divorced; and this prayer rather intimates the desirability of another marriage. This, therefore, must have been written

---

[1] Otto, *Corp. App.* Vol. ix. (Migne, *P. G.* vi.).

[2] See his epigrams in *Anth. Gr.*

[3] Güldenpinning thinks there may be a suggestion of the fatal apple in Sozomen's praise of his sovereign's abstemiousness. I would like to agree, but cannot. *Die Kirchengesch. des Theodoret von Kyrrhos*, pp. 12, 13.

[4] Heraclea Pontica of the maps.

[5] Marcell. *Am. Chron. s. d.; Chron. Pasch. s. d.; Novell. Theod.* xxiii. 5, 21.

before the hope of sons was removed; certainly, therefore, before the closing years of the emperor's reign.

(7) In Book ix, Pulcheria's inclination to virginity is spoken of as expressed in the most solemn way, and with the consecrated gift of a table to signalize it. There is no hint in the work of the marriage with Marcian, suggested by Theodosius on his death-bed, and carried out after his demise. This would indicate that the work was completed before 450.

(8) In ix. 1, he affirms: "That new heresies have not prevailed in our times, we shall find to be due especially to her, as we shall subsequently see." The heresies are those connected with Nestorianism, 428–444, and possibly the return of the Johannists to full communion by the triumphal restoration of Chrysostom's remains in 438; these were to fall within the limits of his work. The Eutychean heresy in its first stage was hostile to Pulcheria's views, while its overthrow was not effected until a year after the death of Theodosius. The close of the Nestorian controversy through the compromise was in 444, and that date would suit well with the fact of mastering the heresy at the very time he was writing this account of Pulcheria.

(9) In ix. 2, he recounts the transfer of the forty martyrs, after a public festival had been appropriately celebrated with fitting honor and pomp, with psalms, " at which I myself was present ; and others who were present can also bear testimony that these things were done in the way described, for almost all of them still survive. And the event occurred much later, when Proclus governed the church of Constantinople." Proclus was elected 434, and continued in office until his death in 447. This transfer must have taken place before 439, the proposed terminus of the history, and very likely a little while after the accession of this long-tried candidate. The time of the writing was at some considerable remove from the event itself, because of his appeal to the survivors as witnesses to the truth of his portrayal, and yet not so far, but that the most of the participants and spectators could still be appealed to. This would correspond very well with the date connected with 443, suggested by the incident in Bithynia, if we allow some interval between the writing of the dedication and Book ix.

(10) In ix. 6, the overthrow of Uldis, 406, is narrated. The settlement of the conquered Sciri as slaves and colonists is enlarged upon. Sozomen himself saw these imperial farmers at their tilling in Bithynia. This may connect itself, possibly, as to the time of the year, and place, with the emperor's progress to Heraclea Pontica. There is evidently an interval between the capture of the Sciri, and their settled work as colonists, when Sozomen visited that region, and between that visit and the writing of the fact. If it corresponded with the imperial progress, it would of course be 443. Taking all these points together, it would seem that the work was begun about the latter part of 443; and that the dedication was written first, because that states the plan of the whole work, including the ninth book, whose record does not meet the intention, there expressed ; moreover, some of the events in Book ix. indicate a considerable interval between the fact and the account of it. When he finished what he wrote, it is not so easy to tell ; it would certainly take him a few years, and the end was reached before any considerable outbreak of the Eutychean heresy; therefore probably in 447, or 448, for the reason that Pulcheria did not conquer that heresy until after her marriage with Marcian ; this date is supported by the fact that the breaking of her vow was unknown to the writer of ix. 1, 3 ; also because the Emperor Theodosius was still alive. The work was the fruit and employment of old age; the style is certainly that of an elderly man, and not that of youth or early maturity.

What were the main objects he had in view in his history?

1. He desired to present the truth with regard to the facts and their results. In i. 1, he affirms: "I will readily transcribe fully from any work that may tend to the elucidation of truth." "Still, as it is requisite, in order to maintain historical accuracy, to pay the strictest attention to the means of eliciting truth, I felt myself bound to examine all writings of this class, according to my ability." This is his professed purpose ; however subjective or churchly his view of truth may be, we must give him the credit for the intention. In i. 1, he appeals

to his readers in this wise : " Let not an impertinent or malignant spirit be imputed to me, for having dwelt upon the disputes of ecclesiastics among themselves, concerning the primacy and pre-eminence of their own heresy. In the first place, as I have already said, a historian ought to regard everything as secondary in importance to truth." And we shall see evidences of his fairness.

2. His history is designed to be a demonstration of Christianity as from God. The vastness of the change wrought by God in the introduction and success of Christianity and the insignificant and mythical themes upon which literature had been wont to exercise itself, prompted him, with his confessed inefficiency, to undertake this line of evidence, in the conviction that God would help his believing incapacity. Hence his work is a record of immediate divine interventions, and extraordinary gifts of the Holy Spirit ; it abounds in visions, miracles, and prophecy. The celestial agents visibly direct affairs ; the flow of vaticination does not cease ; the power to reverse the expected order of events is not suspended. Thus, as to epiphanies of divine, angelic, or sainted beings : In i. 3, is recounted the appearance of the cross unto Constantine ; and in the night during sleep, the manifestation of Christ with a cross, and the instructions given to the emperor. In ii. 1, we have a series of divine interpositions to discover the true cross, and Sozomen remarks in refutation of one explanation, " I do not think that human information is requisite, when God thinks it best to make manifest the same." In ii. 3, the old name, Hestiæ, is changed to Michaelium, because of the reported appearance of the archangel there. The monks are favored with such direct counselors ; Pachomius obeys an angel, who directs him to assemble young men for instruction ; " he was frequently admitted to intercourse with the holy angels." Apollonius yielded to direct divine advice, and withdrew from the desert to a populous region. The cross reappeared in the days of Constantius (iv. 5) ; Julian's life is filled with portents (v. 1, 20, 22 ; vi. 2). A curious bit of speculation occurs in vi. 2 ; in interpreting Julian's alleged use of his blood, he says : " I know not whether the approach of death, as is wont to be the case, when the soul is in the act of being separated from the body, and when it is enabled to behold diviner spectacles than is allotted to men, that Julian might then have beheld Christ. Few allusions have been made to this subject ; and yet I dare not reject this hypothesis as absolutely false, for God often suffers still more improbable and astonishing events to take place, in order to prove that the religion named after Christ is not sustained by human energy." Of Theodore's confession (v. 20) he remarks : " It is said that he was afterwards asked whether he had been sensible of any pain on the rack ; and that he replied he had not been entirely free from suffering, but had his pain assuaged by the attentions of a young man who had stood by him, and had wiped off the perspiration with the finest linen cloth, and supplied him with coolest water, by which he eased the inflammation and refreshed his labors. I am convinced that no man, whatever magnanimity he may possess, is capable without the special assistance of divine Power, of manifesting such entire indifference about the body." In vi. 29, Piammon sees an angel standing near the holy table, and writing down in a book the names of the monks who were present, while he erased the names of those who were absent. Mark had the elements of the holy table administered to him by an angel (vii. 29). Malachion, while journeying with his brothers, was made invisible, and then reappeared, and pursued his way with them (vi. 32). So the portent at Hebdomas was a sign of divine favor to Theodosius the Great (vii. 24) ; the heavenly hosts were the real overthrowers of Gainas (viii. 4) ; Basiliscus the martyr appears to Chrysostom (viii. 28). Pulcheria's celestial directors helps her to find the forty martyrs (ix. 2). The appearance of Zechariah to the serf pointed out the way to the discovery of the prophet's remains (ix. 17). The demoniacal agencies are equally operant, some of which are alluded to in the above passages, but readily yield to prayer and exorcism, if not immediately overthrown by God.

For a demonstration of the same truth, miracles are wrought to effect physical cures, mental troubles, threatened dangers, casting out of demons, silencing philosophers and wordy ecclesiastics, vindicating orthodoxy, reading the thoughts of hypocrites, defeating enemies, sanctifying the sacraments, raising the dead ; and they are the mighty agents for converting philosophers, Jews, pagans, and heretics. They are wrought by the hands of the eminently excellent only ; the gift is associated with a high measure of grace ; for example the bishops Paphnutius (i. 10) and Spyridion (i. 11) are so endowed ; Alexander of Constantinople (i. 14), Eusebius of Emesa (iii. 6), Martin of Tours (iii. 14), Arsacius of Nicomedia (iv. 16), Donatus (vii. 26), Gregory of Neocæsarea (vii. 26), Theotimus of Scythia (vii. 26), Epiphanius of Salamis (vii. 27). In like manner, the monks Antony (i. 13), Amun (i. 14), Eutychianus (i. 14), Macarius the Egyptian, Apollonius, Hilarion, Julian (iii. 14), John, Copres, Helles, Apelles, Eulogius (vi. 28) ; Apollos, John of Diolchus, Benjamin and Pior (vi. 29). The united prayer of a congregation could effect them (vii. 5). The statue of Christ at Paneas, the fountain at Emmaus, the tree at Hermopolis (v. 21), were all miraculous centers. The spot where the Archangel Michael appeared (ii. 3), the places where the head of John the Baptist reposed (vii. 21), the tombs of monks, martyrs, and bishops, — as of Hilarion (iii. 14), Martyrius and Marcianus (iv. 3), Epiphanius (vii. 27), — were replete with restorative virtues. Sozomen had such a miracle wrought upon himself; he believed thoroughly in an uninterrupted stream of charismata; he deemed it necessary for the maintenance of the faith. He was no more credulous than Socrates, or Theodoret, or Evagrius, or Theodore. To criticise him for his belief in this respect is to forget the Christian conscious- ness of the age. And the historic school which seeks to eliminate the volume of testimony, in the assumption that miracles do not fall within the province of history, ignores the first law of that science, which requires the reproduction of all facts, in time and place, whatever they may be, that are affiliated with the evolution of the human will; that other older school which dis- misses all ecclesiastical miracles on the *a priori* assumption that these energies ceased at a time co-ordinate with the death of the Apostles, or at a point not far removed from their age, violates the spirit of induction. These miracles must be tested by evidence, and the laws of super- natural energy, and in no other way. To Sozomen and all his contemporaries the miracle appeared essential both to the proof of the divine origin of Christianity, and to offset and with- stand the influence of the theurgic arts of the philosophers, such as Julianus and many of the Neoplatonists. As he remarks concerning the reply made by Alexander, bishop of Constan- tinople, when he silenced the philosopher by the simple authority of Christ, "It is then right to consider whether it is a greater miracle, that a man, and he a philosopher, should so easily be silenced by a word, or that a stone wall should be cleft by the power of a word, which miracle I have heard some attribute with pride to Julian, surnamed the Chaldean " (i. 18). The gift of prophecy is also represented as sustained throughout this period, and with the same logical aims in view. The monks are especially thus endowed : Antony (i. 13, vi. 5, 6), the two Macarii, Pachomius (iii. 14), Arsacius (iv. 16), John (vi. 28, vii. 22, vii. 28), Theon (vi. 28), Isaac (vi. 40) ; so the bishops Athanasius (iv. 10), Chrysostom and Epiphanius, rather abusively (viii. 15) ; so royal persons, such as the wife of Valens, passively (vi. 16), Pulcheria, directly and passively (ix. 3). The perpetuation of this charism was deemed inherently necessary for the sake of historical continuity, and to prove as well that the faith he loved had been established by God ; equally was it requisite as a holy parallel whereby to gainsay the mantic spirit of Paganism ; as is best illustrated in the silencing of the oracle at Daphne (v. 19), and by his reflections upon the philosopher's tripod devised for finding the successor of Valens (vi. 35). Nor are Socrates, Theodoret, Evagrius, and others any more moderate than Sozomen in this respect.

3. Another aim of his history is to prove that Providence or the divine government is pro- moting the Christian faith directly. The universal order must be interpreting itself distinctly through the Church. The Father must be vindicating the good and punishing the wicked, according to the orthodox category. Sozomen's history is as insistent in this regard as Eliphaz and his philosophic confreres. One must be able to decide infallibly in each case as to cause and effect ; it is a very realistic pragmatism, and is not the exclusive property of Sozomen ; it is a characteristic of all these Church historians.

There is properly enough a recognition of God in history; the sovereign will and the human will are jointly working out the world's order, but it is the attempt to trace the cause and effect immediately and in each case, which is so repulsive and absurd. Some illustrations will show how he brings out this view. In i. 7 the comment made on Constantine's overthrow of Licinius: "From many facts it has often appeared to me that the teaching of the Christians is supported, and its advancement secured, by the Providence of God, and not the least from what then occurred; for at the very moment that Licinius was about to persecute all the churches under him, the war in Bithynia broke out, which ended in a war between him and Constantine, and in which Constantine was so strengthened by Divine assistance, that he was victorious over his enemies by land and by sea." More of detail comes out in the life of Athanasius. Thus in ii. 17, of his election he says: "Alexander, bishop of Alexandria, when about to depart this life, left Athanasius as his successor, in accordance, I am convinced, with the Divine will, directing the vote upon him." And again: "He fled to escape the honor, but he was discovered in his place of concealment by the help of God, who had forecast by Divine manifestations to his blessed predecessors, that the succession was to devolve upon him." His whole career is so viewed in v. 6. There is a large discussion of this subject in vi. 35, where he argues against the plan of pagan philosophers to foretell the future of the empire: "The philosophers, on the other hand, acted as if the deposition and restoration of emperors had depended solely on them; for if the imperial succession was to be considered dependent on the arrangement of the stars, what was requisite but to await the accession of the future emperor, whoever he might be? Or, if the succession was regarded as dependent on the will of God, what right had man to meddle? For it is not the function of human foreknowledge or zeal to understand God's thought; nor if it were right, would it be well for men, even if they be the wisest of all, to think that they can plan better than God." He persists in tracing a connection between God and every event in favor of mechanical goodness or orthodoxy. He follows many opponents, whether heretical or pagan, with the Divine wrath; all these historians do this, — Philostorgius, as well as Evagrius. Sozomen is not nearly so bitter or uncharitable as either of these. He is most atrabilious in the case of Julian, under whom his own family had suffered. As a consequence of this arbitrary pious prag- matism, the most deplorable incompetents are treated as the express favorites of heaven, while the larger-minded pagan or Arian is loaded with contempt. Under this law, too, the evil sides of the orthodox, and the excellences of the pagan, or Arians, are suppressed. The defeats of the Nicene emperors are not mentioned; the victories of the Anti-Nicene are passed by or belittled, while their humiliations are evidence of the impending anger of heaven. In the survey of Helena's life (ii. 2) he says: "It seems to me that so many holy actions demanded a recom- pense, and indeed even in this life she was raised to the summit of magnificence." As to Con- stantine, in ii. 34 he dares say: "He was more successful than any other sovereign in all his undertakings; for he formed no design, I am convinced, without God." When Bishop Felix of Rome died, and Liberius became sole occupant of the see, he construes the fact thus: "This event was no doubt ordained by God, that the seat of Peter might not be dishonored by the occupancy of two bishops; for such an arrangement is a sign of discord, and is foreign to ecclesiastical law" (iv. 15). In all the features of Julian's life, God is visiting him with his unap- peasable anger (vi. 35, v. 21, 22, vi. 1, 2). The election of Nectarius, though it was in viola- tion of ecclesiastical order and an accumulation of ignorant blunders, did not take place without the interposition of Divine strength (vii. 8). Theodosius is portrayed as the prime delight of heaven; thus his simple reliance upon God wins him a hopeless battle with Eugenius (vii. 24). It is so with the whole Theodosian line (viii. 1, ix. 1). Pulcheria has Divine love manifested to her in manifold ways, as does her brother, Theodosius the Younger (ix. 1, 3, 16). Even Alaric is driven by an inexplicable impulse to rebuke the luxury, debauchery, and injustice of the Romans (ix. 6). In ix. 1, he says of his own sovereign: "It appears to me that it was the design of God to show by the events of this period, that piety alone suffices for the salvation of princes ; and that without piety, armies, a powerful empire, and every other resource, are of no avail. The Divine power, which is the guardian of the universe, foresaw that the emperor would be distinguished by his piety, and determined that Pulcheria, his sister, should be the protector of him and of the government." In ix. 16, he explains his secular details in the paragraph : " This is not the proper place to enter into details concerning the deaths of the tyrants ; but I considered it necessary to allude to the circumstance in order to show, that to insure the stability of imperial power, it is sufficient for an emperor to serve God with reverence, which was the course pursued by Honorius." While of his patron he says : " It seems as if God openly manifested His favor towards the present emperor, not only by disposing of warlike affairs in an unexpected way, but also by revealing the sacred bodies of many persons who were of old most distinguished for piety." The whole history is full of this sort of philosophy of its personages. Similarly all natural calamities and the irruption of barbarians are ethically explained, which is correct enough as a general principle ; but these phenomena are punitive or vindicatory of particular deeds. Constantius' course toward Athanasius was heralded by an invasion of the Franks, and by an earthquake in the East (iii. 6). Of Julian he says : " It is, however, very obvious that throughout the reign of this emperor, God gave manifest tokens of His displeasure and permitted many calamities to befall several of the provinces of the Roman Empire. He visited the earth with such fearful earthquakes, that the buildings were shaken, and no more safety could be found within houses than in the open air." Then follow the inundations of the Nile ; the drought and the famine in the empire, and on their heels the pestilences (vi. 2). Under Valens we read : " In the meantime although hail-storms of extraordinary magnitude fell in various places, and although many cities, particularly Nicæa in Bithynia, were shaken by earthquakes, yet Valens the emperor and Eudoxius the bishop paused not in their career, but continued to persecute all Christians who differed from them in opinion " (vi. 10). He does not make the same reflection upon Constantius, when the earthquake at Nicomedia intercepted the meeting of a council (iv. 16) ; Gainas' attempted revolution is " pre-announced by the appearance of a comet directly over the city ; this comet was of extraordinary magnitude, larger, it is said, than any that had previously been seen " (viii. 3). After Chrysostom's exile, " hailstones of extraordinary magnitude fell at Constantinople and in the suburbs of the city. Four days afterwards, the wife of the emperor died. These occurrences were regarded by many as indications of Divine wrath, on account of the persecutions that had been carried on against John " (viii. 27).

But the earthquakes and famines and invasions that happened under Theodosius the Great and Theodosius Junior are not mentioned directly. By such unfair pragmatism Sozomen, as all his fellow-historians, sought to answer the allegations, now more directly affirmed, in the period of barbarian irruption, that the calamities were due to the desertion of the gods. Sulpicius Severus, Augustine, and Orosius built up a somewhat better apology.

4. Another object he kept before him, we will let him state in his own words : " The doctrine of the Catholic Church is shown to be especially the most genuine, since it has been tested frequently by the plots of opposing thinkers ; yet, the disposal of the lot being of God, the Catholic Church has maintained its own ascendancy, has re-assumed its own power, and has led all the churches and the people to the reception of its own truth " (i. 1). Catholicity and Orthodoxy, as defined at Nicæa, are synonymous. The creed of the fathers is final. The Church which spoke in 325 and 381 is the historic and Catholic Church, and the Theodosian line is the Divinely appointed instrument for laying its foundations immovably, the others having failed. Church and State are to be indissolubly wedded. This faith is made mechanically the test of goodness and badness, and this expresses his personal belief.

He speaks of the Scriptures with uniform reverence, and holds to the θεωρία as the method of interpretation, as we see in v. 22, where he says of the Jews : " They were only acquainted with the mere letter of Scripture, and could not, like the Christians and a few of the wisest among the Hebrews, discover the hidden meaning (πρὸς θεωρίαν) " ; yet he speaks with respect (viii. 2) of Chrysostom's way of expounding the sacred records and of his "teacher Diodorus' method, employed in the many books of that bishop," in which he explained the significance of the sacred words and avoided allegory (θεωρία). But when bishops and monks are declared to be skilled in the Scriptures, it is in this mystical sense. His own grandfather was a solver of the amphibolies of the Word, doubtless by this convenient key (v. 5).

The dogmatic standpoint, as we have seen, was traditionalism, toward which the Church gravitated under the dictation of the councils, the influence of bishops like Athanasius, the almost uniform ictus of the Roman see, Ambrose, the Gregories, Basil the Great, Ephraim, Eusebius, and Epiphanius, the majority of monks, and finally the whole force of the State. He opposes all shades of Arianism, as also Apolinarianism; had he completed his work, from what he says of Pulcheria's conquest over heresies, he would have opposed the Nestorian views of the Theotokos. But of Donatism and Cyprianism he has not a word. Of the anthropological struggles of the West there is not a syllable. Here is the place, also, to consider his attitude toward heresies. Sozomen does not assail any phase of Arianism with the intemperate epithets which Eusebius employed to condemn the earlier innovators, or such as abound in Theodoret and Evagrius and later historians. Indeed, he sometimes calls them Christians and members of the Catholic Church. His treatment of the Novatians, while a little offish, is yet generous as compared with other writers, except Socrates, from whom he obtains almost all their history; he devotes much space; he is generally courteous in tone; and when he speaks of the proposed union (iv. 2) between the Catholic Church and that body of believers, he omits the cause of the failure; viz., the reluctance of some legalistic Novatians to acquiesce, — a point which Socrates does not fail to expose. He mentions Montanism (Phrygianism) several times, but with no new facts, save that they were numerous in Phrygia in his day, and had peculiar Paschal usages (i. 6, ii. 18, 32, vii. 18, 19). Of the Gnostic sects, he alludes to the Valentinians only, whose conventicles were repressed by an edict of Constantius (ii. 32). The Manichæans are mentioned only as they are one of the three sects excepted from Gratian's law of toleration (vii. 1). Of the Pricillianists, whose attempt at a world religion falls so wholly within his time, he says nothing. The Quartodecimanians are still numerous and tenacious (vii. 18). He has a bare allusion to the Encratites (v. 11). Of the Origenistic controversy, he has no more to say than he is compelled to, in order to state correctly the conflict between Theophilus and Chrysostom. Over against the Origenists he places the Anthropomorphists (viii. 12). Of Lucifer's separatism, he gives only the rise (iii. 15). With all his emphatic adherence to the current orthodoxy, he must be regarded as the most charitable of historians next to Socrates. Mention has already been made of his kindly disposition toward the Novatians. When writing fully and favorably, as was his duty, about Aëtius (iii. 15), he is constrained to make an apology: "Let it not be accounted strange if I have bestowed commendations upon the leaders or enthusiasts of the above-mentioned heresies. I admire their eloquence and their impressiveness in discourse: I leave their doctrines to be judged by those whose prerogative it is."

On the one hand, we find him insisting on the right of private judgment, as when he discusses the overruling Providence in Julian's life, and especially on the infatuation which led the emperor to Persia in spite of Sallust (vi. 1): "This observation, however, is only inserted lest I should be blamed for omitting it. I leave every one to form his own opinion." So, after discussing the use of penance, he remarks in the following chapter (vii. 17): "Such subjects as the above, however, are best left to the decision of individual judgment." He would also allow latitude in ceremonials (vii. 19), as we shall see. On the other hand, he dreads the progressive and unsettling outcome of the private judgment in exercise. He expresses this fear in iv. 27: "The spirit of innovation is self-laudatory; hence it advanced farther and farther, and crept along to greater novelties. With increasing self-conceit, and in scorn of the fathers, it enacted laws of its own. Nor does it honor the doctrine of the ancients concerning God, but is always excogitating strange dogmas and restlessly adds novelty to novelty, as the events now show."

Of the threatening strategies of free thought in his own day, he devoutly exclaimed : "That new heresies have not prevailed in our times, we shall find to be due especially to her" (Pulcheria) (ix. 1). Consequently he deprecates the deleterious influence of polemics. On the accession of Jovian, he says : "The presidents of the churches now resumed the agitation of doctrinal questions and discussions. They had remained quiet during the reign of Julian, when Christianity itself was endangered, and had unanimously offered up their supplications for the mercy of God. It is thus that men, when attacked by foreign enemies, remain in accord among themselves ; but when external troubles are removed, then internal dissensions creep in" (vi. 4 and in vi. 25).

"Thus do the private animosities of the clergy from time to time greatly injure the Church and divide religion into many heresies ! And this is a proof ; for had George, like Theodotus, received Apolinarius, on his repentance, into communion, I believe that we should never have heard of the heresy that bears his name. Men are prone, when loaded with opprobrium and contempt, to resort to rivalries and innovations ; whereas, when treated with justice, they become moderate and remain in the same position." More emphatic still is his protest in vi. 26 : "Those varying dogmas are the source of innumerable troubles to religion, and many are deterred from embracing Christianity by the diversity of opinion which prevails in matters of doctrine." In the beginning of this same chapter, in speaking of the Eunomians, he delineates them thus : "They do not applaud a good course of life or manner of conduct, or mercy towards the needy, unless exhibited by persons of their own sect, so much as skill in disputation and the power of triumphing in debates." This is a great blow at the *sectores cymini*, and at pride in polemics ; the whole tone is much more liberal than that of the ecclesiastic Theodoret, or even the lawyer Evagrius. Sozomen, like Socrates, represents a generous feeling current among the laymen of Constantinople in court and among the trades and professions. The attitude of the Catholic Church with regard to baptism, he sets forth adequately as trivial, and argues against the Eunomian innovation of one baptism and a change in the formula (vi. 21) : "But whether it was Eunomius or any other person who first made these innovations upon the tradition of baptism, it seems to me that such innovators, whoever they may have been, were alone in danger, according to their own representation, of quitting this life without having received Divine baptism." The argument here is an unusually long one ; with his generation he held to the magical efficacy of the rite. The theory of the sacraments as mysteries or arcana, was one which controlled him throughout, and even limited his fidelity as a historian. Thus in i. 20 : "I thought it necessary to reproduce the very document (the Nicene Creed) concerning these matters, as an example of the truth, in order that posterity might possess in a fixed and clear form, the symbol of that faith which proved pacifying at the time ; but since some pious friends who understood such matters, recommended that these truths ought to be spoken of and heard by the initiated and their initiators only, I agreed with their counsel : for it is not unlikely that some of the uninitiated may read this book : while I have concealed such of the prohibited material as I ought to keep silent about, I have not altogether left the reader ignorant of the opinions held by the Synod." Nor will he repeat the symbol as subjoined to the letter of the council of Antioch (vi. 4) ; and when the Macedonian commission to Liberius make their statement, and the text is given to show their entire acceptance of the Nicene view, Sozomen will not reproduce it. Again in vi. 29, Mark was a monk of "such eminent piety, that Macarius himself, the presbyter of Celliæ, declared that he had never given to him what priests present to the initiated at the holy table ; but that an angel, administering it to him, whose hand up to the forearm, he declared himself to have seen." In viii. 5, in giving the account of a marvelous judgment wrought on a Macedonian wife, who pretended to be a convert to the Nicene views, and thus frequented the orthodox ceremony of the Supper, he remarks, "At the time of the celebration of the mysteries (the initiated will understand what I mean), this woman kept what was given her, and held down her head as if engaged in prayer." In reciting the disturbances at the Easter celebration over the decree of exile against Chrysostom (viii. 21), he says : "They were charged with the commission of such disorderly acts as can be readily conceived by those who have been admitted to the mysteries, but which I consider it requisite to pass over in silence, lest my work should fall into the hands of the uninitiated." Here we have a glimpse of the scope of the arcaña as well as the weakness of the historian in submitting to the advice of narrow friends ; no other historian felt bound to restrict himself in such matters. Sozomen here joined the most extreme sacramentarians of his day. On the weighty matter of discipline, he believes with the Catholic Church in receiving back the penitent into the Church, against Novatian and Donatistic practices. He expresses his opinion at some length, though not so fully as Socrates, in the chapter which relates to the abolition of the penitential presbyter (vii. 16) : " Impecca-bility is a Divine attribute, and belongs not to human nature ; therefore God has decreed that pardon should be extended to the penitent even after many transgressions. As in supplicating for pardon, it is requisite to confess the sin, it seems probable that the priests, from the begin-ning, considered it irksome to make this confession in public, before the whole assembly of the people. They appointed a presbyter of the utmost sanctity and the most undoubted prudence, to act on those occasions : the penitents went to him and confessed their transgressions ; and it was his office to indicate the kind of penance adapted to each sin, and then when satisfaction had been made, to pronounce absolution." He deplores the abolition of the office as the occasion of laxity. The deterrent force of public confession was now lost, and that to the danger of Christian conduct. He sympathizes also with that form of martyrdom which wantonly and ruthlessly assails paganism and is slain in the attempt. The system of relic-worship, so character-istic of any decline of opportunity for heroic action, had set in overwhelmingly, and he believed in it vigorously. Our own age reproduces the same tendency not only in religious, but in secular forms, and among Protestants as well. Thus he commemorates : of Old Testament prophets, Micah and Habakkuk (vii. 29), Zechariah (ix. 17) ; of the preparatory period, the head of John the Baptist (vii. 21) ; of the Apostolic Church, St. Stephen (vii. 29, ix. 16) ; of the martyrs, Babylas (v. 19), Forty Soldiers (ix. 2) ; of the monks, Hilarion (iii. 14), the four brothers (vii. 9). The most prominent of secondary relics is the cross with its inscriptions and nails (ii. 1). The discovery of these is mainly through prayer and heavenly signs ; their pos-session is an object of imperial ambition ; the removal and transportation of them are effected with most gorgeous and reverent pomp ; and the sacred treasures become the agents of endless miracles.

Sozomen, like Socrates and Chrysostom, believes in freedom as to old-time ceremonials. Hé has a chapter on the varieties of religious usage (vii. 19) ; and the record is largely the result of his own inquiry. He remarks in conclusion : " Many other customs are still to be observed in cities and villages ; and those who have been brought up in their observance would, from respect to the great men who instituted and perpetuated these customs, consider it wrong to abolish them. Similar motives must be attributed to those who observe different practices in the celebration of the fast, which has led us into this long digression." From his point of view, uniformity may not encroach upon individualism beyond a certain point. He is certainly quietly and with dignity attacking a party of narrow uniformitarians, who are already pressing for a harmony of all ceremonials in Christendom.

Another feature of the Catholic system that he traces carefully, is the relation between Church and Empire. He devotes more attention to this aspect of polity than to its internal develop-ment ; this latter he touches upon incidentally, and not at all carefully. We have seen how painstakingly he cites the imperial edicts with regard to the Church. The state laws, which at first expressed conciliar decisions, were followed by independent imperial enactments. These, indeed, are at first sporadic, but become more and more the rule. The personal views of Sozomen appear in the narrative, but they are fluctuating. He acquiesces in the imperial convocation of councils, as do all his cotemporaries. On the death of Constantine, in comment-ing upon the hereafter fixed Christian character of the state, he says : " The sacerdotal dignity is not only equal in honor to imperial power, but in sacred places even takes the ascendancy" (ii. 34). With the plan of producing uniformity of religion in the empire, he seems to sympathize (iv. 11). He is indignant at Julian's indifference to the murder of Zeno by the inhabitants of Gaza, and at the deprivations of the Christians, when all their political and personal rights were taken from them (v. 9). To the charge of Libanius, that the man who aimed the dart at Julian was a Christian, and belonged to the race of habitual transgressors of the law, Sozomen replies by defending the regicide : "In the documents above quoted, Libanius clearly states that the emperor fell by the hand of a Christian; and this probably was the truth. It is not unlikely that some of the soldiers who then served in the Roman army might have conceived the idea, since Greeks and all men until this day have praised tyrannicides, for exposing themselves to death in the cause of liberty, and spiritedly standing by their country, their families, and their friends. Still less is he deserving of blame, who for the sake of God and of religion, performed so bold a deed" (vi. 2). This is the highest stand that a lawyer could take in support of individualism. In his view of the exalted prerogatives of the Church, the reply of Valentinian to the bishops, who desired to hold a council, would seem happy. "I am but one of the laity, and have, therefore, no right to interfere in these transactions; let the priests, to whom such matters appertain, assemble where they please" (vi. 7). Theodosius' compulsory course with regard to paganism and orthodoxy, and the choice of Nectarius, are approved. On the other hand, he selected two instances out of many from the life of Ambrose, for the purpose of illustrating how, in God's behalf, that bishop conducted himself towards those in power (vii. 25).

Throughout we find him recognizing the practical headship of Rome ; he expresses himself unconsciously in vi. 22, "The question having been thus decided by the Roman Church, peace was restored and the inquiry ended." This ignores the action of the Synod of Alexandria and that of Constantinople itself, for both had decreed the consubstantiality of the Holy Spirit and opposed the christology of Apolinarius, prior to the action of the Roman Synod. The power delegated to Julius by the council of Sardica (iii. 8), the conflict between the East and the West conducted in mutually arrogant epistles (iii. 10), the subordination of new to old Rome (vii. 9), show the drift toward concentration. Sozomen does not seem to understand the rival movements of Alexandria under Athanasius and Theophilus ; nor the Eastern imperial attempts to elevate Constantinople to the supremacy, nor the mutterings of Antiochan jealousy.

The Church's servility toward the orthodox rulers is fairly expressed, and yet with comparative moderation, by Sozomen. He is an apologist for Constantine, and reflects, as do all the historians, and especially Evagrius in his criticism of Zosimus, the adulations and subterfuges of Eusebius. The religious fluctuation of that emperor is masked ; his crimes are suppressed ; he is made to appear orthodox, even when at his worst Eusebian stage. No wonder that Philostorgius charged the Homoöusians with worshiping Constantine as a god in the ceremonies connected with his image ! Constantius, a vacillating, cruel, incompetent, is also apologized for, but to the damage of his intelligence. Julian, for his years in some respects, one of the most promising and earnest rulers of ancient times, is loaded with obloquy, his highest motives and ideals ridiculed, his victories belittled, his death savagely exulted in. Jovian's and Valentinian's toleration are not understood, but their personal orthodoxy is in so far praised. Valens is looked at through the eyes of his two fierce Cappadocian assailants. His excellences are entirely ignored ; the most inconsequent views are imputed to him while attempting to glorify Basil ; in the sad story of the emperor's dying son, that bishop appears as a brute in his treatment of the agonized father. The stories of heroism attributed to the orthodox are only examples of insufferable insolence ; one must marvel at the patience of Valens, if there be any truth in them. Gratian, that beau-ideal of Western orthodoxy, was really a nose of wax in the hands of Ambrose ; he was esteemed more moderately by the East, and that rather for having called Theodosius to a share in the throne, than for any quality in himself ; but his utter moral collapse, after the magnificent promise of his youth, is wholly veiled from sight. Theodosius the Great is glorified, not for his superior statecraft and generalship, but for his efforts to suppress paganism and heresy. The charges against his private life such as Eunapius and Zosimus suggest, are not hinted at. He is a man of prayer and visions, a relic-worshiper, and a persecutor of pagans and Arians. Great as he certainly was, his distinguishing and conspicuous qualities are passed by. His pitiful children, Arcadius and Honorius, the sorriest quidnuncs of those stormy times, are heroes of piety. Pulcheria, excellent as she was, was not worthy of the excessive flattery poured out upon her; while Anthemius, Troilus, Valerianus, and other noble figures of the day are passed by. The younger Theodosius, with his good training and generally fair endeavor, is delineated in the dedication as the consummate man of all time, while he is a very third-rate soul at best. The eulogies by Socrates (vii. 22 and 42) are just as fulsome. This was the grave sin of the State Church; the Arian State Church did the same for Constantius and Valens; more and more as history reveals the truth concerning many of those idols, does the revulsion increase against a union of two functions which could so degrade both.

The relation of Church and State involves the question of persecution. It is not the history of the endeavor to enforce uniformity, with which we shall concern ourselves, but rather the views Sozomen sets forth, as to the policy of repression. The laws of Constantine suppressing heretics did not affect the Novatians (ii. 32), concerning which justice, he remarks: "The emperor, I believe, willingly relaxed the rigor of the enactment in their favor, for he only desired to strike terror into the minds of his subjects, and had no intention of persecuting them." The punishments inflicted in Constantius' time on the orthodox in Constantinople, both by Macedonius (iv. 23) and Eudoxius (iv. 26), call forth this reflection: "For, if the persecution did not occasion such tortures to the body as preceding ones, it appeared more grievous to all who reflected aright, on account of its disgraceful nature, for both the persecutors and the persecuted belonged to the Church; and the one was all the more disgraceful in that men of the same religion treated their fellows with a degree of cruelty which the ecclesiastical laws prohibit to be manifested towards enemies and strangers." He spares himself the pain of registering all who were ejected from their sees (iv. 27), for no province was without its list of sufferers. The cruelties inflicted by George on pagan and orthodox, furnish a mournful narrative (iv. 30). On the elevation of Julian, a great dread fell upon the Christian world, intensified by the portents which befell him. The series of edicts soon wrought mutual dissension in the Christian ranks, as well as suffering from without. But while Sozomen attributes the refinements of cruelty to Julian, and lays the miseries of the saints at his door as parts of a subtle plan, he nevertheless cannot conceal from himself the absence of direct interference on the part of the State; these calamities were the results of a restoration of the old religion to its ancient union with the State; it was an imperial act; and he is compelled to confess the seeming magnanimity of Julian in certain cases, but even then maligns his motives. The imperial clemency did not arise from any feeling of compassion, but because persecution would only increase the number of Galilean adherents; because he was envious of their glory, did he resort to argument instead of cruelty, and manifest an unexpected benevolence instead of proceeding to rigorous measures (v. 4, 5). "It may be concluded from what has been said, that if Julian shed less blood than preceding persecutors of the Church, and that if he devised fewer punishments for the torture of the body, yet that he was severer in other respects." Nevertheless, this statement is followed by a record of suffering in all quarters of the empire and the impression of purposed directness is given, as if the State had inflicted them, especially when we read that the emperor would not listen to the cautions of Sallust (v. 20). He does not comment on Jovian's toleration, but only rejoices in the return of the Church to ascendency. Unsparing is his picture of the dastardly measures of Valens against the professors of the faith; he regards that persecutor as the special victim of Divine wrath; while, on the other hand, he does not hesitate to call the Arian Goths, who fell under the anger of Athanaric, martyrs (vi. 37). He does not express an opinion as to the partial toleration of Gratian's edict (vii. 1); but in explanation of Theodosius' law forbidding heretics, i.e. all anti-Nicenists, from holding churches and from exercising any clerical function, he says: "Great as were the punishments adjudged by the laws against heretics, they were not always carried into execution; for the emperor had no desire to persecute his subjects; he only desired to enforce uniformity of view about God, through the medium of intimidation. Those who voluntarily renounced heretical opinions, received commendation from him." And it is true that the court practice of persecuting emperors, orthodox or Arian, was utterly in the teeth of their own edicts, and their most intimate counselors were elected without regard to religion. When Justina sought to revive the Arian standard in the West, her treatment of Ambrose is called persecution (vii. 13); but Ambrose's intolerant procedures against the Arians are not even noticed. No quizzical wrinkle disturbs the flow of his narrative in vii. 15, when Theodosius I. gives a heathen temple to the Christians, and the pagans resolve to defend their rights, and do so effectually; but the Christians who perish in that hateful conflict are crowned as martyrs by an imperial edict! For the religious tyranny of Theodosius the Great he is a warm apologist, and disguises the perversion of that principle of freedom for which he pleads most earnestly, when the Arians hold the reins of power, and abuse their opportunity. The contradictions are perfectly apparent and irreconcilable, because uniformity by force has always been impossible. Yet logical men will state the most contradictory reasons, which no quidnunc can refrain from laughing at. Themistius' plea for toleration (vi. 36) in matters of intellectual belief, on the ground of secular diversities in philosophy and from the incomprehensible nature of God, shows the existence of a party who believed in this principle. While Sozomen gives it place, and hailed the Gothic Arians who compelled Valens to cease his oppressions, he has no word of approbation for the proposition or the argument.

5. Another design of his history is stated in i. 1: " I have had to deliberate whether I ought to confine myself to the recital of events connected with the Church under the Roman government; but it seemed more advisable to include, as far as possible, the record of transactions relative to religion among the Persians and barbarians." He regards Christianity as the universal and sole religion, and would trace its extension in all directions. Hence he is the first historian to give us a larger account of religion in Syria and Palestine, introducing us especially to some aspects of Christian life and suffering in Edessa; we are all the more surprised to have no mention of the Church in Africa, and so very little of the Church in the West, except when it comes into close relations with the East, as in the larger controversies, and especially after Arianism threatened to keep its hold upon the Byzantine section of the empire; and the Orient had to cry to the cold and unsympathetic Occident for help, and often in vain. He is also careful to give us some, if not a very original, account of the work of missions. He repeats the story of the Iberians, Armenians, Indians, Saracens, and Goths. He gives us a larger insight into Persia; the errors with which he is charged as swarming, are no more numerous than those of his cotemporaries. Of the large work of Theophilus of Dhu, or the extension of Arianism among the Germanic tribes, he says nothing. Chrysostom's real missionary enterprises are passed by, excepting his expenditure of the funds furnished by Olympias for the redemption and restoration of Isaurian captives (viii. 27). His reflections on the methods of Church extension are more interesting and numerous. Thus, in ii. 5, of the attempt of Constantine to abolish idolatry and introduce the faith, Sozomen says, " Soldiers were not necessary; the courtiers effected it"; he does not consider it advisable to give all the details as to all the lands then won to the state religion. The barbarians he notices as converted through the instrumentality of Christian captives (ii. 6, 7). Armenian influence carried Christianity into Persia (ii. 8). Prodigies, too, are helpful agents (vi. 5, v. 22). The hieroglyphs and crux-symbols discovered in the Egyptian temples led to the repentance of pagans (vii. 15). Sometimes a kingdom will solicit the instruction of an orthodox monk, as in the case of the Saracens (vi. 38). The legal suppressions of paganism facilitate a change of sentiment on the part of many (vii. 15). The very ambitions of their clergy led numbers of the Arians to embrace Nicene views (vii. 17); and the doctrinal discussions among heretics constrain others to embrace a more uniform system of belief (viii. 1). The

efficiency of the monks as evangelists is found in nearly all the biographies of them. On the other hand, he makes confession to the baleful effects of incessant indulgence in polemics. "These varying dogmas are the sources of innumerable troubles to religion ; and many are deterred from embracing Christianity by the diversity of opinion which prevails in matters of doctrine " (vi. 26). This thought of universality, then, is a feature of his history.

6. Another design is to dignify monasticism as the true ethical ideal and goal of Christianity, — as the philosophy which is to supplant all the ancient intellectual strivings of reason, — and he announces this purpose as follows : " Nor is it foreign to ecclesiastical history to introduce in this work an account of those who were the fathers and originators of what is denominated monachism, and of their immediate successors, whose celebrity is well known to us either by observation or report. For I would neither be considered ungracious towards them, nor willing to consign their virtue to oblivion, nor yet be thought ignorant of their history ; but I would wish to leave behind me such a record of their manner of life that others, led by their example, might attain to a blessed and happy end " (i. 1). He is here quietly resisting a school of Christians and politicians who were opposed to the absorbing and destructive qualities of this manner of life ; Athanasius, Basil the Great, Jerome, Chrysostom, had to write in its defense for the same reason, and he sided with these supporters of its virtues, very naturally. He is a full believer in the Divine philosophy which nurtured him ; monasticism with its practical strivings after conformity to the Divine-human Pattern, and its attempt to enthrone the spiritual over the material has a zealous defender in him, of all its rapt and grotesque forms. He determined therefore to make it a unique portion of his history. The discussion of its aims in i. 12 will give us a clue to his own desire to represent it as almost the resultant force in the progress of the Divine kingdom ; one reads the historian's responsive feeling between the lines. This philosophy was the most useful thing received by man from God ; it was superior to all other knowledge, and warranted the neglect of all worldly science ; it strove to eliminate the *adiaphora* from ethics, and to make everything have a moral complexion ; one must be doing good, or else he is doing evil. Its great duties are the discipline of self, the worship of the Creator, and the cultivation of a spirit of other-worldness. These canons and goals are the life of the system. It is the philosophy which is to take the place of the old theoretical schemes ; and it is the great school to fill up the gap made by the decay of the Hellenic universities. The Christian university founded by Theodosius in Sozomen's day, was indeed a blow to this educational ideal. While we may have no accord with his view of this ethical phenomenon, we must concede him the merit of discerning its significance and intent, and allow that he was wise to give us so full an account of its elaboration, and so much detail and scrap of biography ; for it was a dominant element in the history of this time. It formed men and measures. The reproach of Sozomen on this score is wholly a mistake ; he has done us capital service in not neglecting this element, otherwise we could have but little conception of its historical setting, of its patience, its tireless devotion, and we would have to resort to Palladius or Rufinus and the individual biographies. Moreover, it is an uncritical spirit which recoils from dissecting the awful and often repulsive details of legalistic self-denial. After discoursing on the local origin of monasticism and the forms it assumed, we have chapters containing brief sketches of hermits, laurists, and cœnobites (i. 12, 13, 14, iii. 14). The people looked to the monks for the color of their theology (iv. 10). Arianism felt its weakness without them and ineffectually sought their suppression (vi. 20). The Nicene faith uniformly received the support of these communities (vi. 27), to which they remained devoted under all persecutions. Another series of biographies follows in vi. 28–34 : Theophilus (viii. 12) has a preliminary struggle with them to carry forward his plots against John. The royal court itself under Pulcheria's leadership reflected its severe discipline (ix. 13). Sozomen seems also to have studied the rules of various bodies, some of whose details he gives, and indulges in a sort of comparative study of their regulations (vi. 30). Yet with all his implied admiration of the heroes of this system, who went to the almost extreme of abstinence, he remarks in reviewing the

discipline of Theotimus (vii. 26) : " I consider it to be the part of the philosopher to yield to the demand of these appetites from necessity, and not from the love of sensual gratification." It is to be noted that he omits for the most part the immoral forms of monasticism, such as Evagrius gives us a highly rhetorical account of.

7. A more subordinate aim is to present selected secular matters so-called ; he does not consider these to be wholly foreign to the scope of his work. He handles such with considerable largeness in Constantine's life, and keeps up a thread under Constantius and Julian. He is more sparing until he reaches Arcadius and Honorius, and the chapters 3–15 of Book ix. are largely devoted to the Western struggles with usurpers.

8. A final and subordinate aim is the development of imperial law with regard to the Church ; he gives little of purely synodical canons, but remarks, " I consider it necessary, however, to mention the laws enacted for the honor and consolidation of religion, as they constitute a considerable portion of ecclesiastical history."   And in the next chapter, " Having arrived at this point of my history, it would not be right to omit all mention of the laws passed in favor of those individuals in the churches, who had received their freedom " (i. 9). We have already seen how continuously this plan is sustained.

His Method.   1. He is conscious of certain limitations, and expresses them frankly. (*a*) A modest estimate of his own powers (Proemium, i. 1).   (*b*) The excess of material compels him to a constant process of selection (ii. 3, 5, 14, iii. 14, 15, 16, iv. 4, 27, vii. 17. 28, ix. 1.   (*c*) A sense of incapacity to handle some aspects of doctrine (vii. 17).   (*d*) An occasional insufficiency of data to state a positive conclusion (iv. 2, viii. 16).

2. He acknowledges the need of research, and presents his ideal purpose in i. 7 : " I shall record the transactions with which I have been connected, and also those concerning which I have heard from persons who knew or saw the affairs in our own day, or before our own generation.   But I have sought for records of events of earlier date amongst the established laws appertaining to religion, amongst the proceedings of the Synods of the period, amongst the innovations that arose, and in the epistles of kings and priests." His recurring intention was to reproduce the documents just as they were, but he finally decided to epitomize their contents and to present the entire instrument, only when the state of controversy compelled it in order to fairness.   The difficulty in the way of consulting these sources lay in the fact of their dispersion in palaces, churches, and the private libraries of the erudite.   He anticipates criticism by acknowledging that contradictions are likely to appear in his work, not from any fault of his own, but because of the partisan and arbitrary nature of the documents ; he ingenuously confesses that men's passions and conceptions have shaped many of these writings, and that the factious spirit has often been guilty of the willful omission of material, which was not of its side.   He distinctly avers that he felt it his duty to examine all writings of this class according to his ability. Such was his intention.   If now we turn to his actual methods, we can group his ways of accumulating material, somewhat as follows : —

(*a*) His own observation by hearing or sight, and hence knowing, as in ii. 3 ; vii. 19, 28.

(*b*) By obtaining a personally clear knowledge, the medium being undefined, as in the election of Maximus to be bishop of Jerusalem, and Macarius' sympathy therewith ; here his better information was probably due to his Palestinian origin. Ἰστέον μέντοι ὡς οἱ τάδε ἠκριβωκότες, κατὰ γνώμην Μακαρίου γενέσθαί τε καὶ σπουδασθῆναι τῷ πλήθει ταῦτα, ἰσχυρίζονται (ii. 20). As to Serapion and Severianus τὰ μὲν ὧδε ἔγνων (viii. 10). As to Zechariah, where the same phrase occurs (ix. 17). At the close of a universal review of monasticism τάδε ἔγνων ὡς συνέγραψα (iii. 14). As to the Syrian and Persian monks εἰς γνῶσιν ἐμὴν ἦλθον (vi. 34). Ἀλλὰ τὰ μὲν ἀφηγησάμην ἐφ᾽ ὅσον μοι μαθεῖν ἐξεγένετο, περὶ τῶν τότε ἐκκλησιαστικῶν φιλοσόφων (vi. 35).

(*c*) By hearing from those who knew the facts ἅπερ παρὰ ἀκριβῶς ἐπισταμένων ἀκήκοα (ii. 21). As to Arsacius : οἱ παρὰ τῶν Ἀρσάκιον αὐτὸν θεασαμένων ἀκηκοέναι ἔφασαν (iv. 16). As to the mutual prophecies of Epiphanius and John κἀκεῖνον δὲ εἰσέτι νῦν πολλῶν ὄντα τὸν λόγον ἐπυθόμην (viii. 15). As to Atticus : καὶ τὸν μὲν τοιόνδε γενέσθαι φασίν, οἵ γε τὸν ἄνδρα ἔγνωσαν (viii. 27).

(*d*) The correction of a false story by inquiring of trustworthy persons. Thus as to the origin of the Apocalypse of Paul. Ἐρομένῳ δέ μοι περὶ τούτου, ψεῦδος ἔφησεν εἶναι Κίλιξ (vii. 19). As to an accusation against John: τούτου δὲ πρόφασιν ἑτέραν λέγειν οὐκ ἔχω, πλὴν ὅτι ἀψευδής τις οἶμαι πυθανομένῳ περὶ τούτου ἔφη, κ.τ.λ. (viii. 9). The true and twofold causes of difficulty between Theophilus and Isadore: τῶν γε μὴν συγγενομένων τούτοις τότε τοῖς μοναχοῖς ἀνδρὸς οἵου πιστεύεσθαι ἐπυθόμην, κ.τ.λ. (viii. 12).

(*e*) To these may be added the very frequent usage of πυνθάνομαι as a means of expressing his knowledge acquired in any form whatsoever, by hearing, by inquiry, by tradition (i. 21, ii. 8, iii. 14, iv. 25, v. 2, 9, vi. 2 bis, 17, 34 bis, 37, vii. 8, 15, 17, 20, 21, 25, viii. 2, 7, 9, 19).

(*f*) Also his use of ἀκριβόω, showing his effort to attain accurate information, and ἰσχυρίζομαι less frequently, to indicate the strongest confirmation. Both these are used with reserve, and not lightly. Several times he acknowledges his resort to tradition, when he uses the word παρειλήφαμεν, but we cannot always be sure of the form of transmission (iii. 15, 30, vi. 38).

(*g*) Also his reference to those who had more accurate information, or to works whose detail he could not reproduce, or which lay without the province of history (iv. 3).

We see then an ideal and actual plan of research, and a real effort at personal investigation; to deny his frequently iterated language, is to accuse him of deliberate falsehood; and this is palpably unfair; this his honest purpose and work must be borne in mind, in the discussion of his relation to Socrates.

3. As to method in textual criticism, there is none; we find variations in the texts quoted from those of Socrates, Athanasius, and Theodoret, but no more in him than in the rest from one another. When he reports Constantine's speech, he treats it as Thucydides did the orations of his worthies, and as the high-flying Eusebius and the indiscriminating Theodoret do. When he copies a translation from the Greek, he simply says that he gives it just as he found it. On the whole, one is surprised at so fair an agreement in the readings of the documents.

4. There is an entire lack of genuine analytical criticism; the love of allegory (i. 1, ii. 1), the credence given to the Christic sections of Josephus (i. 1), the unquestioning acceptance of Eusebius' turgid statements about Constantine's life, are proofs enough of its absence; and yet Sozomen was careful to present the variety of accounts, so that one might have all points of view, if he did not carefully sift the evidence. This is indeed quite a marked feature of his method. Thus concerning the death of Arius, he gives five different views (ii. 29, 30). He states carefully the varying shades of opinion concerning Marcellus (ii. 33). The two classes of views of the election of Macedonius are recorded and skillfully weighed (iii. 3). The divisions of sentiment after the Synods of Sardica and Philippopolis are accurately grouped (iii. 13). Other instances occur in iii. 14, 18, 23, v. 2, 22, vi. 2, 12, 26, vii. 5, 22. These are but a selection of what is habitual with him, and show a desire to present all sides of a question, and to reflect the divergent convictions of his time about men and measures; but he does not always try to find the just opinion and weigh the testimony; he never tests the validity of his documents, and only a few times tries to decide between clashing judgments, as to which of them rests on a solid foundation of testimony. It is, however, to his credit, when he confesses that his research is baffled, as in iv. 2, with respect to the manner of Paul's death, or suspends his judgment, because the data are insufficient, as in the application to the empress, of Chrysostom's homily on female peccadilloes (viii. 6). Such language shows that he not only sought to ascertain the truth, but to elicit the facts out of conflicting testimony. We may not always think the game worth the powder, but the temper and intent are commendable.

5. Sozomen has a marked zeal for interpreting the events of history; and we can gather these hints of historics, although they do not seem to have been defined as principles in his own mind.

(*a*) He criticises by the rules of traditionalism and monasticism; we find small men given undue prominence, and large ones put far below their proper place (iv. 6, 9, 28, v. 7, 12, vi. 17, 26, vii. 12).

(*b*) He seems to have regarded it his occasional duty to explain the moral intent of a period, of the lives of men, of a special incident; in other words, he used history reflectively and ethically (viii. 4, 12, 17).

(*c*) He is fertile in suggesting motives for which he has no documentary warrant. The entire history of Julian is replete with the insinuation of mean motives (ὡς συμβάλλω). The solitary commendation of him for lowering the price of provisions in Antioch (v. 19) is only a ground for holding him up to ridicule for want of judgment (iii 5, 15, v. 2, 4, 5, 11, 19, 15, 22, vi. 12).

(*d*) He deems it necessary to apologize for his favorites if they are in a questionable position (iii. 18, v. 6, viii. 1).

(*e*) He thinks it right to give recognition to men or measures who have enlisted his admiration (vii. 10).

(*f*) He traces cause and effect in a pragmatic way (vi. 16, 38).

(*g*) He delights in taking prominent figures of a period as the remarkable men who have created a remarkable time, and are Divine instruments, or as objects of Divine protection on account of their piety (iii. 13, 19, iv. 16, v. 13, vi. 17, 26, 27, viii. 3, 4, 6).

(*h*) He dwells at times on characteristics of human nature at play (vi. 4, 26).

(*i*) He gives a favorable explanation of the bad actions of the orthodox (iv. 16).

(*j*) He sometimes introduces speculative explanations or reflections (vi. 2, 4, 37, viii. 5).

6. Chronological method. (1) The imperial reigns are taken as the great periods for the books, and the material is distributed under them; no dates are given, only the names of the emperors. This is stated in the proëmium, and is carried out in the history. (2) He uses the consulates —

(*a*) To mark the beginning and the end of the entire history.

(*b*) Also occasionally to indicate the synchronous occupants of the apostolic sees (i. 2); the convocation of a council (iii. 12, 19, iv. 6, 17, vii. 12); the enthronement of a bishop (iv. 26); the death of an emperor (vii. 29, ix. 1); some general but important event (vii. 5, viii. 4).

(*c*) With this the corresponding year of the emperor is sometimes but rarely given.

(*d*) Another conspicuous chronological system with Sozomen, as in Eusebius, Socrates, and the church historians in general, is to keep up the roll of succession in the greater sees. This had become an essential note of the visible and Catholic Church.

(*e*) Occasionally intervals are indicated as so many years after such and such an event (iii. 5, 11, 12, iv. 1, ix. 1).

(*f*) The length of a reign or of an episcopate, the duration of the life of an emperor or bishop, and of a tendential period are stated, but not often, and without uniformity (iv. 11, v. 1, vii. 5).

(*g*) An unusual number of particles for indefinite time occur as substitutes for an exact method. Nevertheless, one of his main purposes was to narrate his history in strict chronological order, so as to contain the virtue of a chronicle together with a more developed presentation of events. This is almost entirely forgotten, except that the sequence of occurrences is fairly kept up. Yet he does not hesitate to break through even this sequence, when he thinks the collocation of later facts, under the head that he is writing of, may contribute to clearness and completeness, as he directly avers in iii. 3, 14, iv. 10, 11, 12, v. 11, ix. 2. It is no easy task to make a Regesta of Sozomen's history; moreover, he often blunders in the very few dates he gives, as well as in the arrangement of the events themselves; these errors are due to the lack of a fixed system.

7. The contributions to geography are mainly confined to Palestine. Passing more familiar ones, we have a list as follows: Helenopolis (ii. 2), Majuma (ii. 5, v. 3, vii. 28), Anthedon, Bethagathon, Asalea, Thabatha (iii. 14), Diocæsarea (iv. 17), Bethelia (v. 15, vi. 32), Besan-

duca, Capharchobia, Gerara (vi. 32), Botolium (vii. 28), Ceila, Berathsabia with its tomb, Nephsameena (vii. 29), Chaphar Zacharia (ix. 17). Most of these terms are Hebraic or Syrian. Scythopolis is mentioned as abundant in palms (viii. 13). There is no direct, and very little indirect light on the political or ecclesiastical geography of the time; of course the seats of the bishops and of the monks that are enumerated yield a few new names of places. There are equally few hints in the physical features of the empire; the great rains, or hail-storms, or earthquakes are recorded chiefly with regard to their special ethical bearing. The topography of Constantinople has been indicated previously; outside of these, details of Alexandria, Antioch, Cæsarea, Cappadocia are given, but none of them new.

8. Statistics. There is of course no method in the presentation of statistics; there are general proportions, as in ii. 6, iv. 27, v. 15, vi. 20; and special detail, as in the enumeration of monks, iii. 14, vi. 29–34. The best illustration one finds in the account of the Persian martyrs, where there was a distinct effort at registration by Persian, Syrian, and Edessan authorities (ii. 13, 14).

9. Biography is one of the chief constituents of his history. He gives us an account of most of the distinguished Christian masters in theology, in monasticism, martyrdom, oratory, scholarship, administration; and he is refreshingly fair in giving a place to those who were not friendly to his view of the faith. Athanasius may be a chief hero, but Arius is not neglected. Here we may observe that Sozomen makes Aetius the second head of rationalism, and the man who gave it breadth of culture by building the system on the basis of Aristotle (iii. 15, iv. 12); he regards Eunomius as but a reflection of Aetius (vi. 29). This position accorded to Aetius is one deserving special note and study. Philostorgius exalted Eunomius both in his special encomium and in the history. Of course the two Cappadocians, as well as Epiphanius and Chrysostom, are liberally sketched. The imperial biography is fairly full, and a large space is accorded Julian. In every book parts are devoted to the *vitæ sanctorum*, as the best way to set before us the inner life of the Church and the fairest exhibition of Christian character; these monastic sketches are, for the most part, mere glimpses of individuals (a line or two suffices); whereas the more conspicuous founders and organizers, such as Antony, Hilarion, Pachomius, the Macarii, Evagrius, receive a larger recognition. He feels the need of selection in the multiplicity of illustrious characters, and after a sketch of Acacius, Zeno, and Ajax, he says: "I have mentioned these as examples of those who served as priests at this period. It would be a task to enumerate all, when the major part of them were good, and God bore testimony to their lives by readily hearing their prayers and by working many miracles" (vii. 28). Prominent as is the biographical element, and earnestly as he endeavors to substantiate its claims, he confesses, as to Ephraim (iii. 16), "it would require a more experienced hand than mine to furnish a full description of his character and that of the other illustrious men, who, about the same period, had devoted themselves to a life of philosophy; and it is to be regretted that Ephraim did not enter upon this undertaking. The attempt is beyond my powers, for I possess but little knowledge of those great men, or of their exploits."

10. In ecclesiastical culture we have many and important incidental hints, but no direct general chapter except vii. 19; and on special topics, those on the Easter controversy (i. 16, 21, vi. 24, vii. 18, viii. 17) on the penitential presbyter (vii. 16), and on relic worship, are the most significant.

11. Nor is there any methodical statement of growth in the acquisition and exposition of truth; his traditionalism in a measure precluded that, and his acknowledged incapacity to go deeply into the differentiation of these discussions prevented any system; there is no real history of dogma and ethics, except on the external side. He is frank to say: "I leave their doctrines to be judged by those whose right it is. For I have not set forth to record such matters, nor is it befitting in history" (iii. 15); that he does "not profess easily to understand or to expound these matters" (vi. 27); and again, "I should be prolix were I to enter into further particulars,

and under the subject would be by no means an easy one to me, since I have no such dialectic skill " (vii. 17). He furnishes us only with such a statement of doctrine, as sprang out of polemics and councils and the variety of creeds.

12. And so with the history of literature there is no such sustained account of Christian writers and works as in Eusebius ; the second stage of historians did not see fit to be as complete and accurate as their exemplar in this particular, and Photius was left to gather up the fragments for us. What strikes us as peculiar is his confessed ignorance of the works of the greatest theologians. He passes by all the technical writings of Athanasius ; he has no direct knowledge of the works of Hilary, though that might be excused. Of the purely theological works of Basil and Gregory Nazianzen, whom he regards as the pillars of the Nicene faith, he makes no mention ; and indeed makes but the slightest use of their letters and special orations. Of the Arian theologians of all shades, he has no closer knowledge ; he confesses at the outset that he had not read the Thalia (i. 21), but condemns it on Socrates' authority ; and he speaks of Diodorus, bishop of Tarsus, in language that displays unfamiliarity with his treatises (viii. 2).

13. There are no conceptions of the philosophy of history or of historics in general, other than those which have been discussed before.

14. If we pass to the stylistics of Sozomen, we find the quality of the Greek to be excellent ; the dedication is especially studied and rhetorical ; the first chapter of the first book is scarcely inferior in these traits, after which the form becomes more abrupt, after the fashion of an epitomizer, and it is obviously affected by his authorities. The likeness to Xenophon is not continuous, any more than Socrates sustainedly imitates Thucydides, although in elevated conception, Socrates is more in the vein of that philosophic master of history, than Sozomen is a reflection of the writer of the Hellenics. The vocabulary, too, is quite meager ; the same forms of expression occur again and again, yet Photius considers him superior in diction to Socrates,[1] which only one who admires mere form above spirit, can affirm. Certainly it would not be the view of this more subjective age. Of course he reflects the decline of meaning in particles and prepositional prefixes and participial constructions. He does not begin his books with formal prefaces, such as Socrates indulges in ; chapter 1 of Book i. may, however, be regarded as introductory ; and it serves to link Christianity with Judaism. In the distribution of his material there is no system agreeing with his own outline of aims or any other order that is discoverable. The main topics are : Secular affairs, relations of the emperor to Christianity, laws and privileges, missions and persecutions, polemics and irenics, biographies ; but there is no regular discussion of these, either under the reigns or in the books. None of the historians are any better in this regard.

A characteristic of our historian is the admirable generalization and the summaries he pauses to make here and there. The most notable are in iii. 17, a generalized description of the period of the Constantines. iii. 18, a doctrinal summary. iv. 17–19, conciliar movement in the West. iv. 20–22, conciliar movement in the East. iv. 23–25, united results, vi. 6, a succinct comparison of Valens with Valentinian. vi. 10, geographical centers of Nicenism. vi. 21, geographical centers of Arianism and Orthodoxy. vi. 22, geographical distribution of Macedonianism. vi. 26, genesis of Aetianism (Eunomianism). vi. 27, geographical distribution of beliefs. vi. 28–34, geographical grouping of the monks. vii. 2, geographical supremacy of Arianism in the East. vii. 4, geographical survey of religion. vii. 17, divisions of Arianism. viii. 1, summary of Apostolic succession. The selective process is often alluded to (ii. 3, iii. 14, 15, iv. 3, 23, 27, vii. 25, 28, ix. 1) ; and we must confess that he has kept a very just proportion in this way among the subjects he has elected for his narrative.

The Period described.

The work was to have covered the time from 323 to 439, a period of 116 years ; whereas, in fact, he writes continuously only to the death of Honorius as the latest event, 423, and the

---

[1] Myrobib. cod. XXX.

accession of Valentinian III. in 425 ; beyond that in time, but mentioned anticipatively in the narrative (ix. 2), is the transfer of the forty martyrs, which happened certainly after 434, the year of the election of Proclus, therefore probably not far from the proposed limit of his work, say 437 or 438 ; this would give a period of about 114 or 115 years.   He divides the record of this time into nine books, distributed among the emperors.

i. and ii. To Constantine, 323–337=14.

iii. and iv. His sons, 337–361=24.

v. and vi. Julian, Jovian, Valentinian I., Valens, 361–375=17.

vii. and viii. Gratian and Valentinian II., Theodosius I., Arcadius (and Honorius), 375–408=33.

ix. (Honorius) and Theodosius II., 408–437=25.

A noticeable feature, save in the case of Book ix., is the grouping of books by twos, in which the intervals discussed vary from fourteen to thirty-three years.   This grouping seems entirely arbitrary.

For whom he wrote.

The question for whom he wrote has been somewhat obscured by those who regard him simply as a plagiarist.   He evidently turned himself to this task under the conviction that there was need of some such work as his.   He addressed himself chiefly to Christians and not only to monks, because he defers to the narrow views of some friends about the mysteries, — and represses creeds and sacraments, for fear the book might fall into the hands of the uninitiated. He moreover designed his record, not for the more learned classes, but for the instruction of ordinary believers, since he professes uniformly a great modesty in treating the profounder themes of theology and the characters of the more eminent men.   Yet he did not hesitate to submit it to the criticism of his emperor and invited the most erasive and final judgment.   This is probably as far as we may go in the absence of any direct address to specific readers.

The Sources.

I. Those enumerated in his ideal plan (i. 1).

1. The transactions in which he was engaged.

2. The transactions in which others were engaged, who either knew or saw the events in his day, or in prior generations.

3. Laws established concerning religion.

4. Acts of Synods.

5. Record of innovations.

6. Imperial letters.

7. Clerical letters.

II. The sources actually mentioned.   (1) Documents.

(a) Documents actually quoted with text.

The retractation, by Eusebius and Theognis (ii. 16).

The confession of Arius and Euzoius to Constantine (ii. 27).

The Epistle of Constantine to the Synod of Tyre (ii. 28).

Constantine Cæsar to the people of the Catholic Church of the city of Alexandria (iii. 2).

Epistle of the Synod of Jerusalem in behalf of Athanasius (iii. 22).

Ursacius and Valens to Julius (iii. 23).

Ursacius aud Valens to Athanasius (iii. 24).

George of Laodicea to Macedonius, Basilius, Cecropius, and Eugenius (iv. 13); new.

Epistle of Constantius to the church at Antioch (iv. 14); new.

Epistle of the Synod of Ariminum to the Emperor Constantius (iv. 18).

Epistle of Julian to Arsacius, the high-priest of Galatia (v. 16).

Epistle of Julian to the bishops, only a phrase quoted (v. 18); new.

Synod at Antioch, to Jovian (vi. 4).

Eustathius, Silvanus, and Theophilus to Liberius (vi. 11).

Synod of Rome to bishops of Illyricum (vi. 23); first with Sozomen; repeated by Theodoret (*H. E.* ii. 22).

Innocent to John (viii. 26); also in Palladius' Dial.

Innocent to the presbyters, deacons, all the clergy, and the people of the church of Constantinople (viii. 26); also in Palladius' Dial.

There are five imperial letters, four synodical letters, seven episcopal letters, one presbyterial letter, making seventeen in all. This is not nearly so large a number as is given by Socrates, but we must remember the expressed purpose of Sozomen, that, as a rule, he would give abstracts only, and text when in his judgment fairness made it necessary. Of these documents, there are at least three found in no earlier author. In them all, there is only one symbol transcribed, and that is from Arius and Euzoius!

(*b*) Documentary acts of Synods which are mentioned by name.

Acts of the Synod of Tyre (ii. 25).

Acts of the Synod of Seleucia, taken down by tachygraphists (iv. 22).

(*c*) Acts of those Synods only, of which an abstract is recorded.

Alexandria	i. 15.	Seleucia	iv. 22, 23.
Bithynia	i. 15.	Constantinople	iv. 24, 25.
Palestine	i. 15.	Alexandria	v. 12.
Egyptian	i. 16.	Macedonian Council, s. l.	v. 14.
Nicæa	i. 17–23.	Antioch	vi. 4.
Antioch	ii. 19.	Lampsacus	vi. 7.
Tyre	ii. 25.	Nicæa	vi. 8.
Jerusalem	ii. 27.	Macedonian, s. l.	vi. 10, 11.
Constantinople	ii. 29, 33.	Sicily	vi. 12.
Constantinople	iii. 3.	Tyana	vi. 12.
Antioch	iii. 2.	In Caria	vi. 12.
Antioch	iii. 8.	Rome	vi. 23.
Philippopolis	iii. 11.	Pazucomen	vi. 24.
Sardica	iii. 11, 12.	Rome	vi. 25.
Jerusalem	iii. 21, 22.	Antioch (Caria)	vii. 2.
Alexandria	iv. 1.	Constantinople	vii. 7–9.
Sirmium	iv. 6.	Sangurum	vii. 18.
Antioch	iv. 8.	Constantinople	viii. 2.
Milan	iv. 9.	Cyprus	viii. 14.
Antioch	iv. 12.	Of the Oak at Chalcedon	viii. 17.
Ancyra	iv. 13.	Constantinople	viii. 19.
Ariminum	iv. 16–19, 23.	Constantinople	viii. 20.

(*d*) Letters of which an abstract is given, or the general object is stated.

Constantine's Letter to Alexander and Arius	i. 16.	Paul, bishop of Constantinople	iii. 11.
Imperial Letters about the Nicene Council	i. 21, 25.	The bishops of Philippopolis to the bishops of the West	iii. 11.
Constantine to Sapor	ii. 15.	Constans to Constantius	iii. 20.
Constantine to the people of Alexandria	ii. 22.	Constantius to Athanasius	iii. 20.
Constantine to Athanasius	ii. 23.	Constantius to the Alexandrians	iii. 20.
Synod of Tyre to the bishops	ii. 25.	Julius to clergy and people of Alexandria	iii. 20.
Antony's letters to the Emperor	ii. 31.	Constantius to the bishops, presbyters, and to the people of the church of Alexandria	iii. 21.
Constantine's letter to the Alexandrians	ii. 31.	Cyril of Jerusalem to Constantius	iv. 5.
Eusebius to Julius	iii. 7.	Constantius to Athanasius	iv. 9.
Julius, bishop of Rome, to the bishops of the East	iii. 8.	Constantius to Basil of Ancyra	iv. 16.
Synod of Antioch to Julius	iii. 8.	Basil of Ancyra to Constantius	iv. 16.
Constantius to Philip, prefect of Constantinople	iii. 9.	Constantius to Basil	iv. 16.
Bishops of Egypt in favor of Athanasius	iii. 10.	Basil to all the bishops	iv. 16.
Julius to the bishops of Antioch	iii. 10.	Athanasius to a friend	iv. 17.
Constans to Constantius	iii. 10.	Constantius to the Synod of Ariminum	iv. 19.
Constans to Constantius	iii. 11.	Reply of the bishops	iv. 19.
Athanasius to Constans	iii. 11.		

(2) Authors.

(a) Authors from whose works a textual quotation appears.

(b) Authors and works directly referred to as used.

(c) Authors and their works mentioned, but not used.

(d) Hymns of which a line or thought is given.

Unmentioned Authorities.

Sozomen has refrained in large measure from indicating directly his chief authorities for political or ecclesiastical affairs; he has indicated, indeed, some minor springs, as we have seen, but the major ones are passed by. He imitated neither Eusebius, nor Socrates, nor Evagrius in this omission. He does abound in phrases indicative of authorities; thus of the forms of λέγω, λέγουσι, λέγονται, ἔλεγον, ἐλέγετο are used somewhat sparingly, while λέγεται occurs over eighty times, and λόγος about twenty; of φημί, ἔφησεν and φήμη occasionally, while φησί or φασί introduces about thirty statements; εἰρήσθω and εἴρηται also appear in a few cases. One has no assurance of either the method or the validity of the sources from such vague terms, and it is this uncertain and incautious manner that has so often led critics to impeach his general worth, and it must be conceded with some degree of justice; the endless iteration of such words savors of gossip rather than history; this obscurity is not diminished by his persistent οἶμαι and less frequent εἰκάζω.

1. In the discussion of his unmentioned authorities, the first to be considered is Socrates. He is nowhere hinted at, unless under an indefinite " some say," when Sozomen presents a group of opinions.

Socrates preceded Sozomen by a few years, writing his history not long after 439.[1] Sozomen undoubtedly produced his record later, as we have already seen, and it would be just as likely that Socrates should be in the hands of Sozomen as that Philip of Side's contemporary Christian History should have been open to the criticism of Socrates; indeed, the predecessor's work was quite probably an incentive to the task proposed by Sozomen to himself. The internal evidence makes the use sure. We have only to note how Socrates derived his statements about the Novatians from members connected with that body of believers; these very facts are reproduced by Sozomen as Socrates gives them, with the slightest of differences; there is no refutation of this possible. Socrates, therefore, manifestly preceded, and Sozomen employed the material thus amassed.

There are three views of the connection: (1) that Sozomen, excepting a few and not very valuable additions of his own, plagiarized Socrates; (2) that he used the same authorities as Socrates independently, and the points of identity arose from the language of the original in the hands of both; (3) that Socrates was his guide to the chief writers from whom he drew directly with more or less freedom; and when no other light presented itself or was to be found, he would use his path-finder. There is scarcely a more fascinating and genuine field for analytical criticism than this. It should be remarked at the outset that we cannot justly apply this term plagiarism, in its modern sense, to the use of material current in these earlier days of history. There was no more intention to appropriate the work of another in Sozomen, than there was in Socrates, when he fails to note his authority, and yet very evidently has followed him closely; or when Theodoret has taken his stuff from Sozomen, and says nothing about the original. To assail Sozomen as if he were a deliberate thief, and stigmatize him as a feeble reviser of Socrates, is wholly unfair and unwarranted by the general usage of his day and by the facts of the case. In no way can it be proved that Sozomen was a general plagiarist in the opprobrium and iniquity conveyed by the modern use of that term. That Socrates was the finer mind, that he had larger sympathies, that he was concerned to reproduce documents in an ampler degree, that he follows the development of the Church with a sharper and brighter criticism, no one can doubt; he is conspicuously superior in almost every quality of a historian, and confined himself more nearly to the modern idea of which the science should aim to do; but that does not set aside the distinct and supplemental value of Sozomen and his fullness in lines, however zigzag, which had been neglected by others. The acknowledged precedence of Socrates does not warrant us in assailing the fidelity of the lesser light. Since the notes are designed to indicate the relationship between

---

[1] *H. E.* vii. 48.

the two, the passages need not be anticipated here. (2) The second view, that Sozomen made an independent use of the same source which Holzhausen revived, Stäudlin supported, Hefele and Nolte have espoused, seems less tenable than the first. The Novatian material cannot, under any possible conditions, be so explained; the arrangement of the details in eight of the books will not permit any such view. The very corrections of that arrangement require us to be convinced that Socrates was in the corrector's eye; the close resemblance of language in many places where he might easily have expanded from the originals, but preferred to confine himself to the equally meagre tracings of his predecessor, leave no basis for this solution. (3) The third explanation of the interrelation seems thus far the most accurate.[1] Sozomen took Socrates for a guide in the main, (a) as to consecution of events, (b) as to sources, much as students would use a Church history to base their own studies upon. Socrates was a director to the authorities; these Sozomen would use freely; when they failed him, he would take the facts given by Socrates, precisely as he did those which Eusebius or Sabinus furnished, because he had nothing better, and in spite probably of his own inquiries; for let us remember how he insists that he has investigated the originals, and that he had been conscientious in his researches. Now it must be said in further modification of this statement:

(a) That some of the sources obviously consulted by both were doubtless known to Sozomen without Socrates to point them out. Rufinus and Eusebius and Sabinus were known to everybody. In all such cases we may concede an independent reading of those authors, and yet the order in which the subject-matter is arranged is at times more that of his guide-book than of his original.

(b) Moreover, he introduces many new outlines and abstracts, particularly in the transactions of the synods.

(c) He also has independent sources of biography.

(d) His ninth book is wholly unique and entirely out of the leading-strings of the master, for unexplained reasons.

The notes also try to indicate in a measure these more independent traits.

2. The next unmentioned source is Rufinus, in his continuation of Eusebius in two books; this Sozomen certainly read independently of Socrates, very likely in a Greek translation. That author's *Historia Monachorum* also was sifted for a few of the monastic biographies; in these cases there is a closer resemblance to Rufinus than to the parallel sketches of Palladius.

3. Eusebius' Life of Constantine is a primary source for Books i. and ii. In all the events pertaining to that emperor, it is drawn upon freely, just as freely as Socrates employs it, or as Sozomen handles Socrates.

4. Athanasius is also used independently, although in collocating the events, Socrates is followed. There is direct reference to one work only (v. 12), as we have seen. The unmentioned are as follows: —

The Life of St. Antony: *Antonii Vita.*
Epistola de Synodis Arimini in Italia et Seleuciæ in Isauria celebratis.
Epistola ad Serapionem, de morte Arii.
Synodicon; lost.
Tomus ad Antiochenses.
Epistola ad Episcopos Ægypti et Libyæ; ep. encyclica contra Arianos.
Epistola Encyclica ad Episcopos.
Historia Arianorum ad Monachos.
Apologia contra Arianos.
Apologia ad Constantium imperatorem.
Epistolæ heortasticæ.

5. Philostorgius: *Historia Ecclesiastica,* also furnished occasional material, as even the excerpts remaining to us indicate.

---

[1] Jeep: *Quellenuntersuchungen zu den griechischen Kirchenhistorikern,* pp. 137–147.

6. Sabinus: Collection of Synods (Συναγώγη τῶν συνόδων), which is lost; this book was written in the Macedonian and Arian interest; the author is mentioned by Socrates and criticised for his partiality. We can observe how Sozomen used it, where he adds to the statements of Socrates, which the latter had borrowed from that work. These additions are quite frequent in the transactions of the synods; and again a few records of councils, otherwise unknown, are thus preserved for us. We have here a proof of how Sozomen improved on his guide in the details.

7. Philippus of Side; the Christian History (χριστιανικὴ ἱστορία); a few fragments are preserved; Socrates criticises him severely.[1]

8. For the laws, outside of the records alluded to, he probably used the *Codex Gregorianus* and the *Codex Hermogenianus*, his old text-books, and not unlikely the *Codex Theodosianus* (438).

9. Basil the Great: the limited use is indicated by the notes.

10. Gregory Nazianzen: *Orationes contra Julianum*. Other occasional citations are indicated in the notes.

11. Sulpicius Severus: *vita S. Martini* was undoubtedly the source, possibly through a Greek translation of the same, for the summary of that saint's life in iii. 14.
Historia sacra: sometimes there is a hint as if this work had been before him.

12. Palladius: *Historia Lausica* was not so constant a companion as some have suggested; Sozomen has rather borrowed from the sources out of which the bishop of Helenopolis gathered his sketches of the monks.
Dialogus de vita S. Joannis Chrysostomi was used in narrating the incidents of John's life in Book viii. There is no indication of any large draught of Chrysostom's own writings: they may have been used for a few suggestions, contained in the orations before mentioned.

One does not feel sure that Hieronymus or Orosius came under his eye.

He does not seem to have made any direct use of Ammianus Marcellinus (*Res gestæ*), nor of the earlier Latin chroniclers. The points of resemblance with Eutropius (*Breviarium Historiæ Romanæ*) are very doubtful in my judgment; Eunapius (*ex historia excerpta et fragmenta*) seems to have been used in his full form; Zosimus (*Historia*), pretty surely; and for the ninth book, hardly with a doubt the full Olympiodorus, of whom fragments only remain, and yet in that same ninth book there are entirely independent political chapters whose source cannot yet be determined.

The Ninth Book.

The most curious feature of all is Book ix., in the entire change of its method; even were the ecclesiastical affairs to have been presented, he has given here in remarkable excess the events affecting the Western state; he has done it nowhere else; to be sure, he proposes it as a demonstration of the value of imperial piety, and of the ever-present Divine grace, but nowhere else has he done this in so cumulative a form. Some wonderful change came over his purpose, whether that were a fuller view of the relation between state and church, or the desire to deepen the impression of his philosophy of history; or did some imperial domestic catastrophe make him reluctant to dwell upon the sad events which darkened the court he had so glorified?

The grave question arises, Is anything of Book ix. lost?

That it is unfinished cannot be doubted; for (a) In the Proëmium he announces his purpose to carry it to the year A.D. 439, or the seventeenth consulate of Theodosius; but this is not done with any of his ordinary fullness, although his hints reach beyond, as we have seen. (b) In lauding Pulcheria (ix. 1) he remarks, "That new heresies have not prevailed in our time, we shall find to be due especially to her, as we shall subsequently see." Here is the declared purpose of delineating the history of Nestorianism and its overthrow, but there is no appearance of the struggle in the record itself; he altogether passes by Nestorius, as bishop of Constantinople. (c) The

---

[1] *H. E.* vii. 27.

record of the forty martyrs he purposely took out of its normal order, to illustrate the excellence of Pulcheria ; a late event is anticipated, but the whole of what would have been its normal setting is not there. (d) One would naturally expect that a book which had thus far treated mainly of state difficulties would have the usual balance, at least, and that ecclesiastical affairs would have preponderated in the remaining chapters ; but there is only an initial chapter. Seventeen chapters are not his usual tale for a book ; there is an evident break ; the discussion of Nestorianism is not written. Most of all would one expect some allusion to the restoration of Chrysostom under Proclus. (e) In ix. 16, he says, "Among other relics, those of Zechariah, the very ancient prophet, and of Stephen, who was ordained deacon by the Apostles, were discovered ; and it seems incumbent upon me to describe the mode, since the discovery of each was marvelous and divine ; " but he gives only the invention of Zechariah (c. 17). The story of Stephen fails us, and would doubtless have followed immediately. It was his purpose to narrate the story, — this story which Theophanes and Marcellinus mention and Lucianus wrote a book about. (f) In c. ix. 17, this is confirmed ; for he says, "I shall first speak of the relics of the prophet " ; to his second he does not come. (g) The close is abrupt ; one feels instinctively that something is amiss. Hence the work, as we have it, is obviously not complete.

Did he finish it, and is the conclusion lost ?

The mistake into which Gregory I. fell in ascribing to Sozomen the commendation of Theodore of Mopsuestia, with which Theodoret really closes his history, led Baronius to maintain that we did not have the whole of Sozomen ; and others have asserted the same for reasons which are indeed sufficient to prove that the history is unfinished, but not that anything is lost. That we have all that Sozomen wrote is more likely, because the Tripartite History at x. 24 makes the last use of Sozomen at viii. 25 ; it would surely have gone further in its dependence upon him had the later controversy been treated of, since he had been already a chief authority. Nicephorus Callistus, *Historia Ecclesiastica*, xiv. 8, gives the account of the finding of Zechariah in c. 9 ; the story of Stephen in c. 10 ; then the story of the forty martyrs. His source beyond is Socrates, until Evagrius takes up the thread of affairs. If Sozomen had written the more recent events parallel with Socrates, Nicephorus would undoubtedly have followed him as before. Of Theophanes, one cannot speak so confidently. Moreover, we cannot help asking, since we have Socrates, Theodoret, and Evagrius complete, why should Sozomen, who was so admired an author, have suffered any loss? Now, if we have Sozomen entire so far as he wrote, why did he stop where he did? There are no sufficient subjective reasons to be offered. It could scarcely have been in any unfavorable criticism of his prince, for the work seems to have been accepted by his imperial patron ; and there was certainly nothing as objectionable in Sozomen, as in Socrates or in Olympiodorus. Nor is it likely that the unhappiness which invaded the court, the domestic jealousies, which rent its religious as well as connubial peace, or the quarrels over Cyrus or Paulinus or Chrysaphius, in any way restrained him ; for he was beyond some, if not all of these agitations, at the time of his writing, and he had deliberately chosen to ignore such noble personages as Anthemius, Troïlus, Synesius, Aurelianus, and Eudocia, so that we can argue little from his silence, save his manifest jealousy for Pulcheria, and his hostility to certain more liberal tendencies developed under Eudocia. The Nestorian controversy would have been a choice field wherein to exalt the influence of Pulcheria, as he himself suggested. On the whole, one is constrained to believe that Sozomen died before he had completed the record which he had proposed to himself. He must have been nearing his seventieth year when thus suddenly arrested in his chosen study.

The Major Uses made of his Work.

The major uses of him subsequently were by (*a*) Epiphanius Scholasticus, who made a translation into Latin, which Cassiodorus abbreviated, polished, and incorporated in the *Historia Tripartita*.[1]

---

[1] See preface of that work.

(*b*) The deacon Liberatus, in his *Historia Nestorianorum*, used the *Tripartita*.

(*c*) Theophanes, in his *Chronographia*.

(*d*) Theodorus Lector in his *Historia Tripartita*.

(*e*) Nicephorus Callistus, in his *Historia Ecclesiastica* incorporating Theodorus' *Tripartita*.

The Errors.

The errors are numerous, as already suggested by Possevin, on dogmatic grounds; Du Pin, and more recently by Harnack, for historic reasons. They are due to the lack of a systematic chronology, and the blind copying of his authority, especially Socrates, and occasionally to his attempts to correct the order given by his authority.

PART III. — BIBLIOGRAPHY.

A. *Bibliography of Bibliography*.

GESNER: Bibliotheca universalis. s.v. 1545.

POSSEVIN: Apparatus sacer. s.v. 1608.

DU PIN: Nouvelle bibl. d. Auteurs Eccles. Tom. iii. Pt. ii. 189–90. 1690.

SLUTER: Propylæum Historiæ Christianæ, ix. 6, p. 45. 1696.

ITTIG: De bibliothecis patrum apostol. s.v. 1699–1700.

OLEARIUS: Bibliotheca scriptorum eccles. Tom. ii. s.v. 1711.

FABRICIUS: Bibliotheca Græc. Vol. vi. Lib. v. c. 4. xxxi. 1726.

CAVE: Scriptorum Eccles. Hist. Literaria. p. 427. 1740.

WALCH: Bibl. Theol. Tom. iii. p. 114. 1762.

DE BURE: Bibliographie instructive. Nos. 4393–5. 1768.

NODIER: Bibliothéque sacrée gr.-lat. s.v. 1826.

BOOSE: Grundriss der Christl. Liter., § 230. 1828.

CLARKE: Concise view of the succession of Sac. Lit. Vol. ii. p. 225. 1831.

HOFFMANN, S. F. W.: Lexicon Bibliog. s.v. 1833–38.

WALCH, J. G.: Biblioth. Patristica, ii. § 16. 2. ed. Danz. 1834.

VOSSIUS (ed. Westermann): De Historicis Græcis, ii. 20. 1838.

CEILLIER: Hist. Gen. des Auteurs Sacrés. Tom. viii. c. 39. 1858 sqq.

ALZOG: Handb. d. Patrologie. 3d ed. 1876.

NICOLAI: Griech. Literaturgesch. in neuer Bearbeitung. 1874–8.

CHEVALIER: Répertoire des sources hist. d. M. A. s.v. 1877 sqq.

NIRSCHL: Lehrbuch der Patrologie u. Patristik. Vol. iii. c. 4, 235. 1881 sqq.

HARNACK: Herzog R. E., Vol. xiv. s.v. 1884.

——: Encycl. Br., Vol. xxii. s.v. 1887.

THUILLE: Patristisches Handbuch. 1888.

B. *Texts*.

I. *Manuscripts.* — It would indeed be a desirable work to have a uniform apparatus of the codices, not only of Sozomen, but of all the Greek Church historians. Admirable as is Heinchen's survey of Eusebian MSS., it is neither uniform nor complete. No editor of Sozomen from Stephen down, has deemed it necessary to work up the detail even as well as Heinchen. Nolte evidently had the material in hand, but the labor remains to be done. The numbers and positions of many codices have been changed since the days of Valesius, Montfaucon, and Hænelius, and it is impossible to bring harmony out of the differences without direct inspection. It would seem as if no one had consulted some of those mentioned by Montfaucon; e.g. in the Inventarium MSS. monasterii S. Petri Carnutensis, the title is given without number; Socratis, Sozomenis et Theodoreti historia Ecclesiastica, vol. in fol. notat P. sæculo ix. (ii. 1246); and the two described by Hænelius (*a*) Socratis, Sozomenis historia ecclesiastica memb. fol. éxemp. vetus, at Chartres (Fasc. i. col. 130). (*b*) iv. 2, Hermiæ Sozomeni Salaminis, historicæ ecclesiasticæ lib. ix. (Fasc. iii. c. 93) in the Escorial.

II. *Editions of Text.* — 1. The first printed text without translation was by Robert Stephen: Eusebii Pamphili, Ecclesiasticæ historiæ, libri x.; ejusdem de vita Constantini, libri v.; Socratis, libri vii.; Theodoreti episc. Cyrenensis, libri v.; Collectaneorum ex historia ecclesiastica Theodori lectoris, libri ii.; Hermiae Sozomeni, libri ix.; Evagrii, libri vi.; Græce Excud. Rob. Steph. Lutetiæ Parisior. (pridie Cal. Jul.) 1544. Fol.

The sole manuscript at the basis of this edition is the Codex Regius bibliothecæ Parisiensis, n. 1437 (Nolte, 1444) Possevin (App. crit.) says: A Græca vero editio proviget ann. 1545, but this seems a mistake.

2. The next edition of the text was accompanied with a Latin translation; Græce et Latine ex interpretatione J. Christophorsoni et recognitione Suffredi Petri una cum variis lectionibus, J. Christophorsoni, Jos. Scaligeri, Jac. Cuiaci, Jan. Gruteri, Jac. Bongarsii, Col. All. (Geneva) 1612. 2 vols. in fol. This was the text of Stephen with marginal notes of the above [see Hussey, Nolte]. The sources of the notes are not sure.

3. Reprint of Geneva edition: Bibliotheca magna veterum patrum et antiq. Scriptorum eccles. primo a Margarino de la Bigne collecta. Tom. v. has Soc. and Soz. with the Latin of Christophorson and Suff. Petrus. Colon. 1618–22.

4. The edition of Valesius, 1659–1668, with a new translation by himself. Socratis Scholastici et Hermiæ Sozomeni historia ecclesiastica. Henricus Valesius græcum textum collatis MSS. Codicibus emendavit, Latine vertit, et annotationibus illustravit. Adjecta est ad calcem disputatio Archelai Episcopi adversus Manichæum. Parisiis, 1668. Fol. In this edition there are the preface to the reader, explaining his sources; an essay on the life and writings of the historians; and the text is followed by annotations. This edition is conspicuous for the number of codices, more or less accurately collated. The Codex Fuketanus is his chief reliance; the previous annotations were used; he claims to have made no alteration without warrant.

5. Bibliotheca Maxima Veterum Patrum M. de la Bigne, Lugd. 1677. In vol. vii. of this series; this reproduces the Genevan edition.

6. A reprint of Valesius. Eusebii Pamph. Ep. Cæsar. et Theodoreti, Evagrii, Socratis et Sozomeni Historia Ecclesiastica. Gr. Lat. cum notis Valesii. 3 Tomi. Paris, 1678. Fol.

7. A reprint of Valesius. Socratis et Sozomeni historia ecclesiastica. Gr. et Lat. Paris, 1686. Fol.

8. A reprint of Valesius. Historiæ Ecclesiasticæ Eus. Pamph., Soc., Soz., Theodore ti, et Evag. cum excerptis ex historia Philost. et Theod. Lec. Græc. et Lat. c. Annot. H. Valesii. 3 Tomi. Moguntiæ, 1677–79. Fol.

9. Another reprint of Valesius, but from the Mayence edition: Historiæ Ecclesiasticæ Eus., Soc., etc. Græc.-Lat. 3 Tomi. Amst. 1695. Fol.

10. Historiæ ecclesiasticæ Scriptores Græci cum excerptis ex historia Philostorgi et Theodori Lect. Gr. et Lat. c. interpret. H. Valesii. Amst. 1699. Fol. (Georgi.)

11. A separate edition of Socrates and Sozomen, with the usual Valesian apparatus, and the debate of Bishop Archelaus against the Manichæans: Socratis Scholastici et Hermiæ Sozomeni historia ecclesiastica græce et latine. Henricus Valesius Græcum textum collatis MSS. codicibus emendavit, Latine vertit, et Annotationibus illustravit. Adjecta est ad calcem disputatio Archelai Episcopi adversus Manichæum. Ad novissimam editionem Parisiensem castigatissime recusa prostat Amstelodami apud Henricum Wetstenium. 1700.

12. Valesian text as basis and apparatus, with new emendations. General title:
Eusebii Pamphili, Socratis Scholastici, Hermiæ Sozomeni, Theodoreti et Evagrii, Item Philostorgii et Theodori Lectoris quæ extant historiæ ecclesiasticæ græce et latine, in tres tomos distributæ. Henricus Valesius græcum textum ex MSS. codicibus emendavit, latine vertit et Annotationibus illustravit.
Gulielmus Reading novas Elucidationes, præsertim Chronologicas, in hac Editione adjecit. Cantabrigiæ, 1720.
Special title: Socratis Scholastici et Hermiæ Sozomeni historia ecclesiastica græce et latine. Henricus Valesius græcum textum collatis MSS. codicibus emendavit, latine vertit et Adnotationibus illustravit. Adjecta est ad calcem disputatio Archelai Episcopi adversus Manichæum. Hanc Editionem Criticis plurium Eruditorum Observationibus locupletavit Gulielmus Reading. Cantabrigiæ, 1720.
He restores readings of Stephen for some changes made by Valesius; uses Valesius' own manuscript annotations, suggestions of Lowth, Casaubon's variæ lectiones from the codex Jonesianus, and the codex Jonesianus itself. But there is no general collation.

13. Reprint of the Reading edition. 3 vols. Augustæ Taurinorum (Tur:n).

14. Valesian text as basis; partially new apparatus and emendations.
Sozomeni ecclesiastica historia edidit Robertus Hussey, S. T. B. Oxonii: e typographeo academico, 1860. Three volumes, two of text, and the third of annotations. The Latin version is by Valesius.
Hussey died before completing his work; the apparatus was prepared by John Barrow. Besides other not far-reaching collations, Hussey used a codex in the Bodleian, called the codex Barrocianus (B.), and a partial collation of codex Severniensis, which is of inferior value.

15. Reproduction of Reading-Valesius:
Patrologiæ Cursus Completus.
Socratis Scholastici, Hermiæ Sozomeni Historia Ecclesiastica. Henricus Valesius græcum textum collatis MSS. codicibus emendavit, latine vertit notis illustravit; cujus editionem criticis observationibus locupletavit Gul. Reading. Accurante et denuo recognoscente. J. P. Migne. Paris. 1864.

16. The English catalogue announced in August, 1874: Sozomeni Historia Ecclesiastica, edited by Robert Hussey, vol. i., 8°, Macmillan; but it did not appear.

C. *Textual Criticism.*

We have here (1) the apparatus mentioned in the greater editions; (2) the marginal notes and papers of various readings by Bishop Christophorson, Scaliger, Casaubon, Curicius, Gurterius, etc. (3) The solitary work of Dr. Nolte, who, in 1860, wrote a recension of Hussey's edition of Sozomen. Theolog. Q. Schrift. 1861. iii. 417–451; as he had done for Socrates, and did later for Evagrius. He dwells especially on the valuable readings which could be derived from the translation of Epiphanius Scholasticus and from Nicephorus Callistus.

This shows the urgency of collation de novo, and a new edition of the text.

D. *Analytical Criticism.*

Besides the meagre apparatus of the editions, the following works assist in the study, although some are not directly related.

Holzhausen, F. A. Commentatio de fontibus quibus Socrates, Sozomenus ac Theodoretus in scribenda historia sacra usi sunt, adiuncta eorum epicrisi, scripta a Friderico Augusto Holzhausen. Gottingæ, 1825.

Rosenstein, J., in Forschung z. deutsch. Gesch. 1862, i., 166.

Matin: de fontibus Zosimi. Dissert. Berlin, 1865.

Sudhans: de Ratione quæ intercedat inter Zosim. et Amm. cet. relationes. Dissert. Bonn, 1870.

Holden-Egger, Untersuchungen über einige annalist. Quellen z. Gesch. des v. u. vi. Jahrh. Neu. Archiv. d. Gesch. f. alt. deutsch. Gesch. 1876, i. 1.

Güldenpenning, A., Die Quellen zur Geschichte des Kaisers Theod. d. Gr. Dissert. Halle, 1878.

Güldenpenning, A., and Ifland, J.: Der Kaiser Theodosius der Grosse. Halle, 1878. Cf. Harnack in T. L. Z. 1879, 18.

Jeep, Ludwig. Quæstiones Fridericianæ, Dissert. 1881.

Sarrazin, J. V. De Theodoro Lectore Theophanis fonte præcipuo. Dissertatio inauguralis. Lips. 1881.

Jeep. L.: Quellenuntersuchungen zu den Griechischen Kirchenhistorikern. Bes. Abdruck aus dem vierzehnten Supplementbande der Jahrbücher für classische Philologie. Leipzig, 1884.

Güldenpenning, A.: Die Kirchengeschichte des Theodoret von Kyrrhos, eine Untersuchung ihrer Quellen. Halle, 1889.

The above show the sources and their interrelation.

E. *Translations.*

I. *Latin.*— 1. Epiphanius Scholasticus. At the suggestion of Cassiodorus he translated Theodoret, Socrates, and Sozomen. This version, Cassiodorus polished and selected from, for his Historia Ecclesiastica Tripartita. (See Preface to that work.) This was frequently printed. The first edition, Paris, s. a.; Basle, 1523, and after.

2. Eusebii. Pamph. Historia Ecclesiastica c. Sozomeno et Socrate. Basle, 1544. Fol.

This was in the Stephen text. Possevin has severe criticism for Musculus (App. crit.).

3. The same: cum Eus., Soz., Theod. Lect., Evag., et Dorothei Tyri vitis Prophetarum et Apostolorum ex ejusdem Musculi interpretatione et Theodoreti H. E. ex versione Joach. Camerarii. Basle, 1549. Fol.

4. The same in Basle, 1557. Fol.

5. Ecclesiasticæ Scriptores Græci c. Interpretatione lat. Jo. Christophorsoni, recogniti a Suffrido Petro. Col. Agr. 1562. Fol.

Six books of Soz. were by J. C.; the remaining three by S. P.

6. A reprint of (5). Louv. 1569. 8vo.

7. The same with all the translators. Jo. Jacobi Grynæi recognitione atque cum ejus notis. Basle, 1570. Fol.

8. The reprint of (5), according to Possevin: apud hæredis Arnoldi Birckmanni. Basle, 1570. Fol.

9. The reprint of (5), at Paris, 1571. Fol.

10. A reprint of (7). Basle, 1572. Fol.

11. The reprint of (5), Veteres Scriptores Historiæ Ecclesiasticæ Græci. Col. Agr. 1581. Fol.

12. A reprint of (7). Basle, 1587. Fol.

13. Reprint of (3). Basle, 1594. Fol.

14. A new version from new collations and improvements by Grynæus:

Eusebii Pamphili, Ruffini, Socratis, Theodoriti, Sozomeni, Theodori, Evagrii, et Dorothei Ecclesiastica Historia, sex prope secvlorvm res gestas complectens: Latine iam olim a doctissimis viris partim scripta, partim e Græco a clarissimis viris, Vuolfgango Musculo, Joachimo Camerario, et Johanne Christophersono Britanno, eleganter conversa: et nunc ex fide Græcorum codicum sit ut novum opus videri possit, per Joan. Jacobum Grynæum locis obscuris innumeris illustrata, dubijs explicata, mutilis restituta: Chronographia insuper Abrahami Bucholceri, ad

Annum Epochæ Christianæ 1598, et lectionis sacræ historiæ luculenta Methodo exornata.   Cum continuatione in præsentem annum 1611.   Et Indicibus rerum verborumq': lucupletiis.   Basileæ, 1611.   Fol.

The sources for the new readings are not given.

15. Ecclesiasticæ Historiæ Scriptores.   Latine tantum.   Basle, 1612.   Fol   (Georgi.)

16. A reprint of (11).   Coll. All. 1612.   Fol.

17. Ecclesiasticæ historiæ Eusebii.   Soc., Soz., Theodoret, Evag., Latine tantum ex Valesii versione.   Paris, 1677.   Fol.

II. *German.*— 1. Eusebii Pamphili, Sozomeni, Socratis und Theodorets Kirchen Historie durch Hestionem (Caspar Hedio).   Strassb. 1545.   Fol.

This was on the basis of the H. E. Tripartita.

2. A reprint of (1).   Basle, 1607.   Fol.

III. *French.*— 1. General title: Histoire de l'Église.   1675.

Special title for Vol. iii.: Histoire de l'église, écrite par Sozomène.   Traduite par Monsieur Cousin, President en la cour des Monnoyes.   Tome iii.   á Paris, 1676.   4°.

2. Reprint of (1).   Amst. 1686.   6 vols. in 12°.

3. There was a French version of the Tripartite by Ludovicus Cyaneus.   Paris, 1568.   Fol.

4. Possevin (App. Crit. s. Soc.) ascribes a translation of Socrates (including Soz.?) into French in his day to Jacobus Billius Prunæus.

IV. *English.*— 1. An Abridgement of the Ecclesiastical History of Eusebius, Socrates, Sozomen, and Theodoret, translated into English by Samuel Parker.   2 vols.   London, 1707.   8°.

2. A reprint of (1).   London, 1709.   Fol.(?)

3. A third edition: The Ecclesiastical Histories of Eusebius, Socrates, Sozomen, and Theodorit Faithfully Translated and Abridg'd from the Originals.   Together with A brief Account of the Lives of these Historians, and several Useful Notes and Illustrations, and a copious Index.   By Mr. Parker.

The Third edition, carefully Review'd by the Author, and very much Corrected, Improv'd and Enlarg'd.   To which is now added, by a Friend, an Abridgment of the History of Evagrius Scholasticus.   The Whole chiefly design'd for the Use of Young Students in Divinity, and Families Religiously disposed.   London, 1729.   4°.

4. A History of the Church in nine books from A.D. 324 to A.D. 440: a new translation from the Greek, with a memoir of the author.   London, 1846.   8°.

This is in the Bagster series of the Greek Ecclesiastical Historians of the first six centuries.   1843–46.

5. A reprint of (4), Bohn's Ecclesiastical Library.

History of the Church by Sozomen and Philostorgius.   The Ecclesiastical History of Sozomen, comprising a History of the Church, from A.D. 324 to A.D. 440.   Translated from the Greek, with a memoir of the author.

Also the Ecclesiastical History of Philostorgius, as epitomized by Photius, Patriarch of Constantinople.   Translated by Edward Walford, Late Scholar of Balliol College, Oxford.   London, 1855.   8°.

6. A reprint of (4).   London, 1868.   8°.

F. *Historiography.*

The usual Introductions to Church Histories: on the History of Church History; particularly Schröckh, i. 148–9, vii. 188–90.

STAÜDLIN C. F. (Hemsen).   Geschichte und Literatur der Kirchengeschichte.   Hannover, 1827.

BAUR, J. Ch.: Die Epochen der kirchlichen Geschichtschreibung.   Tüb. 1832.

DOWLING, J. G.: An introduction to the critical study of Ecclesiastical History.   London, 1838.

TEN HAAR, B.: de Historiographie der Kerkgeschiedenis.   Utrecht, 1870.

NIRSCHL, JOS.: Propädeutik d. Kirchengeschichte.   Mainz, 1888.

CEILLIER and HARNACK as before.

This is also a field that needs scholars.

G. *Literature.*

[This does not pretend to be exhaustive.]

1. BIOGRAPHICAL.

PHOTIUS: Myrobiblion: codex 30, a few lines of biography and authorship.

SIGEBERT OF GEMBLOUX: de scriptoribus ecclesiasticis (ed. Fabricius), c. 11.

TRITHEMIUS: de Ecclesiasticis scriptoribus (ed. Fabricius), cxxxvi.

HOFFMANN, Jo. JAC.: Lexicon Universale historiam sacram et profanam, etc.   Tom. iv. s.v.

MORERI: le Grand Dictionnaire Historique.   Tom. vi. s.v.

ZEDLER: Universal Lexicon.   Tom. xxxviii. s.v.

WETZER U. WELTE: Lexicon. Art. Kirchengeschichte. vi.[2]
SMITH: Dict. G. R. Biog. and Myth. (Art. by J. C. Means). Vol. iii.
MICHAUD: Biographie Universelle. Tom. xxxix. s.v.
DIDOT FRÈRES: Nouvelle Biographie Géneral. Tom. xliv. s.v.
GLAIRE, J-B.: Dict. univ. des Sciences Ecclesiastiques, s.v.
LICHTENBERGER: Encyclopédie des Sciences Religieuses. Tom. xi. s.v.
SMITH: Art. Vol. iv. Dict. Christ. Biog. Art. by William Milligan.

2. HISTORICAL.

(*a*) THEODORUS LECTOR was the first to have used Sozomen for a Tripartite history, and doubtless alluded to him (cf. Nic. Call. H. E. i. 1).
EVAGRIUS SCHOLASTICUS: H. E. i. Preface.
EPIPHANIUS SCHOLASTICUS and CASSIODORUS in the preface to H. E. Tripartita.
GREGORY the Great mentions him by mistake for Theodoret, in Book vii. of his letters; Ep. 34.
NICEPHORUS CALLISTUS: H. E. i. 1.
BARONIUS: An. Eccl. Vols. iii.–v., ed. 1707.
BELLARMIN-LABBE: Dissertationes philologicæ de Scriptoribus ecclesiasticis. Vol. ii. 371, 372.
PAGI: Critica hist. Chronol. in An. Eccles. Baronii Sæc. iv. 76–292.
TILLEMONT: Histoire des Emper. Rom. vi. 123–7; 613–4.
DU CANGE: Historia Byzantina. Paris, 1680.
GIBBON: Decline and Fall. Vols. ii. iii. Boston, 1862.
HERTZBERG, W.: D. Gesch. Griechenlands unter d. Herrschaft d. Römer. 3 Bde. Halle, 1866–75.
SIEVERS, G. R.: Studien z. Gesch. d. röm. Kaiser. Berlin, 1870.
FINLAY: History of Greece. Vol. i. Oxford, 1877.

(*b*) HOLDER, ALF.: Inventio sanctæ crucis: Actorum Cyriacus, pars i. lat. et gr. &c. Leipzig, 1889.
NESTLE, EBERH.: De Sancta Cruce, ein Beitrag z. christl. Legendengeschichte. Berlin, 1889.
DRÄSEKE, J.: zu Apollinarius v. Laodicea. I. zu den dogmat. Bruchst. des A. II. zur Psalmen-Metaphrase des A. Zwth. xxxi. 469–487. Die Abfassungszeit der Psalm.-Metaphr. des Apoll. ZwTh. xxxii. 108–120.
—— Vitalios von Antiochia u. sein Glaubensbekenntniss. ZWL, 186–201, 1888.
IHM, M.: Studia Ambrosiana. Jahrbücher f. class. Philologie, 1889. Suppl. Bd. xvii. 1, pp. 1–124. rec. Jülicher, Theol. L. Z. 1889, 26.
DRÄSEKE, J.: Apollinarios' von Laodicea Dialoge "Uber d. heil. Dreieinigkeit." TSK 1890, 1, pp. 137–171.
—— Des Apollinarios v. Laodicea Schrift. wider Eunomius. ZKG, xi. 1, 1889.
—— Phöbadius von Agennum und seine Schrift gegen die Arianer. ZWL, 335–343; 391–407. 1889.
BATIFFOL, R.: Fragmente d. Kirchengesch. d. Philostorgius, Röm. Quartalschr. f. christl. Alterthumskunde u. f. Kirchengesch. 1889, 2 and 3.
BATIFFOL, P.: Studia patristica. Études d'ancienne littérature chrétienne. Fasc. 1 (v. d. Wilpert; röm. Quartalschrift 1890, 1; v. Funk; TQS, 1890, 2).

(*c*) GELZER, H.: Sextus Julianus Africanus u. d. byzantin. Chronographie. Leipzig, 1880–85 (ii.); rec. Hilgenfeld, ZwTh, 30, 3, 1887.

(*d*) DE BROGLIE (le duc ALBERT): L'Église et l'Empire romain au IVe siècle. 3 parties. Paris, 1867–9.
PROUDHON, P. J.: Césarisme et Christianisme de l'an 45 avant J.-C. à l'an 476 après. 2 vols. Paris, 1883.
TOZER, H. F.: The Church and the Eastern Empire. London, 1888.
LANGEN, JOS.: Gesch. d. Rom. Kirche bis zum Pontificate Leo's I. Bd. i.; von Leo I. bis Nicolaus I. Bd. ii. Bonn, 1881–5.
WOLFF, P.: Die πρόεδροι auf d. Synode zu Nicäa. ZWL. 1889, 3, pp. 137–151.
BRIGHT, WM.: History of the Church, A.D. 313–451. 2d edition. London, 1869.
NEWMAN, J. H.: Arians of the Fourth Century. 3d edition. London, 1871.
—— Tracts Theological and Ecclesiastical. Nos. ii. and iii. London, 1874.
GWATKIN, H. M.: Studies of Arianism chiefly referring to the character and chronology of the reaction which followed the council of Nicæa. 1882.
—— The Arian Controversy. (Epochs of Church History, Vol. 15.) New York, 1890.
SONNINO, G.: Di uno scisma in Roma à tempi di Valentiniano I. Livorno, 1888.
DRÄSEKE, J.: Der Sieg d. Christenthums in Gaza. ZWL, 20–40. 1888.
BIRT, THDR.: De fide christiana quantum Stilichonis ætate in aula imperatoria occidentali valuerit. Marburg, 1885.

BRIGHT, WM.: Notes on the canons of the first four general councils. London, 1882.

MARTIN, P.: Le Pseudo-Synode connu dans l'histoire sous le nom de Brigandage d'Ephèse, étudié d'après ses actes, retrouvés en syriaque. Paris, 1875.

SCHULTZE, V.: Gesch. d. Untergangs d. Griech.-Röm. Heidenthums. Bd. 1. Jena, 1887; rec. Wissowa: Nuova Centologia, Ser. iii., Vol. xvii. Fasc. 18, 1888. Dtsche. Litztg. 1888, 44. Gwatkin, H. M.: The Engl. Hist. Rev. 1889, Jan.

MARTIN, J. P. P.: Les origines de l'église d'Edesse et des églises syriennes. Paris, 1889.

GÖRRES, J.: D. Christenthum im Sassanidenreich. ZwTh, xxxi. 449–468.

BOISSIER, G.: Études d'histoire religieuse. Le Christianisme et l'invasion des Barbares . . . le lendemain de l'invasion. Revue des deux mondes, 1890. 1er mai, pp. 145–172.

(e) MANSO: Das Leben Constantin d. Grossen. Breslau, 1817.

BURCKHARDT: D. Zeit Constantin's d. Grossen. 2 Aufl. Leipzig, 1880.

KEIM: D. Übertritt Constantin's d. Grossen z. Christenthum. Zürich, 1862.

ZAHN: Constantin d. Grosse u. d. Kirche. Hannover, 1876.

BRIEGER: Konstantin d. Grosse als Religionspolitiker. Gotha, 1880.

GÖRRES, F.: Weitere Beitraege z. Gesch. d. constantinischen Zeitalters. ZwTh, xxxiii., 2, pp. 206–215 1890.

CRIVELLUCCI, A.: Della fide storica di Eusebio nella vita di Constantino, 1889; rec. Schultze: Theol. Litblt. 1889, 9–10.

MARIANO, R.: Constantino Magno e la chiesa cristiana (Nuova Antologia, xxv., fasc. 10; 16 maggio, 1890, pp. 271–299.

MÜCKE, J. F. A.: Flavius Claudius Julianus. 2 abthl. Gotha, 1867–9.

RENDALL, G. H.: The Emperor Julian; Paganism and Christianity. London, 1879.

NEUMANN, K. J.: Prolegomena zu Juliani imperatoris librorum contra Christianos quæ supersunt. Lips. 1880.

———, ——: Juliani Imperatoris Librorum contra Christianos quæ supersunt. Leipzig, 1880.

———, ——: Kaiser Julians Bücher gegen d. Christen. Leipzig, 1880.

KING, C. W.: Julian, the emperor; containing Greg. Nazianzen's two invectives, and Libanius' Monody with Julian's extant theosoph. works. London, 1888.

ZOECKLER, O.: Julianus u. s. christl. Gegner. B. G. 41–48, 101–113. 1888.

SCHWARZ: De vita et de scriptis Juliani Imperatoris. Bonn, 1888; rec. Neumann: TLz, 1889, 5.

LARGAJOLLI, D., e PIETRO PARISIO: Nuovi studi intorno a Guiliano imperatori. Torino, 1889. (Estr. della Riv. di filol. e d'istruz. class. xvii. 7–9.)

STUFFKEN, J. M.: Diss. de Theodosii Magni in rem christianam meritis. Lugd., Bat., 1828.

GÜLDENPENNING, A., IFLAND, J.: D. Kaiser Theodosius d. Gr. Ein Beitrag zur röm. Kaisergeschichte. Halle, 1878.

RICHTER, H.: D. Weström. Reich besonders unter den Kaisern Gratian, Valentinian II., und Maximus. Berlin, 1865.

GÜLDENPENNING, A.; Gesch. d. oström. Reiches unter den Kaisern Arcadius u. Theod. II. Halle, 1885.

(f) PALLMANN: D. Gesch. d. Völkerwanderung v. d. Gothenbekehrung bis z. Tode Alarichs n. d. Quellen dargestellt. 1. Tl. Gotha, 1863. 2. Tl. Weimar, 1864.

WIETERSHEIM, Ed. v.: Gesch. d. Völkerwanderung. 2 Aufl. bes. v. F. Dahn. Leipzig, 1880.

KÜPKE, RUD.: Deutsche Forschungen, Die Anfänge des Königtums bei den Gothen. Berlin, 1859.

ASCHBACH: Gesch. d. Westgothen. Frankfurt, 1827.

MANNERT: Gesch. d. Vandalen. Leipzig, 1785.

PAPENCORDT, FEL.: Gesch. der vandal., Herrschaft in Africa. Berlin, 1837.

PROCOP.: Vandalenkrieg übers, v. Coste. Leipzig, 1885.

SCHMIDT, L.: Aelteste Gesch d. Vandalen. Beitrag. z. Völkerwanderung. Leipzig, 1888.

KLEMM: Attila u. Waltter v. Aquitanien nach d. Geschichte, Sage u. Legende dargestellt. Leipzig, 1827.

HAAGE: Gesch. Attila's. Prgr. Celle, 1862.

THIERRY: Histoire d'Attila et de ses successeurs. Paris, 5 éd. 2 vols., 1874.

DAHN, F.: D. Könige d. Germanen. Würzburg, 1861–70.

ARNOLD, W.: Deutsche Geschichte. Gotha, 1881–3.

(g) HERTZBERG, W.: Gesch. Griechenlands seit d. Absterben d. antiken Lebens (in Heeren u. Ukert 40, iii.). Gotha, 1879.

WALTER, FERD.: Gesch. d. röm. Rechts bis auf Justinian. 2 Tle. 3 Aufl. Bonn, 1860.

KRÜGER, GUST.: Monophysitische Streitigkeiten im Zusammenhange mit der Reichspolitik. Jena, 1884.

BROTHER AZARIAS: Aristotle and the Christian Church. London, 1888.

BOISSIER, G.: Études d'hist. rel. V. L'affaire de l'autel de la Victoire. Rd. m. Juli, 61–90 1888.

SCHICK, C.: D. Stephanskirche der Kaiserin Eudokia bei Jerusalem, 1888. Z. d. Dtsch. Palaestina–Ver. xi. 3–4.

SEECK, O.: Quaestiones de notitia dignitatum. Inaug. Diss. Berlin, 1873.

———, ———: Notitia dignitatum, accedunt notitia urbis Constantinopolitanae et laterculi provinciarum. Berlin, 1876.

HUDEMANN, E. E.: Gesch. d. röm. Postwesens während d. Kaiserzeit. (Calvary's philol. u. archæol. Bibl. Bd. 32.) Berlin, 1875.

LEDRA, A.: Des Publicains et des sociétés vectigalium. Paris, 1876.

MATTHIASS, BERNH.: D. röm. Grundsteuer u. d. Vectigalrecht. Erlangen, 1882.

SEECK, O.: Die Zeitfolge d. Gesetze Constantius. Z. f. Rechtsgeschichte, romanist. Abthl. x. 2, 3, 1–44; 177–251.

(h) AMÉLINEAU, E.: Hist. de S. Pakhôme et de ses communautés (Annales de musée Guiniet. T. 17). (v. J. Réville à Revue de l'hist. des religions. 1890, janv.–févr.)

BARBIER, P.: Vie de S. Athanase. Tours, 1888; rec. Martinor: Études relig., philos., hist. et litt., 1889, févr.; Piolin, P.: Revue des questions hist. 1889, avril.

REYNOLDS, H. R.: Athanasius, his Life and Work. (Church History Series.) London, 1889.

MARTIN, C.: Life of St. Jerome. London, Paul, 1888.

EIRAINER, C.: Der hl. Ephräm d. Syrer. Kempten, 1889. (Rec.: Janetschek, Stud. u. Mitthlgn. aus d. Benedictiner u. Cistercienser Orden, x. Bd. i. 2, 1889; L. Atzberger, Liter. Rundschau f. d. kathol. Deutschland, 1890, 6).

LAMY, T. J.: Études de patrologie orientale. Saint Ephrem. L'Université Catholique NST, iii. 3, mars, 1890. pp. 321–349; iv. 6, juin, pp. 161–190.

WAITZ, G.: Ub. d. Leben u. d. Lehre des Ulfila. Hannover, 1840.

BESSEL, W.: Ueb. d. Leben d. Ulfilas u. d. Beckehrung der Gothen z. Christenthum. Gött. 1860.

SCOTT, C. A. A.: Ulfilas, Apostle of the Goths. London, 1885.

FÖRSTER, TH.: Ambrosius, Bischof v. Mailand. Eine Darstellg. seines Lebens u. Werkens. Halle, 1884.

LUDWIG, F.: Der heil. Joh. Chrysostomos in seinem Verältniss zum byzantinischem Hof. Braunsberg, 1883.

HANSEN: De vita Aetii. Dissert. Dorpat. 1840.

RICHTER: de Stilichone et Rufino. Dissert. Halæ, 1860.

VOLKMANN: Synesius v. Kyrene. Berlin, 1869.

GREGOROVIUS, F.: Athenais, Gesch. e. byzantin. Kaiserin. 2 Aufl. Leipzig, 1882.

PART IV. — CONCLUSION.

The original translation, with its many excellences, seems to belong to an earlier school. It is free both in enlargement and in compression; words at times, and occasionally clauses, are inverted. The editor felt the difficulty of recasting such a flowing style; yet, in spite of the resulting infelicity, he felt constrained to make every possible correction, and these have been very numerous and extended in caption and text.

Sozomen uniformly describes the ancient heathen cult, of whatever form it might be, as Hellenism, and its followers, Hellenists. It seemed advisable to retain the rendering "paganism," which the first translator used toward the middle and the end of his work, although he had not been uniform in the beginning; any other translation would cause a constant confusion between nationality and religion.

In order to give a better impression of the author and text, the spelling of the proper names indicated by the text has been adhered to; the orthography " Novatus " is not a real exception. Where the spelling of a proper name in the caption differs from that of the text, the difference of origin between the two must be borne in mind. To the Pseudo-Nicephorus are due the headings; these variations have been preserved purposely.

The notes have been for the greater part limited to the sources, previous or contemporary. It has not been deemed necessary to load the text with references to the literature, ancient or modern, sufficiently indicated in the Bibliography.   It is just for the editor to say, that while the literature is not unfamiliar to him, he does not believe in the modern German method of annotation and allusion to every book under the sun, to the grave impediment of individual study. Similarly, the dictionaries show the biography and archæology in a better form than can be compressed into a note.   Nor did the editor think it best to introduce into the translation any technical discussion as to the errors of Sozomen.

LIFE AND WRITINGS OF SOZOMEN.

HERMIAS SOZOMEN practiced the law at Constantinople, at the same time with Socrates. His ancestors were not mean; they were originally natives of Palestine, being inhabitants of a village near Gaza, called Bethelia. This village was very populous in times past, and had most stately and ancient churches. But the most glorious structure of them all was the Pantheon, situated on an artificial hill, which was the tower as it were of Bethelia, as Sozomen relates in chap. xv. of his fifth book. The grandfather of Hermias Sozomen was born in that village, and first converted to the Christian faith by Hilarion the monk. For when Alaphion, an inhabitant of the same village, was possessed with a devil, and the Jews and physicians, attempting to cure him, could do him no good by their enchantments, Hilarion, by a bare invocation of the name of God, cast out the devil. Sozomen's grandfather, and Alaphion himself, amazed at this miracle, with their whole families embraced the Christian religion. The grandfather of Sozomen was eminent for his expositions of the Sacred Scriptures, being a person endowed with a polite wit, and an acuteness of understanding; and besides, he was well skilled in literature. Therefore he was highly esteemed by the Christians inhabiting Gaza, Ascalon, and the places adjacent, as being useful and necessary for the propagating of religion, and could easily unloose the knots of the Sacred Scriptures. But Alaphion's descendants excelled others in their sanctity of life, in kindness to the indigent, and in other virtues; and they were the first that built churches and monasteries there, as Sozomen says in the passage above cited, where he also adds, that some holy persons of Alaphion's family were surviving even in his own days, with whom he himself conversed when very young, and concerning whom he promises to speak more afterwards. Most probably he means Salamanes, Phusco, Malchio, and Crispio, brothers, concerning whom he speaks in chap. xxxii. of his sixth book. For he there says that these brethren, instructed in the monastic discipline by Hilarion, were, during the empire of Valens, eminent in the monasteries of Palestine; that they lived near Bethelia, a village in the country of the Gazites, and were descendants of a noble family in those parts. He mentions the same persons in the fifteenth chapter of book viii., where he says that Crispio was Epiphanius's archdeacon. It is evident, therefore, that the brothers were of Alaphion's family. Alaphion, too, was related to Sozomen's grandfather, as we may conjecture; first, because the grandfather of Sozomen is said to have been converted (together with his whole family) to the Christian religion, upon account of Alaphion's wonderful cure, whom Hilarion had healed by calling on the name of Almighty God. Secondly, this conjecture is confirmed by what Sozomen relates, viz., that when he was very young, he conversed familiarly with the aged monks that were of Alaphion's family. And, lastly, from the fact that Sozomen took his name from those persons who were either the sons or grandchildren of Alaphion. For he was called Salamanes Hermias Sozomenus (as Photius declares in his Bibliotheca), from the name of that Salamanes who, as we observed before, was the brother of Phusco, Malchio, and Crispio. Wherefore Nicephorus, and others, are mistaken in supposing that Sozomen had the surname of Salaminius because he was born at Salamis, a city of Cyprus. But we have before shown from Sozomen's own testimony, that he was not born in Cyprus, but in Palestine. For his grandfather was not only a Palestinian, as is above said, but Sozomen himself was also educated in Palestine, in the bosom (so to say) of those monks who were of Alaphion's family. From this education Sozomen seems to have imbibed that most ardent love of a monastic life and discipline, which he declares in so many places of his history. Hence it is, that in his books he is not content to relate who were the fathers and founders of monastic philosophy; but he also carefully relates their successors and disciples, who followed this way of life both in Egypt, Syria, and Palestine, and also in Pontus, Armenia, and Osdroëna. Hence also it is, that in the twelfth chapter of the first book of his history, he has proposed to be read (in the beginning as it were) that gorgeous account of the monastic philosophy. For he supposed that he should have been ungrateful, had he not after this manner at least made a return of thanks to those in whose familiarity he had lived, and from whom, when he was a youth, he had received such eminent examples of a good conversation, as he himself intimates, in the opening of his first book. It is inferred that Sozomen was educated at Gaza, not only from the passage above mentioned, but also from chap. xxviii. of his seventh book, where Sozomen says that he himself had seen Zeno, bishop of Majuma, for this Majuma is a sea-port belonging to the Gazites. Although Zeno was nearly a hundred years old, he was never absent from the morning and evening hymns, unless sickness detained him. After this Sozomen applied himself to the profession of the law. He was a student of the civil law at Berytus, a city of Phœnicia, not far distant from his own country, where there was a famous school of civil law. But he practiced the law at Constantinople, as himself asserts, book ii. chap. iii. And yet he seems not to have been very much employed in pleading of causes; for at the same time that he was an advocate in Constantinople, he wrote his Ecclesiastical History; as may be concluded from his own words in the last-mentioned passage. Before he wrote his nine books of Ecclesiastical History, Sozomen composed a Breviary of Ecclesiastical Affairs, from our Saviour's ascension to the deposition of Licinius. This work was comprised in two books, as himself bears witness in the opening of his first book; but these two books are now lost.

In the composure of his History, Sozomen has made use of a style neither too low nor too high, but one between both, as is most agreeable to a writer of ecclesiastical affairs. Photius prefers Sozomen's style to that of Socrates, and we agree with him in his criticism. But though Sozomen is superior in the elegance of his expression, yet Socrates excels him in judgment. For Socrates judges incomparably well, both of men, and also of ecclesiastical business and affairs; and there is nothing in his works but what is grave and serious, nothing that can be expunged as superfluous. But on the contrary, some passages occur in Sozomen that are trivial and childish. Of this sort is his digression in his first book concerning the building of the city Hemona, and concerning the Argonauts, who carried the ship Argo on their shoulders some furlongs, and also his description of Daphne without the walls of the city Antioch, in chap. xix. of his sixth book; to which we must add that observation of his, concerning the beauty of the body, where he treats of that virgin at whose house the blessed Athanasius was concealed a long while. Lastly, his ninth book contains little else besides warlike events, which ought to have no place in an Ecclesiastical History. Sozomen's style, however, is not without its faults. For the periods of his sentences are only joined together by the particles δὲ and τέ, than which there is nothing more troublesome. Should any one attentively read the epistle in which Sozomen dedicates his work to Theodosius junior, he will find it true that Sozomen was no great orator.

It remains, that we inquire which of these two authors, Socrates or Sozomen, wrote first, and which of them borrowed, or rather stole, from the other. Certainly, since both of them wrote almost the same things of the same transactions, inasmuch as they both began at the same beginning, and concluded their history at the same point (both beginning from the reign of Constantine, and ending at the seventeenth consulate of Theodosius junior), it must needs be true, that one of them robbed the other's desk. This sort of theft was committed by many of the Grecian writers, as Porphyry testifies, Eusebius' Præparatio Evangelica, bk. x. But which was the plagiary, Socrates or Sozomen, it is hard to say, in regard both of them lived in the same times, and both wrote their history in the empire of Theodosius junior. Therefore, in the disquisition of this question, we must make use of conjecture. So Porphyry in the above-mentioned book, since it was uncertain whether Hyperides had stolen from Demosthenes, or Demosthenes from Hyperides, because both had lived in the same time, decided to use conjecture. Let us therefore see upon which of them falls the suspicion of theft. Indeed, this is my sentiment, I suppose that the inferior does frequently steal from the superior, and the junior from the senior. But Sozomen is in my judgment far inferior to Socrates; and he betook himself to writing his history when he was younger than Socrates. For he wrote it whilst he was yet an advocate, as I observed before. Now, the profession of the advocates amongst the Romans was not perpetual, but temporary. Lastly, he that adds something to the other, and sometimes amends the other, seems to have written last. But Sozomen now and then adds some passages to Socrates, and in some places dissents from him, as Photius has observed, and we have hinted in our annotations. Sozomen therefore seems to have written last. And this is the opinion of almost all modern writers, who place Socrates before Sozomen. So Bellarmine in his book "De Scriptoribus Ecclesiasticis"; who is followed by Miræus, Labbæus, and Vossius. Amongst the ancients, Cassiodorus, Photius, and Nicephorus name Socrates in the first place. Although Cassiodorus is found to have varied; for in the preface of the Tripartite History, he inverts the order, and names Theodoret first, ranks Sozomen in the second place, and refers to Socrates as the last. So also Theodorus Lector recounts them in his epistle which he prefixed to his Tripartite History. Thus far concerning Sozomen.

MEMOIR OF SOZOMEN.

———∞⊰⊹⊱∞———

LITTLE more than cursory allusions to SOZOMEN occur in the works of contemporary writers; and the materials for a memoir of his life are therefore at best but few and scanty. We should, in fact, be destitute of almost all knowledge as to his birth, education, mode of life, and private history, had not some information on these points been furnished by himself. In the work before us, the only one which has caused his name to be handed down to posterity, he draws aside the curtain which would otherwise have concealed his origin and parentage, and makes known to us a portion of his family history. He tells us (book v. chap. xv.) that his grandfather was a native of Palestine, and of Pagan parentage; that he, with all his family, was converted to Christianity on witnessing a miracle wrought by St. Hilarion; and that, being possessed of great mental endowments, he afterwards became eminently useful to the men of Gaza and Ascalon, by his extraordinary power in expounding the most obscure passages of Holy Writ.

Our author himself seems to have been born about the beginning of the fifth century. He tells us that in his youth some of the founders of monasticism in Palestine were still living, although they had reached a very advanced period of life, and that he had enjoyed opportunities of intercourse with them. To this circumstance may probably be attributed the tone of reverential admiration in which Sozomen invariably speaks of the ascetic inhabitants of the desert.

The education of Sozomen was conducted with a view to the legal profession; and he studied for some years at Berytus, then noted for its school of law. He afterwards established himself at Constantinople, and, it has been conjectured, held some office at the court of Theodosius the Younger. He is reputed to have possessed some skill in the law, but it is certain that he never attained any eminence in his profession. It is only in the character of an historian that he has rendered himself conspicuous. His first work was an abridgment of Ecclesiastical History, from the ascension of our Lord to the deposition of Licinius (A.D. 324), but this is not extant. The work before us seems to have been commenced about the year 443. It embraces a period of 117 years; namely, from A.D. 323 to A.D. 439. It is generally admitted to have suffered many alterations and mutilations; and this may, in some measure, serve to account for the frequent inaccuracies in point both of narrative and of chronology which pervade the nine books of which it is composed. It is evident, from the very abrupt termination of this history, that it is but a fragmentary portion of a larger work. The precise object of Sozomen in undertaking to write this history is not apparent, as exactly the same ground had previously been gone over by Socrates, if we except the ninth book of the former, which is almost entirely devoted to the political history of the times. The learned Photius prefers the style of Sozomen to that of Socrates; yet Sozomen frequently evinces great deficiency in point of judgment, and on many occasions enlarges upon details which are altogether omitted by Socrates, as unworthy of the dignity of Ecclesiastical History. To us, there is manifest advantage in possessing these separate chronicles of the same events. Facts which might perhaps have been doubted, if not rejected, had they rested upon the sole authority of a single writer, are admitted as unquestionable when authenticated by the combined testimony of Socrates, of Sozomen, and of Theodoret. And, indeed, the very discrepancies which, on several minor points, are discernible in the histories of these writers, are not without their use, inasmuch as they tend to the removal of all suspicion of connivance or collusion.

ADDRESS TO THE EMPEROR THEODOSIUS BY SALA-MINIUS HERMIAS SOZOMEN, AND PROPOSAL FOR AN ECCLESIASTICAL HISTORY.

THE popular saying is, that the former emperors were zealous about some useful matter or other; such as were fond of ornaments, cared for the royal purple, the crown, and the like; those who were studious of letters, composed some mythical work or treatise capable of fascinating its readers; those who were practiced in war, sought to send the weapon straight to the mark, to hit wild beasts, to hurl the spear, or to leap upon the horse. Every one who was devoted to a craft which was pleasing to the rulers announced himself at the palace. One brings a precious stone not easily susceptible of polish; another undertakes to prepare a more brilliant color than the purple robe; one dedicates a poem or treatise; another introduces an expert and strange fashion of armor.

It is considered the greatest and a regal thing for the ruler of the whole people to possess, at least, one of the homely virtues; but no such great estimate has been made of piety, which is, after all, the true ornament of the empire. Thou, however, O most powerful Emperor Theodosius, hast in a word, by God s help, cultivated every virtue. Girt with the purple robe and crown, a symbol of thy dignity to onlookers, thou wearest within always that true ornament of sovereignty, piety and philanthropy. Whence it happens that poets and writers, and the greater part of thy officers as well as the rest of thy subjects, concern themselves on every occasion with thee and thy deeds. And when thou presidest as ruler of contests and judge of discourses, thou art not robbed of thy accuracy by any artificial sound and form, but thou awardest the prize sincerely, observing whether the diction is suitable to the design of the composition; so also with respect to the form of words, divisions, order, unity, phraseology, construction, arguments, thought, and narrative. Thou recompensest the speakers with thy favorable judgment and applause, as well as with golden images, erection of statues, gifts, and every kind of honor. Thou showest greater personal favor toward the speakers than the ancient Cretans did toward the much-sung Homer; or the Alevadæ did to Simonides; or Dionysius, the tyrant of Sicily to Plato, the companion of Socrates; or Philip the Macedonian, to Theopompus the historian; or the Emperor Severus to Oppianus, who related in verse the kinds, nature, and catching of fish. For after the Cretans had rewarded Homer with a thousand *nummi*, they inscribed the amount of the gift on a public column as if to boast of their excessive munificence. The Alevadæ, Dionysius, and Philip were not more reserved than the Cretans, who boasted of their modest and philosophical government, but quickly imitated their column, so that they might not be inferior in their donative. But when Severus bestowed upon Oppianus a golden gift for each line of his moderate verse, he so astonished everybody with his liberality, that the poems of Oppianus are popularly called golden words to this day. Such were the donations of former lovers of learning and discourses. But thou, O Emperor, surpassest any of the ancients in thy liberality to letters, and thou seemest to me to do this not unreasonably. For while thou strivest to conquer all by thy virtues, thou dost also conduct thine own affairs successfully, according to thy thorough knowledge of the story of those ancient affairs, so prosperously directed by the Greeks and Romans. Rumor says that during the day, thou takest military and bodily exercise, and arrangest affairs of state by giving judicial decisions, and by making note of what is necessary, and by observation, both in public and private, of the things which ought to be done; and at night that thou busiest thyself with books. It is a saying, that there serves thee for the study of these works, a lamp which causes the oil to flow automatically into the wick, by means of some mechanism, so that not one of the servants in the palace should be compelled to be taxed with thy labors, and to do violence to nature by fighting against sleep. Thus thou art humane and gentle, both to those near, and to all, since thou dost imitate the Heavenly King who is thy pattern; in that He loves to send rain, and causes the sun to rise on the just and unjust, as well as to furnish other blessings ungrudgingly. As is natural, I hear also that by thy various learning, thou art no less familiar with the nature of stones, and the virtues of roots, and forces of remedies, than Solomon, the wisest son of David; while thou excellest him in virtue; for Solomon became the slave of his pleasures, and did not preserve to the end, that piety which had been for him the source of prosperity and wisdom. But thou, most powerful Emperor, because thou settest thy restraining reason in array against levity, art not only an autocrat of men, but also of the passions of soul and body, as one would naturally suppose. And this, too, ought to be remarked: I understand that thou dost conquer the desire for all food and drink; neither the sweeter figs, to speak poetically, nor any other kind of fruit in its season, can take thee prisoner, except the little that thou dost touch and taste, after thou hast returned thanks to the Maker of all things. Thou art wont to vanquish thirst, stifling heat, and cold by thy daily exercise, so that thou seemest to have self-control as a second nature. Lately, as is well known, thou wast anxious to visit the city of Heraclea in Pontus, and to restore it, prostrated by time, and thou tookest the way in the summer season through Bithynia. When the sun about midday was very fiery, one of the body-guard saw thee, heated with much sweat and clouds of dust, and, as if to do thee a favor, he anticipatingly offered to thee a bowl which reflected brilliantly the rays of the sun; he poured in some sweet drink, and added cold water thereto. But thou, most powerful Emperor, didst receive it, and didst praise the man for his good will, and thou didst make it obvious that thou wouldst soon reward him for his well-wrought deed with royal munificence. But when all the soldiers were wondering with open mouth at the dish, and were counting him blessed who should drink, thou, O noble Emperor, didst return the drink to him and didst command him to use it in whatever way he pleased. So that it seems to me that Alexander, the son of Philip, was surpassed by thy virtue; of whom it is reputed by his admirers, that while he, with the Macedonians, was passing through a waterless place, an anxious soldier found water, drew it, and offered it to Alexander; he would not drink it, but poured out the draught. Therefore, in a word, it is appropriate to call thee, according to Homer, more regal than the kings who preceded thee; for we have heard of some who acquired nothing worthy of admiration, and others who adorned their reign with scarcely one or two deeds. But thou, O most powerful Emperor, hast gathered together all the virtues, and hast excelled every one in piety, philanthropy, courage, prudence, justice, munificence, and a magnanimity befitting royal dignity. And every age will boast of thy rule as alone unstained and pure from murder, beyond all governments that ever existed. Thou teachest thy subjects to pursue serious things with pleasure, so that they show zeal for thee and public affairs, with good will and respect. So that for all these reasons, it has appeared to me, as a writer of Ecclesiastical History, necessary to address myself to thee. For to whom can I do this more appropriately, since I am about to relate the virtue of many devoted men, and the events of the Catholic Church; and since her conflicts with so many enemies lead me to thy threshhold and that of thy fathers? Come thou, who knowest all things and possessest every virtue, especially that piety, which the Divine Word says is the beginning of wisdom, receive from me this writing, and marshal its facts and purify it by thy labors, out of thy accurate knowledge, whether by addition or elimination. For whatever course may seem pleasing to thee, that will be wholly advantageous and brilliant for the readers, nor shall any one put a hand to it after thine approval. My history begins with the third consulate of the Cæsars, Crispus and Constantine, and stretches to thy seventeenth consulship.[1]　I deemed it proper to divide the whole work into nine parts: the first and second books will embrace the ecclesiastical affairs under Constantine; the third and fourth, those under his sons; the fifth and sixth, those under Julian, the cousin of the sons of the great Constantine, and Jovian, and, further, of Valentinian and Valens; the seventh and eighth books, O most powerful Emperor, will open up the affairs under the brothers Gratian and Valentinian, until the proclamation of Theodosius, thy divine grandfather, as far as thy celebrated father Arcadius, together with thy uncle, the most pious and godly Honorius, received the paternal government and shared in the regulation of the Roman world; the ninth book I have devoted to thy Christ-loving and most innocent majesty, which may God always preserve in unbroken good will, triumphing greatly over enemies, and having all things under thy feet and transmitting the holy empire to thy sons' sons with the approbation of Christ, through whom and with whom, be glory to God, and the Father, with the Holy Spirit forever.　Amen.

---

[1] This marks the proposed limits, A.D. 323 to A.D. 439, but he did not carry the narrative further than A.D. 425.

THE ECCLESIASTICAL HISTORY

OF

SALAMINIUS HERMIAS SOZOMENUS.

———◦◦╳◦◦———

BOOK I.

My mind has been often exercised in inquiring how it is that other men are very ready to believe in God the Word, while the Jews are so incredulous, although it was to them that instruction concerning the things of God was, from the beginning, imparted by the prophets, who likewise made them acquainted with the events attendant upon the coming of Christ, before they came to pass.[1] Besides, Abraham, the founder of their nation and of the circumcision, was accounted worthy to be an eye-witness, and the host of the Son of God.[2] And Isaac, his son, was honored as the type of the sacrifice on the cross, for he was led bound to the altar by his father and, as accurate students of the sacred Scriptures affirm, the sufferings of Christ came to pass in like manner. Jacob predicted that the expectation of the nations would be for Christ, as it now is; and he likewise foretold the time in which he came, when he said "the rulers of the Hebrews of the tribe of Judah, the tribal leader, shall fail."[3]

This clearly referred to the reign of Herod, who was an Idumean, on his father's side, and on his mother's, an Arabian, and the Jewish nation was delivered to him by the Roman senate and Augustus Cæsar. And of the rest of the prophets some declared beforehand the birth of Christ, His ineffable conception, the mother remaining a virgin after His birth, His people, and country.[4] Some predicted His divine and marvelous deeds, while others foretold His sufferings, His resurrection from the dead, His ascension into the heavens, and the event accompanying each. But if any be ignorant of these facts it is not difficult to know them by reading the sacred books. Josephus, the son of Matthias, also who was a priest, and was most distinguished among Jews and Romans, may be regarded as a noteworthy witness to the truth concerning Christ[5]; for he hesitates to call Him a man since He wrought marvelous works, and was a teacher of truthful doctrines, but openly calls him Christ; that He was condemned to the death of the cross, and appeared alive again the third day. Nor was Josephus ignorant of numberless other wonderful predictions uttered beforehand by the holy prophets concerning Christ. He further testifies that Christ brought over many to Himself both Greeks and Jews, who continued to love Him, and that the people named after Him had not become extinct. It appears to me that in narrating these things, he all but proclaims that Christ, by comparison of works, is God. As if struck by the miracle, he ran, somehow, a middle course, assailing in no way those who believed in Jesus, but rather agreeing with them.

When I consider this matter it seems reasonably remarkable to me, that the Hebrews did not anticipate, and, before the rest of men, immediately turn to Christianity; for though the Sibyl and some oracles announced beforehand the future of events concerning Christ we are not on this

---

[1] Cf. Eus. *H. E.* i. 4.   [2] Cf. Gen. xviii.
[3] Cf. Gen. xlix. 10.
[4] Isa. vii. 14, foretells that "a virgin shall conceive and bear a son"; but he does not declare, in words, the perpetual virginity of the mother of God. The Roman Catholic Church, however, infers the doctrine from certain types in the Old Testament: such as that of "the bush which burnt with fire, and was not consumed" (Ex. iii. 2).   [5] See Joseph. *Antiq.* xviii. 33; xx. 9, 1.

account to attribute unbelief to all the Greeks. For they were few, who, appearing superior in education, could understand such prophecies, which were, for the most part, in verse, and were declared with more recondite words to the people. Therefore in my judgment, it was the result of the heavenly preknowledge, for the sake of the agreement in future events, that the coming facts were to be made known, not only by his own prophets, but in part also by strangers. Just as a musician, under pressure of a strange melody, may treat the superfluous tones of the chords lightly with his plectrum, or add others to those already existing.

Having now shown that the Hebrews, although in the possession of numerous and more distinct prophecies concerning the coming of Christ, were less willing than the Greeks to embrace the faith that is in Him, let what has been said on the subject suffice. Yet let it by no means be hence accounted contrary to reason that the church should have been mainly built up by the conversion of other nations; for in the first place, it is evident that, in divine and great affairs, God delights to bring to pass changes in a marvelous manner; and then, be it remembered, it was by the exercise of no common virtues that those who, at the very beginning, were at the head of religious affairs, maintained their influence. If they did not, indeed, possess a language sharpened for expression or for beauty of diction, nor the power of convincing their hearers by means of phrases or mathematical demonstrations, yet they did not the less accomplish the work they had undertaken. They gave up their property, neglected their kindred, were stretched upon a cross, and as if endowed with bodies not their own, suffered many and excruciating tortures; neither seduced by the adulation of the people and rulers of any city, nor terrified by their menaces, they clearly evidenced by their conduct, that they were supported in the struggle by the hope of a high reward. So that they, in fact needed not to resort to verbal arguments; for without any effort on their part, their very deeds constrained the inhabitants of every house and of every city to give credit to their testimony, even before they knew wherein it consisted.

Since then so divine and marvelous a change has taken place in the circumstances of men, that ancient cults and national laws have fallen into contempt; since many of the most celebrated writers among the Greeks have tasked their powers of eloquence in describing the Calydonian boar, the bull of Marathon and other similar prodigies, which have really occurred in countries or cities, or have a mystic origin, why should not I rise above myself, and write a history of the Church? For I am persuaded that, as the topic is not the achievements of men, it may appear almost incredible that such a history should be written by me; but, with God, nothing is impossible.

I at first felt strongly inclined to trace the course of events from the very commencement; but on reflecting that similar records of the past up to their own time had been compiled by those wisest of men, Clemens[1] and Hegesippus, successors of the apostles, by Africanus the historian, and by Eusebius, surnamed Pamphilus,[2] a man intimately acquainted with the sacred Scriptures and the writings of the Greek poets and historians, I merely draw up an epitome in two books of all that is recorded to have happened to the churches, from the ascension of Christ to the deposition of Licinius.[3] Now, however, by the help of God, I will endeavor to relate the subsequent events as well.

I shall record the transactions with which I have been connected, and also those concerning which I have heard from persons who knew or saw the affairs in our own day or before our own generation. But I have sought for records of events of earlier date, amongst the established laws appertaining to religion, amongst the proceedings of the synods of the period, amongst the innovations that arose, and in the epistles of kings and priests. Some of these documents are preserved in palaces and churches, and others are dispersed and in the possession of the learned. I thought frequently of transcribing the whole, but on further reflection I deemed it better, on account of the mass of the documents, to give merely a brief synopsis of their contents; yet whenever controverted topics are introduced, I will readily transcribe freely from any work that may tend to the elucidation of truth. If any one who is ignorant of past events should conclude my history to be false, because he meets with conflicting statements in other writings, let him know that since the dogmas of Arius and other more recent hypotheses have been broached, the rulers of the churches, differing in opinion among themselves, have transmitted in writing their own peculiar views, for the benefit of their respective followers; and further, be it remembered, these rulers convened councils and issued what decrees they pleased, often condemning unheard those whose creed was dissimilar to their own, and striving to their utmost to induce the reigning prince and nobles of the time to side with them. Intent upon maintaining the orthodoxy of their own dogmas, the partisans of each sect respectively formed a

---

[1] More probably Clemens Alexandrinus than, as Valesius suggests, Clemens Romanus.
[2] See the *Life of Eusebius*, prefixed to his *Eccles. Hist.* in this series.
[3] These books are not now extant.

collection of such epistles as favored their own heresy, omitting all documents of a contrary tendency. Such are the obstacles by which we are beset in our endeavors to arrive at a conclusion on this subject ! Still, as it is requisite, in order to maintain historical accuracy, to pay the strictest attention to the means of eliciting truth, I felt myself bound to examine all writings of this class according to my ability.

Let not an impertinent or malignant spirit be imputed to me, for having dwelt upon the disputes of ecclesiastics among themselves, concerning the primacy and the pre-eminence of their own heresy. In the first place, as I have already said, an historian ought to regard everything as secondary in importance to truth; moreover, the doctrine of the Catholic Church is shown to be especially the most genuine, since it has been tested frequently by the plots of opposing thinkers; yet, the disposal of the lot being of God, the Catholic Church has maintained its own ascendancy, has reassumed its own power, and has led all the churches and the people to the reception of its own truth.

I have had to deliberate whether I ought to confine myself to the recital of events connected with the Church under the Roman government; but it seemed more advisable to include, as far as possible, the record of transactions relative to religion among the Persians and barbarians. Nor is it foreign to ecclesiastical history to introduce in this work an account of those who were the fathers and originators of what is denominated monachism, and of their immediate successors, whose celebrity is well known to us either by observation or report. For I would neither be considered ungracious[1] towards them, nor willing to consign their virtue to oblivion, nor yet be thought ignorant of their history; but I would wish to leave behind me such a record of their manner of life that others, led by their example, might attain to a blessed and happy end. As the work proceeds, these subjects shall be noted as far as possible.

Invoking the help and propitiousness of God, I now proceed to the narration of events; the present history shall have its beginning from this point.

CHAP. II. — OF THE BISHOPS OF THE LARGE TOWNS IN THE REIGN OF CONSTANTINE ; AND HOW, FROM FEAR OF LICINIUS, CHRISTIANITY WAS PROFESSED CAUTIOUSLY IN THE EAST AS FAR AS LIBYA, WHILE IN THE WEST, THROUGH THE FAVOR OF CONSTANTINE, IT WAS PROFESSED WITH FREEDOM.

DURING the consulate of Constantine Cæsar and Crispus Cæsar, Silvester governed the Church of Rome ; Alexander, that of Alexandria ; and Macarius, that of Jerusalem. Not one, since Romanus,[2] had been appointed over the Church of Antioch on the Orontes ; for the persecution it appears, had prevented the ceremony of ordination from taking place. The bishops assembled at Nicæa not long after were, however, so sensible of the purity of the life and doctrines of Eustathius, that they adjudged him worthy to fill the apostolic see ; although he was then bishop of the neighboring Berœa, they translated him to Antioch.[3]

The Christians of the East, as far as Libya on the borders of Egypt, did not dare to meet openly as a church ; for Licinius had withdrawn his favor from them ; but the Christians of the West, the Greeks, the Macedonians, and the Illyrians, met for worship in safety through the protection of Constantine, who was then at the head of the Roman Empire.[4]

CHAP. III. — BY THE VISION OF THE CROSS, AND BY THE APPEARANCE OF CHRIST, CONSTANTINE IS LED TO EMBRACE CHRISTIANITY. — HE RECEIVES RELIGIOUS INSTRUCTION FROM OUR BRETHREN.

WE have been informed that Constantine was led to honor the Christian religion by the concurrence of several different events, particularly by the appearance of a sign from heaven.

When he first formed the resolution of entering into a war against Maxentius, he was beset with doubts as to the means of carrying on his military operations, and as to the quarter whence he could look for assistance. In the midst of his perplexity, he saw, in a vision, the sight of the cross[5] shining in heaven. He was amazed at the spectacle, but some holy angels who were standing by, exclaimed, "Oh, Constantine ! by this symbol, conquer ! " And it is said that Christ himself appeared to him, and showed him the symbol of the cross, and commanded him to construct one like unto it, and to retain it as his help in battle, as it would insure the victory.

Eusebius, surnamed Pamphilus,[6] affirms that he heard the emperor declare with an oath, as the sun was on the point of inclining about the middle of the day, he and the soldiers who were with him saw in heaven the trophy of the cross

---

[1] It is scarcely fair with Valesius to infer from this passage that Sozomen was a monk himself.

[2] Who this Romanus was is uncertain, as his name does not occur in the catalogue of bishops of Antioch, according to Hieronymus' edition of the *Chronicon*, nor in Nicephorus. In one index at the end of a codex of Eusebius' *History*, in Florence, his name occurs as the twenty-second, in order, and between Philagonius and Eustathius. Theodoret, *H. E.* i. 3, gives the succession Vitalis, Philagonius.   [3] Cf. Soc. i. 23, 24.
[4] For a narrative of the treatment of the Christians by Licinius, and the war between Constantine and Licinius on their account, see Soc. i. 3, 4.
[5] With this chapter, cf. the parallel account in Soc. i. 2.
[6] Cf. Eus. *V. C.* i. 28.

composed of light, and encircled by the following words : " By this sign, conquer."

This vision met him by the way, when he was perplexed as to whither he should lead his army. While he was reflecting on what this could mean, night came ; and when he fell asleep, Christ appeared[1] with the sign which he had seen in heaven, and commanded him to construct a representation of the symbol, and to use it as his help in hostile encounters. There was nothing further to be elucidated ; for the emperor clearly apprehended the necessity of serving God.

At daybreak,[2] he called together the priests of Christ, and questioned them concerning their doctrines. They opened the sacred Scriptures, and expounded the truths relative to Christ, and showed him from the prophets, how the signs which had been predicted, had been fulfilled. The sign which had appeared to him was the symbol, they said, of the victory over hell ; for Christ came among men, was stretched upon the cross, died, and returned to life the third day. On this account, they said, there was hope that at the close of the present dispensation, there would be a general resurrection of the dead, and entrance upon immortality, when those who had led a good life would receive accordingly, and those who had done evil would be punished. Yet, continued they, the means of salvation and of purification from sin are provided ; namely, for the uninitiated,[3] initiation according to the canons of the church ; and for the initiated, abstinence from renewed sin. But as few, even among holy men, are capable of complying with this latter condition, another method of purification is set forth, namely, repentance ; for God, in his love towards man, bestows forgiveness on those who have fallen into sin, on their repentance, and the confirmation of their repentance by good works.

CHAP. IV. — CONSTANTINE COMMANDS THE SIGN OF THE CROSS TO BE CARRIED BEFORE HIM IN BATTLE ; AN EXTRAORDINARY NARRATIVE ABOUT THE BEARERS OF THE SIGN OF THE CROSS.

THE emperor, amazed at the prophecies concerning Christ which were expounded to him by the priests, sent for some skillful artisans, and commanded them to remodel the standard called by the Romans *Labarum*,[4] to convert it into a representation of the cross, and to adorn it with gold and precious stones. This warlike trophy was valued beyond all others ; for it was always wont to be carried before the emperor, and was worshiped by the soldiery. I think that Constantine changed the most honorable

symbol of the Roman power into the sign of Christ, chiefly that by the habit of having it always in view, and of worshiping it, the soldiers might be induced to abandon their ancient forms of superstition, and to recognize the true God, whom the emperor worshiped, as their leader and their help in battle ; for this symbol was always borne in front of his own troops, and was, at the command of the emperor, carried among the phalanxes in the thickest of the fight by an illustrious band of spearmen, of whom each one in turn took the standard upon his shoulders, and paraded it through the ranks. It is said that on one occasion, on an unexpected movement of the hostile forces, the man who held the standard in terror, placed it in the hands of another, and secretly fled from the battle. When he got beyond the reach of the enemy's weapons, he suddenly received a wound and fell, while the man who had stood by the divine symbol remained unhurt, although many weapons were aimed at him ; for the missiles of the enemy, marvelously directed by divine agency, lighted upon the standard, and the bearer thereof, although in the midst of danger, was preserved.

It is also asserted that no soldier who bore this standard in battle ever fell, through any dark calamity, such as is wont to happen to the soldiery in war, or was wounded, or taken prisoner.

CHAP. V. — REFUTATION OF THE ASSERTION THAT CONSTANTINE BECAME A CHRISTIAN IN CONSEQUENCE OF THE MURDER OF HIS SON CRISPUS.

I AM aware that it is reported by the pagans that Constantine, after slaying some of his nearest relations, and particularly after assenting to the murder of his own son Crispus, repented of his evil deeds, and inquired of Sopater,[5] the philosopher, who was then master of the school of Plotinus, concerning the means of purification from guilt. The philosopher — so the story goes — replied that such moral defilement could admit of no purification. The emperor was grieved at this repulse, but happening to meet with some bishops who told him that he would be cleansed from sin, on repentance and on submitting to baptism, he was delighted with their representations, and admired their doctrines, and became a Christian, and led his subjects to the same faith. It appears to me that this story was the invention of persons who desired to vilify the Christian religion. Crispus,[6] on whose account, it is said, Constantine re-

[1] Cf. Eus. *V. C.* i. 29.
[2] id. i. 32.
[3] That is, for the unbaptized and catechumens; the baptized were called the "initiated" (οἱ μεμυημένοι).
[4] Eus. *V. C.* i. 30, 31.

[5] Or Sosipater of Apamea. Cf. Eunap. *V. S.* (Ædesius).
[6] The earlier church historians, except Philost. *H. E.* ii. 4, are silent as to the cause of his death, while the pagan authorities speak freely, but variously; later Christian writers take their statements from the pagans. Cf. Eutrop. *Brev. hist. Rom.* x. 6.

quired purification, did not die till the twentieth year of his father's reign; he held the second place in the empire and bore the name of Cæsar, and many laws, framed with his sanction in favor of Christianity, are still extant. That this was the case can be proved by referring to the dates affixed to these laws, and to the lists of the legislators. It does not appear likely that Sopater had any intercourse with Constantine, whose government was then centered in the regions near the ocean and the Rhine; for his dispute with Maxentius, the governor of Italy, had created so much dissension in the Roman dominions, that it was then no easy matter to dwell in Gaul, in Britain, or in the neighboring countries, in which it is universally admitted Constantine embraced the religion of the Christians, previous to his war with Maxentius, and prior to his return to Rome and Italy: and this is evidenced by the dates of the laws which he enacted in favor of religion. But even granting that Sopater chanced to meet the emperor, or that he had epistolary correspondence with him, it cannot be imagined the philosopher was ignorant that Hercules, the son of Alcmena, obtained purification at Athens by the celebration of the mysteries of Ceres after the murder of his children, and of Iphitus, his guest and friend. That the Greeks held that purification from guilt of this nature could be obtained, is obvious from the instance I have just alleged, and he is a false calumniator who represents that Sopater taught the contrary.

I cannot admit the possibility of the philosopher's having been ignorant of these facts; for he was at that period esteemed the most learned man in Greece.

CHAP. VI. — THE FATHER OF CONSTANTINE ALLOWS THE NAME OF CHRIST TO BE EXTENDED; CONSTANTINE THE GREAT PREPARED IT TO PENETRATE EVERYWHERE.

UNDER the government of Constantine the churches flourished and increased in numbers daily, since they were honored by the good deeds of a benevolent and well-disposed emperor, and otherwise God preserved them from the persecutions and harassments which they had previously encountered. When the churches were suffering from persecution in other parts of the world, Constantius alone, the father of Constantine, accorded the Christians the right of worshiping God without fear. I know of an extraordinary thing done by him, which is worthy of being recorded. He wished to test the fidelity of certain Christians, excellent and good men, who were attached to his palaces. He called them all together, and told them that if they would sacrifice to idols as well as serve

God, they should remain in his service and retain their appointments; but that if they refused compliance with his wishes, they should be sent from the palaces, and should scarcely escape his vengeance. When difference of judgment had divided them into two parties, separating those who consented to abandon their religion from those who preferred the honor of God to their present welfare, the emperor determined upon retaining those who had adhered to their faith as his friends and counselors; but he turned away from the others, whom he regarded as unmanly and impostors, and sent them from his presence, judging that they who had so readily betrayed their God could never be true to their king. Hence it is probable that while Constantius was alive, it did not seem contrary to the laws for the inhabitants of the countries beyond Italy to profess Christianity, that is to say, in Gaul, in Britain, or in the region of the Pyrenean mountains as far as the Western Ocean. When Constantine succeeded to the same government, the affairs of the churches became still more brilliant; for when Maxentius, the son of Herculius, was slain, his share also devolved upon Constantine; and the nations who dwelt by the river Tiber and the Eridanus, which the natives call Padus, those who dwelt by the Aquilis, whither, it is said, the Argo was dragged, and the inhabitants of the coasts of the Tyrrhenian sea were permitted the exercise of their religion without molestation.

When the Argonauts fled from Æetes, they returned homewards by a different route, crossed the sea of Scythia, sailed through some of the rivers there, and so gained the shores of Italy, where they passed the winter and built a city, which they called Emona. The following summer, with the assistance of the people of the country, they dragged the Argo, by means of machinery, the distance of four hundred stadia, and so reached the Aquilis, a river which falls into the Eridanus: the Eridanus itself falls into the Italian sea.

After the battle of Cibalis[1] the Dardanians and the Macedonians, the inhabitants of the banks of the Ister, of Hellas, and the whole nation of Illyria, became subject to Constantine.

CHAP. VII. — CONCERNING THE DISPUTE BETWEEN CONSTANTINE AND LICINIUS HIS BROTHER-IN-LAW ABOUT THE CHRISTIANS, AND HOW LICINIUS WAS CONQUERED BY FORCE AND PUT TO DEATH.

AFTER this reverse, Licinius,[2] who had previously respected the Christians, changed his opinion, and ill-treated many of the priests who

---

[1] One of the battles in which Licinius was routed by Constantine, A.D. 314. Eutrop. *Brev. hist. Rom.* x. 5.
[2] Cf. Soc. i. 3, 4, and especially various parts of Eus. *V. C.*

lived under his government; he also persecuted a multitude of other persons, but especially the soldiers. He was deeply incensed against the Christians on account of his disagreement with Constantine, and thought to wound him by their sufferings for religion, and besides, he suspected that the churches were praying and zealous that Constantine alone should enjoy the sovereign rule. In addition to all this, when on the eve of another battle with Constantine, Licinius, as was wont to be done, made a forecast of the expected war, by sacrifices and oracles, and, deceived by promises of conquest, he returned to the religion of the pagans.

The pagans themselves, too, relate that about this period he consulted the oracle of Apollo Didymus at Miletus, and received an answer concerning the result of the war from the demon, couched in the following verses of Homer:[1]

" Much, old man, do the youths distress thee, warring
    against thee!
Feeble thy strength has become, but thy old age yet shall
    be hardy."

From many facts it has often appeared to me that the teaching of the Christians is supported, and its advancement secured, by the providence of God; and not least from what then occurred; for at the very moment that Licinius was about to persecute all the churches under him, the war in Bithynia broke out, which ended in a war between him and Constantine, and in which Constantine was so strengthened by Divine assistance that he was victorious over his enemies by land and by sea. On the destruction of his fleet and army, Licinius threw himself into Nicomedia, and resided for some time at Thessalonica as a private individual, and was eventually killed there. Such was the end of one who, at the beginning of his reign, had distinguished himself in war and in peace, and who had been honored by receiving the sister of Constantine in marriage.

CHAP. VIII. — LIST OF THE BENEFITS WHICH CONSTANTINE CONFERRED IN THE FREEDOM OF THE CHRISTIANS AND BUILDING OF CHURCHES; AND OTHER DEEDS FOR THE PUBLIC WELFARE.

As soon as the sole government of the Roman empire was vested in Constantine, he issued a public decree[2] commanding all his subjects in the East to honor the Christian religion, carefully to worship the Divine Being, and to recognize that only as Divine which is also essentially so, and which has the power that endures for ever and ever: for he delights to give all good

things ungrudgingly to those who zealously embrace the truth; he meets their undertakings with the best hopes, while misfortunes, whether in peace or in war, whether in public or in private life, befall transgressors. Constantine then added, but without vain boasting, that, God having accounted him as a fitting servant, worthy to reign, he had been led from the British sea to the Eastern provinces in order that the Christian religion might be extended, and that those who, on account of the worship of God had remained steadfast in confessions or martyrdoms, might be advanced to public honors. After making these statements, he entered upon a myriad other details by which he thought his subjects might be drawn to religion. He decreed that all acts and judgments passed by the persecutors of the church against Christianity should be revoked; and commanded that all those who, on account of their confession of Christ, had been sent to banishment — either to the isles or elsewhere, contrary to their own inclination — and all those who had been condemned to labor in the mines, the public works, the harems, the linen factories, or had been enrolled as public functionaries, should be restored to liberty. He removed the stigma of dishonor from those upon whom it had been cast, and permitted those who had been deprived of high appointments in the army, either to reassume their former place, or with an honorable discharge, to enjoy a liberal ease according to their own choice; and when he had recalled all to the enjoyment of their former liberties and customary honors, he likewise restored their possessions. In the case of those who had been slain, and whose property had been confiscated, he enacted that the inheritance should be transferred to the next of kin, or, in default of heirs, to the church belonging to the locality where the estate was situated; and when the inheritance had passed into other hands, and had become either private or national property, he commanded it to be restored. He likewise promised to resort to the fittest and best possible arrangements when the property had been purchased by the exchequer, or had been received therefrom by gift. These measures, as it had been said, having been enacted by the emperor, and ratified by law, were forthwith carried into execution. Christians were thus placed in almost all the principal posts of the Roman government; the worship of false gods was universally prohibited; and the arts of divination, the dedication of statues, and the celebration of pagan festivals were interdicted. Many of the most ancient customs observed in the cities fell into disuse: and among the Egyptians the measure used to indicate the increase of the waters of the Nile was no longer borne into pagan temples, but into churches. The

¹ *Iliad*, viii. 102.
² γράμμα δημόσιον. The decree is given at full length in Eus. *V. C.* ii. 24–42; and the other legislative chapters of Bks. ii. and iv. Cf. Eus. *H. E.* x. 5–7; Soc. i. 18.

spectacle of gladiators was then prohibited among the Romans; and the custom which prevailed among the Phœnicians of Lebanon and Heliopolis of prostituting virgins before marriage, who were accustomed to cohabit in lawful marriage after the first trial of an illicit intercourse, was abolished. Of the houses of prayer, the emperor repaired some which were of sufficient magnitude; others were brilliantly restored by additional length and breadth, and he erected new edifices in places where no building of the kind had existed previously. He furnished the requisite supplies from the imperial treasury, and wrote to the bishops of the cities and the governors of the provinces, desiring them to contribute whatever might be wished, and enjoining submission and zealous obedience to the priests.

The prosperity of religion kept pace with the increased prosperity of the empire. After the war with Licinius, the emperor was successful in battle against foreign nations; he conquered the Sarmatians and the people called Goths, and concluded an advantageous treaty with them. These people dwelt upon the Ister; and as they were very warlike, and always ready in arms both by the multitude and magnitude of their bodies, they kept the other tribes of barbarians in awe, and found antagonists in the Romans alone. It is said that, during this war, Constantine perceived clearly, by means of signs and dreams, that the special protection of Divine Providence had been extended to him. Hence when he had vanquished all those who rose up in battle against him, he evinced his thankfulness to Christ by zealous attention to the concerns of religion, and exhorted the governors to recognize the one true faith and way of salvation. He enacted that part of the funds levied from tributary countries should be forwarded by the various cities to the bishops and clergy, wherever they might be domiciled, and commanded that the law enjoining this gift should be a statute forever. In order to accustom the soldiers to worship God as he did, he had their weapons marked with the symbol of the cross, and he erected a house of prayer in the palace. When he engaged in war, he caused a tent to be borne before him, constructed in the shape of a church, so that in case he or his army might be led into the desert, they might have a sacred edifice in which to praise and worship God, and participate in the mysteries.[1] Priests and deacons followed the tent, who fulfilled the orders about these matters, according to the law of the church. From that period the Roman legions, which now were called by their number, provided each its own tent, with attendant priests and deacons. He also enjoined the observance of the day

termed the Lord's day,[2] which the Jews call the first day of the week, and which the pagans dedicate to the sun, as likewise the day before the seventh, and commanded that no judicial or other business should be transacted on those days, but that God should be served with prayers and supplications. He honored the Lord's day, because on it Christ arose from the dead, and the day above mentioned, because on it he was crucified. He regarded the cross with peculiar reverence, on account both of the power which it conveyed to him in the battles against his enemies, and also of the divine manner in which the symbol had appeared to him. He took away by law the crucifixion customary among the Romans, from the usage of the courts. He commanded that this divine symbol should always be inscribed and stamped whenever coins and images should be struck, and his images, which exist in this very form, still testify to this order. And indeed he strove in everything, particularly in the enactment of laws, to serve God. It appears, too, that he prohibited many flagitious and licentious connections,[3] which till that period had not been forbidden; as one, who cares about it, may see at a glance from these few instances what the laws were, which he established about these points; it appears to me unreasonable now to treat them exhaustively. I consider it necessary, however, to mention the laws enacted for the honor and consolidation of religion, as they constitute a considerable portion of ecclesiastical history. I shall therefore proceed to the recital.

CHAP. IX. — CONSTANTINE ENACTS A LAW IN FAVOR OF CELIBATES AND OF THE CLERGY.

THERE was an ancient Roman law, by which those who were unmarried at the age of twenty-five were not admitted to the same privileges as the married;[4] amongst other clauses in this law, it was specified that those who were not the very nearest kinsmen could gain nothing from a will; and also, that those who were childless were to be deprived of half of any property that might be bequeathed to them. The object of this ancient Roman law was to increase the population of Rome and the subject people, which had been much reduced in numbers by the civil wars, not a long while before this law. The emperor, perceiving that this enactment militated against the interests of those who continued in a state of celibacy and remained childless for the sake of God, and deeming it absurd to attempt the multiplication of the human

---

[1] Μυστηρίων, that is to say, the sacraments of the church.

[2] Eus. V. C. iv. 18, 19.
[3] He probably alludes to the law of Constantine, "de raptu virginum vel viduarum." See Codex Theodos. ix. 24.
[4] The Lex Papia Poppæa. For its origin under Augustus, see Tacit. Ann. iii. 25; Eus. V. C. iv. 26.

species by the care and zeal of man (since nature always receiving increase or decrease according to the fiat from on high), made a law enjoining that the unmarried and childless should have the same advantages as the married. He even bestowed peculiar privileges on those who embraced a life of continence and virginity, and permitted them, contrary to the usage which prevailed throughout the Roman empire, to make a will before they attained the age of puberty; for he believed that those who devoted themselves to the service of God and the cultivation of philosophy would, in all cases, judge aright. For a similar reason the ancient Romans permitted the vestal virgins to make a will as soon as they attained the age of six years. That was the greatest proof of the superior reverence for religion. Constantine exempted the clergy everywhere from taxation, and permitted litigants to appeal to the decision of the bishops if they preferred them to the state rulers.[1] He enacted that their decree should be valid, and as far superior to that of other judges as if pronounced by the emperor himself; that the governors and subordinate military officers should see to the execution of these decrees: and that the definitions made by synods should be irreversible.

Having arrived at this point of my history, it would not be right to omit all mention of the laws passed in favor of those individuals in the churches who had received their freedom. Owing to the strictness of the laws and the unwillingness of masters, there were many difficulties in the way of the acquisition of this better freedom; that is to say, of the freedom of the city of Rome. Constantine therefore made three laws, enacting that all those individuals in the churches, whose freedom should be attested by the priests, should receive the freedom of Rome.[2]

The records of these pious regulations are still extant, it having been the custom to engrave on tablets all laws relating to manumission. Such were the enactments of Constantine; in everything he sought to promote the honor of religion; and religion was valued, not only for its own sake, but also on account of the virtue of those who then participated in it.

CHAP. X. — CONCERNING THE GREAT CONFESSORS WHO SURVIVED.

SINCE the persecution had recently ceased, many excellent Christians, and many of the confessors who had survived, adorned the

churches: among these were Hosius,[3] bishop of Cordova; Amphion,[4] bishop of Epiphania in Cilicia; Maximus, who succeeded Macarius in the church of Jerusalem; and Paphnutius,[5] an Egyptian. It is said by this latter God wrought many miracles, controlling demons, and giving him grace to heal divers kinds of sickness. This Paphnutius, and Maximus, whom we just mentioned, were among the number of confessors whom Maximinus condemned to work in the mines, after having deprived them of the right eye, and the use of the left leg.

CHAP. XI. — ACCOUNT OF ST. SPYRIDON: HIS MODESTY AND STEADFASTNESS.

SPYRIDON,[6] bishop of Trimythun in Cyprus, flourished at this period. To show his virtues, I think the fame which still prevails about him suffices. The wonderful works which he wrought by Divine assistance are, it appears, generally known by those who dwell in the same region. I shall not conceal the facts which have come to me.

He was a peasant, was married, and had children; yet was not, on this account, deficient in spiritual attainments. It is related that one night some wicked men entered his sheepfold, and were in the act of stealing his sheep, when they were suddenly bound, and yet no one bound them. The next day, when he went to the fold, he found them fettered, and released them from their invisible bonds; but he censured them for having preferred to steal what it was lawful for them to win and take, and also for making such a great exertion by night: yet he felt compassion towards them, and, desirous of affording them instruction, so as to induce them to lead a better life, he said to them, " Go, and take this ram with you; for you are wearied with watching, and it is not just that your labor should be so blamed, that you should return empty-handed from my sheepfold." This action is well worthy admiration, but not less so is that which I shall now relate. An individual confided a deposit to the care of his daughter, who was a virgin, and was named Irene. For greater security, she buried it; and it so happened that she died soon after, without mentioning the circumstance to any one. The person to whom the deposit belonged came to ask for it. Spyridon knew not what answer to give

[1] Constantine makes mention of this law in his Epistle to the bishops of Numidia, in Baronius, *A. E.* A.D. 316; n. lxiv.; Eus. *H. E.* x. 7; Cod. Theod. i. 27, de episcopali definitione, 1; xvi. 2, de episcopes ecclesiis et clericis, 2.

[2] Cod. Theod. iv. 7, de manumissionibus inecclesia, 1.

[3] For a further account of Hosius, cf. Soc. i. 7, 13; ii. 20, 29, 31; iii. 7.

[4] Amphion and Lespus are mentioned as bishops of Cilicia in Athan. *Ep. ad Episc. Æg. et Lib.*; another Amphion occurs in Athan. *Ap. cont. Arian,* 7, as bishop in Nicomedia.

[5] Ruf. *H. E.* i. 4; Soc. i. 8, 11; Theodoret, *H. E.* i. 7.

[6] Ruf. *H. E.* i. 5; Soc. i. 8, 12. Ruf. gives the first two stories; Soc. copies and gives credit; Soz. appends three more, and gives credit to himself only throughout. Ruf. had already said, " sed et multa alia ejus feruntur gesta mirabilia, quæ etiam nunc ore omnium celebrantur."

him, so he searched the whole house for it; but not being able to find it, the man wept, tore his hair, and seemed ready to expire. Spyridon, moved with pity, went to the grave, and called the girl by name; and when she answered, he inquired about the deposit. After obtaining the information desired, he returned, found the treasure in the place that had been signified to him, and gave it to the owner. As I have entered upon this subject, it may not be amiss to add this incident also.

It was a custom with this Spyridon to give a certain portion of his fruits to the poor, and to lend another portion to those who wished it as a gratuity; but neither in giving nor taking back did he ever himself distribute or receive: he merely pointed out the storehouse, and told those who resorted to him to take as much as they needed, or to restore what they had borrowed. A certain man who had borrowed in this way, came as though he were about to return it, and when as usual he was directed to replace his loan in the storehouse, he saw an opportunity for an injustice; imagining that the matter would be concealed, he did not liquidate the debt, but fraudulently pretending to have discharged his obligation, he went away as though he had made the return. This, however, could not be long concealed. After some time the man came back again to borrow, and was sent to the storehouse, with permission to measure out for himself as much as he required. Finding the storehouse empty, he went to acquaint Spyridon, and this latter said to him, "I wonder, O man, how it is that you alone have found the storehouse empty and unsupplied with the articles you require: reflect whether you have restored the first loan, since you are in need a second time: were it otherwise, what you seek would not be lacking. Go, trust, and you will find." The man felt the reproof and acknowledged his error. The firmness and the accuracy in the administration of ecclesiastical affairs on the part of this divine man are worthy of admiration. It is said that on one occasion thereafter, the bishops of Cyprus met to consult on some particular emergency. Spyridon was present, as likewise Triphyllius,[1] bishop of the Ledri, a man otherwise eloquent, who on account of practicing the law, had lived alone while at Berytus.[2]

When an assembly had convened, having been requested to address the people, Triphyllius had occasion, in the middle of his discourse, to quote the text, "Take up thy bed and walk,"[3] and he substituted the word "couch" (σκίμπους), for the word "bed" (κράββατος). Spyridon was indignant, and exclaimed, "Art thou greater than he who uttered the word 'bed,' that thou art ashamed to use his words?" When he had said this, he turned from the throne of the priest, and looked towards the people; by this act he taught them to keep the man who is proud of eloquence within bounds; and he was fit to make such a rebuke; for he was reverenced and most illustrious for his works: at the same time he was the superior of that presbyter in age and in the priesthood.

The reception which Spyridon gave to strangers will appear from the following incident. In the quadragesima, it happened that a traveler came upon a journey to visit him on one of those days in which it was his custom to keep a continuous fast with his household,[4] and on the day appointed for tasting food, he would remain without nourishment to mid-day. Perceiving that the stranger was much fatigued, Spyridon said to his daughter, "Come, wash his feet and set meat before him." The virgin replying that there was neither bread nor barley-food in the house, for it would have been superfluous to provide such things at the time of the fast, Spyridon first prayed and asked forgiveness, and bade her to cook some salt pork which chanced to be in the house. When it was prepared, he sat down to table with the stranger, partook of the meat, and told him to follow his example. But the stranger declining, under the plea of being a Christian, he said to him, "It is for that very reason that you ought not to decline partaking of the meat; for the Divine word shows that to the pure all things are pure."[5] Such are the details which I had to relate concerning Spyridon.

CHAP. XII. — ON THE ORGANIZATION OF THE MONKS: ITS ORIGIN AND FOUNDERS.

THOSE who at this period had embraced monasticism[6] were not the least in manifesting the church as most illustrious, and evidencing the truth of their doctrines by their virtuous line of conduct. Indeed, the most useful thing that has been received by man from God is their philosophy.[7] They neglect many branches of mathematics and the technicalities of dialectics, because

---

[1] This Triphyllius is mentioned by Hieron. *de vir. illust.* i. 92, as the author of a commentary on the Song of Solomon, which his biographer had read; and of many other works which had not come into his hands.
[2] Berytus in Phœnicia was celebrated for its school of law, in which, among others, Gregory Thaumaturgus is said to have studied. Biographers, imitating Valesius, have imagined that Sozomen studied there.

[3] Matt. ix. 6.
[4] τῆς τεσσαρακοστῆς ἐνστάσης. While it was Lent and probably Holy Week. See Tertull. *de Pat.* 13, and *de Jejun.* 14.
[5] Tit. i. 15.
[6] On the origin and growth of the monastic system, see Soc. iv. 23, and cf. Gibbon, *Decl. & Fall*, ch. 37, and Bingham's *Christian Antiq.* Bk. vii.; articles in Herz. *R. E.* Bk. iv.; *D. C. A.* Vol. ii.; Ad Harnack: Das Mönchthum, seine Ideale und seine Geschichte.
[7] The verb φιλοσοφεῖν is constantly used by the early Christian historians to signify the practice of asceticism.

they regard such studies as superfluous, and as a useless expenditure of time, seeing that they contribute nothing towards correct living. They apply themselves exclusively to the cultivation of natural and useful science, in order that they may mitigate, if not eradicate, evil. They invariably refrain from accounting any action or principle as good, which occupies a middle place between virtue and vice, for they delight only in what is good. They regard every man as wicked, who, though he abstain from evil, does not do good. For they do not demonstrate virtue by argument, but practice it, and count as nothing the glory current among men. They manfully subjugate the passions of the soul, yielding neither to the necessities of nature, nor succumbing to the weakness of the body. Having possessed the power of the Divine mind, they always look away to the Creator of the whole, night and day worshiping him, and appeasing him by prayers and supplications. By purity of soul and by a life of good works they entered without guilt upon religious observances, and despised purification, lustral vessels, and such ceremonials ; for they think that sins alone are blemishes. They are greater than the external casualties to which we are liable, and hold, as it were, all things under their control : and are not therefore diverted from the path they have selected by the disasters or the necessity which sway the life. They are not distressed when insulted, nor do they defend themselves when suffering from malice ; nor do they lose heart, when pressed by sickness or lack of necessaries, but rather rejoice in such trials and endure them with patience and meekness. They inure themselves through the whole of life to be content with little, and approximate as nearly to God as is possible to human nature. They regard the present life as a journey only, and are not therefore solicitous about acquiring wealth, nor do they provide for the present beyond urgent necessities. They admire the beauty and simplicity of nature, but their hope is placed in heaven and the blessedness of the future. Wholly absorbed in the worship of God, they revolted from obscene language ; and as they had banished evil practices, so they would not allow such things to be even named. They limited, as far as possible, the demands of nature, and compelled the body to be satisfied with moderate supplies. They overcame intemperance by temperance, injustice by justice, and falsehood by truth, and attained the happy medium in all things. They dwelt in harmony and fellowship with their neighbors. They provided for their friends and strangers, imparted to those who were in want, according to their need, and comforted the afflicted. As they were diligent in all things, and zealous in seeking the

supreme good, their instructions, though clothed in modesty and prudence, and devoid of vain and meritricious eloquence, possessed power, like sovereign medicines, in healing the moral diseases of their audience ;. they spoke, too, with fear and reverence, and eschewed all strife, raillery, and anger. Indeed, it is but reasonable to suppress all irrational emotions, and to subdue carnal and natural passions. Elias the prophet and John the Baptist were the authors, as some say, of this sublime philosophy. Philo the Pythagorean [1] relates, that in his time the most virtuous of the Hebrews assembled from all parts of the world, and settled in a tract of country situated on a hill near Lake Mareotis, for the purpose of living as philosophers. He describes their dwellings, their regimen, and their customs, as similar to those which we now meet with among the monks of Egypt. He says that from the moment they began to apply themselves to the study of philosophy, they gave up their property to their relatives, relinquished business and society, and dwelt outside of walls, in fields and in gardens. They had also, he informs us, sacred edifices which were called monasteries, in which they dwelt apart and alone, occupied in celebrating the holy mysteries, and in worshiping God sedulously with psalms and hymns. They never tasted food before sunset, and some only took food every third day, or even at longer intervals. Finally, he says, that on certain days they lay on the ground and abstained from wine and the flesh of animals ; that their food was bread, salt, and hyssop, and their drink, water ; and that there were women among them who had lived as virgins to old age, who, for the love of philosophy, and from their voluntary judgment, practiced celibacy. In this narrative, Philo seems to describe [2] certain Jews who had embraced Christianity, and yet retained the customs of their nation ; for no vestiges of this manner of life are to be found elsewhere : and hence I conclude that this philosophy flourished in Egypt from this period. Others, however, assert that this mode of life originated from the persecutions for the sake of religion, which arose from time to time, and by which many were compelled to flee to the mountains and deserts and forests, and they became used to this kind of living.

CHAP. XIII. — ABOUT ANTONY THE GREAT AND ST. PAUL THE SIMPLE.

WHETHER the Egyptians or others are to be regarded as the founders of this philosophy, it is

---

[1] Valesius would prefer to read " The Platonist."
[2] Cf. Eus. *H. E.* ii. 17, where he attributes to the Christians what is said by Philo concerning the Therapeutæ, as these ascetics were called.

universally admitted that Antony,[1] the great monk, developed this course of life, by morals and befitting exercises, to the summit of exactness and perfection. His fame was so widely spread throughout the deserts of Egypt, that the emperor Constantine, for the reputation of the man's virtue, sought his friendship, honored him with correspondence, and urged him to write about what he might need. He was an Egyptian by race, and belonged to an illustrious family of Coma, which was situated near the Heraclea which is on the Egyptian borders.[2] He was but a youth when he lost his parents; he bestowed his paternal inheritance upon his fellow-villagers, sold the rest of his possessions, and distributed the proceeds among the needy; for he was aware that philosophy does not merely consist in the relinquishment of property, but in the proper distribution of it. He obtained the acquaintance of the devoted men of his time, and emulated the virtues of all. Believing that the practice of goodness would become delightful by habit, though arduous at the outset, he reflected on more intense methods of asceticism, and day by day he augmented it by self-control just as if he were always re-commencing his undertaking. He subdued the voluptuousness of the body by labor, and restrained the passions of the soul by the aid of the Divine wisdom. His food was bread and salt, his drink water, and he never broke his fast till after sunset. He often remained two or more days without eating. He watched, so to speak, throughout the night, and continued in prayer till daybreak. If at any time he indulged in sleep, it was but for a little while on a short mat; but generally the bare earth was his couch. He rejected the practice of anointing with oil, and the use of baths and of similar luxuries likely to relax the tension of the body by moisture; and it is said that he never at any time saw himself naked. He neither possessed nor admired learning, but he valued a good understanding, as being prior to letters and as being the very discoverer of it. He was exceedingly meek and philanthropic, prudent and manly; cheerful in conversation and friendly in disputations, even when others used the controverted topics as occasion for strife. By his own habit and a kind of intelligence he quieted contentiousness when on the increase, and restored them to moderation; he also tempered the ardor of those who conversed with him, and regulated their manners. Although on account of his extraordinary virtues, he had become filled with the Divine foreknowledge, he did not regard foreknowledge

of the future as a virtue, nor did he counsel others to seek this gift rashly, for he considered that no one would be punished or rewarded according to his ignorance or knowledge of futurity; for true blessedness consists in the service of God, and in keeping his laws. "But," said he, "if any man would know the future, let him continually be purified in soul, for then he will have power to walk in the light, and to understand things that are to happen, for God will reveal the future to him." He never suffered himself to be idle, but exhorted all those who seemed disposed to lead a good life, to diligence in labor, to self-examination and confession of sin before Him who created the day and the night; and when they erred, he urged them to record the transgression in writing, that so they might be ashamed of their sins, and be fearful lest any one should find the many things recorded; for he would be fearful, lest if the document were traced to him he should become disclosed to other people as a depraved character. He above all others came forward spiritedly and most zealously for the defense of the injured, and in their cause often resorted to the cities; for many came out to him, and compelled him to intercede for them with the rulers and men in power. All the people felt honored in seeing him, listened with avidity to his discourses, and yielded assent to his arguments; but he preferred to remain unknown and concealed in the deserts. When compelled to visit a city, he never failed to return to the deserts as soon as he had accomplished the work he had undertaken; for, he said, that as fishes are nourished in the water, so the desert is the world prepared for monks; and as fishes die when thrown upon dry land, so monastics lose their gravity when they go into cities. He carried himself obediently and graciously towards all who saw him, and he was careful not to have, nor seem to have, a supercilious nature. I have given this concise account of the manners of Antony, in order that an idea of his philosophy may be formed, by analogy, from the description of his conduct in the desert.

He had many renowned disciples, of whom some flourished in Egypt and Libya, others in Palestine, Syria, and Arabia; not less than their master, did each disciple pass his life with those among whom he dwelt, and regulate his conduct, and instruct many, and wed them unto kindred virtues and philosophy. But it would be difficult for any one to find the companions of Antony or their successors by going carefully through cities and villages to discover them, for they sought concealment more earnestly than many ambitious men, by means of pomp and show, now seek popularity and renown.

We must relate, in chronological order, the

---

[1] Cf. Soc. i. 21, and his reference to the life attributed to Athanasius.
[2] There were two cities of this name, Heraclea the greater and Heraclea the less.

history of the most celebrated disciples of Antony, and particularly that of Paul, surnamed the Simple.[1] It is said that he dwelt in the country, and was married to a beautiful woman, and that having surprised her in the act of adultery, he laughed placidly and affirmed with an oath, that he would live with her no longer ; that he left her with the adulterer, and went immediately to join Antony in the desert. It is further related that he was exceedingly meek and patient : and that, being aged and unaccustomed to monastic severity, Antony put his strength to the proof by various trials, for he was newly come, and detected nothing ignoble ; and that, having given evidence of perfect philosophy, he was sent to live alone, as no longer requiring a teacher. And God himself confirmed the testimony of Antony ; and demonstrated the man to be most illustrious through his deeds, and as greater than even his teacher in vexing and expelling demons.

CHAP. XIV.—ACCOUNT OF ST. AMMON AND EUTY-
CHIUS OF OLYMPUS.

IT was about this period that Ammon,[2] the Egyptian, embraced philosophy. It is said that he was compelled to marry by his family, but that his wife never knew him carnally ; for on the day of their marriage, when they were alone, and when he as the bridegroom was leading her as the bride to his bed, he said to her, " Oh, woman ! our marriage has indeed taken place, but it is not consummated " ; and then he showed her from the Holy Scriptures that it was her chief good to remain a virgin, and entreated that they might live apart. She was convinced by his arguments concerning virginity, but was much distressed by the thought of being separated from him ; and therefore, though occupying a separate bed, he lived with her for eighteen years, during which time he did not neglect the monastic exercises. At the end of this period, the woman whose emulation had been strongly excited by the virtue of her husband, became convinced that it was not just that such a man should, on her account, live in the domestic sphere ; and she considered that it was necessary that each should, for the sake of philosophy, live apart from the other ; and she entreated this of her husband. He therefore took his departure, after having thanked God for the counsel of his wife, and said to her, " Do thou retain this house, and I will make another for myself." He retired to a desert place, south of the Mareotic lake between Scitis and the mountain called Nitria ; and here, during two and twenty years, he devoted himself to philosophy and visited his wife twice every year. This divine man was the founder of the monasteries there, and gathered round him many disciples of note, as the registers of succession show. Many extraordinary events happened to him, which have been accurately fixed by the Egyptian monks, who did very much to commemorate carefully the virtues of the more ancient ascetics, preserved in a succession of unwritten tradition. I will relate such of them as have come to our knowledge.

Ammon and his disciple Theodore, had once occasion to take a journey somewhere, and on the road found it requisite to cross a canal called Lycus. Ammon ordered Theodore to pass over backwards, lest they should witness each other's nudity, and as he was likewise ashamed to see himself naked, he was suddenly, and by a Divine impulse, seized and carried over, and landed on the opposite bank. When Theodore had crossed the water, he perceived that the clothes and feet of the elder were not wet, and inquired the reason ; not receiving a reply, he expostulated strongly on the subject, and at length Ammon, after stipulating that it should not be mentioned during his lifetime, confessed the fact.

Here follows another miracle of the same nature. Some wicked fathers, having brought to him a son, who had been bitten by a mad dog, and was nigh unto death, besought him in their lamentations to heal him. He said to them, " Your son does not require my healing, but if you are willing to restore to your masters the ox you have stolen, he will be healed immediately." And the result was even as had been predicted ; for the ox was restored and the malady of the child removed. It is said that, when Ammon died, Antony saw his spirit ascending into heaven, since the heavenly powers conducted him with the singing of psalms, and on being questioned by his companions as to the cause of his evident astonishment, he did not conceal the matter from them ; for he was seen to survey the sky intently, because of his amazement at the sight of the marvelous spectacle. A short time after, certain persons came from Scitis, and, announcing the hour of Ammon's death, the truth of Antony's prediction was manifested. Thus, as is testified by all good men, each of these holy persons was blessed in a special manner ; the one, by being released from this life ; the other, by being accounted worthy of witnessing so miraculous a spectacle as that which God showed him ; for Antony and Ammon lived at a distance of many days' journey from each other, and the above incident is corroborated by those who were personally acquainted with them both.

---

[1] Ruf. *H. M.* 31; Pall. *H. L.* 27.
[2] Ruf. *H. M.* 30; Pall. *H. L.* 12; Soc. iv. 23.

I am convinced that it was likewise during this reign that Eutychianus[1] embraced philosophy. He fixed his residence in Bithynia, near Olympus. He belonged to the sect of the Novatians,[2] and was a partaker of Divine grace; he healed diseases and wrought miracles, and the fame of his virtuous life induced Constantine to keep his intimacy and friendship. It so happened, that about this period, one of the royal body-guard, who was suspected of plotting against the sovereign, fled, and after search, was apprehended near Olympus. Eutychianus was besought by relatives of the man to intercede on his behalf with the emperor, and in the meantime, to direct that the prisoner's chains might be loosened, lest he should perish beneath their weight. It is related that Eutychianus accordingly sent to the officers who held the man in custody, desiring them to loosen the chains; and that, on their refusal, he went himself to the prison, when the doors, though fastened, opened of their own accord, and the bonds of the prisoner fell off. Eutychianus afterwards repaired to the emperor who was then residing at Byzantium, and easily obtained a pardon, for Constantine was not wont to refuse his requests, because he held the man in very great honor.

I have now given in few words the history of the most illustrious professors of the monastic philosophy. If any one desires more exact information about these men he will find it in the biographies which have been written of very many of them.

CHAP. XV. — THE ARIAN HERESY, ITS ORIGIN, ITS PROGRESS, AND THE CONTENTION WHICH IT OCCASIONED AMONG THE BISHOPS.

ALTHOUGH, as we have shown, religion was in a flourishing condition at this period, yet the churches were disturbed by sore contentions; for under the pretext of piety and of seeking the more perfect discovery of God, certain questions were agitated, which had not, till then, been examined. Arius[3] was the originator of these disputations. He was a presbyter of the church at Alexandria in Egypt, and was at first a zealous thinker about doctrine, and upheld the innovations of Melitius. Eventually, however, he abandoned this latter opinion,[4] and was ordained deacon by Peter, bishop of Alexandria, who afterwards cast him out of the church, because when Peter anathematized the zealots of Melitius and rejected their baptism, Arius assailed

him for these acts and could not be restrained in quietness. After the martyrdom of Peter, Arius asked forgiveness of Achillas, and was restored to his office as deacon, and afterwards elevated to the presbytery. Afterwards Alexander, also, held him in high repute, since he was a most expert logician; for it was said that he was not lacking in such knowledge. He fell into absurd discourses, so that he had the audacity to preach in the church what no one before him had ever suggested; namely, that the Son of God was made out of that which had no prior existence, that there was a period of time in which he existed not; that, as possessing free will, he was capable of vice and virtue, and that he was created and made: to these, many other similar assertions were added as he went forward into the arguments and the details of inquiry. Those who heard these doctrines advanced, blamed Alexander for not opposing the innovations at variance with doctrine. But this bishop deemed it more advisable to leave each party to the free discussion of doubtful topics, so that by persuasion rather than by force, they might cease from contention; hence he sat down as a judge with some of his clergy, and led both sides into a discussion. But it happened on this occasion, as is generally the case in a strife of words, that each party claimed the victory. Arius defended his assertions, but the others contended that the Son is consubstantial and co-eternal with the Father. The council was convened a second time, and the same points contested, but they came to no agreement amongst themselves. During the debate, Alexander seemed to incline first to one party and then to the other[5]; finally, however, he declared himself in favor of those who affirmed that the Son was consubstantial and co-eternal with the Father, and he commanded Arius to receive this doctrine, and to reject his former opinions. Arius, however, would not be persuaded to compliance, and many of the bishops and clergy considered his statement of doctrine to be correct. Alexander, therefore, ejected him and the clergy who concurred with him in sentiment from the church. Those of the parish of Alexandria, who had embraced his opinions, were the presbyters Aithalas, Achillas, Carpones, Sarmates, and Arius,[6] and the deacons Euzoius, Macarius, Julius, Menas, and Helladius. Many of the people, likewise, sided with them: some, because they imagined their doctrines to be of God; others, as frequently happens in similar cases, because they believed them to have

---

[1] Soc. i. 13, who gives his authority as Auxanon, a Novatian.
[2] Eus. H. E. vii. 8; Soc. i. 10; iv. 28, &c.
[3] Eus. V. C. parts of ii. & iii.; Ruf. H. E. i. 1–6; Soc. i. 5–13; Philost. H. E. i. 3–9.
[4] No one else suggests an early connection of Arius with the Melitians.

[5] A doubtful and unsupported assertion. All other testimony makes Alexander steadfast and exact in his definition.
[6] There are variations in names, offices, numbers in attendance, and course of debate in the early as well as later accounts of the controversy.

been ill-treated and unjustly excommunicated. Such being the state of affairs at Alexandria, the partisans of Arius, deeming it prudent to seek the favor of the bishops of other cities, sent legations to them ; they sent a written statement of their doctrines to them, requesting them that, if they considered such sentiments to be of God, they would signify to Alexander that he ought not to molest them ; but that if they disapproved of the doctrines, they should teach them what opinions were necessary to be held. This precaution was of no little advantage to them ; for their tenets became thus universally disseminated, and the questions they had started became matters of debate among all the bishops. Some wrote to Alexander, entreating him not to receive the partisans of Arius into communion unless they repudiated their opinions, while others wrote to urge a contrary line of conduct. When Alexander perceived that many who were revered by the appearance of good conduct, and weighty by the persuasiveness of eloquence, held with the party of Arius, and particularly Eusebius, president of the church of Nicomedia, a man of considerable learning and held in high repute at the palace ; he wrote to the bishops of every church desiring them not to hold communion with them. This measure kindled the zeal of each party the more, and as might have been expected, the contest was increasingly agitated. Eusebius and his partisans had often petitioned Alexander, but could not persuade him ; so that considering themselves insulted, they became indignant and came to a stronger determination to support the doctrine of Arius. A synod having been convened in Bithynia, they wrote to all the bishops, desiring them to hold communion with the Arians, as with those making a true confession, and to require Alexander to hold communion with them likewise. As compliance could not be extorted from Alexander, Arius sent messengers to Paulinas, bishop of Tyre, to Eusebius Pamphilus, who presided over the church of Cæsarea in Palestine, and to Patrophilus, bishop of Scythopolis, soliciting permission for himself and for his adherents, as they had previously attained the rank of presbyters, to form the people who were with them into a church. For it was the custom in Alexandria, as it still is in the present day, that all the churches should be under one bishop, but that each presbyter should have his own church, in which to assemble the people. These three bishops, in concurrence with others who were assembled in Palestine, granted the petition of Arius, and permitted him to assemble the people as before ; but enjoined submission to Alexander, and commanded Arius to strive incessantly to be restored to peace and communion with him.

CHAP. XVI. — CONSTANTINE, HAVING HEARD OF THE STRIFE OF THE BISHOPS, AND THE DIFFERENCE OF OPINION CONCERNING THE PASSOVER, IS GREATLY TROUBLED AND SENDS HOSIUS, A SPANIARD, BISHOP OF CORDOVA, TO ALEXANDRIA, TO ABOLISH THE DISSENSION AMONG THE BISHOPS, AND TO SETTLE THE DISPUTE ABOUT THE PASSOVER.

AFTER there had been many synods held in Egypt, and the contest had still continued to increase in violence, the report of the dissension reached the palace, and Constantine was thereby greatly troubled ; for just at this period, when religion was beginning to be more generally propagated, many were deterred by the difference in doctrines from embracing Christianity. The emperor [1] openly charged Arius and Alexander with having originated this disturbance, and wrote to rebuke them for having made a controversy public which it was in their power to have concealed, and for having contentiously agitated a question which ought never to have been mooted, or upon which, at least, their opinion ought to have been given quietly. He told them that they ought not to have separated from others on account of difference of sentiment concerning certain points of doctrine. For concerning the Divine Providence men ought necessarily to hold one and the same belief ; but the minute researches in this province, especially if they do not bring them to the one opinion, must be retained in secret according to all reason. He exhorted them to put away all loose talk about such points, and to be of one mind ; for he had been not a little grieved, and on this account he had renounced his intention of visiting the cities of the East. It was in this strain that he wrote to Alexander and to Arius, reproving and exhorting them both.

Constantine was also deeply grieved at the diversity of opinion which prevailed concerning the celebration of the Passover ; [2] for some of the cities in the East differed on this point, although they did not withhold from communion with one another ; they kept the festival more according to the manner of the Jews, [3] and as was natural by this divergence, detracted from the splendor of the festal sacrifice. The emperor zealously endeavored to remove both these causes of dissension from the church ; and thinking to be able to remove the evil before it advanced to greater proportions, he sent one who was honored for his faith, his virtuous life, and most approved in those former times for his

[1] Soz. only outlines the letter, given completely in Eus. *V. C.* ii. 64–72 ; of which Soc. quotes the greater part. i. 7.
[2] Eus. *V. C.* iii. 5 ; Soc. i. 8.
[3] They were called Quartodecimanians. Euseb. *H. E.* v. 24 ; Soc. v. 22.

confessions about this doctrine, to reconcile those who were divided on account of doctrine in Egypt, and those who in the East differed about the Passover. This man was Hosius, bishop of Cordova.

CHAP. XVII. — OF THE COUNCIL CONVENED AT NICÆA ON ACCOUNT OF ARIUS.

WHEN it was found that the event did not answer the expectations of the emperor, but that on the contrary, the contention was too great for reconciliation, so that he who had been sent to make peace returned without having accomplished his mission, Constantine convened a synod at Nicæa, in Bithynia, and wrote[1] to the most eminent men of the churches in every country, directing them to be there on an appointed day.[2] Of those who occupied the apostolic sees, the following participated in this conference: Macarius of Jerusalem, Eustathius, who already presided over the church of Antioch on the Orontes; and Alexander of Alexandria near Lake Mareotis. Julius,[3] bishop of Rome, was unable to attend on account of extreme old age; but his place was supplied by Vito and Vicentius, presbyters of his church. Many other excellent and good men from different nations were congregated together, of whom some were celebrated for their learning, their eloquence, and their knowledge of the sacred books, and other discipline; some for the virtuous tenor of their life, and others for the combination of all these qualifications. About three hundred and twenty bishops were present, accompanied by a multitude of presbyters and deacons. There were, likewise, men present who were skilled in dialectics, and ready to assist in the discussions. And as was usually the case on such occasions, many priests resorted to the council for the purpose of transacting their own private affairs;[4] for they considered this a favorable opportunity for rectifying their grievances, and in what points each found fault with the rest, he presented a document to the emperor, wherein he noted the offenses committed against himself. As this course was pursued day after day, the emperor set apart one certain day on which all complaints were to be brought before him. When the appointed time arrived, he took the memorials which had been presented to him, and said, "All these accusations will be brought forward in their own season at the great day of judgment, and will there be judged by the Great Judge of all men;

as to me, I am but a man, and it would be evil in me to take cognizance of such matters, seeing that the accuser and the accused are priests; and the priests ought so to act as never to become amenable to the judgment of others. Imitate, therefore, the divine love and mercy of God, and be ye reconciled to one another; withdraw your accusations against each other; let us be persuaded, and let us devote our attention to those subjects connected with the faith on account of which we are assembled." After this address, in order to make the document of each man nugatory, the emperor commanded the memorials to be burnt, and then appointed a day for solving the doubtful points. But before the appointed time arrived, the bishops assembled together, and having summoned Arius to attend, began to examine the disputed topics, each one amongst them advancing his own opinion. As might have been expected, however, many different questions started out of the investigation: some of the bishops spoke against the introduction of novelties contrary to the faith which had been delivered to them from the beginning. And those especially who had adhered to simplicity of doctrine argued that the faith of God ought to be received without curious inquiries; others, however, contended that ancient opinions ought not to be followed without examination. Many of the bishops who were then assembled, and of the clergy who accompanied them, being remarkable for their dialectic skill, and practiced in such rhetorical methods, became conspicuous, and attracted the notice of the emperor and the court. Of that number Athanasius, who was then a deacon of Alexandria, and had accompanied his bishop Alexander, seemed to have the largest share in the counsel concerning these subjects.

CHAP. XVIII. — TWO PHILOSOPHERS ARE CONVERTED TO THE FAITH BY THE SIMPLICITY OF TWO OLD MEN WITH WHOM THEY HOLD A DISPUTATION.

WHILE these disputations were being carried on, certain of the pagan philosophers became desirous of taking part in them; some, because they wished for information as to the doctrine that was inculcated; and others, because, feeling incensed against the Christians on account of the recent suppression of the pagan religion, wished to convert the inquiry about doctrine into a strife about words, so as to introduce dissensions among them, and to make them appear as holding contradictory opinions. It is related that one of these philosophers, priding himself on his acknowledged superiority of eloquence, began to ridicule the priests, and thereby roused the indignation of a simple old man, highly esteemed

---

[1] Eus. *V. C.* iii. 6.
[2] Eus. *V. C.* iii. 7–11; Soc. i. 8; Ruf. *H. E.* i. 2. The variations and additions of Theodoret are very noteworthy. *H. E.* i. 7.
[3] Mistake for Silvester. Cf. ii. 20.
[4] Ruf. *H. E.* i. 2; Soc. i. 8. Soz. here makes, as usual, a free use of the speech as reported by Rufinus.

as a confessor, who, although unskilled in logical refinements and wordiness, undertook to oppose him. The less serious of those who knew the confessor, raised a laugh[1] at his expense for engaging in such an undertaking; but the more thoughtful felt anxious lest, in opposing so eloquent a man, he should only render himself ridiculous; yet his influence was so great, and his reputation so high among them, that they could not forbid his engaging in the debate; and he accordingly delivered himself in the following terms: "In the name of Jesus Christ, O philosopher, hearken to me. There is one God, the maker of heaven and earth, and of all things visible and invisible. He made all things by the power of the Word, and established them by the holiness of His Spirit. The Word, whom we call the Son of God, seeing that man was sunk in error and living like unto the beasts, pitied him, and vouchsafed to be born of woman, to hold intercourse with men, and to die for them. And He will come again to judge each of us as to the deeds of this present life. We believe these things to be true with all simplicity. Do not, therefore, expend your labor in vain by striving to disprove facts which can only be understood by faith or by scrutinizing the manner in which these things did or did not come to pass. Answer me, dost thou believe?" The philosopher, astonished at what had occurred, replied, "I believe"; and having thanked the old man for having overcome him in argument, he began to teach the same doctrines to others. He exhorted those who still held his former sentiments to adopt the views he had embraced, assuring them on oath, that he had been impelled to embrace Christianity by a certain inexplicable impulse.

It is said that a similar miracle was performed by Alexander, who governed the church of Constantinople. When Constantine returned to Byzantium, certain philosophers came to him to complain of the innovations in religion, and particularly of his having introduced a new form of worship into the state, contrary to that followed by his forefathers, and by all who were formerly in power, whether among the Greeks or the Romans. They likewise desired to hold a disputation on the doctrine with Alexander the bishop; and he, although unskilled in such argumentative contests, and perhaps persuaded by his life, seeing that he was an excellent and good man, accepted the struggle at the command of the emperor. When the philosophers were assembled, since every one wished to engage in the discussion, he requested that one whom they esteemed worthy might be chosen as spokesman, while the others were to

remain silent. When one of the philosophers began to open the debate, Alexander said to him, "I command thee in the name of Jesus Christ not to speak." The man was instantaneously silenced. It is then right to consider whether it is a greater miracle that a man, and he a philosopher, should so easily be silenced by a word, or that a stone-wall should be cleft by the power of a word, which miracle I have heard some attribute to Julian, surnamed the Chaldean.[2] I have understood that these events happened in the way above narrated.

CHAP. XIX. — WHEN THE COUNCIL WAS ASSEMBLED, THE EMPEROR DELIVERED A PUBLIC ADDRESS.

THE bishops held long consultations; and after summoning Arius before them, they made an accurate test of his propositions; they were intently on their guard, not to come to a vote on either side. When at length the appointed day arrived on which it had been decided to settle the doubtful points, they assembled together[3] in the palace, because the emperor had signified his intention of taking part in the deliberations. When he was in the same place with the priests, he passed through to the head of the conference, and seated himself on the throne which had been prepared for him, and the synod was then commanded to be seated; for seats had been arranged on either side along the walls of the palatial rooms, for it was the largest, and excelled the other chambers.

After they were seated, Eusebius Pamphilus arose and delivered an oration[4] in honor of the emperor, returning thanks to God on his account. When he had ceased speaking, and silence was restored, the emperor delivered himself in the following words: "I give thanks to God for all things, but particularly, O friends, for being permitted to see your conference. And the event has exceeded my prayer, in that so many priests of Christ have been conducted into the same place; now, it is my desire that you should be of one mind and be partakers of a consentient judgment, for I deem dissension in the Church of God as more dangerous than any other evil. Therefore when it was announced, and I understood you were in discord, an unwholesome thing to hear, I was deeply pained in soul; and least of all does it profit you, since you are the conductors of divine worship and arbiters of peace.

---

[1] Ruf. H. E. i. 3; Soc. i. 8. Soz. gives a free rendering of Ruf.

[2] Suidas says he was a philosopher, and the father of Julian, called the Theurgist. He was the author of a work concerning demons, in four books. The son, who flourished under Marcus Aurelius, was so skilled in the magic art, that he called down rain from heaven, when the Roman soldiers were perishing from thirst. Arnuphis, an Egyptian philosopher, was said to have wrought a similar miracle. Suidas, s. v. [3] Eus. V. C. iii. 10–12. [4] Theodoret, H. E. i. 7, places this oration in the mouth of Eustathius, bishop of Antioch. The variations in the speech as recorded by Sozomen, show his classic view of reporting. Theodoret's report of Constantine's address is equally divergent.

On this account it is, that I have called you together in a holy Synod, and being both your emperor and your fellow-physician, I seek for you a favor which is acceptable to our common Lord, and as honorable for me to receive, as for you to grant. The favor which I seek is, that you examine the causes of the strife, and put a consentient and peaceful end thereto ; so that I may triumph with you over the envious demon, who excited this internal revolt because he was provoked to see our external enemies and tyrants under our feet, and envied our good estate." The emperor pronounced this discourse in Latin, and the interpretation was supplied by one at his side.

CHAP. XX. — AFTER HAVING GIVEN AUDIENCE TO BOTH PARTIES, THE EMPEROR CONDEMNED THE FOLLOWERS OF ARIUS AND BANISHED THEM.

THE next debate by the priests turned upon doctrine.[1] The emperor gave patient attention to the speeches of both parties ; he applauded those who spoke well, rebuked those who displayed a tendency to altercation, and according to his apprehension of what he heard, for he was not wholly unpracticed in the Greek tongue, he addressed himself with kindness to each one. Finally all the priests agreed with one another and conceded that the Son is consubstantial with the Father. At the commencement of the conference there were but seventeen who praised the opinion of Arius, but eventually the majority of these yielded assent to the general view. To this judgment the emperor likewise deferred, for he regarded the unanimity of the conference to be a divine approbation ; and he ordained that any one who should be rebellious thereto, should forthwith be sent into banishment, as guilty of endeavoring to overthrow the Divine definitions. I had thought it necessary to reproduce the very document concerning the matter, as an example of the truth, in order that posterity might possess in a fixed and clear form the symbol of the faith which proved pacificatory at the time ; but since some pious friends, who understood such matters, recommended that these truths ought to be spoken of and heard by the initiated and their initiators[2] only, I agreed with their council ; for it is not unlikely that some of the uninitiated may read this book. While I have concealed such of the prohibited material as I ought to keep silent about, I have not altogether left the reader ignorant of the opinions held by the synod.

CHAP. XXI. — WHAT THE COUNCIL DETERMINED ABOUT ARIUS ; THE CONDEMNATION OF HIS FOLLOWERS ; HIS WRITINGS ARE TO BE BURNT ; CERTAIN OF THE HIGH PRIESTS DIFFER FROM THE COUNCIL ; THE SETTLEMENT OF THE PASSOVER.

IT ought to be known, that they affirmed the Son to be consubstantial with the Father ; and that those are to be excommunicated and voted aliens to the Catholic Church, who assert that there was a time in which the Son existed not, and before He was begotten He was not, and that He was made from what had no existence, and that He is of another hypostasis or substance from the Father, and that He is subject to change or mutation. This decision was sanctioned by Eusebius, bishop of Nicomedia ; by Theognis, bishop of Nicæa ; by Maris, bishop of Chalcedon ; by Patrophilus, bishop of Scythopolis ; and by Secundus, bishop of Ptolemais in Libya.[3] Eusebius Pamphilus, however, withheld his assent for a little while, but on further examination assented.[4] The council excommunicated Arius and his adherents, and prohibited his entering Alexandria. The words in which his opinions were couched were likewise condemned, as also a work entitled "Thalia," which he had written on the subject. I have not read this book, but I understand that it is of a loose character, resembling in license Sotadus.[5] It ought to be known that although Eusebius, bishop of Nicomedia, and Theognis, bishop of Nicæa, assented to the document of this faith set forth by the council, they neither agreed nor subscribed to the deposition of Arius. The emperor punished Arius with exile, and dispatched edicts to the bishops and people of every country, denouncing him and his adherents as ungodly, and commanding that their books should be destroyed, in order that no remembrance of him or of the doctrine which he had broached might remain. Whoever should be found secreting his writings and who should not burn them immediately on the accusation, should undergo the penalty of death, and suffer capital punishment. The emperor wrote letters to every city against Arius and those who had received his doctrines, and commanded Eusebius and Theognis to quit the cities whereof they were bishops ; he addressed himself in particular to the church of Nicomedia, urging it to adhere to the faith which had been set forth by the council, to elect orthodox bishops, to obey them, and to let the

---

[1] Eus. *V. C.* iii. 13, 14 ; Soc. i. 8.
[2] μυσται και μυσταγωγοί, as applied to the Christian mysteries. The principle here adduced is different from that which ruled with Ruf. *H. E.* i. 6 ; Soc. i. 8.

[3] There are variations in the earlier writers as to the number and names of the excommunicated and banished.
[4] Eusebius' attempt at straddling amounts to prevarication here, and later ; Soc. i. 8 copied by the later historians.
[5] Cf. Soc. i. 9 ; both borrowed their criticism from Athan. *Or. cont. Arian.* i. 4, etc.

past fall into oblivion ; and he threatened with punishment those who should venture to speak well of the exiled bishops, or to adopt their sentiments. In these and in other letters, he manifested resentment against Eusebius, because he had previously adopted the opinions of the tyrant, and had engaged in his plots. In accordance with the imperial edicts, Eusebius and Theognis were ejected from the churches which they held, and Amphion received that of Nicomedia, and Chrestus that of Nicæa. On the termination of this doctrinal controversy, the council decided that the Paschal feast should be celebrated at the same time in every place.[1]

CHAP. XXII. — ACESIUS, BISHOP OF THE NOVATIANS, IS SUMMONED BY THE EMPEROR TO BE PRESENT AT THE FIRST COUNCIL.

IT is related, that the emperor, under the impulse of an ardent desire to see harmony re-established among Christians, summoned Acesius, bishop of the church of the Novatians,[2] to the council, placed before him the definition of the faith and of the feast, which had already been confirmed by the signatures of the bishops, and asked whether he could agree thereto. Acesius answered that their exposition defined no new doctrine, and that he accorded in opinion with the Synod, and that he had from the beginning held these sentiments with respect both to the faith and to the feast. "Why, then," said the emperor, "do you keep aloof from communion with others, if you are of one mind with them?" He replied that the dissension first broke out under Decius, between Novatius and Cornelius,[3] and that he considered such persons unworthy of communion who, after baptism, had fallen into those sins which the Scriptures declare to be unto death ;[4] for that the remission of those sins, he thought, depended on the authority of God only, and not on the priests. The emperor replied, by saying, "O Acesius, take a ladder and ascend alone to heaven." By this speech I do not imagine the emperor intended to praise Acesius, but rather to blame him, because, being but a man, he fancied himself exempt from sin.[5]

CHAP. XXIII. — CANONS APPOINTED BY THE COUNCIL ; PAPHNUTIUS, A CERTAIN CONFESSOR, RESTRAINS THE COUNCIL FROM FORMING A CANON ENJOINING CELIBACY TO ALL WHO WERE ABOUT TO BE HONORED WITH THE PRIESTHOOD.

ZEALOUS of reforming the life of those who were engaged about the churches, the Synod

enacted laws which were called canons.[6] While they were deliberating about this, some thought that a law ought to be passed enacting that bishops and presbyters, deacons and sub-deacons, should hold no intercourse with the wife they had espoused before they entered the priesthood ; but Paphnutius,[7] the confessor, stood up and testified against this proposition ; he said that marriage was honorable and chaste, and that cohabitation with their own wives was chastity, and advised the Synod not to frame such a law, for it would be difficult to bear, and might serve as an occasion of incontinence to them and their wives ; and he reminded them, that according to the ancient tradition of the church, those who were unmarried when they took part in the communion of sacred orders, were required to remain so, but that those who were married, were not to put away their wives. Such was the advice of Paphnutius, although he was himself unmarried, and in accordance with it, the Synod concurred in his counsel, enacted no law about it, but left the matter to the decision of individual judgment, and not to compulsion. The Synod, however, enacted other laws regulating the government of the Church ; and these laws may easily be found, as they are in the possession of many individuals.

CHAP. XXIV. — CONCERNING MELITIUS ; THE EXCELLENT DIRECTIONS MADE BY THE HOLY COUNCIL IN HIS COMPLICATIONS.

AFTER an investigation had been made into the conduct of Melitius when in Egypt, the Synod sentenced him to reside in Lycus,[8] and to retain only the name of bishop ; and prohibited him from ordaining any one either in a city or a village. Those who had previously been ordained by him, were permitted by this law, to remain in communion and in the ministry, but were to be accounted secondary in point of dignity to the clergy in church and parish.[9] When by death an appointment became vacant, they were allowed to succeed to it, if deemed worthy, by the vote of the multitude, but in this case, were to be ordained by the bishop of the Church of Alexandria, for they were interdicted from exercising any power or influence in elections. This regulation appeared just to the Synod,

---

[1] Eus. V. C. iii. 14–24 ; Soc. i. 8, 9.
[2] Soc. i. 10, who derived it from Auxanon, a presbyter, who accompanied Acesius to Nice. Cf. i. 13.
[3] Eus. H. E. vi. 43–46.   [4] 1 John v. 16.
[5] Socrates' statement of the source of his information is passed over, as well as his criticism of prejudiced historians. The comment substituted by Soz. is, nevertheless, a partially correct interpretation.
[6] Soc. i. 11. Cf. the perverted text of the Canones Nicæni, in Ruf. H. E. i. 6.
[7] Soc. i. 11.
[8] Lycus (Lycopolis) is not named in the letter of the Synod, which says simply that he should reside in his own city. Soz. took the fact from Athan. Apol. cont. Arian. 71, where Melitius, in the brief to Alexander, calls himself bishop of Lycus. This is a proof of our historian's use of the same documents to amplify the statements of Socrates.
[9] Soc. i. 9, for text of the letter.

for Melitius[1] and his followers had manifested great rashness and temerity in administering ordination ; so that it also deprived the ordinations which differed from those of Peter of all consideration. He, when he conducted the Alexandrian Church, fled on account of the persecution then raging, but afterwards suffered martyrdom.

CHAP. XXV. — THE EMPEROR PREPARED A PUBLIC TABLE FOR THE SYNOD, AFTER INVITING ITS MEMBERS TO CONSTANTINOPLE, AND HONORING THEM WITH GIFTS. HE EXHORTED ALL TO BE OF ONE MIND, AND FORWARDED TO ALEXANDRIA AND EVERY OTHER PLACE THE DECREES OF THE HOLY SYNOD.

AT the very time that these decrees were passed by the council, the twentieth anniversary[2] of the reign of Constantine was celebrated ; for it was a Roman custom to have a feast on the tenth year of every reign. The emperor, there-fore, thought it to be opportune, and invited the Synod to the festival, and presented suitable gifts to them ; and when they prepared to return home, he called them all together, and exhorted them to be of one mind about the faith and at peace among themselves, so that no dissensions might henceforth creep in among them. After many other similar exhortations, he concluded by commanding them to be diligent in prayer, and always to supplicate God for himself, his children, and the empire, and after he had thus addressed those who had come to Nicæa, he bade them farewell. He wrote to the churches in every city, in order that he might make plain to those who had not been present, what had been rectified by the Synod ; and especially to the Church of Alexandria he wrote more than this ; urging them to lay aside all dissent, and to be harmonious in the faith issued by the Synod ; for this could be nothing else than the judgment of God, since it was established by the Holy Spirit from the concurrence of so many and such illustrious high priests, and approved after accurate inquiry and test of all the doubtful points.

[1] The best text reads Melitius, not Meletius, so Athanas. and Soc.; usually the books write Meletius and Meletians. We follow the reading.
[2] This feast, called Vicennalia, is mentioned in Eus. *V. C.* iii. 15, 16.

BOOK II.

WHEN the business at Nicæa had been transacted as above related, the priests returned home. The emperor rejoiced exceedingly at the restoration of unity of opinion in the Catholic Church, and desirous of expressing in behalf of himself, his children, and the empire, the gratitude towards God which the unanimity of the bishops inspired, he directed that a house of prayer should be erected to God at Jerusalem[1] near the place called Calvary. At the same time his mother Helena repaired to the city for the purpose of offering up prayer, and of visiting the sacred places. Her zeal for Christianity made her anxious to find the wood which had formed the adorable cross. But it was no easy matter to discover either this relic or the Lord's sepulchre; for the Pagans, who in former times had persecuted the Church,[2] and who, at the first promulgation of Christianity, had had recourse to every artifice to exterminate it, had concealed that spot under much heaped up earth, and elevated what before was quite depressed, as it looks now, and the more effectually to conceal them, had enclosed the entire place of the resurrection and Mount Calvary within a wall, and had, moreover, ornamented the whole locality, and paved it with stone. They also erected a temple to Aphrodite, and set up a little image, so that those who repaired thither to worship Christ would appear to bow the knee to Aphrodite, and that thus the true cause of offering worship in that place would, in course of time, be forgotten; and that as Christians would not dare fearlessly to frequent the place or to point it out to others, the temple and statue would come to be regarded as exclusively appertaining to the Pagans. At length, however, the place was discovered, and the fraud about it so zealously maintained was detected; some say that the facts were first disclosed by a Hebrew who dwelt in the East, and who derived his information from some documents which had come to him by paternal inheritance; but it seems more accordant with truth to suppose that God revealed the fact by means of signs and dreams; for I do not think that human information is requisite when God thinks it best to make manifest the same. When by command of the emperor the place was excavated deeply, the cave whence our Lord arose from the dead was discovered; and at no great distance, three crosses were found and another separate piece of wood, on which were inscribed in white letters in Hebrew, in Greek, and in Latin, the following words: "Jesus of Nazareth, the king of the Jews." These words, as the sacred book of the gospels relates, were placed by command of Pilate, governor of Judæa, over the head of Christ. There yet, however, remained a difficulty in distinguishing the Divine cross from the others; for the inscription had been wrenched from it and thrown aside, and the cross itself had been cast aside with the others, without any distinction, when the bodies of the crucified were taken down. For according to history, the soldiers found Jesus dead upon the cross, and they took him down, and gave him up to be buried; while, in order to accelerate the death of the two thieves, who were crucified on either hand, they broke their legs, and then took down the crosses, and flung them out of the way. It was no concern of theirs to deposit the crosses in their first order; for it was growing late, and as the men were dead, they did not think it worth while to remain to attend to the crosses. A more Divine information than could be furnished by man was therefore necessary in order to distinguish the Divine cross from the others, and this revelation was given in the following manner: There was a certain lady of rank in Jerusalem who was afflicted with a most grievous and incurable disease; Macarius, bishop of Jerusalem, accompanied by the mother of the emperor and her attendants, repaired to her bedside. After engaging in prayer, Macarius signified by signs to the spectators that the Divine cross would be the one which, on being brought in contact with the invalid, should remove the disease. He approached her in turn with each of the crosses;

---

[1] Eus. *V. C.* iii. 25-40; Soc. i. 9, Letter to Macarius, bishop of Jerusalem.
[2] Ruf. *H. E.* i. 7, 8; Soc. *H. E.* I. 17; Sulp. Sev. *H. S.* ii. 33, 34, another story of the identification. Soz. furnishes an additional story about the discovery, which he, however, confutes.

but when two of the crosses were laid on her, it seemed but folly and mockery to her for she was at the gates of death. When, however, the third cross was in like manner brought to her, she suddenly opened her eyes, regained her strength, and immediately sprang from her bed, well. It is said that a dead person was, in the same way, restored to life. The venerated wood having been thus identified, the greater portion of it was deposited in a silver case, in which it is still preserved in Jerusalem : but the empress sent part of it to her son Constantine, together with the nails by which the body of Christ had been fastened. Of these, it is related, the emperor had a head-piece and bit made for his horse, according to the prophecy of Zechariah, who referred to this period when he said, " that which shall be upon the bit of the horse shall be holy to the Lord Almighty." [1] These things, indeed, were formerly known to the sacred prophets, and predicted by them, and at length, when it seemed to God that they should be manifested, were confirmed by wonderful works. Nor does this appear so marvelous when it is remembered that, even among the Pagans, it was confessed that the Sibyl had predicted that thus it should be, —

" Oh most blessed tree, on which our Lord was hung." [2]

Our most zealous adversaries cannot deny the truth of this fact, and it is hence evident that a pre-manifestation was made of the wood of the cross, and of the adoration ($\sigma\acute{\epsilon}\beta\alpha\varsigma$) it received.

The above incidents we have related precisely as they were delivered to us by men of great accuracy, by whom the information was derived by succession from father to son ; and others have recorded the same events in writing for the benefit of posterity.

CHAP. II. — CONCERNING HELENA, THE MOTHER OF THE EMPEROR ; SHE VISITED JERUSALEM, BUILT TEMPLES IN THAT CITY, AND PERFORMED OTHER GODLY WORKS : HER DEATH.

ABOUT this period, the emperor, having determined upon erecting a temple in honor of God, charged the governors to see that the work was executed in the most magnificent and costly manner possible. His mother Helena also erected two temples, [3] the one at Bethlehem near the cave where Christ was born, the other on ridges of the Mount of Olives, whence He was taken up to heaven. Many other acts show her piety and religiousness, among which the following is not the least remarkable : During her residence at Jerusalem, it is related that she assembled the sacred virgins at a feast, ministered to them at supper, presented them with food, poured water on their hands, and performed other similar services customary to those who wait upon guests. When she visited the cities of the East, she bestowed befitting gifts on the churches in every town, enriched those individuals who had been deprived of their possessions, supplied ungrudgingly the necessities of the poor, and restored to liberty those who had been long imprisoned, or condemned to exile or the mines. It seems to me that so many holy actions demanded a recompense ; and indeed, even in this life, she was raised to the summit of magnificence and splendor ; she was proclaimed Augusta ; her image was stamped on golden coins, and she was invested by her son with authority over the imperial treasury to give it according to her judgment. Her death, too, was glorious ; for when, at the age of eighty, she quitted this life, she left her son and her descendants (like her of the race of Cæsar), masters of the Roman world. And if there be any advantage in such fame — forgetfulness did not conceal her though she was dead — the coming age has the pledge of her perpetual memory ; for two cities are named after her, the one in Bithynia, and the other in Palestine. [4] Such is the history of Helena.

CHAP. III. — TEMPLES BUILT BY CONSTANTINE THE GREAT ; THE CITY CALLED BY HIS NAME ; ITS FOUNDING ; THE BUILDINGS WITHIN IT ; THE TEMPLE OF MICHAEL THE ARCHSOLDIER, IN THE SOSTHENIUM, AND THE MIRACLES WHICH HAVE OCCURRED THERE.

THE emperor, [5] always intent on the advancement of religion, erected the most beautiful temples to God in every place, particularly in metropolises, such as Nicomedia in Bithynia, Antioch on the river Orontes, and Byzantium. He greatly improved this latter city, and constituted it the equal of Rome in power, and participation in the government ; for, when he had settled the affairs of the empire according to his own mind, and had rectified foreign affairs by wars and treaties, he resolved upon founding a city which should be called by his own name, and should be equal in celebrity to Rome. With this intention, he repaired to a plain at the foot of Troy, near the Hellespont, above the tomb of Ajax, where, it is said, the Achaians had their naval stations and tents while besieging Troy ; and here he laid the plan of a large and beautiful city, and built the gates on

---

[1] Zech. xiv. 20. (LXX.)   [2] Sib. Or. vi. 26.
[3] Eus. *V. C.* iii. 41, 47; Soc. i. 17.

[4] Helenopolis in Palestine not mentioned by Soc. i. 17, 18. Was the site of this city at the convent of Mt. Carmel or at St. Helena's towers, near the Scala Tyriorum? For the Bithynian city, cf. Procopius, *de Ædificiis* v. 2; cf. also Philost. ii. 12; Eus. *Chronicon* (Hieron.), under A.D. 331.
[5] Eus. *V. C.* iii. 50-58; iv. 58; Soc. i. 18; Zos. ii. 30-32.

an elevated spot of ground, whence they are still visible from the sea to those sailing by. But when he had advanced thus far, God appeared to him by night, and commanded him to seek another spot. Led by the hand of God, he arrived at Byzantium in Thrace, beyond Chalcedon in Bithynia, and here he was desired to build his city and to render it worthy of the name of Constantine. In obedience to the words of God, he therefore enlarged the city formerly called Byzantium, and surrounded it with high walls. He also erected magnificent dwelling houses southward through the regions. Since he was aware that the former population was insufficient for so great a city, he peopled it with men of rank and their households, whom he summoned hither from the elder Rome and from other countries. He imposed taxes to cover the expenses of building and adorning the city, and of supplying its inhabitants with food, and providing the city with all the other requisites. He adorned it sumptuously with a hippodrome, fountains, porticos, and other structures. He named it New Rome and Constantinople, and constituted it the imperial capital for all the inhabitants of the North, the South, the East, and the shores of the Mediterranean, from the cities on the Ister and from Epidamnus and the Ionian gulf, to Cyrene and that part of Libya called Borium.

He constructed another council house which they call senate ; he ordered the same honors and festal days as those customary to the other Romans, and he did not fail studiously to make the city which bore his name equal in every respect to that of Rome in Italy ; nor were his wishes thwarted ; for by the assistance of God, it had to be confessed as great in population and wealth. I know of no cause to account for this extraordinary aggrandizement, unless it be the piety of the builder and of the inhabitants, and their compassion and liberality towards the poor. The zeal they manifested for the Christian faith was so great that many of the Jewish inhabitants and most of the Greeks were converted. As this city became the capital of the empire during the period of religious prosperity, it was not polluted by altars, Grecian temples, nor sacrifices ; and although Julian authorized the introduction of idolatry for a short space of time, it soon afterwards became extinct. Constantine further honored this newly compacted city of Christ, named after himself, by adorning it with numerous and magnificent houses of prayer. And the Deity also co-operated with the spirit of the emperor, and by Divine manifestations persuaded men that these prayer houses in the city were holy and salvatory. According to the general opinion of foreigners and citizens, the most remarkable church was that built in a place formerly called Hestiæ. This place, which is now called Michælium, lies to the right of those who sail from Pontus to Constantinople, and is about thirty-five stadia distant from the latter city by water, but if you make the circuit of the bay, the journey between them is seventy stadia and upwards. This place obtained the name which now prevails, because it is believed that Michael, the Divine archangel, once appeared there. And I also affirm that this is true, because I myself received the greatest benefits, and the experience of really helpful deeds on the part of many others proves this to be so. For some who had fallen into fearful reverses or unavoidable dangers, others with disease and unknown sufferings, there prayed to God, and met with a change in their misfortunes. I should be prolix were I to give details of circumstance and person. But I cannot omit mentioning the case of Aquilinus, who is even at the present time residing with us, and who is an advocate in the same court of justice as that to which we belong.[1] I shall relate what I heard from him concerning this occurrence and what I saw. Being attacked with a severe fever, arising from a yellowish bile, the physicians gave him some foreign drug to drink. This he vomited, and, by the effort of vomiting, diffused the bile, which tinged his countenance with a yellow color. Hence he had to vomit all his food and drink. For a long time he remained in this state ; and since his nourishment would not be quiet in him, the skill of the physicians was at a loss for the suffering. Finding that he was already half dead, he commanded his servant to carry him to the house of prayer ; for he affirmed earnestly that there he would either die or be freed from his disease. While he was lying there, a Divine Power appeared to him by night, and commanded him to dip his foot in a confection made of honey, wine, and pepper. The man did so, and was freed from his complaint, although the prescription was contrary to the professional rules of the physicians, a confection of so very hot a nature being considered adverse to a bilious disorder. I have also heard that Probianus, one of the physicians of the palace, who was suffering greatly from a disease in the feet, likewise met with deliverance from sickness at this place, and was accounted worthy of being visited with a wonderful and Divine vision. He had formerly been attached to the Pagan superstitions, but afterwards became a Christian ; yet, while he admitted in one way or another the probability of the rest of our doctrines, he could not understand how, by the

---

[1] ἀγορεύοντι. This shows that Sozomen was an advocate in the law courts at the very time of his writing this history.

Divine cross, the salvation of all is effected. While his mind was in doubt on this subject, the symbol of the cross, which lay on the altar of this church, was pointed out to him in the Divine vision, and he heard a voice openly declaring, that, as Christ had been crucified on the cross, the necessities of the human race or of individuals, whatsoever they might be, could not be met by the ministration of Divine angels or of pious and good men; for that there was no power to rectify apart from the venerated cross. I have only recorded a few of the incidents which I know to have taken place in this temple, because there is not time to recount them all.

CHAP. IV. — WHAT CONSTANTINE THE GREAT EF-
FECTED ABOUT THE OAK IN MAMRE; HE ALSO
BUILT A TEMPLE.

I CONSIDER it necessary to detail the proceedings of Constantine in relation to what is called the oak of Mamre.[1] This place is now called Terebinthus, and is about fifteen stadia distant from Hebron, which lies to the south, but is two hundred and fifty stadia distant from Jerusalem. It is recorded that here the Son of God appeared to Abraham, with two angels, who had been sent against Sodom, and foretold the birth of his son. Here the inhabitants of the country and of the regions round Palestine, the Phœnicians, and the Arabians, assemble annually during the summer season to keep a brilliant feast; and many others, both buyers and sellers, resort thither on account of the fair. Indeed, this feast is diligently frequented by all nations: by the Jews, because they boast of their descent from the patriarch Abraham; by the Pagans, because angels there appeared to men; and by Christians, because He who for the salvation of mankind was born of a virgin, afterwards manifested Himself there to a godly man. This place was moreover honored fittingly with religious exercises. Here some prayed to the God of all; some called upon the angels, poured out wine, burnt incense, or offered an ox, or he-goat, a sheep, or a cock. Each one made some beautiful product of his labor, and after carefully husbanding it through the entire year, he offered it according to promise as provision for that feast, both for himself and his dependents. And either from honor to the place, or from fear of Divine wrath, they all abstained from coming near their wives, although during the feast these were more than ordinarily studious of their beauty and adornment. Nor, if they chanced to appear and to take part in the public processions, did they act at all licentiously. Nor did they behave imprudently in any other respect, although the tents were contiguous to each other, and they all lay promiscuously together. The place is open country, and arable, and without houses, with the exception of the buildings around Abraham's old oak and the well he prepared. No one during the time of the feast drew water from that well; for according to Pagan usage, some placed burning lamps near it; some poured out wine, or cast in cakes; and others, coins, myrrh, or incense. Hence, as I suppose, the water was rendered useless by commixture with the things cast into it. Once whilst these customs were being celebrated by the Pagans, after the aforesaid manner, and as was the established usage with hilarity, the mother-in-law[2] of Constantine was present for prayer, and apprised the emperor of what was being done. On receiving this information, he rebuked the bishops of Palestine in no measured terms, because they had neglected their duty, and had permitted a holy place to be defiled by impure libations and sacrifices; and he expressed his godly censure in an epistle which he wrote on the subject to Macarius, bishop of Jerusalem, to Eusebius Pamphilus, and to the bishops of Palestine. He commanded these bishops to hold a conference on this subject with the Phœnician bishops, and issue directions for the demolition, from the foundations, of the altar formerly erected there, the destruction of the carved images by fire, and the erection of a church worthy of so ancient and so holy a place. The emperor finally enjoined, that no libations or sacrifices should be offered on the spot, but that it should be exclusively devoted to the worship of God according to the law of the Church; and that if any attempt should be made to restore the former rites, the bishops were to inform against the delinquent, in order that he might be subjected to the greatest punishment. The governors and priests of Christ strictly enforced the injunctions contained in the emperor's letter.

CHAP. V. — CONSTANTINE DESTROYED THE PLACES
DEDICATED TO THE IDOLS, AND PERSUADED THE
PEOPLE TO PREFER CHRISTIANITY.

As many nations and cities throughout the whole realm of his subjects retained a feeling of fear and veneration towards their vain idols, which led them to disregard the doctrines of the Christians, and to have a care for their ancient customs, and the manners and feasts of their fathers, it appeared necessary to the emperor to teach the governors to suppress their superstitious rites of worship. He thought that this would be easily accomplished if he could get

---

[1] Eus. *V. C.* iii. 51–53; Soc. i. 18. As a native of Palestine, Soz. here adds local details.

[2] Eutropia, the mother of Fausta.

them to despise their temples and the images contained therein.[1] To carry this project into execution he did not require military aid; for Christian men belonging to the palace went from city to city bearing imperial letters. The people were induced to remain passive from the fear that, if they resisted these edicts, they, their children, and their wives, would be exposed to evil. The vergers and the priests, being unsupported by the multitude, brought out their most precious treasures, and the idols called διοπετῆ,[2] and through these servitors, the gifts were drawn forth from the shrines and the hidden recesses in the temples. The spots previously inaccessible, and known only to the priests, were made accessible to all who desired to enter. Such of the images as were constructed of precious material, and whatever else was valuable, were purified by fire, and became public property. The brazen images which were skillfully wrought were carried to the city, named after the emperor, and placed there as objects of embellishment, where they may still be seen in public places, as in the streets, the hippodrome, and the palaces. Amongst them was the statue of Apollo which was in the seat of the oracle of the Pytheness, and likewise the statues of the Muses from Helicon, the tripods from Delphos, and the much extolled Pan, which Pausanias the Lacedæmonian and the Grecian cities had devoted, — after the war against the Medes.

As to the temples, some were stripped of their doors, others of their roofs, and others were neglected, allowed to fall into ruin, or destroyed. The temple of Æsculapius in Ægis, a city of Cilicia, and that of Venus at Aphaca, near Mount Lebanon and the River Adonis, were then undermined and entirely destroyed. Both of these temples were most highly honored and reverenced by the ancients; as the Ægeatæ were wont to say, that those among them who were weakened in body were delivered from diseases because the demon manifested himself by night, and healed them. And at Aphaca, it was believed that on a certain prayer being uttered on a given day, a fire like a star descended from the top of Lebanon and sunk into the neighboring river; they affirmed that this was Urania, for they call Aphrodite by this name. The efforts of the emperor succeeded to the utmost of his anticipations; for on beholding the objects of their former reverence and fear boldly cast down and stuffed with straw and hay, the people were led to despise what they had previously venerated, and to blame the erroneous opinion of their ances-

tors. Others, envious at the honor in which Christians were held by the emperor, deemed it necessary to imitate the acts of the ruler; others devoted themselves to an examination of Christianity, and by means of signs, of dreams, or of conferences with bishops and monks, were convinced that it was better to become Christians. From this period, nations and citizens spontaneously renounced their former opinion. At that time a port of Gaza, called Majuma, wherein superstition and ancient ceremonies had been hitherto admired, turned unitedly with all its inhabitants to Christianity. The emperor, in order to reward their piety, deemed them worthy of the greatest honor, and distinguished the place as a city, a status it had not previously enjoyed, and named it Constantia: thus honoring the spot on account of its piety, by bestowing on it the name of the dearest of his children. On the same account, also, Constantine in Phœnicia is known to have received its name from the emperor. But it would not be convenient to record every instance of this kind, for many other cities about this time went over to religion, and spontaneously, without any command of the emperor, destroyed the adjacent temples and statues, and erected houses of prayer.

CHAP. VI. — THE REASON WHY UNDER CONSTANTINE, THE NAME OF CHRIST WAS SPREAD THROUGHOUT THE WHOLE WORLD.

THE church having been in this manner spread throughout the whole Roman world, religion was introduced even among the barbarians themselves.[3] The tribes on both sides of the Rhine were Christianized, as likewise the Celts and the Gauls who dwelt upon the most distant shores of the ocean; the Goths, too, and such tribes as were contiguous to them, who formerly dwelt on either of the high shores of the Danube, had long shared in the Christian faith, and had changed into a gentler and more rational observance. Almost all the barbarians had professed to hold the Christian doctrine in honor, from the time of the wars between the Romans and foreign tribes, under the government of Gallienus and the emperors who succeeded him. For when an unspeakable multitude of mixed nations passed over from Thrace into Asia and overran it, and when other barbarians from the various regions did the same things to the adjacent Romans, many priests of Christ who had been taken captive, dwelt among these tribes; and during their residence among them, healed the sick, and cleansed those who were possessed of demons, by the name of Christ only, and by

[1] Eus. V. C. iii. 54–58; iv. 38; Soc. i. 18; Zos. ii. 31.
[2] i.e. "sent down from Jupiter." Such were the Palladium of Troy, the Ancile at Rome, and "the image" of Diana, "which fell down from Jupiter," mentioned in Acts xix. 35.
[3] Irenæus adv. Hæres i. 3 (ed. Harvey); Philost. ii. 5, 6.

calling on the Son of God ; moreover they led [1] a blameless life, and excited envy by their virtues. The barbarians, amazed at the conduct and wonderful works of these men, thought that it would be prudent on their part, and pleasing to the Deity, if they should imitate those whom they saw were better ; and, like them, would render homage to God. When teachers as to what should be done, had been proposed to them, the people were taught and baptized, and subsequently were gathered into churches.

CHAP. VII. — HOW THE IBERIANS RECEIVED THE FAITH OF CHRIST.

It is said that during this reign the Iberians,[2] a large and warlike barbarian nation, confessed Christ.[3] They dwelt to the north beyond Armenia. A Christian woman, who had been taken captive, induced them to renounce the religion of their fathers. She was very faithful and godly, and did not, amongst foreigners, remit her accustomed routine of religious duty. To fast, to pray night and day, and to praise God, constituted her delight. The barbarians inquired as to the motives of her endurance : she simply answered, that it was necessary in this way to worship the Son of God ; but the name of Him who was to be worshiped, and the manner of worshiping, appeared strange to them. It happened that a boy of the country was taken ill, and his mother, according to the custom of the Iberians, took him around from house to house, in hope that some one might be found capable of curing the disease, and the change from the suffering might be easy for the afflicted. As no one capable of healing him could be found, the boy was brought to the captive, and she said, "as to medicines, I have neither experience nor knowledge, nor am I acquainted with the mode of applying ointments or plasters ; but, O woman, I believe that Christ whom I worship, the true and great God, will become the Saviour of thy child." Then she prayed for him immediately and freed him from the disease, although just before it was believed that he was about to die. A little while after, the wife of the governor of the nation was, by an incurable disease, brought nigh unto death ; yet she too was saved in the same manner. And thus did this captive teach the knowledge of Christ, by introducing Him as the dispenser of health, and as the Lord of life, of empire, and of all things. The governor's wife, convinced by her own personal experience, believed the words of the captive, embraced the Christian religion, and held the woman in much honor. The king, astonished at the celerity of the cure, and the miraculousness and healing of faith, learned the cause from his wife, and commanded that the captive should be rewarded with gifts. "Of gifts," said the queen, "her estimate is very low, whatever may be their value ; she makes much of the service she renders to her God only. Therefore if we wish to gratify her, or desire to do what is safe and right, let us also worship God, who is mighty and a Saviour, and who, at His will, gives continuance unto kings, casts down the high, renders the illustrious abject, and saves those in terrible straits." The queen continued to argue in this excellent manner, but the sovereign of Iberia remained in doubt and unconvinced, as he reflected on the novelty of the matters, and also respected the religion of his fathers. A little while after, he went into the woods with his attendants, on a hunting excursion ; all of a sudden thick clouds arose, and a heavy air was everywhere diffused by them, so as to conceal the heavens and the sun ; profound night and great darkness pervaded the wood. Since each of the hunters was alarmed for his own safety, they scattered in different directions. The king, while thus wandering alone, thought of Christ, as men are wont to do in times of danger. He determined that if he should be delivered from his present emergency, he would walk before God and worship Him. At the very instant that these thoughts were upon his mind, the darkness was dissipated, the air became serene, the rays of the sun penetrated into the wood, and the king went out in safety. He informed his wife of the event that had befallen him, sent for the captive, and commanded her to teach him in what way he ought to worship Christ. When she had given as much instruction as it was right for a woman to say and do, he called together his subjects and declared to them plainly the Divine mercies which had been vouchsafed to himself and to his wife, and although uninitiated, he declared to his people the doctrines of Christ. The whole nation was persuaded to embrace Christianity, the men being convinced by the representations of the king, and the women by those of the queen and the captive. And speedily with the general consent of the entire nation, they prepared most zealously to build a church. When the external walls were completed, machines were brought to raise up the columns, and fix them upon their pedestals. It is related, that when the first and second columns had been righted by these means, great difficulty was found in fixing the third column, neither art nor physical strength being of any

---

[1] πολιτείαν ἄμεμπτον ἐφιλοσόφουν. The Christian life, and especially the monastic, was regarded as the true philosophy.
[2] By the Iberians we are to understand, not the people of Spain (for they had a church among them as early as the time of Irenæus ; see adv. Hæres. i. 3, ed. Harvey), but the people of that name in Asia. Cf. Soç. i. 20, who says these Iberians migrated from Spain.
[3] Ruf. H. E. i. 10 ; Soc. i. 20 ; Soz. takes directly from Ruf.

avail, although many were present to assist in the pulling. When evening came on, the female captive remained alone on the spot, and she continued there throughout the night, interceding with God that the erection of the columns might be easily accomplished, especially as all the rest had taken their departure distressed at the failure ; for the column was only half raised, and remained standing, and one end of it was so embedded in its foundations that it was impossible to move it downward. It was God's will that by this, as well as by the preceding miracle, the Iberians should be still further confirmed about the Deity. Early in the morning, when they were present at the church, they beheld a wonderful spectacle, which seemed to them as a dream. The column, which on the day before had been immovable, now appeared erect, and elevated a small space above its proper base. All present were struck with admiration, and confessed, with one consent, that Christ alone is the true God. Whilst they were all looking on, the column slipped quietly and spontaneously, and was adjusted as by machinery on its base. The other columns were then erected with ease, and the Iberians completed the structure with greater alacrity. The church having been thus speedily built, the Iberians, at the recommendation of the captive, sent ambassadors to the Emperor Constantine, bearing proposals for alliance and treaties, and requesting that priests might be sent to their nation. On their arrival, the ambassadors related the events that had occurred, and how the whole nation with much care worshiped Christ. The emperor of the Romans was delighted with the embassy, and after acceding to every request that was proffered, dismissed the ambassadors. Thus did the Iberians receive the knowledge of Christ, and until this day they worship him carefully.

CHAP. VIII. — HOW THE ARMENIANS AND PERSIANS EMBRACED CHRISTIANITY.

SUBSEQUENTLY the Christian religion became known to the neighboring tribes and was very greatly disseminated.[1] The Armenians, I have understood, were the first to embrace Christianity.[2] It is said that Tiridates, then the sovereign of that nation, became a Christian by means of a marvelous Divine sign which was wrought in his own house ; and that he issued commands to all the subjects, by a herald, to adopt the

same religion.[3] I think that the beginning of the conversion of the Persians[4] was owing to their intercourse with the Osroenians and Armenians ; for it is likely that they would converse with such Divine men and make experience of their virtue.

CHAP. IX. — SAPOR KING OF PERSIA IS EXCITED AGAINST THE CHRISTIANS. SYMEON, BISHOP OF PERSIA, AND USTHAZANES, A EUNUCH, SUFFER THE AGONY OF MARTYRDOM.

WHEN, in course of time, the Christians increased in number, and began to form churches, and appointed priests and deacons, the Magi, who as a priestly tribe had from the beginning in successive generations acted as the guardians of the Persian religion, became deeply incensed against them.[5] The Jews, who through envy are in some way naturally opposed to the Christian religion, were likewise offended. They therefore brought accusations before Sapor, the reigning sovereign, against Symeon, who was then archbishop of Seleucia and Ctesiphon, royal cities of Persia, and charged him with being a friend of the Cæsar of the Romans, and with communicating the affairs of the Persians to him. Sapor believed these accusations, and at first, ground the Christians with excessive taxes, although he knew that the generality of them had voluntarily embraced poverty. He entrusted the exaction to cruel men, hoping that, by the want of necessaries, and the atrocity of the exactors, they might be compelled to abjure their religion ; for this was his aim. Afterwards, however, he commanded that the priests and conductors of the worship of God should be slain with the sword. The churches were demolished, their vessels were deposited in the treasury, and Symeon was arrested as a traitor to the kingdom and the religion of the Persians. Thus the Magi, with the co-operation of the Jews, quickly destroyed the houses of prayer. Symeon, on his apprehension, was bound with chains, and brought before the king. There the man evinced his excellence and courage ; for when Sapor commanded that he should be led away to the torture, he did not fear, and would not prostrate himself. The king, greatly exasperated, demanded why he did not prostrate himself as he had done formerly. Symeon replied, "Formerly I was not led away bound in order that I might abjure the truth of God, and there-

---

[1] This paragraph is regarded by Valesius as spurious.
[2] The source of this chapter certainly is not Moses Chorenensis. Tiridates III. reigned A.D. 286-342. At first a persecutor, through Gregory the Illuminator he became a Christian. Yet parts of Armenia were Christianized much earlier. Dionysius bishop of Alexandria wrote a letter on Repentance to the Armenians in the reign of Gallus. Eus. *H. E.* vi. 46. Cf. Agathangelas, History of Tiridates the Great, and the preaching of Gregory the Illuminator.

[3] Here follows in the Greek text a repetition, word for word, of the first two lines of this chapter, which seem to be superfluous, if we do not reject the paragraph above.
[4] Soz. is wrong in attributing the conversion of Persia to Armenia.
[5] The source for chaps. 9-14 must be some early translation of *Acta Persarum*, which the Syrians, especially those of Edessa, made; cf. chap. 14. Soz. is independent. The persecution began under Shapur II. A.D. 343.

fore I did not then object to pay the customary respect to royalty; but now it would not be proper for me to do so; for I stand here in defense of godliness and of our opinion." When he ceased speaking, the king commanded him to worship the sun, promising, as an inducement, to bestow gifts upon him, and to hold him in honor; but on the other hand, threatening, in case of non-compliance, to visit him and the whole body of Christians with destruction. When the king found that he neither frightened him by menaces, nor caused him to relax by promises, and that Symeon remained firm and refused to worship the sun, or to betray his religion, he commanded him to be put in bonds for a while, probably imagining that he would change his mind.

When Symeon was being conducted to prison, Usthazanes, an aged eunuch, the foster-father of Sapor and superintendent of the palace, who happened to be sitting at the gates of the palace, arose to do him reverence. Symeon reproachfully forbade him in a loud and haughty voice, averted his countenance, and passed by; for the eunuch had been formerly a Christian, but had recently yielded to authority, and had worshiped the sun. This conduct so affected the eunuch that he wept aloud, laid aside the white garment with which he was robed, and clothed himself, as a mourner, in black. He then seated himself in front of the palace, crying and groaning, and saying, "Woe is me! What must not await me since I have denied God; and on this account Symeon, formerly my familiar friend, does not think me worthy of being spoken to, but turns away and hastens from me." When Sapor heard of what had occurred, he called the eunuch to him, and inquired into the cause of his grief, and asked him whether any calamity had befallen his family. Usthazanes replied and said, "O king, nothing has occurred to my family; but I would rather have suffered any other affliction whatsoever than that which has befallen me, and it would have been easy to bear. Now I mourn because I am alive, and ought to have been dead long ago; yet I still see the sun which, not voluntarily, but to please thee, I professed to worship. Therefore, on both accounts, it is just that I should die, for I have been a betrayer of Christ, and a deceiver of thee." He then swore by the Maker of heaven and earth, that he would never swerve from his convictions. Sapor, astonished at the wonderful conversion of the eunuch, was still more enraged against the Christians, as if they had effected it by enchantments. Still, he spared the old man, and strove with all his strength, by alternate gentleness and harshness, to bring him over to his own sentiments. But finding that his efforts were useless, and that Usthazanes persisted in declaring that he would

never be so foolish as to worship the creature instead of the creator, he became inflamed with passion, and commanded that the eunuch's head should be struck off with a sword. When the executioners came forward to perform their office, Usthazanes requested them to wait a little, that he might communicate something to the king. He then called one of the most faithful eunuchs, and bade him say to Sapor, "From my youth until now I have been well affected, O king, to your house, and have ministered with fitting diligence to your father and yourself. I need no witnesses to corroborate my statements; these facts are well established. For all the matters wherein at divers times I have gladly served you, grant me this reward; let it not be imagined by those who are ignorant of the circumstances, that I have incurred this punishment by acts of unfaithfulness against the kingdom, or by the commission of any other crime; but let it be published and proclaimed abroad by a herald, that Usthazanes loses his head for no knavery that he has ever committed in the palaces, but for being a Christian, and for refusing to obey the king in denying his own God." The eunuch delivered this message, and Sapor, according to the request of Usthazanes, commanded a herald to make the desired proclamation; for the king imagined that others would be easily deterred from embracing Christianity, by reflecting that he who sacrificed his aged foster-father and esteemed household servant, would assuredly spare no other Christian. Usthazanes, however, believed that as by his timidity in consenting to worship the sun, he had caused many Christians to fear, so now, by the diligent proclamation of the cause of his sufferings, many might be edified by learning that he died for the sake of religion, and so became imitators of his fortitude.

CHAP. X. — CHRISTIANS SLAIN BY SAPOR IN PERSIA.

IN this manner the honorable life of Usthazanes was terminated, and when the intelligence was brought to Symeon in the prison, he offered thanksgiving to God on his account. The following day, which happened to be the sixth day of the week, and likewise the day on which, as immediately preceding the festival of the resurrection, the annual memorial of the passion of the Saviour is celebrated, the king issued orders for the decapitation of Symeon; for he had again been conducted to the palace from the prison, had reasoned most nobly with Sapor on points of doctrine, and had expressed a determination never to worship either the king or the sun. On the same day a hundred other prisoners were ordered to be slain. Symeon beheld their execution, and last of all he was put to death. Amongst these victims were bishops, presbyters, and other clergy of different grades. As they were being led out to execution, the chief of the Magi approached them, and asked them whether they would preserve their lives by conforming to the religion of the king and by worshiping the sun. As none of them would comply with this condition, they were conducted to the place of execution, and the executioners applied themselves to the task of slaying these martyrs. Symeon, standing by those who were to be slain, exhorted them to constancy, and reasoned concerning death, and the resurrection, and piety, and showed them from the sacred Scriptures that a death like theirs is true life; whereas to live, and through fear to deny God, is as truly death. He told them, too, that even if no one were to slay them, death would inevitably overtake them; for our death is a natural consequence of our birth. The things after those of this life are perpetual, and do not happen alike to all men; but as if measured by some rule, they must give an accurate account of the course of life here. Each one who did well, will receive immortal rewards and will escape the punishments of those who did the opposite. He likewise told them that the greatest and happiest of all good actions is to die for the cause of God. While Symeon was pursuing such themes, and like a household attendant, was exhorting them about the manner in which they were to go into the conflicts, each one listened and spiritedly went to the slaughter. After the executioner had despatched a hundred, Symeon himself was slain; and Abedechalaas and Anannias, two aged presbyters of his own church, who had been his fellow-prisoners, suffered with him.[1]

CHAP. XI. — PUSICES, SUPERINTENDENT OF THE ARTISANS OF SAPOR.

PUSICES, the superintendent of the king's artisans, was present at the execution; perceiving that Anannias trembled as the necessary preparations for his death were being made, he said to him, "O old man, close your eyes for a little while and be of good courage, for you will soon behold the light of Christ." No sooner had he uttered these words than he was arrested and conducted before the king; and as he frankly avowed himself a Christian, and spoke with great freedom to the king concerning his opinion and the martyrs, he was condemned to an extraordinary and most cruel death, because it was not lawful to address the king with such boldness. The executioners pierced the muscles of his neck in such a manner as to extract his tongue. On the charge of some persons, his

daughter, who had devoted herself to a life of holy virginity, was arraigned and executed at the same time. The following year, on the day on which the passion of Christ was commemorated, and when preparations were being made for the celebration of the festival commemorative of his resurrection from the dead, Sapor issued a most cruel edict throughout Persia, condemning to death all those who should confess themselves to be Christians. It is said that a greater number of Christians suffered by the sword; for the Magi sought diligently in the cities and villages for those who had concealed themselves; and many voluntarily surrendered themselves, lest they should appear, by their silence, to deny Christ. Of the Christians who were thus unsparingly sacrificed, many who were attached to the palace were slain, and amongst these was Azades,[2] a eunuch, who was especially beloved by the king. On hearing of his death, Sapor was overwhelmed with grief, and put a stop to the general slaughter of the Christians; and he directed that the teachers of religion should alone be slain.

CHAP. XII. — TARBULA, THE SISTER OF SYMEON, AND HER MARTYRDOM.

ABOUT the same period, the queen was attacked with a disease, and Tarbula, the sister of Symeon the bishop, a holy virgin, was arrested with her servant, who shared in the same mode of life, as likewise a sister of Tarbula, who, after the death of her husband, abjured marriage, and led a similar career. The cause of their arrest was the charge of the Jews, who reported that they had injured the queen by their enchantments, on account of their rage at the death of Symeon. As invalids easily give credit to the most repulsive representations, the queen believed the charge, and especially because it emanated from the Jews, since she had embraced their sentiments, and lived in the observance of the Jewish rites, for she had great confidence in their veracity and in their attachment to herself. The Magi having seized Tarbula and her companions, condemned them to death; and after having sawn them asunder, they fastened them up to poles and made the queen pass through the midst of the poles as a medium for turning away the disease. It is said that this Tarbula was beautiful and very stately in form, and that one of the Magi, having become deeply enamored with her, secretly sent a proposal for intercourse, and promised as a reward to save her and her companions if she would consent. But she would give no ear to

---

[1] The attempt to fix the date as Pagi, *Ap.* 21, 349, has no historical warrant; see Pagi, under 343 iii.

[2] Assemanus, *Bibl. Orient.* t. i. 189, speaks of Azades as the eunuch of Artascirus, ruler of Adiabene, who was a cousin of Sapor.

his licentiousness, and treated the Magi with scorn, and rebuked his lust. She would rather prefer courageously to die than to betray her virginity.

As it was ordained by the edict of Sapor, which we mentioned above, that the Christians should not be slaughtered indiscriminately, but that the priests and teachers of the opinions should be slain, the Magi and Arch-Magi traversed the whole country of Persia, studiously maltreating the bishops and presbyters. They sought them especially in the country of Adiabene, a part of the Persian dominions, because it was wholly Christianized.

CHAP. XIII. — MARTYRDOM OF ST. ACEPSIMAS AND OF HIS COMPANIONS.

ABOUT this period they arrested Acepsimas the bishop, and many of his clergy. After having taken counsel together, they satisfied themselves with the hunt after the leader only ; they dismissed the rest after they had taken away their property. James, however, who was one of the presbyters, voluntarily followed Acepsimas, obtained permission from the Magi to share his prison, and spiritedly ministered to the old man, lightened his misfortunes as far as he was able, and dressed his wounds ; for not long after his apprehension, the Magi had injuriously tortured him with raw thongs in forcing him to worship the sun ; and on his refusal to do so had retained him again in bonds. Two presbyters named Aithalas and James, and two deacons, by name Azadanes and Abdiesus, after being scourged most injuriously by the Magi, were compelled to live in prison, on account of their opinions. After a long time had elapsed, the great Arch-Magi communicated to the king the facts about them to be punished ; and having received permission to deal with them as he pleased, unless they would consent to worship the sun, he made known this decision of Sapor's to the prisoners. They replied openly, that they would never betray the cause of Christ nor worship the sun ; he tortured them unsparingly. Acepsimas persevered in the manly confession of his faith, till death put an end to his torments. Certain Armenians, whom the Persians retained as hostages, secretly carried away his body and buried it. The other prisoners, although not less scourged, lived as by a miracle, and as they would not change their judgment, were again put in bonds. Among these was Aithalas, who was stretched out while thus beaten, and his arms were torn out of his shoulders by the very great wrench ; and he carried his hands about as dead and swinging loosely, so that others had to convey food to his mouth. Under this rule, an innumerable

multitude of presbyters, deacons, monks, holy virgins, and others who served the churches and were set apart for its dogma, terminated their lives by martyrdom. The following are the names of the bishops, so far as I have been able to ascertain : Barbasymes, Paulus, Gaddiabes, Sabinus, Mareas, Mocius, John, Hormisdas, Papas, James, Romas, Maares, Agas, Bochres, Abdas, Abdiesus, John, Abramins, Agdelas, Sapores, Isaac, and Dausas. The latter had been made prisoner by the Persians, and brought from a place named Zabdæus.[1] He died about this time in defense of the dogma ; and Mareabdes, a chorepiscopus, and about two hundred and fifty of his clergy, who had also been captured by the Persians, suffered with him.

CHAP. XIV. — THE MARTYRDOM OF BISHOP MILLES AND HIS CONDUCT. SIXTEEN THOUSAND DISTINGUISHED MEN IN PERSIA SUFFER MARTYRDOM UNDER SAPOR, BESIDES OBSCURE INDIVIDUALS.

ABOUT this period Milles suffered martyrdom. He originally served the Persians in a military capacity, but afterwards abandoned that vocation, in order to embrace the apostolical mode of life. It is related that he was ordained bishop over a Persian city, and he underwent a variety of sufferings, and endured wounds and drawings ; and that, failing in his efforts to convert the inhabitants to Christianity, he uttered imprecations against the city, and departed. Not long after, some of the principal citizens offended the king, and an army with three hundred elephants was sent against them ; the city was utterly demolished and its land was ploughed and sown. Milles, taking with him only his wallet, in which was the holy Book of the Gospels, repaired to Jerusalem in prayer ; thence he proceeded to Egypt in order to see the monks. The extraordinary and admirable works which we have heard that he accomplished, are attested by the Syrians, who have written an account of his actions and life. For my own part, I think that I have said enough of him and of the other martyrs who suffered in Persia during the reign of Sapor ; for it would be difficult to relate in detail every circumstance respecting them, such as their names, their country, the mode of completing their martyrdom, and the species of torture to which they were subjected ; for they are innumerable, since such methods are jealously affected by the Persians, even to the extreme of cruelty. I shall briefly state that the number of men and women whose names have been ascertained, and who were martyred at this period, have been computed to be sixteen thousand ; while the multitude outside of these is beyond enumeration, and

---

[1] Am. Marcell. 20. 7, 1, Zabdiceni; 25. 7, 9, Zabdicena.

on this account to reckon off their names appeared difficult to the Persians and Syrians and to the inhabitants of Edessa, who have devoted much care to this matter.

CHAP. XV. — CONSTANTINE WRITES TO SAPOR TO STAY THE PERSECUTION OF THE CHRISTIANS.

CONSTANTINE the Roman emperor was angry, and bore it ill when he heard of the sufferings to which the Christians were exposed in Persia. He desired most anxiously to render them assistance, yet knew not in what way to effect this object. About this time some ambassadors from the Persian king arrived at his court, and after granting their requests and dismissing them, he thought it would be a favorable opportunity to address Sapor in behalf of the Christians in Persia, and wrote to him,[1] confessing that it would be a very great and forever indescribable favor, if he would be humane to those who admired the teaching of the Christians under him. "There is nothing in their religion," said he, " of a reprehensible nature ; by bloodless prayers alone do they offer supplication to God, for he delighteth not in the outpouring of blood, but taketh pleasure only in a pure soul devoted to virtue and to religion ; so that they who believe these things are worthy of commendation." The emperor then assured Sapor that God would be propitious to him if he treated the Christians with lenity, and adduced the example of Valerian and of himself in proof thereof. He had himself, by faith in Christ, and by the aid of Divine inclination, come forth from the shores of the Western ocean, and reduced to obedience the whole of the Roman world, and had terminated many wars against foreigners and usurpers ; and yet had never had recourse to sacrifices or divinations, but had for victory used only the symbol of the Cross at the head of his own armies, and prayer pure from blood and defilement. The reign of Valerian was prosperous so long as he refrained from persecuting the Church ; but he afterwards commenced a persecution against the Christians, and was delivered by Divine vengeance into the hands of the Persians, who took him prisoner and put him to a cruel death."

It was in this strain that Constantine wrote to Sapor, urging him to be well-disposed to this religion ; for the emperor extended his watchful care over all the Christians of every region, whether Roman or foreign.

CHAP. XVI. — EUSEBIUS AND THEOGNIS WHO AT THE COUNCIL OF NICE HAD ASSENTED TO THE WRITINGS OF ARIUS RESTORED TO THEIR OWN SEES.

NOT long after the council of Nice, Arius was recalled from exile ; but the prohibition to enter Alexandria was unrevoked. It shall be related in the proper place how he strove to obtain permission to return to Egypt. Not long after, Eusebius, bishop of Nicomedia, and Theognis, bishop of Nicæa, regained possession of their churches after expelling Amphion and Chrestos who had been ordained in their stead.[2] They owed their restoration to a document which they had presented to the bishops, containing a retractation : "Although we have been condemned without a trial by your piety, we deemed it right to remain silent concerning the judgment passed by your piety. But as it would be absurd to remain longer silent, when silence is regarded as a proof of the truth of the calumniators, we now declare to you that we too agree in this faith, and after a diligent examination of the thought in the word 'consubstantial,' we are wholly intent upon preserving peace, and that we never pursued any heresy. Having proposed for the safety of the churches such argument[3] as occurred to us, and having been fully convinced, and fully convincing those who ought to have been persuaded by us, we undersigned the creed ; but we did not subscribe to the anathema, not because we impugned the creed, but because we did not believe the accused to be what he was represented to us ; the letters we had received from him, and the arguments he had delivered in our presence, fully satisfying us that he was not such an one. Would that the holy Synod were convinced that we are not bent on opposing, but are accordant with the points accurately defined by you, and by this document, we do attest our assent thereto : and this is not because we are wearied of exile, but because we wish to avert all suspicion of heresy ; for if you will condescend to admit us now into your presence, you will find us in all points of the same sentiments as yourselves, and obedient to your decisions, and then it shall seem good to your piety to be merciful to him who was accused on these points and to have him recalled. If the party amenable to justice has been recalled and has defended himself from the charge made, it would be absurd, were we by our silence to con-

[1] The Embassy is spoken of in Eus. V. C. iv. 8; the letter of Constantine to Shapûr, iv. 9–13. But Soz. is mistaken about its date; for it was written before Sapor had commenced his persecution of the Christians. As usual, Soz. quotes briefly, and with no regard to the language and little to the thought. Theodoret, H. E. i. 25 (24), is accurate. For further relations of Constantine with Persia, cf. Eus. V. C. iv. 56, 57.

[2] Cf. Soc. i. 14. The variations of text are slight. Is the original from Sabinus' ἡ συναγωγὴ τῶν συνοδικῶν?
[3] The facts (as we learn from the Epistle of Eusebius of Cæsarea, which is given by Soc. i. 8, and Theodoret, H. E. i. 12) are as follows: The bishops, who demurred to the term ὁμοούσιον, as defined in the Nicene symbol, proposed another alleged older Antiochan form to the Synod. But the Nicene Fathers rejected it, and refused to depart from their own definition. Eusebius Pamphilus and his party then signed the Catholic and Orthodox creed, for fear of the emperor and other motives.

firm the reports that calumny had spread against us. We beseech you then, as befits your piety, dear to Christ, that you memorialize our emperor, most beloved of God, and that you hand over our petition, and that you counsel quickly, what is agreeable to you concerning us." It was by these means that Eusebius and Theognis, after their change of sentiment, were reinstated in their churches.

CHAP. XVII. — ON THE DEATH OF ALEXANDER, BISHOP OF ALEXANDRIA, AT HIS SUGGESTION, ATHANASIUS RECEIVES THE THRONE ; AND AN ACCOUNT OF HIS YOUTH ; HOW HE WAS A SELF-TAUGHT PRIEST, AND BELOVED BY ANTONY THE GREAT.

ABOUT this period[1] Alexander, bishop of Alexandria, when about to depart this life, left Athanasius as his successor, in accordance, I am convinced, with the Divine will directing the vote upon him. It is said that Athanasius at first sought to avoid the honor by flight, but that he, although unwilling, was afterwards constrained by Alexander to accept the bishopric. This is testified by Apolinarius, the Syrian,[2] in the following terms : " In all these matters much disturbance was excited by impiety, but its first effects were felt by the blessed teacher of this man, who was at hand as an assistant, and behaved as a son would to his father. Afterwards this holy man himself underwent the same experience, for when appointed to the episcopal succession he fled to escape the honor ; but he was discovered in his place of concealment by the help of God, who had forecast by Divine manifestations to his blessed predecessor, that the succession was to devolve upon him. For when Alexander was on the point of death, he called upon Athanasius, who was then absent. One who bore the same name, and who happened to be present, on hearing him call this way, answered him ; but to him Alexander was silent, since he was not summoning this man. Again he called, and as it often happens, the one present kept still, and so the absent one was disclosed. Moreover, the blessed Alexander prophetically exclaimed, 'O Athanasius, thou thinkest to escape, but thou wilt not escape'; meaning that Athanasius would be called to the conflict." Such is the account given by Apolinarius respecting Athanasius.

The Arians assert that after the death of Alexander, the respective followers of that bishop and of Melitius held communion together, and fifty-four bishops from Thebes, and other parts of Egypt, assembled together, and agreed by oath to choose by a common vote, the man who could advantageously administer the Church of Alexandria ; but that seven[3] of the bishops, in violation of their oath, and contrary to the opinion of all, secretly ordained Athanasius ; and that on this account many of the people and of the Egyptian clergy seceded from communion with him. For my part, I am convinced that it was by Divine appointment that Athanasius succeeded to the high-priesthood ; for he was eloquent and intelligent, and capable of opposing plots, and of such a man the times had the greatest need. He displayed great aptitude in the exercise of the ecclesiastical functions and fitness for the priesthood, and was, so to speak, from his earliest years, self-taught. It is said that the following incident occurred to him in his youth.[4] It was the custom of the Alexandrians to celebrate with great pomp an annual festival in honor of one of their bishops named Peter, who had suffered martyrdom. Alexander, who then conducted the church, engaged in the celebration of this festival, and after having completed the worship, he remained on the spot, awaiting the arrival of some guests whom he expected to breakfast. In the meantime he chanced to cast his eyes towards the sea, and perceived some children playing on the shore, and amusing themselves by imitating the bishop and the ceremonies of the Church. At first he considered the mimicry as innocent, and took pleasure in witnessing it ; but when they touched upon the unutterable, he was troubled, and communicated the matter to the chief of the clergy. The children were called together and questioned as to the game at which they were playing, and as to what they did and said when engaged in this amusement. At first they through fear denied ; but when Alexander threatened them with torture, they confessed that Athanasius was their bishop and leader, and that many children who had not been initiated had been baptized by him. Alexander carefully inquired what the priest of their play was in the habit of saying or doing, and what they answered or were taught. On finding that the exact routine of the Church had been accurately observed by them, he consulted the priests around him on the subject, and decided that it would be unnecessary to rebaptize those who, in their simplicity, had been judged worthy of the Divine grace. He therefore merely performed for them such offices as it is lawful only for those who are consecrated to initiating the mysteries. He then took Athanasius and the other children, who had playfully acted as pres-

---

[1] About five months after the council of Nicæa, according to a statement of Athan. *Apol. cont. Arian.* 59.
[2] This quotation is first made by Soz., and is found nowhere else.

[3] See the refutation of the calumny in Athan. *Apol. cont. Arian.* 6, where the acts of the vindicatory synod are given, 3 sqq. Cf. Philost. ii. 11, gives a different account from the Arian point of view; probably the whole story is from Sabinus.
[4] Ruf. *H. E.* i. 14. Cf. Soc. i. 15, who credits Ruf. with the story.

byters and deacons, to their own relations under God as a witness that they might be brought up for the Church, and for leadership in what they had imitated. Not long after, he took Athanasius as his table companion and secretary. He had been well educated, was versed in grammar and rhetoric, and already when he came to man's estate, and before he attained the bishopric, he gave proof to those conversing with him of his being a man of wisdom and intellectuality. But when,[1] on the death of Alexander, the succession devolved upon him, his reputation was greatly increased, and was sustained by his own private virtues and by the testimony of the monk, Antony the Great. This monk repaired to him when he requested his presence, visited the cities, accompanied him to the churches, and agreed with him in opinion concerning the Godhead. He evinced unlimited friendship towards him, and avoided the society of his enemies and opponents.

CHAP. XVIII. — THE ARIANS AND MELITIANS CONFER CELEBRITY ON ATHANASIUS ; CONCERNING EUSEBIUS, AND HIS REQUEST OF ATHANASIUS TO ADMIT ARIUS TO COMMUNION ; CONCERNING THE TERM " CONSUBSTANTIAL " ; EUSEBIUS PAMPHILUS AND EUSTATHIUS, BISHOP OF ANTIOCH, CREATE TUMULTS ABOVE ALL THE REST.

THE reputation of Athanasius was, however, especially increased by the Arians and Melitians ;[2] although always plotting, they never appeared rightly to catch and make him a prisoner. In the first place, Eusebius wrote to urge him to receive the Arians into communion, and threatened, without writing it, to ill-treat him should he refuse to do so. But as Athanasius would not yield to his representation, but maintained that those who had devised a heresy in innovating upon the truth, and who had been condemned by the council of Nice, ought not to be received into the Church, Eusebius contrived to interest the emperor in favor of Arius, and so procured his return. I shall state a little further on how all these events came to pass.[3]

At this period, the bishops had another tumultuous dispute among themselves, concerning the precise meaning of the term " consubstantial."[4] Some thought that this term could not be admitted without blasphemy ; that it implied the non-existence of the Son of God ; and that it involved the error of Montanus and Sabellius. Those, on the other hand, who defended the

term, regarded their opponents as Greeks (or pagans), and considered that their sentiments led to polytheism. Eusebius, surnamed Pamphilus, and Eustathius, bishop of Antioch, took the lead in this dispute. They both confessed the Son of God to exist hypostatically, and yet they contended together as if they had misunderstood each other. Eustathius accused Eusebius of altering the doctrines ratified by the council of Nicæa, while the latter declared that he approved of all the Nicæan doctrines, and reproached Eustathius for cleaving to the heresy of Sabellius.

CHAP. XIX. — SYNOD OF ANTIOCH ; UNJUST DEPOSITION OF EUSTATHIUS ; EUPHRONIUS RECEIVES THE THRONE ; CONSTANTINE THE GREAT WRITES TO THE SYNOD AND TO EUSEBIUS PAMPHILUS, WHO REFUSES THE BISHOPRIC OF ANTIOCH.

A SYNOD having been convened at Antioch, Eustathius was deprived of the church of that city.[5] It was most generally believed that he was deposed merely on account of his adherence to the faith of the council of Nicæa, and on account of his having accused Eusebius, Paulinus, bishop of Tyre, and Patrophilus, bishop of Scythopolis (whose sentiments were adopted by the Eastern priests), of favoring the heresy of Arius. The pretext resorted to for his deposition, however, was, that he had defiled the priesthood by unholy deeds. His deposition excited so great a sedition at Antioch, that the people were on the point of taking up arms, and the whole city was in a state of commotion. This greatly injured him in the opinion of the emperor ; for when he understood what had happened, and that the people of that church were divided into two parties, he was much enraged, and regarded him with suspicion as the author of the tumult. The emperor, however, sent an illustrious officer of his palace, invested with full authority, to calm the populace, and put an end to the disturbance, without having recourse to violence or injury.

Those who had deposed Eustathius, and who on this account were assembled in Antioch, imagining that their sentiments would be universally received, if they could succeed in placing óver the Church of Antioch one of their own opinion, who was known to the emperor, and held in repute for learning and eloquence, and that they could obtain the obedience of the rest, fixed their thoughts upon Eusebius Pamphilus for that see. They wrote to the emperor upon this subject, and stated that this course would be highly acceptable to the people. He had,

---

[1] From the *Life of Antony*, attributed to Athanasius, which Evagrius, a presbyter of Antioch, translated into Latin. Ruf. *H. E.* i. 8, *Hieron. de vir. illust.* 87, 88, 125.
[2] Source here is Soc. i. 23, but abridged.   [3] See chap. 22.
[4] Soc. again the source, but abridged; the matter is entirely the fruit of his own research, as Soc. states in this chapter (chap. i. 23). Cf. Eus. *V. C.* iii. 23.

[5] Eus. *V. C.* iii. 59–62; Soc. i. 24; Philost. ii. 7. Soz. has additional details, especially of names. Very likely, therefore, Soc. and Soz. have drawn from the same source.

in fact, been sought by all the clergy and laity who were inimical to Eustathius. Eusebius, however, wrote to the emperor refusing the dignity. The emperor approved of his refusal with praise; for there was an ecclesiastical law prohibiting the removal of a bishop from one bishopric to another. He wrote to the people and to Eusebius, adopting his judgment and calling him happy, because he was worthy to hold the bishopric not only of one single city, but of the world. The emperor also wrote to the people of the Church of Antioch concerning like-mindedness, and told them that they ought not to desire the bishops of other regions, even as they ought not to covet the possessions of others. In addition to these, he despatched another epistle to the Synod, in private session, and similarly commended Eusebius as in the letter to him for having refused the bishopric; and being convinced that Euphronius, a presbyter of Cappadocia, and George of Arethusa were men approved in creed, he commanded the bishops to decide for one or other of them, or for whomsoever might appear worthy of the honor, and to ordain a president for the Church of Antioch. On the receipt of these letters from the emperor, Euphronius was ordained; and I have heard that Eustathius bore this unjust calumny calmly, judging it to be better, as he was a man who, besides his virtues and excellent qualities, was justly admired on account of his fine eloquence, as is evidenced by his transmitted works, which are highly approved for their choice of words, flavor of expression, temperateness of sentiments, elegance and grace of narration.

CHAP. XX. — CONCERNING MAXIMUS, WHO SUCCEEDED MACARIUS IN THE SEE OF JERUSALEM.

ABOUT this time Mark,[1] who had succeeded Silvester, and who had held the episcopal sway during a short period, died, and Julius was raised to the see of Rome. Maximus succeeded Macarius in the bishopric of Jerusalem.[2] It is said that Macarius had ordained him bishop over the church of Diospolis, but that the members of the church of Jerusalem insisted upon his remaining among them. For since he was a confessor, and otherwise excellent, he was secretly chosen beforehand in the approbation of the people for their bishopric, after that Macarius should die. The dread of offending the people and exciting an insurrection led to the election of another bishop over Diospolis,

and Maximus remained in Jerusalem, and exercised the priestly functions conjointly with Macarius; and after the death of this latter, he governed that church. It is, however, well known to those who are accurately acquainted with these circumstances, that Macarius concurred with the people in their desire to retain Maximus; for it is said that he regretted the ordination of Maximus, and thought that he ought necessarily to have been reserved for his own succession on account of his holding right views concerning God and his confession, which had so endeared him to the people. He likewise feared that, at his death, the adherents of Eusebius and Patrophilus, who had embraced Arianism, would take that opportunity to place one of their own views in his see; for even while Macarius was living, they had attempted to introduce some innovations, but since they were to be separated from him, they on this account kept quiet.

CHAP. XXI. — THE MELITIANS AND THE ARIANS AGREE IN SENTIMENT; EUSEBIUS AND THEOGNIS ENDEAVOR TO INFLAME ANEW THE DISEASE OF ARIUS.

IN the meantime the contention which had been stirred in the beginning among the Egyptians, could not be quelled.[3] The Arian heresy had been positively condemned by the council of Nice, while the followers of Melitius had been admitted into communion under the stipulations above stated. When Alexander returned to Egypt, Melitius delivered up to him the churches whose government he had unlawfully usurped, and returned to Lycus. Not long after, finding his end approaching, he nominated John, one of his most intimate friends, as his successor, contrary to the decree of the Nicæan Council, and thus fresh cause of discord in the churches was produced. When the Arians perceived that the Melitians were introducing innovations, they also harassed the churches. For, as frequently occurs in similar disturbances, some applauded the opinion of Arius, while others contended that those who had been ordained by Melitius ought to govern the churches. These two bodies of sectarians had hitherto been opposed to each other, but on perceiving that the priests of the Catholic Church were followed by the multitude, they became jealous and formed an alliance together, and manifested a common enmity to the clergy of Alexandria. Their measures of attack and defense were so long carried on in concert, that in process of time the Melitians were generally called Arians in

---

[1] Marcus is not mentioned by Soc. or Theodoret, only by the Latins. The order is correct, whereas in i. 17 Julius is mistakenly made to do duty for Silvester.
[2] This whole chapter is from an unknown source, and shows familiarity with Palestinian history.

[3] This chapter is also unique with Soz., both as to the Melitians and Eusebius. The Melitian opposition is evident from Soc. i. 27.

Egypt, although they only dissent on questions of the presidency of the churches, while the Arians hold the same opinions concerning God as Arius. Although they individually denied one another's tenets, yet they dissimulated in contradiction of their own view, in order to attain an underhanded agreement in the fellowship of their enmity; at the same time each one expected to prevail easily in what he desired. From this period, however, the Melitians after the discussion on those topics, received the Arian doctrines, and held the same opinion as Arius concerning God. This revived the original controversy concerning Arius, and some of the laity and clergy seceded from communion with the others. The dispute concerning the doctrines of Arius was rekindled once more in other cities, and particularly in Bithynia and Hellespontus, and in the city of Constantinople. In short, it is said that Eusebius, bishop of Nicomedia, and Theognis, bishop of Nicæa, bribed the notary to whom the emperor had intrusted the custody of the documents of the Nicæan Council, effaced their signatures, and attempted openly to teach that the Son is not to be considered consubstantial with the Father. Eusebius was accused of these irregularities before the emperor, and he replied with great boldness as he showed part of his clothing. "If this robe," said he, "had been cut asunder in my presence, I could not affirm the fragments to be all of the same substance." The emperor was much grieved at these disputes, for he had believed that questions of this nature had been finally decided by the council of Nicæa, but contrary to his hopes he saw them again agitated. He more especially regretted that Eusebius and Theognis had received certain Alexandrians into communion,[1] although the Synod had recommended them to repent on account of their heterodox opinions, and although he had himself condemned them to banishment from their native land, as being the exciters of sedition.[2] It is asserted by some, that it was for the above reasons that the emperor in anger exiled Eusebius and Theognis; but as I have already stated, I have derived my information from those who are intimately acquainted with these matters.

CHAP. XXII. — THE VAIN MACHINATIONS OF THE ARIANS AND MELITIANS AGAINST ST. ATHANASIUS.

THE various calamities which befell Athanasius were primarily occasioned by Eusebius and Theognis.[3] As they possessed great freedom of speech and influence with the emperor, they strove for the recall of Arius, with whom they were on terms of concord and friendship, to Alexandria, and at the same time the expulsion from the Church of him who was opposed to them. They accused him before Constantine of being the author of all the seditions and troubles that agitated the Church, and of excluding those who were desirous of joining the Church; and alleged that unanimity would be restored were he alone to be removed. The accusations against him were substantiated by many bishops and clergy who were with John, and who sedulously obtained access to the emperor; they pretended to great orthodoxy, and imputed to Athanasius and the bishops of his party all the bloodshed, bonds, unjust blows, wounds, and conflagrations of churches. But when Athanasius demonstrated to the emperor the illegality of the ordination of John's adherents, their innovations of the decrees of the Nicæan Council, and the unsoundness of their faith, and the insults offered to those who held right opinions about God, Constantine was at a loss to know whom to believe. Since there were such mutual allegations, and many accusations were frequently stirred up by each party, and since he was earnestly anxious to restore the likemindedness of the people, he wrote to Athanasius that no one should be shut out. If this should be betrayed to the last, he would send regardless of consequences, one who should expel him from the city of Alexandria. If any one should desire to see this letter of the emperor's, he will here find the portion of it relating to this affair: "As you are now acquainted with my will, which is, that to all who desire to enter the Church you should offer an unhindered entrance. For should I hear that any who are willing to join the Church, have been debarred or hindered therefrom by you, I shall send at once an officer who shall remove you, according to my command, and shall transfer you to some other place." Athanasius, however, wrote to the emperor and convinced him that the Arians ought not to be received into communion by the Catholic Church; and Eusebius, perceiving that his schemes could never be carried into execution while Athanasius strove in opposition, determined to resort to any means in order to get rid of him. But as he could not find a sufficient pretext for effecting this design, he promised the Melitians to interest the emperor and those in power in their favor, if they would bring an accusation against Athanasius. Accordingly, came the first indictment that he had imposed upon the Egyptians a tax on linen

---

[1] Soz. has taken this from the Epistle of Constantine to the Nicomedians against Eusebius and Theognis. This is preserved by Theodoret, *H. E.* i. 20. Theodoret gives the full text; he and Soz. both obtained it from some such collection as that of Sabinus.

[2] Cf. Athan. *Apol. cont. Arian.* 7 (in the letter of the Alexandrian Synod).

[3] Athan. *Apol. cont. Arian.* 6; Soc. i. 27; Theod. *H. E.* i. 26, 27. Soz. works independently from the same sources.

tunics, and that such a tribute had been exacted from the accusers. Apis[1] and Macarius, presbyters of the Church of Athanasius, who then happened to be at court, clearly proved the persistent accusation to be false. On being summoned to answer for the offense, Athanasius was further accused of having conspired against the emperor, and of having sent, for this purpose, a casket of gold to one Philumen. The emperor detected the calumny of his accusers, sent Athanasius home, and wrote to the people of Alexandria to testify that their bishop possessed great moderation and a correct faith; that he had gladly met him, and recognized him to be a man of God; and that, as envy had been the sole cause of his indictment, he had appeared to better advantage than his accusers; and having heard that the Arian and Melitian sectarians had excited dissensions in Egypt, the emperor, in the same epistle, exhorted the multitude to look to God, to take heed unto his judgments, to be well disposed toward one another, to prosecute with all their might those who plotted against their like-mindedness; thus the emperor wrote to the people, exhorting them all to like-mindedness, and striving to prevent divisions in the Church.

CHAP. XXIII. — CALUMNY RESPECTING ST. ATHANASIUS AND THE HAND OF ARSENIUS.

THE Melitians, on the failure of their first attempt, secretly concocted other indictments against Athanasius.[2] On the one hand they charged him with breaking a sacred chalice, and on the other with having slain one Arsenius, and with having cut off his arm and retained it for magical purposes. It is said that this Arsenius was one of the clergy,[3] but that, having committed some crime, he fled to a place of concealment for fear of being convicted and punished by his bishop. The enemies of Athanasius devised the most serious attack for this occurrence. They sought Arsenius with great diligence, and found him; they showed him great kindness, promised to secure for him every good-will and safety, and conducted him secretly to Patrines,[4] a presbyter of a monastery, who was one of their confederates, and of the same interest as themselves. After having thus carefully concealed him, they diligently spread the report in the market-places and public assemblies that he had been slain by Athanasius. They also bribed John, a monk, to corroborate the accusation. As this evil report was universally circulated, and had even reached the ears of the emperor, Athanasius, being apprehensive that it would be difficult to defend his cause before judges whose minds were prejudiced by such false rumors, resorted to stratagems akin to those of his adversaries. He did everything in his power to prevent truth from being obscured by their attacks; but the multitude could not be convinced, on account of the non-appearance of Arsenius. Reflecting, therefore, that the suspicion which rested upon him could not be removed except by proving that Arsenius, who was said to be dead, was still alive, he sent a most trustworthy deacon in quest of him. The deacon went to Thebes, and ascertained from the declaration of some monks where he was living. And when he came to Patrines, with whom he had been concealed, he found that Arsenius was not there; for on the first intelligence of the arrival of the deacon he had been conveyed to Lower Egypt. The deacon arrested Patrines, and conducted him to Alexandria, as also Elias, one of his associates, who was said to have been the person who conveyed Arsenius elsewhere. He delivered them both to the commander of the Egyptian forces, and they confessed that Arsenius was still alive, that he had been secretly concealed in their house, and that he was now living in Egypt. Athanasius took care that all these facts should be reported to Constantine. The emperor wrote back to him, desiring him to attend to the due performance of the priestly functions, and the maintenance of order and piety among the people, and not to be disquieted by the machinations of the Melitians, it being evident that envy alone was the cause of the false indictments which were circulated against him and the disturbance in the churches. The emperor added that, for the future, he should not give place to such reports; and that, unless the calumniators preserved the peace, he should certainly subject them to the rigor of the state laws, and let justice have its course, as they had not only unjustly plotted against the innocent, but had also shamefully abused the good order and piety of the Church. Such was the strain of the emperor's letter to Athanasius; and he further commanded that it should be read aloud before the public, in order that they might all be made acquainted with his intentions. The Melitians were alarmed at these menaces, and became more quiet for a while, because they viewed with anxiety the threat of the ruler. The churches throughout Egypt enjoyed profound peace, and, directed by the presidency of this great priest, it daily increased in numbers by the conversion of multitudes of pagans and other heretics.

[1] Soc. i. 27, Alypius; Athan. *Apol. cont. Arian.* 60, where a part of the Epistle of the emperor Constantine is given, and in this Apis and Macarius are mentioned; here is an instance how Soz. corrects Soc.
[2] Athan. *Apol. cont. Arian.* 63; Ruf. *H. E.* i. 15-17; Soc. i. 27. Independent workers of the same and other material.
[3] He was bishop of the city of Hypselitæ, according to the caption of his letter to Athan. See *Apol. cont. Arian.* 69.
[4] Athan. calls him Pinnes, presbyter of a mansio (not monastery) of Ptemencyrceus. See his letter to John in the *Apol. cont. Arian.* 67. How did Soz. change this name to Patrines?

CHAP. XXIV. — SOME INDIAN NATIONS RECEIVED CHRISTIANITY AT THAT TIME THROUGH THE INSTRUMENTALITY OF TWO CAPTIVES, FRUMENTIUS AND EDESIUS.

WE have heard that about this period some of the most distant of the nations that we call Indians, to whom the preaching of Bartholomew was unknown, shared in our doctrine, through Frumentius,[1] who became a priest and teacher of the sacred learning among them. But in order that we may know, even by the marvel of what happened in India, that the doctrine of the Christians ought to be received as a system not from man, as it seems a tissue of miracles to some, it is necessary to relate the reason for the ordination of Frumentius. It was as follows: The most celebrated philosophers among the Greeks explored unknown cities and regions. Plato, the friend of Socrates, dwelt for a time among the Egyptians, in order to acquaint himself with their manners and customs. He likewise sailed to Sicily for the sight of its craters, whence, as from a fountain, spontaneously issued streams of fire, which frequently overflowing, rushed like a river and consumed the neighboring regions, so that even yet many fields appear burnt and cannot be sown or planted with trees, just as they narrate about the land of Sodom. These craters were likewise explored by Empedocles, a man highly celebrated for philosophy among the Greeks, and who has expounded his knowledge in heroic verse. He set out to investigate this fiery eruption, when either because he thought such a mode of death preferable to any other, or because, to speak more truthfully, he perhaps knew not wherefore he should seek to terminate his life in this manner, he leaped into the fire and perished. Democritus of Coös explored many cities and climates and nations, and he says concerning himself that eighty years of his life were spent in traveling through foreign lands. Besides these philosophers, thousands of wise men among the Greeks, ancient and modern, devoted themselves to this travel. In emulation, Meropius, a philosopher of Tyre in Phœnicia, journeyed as far as India. They say he was accompanied by two youths, named Frumentius and Edesius; they were his relatives; he conducted their rhetorical training, and educated them liberally. After exploring India as much as possible, he set out for home, and embarked in a vessel which was on the point of sailing for Egypt. It happened that, from want of water or some other necessary, the vessel was obliged to stop at some port, and the Indians rushed upon it and murdered all, Meropius in-

cluded. These Indians had just thrown off their alliance with the Romans; they took the boys as living captives, because they pitied their youth, and conducted them to their king. He appointed the younger one his cup-bearer; the older, Frumentius, he put over his house and made him administrator of his treasures; for he perceived that he was intelligent and very capable in business. These youths served the king usefully and faithfully during a long course of years, and when he felt his end approaching, his son and wife surviving, he rewarded the good-will of the servants with liberty, and permitted them to go where they pleased. They were anxious to return to Tyre, where their relatives resided; but the king's son being a minor, his mother besought them to remain for a little while and take charge of public affairs, until her son reached the years of manhood. They yielded to her entreaties, and directed the affairs of the kingdom and of the government of the Indies. Frumentius, by some Divine impulse, perhaps because God moved him spontaneously, inquired whether there were any Christians in India, or Romans among the merchants, who had sailed thither. Having succeeded in finding the objects of his inquiry, he summoned them into his presence, treated them with love and friendliness, and convened them for prayer, and the assembly was conducted after the Roman usage; and when he had built houses of prayer, he encouraged them to honor God continually.

When the king's son attained the age of manhood, Frumentius and Edesius besought him and the queen, and not without difficulty persuaded the rulers to be separated from themselves, and having parted as friends, they went back as Roman subjects. Edesius went to Tyre to see his relatives, and was soon after advanced to the dignity of presbyter. Frumentius, however, instead of returning to Phœnicia, repaired to Alexandria; for with him patriotism and filial piety were subordinate to religious zeal. He conferred with Athanasius, the head of the Alexandrian Church, described to him the state of affairs in India, and the necessity of appointing a bishop over the Christians located in that country. Athanasius assembled the endemic priests, and consulted with them on the subject; and he ordained Frumentius bishop of India, since he was peculiarly qualified and apt to do much service among those among whom he was the first to manifest the name of Christian, and the seed of the participation in the doctrine was sown.[2] Frumentius, therefore, returned to India, and, it is said, discharged the priestly functions so admirably that he became an object of uni-

---

[1] Ruf. i. 9, who gathered the facts from Edesius himself. Cf. Soc. i. 19. Soz. substitutes the scientific order of Plato, Empedocles, and Democritus for that of Metrodorus. The story is briefly reported by Theodoret, H. E. i. 23.

[2] Athan. Apol. ad Const. 29–31. Frumentius was called the Abba Salama of Αὐξούμις (Axum). Cf. Historia Ethiopica, Ludolf; Nic. Call. repeats this story of Rufinus in his H. E. i. 37, with which compare the narrative in xvii. 32.

versal admiration, and was revered as no less than an apostle. God highly honored him, enabling him to perform many wonderful cures, and to work signs and wonders. Such was the origin of the Indian priesthood.

CHAP. XXV. — COUNCIL OF TYRE ; ILLEGAL DEPOSITION OF ST. ATHANASIUS.

THE plots of the enemies of Athanasius involved him in fresh troubles, excited the hatred of the emperor against him, and stirred up a multitude of accusers. Wearied by their importunity, the emperor convened a council at Cæsarea in Palestine. Athanasius was summoned thither; but fearing the artifices of Eusebius, bishop of the city, of Eusebius, bishop of Nicomedia, and of their party, he refused to attend, and for thirty months, although pressed to attend, persisted in his refusal. At the end of that period, however, he was forced more urgently and repaired to Tyre, where a great number of the bishops of the East were assembled,[1] who commanded him to undergo the charges of those who accused him. Of John's party, Callinicus, a bishop, and a certain Ischurias, accused him of breaking a mystical chalice and of throwing down an episcopal chair; and of often causing Ischurias, although he was a presbyter, to be loaded with chains; and by falsely informing Hyginus, governor of Egypt, that he had cast stones at the statues of the emperor; of occasioning his being thrown into prison; of deposing Callinicus, bishop of the Catholic Church at Pelusium, and of saying that he would debar him from fellowship unless he could remove certain suspicions concerning his having broken a mystical chalice; of committing the Church of Pelusium to Mark, a deposed presbyter; and of placing Callinicus under a military guard, and of putting him under judicial tortures. Euplus, Pachomius, Isaac, Achillas,[2] and Hermæon, bishops of John's party, accused him of inflicting blows. They all concurred in maintaining that he obtained the episcopal dignity by means of the perjury of certain individuals, it having been decreed that no one should receive ordination, who could not clear himself of any crime laid to his charge. They further alleged, that having been deceived by him, they had separated themselves from communion with him, and that, so far from satisfying their scruples, he had treated them with violence and thrown them into prison.

Further, the affair of Arsenius was again agitated; and as generally happens in such a studiously concocted plot, many even of those considered his friends loomed up unexpectedly as accusers. A document was then read, containing popular complaints that the people of Alexandria could not continue their attendance at church on his account. Athanasius, having been urged to justify himself, presented himself repeatedly before the tribunal; successfully repelled some of the allegations, and requested delay for investigation as to the others. He was exceedingly perplexed when he reflected on the favor in which his accusers were held by his judges, on the number of witnesses belonging to the sects of Arius and Melitius who appeared against him, and on the indulgence that was manifested towards the informers, whose allegations had been overcome. And especially in the indictment concerning Arsenius, whose arm he was charged with having cut off for purposes of magic, and in the indictment concerning a certain woman to whom he was charged with having given gifts for uncleanness, and with having corrupted her by night, although she was unwilling. Both these indictments were proved to be ridiculous and full of false espionage. When this female made the deposition before the bishops, Timothy, a presbyter of Alexandria, who stood by Athanasius, approached her according to a plan he had secretly concerted, and said to her, " Did I then, O woman, violate your chastity? "[3] She replied, " But didst thou not? " and mentioned the place and the attendant circumstances, in which she had been forced. He likewise led Arsenius into the midst of them, showed both his hands to the judges, and requested them to make the accusers account for the arm which they had exhibited. For it happened that Arsenius, either driven by a Divine influence, or, as it is said, having been concealed by the plans of Athanasius, when the danger to that bishop on his account was announced, escaped by night, and arrived at Tyre the day before the trial. But these allegations having been thus summarily dismissed, so that no defense was necessary, no mention of the first was made in the transactions ; most probably, I think, because the whole affair was considered too indecorous and absurd for insertion. As to the second, the accusers strove to justify themselves by saying that a bishop under the jurisdiction of Athanasius, named Plusian,[4] had, at the command of his chief, burnt the house of Arsenius, fastened him to a column, and maltreated him with thongs, and then chained him in a cell. They further stated that Arsenius escaped from the

---

[1] Eus. V. C. iv. 41, 42; the letter in 42 has a late addition in Theodoret, H. E. i. 29 (27); Athan. Apol. cont. Arian. 8-12, 71-83; Ruf. H. E. i. 16, 17; Soc. i. 27-32.
[2] In the brief by Melitius, Achilles and Hermæon are given as bishops respectively of Cusæ and Cynus (Cynopolis) Athan. Apol. cont. Arian. 71.

[3] Ruf. H. E. i. 17.
[4] Mention is made of a bishop of this name in the Epistle of Arsenius to Athanasius, which is preserved in the Apol. cont. Arian. 69.

cell through a window, and while he was sought for remained a while in concealment; that as he did not appear, they naturally supposed him to be dead; that the reputation he had acquired as a man and confessor, had endeared him to the bishops of John's party; and that they sought for him, and applied on his behalf to the magistrates.

Athanasius was filled with apprehension when he reflected on these subjects, and began to suspect that his enemies were secretly scheming to effect his ruin. After several sessions, when the Synod was filled with tumult and confusion, and the accusers and a multitude of persons around the tribunal were crying aloud that Athanasius ought to be deposed as a sorcerer and a ruffian, and as being utterly unworthy the priesthood, the officers, who had been appointed by the emperor to be present at the Synod for the maintenance of order, compelled the accused to quit the judgment hall secretly; for they feared lest they might become his murderers, as is apt to be the case in the rush of a tumult. On finding that he could not remain in Tyre without peril of his life, and that there was no hope of obtaining justice against his numerous accusers, from judges who were inimical to him, he fled to Constantinople. The Synod condemned him during his absence, deposed him from the bishopric, and prohibited his residing at Alexandria, lest, said they, he should excite disturbances and seditions. John and all his adherents were restored to communion, as if they had been unjustly suffering wrongs, and each was reinstated in his own clerical rank. The bishops then gave an account of their proceedings to the emperor, and wrote to the bishops of all regions, enjoining them not to receive Athanasius into fellowship, and not to write to him or receive letters from him, as one who had been convicted of the crimes which they had investigated, and on account of his flight, as also guilty in those indictments which had not been tried. They likewise declared, in this epistle, that they had been obliged to pass such condemnation upon him, because, when commanded by the emperor the preceding year to repair to the bishops of the East, who were assembled at Cæsarea, he disobeyed the injunction, kept the bishops waiting for him, and set at naught the commands of the ruler. They also deposed that when the bishops had assembled at Tyre, he went to that city, attended by a large retinue, for the purpose of exciting disturbances and tumults in the Synod; that when there, he sometimes refused to reply to the charges preferred against him; sometimes insulted the bishops individually; when summoned by them, sometimes not obeying, at others not deigning to be judged. They specified in the same

letter, that he was manifestly guilty of having broken a mystical chalice, and that this fact was attested by Theognis, bishop of Nicæa; by Maris, bishop of Chalcedonia; by Theodore, bishop of Heraclea; by Valentinus and Ursacius; and by Macedonius, who had been sent to the village in Egypt, where the chalice was said to have been broken, in order to ascertain the truth. Thus did the bishops detail successively each of the allegations against Athanasius, with the same art to which sophists resort when they desire to heighten the effect of their calumnies. Many of the priests, however, who were present at the trial, perceived the injustice of the accusation. It is related that Paphnutius, the confessor,[1] who was present at the Synod, arose, and took the hand of Maximus, the bishop of Jerusalem, to lead him away, as if those who were confessors, and had their eyes dug out for the sake of piety, ought not to participate in an assembly of wicked men.

CHAP. XXVI. — ERECTION OF A TEMPLE BY CONSTANTINE THE GREAT AT GOLGOTHA, IN JERUSALEM; ITS DEDICATION.

THE temple,[2] called the "Great Martyrium," which was built in the place of the skull at Jerusalem, was completed about the thirtieth year[3] of the reign of Constantine; and Marianus, an official, who was a short-hand writer of the emperor, came to Tyre and delivered a letter from the emperor to the council, commanding them to repair quickly to Jerusalem, in order to consecrate the temple. Although this had been previously determined upon, yet the emperor deemed it necessary that the disputes which prevailed among the bishops who had been convened at Tyre should be first adjusted, and that they should be purged of all discord and grief before going to the consecration of the temple. For it is fitting to such a festival for the priests to be like-minded. When the bishops arrived at Jerusalem, the temple was therefore consecrated, as likewise numerous ornaments and gifts, which were sent by the emperor and are still preserved in the sacred edifice; their costliness and magnificence is such that they cannot be looked upon without exciting wonder. Since that period the anniversary of the consecration has been celebrated with great pomp by the church of Jerusalem;[4] the festival continues eight days, initiation by baptism is administered, and people from every

---

[1] This is in Ruf. H. E. i. 17. He also signs the first letter of the Egyptian bishops at Tyre to Dionysius; Athan. Apol. cont. Arian. 79; he presumably subscribed to the second. Ibid.
[2] Eus. V. C. iv. 43–47; Athan. Apol. cont. Arian. 84; Soc. i. 33. Cf. Theodoret, H. E. i. 31 (29). Soz.'s account is better than that of either Soc. or Theodoret.
[3] A.D. 335.   [4] Sept. 13.

region under the sun resort to Jerusalem during this festival, and visit the sacred places.

CHAP. XXVII. — CONCERNING THE PRESBYTER BY WHOM CONSTANTINE WAS PERSUADED TO RECALL ARIUS AND EUZOIUS FROM EXILE; THE TRACTATE CONCERNING HIS POSSIBLY PIOUS FAITH, AND HOW ARIUS WAS AGAIN RECEIVED BY THE SYNOD ASSEMBLED AT JERUSALEM.

THE bishops who had embraced the sentiments of Arius found a favorable opportunity of restoring him and Euzoius to communion, by zealously striving to have a council in the city of Jerusalem. They effected their design in the following manner [1] : —

A certain presbyter who was a great admirer of the Arian doctrines, was on terms of intimacy with the emperor's sister. At first he concealed his sentiments; but as he frequently visited and became by degrees more familiar with Constantia, for such was the name of the sister of Constantine, he took courage to represent to her that Arius was unjustly exiled from his country, and cast out from the Church, through the jealousy and personal enmity of Alexander, bishop of the Alexandrian Church. He said that his jealousy had been excited by the esteem which the people manifested towards Arius.

Constantia believed these representations to be true, yet took no steps in her lifetime to innovate upon the decrees of Nicæa. Being attacked with a disease which threatened to terminate in death, she besought her brother, who went to visit her, to grant what she was about to ask, as a last favor; this request was, to receive the above mentioned presbyter on terms of intimacy, and to rely upon him as a man who had correct opinions about the Divinity. "For my part," she added, "I am drawing nigh to death, and am no longer interested in the concerns of this life; the only apprehension I now feel, arises from dread lest you should incur the wrath of God and suffer any calamity, or the loss of your empire, since you have been induced to condemn just and good men wrongfully to perpetual banishment." From that period the emperor received the presbyter into favor, and after permitting him to speak freely with him and to commune on the same topics concerning which his sister had given her command, deemed it necessary to subject the case of Arius to a fresh examination; it is probable that, in forming this decision, the emperor was either influenced by a belief in the credibility of the attacks, or by the desire of gratifying his sister. It was not long before he recalled Arius from exile,[2] and demanded of him a written exposition of his faith concerning the Godhead. Arius avoided making use of the new terms which he had previously devised, and constructed another exposition by using simple terms, and such as were recognized by the sacred Scriptures; he declared upon oath, that he held the doctrines set forth in this exposition, that he both felt these statements *ex animo* and had no other thought than these. It was as follows:[3] "Arius and Euzoius, presbyters, to Constantine, our most pious emperor and most beloved of God.

"According as your piety, beloved of God, commanded, O sovereign emperor, we here furnish a written statement of our own faith, and we protest before God that we, and all those who are with us, believe what is here set forth.

"We believe in one God, the Father Almighty, and in His Son the Lord Jesus Christ, who was begotten from Him before all ages, God the Word, by whom all things were made, whether things in heaven or things on earth; He came and took upon Him flesh, suffered and rose again, and ascended into heaven, whence He will again come to judge the quick and the dead.

"We believe in the Holy Ghost, in the resurrection of the body, in the life to come, in the kingdom of heaven, and in one Catholic Church of God, established throughout the earth. We have received this faith from the Holy Gospels, in which the Lord says to His disciples, 'Go forth and teach all nations, baptizing them in the name of the Father, and of the Son, and of the Holy Ghost.' If we do not so believe this, and if we do not truly receive the doctrines concerning the Father, the Son, and the Holy Ghost, as they are taught by the whole Catholic Church and by the sacred Scriptures, as we believe in every point, let God be our judge, both now and in the day which is to come. Wherefore we appeal to your piety, O our emperor most beloved of God, that, as we are enrolled among the members of the clergy, and as we hold the faith and thought of the Church and of the sacred Scriptures, we may be openly reconciled to our mother, the Church, through your peacemaking and pious piety; so that useless questions and disputes may be cast aside, and that we and the Church may dwell together in peace, and we all in common may offer the customary prayer for your peaceful and pious empire and for your entire family."

Many considered this declaration of faith as an artful compilation, and as bearing the appearance of difference in expression, while, in reality, it supported the doctrine of Arius; the terms in which it was couched being so vague

---

[1] Ruf. *H. E.* i. 11; Soc. i. 25, 26, 33.
[2] This letter of the emperor is in Soc. i. 25.

[3] Soc. i. 26, verbal variations. Both probably from Sabinus.

that it was susceptible of diverse interpretations. The emperor imagined that Arius and Euzoius were of the same sentiments as the bishops of the council of Nicæa, and was delighted over the affair. He did not, however, attempt to restore them to communion without the judgment and approval of those who are, by the law of the Church, masters in these matters. He, therefore, sends them to the bishops who were then assembled at Jerusalem, and wrote, desiring them to examine the declaration of faith submitted by Arius and Euzoius, and so to influence the Synod that, whether they found that their doctrine was orthodox, and that the jealousy of their enemies had been the sole cause of their condemnation, or that, without having reason to blame those who had condemned them, they had changed their minds, a humane decision might, in either case, be accorded them. Those who had long been zealous for this, seized the opportunity under cover of the emperor's letter, and received him into fellowship. They wrote immediately to the emperor himself, to the Church of Alexandria, and to the bishops and clergy of Egypt, of Thebes, and of Libya, earnestly exhorting them to receive Arius and Euzoius into communion, since the emperor bore witness to the correctness of their faith, in one of his own epistles, and since the judgment of the emperor had been confirmed by the vote of the Synod.[1]

These were the subjects which were zealously discussed by the Synod of Jerusalem.

CHAP. XXVIII. — LETTER FROM THE EMPEROR CONSTANTINE TO THE SYNOD OF TYRE, AND EXILE OF ST. ATHANASIUS THROUGH THE MACHINATION OF THE ARIAN FACTION.

ATHANASIUS, after having fled from Tyre, repaired[2] to Constantinople, and on coming to the emperor Constantine, complained of what he had suffered, in presence of the bishops who had condemned him, and besought him to permit the decrees of the council of Tyre to be submitted for examination before the emperor. Constantine regarded this request as reasonable, and wrote in the following terms to the bishops assembled at Tyre : —

" I know not what has been enacted in confusion and vehemence by your Synod ; but it appears that, from some disturbing disorder, decrees which are not in conformity with truth have been enacted, and that your constant irritation of one another evidently prevented you from considering what is pleasing to God. But it will be the work of Divine Providence to scatter the evils which have been drawn out of this contentiousness, and to manifest to us clearly whether you have not been misled in your judgment by motives of private friendship or aversion. I therefore command that you all come here to my piety without delay, in order that we may receive an exact account of your transactions. I will explain to you the cause of my writing to you in this strain, and you will know from what follows, why I summon you before myself through this document. As I was returning on horseback to that city which bears my name, and which I regard as my much prospered country, Athanasius, the bishop, presented himself so unexpectedly in the middle of the highway, with certain individuals who accompanied him, that I felt exceedingly surprised at beholding him. God, who sees all things, is my witness, that at first I did not know who he was, but that some of my attendants having ascertained this point, and the injustice which he had suffered, gave me the necessary information. I did not on this occasion grant him an interview. He, however, persevered in requesting an audience ; and although I refused him, and was on the point of commanding that he should be removed from my presence, he told me with more boldness, that he sought no other favor of me than that I should summon you hither, in order that he might in your presence complain of what he had suffered unnecessarily. As this request appears reasonable and timely, I deemed it right to address you in this strain, and to command all of you who were convened at the Synod of Tyre to hasten to the court of our clemency, so that you may demonstrate by your works, the purity and inflexibility of your decisions before me, whom you cannot refuse to acknowledge as a genuine servant of God. By my zeal in His service, peace has been established throughout the world, and the name of God is genuinely praised among the barbarians, who till now were in ignorance of the truth ; and it is evident that whoever is ignorant of the truth knows not God. Notwithstanding, as is above stated, the barbarians have, through my instrumentality, learnt to know genuinely and to worship God ; for they perceived that everywhere, and on all occasions, his protection rested on me ; and they reverence God the more deeply because they fear my power. But we who have to announce the mysteries of forbearance (for I will not say that we keep them), we, I say, ought not to do anything that can tend to dissension or hatred, or, to speak plainly, to the destruction of the human race. Come, then, to us, as I have said, with all diligence, and be assured that I shall do everything in my power to preserve all the particularly infallible parts of the law of God in a way that no fault or heterodoxy can be fabri-

[1] Ruf. *H. E*, i. 11; Soc. i. 33. For the letter of the Synod, cf. Athan. *de Synodis*, 21; a part is also given in *Apol. cont. Arian.* 84.
[2] This letter is given in Athan. *Apol. cont. Arian.* 86; Soc. i. 33-35.

cated; while those enemies of the law who, under the guise of the Holy Name, endeavor to introduce variant and differing blasphemies, have been openly scattered, utterly crushed, and wholly suppressed."

This letter of the emperor so excited the fears of some of the bishops that they set off on their journey homewards. But Eusebius, bishop of Nicomedia, and his partisans, went to the emperor, and represented that the Synod of Tyre had enacted no decrees against Athanasius but what were founded on justice. They brought forward as witnesses Theognis, Maris, Theodore, Valens, and Ursacius, and deposed that he had broken the mystical cup, and after uttering many other calumnies, they prevailed with their accusations. The emperor, either believing their statements to be true, or imagining that unanimity would be restored among the bishops if Athanasius were removed, exiled him to Treves, in Western Gaul; and thither, therefore, he was conducted.

CHAP. XXIX. — ALEXANDER, BISHOP OF CONSTANTINOPLE; HIS REFUSAL TO RECEIVE ARIUS INTO COMMUNION; ARIUS IS BURST ASUNDER WHILE SEEKING NATURAL RELIEF.

AFTER the Synod of Jerusalem, Arius went to Egypt,[1] but as he could not obtain permission to hold communion with the Church of Alexandria, he returned to Constantinople. As all those who had embraced his sentiments, and those who were attached to Eusebius, bishop of Nicomedia, had assembled cunningly in that city for the purpose of holding a council, Alexander, who was then ordering the see of Constantinople, used every effort to dissolve the council. But as his endeavors were frustrated, he openly refused all covenant with Arius, affirming that it was neither just nor according to ecclesiastical canons, to make powerless their own vote, and that of those bishops who had been assembled at Nicæa, from nearly every region under the sun. When the partisans of Eusebius perceived that their arguments produced no effect on Alexander, they had recourse to contumely, and threatened that unless he would receive Arius into communion on a stated day, he should be expelled from the church, and that another should be elected in his place who would be willing to hold communion with Arius. They then separated, the partisans of Eusebius, to await the time they had fixed for carrying their menaces into execution, and Alexander to pray that the words of Eusebius might be prevented from being carried into deed. His chief source of fear arose from the fact that the emperor had been persuaded to give way. On the day before the appointed day he prostrated himself before the altar, and continued all the night in prayer to God, that his enemies might be prevented from carrying their schemes into execution against him. Late in the afternoon, Arius, being seized suddenly with pain in the stomach, was compelled to repair to the public place set apart for emergencies of this nature. As some time passed away without his coming out, some persons, who were waiting for him outside, entered, and found him dead and still sitting upon the seat. When his death became known, all people did not view the occurrence under the same aspect. Some believed that he died at that very hour, seized by a sudden disease of the heart, or suffering weakness from his joy over the fact that his matters were falling out according to his mind; others imagined that this mode of death was inflicted on him in judgment, on account of his impiety. Those who held his sentiments were of opinion that his death was brought about by magical arts. It will not be out of place to quote what Athanasius, bishop of Alexandria, stated on the subject. The following is his narrative: —

CHAP. XXX. — ACCOUNT GIVEN BY THE GREAT ATHANASIUS OF THE DEATH OF ARIUS.

"ARIUS,[2] the author of the heresy and the associate of Eusebius, having been summoned before the most blessed Constantine Augustus, at the solicitation of the partisans of Eusebius, was desired to give in writing an exposition of his faith. He drew up this document with great artfulness, and like the devil, concealed his impious assertions beneath the simple words of Scripture. The most blessed Constantine said to him, 'If you have no other points in mind than these, render testimony to the truth; for if you perjure yourself, the Lord will punish you'; and the wretched man swore that he neither held nor conceived any sentiments except those now specified in the document, even if he had ever affirmed otherwise; soon after he went out, and judgment was visited upon him; for he bent forwards and burst in the middle. With all men the common end of life is death. We must not blame a man, even if he be an enemy, merely because he died, for it is uncertain whether we shall live to the evening. But the end of Arius was so singular that it seems worthy of some remark. The partisans of Eusebius threatened to reinstate

---

[1] Ruf. *H. E.* i. 12, 13; Soc. i. 37, 38; Athan. *Ep. ad Serapion*, and *ad Episcop. Ægypt. et Lib.* 19. Soz. follows Athan. and Ruf. Athan. says he derived his statements from Macarius, a presbyter, an eye-witness of some of the events narrated in this chapter and the next.

[2] Cf. Athan. *Ep. ad Episc. Ægypt. et Lib.* 18, 19; cf. Athan. *Ep. ad Serapion*, which treats of the death of Arius.

him in the church, and Alexander, bishop of Constantinople, opposed their intention; Arius placed his confidence in the power and menaces of Eusebius; for it was the Sabbath, and he expected the next day to be readmitted. The dispute ran high; the partisans of Eusebius were loud in their menaces, while Alexander had recourse to prayer. The Lord was the judge, and declared himself against the unjust. A little before sunset Arius was compelled by a want of nature to enter the place appointed for such emergencies, and here he lost at once both restoration to communion and his life. The most blessed Constantine was amazed when he heard of this occurrence, and regarded it as the proof of perjury. It then became evident to every one that the menaces of Eusebius were absolutely futile, and that the expectations of Arius were vain. It also became manifest that the Arian madness could not be fellowshipped by the Saviour both here and in the church of the Firstborn. Is it not then astonishing that some are still found who seek to exculpate him whom the Lord condemned, and to defend that heresy which the Lord proved to be unworthy of fellowship, by not permitting its author to enter the church? We have been duly informed that this was the mode of the death of Arius." It is said that for a long period subsequently no one would make use of the seat on which he died. Those who were compelled by necessities of nature, as is wont to be the case in a crowd, to visit the public place, when they entered, spoke to one another to avoid the seat, and the place was shunned afterwards, because Arius had there received the punishment of his impiety. At a later time a certain rich and powerful man, who had embraced the Arian tenets, bought the place of the public, and built a house on the spot, in order that the occurrence might fall into oblivion, and that there might be no perpetual memorial of the death of Arius.

CHAP. XXXI. — EVENTS WHICH OCCURRED IN ALEXANDRIA AFTER THE DEATH OF ARIUS. LETTER OF CONSTANTINE THE GREAT TO THE CHURCH THERE.

THE death of Arius did not terminate the doctrinal dispute which he had originated.[1] Those who adhered to his sentiments did not cease from plotting against those who maintained opposite opinions. The people of Alexandria loudly complained of the exile of Athanasius, and offered up supplications for his return; and Antony, the celebrated monk, wrote frequently to the emperor to entreat him to attach no credit to the insinuations of the Meli-

tians, but to reject their accusations as calumnies; yet the emperor was not convinced by these arguments, and wrote to the Alexandrians, accusing them of folly and of disorderly conduct. He commanded the clergy and the holy virgins to remain quiet, and declared that he would not change his mind nor recall Athanasius, whom, he said, he regarded as an exciter of sedition, justly condemned by the judgment of the Church. He replied to Antony, by stating that he ought not to overlook the decree of the Synod; for even if some few of the bishops, he said, were actuated by ill-will or the desire to oblige others, it scarcely seems credible that so many prudent and excellent bishops could have been impelled by such motives; and, he added, that Athanasius was contumelious and arrogant, and the cause of dissension and sedition. The enemies of Athanasius accused him the more especially of these crimes, because they knew that the emperor regarded them with peculiar aversion. When he heard that the Church was split into two factions, of which one supported Athanasius and the other John, he was transported with indignation, and exiled John himself. This John had succeeded Melitius, and had, with those who held the same sentiments as himself, been restored to communion and reestablished in the clerical functions by the Synod of Tyre. His banishment was contrary to the wishes of the enemies of Athanasius, yet it was done, and the decrees of the Synod of Tyre did not benefit John, for the emperor was beyond supplication or petition of any kind with respect to any one who was suspected of stirring up Christian people to sedition or dissension.

CHAP. XXXII. — CONSTANTINE ENACTS A LAW AGAINST ALL HERESIES, AND PROHIBITS THE PEOPLE FROM HOLDING CHURCH IN ANY PLACE BUT THE CATHOLIC CHURCH, AND THUS THE GREATER NUMBER OF HERESIES DISAPPEAR. THE ARIANS WHO SIDED WITH EUSEBIUS OF NICOMEDIA, ARTFULLY ATTEMPTED TO OBLITERATE THE TERM "CONSUBSTANTIAL."

ALTHOUGH the doctrine of Arius was zealously supported by many persons in disputations,[2] a party had not as yet been formed to whom the name of Arians could be applied as a distinctive appellation; for all assembled together as a church and held communion with each other, with the exception of the Novatians, those called Phrygians, the Valentinians, the Marcionites, the Paulianians, and some few others who adhered to already invented heresies. The emperor, however, enacted a law that their own

---

[1] This chapter has no parallel in the present sources.

[2] This chapter, outside of the law of Constantine against the heretics (Eus. V. C. iii. 64), consists of Soz.'s reflections on the state of the heresies.

houses of prayer should be abolished ; and that they should meet in the churches, and not hold church in private houses, or in public places. He deemed it better to hold fellowship in the Catholic Church, and he advised them to assemble in her walls. By means of this law, almost all the heresies, I believe, disappeared. During the reign of preceding emperors, all who worshiped Christ, however they might have differed from each other in opinion, received the same treatment from the pagans, and were persecuted with equal cruelty. These common calamities, to which they were all equally liable, prevented them from prosecuting any close inquiries as to the differences of opinion which existed among themselves ; it was therefore easy for the members of each party to hold church by themselves, and by continually conferring with one another, however few they might have been in number, they were not disrupted. But after this law was passed they could not assemble in public, because it was forbidden ; nor could they hold their assemblies in secret, for they were watched by the bishops and clergy of their city. Hence the greater number of these sectarians were led, by fear of consequences, to join themselves to the Catholic Church. Those who adhered to their original sentiments did not, at their death, leave any disciples to propagate their heresy, for they could neither come together into the same place, nor were they able to teach in security those of the same opinions. On account either of the absurdity of the heretical dogmas, or of the utter ignorance of those who devised and taught them, the respective followers of each heresy were, from the beginning, very few in number. The Novatians alone,[1] who had obtained good leaders, and who entertained the same opinions respecting the Divinity as the Catholic Church, were numerous, from the beginning, and remained so, not being much injured by this law ; the emperor, I believe, willingly relaxed in their favor the rigor of the enactment, for he only desired to strike terror into the minds of his subjects, and had no intention of persecuting them. Acesius, who was then the bishop of this heresy in Constantinople, was much esteemed by the emperor on account of his virtuous life ; and it is probable that it was for his sake that the church which he governed met with protection. The Phrygians suffered the same treatment as the other heretics in all the Roman provinces except Phrygia and the neighboring regions, for here they had, since the time of Montanus, existed in great numbers, and do so to the present day.

About this time the partisans of Eusebius, bishop of Nicomedia, and of Theognis, bishop of Nicæa, began to make innovations in writing upon the confession set forth by the Nicæan Council. They did not venture to reject openly the assertion that the Son is consubstantial with the Father, because this assertion was maintained by the emperer ; but they propounded another document, and signified to the Eastern bishops that they received the terms of the Nicæan doctrine with verbal interpretations. From this declaration and reflection, the former dispute lapsed into fresh discussion, and what seemed to have been put at rest was again set in motion.

CHAP. XXXIII. — MARCELLUS BISHOP OF ANCYRA ; HIS HERESY AND DEPOSITION.

AT the same period, Marcellus, bishop of Ancyra,[2] in Galatia, was deposed and cast out of the Church by the bishops assembled at Constantinople, because he had introduced some new doctrines, whereby he taught that the existence of the Son of God commenced when He was born of Mary, and that His kingdom would have an end ; he had, moreover, drawn up a written document wherein these views were propounded. Basil, a man of great eloquence and learning, was invested with the bishopric of the parish of Galatia. They also wrote to the churches in the neighboring regions, to desire them to search for the copies of the book[3] written by Marcellus, and to destroy them, and to lead back any whom they might find to have embraced his sentiments. They stated that the work was too voluminous to admit of their transcribing the whole in their epistle, but that they inserted quotations of certain passages in order to prove that the doctrines which they had condemned were there advocated. Some persons, however, maintained that Marcellus had merely propounded a few questions which had been misconstrued by the adherents of Eusebius, and represented to the emperor as actual confessions. Eusebius and his partisans were much irritated against Marcellus, because he had not consented to the definitions propounded by the Synod in Phœnicia, nor to the regulations which had been made in favor of Arius at Jerusalem ; and had likewise refused to attend at the consecration of the Great Martyrium, in order to avoid communion with them. In their letter to the emperor, they dwelt largely upon this latter circumstance, and brought it forward

---

[1] Sozomen speaks with favor of the Novatians, though not with the earnestness of Socrates.

[2] Soc. i. 36. Soz. has more detail as to Asterius, and better order; both probably took from the same source. Compare the attitude of Athan. toward Marcellus.

[3] Hil. *Fragm.* ii. 22, gives the title of this work as *de Subjectione Domini Christi.* Eus. Pamp. wrote a refutation of this book.

as a charge, alleging that it was a personal insult to him to refuse attendance at the consecration of the temple which he had constructed at Jerusalem. The motive by which Marcellus was induced to write this work was that Asterius, who was a sophist and a native of Cappadocia, had written a treatise in defense of the Arian doctrines, and had read it in various cities, and to the bishops, and likewise at several Synods where he had attended. Marcellus undertook to refute his arguments, and while thus engaged, he, either deliberately or unintentionally, fell into the opinions of Paul of Samosata. He was afterwards, however, reinstated in his bishopric by the Synod of Sardis, after having proved that he did not hold such sentiments.

CHAP. XXXIV. — DEATH OF CONSTANTINE THE GREAT ; HE DIED AFTER BAPTISM AND WAS BURIED IN THE TEMPLE OF THE HOLY APOSTLES.

THE emperor had already divided the empire among his sons, who were styled Cæsars.[1] To Constantine and Constans he awarded the western regions ; and to Constantius, the eastern ; and as he was indisposed, and required to have recourse to bathing, he repaired for that purpose to Helenopolis, a city of Bithynia. His malady, however, increased, and he went to Nicomedia, and was initiated into holy baptism in one of the suburbs of that city. After the ceremony he was filled with joy, and returned thanks to God. He then confirmed the division of the empire among his sons, according to his former allotment, and bestowed certain privileges on old Rome and on the city named after himself. He placed his testament in the hands of the presbyter who constantly extolled Arius, and who had been recommended to him as a man

of virtuous life by his sister Constantia in her last moments, and commanded him with an added oath to deliver it to Constantius on his return, for neither Constantius nor the other Cæsars were with their dying father. After making these arrangements, Constantine survived but a few days ; he died in the sixty-fifth year of his age, and the thirty-first of his reign. He was a powerful protector of the Christian religion, and was the first of the emperors who began to be zealous for the Church, and to bestow upon her high benefactions. He was more successful than any other sovereign in all his undertakings ; for he formed no design, I am convinced, without God. He was victorious in his wars against the Goths and Sarmatians, and, indeed, in all his military enterprises ; and he changed the form of government according to his own mind with so much ease, that he created another senate and another imperial city, to which he gave his own name. He assailed the pagan religion, and in a little while subverted it, although it had prevailed for ages among the princes and the people.

After the death of Constantine, his body was placed in a golden coffin, conveyed to Constantinople, and deposited on a certain platform in the palace ; the same honor and ceremonial were observed, by those who were in the palace, as were accorded to him while living. On hearing of his father's death, Constantius, who was then in the East, hastened to Constantinople, and interred the royal remains with the utmost magnificence, and deposited them in the tomb which had been constructed by order of the deceased in the Church of the Apostles. From this period it became the custom to deposit the remains of subsequent Christian emperors in the same place of interment ; and here bishops, likewise, were buried, for the hierarchical dignity is not only equal in honor to imperial power, but, in sacred places, even takes the ascendancy.

[1] Eus. V. C. iv. 61–75; Ruf. H. E. i. 11; Soc. i. 38–40; cf. Philost. ii. 16, 17. Cf. Eutrop. Brev. hist. Rom. x. 7, 8.

BOOK III.

WE have now seen what events transpired in
the churches during the reign of Constantine.[1]
On his death the doctrine which had been set
forth at Nicæa, was subjected to renewed examination. Although this doctrine was not universally approved, no one, during the life of
Constantine, had dared to reject it openly. At
his death, however, many renounced this opinion,
especially those who had previously been suspected of treachery. Of all these Eusebius and
Theognis, bishops of the province of Bithynia,
did everything in their power to give predominance to the tenets of Arius. They believed
that this object would be easily accomplished,
if the return of Athanasius from exile could
be prevented, and by giving the government
of the Egyptian churches to a bishop of like
opinion with them. They found an efficient
coadjutor in the presbyter who had obtained
from Constantine the recall of Arius. He was
held in high esteem by the emperor Constantius,
on account of the service he had rendered in
delivering to him the testament of his father;
since he was trusted, he boldly seized the opportunities, until he became an intimate of the emperor's wife, and of the powerful eunuchs of
the women's sleeping apartments. At this
period Eusebius[2] was appointed to superintend
the concerns of the royal household, and being
zealously attached to Arianism, he induced the
empress and many of the persons belonging to
the court to adopt the same sentiments. Hence
disputations concerning doctrines again became
prevalent, both in private and in public, and
revilings and animosities were renewed. This
state of things was in accordance with the views
of Theognis and his partisans.

CHAP. II. — RETURN OF ATHANASIUS THE GREAT
FROM ROME ; LETTER OF CONSTANTINE CÆSAR,
SON OF CONSTANTINE THE GREAT ; RENEWED
MACHINATIONS OF THE ARIANS AGAINST ATHA-
NASIUS ; ACACIUS OF BERRŒA ; WAR BETWEEN
CONSTANS AND CONSTANTINE.

AT this period Athanasius returned from Gaul
to Alexandria.[3] It is said that Constantine intended to have recalled him, and that in his
testament he even gave orders to that effect.
But as he was prevented by death from performing his intention, his son who bore his
name, and who was then commanding in Western Gaul, recalled Athanasius, and wrote a letter
on the subject to the people of Alexandria.
Having met with a copy of this letter translated
from the Latin into Greek, I shall insert it precisely as I found it. It is as follows : —

"Constantine Cæsar, to the people of the
Catholic Church in the city of Alexandria.[4]

"You cannot, I believe, be unacquainted with
the fact that Athanasius, the interpreter of the
venerated law, since the cruelty of his blood-
thirsty and hostile enemies continued, to the
danger of his sacred person, was sent for a time
into Gaul in order that he might not incur irre-
trievable extremities through the perversity of
these worthless opponents ; in order then to
make this danger futile, he was taken out of the
jaws of the men, who pressed upon him, and
was commanded to live near me, so that in the
city where he dwelt, he might be amply furnished with all necessaries ; but his virtue is
so famous and extraordinary, because he is
confident of Divine aid, that he sets at naught
all the rougher burdens of fortune. Our lord
and my father, Constantine Augustus, of blessed
memory, intended to have reinstated this bishop
in his own place, and thus especially to have
restored him to your much beloved piety ; but,
since he was anticipated by the human lot, and
died before fulfilling his intention, I, as his successor, purpose to carry into execution the design
of the emperor of Divine memory. Athanasius
will inform you, when he shall see your face, in
how great reverence he was held by me. Nor
is it surprising that I should have acted as I
have done towards him, for the image of your
own desire and the appearance of so noble a
man, moved and impelled me to this step. May
Divine Providence watch over you, my beloved
brethren."

In consequence of this letter from the emper-
or Athanasius went home, and resumed the government of the Egyptian churches. Those who
were attached to the Arian doctrines were thrown

---

[1] This section is manifestly an abridgment of Soc. ii. 2.
[2] This Eusebius was a eunuch, who was now made chief cham-
berlain, and became a disciple of the alleged presbyter.

[3] This chapter follows the order of Soc. ii. 2–5. Cf. Philost.
ii. 18.
[4] This letter is translated in Athan. *Apol. cont. Arian.* 87; the
original was in Latin, and Athan. probably translated it.

into consternation and could not keep the peace ; they excited continuous seditions, and had recourse to other machinations against him. The partisans of Eusebius accused him before the emperor of being a seditious person, and of having reversed the decree of exile, contrary to the laws of the church, and without the consent of the bishops. I shall presently relate in the proper place, how, by their intrigues, Athanasius was again expelled from Alexandria.

Eusebius, surnamed Pamphilus, died[1] about this period, and Acacius succeeded to the bishopric of Cæsarea in Palestine. He was a zealous imitator of Eusebius because he had been instructed by him in the Sacred Word ; he possessed a capable mind and was polished in expression, so that he left many writings worthy of commendation. Not long after,[2] the emperor Constantine declared war against his brother Constans at Aquileia,[3] and was slain by his own generals. The Roman Empire was divided between the surviving brothers ; the West fell to the lot of Constans and the East to Constantius.

CHAP. III. — PAUL, BISHOP OF CONSTANTINOPLE, AND MACEDONIUS, THE PNEUMATOMACHIAN.

ALEXANDER died[4] about this time, and Paul succeeded to the high priesthood of Constantinople. The followers of Arius and Macedonius assert that he took possession at his own motion, and against the advice of Eusebius, bishop of Nicomedia, or of Theodore, bishop of Heraclea, in Thrace ; upon whom, as being the nearest bishops, the right of conferring ordination devolved. Many, however, maintain, on the testimony of Alexander, whom he succeeded, that he was ordained by the bishops who were then assembled at Constantinople.[5] For when Alexander, who was ninety-eight years of age, and who had conducted the episcopal office vigorously for twenty-three years, was at the point of death, his clergy asked him to whom he wished to turn over his church. " If," replied he, " you seek a man good in Divine matters and one who is apt to teach you, have Paul. But if you desire one who is conversant with public affairs, and with the councils of rulers, Macedonius is better." The Macedonians themselves admit that this testimony was given by Alexander ; but they say that Paul was more skilled in the transaction of business and the art of eloquence ; but they put emphasis for Macedonius, on the

testimony of his life ; and they accuse Paul of having been addicted to effeminacy and an indifferent conduct.[6] It appears, however, from their own acknowledgment, that Paul was a man of eloquence, and brilliant in teaching the Church. Events proved that he was not competent to combat the casualties of life, or to hold intercourse with those in power ; for he was never successful in subverting the machinations of his enemies,[7] like those who are adroit in the management of affairs. Although he was greatly beloved by the people, he suffered severely from the treachery of those who then rejected the doctrine which prevailed at Nicæa. In the first place, he was expelled from the church of Constantinople, as if some accusation of misconduct had been established against him.[7] He was then condemned to banishment, and finally, it is said, fell a victim to the devices of his enemies, and was strangled. But these latter events took place at a subsequent period.

CHAP. IV. — A SEDITION WAS EXCITED ON THE ORDINATION OF PAUL.

THE ordination of Paul occasioned a great commotion in the Church of Constantinople.[8] During the life of Alexander, the Arians did not act very openly ; for the people by being attentive to him were well governed and honored Divine things, and especially believed that the unexpected occurrence which befell Arius, whom they believed met such a death, was the Divine wrath, drawn down by the imprecations of Alexander. After the death of this bishop, however, the people became divided into two parties, and disputes and contests concerning doctrines were openly carried on. The adherents of Arius desired the ordination of Macedonius, while those who maintained that the Son is consubstantial with the Father wished to have Paul as their bishop ; and this latter party prevailed. After the ordination of Paul, the emperor, who chanced to be away from home, returned to Constantinople, and manifested as much displeasure at what had taken place as though the bishopric had been conferred upon an unworthy man. Through the machinations of the enemies of Paul a Synod was convened, and he was expelled from the Church. It handed over the Church of Constantinople to Eusebius, bishop of Nicomedia.

---

[1] Soc. ii. 4.　　[2] Soc. ii. 5.

[3] The mention of Aquileia, which is omitted by Socrates, shows consultation with another source. The statement of the agents in his death is different also.

[4] Cf. Soc. ii. 6. While the order of events is the same, Soz. had a different source, for he makes additions. Cf. Athan. *Hist. Arian.* 7.　　[5] An endemic Synod.

[6] ἀδιάφορος βίος, literally " an indifferent life." St. Nilus, St. Basil, and others of the Christian Fathers use this phrase as opposed to an ascetic life.

[7] He had been originally accused by his presbyter Macedonius. The accusation, according to Theodoret, after his restoration was sedition (*H. E.* ii. 5), the crime usually imputed to the homoousians. Cf. Athan. *Hist. Arian.*

[8] Soc. ii. 6, 7.

CHAP. V. — THE PARTIAL COUNCIL OF ANTIOCH ; IT DEPOSED ATHANASIUS ; IT SUBSTITUTED GREGORY ; ITS TWO STATEMENTS OF THE FAITH ; THOSE WHO AGREED WITH THEM.

SOON after these occurrences, the emperor went to Antioch, a city of Syria.[1] Here a church had already been completed, which excelled in size and beauty. Constantine began to build it during his lifetime, and as the structure had been just finished by his son Constantius, it was deemed a favorable opportunity by the partisans of Eusebius, who of old were zealous for it, to convene a council. They, therefore, with those from various regions who held their sentiments, met together in Antioch ;[2] their bishops were about ninety-seven in number. Their professed object was the consecration of the newly finished church ; but they intended nothing else than the abolition of the decrees of the Nicæan Council, and this was fully proved by the sequel. The Church of Antioch was then governed by Placetus,[3] who had succeeded Euphronius. The death of Constantine the Great had taken place about five years prior to this period. When all the bishops had assembled in the presence of the emperor Constantius, the majority expressed great indignation, and vigorously accused Athanasius of having contemned the sacerdotal regulation which they had enacted,[4] and taken possession of the bishopric of Alexandria without first obtaining the sanction of a council. They also deposed that he was the cause of the death of several persons, who fell in a sedition excited by his return ; and that many others had on the same occasion been arrested and delivered up to the judicial tribunals. By these accusations they contrived to cast odium on Athanasius, and it was decreed that Gregory should be invested with the government of the Church of Alexandria. They then turned to the discussion of doctrinal questions, and found no fault with the decrees of the council of Nice. They dispatched letters to the bishops of every city, in which they declared that, as they were bishops themselves, they had not followed Arius. " For how," said they, " could we have been followers of him, when he was but a presbyter,[5] and we were placed above him?" Since they were the testers of his faith, they had readily received him ; and they believed in the faith which had from the beginning been handed down by tradition. This they further explained at the bottom of their letter, but without mentioning the substance of the Father or the Son, or the term consubstantial. They resorted, in fact, to such ambiguity of expression, that neither the Arians nor the followers of the decrees of the Nicæan Council could call the arrangement of their words into question, as though they were ignorant of the holy Scriptures. They purposely avoided all forms of expression which were rejected by either party, and only made use of those which were universally admitted. They confessed[6] that the Son is with the Father, that He is the only begotten One, and that He is God, and existed before all things ; and that He took flesh upon Him, and fulfilled the will of His Father. They confessed these and similar truths, but they did not describe the doctrine of the Son being co-eternal or consubstantial with the Father, or the opposite. They subsequently changed their minds, it appears, about this formulary, and issued another,[7] which, I think, very nearly resembled that of the council of Nice, unless, indeed, some secret meaning be attached to the words which is not apparent to me. Although they refrained — I know not from what motive — from saying that the Son is consubstantial, they confessed that He is immutable, that His Divinity is not susceptible of change, that He is the perfect image of the substance, and counsel, and power, and glory of the Father, and that He is the first-born of every creature. They stated that they had found this formulary of faith, and that it was entirely written by Lucianus,[8] who was martyred in Nicomedia, and who was a man highly approved and exceedingly accurate in the sacred Scriptures. I know not whether this statement was really true, or whether they merely advanced it in order to give weight to their own document, by connecting with it the dignity of a martyr. Not only did Eusebius (who, on the expulsion of Paul, had been transferred from Nicomedia to the throne of Constantinople) participate in this council, but likewise Acacius, the successor of Eusebius Pamphilus, Patrophilus, bishop of Scythopolis, Theodore, bishop of Heraclea, formerly called Perinthus, Eudoxius, bishop of Germanicia, who subsequently directed the Church of Constantinople after Macedonius, and Gregory, who had been chosen to preside over the Church of Alexandria. It was universally acknowledged that all these bishops held the same sentiments, such as Dianius,[9] bishop of Cæsarea in Cappadocia, George, bishop of Laodicea in Syria, and many others who acted as bishops over metropolitan and other distinguished churches.

---

[1] Soc. ii. 7.
[2] Soc. ii. 8-10. Soz. with independent matter borrows from the same sources as Soc., one of which is Athan. de Synodis, 22-25.
[3] Also called Flaccillus. Soc. ii. 8.
[4] Cf. Soc. ii. 10. [5] Athan. de Synodis, 22.
[6] This creed is given in Athan. de Synodis, 23. Cf. Soc. ii. 10; here only in a suggestion and criticism.
[7] Theophronius' statement is passed over, and the final creed is here given in summary. Athan. de Synodis, 24, 25.
[8] This person was a presbyter of Antioch. Cf. vi. 12; Philost. ii. 12-14; Eus. H. E. ix. 6.
[9] He is also called Dianœus.

CHAP. VI. — EUSEBIUS SURNAMED EMESENUS; GREGORY ACCEPTED ALEXANDRIA; ATHANASIUS SEEKS REFUGE IN ROME.

EUSEBIUS, surnamed Emesenus, likewise attended the council.[1] He sprang from a noble family of Edessa, a city of Osroënæ. According to the custom of his country, he had from his youth upwards, learned the Holy Word, and was afterwards made acquainted with the learning of the Greeks, by the teachers who then frequented his native city. He subsequently acquired a more intimate knowledge of sacred literature, under the guidance of Eusebius Pamphilus and Patrophilus, the president of Scythopolis. He went to Antioch at the time that Eustathius was deposed on the accusation of Cyrus, and lived with Euphronius, his successor, on terms of intimacy. He fled to escape being invested with the priestly dignity, went to Alexandria, and frequented the schools of the philosophers. After acquainting himself with their mode of discipline, he returned to Antioch and dwelt with Placetus, the successor of Euphronius. During the time that the council was held in that city, Eusebius, bishop of Constantinople, entreated him to accept the see of Alexandria; for it was thought that, by his great reputation for sanctity and consummate eloquence, he would easily supplant Athanasius in the esteem of the Egyptians. He, however, refused the ordination, on the plea that he could otherwise only incur the ready hatred of the Alexandrians, who would have no other bishop but Athanasius. Gregory was, therefore, appointed to the church of Alexandria, and Eusebius to that of Emesa.

There he suffered from a sedition; for the people accused him of practicing that variety of astronomy which is called astrological, and being obliged to seek safety by flight, he repaired to Laodicea, and dwelt with George, bishop of that city, who was his particular friend. He afterwards accompanied this bishop to Antioch, and obtained permission from the bishops Placetus and Narcissus to return to Emesa. He was much esteemed by the emperor Constantius, and attended him in his military expedition against the Persians. It is said that God wrought miracles through his instrumentality, as is testified by George of Laodicea,[2] who has related these and other incidents about him.

But although he was endowed with so many exalted qualities, he could not escape the jealousy of those who are irritated by witnessing the virtues of others. He endured the censure of having embraced the doctrines of Sabellius. At the present time, however, he voted with the bishops who had been convened at Antioch. It is said that Maximus, bishop of Jerusalem, purposely, kept aloof from this council, because he repented having unawares consented to the deposition of Athanasius.[3] The manager of the Roman see, nor any representative from the east of Italy, nor from the parts beyond Rome were present at Antioch.[4] At the same period of time, the Franks devastated Western Gaul; and the provinces of the East, and more particularly Antioch after the Synod, were visited by tremendous earthquakes.[5] After the Synod, Gregory repaired to Alexandria with a large body of soldiers, who were enjoined to provide an undisturbed and safe entrance into the city: the Arians also, who were anxious for the expulsion of Athanasius, sided with him. Athanasius, fearful lest the people should be exposed to sufferings on his account,[6] assembled them by night in the church, and when the soldiers came to take possession of the church, prayers having been concluded, he first ordered a psalm to be sung. During the chanting of this psalm the soldiers remained without and quietly awaited its conclusion, and in the meantime Athanasius passed under the singers and secretly made his escape, and fled to Rome. In this manner Gregory possessed himself of the see of Alexandria. The indignation of the people was aroused, and they burnt the church which bore the name of Dionysius, one of their former bishops.

CHAP. VII. — HIGH PRIESTS OF ROME AND OF CONSTANTINOPLE; RESTORATION OF PAUL AFTER EUSEBIUS; THE SLAUGHTER OF HERMOGENES, A GENERAL OF THE ARMY; CONSTANTIUS CAME FROM ANTIOCH AND REMOVED PAUL, AND WAS WRATHFULLY DISPOSED TOWARD THE CITY; HE ALLOWED MACEDONIUS TO BE IN DOUBT, AND RETURNED TO ANTIOCH.

THUS were the schemes of those who upheld various heresies in opposition to truth successfully carried into execution; and thus did they depose those bishops who strenuously maintained throughout the East the supremacy of the doctrines of the Nicæan Council. These heretics had taken possession of the most important sees, such as Alexandria in Egypt, Antioch in Syria, and the imperial city of the Hellespont, and they held all the persuaded bishops in subjection. The ruler of the Church at Rome and all the priests of the West regarded these deeds as a personal insult; for they had accorded from the beginning with all the decisions in the vote made by those convened at Nice, nor did they now cease from that way of thinking. On the arrival of Athanasius, they received him

---

[1] From his life by George, bishop of Laodicea. Cf. Soc. ii. 9.
[2] Soc. also quotes him (ii. 9), and says he wrote an Encomium of Eusebius Emesenus, ii. 24

[3] Soc. ii. 8.   [4] Soc. ii. 8.   [5] Soc. ii. 10.
[6] Athan. Ep. Encyc. 2–7; Apol. cont. Arian. 30; Hist. Arian. 10–14, 57, 74; Soc. ii. 11.

kindly, and espoused his cause among themselves. Irritated at this interference, Eusebius
wrote to Julius, exhorting him to constitute himself a judge of the decrees that had been
enacted against Athanasius by the council of
Tyre.[1] But before he had been able to ascertain
the sentiments of Julius, and, indeed, not long
after the council of Antioch, Eusebius died.
Immediately upon this event, those citizens of
Constantinople who maintained the doctrines of
the Nicæan Council, conducted Paul to the
church. At the same time those of the opposing multitude seized this occasion and came
together in another church, among whom were
the adherents of Theognis, bishop of Nicæa, of
Theodore, bishop of Heraclea, and others of the
same party who chanced to be present, and they
ordained Macedonius bishop of Constantinople.
This excited frequent seditions in the city which
assumed all the appearance of a war, for the people fell upon one another, and many perished.
The city was filled with tumult, so that the emperor, who was then at Antioch, on hearing of
what had occurred, was moved to wrath, and issued
a decree for the expulsion of Paul. Hermogenes,
general of the cavalry, endeavored to put this
edict of the emperor's into execution ; for having
been sent to Thrace, he had, on the journey, to
pass by Constantinople, and he thought, by
means of his army, to eject Paul from the church
by force. But the people, instead of yielding,
met him with open resistance, and while the
soldiers, in order to carry out the orders they
had received, attempted still greater violence,
the insurgents entered the house of Hermogenes, set fire to it, killed him, and attaching a
cord to his body, dragged it through the city.[2]
The emperor had no sooner received this intelligence than he took horse for Constantinople, in order to punish the people. But he
spared them when he saw them coming to meet
him with tears and supplications. He deprived
the city of about half of the corn which his
father, Constantine, had granted them annually
out of the public treasury from the tributes of
Egypt, probably from the idea that luxury and
excess made the populace idle and disposed to
sedition. He turned his anger against Paul and
commanded his expulsion from the city. He
manifested great displeasure against Macedonius also, because he was the occasion of the
murder of the general and of other individuals ;
and also, because he had been ordained without first obtaining his sanction. He, however,
returned to Antioch, without having either confirmed or dissolved his ordination. Meanwhile
the zealots of the Arian tenets deposed Gregory,
because he was indifferent in the support of

their doctrines, and had moreover incurred the
ill-will of the Alexandrians on account of the
calamities which had befallen the city at his
entrance, especially the conflagration of the
church. They elected George, a native of
Cappadocia, in his stead ;[3] this new bishop was
admired on account of his activity and his zeal
in support of the Arian dogma.

CHAP. VIII. — ARRIVAL OF THE EASTERN HIGH
PRIESTS AT ROME ; LETTER OF JULIUS, BISHOP
OF ROME, CONCERNING THEM ; BY MEANS OF
THE LETTERS OF JULIUS, PAUL AND ATHANASIUS
RECEIVE THEIR OWN SEES ; CONTENTS OF THE
LETTER FROM THE ARCHPRIESTS OF THE EAST TO
JULIUS.

ATHANASIUS, on leaving Alexandria, had fled to
Rome.[4] Paul, bishop of Constantinople, Marcellus, bishop of Ancyra, and Asclepas, bishop of
Gaza, repaired thither at the same time. Asclepas,
who was opposed to the Arians and had therefore been deposed, after having been accused
by some of the heterodox of having thrown
down an altar ; Quintianus had been appointed
in his stead over the Church of Gaza. Lucius also,
bishop of Adrianople, who had been deposed
from the church under his care on another
charge, was dwelling at this period in Rome. The
Roman bishop, on learning the accusation against
each individual, and on finding that they held
the same sentiments about the Nicæan dogmas,
admitted them to communion as of like orthodoxy ; and as the care for all was fitting to the
dignity of his see, he restored them all to their
own churches. He wrote to the bishops of the
East, and rebuked them for having judged these
bishops unjustly, and for harassing the Churches
by abandoning the Nicæan doctrines. He summoned a few among them to appear before him
on an appointed day, in order to account to him
for the sentence they had passed, and threatened
to bear with them no longer, unless they would
cease to make innovations. This was the tenor
of his letters. Athanasius and Paul were reinstated in their respective sees, and forwarded
the letter of Julius to the bishops of the East.
The bishops could scarcely brook such documents, and they assembled together at Antioch,[5]
and framed a reply to Julius, beautifully expressed and composed with great legal skill, yet
filled with considerable irony and indulging in
the strongest threats. They confessed in this
epistle, that the Church of Rome was entitled
to universal honor, because it was the school of
the apostles, and had become the metropolis of

[1] Soc. ii. 11–14; Athan. *Apol. cont. Arian.* 22.
[2] Cf. Am. Marcel. xiv. 10. 2.

[3] Soc. ii. 14. Cf. Philost. iii. 3.
[4] *Apol. cont. Arian.* 20–35; Soc. ii. 15. Soz. is more extended
than Soc.
[5] From Sabinus? Cf. Soc. ii. 15.

piety from the outset, although the introducers
of the doctrine had settled there from the East.
They added that the second place in point of
honor ought not to be assigned to them, because
they did not have the advantage of size or number in their churches; for they excelled the
Romans in virtue and determination. They
called Julius to account for having admitted the
followers of Athanasius into communion, and
expressed their indignation against him for having insulted their Synod and abrogated their
decrees, and they assailed his transactions as
unjust and discordant with ecclesiastical right.
After these censures and protestations against
such grievances, they proceeded to state, that if
Julius would acknowledge the deposition of the
bishops whom they had expelled, and the substitution of those whom they had ordained in
their stead, they would promise peace and fellowship; but that, unless he would accede to
these terms, they would openly declare their
opposition. They added that the priests who
had preceded them in the government of the
Eastern churches had offered no opposition to
the deposition of Novatian, by the Church of
Rome. They made no allusion in their letter
to any deviations they had manifested from the
doctrines of the council of Nice, but merely
stated they had various reasons to allege in justification of the course they had pursued, and that
they considered it unnecessary to enter at that
time upon any defense of their conduct, as they
were suspected of having violated justice in
every respect.

CHAP. IX. — EJECTION OF PAUL AND ATHANASIUS;
MACEDONIUS IS INVESTED WITH THE GOVERN-
MENT OF THE CHURCH OF CONSTANTINOPLE.

AFTER having written in this strain to Julius,
the bishops of the East brought accusations
against those whom they had deposed before
the emperor Constantius.[1] Accordingly, the emperor, who was then at Antioch, wrote to Philip,
the prefect of Constantinople, commanding him
to surrender the Church to Macedonius, and to
expel Paul from the city. The prefect feared
the commotion among the people, and before
the order of the emperor could be divulged, he
repaired to the public bath which is called
Zeuxippus, a conspicuous and large structure,
and summoned Paul, as if he wished to converse
with him on some affairs of general interest; as
soon as he had arrived, he showed him the edict
of the emperor. Paul was, according to orders,
secretly conducted through the palace contiguous to the bath, to the seaside, and placed on

board a vessel and was sent to Thessalonica,
whence, it is said, his ancestors originally came.
He was strictly prohibited from approaching the
Eastern regions, but was not forbidden to visit
Illyria and the remoter provinces.

On quitting the court room, Philip, accompanied by Macedonius, proceeded to the church.
The people, who had in the meantime been assembling together in untold numbers, quickly
filled the church, and the two parties into which
they were divided, namely, the supporters of the
Arian heresy and the followers of Paul respectively, strove to take possession of the building.
When the prefect and Macedonius arrived at the
gates of the church, the soldiers endeavored to
force back the people, in order to make way for
these dignitaries, but as they were so crowded
together, it was impossible for them to recede,
since they were closely packed to the farthest
point, or to make way; the soldiers, under the impression that the crowd was unwilling to retire,
slew many with their swords, and a great number
were killed by being trampled upon. The edict
of the emperor was thus accomplished, and
Macedonius received the Churches, while Paul
was unexpectedly ejected from the Church in
Constantinople.

Athanasius in the meantime had fled, and concealed himself, fearing the menace of the emperor Constantius, for he had threatened to punish
him with death; for the heterodox had made the
emperor believe that he was a seditious person,
and that he had, on his return to the bishopric,
occasioned the death of several persons. But
the anger of the emperor had been chiefly excited by the representation that Athanasius had
sold the provisions which the emperor Constantine had bestowed on the poor of Alexandria,
and had appropriated the price.

CHAP. X. — THE BISHOP OF ROME WRITES TO THE
BISHOPS OF THE EAST IN FAVOR OF ATHANASIUS,
AND THEY SEND AN EMBASSY TO ROME WHO, WITH
THE BISHOP OF ROME, ARE TO INVESTIGATE THE
CHARGES AGAINST THE EASTERN BISHOPS; THIS
DEPUTATION IS DISMISSED BY CONSTANS, THE
CÆSAR.

THE bishops of Egypt,[2] having sent a declaration in writing that these allegations were false,
and Julius having been apprised that Athanasius
was far from being in safety in Egypt, sent for
him to his own city. He replied at the same
time to the letter of the bishops who were convened at Antioch, for just then he happened to
have received their epistle,[3] and accused them
of having clandestinely introduced innovations

[1] Soc. ii. 16, 17; Athan. *Hist. Arian.* 7; and *Apol. de fuga sua*, 3, 6-8. Cf. Theodoret, *H. E.* ii. 5.

[2] Athan. *Apol. cont. Arian.* 3-19.
[3] *Id.* 20-35, 36; Soc. ii. 17, 18. Soz. gives more points. Soc. accuses Sabinus of omitting the Julian letters.

contrary to the dogmas of the Nicene council, and of having violated the laws of the Church, by neglecting to invite him to join their Synod; for he alleged that there is a sacerdotal canon which declares that whatever is enacted contrary to the judgment of the bishop of Rome is null. He also reproached them for having deviated from justice in all their proceedings against Athanasius, both at Tyre and Mareotis, and stated that the decrees enacted at the former city had been annulled, on account of the calumny concerning the hand of Arsenius, and at the latter city, on account of the absence of Athanasius. Last of all he reprehended the arrogant style of their epistle.

Julius was induced by all these reasons to undertake the defense of Athanasius and of Paul: the latter had arrived in Italy not long previously, and had lamented bitterly these calamities. When Julius perceived that what he had written to those who held the sacerdotal dignity in the East was of no avail, he made the matter known to Constans the emperor. Accordingly, Constans wrote to his brother Constantius, requesting him to send some of the bishops of the East, that they might assign a reason for the edicts of deposition which they had passed. Three bishops were selected for this purpose; namely, Narcissus, bishop of Irenopolis, in Cilicia; Theodore, bishop of Heraclea, in Thrace; and Mark, bishop of Arethusa, in Syria. On their arrival in Italy, they strove to justify their actions and to persuade the emperor that the sentence passed by the Eastern Synod was just. Being required to produce a statement of their belief, they concealed the formulary they had drawn up at Antioch, and presented another written confession[1] which was equally at variance with the doctrines approved at Nicæa. Constans perceived that they had unjustly entrapped both Paul and Athanasius, and had ejected them from communion, not for charges against his conduct, as the depositions held, but simply on account of differences in doctrine; and he accordingly dismissed the deputation without giving any credit to the representations for which they had come.

CHAP. XI. — THE LONG FORMULARY AND THE ENACTMENTS ISSUED BY THE SYNOD OF SARDICA. JULIUS, BISHOP OF ROME, AND HOSIUS, THE SPANISH BISHOP, DEPOSED BY THE BISHOPS OF THE EAST, BECAUSE THEY HELD COMMUNION WITH ATHANASIUS AND THE REST.

THREE years afterwards, the bishops of the East[2] sent to those of the West a formulary of faith, which, because it had been framed with verbiage and thoughts in excess of any former confession, was called μακρόστιχος ἔκθεσις.[3] In this formulary they made no mention of the substance of God, but those are excommunicated who maintain that the Son arose out of what had no previous existence, or that He is of another hypostasis, and not of God, or that there was a time or an age in which He existed not. Eudoxius, who was still bishop of Germanicia, Martyrius, and Macedonius, carried this document, but the Western priests did not entertain it; for they declared that they felt fully satisfied with the doctrines established at Nicæa, and thought it entirely unnecessary to be too curious about such points.

After the Emperor Constans[4] had requested his brother to reinstate the followers of Athanasius in their sees, and had found his application to be unavailing, on account of the counteracting influence of those who adopted a hostile heresy; and when, moreover, the party of Athanasius and Paul entreated Constans to assemble a Synod on account of the plots for the abolition of orthodox doctrines, both the emperors were of the opinion that the bishops of the East and of the West should be convened on a certain day at Sardica, a city of Illyria. The bishops of the East, who had previously assembled at Philippopolis, a city of Thrace, wrote to the bishops of the West, who had already assembled at Sardica, that they would not join them, unless they would eject the followers of Athanasius from their assembly, and from communion with them, because they had been deposed. They afterwards went to Sardica, but declared they would not enter the church, while those who had been deposed by them were admitted thither. The bishops of the West replied, that they never had ejected them, and that they would not yield this now, particularly as Julius, bishop of Rome, after having investigated the case, had not condemned them, and that besides, they were present and ready to justify themselves and to refute again the offenses imputed to them. These declarations, however, were of no avail; and since the time they had appointed for the adjustment of their differences, concerning which they had convened, had expired, they finally wrote letters to one another on these points, and by these they were led to an increase of their previous ill-will. And after they had convened separately, they brought forward opposite decisions; for the Eastern bishops confirmed the sentences they had already enacted against Athanasius, Paul, Marcellus, and Asclepas, and deposed Julius, bishop of Rome,

[1] Athan. *de Synodis*, 25, and given in full by Soc. ii. 18.
[2] Athan. *de Synodis*, 26, in ten heads, and given by Soc. ii. 19, and with like introduction.

[3] For the whole section, Soc. ii. 19, 20; Athan. *de Synodis*, 26. Cf. Hil. *Frag.* ii. and iii.; Sulp. Sev. *H. S.* ii. 36.
[4] Soc. ii. 20, but Soz. has other details.

because he had been the first to admit those who had been condemned by them, into communion ; and Hosius, the confessor, was also deposed, partly for the same reason, and partly because he was the friend of Paulinus and Eustathius, the rulers of the church in Antioch. Maximus, bishop of Treves, was deposed, because he had been among the first who had received Paul into communion, and had been the cause of his returning to Constantinople, and because he had excluded from communion the Eastern bishops who had repaired to Gaul. Besides the above, they likewise deposed Protogenes, bishop of Sardica, and Gaudentius ;[1] the one because he favored Marcellus, although he had previously condemned him, and the other because he had adopted a different line of conduct from that of Cyriacus, his predecessor, and had supported many individuals then deposed by them. After issuing these sentences, they made known to the bishops of every region, that they were not to hold communion with those who were deposed, and that they were not to write to them, nor to receive letters from them. They likewise commanded them to believe what was said concerning God in the formulary which they subjoined to their letter, and in which no mention was made of the term " consubstantial," but in which, those were excommunicated who said there are three Gods, or that Christ is not God, or that the Father, the Son, and the Holy Ghost are the same, or that the Son is unbegotten, or that there was a time or an age in which He existed not.[2]

CHAP. XII. — THE BISHOPS OF THE PARTY OF JULIUS AND HOSIUS HELD ANOTHER SESSION AND DEPOSED THE EASTERN HIGH PRIESTS, AND ALSO MADE A FORMULARY OF FAITH.

THE adherents of Hosius,[3] in the meantime, assembled together, and declared them innocent : Athanasius, because unjust machinations had been carried on against him by those who had convened at Tyre ; and Marcellus, because he did not hold the opinions with which he was charged ; and Asclepas, because he had been re-established in his diocese by the vote of Eusebius Pamphilus and of many other judges ; that this was true he proved by the records of the trial ; and lastly, Lucius, because his accusers had fled. They wrote to the parishes of each of the acquitted, commanding them to receive and recognize their bishops. They stated that Gregory had not been nominated by them bishop of

Alexandria ; nor Basil, bishop of Ancyra ; nor Quintianus, bishop of Gaza ; and that they had not received these men into communion, and did not even account them Christians. They deposed from the episcopates, Theodore, bishop of Thrace ; Narcissus, bishop of Irenopolis ; Acacius, bishop of Cæsarea, in Palestine ; Menophantus, bishop of Ephesus ; Ursacius, bishop of Sigidunus in Mœsia ; Valens, bishop of Mursia in Pannonia ; and George, bishop of Laodicea, although this latter had not attended the Synod with the Eastern bishops. They ejected the above-named individuals from the priesthood and from communion, because they separated the Son from the substance of the Father, and had received those who had been formerly deposed on account of their holding the Arian heresy, and had, moreover, promoted them to the highest offices in the service of God. After they had excided them for these perversions and decreed them to be aliens to the Catholic Church, they afterwards wrote to the bishops of every nation,[4] commanding them to confirm these decrees, and to be of one mind on doctrinal subjects with themselves. They likewise compiled another document of faith, which was more copious than that of Nicæa, although the same thought was carefully preserved, and very little change was made in the words of that instrument. Hosius and Protogenes, who held the first rank among the Western bishops assembled at Sardica, fearing perhaps lest they should be suspected of making any innovations upon the doctrines of the Nicene council, wrote to Julius,[5] and testified that they were firmly attached to these doctrines, but, pressed by the need of perspicuity, they had to expand the identical thought, in order that the Arians might not take advantage of the brevity of the document, to draw those who were unskilled in dialectics into some absurdity. When what I have related had been transacted by each party, the conference was dissolved, and the members returned to their respective homes. This Synod was held during the consulate of Rufinus and Eusebius, and about eleven years after the death of Constantine.[6] There were about three hundred[7] bishops of cities in the West, and upwards of seventy-six Eastern bishops, among whom was Ischyrion, who had been appointed bishop of Mareotis by the enemies of Athanasius.

CHAP. XIII. — AFTER THE SYNOD, THE EAST AND THE WEST ARE SEPARATED ; THE WEST NOBLY

---

[1] He was bishop of Naïssus in Mœsia Superior.
[2] This section concerning the Synod of the Eastern bishops is probably from Sabinus. Cf. Hil. *Frag.* iii.
[3] Athan. *Apol. cont. Arian.* 36–50 ; Hil. *Frag.* ii. and iii.; Soc. ii. 20, 22. Cf. Sulp. Sev. *H. S.* ii. 36. Soz. used the same source as Soc., but independently.

[4] This letter is in Athan. *Apol. cont. Arian.* 44–49; and cf. Theod. *H. E.* ii. 8; Hil. *Frag.* ii.
[5] This epistle is nowhere extant. Güldenpenning suggests Sabinus as the source, but hardly from the statement which Socrates makes as to Sabinian partiality.
[6] A.D. 347–8. But A.D. 344 is probably the true date.
[7] So Soc.; but Theodoret says 250, ii. 7.

ADHERES TO THE FAITH OF THE NICENE COUN-
CIL, WHILE THE EAST IS DISTURBED BY CON-
TENTION HERE AND THERE OVER THIS DOGMA.

AFTER this Synod, the Eastern and the Western churches ceased to maintain the intercourse
which usually exists among people of the same
faith, and refrained from holding communion
with each other.[1] The Christians of the West
separated themselves from all as far as Thrace ;
those of the East as far as Illyria. This divided
state of the churches was mixed, as might be
supposed, with dissentient views and calumnies.
Although they had previously differed on doctrinal subjects, yet the evil had attained no great
height, for they had still held communion together and were wont to have kindred feelings.
The Church throughout the whole of the West
in its entirety regulated itself by the doctrines
of the Fathers, and kept aloof from all contentions and hair-splitting about dogma. Although Auxentius, who had become bishop of
Milan, and Valens and Ursacius, bishops of
Pannonia, had endeavored to lead that part
of the empire into the Arian doctrines, their
efforts had been carefully anticipated by the
president of the Roman see and the other
priests, who cut out the seeds of such a troublesome heresy. As to the Eastern Church, although it had been racked by dissension since
the time of the council of Antioch, and although
it had already openly differed from the Nicæan
form of belief, yet I think it is true that the
opinion of the majority united in the same
thought, and confessed the Son to be of the substance of the Father. There were some, however, who were fond of wrangling and battled
against the term " consubstantial " ; for those who
had been opposed to the word at the beginning,
thought, as I infer, and as happens to most people, that it would be a disgrace to appear as
conquered. Others were finally convinced of the
truth of the doctrines concerning God, by the
habit of frequent disputation on these themes,
and ever afterwards continued firmly attached to
them. Others again, being aware that contentions ought not to arise, inclined toward that
which was gratifying to each of the sides, on
account of the influence, either of friendship or
they were swayed by the various causes which
often induce men to embrace what they ought
to reject, and to act without boldness, in circumstances which require thorough conviction.
Many others, accounting it absurd to consume
their time in altercations about words, quietly
adopted the sentiments inculcated by the council of Nicæa. Paul, bishop of Constantinople,
Athanasius, bishop of Alexandria, the entire

multitude of monks, Antony the Great, who still
survived, his disciples, and a great number of
Egyptians and of other places in the Roman
territory, firmly and openly maintained the doctrines of the Nicæan council throughout the
other regions of the East. As I have been led to
allude to the monks, I shall briefly mention those
who flourished during the reign of Constantius.

CHAP. XIV. — OF THE HOLY MEN WHO FLOUR-
ISHED ABOUT THIS TIME IN EGYPT, NAMELY,
ANTONY, THE TWO MACARIUSES, HERACLIUS,
CRONIUS, PAPHNUTIUS, PUTUBASTUS, ARSISIUS,
SERAPION, PITURION, PACHOMIUS, APOLLONIUS,
ANUPH, HILARION, AND A REGISTER OF MANY
OTHER SAINTS.

I SHALL commence my recital[2] with Egypt
and the two men named Macarius, who were the
celebrated chiefs of Scetis and of the neighboring mountain ; the one was a native of Egypt,
the other was called *Politicus*, because he was a
citizen and was of Alexandrian origin. They
were both so wonderfully endowed with Divine
knowledge and philosophy, that the demons regarded them with terror, and they wrought many
extraordinary works and miraculous cures. The
Egyptian, the story says, restored a dead man to
life, in order to convince a heretic of the truth
of the resurrection from the dead. He lived
about ninety years, sixty of which he passed in
the deserts. When in his youth he commenced
the study of philosophy, he progressed so rapidly,
that the monks surnamed him " *old child*," and
at the age of forty he was ordained presbyter.
The other Macarius became a presbyter at a later
period of his life ; he was proficient in all the
exercises of asceticism, some of which he devised
himself, and what particulars he heard among
other ascetics, he carried through to success in
every form, so that by thoroughly drying up his
skin, the hairs of his beard ceased to grow.
Pambo, Heraclides, Cronius, Paphnutius, Putubastus, Arsisius, Serapion the Great, Piturion, who
dwelt near Thebes, and Pachomius, the founder
of the monks called the Tabennesians, flourished
at the same place and period. The attire and
government of this sect differed in some respects
from those of other monks. Its members were,
however, devoted to virtue, they contemned the
things of earth, excited the soul to heavenly contemplation, and prepared it to quit the body
with joy. They were clothed in skins in remembrance of Elias, it appears to me, because they

---

[1] Soc. ii. 22. The rest of the chapter is marked by an independent survey of the division.

[2] This chapter is made up from a great variety of sources, as
well as personal observation. Prominent among these are Ruf.
H. M. and *H. E.*; Pall. *H. L.*; Syrian biographies; Ephraim
Syrus, *Vita Juliani*; Athan. *Vita Antonii*; Timotheus' collection of monastic biography, mentioned in Soz. vi. 29; Hieron. *de
vir. illust.*; Evagrius Ponticus, *Gnosticus;* Philippus of Side,
Historia Christiana; Sulp. Sev. *de Vita Martini*.

thought that the virtue of the prophet would be thus always retained in their memory, and that they would be enabled, like him to resist manfully the seductions of amorous pleasures, to be influenced by similar zeal, and be incited to the practice of sobriety by the hope of an equal reward. It is said that the peculiar vestments of these Egyptian monks had reference to some secret connected with their philosophy, and did not differ from those of others without some adequate cause. They wore their tunics without sleeves, in order to teach that the hands ought not to be ready to do presumptuous evil. They wore a covering on their heads called a cowl, to show that they ought to live with the same innocence and purity as infants who are nourished with milk, and wear a covering of the same form. Their girdle, and a species of scarf, which they wear across the loins, shoulders, and arms, admonish them that they ought to be always ready in the service and work of God. I am aware that other reasons have been assigned for their peculiarity of attire, but what I have said appears to me to be sufficient. It is said that Pachomius at first practiced philosophy alone in a cave, but that a holy angel appeared to him, and commanded him to call together some young monks, and live with them, for he had succeeded well in pursuing philosophy by himself, and to train them by the laws which were about to be delivered to him, and now he was to possess and benefit many as a leader of communities. A tablet was then given to him, which is still carefully preserved. Upon this tablet were inscribed injunctions by which he was bound to permit every one to eat, to drink, to work, and to fast, according to his capabilities of so doing; those who ate heartily were to be subjected to arduous labor, and the ascetic were to have more easy tasks assigned them; he was commanded to have many cells erected, in each of which three monks were to dwell, who were to take their meals at a common refectory in silence, and to sit around the table with a veil thrown over the face, so that they might not be able to see each other or anything but the table and what was set before them; they were not to admit strangers to eat with them, with the exception of travelers, to whom they were to show hospitality; those who desired to live with them, were first to undergo a probation of three years, during which time the most laborious tasks were to be done, and, by this method they could share in their community. They were to clothe themselves in skins, and to wear woolen tiaras adorned with purple nails, and linen tunics and girdles. They were to sleep in their tunics and garments of skin, reclining on long chairs specially constructed by being closed on each side, so that it could hold the material of each couch. On the first and last days of the week they were to approach the altar for

the communion in the holy mysteries, and were then to unloose their girdles and throw off their robes of skin. They were to pray twelve times every day and as often during the evening, and were to offer up the same number of prayers during the night. At the ninth hour they were to pray thrice, and when about to partake of food they were to sing a psalm before each prayer. The whole community was to be divided into twenty-four classes, each of which was to be distinguished by one of the letters of the Greek alphabet, and so that each might have a cognomen fitting to the grade of its conduct and habit. Thus the name of Iota was given to the more simple, and that of Zeta or of Xi to the crooked, and the names of the other letters were chosen according as the purpose of the order most fittingly answered the form of the letter.

These were the laws[1] by which Pachomius ruled his own disciples. He was a man who loved men and was beloved of God, so that he could foreknow future events, and was frequently admitted to intercourse with the holy angels. He resided at Tabenna, in Thebais, and hence the name Tabennesians, which still continues. By adopting these rules for their government, they became very renowned, and in process of time increased so vastly, that they reached to the number of seven thousand men. But the community on the island of Tabenna with which Pachomius lived, consisted of about thirteen hundred; the others resided in the Thebais and the rest of Egypt. They all observed one and the same rule of life, and possessed everything in common. They regarded the community established in the island of Tabenna as their mother, and the rulers of it as their fathers and their princes.

About the same period, Apollonius became celebrated by his profession of monastic philosophy. It is said that from the age of fifteen he devoted himself to philosophy in the deserts, and that when he attained the age of forty, he went according to a Divine command he then received, to dwell in regions inhabited by men. He had likewise a community in the Thebais. He was greatly beloved of God, and was endowed with the power of performing miraculous cures and notable works. He was exact in the observance of duty, and instructed others in philosophy with great goodness and kindness. He was acceptable to such a degree in his prayers, that nothing of what he asked from God was denied him, but he was so wise that he always proffered prudent requests and such as the Divine Being is ever ready to grant.

I believe that Anuph the divine, lived about this period. I have been informed that from the time of the persecution, when he first

---

[1] See the Collection of Regulæ and Precepts, as translated by Hieron. ii. p. 66 sqq.

avowed his attachment to Christianity, he never uttered a falsehood, nor desired the things of earth. All his prayers and supplications to God were duly answered, and he was instructed by a holy angel in every virtue. Let, however, what we have said of the Egyptian monks suffice.

The same species of philosophy was about this time cultivated in Palestine, after being learned in Egypt, and Hilarion the divine then acquired great celebrity. He was a native of Thabatha,[1] a village situated near the town of Gaza, towards the south, and hard by a torrent which falls into the sea, and received the same name as the village, from the people of that country. When he was studying grammar at Alexandria, he went out into the desert to see the monk Antony the Great, and in his company he learned to adopt a like philosophy. After spending a short time there, he returned to his own country, because he was not allowed to be as quiet as he wished, on account of the multitudes who flocked around Antony. On finding his parents dead, he distributed his patrimony among his brethren and the poor, and without reserving anything whatever for himself, he went to dwell in a desert situated near the sea, and about twenty stadia from his native village. His cell residence was a very little house, and was constructed of bricks, chips and broken tiles, and was of such a breadth, height, and length that no one could stand in it without bending the head, or lie down in it without drawing up the feet; for in everything he strove to accustom himself to hardship and to the subjugation of luxurious ease. To none of those we have known did he yield in the high reach of his unboastful and approved temperance. He contended against hunger and thirst, cold and heat, and other afflictions of the body and of the soul. He was earnest in conduct, grave in discourse, and with a good memory and accurate attainment in Sacred Writ. He was so beloved by God, that even now many afflicted and possessed people are healed at his tomb. It is remarkable that he was first interred in the island of Cyprus, but that his remains are now deposited in Palestine; for it so happened, that he died during his residence in Cyprus, and was buried by the inhabitants with great honor and respect. But Hesychas, one of the most renowned of his disciples, stole the body, conveyed it to Palestine, and interred it in his own monastery. From that period, the inhabitants conducted a public and brilliant festival yearly; for it is the custom in Palestine to bestow this honor on those among them, who have attained renown by their goodness, such as Aurelius, Anthedonius, Alexion, a native of Bethagathon, and Alaphion, a native of Asalea, who, during the reign of Constantius, lived religiously and courageously in the practice of philosophy, and by their personal virtues they caused a considerable increase to the faith among the cities and villages that were still under the pagan superstition.

About the same period, Julian practiced philosophy near Edessa; he attempted a very severe and incorporeal method of life so that he seemed to consist of bones and skin without flesh. The setting forth of the history is due to Ephraim, the Syrian writer, who wrote the story of Julian's life. God himself confirmed the high opinion which men had formed of him; for He bestowed on him the power of expelling demons and of healing all kinds of diseases, without having recourse to drugs, but simply by prayer.

Besides the above, many other ecclesiastical philosophers flourished in the territories of Edessa and Amida, and about the mountain called Gaugalius; among these were Daniel and Simeon. But I shall now say nothing further of the Syrian monks; I shall further on, if God will, describe them more fully.[2]

It is said that Eustathius,[3] who governed the church of Sebaste in Armenia, founded a society of monks in Armenia, Paphlagonia, and Pontus, and became the author of a zealous discipline, both as to what meats were to be partaken of or to be avoided, what garments were to be worn, and what customs and exact course of conduct were to be adopted. Some assert that he was the author of the ascetic treatises commonly attributed to Basil of Cappadocia. It is said that his great exactness led him into certain extravagances which were altogether contrary to the laws of the Church. Many persons, however, justify him from this accusation, and throw the blame upon some of his disciples, who condemned marriage, refused to pray to God in the houses of married persons, despised married presbyters, fasted on Lord's days, held their assemblies in private houses, denounced the rich as altogether without part in the kingdom of God, contemned those who partook of animal food. They did not retain the customary tunics and stoles for their dress, but used a strange and unwonted garb, and made many other innovations. Many women were deluded by them, and left their husbands; but, not being able to practice continence, they fell into adultery. Other women, under the pretext of religion, cut off their hair, and behaved otherwise than is fitting to a woman, by arraying themselves in men's apparel. The bishops of the neighborhood of Gangroe, the metropolis

---

[1] According to Hieronymus, *Vita Hilaronis*, 2, Hilarion was born in the village of Thabatha, which is about five miles from Gaza; Thebasa, according to Niceph. ix. 15.

[2] See below, chap. 16, and vi. 34.
[3] Soc. ii. 43.

of Paphlagonia, assembled themselves together, and declared that all those who imbibed these opinions should be aliens to the Catholic Church, unless, according to the definitions of the Synod, they would renounce each of the aforesaid customs. It is said that from that time, Eustathius exchanged his clothing for the stole, and made his journeys habited like other priests, thus proving that he had not introduced and practiced these novelties out of self-will, but for the sake of a godly asceticism. He was as renowned for his discourses as for the purity of his life. To confess the truth, he was not eloquent, nor had he ever studied the art of eloquence; yet he had admirable sense and a high capacity of persuasion, so that he induced several men and women, who were living in fornication, to enter upon a temperate and earnest course of life. It is related that a certain man and woman, who, according to the custom of the Church, had devoted themselves to a life of virginity, were accused of cohabiting together. He strove to make them cease from their intercourse; finding that his remonstrances produced no effect upon them, he sighed deeply, and said, that a woman who had been legally married had, on one occasion, heard him discourse on the advantage of continence, and was thereby so deeply affected that she voluntarily abstained from legitimate intercourse with her own husband, and that the weakness of his powers of conviction was, on the other hand, attested by the fact, that the parties above mentioned persisted in their illegal course. Such were the men who originated the practice of monastic discipline in the regions above mentioned.

Although the Thracians, the Illyrians, and the other European nations were still inexperienced in monastic communities, yet they were not altogether lacking in men devoted to philosophy. Of these, Martin,[1] the descendant of a noble family of Saboria in Pannonia, was the most illustrious. He was originally a noted warrior, and the commander of armies; but, accounting the service of God to be a more honorable profession, he embraced a life of philosophy, and lived, in the first place, in Illyria. Here he zealously defended the orthodox doctrines against the attacks of the Arian bishops, and after being plotted against and frequently beaten by the people, he was driven from the country. He then went to Milan, and dwelt alone. He was soon, however, obliged to quit his place of retreat on account of the machinations of Auxentius, bishop of that region, who did not hold soundly to the Nicene faith; and he went to an island called Gallenaria, where he remained for some time, satisfying himself with roots of plants. Gallenaria is a small and unin-

habited island lying in the Tyrrhenian Sea. Martin was afterwards appointed bishop of the church of Tarracinæ (Tours). He was so richly endowed with miraculous gifts that he restored a dead man to life, and performed other signs as wonderful as those wrought by the apostles. We have heard that Hilary, a man divine in his life and conversation, lived about the same time, and in the same country; like Martin, he was obliged to flee from his place of abode, on account of his zeal in defense of the faith.

I have now related what I have been able to ascertain concerning the individuals who practiced philosophy in piety and ecclesiastical rites. There were many others who were noted in the churches about the same period on account of their great eloquence, and among these the most distinguished were, Eusebius, who administered the priestly office at Emesa; Titus, bishop of Bostra; Serapion, bishop of Thmuis; Basil, bishop of Ancyra; Eudoxius, bishop of Germanicia; Acacius, bishop of Cæsarea; and Cyril, who controlled the see of Jerusalem. A proof of their education is in the books they have written and left behind, and the many things worthy of record.

CHAP. XV.— DIDYMUS THE BLIND, AND AETIUS THE HERETIC.

DIDYMUS,[2] an ecclesiastical writer and president of the school of sacred learning in Alexandria, flourished about the same period. He was acquainted with every branch of science, and was conversant with poetry and rhetoric, with astronomy and geometry, with arithmetic, and with the various theories of philosophy. He had acquired all this knowledge by the efforts of his own mind, aided by the sense of hearing, for he became blind during his first attempt at learning the rudiments. When he had advanced to youth, he manifested an ardent desire to acquire speech and training, and for this purpose he frequented the teachers of these branches, but learned by hearing only, where he made such rapid progress that he speedily comprehended the difficult theorems in mathematics. It is said that he learned the letters of the alphabet by means of tablets in which they were engraved, and which he felt with his fingers; and that he made himself acquainted with syllables and words by the force of attention and memory, and by listening attentively to the sounds. His was a very extraordinary case, and many persons resorted to Alexandria for the express purpose of hearing, or, at least, of seeing him. His firmness in defending the doctrines of the

1 Sulp. Sev. *Vita Martini*.

2 Ruf. *H. E.* ii. 7; i. 30, 31; Soc. iv. 25; iii. 10; ii. 35; Hieron. *de vir. illust.* c. cix.

Nicæan council was extremely displeasing to the Arians. He easily carried conviction to the minds of his audience by persuasion rather than by power of reasoning, and he constituted each one a judge of the ambiguous points. He was much sought after by the members of the Catholic Church, and was praised by the orders of monks in Egypt, and by Antòny the Great.

It is related that when Antony left the desert and repaired to Alexandria to give his testimony in favor of the doctrines of Athanasius, he said to Didymus, " It is not a severe thing, nor does it deserve to be grieved over, O Didymus, that you are deprived of the organs of sight which are possessed by rats, mice, and the lowest animals ; but it is a great blessing to possess eyes like angels, whereby you can contemplate keenly the Divine Being, and see accurately the true knowledge." In Italy and its territories, Eusebius and Hilary, whom I have already mentioned, were conspicuous for strength in the use of their native tongue, whose treatises [1] concerning the faith and against the heterodox, they say, were approvingly circulated. Lucifer, as the story goes, was the founder of a heresy which bears his name,[2] and flourished at this period. Aetius [3] was likewise held in high estimation among the heterodox ; he was a dialectician, apt in syllogism and proficient in disputation, and a diligent student of such forms, but without art. He reasoned so boldly concerning the nature of God, that many persons gave him the name of " Atheist." It is said that he was originally a physician of Antioch in Syria, and that, as he frequently attended meetings of the churches, and thought over the Sacred Scriptures, he became acquainted with Gallus, who was then Cæsar, and who honored religion much and cherished its professors. It seems likely that, as Aetius obtained the esteem of Cæsar by means of these disputations, he devoted himself the more assiduously to these pursuits, in order to progress in the favor of the emperor. It is said that he was versed in the philosophy of Aristotle, and frequented the schools in which it was taught at Alexandria.

Besides the individuals above specified, there were many others in the churches who were capable of instructing the people and of reasoning concerning the doctrines of the Holy Scriptures. It would be too great a task to attempt to name them all. Let it not be accounted strange, if I have bestowed commendations upon the leaders or enthusiasts of the above-mentioned heresies. I admire their eloquence, and their impressiveness in discourse. I leave their doctrines to be judged by those whose right it is. For I have not been set forth to record such matters, nor is it befitting in history ; I have only to give an account of events as they happened, not supplementing my own additions. Of those who at that time became most distinguished in education and discourse and who used the Roman and Greek languages, I have enumerated in the above narrative as many as I have received an account of.

CHAP. XVI. — CONCERNING ST. EPHRAIM.

EPHRAIM the Syrian [4] was entitled to the highest honors, and was the greatest ornament of the Catholic Church. He was a native of Nisibis, or his family was of the neighboring territory. He devoted his life to monastic philosophy ; and although he received no instruction, he became, contrary to all expectation, so proficient in the learning and language of the Syrians, that he comprehended with ease the most abstruse theorems of philosophy. His style of writing was so replete with splendid oratory and with richness and temperateness of thought that he surpassed the most approved writers of Greece. If the works of these writers were to be translated into Syriac, or any other language, and divested, as it were, of the beauties of the Greek language, they would retain little of their original elegance and value. The productions of Ephraim have not this disadvantage : they were translated into Greek during his life, and translations are even now being made, and yet they preserve much of their original force, so that his works are not less admired when read in Greek than when read in Syriac. Basil, who was subsequently bishop of the metropolis of Cappadocia, was a great admirer of Ephraim, and was astonished at his erudition. The opinion of Basil, who is universally confessed to have been the most eloquent man of his age, is a stronger testimony, I think, to the merit of Ephraim, than anything that could be indited to his praise. It is said that he wrote three hundred thousand verses, and that he had many disciples who were zealously attached to his doctrines. The most celebrated of his disciples were Abbas, Zenobius, Abraham, Maras, and Simeon, in whom the Syrians and whoever among them pursued accurate learning make a great boast. Paulanas and Aranad are praised for their finished speech, although reported to have deviated from sound doctrine.

I am not ignorant that there were some very learned men who formerly flourished in Osroëne, as, for instance, Bardasanes, who devised a heresy designated by his name,[5] and Harmonius, his

---

[1] He alludes to the treatises of Hilary against the Arians and Auxentius, and against Constantius.

[2] That, namely, of the Luciferians. Cf. Soc. iii. 9.

[3] Cf. Soc. ii. 35; Philost. iii. 15–20; supplementa from Phot. cod. 40; fragmenta from Suidas, s.v.

[4] See below, vi. 34. This chapter is independent. Theod. iv. 29 has Soz. before him, and possibly also the same original. Cf. Hieron. de vir. illust. cxv.   [5] Cf. Euseb. H. E. iv. 30.

son. It is related that this latter was deeply versed in Grecian erudition, and was the first to subdue his native tongue to meters and musical laws; these verses he delivered to the choirs, and even now the Syrians frequently sing, not the precise copies by Harmonius, but the same melodies. For as Harmonius was not altogether free from the errors of his father, and entertained various opinions concerning the soul, the generation and destruction of the body, and the regeneration which are taught by the Greek philosophers, he introduced some of these sentiments into the lyrical songs which he composed. When Ephraim perceived that the Syrians were charmed with the elegance of the diction and the rhythm of the melody, he became apprehensive, lest they should imbibe the same opinions; and therefore, although he was ignorant of Grecian learning, he applied himself to the understanding of the metres of Harmonius, and composed similar poems in accordance with the doctrines of the Church, and wrought also in sacred hymns and in the praises of passionless men. From that period the Syrians sang the odes of Ephraim according to the law of the ode established by Harmonius. The execution of this work is alone sufficient to attest the natural endowments of Ephraim. He was as celebrated for the good actions he performed as for the rigid course of discipline he pursued. He was particularly fond of tranquillity. He was so serious and so careful to avoid giving occasion to calumny, that he refrained from the very sight of women. It is related that a female of careless life, who was either desirous of tempting him, or who had been bribed for the purpose, contrived on one occasion to meet him face to face, and fixed her eyes intently upon him; he rebuked her, and commanded her to look down upon the ground, "Wherefore should I obey your injunction," replied the woman; "for I was born not of the earth, but of you? It would be more just if you were to look down upon the earth whence you sprang, while I look upon you, as I was born of you." Ephraim, astonished at the little woman, recorded the whole transaction in a book, which most Syrians regard as one of the best of his productions. It is also said of him, that, although he was naturally prone to passion, he never exhibited angry feeling toward any one from the period of his embracing a monastic life. It once happened that after he had, according to custom, been fasting several days, his attendant, in presenting some food to him, let fall the dish on which it was placed. Ephraim, perceiving that he was overwhelmed with shame and terror, said to him, "Take courage; we will go to the food as the food does not come to us"; and he immediately seated himself beside the fragments of the dish, and ate his supper. What I am about to relate will suffice to show that he was totally exempt from the love of vainglory. He was appointed bishop of some town, and attempts were made to convey him away for the purpose of ordaining him. As soon as he became aware of what was intended, he ran to the market-place, and showed himself as a madman by stepping in a disorderly way, dragging his clothes along, and eating in public. Those who had come to carry him away to be their bishop, on seeing him in this state, believed that he was out of his mind, and departed; and he, meeting with an opportunity for effecting his escape, remained in concealment until another had been ordained in his place. What I have now said concerning Ephraim must suffice, although his own countrymen relate many other anecdotes of him. Yet his conduct on one occasion, shortly before his death, appears to me so worthy of remembrance that I shall record it here. The city of Edessa being severely visited by famine, he quitted the solitary cell in which he pursued philosophy, and rebuked the rich for permitting the poor to die around them, instead of imparting to them of their superfluities; and he represented to them by his philosophy, that the wealth which they were treasuring up so carefully would turn to their own condemnation, and to the ruin of the soul, which is of more value than all riches, and the body itself and all other values, and he proved that they were putting no estimate upon their souls, because of their actions. The rich men, revering the man and his words, replied, "We are not intent upon hoarding our wealth, but we know of no one to whom we can confide the distribution of our goods, for all are prone to seek after lucre, and to betray the trust placed in them." "What think you of me?" asked Ephraim. On their admitting that they considered him an efficient, excellent, and good man, and worthy, and that he was exactly what his reputation confirmed, he offered to undertake the distribution of their alms. As soon as he received their money, he had about three hundred beds fitted up in the public porches; and here he tended those who were ill and suffering from the effects of the famine, whether they were foreigners or natives of the surrounding country. On the cessation of the famine he returned to the cell in which he had previously dwelt; and, after the lapse of a few days, he expired. He attained no higher clerical degree than that of deacon, although he became no less famous for his virtue than those who are ordained to the priesthood and are admired for the conversation of a good life and for learning. I have now given some account of the virtue of Ephraim. It would require a more experienced hand than mine, to furnish a full description of his character and that of the other illustrious men who, about the same period, had devoted themselves to a life and career of philosophy ; and for some things, it would require such a writer as he himself was. The attempt is beyond my powers by reason of weakness of language, and ignorance of the men themselves and their exploits. Some of them concealed themselves in the deserts. Others, who lived in the intercourse of cities, strove to preserve a mean appearance, and to seem as if they differed in no respect from the multitude, working out their virtue, concealing a true estimate of themselves, that they might avoid the praises of others. For as they were intent upon the exchange of future benefits, they made God alone the witness of their thoughts, and had no concern for outward glory.

CHAP. XVII.— TRANSACTIONS OF THAT PERIOD, AND PROGRESS OF CHRISTIAN DOCTRINE THROUGH THE JOINT EFFORTS OF EMPERORS AND ARCH-PRIESTS.

THOSE who presided over the churches at this period were noted for personal conduct, and, as might be expected, the people whom they governed were earnestly attached to the worship of Christ.[1] Religion daily progressed, by the zeal, virtue, and wonderful works of the priests, and of the ecclesiastical philosophers, who attracted the attention of the pagans, and led them to renounce their superstitions. The emperors who then occupied the throne were as zealous as was their father in protecting the churches, and they granted honors and tax exemptions to the clergy, their children, and their slaves. They confirmed the laws enacted by their father, and enforced new ones prohibiting the offering of sacrifice, the worship of images, or any other pagan observance. They commanded that all temples, whether in cities or in the country, should be closed. Some of these temples were presented to the churches, when either the ground they stood on or the materials for building were required. The greatest possible care was bestowed upon the houses of prayer, those which had been defaced by time were repaired, and others were erected from the foundations in a style of extraordinary magnificence. The church of Emesa is one most worthy to see and famous for its beauty. The Jews were strictly forbidden to purchase a slave belonging to any other heresy than their own. If they transgressed this law, the slave was confiscated[2] to the public ; but if they administered to him the Jewish rite

of circumcision, the penalties were death and total confiscation of property. For, as the emperors were desirous of promoting by every means the spread of Christianity, they deemed it necessary to prevent the Jews from proselyting those whose ancestors were of another religion, and those who were holding the hope of professing Christianity were carefully reserved for the Church ; for it was from the pagan multitudes that the Christian religion increased.

CHAP. XVIII. — CONCERNING THE DOCTRINES HELD BY THE SONS OF CONSTANTINE. DISTINCTION BETWEEN THE TERMS " HOMOOUSIOS " AND " HOMOIOUSIOS." WHENCE IT CAME THAT CONSTANTIUS QUICKLY ABANDONED THE CORRECT FAITH.

THE emperors[3] had, from the beginning, preserved their father's view about doctrine ; for they both favored the Nicene form of belief. Constans maintained these opinions till his death ; Constantius held a similar view for some time ; he, however, renounced his former sentiments when the term " consubstantial " was calumniated, yet he did not altogether refrain from confessing that the Son is of like substance with the Father. The followers of Eusebius, and other bishops of the East, who were admired for their speech and life, made a distinction, as we know, between the term " consubstantial " (homoousios) and the expression " of like substance," which latter they designated by the term, " homoiousios." They say that the term " consubstantial " (homoousios) properly belongs to corporeal beings, such as men and other animals, trees and plants, whose participation and origin is in like things ; but that the term " homoiousios " appertains exclusively to incorporeal beings, such as God and the angels, of each one of whom a conception is formed according to his own peculiar substance. The Emperor Constantius was deceived by this distinction ; and although I am certain that he retained the same doctrines as those held by his father and brother, yet he adopted a change of phraseology, and, instead of using the term " homoousios," made use of the term " homoiousios." The teachers to whom we have alluded maintained that it was necessary to be thus precise in the use of terms, and that otherwise we should be in danger of conceiving that to be a body which is incorporeal. Many, however, regard this distinction as an absurdity, " for," say they, " the things which are conceived by the mind can be

---

[1] This chapter is an independent view, and also groups the laws under Constantius. Cf. Cod. Theod.
[2] δημόσιον οἰκέτην εἶναι. The early interpreters understood these words as referring to the Jewish offender, and not to the slave.

But the law itself is extant in Cod. Theod. xvi. 91, 2, and is entitled Ne Christianum Mancipium Judæus habeat. The second law begins: Si aliquis Judæorum, mancipium sectæ alterius seu nationis crediderit comparandum, mancipium fisco protenus vindicetur.
[3] An independent survey of the imperial and clerical views.

designated only by names derived from things which are seen ; and there is no danger in the use of words, provided that there be no error about the idea.

CHAP. XIX. — FURTHER PARTICULARS CONCERNING THE TERM "CONSUBSTANTIAL." COUNCIL OF ARIMINUM, THE MANNER, SOURCE, AND REASON OF ITS CONVENTION.

IT is not surprising that the Emperor Constantius was induced to adopt the use of the term " *homoiousios*," for it was admitted by many priests who conformed to the doctrines of the Nicæan council.[1] Many use the two words indifferently, to convey the same meaning. Hence, it appears to me, that the Arians departed greatly from the truth when they affirmed that, after the council of Nicæa, many of the priests, among whom were Eusebius and Theognis, refused to admit that the Son is consubstantial with the Father, and that Constantine was in consequence so indignant, that he condemned them to banishment. They say that it was afterwards revealed to his sister by a dream or a vision from God, that these bishops held orthodox doctrines and had suffered unjustly ; and that the emperor thereupon recalled them, and demanded of them wherefore they had departed from the Nicene doctrines, since they had been participants in the document concerning the faith which had been there framed ; and that they urged in reply that they had not assented to those doctrines from conviction, but from the fear that, if the disputes then existing were prolonged, the emperor, who was then just beginning to embrace Christianity, and who was yet unbaptized, might be impelled to return to Paganism, as seemed likely, and to persecute the Church. They assert that Constantine was pleased with this defense, and determined upon convening another council ; but that, being prevented by death from carrying his scheme into execution, the task devolved upon his eldest son, Constantius, to whom he represented that it would avail him nothing to be possessed of imperial power, unless he could establish uniformity of worship throughout his empire ; and Constantius they say, at the instigation of his father, convened a council at Ariminum.[2] This story is easily seen to be a gross fabrication, for the council was convened during the consulate of Hypatius and Eusebius, and twenty-two years after Constantius had, on the death of his father, succeeded to the empire. Now, during this interval of twenty-two years, many councils were held, in which debates were carried on concern-

ing the terms "*homoousios*" and "*homoiousios.*" No one, it appears, ventured to deny that the Son is of like substance[3] with the Father, until Aetius, by starting a contrary opinion, so offended the emperor that, in order to arrest the course of the heresy, he commanded the priests to assemble themselves together at Ariminum and at Seleucia. Thus the true cause of this council being convened was not the command of Constantine,[4] but the question agitated by Aetius. And this will become still more apparent by what we shall hereafter relate.

CHAP XX. — ATHANASIUS AGAIN REINSTATED BY THE LETTER OF CONSTANTIUS, AND RECEIVES HIS SEE. THE ARCH-PRIESTS OF ANTIOCH. QUESTION PUT BY CONSTANTIUS TO ATHANASIUS. THE PRAISE OF GOD IN HYMNS.

WHEN Constans was apprised of what had been enacted at Sardica, he wrote[5] to his brother to request him to restore the followers of Athanasius and Paul to their own churches. As Constantius seemed to hesitate, he wrote again, and threatened him with war, unless he would consent to receive the bishops. Constantius, after conferring on the subject with the bishops of the East, judged that it would be foolish to excite on this account the horrors of civil war. He therefore recalled Athanasius from Italy, and sent public carriages to convey him on his return homewards, and wrote several letters requesting his speedy return. Athanasius, who was then residing at Aquilea, on receiving the letters of Constantius, repaired to Rome to take leave of Julius and his friends. Julius parted from him with great demonstrations of friendship, and gave him a letter addressed to the clergy and people of Alexandria, in which he spoke of him as a wonderful man, deserving of renown by the numerous trials he had undergone, and congratulated the church of Alexandria on the return of so good a priest, and exhorted them to follow his doctrines.

He then proceeded to Antioch in Syria, where the emperor was then residing. Leontius presided over the churches of that region ; for after the flight of Eustathius, those who held heretical sentiments had seized the see of Antioch. The first bishop they appointed was Euphronius ; to him succeeded Placetus ; and afterwards Stephen. This latter was deposed as being unworthy of the dignity, and Leontius obtained the bishopric. Athanasius avoided him as a heretic, and communed with those who were

---

[1] An independent chapter on the true cause of division and the origin of the council of Ariminum. Cf. Athan. *Ep. de Synodis.*
[2] Cf. Soc. ii. 37.

[3] κατ᾿ οὐσίαν ἀνόμοιον is the right correction of Valesius.
[4] A mistake for Constantius.
[5] Athan. *Apol. cont. Arian.* 51–56; *Hist. Arian.* 15, 16; Ruf. i. 19; Soc. ii. 22, 23, who gives texts from Athanasius of the second letter of Constans (in part); those of Constantius to Athanasius; and Julius to the Alexandrians. Philost. iii. 13.

called Eustathians, who assembled in a private house. Since he found that Constantius was well disposed, and agreeable, and it looked as if the emperor would restore his own church to him, Constantius, at the instigation of the leaders of the opposing heresy, replied as follows: "I am ready to perform all that I promised when I recalled you; but it is just that you should in return grant me a favor, and that is, that you yield one of the numerous churches which are under your sway to those who are averse to holding communion with you." Athanasius replied: "O emperor, it is exceedingly just and necessary to obey your commands, and I will not gainsay, but as in the city of Antioch there are many who eschew communion between the heterodox and ourselves, I seek a like favor that one church may be conceded to us, and that we may assemble there in safety." As the request of Athanasius appeared reasonable to the emperor, the heterodox deemed it more politic to keep quiet; for they reflected that their peculiar opinions could never gain any ground in Alexandria, on account of Athanasius, who was able both to retain those who held the same sentiments as himself, and lead those of contrary opinions; and that, moreover, if they gave up one of the churches of Antioch, the Eustathians, who were very numerous, would assemble together, and then probably attempt innovations, since it would be possible for them without risk to retain those whom they held. Besides, the heterodox perceived that, although the government of the churches was in their hands, all the clergy and people did not conform to their doctrines.[1] When they sang hymns to God, they were, according to custom, divided into choirs, and, at the end of the odes, each one declared what were his own peculiar sentiments. Some offered praise to "the Father *and* the Son," regarding them as co-equal in glory; others glorified "The Father *by* the Son," to denote by the insertion of the preposition that they considered the Son to be inferior to the Father. While these occurrences took place, Leontius, the bishop of the opposite faction, who then presided over the see of Antioch, did not dare to prohibit the singing of hymns to God which were in accordance with the tradition of the Nicæan Synod, for he feared to excite an insurrection of the people. It is related, however, that he once raised his hand to his head, the hairs of which were quite white, and said, "When this snow is dissolved, there will be plenty of mud." By this he intended to signify that, after his death, the different modes of singing hymns would give rise to great seditions, and that his successors would not show the same consideration to the people which he had manifested.

CHAP. XXI. — LETTER OF CONSTANTIUS TO THE EGYPTIANS IN BEHALF OF ATHANASIUS. SYNOD OF JERUSALEM.

THE emperor, on sending back[2] Athanasius to Egypt, wrote in his favor to the bishops and presbyters of that country, and to the people of the church of Alexandria; he testified to the integrity of his conduct and the virtue of his manners, and exhorted them to be of one mind, and to unite in prayer and service to God under his guidance. He added that, if any evil-disposed persons should excite disturbances, they should receive the punishment awarded by the laws for such offenses. He also commanded that the former decrees he had enacted against Athanasius, and those who were in communion with him, should be effaced from the public registers, and that his clergy should be admitted to the same exemptions they had previously enjoyed; and edicts to this effect were dispatched to the governors of Egypt and Libya.

Immediately on his arrival in Egypt, Athanasius displaced those whom he knew to be attached to Arianism, and placed the government of the Church and the confession of the Nicæan council in the hands of those whom he approved, and he exhorted them to hold to this with earnestness. It was said at that time, that, when he was traveling through other countries, he effected the same change, if he happened to visit churches which were under the Arians. He was certainly accused of having dared to perform the ceremony of ordination in cities where he had no right to do so. But because he had effected his return, although his enemies were unwilling, and it did not seem that he could be easily cast under suspicion, in that he was honored with the friendship of the Emperor Constans, he was regarded with greater consideration than before. Many bishops, who had previously been at enmity with him, received him into communion, particularly those of Palestine. When he at that time visited these latter, they received him kindly. They held a Synod at Jerusalem, and Maximus and the others wrote the following letter in his favor.

CHAP. XXII. — EPISTLE WRITTEN BY THE SYNOD OF JERUSALEM IN FAVOR OF ATHANASIUS.

"THE holy Synod assembled at Jerusalem, to the presbyters, deacons, and people of Egypt, Libya, and Alexandria, our beloved and most cherished brethren, greeting in the Lord.[3]

---

[1] Here he uses Athan. *Historia Arian.* 28; *Apol. de fuga sua,* 26. Theodoret, too, in his sketch of Leontius, *H. E.* ii. 24, quotes briefly from Athan. Cf. Philost. iii. 13.

[2] Athan. *Apol. cont. Arian.* 54–56; *Hist. Arian.* 23; these are given in Soc. ii. 23; and for the Synod of Jerusalem, ii. 24; Ruf. i. 19.
[3] From Athan. *Apol. cont. Arian.* 57, where also the names of the subscribers are given.

"We can never, O beloved, return adequate thanks to God, the Creator of all things, for the wonderful works he has now accomplished, particularly for the blessings He has conferred on your churches by the restoration of Athanasius, your shepherd and lord, and our fellow-minister. Who could have hoped to have ever seen this with his eyes, which now you are realizing in deed? But truly your prayers have been heard by the God of the universe who is concerned for His Church, and who has regarded your tears and complaint, and on this account has heard your requests. For you were scattered abroad and rent like sheep without a pastor. Therefore, the true Shepherd, who from heaven watched over you, and who is concerned for His own sheep, has restored to you him whom you desired. Behold, we do all things for the peace of the Church, and are influenced by love like yours. Therefore we received and embraced your pastor, and, having held communion with you through him, we dispatch this address and our eucharistic prayers that you may know how we are united by the bond of love to him and you. It is right that you should pray for the piety of the emperors most beloved of God, who having recognized your desire about him and his purity determined to restore him to you with every honor. Receive him, then, with uplifted hands, and be zealous to send aloft the requisite eucharistic prayers in his behalf to the God who has conferred these benefits upon you; and may you ever rejoice with God, and glorify the Lord in Christ Jesus our Lord, by whom be glory to the Father throughout all ages. Amen."

CHAP. XXIII. — VALENS AND URSACIUS, WHO BELONGED TO THE ARIAN FACTION, CONFESS TO THE BISHOP OF ROME THAT THEY HAD MADE FALSE CHARGES AGAINST ATHANASIUS.

SUCH was the letter written by the Synod convened in Palestine. Some time after Athanasius had the satisfaction of seeing the injustice of the sentence enacted against him by the council of Tyre publicly recognized.[1] Valens and Ursacius, who had been sent with Theognis and his followers to obtain information in Mareotis, as we before mentioned, concerning the holy cup which Ischyrion had accused Athanasius of having broken, wrote the following retraction to Julius, bishop of Rome: —

"Ursacius and Valens, to the most blessed Lord Pope Julius.

"Since we previously, as is well known, made many various charges against Athanasius, the bishop, by our letters, and although we have been urged persistently by the epistles of your excellency in this matter which we publicly alleged and have not been able to give a reason for our accusation, therefore, we now confess to your excellency in the presence of all the presbyters, our brethren, that all that you have heard concerning the aforesaid Athanasius is utterly false and fictitious, and in every way foreign to his nature. For this reason, we joyfully enter into communion with him, particularly as your piety in accordance with your implanted love of goodness has granted forgiveness to us for our error. Moreover, we declare unto you that if the bishops of the East, or even Athanasius himself, should at any time malignantly summon us to judgment, we would not sever ourselves from your judgment and disposition about the case. We now and ever shall anathematize, as we formerly did in the memorial which we presented at Milan, the heretic Arius and his followers, who say that there was a time, in which the Son existed not, and that Christ is from that which had no existence, and who deny that Christ was God and the Son of God before all ages. We again protest, in our own handwriting, that we shall ever condemn the aforesaid Arian heresy, and its originators.

"I, Ursacius, sign this confession with my own signature. In like manner also Valens."

This was the confession which they sent to Julius. It is also necessary to append to it their letter to Athanasius: it is as follows: —

CHAP. XXIV. — LETTER OF CONCILIATION FROM VALENS AND URSACIUS TO THE GREAT ATHANASIUS. RESTORATION OF THE OTHER EASTERN BISHOPS TO THEIR OWN SEES. EJECTION OF MACEDONIUS AGAIN; AND ACCESSION OF PAUL TO THE SEE.

"THE bishops, Ursacius and Valens, to Athanasius, our brother in the Lord.[2]

"We take the opportunity of the departure of Museus, our brother and fellow-presbyter, who is going to your esteemed self, O beloved brother, to send you amplest greeting from Aquileia through him, and hope that our letter will find you in good health. You will afford us great encouragement if you will write us a reply to this letter. Know that we are at peace and in ecclesiastical communion with you."

Athanasius therefore returned under such circumstances from the West to Egypt. Paul, Marcellus, Asclepas, and Lucius, whom the edict of the emperor had returned from exile, received their own sees. Immediately on the return of Paul to Constantinople Macedonius retired, and held church in private. There was a great tumult at Ancyra on the deposition of Basil from the church there, and the reinstallation of Marcellus. The other bishops were reinstated in their churches without difficulty.[3]

---

[1] From Athan. *Apol. cont. Arian.* 58; Soc. ii. 24, only an allusion; Hil. *Fragm.* ii. 20; Sulp. Sev. *H. S.* ii. 36.

[2] Athan. *Apol. cont. Arian.* 58; Hil. *Fragm.* ii. 20.
[3] Soc. ii. 23.

BOOK IV.

CHAP. I. — DEATH OF CONSTANS CÆSAR. OCCURRENCES WHICH TOOK PLACE IN ROME.

FOUR years after the council of Sardica,[1] Constans was killed in Western Gaul.[2] Magnentius, who had plotted his murder, reduced the entire government of Constans under his own sway. In the meantime Vetranio was proclaimed emperor at Sirmium, by the Illyrian troops. Nepotian, the son of the late emperor's sister, gathered about him a body of gladiators, and wrangled for the imperial power, and ancient Rome had the greatest share of these evils. Nepotian, however, was put to death by the soldiers of Magnentius.[3] Constantius, finding himself the sole master of the empire, was proclaimed sole ruler, and hastened to depose the tyrants. In the meantime, Athanasius, having arrived in Alexandria, prepared to convene a Synod of the Egyptian bishops, and had the enactments confirmed which had been passed at Sardica, and in Palestine, in his favor.

CHAP. II. — CONSTANTIUS AGAIN EJECTS ATHANASIUS, AND BANISHES THOSE WHO REPRESENTED THE HOMOOUSIAN DOCTRINE. DEATH OF PAUL, BISHOP OF CONSTANTINOPLE. MACEDONIUS : HIS SECOND USURPATION OF THE SEE, AND HIS EVIL DEEDS.

THE emperor,[4] deceived by the calumnies of the heterodox, changed his mind, and, in opposition to the decrees of the council of Sardica, exiled the bishops whom he had previously restored. Marcellus was again deposed, and Basil re-acquired possession of the bishopric of Ancyra. Lucius was thrown into prison, and died there. Paul was condemned to perpetual banishment, and was conveyed to Cucusum, in Armenia, where he died. I have never, however, been able to ascertain whether or not he died a natural death. It is still reported, that he was strangled by the adherents of Macedonius.[5] As soon as he was sent into exile, Macedonius seized the government of his church ; and, being aided by several orders of monks whom he had incorporated at Constantinople, and by alliances with many of the neighboring bishops, he commenced, it is said, a persecution against those who held the sentiments of Paul. He ejected them, in the first place, from the church, and then compelled them to enter into communion with himself. Many perished from wounds received in the struggle ; some were deprived of their possessions ; some, of the rights of citizenship ; and others were branded on the forehead with an iron instrument, in order that they might be stamped as infamous. The emperor was displeased when he heard of these transactions, and imputed the blame of them to Macedonius and his adherents.

CHAP. III. — MARTYRDOM OF THE HOLY NOTARIES.

THE persecution increased in violence,[6] and led to deeds of blood. Martyrius and Marcian were among those who were slain. They had lived in Paul's house,[7] and were delivered up by Macedonius to the governor, as having been guilty of the murder of Hermogenes, and of exciting the former sedition against him. Martyrius was a sub-deacon, and Marcian a singer and a reader of Holy Scripture. Their tomb is famous, and is situated before the walls of Constantinople, as a memorial of the martyrs ; it is placed in a house of prayer, which was commenced by John and completed by Sisinnius ; these both afterwards presided over the church of Constantinople. For they who had been unworthily adjudged to have no part in the honors of martyrdom, were honored by God, because the very place where those conducted to death had been decapitated, and which previously was not approached on account of ghosts, was now purified, and those who were under the influence of demons were released from the disease, and many other notable miracles were wrought at the tomb. These are the particulars which should be stated concerning Martyrius and Marcian. If what I have related appears

[1] According to Soz. A.D. 351, really A.D. 350.
[2] Ruf. *H. E.* i. 19; Soc. ii. 25, 26. Soz. here condenses Soc. Cf. Athan. *Apol. ad. Imp. Constantium.*
[3] Zos. ii. 41–53; Am. Marcel. xv. 1, 2; Petrus Patricius, *Historia,* 14; Eutrop. *Brev. Hist. Rom.* x. 9–11.
[4] Soc. ii. 26, 27; Athan. *Hist. Arian.* 7; *Apol. de fuga sua,* 3; cf. Theodoret, *H. E.* ii. 5.
[5] See preceding references; Athan. is decided.

[6] An independent chapter.
[7] Niceph. Coll. *H. E.* ix. 30 adds that they were the notaries of Paul; hence the caption. The memory of these martyrs is celebrated in the Greek Church under the name of the Notaries, on the 25th of October.

to be scarcely credible, it is easy to apply for further information to those who are more accurately acquainted with the circumstances ; and perhaps far more wonderful things are related concerning them than those which I have detailed.

CHAP. IV. — CAMPAIGN OF CONSTANTIUS IN SIRMIUM, AND DETAILS CONCERNING VETRANIO AND MAGNENTIUS. GALLUS RECEIVES THE TITLE OF CÆSAR, AND IS SENT TO THE EAST.

ON the expulsion of Athanasius, which took place about this period, George persecuted[1] all those throughout Egypt who refused to conform to his sentiments. The emperor marched into Illyria, and entered Sirmium, whither Vetranio had repaired by appointment. The soldiers who had proclaimed him emperor suddenly changed their mind, and saluted Constantius as sole sovereign, and as Augustus, for both the emperor and his supporters, strove for this very action. Vetranio perceived that he was betrayed, and threw himself as a suppliant at the feet of Constantius. Constantius pitied him indeed, but stripped him of the imperial ornaments and purple, obliged him to return to private life, liberally provided for his wants out of the public treasury, and told him that it was more seemly to an old man to abstain from the cares of empire and to live in quietude. After terminating these arrangements in favor of Vetranio, Constantius sent a large army into Italy against Magnentius. He then conferred the title of Cæsar on his cousin Gallus, and sent him into Syria to defend the provinces of the East.

CHAP. V. — CYRIL DIRECTS THE SACERDOTAL OFFICE AFTER MAXIMUS, AND THE LARGEST FORM OF THE CROSS, SURPASSING THE SUN IN SPLENDOR, AGAIN APPEARS IN THE HEAVENS, AND IS VISIBLE DURING SEVERAL DAYS.

AT the time that Cyril administered the church of Jerusalem after Maximus, the sign of the cross appeared in the heavens. It shone brilliantly, not with divergent rays like a comet, but with the concentration of a great deal of light, apparently dense and yet transparent. Its length was about fifteen stadia from Calvary to the Mount of Olives, and its breadth was in proportion to its length. So extraordinary a phenomenon excited universal terror. Men, women, and children left their houses, the market-place, or their respective employments, and ran to the church, where they sang hymns to Christ together, and voluntarily confessed their belief in God. The intelligence disturbed in no little measure our entire dominions, and this happened rapidly ; for, as the custom was, there were travelers from every part of the world, so to speak, who were dwelling at Jerusalem for prayer, or to visit its places of interest, these were spectators of the sign, and divulged the facts to their friends at home. The emperor was made acquainted with the occurrence, partly by numerous reports concerning it which were then current, and partly by a letter from Cyril[2] the bishop. It was said that this prodigy was a fulfillment of an ancient prophecy contained in the Holy Scriptures. It was the means of the conversion of many pagans and Jews to Christianity.

CHAP. VI. — PHOTINUS, BISHOP OF SIRMIUM. HIS HERESY, AND THE COUNCIL CONVENED AT SIRMIUM IN OPPOSITION THERETO. THE THREE FORMULARIES OF FAITH. THIS AGITATOR OF EMPTY IDEAS WAS REFUTED BY BASIL OF ANCYRA. AFTER HIS DEPOSITION PHOTINUS, ALTHOUGH SOLICITED, DECLINED RECONCILIATION.

ABOUT this time,[3] Photinus, who administered the church of Sirmium, laid before the emperor, who was then staying at that city, a heresy which he had originated some time previously. His natural ease of utterance and powers of persuasion enabled him to lead many into his own way of thinking. He acknowledged that there was one God Almighty, by whose own word all things were created, but would not admit that the generation and existence of the Son was before all ages ; on the contrary, he alleged that Christ derived His existence from Mary. As soon as this opinion was divulged, it excited the indignation of the Western and of the Eastern bishops, and they considered it in common as an innovation of each one's particular belief, for it was equally opposed by those who maintained the doctrines of the Nicæan council, and by those who favored the tenets of Arius. The emperor also regarded the heresy with aversion, and convened a council at Sirmium, where he was then residing. Of the Eastern bishops, George, who governed the church of Alexandria, Basil, bishop of Ancyra, and Mark, bishop of Arethusa, were present at this council ; and among the Western

1 Eutrop. *Brev. Hist. Rom.* x. 11, 12; Zos. ii. 44, 45; Athan. *Apol. de fuga sua*, 6, 7; *Ep. ad Episc. Æg. et Lib.* 7; Soc. ii. 25-29; Ruf. *H. E.* i. 19; Philost. iii. 22, 25.

2 The letter here alluded to by Sozomen was addressed by Cyril of Jerusalem to Constantius, and is extant among his works. C. 1165, *M. P. G.* 33; cf. Soc. ii. 28; Philost. iii. 26; Hieron. *Chron. Eus.* s. A.D. 357.

3 Athan. *de Synodis*, 8, 9; Soc. ii. 29-31, 37; Sulp. Sev. *H. S.* ii. 36, 37.

bishops were Valens, bishop of Mursa, and Hosius the Confessor. This latter, who had attended the council of Nicæa, was unwillingly a participant of this; he had not long previously been condemned to banishment through the machinations of the Arians; he was summoned to the council of Sirmium by the command of the emperor extorted by the Arians, who believed that their party would be strengthened, if they could gain over, either by persuasion or force, a man held in universal admiration and esteem, as was Hosius. The period at which the council was convened at Sirmium, was the year after the expiration of the consulate of Sergius and Nigrinian; and during this year there were no consuls either in the East or the West, owing to the insurrections excited by the tyrants. Photinus was deposed by this council, because he was accused of countenancing the errors of Sabellius and Paul of Samosata. The council then proceeded to draw up three formularies of faith in addition to the previous confessions, of which one was written in Greek, and the others in Latin. But they did not agree with one another, nor with any other of the former expositions of doctrine, either in word or import. It is not said in the Greek formulary,[1] that the Son is consubstantial, or of like substance, with the Father, but it is there declared, that those who maintain that the Son had no commencement, or that He proceeded from an expansion of the substance of the Father, or that He is united to the Father without being subject to Him, are excommunicated. In one of the Roman formularies,[2] it is forbidden to say, of the essence of the Godhead which the Romans call substance, that the Son is either consubstantial, or of like substance with the Father, as such statements do not occur in the Holy Scriptures, and are beyond the reach of the understanding and knowledge of men. It is said, that the Father must be recognized as superior to the Son in honor, in dignity, in divinity, and in the relationship suggested by His name of Father; and that it must be confessed that the Son, like all created beings, is subject to the Father, that the Father had no commencement, and that the generation of the Son is unknown to all save the Father. It is related, that when this formulary was completed, the bishops became aware of the errors it contained, and endeavored to withdraw it from the public, and to correct it; and that the emperor threatened to punish those who should retain or conceal any of the copies that had been made of it. But having been once published, no efforts were adequate to suppress it altogether.

The third formulary[3] is of the same import as the others. It prohibits the use of the term "substance" on account of the terms used in Latin, while the Greek term having been used with too much simplicity by the Fathers, and having been a cause of offense to many of the unlearned multitude, because it was not to be found in the Scriptures, "we have deemed it right totally to reject the use of it: and we would enjoin the omission of all mention of the term in allusion to the Godhead, for it is nowhere said in the Holy Scriptures, that the Father, Son, and Holy Ghost are of the same substance, where the word person is written. But we say, in conformity with the Holy Scriptures, that the Son is like unto the Father."

Such was the decision arrived at in the presence of the emperor concerning the faith. Hosius at first refused to assent to it. Compulsion, however, was resorted to; and being extremely old, he sunk, as it is reported, beneath the blows that were inflicted on him, and yielded his consent and signature.

After the deposition of Photinus, the Synod thought it expedient to try whether it were not somehow possible to persuade him to change his views. But when the bishop urged him, and promised to restore his bishopric if he would renounce his own dogma, and vote for their formulary, he would not acquiesce, but challenged them to a discussion. On the day appointed for this purpose, the bishops, therefore, assembled with the judges who had been appointed by the emperor to preside at their meetings, and who, in point of eloquence and dignity, held the first rank in the palace. Basil, bishop of Ancyra, was selected to commence the disputation against Photinus. The conflict lasted a long time, on account of the numerous questions started and the answers given by each party, and which were immediately taken down in short-hand; but finally the victory declared itself in favor of Basil. Photinus was condemned and banished, but did not cease on that account from enlarging his own dogma. He wrote and published many works in Greek and Latin, in which he endeavored to show that all opinions, except his own, were erroneous. I have now concluded all that I had to say concerning Photinus and the heresy to which his name was affixed.

CHAP. VII. — DEATH OF THE TYRANTS MAGNENTIUS AND SILVANUS THE APOSTATE. SEDITION OF THE JEWS IN PALESTINE. GALLUS CÆSAR IS SLAIN, ON SUSPICION OF REVOLUTION.

In the meantime,[4] Magnentius made himself

---

[1] Soc. ii. 30, text.
[2] Soc. ii. 30, Latin text translated into Greek.
[3] Athan. de Synodis, 8; Soc. ii. 37, text translated into Greek.
[4] Soc. ii. 32–34; cf. Philost. iii. 26–28; iv. 1; Orosius, vii. 29;

master of ancient Rome, and put numbers of the senators, and of the people, to death. Hearing that the troops of Constantius were approaching, he retired into Gaul; and here the two parties had frequent encounters, in which sometimes the one and sometimes the other was victorious. At length, however, Magnentius was defeated, and fled to Mursa, which is the fortress of this Gaul, and when he saw that his soldiers were dispirited because they had been defeated, he stood on an elevated spot and endeavored to revive their courage. But, although they addressed Magnentius with the acclamations usually paid to emperors, and were ready to shout at his public appearance, they secretly and without premeditation shouted for Constantius as emperor in place of Magnentius. Magnentius, concluding from this circumstance, that he was not destined by God to hold the reins of empire, endeavored to retreat from the fortress to some distant place. But he was pursued by the troops of Constantius, and being overtaken at a spot called Mount Seleucus, he escaped alone from the encounter, and fled to Lugduna. On his arrival there, he slew his own mother and his brother, whom he had named Cæsar; and lastly, he killed himself.[1] Not long after, Decentius, another of his brothers, put an end to his own existence. Still the public tumults were not quelled; for not long after, Silvanus assumed the supreme authority in Gaul; but he was put to death immediately by the generals of Constantius.

The Jews of Diocæsarea also overran Palestine and the neighboring territories; they took up arms with the design of shaking off the Roman yoke.[2] On hearing of their insurrection, Gallus Cæsar, who was then at Antioch, sent troops against them, defeated them, and destroyed Diocæsarea. Gallus, intoxicated with success, could not bear his prosperity, but aspired to the supreme power, and he slew Magnus, the quæstor, and Domitian, the prefect of the East, because they apprised the emperor of his innovations. The anger of Constantius was excited; and he summoned him to his presence. Gallus did not dare to refuse obedience, and set out on his journey. When, however, he reached the island Elavona he was killed by the emperor's order; this event occurred in the third year of his consulate, and the seventh of Constantius.[3]

CHAP. VIII.— ARRIVAL OF CONSTANTIUS AT ROME. A COUNCIL HELD IN ITALY. ACCOUNT OF WHAT HAPPENED TO ATHANASIUS THE GREAT THROUGH THE MACHINATIONS OF THE ARIANS.

On the death of the tyrants,[4] Constantius anticipated the restoration of peace and cessation of tumults, and quitted Sirmium in order to return to ancient Rome, and to enjoy the honor of a triumph after his victory over the tyrants. He likewise intended to bring the Eastern and the Western bishops, if possible, to one mind concerning doctrine, by convening a council in Italy. Julius died about this period, after having governed the church of Rome during twenty-five years;[5] and Liberius succeeded him. Those who were opposed to the doctrines of the Nicæan council thought this a favorable opportunity to calumniate the bishops whom they had deposed, and to procure their ejection from the church as abettors of false doctrine, and as disturbers of the public peace; and to accuse them of having sought, during the life of Constans, to excite a misunderstanding between the emperors; and it was true, as we related above,[6] that Constans menaced his brother with war unless he would consent to receive the orthodox bishops. Their efforts were principally directed against Athanasius, towards whom they entertained so great an aversion that, even when he was protected by Constans, and enjoyed the friendship of Constantius, they could not conceal their enmity. Narcissus, bishop of Cilicia, Theodore, bishop of Thrace, Eugenius, bishop of Nicæa, Patrophilus, bishop of Scythopolis, Menophantes, bishop of Ephesus, and other bishops, to the number of thirty, assembled themselves in Antioch,[7] and wrote a letter to all the bishops of every region, in which they stated that Athanasius had returned to his bishopric in violation of the rules of the Church, that he had not justified himself in any council, and that he was only supported by some of his own faction; and they exhorted them not to hold communion with him, nor to write to him, but to enter into communion with George, who had been ordained to succeed him. Athanasius only contemned these proceedings; but he was about to undergo greater trials than any he had yet experienced. Immediately on the death of Magnentius, and as soon as Constantius found himself sole master of the Roman Empire, he directed all his efforts to induce the bishops of the West to admit that the Son is of like substance with the Father. In carrying out this scheme, however, he did not, in the first place, resort to compulsion, but endeavored by persuasion to obtain the concurrence of the other bishops in the decrees of the Eastern bishops against Athanasius; for he thought that if he could

---

language and order like Soz.; Sulp. Sev. *H. S.* ii. 38; Am. Marcel. xiv. 1, 7-9, 11; Zos. ii. 45-55; Eutrop. *Brev. hist. Rom.* x. 12, 13.
[1] A.D. 353.   [2] Soc. ii. 33, 34.   [3] A.D. 353.

[4] Independent chapter.
[5] Sozomen is mistaken in saying twenty-five years; he was bishop from A.D. 337-352, fifteen years; this error is due to his earlier confusion of Julius and Silvester.
[6] See above, iii. 20.
[7] Sozomen is the only historian who makes mention of this Synod at Antioch in Syria; probably from Sabinus.

bring them to be of one mind on this point, it would be easy for him to regulate aright the affairs connected with religion.

CHAP. IX. — COUNCIL OF MILAN.   FLIGHT OF ATHANASIUS.

THE emperor[1] was extremely urgent to convene a council in Milan, yet few of the Eastern bishops repaired thither; some, it appears, excused themselves from attendance under the plea of illness; others, on account of the length and difficulties of the journey. There were, however, upwards of three hundred of the Western bishops at the council. The Eastern bishops insisted that Athanasius should be condemned to banishment, and expelled from Alexandria; and the others, either from fear, fraud, or ignorance, assented to the measure. Dionysius, bishop of Alba, the metropolis of Italy, Eusebius, bishop of Vercella in Liguria, Paulinus, bishop of Treves, Rhodanus,[2] and Lucifer, were the only bishops who protested against this decision; and they declared that Athanasius ought not to be condemned on such slight pretexts; and that the evil would not cease with his condemnation; but that those who supported the orthodox doctrines concerning the Godhead would be forthwith subjected to a plot. They represented that the whole measure was a scheme concerted by the emperor and the Arians with the view of suppressing the Nicene faith. Their boldness was punished by an edict of immediate banishment, and Hilary was exiled with them. The result too plainly showed for what purpose the council of Milan had been convened. For the councils which were held shortly after at Ariminum and Seleucia were evidently designed to change the doctrines established by the Nicæan council, as I shall directly show.

Athanasius, being apprised that plots had been formed against him at court, deemed it prudent not to repair to the emperor himself, as he knew that his life would be thereby endangered, nor did he think that it would be of any avail. He, however, selected five of the Egyptian bishops, among whom was Serapion, bishop of Thumis, a prelate distinguished by the wonderful sanctity of his life and the power of his eloquence, and sent them with three presbyters of the Church to the emperor, who was then in the West. They were directed to attempt, if possible, to conciliate the emperor; to reply, if requisite, to the calumnies of the hostile party; and to take such measures as they deemed most advisable for the welfare of the Church and himself. Shortly after they had embarked on their voyage, Athanasius received some letters from the emperor, summoning him to the palace. Athanasius and all the people of the Church were greatly troubled at this command; for they considered that no safety could be enjoyed when acting either in obedience or in disobedience to an emperor of heterodox sentiments. It was, however, determined that he should remain at Alexandria, and the bearer of the letters quitted the city without having effected anything. The following summer, another messenger from the emperor arrived with the governors of the provinces, and he was charged to urge the departure of Athanasius from the city, and to act with hostility against the clergy. When he perceived, however, that the people of the Church were full of courage, and ready to take up arms, he also departed from the city without accomplishing his mission. Not long after, troops, called the Roman legions, which were quartered in Egypt and Libya, marched into Alexandria. As it was reported that Athanasius was concealed in the church known by the name "Theonas," the commander of the troops, and Hilary,[3] whom the emperor had again intrusted with the transaction of this affair, caused the doors of the church to be burst open, and thus effected their entrance; but they did not find Athanasius within the walls, although they sought for him everywhere. It is said that he escaped this and many other perils by the Divine interposition; and that God had disclosed this previously; directly as he went out, the soldiers took the doors of the church, and were within a little of seizing him.

CHAP. X. — DIVERS MACHINATIONS OF THE ARIANS AGAINST ATHANASIUS, AND HIS ESCAPE FROM VARIOUS DANGERS THROUGH DIVINE INTERPOSITION.   EVIL DEEDS PERPETRATED BY GEORGE IN EGYPT AFTER THE EXPULSION OF ATHANASIUS.

THERE is no doubt but that Athanasius was beloved of God, and endowed with the gift of foreseeing the future.[4] More wonderful facts than those which we have related might be adduced to prove his intimate acquaintance with futurity. It happened that during the life of Constans, the Emperor Constantius was once determined upon ill-treating this holy man; but Athanasius fled, and concealed himself with some one of his acquaintances. He lived for a long time in a subterranean and sunless dwelling, which

---

[1] Ruf. *H. E.* i. 19, 20; Athan. *Hist. Arian.* 31–46, and probably the lost letter of consecration addressed to the nuns; Theodoret, *H. E.* ii. 14, 15; Soc. ii. 36; Sulp. Sev. *H. S.* ii. 39.
[2] Or, as Rufinus and Sulpicius Severus call him, Rhodanius. Socrates omits Rhodanus and Lucifer, and does not mention Hilary. Sozomen evidently used Rufinus. Rhodanus was bishop of Toulouse. Sulp. Sev. *H. S.* ii. 39.

[3] The general was Syrianus; Hilary was notary to the Emperor Constantius, and was sent by him to expel Athanasius from Alexandria. On the whole passage, see Athan. *Apol. ad Const. imp.* 19–25; *Apol. de fuga sua*, 24.
[4] Ruf. *H. E.* i. 18, 33, 34; Soc. ii. 45; iii. 14; Sozomen groups these stories without regard to time; see next chapter; he has some independent material.

had been used as a reservoir for water. No one knew where he was concealed except a serving-woman, who seemed faithful, and who waited upon him. As the heterodox, however, were anxiously intent upon taking Athanasius alive, it appears that, by means of gifts or promises, they at length succeeded in corrupting the attendant. But Athanasius was forewarned by God of her treachery, and effected his escape from the place. The servant was punished for having made a false deposition against her masters, while they, on their part, fled the country; for it was accounted no venial crime by the heterodox to receive or to conceal Athanasius, but was, on the contrary, regarded as an act of disobedience against the express commands of the emperor, and as a crime against the empire, and was visited as such by the civil tribunals. It has come to my hearing that Athanasius was saved on another occasion in a similar manner. He was again obliged for the same reason to flee for his life; and he set sail up the Nile[1] with the design of retreating to the further districts of Egypt, but his enemies received intelligence of his intention, and pursued him. Being forewarned of God that he would be pursued, he announced it to his fellow-passengers, and commanded them to return to Alexandria. While he sailed down the river, his plotters rowed by. He reached Alexandria in safety, and effectually concealed himself in the midst of its similar and numerous houses. His success in avoiding these and many other perils led to his being accused of sorcery by the pagan and the heterodox. It is reported, that once, as he was passing through the city, a crow was heard to caw, and that a number of pagans who happened to be on the spot, asked him in derision what the crow was saying. He replied, smiling, "It utters the sound cras, the meaning of which in the Latin language is, 'to-morrow'; and it has hereby announced to you that the morrow will not be propitious to you; for it indicates that you will be forbidden by the Roman emperor to celebrate your festival to-morrow." Although this prediction of Athanasius appeared to be absurd, it was fulfilled; for the following day edicts were transmitted to the governors from the emperor, by which it was commanded that the pagans were not to be permitted to assemble in the temples to perform their usual ceremonies, nor to celebrate their festival; and thus was abolished the most solemn and magnificent feast which the pagans had retained. What I have said is sufficient to show that this holy man was endowed with the gift of prophecy.

After Athanasius had escaped, in the manner we have described, from those who sought to arrest him, his clergy and people remained for some time in possession of the churches; but eventually, the governor of Egypt and the commander of the army forcibly ejected all those who maintained the sentiments of Athanasius, in order to deliver up the government of the churches to those who favored George, whose arrival was then expected. Not long after he reached the city, and the churches were placed under his authority. He ruled by force rather than by priestly moderation; and as he strove to strike terror into the minds of the people, and carried on a cruel persecution against the followers of Athanasius, and, moreover, imprisoned and maimed many men and women, he was accounted a tyrant. For these reasons he fell into a universal hate; the people were so deeply incensed at his conduct, that they rushed into the church, and would have torn him to pieces; in such an extremity of danger, he escaped with difficulty, and fled to the emperor. Those who held the sentiments of Athanasius then took possession of the churches. But they did not long retain the mastery of them; for the commander of the troops in Egypt came and restored the churches to the partisans of George. An imperial shorthand writer of the notary class was afterwards sent to punish the leaders of the sedition, and he tortured and scourged many of the citizens. When George returned a little while after, he was more formidable, it appears, than ever, and was regarded with greater aversion than before, for he instigated the emperor to the perpetration of many evil deeds; and besides, the monks of Egypt openly declared him to be perfidious and inflated with arrogance. The opinions of these monks were always adopted by the people, and their testimony was universally received, because they were noted for their virtue and the philosophical tenor of their lives.

CHAP. XI. — LIBERIUS, BISHOP OF ROME, AND THE CAUSE OF HIS BEING EXILED BY CONSTANTIUS. FELIX HIS SUCCESSOR.

ALTHOUGH what I have recorded did not occur to Athanasius and the church of Alexandria, at the same period of time after the death of Constans, yet I deemed it right, for the sake of greater clearness, to relate all these events collectively. The council of Milan[2] was dissolved without any business having been transacted, and the emperor condemned to banishment all those who had opposed the designs of the enemies of Athanasius. As Constantius

---

[1] Soc. iii. 14.

[2] Athan. *Hist. Arian.* 31–46; Ruf. *H. E.* i. 21; Soc. ii. 36; Sulp. Sev. *H. S.* ii. 39; cf. Theodoret, *H. E.* ii. 16, dialogue between the emperor and Liberius; Am. Marcel. xv. 7.

wished to establish uniformity of doctrine throughout the Church, and to unite the priesthood in the maintenance of the same sentiments, he formed a plan to convene the bishops of every religion to a council, to be held in the West. He was aware of the difficulty of carrying this scheme into execution, arising from the vast extent of land and seas which some of the bishops would have to traverse, yet he did not altogether despair of success. While this project was occupying his mind, and before he prepared to make his triumphal entrance into Rome, he sent for Liberius, the bishop of Rome, and strove to persuade him to conformity of sentiment with the priests by whom he was attended, amongst whom was Eudoxius. As Liberius, however, refused compliance, and protested that he would never yield on this point, the emperor banished him to Berœa, in Thrace. It is alleged, that another pretext for the banishment of Liberius was, that he would not withdraw from communion with Athanasius, but manfully opposed the emperor, who insisted that Athanasius had injured the Church, had occasioned the death of the elder of his two brothers,[1] and had sown the seeds of enmity between Constans and himself. As the emperor revived all the decrees which had been enacted against Athanasius by various councils, and particularly by that of Tyre, Liberius told him that no regard ought to be paid to edicts which were issued from motives of hatred, of favor, or of fear. He desired that the bishops of every region should be made to sign the formulary of faith compiled at Nicæa, and that those bishops who had been exiled on account of their adherence to it should be recalled. He suggested that after these matters were righted all the bishops should, at their own expense, and without being furnished either with public conveyances or money, so as not to seem burdensome and destructive, proceed to Alexandria, and make an accurate test of the truth, which could be more easily instituted at that city than elsewhere, as the injured and those who had inflicted injury as well as the confuters of the charges dwelt there. He then exhibited the letter written by Valens and Ursacius to Julius, his predecessor in the Roman see, in which they solicited his forgiveness, and acknowledged that the depositions brought against Athanasius, at the Mareotis, were false ; and he besought the emperor not to condemn Athanasius during his absence, nor to give credit to enactments which were evidently obtained by the machinations of his enemies. With respect to the alleged injuries which had been inflicted on his two brothers, he entreated the emperor not

to revenge himself by the hands of priests who had been set apart by God, not for the execution of vengeance, but for sanctification, and the performance of just and benevolent actions.

The emperor perceiving that Liberius was not disposed to comply with his mandate, commanded that he should be conveyed to Thrace, unless he would change his mind within two days. "To me, O emperor," replied Liberius, "there is no need of deliberation ; my resolution has long been formed and decided, and I am ready to go forth to exile." It is said, that when he was being conducted to banishment, the emperor sent him five hundred pieces of gold ; he, however, refused to receive them, and said to the messenger who brought them, "Go, and tell him who sent this gold to give it to the flatterers and hypocrites[2] who surround him, for their insatiable cupidity plunges them into a state of perpetual want which can never be relieved. Christ, who is in all respects,[3] like unto his Father, supplies us with food and with all good things."

Liberius having for the above reasons been deposed from the Roman church, his government was transferred to Felix, a deacon of the clergy there. It is said that Felix always continued in adherence to the Nicene faith ; and that, with respect to his conduct in religious matters he was blameless. The only thing alleged against him was, that, prior to his ordination, he held communion with the heterodox. When the emperor entered Rome, the people loudly demanded Liberius, and besought his return ; after consulting with the bishops who were with him, he replied that he would recall Liberius and restore him to the people, if he would consent to embrace the same sentiments as those held by the priests of the court.

CHAP. XII. — AETIUS, THE SYRIAN, AND EUDOXIUS, THE SUCCESSOR OF LEONTIUS IN ANTIOCH. CONCERNING THE TERM "CONSUBSTANTIAL."

ABOUT this time,[4] Aetius broached his peculiar opinions concerning the Godhead. He was then deacon of the church of Antioch, and had been ordained by Leontius.[5] He maintained, like Arius, that the Son is a created being, that He was created out of nothing, and that He is dissimilar from the Father. As he was extremely addicted to contention, very bold in his assertions on theological subjects, and prone to have

---

[1] The dialogue is preserved in Theodoret, *H. E.* ii. 16. Cf. Hil. *Fragm.* v., vi.

[2] He means the Arian bishops. It is like the terms Athanasius employs.
[3] One would have expected from Liberius "the same," i.e. ὁμός instead of ὅμοιος.
[4] iii. 15, and references there; Athan. *de Synodis*, 8, 38; Soc. ii. 35, 36; cf. Theodoret, *H. E.* ii. 24.
[5] So also says Socrates. But Epiphanius asserts that he was ordained by George of Alexandria in Taurus. *Adv. hæres.* iii. 1, 38 (*hæres.* lxxiii.).

recourse to a very subtle mode of argumentation, he was accounted a heretic, even by those who held the same sentiments as himself. When he had been, for this reason, excommunicated by the heterodox, he feigned a refusal to hold communion with them, because they had unjustly admitted Arius into communion after he had perjured himself by declaring to the Emperor Constantine that he maintained the doctrines of the council of Nicæa. Such is the account given of Aetius.

While the emperor was in the West, tidings arrived of the death of Leontius, bishop of Antioch. Eudoxius requested permission of the emperor to return to Syria, that he might superintend the affairs of that church. On permission being granted, he repaired with all speed to Antioch, and installed himself as bishop of that city without the sanction of George, bishop of Laodicea; of Mark, bishop of Arethusa; of the other Syrian bishops; or of any other bishop to whom the right of ordination pertained. It was reported that he acted with the concurrence of the emperor, and of the eunuchs belonging to the palace, who, like Eudoxius, favored the doctrines of Aetius, and believed that the Son is dissimilar from the Father. When Eudoxius found himself in possession of the church of Antioch, he ventured to uphold this heresy openly. He assembled in Antioch all those who held the same opinions as himself, among whom was Acacius, bishop of Tyre, and rejected the terms, " of like substance," and " consubstantial," under the pretext that they had been denounced by the Western bishops. For Hosius, with some of the priests there, had certainly, with the view of arresting the contention excited by Valens, Ursacius, and Germanius,[1] consented, though by compulsion,[2] at Sirmium, as it is reported, to refrain from the use of the terms " consubstantial" and " of like substance," because such terms do not occur in the Holy Scriptures, and are beyond the understanding of men.[3] They[4] sent an epistle to the bishops as though these sustained the writings of Hosius on this point, and conveyed their thanks to Valens, Ursacius, and Germanius, because they had given the impulse of right views to the Western bishops.

CHAP. XIII.— INNOVATIONS OF EUDOXIUS CENSURED IN A LETTER WRITTEN BY GEORGE, BISHOP OF LAODICEA. DEPUTATION FROM THE COUNCIL OF ANCYRA TO CONSTANTIUS.

AFTER Eudoxius had introduced these new doctrines, many members of the church of Antioch, who were opposed to them, were excommunicated.[5] George, bishop of Laodicea, gave them a letter to take to the bishops who had been invited from the neighboring towns of Ancyra in Galatia by Basil, for the purpose of consecrating a church which he had erected. This letter was as follows : —

" George, to his most honored lords Macedonius, Basil, Cecropius, and Eugenius, sends greeting in the Lord.

" Nearly the whole city has suffered from the shipwreck of Aetius. The disciples of this wicked man, whom you contemned, have been encouraged by Eudoxius, and promoted by him to clerical appointments, and Aetius himself has been raised to the highest honor. Go, then, to the assistance of this great city, lest by its shipwreck the whole world should be submerged. Assemble yourselves together, and solicit the signatures of other bishops, that Aetius may be ejected from the church of Antioch, and that his disciples who have been manipulated beforehand into the lists of the clergy by Eudoxius, may be cut off. If Eudoxius persist in affirming with Aetius, that the Son is dissimilar from the Father, and in preferring those who uphold this dogma to those who reject it, the city of Antioch is lost to you." Such was the strain of George's letter.

The bishops who were assembled at Ancyra clearly perceived by the enactments of Eudoxius at Antioch, that he contemplated the introduction of innovations in doctrine; they apprised the emperor of this fact, and besought him that the doctrine established at Sardica, at Sirmium, and at other councils, might be confirmed, and especially the dogma that the Son is of like substance with the Father. In order to proffer this request to the emperor, they sent to him a deputation composed of the following bishops : Basil, bishop of Ancyra; Eustathius, bishop of Sebaste ; Eleusius, bishop of Cyzicus ; and Leontius, the presbyter of the imperial bedchamber. On their arrival at the palace, they found that Asphalius, a presbyter of Antioch, and a zealot of the Aetian heresy, was on the point of taking his departure, after having terminated the business for which he undertook the journey and having obtained a letter from the emperor. On receiving, however, the intelligence concerning the heresy conveyed by the deputation from Ancyra, Constantius condemned Eudoxius and his followers, withdrew the letter he had confided to Asphalius, and wrote the following one : —

---

[1] Otherwise called Germinius. He was afterwards promoted to the bishopric of Sirmium, according to Athan. *Hist. Arian.* 74; cf. *de Synodis*, 1, 8.
[2] See, above, chap. vi. near the end.
[3] Athanasius also excuses the lapse of Hosius on the ground that he acted under compulsion.
[4] Not the individual letter of Eudoxius, according to some readings, but of the Synod of Antioch.

[5] Philost. iv. 4-6, 8; x. 12; and fragment in Suidas s. Eudoxius; Athan. *Hist. Arian.* 4, 5; Hil. *de Synod.* 8, 9, 90; Soc. ii. 37, 40; Theodoret, *H. E.* ii. 25, 26.

CHAP. XIV. — LETTER OF THE EMPEROR CONSTAN-
TIUS AGAINST EUDOXIUS AND HIS PARTISANS.

" CONSTANTIUS AUGUSTUS the Conqueror, to
the holy church in Antioch.[1]

" Eudoxius came without our authority ; let no
one suppose that he had it, for we are far from regarding such persons with favor. If they have
recourse to deceit with others in transactions like
this, they give evidence that they will refine
away the truth in still higher things. For from
what will they voluntarily refrain, who, for the
sake of power, follow the round of the cities,
leaping from one to another, as a kind of wan-
derer, prying into every nook, led by the desire
for more ? It is reported that there are among
these people certain quacks and sophists, whose
very names are scarcely to be tolerated, and
whose deeds are evil and most impious. You
all know to what set of people I allude ; for you
are all thoroughly acquainted with the doctrines
of Aetius and the heresy which he has cultivated.
He and his followers have devoted themselves
exclusively to the task of corrupting the people ;
and these clever fellows have had the audacity
to publish that we approved of their ordination.
Such is the report they circulate, after the manner of those who talk overmuch ; but it is not
true, and, indeed, far removed from the truth.
Recall to your recollection the words of which
we made use, when we first made a declaration
of our belief ; for we confessed that our Saviour
is the Son of God, and of like substance with
the Father. But these people, who have the
audacity to set forth whatever enters their imagination, concerning the Godhead, are not far removed from atheism ; and they strive, moreover,
to propagate their opinions among others. We
are convinced that their iniquitous proceedings
will fall back upon their own heads. In the
meantime, it is sufficient to eject them from
synods and from ordinary conference ; for I will
not now allude to the chastisements which must
hereafter overtake them, unless they will desist
from their madness. How great is the evil they
perpetrate, when they collect together the most
wicked persons, as if by an edict, and they select
the leaders of heresy for the clergy, thus debas-
ing the reverend order as though they were allowed to do what they please ! Who can bear
with people who fill the cities with impiety, who
secrete impurity in the most distant regions,
and who delight in nothing but in injuring the
righteous ? What an evil-working unity it is,
which limps forward to enthrone itself in the
diviner seats ! Now is the time for those who
have imbibed the truth to come forward into the
light, and whoever were previously restrained
through fear, and now would escape from con-
ventionalism, let them step into the middle ; for
the artifices of these evil men have been thoroughly confuted, and no sort of device can be
invented which will deliver them from acting
impiously. It is the duty of good men to retain
the faith of the Fathers, and, so to speak, to
augment it, without busying themselves with
other matters. I earnestly exhort those who
have escaped, though but recently, from the precipice of this heresy, to assent to the decrees
which the bishops who are wise in divine learning, have rightly determined for the better."

Thus we see that the heresy usually denominated Anomian was within a little of becoming
predominant at this period.

CHAP. XV. — THE EMPEROR CONSTANTIUS REPAIRS
TO SIRMIUM, RECALLS LIBERIUS, AND RESTORES
HIM TO THE CHURCH OF ROME ; HE ALSO COM-
MANDS FELIX TO ASSIST LIBERIUS IN THE SACER-
DOTAL OFFICE.

NOT long after these events, the emperor
returned to Sirmium from Rome ; on receiving a
deputation from the Western bishops, he recalled
Liberius from Berœa.[2] Constantius urged him,
in the presence of the deputies of the Eastern
bishops, and of the other priests who were at
the camp, to confess that the Son is not of the
same substance as the Father. He was instigated
to this measure by Basil, Eustathius, and Eusebius, who possessed great influence over him.
They had formed a compilation, in one document, of the decrees against Paul of Samosata,
and Photinus, bishop of Sirmium ; to which
they subjoined a formulary of faith drawn up at
Antioch at the consecration of the church, as if
certain persons had, under the pretext of the
term " consubstantial," attempted to establish a
heresy of their own. Liberius, Athanasius, Alexander, Severianus, and Crescens, a priest of Africa, were induced to assent to this document, as
were likewise Ursacius, Germanius, bishop of
Sirmium, Valens, bishop of Mursa, and as many
of the Eastern bishops as were present. They
partially approved of a confession of faith drawn
up by Liberius, in which he declared that those
who affirm that the Son is not like unto the
Father in substance and in all other respects,
are excommunicated. For when Eudoxius and
his partisans at Antioch, who favored the heresy
of Aetius, received the letter of Hosius, they
circulated the report that Liberius had renounced
the term " consubstantial," and had admitted

---

[1] Independent document. Cf. Theodoret, ii. 26, who alludes to the
first part of this letter, then apparently mixes another one by Constantius with it.

[2] Athan. *Hist. Arian.* 35–41; Epistles of Liberius, *M. P. L.* 8;
Hil. *Fragm.* iv.–vi.; Theodoret, *H. E.* ii. 17; Ruf. i. 22; Philost. iv.
3; Soc. ii. 37; Sulp. Sev. *H. S.* ii. 39. Many independent details.

that the Son is dissimilar from the Father. After these enactments had been made by the Western bishops, the emperor permitted Liberius to return to Rome. The bishops who were then convened at Sirmium[1] wrote to Felix, who governed the Roman church, and to the other bishops, desiring them to receive Liberius. They directed that both should share the apostolical throne and discharge the priestly duties in common, with harmony of mind; and that whatever illegalities might have occurred in the ordination of Felix, or the banishment of Liberius, might be buried in oblivion. The people of Rome regarded Liberius as a very excellent man, and esteemed him highly on account of the courage he had evinced in opposing the emperor, so that they had even excited seditions on his account, and had gone so far as to shed blood. Felix survived but a short time; and Liberius found himself in sole possession of the church. This event was, no doubt, ordained by God, that the seat of Peter might not be dishonored by the occupancy of two bishops; for such an arrangement is a sign of discord, and is foreign to ecclesiastical law.

CHAP. XVI. — THE EMPEROR PURPOSED, ON ACCOUNT OF THE HERESY OF AETIUS AND THE INNOVATIONS IN ANTIOCH, TO CONVENE A COUNCIL AT NICO-MEDIA; BUT AS AN EARTHQUAKE TOOK PLACE IN THAT CITY, AND MANY OTHER AFFAIRS INTERVENED, THE COUNCIL WAS FIRST CONVENED AT NICÆA, AND AFTERWARDS AT ARIMINUM AND SELEUCIA. ACCOUNT OF ARSACIUS, THE CONFESSOR.

SUCH were the events which transpired at Sirmium. It seemed at this period as if, from the fear of displeasing the emperor, the Eastern and Western Churches had united in the profession of the same doctrine. The emperor had determined upon convening a council at Nicæa to take into consideration the innovations introduced at Antioch, and the heresy of Aetius.[2] As Basil, however, and his party were averse to the council being held in this city, because doctrinal questions had previously been agitated there, it was determined to hold the council at Nicomedia in Bithynia; and edicts were issued, summoning the most intelligent and eloquent bishops of every nation to repair thither punctually on an appointed day, so that it might be the privilege of all the priests of the state to share in the Synod and to be present at its decisions. The great number of these bishops had commenced their journey when the calamity

that had come upon Nicomedia was reported, and that God had shaken the entire city to its foundations. Since the story of the destruction of the city everywhere prevailed and grew, the bishops arrested their journey; for as is usual in such cases, far more was rumored to those at a distance, than had actually occurred. It was reported that Nicæa, Perinthus, and the neighboring cities, even Constantinople, had been involved in the same catastrophe. The orthodox bishops were grieved immoderately at this occurrence; for the enemies of religion took occasion, on the overthrow of a magnificent church, to represent to the emperor that a multitude of bishops, men, women, and children fled to the church in the hope of their finding safety, and that they all perished. This report was not true. The earthquake occurred at the second hour of the day, at which time there was no assembly in the church. The only bishops who were killed were Cecropius, bishop of Nicomedia, and a bishop from the Bosphorus, and they were outside of the church when the fatal accident happened. The city was shaken in an instant of time, so that the people had not the power, even if they had the wish, to seek safety by flight; at the first experience of danger, they were either preserved, or they perished on the spot where they were standing.[3]

It is said that this calamity was predicted by Arsacius.[4] He was a Persian, and a soldier who was employed in tending the emperor's lions; but during the reign of Licinius he became a noted confessor, and left the army. He then went to the citadel of Nicomedia, and led the life of a monastic philosopher within its walls. Here a vision from heaven appeared to him, and he was commanded to quit the city immediately, that he might be saved from the calamity about to happen. He ran with the utmost earnestness to the church, and besought the clergy to offer supplications to God that His anger might be turned away. But, finding that far from being believed by them, he was regarded with ridicule, and as disclosing unlooked-for sufferings, he returned to his tower, and prostrated himself on the ground in prayer. Just at this moment the earthquake occurred, and many perished. Those who were spared fled into the country and the desert. And as happens in a prosperous and large city, there were fires in the brasiers and extinguishers of every house, and in the ovens of the baths, and in the furnaces of all who use fire in the arts; and when the framework fell in ruin, the flame was hemmed in by the stuff, and of course there was dry wood commingled, much of which was oily, — this served as a con-

---

[1] The fourth Sirmium council, A.D. 358.
[2] Philost. iv. 10, 11; Athan. *de Synodis*, 2–7; Soc. ii. 37, 39; cf. Theodoret, *H. E.* ii. 18, 26. Soz.'s facts are more voluminous, and the grouping independent.

[3] Cf. Am. Marcell. xvii. 7; Idatius under 358 in *Descriptio Consulum*.
[4] A story from tradition by Soz.

tribution to the rapid conflagration, and nourished the fire without stint ; the flame creeping everywhere, and attaching to itself all circumjacent material, made the entire city, so to speak, one mass of fire. It being impossible to obtain access to the houses, those who had been saved from the earthquake rushed to the citadel. Arsacius was found dead in the unshaken tower, and prostrated on the ground, in the same posture in which he had begun to pray. It was said that he had supplicated God to permit him to die, because he preferred death to beholding the destruction of a city in which he had first known Christ, and practiced monastical philosophy. As I have been led to speak of this good man, it is well to mention that he was endowed by God with the power of exorcising demons and of purifying those troubled by them. A man possessed with a demon once ran through the market-place with a naked sword in his hand. The people fled from him, and the whole city was in confusion. Arsacius went out to meet him, and called upon the name of Christ, and at that name the demon was expelled, and the man restored to sanity. Besides the above, Arsacius performed many other actions beyond the power and skill of man. There was a dragon, or some other species of reptile, which had entrenched itself in a cavity of the roadside, and which destroyed those who passed by, with its breath. Arsacius went to the spot and engaged in prayer, and the serpent voluntarily crept forth from its hole, dashed its head against the ground, and killed itself. All these details I have obtained from persons who heard them stated by those who had seen Arsacius.

As the bishops were deterred from continuing their journey by the intelligence of the calamity which had occurred at Nicomedia, some awaited the further commands of the emperor, and others declared their opinions concerning the faith in letters which they wrote on the subject. The emperor hesitates as to what measures ought to be adopted, and writes to consult Basil as to whether a council ought to be convened. In his reply, it appears, Basil commended his piety, and tried to console him for the destruction of Nicomedia by examples drawn from the Holy Scriptures ; he exhorted him, for the sake of religion, to hasten the Synod ; and not to drop such a proof of his zeal for religion, and not to dismiss the priests who had been gathered together for this purpose, and had already set forth and were on their way, until some business had been transacted. He also suggested that the council might be held at Nicæa instead of Nicomedia, so that the disputed points might be finally decided on the very spot where they had been first called

in question. Basil, in writing to this effect, believed that the emperor would be pleased with this proposition, as he had himself originally suggested the propriety of holding the council at Nicæa. On receiving this epistle from Basil, the emperor commanded that, at the commencement of summer, the bishops should assemble together at Nicæa, with the exception of those who were laboring under bodily infirmity ; and these latter were to depute presbyters and deacons to make known their sentiments and to consult together on contested points of doctrine, and arrive at the same decision concerning all points at issue. He ordained that ten delegates should be selected from the Western churches, and as many from the Eastern, to take cognizance of the enactments that might be issued, and to decide whether they were in accordance with the Holy Scriptures, and also to exercise a general superintendence over the transactions of the council. After further consultation the emperor enacted that the bishops should remain where they might be residing, or in their own churches, until it had been decided where the council was to be held, and until they received notice to repair thither. He then writes to Basil, and directs him to inquire by letter of the Eastern bishops, where they would advise the council to be held, so that a public announcement might be made at the commencement of spring ; for the emperor was of opinion that it was not advisable to convene the council at Nicæa, on account of the earthquake which had recently occurred in the province. Basil wrote to the bishops of every province, urging them to deliberate together, and to decide quickly upon the locality in which it would be most expedient to hold the council, and he prefixed a copy of the emperor's letter to his epistle. As is frequently the case in similar circumstances, the bishops were divided in opinion on the subject, and Basil repaired to the emperor, who was then at Sirmium. He found several bishops at that city who had gone thither on their own private affairs, and among them were Mark, bishop of Arethusa, and George, who had been appointed to preside over the church of Alexandria. When at length it was decided that the council should be held in Seleucia, a city of Isauria, by Valens and his adherents, for Valens was then sojourning in Sirmium ; since they favored the heresy of the Anomians, they urged the bishops who were present at the military court, to subscribe to a formulary of the faith which had been prepared, and in which there was no mention of the term "substance." But while preparations were being zealously made for convening the council, Eudoxius and Acacius, Ursacius and Valens, with their followers, reflected that, while many of the bishops were attached to the Nicene faith, and others favored the formulary drawn up at the consecration of the church of Antioch, yet that both parties retained the use of the term "substance," and maintained that the Son was, in every respect, like unto the Father; and being aware that if both parties assembled together in one place they would readily condemn the doctrines of Aetius, as being contrary to their respective creeds, they so contrived matters that the bishops of the West were convened at Ariminum, and those of the East at Seleucia, a city of Isauria. As it is easier to convince a few than a great many individuals, they conceived that they might possibly lead both parties to favor their sentiments by dealing with them separately, or that they might, at any rate, succeed with one, so that their heresy might not incur universal condemnation. They accomplished this through Eusebius, a eunuch who was superintendent of the imperial house: he was on terms of friendship with Eudoxius, and upheld the same doctrines, and many of those in power were seeking to conciliate this very Eusebius.

CHAP. XVII. — PROCEEDINGS OF THE COUNCIL OF ARIMINUM.

THE emperor[1] was persuaded that it would not be desirable for the public, on account of the expense, nor advantageous to the bishops, on account of the length of the journey, to convene them all to the same place for the purpose of holding a council. He therefore writes to the bishops who were then at Ariminum, as well as to those who were then at Seleucia, and directed them to enter upon an investigation of contested points concerning the faith, and then to turn their attention to the complaints of Cyril, bishop of Jerusalem, and of other bishops who had remonstrated against the injustice of the decrees of deposition and banishment which had been issued against them, and to examine the legality of various sentences which had been enacted against other bishops. There were, in fact, several accusations pending against different bishops. George was accused by the Egyptians of rapine and violence. Finally, the emperor commanded that ten deputies should be sent to him from each council, to inform him of their respective proceedings.

In accordance with this edict, the bishops assembled at the appointed cities. The Synod at Ariminum first commenced proceedings;[2] it consisted of about four hundred members. Those who regarded Athanasius with the greatest enmity, were of opinion that there was nothing further to be decreed against him. When they

had entered upon the investigation of doctrinal questions, Valens and Ursacius, supported by Germenius, Auxentius, Caius, and Demophilus, advanced into the middle of the assembly, and demanded that all the formularies of the faith which had been previously compiled should be suppressed, and that the formulary which they had but a short time previously set forth in the Latin language at Sirmium should be alone retained. In this formulary it was taught, according to Scripture, that the Son is like unto the Father; but no mention was made of the substance of God. They declared that this formulary had been approved by the emperor, and that it was incumbent upon the council to adopt it, instead of consulting too scrupulously the individual opinions of every member of the council, so that disputes and divisions might not spring up, were the terms to be delivered up to debate and accurate proof. They added that it would better enable those who were more ignorant of the art of discourse to have a right conception of God, than were they to introduce novelties in terms, so akin to disputatious jugglery. By these representations, they designed to denounce the use of the term "consubstantial," because they said it was not found in the Holy Scriptures, and was obscure to the multitude; and, instead of this term, they wished to substitute the expression that "the Son is like unto the Father in all things," which is borne out by the Holy Scriptures. After they had read their formulary containing the above representations, many of the bishops told them that no new formulary of the faith ought to be set forth, that those which had been previously compiled were quite sufficient for all purposes, and that they were met together for the express purpose of preventing all innovations. These bishops then urged those who had compiled and read the formulary to declare publicly their condemnation of the Arian doctrine, as the cause of all the troubles which had agitated the churches of every region. Ursacius and Valens, Germenius and Auxentius, Demophilus and Caius, having protested against this protestation, the council commanded that the expositions of the other heresies should be read, and likewise that set forth at Nicæa; so that those formularies which favored divers heresies might be condemned, and those which were in accordance with the Nicene doctrines might be approved; in order that there might be no further ground for dispute, and no future necessity for councils, but that an efficient decision might be formed.[3] They remarked that it was absurd to compose so many formularies, as if they had but just commenced to become acquainted with the faith, and as if

---

[1] Athan. *de Synodis*, 8–11; Soc. ii. 37; Ruf. i. 21; Philost. *H. E.* iv. 10; Theodoret, *H. E.* ii. 18.
[2] A.D. 359.

[3] This speech is quoted directly in Soc. ii. 37.

they wished to slight the ancient traditions of the Church, by which the churches had been governed by themselves, and by their predecessors, many of whom had witnessed a good confession, and had received the crown of martyrdom. Such were the arguments adduced by these bishops, to prove that no innovations ought to be attempted. As Valens and Ursacius and their partisans refused to be convinced by these arguments, but persisted in advocating the adoption of their own formulary, they were deposed, and it was decided that their formulary should be rejected. It was remarked that the declaration at the commencement of this formulary, of its having been compiled at Sirmium, in the presence of Constantius, "the eternal Augustus," and during the consulate of Eusebius and Hypatius, was an absurdity. Athanasius made the same remark, in a letter addressed to one of his friends,[1] and said that it was ridiculous to term Constantius the eternal emperor, and yet to shrink from acknowledging the Son of God to be eternal; he also ridiculed the date affixed to the formulary, as though condemnation were meant to be thrown on the faith of former ages, as well as on those who had, before that period, been initiated into the faith.

After these events had transpired at Ariminum, Valens and Ursacius, together with their adherents, irritated at their deposition, repaired with all haste to the emperor.

CHAP. XVIII. — LETTER FROM THE COUNCIL AT ARIMINUM TO THE EMPEROR CONSTANTIUS.

THE Synod selected twenty bishops,[2] and sent them on an embassy to the emperor, with the following letter, which has been translated from Latin into Greek : — [3]

"We believe that it is by the command of God, as well as by the arrangement of your piety, that we have been led from all the cities of the West, to assemble at Ariminum, for the purpose of declaring the faith of the Catholic Church, and of detecting those who have set forth heresies in opposition to it. After a protracted investigation, we have come to the conclusion that it is best to preserve that faith which has been continuous from antiquity, and which was preached by the prophets, the evangelists, the apostles of our Lord Jesus Christ, the Guardian of your empire, and Protector of your strength, by holding on thereto and guarding it to the end. It would have been absurd, as well as illegal, to have introduced any change in the doctrines which were so rightly and so justly

propounded by the bishops at Nicæa, with the concurrence of the most illustrious Constantine, the emperor and your father, whose teaching and thought has gone forth and been preached in the universal hearing and reflection of men ; and it is the antagonist and destroyer of the Arian heresy ; through whose agency not only that deflection from the faith, but all others have been destroyed. There is great danger in adding to, or in taking away from, these doctrines ; nor can the slightest alteration be made in any one of them, without giving an opportunity to the adversaries to do what they list. Ursacius and Valens, after having been suspected of participating in and advising about the Arian doctrine, were cut off from communion with us. In the hope of being restored to communion, they confessed their error, and obtained forgiveness, as their own writings testify, through which they were spared and received a pardon from the charges. The occasion on which the edict of forgiveness was conceded, was at the council of Milan, when the presbyters of the Roman church were also present.

"Since we know that the formulary of the faith set forth at Nicæa was compiled with the greatest care and accuracy, in the presence of Constantine, of worthy memory, who maintained it throughout his life, and at his baptism, and when he departed to enjoy the merited peace of heaven, we judge that it would be absurd to attempt any alteration in it, and to overlook so many holy confessors and martyrs, and the writers and authors of this dogma, who have bestowed much thought upon it, and have perpetuated the ancient decree of the Catholic Church. God has transmitted the knowledge of their faith to the time in which you live, through our Lord Jesus Christ, by whom you reign and rule the world. Again have these wretched men, who are lamentable, to our way of thinking, announced themselves as heralds of an impious view with unlawful rashness, and have attempted to overturn the entire system of truth. For according to your injunction, the Synod was convened, and these men laid bare the view of their own deceit ; for they attempted an innovation which they introduced with knavery and disturbance, and they found some companions whom they captured for this nefarious transaction ; viz. Germanius, Auxentius, and Caius, who caused contention and discord. The teaching of these men, although it was uniform, exceeded the entire range of blasphemies. As they perceived that they were after all not of the same heresy, and that they did not think alike in any of the points of their evil suggestions, they went over to our symbol, so that it might appear as some other document. The time was indeed brief, but it was sufficient to refute their opinions.

1 Athan. de Synodis, 3 ; quoted by Soc. ii. 37.
2 The emperor had requested ten ; cf. also ii. 23.
3 Athan. de Synodis, c. 10 ; Hil. Fragm. viii., Latin form ; Soc. ii. 37 ; Theod. ii 19.

In order that the affairs of the Church might not be wrecked by them and that the disturbance and tumult which tossed everything to and fro might be restrained, it appeared the safe thing to preserve the ancient and immovable definitions, and to eject the aforesaid persons from communion with us. We have, for this reason, sent our re-instructed deputies to your Clemency, and have furnished them with letters, declaratory of the sentiments of the council. These deputies have been especially charged by us to maintain the truths which were defined rightly by the founders, and to instruct your Holiness as to the falsity of the assertion of Valens and Ursacius, that a few changes in righteous truths would produce peace in the Church. For how can peace be reproduced by those who destroy peace? They would be more likely to introduce contention and disturbance into the other cities and into the Church of Rome. We therefore entreat your Clemency to consider our deputies with gentle audience and mild look, and not to allow the dead to be dishonored by any novel changes. We pray you to permit us to remain in the definitions and decrees which we received from our ancestors, who, we would affirm, did their work with ready minds, with prudence, and with the Holy Spirit. For these innovations not only lead believers to infidelity, but also delude unbelievers to immaturity. We likewise entreat you to command that the bishops who are now absent from their churches, and of whom some are laboring under the infirmities of old age, and others under the privations of poverty, may be furnished with the means of returning to their own homes, in order that the churches may not be longer deprived of their ministry.

" Again, we beseech you that nothing be taken away from the former decisions, or added to them; let all remain unchanged, even as it has been preserved from the piety of your father to the present time; so that we may not in future be fatigued, and be compelled to become strangers to our own parishes, but that bishops and people may dwell together in peace, and be able to devote themselves to prayer and supplication for your own personal salvation and empire and peace, which may the Deity graciously vouchsafe to you uninterruptedly.

" Our deputies will show you the signatures and the names of the bishops, and some of them will offer instruction to your Holiness out of the Sacred Scriptures."

CHAP. XIX. CONCERNING THE DEPUTIES OF THE
    COUNCIL AND THE EMPEROR'S LETTER; AGREE-
    MENT OF THE ADHERENTS OF URSACIUS AND
    VALENS AFTERWARDS WITH THE LETTER PUT
    FORTH; EXILE OF THE ARCHBISHOPS. CON-

CERNING THE SYNOD AT NICÆA, AND THE REASON WHY THE SYNOD WAS HELD IN ARIMINUM.

WE have now transcribed the letter of the council of Ariminum. Ursacius and Valens, with their adherents, anticipating the arrival of the deputies of the council, showed to the emperor the document which they had read, and calumniated the council.[1] The emperor was displeased at the rejection of this formulary, as it had been composed in his presence at Sirmium, and he therefore treated Ursacius and Valens with honor; while, on the other hand, he manifested great contempt towards the deputies, and even delayed granting them an audience. At length, however, he wrote to the Synod, and informed them that an expedition which he was compelled to undertake against the barbarians prevented him from conferring with the deputies; and that he had, therefore, commanded them to remain at Adrianople until his return, in order that, when public business had been dismissed, his mind might be at liberty to hear and test the representations of the deputies; " for it is right," he said, " to bring to the investigation of Divine subjects, a mind unfettered by other cares." Such was the strain of his letter.[2]

The bishops replied that they could never depart from the decision they had formed, as they had before declared in writing, and had charged their deputies to declare; and they besought him to regard them with favor, and to give audience to their deputies, and to read their letter. They told him that it must appear grievous to him that so many churches should be deprived of their bishops; and that, if agreeable to him, they would return to their churches before the winter. After writing this letter, which was full of supplications and entreaties, the bishops waited for a time for a reply; but as no answer was granted them, they afterwards returned to their own cities.

What I have above stated clearly proves that the bishops who were convened at Ariminum confirmed the decrees which had of old been set forth at Nicæa. Let us now consider how it was that they eventually assented to the formulary of faith compiled by Valens and Ursacius and their followers. Various accounts have been given me of this transaction. Some say that the emperor was offended at the bishops having departed from Ariminum without his permission, and allowed Valens and his partisans to govern the churches of the West according to their own will, to set forth their own formulary, to eject

[1] In addition to the references in 18, Athan. de Synodis, 55; Ep. ad. Afros episcopos, 3, 4. Documents reproduced in Soc. ii. 37.
[2] The reply of the bishops to Constantius, also reproduced in Theodoret, H. E. ii. 20, from Athan. de Synodis, 55. Soz. presents the best general grouping of the facts.

those who refused to sign it from the churches, and to ordain others in their place. They say that, taking advantage of this power, Valens compelled some of the bishops to sign the formulary, and that he drove many who refused compliance, from their churches, and first of all Liberius, bishop of Rome. It is further asserted that when Valens and his adherents had acted in this manner in Italy, they resolved to handle the Eastern churches in the same way. As these persecutors were passing through Thrace, they stopped, it is said, at Nicæa, a city of that province. They there convened a council, and read the formulary of Ariminum, which they had translated into the Greek language, and by representing that it had been approved by a general council, they obtained its adoption at Nicæa; they then cunningly denominated it the Nicæan formulary of faith, in order, by the resemblance of names, to deceive the simple, and cause it to be mistaken for the ancient formulary set forth by the Nicæan council. Such is the account given by some parties. Others say that the bishops who were convened at the council of Ariminum were wearied by their detention in that city, as the emperor neither honored them with a reply to their letter, nor granted them permission to return to their own churches; and that, at this juncture, those who had espoused the opposite heresy represented to them that it was not right that divisions should exist between the priests of the whole world for the sake of one word, and that it was only requisite to admit that the Son is like unto the Father in order to put an end to all disputes; for that the bishops of the East would never rest until the term "substance" was rejected. By these representations, it is said, the members of the council were at length persuaded to assent to the formulary which Ursacius had so sedulously pressed upon them. Ursacius and his partisans, being apprehensive lest the deputies sent by the council to the emperor should declare what firmness was in the first place evinced by the Western bishops, and should expose the true cause of the rejection of the term "consubstantial," detained these deputies at Nicæa in Thrace throughout the winter, under the pretext that no public conveyance could be then obtained, and that the roads were in a bad state for traveling; and they then induced them, it is said, to translate the formulary they had accepted from Latin into Greek, and to send it to the Eastern bishops. By this means, they anticipated that the formulary would produce the impression they intended without the fraud being detected; for there was no one to testify that the members of the council of Ariminum had not voluntarily rejected the term "substance" from deference to the Eastern bishops, who were averse to the use of that word. But this was evidently a false account; for all the members of the council, with the exception of a few, maintained strenuously that the Son is like unto the Father in substance, and the only differences of opinion existing between them were that some said that the Son is of the same substance as the Father, while others asserted that he is of like substance with the Father. Some state this matter in one form, others in a different one.

CHAP. XX. — EVENTS WHICH TOOK PLACE IN THE EASTERN CHURCHES: MARATHONIUS, ELEUSIUS OF CYZICUS, AND MACEDONIUS EXPEL THOSE WHO MAINTAIN THE TERM "CONSUBSTANTIAL." CONCERNING THE CHURCHES OF THE NOVATIANS; HOW ONE CHURCH WAS TRANSPORTED; THE NOVATIANS ENTER INTO COMMUNION WITH THE ORTHODOX.

WHILE the events I have above related were taking place in Italy, the East, even before the council of Seleucia had been constituted, was the theatre of great disturbances.[1] The adherents of Acacius and Patrophilus, having ejected Maximus, turned over the church of Jerusalem to Cyril. Macedonius harassed Constantinople and the neighboring cities; he was abetted by Eleusius and Marathonius. This latter was originally a deacon in his own church, and was a zealous superintendent of the poor of the monastical dwellings inhabited by men and women, and Macedonius raised him to the bishopric of Nicomedia. Eleusius, who, not without distinction, was formerly attached to the military service of the palace, had been ordained bishop of Cyzicus. It is said that Eleusius and Marathonius were both good men in their conduct, but that they were zealous in persecuting those who maintained that the Son is of the same substance as the Father, although they were not so distinctly cruel as Macedonius, who not only expelled those who refused to hold communion with him, but imprisoned some, and dragged others before the tribunals. In many cases he compelled the unwilling to communion. He seized children and women who had not been initiated and initiated them, and destroyed many churches in different places, under the pretext that the emperor had commanded the demolition of all houses of prayer in which the Son was recognized to be of the same substance as the Father.

Under this pretext the church of the Novatians at Constantinople, situated in that part of the city called Pelargus, was destroyed. It is related that these heretics performed a courageous action with the aid of the members of the

---

[1] Soc. ii. 38, from which the most of this chapter is derived; a few details in addition are given by Soz. Cf. Theodoret, *H. E.* ii. 26.

Catholic Church, with whom they made common cause. When those who were employed to destroy this church were about to commence the work of demolition, the Novatians assembled themselves together ; some tore down the materials, and others conveyed them to a suburb of the city called Sycæ. They quickly achieved this task ; for men, women, and children participated in it, and by offering their labor to God they were extraordinarily inspirited. By the exercise of this zeal the church was soon renewed, and, from this circumstance, received the name of Anastasia. After the death of Constantius, Julian, his successor, granted to the Novatians the ground which they had previously possessed, and permitted them to rebuild their church. The people spiritedly took advantage of this permission, and transported the identical materials of the former edifice from Sycæ. But this happened at a later period of time than that which we are now reviewing. At this period a union was nearly effected between the Novatian and Catholic churches ; for as they held the same opinions concerning the Godhead, and were subjected to a common persecution, the members of both churches assembled and prayed together. The Catholics then possessed no houses of prayer, for the Arians had wrested them from them. It appears, too, that from the frequent intercourse between the members of each church, they reasoned that the differences between them were vain, and they resolved to commune with one another. A reconciliation would certainly have been effected, I think, had not the desire of the multitude been frustrated by the slander of a few individuals, who asserted that there was an ancient law prohibiting the union of the churches.

CHAP. XXI. — PROCEEDINGS OF MACEDONIUS IN MANTINIUM. HIS REMOVAL FROM HIS SEE WHEN HE ATTEMPTED TO REMOVE THE COFFIN OF CONSTANTINE THE GREAT. JULIAN WAS PRONOUNCED CÆSAR.

ABOUT the same time Eleusius wholly demolished the church of the Novatians in Cyzicus.[1] The inhabitants of other parts of Paphlagonia, and particularly of Mantinium, were subjected to similar persecutions. Macedonius, having been apprised that the majority of these people were followers of Novatus, and that the ecclesiastical power was not of itself sufficiently strong to expel them, persuaded the emperor to send four cohorts against them. For he imagined that men who are unaccustomed to arms would, on the first appearance of soldiers, be seized with terror, and conform to his sentiments. But it happened otherwise, for the people of Manti-

nium armed themselves with sickles and axes and whatever other weapons chanced to be at hand, and marched against the military. A severe conflict ensued, and many of the Paphlagonians fell, but nearly all the soldiers were slain. Many of the friends of Macedonius blamed him for having occasioned so great a disaster, and the emperor was displeased, and regarded him with less favor than before. Inimical feelings were engendered still more strongly by another occurrence. Macedonius contemplated the removal of the coffin of the Emperor Constantine, as the structure in which it had been concealed was falling into ruin. The people were divided in opinion on this subject : some concurred in the design, and others opposed it, deeming it impious and similar to digging up a grave. Those who maintained the Nicene doctrines were of the latter sentiment, and insisted that no indignity should be offered to the body of Constantine, as that emperor had held the same doctrines as themselves. They were besides, I can readily imagine, eager to oppose the projects of Macedonius. However, without further delay, Macedonius caused the coffin to be conveyed to the same church in which the tomb of Acacius the martyr is placed. The people, divided into two factions, the one approving, the other condemning the deed, rushed upon each other in the same church, and so much carnage ensued that the house of prayer and the adjoining place were filled with blood and slaughtered bodies. The emperor, who was then in the West, was deeply incensed on hearing of this occurrence ; and he blamed Macedonius as the cause of the indignity offered to his father, and of the slaughter of the people.

The emperor had determined to visit the East, and held on his way ; he conferred the title of Cæsar on his cousin Julian, and sent him to Western Gaul.

CHAP. XXII. — COUNCIL OF SELEUCIA.

ABOUT the same period the Eastern bishops assembled,[2] to the number of about one hundred and sixty, in Seleucia, a city of Isauria. This was during the consultate of Eusebius and Hypatius. Leonas, who held a brilliant military office at the palace, repaired to this council at the command of Constantius, so that the doctrinal confession might be conducted in his presence. Lauricius, the military governor of the province, was present to prepare whatever might be necessary ; for the letter of the emperor had commanded him to render this service. At the

---

[1] Soc. ii. 38; order and detail from Socrates.

[2] Soz. alludes to the original acts of the Synod at the end, and Soc. ii. 39, to Sabinus' collection. Sabinus probably reported the exact originals. Athan. *de Synodis*, 12, 13; Hil. *contra Constantium*, 12; Philost. iv. 11; Sulp. Sev. *H. S.* ii. 42. Cf. Theodoret, *H. E.* ii. 26; Athan. *de Synodis*, 29.

first session of this council, several of the bishops were absent, and among others, Patrophilus, bishop of Scythopolis; Macedonius, bishop of Constantinople; and Basil, bishop of Ancyra. They resorted to divers pretexts in justification of their non-attendance. Patrophilus alleged in excuse a complaint in the eyes, and Macedonius pleaded indisposition; but it was suspected they had absented themselves from the fear that various accusations would be brought against them. As the other bishops refused to enter upon the investigation of disputed points during their absence, Leonas commanded them to proceed at once to the examination of the questions that had been agitated. Thus some were of opinion that it was necessary to commence with the discussion of doctrinal topics, while others maintained that inquiries ought first to be instituted into the conduct of those among them against whom accusations had been laid, as had been the case with Cyril, bishop of Jerusalem, Eustathius, bishop of Sebaste, and others. The ambiguity of the emperor's letters, which sometimes prescribed one course and sometimes another, gave rise to this dispute. The contention arising from this source became so fierce, that all union was destroyed between them, and they became divided into two parties. However, the advice of those who wished to commence with the examination of doctrine, prevailed. When they proceeded to the investigation of terms, some desired to reject the use of the term "substance," and appealed to the authority of the formulary of faith which had not long previously been compiled by Mark[1] at Sirmium, and had been received by the bishops who were at the court, among whom was Basil,[2] bishop of Ancyra. Many others were anxious for the adoption of the formulary of faith drawn up at the dedication of the church of Antioch. To the first of these parties belonged Eudoxius, Acacius, Patrophilus, George, bishop of Alexandria, Uranius, bishop of Tyre, and thirty-two other bishops. The latter party was supported by George, bishop of Laodicea, in Syria; by Eleusius, bishop of Cyzicus; by Sophronius, bishop of Pompeiopolis, in Paphlagonia; with these the majority agreed. It was suspected, and with reason, that Acacius and his partisans absented themselves on account of the difference between their sentiments and those of the aforesaid bishops, and also because they desired to evade the investigation of certain accusations which had been brought against them; for, although they had previously acknowledged in writing to Macedonius, bishop of Constantinople, that the Son is in all respects like unto the Father, and of the same substance, now they

fought entirely shy of their former professions. After prolonged disputations and contention, Silvanus, bishop of Tarsus, declared, in a loud and peremptory tone, that no new formulary of faith ought to be introduced but that which had been approved at Antioch, and this alone ought to prevail. As this proposition was repugnant to the followers of Acacius, they withdrew, and the other bishops read the formulary of Antioch. The following day these bishops assembled in the church, closed the doors, and privately confirmed this formulary. Acacius condemned this proceeding, and laid the formulary which he advocated before Leonas and Lauricius privately. Three days afterwards the same bishops reassembled, and were joined by Macedonius and Basil, who had been previously absent. Acacius and his partisans declared that they would take no part in the proceedings of the council until those who had been deposed and accused had quitted the assembly. His demand was complied with; for the bishops of the opposite party were determined that he should have no pretext for dissolving the council, which was evidently his object, in order to prevent the impending examination of the heresy of Aetius, and of the accusations which had been brought against himself and his partisans. When all the members were assembled, Leonas stated that he held a document which had been handed to him by the partisans of Acacius; it was their formulary of faith, with introductory remarks. None of the other bishops knew anything about it; for Leonas, who was of the same sentiment as Acacius, had willingly kept the whole matter a secret. When this document[3] was read, the whole assembly was filled with tumult; for some of the statements it contained were to the effect that, though the emperor had prohibited the introduction of any term into the formularies of faith which was not found in the Sacred Scriptures, yet that bishops who had been deposed, having been brought from various provinces to the assembly, with others who had been illegally ordained, the council had been thrown into confusion, and that some of the members had been insulted, and others prevented from speaking. It was added that Acacius and his partisans did not reject the formulary which had been compiled at Antioch, although those who had assembled in that city had drawn it up for the express purpose of meeting the difficulty which had just then arisen; but that, as the terms "consubstantial" and "of similar substance" had grieved some individuals, and that, as it had been recently asserted that the Son is dissimilar from the Father, it was necessary, on this account, to reject the terms "consubstan-

---

[1] The author of the first formulary of Sirmium is here given by Soz. Soc. stated it, ii. 30.   [2] See above, 16.   [3] Given by Soc. ii. 40.

tial" and a "similar substance," which do not occur in Scripture, to condemn the term "dissimilar," and to confess clearly that the Son is like unto the Father; for He is, as the Apostle Paul somewhere says, "the image of the invisible God." These prefatory observations were followed by a formulary, which was neither conformable with that of Nicæa, nor with that of Antioch, and which was so artfully worded that the followers of Arius and of Aetius would not appear to be in error if they should thus state their faith. In this formulary, the words used by those who had convened at Nicæa, in condemnation of the Arian doctrine, were omitted, and the declarations of the council of Antioch, concerning the immutability of the Deity of the Son, and concerning His being the unchangeable image of the substance, the counsel, and the power, and the glory of the Father, were passed over in silence, and belief was simply expressed in the Father, in the Son, and in the Holy Ghost; and after bestowing some vulgar epithets on a few individuals who had never entered into any doctrinal contention on one side or the other, all those who entertained any other opinions than those set forth in this formulary were declared to be aliens to the Catholic Church. Such were the contents of the document presented by Leonas, and which had been signed by Acacius, and by those who had adopted his sentiments. After it had been read, Sophronius, a bishop of Paphlagonia, exclaimed, "If we daily receive the opinions of individuals as a statement of the faith, we shall fail in attaining precision of the truth." Acacius having retorted that it was not forbidden to compile new formularies, as that of Nicæa had been once and frequently altered, Eleusius replied as follows: "But the council has not now met for the purpose of learning what is already known, or of accepting any other formulary than that which has been already approved by those who assembled at Antioch; and, moreover, living and dying, we will adhere to this formulary." The dispute having taken this turn, they entered upon another inquiry, and asked the partisans of Acacius, in what they considered the Son to be like unto the Father. They replied that the Son is similar in will only, but not in substance, and the others thereupon insisted that He is similar in substance, and convicted Acacius, by a work which he had formerly written, that he had once been of their opinion. Acacius replied that he ought not to be judged from his own writings; and the dispute had continued with heat for some time, when Eleusius, bishop of Cyzicus, spoke as follows: "It matters little to the council whether Mark or Basil has transgressed in any way, or whether they or the adherents of Acacius have any accusation to bring against each other;

neither does the trouble devolve upon the council of examining whether their formulary be commendable or otherwise; it is enough to maintain the formulary which has been already confirmed at Antioch by ninety-seven priests; and if any one desire to introduce any doctrine which is not contained therein, he ought to be held as an alien to religion and the Church." Those who were of his sentiments applauded his speech; and the assembly then arose and separated. The following day, the partisans of Acacius and of George refused to attend the council; and Leonas, who had now openly declared himself to be of their sentiments, likewise refused, in spite of all entreaties, to repair thither. Those who were deputed to request his attendance found the partisans of Acacius in his house; and he declined their invitation, under the plea that too much discord prevailed in the council, and that he had only been commanded by the emperor to attend the council in case of unanimity among the members. Much time was consumed in this way; and the partisans of Acacius were frequently solicited by the other bishops to attend the assemblies; but they sometimes demanded a special conference in the house of Leonas, and sometimes alleged that they had been commissioned by the emperor to judge those who had been accused; for they would not receive the creed adopted by the other bishops, nor clear themselves of the crimes of which they had been accused; neither would they examine the case of Cyril, whom they had deposed; and there was no one to compel them to do so. The council, however, eventually deposed George, bishop of Alexandria; Acacius, bishop of Cæsarea; Uranius, bishop of Tyre; Patrophilus, bishop of Scythopolis; and Eudoxius, bishop of Antioch; and several other prelates. Many persons were likewise put out of communion until they could purge themselves of the crimes imputed to them. The transactions were conveyed in writing to the parish of each of the clergy. Adrian,[1] a presbyter of Antioch, was ordained bishop over that church, in room of Eudoxius; but the partisans of Acacius arrested him and delivered him over to Leonas and Lauricius. They committed him into the custody of the soldiers, but afterwards sent him into exile.

We have now given a brief account of the termination of the council of Seleucia. Those who desire more detailed information must seek it in the acts of the council,[2] which have been transcribed by attendant shorthand writers.

CHAP. XXIII. — ACACIUS AND AETIUS; AND HOW THE DEPUTIES OF THE TWO COUNCILS OF ARIMINUM

---

[1] Mistake for Annianus, as given in 24.
[2] Soc. refers anxious readers to the collection by Sabinus, ii. 39.

AND OF SELEUCIA WERE LED BY THE EMPEROR
TO ACCEPT THE SAME DOCTRINES.

IMMEDIATELY after the above transactions, the
adherents of Acacius repaired to the emperor;[1]
but the other bishops returned to their respective homes.   The ten bishops who had been
unanimously chosen as deputies to the emperor,
met, on their arrival at the court, the ten
deputies[2] of the council of Ariminum, and likewise the partisans of Acacius.   These latter had
gained over to their cause the chief men attached
to the palace, and, through their influence, had
secured the favor of the emperor.   It was
reported that some of these proselytes had
espoused the sentiments of Acacius at some
previous period; that some were bribed by
means of the wealth belonging to the churches;
and that others were seduced by the subtilty of
the arguments presented to them, and by the
dignity of the persuader.   Acacius was, in fact,
no common character; by nature he was gifted
with great powers of intellect and eloquence,
and he exhibited no want of skill or of address
in the accomplishment of his schemes.   He was
the president of an illustrious church, and could
boast of Eusebius Pamphilus as his teacher,
whom he succeeded in the episcopate, and was
more honorably known than any other man by
the reputation and succession of his books.
Endowed with all these advantages, he succeeded with ease in whatever he undertook.
As there were at this period at Constantinople all together twenty deputies, ten from each
council, besides many other bishops, who, from
various motives, had repaired to the city, Honoratus,[3] whom the emperor, before his departure
to the West, had constituted chief governor of
Constantinople, received directions to examine,
in the presence of the exarchs of the great council, the reports circulated concerning Aetius and
his heresy.   Constantius, with some of the rulers,
eventually undertook the investigation of this
case; and as it was proved that Aetius had
introduced dogmas essentially opposed to the
faith, the emperor and the other judges were
offended at his blasphemous statements.   It is
said that the partisans of Acacius at first feigned
ignorance of this heresy, for the purpose of
inducing the emperor and those around him to
take cognizance of it; for they imagined that
the eloquence of Aetius would be irresistible;
that he would infallibly succeed in convincing
his auditory; and that his heresy would conquer
the unwilling.   When, however, the result proved
the futility of their expectations, they demanded

that the formulary of faith accepted by the council of Ariminum should receive the sanction of
the deputies from the council of Seleucia.   As
these latter protested that they would never renounce the use of the term "substance," the
Acacians declared to them upon oath that they
did not hold the Son to be, in substance, dissimilar from the Father; but that, on the contrary, they were ready to denounce this opinion
as heresy.   They added that they esteemed the
formulary compiled by the Western bishops at
Ariminum the more highly, because the word
"substance" had been unexpectedly expunged
from it; because, they said, if this formulary
were to be received, there would be no further
mention, either of the word "substance" or of
the term "consubstantial," to which many of the
Western priests were, from their reverence for
the Nicæan council, peculiarly attached.
It was for these reasons that the emperor approved of the formulary; and when he recalled
to mind the great number of bishops who had
been convened at Ariminum, and reflected that
there is no error in saying either that "the Son
is like unto the Father" or "of the same substance as the Father"; and when he further considered that no difference in signification would
ensue, if, for terms which do not occur in Scripture, other equivalent and uncontrovertible expressions were to be substituted (such, for instance,
as the word "similar"), he determined upon giving his sanction to the formulary.   Such being
his own sentiments, he commanded the bishops
to accept the formulary.   The next day preparations were made for the pompous ceremony of
proclaiming him consul, which, according to the
Roman custom, took place in the beginning of
the month of January, and the whole of that day
and part of the ensuing night the emperor spent
with the bishops, and at length succeeded in persuading the deputies of the council of Seleucia to
receive the formulary transmitted from Ariminum.

CHAP. XXIV. — FORMULARY OF THE COUNCIL OF
ARIMINUM APPROVED BY THE ACACIANS.   LIST OF
THE DEPOSED CHIEF-PRIESTS, AND THE CAUSES
OF THEIR CONDEMNATION.

THE partisans of Acacius[4] remained some time
at Constantinople, and invited thither several
bishops of Bithynia, among whom were Maris,
bishop of Chalcedon, and Ulfilas, bishop of the
Goths.   These prelates having assembled together, in number about fifty, they confirmed
the formulary read at the council of Ariminum,
adding this provision, that the terms "substance"

---

[1] A few hints in Philost. iv. 12; Soc. ii. 41.   Cf. Sulp. Sev. H. S.
ii. 43–45; Theodoret, H. E. ii. 27.   But the main part is independent.
[2] Cf. iv. 18; twenty.   Philost. tells us that Acacius prepared the
minutes of this Synod.
[3] Concerning this Honoratus see the *Descriptio Consulum* of
Idatius.

[4] The acts of this Synod of Constantinople were written by
Acacius. Cf. Philost. iv. 12.   Further, cf. Philost. iv. 12, v. 1;
Athan. *de Synodis*, 30, the formulary; Soc. ii. 41 (with the revised
formulary), 42, 43; Theodoret, H. E. ii. 27, 28.   Soz. enlarges on
the depositions, giving us much new material; Theodoret gives a
letter against Aetius (from Sabinus?).

and "hypostasis" should never again be used in reference to God. They also declared that all other formularies set forth in times past, as likewise those that might be compiled at any future period, should be condemned. They then deposed Aetius from his office of deacon, because he had written works full of contention and of a species of vain knowledge opposed to the ecclesiastical vocation; because he had used in writing and in disputation several impious expressions; and because he had been the occasion of troubles and seditions in the Church. It was alleged by many that they did not depose him willingly, but merely because they wished to remove all suspicion from the mind of the emperor which he had with regard to them, for they had been accused of holding Aetian views. Those who held these sentiments took advantage of the resentment with which, for reasons above mentioned, the emperor regarded Macedonius, and they accordingly deposed him, and likewise Eleusius, bishop of Cyzicus; Basil, bishop of Ancyra; Heortasius, bishop of Sardis; and Dracontius, bishop of Pergamus. Although they differed about doctrine from those bishops, yet in deposing them, no blame was thrown upon their faith, but charges were alleged against them in common with all, that they had disturbed the peace and violated the laws of the Church. They specified, in particular, that when the presbyter Diogenes was traveling from Alexandria to Ancyra, Basil seized his papers, and struck him; they also deposed that Basil had, without trial, delivered over many of the clergy from Antioch, from the banks of the Euphrates, and from Cilicia, Galatia, and Asia, to the rulers of the provinces, to be exiled and subjected to cruel punishments, so that many had been loaded with chains, and had been compelled to bribe the soldiers, who were conducting them away, not to ill-use them. They added that, on one occasion, when the emperor had commanded Aetius and some of his followers to be led before Cecropius, that they might answer to him for various accusations laid to their charge, Basil recommended the person who was intrusted with the execution of this edict, to act according to the dictates of his own judgment. They said that he wrote directions to Hermogenes,[1] the prefect and governor of Syria, stating who were to be banished, and whither they were to be sent; and that, when the exiles were recalled by the emperor, he would not consent to their return, but opposed himself to the wishes of the rulers and of the priests. They further deposed that Basil had excited the clergy of Sirimium against Germanius; and that, although he stated in writing that he had admitted Germanius, Valens, and Ursacius into commun-

ion, he had placed them as criminals before the tribunal of the African bishops; and that, when taxed with this deed, he had denied it, and perjured himself; and that, when he was afterwards convicted, he strove to justify his perjury by sophistical reasoning. They added, that he had been the cause of contention and of sedition in Illyria, Italy, Africa, and in the Roman church; that he had thrown a servant into prison to compel her to bear false witness against her mistress; that he had baptized a man of loose life, who lived in illicit intercourse with a woman, and had promoted him to be a deacon; that he had neglected to excommunicate a quack-doctor who had occasioned the death of several persons; and that he and some of the clergy had bound themselves by oath before the holy table, not to bring accusations against each other. This, they said, was an artifice adopted by the president of the clergy to shield himself from the accusations of his plaintiffs. In short, such were the reasons they specified for the deposition of Basil. Eustathius, they said, was deposed because, when a presbyter, he had been condemned, and put away from the communion of prayers by Eulalius, his own father, who was bishop of the church of Cæsarea, in Cappadocia; and also because he had been excommunicated by a council held at Neocæsarea, a city of Pontus, and deposed by Eusebius, bishop of Constantinople, for unfaithfulness in the discharge of certain duties that had devolved upon him. He had also been deprived of his bishopric by those who were convened in Gangroe, on account of his having taught, acted, and thought contrary to sound doctrine. He had been convicted of perjury by the council of Antioch. He had likewise endeavored to reverse the decrees of those convened at Melitina; and, although he was guilty of many crimes, he had the assurance to aspire to be judge over the others, and to stigmatize them as heretics. They deposed Eleusius because he had raised inconsiderately one Heraclius, a native of Tyre, to be a deacon; this man had been a priest of Hercules at Tyre, had been accused of and tried for sorcery, and, therefore, had retired to Cyzicus and feigned conversion to Christianity; and moreover, Eleusius, after having been apprised of these circumstances, had not driven him from the Church. He had also, without inquiry, ordained certain individuals, who had come to Cyzicus, after they had been condemned by Maris, bishop of Chalcedonia, who participated in this council. Heortasius was deposed because he had been ordained bishop of Sardis without the sanction of the bishops of Lydia. They deposed Dracontius, bishop of Pergamus, because he had previously held another bishopric in Galatia, and because, they stated, he had on both occa-

[1] Further mention is made of this Hermogenes by Am. Marcell. xix. 12, 6; xxi. 6, 9.

sions been unlawfully ordained. After these transactions, a second assembly of the council was held, and Silvanus, bishop of Tarsus, Sophronius, bishop of Pompeiopolis in Paphlagonia, Elpidius, bishop of Satala, and Neonas, bishop of Seleucia in Isauria, were deposed. The reason they assigned for the deposition of Silvanus was, that he had constituted himself the leader of a foolish party in Seleucia and Constantinople; he had, besides, constituted Theophilus as president of the church of Castabala, who had been previously ordained bishop of Eleutheropolis by the bishops of Palestine, and who had promised upon oath that he would never accept any other bishopric without their permission. Sophronius was deposed on account of his avarice, and on account of his having sold some of the offerings presented to the church, for his own profit; besides, after he had received a first and second summons to appear before the council, he could, at last, be scarcely induced to make his appearance, and then, instead of replying to the accusations brought against him, he appealed to other judges. Neonas was deposed for having resorted to violence in his endeavors to procure the ordination in his own church, of Annianus, who had been appointed bishop of Antioch,[1] and for having ordained as bishops certain individuals who had previously been engaged in politics, and who were utterly ignorant of the Holy Scriptures and of ecclesiastical canons, and who, after their ordination, preferred the enjoyment of their property to that of the priestly dignity, and declared in writing that they would rather take charge of their own possessions than to discharge the episcopal functions without them. Elpidius was deposed because he had participated in the malpractices of Basil, and had occasioned great disorders; and because he had, contrary to the decrees of the council of Melitina, restored to his former rank in the presbytery a man named Eusebius, who had been deposed for having created Nectaria a deaconess, after she had been excommunicated on account of violating agreements and oaths; and to confer this honor upon her was clearly contrary to the laws of the Church.

CHAP. XXV. — CAUSES OF THE DEPOSITION OF CYRIL, BISHOP OF JERUSALEM. MUTUAL DISSENSIONS AMONG THE BISHOPS. MELITIUS IS ORDAINED BY THE ARIANS, AND SUPPLANTS EUSTATHIUS IN THE BISHOPRIC OF SEBASTE.

BESIDES the prelates above mentioned, Cyril, bishop of Jerusalem, was deposed[2] because he had admitted Eustathius and Elpidius into communion, after they had opposed the decrees enacted by those convened at Melitina, among whom was Cyril himself; and because he had also received Basil and George, bishop of Laodicea, into communion after their deposition in Palestine. When Cyril was first installed in the bishopric of Jerusalem, he had a dispute with Acacius, bishop of Cæsarea, concerning his rights as a Metropolitan, which he claimed on the ground of his bishopric being an apostolic see. This dispute excited feelings of enmity between the two bishops, and they mutually accused each other of unsoundness of doctrine concerning the Godhead. In fact, they had both been suspected previously; the one, that is, Acacius, of favoring the heresy of Arius; and the other, of siding with those who maintain that the Son is in substance like unto the Father. Acacius being thus inimically disposed towards Cyril, and finding himself supported by the bishops of the province, who were of the same sentiments as himself, contrived to depose Cyril under the following pretext. Jerusalem and the neighboring country was at one time visited with a famine, and the poor appealed in great multitudes to Cyril, as their bishop, for necessary food. As he had no money to purchase the requisite provisions, he sold for this purpose the veil and sacred ornaments of the church. It is said that a man, having recognized an offering which he had presented at the altar as forming part of the costume of an actress, made it his business to inquire whence it was procured; and ascertained that a merchant had sold it to the actress, and that the bishop had sold it to the merchant. It was under this pretext that Acacius deposed Cyril.

And on inquiry I find these to be the facts. It is said that the Acacians then expelled from Constantinople all the bishops above mentioned who had been deposed. Ten bishops of their own party who had refused to subscribe to these edicts of deposition, were separated from the others, and were interdicted from performing the functions of the ministry or ruling their churches until they consented to give their signatures. It was enacted that unless they complied within six months,[3] and yielded their assent to all the decrees of the council, they should be deposed, and that the bishops of every province should be summoned to elect other bishops in their stead. After these determinations and deeds, letters were then sent to all the bishops and clergy, to observe and fulfill its decrees.

As a consequence, not long after, some of the Eudoxian party were substituted here and there. Eudoxius himself took possession of the bishopric of Macedonius; Athanasius was placed over the church of Basil; and Eunomius, who was

---

[1] Cf. iv. 22.   [2] See references to previous chapter.

[3] See the abrogation of the time-limit through a Synod convened by Eudoxius. Philost. vii. 6.

subsequently the leader of a heresy bearing his name, took the see of Eleusius; and Meletius was appointed to the church of Sebaste, instead of Eustathius.

CHAP. XXVI. — DEATH OF MACEDONIUS, BISHOP OF CONSTANTINOPLE. WHAT EUDOXIUS SAID IN HIS TEACHING. EUDOXIUS AND ACACIUS STRENU- OUSLY SOUGHT THE ABOLITION OF THE FORMULA- RIES OF FAITH SET FORTH AT NICÆA AND AT ARIMINUM; TROUBLES WHICH THENCE AROSE IN THE CHURCHES.

MACEDONIUS,[1] on his expulsion from the church of Constantinople, retired to one of the suburbs of the city, where he died. Eudoxius took pos- session of his church in the tenth year of the consulate of Constantius, and the third of Julian, surnamed Cæsar. It is related that, at the dedication of the great church called "Sophia," when he rose to teach the people, he commenced his discourse with the following proposition: "The Father is impious, the Son is pious"; and that, as these words excited a great commo- tion among the people, he added, "Be calm; the Father is impious, because he worships no one; the Son is pious, because he worships the Father." On this explanation, he threw his au- dience into laughter. Eudoxius and Acacius jointly exerted themselves to the utmost in en- deavoring to cause the edicts of the Nicene Council to fall into oblivion. They sent the for- mulary read at Ariminum with various explana- tory additions of their own, to every province of the empire, and procured from the emperor an edict for the banishment of all who should refuse to subscribe to it. But this undertaking, which appeared to them so easy of execution, was the be- ginning of the greatest calamities, for it excited commotions throughout the empire, and entailed upon the Church in every region a persecution more grievous than those which it had suffered under the pagan emperors.[2] For if this persecu- tion did not occasion such tortures to the body as the preceding ones, it appeared more grievous to all who reflected aright, on account of its disgraceful nature; for both the persecutors and the persecuted belonged to the Church; and the one was all the more disgraceful in that men of the same religion treated their fellows with a degree of cruelty which the ecclesiastical laws prohibit to be manifested towards enemies and strangers.

CHAP. XXVII. — MACEDONIUS, AFTER HIS REJECTION FROM HIS SEE, BLASPHEMES AGAINST THE HOLY

SPIRIT; PROPAGATION OF HIS HERESY THROUGH THE INSTRUMENTALITY OF MARATHONIUS AND OTHERS.

THE spirit of innovation is self-laudatory,[3] and hence it advanced further and further, and crept along to greater novelties with increasing self- conceit, and in scorn of the fathers it enacted laws of its own, nor does it honor the doctrines of the ancients concerning God, but is always thinking out strange dogmas and restlessly adds novelty to novelty as the events now show. For after Macedonius had been deposed from the church of Constantinople, he renounced the tenets of Acacius and Eudoxius.[4] He began to teach that the Son is God, and that He is in all respects and in substance like unto the Father. But he affirmed that the Holy Ghost is not a participant of the same dignities, and designated Him a minister and a servant, and applied to Him whatever could, without error, be said of the holy angels. This doctrine was embraced by Eleusius, Eustathius, and by all the other bishops who had been deposed at Constantinople, by the partisans of the opposite heresy. Their example was quickly followed by no small part of the people of Constantinople, Bithynia, Thrace, the Hellespont, and of the neighboring provinces. For their mode of life had no little influence, and to this do the people give special attention. They assumed great gravity of demeanor, and their discipline was like that of the monks; their conversation was plain and of a style fitted to persuade. It is said that all these qualifications were united in Marathonius. He originally held a public appointment in the army, under the command of the prefect. After amassing some money in this employment, he quit military sci- ence, and undertook the superintendence of the establishments for the relief of the sick and the destitute. Afterwards, at the suggestion of Eusta- thius, bishop of Sebaste, he embraced an ascetic mode of life, and founded a monastical institu- tion in Constantinople which exists to the present day. He brought so much zeal, and so much of his own wealth to the support of the aforesaid heresy, that the Macedonians were by many termed Marathonians, and it seems to me not without reason; for it appears that he alone, to- gether with his institutions, was the cause that it was not altogether extinguished in Constantino- ple. In fact, after the deposition of Macedonius, the Macedonians possessed neither churches nor bishops until the reign of Arcadius.[5]

The Arians, who drove out of the churches and rigorously persecuted all who held different

[1] Soc. ii. 43; Ruf. H. E. i. 21. Soz. has independent details.
[2] Cf. with Ruf. H. E. i. 21.
[3] Soc. ii. 45; Ruf. H. E. ii. 25; Theodoret, H. E. ii. 6. Soz. independent.
[4] Cf. Philost. iv. 9.
[5] After A.D. 395. Yet according to vii. 2, the Macedonians took advantage of the Gratian law and repossessed the churches from which Valens had ejected them.

sentiments from themselves, deprived them of all these privileges. It would be no easy task to enumerate the names of the priests who were at this period ejected from their own cities; for I believe that no province of the empire was exempted from such a calamity.

CHAP. XXVIII. — THE ARIANS, UNDER THE IMPRESSION THAT THE DIVINE MELETIUS UPHELD THEIR SENTIMENTS, TRANSLATE HIM FROM SEBASTE TO ANTIOCH. ON HIS BOLD CONFESSION OF THE ORTHODOX DOCTRINES, THEY WERE CONFOUNDED, AND AFTER THEY HAD DEPOSED HIM THEY PLACED EUZOIUS IN THE SEE. MELETIUS FORMED HIS OWN CHURCH : BUT THOSE WHO HELD TO CONSUBSTANTIALITY TURNED AWAY FROM HIM BECAUSE HE HAD BEEN ORDAINED BY ARIANS.

AT the period that Eudoxius obtained the government of the church of Constantinople,[1] there were many aspirants to the see of Antioch; and as is frequently the case under such circumstances, contentions and seditions divided the clergy and the people of that church.

Each party was anxious to commit the government of the church to a bishop of its own persuasion; for interminable disputes concerning doctrine were rampant among them, and they could not agree as to the mode of singing psalms; and, as has been before stated, psalms were sung by each individual, in conformity with his own peculiar creed. Such being the state of the church at Antioch, the partisans of Eudoxius thought it would be well to intrust the bishopric of that city to Meletius, then bishop of Sebaste, he being possessed of great and persuasive eloquence, of excellent life, and above all, as they imagined, being of like opinions with themselves. They believed that his reputation would attract the inhabitants of Antioch and of the neighboring cities to conform to their heresy, particularly those called Eustathians, who had adhered invariably to the Nicene doctrines. But their expectations were utterly frustrated. It is said that on his first arrival in Antioch, an immense multitude, composed of Arians, and of those who were in communion with Paulinus, flocked around him. Some wished to see the man because his fame was great, even before his coming; others were anxious to hear what he had to say, and to ascertain the nature of his opinions; for a report had been spread abroad which was afterwards proved to be true, that he maintained the doctrines of those convened at Nicæa. In his first discourses he confined himself to instructing the people in what we call

ethics; afterwards, however, he openly declared that the Son is of the same substance as the Father. It is said that at these words, the archdeacon of the church, who was then one of the clergy there, stretched out his hand, and covered the mouth of the preacher; but that he continued to explain his sentiments more clearly by means of his fingers than he could by language. He extended three fingers only towards the people, closed them, and then allowed only one finger to remain extended, and thus expressed by signs what he was prevented from uttering. As the archdeacon, in his embarrassment, seized the hand, he released the mouth; the tongue was free, and Meletius declared his opinion still more clearly and with a loud voice, and exhorted his auditors to adhere to the tenets of the council of Nicæa, and he testified to his hearers that those who held other views deviated from the truth. As he persisted in the enunciation of the same sentiments, either by word of mouth or by means of signs, when the archdeacon closed his mouth, a contention between both sides occurred, not unlike that of the pancratium; the followers of Eustathius shouted aloud and rejoiced and leaped, while the Arians were cast down. Eudoxius and his partisans were transported with indignation at this discourse, and contrived by their machinations to expel Meletius from Antioch. Soon afterwards, however, they recalled him, for they fancied he had renounced his former sentiments and had espoused theirs. As, however, it soon became apparent that his devotion to the Nicene doctrines was firm and unalterable, he was ejected from the church, and banished by order of the emperor; and the see of Antioch was conferred on Euzoius, who had formerly been banished with Arius. The followers of Meletius separated themselves from the Arians, and held their assemblies apart, for those who had from the beginning maintained that the Son is consubstantial with the Father refused to admit them into communion, because Meletius had been ordained by Arian bishops, and because his followers had been baptized by Arian priests. For this reason they were separated, although holding the same views.

The emperor having been informed that an insurrection was about to arise in Persia, repaired to Antioch.

CHAP. XXIX. — THE PARTISANS OF ACACIUS AGAIN DO NOT REMAIN QUIET, BUT STRIVE TO ABOLISH THE TERM " CONSUBSTANTIAL," AND TO CONFIRM THE HERESY OF ARIUS.

THE partisans of Acacius[2] were not able to

---

[1] Soc. ii. 44. The order is the same in Soz., but with many new details. Philost. v. 1, 5; Ruf. *H. E.* i. 24. Cf. Theodoret, *H. E.* ii. 31.

[2] Soc. ii. 45. Soz. and he are much alike, but yet each has independent statements; both evidently draw from the same source. Athan. *de Synodis*, 31; Ruf. *H. E.* i. 25.

remain in tranquillity ; and they therefore assembled together with a few others in Antioch, and condemned the decrees which they had themselves enacted. They decided to erase the term "similar" from the formulary which had been read at Ariminum and at Constantinople, and affirmed that in all respects, in substance and in will, the Son is dissimilar from the Father, and that He proceeded from what had no previous existence, even as Arius had taught from the commencement. They were joined by the partisans of Aetius, who had been the first after Arius to venture openly upon the profession of these opinions ; hence Aetius was called atheist, and his approvers, Anomians and Exucontians.

When those who maintained the Nicene doctrines demanded of the Acacians how they could say that the Son is dissimilar from the Father, and that He proceeded out of nothing, when it was affirmed in their own formulary that He is "God of God," they replied that the Apostle Paul had declared that "All things are of God,"[1] and that the Son is included in the term "all things"; and that it was in this sense, and in accordance with the Sacred Scriptures, that the expressions in their formulary were to be understood. Such were the equivocations and sophistry to which they had recourse. At length, finding that they could advance no efficient argument to justify themselves in the opinion of those who pressed them on this point, they withdrew from the assembly, after the formulary of Constantinople had been read a second time, and returned to their own cities.

[1] I Cor. xi. 12.

CHAP. XXX. — GEORGE, BISHOP OF ANTIOCH, AND THE CHIEF-PRIESTS OF JERUSALEM. THREE CHIEF-PRIESTS SUCCESSIVELY SUCCEED CYRIL ; RESTORATION OF CYRIL TO THE SEE OF JERUSALEM.

DURING this period,[2] Athanasius was obliged to remain in concealment, and George returned to Alexandria, and commenced a cruel persecution against the pagans, and against the Christians who differed from him in opinion. He compelled both parties to offer worship in the mode he indicated, and where opposition was made, he enforced obedience by compulsion. He was hated by the rulers because he scorned them and was giving orders to the officers ; and the multitude detested him on account of his tyranny, for his power was greater than all the rest. The pagans regarded him with even greater aversion than the Christians, because he prohibited them from offering sacrifices, and from celebrating their ancestral festivals ; and because he had on one occasion, introduced the governor of Egypt[3] and armed soldiery into the city, and despoiled their images, votives and temple ornaments. This was, in fact, the cause of his death, on which I will dwell.

On the deposition of Cyril, Erennius obtained the church of Jerusalem ;[4] he was succeeded by Heraclius, and to Heraclius succeeded Hilarius ; for we have gathered from tradition that in that period these persons administered the church there, until the reign of Theodosius, when Cyril was once more restored to his own see.

[2] Soc. ii. 45. Soz. has some order, but varying points.
[3] Namely, Artemius, who was afterwards martyred under Julian. Am. Marcel. xxii. 11. 3–8.
[4] Soc. iv. 25. Epiphanius (adv. Hæres, ii. 3, 10; Hæres, lxvi.), places another Cyril after Herennius. Soc. calls Erennius, Arrenius.

BOOK V.

Such were the transactions which took[1] place in the Eastern Church. In the meantime, however, Julian, the Cæsar, attacked and conquered the barbarians who dwelt on the banks of the Rhine; many he killed, and others he took prisoners. As the victory added greatly to his fame, and as his moderation and gentleness had endeared him to the troops, they proclaimed him Augustus. Far from making an excuse to Constantius for this act, he exchanged the officers who had been elected by Constantius, and industriously circulated letters wherein Constantius had solicited the barbarians to enter the Roman territories, and aid him against Magnentius. He then suddenly changed his religion, and although he had previously confessed Christianity, he declared himself high-priest, frequented the pagan temples, offered sacrifices, and invited his subjects to adopt that form of worship.

As an invasion of Roman territory by the Persians was expected, and as Constantius had on this account repaired to Syria, Julian conceived that he might without battle render himself master of Illyricum; he therefore set out on his journey to this province, under pretense that he intended to present an apology to Constantius for having, without his sanction, received the symbols of imperial power. It is said, that when he arrived on the borders of Illyria, the vines appeared full of green grapes, although the time of the vintage was past, and the Pleiades had set; and that there fell upon his followers a dashing of the dew from the atmosphere, of which each drop was stamped with the sign of the cross. He and many of those with him regarded the grapes appearing out of season as a favorable omen; while the dew had made that figure by chance on the garments upon which it happened to fall.

Others thought that of the two symbols, the one of the green grapes signified that the emperor would die prematurely, and his reign would be very short; while the second sign, that of the crosses formed by the drops of dew, indicated that the Christian religion is from heaven, and that all persons ought to receive the sign of the cross. I am, for my own part, convinced that those who regarded these two phenomena as unfavorable omens for Julian, were not mistaken; and the progress of time proved the accuracy of their opinion.

When Constantius heard that Julian was marching against him at the head of an army, he abandoned his intended expedition against the Persians, and departed for Constantinople; but he died on the journey, when he had arrived as far as Mopsucrenæ, which lies near the Taurus, between Cilicia and Cappadocia.

He died in the forty-fifth year of his age, after reigning thirteen years conjointly with his father Constantine, and twenty-five years after the death of that emperor.

A little while after the decease of Constantius, Julian, who had already made himself master of Thrace, entered Constantinople and was proclaimed emperor. Pagans assert that diviners and demons had predicted the death of Constantius, and the change in affairs, before his departure for Galatia, and had advised him to undertake the expedition. This might have been regarded as a true prediction, had not the life of Julian been terminated so shortly afterwards, and when he had only tasted the imperial power as in a dream. But it appears to me absurd to believe that, after he had heard the death of Constantius predicted, and had been warned that it would be his own fate to fall in battle by the hands of the Persians, he should have leaped into manifest death, — offering him no other fame in the world than that of lack of counsel, and poor generalship, — and who, had he lived, would probably have suffered the greater part of the Roman territories to fall under the Persian yoke. This observation, however, is only inserted lest I should be blamed for omitting it. I leave every one to form his own opinion.

CHAP. II. — THE LIFE, EDUCATION, AND TRAINING OF JULIAN, AND HIS ACCESSION TO THE EMPIRE.

Immediately after the death of Constantius,[2]

---

[1] Soc. ii. 47, and iii. 1; Ruf. *H. E.* i. 26; Orosius, vii. 29, 30; Philost. vi. 5, 6. Soz. has much that is independent. Cf. Eunapius, Zos., and Am. Marcel. under the reigns of Constantius and Julian. Eutrop. *Brev. Hist. Rom.* x. 14, 15.

[2] Soc. iii. 1. Much the same order is followed by Soz., but with

the dread of a persecution arose in the Church, and Christians suffered more anguish from the anticipation of this calamity than they would have experienced from its actual occurrence. This state of feeling proceeded from the fact that a long interval had made them unaccustomed to such dangers, and from the remembrance of the tortures which had been exercised by the tyrants upon their fathers, and from their knowledge of the hatred with which the emperor regarded their doctrines. It is said that he openly renounced the faith of Christ so entirely, that he by sacrifices and expiations, which the pagans call renunciatory, and by the blood of animals, purged himself of our baptism. From that period he employed himself in auguries and in the celebration of the pagan rites, both publicly and privately. It is related[1] that one day, as he was inspecting the entrails of a victim, he beheld among them a cross encompassed with a crown. This appearance terrified those who were assisting in the ceremony, for they judged that it indicated the strength of religion, and the eternal duration of the Christian doctrines; inasmuch as the crown by which it was encircled is the symbol of victory, and because of its continuity, for the circle beginning everywhere and ending in itself, has no limits in any direction. The chief augur commanded Julian to be of good cheer, because in his judgment the victims were propitious, and since they surrounded the symbol of the Christian doctrine, and was indeed pushing into it, so that it would not spread and expand itself where it wished, since it was limited by the circumference of the circle.

I have also heard that one day Julian descended into a most noted and terrific adytum,[2] either for the purpose of participating in some initiation, or of consulting an oracle; and that, by means of machinery which is devised for this end, or of enchantments, such frightful specters were projected suddenly before him, that through perturbation and fear, he became forgetful of those who were present, for he had turned to his new religion when already a man, and so unconsciously fell into his earlier habit, and signed himself with the symbol of Christ, just as the Christian encompassed with untried dangers is wont to do. Immediately the specters disappeared and their designs were frustrated. The initiator was at first surprised at this, but when apprised of the cause of the flight of the demons, he declared that the act was a profanation; and after exhorting the emperor to be courageous and to have no recourse in deed or thought to anything connected with the Christian religion, he again

conducted him to the initiation. The zeal of the king for such matters saddened the Christians not a little and made them extremely anxious, more especially as he had been himself formerly a Christian. He was born of pious parents, had been initiated in infancy according to the custom of the Church, and had been brought up in the knowledge of the Holy Scriptures, and was nurtured by bishops and men of the Church. He and Gallus were the sons of Constantius, the brother by the same father of Constantine the emperor, and of Dalmatius. Dalmatius had a son of the same name, who was declared Cæsar, and was slain by the soldiery after the death of Constantine. His fate would have been shared by Gallus and Julian, who were then orphans, had not Gallus been spared on account of a disease under which he was laboring, and from which, it was supposed, that he would soon naturally die; and Julian, on account of his extreme youth, for he was but eight years of age. After this wonderful preservation, a residence was assigned to the two brothers in a palace called Macellum, situated in Cappadocia; this imperial post was near Mount Argeus, and not far from Cæsarea; it contained a magnificent palace and was adorned with baths, gardens, and perennial fountains. Here they were cultured and educated in a manner corresponding to the dignity of their birth; they were taught the sciences and bodily exercises befitting their age, by masters of languages and interpreters of the Holy Scriptures, so that they were enrolled among the clergy, and read the ecclesiastical books to the people. Their habits and actions indicated no dereliction from piety. They respected the clergy and other good people and persons zealous for doctrine; they repaired regularly to church and rendered due homage to the tombs of the martyrs.

It is said that they undertook to deposit the tomb of St. Mammas[3] the martyr in a large edifice, and to divide the labor between themselves, and that while they were trying to excel one another in a rivalry of honor, an event occurred which was so astonishing that it would indeed be utterly incredible were it not for the testimony of many who are still among us, who heard it from those who were eyewitnesses of the transaction.

The part of the edifice upon which Gallus labored advanced rapidly and according to wish, but of the section upon which Julian labored, a part fell into ruin; another was projected upward from the earth; a third immediately on its touching the foundation could not be held

the addition of many details. Greg. Naz. adv. Julianum, i. and ii. Invectiva; Eunapius, Excerpt, i. 1, 2; Excerpt, ii. 1-24; Zos. ii. 45; iii. 2-29, 34. Am. Marcel. xv.-xxiv. Theodoret, H. E. iii. 2, 3, follows Soz. succinctly.   [1] Greg. Naz. Or. cont. Julianum, i. 54.
[2] Greg. Naz. cont. Julianum, 1 inv. 55.

[3] Under Aurelian, A.D. 274. The Greeks celebrate him Sept. 2; Latins, Aug. 17. He is said by Greg. Naz. (Orat. 44, 12), and by Basil (Hom. 23, on St. Mammas) to have been a shepherd and also a martyr. The miraculous story here related is given also by Greg. Naz. in his First Oration against Julian, 25, though he does not mention the martyr's name.

upright, but was hurled backward as if some resistant and strong force from beneath were pushing against it.

This was universally regarded as a prodigy. The people, however, drew no conclusion from it till subsequent events manifested its import. There were a few who from that moment doubted the reality of Julian's religion, and suspected that he only made an outward profession of piety for fear of displeasing the emperor, who was then a Christian, and that he concealed his own sentiments because it was not safe to divulge them. It is asserted that he was first secretly led to renounce the religion of his fathers by his intercourse with diviners; for when the resentment of Constantius against the two brothers was abated, Gallus went to Asia, and took up his residence in Ephesus, where the greater part of his property was situated; and Julian repaired to Constantinople, and frequented the schools, where his fine natural abilities and ready attainments in the sciences did not remain concealed. He appeared in public in the garb of a private individual, and had much company; but because he was related to the emperor and was capable of conducting affairs and was expected to become emperor, considerable talk about him to this effect was prevalent, as is wont to be the case in a populous and imperial city, he was commanded to retire to Nicomedia.

Here he became acquainted with Maximus, an Ephesian philosopher,[1] who instructed him in philosophy, and inspired him with hatred towards the Christian religion, and moreover assured him that the much talked of prophecy about him was true. Julian, as happens in many cases, while suffering in anticipation of severe circumstances, was softened by these favorable hopes and held Maximus as his friend. As these occurrences reached the ears of Constantius, Julian became apprehensive, and accordingly shaved himself, and adopted externally the monkish mode of life, while he secretly held to the other religion.

When he arrived at the age of manhood, he was more readily infatuated, and yet was anxious about these tendencies; and admiring the art (if there be such an art) of predicting the future, he thought the knowledge of it necessary; he advanced to such experiments as are not lawful for Christians. From this period he had as his friends those who followed this art. In this opinion, he came into Asia from Nicomedia, and there consorting with men of such practices, he became more ardent in the pursuit of divination. When Gallus, his brother, who had been established as Cæsar, was put to death on being accused of revolution, Constantius also suspected Julian of cherishing the love of empire, and therefore put him under the custody of guards.

Eusebia, the wife of Constantius, obtained for him permission to retire to Athens; and he accordingly settled there, under pretext of attending the pagan exercises and schools; but as rumor says, he communed with diviners concerning his future prospects. Constantius recalled him, and proclaimed him Cæsar, promised him his sister Constantia[2] in marriage, and sent him to Gaul; for the barbarians whose aid had been hired by Constantius previously against Magnentius, finding that their services were not required, had portioned out that country. As Julian was very young, generals, to whom the prudential affairs were turned over, were sent with him; but as these generals abandoned themselves to pleasure, he was present as Cæsar, and provided for the war. He confirmed his soldiers in their spirit for battle, and urged them in other ways to incur danger; he also ordered that a fixed reward should be given to each one who should slay a barbarian. After he had thus secured the affections of the soldiery, he wrote to Constantius, acquainting him with the levity of the generals; and when another general had been sent, he attacked the barbarians, and obtained the victory. They sent embassies to beg for peace, and showed the letter in which Constantius had requested them to enter the Roman dominions. He purposely delayed to send the ambassador back; he attacked a number of the enemy unexpectedly and conquered them.

Some have said that Constantius, with designed enmity, committed this campaign to him;[3] but this does not appear probable to me. For, as it rested with Constantius alone to nominate him Cæsar, why did he confer that title upon him? Why did he give him his sister in marriage, or hear his complaints against the inefficient generals, and send a competent one in their stead in order to complete the war, if he were not friendly to Julian?

But as I conjecture, he conferred on him the title of Cæsar because he was well disposed to Julian; but that after Julian had, without his sanction, been proclaimed emperor, he plotted against him through the barbarians on the Rhine; and this, I think, resulted either from the dread that Julian would seek revenge for the ill-treatment he and his brother Gallus had experienced during their youth, or as would be natural, from jealousy of his attaining similar honor. But a great variety of opinions are entertained on this subject.

---

[1] See Eunap. *V. S. vita Maximi;* Julian wrote four letters to him, *Op. Ep.* 15, 16, 38, 39; to be distinguished from another teacher of Julian, Maximus of Epirus.

[2] Sozomen is mistaken here, as Constantia was married to Gallus Cæsar, the brother of Julian. Soc. iii. 1, and Am. Marcel. xv. 8, 18, give Helena as the name of Julian's wife.

[3] As Eunapius, *Exc.* ii. 3.

CHAP. III. — JULIAN, ON HIS SETTLEMENT IN THE EMPIRE, BEGAN QUIETLY TO STIR UP OPPOSITION TO CHRISTIANITY, AND TO INTRODUCE PAGANISM ARTFULLY.

WHEN Julian found himself sole possessor of the empire,[1] he commanded that all the pagan temples should be reopened throughout the East; that those which had been neglected should be repaired; that those which had fallen into ruins should be rebuilt, and that the altars should be restored. He assigned considerable money for this purpose; he restored the customs of antiquity and the ancestral ceremonies in the cities, and the practice of offering sacrifice.

He himself offered libations openly and publicly sacrificed; bestowed honors on those who were zealous in the performance of these ceremonies; restored the initiators and the priests, the hierophants and the servants of the images, to their old privileges; and confirmed the legislation of former emperors in their behalf; he conceded exemption from duties and from other burdens as was their previous right; he restored the provisions, which had been abolished, to the temple guardians, and commanded them to be pure from meats, and to abstain from whatever according to pagan saying was befitting him who had announced his purpose of leading a pure life.

He also ordered that the nilometer and the symbols and the former ancestral tablets should be cared for in the temple of Serapis, instead of being deposited, according to the regulation, established by Constantine, in the church. He wrote frequently to the inhabitants of those cities in which he knew paganism was nourished, and urged them to ask what gifts they might desire. Towards the Christians, on the contrary, he openly manifested his aversion, refusing to honor them with his presence, or to receive their deputies who were delegated to report about grievances.

When the inhabitants of Nisibis sent to implore his aid against the Persians, who were on the point of invading the Roman territories, he refused to assist them because they were wholly Christianized, and would neither reopen their temples nor resort to the sacred places; he threatened that he would not help them, nor receive their embassy, nor approach to enter their city before he should hear that they had returned to paganism.

He likewise accused the inhabitants of Constantia in Palestine, of attachment to Christianity, and rendered their city tributary to that of Gaza. Constantia, as we stated before, was formerly called Majuma, and was used as a harbor for the vessels of Gaza; but on hearing that the majority of its inhabitants were Christians, Constantine elevated it to the dignity of a city, and conferred upon it the name of his own son, and a separate form of government; for he considered that it ought not to be dependent on Gaza, a city addicted to pagan rites. On the accession of Julian, the citizens of Gaza went to law against those of Constantia. The emperor himself sat as judge, and decided in favor of Gaza, and commanded that Constantia should be an appendage to that city, although it was situated at a distance of twenty stadia.

Its former name having been abolished by him, it has since been denominated the maritime region of Gaza. They have now the same city magistrates, military officers, and public regulations. With respect to ecclesiastical concerns, however, they may still be regarded as two cities. They have each their own bishop and their own clergy; they celebrate festivals in honor of their respective martyrs, and in memory of the priests who successively ruled them; and the boundaries of the adjacent fields by which the altars belonging to the bishops are divided, are still preserved.

It happened within our own remembrance that an attempt was made by the bishop of Gaza, on the death of the president of the church at Majuma, to unite the clergy of that town with those under his own jurisdiction; and the plea he advanced was, that it was not lawful for two bishops to preside over one city. The inhabitants of Majuma opposed this scheme, and the council of the province took cognizance of the dispute, and ordained another bishop. The council decided that it was altogether right for those who had been deemed worthy of the honors of a city on account of their piety, not to be deprived of the privilege conferred upon the priesthood and rank of their churches, through the decision of a pagan emperor, who had taken a different ground of action.

But these events occurred at a later period than that now under review.

CHAP. IV. — JULIAN INFLICTED EVILS UPON THE INHABITANTS OF CÆSAREA. BOLD FIDELITY OF MARIS, BISHOP OF CHALCEDON.

ABOUT the same time, the emperor erased Cæsarea,[2] the large and wealthy metropolis of Cappadocia, situated near Mount Argeus, from the catalogue of cities, and even deprived it of the name of Cæsarea, which had been conferred upon it during the reign of Claudius Cæsar, its former name having been Mazaca.[3] He had

---

[1] An independent chapter; cf. Theodoret, H. E. iii. 6, 7.

[2] The record is unique with Soz. Cf. the allusion in Greg. Naz. Or. cont. Julianum, i. 92; and Am. Marcel. xx. 9. 1, 2 (Mazaca).
[3] Am. Marcel. in quotation above; and Philost. ix. 12, who says that the original name of Cæsarea was Mazaca, from Mosoch, afterwards changed into Mazaca by inflection.

long regarded the inhabitants of this city with extreme aversion, because they were zealously attached to Christianity, and had formerly destroyed the temple of the ancestral Apollo and that of Jupiter, the tutelar deity of the city. The temple dedicated to Fortune,[1] the only one remaining in the city, was overturned by the Christians after his accession; and on hearing of the deed, he hated the entire city intensely and could scarce endure it. He also •blamed the pagans, who were few in number, but who ought, he said, to have hastened to the temple, and, if necessary, to have suffered cheerfully for Fortune. He caused all possessions and money belonging to the churches of the city and suburbs of Cæsarea to be rigorously sought out and carried away; about three hundred pounds of gold, obtained from this source, were conveyed to the public treasury. He also commanded that all the clergy should be enrolled among the troops under the governor of the province, which is accounted the most arduous and least honorable service among the Romans.

He ordered the Christian populace to be numbered, women and children inclusive, and imposed taxes upon them as onerous as those to which villages are subjected.

He further threatened that, unless their temples were speedily re-erected, his wrath would not be appeased, but would be visited on the city, until none of the Galileans remained in existence; for this was the name which, in derision, he was wont to give to the Christians. There is no doubt but that his menaces would have been fully executed had not death quickly intervened.

It was not from any feeling of compassion towards the Christians that he treated them at first with greater humanity than had been evinced by former persecutors, but because he had discovered that paganism had derived no advantage from their tortures, while Christianity had been especially increased, and had become more honored by the fortitude of those who died in defense of the faith.

It was simply from envy of their glory, that instead of employing fire and the sword against them, and maltreating their bodies like former persecutors, and instead of casting them into the sea, or burying them alive in order to compel them to a change of sentiment, he had recourse to argument and persuasion, and sought by these means to reduce them to paganism; he expected to gain his ends more easily by abandoning all violent measures, and by the manifestation of unexpected benevolence. It is said that on one occasion, when he

was sacrificing in the temple of Fortune at Constantinople, Maris,[2] bishop of Chalcedon, presented himself before him, and publicly rebuked him as an irreligous man, an atheist, and an apostate. Julian had nothing in return to reproach him with except his blindness, for his sight was impaired by old age, and he was led by a child. According to his usual custom of uttering blasphemies against Christ, Julian afterward added in derision, "The Galilean, thy God, will not cure thee." Maris replied, 'I thank God for my blindness, since it prevents me from beholding one who has fallen away from our religion." Julian passed on without giving a reply, for he considered that paganism would be more advanced by a personal and unexpected exhibition of patience and mildness towards Christians.

CHAP. V. — JULIAN RESTORES LIBERTY TO THE CHRISTIANS, IN ORDER TO EXECUTE FURTHER TROUBLES IN THE CHURCH. THE EVIL TREATMENT OF CHRISTIANS HE DEVISED.

IT was from these motives that Julian recalled from exile[3] all Christians who, during the reign of Constantius, had been banished on account of their religious sentiments, and restored to them their property that had been confiscated by law. He charged the people not to commit any act of injustice against the Christians, not to insult them, and not to constrain them to offer sacrifice unwillingly. He commanded that if they should of their own accord desire to draw near the altars, they were first to appease the wrath of the demons, whom the pagans regard as capable of averting evil, and to purify themselves by the customary course of expiations. He deprived the clergy, however, of the immunities, honors, and provisions which Constantine had conferred;[4] repealed the laws which had been enacted in their favor, and reinforced their statute liabilities. He even compelled the virgins and widows, who, on account of their poverty, were reckoned among the clergy, to refund the provision which had been assigned them from public sources. For when Constantine adjusted the temporal concerns of the Church, he devoted a sufficient portion of the taxes raised upon every city, to the support of the clergy everywhere; and to ensure the stability of this arrangement he enacted a law which has continued in force from the death of Julian to the present day. They say these transactions were very cruel and rigorous, as appears by the receipts given by the receivers of the money to those from whom it had been extorted, and

---

[1] Τὸ Τυχεῖον was the Byzantine term for the temple of the city genius. This one is mentioned by Greg. Naz. *Or. cont. Julianum*, i. 92, as Τύχη; similarly in *Or.* xviii. 34.

[2] Concerning this Maris, see Soc. iii. 12.
[3] Soc. iii. 11; Philost. vi. 7, vii. 4.
[4] Eus. *V. C.* ii. 30–42.

which were designed to show that the property received in accordance with the law of Constantine had been refunded.

Nothing, however, could diminish the enmity of the ruler against religion. In the intensity of his hatred against the faith, he seized every opportunity to ruin the Church. He deprived it of its property, votives, and sacred vessels, and condemned those who had demolished temples during the reign of Constantine and Constantius, to rebuild them, or to defray the expenses of their re-erection. On this ground, since they were unable to pay the sums and also on account of the inquisition for sacred money, many of the priests, clergy, and the other Christians were cruelly tortured and cast into prison.

It may be concluded from what has been said, that if Julian shed less blood than preceding persecutors of the Church, and that if he devised fewer punishments for the torture of the body, yet that he was severer in other respects; for he appears as inflicting evil upon it in every way, except that he recalled the priests who had been condemned to banishment by the Emperor Constantius; but it is said he issued this order in their behalf, not out of mercy, but that through contention among themselves, the churches might be involved in fraternal strife, and might fail of her own rights, or because he wanted to asperse Constantius; for he supposed that he could render the dead monarch odious to almost all his subjects, by favoring the pagans who were of the same sentiments as himself, and by showing compassion to those who had suffered for Christ, as having been treated unjustly. He expelled the eunuchs from the palaces, because the late emperor had been well affected towards them. He condemned Eusebius, the governor of the imperial court, to death, from a suspicion he entertained that it was at his suggestion that Gallus his brother had been slain. He recalled Aetius, the leader of the Eunomian heresy,[1] from the region whither Constantius had banished him, who had been otherwise suspected on account of his intimacy with Gallus; and to him Julian sent letters full of benignity, and furnished him with public conveyances. For a similar reason he condemned Eleusius, bishop of Cyzicus, under the heaviest penalty, to rebuild, within two months, and at his own expense, a church belonging to the Novatians which he had destroyed under Constantius. Many other things might be found which he did from hatred to his predecessor, either himself effecting these or permitting others to accomplish them.

BEAUTIFUL VIRGIN, REAPPEARS AT THAT TIME IN PUBLIC, AND ENTERS THE CHURCH OF ALEXANDRIA.

At this period, Athanasius, who had long remained in concealment, having heard of the death of Constantius, appeared by night in the church at Alexandria.[2] His unexpected appearance excited the greatest astonishment. He had escaped falling into the hands of the governor of Egypt, who, at the command of the emperor, and at the request of the friends of George, had formed plans to arrest him, as before stated, and had concealed himself in the house of a holy virgin in Alexandria. It is said that she was endowed with such extraordinary beauty, that those who beheld her regarded her as a phenomenon of nature; and that men who possessed continence and prudence, kept aloof from her in order that no blame might be attached to them by the suspicious. She was in the very flower of youth and was exceedingly modest and prudent, qualities which are wont alone to adorn the body even to a refinement of beauty when nature may not be helpful with the gift. For it is not true, as some assert, that "as is the body, so is the soul." On the contrary, the habit of the body is imaged forth by the operation of the soul, and any one who is active in any way whatever will appear to be of that nature as long as he may be thus actively engaged.

This is a truth I think admitted by all who have accurately investigated the subject. It is related that Athanasius sought refuge in the house of this holy virgin by the revelation of God, who designed to save him in this manner. When I reflect on the result which ensued, I cannot doubt but that all the events were directed by God; so that the relatives of Athanasius might not have distress if any one had attempted to trouble them about him, and had they been compelled to swear. There was nothing to excite suspicion of a priest being concealed in the house of so lovely a virgin. However, she had the courage to receive him, and through her prudence preserved his life. She was his most faithful keeper and assiduous servant; for she washed his feet and brought him food, and she alone served in every other necessity, which nature demands in her exacting uses; the books he stood in need of she cared for through the help of others; during the long time in which these services were rendered, none of the inhabitants of Alexandria knew anything about it.

CHAP. VI. — ATHANASIUS, AFTER HAVING BEEN SEVEN YEARS CONCEALED IN THE HOUSE OF A WISE AND

CHAP. VII. — VIOLENT DEATH AND TRIUMPH OF GEORGE, BISHOP OF ALEXANDRIA. THE RESULT

---

[1] *Juliani Op. Ep.* 31, a letter from him to Aetius.

[2] Pallad. *H. I.* 136; cf. Soc. iii. 4; cf. *Chronicon prævium* to Festal letters, under A.D. 360.

OF CERTAIN OCCURRENCES IN THE TEMPLE OF MITHRA. LETTER OF JULIAN ON THIS AGGRAVATED CIRCUMSTANCE.

AFTER Athanasius had been preserved in this wise and appeared suddenly in the church, no one knew whence he came.[1] The people of Alexandria, however, rejoiced at his return, and restored his churches to him.

The Arians, being thus expelled from the churches, were compelled to hold their assemblies in private houses, and constituted Lucius, in the place of George, as the bishop of their heresy. George had been already slain; for when the magistrates had announced to the public the decease of Constantius, and that Julian was sole ruler, the pagans of Alexandria rose up in sedition. They attacked George with shouts and reproaches as if they would kill him at once. The repellants of this precipitate attack, then put him in prison; a little while after they rushed, early in the morning, to the prison, killed him, flung the corpse upon a camel, and after exposing it to every insult during the day, burnt it at nightfall. I am not ignorant that the Arian heretics assert that George received this cruel treatment from the followers of Athanasius; but it seems to me more probable that the perpetrators of these deeds were the pagans; for they had more cause than any other body of men to hate him, especially on account of the insults he offered their images and their temples; and having, morever, prohibited them from sacrificing, or performing the ancestral rites. Besides, the influence he had acquired in the palaces intensified the hatred towards him; and as the people are wont to feel towards those in power, they regarded him as unendurable.

A calamity had also taken place at a spot called Mithrium; it was originally a desert, and Constantius had bestowed it on the church of Alexandria. While George was clearing the ground, in order to erect a house of prayer, an adytum was discovered. In it were found idols and certain instruments for initiation or perfection which seemed ludicrous and strange to the beholders. The Christians caused them to be publicly exhibited, and made a procession in order to nettle the pagans; but the pagans gathered a multitude together, and rushed upon and attacked the Christians, after arming themselves with swords, stones, and whatever weapon came first to hand. They slew many of the Christians, and, in derision of their religion, crucified others, and they left many wounded.

This led to the abandonment of the work that had been commenced by the Christians, while the pagans murdered George as soon as they had heard of the accession of Julian to the empire. This fact is admitted by that emperor himself, which he would not have confessed unless he had been forced by the truth; for he would rather, I think, have had the Christians, whoever they were, than the pagans to be the murderers of George; but it could not be concealed. It is apparent in the letter which he wrote on the subject to the inhabitants of Alexandria,[2] wherein he expresses severe opinions. In this epistle he only censures and passes over the punishment; for he said that he feared Serapis, their tutelary divinity, and Alexander their founder, and Julian, his own uncle, who formerly was governor of Egypt and of Alexandria. This latter was so favorable to paganism and hated Christianity so exceedingly, that contrary to the wishes of the emperor, he persecuted the Christians unto death.

CHAP. VIII. — CONCERNING THEODORE, THE KEEPER OF THE SACRED VESSELS OF ANTIOCH. HOW JULIAN, THE UNCLE OF THE TRAITOR, ON ACCOUNT OF THESE VESSELS, FALLS A PREY TO WORMS.

IT is said that when Julian, the uncle of the emperor,[3] was intent upon removing the votive gifts of the church of Antioch, which were many and costly, and placing them in the imperial treasury, and also closing the places of prayer, all the clergy fled. One presbyter, by name Theodoritus, alone did not leave the city; Julian seized him, as the keeper of the treasures, and as capable of giving information concerning them, and maltreated him terribly; finally he ordered him to be slain with the sword, after he had responded bravely under every torture and had been well approved by his doctrinal confessions. When Julian had made a booty of the sacred vessels, he flung them upon the ground and began to mock; after blaspheming Christ as much as he wished, he sat upon the vessels and augmented his insulting acts. Immediately his genitals and rectum were corrupted; their flesh became putrescent, and was changed into worms. The disease was beyond the skill of the physicians. However, from reverence and fear for the emperor, they resorted to experiments with all manner of drugs, and the most costly and the fattest birds were slain, and their fat was applied to the corrupted parts, in the hope that the worms might be thereby attracted to the surface, but this was of no effect;

---

[1] Soc. iii. 2–4. Cf. Philost. vii. 2; Am. Marcel. xxii. 11. 3–11; Athan. *Ep. ad. Episc.* 7; *Hist. Arian.* 51, 72, 75, etc.; *Juliani Op. Epp.* 8, 9, 10, 36, 45, 55.

[2] Text given by Soc. iii. 3; cf. *Juliani Op. Ep.* 10.
[3] Philost. vii. 10, variations; Theodoret, iii. 12, 13. Cf. Am. Marcel. xxiii. 1. 4–6.

for being deep buried, they crept into the living flesh, and did not cease their gnawing until they put an end to his life. It seemed that this calamity was an infliction of Divine wrath, because the keeper of the imperial treasures, and other of the chief officers of the court who had made sport of the Church, died in an extraordinary and dreadful manner,[1] as if condemned by Divine wrath.

CHAP. IX. — MARTYRDOM OF THE SAINTS EUSEBIUS, NESTABUS, AND ZENO IN THE CITY OF GAZA.

As I have advanced thus far in my history, and have given an account of the death of George and of Theodoritus, I deem it right to relate some particulars concerning the death of the three brethren, Eusebius, Nestabus, and Zeno.[2] The inhabitants of Gaza, being inflamed with rage against them, dragged them from their house, in which they had concealed themselves, and cast them into prison, and beat them. They then assembled in the theater, and cried out loudly against them, declaring that they had committed sacrilege in their temple, and had used the past opportunity for the injury and insult of paganism. By these shouts and by instigating one another to the murder of the brethren, they were filled with fury; and when they had been mutually incited, as a crowd in revolt is wont to do, they rushed to the prison. They handled the men very cruelly; sometimes with the face and sometimes with the back upon the ground, the victims were dragged along, and were dashed to pieces by the pavement. I have been told that even women quitted their distaffs and pierced them with the weaving-spindles, and that the cooks in the markets snatched from their stands the boiling pots foaming with hot water and poured it over the victims, or perforated them with spits. When they had torn the flesh from them and crushed in their skulls, so that the brain ran out on the ground, their bodies were dragged out of the city and flung on the spot generally used as a receptacle for the carcasses of beasts; then a large fire was lighted, and they burned the bodies; the remnant of the bones not consumed by the fire was mixed with those of camels and asses, that they might not be found easily. But they were not long concealed; for a Christian woman, who was an inhabitant, though not a native of Gaza, collected the bones at night by the direction of God. She put them in an earthen pot and gave them to Zeno, their cousin, to keep, for

thus God had informed her in a dream, and also had indicated to the woman where the man lived: and before she saw him, he was shown to her, for she was previously unacquainted with Zeno; and when the persecution had been agitated recently he remained concealed. He was within a little of being seized by the people of Gaza and being put to death; but he had effected his escape while the people were occupied in the murder of his cousins, and had fled to Anthedon, a maritime city, about twenty stadia from Gaza and similarly favorable to paganism and devoted to idolatry. When the inhabitants of this city discovered that he was a Christian, they beat him terribly on the back with rods and drove him out of the city. He then fled to the harbor of Gaza and concealed himself; and here the woman found him and gave him the remains. He kept them carefully in his house until the reign of Theodosius, when he was ordained bishop; and he erected a house of prayer beyond the walls of the city, placed an altar there, and deposited the bones of the martyrs near those of Nestor, the Confessor. Nestor had been on terms of intimacy with his cousins, and was seized with them by the people of Gaza, imprisoned, and scourged. But those who dragged him through the city were affected by his personal beauty; and, struck with compassion, they cast him, before he was quite dead, out of the city. Some persons found him, and carried him to the house of Zeno, where he expired during the dressing of his cuts and wounds. When the inhabitants of Gaza began to reflect on the enormity of their crime, they trembled lest the emperor should take vengeance on them.

It was reported that the emperor was filled with indignation, and had determined upon punishing the decuria; but this report was false, and had no foundation save in the fears and self-accusations of the criminals. Julian, far from evincing as much anger against them as he had manifested against the Alexandrians on the murder of George, did not even write to rebuke the people of Gaza. On the contrary, he deposed the governor of the province, and held him as a suspect, and represented that clemency alone prevented his being put to death. The crime imputed to him was, that of having arrested some of the inhabitants of Gaza, who were reported to have begun the sedition and murders, and of having imprisoned them until judgment could be passed upon them in accordance with the laws. "For what right had he," asked the emperor, "to arrest the citizens merely for retaliating on a few Galileans the injuries that had been inflicted on them and their gods?" This, it is said, was the fact in the case.

CHAP. X. — CONCERNING ST. HILARION AND THE VIRGINS IN HELIOPOLIS WHO WERE DESTROYED BY SWINE. STRANGE MARTYRDOM OF MARK, BISHOP OF ARETHUSA.

At the same period the inhabitants of Gaza sought for the monk Hilarion; but he had fled to Sicily.[1] Here he employed himself in collecting wood in the deserts and on the mountains, which he carried on his shoulders for sale in the cities, and, by these means, obtained sufficient food for the support of the body. But as he was at length recognized by a man of quality whom he had dispossessed of a demon, he retired to Dalmatia, where, by the power of God, he performed numerous miracles, and through prayer, repressed an inundation of the sea and restored the waves to their proper bounds, and again departed, for it was no joy to him to live among those who praised him; but when he changed his place of abode, he was desirous of being unobserved and by frequent migrations to be rid of the fame which prevailed about him. Eventually he sailed for the island of Cyprus, but touched at Paphos, and, at the entreaty of the bishop of Cyprus, he loved the life there and practiced philosophy at a place called Charburis.

Here he only escaped martyrdom by flight; for he fled in compliance with the Divine precept which commands us not to expose ourselves to persecution; but that if we fall into the hands of persecutors, to overcome by our own fortitude the violence of our oppressors.

The inhabitants of Gaza and of Alexandria were not the only citizens who exercised such atrocities against the Christians as those I have described. The inhabitants of Heliopolis, near Mount Libanus, and of Arethusa in Syria, seem to have surpassed them in excess of cruelty.[2] The former were guilty of an act of barbarity which could scarcely be credited, had it not been corroborated by the testimony of those who witnessed it. They stripped the holy virgins, who had never been looked upon by the multitude, of their garments, and exposed them in a state of nudity as a public spectacle and objects of insult. After numerous other inflictions they at last shaved them, ripped them open, and concealed in their viscera the food usually given to pigs; and since the swine could not distinguish, but were impelled by the need of their customary food, they also tore in pieces the human flesh.

I am convinced that the citizens of Heliopolis perpetrated this barbarity against the holy virgins on account of the prohibition of the ancient custom of yielding up virgins to prostitution with any chance comer before being united in marriage to their betrothed. This custom was prohibited by a law enacted by Constantine, after he had destroyed the temple of Venus at Heliopolis, and erected a church upon its ruins.[3]

Mark, bishop of Arethusa,[4] an old man and venerable for his gray hairs and life, was put to a very cruel death by the inhabitants of that city, who had long entertained inimical feelings against him, because, during the reign of Constantine, he had more spiritedly than persuasively elevated the pagans to Christianity, and had demolished a most sacred and magnificent temple. On the accession of Julian he saw that the people were excited against the bishop; an edict was issued commanding the bishop either to defray the expenses of its re-erection, or to rebuild the temple. Reflecting that the one was impossible and the other unlawful for a Christian and still less for a priest, he at first fled from the city. On hearing, however, that many were suffering on his account, that some were dragged before the tribunals and others tortured, he returned, and offered to suffer whatever the multitude might choose to inflict upon him. The entire people, instead of admiring him the more as having manifested a deed befitting a philosopher, conceived that he was actuated by contempt towards them, and rushed upon him, dragged him through the streets, pressing and plucking and beating whatever member each one happened upon. People of each sex and of all ages joined with alacrity and fury in this atrocious proceeding. His ears were severed by fine ropes; the boys who frequented the schools made game of him by tossing him aloft and rolling him over and over, sending him forward, catching him up, and unsparingly piercing him with their styles. When his whole body was covered with wounds, and he nevertheless was still breathing, they anointed him with honey and a certain mixture, and placing him in a fish-basket made of woven rushes, raised him up on an eminence. It is said that while he was in this position, and the wasps and bees lit upon him and consumed his flesh, he told the inhabitants of Arethusa that he was raised up above them, and could look down upon them below him, and that this reminded him of the difference that would exist between them in the life to come. It is also related that the prefect[5] who, although a pagan, was of such noble conduct that his memory is still honored in that country, admired the self-control of Mark, and boldly uttered reproaches against the emperor for allowing himself to be

---

[1] Hieron. *Vita Hilarionis* (divergent on some points).
[2] Greg. Naz. *Or. cont. Julianum*, i. 86, 87.
[3] Eus. *V. C.* iii. 58.
[4] Greg. Naz. *Or. cont. Julianum*, i. 88–90.
[5] He means Sallustius, who was at this time præfectus prætorio Orientis, to be distinguished from another Sallustius, who was præfectus prætorio Galliæ.

vanquished by an old man, who was exposed to innumerable tortures; and he added that such proceedings reflected ridicule on the emperor, while the names of the persecuted were at the same time rendered illustrious. Thus did the blessed one[1] endure all the torments inflicted upon him by the inhabitants of Arethusa with such unshaken fortitude that even the pagans praised him.

CHAP. XI. — CONCERNING MACEDONIUS, THEODULUS, GRATIAN, BUSIRIS, BASIL, AND EUPSYCHIUS, WHO SUFFERED MARTYRDOM IN THOSE TIMES.

ABOUT the same period, Macedonius, Theodulus, and Tatian, who were Phrygians by birth, courageously endured martyrdom.[2] A temple of Misos, a city of Phrygia, having been reopened by the governor of the province, after it had been closed many years, these martyrs entered therein by night, and destroyed the images. As other individuals were arrested, and were on the point of being punished for the deed, they avowed themselves the actors in the transaction. They might have escaped all further punishment by offering sacrifices to idols; but the governor could not persuade them to accept acquittal on these terms. His persuasions being ineffectual, he maltreated them in a variety of forms, and finally extended them on a gridiron, beneath which a fire had been lighted. While they were being consumed, they said to the governor, "Amachus (for that was his name), "if you desire cooked flesh, give orders that our bodies may be turned with the other side to the fire, in order that we may not seem, to your taste, half cooked." Thus did these men nobly endure and lay down their life amid the punishments.

It is said that Busiris also obtained renown at Ancyra, a city of Galatia, by his brilliant and most manly confession of religion. He belonged to the heresy denominated Eucratites; the governor of the province apprehended and designed to maltreat him for ridiculing the pagans. He led him forth publicly to the torture chamber and commanded that he should be elevated. Busiris raised both hands to his head so as to leave his sides exposed, and told the governor that it would be useless for the executioners to lift him up to the instrument of torture and afterwards to lower him, as he was ready without this to yield to the tortures as much as might be desired. The governor was surprised at this proposition; but his astonishment was increased by what followed, for Busiris remained firm, holding up both hands and receiving the blows while his sides were being torn with hooks, according to the governor's direction. Immediately afterwards, Busiris was consigned to prison, but was released not long subsequently, on the announcement of the death of Julian. He lived till the reign of Theodosius, renounced his former heresy, and joined the Catholic Church.

It is said that about this period, Basil,[3] presbyter of the church of Ancyra, and Eupsychius,[4] a noble of Cæsarea in Cappadocia, who had but just taken to himself a wife and was still a bridegroom, terminated their lives by martyrdom. I believe that Eupsychius was condemned in consequence of the demolition of the temple of Fortune, which, as I have already stated, excited the anger of the emperor against all the inhabitants of Cæsarea. Indeed, all the actors in this transaction were condemned, some to death, and others to banishment. Basil had long manifested great zeal in defense of the faith, and had opposed the Arians during the reign of Constantius; hence the partisans of Eudoxius had prohibited him from holding public assemblies. On the accession of Julian, however, he traveled hither and thither, publicly and openly exhorting the Christians to cleave to their own doctrines, and to refrain from defiling themselves with pagan sacrifices and libations. He urged them to account as nothing the honors which the emperor might bestow upon them, such honors being but of short duration, and leading to eternal infamy. His zeal had already rendered him an object of suspicion and of hatred to the pagans, when one day he chanced to pass by and see them offering sacrifice. He sighed deeply, and uttered a prayer to the effect that no Christian might be suffered to fall into similar delusion. He was seized on the spot, and conveyed to the governor of the province. Many tortures were inflicted on him; and in the manly endurance of this anguish he received the crown of martyrdom.

Even if these cruelties were perpetrated contrary to the will of the emperor, yet they serve to prove that his reign was signalized by martyrs neither ignoble nor few.

For the sake of clearness, I have related all these occurrences collectively, although the martyrdoms really occurred at different periods.

CHAP. XII. — CONCERNING LUCIFER AND EUSEBIUS, BISHOPS OF THE WEST. EUSEBIUS WITH ATHANASIUS THE GREAT AND OTHER BISHOPS COLLECT A COUNCIL AT ALEXANDRIA, AND CONFIRM THE NICENE FAITH BY DEFINING THE CONSUBSTAN-

---

[1] Most likely this was the same Mark, bishop of Arethusa, mentioned in iii. 10; iv. 6, 12, 16, 22.
[2] For the Phrygians, Soc. iii. 15.

[3] Independent with Soz.
[4] Basil, M. *Ep.* c.; Greg. Naz. *Ep.* lviii.

TIALITY OF THE SPIRIT WITH THE FATHER AND THE SON. THEIR DECREE CONCERNING SUBSTANCE AND HYPOSTASIS.

AFTER the return of Athanasius, Lucifer, bishop of Cagliari in Sardinia, and Eusebius, bishop of Vercelli, a city of Liguria in Italy, returned from the upper Thebais.[1] They had been condemned by Constantius to perpetual exile in that country. For the regulation and general systematizing of ecclesiastical affairs, Eusebius came to Alexandria, and there, in concert with Athanasius, to hold a council for the purpose of confirming the Nicene doctrines.

Lucifer sent a deacon with Eusebius to take his place in the council, and went himself to Antioch, to visit the church there in its disturbances.

A schism had been excited by the Arians, then under the guidance of Euzoius, and by the followers of Meletius, who, as I have above stated, were at variance even with those who held the same opinions as themselves. As Meletius had not then returned from exile, Lucifer ordained Paulinus bishop.[2]

In the meantime, the bishops of many cities had assembled in Alexandria with Athanasius and Eusebius, and had confirmed the Nicene doctrines. They confessed that the Holy Ghost is of the same substance as the Father and the Son, and they made use of the term "Trinity."

They declared that the human nature assumed by God the Word is to be regarded as consisting of not a perfect body only, but also of a perfect soul, even as was taught by the ancient Church philosophers. As the Church had been agitated by questions concerning the terms "substance" and "hypostasis," and the contentions and disputes about these words had been frequent, they decreed, and, as I think, wisely, that these terms should not henceforth at the beginning be used in reference to God, except in refutation of the Sabellian tenet; lest from the paucity of terms, one and the same thing might appear to be called by three names; but that one might understand each by its peculiar term in a threefold way.

These were the decrees passed by the bishops convened at Alexandria. Athanasius read in the council the document about his flight which he had written in order to justify himself.[3]

CHAP. XIII. — CONCERNING PAULINUS AND MELETIUS, CHIEF-PRIESTS OF ANTIOCH ; HOW EUSEBIUS

AND LUCIFER ANTAGONIZED ONE ANOTHER ; EUSEBIUS AND HILARIUS DEFEND THE NICENE FAITH.

ON the termination of the council, Eusebius repaired to Antioch and found dissension prevailing among the people.[4] Those who were attached to Meletius would not join Paulinus, but held their assemblies apart. Eusebius was much grieved at the state of affairs ; for the ordination ought not to have taken place without the unanimous consent of the people ; yet, from respect towards Lucifer, he did not openly express his dissatisfaction.

He refused to hold communion with either party, but promised to redress their respective grievances by means of a council. While he was thus striving to restore concord and unanimity, Meletius returned from exile, and, finding that those who held his sentiments had seceded from the other party, he held meetings with them beyond the walls of the city. Paulinus, in the meantime, assembled his own party within the city ; for his mildness, his virtuous life, and his advanced age had so far won the respect of Euzoius, the Arian president, that, instead of being expelled from the city, a church had been assigned him for his own use. Eusebius, on finding all his endeavors for the restoration of concord frustrated, quitted Antioch. Lucifer fancied himself injured by him, because he had refused to approve the ordination of Paulinus ; and, in displeasure, seceded from communion with him. As if purely from the desire of contention, Lucifer then began to cast aspersions on the enactments of the council of Alexandria ; and in this way he seems to have originated the heresy which has been called after him, Luciferian.

Those who espoused his cause seceded from the church ; but, although he was deeply chagrined at the aspect affairs had taken, yet, because he had deputed a deacon to accompany Eusebius in lieu of himself, he yielded to the decrees of the council of Alexandria, and conformed to the doctrines of the Catholic Church. About this period he repaired to Sardinia.

In the meantime Eusebius traversed the Eastern provinces, restored those who had declined from the faith, and taught them what it was necessary to believe. After passing through Illyria, he went to Italy, and there he met with Hilarius, bishop of Poictiers[5] in Aquitania. Hilarius had returned from exile before Eusebius, and had taught the Italians and the Gauls what doctrines they had to receive, and what to reject ; he expressed himself with great eloquence in the Latin tongue, and wrote many

[1] Athan. *Hist. Arian.* 33; *Apol. de fuga sua,* 4. The whole of the *Tomus ad Antioch.;* Soc. iii. 5-8; Ruf. *H. E.* i. 27-30; Theodoret, *H. E.* iii. 4, 5.
[2] Soc. iii. 6.
[3] Soc. gives a considerable extract, iii. 8, from Athan. *Apol. de fuga sua.*

[4] Ruf. *H. E.* i. 30, 31; Soc. iii. 9, 10. Cf. Theodoret, *H. E.* iii. 4, 5; Sulp. Sev. *H. S.* ii. 45.
[5] Soc. iii. 10, who says his source is Sabinus, ἐν τῇ συναγωγῇ τῶν συνοδικῶν.

admirable works, it is said, in refutation of the Arian dogmas. Thus did Hilarius and Eusebius maintain the doctrines of the Nicæan council in the regions of the West.

CHAP. XIV. — THE PARTISANS OF MACEDONIUS DISPUTED WITH THE ARIANS CONCERNING ACACIUS.

AT this period the adherents of Macedonius, among whom were Eleusius, Eustathius, and Sophronius, who now began openly to be called Macedonians, as constituting a distinct sect, adopted the bold measure on the death of Constantius, of calling together those of their own sentiments who had been convened at Seleucia, and of holding several councils. They condemned the partisans of Acacius and the faith which had been established at Ariminum, and confirmed the doctrines which had been set forth at Antioch, and afterwards approved at Seleucia.

When interrogated as to the cause of their dispute with the partisans of Acacius, with whom, as being of the same sentiments as themselves, they had formerly held communion, they replied by the mouth of Sophronius,[1] a bishop of Paphlagonia, that while the Christians in the West maintained the use of the term "consubstantial," the followers of Aetius in the East upheld the dogma of dissimilarity as to substance ; and that the former party irregularly wove together into a unity the distinct persons of the Father and of the Son, by their use of the term "consubstantial," and that the latter party represented too great a difference as existing in the relationship between the nature of the Father and of the Son ; but that they themselves preserved the mean between the two extremes, and avoided both errors, by religiously maintaining that in hypostasis, the Son is like unto the Father. It was by such representations as these that the Macedonians vindicated themselves from blame.

CHAP. XV. — ATHANASIUS IS AGAIN BANISHED ; CONCERNING ELEUSIUS, BISHOP OF CYZICUS, AND TITUS, BISHOP OF BOSTRA ; MENTION OF THE ANCESTORS OF THE AUTHOR.

THE emperor,[2] on being informed that Athanasius held meetings in the church of Alexandria, and taught the people boldly, and converted many pagans to Christianity, commanded him, under the severest penalties, to depart from Alexandria.[3] The pretext made use of for enforcing this edict, was that Athanasius, after having been banished by Constantius, had reassumed his episcopal see without the sanction of the reigning emperor ; for Julian declared that he had never contemplated restoring the bishops who had been exiled by Constantius to their ecclesiastical functions, but only to their native land. On the announcement of the command enjoining his immediate departure, Athanasius said to the Christian multitudes who stood weeping around him, " Be of good courage ; it is but a cloud which will speedily be dispersed." After these words he bade farewell ; he then committed the care of the church to the most zealous of his friends and quitted Alexandria.

About the same period, the inhabitants of Cyzicus sent an embassy to the emperor to lay before him some of their private affairs, and particularly to entreat the restoration of the pagan temples. He applauded their forethought, and promised to grant all their requests. He expelled Eleusius, the bishop of their city, because he had destroyed some temples, and desecrated the sacred areas with contumely, provided houses for the support of widows, erected buildings for holy virgins, and induced pagans to abandon their ancestral rites.

The emperor prohibited some foreign Christians, who had accompanied him, from entering the city of Cyzicus, from the apprehension, it appears, that they would, in conjunction with the Christians within the city, excite a sedition on account of religion. There were many persons gathered with them who also held like religious views with the Christians of the city, and who were engaged in woolen manufactures for the state, and were coiners of money. They were numerous, and were divided into two populous classes ; they had received permission from preceding emperors to dwell, with their wives and possessions, in Cyzicus, provided that they annually handed over to the public treasury a supply of clothes for the soldiery and of newly coined money.

Although Julian was anxious to advance paganism by every means, yet he deemed it the height of imprudence to employ force or vengeance against those who refused to sacrifice. Besides, there were so many Christians in every city that it would have been no easy task for the rulers even to number them. He did not even forbid them to assemble together for worship, as he was aware that when freedom of the will is called into question, constraint is utterly useless. He expelled the clergy and presidents of the churches from all the cities, in order to put an end to these assemblies, saying truly that by their absence the gatherings of the people would be effectually dissolved, if indeed

---

[1] Soc. iii. 10, gives a direct extract; Soz. leaves out some words purposely.
[2] Soc. iii. 13, 14; Ruf. H.E. i. 32–34; all remotely; much new material in this chapter. Cf. Theodoret, H. E. iii. 9; Athan. Ep. Heort., under 363.
[3] The edict of Julian, in Juliani Op. Ep. xxvi.

there were none to convene the churches, and none to teach or to dispense the mysteries, religion itself would, in the course of time, fall into oblivion. The pretext which he advanced for these proceedings was, that the clergy were the leaders of sedition among the people. Under this plea, he expelled Eleusius and his friends from Cyzicus, although there was not even a symptom nor expectation of sedition in that city. He also publicly called upon the citizens of Bostra[1] to expel Titus, their bishop. It appears that the emperor had threatened to impeach Titus and the other clergy as the authors of any sedition that might arise among the people, and that Titus had thereupon written, stating to him that although the Christians were near the pagans in number, yet that, in accordance with his exhortations, they were disposed to remain quiet, and were not likely to rise up in sedition. Julian, with the view of not exciting the enmity of the inhabitants of Bostra against Titus, represented, in a letter which he addressed to them, that their bishop had advanced a calumny against them, by stating that it was in accordance with his exhortations rather than with their own inclination that they refrained from sedition; and Julian exhorted them to expel him from their city as a public enemy.

It appears that the Christians were subjected to similar injustice in other places; sometimes by the command of the emperor, and sometimes by the wrath and impetuosity of the populace. The blame of these transactions may be justly imputed to the ruler; for he did not bring under the force of law the transgressors of law, but out of his hatred to the Christian religion, he only visited the perpetrators of such deeds with verbal rebukes, while, by his actions, he urged them on in the same course. Hence although not absolutely persecuted by the emperor, the Christians were obliged to flee from city to city and village to village. My grandfather and many of my ancestors were compelled to flee in this manner. My grandfather was of pagan parentage; and, with his own family and that of Alaphion, had been the first to embrace Christianity in Bethelia, a populous town near Gaza, in which there are temples highly reverenced by the people of the country, on account of their antiquity and structural excellence. The most celebrated of these temples is the Pantheon, built on an artificial eminence commanding a view of the whole town. The conjecture is that the place received its name from the temple, that the original name given to this temple was in the Syriac language, and that this name was afterwards rendered into Greek and

expressed by a word which signifies that the temple is the residence of all the gods.

It is said that the above-mentioned families were converted through the instrumentality of the monk Hilarion. Alaphion, it appears, was possessed of a devil; and neither the pagans nor the Jews could, by any incantations and enchantments, deliver him from this affliction; but Hilarion, by simply calling on the name of Christ, expelled the demon, and Alaphion, with his whole family, immediately embraced Christianity.

My grandfather was endowed with great natural ability, which he applied with success to the explanation of the Sacred Scriptures; he had made some attainments in general knowledge, and was not ignorant of arithmetic. He was much beloved by the Christians of Ascalon, of Gaza, and of the surrounding country; and was regarded as necessary to religion, on account of his gift in expounding the doubtful points of Scripture. No one can speak in adequate terms of the virtues of the other[2] family. The first churches and monasteries erected in that country were founded by members of this family and supported by their power and beneficence towards strangers and the needy. Some good men belonging to this family have flourished even in our own days; and in my youth I saw some of them, but they were then very aged. I shall have occasion to say more concerning them in the course of my history.[3]

CHAP. XVI. — EFFORTS OF JULIAN TO ESTABLISH PAGANISM AND TO ABOLISH OUR USAGES. THE EPISTLE WHICH HE SENT TO THE PAGAN HIGH-PRIESTS.

THE emperor[4] was deeply grieved at finding that all his efforts to secure the predominance of paganism were utterly ineffectual, and at seeing Christianity excelling in repute; for although the gates of the temples were kept open, although sacrifices were offered, and the observance of ancient festivals restored in all the cities, yet he was far from being satisfied; for he could plainly foresee that, on the withdrawal of his influence, a change in the whole aspect of affairs would speedily take place. He was particularly chagrined on discovering that the wives, children, and servants of many of the pagan priests had been converted to Christianity. On reflecting that one main support of the Christian religion was the life and behavior of its professors, he determined to introduce into the pagan temples the order and discipline of Christianity, to insti-

---

[1] *Juliani Op. Ep.* lii. Julianus Bostrenis.

[2] He probably means that of Alaphion.
[3] He means Salamines, Phuscon, Malachion, and Crispion, whom he mentions below, vi. 32.
[4] Independent with Soz.

tute various orders and degrees of ministry, to appoint teachers and readers to give instruction in pagan doctrines and exhortations, and to command that prayers should be offered on certain days at stated hours. He moreover resolved to found monasteries for the accommodation of men and women who desired to live in philosophical retirement, as likewise hospitals for the relief of strangers and of the poor and for other philanthropical purposes. He wished to introduce among the pagans the Christian system of penance for voluntary and involuntary transgressions; but the point of ecclesiastical discipline which he chiefly admired, and desired to establish among the pagans, was the custom among the bishops to give letters of recommendation to those who traveled to foreign lands, wherein they commended them to the hospitality and kindness of other bishops, in all places, and under all contingencies. In this way did Julian strive to ingraft the customs of Christianity upon paganism. But if what I have stated appears to be incredible, I need not go far in search of proofs to corroborate my assertions; for I can produce a letter written by the emperor himself on the subject. He writes as follows:[1]—

"To Arsacius, High-Priest of Galatia. Paganism has not yet reached the degree of prosperity that might be desired, owing to the conduct of its votaries. The worship of the gods, however, is conducted on the grandest and most magnificent scale, so far exceeding our very prayer and hope; let our Adrastea be propitious to these words, for no one could have dared to look for so extensive and so surprising a change as that which we have witnessed within a very short space of time. But are we to rest satisfied with what has been already effected? Ought we not rather to consider that the progress of Atheism has been principally owing to the humanity evinced by Christians towards strangers, to the reverence they have manifested towards the dead, and to the delusive gravity which they have assumed in their life? It is requisite that each of us should be diligent in the discharge of duty: I do not refer to you alone, as that would not suffice, but to all the priests of Galatia.

"You must either put them to shame, or try the power of persuasion, or else deprive them of their sacerdotal offices, if they do not with their wives, their children, and their servants join in the service of the gods, or if they support the servants, sons, or wives of the Galileans in treating the gods impiously and in preferring Atheism to piety. Then exhort the priests not to frequent theaters, not to drink at taverns, and not to engage in any trade, or practice any nefarious art.

"Honor those who yield to your remonstrances, and expel those who disregard them. Establish hostelries in every city, so that strangers from neighboring and foreign countries may reap the benefit of our philanthropy, according to their respective need.

"I have provided means to meet the necessary expenditure, and have issued directions throughout the whole of Galatia, that you should be furnished annually with thirty thousand bushels of corn and sixty thousand measures of wine, of which the fifth part is to be devoted to the support of the poor who attend upon the priests; and the rest to be distributed among strangers and our own poor. For, while there are no persons in need among the Jews, and while even the impious Galileans provide not only for those of their own party who are in want, but also for those who hold with us, it would indeed be disgraceful if we were to allow our own people to suffer from poverty.

"Teach the pagans to co-operate in this work of benevolence, and let the first-fruits of the pagan towns be offered to the gods.

"Habituate the pagans to the exercise of this liberality, by showing them how such conduct is sanctioned by the practice of remote antiquity; for Homer[2] represents Eumæus as saying,—

'My guest! I should offend, treating with scorn
The stranger, though a poorer should arrive
Than even thyself; for all the poor that are,
And all the strangers are the care of Jove.'

"Let us not permit others to excel us in good deeds; let us not dishonor ourselves by violence, but rather let us be foremost in piety towards the gods. If I hear that you act according to my directions, I shall be full of joy. Do not often visit the governors at their own houses, but write to them frequently. When they enter the city, let no priest go to meet them; and let not the priest accompany them further than the vestibule when they repair to the temple of the gods; neither let any soldiers march before them on such occasions; but let those follow them who will. For as soon as they have entered within the sacred bounds, they are but private individuals; for there it is your duty, as you well know, to preside, according to the divine decree. Those who humbly conform to this law manifest that they possess true religion; whereas those who contemn it are proud and vainglorious.

"I am ready to render assistance to the inhabitants of Pessinus, provided that they will propitiate the mother of the gods; but if they neglect this duty, they will incur my utmost displeasure.

[1] *Juliani Op. Ep.* xlix.

[2] *Odyss.* xiv. 56.

'I should myself transgress,
Receiving here, and giving conduct hence
To one detested by the gods as these.'[1]

"Convince them, therefore, that if they desire my assistance, they must offer up supplications to the mother of the gods."

CHAP. XVII. — IN ORDER THAT HE MIGHT NOT BE THOUGHT TYRANNICAL, JULIAN PROCEEDS ARTFULLY AGAINST THE CHRISTIANS. ABOLITION OF THE SIGN OF THE CROSS. HE MAKES THE SOLDIERY SACRIFICE, ALTHOUGH THEY WERE UNWILLING.

WHEN Julian acted and wrote in the manner aforesaid, he expected that he would by these means easily induce his subjects to change their religious opinions.[2] Although he earnestly desired to abolish the Christian religion, yet he plainly was ashamed to employ violent measures, lest he should be accounted tyrannical. He used every means, however, that could possibly be devised to lead his subjects back to paganism; and he was more especially urgent with the soldiery, whom he sometimes addressed individually and sometimes through the medium of their officers. To habituate them in all things to the worship of the gods, he restored the ancient form of the standard of the Roman armies,[3] which, as we have already stated, Constantine had, at the command of God, converted into the sign of the cross. Julian also[4] caused to be painted, in juxtaposition with his own figure, on the public pictures, a representation either of Jupiter coming out of heaven and presenting to him the symbols of imperial power, a crown or a purple robe, or else of Mars, or of Mercury, with their eyes intently fixed upon him, as if to express their admiration of his eloquence and military skill. He placed the pictures of the gods in juxtaposition with his own, in order that the people might secretly be led to worship them under the pretext of rendering due honor to him; he abused ancient usages, and endeavored to conceal his purpose from his subjects. He considered that if they would yield obedience on this point, they would be the more ready to obey him on every other occasion; but that if they ventured to refuse obedience, he would have reason to punish them, as infringers of the Roman customs and offenders against the emperor and the state. There were but very few (and the law had its course against them) who, seeing through his designs, refused to render the customary homage

to his pictures; but the multitude, through ignorance or simplicity, conformed as usual to the ancient regulation, and thoughtlessly paid homage to his image. The emperor derived but little advantage from this artifice; yet he did not cease from his efforts to effect a change in religion.

The next machination to which he had recourse was less subtle and more violent than the former one; and the fortitude of many soldiers attached to the court was thereby tested. When the stated day came round for giving money to the troops,[5] which day generally fell upon the anniversary of some festival among the Romans, such as that of the birth of the emperor, or the foundation of some royal city, Julian reflected that soldiers are naturally thoughtless and simple, and disposed to be covetous of money, and therefore concluded that it would be a favorable opportunity to seduce them to the worship of the gods. Accordingly, as each soldier approached to receive the money, he was commanded to offer sacrifice, fire and incense having been previously placed for this purpose near the emperor, according to an ancient Roman custom. Some of the soldiers had the courage to refuse to offer sacrifice and receive the gold; others were so habituated to the observance of the law and custom that they conformed to it, without imagining that they were committing sin. Others, again, deluded by the luster of the gold, or compelled by fear and consideration on account of the test which was immediately in sight, complied with the pagan rite, and suffered themselves to fall into the temptation from which they ought to have fled.

It is related that, as some of them who had ignorantly fallen into this sin were seated at table, and drinking to each other, one among them happened to mention the name of Christ over the cups. Another of the guests immediately exclaimed: "It is extraordinary that you should call upon Christ, when, but a short time ago, you denied him for the sake of the emperor's gift, by throwing incense into the fire." On hearing this observation, they all became suddenly conscious of the sin they had committed; they rose from table and rushed into the public streets, where they screamed and wept and called upon all men to witness that they were and would remain Christians, and that they had offered incense unawares, and with the hand alone, and not with the assent of the judgment. They then presented themselves before the emperor, threw back his gold, and courageously asked him to take back his own gift, and besought him to put them to death, protesting that they would never renounce their sentiments,

---

[1] Odyss. x. 74.
[2] Soc. iii. 13; Ruf. H. E. i. 32; Greg. Naz. cont. Jul. i. 66, 80, 84; Theodoret, H. E. iii. 16, 17
[3] Greg. Naz. Or. cont. Jul. i. 66.   [4] Id. 80, 81.

[5] Greg. Naz. Or. cont. Jul. i. 82–84; Theodoret, H. E. iii. 17; the variations.

whatever torments might, in consequence of the sin committed by their hand, be inflicted on the other parts of their body for the sake of Christ.

Whatever displeasure the emperor might have felt against them, he refrained from slaying them, lest they should enjoy the honor of martyrdom; he therefore merely deprived them of their military commission and dismissed them from the palace.

CHAP. XVIII. — HE PROHIBITED THE CHRISTIANS FROM THE MARKETS AND FROM THE JUDICIAL SEATS AND FROM SHARING IN GREEK EDUCATION. RESISTANCE OF BASIL THE GREAT, GREGORY THE THEOLOGIAN, AND APOLINARIUS TO THIS DECREE. THEY RAPIDLY TRANSLATE THE SCRIPTURE INTO GREEK MODES OF EXPRESSION. APOLINARIUS AND GREGORY NAZIANZEN DO THIS MORE THAN BASIL, THE ONE IN A RHETORICAL VEIN, THE OTHER IN EPIC STYLE AND IN IMITATION OF EVERY POET.

JULIAN entertained the same sentiments as those above described towards all Christians, as he manifested whenever an opportunity was offered. Those who refused to sacrifice to the gods, although perfectly blameless in other respects, were deprived of the rights of citizenship,[1] and of the privilege of participating in assemblies, and in the forum; and he would not allow them to be judges or magistrates, or to share in offices.

He forbade the children of Christians from frequenting the public schools, and from being instructed in the writings of the Greek poets and authors.[2] He entertained great resentment against Apolinarius the Syrian, a man of manifold knowledge and philological attainments, against Basil and Gregory, natives of Cappadocia, the most celebrated orators of the time, and against other learned and eloquent men, of whom some were attached to the Nicene doctrines, and others to the dogmas of Arius. His sole motive for excluding the children of Christian parents from instruction in the learning of the Greeks, was because he considered such studies conducive to the acquisition of argumentative and persuasive power. Apolinarius, therefore, employed his great learning and ingenuity in the production of a heroic epic on the antiquities of the Hebrews to the reign of Saul, as a substitute for the poem of Homer. He divided this work into twenty-four parts, to each of which he appended the name of one of the letters of the Greek alphabet, according to their number and order. He also wrote comedies in imitation of Menander, tragedies resem-

bling those of Euripides, and odes on the model of Pindar. In short, taking themes of the entire circle of knowledge from the Scriptures, he produced within a very brief space of time, a set of works which in manner, expression, character, and arrangement are well approved as similar to the Greek literatures and which were equal in number and in force. Were it not for the extreme partiality with which the productions of antiquity are regarded, I doubt not but that the writings of Apolinarius would be held in as much estimation as those of the ancients.[3]

The comprehensiveness of his intellect is more especially to be admired; for he excelled in every branch of literature, whereas ancient writers were proficient only in one. He wrote a very remarkable work entitled "The Truth"[4] against the emperor and the pagan philosophers, in which he clearly proved, without any appeal to the authority of Scripture, that they were far from having attained right opinions of God. The emperor, for the purpose of casting ridicule on works of this nature, wrote to the bishops in the following words: "I have read, I have understood, and I have condemned."[5] To this they sent the following reply, "You have read, but you have not understood; for, had you understood, you would not have condemned."

Some have attributed this letter to Basil, the president of the church in Cappadocia, and perhaps not without reason; but whether dictated by him or by another, it fully displays the magnanimity and learning of the writer.

CHAP. XIX. — WORK WRITTEN BY JULIAN ENTITLED "AVERSION TO BEARDS." DAPHNE IN ANTIOCH, A FULL DESCRIPTION OF IT. TRANSLATION OF THE REMAINS OF BABYLAS, THE HOLY MARTYR.

JULIAN,[6] having determined upon undertaking a war against Persia, repaired to Antioch in Syria. The people loudly complained, that, although provisions were very abundant the price affixed to them was very high. Accordingly, the emperor, from liberality, as I believe, towards the people, reduced the price of provisions to so low a scale that the vendors fled the city.

A scarcity in consequence ensued, for which the people blamed the emperor; and their resentment found vent in ridiculing the length of his beard, and the bulls which he had had stamped upon his coins; and they satirically

---

[1] *Juliani Op. Ep.* xlii.; Soc. iii. 13.
[2] Greg. Naz. *Or. cont. Jul.* i. 101-124; Ruf. *H. E.* i. 32: Theodoret, *H. E.* iii. 8.

[3] The question about the nature of Christian culture has Socrates on the side of the humanities, iii. 16, where there is an extended argument in defense of a return to the study of Greek literature. Sozomen is somewhat on the fence, but inclining towards the opposite view.
[4] Apolinarius (Apollinaris), bishop of Hierapolis, also wrote a treatise with the same name. See Euseb. *H. E.* iv. 27, and Phot. *Bibl.*, Cod. 145.
[5] *Ep.* 77, formerly falsely ascribed to Julian.
[6] Soc. iii. 17, 18; Ruf. *H. E.* i. 35; Philost. vii. 8; Theodoret, iii. 10; Am. Marcel. xxii. 14. 1-3.

remarked, that he upset the world in the same way that his priests, when offering sacrifice, threw down the victims.

At first his displeasure was excited, and he threatened to punish them and prepared to depart for Tarsus. Afterwards, however, he suppressed his feelings of indignation, and repaid their ridicule by words alone; he composed a very elegant work under the title of "Aversion to Beards," which he sent to them. He treated the Christians of the city precisely in the same manner as at other places, and endeavored, as far as possible, to promote the extension of paganism.

I shall here recount some of the details connected with the tomb of Babylas, the martyr, and certain occurrences which took place about this period in the temple of Apollo at Daphne.

Daphne is a suburb of Antioch, and is planted with cypresses and other trees, beneath which all kinds of flowers flourish in their season. The branches of these trees are so thick and interlaced that they may be said to form a roof rather than merely to afford shade, and the rays of the sun can never pierce through them to the soil beneath. It is made delicious and exceedingly lovely by the richness and beauty of the waters, the temperateness of the air, and the breath of friendly winds. The Greeks invent the myth that Daphne, the daughter of the river Ladon, was here changed into a tree which bears her name, while she was fleeing from Arcadia, to evade the love of Apollo. The passion of Apollo was not diminished, they say, by this transformation; he made a crown of the leaves of his beloved and embraced the tree. He afterwards often fixed his residence on this spot, as being dearer to him than any other place.

Men of grave temperament, however, considered it disgraceful to approach this suburb; for the position and nature of the place seemed to excite voluptuous feelings; and the substance of the fable itself being erotic, afforded a measurable impulse and redoubled the passions among corrupt youths. They, who furnished this myth as an excuse, were greatly inflamed and gave way without constraint to profligate deeds, incapable of being continent themselves, or of enduring the presence of those who were continent. Any one who dwelt at Daphne without a mistress was regarded as callous and ungracious, and was shunned as an abominable and abhorrent thing. The pagans likewise manifested great reverence for this place on account of a very beautiful statue of the Daphnic Apollo which stood here, as also a magnificent and costly temple, supposed to have been built by Seleucus, the father of Antiochus, who gave his name to the city of Antioch. Those who attach credit to fables of this kind believe that a stream flows from the fountain Castalia which confers the power of predicting the future, and which is similar in its name and powers to the fountain of Delphi. It is related that Adrian here received intimation of his future greatness, when he was but a private individual; and that he dipped a leaf of the laurel into the water and found written thereon an account of his destiny. When he became emperor, it is said, he commanded the fountain to be closed, in order that no one might be enabled to pry into the knowledge of the future. But I leave this subject to those who are more accurately acquainted with mythology than I am.

When Gallus, the brother of Julian, had been declared Cæsar by Constantius, and had fixed his residence at Antioch, his zeal for the Christian religion and his veneration for the memory of the martyrs determined him to purge the place of the pagan superstition and the outrages of profligates. He considered that the readiest method of effecting this object would be to erect a house of prayer in the temple and to transfer thither the tomb of Babylas, the martyr, who had, with great reputation to himself, presided over the church of Antioch, and suffered martyrdom. It is said that from the time of this translation, the demon ceased to utter oracles. This silence was at first attributed to the neglect into which his service was allowed to fall and to the omission of the former cult; but results proved that it was occasioned solely by the presence of the holy martyr. The silence continued unbroken even when Julian was the sole ruler of the Roman Empire, although libations, incense, and victims were offered in abundance to the demon; for when eventually the oracle itself spoke and indicated the cause of its previous silence, the emperor himself entered the temple for the purpose of consulting the oracle, and offering up gifts and sacrifices with entreaties to grant a reply. The demon did not openly admit that the hindrance was occasioned by the tomb of Babylas, the martyr, but he stated that the place was filled with dead bodies, and that this prevented the oracle from speaking.

Although many interments had taken place at Daphne, the emperor perceived that it was the presence of Babylas, the martyr, alone which had silenced the oracle, and he commanded his tomb to be removed. The Christians, therefore, assembled together and conveyed the coffin to the city, about forty stadia distant, and deposited it in the place where it is still preserved, and to which the name of the martyr has been given. It is said that men and women, young men and maidens, old men and children drew the casket, and encouraged one another by singing psalms as they went along the road, apparently for the purpose of lightening their labor, but in truth because they were transported by zeal and spirit for their kindred religious belief, which the emperor had opposed. The best singers sang first, and the multitude replied in chorus, and the following was the burden of their song : " Confounded are all they who worship graven images, who boast themselves in idols."

CHAP. XX. — IN CONSEQUENCE OF THE TRANS-
LATION, MANY OF THE CHRISTIANS ARE ILL-
TREATED. THEODORE THE CONFESSOR. TEMPLE
OF APOLLO AT DAPHNE DESTROYED BY FIRE
FALLING FROM HEAVEN.

THE transaction above related[1] excited the indignation of the emperor as much as if an insult had been offered him, and he determined upon punishing the Christians ; but Sallust, a prætorian prefect, although a pagan, tried to dissuade him from this measure. The emperor, however, could not be appeased, and Sallust was compelled to execute his mandate, and arrest and imprison many Christians. One of the first whom he arrested was a young man named Theodore, who was immediately stretched upon the rack ; but although his flesh was lacerated by the application of the nails, he addressed no supplication to Sallust, nor did he implore a diminution of his torments ; on the contrary, he seemed as insensible to pain as if he had been merely a spectator of the sufferings of another, and bravely received the wounds ; and he sang the same psalm which he had joined in singing the day before, to show that he did not repent of the act for which he had been condemned. The prefect, struck with admiration at the fortitude of the young man, went to the emperor and told him that, unless he would desist speedily from the measure he had undertaken, he and his party would be exposed to ridicule while the Christians would acquire more glory. This representation produced its effect, and the Christians who had been arrested were set at liberty. It is said[2] that Theodore was afterwards asked whether he had been sensible of any pain while on the rack ; and that he replied that he had not been entirely free from suffering, but had his pains assuaged by the attentions of a young man who had stood by him, and who had wiped off the perspiration with the finest linen cloth, and supplied him with coolest water by which he eased the inflammation and refreshed his labors. I am convinced that no man, whatever mag-

nanimity he may possess, is capable, without the special assistance of Divine Power, of manifesting such entire indifference about the body.

The body of the martyr Babylas was, for the reasons aforesaid, removed to Daphne, and was subsequently conveyed elsewhere. Soon after it had been taken away, fire suddenly fell upon the temple of the Daphnic Apollo, the roof and the very statue of the god were burned, and the naked walls, with the columns on which the portico and the back part of the edifice had rested, alone escaped the conflagration.[3] The Christians believed that the prayers of the martyr had drawn down fire from heaven upon the demon ; but the pagans reported the Christians as having set fire to the place. This suspicion gained ground ; and the priest of Apollo was brought before the tribunal of justice to render up the names of those who had dared the incendiary act ; but though bound and subjected to the most cruel tortures, he did not name any one.

Hence the Christians were more fully convinced than before, that it was not by the deed of man, but by the wrath of God, that fire was poured down from heaven upon the temple. Such were the occurrences which then took place. The emperor, as I conjecture, on hearing that the calamity at Daphne had been occasioned by the martyr Babylas, and on being further informed that the honored remains of the martyrs were preserved in several houses of prayer near the temple of the Apollo Didymus, which is situated close to the city of Miletus, wrote to the governor of Caria, commanding him to destroy with fire all such edifices as were furnished with a roof and an altar, and to throw down from their very foundations the houses of prayer which were incomplete in these respects.

CHAP. XXI. — OF THE STATUE OF CHRIST IN
PANEAS WHICH JULIAN OVERTHREW AND MADE
VALUELESS ; HE ERECTED HIS OWN STATUE ;
THIS WAS OVERTHROWN BY A THUNDER-BOLT
AND DESTROYED. FOUNTAIN OF EMMAUS IN
WHICH CHRIST WASHED HIS FEET. CONCERN-
ING THE TREE PERSIS, WHICH WORSHIPED
CHRIST IN EGYPT, AND THE WONDERS WROUGHT
THROUGH IT.

AMONG so many remarkable events which occurred during the reign of Julian, I must not omit to mention one which affords a sign of the power of Christ, and proof of the Divine wrath against the emperor.[4]

Having heard that at Cæsarea Philippi, otherwise called Paneas, a city of Phœnicia, there was a celebrated statue of Christ which had been erected by a woman whom the Lord had

1 Ruf. *H. E.* i. 36; Soc. iii. 19; Theodoret, *H. E.* iii. 11; Am. Marcel. xxii. 13.
2 Rufinus saw Theodore at Antioch, and asked him this question, Ruf. i. 36; and Soc. shows the source from which he borrowed the story by affirming that Rufinus, author of an ecclesiastical history in Latin, had this interview with Theodore.
3 Am. Marcel. xxii. 13. 1-3.
4 Philost. vii. 3, who was eyewitness.

cured of a flow of blood,[1] Julian commanded it to be taken down and a statue of himself erected in its place ; but a violent fire from heaven fell upon it and broke off the parts contiguous to the breast ; the head and neck were thrown prostrate, and it was transfixed to the ground with the face downwards at the point where the fracture of the bust was ; and it has stood in that fashion from that day until now, full of the rust of the lightning. The statue of Christ was dragged around the city and mutilated by the pagans ; but the Christians recovered the fragments, and deposited the statue in the church in which it is still preserved. Eusebius relates, that at the base of this statue grew an herb which was unknown to the physicians and empirics, but was efficacious in the cure of all disorders. It does not appear a matter of astonishment to me, that, after God had vouchsafed to dwell with men, he should condescend to bestow benefits upon them.

It appears that innumerable other miracles were wrought in different cities and villages ; accounts have been accurately preserved by the inhabitants of these places only, because they learned them from ancestral tradition ; and how true this is, I will at once show. There is a city now called Nicopolis, in Palestine, which was formerly only a village, and which was mentioned by the divine book of the Gospel under the name of Emmaus.[2] The name of Nicoplis was given to this place by the Romans after the conquest of Jerusalem and the victory over the Jews. Just beyond the city where three roads meet, is the spot where Christ, after His resurrection, said farewell to Cleopas and his companion, as if he were going to another village ; and here is a healing fountain in which men and other living creatures afflicted with different diseases wash away their sufferings ; for it is said that when Christ together with His disciples came from a journey to this fountain, they bathed their feet therein, and, from that time the water became a cure for disorders.

At Hermopolis, in the Thebais, is a tree called Persis, of which the branches, the leaves, and the least portion of the bark, are said to heal diseases, when touched by the sick ; for it is related by the Egyptians that when Joseph fled with Christ and Mary, the holy mother of God, from the wrath of Herod, they went to Hermopolis ; when entering at the gate, this largest tree, as if not enduring the advent of Christ, inclined to the ground and worshiped Him. I relate precisely what I have heard from many sources concerning this tree. I think that this phenomenon was a sign of the presence of God in the city ; or perhaps, as seems most probable, the

tree, which had been worshiped by the inhabitants, after the pagan custom, was shaken, because the demon, who had been an object of worship, started up at sight of Him who was manifested for purification from such agencies. It was moved of its own accord ; for at the presence of Christ the idols of Egypt were shaken, even as Isaiah[3] the prophet had foretold. On the expulsion of the demon, the tree was permitted to remain as a monument of what had occurred, and was endued with the property of healing those who believed.

The inhabitants of Egypt and of Palestine testify to the truth of these events, which took place among themselves.

CHAP. XXII.— FROM AVERSION TO THE CHRISTIANS, JULIAN GRANTED PERMISSION TO THE JEWS TO REBUILD THE TEMPLE AT JERUSALEM ; IN EVERY ENDEAVOR TO PUT THEIR HANDS TO THE WORK, FIRE SPRANG UPWARD AND KILLED MANY. ABOUT THE SIGN OF THE CROSS WHICH APPEARED ON THE CLOTHING OF THOSE WHO HAD EXERTED THEMSELVES IN THIS WORK.

THOUGH the emperor[4] hated and opressed the Christians, he manifested benevolence and humanity towards the Jews. He wrote[5] to the Jewish patriarchs and leaders, as well as to the people, requesting them to pray for him, and for the prosperity of the empire. In taking this step he was not actuated, I am convinced, by any respect for their religion ; for he was aware that it is, so to speak, the mother of the Christian religion, and he knew that both religions rest upon the authority of the patriarchs and the prophets ; but he thought to grieve the Christians by favoring the Jews, who are their most inveterate enemies. But perhaps he also calculated upon persuading the Jews to embrace paganism and sacrifices ; for they were only acquainted with the mere letter of Scripture, and could not, like the Christians and a few of the wisest among the Hebrews, discern the hidden meaning.

Events proved that this was his real motive ; for he sent for some of the chiefs of the race and exhorted them to return to the observance of the laws of Moses and the customs of their fathers. On their replying that because the temple in Jerusalem was overturned, it was neither lawful nor ancestral to do this in another place than the metropolis out of which they had been cast, he gave them public money, commanded them to rebuild the temple, and to practice the cult similar to that of their ances-

---

[1] Eus. H. E. vii. 18.　　[2] Luke xxiv. 13.

[3] Ch. xix. 1.
[4] Ruf. H. E. i. 37–39; Philost. vii. 14; Soc. iii. 20; Theodoret, H. E. iii. 20; Greg. Naz. Or. cont. Jul. ii. 3, 4; and particularly Am. Marcel. xxiii. 1. 1–3.
[5] Juliani Op. Ep. xxv., ad Judæorum nationem.

tors, by sacrificing after the ancient way. The Jews entered upon the undertaking, without reflecting that, according to the prediction of the holy prophets, it could not be accomplished. They sought for the most skillful artisans, collected materials, cleared the ground, and entered so earnestly upon the task, that even the women carried heaps of earth, and brought their necklaces and other female ornaments towards defraying the expense. The emperor, the other pagans, and all the Jews, regarded every other undertaking as secondary in importance to this. Although the pagans were not well-disposed towards the Jews, yet 'they assisted them in this enterprise, because they reckoned upon its ultimate success, and hoped by this means to falsify the prophecies of Christ. Besides this motive, the Jews themselves were impelled by the consideration that the time had arrived for rebuilding their temple. When they had removed the ruins of the former building, they dug up the ground and cleared away its foundation ; it is said that on the following day when they were about to lay the first foundation, a great earthquake occurred, and by the violent agitation of the earth, stones were thrown up from the depths, by which those of the Jews who were engaged in the work were wounded, as likewise those who were merely looking on. The houses and public porticos, near the site of the temple, in which they had diverted themselves, were suddenly thrown down ; many were caught thereby, some perished immediately, others were found half dead and mutilated of hands or legs, others were injured in other parts of the body. When God caused the earthquake to cease, the workmen who survived again returned to their task, partly because such was the edict of the emperor, and partly because they were themselves interested in the undertaking. Men often, in endeavoring to gratify their own passions, seek what is injurious to them, reject what would be truly advantageous, and are deluded by the idea that nothing is really useful except what is agreeable to them. When once led astray by this error, they are no longer able to act in a manner conducive to their own interests, or to take warning by the calamities which are visited upon them.

The Jews, I believe, were just in this state ; for, instead of regarding this unexpected earthquake as a manifest indication that God was opposed to the re-erection of their temple, they proceeded to recommence the work. But all parties relate, that they had scarcely returned to the undertaking, when fire burst suddenly from the foundations of the temple, and consumed several of the workmen.

This fact is fearlessly stated, and believed by all ; the only discrepancy in the narrative is that some maintain that flame burst from the interior of the temple, as the workmen were striving to force an entrance, while others say that the fire proceeded directly from the earth. In whichever way the phenomenon might have occurred, it is equally wonderful. A more tangible and still more extraordinary prodigy ensued ; suddenly the sign of the cross appeared spontaneously on the garments of the persons engaged in the undertaking. These crosses were disposed like stars, and appeared the work of art. Many were hence led to confess that Christ is God, and that the rebuilding of the temple was not pleasing to Him ; others presented themselves in the church, were initiated, and besought Christ, with hymns and supplications, to pardon their transgression. If any one does not feel disposed to believe my narrative, let him go and be convinced by those who heard the facts I have related from the eyewitnesses of them, for they are still alive. Let him inquire, also, of the Jews and pagans who left the work in an incomplete state, or who, to speak more accurately, were able to commence it.

BOOK VI.

I HAVE narrated in the preceding book the occurrences which took place in the Church, during the reign of Julian.[1] This emperor, having determined to carry on the war with Persia, made a rapid transit across the Euphrates in the beginning of spring, and, passing by Edessa from hatred to the inhabitants, who had long professed Christianity, he went on to Carræ, where there was a temple of Jupiter, in which he offered up sacrifice and prayer. He then selected twenty thousand armed men from among his troops, and sent them towards the Tigris, in order that they might guard those regions, and also be ready to join him, in case he should require their assistance. He then wrote to Arsacius, king of Armenia, one of the Roman allies, to bespeak his aid in the war. In this letter Julian manifested the most unbounded arrogance; he boasted of the high qualities which had, he said, rendered him worthy of the empire, and acceptable to the gods for whom he cared; he reviled Constantius, his predecessor, as an effeminate and impious emperor, and threatened Arsacius in a grossly insulting way; and since he understood that he was a Christian, he intensified his insults, or eagerly and largely uttered unlawful blasphemies against Christ, for he was wont to dare this in every case. He told Arsacius that unless he acted according to his directions, the God in whom he trusted would not be able to defend him from his vengeance. When he considered that all his arrangements had been duly made, he led his army through Assyria.

He took a great many towns and fortresses, either through treachery or by battle, and thoughtlessly proceeded onwards, without reflecting that he would have to return by the same route. He pillaged every place he approached, and pulled down or burnt the granaries and storehouses. As he was journeying up the Euphrates, he arrived at Ctesiphon, a very large city, whither the Persian monarchs have now transferred their residence from Babylon. The Tigris flows near this spot. As he was prevented from reaching the city with his ships, by a part of the land which separated it from the river, he judged that either he must pursue his journey by water, or quit his ships and go to Ctesiphon by land; and he interrogated the prisoners on the subject. Having ascertained from them that there was a canal which had been blocked up in the course of time, he caused it to be cleared out, and, having thus effected a communication between the Euphrates and the Tigris, he proceeded towards the city, his ships floating along by the side of his army. But the Persians appeared on the banks of the Tigris with a formidable display of horse and many armed troops, of elephants, and of horses; and Julian became conscious that his army was besieged between two great rivers, and was in danger of perishing, either by remaining in its present position, or by retreating through the cities and villages which he had so utterly devastated that no provisions were attainable; therefore he summoned the soldiers to see horse-races, and proposed rewards to the fleetest racers. In the meantime he commanded the officers of the ships to throw over the provisions and baggage of the army, so that the soldiers, seeing themselves in danger by the want of necessaries, might turn about boldly and fight their enemies more desperately. After supper he sent for the generals and tribunes and commanded the embarkation of the troops. They sailed along the Tigris during the night and came at once to the opposite banks and disembarked; but their departure was perceived by some of the Persians, who exhorted one another to oppose them, but those still asleep the Romans readily overcame.

At daybreak, the two armies engaged in battle; and after much bloodshed on both sides, the Romans returned by the river, and encamped near Ctesiphon. The emperor, being no longer desirous of proceeding further, burnt his vessels, as he considered that they required too many soldiers to guard them; and he then commenced his retreat along the Tigris, which was to his left. The prisoners, who acted as guides to the Romans, led them to a fertile country where

¹ Philost. vii. 15; Eutrop. *Brev. hist. rom.* x. 16; Eunap. *Fr.* ii. 15-19; Am. Marcel. xxiii. and xxiv.; Ruf. i. 36; Soc. iii. 21; Greg. Naz. *Or. cont. Jul.* ii. 8-15; Zos. iii. 12-30; Orosius, vii. 30.

they found abundance of provisions. Soon after, an old man who had resolved to die for the liberty of Persia, allowed himself to be taken prisoner, and was brought before the emperor. On being questioned as to the route, and seeming to speak the truth, he persuaded them to follow him as capable of transporting the army very speedily to the Roman frontiers. He observed that for the space of three or four days' journey this road would be difficult, and that it would be necessary to carry provisions during that time, as the surrounding country was sterile. The emperor was deceived by the discourse of this wise old man, and approved the march by this route. On advancing further, after the lapse of three days, they were cast upon an uncultivated region. The old prisoner was put to torture. He confessed that he had exposed himself voluntarily to death for the sake of his country, and was therefore prepared to endure any sufferings that could be inflicted on him.

The Roman troops were now worn out by the length of the journey and the scarcity of provisions, and the Persians chose this moment to attack them.

In the heat of the conflict which ensued, a violent wind arose; and the sky and the sun were totally concealed by the clouds, while the air was at the same time mixed with dust. During the darkness which was thus produced, a horseman, riding at full gallop, directed his lance against the emperor, and wounded him mortally. After throwing Julian from his horse, the unknown assailant secretly went away. Some conjectured that he was a Persian; others, that he was a Saracen. There are those who insist that he who struck the blow was a Roman soldier, who was indignant at the imprudence and temerity which the emperor had manifested in exposing his army to such peril. Libanius,[1] the sophist, a native of Syria, the most intimate friend of Julian, expressed himself in the following terms concerning the person who had committed the deed: " You desire to know by whom the emperor was slain. I know not his name. We have a proof, however, that the murderer was not one of the enemies; for no one came forward to claim the reward, although the king of Persia caused proclamation to be made, by a herald, of the honors to be awarded to him who had performed the deed. We are surely beholden to the enemy for not arrogating to themselves the glory of the action, but for leaving it to us to seek the slayer among ourselves.

" Those who sought his death were those who lived in habitual transgression of the laws, and who had formerly conspired against him, and who therefore perpetrated the deed as soon as they could find an opportunity. They were impelled by the desire of obtaining a greater degree of freedom from all control than they could enjoy under his government; and they were, perhaps, mainly stimulated by their indignation at the attachment of the emperor to the service of the gods, to which they were averse."

CHAP. II. — HE PERISHED UNDER DIVINE WRATH. VISIONS OF THE EMPEROR'S DEATH SEEN BY VARIOUS INDIVIDUALS. REPLY OF THE CARPENTER'S SON; JULIAN TOSSED HIS BLOOD ALOFT TO CHRIST. CALAMITIES WHICH JULIAN ENTAILED UPON THE ROMANS.

IN the document above quoted, Libanius clearly states that the emperor fell by the hand of a Christian; and this, probably, was the truth.[2] It is not unlikely that some of the soldiers who then served in the Roman army might have conceived the idea, since Greeks and all men until this day have praised tyrannicides for exposing themselves to death in the cause of liberty, and spiritedly standing by their country, their families, and their friends. Still less is he deserving of blame, who, for the sake of God and of religion, performed so bold a deed. Beyond this I know nothing accurately concerning the men who committed this murder besides what I have narrated. All men, however, concur in receiving the account which has been handed down to us, and which evidences his death to have been the result of Divine wrath. A proof of this is the Divine vision which one of his friends had, which I will now proceed to describe. He had, it is related, traveled into Persia, with the intention of joining the emperor. While on the road, he found himself so far from any habitation that he was obliged, on one night, to sleep in a church. He saw, during that night, either in a dream or a vision, all the apostles and prophets assembled together, and complaining of the injuries which the emperor had inflicted on the Church, and consulting concerning the best measures to be adopted. After much deliberation and embarrassment two individuals arose in the midst of the assembly, desired the others to be of good cheer, and left the company hastily, as if to deprive Julian of the imperial power. He who was the spectator of this marvel did not attempt to pursue his journey, but awaited, in horrible suspense, the conclusion of this revelation. He laid himself down to sleep again, in the same place, and again he saw the same assembly; the two individuals who had appeared to depart the preceding night to effect their purpose against

[1] Libanii Op. vol. ii. p. 614, ed. Reisk. Cf. Soc. iii. 22, 23; a summary and refutation of Libanius.   [2] Independent chapter. Cf. Ephr. Syr. Carmina adv. Julianum, ed. Overbeck.

Julian, suddenly returned and announced his death to the others.

On the same day a vision was sent to Didymus, an ecclesiastical philosopher, who dwelt at Alexandria; and who, being deeply grieved at the errors of Julian and his persecution of the churches, fasted and offered up supplications to God continually on this account. From the effects of anxiety and want of food during the previous night, he fell asleep while sitting in his chair. Then being, as it were, in an ecstasy, he beheld white horses traversing the air, and heard a voice saying to those who were riding thereon, " Go and tell Didymus that Julian has been slain just at this hour; let him communicate this intelligence to Athanasius, the bishop, and let him arise and eat." I have been credibly informed that the friend of Julian and the philosopher beheld those things. Results proved that neither of them were far from having witnessed the truth. But if these instances do not suffice to prove that the death of Julian was the effect of Divine wrath on account of his persecution of the Church, let the prediction of one of the ecclesiastics be called to mind.[1] When Julian was preparing to enter upon the war against the Persians, he threatened that on the termination of the war he would treat the Christians with severity, and boasted that the Son of the Carpenter would be unable to aid them; the ecclesiastic above mentioned thereupon rejoined, that the Son of the Carpenter was then preparing him a wooden coffin in view of his death.

Julian himself was well aware whence the mortal stroke proceeded, and what was the cause of its infliction; for, it is said, when he was wounded, he took some of the blood that flowed from the wound, and threw it up into the air, as if he had seen Jesus Christ appearing, and intended to throw it at him, in order to reproach him with his slaughter. Others say that he was angry with the sun because it had favored the Persians, and had not rescued him, although, according to the doctrine of the astronomers, it had presided at his birth; and that it was to express his indignation against this luminary that he took blood in his hand and flung it upwards in the air.[2]

I know not whether, on the approach of death, as is wont to be the case when the soul is in the act of being separated from the body and when it is enabled to behold diviner spectacles than are allotted to men, and so Julian might have beheld Christ. Few allusions have been made to this subject, and yet I dare not reject this hypothesis as absolutely false; for God often suffers still more improbable and astonishing

events to take place in order to prove that the religion named after Christ is not sustained by human energy. It is, however, very obvious that, throughout the reign of this emperor, God gave manifest tokens of His displeasure, and permitted many calamities to befall several of the provinces of the Roman Empire. He visited the earth with such fearful earthquakes, that the buildings were shaken, and no more safety could be found within the houses than in the open air. From what I have heard, I conjecture that it was during the reign of this emperor, or, at least, when he occupied the second place in the government, that a great calamity occurred near Alexandria in Egypt,[3] when the sea receded and again passed beyond its boundaries from the reflux waves, and deluged a great deal of the land, so that on the retreat of the waters, the sea-skiffs were found lodged on the roofs of the houses. The anniversary of this inundation, which they call the birthday of an earthquake, is still commemorated at Alexandria by a yearly festival; a general illumination is made throughout the city; they offer thankful prayers to God, and celebrate the day very brilliantly and piously. An excessive drought also occurred during this reign; the plants perished and the air was corrupted; and for want of proper sustenance, men were obliged to have recourse to the food usually eaten by other animals.

The famine introduced peculiar diseases, by which many lives were lost. Such was the state of the empire during the administration of Julian.

CHAP. III.—THE REIGN OF JOVIAN; HE INTRODUCED MANY LAWS WHICH HE CARRIED OUT IN HIS GOVERNMENT.

AFTER the decease of Julian, the government of the empire was, by the unanimous consent of the troops, tendered to Jovian.[4] When the army was about to proclaim him emperor, he announced himself to be a Christian and refused the sovereignty, nor would he receive the symbols of empire; but when the soldiers discovered the cause of his refusal, they loudly proclaimed that they were themselves Christians.

The dangerous and disturbed condition in which affairs had been left by Julian's strategy, and the sufferings of the army from famine in an enemy's country, compelled Jovian to conclude a peace with the Persians, and to cede to them some territories which had been formerly tributary to the Romans. Having learned from experience that the impiety of his predecessor

---

[1] Theodoret, H. E. iii. 23 (a pedagogue).
[2] Cf. version by Philost. vii. 15.

[3] A mistake; it occurred under Valentian and Valens. Am. Marcel. xxvi. 10. 15-19. Idatius: Descr. Consulum, under A.D. 385 (July 21).
[4] Soc. iii. 22; Ruf. H. E. ii. 1; Philost. viii. 1, 5. Cf. Theodoret, iv. 1, 2, 4; Eutrop. Brev. hist. rom. x. 17, 18; Zos. iii. 30-35; Am. Marcel. xxv. 5. 4-10.

had excited the wrath of God, and given rise to public calamities, he wrote without delay to the governors of the provinces, directing that the people should assemble together without fear in the churches, that they should serve God with reverence, and that they should receive the Christian faith as the only true religion. He restored to the churches and the clergy, to the widows and the virgins, the same immunities and every former dotation for the advantage and honor of religion, which had been granted by Constantine and his sons, and afterwards withdrawn by Julian. He commanded Secundus,[1] who was then a prætorian prefect, to constitute it a capital crime to marry any of the holy virgins, or even to regard them with unchaste desires and to carry them off.

He enacted this law[2] on account of the wickedness which had prevailed during the reign of Julian ; for many had taken wives from among the holy virgins, and, either by force or guile, had completely corrupted them ; and thence had proceeded that indulgence of disgraceful lusts with impunity, which always occur when religion is abused.

CHAP. IV. — TROUBLES AGAIN ARISE IN THE CHURCHES ; SYNOD OF ANTIOCH, IN WHICH THE NICENE FAITH IS CONFIRMED ; THE POINTS WHICH THIS IMPORTANT SYNOD WROTE ABOUT TO JOVIAN.

THE presidents of the churches now resumed the agitation of doctrinal questions and discussions.[3] They had remained quiet during the reign of Julian when Christianity itself was endangered, and had unanimously offered up their supplications for the mercy of God. It is thus that men, when attacked by foreign enemies, remain in accord among themselves ; but, when external troubles are removed, then internal dissensions creep in ; this, however, is not a proper place for the citation of the numerous examples in governments and nations which history affords of this fact.

At this period Basil, bishop of Ancyra, Silvanus, bishop of Tarsus, Sophronius, bishop of Pompeiopolis, and others of their party who regarded the heresy of the Anomians, so-called, with the utmost aversion, and received the term " similar as to substance," instead of the term " consubstantial," wrote a treatise to the emperor ; and after expressing their thankfulness to God for his accession to the empire, besought him to confirm the decrees issued at Ariminum and Se-

leucia, and to annul what had been established merely by the zeal and power of certain individuals.

They also entreated that, if division, which existed on account of the Synods, should still prevail in the churches, the bishops from every region might be convened alone in some place indicated by the emperor, and not be permitted to assemble elsewhere and issue decrees at variance with each other, as had been done during the reign of Constantius. They added that they had not gone to visit him at his camp, because they were fearful of being burdensome to him ; but that if he desired to see them, they would gladly repair to him, and defray all the expenses attendant on the journey themselves. Such was the document written to the Emperor Jovian.

At this juncture a council was convened at Antioch in Syria ; the form of belief established by the council of Nicæa was confirmed ; and it was decided that the Son is incontrovertibly of the same substance as the Father. Meletius, who then governed the church of Antioch ; Eusebius, bishop of Samosata ; Pelagius, bishop of Laodicea in Syria ; Acacius, bishop of Cæsarea in Palestine ; Irenius, bishop of Gaza ; and Athanasius, bishop of Ancyra, took part in this council.

On the termination of the council they acquainted the emperor with the transactions that had taken place, by dispatching the following letter :[4] —

" To the most religious and God-beloved Augustus, our Sovereign Jovian, the Conqueror, from the bishops assembled from divers regions, at Antioch.

" We know, O emperor, well-beloved of God, that your piety is fully intent upon maintaining peace and concord in the Church ; neither are we ignorant that you have well received the impress of the chief point of such unity, viz., the true and orthodox faith.

" Lest, therefore, we should be reckoned among those who assail these doctrines of truth, we attest to your piety that we receive and maintain the form of belief which was anciently set forth by the holy council of Nicæa. Now, although the term ' consubstantial ' appears strange to some persons, yet it was safely interpreted by the Fathers, and signifies that the Son was begotten of the substance of the Father. This term does not convey the idea of unbroken generation ; neither does it coincide with the use which the Greeks make of the word ' substance,' but it is calculated to withstand the impious and rash allegation of Arius, that the Son proceeded from what had had no previous existence. The Anomians who have just sprung

---

[1] This is Sallustius, the prefectus prætorio of the Oriens, who bore the name Secundus.
[2] This constitution of Jovian is extant in *Cod. Theod.* ix. 25 ; *de raptu, vel matrimonio sanctimonialium virginum vel viduarum*, 2.
[3] Soc. iii. 24, 25 ; Philost. viii. 5 ; Theodoret, *H. E.* iv. 2, 4.

[4] From Sabinus, according to Soc. iv. 25, who also gives the text.

up have the shameless boldness to maintain this word to the grief of the concord of the Church. We subjoin to this letter a copy of the formulary of faith adopted by the bishops assembled at Nicæa, which we also cherish."

Such were the decisions formed by the priests convened at Antioch; and they appended to their letter a copy of the Nicene formulary of faith.

CHAP. V. — ATHANASIUS THE GREAT IS VERY HIGHLY ESTEEMED BY THE EMPEROR, AND RULES OVER THE CHURCHES OF EGYPT. VISION OF ANTONY THE GREAT.

AT this period,[1] Athanasius, who governed the see of Alexandria, and some of his friends, deemed it requisite, as the emperor was a Christian, to repair to his court.[2] Accordingly Athanasius went to Antioch, and laid such matters before the emperor as he deemed expedient. Others, however, say that the emperor sent for him in order to consult him concerning the affairs relative to religion and the right tenet. When the business of the Church had as far as possible been transacted, Athanasius began to think of returning.

Euzoius, bishop of the Arian heresy in Antioch, endeavored to install Probatius, a eunuch who held the same sentiments as himself, in Alexandria. The whole party of Euzoius conspired with him to effect this design; and Lucius, a citizen of Alexandria, who had been ordained presbyter by George, endeavored to prejudice the emperor against Athanasius, by representing[3] that he had been accused of divers crimes and had been condemned to perpetual banishment by preceding emperors, as the author of the dissensions and troubles of the Church concerning the Divine Being. Lucius likewise besought Jovian to appoint another bishop over the church of Alexandria. The emperor, since he knew the plots which had happened against Athanasius, attached no credit to the calumny, and with threatening, commanded Lucius to retire quietly; he also ordered Probatius and the other eunuchs belonging to his palace, whom he regarded as the originators of these troubles, to act more advisedly. From that period Jovian manifested the greatest friendship towards Athanasius, and sent him back to Egypt, with directions to govern the churches and people of that country as he might think fit. It is also said that he passed commendations on the virtue of the bishop, on his life, his intellectual endowments, and his eloquence.

Thus, after having been exposed to opposition for a long while, as has been narrated in the former books, was the Nicene faith fully reestablished under the present government; but further embarrassment awaited it within a very short period. For, as it appeared afterwards, the whole of the prediction of Antony the Monk was not fulfilled by the occurrences which befell the Church during the reign of Constantius; part thereof was not accomplished until the reign of Valens. It is said that before the Arians got control of the churches during the reign of Constantius, Antony had a dream in which he saw mules kicking the altar with their hoofs and overturning the holy table. On awakening, he immediately predicted that the Church would be troubled by the introduction of spurious and mixed doctrines, and by the rebellion of the heterodox. The truth of this prediction was evidenced by the events which occurred before and after the period now under review.

CHAP. VI. — DEATH OF JOVIAN; THE LIFE OF VALENTINIAN, AND HIS CONFIDENCE IN GOD; HOW HE WAS ADVANCED TO THE THRONE AND SELECTED HIS BROTHER VALENS TO REIGN WITH HIM; THE DIFFERENCES OF BOTH.

AFTER Jovian had reigned about eight months, he died suddenly at Dadastana, a town of Bithynia, while on his road to Constantinople.[4] Some say that his death was occasioned by eating too plentiful a supper; others attribute it to the dampness of the chamber in which he slept; for it had been recently plastered with unslaked lime, and quantities of coals had been burnt in it during the winter for a preventive; the walls had become damp and were exceedingly moist.

On the arrival of the troops at Nicæa in Bithynia, they proclaimed Valentinian emperor. He was a good man and capable of holding the reins of the empire. He had not long returned from banishment; for it is said that Julian, immediately on his accession to the empire, erased the name of Valentinian from the Jovian legions, as they were called, and condemned him to perpetual banishment, under the pretext that he had failed in his duty of leading out the soldiers under his command against the enemy. The true reason of his condemnation, however, was the following: When Julian was in Gaul, he went one day to a temple to offer incense. Valentinian[5] accompanied him, according to an ancient Roman law, which still prevails, and which enacted that the leader of the Jovians and

---

[1] A largely independent chapter. Cf. Soc. iii. 24; Philost. viii. 6.
[2] This may have a connection with Theodoret, iv. 2, 3; Athanas. *Ep. ad Jovianum imp.*, where several petitions and interlocutions of the Arians with Jovian against Athanasius are given.
[3] The accusations made by the Arians, Lucius and Bernicianus. See preceding reference to *Ep. ad Jovianum*, 4.

[4] Philost. viii. 8; Soc. iii. 26; iv. 1; Ruf. ii. 1, 2. Cf. Theodoret, *H. E.* iv. 5, 6; Eudox. *Brev. hist. rom.* x. 18; Zos. iii. 35, 36; Am. Marcel. xxv. 10, 12-17; Jovian, xxvi. 1-4, accession of Valentinian and choice of Valens.
[5] Philost. vii. 7; Theodoret, *H. E.* iii. 16.

the Herculeans (that is to say, the legions of soldiers who have received this appellation in honor of Jupiter and of Hercules) should always attend the emperor as his body-guard. When they were about to enter the temple, the priest, in accordance with the pagan custom, sprinkled water upon them with the branch of a tree. A drop fell upon the robe of Valentinian; he scarcely could restrain himself, for he was a Christian, and he rebuked his asperser; it is even said that he cut off, in view of the emperor, the portion of the garment on which the water had fallen, and flung it from him. From that moment Julian entertained inimical feelings against him, and soon after banished him to Melitine in Armenia, under the plea of misconduct in military affairs; for he would not have religion regarded as the cause of the decree, lest Valentinian should be accounted a martyr or a confessor. Julian treated other Christians, as we have already stated, in the same manner; for, as was said before, he perceived that to subject them to hazards only added to their reputation, and tended to the consolidation of their religion. As soon as Jovian succeeded to the throne, Valentinian was recalled from banishment to Nicæa; but the death of the emperor in the meantime took place, and Valentinian, by the unanimous consent of the troops and those who held the chief positions in the government, was appointed his successor. When he was invested with the symbols of imperial power, the soldiers cried out that it was necessary to elect some one to share the burden of government. To this proposition, Valentinian made the following reply: "It depended on you alone, O soldiers, to proclaim me emperor; but now that you have elected me, it depends not upon you, but upon me, to perform what you demand. Remain quiet, as subjects ought to do, and leave me to act as an emperor in attending to the public affairs."

Not long after this refusal to comply with the demand of the soldiery, he repaired to Constantinople, and proclaimed his brother emperor. He gave him the East as his share of the empire, and reserved to himself the regions along the Western Ocean, from Illyria to the furthest coasts of Libya. Both the brothers were Christians, but they differed in opinion and disposition. For Valens, when he was baptized, employed Eudoxius as his initiator, and was zealously attached to the doctrines of Arius, and would readily have compelled all mankind by force to yield to them. Valentinian, on the other hand, maintained the faith of the council of Nicæa, and favored those who upheld the same sentiments, without molesting those who entertained other opinions.

CHAP. VII. — TROUBLES AGAIN ARISE IN THE CHURCHES, AND THE SYNOD OF LAMPSACUS IS HELD. THE ARIANS WHO SUPPORTED EUDOXIUS PREVAIL AND EJECT THE ORTHODOX FROM THE CHURCHES. AMONG THE EJECTED IS MELETIUS OF ANTIOCH.

WHEN Valentinian was journeying from Constantinople to Rome,[1] he had to pass through Thrace; and the bishops of Hellespontus and of Bithynia, with others, who maintained that the Son is consubstantial with the Father, dispatched Hypatian, bishop of Heraclea in Perinthus, to meet him, and to request permission to assemble themselves together for deliberation on questions of doctrine.

When Hypatian had delivered the message with which he was intrusted, Valentinian made the following reply: "I am but one of the laity, and have therefore no right to interfere in these transactions; let the priests, to whom such matters appertain, assemble where they please." On receiving this answer through Hypatian, their deputy, the bishops assembled at Lampsacus.

After having conferred together for the space of two months, they annulled all that had been decreed at Constantinople, through the machinations of the partisans of Eudoxius and Acacius. They likewise declared null and void the formulary of faith which had been circulated under the false assertion that it was the compilation of the Western bishops, and to which the signatures of many bishops had been obtained, by the promise that the dogma of dissimilarity as to substance should be condemned, — a promise which had never been performed.

They decreed that the doctrine of the Son being in substance like unto the Father, should have the ascendancy; for they said that it was necessary to resort to the use of the term "like" as indicative of the hypostases of the Godhead. They agreed that the form of belief which had been confessed at Seleucia, and set forth at the dedication of the church of Antioch, should be maintained by all the churches.

They directed that all the bishops who had been deposed by those who hold that the Son is dissimilar from the Father, should forthwith be reinstated in their sees, as having been unjustly ejected from their churches. They declared that if any wished to bring accusations against them, they would be permitted to do so, but under the penalty of incurring the same punishment as that due to the alleged crime, should the accusation prove to be false. The orthodox bishops of the province and of the neighboring countries were to preside as judges, and to assemble in the church, with the witnesses who were to make the depositions.

After making these decisions, the bishops

[1] Soc. iv. 2, 4. Soz. is much fuller; probably from Sabinus.

summoned the partisans of Eudoxius, and exhorted them to repentance; but as they would give no heed to these remonstrances, the decrees enacted by the council were sent to all the churches. Judging that Eudoxius would be likely to endeavor to persuade the emperor to side with him, and would calumniate them, they determined to be beforehand with him, and to send an account of their proceedings in Lampsacus to the court.

Their deputies met the Emperor Valens as he was returning from Heraclea to Thrace, where he had been traveling in company with his brother, who had gone on to Old Rome.

Eudoxius, however, had previously gained over the emperor and his courtiers to his own sentiments; so that when the deputies of the council of Lampsacus presented themselves before Valens, he merely exhorted them not to be at variance with Eudoxius. The deputies replied by reminding him of the artifices to which Eudoxius had resorted at Constantinople, and of his machinations to annul the decrees of the council of Seleucia; and these representations kindled the wrath of Valens to such a pitch, that he condemned the deputies to banishment, and made over the churches to the partisans of Eudoxius. He then passed over into Syria, for he feared lest the Persians should break the truce which they had concluded with Jovian for thirty years. On finding, however, that the Persians were not disposed to insurrection, he fixed his residence at Antioch. He sent Meletius, the bishop, into banishment, but spared Paul, because he admired the sanctity of his life. Those who were not in communion with Euzoius were either ejected from the churches, or maltreated and harassed in some other form.

CHAP. VIII.—REVOLT AND EXTRAORDINARY DEATH OF PROCOPIUS. ELEUSIUS, BISHOP OF CYZICUS, AND EUNOMIUS, THE HERETIC. EUNOMIUS SUCCEEDS ELEUSIUS.

IT is probable that a severe persecution might have ensued at this juncture, had not Procopius commenced a civil war.[1] As he began to play the tyrant at Constantinople, he soon collected a large army, and marched against Valens.

The latter quitted Syria, and met Procopius near Nacolia, a city of Phrygia, and captured him alive through the treachery of Agelon and Gomarius, two of his generals.

Valens put him and his betrayers to a cruel death; and although it is said that he had sworn to show favor to the two generals, he caused them to be sawn asunder.

He commanded Procopius to be fastened by the legs to two trees which had been bent to the ground, and he allowed these to spring up; when the trees were left to resume their natural position, the victim was torn in twain.

On the termination of this war, Valens retired to Nicæa, and finding himself in possession of profound tranquillity, he again began to molest those who differed from him in opinion concerning the Divine nature.

His anger was unbounded against the bishops of the council of Lampsacus, because they had condemned the Arian bishops and the formulary of faith set forth at Ariminum.

While under the influence of these resentful feelings, he summoned Eleusius from Syria, and having called together a Synod of bishops who held his own sentiments, he endeavored to compel him to assent to their doctrines. Eleusius at first manfully refused compliance. But afterwards, from the dread of exile and deprivation of his property, as was threatened by the emperor, he yielded to the mandate. He soon repented of his weakness, and on his return to Cyzicus he made a public confession of his fault in the church, and urged the people to choose another bishop, for he said that he could not discharge the duties of a priesthood after having been a traitor to his own doctrine. The citizens respected his conduct and were especially well-disposed to him, so that they did not choose to have another bishop. Eudoxius, president of the Arians in Constantinople, however, ordained Eunomius as bishop of Cyzicus; for he expected that by his great powers of eloquence Eunomius would easily draw the people of Cyzicus over to his own sentiments. On his arrival at that city he expelled Eleusius, for he was furnished with an imperial edict to that effect, and took possession of the churches himself.

The followers of Eleusius built a house of prayer without the walls of the city, and here they held their assemblies. I shall soon again have occasion to revert to Eunomius and the heresy which bears his name.

CHAP. IX.— SUFFERINGS OF THOSE WHO MAINTAINED THE NICENE FAITH. AGELIUS, THE RULER OF THE NOVATIANS.

THE Christians who represented the Nicene doctrines and the followers of the Novatian views[2] were treated with equal severity in the city of Constantinople.

They were all ultimately expelled from the city; and the churches of the Novatians were closed by order of the emperor. The other party had no churches to be closed, having been

[1] Soc. iv. 5-7; Philost. ix. 5; Eunap. *Fr.* i. 5; ii. 28; Am. Marcel. xxvi. 5-10; Zos. iv. 4-8.

[2] Soc. iv. 9, the source.

deprived of them all during the reign of Constantius.

At this period, Agelius who, from the time of Constantius, had governed the church of the Novatians at Constantinople, was condemned to banishment. It is said that he was especially remarkable for his course of life according to the ecclesiastical laws. With respect to his mode of life, he had attained to the highest degree of philosophy, namely, freedom from worldly possessions; this was evidenced by his daily conduct; he had but one tunic, and always walked barefooted. Not long after his banishment, he was recalled, received the churches under him, and boldly convened churches through the influence of Marcian, a man of extraordinary virtue and eloquence, who had formerly been enrolled among the troops of the palace, but at this period was a presbyter of the Novatian heresy, and the teacher of grammar to Anastasia and Carosa,[1] the daughters of the emperor. There are still baths at Constantinople which bear the names of these princesses. It was for the sake of Marcian alone that the privilege above-mentioned was conceded to the Novatians.

CHAP. X. — CONCERNING VALENTINIAN THE YOUNGER AND GRATIAN. PERSECUTION UNDER VALENS. THE HOMOOUSIANS, BEING OPPRESSED BY THE ARIANS AND MACEDONIANS, SEND AN EMBASSY TO ROME.[2]

ABOUT this period, a son was born to Valentinian in the West, to whom the emperor gave his own name. Not long after, he proclaimed his son Gratian emperor; this prince was born before his father held the government.

In the meantime, although hailstones of extraordinary magnitude fell in various places, and although many cities, particularly Nicæa in Bithynia, were shaken by earthquakes, yet Valens, the emperor, and Eudoxius, the bishop, paused not in their career, but continued to persecute all Christians who differed from them in opinion. They succeeded to the utmost of their expectations in their machinations against those who adhered to the Nicene doctrines; for throughout the greater time of Valens' rule, particularly in Thrace, Bithynia, and the Hellespont, and still further beyond, these Christians had neither churches nor priests. Valens and Eudoxius then directed their resentment against

the Macedonians, who were more in number than the Christians above mentioned in that region, and persecuted them without measure.

The Macedonians, in apprehension of further sufferings, sent deputies to various cities, and finally agreed to have recourse to Valentinian and to the bishop of Rome rather than share in the faith of Eudoxius and Valens and their followers; and when this seemed favorable for execution, they selected three of their own number, — Eustathius, bishop of Sebaste; Silvanus, bishop of Tarsus; and Theophilus, bishop of Castabalis, — and sent them to the Emperor Valentinian; they likewise intrusted them with a letter, addressed to Liberius, bishop of Rome, and to the other priests of the West, in which they entreated them as prelates who had adhered to the faith approved and confirmed by the apostles, and who before others ought to watch over religion, to receive their deputies with all confirmation, and to confer with them about what should be done in the interval until the affairs of the Church could be approvedly set in order.

When the deputies arrived in Italy, they found that the emperor was in Gaul, engaged in war against the barbarians. As they considered that it would be perilous to visit the seat of war in Gaul, they delivered their letter to Liberius.[3] After having conferred with him concerning the objects of their embassy, they condemned Arius and those who held and taught his doctrines; they renounced all heresies opposed to the faith established at Nicæa; and received the term "consubstantial," as being a word that conveys the same signification as the expression "like in substance." When they had presented a confession of faith, analogous to the above, to Liberius, he received them into communion with himself, and wrote to the bishops of the East, commending the orthodoxy of their faith, and detailing what had passed in the conference he had held with them. The confession of faith made by Eustathius and his companions was as follows : —

CHAP. XI. — THE CONFESSION OF EUSTATHIUS, SILVANUS, AND THEOPHILUS, THE DEPUTIES OF THE MACEDONIANS, TO LIBERIUS, BISHOP OF ROME.

"To Liberius, our Lord and Brother, and Fellow-minister — Eustathius, Silvanus, and Theophilus send greeting in the Lord.[4]

"On account of the mad opinions of the heretics who do not cease to keep on sowing scandals for the Catholic churches, we who nul-

---

[1] According to Am. Marcel. xxvi. 6, 14, the Anastasian baths were so called after a sister of Constantine. But Soz. supposes that there were baths in his day named after the sisters, not the one, but both. Soc. says only Anastasia. Cf. Idatius, *Desc. Coss. s.* A.D. 375. His cons. thermæ Carosianæ dedicatæ sunt agente præfecto V. C. Vendalonis Magno.

[2] Valesius remarks that the title of this chapter is incorrect, and that it was the Macedonians, and not the orthodox Christians, who sent the embassy to Rome.

[3] Soc. iv. 10, 11, 12, from whom Soz. seems to have compressed.

[4] Soc. iv. 12. Soz. has only half of the document with a number of variations.

lify their every attack confess the Synod which was held at Lampsacus, the one at Smyrna and the councils held in other places, by the orthodox bishops. We have furnished letters and sent on an embassy to your Goodness, as likewise to all the other bishops of Italy and of the West, to confirm and preserve the Catholic faith, which was established at the holy council of Nicæa, by the blessed Constantine and three hundred and eighteen God-fearing fathers.

"This remains, by an unmixed and immovable settlement, until now, and will remain perpetually; in which the term 'consubstantial' is fixed in all holiness and piety in testimony against the perverseness of Arius. We confess, each with his own hand, that we with'the aforesaid have always held this same faith, that we still hold it, and that we shall adhere to it to the last. We condemn Arius, his impious dogmas, and his disciples. We also condemn the heresies of Patropasianus,[1] of Photinus, of Marcellus, of Paul of Samosata, and all who maintain such doctrines themselves. We anathematize all heresies opposed to the aforesaid faith established by the saintly fathers at Nicæa. We anathematize Arius especially, and condemn all such decrees as were enacted at Ariminum, in opposition to the aforesaid faith established by the holy council of Nicæa. We were formerly deluded by the guile and perjury of certain parties, and subscribed to these decrees when they were transmitted to Constantinople from Nicæa, a city of Thrace."

After this confession they subjoined a copy of the entire formulary of Nicæa to their own creed, and, having received from Liberius a written account of all that they had transacted, they sailed to Sicily.

CHAP. XII. — COUNCILS OF SICILY AND OF TYANA. THE SYNOD WHICH WAS EXPECTED TO BE HELD IN CILICIA IS DISSOLVED BY VALENS. THE PERSECUTION AT THAT TIME. ATHANASIUS THE GREAT FLEES AGAIN, AND IS IN CONCEALMENT; BY THE LETTER OF VALENS HE REAPPEARS, AND GOVERNS THE CHURCHES IN EGYPT.

A COUNCIL was convened at Sicily;[2] and after the same doctrines had been confirmed as those set forth in the confession of the deputies, the assembly was dissolved.

At the same time, a council was held at Tyana; and Eusebius, bishop of Cæsarea in Cappadocia, Athanasius, bishop of Ancyra, Pelagius, bishop of Laodicea, Zeno, bishop of Tyre, Paul, bishop of Emesa, Otreus, bishop of Melitene, and Gregory, bishop of Nazianzen, were present with many others, who, during the reign of Jovian, had assembled at Antioch, and determined to maintain the doctrine of the Son being consubstantial with the Father. The letters of Liberius and the Western bishops were read at this council. These letters afforded high satisfaction to the members of the council; and they wrote to all the churches, desiring them to peruse the decrees of the bishops in Asia,[2] and the documents written by Liberius and the bishops of Italy, of Africa, of. Gaul, and of Sicily, which had been intrusted to the deputies of the council of Lampsacus. They urged them to reflect on the great number of persons by whom these documents had been drawn up, and who were far more in number than the members of the council of Ariminum, and exhorted them to be of one mind, and to enter into communion with them, to signify the same by writing, and finally to assemble together at Tarsus in Cilicia before the end of the spring. On a fixed date which they prescribed, they urged one another to convene. On the approach of the appointed day, when the Synod was on the point of assembling at Tarsus, about thirty-four of the Asiatic bishops came together in Caria, in the province of Asia, commended the design of establishing uniformity of belief in the Church, but objected to the term "consubstantial," and insisted that the formularies of faith set forth by the councils of Antioch and Seleucia, and maintained by Lucian, the martyr, and by many of their predecessors, with dangers and tensions, ought to obtain the ascendancy over all others.

The emperor, at the instigation of Eudoxius, prevented by letter the council from being convened in Cilicia, and even prohibited it under severe penalties. He also wrote to the governors of the provinces, commanding them to eject all bishops from their churches who had been banished by Constantine[3] and who had again taken up their priesthood under the Emperor Julian. On account of this order, those who were at the head of the government of Egypt were anxious to deprive Athanasius of his bishopric and expel him from the city; for no light punishment was inserted in the imperial letters; for unless the injunctions were fulfilled, all the magistrates equally, and the soldiers under them, and counselors were condemned to the payment of much money and also threatened with bodily maltreatment.[4]

The majority of Christians of the city, however, assembled and besought the governor not to banish Athanasius without further consideration of the terms of the imperial letter, which merely specified all bishops who had been

---

[1] A curious blunder.
[2] Soc. iv. 12, 13, 20. Soz. has much more acts and details. Sabinus is probably a chief source, though not the only one. Soc. iv. 12, at end.

[2] Text reads ἀνὰ τὴν Ἀσίαν; it is wrong to substitute δύσιν.
[3] Obviously an error in the text, for Constantius. See below, where the name is given correctly.
[4] Cf. *Chronicon*, prefacing the Festal letters of Athan. from A.D. 365 on.

banished by Constantius and recalled by Julian ; and it was manifest that Athanasius was not of this number, inasmuch as he had been recalled by Constantius and had resumed his bishopric ; but Julian, at the very time that all the other bishops had been recalled, persecuted him, and finally Jovian recalled him. The governor was by no means convinced by these arguments ; nevertheless, he restrained himself and did not give way to the use of force. The people ran together from every quarter ; there was much commotion and perturbation throughout the city ; an insurrection was expected ; he therefore advised the emperor of the facts and allowed the bishop to remain in the city. Some days afterwards, when the popular excitement had seemingly abated, Athanasius secretly quitted the city at dusk, and concealed himself somewhere. The very same night, the governor of Egypt and the military chief took possession of the church in which Athanasius generally dwelt, and sought him in every part of the edifice, and even on the roof, but in vain ; for they had calculated upon seizing the moment when the popular commotion had partially subsided, and when the whole city was wrapt in sleep, to execute the mandate of the emperor, and to transport Athanasius quietly from the city.

Not to have found Athanasius naturally excited universal astonishment. Some attributed his escape to a special revelation from above ; others to the advice of some of his followers ; both had the same result ; but more than human prudence seems to have been requisite to foresee and to avoid such a plot. Some say, that as soon as the people gave indications of being disposed to sedition, he concealed himself among the tombs of his ancestors, being apprehensive lest he should be regarded as the cause of any disturbances that might ensue ; and that he afterwards retreated to some other place of concealment.

The Emperor Valens, soon after, wrote to grant permission for him to return and hold his church. It is very doubtful, whether, in making this concession, Valens acted according to his own inclination. I rather imagine that, on reflecting on the esteem in which Athanasius was universally held, he feared to excite the displeasure of the Emperor Valentinian, who was well-known to be attached to the Nicene doctrines ; or perhaps he was apprehensive of a commotion on the part of the many admirers of the bishop, lest some innovation might injure the public affairs.

I also believe that the Arian presidents did not, on this occasion, plead' very vehemently against Athanasius ; for they considered that, if he were ejected from the city, he would probably traduce them to the emperors and then

would have an occasion for conference with respect to them, and might possibly succeed in persuading Valens to adopt his own sentiments, and in arousing the anger of the like-minded Valentinian against themselves.

They were greatly troubled by the evidences of the virtue and courage of Athanasius, which had been afforded by the events which had transpired during the reign of Constantius. He had, in fact, so skilfully evaded the plots of his enemies, that they had been constrained to consent to his reinstallation in the government of the churches of Egypt ; and yet he could scarcely be induced to return from Italy, although letters had been dispatched by Constantius to that effect.

I am convinced that it was solely from these reasons that Athanasius was not expelled from his church like the other bishops, who were subjected to as cruel a persecution as ever was inflicted by pagans.

Those who would not change their doctrinal tenets were banished ; their houses of prayer were taken from them, and placed in the possession of those who held opposite sentiments. Egypt alone was, during the life of Athanasius, exempted from this persecution.

CHAP. XIII. — DEMOPHILUS, AN ARIAN, BECAME BISHOP OF CONSTANTINOPLE AFTER EUDOXIUS. THE PIOUS ELECT EVAGRIUS. ACCOUNT OF THE PERSECUTION WHICH ENSUED.

ABOUT this time the Emperor Valens went to Antioch on the Orontes ; while he was on his journey Eudoxius died, after having governed the churches of Constantinople during the space of eleven years.[1] Demophilus was immediately ordained as his successor by the Arian bishops. The followers of the Nicene doctrines, believing that the course of events was in their power, elected Evagrius as their bishop. He had been ordained by Eustathius, who had formerly governed the church of Antioch in Syria, and who having been recalled from banishment by Jovian, lived in a private manner at Constantinople, and devoted himself to the instruction of those who held his sentiments, exhorting them to perseverance in their view of the Divine Being. The Arian heretics were stirred to revolt, and commenced a violent persecution against those who had participated in the ordination of Evagrius. The Emperor Valens, who was then at Nicomedia, on being apprised of the occurrences that had taken place in Constantinople since the death of Eudoxius, was fearful lest any interest of the city should suffer by sedition, and therefore sent thither as many troops as he thought requisite to preserve tranquillity.

1 Soc. iv. 13-15 ; Philost. ix. 4-10.

Eustathius was arrested by his command and banished to Bizya, a city of Thrace, and Evagrius was exiled to some other region. And such was the manner of this event.

CHAP. XIV. — ACCOUNT OF THE EIGHTY PIOUS DELEGATES IN NICOMEDIA, WHOM VALENS BURNED WITH THE VESSEL IN MID-SEA.

THE Arians, as is customary with the prosperous, because more insolent,[1] persecuted unmercifully all Christians whose religious sentiments were opposed to their own.

These Christians being exposed to bodily injuries, and betrayed to magistrates and prisons, and finding themselves moreover gradually impoverished by the frequent fines, were at length compelled to appeal for redress to the emperor. Although exceedingly angry, the emperor did not openly manifest any wrath, but secretly commanded the prefect to seize and slay the whole deputation. But the prefect, being apprehensive that a whole popular insurrection would be excited if he were to put so many good and religious men to death without any of the forms of justice, pretended that they were to be sent into exile, and under this pretext compelled them to embark on board a ship, to which they assented with the most perfect resignation. When they had sailed to about the center of the bay, which was called Astacius, the sailors, according to the orders they had received, set fire to the vessel and leaped into the tender. A wind arising, the ship was blown along to Dacibiza, a place on the sea-coast of Bithynia; but no sooner had it neared the shore, than it was utterly consumed with all the men on board.

CHAP. XV. — DISPUTES BETWEEN EUSEBIUS, BISHOP OF CÆSAREA, AND BASIL THE GREAT. HENCE THE ARIANS TOOK COURAGE AND CAME TO CÆSAREA, AND WERE REPULSED.

WHEN Valens quitted Nicomedia, he went on to Antioch;[2] and in passing through Cappadocia he did all in his power, according to custom, to injure the orthodox and to deliver up the churches to the Arians. He thought to accomplish his designs the more easily on account of a dispute[3] which was then pending between Basil and Eusebius, who then governed the church of Cæsarea. This dissension had been the cause of Basil's departing from Pontus, where he lived conjointly with some monks who pursued the philosophy. The people and some of the most powerful and the wisest men in the city began to regard Eusebius with suspicion, particularly as they considered him the cause of the withdrawal of one who was equally celebrated for his piety and his eloquence; and they accordingly began to plan a secession and the holding of separate church. In the meantime Basil, fearing to be a source of further trouble to the Church, which was already rent by the dissensions of heretics, remained in retirement in the monasteries at Pontus. The emperor and the bishops of the Arian heresy, who were always attached to his suite, were more inspirited in their designs by the absence of Basil and the hatred of the people towards Eusebius. But the event was contrary to their judgment. On the first intelligence of the intention of the emperor to pass through Cappadocia, Basil quitted Pontus and returned to Cæsarea, where he effected a reconciliation with Eusebius, and by his eloquence he opportunely aided the Church. The projects of Valens were thus defeated, and he returned with his bishops without having accomplished any of his designs.

CHAP. XVI. — BASIL BECOMES BISHOP OF CÆSAREA AFTER EUSEBIUS; HIS BOLDNESS TOWARDS THE EMPEROR AND THE PREFECT.

SOME time after, the emperor again visited Cappadocia, and found that Basil was administering the churches there after the death of Eusebius.[4] He thought of expelling him, but was unwillingly restrained from his intention. It is said that the night after he had formed his plans his wife was disturbed by a frightful dream, and that his only son Galates was cut off by a rapid disease. The death of this son was universally attributed to the vengeance of God as a punishment of his parents for the machinations that had been carried on against Basil. Valens himself was of this opinion, and, after the death of his son, offered no further molestation to the bishop.

When the prince was sinking under the disease, and at the point of death, the emperor sent for Basil and requested him to pray to God for his son's recovery. For as soon as Valens had arrived at Cæsarea, the prefect had sent for Basil and commanded him to embrace the religious sentiments of the emperor, menacing him with death in case of non-compliance. Basil replied that it would be great gain to him and the grant of the highest favor to be delivered as quickly as possible from the bondage of the body. The prefect gave him the rest of the day and the approaching night for deliberation, and advised him not to rush imprudently into

---

[1] Soc. iv. 16. Cf. Theodoret, *H. E.* iv. 24.
[2] Independent chapter.
[3] Concerning this difference, see Greg. Naz. *Or.* xliii. 27-37, in praise of Basil.

[4] Greg. Naz. *Or.* xliii. 44-57; Greg. Nyss. *contra Eunomium,* ii. 290-295; Ruf. ii. 9; Soc. iv. 26. Cf. Theodoret, iv. 19.

obvious danger, but that he should come on the day after and declare his opinion. "I do not require to deliberate," replied Basil. "My determination will be the same to-morrow as it is to-day; for since I am a creature I can never be induced to worship that which is similar to myself and worship it as God; neither will I conform to your religion, nor to that of the emperor. Although your distinction may be great, and although you have the honor of ruling no inconsiderable portion of the empire, yet I ought not on these accounts to seek to please men, and, at the same time, belittle that Divine faith which neither loss of goods, nor exile, nor condemnation to death would ever impel me to betray. Inflictions of this nature have never excited in my mind one pang of sorrow. I possess nothing but a cloak and a few books. I dwell on the earth as a traveler. The body through its weakness would have the better of all sensation and torture after the first blow."

The prefect admired the courage evinced in this bold reply, and communicated the circumstance to the emperor. On the festival of the Epiphany, the emperor repaired to the church, with the rulers and his guards, presented gifts at the holy table, and held a conference with Basil, whose wisdom and whose order and arrangement in the conduct of the priesthood and the church elicited his praise.

Not long after, however, the calumny of his enemies prevailed, and Basil was condemned to banishment. The night for the execution of the edict was at hand; the son of the emperor suddenly fell ill with a pressing and dangerous fever. The father prostrated himself on the earth and wept over the son who was still alive, and not knowing what other measures to take towards effecting the recovery of his son, he dispatched some of his attendants to Basil to come and visit the prostrate child; because he himself feared to summon the bishop, on account of the injury just inflicted upon him. Immediately on the arrival of Basil, the boy began to rally; so that many maintain that his recovery would have been complete, had not some heretics been summoned to pray with Basil for the restoration of the boy. It is said that the prefect, likewise, fell ill; but that on his repentance, and on prayer being offered to God, he was restored to health. The instances above adduced are quite inadequate to convey an idea of the wonderful endowments of Basil; his extreme addiction to the philosophic life and astonishing powers of eloquence attracted great celebrity.

CHAP. XVII. — FRIENDSHIP OF BASIL AND OF GREGORY, THE THEOLOGIAN; BEING PEERS IN WISDOM, THEY DEFEND THE NICENE DOCTRINES.

BASIL and Gregory were contemporaries, and they were recognized to be equally intent, so to speak, upon the cultivation of the virtues.[1] They[2] had both studied in their youth at Athens, under Himerius and Proæresius, the most approved sophists of the age; and afterwards at Antioch, under Libanius, the Syrian. But as they subsequently conceived a contempt for sophistry and the study of the law, they determined to study philosophy according to the law of the Church. After having spent some time in the pursuit of the sciences, taught by pagan philosophers, they entered upon the study of the commentaries which Origen and the best approved authors who lived before and after his time, have written in explanation of the Sacred Scriptures.

They rendered great assistance to those who, like themselves, maintained the Nicene doctrines, for they manfully opposed the dogmas of the Arians, proving that these heretics did not rightly understand either the data upon which they proceeded, nor the opinions of Origen, upon which they mainly depended. These two holy men divided the perils of their undertaking, either by mutual agreement, or, as I have been informed, by lot. The cities in the neighborhood of Pontus fell to the lot of Basil; and here he founded numerous monasteries, and, by teaching the people, he persuaded them to hold like views with himself. After the death of his father, Gregory acted as bishop of the small city of Nazianzus,[3] but resided on that account in a variety of places, and especially at Constantinople. Not long after he was appointed by the vote of many priests to act as president of the people there; for there was then neither bishop nor church in Constantinople, and the doctrines of the council of Nicæa were almost extinct.

CHAP. XVIII. — THE PERSECUTION WHICH OCCURRED AT ANTIOCH, ON THE ORONTES. THE PLACE OF PRAYER IN EDESSA, CALLED AFTER THE APOSTLE THOMAS; THE ASSEMBLY THERE, AND CONFESSION OF THE INHABITANTS OF EDESSA.

THE emperor went to Antioch, and entirely ejected from the churches of that city and of the neighboring cities all those who adhered to the Nicene doctrines;[4] moreover, he oppressed them with manifold punishments; as some affirm, he commanded many to be put to death in various ways, and caused others to be cast into the river Orontes. Having heard that there was a magnificent oratory at Edessa, named after

---

[1] Chrysostom, de Sacerdotio, i. 1-7.
[2] Soc. iv. 26; Ruf. ii. 9. Cf. Theodoret, H. E. iv. 30.
[3] He had been coadjutor bishop during his father's lifetime.
[4] Ruf. ii. 5; Soc. iv. 17, 18. Soz. resembles Soc. in both incidents. Soc. resembles Ruf. in the Edessa story; neither mention the prefect's name, as does Soz. Philost. ix. 11; Theodoret, H. E. iv. 17.

the Apostle Thomas, he went to see it. He beheld the members of the Catholic Church assembled for worship in the plain before the walls of the city; for there, too, they had been deprived of their houses of prayer. It is said that the emperor reproached the prefect thoroughly and struck him on the jaw with his fist for having permitted these congregations contrary to his edict. Modestus (for this was the name of the prefect), although he was himself a heretic, secretly warned the people of Edessa not to meet for prayer on the accustomed spot the next day; for he had received orders from the emperor to punish all who should be seized. He uttered such threats with the forethought that none, or at least but a few, would incur danger, and with the desire to appease the wrath of the monarch. But the people of Edessa, totally disregarding the threat, ran together with more than their customary zeal, and filled the usual place of meeting.

Modestus, on being apprised of their proceedings, was undecided as to what measures ought to be adopted, and repaired in embarrassment to the plain with the throng. A woman, leading a child by the hand, and trailing her mantle in a way unbefitting the decency of women, forced her way through the files of the soldiers who were conducted by the prefect, as if bent upon some affair of importance. Modestus remarked her conduct, ordered her to be arrested, and summoned her into his presence, to inquire the cause of her running. She replied that she was hastening to the plain where the members of the Catholic Church were assembled. "Know you not," replied Modestus, "that the prefect is on his way thither for the purpose of condemning to death all who are found on the spot?" "I have heard so," replied she, "and this is the very reason of my haste; for I am fearful of arriving too late, and thus losing the honor of martyrdom for God." The governor having asked her why she took her child with her, she replied, "In order that he may share in the common suffering, and participate in the same reward." Modestus, struck with astonishment at the courage of this woman, went to the emperor, and, acquainting him with what had occurred, persuaded him not to carry out a design which he showed to be disgraceful and disastrous. Thus was the Christian faith confessed by the whole city of Edessa.

CHAP. XIX. — DEATH OF THE GREAT ATHANASIUS; THE ELEVATION OF LUCIUS, WHO WAS ARIAN-MINDED, TO THE SEE; THE NUMEROUS CALAMITIES HE BROUGHT UPON THE CHURCHES IN EGYPT; PETER, WHO SERVED AFTER ATHANASIUS, PASSED OVER TO ROME.

ATHANASIUS, bishop of the church of Alexandria, died about this period, after having completed his high-priesthood in about forty-six years.[1] The Arians having received early intelligence of his death, Euzoius, president of the Arians at Antioch, and Magnus, the chief treasurer, were sent by the emperor, and lost no time in seizing and imprisoning Peter, whom Athanasius had appointed to succeed him in the bishopric; and they forthwith transferred the government of the church to Lucius.

Hence those in Egypt suffered more grievously than those in other places, and misfortunes piled upon misfortunes oppressed the members of the Catholic Church; for as soon as Lucius settled in Alexandria, he attempted to take possession of the churches; he met with opposition from the people, and the clergy and holy virgins were accused as originators of the sedition. Some made their escape as if the city had fallen into the hands of an enemy; others were seized and imprisoned. Some of the prisoners were afterwards dragged from the dungeons to be torn with hooks and thongs, while others were burned by means of flaming torches. It seemed wonderful how they could possibly survive the tortures to which they were subjected. Banishment or even death itself would have been preferable to such sufferings. Peter, the bishop, made his escape from prison; and embarking on board a ship, proceeded to Rome, the bishop of which church held the same sentiments as himself. Thus the Arians, although not many in number, remained in possession of the churches. At the same time, an edict was issued by the emperor, enacting that as many of the followers of the Nicene doctrines should be ejected from Alexandria and the rest of Egypt, as might be directed by Lucius. Euzoius, having thus accomplished all his designs, returned to Antioch.

CHAP. XX.—PERSECUTION OF THE EGYPTIAN MONKS, AND OF THE DISCIPLES OF ST. ANTONY. THEY WERE ENCLOSED IN A CERTAIN ISLAND ON ACCOUNT OF THEIR ORTHODOXY; THE MIRACLES WHICH THEY WROUGHT.

LUCIUS went with the general of the soldiers in Egypt, against the monks in the desert;[2] for he imagined that if he could overcome their opposition by interrupting the tranquillity which

---

[1] Ruf. ii. 3; Soc. iv. 20-22. In c. 22 he mentions a letter of Peter to the churches, giving an account of the persecutions; and that Sabinus records none of these things. Cf. Theodoret, *H. E.* iv. 20-22. In c. 22 a part of Peter's letter is given. Hieron. *de vir. illust.* lxxxvii.; Greg. Naz. *Or.* xxi. *in laudem Magni Athanasii episcopi Alexandrini.*

[2] Ruf. ii. 3, 4; Soc. iv. 22, 24; Theodoret, *H. E.* iv. 21, 22; *Chronicon prævium* to the Vestal letters, from A.D. 367 to 373, and *Chronicon acephalum*, 15-19; Greg. Naz. *Or.* xxv. 11-14, xxxiv. 3; *Cod. Theod.* xvi. 1, 2; *Pœmata*, 12, *de seipso et de episcopis.*

they loved, he would meet with fewer obstacles in drawing over to his party the Christians who inhabited the cities. The monasteries of this country were governed by several individuals of eminent sanctity, who were strenuously opposed to the heresy of Arius. The people, who were neither willing nor competent to enter upon the investigation of doctrinal questions, received their opinions from them, and thought with them; for they were persuaded that men whose virtue was manifested by their deeds were in possession of truth. We have heard that the leaders of these Egyptian ascetics were two men of the name of Macarius, of whom mention has already been made,[1] Pambo and Heraclides, and other disciples of Antony.

On reflecting that the Arians could never succeed in establishing an ascendency over the Catholic Church, unless the monks could be drawn over to their party, Lucius determined to have recourse to force to compel the monks to side with him, since he was unable to persuade them. But here again his scheme failed; for the monks were prepared to subject their necks to the sword rather than to swerve from the Nicene doctrines. It is related that, at the very time that the soldiers were about to attack them, a man whose limbs were withered and who was unable to stand on his feet was carried to them; and that when they had anointed him with oil, and commanded him in the name of Christ, whom Lucius persecuted, to arise and go to his house, he suddenly became whole. This miraculous cure openly manifested the necessity of adopting the sentiments of those to whom God himself had testified as possessing the truth, while Lucius was condemned, in that God heard their prayers and had healed the sick.

But the plotters against the monks were not led to repentance by this miracle; on the contrary, they arrested these holy men by night, and conveyed them to an island of Egypt, concealed in the swamps. The inhabitants of this island had never heard of the Christian faith, and were devoted to the service of demons: the island contained a temple of great antiquity which was held in great reverence. It is said that when the monks landed on the island, the daughter of the priest, who was possessed of a devil, went to them. The girl ran screaming towards them; and the people of the island, astonished at her sudden and strange conduct, followed. When she drew near the ship in which were the holy messengers, she flung herself pleadingly upon the ground, and exclaimed supplicatingly in a loud voice, "Wherefore are you come to us, O servants of the great God? for we have long dwelt in this island as our residence; we have

troubled no one. Unknown to men, we have concealed ourselves here, and are everywhere surrounded by these marshes. If, however, it please you, accept our possessions, and fix your abode here; we will quit the island."

Such were her utterances. Macarius and his companions rebuked the demon, and the girl became sane. Her father and all her house, with the inhabitants of the island, immediately embraced Christianity, and after demolishing their temple, they transformed it into a church. On these occurrences being reported at Alexandria, Lucius was overcome with immoderate grief; and, fearing lest he should incur the hatred of his own partisans, and be accused of warring against God, and not against man, he sent secret orders for Macarius and his companions to be re-conveyed to their own dwellings in the wilderness. Thus did Lucius occasion troubles and commotions in Egypt.

About the same period, Didymus the philosopher and several other illustrious men acquired great renown. Struck by their virtue, and by that of the monks, the people followed their doctrines and opposed those of the partisans of Lucius.

The Arians, though not so strong in point of numbers as the other party, grievously persecuted the church of Egypt.

CHAP. XXI. — LIST OF THE PLACES IN WHICH THE NICENE DOCTRINES WERE REPRESENTED; FAITH MANIFESTED BY THE SCYTHIANS; VETRANIO, THE LEADER OF THIS RACE.

ARIANISM met with similar opposition at the same period in Osröene; but in the Cappadocias, Providence allotted such a divine and educated pair of men, — Basil, the bishop of Cæsarea in that country, and Gregory, bishop of Nazianzen.[2] Syria and the neighboring provinces, and more especially the city of Antioch, were plunged into confusion and disorder; for the Arians were very numerous in these parts, and had possession of the churches. The members of the Catholic Church were not, however, few in number. They were called Eustathians and Paulinists, and were under the guidance of Paulinus and Meletius, as has been before stated. It was through their instrumentality that the church of Antioch was preserved from the encroachments of the Arians, and enabled to resist the zeal of the emperor and of those in power about him. Indeed, it appears that in all the churches which were governed by brave men, the people did not deviate from their former opinions.

It is said that this was the cause of the firmness with which the Scythians adhered to their

---

[1] In iii. 14; Pallad. *H. L.* xix., xx.

[2] This is an independent chapter. Cf. Theodoret, *H. E.* iv. 35.

faith. There are in this country a great number of cities, villages, and fortresses. The metropolis is called Tomi; it is a large and populous city, and lies on the sea-shore to the left of one sailing to the sea, called the Euxine.

According to an ancient custom which still prevails, all the churches of the whole country are under the sway of one bishop.[1]

Vetranio ruled over these churches at the period that the emperor visited Tomi. Valens repaired to the church, and strove, according to his usual custom, to gain over the bishop to the heresy of Arius; but this latter manfully opposed his arguments, and after a courageous defense of the Nicene doctrines, quitted the emperor and proceeded to another church, whither he was followed by the people. Almost the entire city had crowded to see the emperor, for they expected that something extraordinary would result from this interview with the bishop.

Valens was extremely offended at being left alone in the church with his attendants, and in resentment, condemned Vetranio to banishment. Not long after, however, he recalled him, because, I believe, he apprehended an insurrection; for the Scythians were offended at the absence of their bishop.

He well knew that the Scythians were a courageous nation, and that their country, by the position of its places, possessed many natural advantages which rendered it necessary to the Roman Empire, for it served as a barrier to ward off the barbarians.

Thus was the intention of the ruler openly frustrated by Vetranio. The Scythians themselves testify that he was good in all other respects and eminent for the virtue of his life.

The resentment of the emperor was visited upon all the clergy except those of the Western churches; for Valentinian, who reigned over the Western regions, was an admirer of the Nicene doctrines, and was imbued with so much reverence for religion, that he never imposed any commands upon the priests, nor ever attempted to introduce any alteration for better or for worse in ecclesiastical regulations. Although he had become one of the best of emperors, and had shown his capacity to rule affairs, he considered that ecclesiastical matters were beyond the range of his jurisdiction.

CHAP. XXII. — AT THAT TIME, THE DOCTRINE OF THE HOLY GHOST WAS AGITATED, AND IT WAS DECIDED THAT HE IS TO BE CONSIDERED CONSUBSTANTIAL WITH THE FATHER AND THE SON.

A QUESTION was renewed at this juncture which had previously excited much inquiry and now more; namely, whether the Holy Ghost is or is not to be considered consubstantial with the Father and the Son.[2]

Many contentions and debates ensued on this subject, similar to those which had been held concerning the nature of God the Word. Those who asserted that the Son is dissimilar from the Father, and those who insisted that He is similar in substance to the Father, came to one common opinion concerning the Holy Ghost; for both parties maintained that the Holy Ghost differs in substance, and that He is but the Minister and the third in point of order, honor, and substance. Those, on the contrary, who believed that the Son is consubstantial with the Father, held also the same view about the Spirit. This doctrine was nobly maintained in Syria by Apolinarius, bishop of Laodicea; in Egypt by Athanasius,[3] the bishop; in Cappadocia and in the churches of Pontus by Basil[4] and Gregory.[5] The bishop of Rome, on learning that this question was agitated with great acrimony, and that it of course was augmented daily by controversies, wrote to the churches of the East and urged them to receive the doctrine upheld by the Western clergy; namely, that the three Persons of the Trinity are of the same substance and of equal dignity. The question having been thus decided by the Roman churches, peace was restored, and the inquiry appeared to have an end.

CHAP. XXIII. — DEATH OF LIBERIUS, BISHOP OF ROME. HE IS SUCCEEDED BY DAMASUS AND SYRICIUS.[6] ORTHODOX DOCTRINES PREVAIL EVERYWHERE THROUGHOUT THE WEST, EXCEPT AT MILAN, WHERE AUXENTIUS IS THE HIGH-PRIEST. SYNOD HELD AT ROME, BY WHICH AUXENTIUS IS DEPOSED; THE DEFINITION WHICH IT SENT BY LETTER.

ABOUT this period Liberius died,[7] and Damasus succeeded to the see of Rome.[8] A deacon named Ursicius, who had obtained some votes in his favor, but could not endure the defeat, therefore caused himself to be clandestinely ordained by some bishops of little note, and endeavored to create a division among the people and to hold a separate church. He succeeded in effecting this division, and some of the people respected him as bishop, while the rest adhered to Damasus. This gave rise

---

[1] Sozomen repeats this below, in vii. 19, where he recounts the various local customs prevailing in the ecclesiastical system.

[2] This chapter seems curiously out of place after the history of the Macedonians and that of the Synod of Alexandria. Cf. Soc. ii. 45, iii. 7.
[3] Athan. *Epp.* i., iii., iv., ad Serapionem, contra illos qui blasphemant et dicunt spiritum sanctum rem creatam esse.
[4] Bas. *adv. Eunomium,* iii., v.; Lib. *de Spiritu Sancto.*
[5] Greg. Naz. *Or.* xxxi., xxxiv., xli.
[6] For Ursicius.
[7] A.D. 366, Sept. 24.
[8] Soc. iv. 29; Ruf. *H. E.* ii. 10. Soz. omits the name of the prefect.

to much contention and revolt among the people, which at length proceeded to the evil of wounds and murder. The prefect of Rome was obliged to interfere, and to punish many of the people and of the clergy; and he put an end to the attempt of Ursicius.[1]

With respect to doctrine, however, no dissension arose either at Rome or in any other of the Western churches. The people unanimously adhered to the form of belief established at Nicæa, and regarded the three persons of the Trinity as equal in dignity and in power.

Auxentius and his followers differed from the others in opinion; he was then president of the church in Milan, and, in conjunction with a few partisans, was intent upon the introduction of innovations, and the maintenance of the Arian dogma of the dissimilarity of the Son and of the Holy Ghost, according to the inquiry which had last sprung up, in opposition to the unanimous agreement of the Western priests. The bishops of Gaul and of Venetia having reported that similar attempts to disturb the peace of the Church were being made by others among them, the bishops of several provinces assembled not long after at Rome, and decreed that Auxentius and those who held his sentiments should be aliens from their communion. They confirmed the traditional faith established by the council of Nicæa, and annulled all the decrees that had been issued at Ariminum contrary to that faith, under the plea that these decrees had not received the assent of the bishop of Rome, nor of other bishops who agreed with them, and that many who had been present at the Synod, had disapproved of the enactments there made by them. That such was the decision really formed by the Synod is testified by the epistle[2] addressed by Damasus, the Roman bishop, and the rest of the assembly, to the bishops of Illyria. It is as follows:[3] —

"Damasus, Valerius,[4] and the other bishops of the holy assembly convened at Rome to the dearly beloved brethren settled in Illyria, greeting in the Lord.

"We believe that you uphold and teach to the people our holy faith, which is founded on the doctrine of the apostles. This faith differs in no respect from that defined by the Fathers; neither is it allowable for the priests of God, whose right it is to instruct the wise, to have any other thought. We have, however, been informed by some of our brethren of Gaul and of Venice, that certain individuals are bent upon the introduction of heresy.

"All bishops should diligently guard against this evil, lest some of their flock should be led by inexperience, and others by simplicity, to oppose the proper interpretations.

"Those who devise strange doctrines ought not to be followed; but the opinions of our fathers ought to be retained, whatever may be the diversity of judgment around us.

"Hence Auxentius, bishop of Milan, has been publicly declared to be condemned pre-eminently in this matter. It is right, therefore, that all the teachers of the Roman world should be of one mind, and not pollute the faith by divers conflicting doctrines.

"For when the malice of the heretics first began to mature itself, as the blasphemy of the Arians has even now done, — may it be far from us, — our fathers to the number of three hundred and eighteen elect, after making an investigation in Nicæa, erected the wall against the weapons of the devil, and repelled the deadly poison by this antidote.

"This antidote consists in the belief, that the Father and the Son have one Godhead, one virtue, and one substance ($\chi\rho\tilde{\eta}\mu\alpha$). It is also requisite to believe that the Holy Ghost is of the same hypostasis. We have decreed that those who hold any other doctrines are to be aliens from our communion.

"Some have decreed to discolor this saving definition and adorable view; but in the very beginning, some of the persons who made the innovation at the council of Ariminum, or who were compelled to vote for the change, have since, in some measure, made amends by confessing that they were deceived by certain specious arguments, which did not appear to them to be contrary to the principles laid down by our fathers at Nicæa. The number of individuals congregated at the council of Ariminum proves nothing in prejudice of orthodox doctrines; for the council was held without the sanction of the bishops at Rome, whose opinion, before that of all others, ought to have been received, and without the assent either of Vincentius, who during a very long series of years guarded the episcopate without spot, or of many other bishops who agreed with those last mentioned.

"Besides, as has been before stated, those very persons who seemed inclined to something illusory, testified their disapprobation of their own proceedings as soon as they made use of a better judgment. Therefore your purity must see that this alone is the faith which was established at Nicæa upon the authority of the apostles, and which must ever be retained inviolate, and that all bishops, whether of the East, or of the West, who profess the Catholic religion, ought to consider it an honor to be in communion with us. We believe that it will not be long

[1] Cf. Am. Marcel. xxvii. 3. 12–15.
[2] This epistle is first given by Soz.; it is repeated in Theodoret, H. E. ii. 22. The Synod was held A.D. 369.
[3] All these prefatory details are unique with Soz.
[4] He was bishop of Aquileia. Theodoret calls him Valerianus.

before those who maintain other sentiments will be excluded from communion, and deprived of the name and dignity of bishop; so that the people who are now oppressed by the yoke of those pernicious and deceitful principles, may have liberty to breathe. For it is not in the power of these bishops to rectify the error of the people, inasmuch as they are themselves held by error. Let, therefore, the opinion of your honor also be in accord with all the priests of God, in which we believe you to be holy and firm. That we ought so to believe along with you will be proved by the exchange of letters with your love."

CHAP. XXIV. — CONCERNING ST. AMBROSE AND HIS ELEVATION TO THE HIGH PRIESTHOOD; HOW HE PERSUADED THE PEOPLE TO PRACTICE PIETY. THE NOVATIANS OF PHRYGIA AND THE PASSOVER.

THE clergy of the West having thus anticipated the designs of those who sought to introduce innovations among them,[1] carefully continued to preserve the inviolability of the faith which had from the beginning been handed down to them. With the solitary exception of Auxentius and his partisans, there were no individuals among them who entertained heterodox opinions. Auxentius, however, did not live long after this period. At his death a sedition arose among the people concerning the choice of a bishop for the church of Milan, and the city was in danger. Those who had aspired to the bishopric, and been defeated in their expectations, were loud in their menaces, as is usual in such commotions.

Ambrosius, who was then the governor of the province, being fearful of the movement of the people, went to the church, and exhorted the people to cease from contention, to remember the laws, and to re-establish concord and the prosperity which springs from peace. Before he had ceased speaking, all his auditors at once suppressed the angry feelings by which they had been mutually agitated against each other, and directed the vote of the bishopric upon him, as a fulfillment of his counsel to harmony. They exhorted him to be baptized, for he was still uninitiated, and begged him to receive the priesthood. After he had refused and declined, and unfeignedly fled the business, the people still insisted, and declared that the contention would never be appeased unless he would accede to their wishes; and at length intelligence of these transactions was conveyed to the court. It is said that the Emperor Valentinian prayed, and returned thanks to God that the very man whom he had appointed governor had been chosen to fill a priestly office. When he was informed of the earnest desires of the people and the refusal of Ambrosius, he inferred that events had been so ordered by God for the purpose of restoring peace to the church of Milan, and commanded that Ambrosius should be ordained as quickly as possible.[2] He was initiated and ordained at the same time, and forthwith proceeded to bring the church under his sway to unanimity of opinion concerning the Divine nature; for, while under the guidance of Auxentius, it had long been rent by dissensions on this subject. We shall hereafter have occasion to speak of the conduct of Ambrosius after his ordination, and of the courageous and holy manner in which he discharged the functions of the priesthood.

About this period, the Novatians of Phrygia, contrary to their ancient custom, began to celebrate the festival of the Passover on the same day as the Jews. Novatius, the originator of their heresy, refused to receive those who repented of their sins into communion, and it was in this respect alone that he innovated upon the established doctrine. But he and those who succeeded him celebrated the feast of the Passover after the vernal equinox, according to the custom of the Roman church. Some Novatian bishops, however, assembled about this time at Pazi, a town of Phrygia, near the source of the river Sangarus, and agreeing not to follow, in this point of discipline, the practice of those who differed in doctrine from them, established a new law; they determined upon keeping the feast of unleavened bread, and upon celebrating the Passover on the same days as the Jews. Agelius, the bishop of the Novatians at Constantinople, and the bishops of the Novatians at Nicæa, Nicomedia, and Cotyæum, a noted city of Phrygia, did not take part in this Synod, although the Novatians consider them to be lords and colophons, so to speak, of the transactions affecting their heresy and their churches. How for this reason, these innovators advanced into divergence, and having cut themselves off, formed a separate church, I will speak of at the right time.

CHAP. XXV. — CONCERNING APOLINARIUS: FATHER AND SON OF THAT NAME. VITALIANUS, THE PRESBYTER. ON BEING DISLODGED FROM ONE KIND OF HERESY, THEY INCLINE TO OTHERS.

ABOUT this period, Apolinarius openly devised a heresy, to which his name has since been given.[3] He induced many persons to secede from the Church, and formed separate

---

[1] Ruf. *H. E.* ii. 11; Soc. iv. 28, 30. Cf. Theodoret, *H. E.* iv. 6, 7.

[2] A.D. 374, December.
[3] Ruf. *H. E.* ii. 20; Soc. ii. 46, iii. 16. Cf. Theodoret, *H. E.* v. 3, 4. Soz. has much independent material.

assemblies. Vitalius, a presbyter of Antioch, and one of the priests of Meletius, concurred with him in the confirmation of his peculiar opinion. In other respects, Vitalius was conspicuous in life and conduct, and was zealous in watching over those committed to his pastoral superintendence; hence he was greatly revered by the people. He seceded from communion with Meletius, joined Apolinarius and presided over those at Antioch who had embraced the same opinions; by the sanctity of his life he attracted a great number of followers, who are still called Vitalians by the citizens of Antioch. It is said he was led to secede from the Church from resentment at the contempt that was manifested towards him by Flavian, then one of his fellow-presbyters, but who was afterwards raised to the bishopric of Antioch. Flavian having prevented him from holding his customary interview with the bishop, he fancied himself despised and entered into communion with Apolinarius, and held him as his friend. From that period the members of this sect have formed separate churches in various cities, under their own bishops, and have established laws differing from those of the Catholic Church. Besides the customary sacred order, they sang some metrical songs composed by Apolinarius; for, in addition to his other learning he was a poet, and skilled in a great variety of meters, and by their sweetness he induced many to cleave to him. Men sang his strains at convivial meetings and at their daily labor, and women sang them while engaged at the loom. But, whether his tender poems were adapted for holidays, festivals, or other occasions, they were all alike to the praise and glory of God. Damasus, bishop of Rome, and Peter, bishop of Alexandria, were the first to learn that the heresy was creeping among the people, and at a council held at Rome [1] they voted it to be foreign to the Catholic Church. It is said that it was as much from narrowness of mind as from any other cause that Apolinarius made an innovation in doctrine. For when Athanasius, who administered the church of Alexandria, was on his road back to Egypt from the place whither he had been banished by Constantine, he had to pass through Laodicea, and that while in that city he formed an intimacy with Apolinarius, which terminated in the strictest friendship. As, however, the heterodox considered it disgraceful to hold communion with Athanasius, George, the bishop of the Arians in that city, ejected Apolinarius in a very insulting manner from the church, under the plea that he had received Athanasius contrary to the canons and holy laws. The bishop did not rest here, but reproached him with crimes which he had committed and repented of at a remote period. For when Theodotus, the predecessor of George, regulated the church of Laodicea, Epiphanius, the sophist, recited a hymn which he had composed in honor of Dionysus. Apolinarius, who was then a youth and a pupil of Epiphanius, went to hear the recitation, accompanied by his father, whose name also was Apolinarius, and who was a noted grammarian. After the exordium, Epiphanius, according to the custom always observed at the public recitation of hymns, directed the uninitiated and the profane to go out of doors. But neither Apolinarius the younger nor the elder, nor, indeed, any of the Christians who were present, left the audience. When Theodotus, the bishop, heard that they had been present during the recitation, he was exceedingly displeased; he, however, pardoned the laymen who had committed this error, after they had received a moderate reproof. With respect to Apolinarius, father and son, he convicted them both publicly of their sin, and ejected them from the church; for they both belonged to the clergy, the father being a presbyter, and the son a reader of the Holy Scriptures. After some time had elapsed, and when the father and son had evinced by tears and fasting a degree of repentance adequate to their transgression, Theodotus restored them to their offices in the church. When George received the same bishopric, he excommunicated Apolinarius, and treated him as alien to the Church on account of his having, as before stated, received Athanasius into communion. It is said that Apolinarius besought him repeatedly to restore him to communion, but that he was inexorable. Apolinarius, overcome with grief, disturbed the Church, and by innovations in doctrines introduced the aforesaid heresy; [2] and he thought by means of his eloquence to revenge himself on his enemy by proving that George had deposed one who was more deeply acquainted with the Sacred Scriptures than himself. Thus do the private animosities of the clergy from time to time greatly injure the Church, and divide religion into many heresies. And this is a proof; for had George, like Theodotus, received Apolinarius on his repentance into communion, I believe that we should never have heard of the heresy that bears his name. Men are prone, when loaded with opprobrium and contempt, to resort to rivalries and innovations; whereas when treated with justice, they become moderate, and remain in the same position.

CHAP. XXVI. — EUNOMIUS AND HIS TEACHER AETIUS, THEIR AFFAIRS AND DOCTRINES. THEY WERE

---

[1] Held A.D. 377 (Rade), 374 (Hefele). The letters of Damasus, "Illud sane miramur," "non nobis quidquam," refer to this subject.

[2] Athan. *Tomus ad Antioch.* 7, 8; *Ep. ad Epictetum; De incarnatione Domini nostri Jesu Christi contra Apollinarium.*

THE FIRST WHO BROACHED ONE IMMERSION FOR THE BAPTISM.

ABOUT this time, Eunomius,[1] who had held the church in Cyzicus in place of Eleusius, and who presided over the Arian heresy, devised another heresy besides this, which some have called by his name, but which is sometimes denominated the Anomian heresy. Some assert that Eunomius was the first who ventured to maintain that divine baptism ought to be performed by one immersion, and to corrupt, in this manner, the apostolical tradition which has been carefully handed down to the present day. He invented, it is said, a mode of discipline contrary to that of the Church, and disguised the innovation under gravity and greater severity. He was an artist in words and contentions, and delighted in arguments. The generality of those who entertain his sentiments have the same predilections. They do not applaud a good course of life or manner, or mercy towards the needy, unless exhibited by persons of their own sect, so much as skill in disputation and the power of triumphing in debates. Persons possessed of these accomplishments are accounted pious above all others among them. Others assert, I believe more truthfully, that Theophronius, a native of Cappadocia, and Eutychius, both zealous propagators of this heresy, seceded from communion with Eunomius during the succeeding reign, and innovated about the other doctrines of Eunomius and about the divine baptism. They asserted that baptism ought not to be administered in the name of the Trinity, but in the name of the death of Christ. It appears that Eunomius broached no new opinion on the subject, but was from the beginning firmly attached to the sentiments of Arius, and remained so. After his elevation to the bishopric of Cyzicus, he was accused by his own clergy of introducing innovations in doctrine. Eudoxius, ruler of the Arian heresy at Constantinople, summoned him and obliged him to give an account of his doctrines to the people; finding, however, no fault in him, Eudoxius exhorted him to return to Cyzicus. Eunomius, however, replied, that he could not remain with people who regarded him with suspicion; and, it is said, seized the opportunity for secession, although it seems that, in taking this step he was really actuated by the resentment he felt at the refusal which Aetius, his teacher, had met with, of being received into communion. Eunomius, it is added, dwelt with Aetius, and never deviated from his original sentiments. Such are the conflicting accounts of various individuals; some narrate the circumstances in one way, and some in another. But whether it was Eunomius, or any other person, who first made these innovations upon the tradition of baptism, it seems to me that such innovators, whoever they may have been, were alone in danger, according to their own representation, of quitting this life without having received the divine baptism; for if, after they had been baptized according to the mode recommended from the beginning, they found it impossible to rebaptize themselves, it must be admitted that they introduced a practice to which they had not themselves submitted, and thus undertook to administer to others what had never been administered to them by themselves nor by others. Thus, after having laid down the dogma by some non-existent principle and private assumption, they proceeded to bestow upon others what they had not themselves received. The absurdity of this assumption is manifest from their own confession; for they admit that the uninitiated have not the power to baptize others. Now, according to their opinion, he who has not been baptized in conformity with their tradition is unbaptized as one not properly initiated, and they confirm this opinion by their practice, inasmuch as they rebaptize all those who join their sect, although previously initiated according to the tradition of the Catholic Church. These varying dogmas are the sources of innumerable troubles to religion; and many are deterred from embracing Christianity by the diversity of opinion which prevails in matters of doctrine.

The disputes daily became stronger, and, as in the beginning of heresies, they grew; for they had leaders who were not deficient in zeal or power of words; indeed, it appears that the greater part of the Catholic Church would have been subverted by this heresy, had it not found opponents in Basil and Gregory, the Cappadocians. The reign of Theodosius began a little while after; he banished the founders of heretical sects from the populous parts of the empire to the more desert regions.

But, lest those who read my history should be ignorant of the precise nature of the two heresies to which I have more especially alluded, I think it necessary to state that Aetius, the Syrian, was the originator of the heresy usually attributed to Eunomius; and that, like Arius, he maintained that the Son is dissimilar from the Father, that He is a created being, and was created out of what had no previous existence. Those who held these views were formerly called Aetians; but afterwards, during the reign of Constantius, when, as we have stated, some parties maintained that the Son is consubstantial with the Father, and others that He is like in substance to the Father, and

---

[1] Philost. many sections, especially from vi. to x. 4; he says in iii. 21, that he had written an encomium of Eunomius. Soc. iv. 7, 13, v. 24. The many opinions gathered up by Soz. were probably contributed by Sabinus. There is more original judgment in this chapter than in any other. Cf. the great treatises of Basil and Greg. Nyssa against Eunomius.

when the council of Ariminum had decreed that the Son is only to be considered like unto the Father, Aetius was condemned to banishment, as guilty of impiety and blasphemy against God. For some time subsequently his heresy seemed to have been suppressed; for neither any other man of note, nor even Eunomius, ventured openly upon undertaking its defense. But when Eunomius was raised to the church of Cyzicus in place of Eleusius, he could no longer quietly restrain himself, and in open debate he brought forward again the tenets of Aetius. Hence, as it often happens that the names of the original founders of heretical sects pass into oblivion, the followers of Eunomius were designated by his own name, although he merely renewed the heresy of Aetius, and promulgated it with greater boldness than was done by him who first handed it down.

CHAP. XXVII. — ACCOUNT GIVEN, BY GREGORY THE THEOLOGIAN, OF APOLINARIUS AND EUNOMIUS, IN A LETTER TO NECTARIUS. THEIR HERESY WAS DISTINGUISHED BY THE PHILOSOPHY OF THE MONKS WHO WERE THEN LIVING, FOR THE HERESY OF THESE TWO HELD NEARLY THE ENTIRE EAST.

IT is obvious that Eunomius and Aetius held the same opinions. In several passages of his writings, Eunomius boasts and frequently testifies that Aetius was his instructor. Gregory, bishop of Nazianzen, speaks in the following terms of Apolinarius in a letter addressed to Nectarius, the leader of the church in Constantinople:[1] "Eunomius, who is a constant source of trouble among us, is not content with being a burden to us himself, but would consider himself to blame if he did not strive to drag every one with him to the destruction whither he is hastening. Such conduct, however, may be tolerated in some degree. The most grievous calamity against which the Church has now to struggle arises from the audacity of the Apolinarians. I know not how your Holiness could have agreed that they should be as free to hold meetings as we ourselves. You have been fully instructed by the grace of God, in the Divine mysteries, and not only understand the defense of the Word of God, but also whatever innovations have been made by heretics against the sound faith; yet it may not be amiss for your revered Excellency to hear from our narrowness, that a book written by Apolinarius has fallen into my hands, in which the proposition surpasses all forms of heretical pravity. He affirms that the flesh assumed for the transformation of our nature, under the dispensation of the only begotten Son of God was not acquired for this end; but that this carnal nature existed in the Son from the beginning. He substantiates this evil hypothesis by a misapplication of the following words of Scripture : 'No man hath ascended up into heaven.'[2] He alleges from this text, that Christ was the Son of man before He descended from heaven, and that when He did descend, He brought with Him His own flesh which He had already possessed in heaven which was before the ages and essentially united. He also states another apostolic saying: 'The second man is from heaven.'[3] He, moreover, maintains that the man who came down from heaven was destitute of intellect ($\nu o \hat{v} s$), but that the Deity of the only begotten Son fulfilled the nature of intellect, and constituted the third part of the human compound. The body and soul ($\psi v \chi \dot{\eta}$) formed two parts, as in other men, but there was no intellect, but the Word of God filled the place of intellect. Nor does this end the awful spectacle; for the most grievous point of the heresy is, that he asserts that the only-begotten God, the Judge of all men, the Giver of life, and the Destroyer of death, is Himself subject to death; that He suffered in His own Godhead, and that in the resurrection of the body in the third day, the Godhead also was raised from the dead with the body; and that it was raised again from the dead by the Father. It would take too long to recount all the other extravagant doctrines propounded by these heretics." What I have said may, I think, suffice to show the nature of the sentiments maintained by Apolinarius and Eunomius. If any one desire more detailed information, I can only refer him to the works on the subject written either by them or by others concerning these men. I do not profess easily to understand or to expound these matters, as it seems to me the fact that these dogmas did not prevail and make further advance is to be attributed, in addition to the causes mentioned, especially to the monks of that period; for all those philosophers in Syria, Cappadocia, and the neighboring provinces, were sincerely attached to the Nicene faith. The eastern regions, however, from Cilicia to Phœnicia, were endangered by the heresy of Apolinarius. The heresy of Eunomius was spread from Cilicia and the mountains of Taurus as far as the Hellespont and Constantinople. These two heretics found it easy to attract to their respective parties the persons among whom they dwelt, and those of the neighborhood. But the same fate awaited them that had been experienced by the Arians; for the people admired the monks who manifested their virtue by works and believed that they held right opin-

---

[1] Greg. Naz. *Ep.* ccii., quoted in part.   [2] John iii. 13.   [3] 1 Cor. xv. 47.

ions, while they turned away from those who held other opinions, as impious and as holding spurious doctrines. In the same way the Egyptians were led by the monks to oppose the Arians.

CHAP. XXVIII. — OF THE HOLY MEN WHO FLOUR-
ISHED AT THIS PERIOD IN EGYPT. JOHN, OR,
AMON,[1] BENUS, THEONAS, COPRES, HELLES,
ELIAS, APELLES, ISIDORE, SERAPION, DIOSCORUS,
AND EULOGIUS.

As this period was distinguished by many holy men,[2] who devoted themselves to a life of philosophy, it seems requisite to give some account of them, for in that time there flourished a very great abundance of men beloved of God. There was not, it appears, a more celebrated man in Egypt than John. He had received from God the power of discerning the future and the most hidden things as clearly as the ancient prophets, and he had, moreover, the gift of healing those who suffered with incurable afflictions and diseases. Or was another eminent man of this period; he had lived in solitude from his earliest youth, occupying himself continually in singing the praises of God. He subsisted on herbs and roots, and his drink was water, when he could find it. In his old age he went, by the command of God, to Thebaïs, where he presided over several monasteries, nor was he without part in divine works. By means of prayer alone he expelled diseases and devils. He knew nothing of letters, nor did he need books to support his memory; for whatever he received into his mind was never afterwards forgotten.

Ammon, the leader of the monks called Tabennesiotians, dwelt in the same region, and was followed by about three thousand disciples. Benus and Theonas likewise presided over monastic orders, and possessed the gift of foreknowledge and of prophecy. It is said that though Theonas was versed in all the learning of the Egyptians, the Greeks, and the Romans, he practiced silence for the space of thirty years. Benus was never seen to manifest any signs of anger, and never heard to swear, or to utter a false, a vain, a rash, or a useless word.

Copres, Helles, and Elias also flourished at this period. It is said that Copres had received from God the power of healing sickness and divers diseases, and of overcoming demons. Helles had from his youth upwards been trained in the monastic life, and he wrought many wonderful works. He could carry fire in his bosom without burning his clothes. He excited

his fellow-monks to the practice of virtue by representing that with a good conduct, the display of miracles would follow. Elias, who practiced philosophy near the city of Antinoüs, was at this period about a hundred and ten years of age; before this he said he had passed seventy years alone in the desert. Notwithstanding his advanced age, he was unremitting in the practice of fasting and courageous discipline.

Apelles flourished at the same period, and performed numerous miracles in the Egyptian monasteries, near the city of Acoris. He at one time worked as a smith, for this was his trade; and one night the devil undertook to tempt him to incontinence, by appearing before him in the form of a beautiful woman; Apelles, however, seized the iron which was heating in the furnace, and burnt the face of the devil, who screamed like a wild bird and ran away.

Isidore, Serapion, and Dioscorus, at this period, were among the most celebrated fathers of the monks. Isidore caused his monastery to be closed, so that no one could obtain egress or ingress, and supplied the wants of those within the walls. Serapion lived in the neighborhood of Arsenoites, and had about a thousand monks under his guidance. He taught all to earn their provisions by their labors and to provide for others who were poor. During harvest-time they busied themselves in reaping for pay; they set aside sufficient corn for their own use, and shared it with the rest of the monks. Dioscorus had not more than a hundred disciples; he was a presbyter, and applied himself with great exactness to the duties of his priesthood; he examined and carefully questioned those who presented themselves as candidates for participation in the holy mysteries, so that they might purify their minds and not be without a consciousness of any evil they might have committed. The presbyter Eulogius was still more scrupulous in the dispensation of the Divine mysteries. It is said that, when he was officiating in the priestly office, he could discern what was in the minds of those who came to him, so that he could clearly detect sin, and the secret thoughts of each one of his audience. He excluded from the altar all who had perpetrated crime or formed evil resolutions, and publicly convicted them of sin; but, on their purifying themselves by repentance, he again received them into communion.

CHAP. XXIX. — CONCERNING THE MONKS OF THE-
BAÏS : APOLLOS, DOROTHEUS ; CONCERNING PIAM-
MON, JOHN, MARK, MACARIUS, APOLLODORUS,
MOSES, PAUL, WHO WAS IN FERMA, PACHO,
STEPHEN, AND PIOR.

---

[1] Ammon in the text.
[2] This chapter is probably built on Timothy, bishop of Alexandria's collection; see next chapter. Cf. Ruf. *H. M.*, with whose order it agrees better than with the series in Palladius, *H. L.;* cf. Ruf. *H. E.* ii. 8.

Apollos flourished about the same period in Thebaïs. He early devoted himself to a life of philosophy; and after having passed forty years in the desert, he shut himself up, by the command of God, in a cave formed at the foot of a mountain, near a very populous district. By the multitude of his miracles, he soon became distinguished, and was the head of many monks; for he directed them profitably by his instructions. Timothy, who conducted the church of Alexandria, has given us a history of his method of discipline and of what divine and marvelous deeds he was a worker; he also narrates the lives of other approved monks, many of whom I have mentioned.[1]

In that time many good monks, to the number of about two thousand, preached philosophy in the neighborhood of Alexandria; some in a district called the Hermitage, and others more towards Mareotis and Libya. Dorotheus, a native of Thebes, was among the most celebrated of these monks. He spent the day in collecting stones upon the seashore, which he used in erecting cells to be given to those who were unable to build them. During the night, he employed himself in weaving baskets of palm leaves; and these he sold, to obtain the means of subsistence. He ate six ounces of bread with a few vegetables daily, and drank nothing but water. Having accustomed himself to this extreme abstinence from his youth, he continued to observe it in old age. He was never seen to recline on a mat or a bed, nor even to place his limbs in an easy attitude, or willingly to surrender himself to sleep. Sometimes, from natural lassitude, his eyes would involuntarily close when he was at his daily labor or his meals; and when nodding during his eating, the food would fall from his mouth. One day, being utterly overcome by drowsiness, he fell down on the mat; he was displeased at finding himself in this position, and said, in an undertone of voice, "If angels are persuaded to sleep, you will persuade also the zealous." Perhaps he might have said this to himself, or perhaps to the demon who had become an impediment to his zealous exercises. He was once asked by a person who came to him while he was exhausting himself, why he destroyed his body. "Because it destroys me," was his reply.

Piammon and John presided over two celebrated Egyptian monasteries near Diolcus. They were presbyters who discharged their priesthood very carefully and reverently. It is said that one day, when Piammon was officiating as priest, he beheld an angel standing near the holy table and writing down in a book the names of the monks who were present, while he erased the names of those who were absent. John had received from God such power over sufferings and diseases, that he healed the gouty and restored the paralytic.

A very old man, named Benjamin, was practicing philosophy very brilliantly about this period, in the desert near Scetis. God had bestowed upon him the power of relieving the sick of every disease without medicine, by the touch only of his hand, or by means of a little oil consecrated by prayer. The story is, that he was attacked by a dropsy, and his body was swollen to such a size that it became necessary, in order to carry him from his cell, to enlarge the door. As his malady would not admit of his lying in a recumbent posture, he remained, during eight months, seated on a very large skin, and continued to heal the sick, without regretting that his own recovery was not effected. He comforted those who came to visit him, and requested them to pray for his soul; adding that he cared little for his body, for it had been of no service to him when in health, and could not, now that it was diseased, be of any injury to him.

About the same time the celebrated Mark, Marcarius the younger, Apollonius, and Moses, an Egyptian, dwelt at Scetis. It is said that Mark was, from his youth upwards, distinguished by extreme mildness and prudence; he committed the Sacred Scriptures to memory, and manifested such eminent piety that Macarius himself, the presbyter of Celliæ,[2] declared that he had never given to him what priests present to the initiated at the holy table, but that an angel administered it to him whose hand up to the forearm he declares himself to have seen.

Macarius had received from God the power of dispelling demons. A murder which he had unintentionally committed was the original cause of his embracing a life of philosophy. He was a shepherd, and led his flock to graze on the banks of Lake Mareotis, when in sport he slew one of his companions. Fearful of being delivered up to justice, he fled to the desert. Here he concealed himself during three years, and afterwards erected a small dwelling on the spot, in which he dwelt twenty-five years. He was accustomed to say that he owed much to the calamity that had befallen him in early life, and even called the unintentional murder he had committed a salutary deed, inasmuch as it had been the cause of his embracing philosophy and a blessed mode of life.

Apollonius, after passing his life in the pursuits of commerce, retired in his old age to Scetis. On reflecting that he was too old to

---

[1] Here we learn that Timothy furnished the storehouse for this monastic biography. The stories of this chapter are probably also borrowed from him, at least in part. There is a more conspicuous divergence from Palladius and Rufinus.

[2] Ruf. *H. M.* 22; the place was thus named from the number of cells located there.

learn writing or any other art, he purchased with his own money a supply of every kind of drug, and of food suited for the sick, some of which he carried until the ninth hour to the door of every monastery, for the relief of those who were suffering from disease. Finding this practice advantageous to himself, he adopted this mode of life; and when he felt death approaching he delivered his drugs to one whom he exhorted to go and do as he had done.

Moses was originally a slave, but was driven from his master's house on account of his immorality. He joined some robbers, and became leader of the band. After having perpetrated many evil deeds and dared some murders, by some sudden conversion he embraced the monastic life, and attained the highest point of philosophy. As the healthful and vigorous habit of body which had been induced by his former avocations acted as a stimulus to his imagination and excited a desire for pleasure, he resorted to every possible means of macerating his body; thus, he subsisted on a little bread without cooked food, subjected himself to severe labor, and prayed fifty times daily; he prayed standing, without bending his knees or closing his eyes in sleep. He sometimes went during the night to the cells of the monks and secretly filled their pitchers with water, and this was very laborious, for he had sometimes to go ten, sometimes twenty, and sometimes thirty and more, stadia in quest of water. Notwithstanding all his efforts to macerate his body, it was long before he could subdue his natural vigor of constitution. It is reported that robbers once broke into the dwelling where he was practicing philosophy; he seized and bound them, threw the four men across his shoulders, and bore them to the church, that the monks who were there assembled might deal with them as they thought fit, for he did not consider himself authorized to punish any one. For they say so sudden a conversion from vice to virtue was never before witnessed, nor such rapid attainments in monastical philosophy. Hence God rendered him an object of dread to the demons, and he was ordained presbyter over the monks at Scetis. After a life spent in this manner, he died at the age of seventy-five, leaving behind him numerous eminent disciples.

Paul, Pachon, Stephen, and Moses, of whom the two latter were Libyans, and Pior, who was an Egyptian, flourished during this reign. Paul dwelt at Ferme, a mountain of Scetis, and presided over five hundred ascetics. He did not labor with his hands, neither did he receive alms of any one, except such food as was necessary for his subsistence. He did nothing but pray, and daily offered up to God three hundred prayers. He placed three hundred pebbles in his bosom, for fear of omitting any of these prayers; and, at the conclusion of each, he took away one of the pebbles. When there were no pebbles remaining, he knew that he had gone through the whole course of his prescribed prayers.

Pachon also flourished during this period at Scetis. He followed this career from youth to extreme old age, without ever being found unmanly in self-control by the appetites of the body, the passions of the soul, or a demon, — in short, in all those things which the philosopher should conquer.

Stephen dwelt at Mareotis near Marmarica. During sixty years, through exactness, he attained the perfection of asceticism, became very noted as a monk, and was intimate with Antony the Great. He was very mild and prudent, and his usual style of conversation was sweet and profitable, and well calculated to comfort the souls of the afflicted, to transform them into good spirits, if even they had previously been depressed by griefs which seemed necessary. He behaved similarly about his own afflictions. He was troubled with a severe and incurable ulcer, and surgeons were employed to operate upon the diseased members. During the operation Stephen employed himself in weaving palm leaves, and exhorted those who were around him not to concern themselves about his sufferings. He told them to have no other thought than that God does nothing but for our good, and that his affliction would tend to his real welfare, inasmuch as it would perhaps atone for his sins, it being better to be judged in this life than in the life to come.

Moses was celebrated for his meekness, his love, and his power of healing of sufferings by prayer. Pior determined, from his youth, to devote himself to a life of philosophy; and, with this view, quitted his father's house after having made a vow that he would never again look upon any of his relations. After fifty years had expired, one of his sisters heard that he was still alive, and she was so transported with joy at this unexpected intelligence, that she could not rest till she had seen him. The bishop of the place where she resided was so affected by the groans and tears of the aged woman, that he wrote to the leaders of the monks in the desert of Scetis, desiring them to send Pior to him. The superiors accordingly directed him to repair to the city of his birth, and he could not say nay, for disobedience was regarded as unlawful by the monks of Egypt, and I think also by other monks. He went with another monk to the door of his father's house, and caused himself to be announced. When he heard the door being opened, he closed his eyes, and calling his sister by name, he said to her, " I am Pior, your brother; look at me as much as you please."

His sister was delighted beyond measure at again beholding him, and returned thanks to God. He prayed at the door where he stood, and then returned to the place where he lived; there he dug a well, and found that the water was bitter, but he persevered in the use of it till his death. Then the height to which he had carried his self-denial was known; for after he died, several attempted to practice philosophy in the place where he had dwelt, but found it impossible to remain there. I am convinced that, had it not been for the principles of philosophy which he had espoused, he could easily have changed the water to a sweet taste by prayer; for he caused water to flow in a spot where none had existed previously. It is said that some monks, under the guidance of Moses, undertook to dig a well, but the expected vein did not appear, nor did any depth yield the water, and they were about to abandon the task, when, about midday, Pior joined them; he first embraced them, and then rebuked their want of faith and littleness of soul; he then descended into the pit they had excavated; and, after engaging in prayer, struck the ground thrice with a rod. A spring of water soon after rose to the surface, and filled the whole excavation. After prayer, Pior departed; and though the monks urged him to break his fast with them, he refused, alleging that he had not been sent to them for that purpose, but merely in order to perform the act he had effected.[1]

CHAP. XXX. — MONKS OF SCETIS: ORIGEN, DIDYMUS, CRONION, ORSISIUS, PUTUBATUS, ARSION, SERAPION, AMMON, EUSEBIUS, AND DIOSCORUS, THE BRETHREN·WHO ARE CALLED LONG, AND EVAGRIUS THE PHILOSOPHER.

AT this period, Origen, one of the disciples of Antony the Great, was still living at a great age, in the monasteries of Scetis.[2] Also, Didymus, and Cronion, who was about one hundred and ten years of age, Arsisius the Great, Putubatus, Arsion, and Serapion, all of whom had been contemporary with Antony the Great. They had grown old in the exercise of philosophy, and were at this period presiding over the monasteries. There were some holy men among them who were young and middle aged, but who were celebrated for their excellent and good qualities. Among these were Ammonius, Eusebius, and Dioscorus. They were brothers, but on account of their height of stature were called the "Long Brothers."[3] It is said that Ammon

attained the summit of philosophy, and consequently overcame the love of ease and pleasure. He was very studious, and had read the works of Origen, of Didymus, and of other ecclesiastical writers. From his youth to the day of his death he never tasted anything, with the exception of bread, that had been prepared by means of fire. He was once chosen to be ordained bishop; and after urging every argument that could be devised in rejection of the honor, but in vain, he cut off one of his ears, and said to those who had come for him, "Go away. Henceforward the priestly law forbids my ordination, for the person of a priest should be perfect." Those who had been sent for him accordingly departed; but, on ascertaining that the Church does not observe the Jewish law in requiring a priest to be perfect in all his members, but merely requires him to be irreprehensible in point of morals, they returned to Ammon, and endeavored to take him by force. He protested to them that, if they attempted any violence against him, he would cut out his tongue; and, terrified at this menace, they immediately took their departure. Ammon was ever after surnamed Parotes. Some time afterwards, during the ensuing reign, the wise Evagrius formed an intimacy with him. Evagrius[4] was a wise man, powerful in thought and in word, and skillful in discerning the arguments which led to virtue and to vice, and capable in urging others to imitate the one, and to eschew the other. His eloquence is fully attested by the works he has left behind him.[5] With respect to his moral character, it is said that he was totally free from all pride or superciliousness, so that he was not elated when just commendations were awarded him, nor displeased when unjust reproaches were brought against him. He was a citizen of Iberia, near the Euxine. He had philosophized and studied the Sacred Scriptures under Gregory, bishop of Nazianzen, and had filled the office of archdeacon when Gregory administered the church in Constantinople. He was handsome in person, and careful in his mode of attire; and hence an acquaintanceship he had formed with a certain lady excited the jealousy of her husband, who plotted his death. While the plot was about being carried forward into deed, God sent him while sleeping, a fearful and saving vision in a dream. It appeared to him that he had been arrested in the act of committing some crime, and that he was bound hand and foot in irons. As he was being led before the magistrates to receive the sentence of condemnation, a man who held in his hand the book of the Holy Gospels addressed him, and promised to deliver him from his bonds, and confirmed this

---

[1] See another story of Pior in Soc. iv. 23.
[2] This chapter may have its basis in the collection of Timothy. Cf. Palladius, *H. L.*, for some of the biographies.
[3] Cf. viii. 12 sqq.

[4] Cf. also Soc. iv. 23.   [5] PGM. xl.

with an oath, provided he would quit the city. Evagrius touched the book, and made oath that he would do so. Immediately his chains appeared to fall off, and he awoke. He was convinced by this divine dream, and fled the danger. He resolved upon devoting himself to a life of asceticism, and proceeded from Constantinople to Jerusalem. Some time after he went to visit the philosophers of Scetis, and gladly determined to live there.

CHAP. XXXI. — CONCERNING THE MONKS OF NITRIA, AND THE MONASTERIES CALLED CELLS; ABOUT THE ONE IN RHINOCORURA; ABOUT MELAS, DIONYSIUS, AND SOLON.

THEY call this place Nitria. It is inhabited by a great number of persons devoted to a life of philosophy, and derives its name from its vicinity to a village in which nitre is gathered. It contains about fifty monasteries, built tolerably near to each other, some of which are inhabited by monks who live together in society, and others by monks who have adopted a solitary mode of existence. More in the interior of the desert, about seventy stadia from this locality, is another place called Cellia,[1] throughout which numerous little dwellings are dispersed hither and thither, and hence its name; but at such a distance that those who dwell in them can neither see nor hear each other. They assemble together on the first and last days of each week; and if any monk happen to be absent, it is evident that he has been left behind involuntarily, having been hindered by suffering some disease; they do not all go immediately to see and nurse him, but each one in turn at different times, and bearing whatever each has suitable for disease. Except for such a cause, they seldom converse together, unless, indeed, there be one among them capable of communicating further knowledge concerning God and the salvation of the soul. Those who dwell in the cells are those who have attained the summit of philosophy, and who are therefore able to regulate their own conduct, to live alone, and are separated from the others for the sake of quietude. This is what I had briefly to state concerning Scetis and its philosophers. Some one would probably censure my writing as prolix, were I to enter into further details concerning their mode of life; for they have established individual courses of life, labors, customs, exercises, abstinence, and time, divided naturally according to the age of the individual.

Rhinocorura was also celebrated at this period, an account of the holy men, not from abroad, but who were natives of the place. I have heard[2] that the most eminent philosophers among them were Melas, who then administered the church of the country; Dionysius, who presided over a monastery situated to the north of the city; and Solon, the brother and successor to the bishopric of Melas. It is said that when the decree for the ejection of all priests opposed to Arianism was issued, the officers appointed to apprehend Melas found him engaged as the lowest servant, in trimming the lights of the church, with a girdle soiled with oil on his cloak, and carrying the wicks. When they asked him for the bishop, he replied that he was within, and that he would conduct them to him. As they were fatigued with their journey, he led them to the episcopal dwelling, made them sit down at table, and gave them to eat of such things as he had. After the repast, he supplied them with water to wash their hands; for he served the guests, and then told them who he was. Amazed at his conduct, they confessed the mission on which they had arrived; but from respect to him, gave him full liberty to go wherever he would. He, however, replied that he would not shrink from the sufferings to which the other bishops who maintained the same sentiments as himself were exposed, and that he was willing to go into exile. Having philosophized from his youth, he had exercised himself in all the monastic virtues.

Solon quitted the pursuits of commerce to embrace a monastic life, a measure which tended greatly to his welfare; for under the instruction of his brother and other ascetics, he progressed rapidly in piety towards God, and in goodness towards his neighbor. The church of Rhinocorura having been thus, from the beginning, under the guidance of such exemplary bishops, never afterwards swerved from their precepts, and produced good men. The clergy of this church dwell in one house, sit at the same table, and have everything in common.

CHAP. XXXII. — MONKS OF PALESTINE: HESYCAS, EPIPHANIUS, WHO WAS AFTERWARDS IN CYPRUS, AMMONIUS, AND SILVANUS.

MANY monastical institutions flourished in Palestine.[3] Many of those whom I enumerated under the reign of Constantius were still cultivating the science. They and their associates attained the summit of philosophical perfection, and added still greater reputation to their monasteries; and among them Hesycas,[4] a companion of Hilarion, and Epiphanius, afterwards bishop of Salamis in Cyprus, deserve to be particularly noticed. Hesycas devoted himself to a life of

---

[1] See above, note on c. 29. For Nitria and Cellia, see Ruf. H. M. 21, 22; Pallad. H. L. 69.

[2] This is independent.
[3] This chapter is probably derived from local Palestinian biographies familiar to him as a native.
[4] Hesychius, Hieron. Vit. Hil.

philosophy in the same locality where his master had formerly resided; and Epiphanius[1] fixed his abode near the village of Besauduc, which was his birthplace, in the government of Eleutheropolis. Having been instructed from his youth by the most celebrated ascetics, and having on this account passed the most of his time in Egypt, Epiphanius became most celebrated in Egypt and Palestine by his attainments in monastic philosophy, and was chosen by the inhabitants of Cyprus to act as bishop of the metropolis of their island. Hence he is, I think, the most revered man under the whole heaven, so to speak; for he fulfilled his priesthood in the concourse of a large city and in a seaport; and when he threw himself into civil affairs, he conducted them with so much virtue that he became known in a little while to all citizens and every variety of foreigner; to some, because they had seen the man himself, and had experience of his manner of living; and to others, who had learned it from these spectators. Before he went to Cyprus, he resided for some time, during the present reign, in Palestine.

At the same period in the monasteries, Salamines, Phuscon, Malachion, and Crispion, four brethren, were highly distinguished: they practiced philosophy near Bethelia, a village of Gaza; they were of a resident noble family, and had been instructed in philosophy by Hilarion. It is related that the brothers were once journeying homewards, when Malachion was suddenly snatched away and became invisible; soon afterwards, however, he reappeared and continued the journey with his brothers. He did not long survive this occurrence, but died in the flower of his youth. He was not behind men of advanced age in the philosophy of virtuous life and of piety.

Ammonius lived at a distance of ten stadia from those last mentioned; he dwelt near Capharcobra, the place of his birth, a town of Gaza. He was very exact and courageous in carrying through asceticism. I think that Silvanus, a native of Palestine, to whom, on account of his high virtue, an angel was once seen to minister, practiced philosophy about the same time in Egypt. Then he lived at Mount Sinai, and afterwards founded at Gerari, in the wady, a very extensive and most noted cœnobium for many good men, over which the excellent Zacharias subsequently presided.

CHAP. XXXIII. — MONKS OF SYRIA AND PERSIA: BATTHEUS, EUSEBIUS, BARGES, HALAS, ABBO, LAZARUS, ABDALEUS, ZENO, HELIODORUS, EUSEBIUS OF CARRÆ, PROTOGENES, AND AONES.

LET us pass thence to Syria and Persia,[2] the parts adjacent to Syria. We shall find that the monks of these countries emulated those of Egypt in the practice of philosophy. Battheus, Eusebius, Barges, Halas, Abbos, Lazarus, who attained the episcopal dignity, Abdaleus, Zeno, and Heliodorus, flourished in Nisibis, near the mountain called Sigoron. When they first entered upon the philosophic career, they were denominated shepherds, because they had no houses, ate neither bread nor meat, and drank no wine; but dwelt constantly on the mountains, and passed their time in praising God by prayers and hymns, according to the law of the Church. At the usual hours of meals, they each took a sickle, and went to the mountain to cut some grass on the mountains, as though they were flocks in pasture; and this served for their repast. Such was their course of philosophy. Eusebius voluntarily shut himself up in a cell to philosophize, near Carræ.[3] Protogenes dwelt in the same locality, and ruled the church there after Vitus who was then bishop. This is the celebrated Vitus of whom they say that when the Emperor Constantine first saw him, he confessed that God had frequently shown this man in appearances to him and enjoined him to obey implicitly what he should say. Aones had a monastery in Phadana; this was the spot where Jacob, the grandson of Abraham, on his journey from Palestine, met the damsel whom he afterwards married, and where he rolled away the stone, that her flock might drink of the water of the well. It is said that Aones was the first who introduced the life apart from all men, and the severe philosophy into Syria, just as it was first introduced by Antony into Egypt.

CHAP. XXXIV. — MONKS OF EDESSA: JULIANUS, EPHRAIM SYRUS, BARUS, AND EULOGIUS; FURTHER, THE MONKS OF CŒLE-SYRIA: VALENTINUS, THEODORE, MEROSAS, BASSUS, BASSONIUS; AND THE HOLY MEN OF GALATIA AND CAPPADOCIA, AND ELSEWHERE; WHY THOSE SAINTS UNTIL RECENTLY WERE LONG-LIVED.

GADDANAS and Azizus dwelt with Aones, and emulated his virtues.[4] Ephraim the Syrian, who was an historian, and has been noticed[5] in our own recital of events under the reign of Constantius, was the most renowned philosopher in this time, together with Julian, in the neighborhood of Edessa and its adjacent regions. Barses[6] and Eulogius were both, at a later period than that to which we are referring, ordained

---

[2] Again, presumably, from Syrian biographies. Theodoret, *H. E.* iv. 28, has but one identical name; and the same is true of his *Historia Religiosa.* Battheus, Halas, and Heliodorus are repeated in the following chapter.
[3] Cf. Basil, *Ep.* cclv.
[4] From Syrian biographies.
[5] See above, iii. 14, 16.
[6] Basil, *Ep.* cclxvii.

bishops, but not of any city; for the title was merely an honorary one, conferred on them as a compensation for their excellent conduct; and they were ordained in their own monasteries. Lazarus, to whom we have already alluded, was ordained bishop in the same manner. Such were the most celebrated philosophers of asceticism who flourished in Syria, Persia, and the neighboring countries, so far, at least, as I have been able to ascertain. The course common to all, so to speak, consisted in diligent attention to the state of the soul, which by means of fasting, prayer, and hymns to God, they kept in constant preparation to quit the things of this world. They devoted the greater part of their time to these holy exercises, and they wholly despised worldly possessions, temporal affairs, and the ease and adornment of the body. Some of the monks carried their self-denial to an extraordinary height. Battheus, for instance, by excessive abstinence and fasting, had worms crawl from his teeth; Halas, again, had not tasted bread for eighty years; and Heliodorus passed many nights without yielding to sleep, and added thereto seven days of fasting.

Although Cœle-Syria and Upper Syria, with the exception of the city of Antioch, was slowly converted to Christianity, it was not lacking in ecclesiastical philosophers, whose conduct appeared the more heroic from their having to encounter the enmity and hatred of the inhabitants of the place. And they nobly refrained from resistance, or resorting to the law, but spiritedly endured the insults and blows inflicted by the pagans. Such, I found, was the course pursued by Valentian, who, according to some accounts, was born at Emesa, but according to others, at Arethusa. Another individual of the same name distinguished himself by similar conduct, as likewise Theodore. Both were from Titti, which is of the nome of the Apameans; not less distinguished were Marosas, a native of Nechilis, Bassus, Bassones, and Paul. This latter was from the village of Telmison. He founded many communities in many places, and introduced the method essential to the knowledge of philosophy, and finally established the greatest and most distinguished community of monks in a place called Jugatum. Here, after a long and honorable life, he died, and was interred. Some of the monks who have practiced philosophy in a distinguished and divine way have survived to our own days; indeed, most of those to whom allusion has been made enjoyed a very long term of existence; and I am convinced that God added to the length of their days for the express purpose of furthering the interests of religion. They were instrumental in leading nearly the whole Syrian nation, and most of the Persians and Saracens, to the proper religion, and caused them to cease from

paganism. After beginning the monastic philosophy there, they brought forward many like themselves.

I suppose that Galatia, Cappadocia, and the neighboring provinces contained many other ecclesiastical philosophers at that time, for these regions formerly had zealously embraced our doctrine. These monks, for the most part, dwelt in communities in cities and villages, for they did not habituate themselves to the tradition of their predecessors. The severity of the winter, which is always a natural feature of that country, would probably make a hermit life impracticable. Leontius and Prapidius were, I understand, the most celebrated of these monks. The former afterwards administered the church of Ancyra, and the latter, a man of very advanced age, performed the episcopal functions in several villages. He also presided over the Basileias, the most celebrated hospice for the poor. It was established by Basil, bishop of Cæsarea, from whom it received its name in the beginning, and retains it until to-day.

CHAP. XXXV. — THE WOODEN TRIPOD AND THE SUCCESSION OF THE EMPEROR, THROUGH A KNOWLEDGE OF ITS LETTERS. DESTRUCTION OF THE PHILOSOPHERS; ASTRONOMY.

SUCH is the information which I have been enabled to collect concerning the ecclesiastical philosophers of that time. As to the pagans, they were nearly all exterminated about the period to which we have been referring.[1] Some among them, who were reputed to excel in philosophy, and who viewed with extreme displeasure the progress of the Christian religion, were devising who would be the successor of Valens on the throne of the Roman Empire, and resorted to every variety of mantic art for the purpose of attaining this insight into futurity. After various incantations, they constructed a tripod of laurel wood, and they wound up with the invocations and words to which they are accustomed; so that the name of the emperor might be shown by the collection of letters which were indicated, letter by letter, through the machinery of the tripod and the prophecy. They were gaping with open mouth for Theodore, a man who held a distinguished military appointment in the palace. He was a pagan and a learned man. The disposition of the letters, coming as far as the delta of his name, deceived the philosophers. They hence expected that Theodore would very soon be the emperor. When their undertaking was informed upon, Valens was as unbearably incensed, as if a conspiracy had been formed against his safety.

---

[1] Philost. ix. 15; Eunap. *Fragm.* ii. 32, 33; Am. Marcel. xxix. 1. 29–44; Zos. iv. 13; Soc. iv. 19.

Therefore all were arrested ; Theodore and the constructors of the tripod were commanded to be put to death, some with fire, others with the sword. Likewise for the same reason the most brilliant philosophers of the empire were slain ; since the wrath of the emperor was unchecked, the death penalty advanced even to those who were not philosophers, but who wore garments similar to theirs ; hence those who applied themselves to other pursuits would not clothe themselves with the crocotium or tribonium, on account of the suspicion and fear of danger, so that they might not seem to be pursuing magic and sorcery. I do not in the least think that the emperor will be more blamed by right-thinking people for such wrath and cruelty than the philosophers, for their rashness and their unphilosophical undertaking. The emperor, absurdly supposing that he could put his successor to death, spared neither those who had prophesied nor the subject of their prophecy, as they say he did not spare those who bore the same name of Theodore, — and some were men of distinction, — whether they were precisely the same or similar in beginning with θ and ending with δ. The philosophers, on the other hand, acted as if the deposition and restoration of emperors had depended solely on them ; for if the imperial succession was to be considered dependent on the arrangement of the stars, what was requisite but to await the accession of the future emperor, whoever he might be ? or if the succession was regarded as dependent on the will of God, what right had man to meddle ? For it is not the function of human foreknowledge or zeal to understand God's thought ; nor if it were right, would it be well for men, even if they be the wisest of all, to think that they can plan better than God. If it were merely from rash curiosity to discern the things of futurity that they showed such lack of judgment as to be ready to be caught in danger, and to despise the laws anciently established among the Romans, and at a time when it was not dangerous to conduct pagan worship and to sacrifice ; in this they thought differently from Socrates ; for when unjustly condemned to drink poison, he refused to save himself by violating the laws in which he had been born and educated, nor would he escape from prison, although it was in his power to do so.

CHAP. XXXVI. — EXPEDITION AGAINST THE SARMATIANS ; DEATH OF VALENTINIAN IN ROME ; VALENTINIAN THE YOUNGER PROCLAIMED ; PERSECUTION OF THE PRIESTS ; ORATION OF THE PHILOSOPHER THEMISTIUS, ON ACCOUNT OF WHICH VALENS WAS DISPOSED TO TREAT THOSE WHO DIFFERED FROM HIM MORE HUMANELY.

SUCH subjects as the above, however, are best left to the examination and decision of individual judgment.

The Sarmatians [1] having invaded the western parts of the empire, Valentinian levied an army to oppose them. As soon, however, as they heard of the number and strength of the troops raised against them, they sent an embassy to solicit peace. When the ambassadors were ushered into the presence of Valentinian, he asked them whether all the Sarmatians were similar to them. On their replying that the principal men of the nation had been selected to form the embassy, the emperor exclaimed, in great fury, " A terrible thing do our subjects endure, and a calamity is surrounding the Roman government, if the Sarmatians, a barbarous race, of whom these are your best men, do not love to abide by themselves, but are emboldened to invade my government, and presume to make war at all against the Romans." He spoke in this strain for some time in a very high pitch of voice, and his rage was so violent and so unbounded, that at length he burst simultaneously a blood-vessel and an artery. He lost, in consequence, a great quantity of blood, and expired soon after in a fortress of Gaul.[2] He was about fifty-four years of age, and had, during thirteen years, guided the reins of government with good results and much distinction. Six days after his death his youngest son, who bore the same name as himself, was proclaimed emperor by the soldiers ; and soon afterwards Valens and Gratian, his brother, formally assented to this election, although they were at first irritated at the soldiers having transferred the symbols of government to him without their previous consent.

During this period Valens had fixed his residence at Antioch in Syria, and became more hostile to those who differed from him in opinion concerning the divine nature, and he vexed them more severely and persecuted them. The philosopher Themistius pronounced an oration in his presence, in which he admonished him that he ought not to wonder at the dissension concerning ecclesiastical doctrines, for it was more moderate and less than among the pagans, for the opinions among them are multiform ; and that, in the number of dogmas leading to perpetual disputes, necessarily the difference about them makes more contentions and discussions ; and accordingly it might probably be pleasing to God not to be so easily known, and to have a divergence of opinion, so that each might fear Him the rather, since an accurate knowledge of Him is so unattainable. And in the attempt to summarize this vastness, one would tend to conclude how great He is and how good He is.[3]

[1] Soc. iv. 31, 32; Ruf. *H. E.* ii. 12; Philost. ix. 16.
[2] Am. Marcel. xxx. 6, 1–4; Zos. iv. 17; Orosius, vii. 32.
[3] The extant oration, xii., on this theme was addressed to Valens at an earlier date.

CHAP. XXXVII. — CONCERNING THE BARBARIANS BE-
YOND THE DANUBE, WHO WERE DRIVEN OUT BY
THE HUNS, AND ADVANCED TO THE ROMANS, AND
THEIR CONVERSION TO CHRISTIANITY; ULPHILAS
AND ATHANARICHUS; OCCURRENCES BETWEEN
THEM; WHENCE THE GOTHS RECEIVED ARIANISM.

THIS remarkable oration of Themistius disposed the emperor to be somewhat more
humane, and the punishments became in consequence less severe than before. He would
not have wholly withdrawn his wrath from the
priests unless the anxieties of public affairs had
supervened, and not permitted him to pursue
them further.[1] For the Goths, who inhabited
the regions beyond the Ister, and had conquered
other barbarians, having been vanquished and
driven from their country by the Huns, had
passed over into the Roman boundaries. The
Huns, it is said, were unknown to the Thracians
of the Ister and the Goths before this period;
for though they were dwelling secretly near to
one another, a lake of vast extent was between
them, and the inhabitants on each side of the
lake respectively imagined that their own country was situated at the extremity of the earth,
and that there was nothing beyond them but
the sea and water. It so happened, however,
that an ox, tormented by insects, plunged into
the lake, and was pursued by the herdsman;
who, perceiving for the first time that the opposite bank was inhabited, made known the circumstance to his fellow-tribesmen. Some, however,
relate that a stag was fleeing, and showed some of
the hunters who were of the race of the Huns the
way which was concealed superficially by the
water. On arriving at the opposite bank, the hunters were struck with the beauty of the country, the
serenity of the air, and the adaptedness for cultivation; and they reported what they had seen
to their king. The Huns then made an attempt
to attack the Goths with a few soldiers; but they
afterwards raised a powerful army, conquered
the Goths in battle, and took possession of their
whole country. The vanquished nation, being
pursued by their enemies, crossed over into the
Roman territories. They passed over the river,
and dispatched an embassy to the emperor,
assuring him of their co-operation in any warfare in which he might engage, provided that
he would assign a portion of land for them to
inhabit. Ulphilas, the bishop of the nation,
was the chief of the embassy. The object of
his embassy was fully accomplished, and the
Goths were permitted to take up their abode
in Thrace. Soon after contentions broke out
among them, which led to their division into
two parts, one of which was headed by Athanaric, and the other by Phritigernes. They took
up arms against each other, and Phritigernes
was vanquished, and implored the assistance
of the Romans. The emperor having commanded the troops in Thrace to assist and to
ally with him, a second battle was fought, and
Athanaric and his party were put to flight. In
acknowledgment of the timely succor afforded
by Valens, and in proof of his fidelity to the
Romans, Phritigernes embraced the religion of
the emperor, and persuaded the barbarians over
whom he ruled to follow his example. It does
not, however, appear to me that this is the only
reason that can be advanced to account for the
Goths having retained, even to the present day,
the tenets of Arianism. For Ulphilas, their
bishop, originally held no opinions at variance
with those of the Catholic Church; for during
the reign of Constantius, though he took part,
as I am convinced, from thoughtlessness, at
the council of Constantinople, in conjunction
with Eudoxius and Acacius, yet he did not
swerve from the doctrines of the Nicæan council. He afterwards, it appears, returned to
Constantinople, and, it is said, entered into disputations on doctrinal topics with the chiefs of
the Arian faction; and they promised to lay his
requests before the emperor, and forward the
object of his embassy, if he would conform to
their opinions. Compelled by the urgency of
the occasion, or, possibly, thinking that it was
better to hold such views concerning the Divine
nature, Ulphilas entered into communion with
the Arians, and separated himself and his whole
nation from all connection with the Catholic
Church. For as he had instructed the Goths in
the elements of religion, and through him they
shared in a gentler mode of life, they placed
the most implicit confidence in his directions,
and were firmly convinced that he could neither
do nor say anything that was evil. He had, in
fact, given many signal proofs of the greatness
of his virtue. He had exposed himself to
innumerable perils in defense of the faith,
during the period that the aforesaid barbarians
were given to pagan worship. He taught them
the use of letters, and translated the Sacred
Scriptures into their own language. It was on
this account, that the barbarians on the banks of
the Ister followed the tenets of Arius. At the
same period, there were many of the subjects of
Phritigernes who testified to Christ, and were
martyred. Athanaric resented that his subjects
had become Christian under the persuasion of
Ulphilas; and because they had abandoned the
cult of their fathers, he subjected many individuals to many punishments; some he put to
death after they had been dragged before tribunals and had nobly confessed the doctrine, and

---

[1] Soc. iv. 32–35; Philost. ii. 5, ix. 16, 17. Cf. Theodoret, *H. E.*
iv. 37; Eunap. *Fr.* i. 5, 6, ii. 34; Am. Marcel. parts of xxvii., xxx.,
xxxi.; Zos. iv. 10 sqq.

others were slain without being permitted to utter a single word in their own defense. It is said that the officers appointed by Athanaric to execute his cruel mandates, caused a statue to be constructed, which they placed on a chariot, and had it conveyed to the tents of those who were suspected of having embraced Christianity, and who were therefore commanded to worship the statue and offer sacrifice; if they refused to do so, the men and the tents were burnt together. But I have heard that an outrage of still greater atrocity was perpetrated at this period. Many refused to obey those who were compelling them by force to sacrifice. Among them were men and women; of the latter some were leading their little children, others were nourishing their new-born infants at the breast; they fled to their church, which was a tent. The pagans set fire to it, and all were destroyed.

The Goths were not long in making peace among themselves; and in unreasonable excitement, they then began to ravage Thrace and to pillage the cities and villages. Valens, on inquiry, learned by experiment how great a mistake he had made; for he had calculated that the Goths would always be useful to the empire and formidable to its enemies, and had therefore neglected the reinforcement of the Roman ranks. He had taken gold from the cities and villages under the Romans, instead of the usual complement of men for the military service. On his expectation being thus frustrated, he quitted Antioch and hastened to Constantinople. Hence the persecution which he had been carrying on against Christians differing in opinion from himself, had a truce. Euzoius, president of the Arians, died, and Dorotheus was proposed for his government.

CHAP. XXXVIII. — CONCERNING MANIA, THE PHYLARCH OF THE SARACENS. WHEN THE TREATY WITH THE ROMANS WAS DISSOLVED, MOSES, THEIR BISHOP, WHO HAD BEEN ORDAINED BY THE CHRISTIANS, RENEWED IT. NARRATIVE CONCERNING THE ISHMAELITES AND THE SARACENS, AND THEIR GOODS; AND HOW THEY BEGAN TO BE CHRISTIANIZED THROUGH ZOCOMUS, THEIR PHYLARCH.

ABOUT this period the king of the Saracens died,[1] and the peace which had previously existed between that nation and the Romans was dissolved. Mania,[2] the widow of the late monarch, after attaining to the government of her race, led her troops into Phœnicia and Pales-

tine, as far as the regions of Egypt lying to the left of those who sail towards the source of the Nile, and which are generally denominated Arabia. This war was by no means a contemptible one, although conducted by a woman. The Romans, it is said, considered it so arduous and so perilous, that the general of the Phœnician troops applied for assistance to the general of the entire cavalry and infantry of the East. This latter ridiculed the summons, and undertook to give battle alone. He accordingly attacked Mania, who commanded her own troops in person; and he was rescued with difficulty by the general of the troops of Palestine and Phœnicia. Perceiving the extremity of the danger, this general deemed it unnecessary to obey the orders he had received to keep aloof from the combat; he therefore rushed upon the barbarians, and furnished his superior an opportunity for safe retreat, while he himself yielded ground and shot at those who fled, and beat off with his arrows the enemies who were pressing upon him. This occurrence is still held in remembrance among the people of the country, and is celebrated in songs by the Saracens.

As the war was still pursued with vigor, the Romans found it necessary to send an embassy to Mania to solicit peace. It is said that she refused to comply with the request of the embassy, unless consent were given for the ordination of a certain man named Moses, who practiced philosophy in a neighboring desert, as bishop over her subjects. This Moses was a man of virtuous life, and noted for performing the divine and miraculous signs. On these conditions being announced to the emperor, the chiefs of the army were commanded to seize Moses, and conduct him to Lucius. The monk exclaimed, in the presence of the rulers and the assembled people, "I am not worthy of the honor of bearing the name and dignity of chief priest; but if, notwithstanding my unworthiness God destines me to this office, I take Him to witness who created the heavens and the earth, that I will not be ordained by the imposition of the hands of Lucius, which are defiled with the blood of holy men." Lucius immediately rejoined, "If you are unacquainted with the nature of my creed, you do wrong in judging me before you are in possession of all the circumstances of the case. If you have been prejudiced by the calumnies that have been circulated against me, at least allow me to declare to you what are my sentiments; and do you be the judge of them." "Your creed is already well known to me," replied Moses; "and its nature is testified by bishops, presbyters, and deacons, who are suffering grievously in exile, and the mines. It is clear that your sentiments are opposed to the faith of Christ, and to all

---

[1] Ruf. *H. E.* ii. 6; Soc. iv. 36. Cf. Theodoret, *H. E.* iv. 23; yet Soz. has original detail in the story of Mania, and appends the story of Zocomus.   [2] Otherwise called Mavia.

orthodox doctrines concerning the Godhead." [1] Having again protested, upon oath, that he would not receive ordination from them, he went to the Saracens. He reconciled them to the Romans, and converted many to Christianity, and passed his life among them as a priest, although he found few who shared in his belief.

This is the tribe which took its origin and had its name from Ishmael, the son of Abraham; and the ancients called them Ishmaelites after their progenitor. As their mother Hagar was a slave, they afterwards, to conceal the opprobrium of their origin, assumed the name of Saracens, as if they were descended from Sara, the wife of Abraham. Such being their origin, they practice circumcision like the Jews, refrain from the use of pork, and observe many other Jewish rites and customs. If, indeed, they deviate in any respect from the observances of that nation, it must be ascribed to the lapse of time, and to their intercourse with the neighboring nations. Moses, who lived many centuries after Abraham, only legislated for those whom he led out of Egypt. The inhabitants of the neighboring countries, being strongly addicted to superstition, probably soon corrupted the laws imposed upon them by their forefather Ishmael. The ancient Hebrews had their community life under this law only, using therefore unwritten customs, before the Mosaic legislation. These people certainly served the same gods as the neighboring nations, honoring and naming them similarly, so that by this likeness with their forefathers in religion, there is evidenced their departure from the laws of their forefathers. As is usual, in the lapse of time, their ancient customs fell into oblivion, and other practices gradually got the precedence among them. Some of their tribe afterwards happening to come in contact with the Jews, gathered from them the facts of their true origin, returned to their kinsmen, and inclined to the Hebrew customs and laws. From that time on, until now, many of them regulate their lives according to the Jewish precepts. Some of the Saracens were converted to Christianity not long before the present reign. They shared in the faith of Christ by intercourse with the priests and monks who dwelt near them, and practiced philosophy in the neighboring deserts, and who were distinguished by the excellence of their life, and by their miraculous works. It is said that a whole tribe, and Zocomus, their chief, were converted to Christianity and baptized about this period, under the following circumstances: Zocomus was childless, and went to a certain monk of great celebrity to complain to him of this calamity; for among the Saracens, and I believe other barbarian nations, it was

accounted of great importance to have children. The monk desired Zocomus to be of good cheer, engaged in prayer on his behalf, and sent him away with the promise that if he would believe in Christ, he would have a son. When this promise was confirmed by God, and when a son was born to him, Zocomus was initiated, and all his subjects with him. From that period this tribe was peculiarly fortunate, and became strong in point of number, and formidable to the Persians as well as to the other Saracens. Such are the details that I have been enabled to collect concerning the conversion of the Saracens and their first bishop.

CHAP. XXXIX. — PETER, HAVING RETURNED FROM ROME, REGAINS THE CHURCHES OF EGYPT, AFTER LUCIUS HAD GIVEN WAY; EXPEDITION OF VALENS INTO THE WEST AGAINST THE SCYTHIANS.

THOSE in every city who maintained the Nicene doctrine now began to take courage, and more particularly the inhabitants of Alexandria in Egypt. Peter [2] had returned thither from Rome with a letter from Damasus, confirmatory of the tenets of Nicæa and of his own ordination; and he was installed in the government of the churches in the place of Lucius, who sailed away to Constantinople after his eviction. The Emperor Valens very naturally was so distracted by other affairs, that he had no leisure to attend to these transactions. He had no sooner arrived at Constantinople than he incurred the suspicion and hatred of the people. The barbarians were pillaging Thrace, and were even advancing to the very suburbs, and attempted to make an assault on the very walls, with no one to hinder them. The city was indignant at this inertness; and the people even charged the emperor with being a party to their attack, because he did not sally forth, but delayed offering battle. At length, when he was present at the sports of the Hippodrome, the people openly and loudly accused him of neglecting the affairs of the state, and demanded arms that they might fight in their own defense. Valens, offended at these reproaches, immediately undertook an expedition against the barbarians; but he threatened to punish the insolence of the people on his return, and also to take vengeance on them for having formerly supported the tyrant Procopius.

CHAP. XL. — SAINT ISAAC, THE MONK, PREDICTS THE DEATH OF VALENS. VALENS IN HIS FLIGHT ENTERS A CHAFF-HOUSE, IS CONSUMED, AND SO YIELDS UP HIS LIFE.

WHEN Valens was on the point of departing

---

[1] See above, vi. 19, 20.

[2] Soc. iv. 37, 38; Eunap. *Fr.* i. 6; Am. Marcel. xxxi. 11. 1-5; Zos. iv. 22-24.

from Constantinople,[1] Isaac, a monk of great virtue, who feared no danger in the cause of God, presented himself before him, and addressed him in the following words: "Give back, O emperor, to the orthodox, and to those who maintain the Nicene doctrines, the churches of which you have deprived them, and the victory will be yours." The emperor was offended at this act of boldness, and commanded that Isaac should be arrested and kept in chains until his return, when he meant to bring him to justice for his temerity. Isaac, however, replied, "You will not return unless you restore the churches." And so in fact it came to pass. For when Valens marched out with his army, the Goths retreated while pursued. In his advances he passed by Thrace, and came to Adrianople. When at not great distance from the barbarians, he found them encamped in a secure position; and yet he had the rashness to attack them before he had arranged his own legions in proper order. His cavalry was dispersed, his infantry compelled to retreat; and, pursued by the enemy, he dismounted from his horse, and with a few attendants entered into a small house or tower, where he secreted himself. The barbarians were in full pursuit, and went beyond the tower, not suspecting that he had selected it for his place of concealment. As the last detachment of the barbarians was passing by the tower, the attendants of the emperor let fly a volley of arrows from their covert, which immediately led to the exclamation that Valens was concealed within the building. Those who were a little in advance heard this exclamation, and made known the news with a shout to those companions who were in advance of them; and thus the news was conveyed till it reached the detachments which were foremost in the pursuit. They returned, and encompassed the tower. They collected vast quantities of wood from the country around, which they piled up against the tower, and finally set fire to the mass. A wind which had happened to arise favored the progress of the conflagration; and in a short period the tower, with all that it contained, including the emperor and his attendants, was utterly destroyed. Valens was fifty years of age. He had reigned thirteen years conjointly with his brother, and three by himself.

[1] Philost. ix. 17; Soc. iv. 38; Ruf. *H. E.* ii. 13. Cf. Theodoret, *H. E.* iv. 31-36; Eunap. *Fr.* i. 6; ii. 40, 41; Am. Marcel. xxxi. 11-14; Zos. iv. 24. Soz. has wrought with some other material as well.

BOOK VII.

SUCH was the fate of Valens. The barbarians,[1] flushed with victory, overran Thrace, and advanced to the gates of Constantinople. In this emergency, a few of the confederate Saracens sent by Mavia, together with many of the populace, were of great service. It is reported that Dominica, wife of Valens, furnished money out of the public treasury, and some of the people, after hastily arming themselves, attacked the barbarians, and drove them from the city.

Gratian, who at this period reigned conjointly with his brother over the whole Roman Empire, disapproved of the late persecution that had been carried on to check the diversity in religious creeds, and recalled all those who had been banished on account of their religion. He also enacted a law by which it was decreed that every individual should be freely permitted the exercise of his own religion, and should be allowed to hold assemblies, with the exception of the Manichæans and the followers of Photinus and Eunomius.[2]

ON reflecting that, while it was indispensably requisite to check the incursions of the barbarians of the Ister in Illyria and Thrace, his presence was equally necessary in Gaul to repel the inroads of the Alemanni, Gratian associated Theodosius[3] with himself at Sirmich, in the government of the empire. Theodosius belonged to an illustrious family of the Pyrenees in Iberia, and had acquired so much renown in war, that before he was raised to the imperial power, he was universally considered capable of guiding the reins of the empire.

At this period all the churches of the East, with the exception of that of Jerusalem, were in the hands of the Arians. The Macedonians differed but little in opinion from those who maintained the doctrine of Nicæa, and held intercourse and communion with them in all the cities; and this had been more especially the case with the Macedonians of Constantinople, ever since their reconciliation with Liberius. But after the enactment of Gratian's law, some bishops of the Macedonian heresy took courage and repossessed the churches from which they had been ejected by Valens. They assembled together at Antioch in Caria, and protested that the Son is not to be declared " consubstantial " with the Father, but only like unto Him in substance. From that period, many of the Macedonians seceded from the others, and held separate churches; while others, condemning this opposition and contentiousness of those who had made these decisions, united themselves still more firmly with the followers of the Nicene doctrines.

Many of the bishops who had been banished by Valens, and who were recalled about this period in consequence of the law of Gratian, manifested no ambition to be restored to the highest offices of the Church; but they preferred the unity of the people, and therefore begged the Arian bishops to retain the posts they occupied, and not to rend by dissension the Church, which had been transmitted by God and the apostles as one, but which contentiousness and ambition for precedence had divided into many parts. Eulalius, bishop of Amasia in Pontus, was one of those who pursued this course of conduct. It is said that when he returned from exile, he found that his church was presided over by an Arian bishop, and that scarcely fifty inhabitants of the city had submitted to the control of this new bishop. Eulalius, desiring unity above all other considerations, offered to take part·with the Arian bishop in the government of the church, and expressly agreed to allow him the precedence. But as the Arian would not comply with this proposition, it was not long before he found himself deserted by the few who had followed him, and who went over to the other party.

[1] Soc. v. 1, 2; Ruf. *H. E.* ii. 13. Cf. Theodoret, *H. E.* v. 1, 2; Eunap. *Fragm.* i. 6.
[2] *Cod. Theod.* xvi, v. 388. 5–16; the legislation from A.D. 379–388.
[3] Soc. v. 2–4; Philost. ix. 17;·Ruf. *H. E.* ii. 14. Cf. Theodoret, *H. E.* v. 5–7. Soz. has other material; Zos. iv. 24. Cf. Eunap. *Fragm.* ii. 42, for an opposite view of Theodosius.

CHAP. III. — CONCERNING ST. MELETIUS AND PAU-
LINUS, BISHOP OF ANTIOCH. THEIR OATH RE-
SPECTING THE EPISCOPAL SEE.

In consequence of this law, Meletius returned about this period to Antioch in Syria; and his presence gave rise to great contention among the people.[1] Paulinus, whom Valens, from veneration for his piety, had not ventured to banish, was still alive. The partisans of Meletius, therefore, proposed his association with Paulinus, who condemned the ordination of Meletius, because it had been conferred by Arian bishops; and yet the supporters of Meletius went forward by force into the work they had devised; for they were not few in number, and so placed Meletius on the episcopal throne in one of the suburban churches. The mutual animosity of the two parties increased, and sedition was expected, had not a remarkable plan for the restoration of concord prevailed. For it seemed best, to take oaths from those who were considered elegible, or who were expected to occupy the episcopal see of that place. Of these there were five besides Flavian. These promised that they would neither strive for, nor accept the episcopate should an ordination take place among them during the life of Paulinus and Meletius, and that in the event of the decease of either of these great men, the other alone should succeed to the bishopric. On their ratifying this promise with oaths, unanimity was restored among almost all the people; a few of the Luciferites still diverged because Meletius had been ordained by heretics. On the termination of this contest, Meletius proceeded to Constantinople, where many other bishops had assembled together to deliberate on the necessity of translating Gregory from the bishopric of Nazianzen to that of this city.

CHAP. IV. — REIGN OF THEODOSIUS THE GREAT; HE WAS INITIATED INTO DIVINE BAPTISM BY ASCHOLIUS, BISHOP OF THESSALONICA. THE LETTERS HE ADDRESSED TO THOSE WHO DID NOT HOLD THE DEFINITION OF THE COUNCIL OF NICE.

As Gaul was about this period infested by the incursions of the Alemanni,[2] Gratian returned to his paternal dominions, which he had reserved for himself and his brother, when he bestowed the government of Illyria and of the Eastern provinces upon Theodosius. He effected his purpose with regard to the barbarians; and Theodosius was equally successful against the tribes from the banks of the Ister; he defeated them, compelled them to sue for peace, and, after accepting hostages from them, pro-

ceeded to Thessalonica. He fell ill while in this city, and after receiving instruction from Ascholius, the bishop, he was initiated, and was soon after restored to health. The parents of Theodosius were Christians, and were attached to the Nicene doctrines; he was pleased with Ascholius, who maintained the same doctrines, and was, in a word, endowed with every virtue of the priesthood. He also rejoiced at finding that the Arian heresy had not been participated in by Illyria.[3] He inquired concerning the religious sentiments which were prevalent in the other provinces, and ascertained that, as far as Macedonia,[4] all the churches were like minded, and all held that equal homage ought to be rendered to God the Word, and to the Holy Ghost, as to God the Father; but that towards the East, and particularly at Constantinople, the people were divided into many different heresies. Reflecting that it would be better to propound his own religious views to his subjects, so as not to appear to be using force by commanding the unwilling subject to worship contrary to his judgment, Theodosius enacted a law at Thessalonica, which he caused to be published at Constantinople, well knowing that the rescript would speedily become public to all the other cities, if issued from that city, which is as a citadel of the whole empire. He made known by this law his intention of leading all his subjects to the reception of that faith which Peter, the chief of the apostles, had, from the beginning, preached to the Romans, and which was professed by Damasus, bishop of Rome, and by Peter, bishop of Alexandria. He enacted[5] that the title of "Catholic Church" should be exclusively confined to those who rendered equal homage to the Three Persons of the Trinity, and that those individuals who entertained opposite opinions should be treated as heretics, regarded with contempt, and delivered over to punishment.

CHAP. V. — GREGORY, THE THEOLOGIAN, RECEIVES FROM THEODOSIUS THE GOVERNMENT OF THE CHURCHES. EXPULSION OF DEMOPHILUS, AND OF ALL WHO DENY THAT THE SON IS "CONSUBSTANTIAL" WITH THE FATHER.

Soon after the enactment of this law, Theodosius went to Constantinople.[6] The Arians, under the guidance of Demophilus, still retained possession of the churches. Gregory of Nazianzen presided over those who maintain the "consubstantiality" of the Holy Trinity, and

[1] Soc. v. 5; Ruf. H. E. ii. 21; Theodoret, H. E. v. 3.
[2] Soc. v. 6; Philost. ix. 19. Independent points by Soz. Cf. Zos. iv. 25-27; cf. Eunap. Fragm. i. 7, ii. 43-46.
[3] The same testimony is given by Basil, in his letter to Valerianus, bishop of Illyria, Ep. xci., and in the letter to the Neo-Cæsareans, Ep. cciv.
[4] This is also plain from the acts of the council of Aquileia, A.D. 381. Hard. vol. i.
[5] Cod. Theod. xvi., under "de Fide Catholica," 2.
[6] Soc. v. 6; Philost. ix. 19; Theodoret, H. E. v. 8; Marcellinus Comes, Chronicon, s. A.D. 380.

assembled them together in a little dwelling, which had been altered into the form of a house of prayer, by those who held the same opinions and had a like form of worship. It subsequently became one of the most conspicuous in the city, and is so now, not only for the beauty and number of its structures, but also for the advantages accruing to it from the visible manifestations of God. For the power of God was there manifested, and was helpful both in waking visions and in dreams, often for the relief of many diseases and for those afflicted by some sudden transmutation in their affairs. The power was accredited to Mary, the Mother of God, the holy virgin, for she does manifest herself in this way. The name of Anastasia was given to this church, because, as I believe, the Nicene doctrines which were fallen into disuse in Constantinople, and, so to speak, buried by reason of the power of the heterodox, arose from the dead and were again quickened through the discourses of Gregory; or, as I have heard, some affirm with assurance that one day, when the people were met together for worship in this edifice, a pregnant woman fell from the highest gallery, and was found dead on the spot; but that, at the prayer of the whole congregation, she was restored to life, and she and the infant were saved. On account of the occurrence of this divine marvel, the place, as some assert, obtained its name.

The emperor sent to command Demophilus to conform to the doctrines of Nicæa, and to lead the people to embrace the same sentiments, or else to vacate the churches. Demophilus assembled the people, acquainted them with the imperial edict, and informed them that it was his intention to hold a church the next day without the walls of the city, in accordance, he said, with the Divine law, which commands us when we are persecuted in one city to "flee unto another."[1] From that day he always held church without the city with Lucius, who was formerly the bishop of the Arians at Alexandria; and who, after having been expelled, as above related, from that city, fled to Constantinople and fixed his residence there. When Demophilus and his followers had quitted the church, the emperor entered therein and engaged in prayer; and from that period those who maintained the consubstantiality of the Holy Trinity held possession of the houses of prayer. These events occurred in the fifth year of the consulate of Gratian, and in the first of that of Theodosius, and after the churches had been during forty years in the hands of the Arians.

CHAP. VI. — CONCERNING THE ARIANS; AND FURTHER, THE SUCCESS OF EUNOMIUS. BOLDNESS OF ST. AMPHILOCHIUS TOWARD THE EMPEROR.

THE Arians, who were still very strong in point of numbers,[2] and who, through the protection formerly granted by Constantius and Valens, were still convening without fear, and discoursing publicly concerning God and the Divine nature, now determined upon making an attempt to gain over the emperor to their party, through the intervention of individuals of their sect who held appointments at court; and they entertained hopes of succeeding in this project, as well as they had succeeded in the case of Constantius. These machinations excited great anxiety and fear among the members of the Catholic Church; but the chief cause of their apprehension was the reasoning power of Eunomius. It appears that, during the reign of Valens, Eunomius had some dispute with his own clergy at Cyzicus, and had in consequence seceded from the Arians, and retired to Bithynia, near Constantinople. Here multitudes resorted to him; some also gathered from different quarters, a few with the design of testing his principles, and others merely from the desire of listening to his discourses. His reputation reached the ears of the emperor, who would gladly have held a conference with him. But the Empress Flacilla[3] studiously prevented an interview from taking place between them; for she was the most faithful guard of the Nicene doctrines, and feared least Eunomius might, by his powers of disputation, induce a change in the sentiments of the emperor.

In the meantime, while these intrigues were being carried on by each party, it is said that the bishops then residing in Constantinople went to the emperor, to render him the customary salutations. An old priest from a city of little note,[4] and who was simple and unworldly, yet well instructed in Divine subjects, formed one of this party. The rest saluted the emperor with uncovered head and very reverently. The aged priest greeted him in the same form; but, instead of rendering equal honor to the prince, who was seated beside his father, the old priest approached him, patted him familiarly, and called him his dear child. The emperor was incensed and enraged at the indignity offered to his son, in that he had not been accorded like honor; and commanded that the old man should be thrust from his presence with violence. While being pushed away, hither and thither, however, the old priest turned around and exclaimed, "Reflect, O emperor, on the wrath of the Heavenly Father against those who do not honor His Son as Himself, and who have the audacity to assert that the Son is inferior to the

---

[1] Matt. x. 23.

[2] Independent chapter. Cf. Philost. ix. 13, 14.
[3] She was the first, and not the second, wife of Theodosius, and the mother of Arcadius and Honorius. Her funeral panegyric was delivered by Gregory of Nyssa (vol. iii. 877), as well as that of her daughter Pulcheria, (id. 863). Cf. Philost. x. 7 (Placidia).
[4] Theodoret, H. E. v. 16, refers this incident to Amphilochius, bishop of Iconium and Nicephorus follows him, xii. 9.

Father." The emperor felt the force of this observation, recalled the priest, apologized to him for what had occurred, and confessed that he had spoken the truth. The emperor was henceforward less disposed to hold intercourse with heretics, and he prohibited contests and assemblies in the markets. He made it dangerous to hold discussions of this kind about the substance and nature of God, by enacting a law, and defining the punishments in this matter.[1]

CHAP. VII. — CONCERNING THE SECOND HOLY GENERAL COUNCIL, AND THE PLACE AND CAUSE OF ITS CONVENTION. ABDICATION OF GREGORY THE THEOLOGIAN.

THE emperor soon after convened a council of orthodox bishops, for the purpose of confirming the decrees of Nicæa, and of electing a bishop to the vacant see of Constantinople.[2] He likewise summoned the Macedonians to this assembly; for as their doctrines differed but little from those of the Catholic Church, he judged that it would be easy to effect a reunion with them. About a hundred and fifty bishops who maintained the consubstantiality of the Holy Trinity, were present at this council, as likewise thirty-six of the Macedonian bishops, chiefly from the cities of the Hellespont; of whom the principal were Eleusius, bishop of Cyzicus, and Marcian, bishop of Lampsacus. The other party was under the guidance of Timothy, who had succeeded his brother Peter in the see of Alexandria; of Meletius, bishop of Antioch, who had repaired to Constantinople a short time previously, on account of the election of Gregory, and of Cyril, bishop of Jerusalem, who had at this period renounced the tenets of the Macedonians which he previously held. Ascholius, bishop of Thessalonica, Diodorus, bishop of Tarsus, and Acacius, bishop of Berea, were also present at the council. These latter unanimously maintained the decrees of Nicæa, and urged Eleusius and his partisans to conform to these sentiments, reminding them, at the same time, of the embassy they had formerly deputed to Liberius, and of the confession they conveyed to him through the medium of Eustathius, Silvanus, and Theophilus, as has been narrated. The Macedonians, however, declared openly that they would never admit the Son to be of the same substance as the Father, whatever confession they might formerly have made to Liberius, and immediately withdrew. They then wrote to those of their adherents in every city, exhorting them not to conform to the doctrines of Nicæa.

The bishops who remained at Constantinople now turned their attention to the election of a prelate to the see of that city. It is said that the emperor, from profound admiration of the sanctity and eloquence of Gregory, judged that he was worthy of this bishopric, and that, from reverence of his virtue, the greater number of the Synod was of the same opinion. Gregory at first consented to accept the presidency of the church of Constantinople; but afterwards, on ascertaining that some of the bishops, particularly those of Egpyt, objected to the election, he withdrew his consent. For my part, this wisest of men is worthy of admiration, not only for universal qualifications, but not the least for his conduct under the present circumstances. His eloquence did not inspire him with pride, nor did vainglory lead him to desire the control of a church, which he had received when it was no longer in danger. He surrendered his appointment to the bishops when it was required of him, and never complained of his many labors, or of the dangers he had incurred in the suppression of heresies. Had he retained possession of the bishopric of Constantinople, it would have been no detriment to the interests of any individual, as another bishop had been appointed in his stead at Nazianzen. But the council, in strict obedience to the laws of the fathers and ecclesiastical order, withdrew from him, with his own acquiescence, the deposit which had been confided to him, without making an exception in favor of so eminent a man. The emperor and the priests therefore proceeded to the election of another bishop, which they regarded as the most important affair then requiring attention; and the emperor was urgent that diligent investigations might be instituted, so that the most excellent and best individual might be intrusted with the highpriesthood of the great and royal city. The council, however, was divided in sentiment; for each of the members desired to see one of his own friends ordained over the church.

CHAP. VIII. — ELECTION OF NECTARIUS TO THE SEE OF CONSTANTINOPLE; HIS BIRTHPLACE AND EDUCATION.

A CERTAIN man of Tarsus in Cilicia, of the illustrious order of senator, was at this period residing at Constantinople.[3] Being about to return to his own country, he called upon Diodorus, bishop of Tarsus, to inquire whether he had any letters to send by him. Diodorus was fully intent upon the ordination, which was the subject then engrossing universal attention of the men. He had no sooner seen Nectarius than he considered him worthy of the bishopric,

[1] Cod. Theod. xvi. iv. De his, qui super religione contendunt, 2.
[2] Soc. v. 7, 8; cf. Theodoret, H. E. v. 7, 8; Ruf. H. E. ii. 19; Marcell. Chron. s. A.D. 381.
[3] Soc. v. 8; cf. Theodoret, H. E. v. 8; Marcell. s. A.D. 381. Soz. is entirely independent.

and straightway determined this in his own mind as he reflected on the venerable age of the man, his form so befitting a priest, and the suavity of his manners. He conducted him, as if upon some other business, to the bishop of Antioch, and requested him to use his influence to procure this election. The bishop of Antioch derided this request, for the names of the most eminent men had already been proposed for consideration. He, however, called Nectarius to him, and desired him to remain for a short time with him. Some time after, the emperor commanded the priests to draw up a list of the names of those whom they thought worthy of the ordination, reserving to himself the right of choosing any one of those whose names were thus submitted to him. All the bishops complied with this mandate; and, among the others, the bishop of Antioch wrote down the names of those whom he proposed as candidates for the bishopric, and, at the end of his list, from consideration for Diodorus, he inserted the name of Nectarius. The emperor read the list of those inscribed and stopped at the name of Nectarius at the end of the document, on which he placed his finger, and seemed for some time lost in reflection; ran it up to the beginning, and again went through the whole, and chose Nectarius. This nomination excited great astonishment, and all the people were anxious to ascertain who Nectarius was, his manner of life, and birthplace. When they heard that he had not been initiated, their amazement was increased at the decision of the emperor. I believe that Diodorus himself was not aware that Nectarius had not been baptized; for, had he been acquainted with this fact, he would not have ventured to give his vote for the priesthood to one uninitiated. It appears reasonable to suppose, that on perceiving that Nectarius was of advanced age, he took it for granted that he had been initiated long previously. But these events did not take place without the interposition of God. For when the emperor was informed that Nectarius had not been initiated, he remained of the same opinion, although opposed ·by many priests. When at last, consent had been given to the imperial mandate, Nectarius was initiated, and while yet clad in his initiatory robes, was proclaimed bishop of Constantinople by the unanimous voice of the Synod. Many have conjectured that the emperor was led to make this election by a Divine revelation. I shall not decide whether this conjecture be true or false; but I feel convinced, when I reflect on the extraordinary circumstances attending this ordination, that the events were not brought about without the Divine strength; and that God led this mild and virtuous and excellent man into the priesthood. Such are the details which I have been able to ascertain concerning the ordination of Nectarius.

CHAP. IX. — DECREES OF THE SECOND GENERAL COUNCIL. MAXIMUS, THE CYNICAL PHILOSOPHER.

AFTER these transactions, Nectarius and the other priests assembled together,[1] and decreed that the faith established by the council of Nicæa should remain dominant, and that all heresies should be condemned; that the churches everywhere should be governed according to the ancient canons; that each bishop should remain in his own church, and not go elsewhere under any light pretext; or, without invitation, perform ordinations in which he had no right to interfere, as had frequently been the case in the Catholic Church during the times of persecution. They likewise decreed that the affairs of each church should be subjected to the investigation and control of a council of the province; and that the bishop of Constantinople should rank next in point of precedence to the bishop of Rome, as occupying the see of New Rome; for Constantinople was not only already favored with this appellation, but was also in the enjoyment of many privileges, — such as a senate of its own, and the division of the citizens into ranks and orders; it was also governed by its own magistrates, and possessed contracts, laws, and immunities in equal degree with those of Rome in Italy.

The council also decreed that Maximus had not been nor was now a bishop; and that those individuals whom he had ordained were not of the clergy; and that all that had been done by him, or in his name, was null and void. Maximus was a native of Alexandria, and, by profession, a cynical philosopher. He was zealously attached to the Nicene doctrines, and had been secretly ordained bishop of Constantinople by bishops who had assembled in that city from Egypt.

Such were the decrees of the council. They were confirmed by the emperor, who enacted[2] that the faith established at Nicæa should be dominant, and that the churches everywhere should be placed in the hands of those who acknowledged one and the same Godhead in the hypostasis of three Persons of equal honor and of equal power; namely, the Father, the Son, and the Holy Ghost. To designate them still more precisely, the emperor declared that he referred to those who held communion with Nectarius, at Constantinople, and with Timothy, bishop of Alexandria, in Egypt; in the churches of the East with Diodorus, bishop of Tarsus,

---

[1] Soc. v. 8; cf. Theodoret, H. E. v. 8, 9. The latter chapter gives the text of the letter of this Synod to the Synod of Rome. Soz. is here independent.
[2] Cod. Theod. xvi. 3.

and in Syria with Pelagius, bishop of Laodicea, and in Asia with Amphilochius, president of the churches in Iconium ; to those in the cities by the Pontus, from Bithynia to Armenia, who held communion with Helladius, bishop of the church of Cæsarea in Cappadocia ; with Gregory, bishop of Nyssa ; and with Otreinus, bishop of Melitine ; and to the cities of Thrace and Scythia, who held communion with Terentius, bishop of Tomi, and with Martyrius, bishop of Marcianopolis. The emperor was personally acquainted with all these bishops, and had ascertained that they governed their respective churches wisely and piously. After these transactions, the council was dissolved, and each of the bishops returned homewards.

CHAP. X. — CONCERNING MARTYRIUS OF CILICIA. TRANSLATION OF THE REMAINS OF ST. PAUL THE CONFESSOR, AND OF MELETIUS, BISHOP OF ANTIOCH.

NECTARIUS made himself acquainted with the routine of sacerdotal ceremonies under the instruction of Cyriacus,[1] bishop of Adana, whom he had requested Diodorus, bishop of Tarsus, to leave with him for a short period. Nectarius also retained several other Cilicians with him, amongst whom was Martyrius, his physician, who had been a witness of the irregularities of his youth. Nectarius was desirous of ordaining him deacon ; but Martyrius refused the honor under the plea of his own unworthiness of such a divine service, and called upon Nectarius himself to witness as to the course of his past life. To this Nectarius replied as follows : "Although I am now a priest, do you not know that my past career was a more guilty one than yours, inasmuch as you were but an instrument in my numerous profligacies?" "But you, O blessed one," replied Martyrius, "were cleansed by baptism, and were then accounted worthy of the priesthood. Both these ordinances are appointed by the Divine law for purification from sin, and it seems to me that you now differ in no respect from a new-born infant ; but I long ago received holy baptism, and have since continued in the same abusive course." It was under this plea that he excused himself from receiving ordination ; and I commend the man for his refusal, and therefore would give him a part in my history.

The Emperor Theodosius, on being informed of various events connected with Paul,[2] formerly bishop of Constantinople, caused his body to be removed to the church erected by Macedonius, his enemy, and buried there. This temple is a spacious and most distinguished edifice, and is still named after Paul. Hence many persons who are ignorant of the facts of the case, particularly women and the mass of the people, imagine that Paul, the apostle, is interred therein. The remains of Meletius were at the same time conveyed to Antioch, and deposited near the tomb of Babylas the martyr. It is said that through every public way, by the command of the emperor, the relics were received within the walls in every city, contrary to Roman custom, and were honored with singing of psalms antiphonally in such places, until they were transferred to Antioch.

CHAP. XI. — ORDINATION OF FLAVIAN AS BISHOP OF ANTIOCH, AND SUBSEQUENT OCCURRENCES ON ACCOUNT OF THE OATH.

AFTER the pompous interment of the remains of Meletius, Flavian was ordained in his stead, and that, too, in direct violation of the oath he had taken ;[3] for Paulinus was still alive. This gave rise to fresh troubles in the church of Antioch. Many persons refused to maintain communion with Flavian, and held their church apart with Paulinus. Even the priests differed among themselves on this subject. The Egyptians, Arabians, and Cypriots were indignant at the injustice that had been manifested towards Paulinus. On the other hand, the Syrians, the Palestinians, the Phœnicians, and the greater part of Armenia, Cappadocia, Galatia, and Pontus, sided with Flavian. The bishop of Rome, and all the Western priests, regarded the conduct of Flavian with the utmost displeasure. They addressed the customary epistles, called synodical, to Paulinus as bishop of Antioch, and took no notice of Flavian. They also withdrew from communion with Diodorus, bishop of Tarsus, and Acacius, bishop of Berea, because they had ordained Flavian.[4] To take further cognizance of the affair, the Western bishops and the Emperor Gratian wrote to the bishops of the East, and summoned them to attend a council in the West.

CHAP. XII. — PROJECT OF THEODOSIUS TO UNIFY ALL THE HERESIES. THE PROPOSITIONS MADE BY AGELIUS AND SISINIUS, THE NOVATIANS. AT ANOTHER SYNOD, THE EMPEROR RECEIVED THOSE ONLY WHO REPRESENT CONSUBSTANTIALITY ; THOSE WHO HELD A DIFFERENT VIEW HE EJECTED FROM THE CHURCHES.

ALTHOUGH all the houses of prayer were at this period in the possession of the Catholic Church, many troubles occurred in various parts

---

[1] Most of this chapter is independent with Soz.
[2] Soc. v. 9. Soz. is independent.

[3] Soc. v. 9; cf. Theodoret, *H. E.* v. 23.
[4] Ambrose, and other bishops of Italy, convened in an undesignated Synod, condemned Nectarius, both for his part in this procedure and also as improperly ordained. Hard. i. c. 844.

of the empire, instigated by the Arians.[1] The Emperor Theodosius, therefore, soon after the council above mentioned, again summoned together the presidents of the sects which were flourishing, in order that they might either bring others to their own state of conviction on disputed topics, or be convinced themselves; for he imagined that all would be brought to oneness of opinion, if a free discussion were entered into, concerning ambiguous points of doctrine. The council, therefore, was convened. This occurred in the year of the second consulate of Merobaudes, and the first of Saturninus, and at the same period that Arcadius was associated with his father in the government of the empire. Theodosius sent for Nectarius, consulted with him concerning the coming Synod, and commanded him to introduce the discussion of all questions which had given rise to heresies, so that the church of the believers in Christ might be one, and might agree on the doctrine according to which piety ought to be observed. When Nectarius returned home, feeling anxious about the affair confided to him, he made known the mandate of the emperor to Agelius, the president of the church of the Novatians, who held the same religious sentiments as himself. Agelius proved the virtue of his life by works, but was unaccustomed to the finesse and deception of words; he therefore proposed as a substitute, one of his readers, by name Sisinius, who afterwards succeeded him as bishop, a man who could see what was practical, and could debate, if that were necessary. Sisinius possessed powers of intellect and of expression; he had an accurate knowledge of the interpretation of the Holy Scriptures, and was well acquainted with profane and with ecclesiastical literature. He proposed that all disputation with the heterodox, as being a fruitful source of contention and war, should be avoided; but recommended that inquiries should rather be instituted, as to whether the heretics admitted the testimony of the expositors and teachers of the sacred words, who lived before the Church was rent in division. " If they reject the testimony of these great men," said he, " they will be condemned by their own followers; but if they admit their authority as being adequate to resolve ambiguous points of doctrine, we will produce their books." For Sisinius was well aware that, as the ancients recognized the Son to be eternal like the Father, they had never presumed to assert that He had had an origin from some beginning. This suggestion received the approbation of Nectarius, and afterwards of the emperor; and investigations were set on foot as to the opinions entertained by heretics concerning the ancient interpreters of

Scripture. As it was found that the heretics professed to hold these early writers in great admiration, the emperor asked them openly whether they would defer to the authority of the aforesaid on controverted topics, and test their own doctrines by the sentiments propounded in those works. This proposition excited great contention among the leaders of the various heretical sects, for they did not all hold the same view about the books of the ancients; the emperor knew that they were convicted by the debates over their own words alone, and withdrew the proposition. He blamed them for their opinion, and commanded each party to draw up a written exposition of its own creed. On the day appointed for the presentation of these documents, Nectarius and Agelius appeared at the palace, as representatives of those who maintain the consubstantiality of the Holy Trinity; Demophilus, the Arian president, came forward as the deputy of the Arians; Eunomius represented the Eunomians; and Eleusius, bishop of Cyzicus, appeared for the sectarians denominated Macedonians. The emperor, after receiving their formularies, expressed himself in favor of that one alone in which consubstantiality of the Trinity was recognized, and destroyed the others. The interests of the Novatians were not affected by this transaction, for they held the same doctrines as the Catholic Church concerning the Divine nature. The members of the other sects were indignant with the priests for having entered into unwise disputations in the presence of the emperor. Many renounced their former opinions, and embraced the authorized form of religion. The emperor enacted a law, prohibiting heretics from holding churches, from giving public instructions in the faith, and from conferring ordination on bishops or others.[2] Some of the heterodox were expelled from the cities and villages, while others were disgraced and deprived of the privileges enjoyed by other subjects of the empire. Great as were the punishments adjudged by the laws against heretics, they were not always carried into execution, for the emperor had no desire to persecute his subjects; he only desired to enforce uniformity of view about God through the medium of intimidation. Those who voluntarily renounced heretical opinions received commendation from him.

CHAP. XIII. — MAXIMUS THE TYRANT.   CONCERNING THE OCCURRENCES BETWEEN THE EMPRESS JUSTINA AND ST. AMBROSE.   THE EMPEROR GRATIAN WAS KILLED BY GUILE.   VALENTINIAN AND HIS MOTHER FLED TO THEODOSIUS IN THESSALONICA.

As the Emperor Gratian was at this period

---

[1] Soc. v. 10, from whom Soz. borrows his facts.

[2] Cod. Theod. xvi. 5, 15.

occupied with a war against the Alamanni,[1] Maximus quitted Britain, with the design of usurping the imperial power. Valentinian was then residing in Italy, but as he was a minor, the affairs of state were transacted by Probus, a prætorian prefect, who had formerly been consul.

Justina, the mother of the emperor, having espoused the Arian heresy, persecuted Ambrose, bishop of Milan, and disquieted the churches by her efforts to introduce alterations in the Nicene doctrines, and to obtain the predominance of the form of belief set forth at Ariminum. She was incensed against Ambrose because he strenuously opposed her attempts at innovation, and she represented to her son that he had insulted her. Valentinian believed this calumny, and, determined to avenge the supposed wrongs of his mother, he sent a party of soldiers against the church. On their reaching the temple, they forced their way into the interior, arrested Ambrose, and were about to lead him into exile at that very moment, when the people assembled in crowds at the church, and evinced a resolution to die rather than submit to the banishment of their priest. Justina was still further incensed at this occurrence ; and with a view of enforcing her project by law, she sent for Menivolus,[2] one of the legal secretaries, and commanded him to draw up, as quickly as possible, an edict confirmatory of the decrees of Ariminum. Menivolus, being firmly attached to the Catholic Church, refused to write the document, and the empress tried to bribe him by promises of greater honors. He still, however, refused compliance, and, tearing off his belt, he threw it at the feet of Justina, and declared that he would neither retain his present office, nor accept of promotion, as the reward of impiety. As he remained firm in his refusal, others were intrusted with the compilation of the law. By this law, all who conformed to the doctrines set forth at Ariminum and ratified at Constantinople were exhorted to convene boldly ; and it was enacted that death should be the punishment of those who should hinder or be running counter to this law of the emperor. While the mother of the emperor was planning the means of carrying this cruel law into execution, intelligence was brought of the murder of Gratian, through the treachery of Andragathius, the general of Maximus. Andragathius obtained possession of the imperial chariot, and sent word to the emperor that his consort was traveling towards his camp. Gratian, who was but recently married and youthful, as well as passionately attached to his wife, hastened incautiously across the river, and in his anxiety to meet her fell without forethought into the hands

of Andragathius ; he was seized, and, in a little while, put to death. He was in the twenty-fourth year of his age, and had reigned fifteen years. This calamity quieted Justina's wrath against Ambrose.

Maximus, in the meantime, raised a large army of Britons, neighboring Gauls, Celts, and other nations, and marched into Italy. The pretext which he advanced for this measure was, that he desired to prevent the introduction of innovations in the ancient form of religion and of ecclesiastical order ; but he was in reality actuated by the desire of dispelling any suspicion that might have been excited as to his aspirations after tyranny. He was watching and intriguing for the imperial rule in such a way that it might appear as if he had acquired the Roman government by law, and not by force. Valentinian was compelled by the exigencies of the times to recognize the symbols of his rule ; but soon after, in fear of suffering, fled with his mother Justina, and Probus, the prætorian prefect in Italy, to Thessalonica.

CHAP. XIV. — BIRTH OF HONORIUS. THEODOSIUS LEAVES ARCADIUS AT CONSTANTINOPLE, AND PROCEEDS TO ITALY. SUCCESSION OF THE NOVATIAN AND OTHER PATRIARCHS. AUDACITY OF THE ARIANS. THEODOSIUS, AFTER DESTROYING THE TYRANT, CELEBRATES A MAGNIFICENT TRIUMPH IN ROME.

WHILE Theodosius was making preparations for a war against Maximus, his son Honorius was born.[3] On the completion of these warlike preparations, he left his son Arcadius to govern at Constantinople, and proceeded to Thessalonica, where he received Valentinian. He refused either to dismiss openly, or to give audience to the embassy sent by Maximus, but continued his journey at the head of his troops towards Italy.

About this period, Agelius, bishop of the Novatians at Constantinople, feeling his end approaching, nominated Sisinius, one of the presbyters of his church, as his successor. The people, however, murmured that the preference had not rather been given to Marcian, who was noted on account of his piety, and Agelius therefore ordained him, and addressed the people who were assembled in the church in the following words : " After me you shall have Marcian for your bishop, and after him, Sisinius." Agelius died soon after he had uttered these words. He had governed his church forty years with the greatest approbation from his own heretical party ; and some assert that during the times of Pagan persecution, he had openly confessed the name of Christ.

[1] Ruf. H. E. ii. 14-16; Philost. x. 5, 7; Soc. v. 11. Cf. Theodoret, H. E. v. 12, 13; Eunap. Fragm. ii. 48; Zos. iv. 42, 43.
[2] In Ruf. H. E. ii. 16, Benevolus.

[3] Soc. v. 12-14, 21, is the main source for Soz. Cf. Ruf. H. E. ii. 17; Philost. x. 8, 9, 11; Theodoret, H. E. v. 15; Zos. iv. 45-47.

Not long after Timothy and Cyril died; Theophilus succeeded to the see of Alexandria, and John to that of Jerusalem. Demophilus, leader of the Arians at Constantinople, likewise died, and was succeeded by Marinus of Thrace; but he was superseded by Dorotheus, who soon after arrived from Antioch in Syria, and who was considered by his sect to be better qualified for the office than Marinus.

Theodosius, having in the meantime entered Italy, various conflicting reports were spread as to the success of his arms. It was rumored among the Arians that the greater part of his army had been cut to pieces in battle, and that he himself had been captured by the tyrant; and assuming this report to be true, these sectarians became bold and ran to the house of Nectarius and set it on fire, from indignation at the power which the bishop had obtained over the churches. The emperor, however, carried out his purpose in the war, for the soldiers of Maximus, impelled by fear of the preparations against them, or treachery, seized and slew the tyrant. Andragathius, the murderer of Gratian, no sooner heard of the death of Maximus, than he leaped into the river with his armor, and perished. The war having been thus terminated, and the death of Gratian avenged, Theodosius, accompanied by Valentinian, celebrated a triumph in Rome, and restored order in the churches of Italy, for the Empress Justina was dead.

CHAP. XV. — FLAVIAN AND EVAGRIUS, BISHOPS OF ANTIOCH. THE EVENTS AT ALEXANDRIA UPON THE DESTRUCTION OF THE TEMPLE OF DIONYSUS. THE SERAPEUM AND THE OTHER IDOLATROUS TEMPLES WHICH WERE DESTROYED.

PAULINUS,[1] bishop of Antioch, died about this period, and those who had been convened into a church with him persisted in their aversion to Flavian, although his religious sentiments were precisely the same as their own, because he had violated the oath he had formerly made to Meletius. They, therefore, elected Evagrius as their bishop. Evagrius did not long survive this appointment, and although Flavian prevented the election of another bishop, those who had seceded from communion with him, still continued to hold their assemblies apart.

About this period, the bishop of Alexandria, to whom the temple of Dionysus had, at his own request, been granted by the emperor, converted the edifice into a church. The statues were removed, the adyta were exposed; and, in order to cast contumely on the pagan mysteries, he made a procession for the display of these ob-

jects; the phalli, and whatever other object had been concealed in the adyta which really was, or seemed to be, ridiculous, he made a public exhibition of. The pagans, amazed at so unexpected an exposure, could not suffer it in silence, but conspired together to attack the Christians. They killed many of the Christians, wounded others, and seized the Serapion, a temple which was conspicuous for beauty and vastness and which was seated on an eminence. This they converted into a temporary citadel; and hither they conveyed many of the Christians, put them to the torture, and compelled them to offer sacrifice. Those who refused compliance were crucified, had both legs broken, or were put to death in some cruel manner. When the sedition had prevailed for some time, the rulers came and urged the people to remember the laws, to lay down their arms, and to give up the Serapion. There came then Romanus, the general of the military legions in Egypt; and Evagrius was the prefect of Alexandria.[2] As their efforts, however, to reduce the people to submission were utterly in vain, they made known what had transpired to the emperor. Those who had shut themselves up in the Serapion prepared a more spirited resistance, from fear of the punishment that they knew would await their audacious proceedings, and they were further instigated to revolt by the inflammatory discourses of a man named Olympius, attired in the garments of a philosopher, who told them that they ought to die rather than neglect the gods of their fathers. Perceiving that they were greatly dispirited by the destruction of the idolatrous statues, he assured them that such a circumstance did not warrant their renouncing their religion; for that the statues were composed of corruptible materials, and were mere pictures, and therefore would disappear; whereas, the powers which had dwelt within them, had flown to heaven. By such representations as these, he retained the multitude with him in the Serapion.

When the emperor was informed of these occurrences, he declared that the Christians who had been slain were blessed, inasmuch as they had been admitted to the honor of martyrdom, and had suffered in defense of the faith. He offered free pardon[3] to those who had slain them, hoping that by this act of clemency they would be the more readily induced to embrace Christianity; and he commanded the demolition of the temples in Alexandria which had been the cause of the popular sedition. It is said

---

[1] Soc. v. 15-17; Ruf. ii. *H. E.* ii. 21-24; Theodoret, *H. E.* v. 21-23; many independent points in Soz.

[2] *Cod. Theod.* xvi. 10, 11.
[3] The opinion of St. Augustine (*Ep.* 158, *ad Marcell.*) is here quoted by Valesius: "lest the sufferings of the servants of God, which ought to be held in esteem in the Church, be defiled by the blood of their enemies." See, also, below, the death of Marcellus of Apamea.

that, when this imperial edict was read in public, the Christians uttered loud shouts of joy, because the emperor laid the odium of what had occurred upon the pagans. The people who were guarding the Serapion were so terrified at hearing these shouts, that they took to flight, and the Christians immediately obtained possession of the spot, which they have retained ever since. I have been informed that, on the night preceding this occurrence, Olympius heard the voice of one singing hallelujah in the Serapion. The doors were shut and everything was still; and as he could see no one, but could only hear the voice of the singer, he at once understood what the sign signified; and unknown to any one he quitted the Serapion and embarked for Italy. It is said that when the temple was being demolished, some stones were found, on which were hieroglyphic characters in the form of a cross, which on being submitted to the inspection of the learned, were interpreted as signifying the life to come.[1] These characters led to the conversion of several of the pagans, as did likewise other inscriptions found in the same place, and which contained predictions of the destruction of the temple. It was thus that the Serapion was taken, and, a little while after, converted into a church; it received the name of the Emperor Arcadius.

There were still pagans in many cities, who contended zealously in behalf of their temples; as, for instance, the inhabitants of Petræa and of Areopolis, in Arabia; of Raphi and Gaza, in Palestine; of Heriopolis in Phœnicia; and of Apamea, on the river Axius, in Syria. I have been informed that the inhabitants of the last-named city often armed the men of Galilee and the peasants of Lebanon in defense of their temples; and that at last, they even carried their audacity to such a height, as to slay a bishop named Marcellus. This bishop had commanded the demolition of all the temples in the city and villages, under the supposition that it would not be easy otherwise for them to be converted from their former religion. Having heard that there was a very spacious temple at Aulon, a district of Apamea, he repaired thither with a body of soldiers and gladiators. He stationed himself at a distance from the scene of conflict, beyond the reach of the arrows; for he was afflicted with the gout, and was unable to fight, to pursue, or to flee. Whilst the soldiers and gladiators were engaged in the assault against the temple, some pagans, discovering that he was alone, hastened to the place where he was separated from the combat; they arose suddenly and seized him, and burnt him alive. The perpetrators of this deed were not then

known, but, in course of time, they were detected, and the sons of Marcellus determined upon avenging his death. The council of the province, however, prohibited them from executing this design, and declared that it was not just that the relatives or friends of Marcellus should seek to avenge his death; when they should rather return thanks to God for having accounted him worthy to die in such a cause.

CHAP. XVI. — IN WHAT MANNER, AND FROM WHAT CAUSE, THE FUNCTIONS OF THE PRESBYTER, APPOINTED TO PRESIDE OVER THE IMPOSITION OF PENANCE, WERE ABOLISHED. DISSERTATION ON THE MODE OF IMPOSING PENANCE.

NECTARIUS, about this period, abolished the office of the presbyter whose duty it was to preside over the imposition of penance; and this is the first instance of the suppression of this office in the Church.[2] This example was followed by the bishops of every region. Various accounts have been given of the nature, the origin, and the cause of the abolition of this office. I shall state my own views on the subject. Impeccability is a Divine attribute, and belongs not to human nature; therefore God has decreed that pardon should be extended to the penitent, even after many transgressions. As in supplicating for pardon, it is requisite to confess the sin, it seems probable that the priests, from the beginning, considered it irksome to make this confession in public, before the whole assembly of the people. They therefore appointed a presbyter, of the utmost sanctity, and the most undoubted prudence, to act on these occasions; the penitents went to him, and confessed their transgressions; and it was his office to indicate the kind of penance adapted to each sin, and then when satisfaction had been made, to pronounce absolution. As the custom of doing penance never gained ground among the Novatians, regulations of this nature were of course unnecessary among them; but the custom prevailed among all other heretics, and prevails even to the present day. It is observed with great rigor by the Western churches,[3] particularly at Rome, where there is a place appropriated to the reception of penitents, in which spot they stand and mourn until the completion of the services, for it is not lawful for them to take part in the mysteries; then they cast themselves, with groans and lamentations, prostrate on the ground. The bishop conducts the ceremony, sheds tears, and prostrates himself in like manner; and all the people burst into tears, and groan aloud. Afterwards, the bishop rises first from the ground, and raises up the others; he offers up prayer on be-

---

[1] Ruf. *H. E.* ii. 29; Soc. v. 17.

[2] Soc. v. 19; yet Soz.'s account and setting is different.
[3] The Western Church preserved the earlier discipline.

half of the penitents, and then dismisses them. Each of the penitents subjects himself in private to voluntary suffering, either by fastings, by abstaining from the bath or from divers kinds of meats, or by other prescribed means, until a certain period appointed by the bishop. When the time arrives, he is made free from the consequences of his sin, and assembles at the church with the people. The Roman priests have carefully observed this custom from the beginning to the present time. In the church at Constantinople, a presbyter was always appointed to preside over the penitents, until a lady of the nobility made a deposition to the effect, that when she resorted as a penitent to the presbyter, to fast and offer supplications to God, and tarried for that purpose, in the church, a rape had been committed on her person by the deacon. Great displeasure was manifested by the people when this occurrence was made known to them, on account of the discredit that would result to the church; and the priests, in particular, were thereby greatly scandalized. Nectarius, after much hesitation as to what means ought to be adopted, deposed the deacon; and, at the advice of certain persons, who urged the necessity of leaving each individual to examine himself before participating in the sacred mysteries, he abolished the office of the presbyter presiding over penance. From that period, therefore, the performance of penance fell into disuse; and it seems to me, that extreme laxity of principle was thus substituted for the severity and rigor of antiquity. Under the ancient system, I think, offences were of rarer occurrence; for people were deterred from their commission, by the dread of confessing them, and of exposing them to the scrutiny of a severe judge. I believe it was from similar considerations, that the Emperor Theodosius, who was always zealous in promoting the glory of the Church, issued a law,[1] enacting that women should not be admitted into the ministry, unless they had had children, and were upwards of sixty years of age, according to the precept of the Apostle Paul.[2] By this law it was also decreed, that women who had shaved their heads should be ejected from the churches; and that the bishop by whom such women were admitted should be deposed from the bishopric.

CHAP. XVII. — BANISHMENT OF EUNOMIUS BY THEODOSIUS THE GREAT. THEOPHRONIUS, HIS SUCCESSOR; OF EUTYCHUS, AND OF DOROTHEUS, AND THEIR HERESIES; OF THOSE CALLED PSATHYRIANS; DIVISION OF THE ARIANS INTO DIFFERENT PARTIES; THOSE IN CONSTANTINOPLE WERE MORE LIMITED.

SUCH subjects as the above, however, are best left to the decision of individual judgment.

The emperor, about this period, condemned Eunomius to banishment.[3] This heretic had fixed his residence in the suburbs of Constantinople, and held frequent churches in private houses, where he read his own writings. He induced many to embrace his sentiments, so that the sectarians, who were named after him, became very numerous. He died not long after his banishment, and was interred at Dacora, his birthplace, a village of Cappadocia, situated near Mount Argeus, in the territory of Cæsarea. Theophronius, who was also a native of Cappadocia, and who had been his disciple, continued to promulgate his doctrines. Having gotten a smattering, through the writings of Aristotle, he composed an introduction to the study of the syllogisms in them, which he entitled "Exercises for the Mind." But he afterwards engaged, I have understood, in many unprofitable disputations, and soon ceased to confine himself to the doctrines of his master. But being eager for new things, he endeavored to prove, from the terms which are placed in the Sacred Scriptures, that though God foreknows that which is not, and knows that which is, and remembers what has happened, he does not always have that knowledge in the same manner with respect to the future and present, and changes his knowledge of the past. As this hypothesis appeared positively absurd to the Eunomians, they excommunicated him from their church; and he constituted himself the leader of a new sect, called, after his name, Theophronians. Not long after, Eutychus, one of the Eunomians, originated another sect in Constantinople, to which his own name was given. For the question had been proposed, as to whether the Son of God is or is not acquainted with the last hour; and for its solution, the words of the evangelist were quoted, in which it is stated that the day and hour are known only to the Father.[4] Eutychus, however, contended that this knowledge belongs also to the Son, inasmuch as He has received all things from the Father. The Eunomian presidents, having condemned this opinion, he seceded from communion with them, and went to join Eunomius in his place of banishment. A deacon, and some other individuals, who had been dispatched from Constantinople to accuse Eutychus, and, if necessary, to oppose him in argument, arrived first at the place of destination. When Eunomius was made acquainted with the object of their journey, he expressed himself in favor of the sentiments propounded by Eutychus; and, on his arrival, prayed with him, although it was not lawful to

[1] Cod. Theod. xvi. 2. 27.
[2] 1 Tim. v. 9. Cf. change in Justinian, Novell. 123. 13.

[3] Soc. v. 20, 23, 24; Philost. x. 6. Soz. has some independent points.   [4] Matt. xxiv. 36.

pray with any one who travels unprovided with letters written in sacred characters, attesting his being in communion. Eunomius died soon after this contention; and the Eunomian president, at Constantinople, refused to receive Eutychus into communion; for he antagonized him from jealousy because he was not even of clerical rank, and because he could not answer his arguments, and did not find it possible to solve his problems. Eutychus, therefore, separated those who had espoused his sentiments into a personal heresy. Many assert that he and Theophronius were the first who propounded the peculiar views entertained by the Eunomians concerning divine baptism. The above is a brief account of such details as I have been able to give in order to afford a succinct knowledge of the causes which led the Eunomians to be divided among themselves. I should be prolix were I to enter into further particulars; and, indeed, the subject would be by no means an easy one to me, since I have no such dialectic skill.

The following question was, in the meantime, agitated among the Arians of Constantinople: Prior to the existence of the Son (whom they regard as having proceeded out of nothing), is God to be termed the Father? Dorotheus, who had been summoned from Antioch to rule over them in the place of Marinus, was of opinion that God could not have been called the Father prior to the existence of the Son, because the name of Father has a necessary connection with that of Son. Marinus, on the other hand, maintained that the Father was the Father, even when the Son existed not; and he advanced this opinion either from conviction, or else from the desire of contention, and from jealousy at the preference that had been shown to Dorotheus in the Church. The Arians were thus divided into two parties; Dorotheus and his followers retained possession of the houses of prayer, while Marinus, and those who seceded with him, erected new edifices in which to hold their own churches. The name " Psathyrians " and " Goths " were given to the partisans of Marinus; Psathyrians, because Theoctistus, a certain cake-vender ($\psi\alpha\theta\nu\rho\sigma\pi\dot\omega\lambda\eta\varsigma$) was a zealous advocate of their opinions; and Goths, because their sentiments were approved by Selinus, bishop of that nation. Almost all these barbarians followed the instructions of Selinus, and they gathered in churches with the followers of Marinus. The Goths were drawn to Selinus particularly because he had formerly been the secretary of Ulphilas, and had succeeded him as bishop. He was capable of teaching in their churches, not only in the vernacular, but also in the Greek language.

Soon after a contest for precedency arose between Marinus and Agapius, whom Marinus himself had ordained bishop over the Arians at Ephesus; and in the quarrel which ensued, the Goths took the part of Agapius. It is said that many of the Arian clergy of that city were so much irritated through the ambition displayed by these two bishops, that they communed with the Catholic Church. Such was the origin of the division of the Arians into two factions, — a division which still subsists; so that, in every city, they have separate churches. The Arians at Constantinople, however, after a separation of thirty-five years, were reconciled to each other by Plinthas, formerly a consul,[1] general of the cavalry and infantry, a man possessed of great influence at court. To prevent the revival of the former dissensions among them, the question which had been the cause of the division was forbidden to be mooted. And these occurrences took place later.

CHAP. XVIII. — ANOTHER HERESY, THAT OF THE SABBATIANS, IS ORIGINATED BY THE NOVATIANS. THEIR SYNOD IN SANGARUS. ACCOUNT IN GREATER DETAIL OF THE EASTER FESTIVAL.

A DIVISION arose during the same reign among the Novatians[2] concerning the celebration of the festival of Easter, and from this dispute originated another, called the Sabbatian. Sabbatius, who, with Theoctistus and Macarius, had been ordained presbyter by Marcian, adopted the opinion of the co-presbyters, who had been convened at Pazoucoma[3] during the reign of Valens, and maintained that the feast of the Passover (Easter) ought to be celebrated by Christians as by Jews. He seceded from the Church at first for the purpose of exercising greater austerity, for he professed to adopt a very austere mode of life. He also declared that one motive of his secession was, that many persons who participated in the mysteries appeared to him to be unworthy of the honor. When, however, his design of introducing innovations was detected, Marcian expressed his regret at having ordained him, and, it is said, was often heard to exclaim that he would rather have laid his hands upon thorns than upon the head of Sabbatius. Perceiving that the people of his diocese were being rent into two factions, Marcian summoned all the bishops of his own persuasion to Sangarus, a town of Bithynia, near the seashore, not far from the city of Helenopolis. When they had assembled, they summoned Sabbatius, and asked him to state the cause of his grievance; and as he merely complained of the diversity prevailing in regard to the feast, they suspected that he made this a pretext to disguise his love of precedency, and made him

---

[1] He held the consulate with Monaxius, A.D. 419.
[2] Soc. v. 21, 22. Soz. has independent material.
[3] $\Pi\alpha\zeta\sigma\nu\kappa\dot\omega\mu\eta$; Soc. $\dot\epsilon\nu$ $\Pi\dot\alpha\zeta\phi$ $\kappa\dot\omega\mu\eta$.

declare upon oath that he would never accept the episcopal office. When he had taken the required oath, all were of the same opinion, and they voted to hold the church together, for the difference prevailing in the celebration of the Paschal feast ought by no means to be made an occasion for separation from communion; and they decided that each individual should be at liberty to observe the feast according to his own judgment. They enacted a canon on the subject, which they styled the "Indifferent (ἀδιά-φορος) Canon." Such were the transactions of the assembly at Sangarus. From that period Sabbatius adhered to the usage of the Jews; and unless all happened to observe the feast at the same time, he fasted, according to the custom, but in advance, and celebrated the Passover with the usual prescriptions by himself. He passed the Saturday, from the evening to the appointed time, in watching and in offering up the prescribed prayers; and on the following day he assembled with the multitude, and partook of the mysteries. This mode of observing the feast was at first unnoticed by the people; but as, in process of time, it began to attract observation, and to become more generally known, he found a great many imitators, particularly in Phrygia and Galatia, to whom this celebration of the feast became a national custom. Eventually he openly seceded from communion, and became the bishop of those who had espoused his sentiments, as we shall have occasion to show in the proper place.

I am, for my own part, astonished that Sabbatius and his followers attempted to introduce this innovation. The ancient Hebrews, as is related by Eusebius,[1] on the testimony of Philo, Josephus, Aristobulus, and several others, offered the sacrifices after the vernal equinox, when the sun is in the first sign of the zodiac, called by the Greeks the Ram, and when the moon is in the opposite quarter of the heavens, and in the fourteenth day of her age. Even the Novatians themselves, who have studied the subject with some accuracy, declare that the founder of their heresy and his first disciples did not follow this custom, which was introduced for the first time by those who assembled at Pazoucoma; and that at old Rome the members of this sect still observe the same practice as the Romans, who have not deviated from their original usage in this particular, the custom having been handed down to them by the holy apostles Peter and Paul. Further, the Samaritans, who are scrupulous observers of the laws of Moses, never celebrate this festival till the first-fruits have reached maturity; they say it is, in the law, called the Feast of First-Fruits, and before these appear, it is not lawful to observe the feast; and, therefore, necessarily the vernal equinox must precede. Hence arises my astonishment that those who profess to adopt the Jewish custom in the celebration of this feast, do not conform to the ancient practice of the Jews. With the exception of the people above mentioned, and the Quartodecimani of Asia, all heresies, I believe, celebrate the Passover in the same manner as the Romans and the Egyptians. The Quartodecimani are so called because they observe this festival, like the Jews, on the fourteenth day of the moon, and hence their name. The Novatians observe the day of the resurrection. They follow the custom of the Jews and the Quartodecimani, except when the fourteenth day of the moon falls upon the first day of the week, in which case they celebrate the feast so many days after the Jews, as there are intervening days between the fourteenth day of the moon and the following Lord's day. The Montanists, who are called Pepuzites and Phrygians, celebrate the Passover according to a strange fashion which they introduced. They blame those who regulate the time of observing the feast according to the course of the moon, and affirm that it is right to attend exclusively to the cycles of the sun. They reckon each month to consist of thirty days, and account the day after the vernal equinox as the first day of the year, which, according to the Roman method of computation, would be called the ninth day before the calends of April. It was on this day, they say, that the two great luminaries appointed for the indication of times and of years were created. This they prove by the fact that every eight years the sun and the moon meet together in the same point of the heavens. The moon's cycle of eight years is accomplished in ninety-nine months, and in two thousand nine hundred and twenty-two days; and during that time there are eight revolutions made by the sun, each comprising three hundred and sixty-five days, and the fourth part of a day. For they compute the day of the creation of the sun, mentioned in Sacred Writ, to have been the fourteenth day of the moon, occurring after the ninth day before the calends of the month of April, and answering to the eighth day prior to ides of the same month. They always celebrate the Passover on this day, when it falls on the day of the resurrection; otherwise they celebrate it on the following Lord's day; for it is written according to their assertion that the feast may be held on any day between the fourteenth and twenty-first.

CHAP. XIX. — A LIST WORTHY OF STUDY, GIVEN BY THE HISTORIAN, OF CUSTOMS AMONG DIFFERENT NATIONS AND CHURCHES.

---

[1] Eus. *H. E.* vii. 32. Extracts from the canons of Anatolius.

WE have now described the various usages that prevailed in the celebration of the Passover.[1] It appears to me that Victor, bishop of Rome, and Polycarp, bishop of Smyrna, came to a very wise decision on the controversy that had arisen between them.[2] For as the bishops of the West did not deem it necessary to dishonor the tradition handed down to them by Peter and by Paul, and as, on the other hand, the Asiatic bishops persisted in following the rules laid down by John the evangelist, they unanimously agreed to continue in the observance of the festival according to their respective customs, without separation from communion with each other. They faithfully and justly assumed, that those who accorded in the essentials of worship ought not to separate from one another on account of customs. For exactly similar traditions on every point are to be found in all the churches, even though they hold the same opinions. There are, for instance, many cities in Scythia, and yet they all have but one bishop; whereas, in other nations a bishop serves as priest even over a village, as I have myself observed in Arabia, and in Cyprus, and among the Novatians and Montanists of Phrygia. Again, there are even now but seven deacons at Rome, answering precisely to the number ordained by the apostles, of whom Stephen was the first martyr; whereas, in other churches, the number of deacons is a matter of indifference. At Rome hallelujah is sung once annually, namely, on the first day of the festival of the Passover; so that it is a common thing among the Romans to swear by the fact of hearing or singing this hymn. In that city the people are not taught by the bishop, nor by any one in the Church. At Alexandria the bishop of the city alone teaches the people, and it is said that this custom has prevailed there ever since the days of Arius, who, though but a presbyter, broached a new doctrine. Another strange custom also prevails at Alexandria which I have never witnessed nor heard of elsewhere, and this is, that when the Gospel is read the bishop does not rise from his seat. The archdeacon alone reads the Gospel in this city, whereas in some places it is read by the deacons, and in many churches only by the priests; while on noted days it is read by the bishops, as, for instance, at Constantinople, on the first day of the festival of the resurrection.[3] In some churches the interval called Quadragesima, which occurs before this festival, and is devoted by the people to fasting, is made to consist of six weeks; and this is the case in Illyria and the Western regions, in Libya, throughout Egypt, and in Palestine; whereas it is made to comprise seven weeks at Constantinople, and in the neighboring provinces as far as Phœnicia. In some churches the people fast three alternate weeks, during the space of six or seven weeks, whereas in others they fast continuously during the three weeks immediately preceding the festival. Some people, as the Montanists, only fast two weeks. Assemblies are not held in all churches on the same time or manner. The people of Constantinople, and almost everywhere, assemble together on the Sabbath, as well as on the first day of the week, which custom is never observed at Rome or at Alexandria. There are several cities and villages in Egypt where, contrary to the usage established elsewhere, the people meet together on Sabbath evenings, and, although they have dined previously, partake of the mysteries. The same prayers and psalms are not recited nor the same lections read on the same occasions in all churches. Thus the book entitled "The Apocalypse of Peter," which was considered altogether spurious by the ancients, is still read in some of the churches of Palestine, on the day of preparation, when the people observe a fast in memory of the passion of the Saviour. So the work entitled "The Apocalypse of the Apostle Paul," though unrecognized by the ancients, is still esteemed by most of the monks. Some persons affirm that the book was found during this reign, by Divine revelation, in a marble box, buried beneath the soil in the house of Paul at Tarsus in Cilicia. I have been informed that this report is false by Cilix, a presbyter of the church in Tarsus, a man of very advanced age, as is indicated by his gray hairs, who says that no such occurrence is known among them, and wonders if the heretics did not invent the story. What I have said upon this subject must now suffice. Many other customs are still to be observed in cities and villages; and those who have been brought up in their observance would, from respect to the great men who instituted and perpetuated these customs, consider it wrong to abolish them. Similar motives must be attributed to those who observe different practices in the celebration of the feast which has led us into this long digression.

CHAP. XX. — EXTENSION OF OUR DOCTRINES, AND COMPLETE DEMOLITION OF IDOLATROUS TEMPLES. INUNDATION OF THE NILE.

WHILE the heretics were disrupted among themselves, the Catholic Church increased more and more by many accessions from the heterodox, on account of the dissensions among them and

---

[1] Soc. v. 22. Soz. has much new matter of his own.
[2] Eus. H. E. iv. 14 (from Irenæus). Not Victor, but Anicetus; the conflict of Victor was with Polycrates, bishop of Ephesus. Eus. H. E. v. 24.
[3] Nicephorus (xii. 34) declares that this custom lasted down to his own day; and that it was practiced also on the 1st of January, as well as at Easter.

especially from multitudes of pagans.[1] The emperor having observed that the practice of idolatry had been greatly promoted by the facility of constant ingress and egress to and from the temple, directed the entrances of all temples to be closed; and eventually he commanded the demolition of many of these edifices.[2] When the pagans found themselves deprived of their own houses of prayer, they began to frequent our churches; for they did not dare to offer sacrifices after the pagan form in secret, for it was dangerous, since the sacrifice was under the penalty of death and of confiscation of property.

It is said that the river of Egypt did not overflow its banks this year at the proper season; and that the Egyptians angrily ascribed this circumstance to the prohibition of sacrifices to it, according to the ancestral law. The governor of the province, apprehensive lest the general discontent should terminate in sedition, sent a message to the emperor on the subject. But the emperor, far from attaching more importance to the temporary fertility produced by the Nile, than to the fidelity he owed to God and the interests of religion, replied as follows: "Let that river cease to flow, if enchantments are requisite to insure the regularity of its course; or if it delights in sacrifices, or if blood must be mingled with the waters that derive their source from the paradise of God." Soon afterwards, the Nile overflowed its banks with such violence, that the highest eminences were submerged. When it reached the farthest limit and almost had attained the fullest measure, the water did not the less press upward, so that the Egyptians were thrown into the contrary fear. The dread was lest the city of Alexandria and part of Libya should be submerged. The pagans of Alexandria, irritated at this unexpected occurrence, exclaimed in derision at the public theatres, that the river, like an old man or fool, could not moderate its proceedings. Many of the Egyptians were hence induced to abandon the superstitions of their forefathers, and embrace Christianity. These incidents are given as I have learned them.

CHAP. XXI. — DISCOVERY OF THE HONORED HEAD OF THE FORERUNNER OF OUR LORD, AND THE EVENTS ABOUT IT.

ABOUT this time the head of John the Baptist, which Herodias had asked of Herod the tetrarch, was removed to Constantinople.[3] It is said that it was discovered by some monks of the Macedonian heresy, who originally dwelt at Constantinople, and afterwards fixed their abode in Cilicia. Mardonius, the first eunuch of the palace, made known this discovery at court, during the preceding reign; and Valens commanded that the relic should be removed to Constantinople. The officers appointed to carry it thither, placed it in a public chariot, and proceeded with it as far as Pantichium, a district in the territory of Chalcedon. Here the mules of the chariot suddenly stopped; and neither the application of the lash, nor the threats of the hostlers, could induce them to advance further. So extraordinary an event was considered by all, and even by the emperor himself, to be of God; and the holy head was therefore deposited at Cosilaos, a village in the neighborhood, which belonged to Mardonius. Soon after, the Emperor Theodosius, impelled by an impulse from God, or from the prophet, repaired to the village. He determined upon removing the remains of the Baptist, and it is said met with no opposition, except from a holy virgin, Matrona, who had been the servant and guardian of the relic. He laid aside all authority and force, and after many entreaties, extorted a reluctant consent from her to remove the head; for she bore in mind what had occurred at the period when Valens commanded its removal. The emperor placed it, with the box in which it was encased, in his purple robe, and conveyed it to a place called Hebdomos, in the suburbs of Constantinople, where he erected a spacious and magnificent temple. The woman who had been appointed to the charge of the relic could not be persuaded by the emperor to renounce her religious sentiments, although he had recourse to entreaty and promises; for she was, it appears, of the Macedonian heresy. A presbyter of the same tendency, named Vincent, who also took charge of the coffin of the prophet, and performed the sacerdotal functions over it, followed the religious opinions of the emperor, and entered into communion with the Catholic Church. He had taken an oath, as the Macedonians affirm, never to swerve from their doctrines; but he afterwards openly declared that, if the Baptist would follow the emperor, he also would enter into communion with him and be separated. He was a Persian, and had left his country in company with a relative named Addas, during the reign of Constantius, in order to avoid the persecution which the Christians were then suffering in Persia. On his arrival in the Roman territories, he was placed in the ranks of the clergy, and advanced to the office of presbyter. Addas married and rendered great service to the Church. He left a son named Auxentius, who was noted for his very faithful piety, his zeal for his friends, the moderation of his life, his love of letters, and the greatness of his attainments

[1] Independent chapter. Cf. Ruf. *H. E.* ii. 19; Theodoret, *H. E.* v. 21; Zos. iv. 28, 29.   [2] *Cod. Theod.* xvi. 10, 12.
[3] An independent chapter. Cf. Philost. vii. 4; Theodoret, *H. E.* iii. 7; Marcell. *Chron.* A.D. 453; Ruf. *H. E.* ii. 28.

in pagan and ecclesiastical literature. He was modest and retiring in deportment, although admitted to familiarity with the emperor and the courtiers, and possessed of a very illustrious appointment. His memory is still revered by the monks and zealous men, who were all acquainted with him. The woman who had been entrusted with the relic remained during the rest of her life at Cosilaos. She was greatly distinguished by her piety and wisdom, and instructed many holy virgins; and I have been assured that many still survive who reflect the honorable character which was the result of training under Matrona.

CHAP. XXII. — DEATH OF VALENTINIAN THE YOUNGER, EMPEROR IN ROME, THROUGH STRANGLING. THE TYRANT EUGENIUS. PROPHECY OF JOHN, THE MONK OF THEBAÏS.

WHILE Theodosius was thus occupied in the wise and peaceful government of his subjects in the East, and in the service of God, intelligence was brought that Valentinian had been strangled.[1] Some say that he was put to death by the eunuchs of the bedchamber, at the solicitation of Arbogastes, a military chief, and of certain courtiers, who were displeased because the young prince had begun to walk in the footsteps of his father, concerning the government, and contrary to the opinions approved by them. Others assert, however, that Valentinian committed the fatal deed with his own hands, because he found himself impeded in attempting deeds which are not lawful in one of his years; and on this account he did not deem it worth while to live; for although an emperor, he was not allowed to do what he wished. It is said that the boy was noble in person, and excellent in royal manners; and that, had he lived to the age of manhood, he would have shown himself worthy of holding the reins of empire, and would have surpassed his father in magnanimity and justice. But though endowed with these promising qualities, he died in the manner above related.

A certain man named Eugenius, who was by no means sincere in his professions of Christianity, aspired to sovereignty, and assumed the symbols of imperial power. He was hoping to succeed in the attempt safely; for he was led by the predictions of individuals who professed to foresee the future, by the examination of the entrails and livers of animals and the course of the stars. Men of the highest rank among the Romans were addicted to these superstitions. Flavian, then a prætorian prefect, a learned man, and one who appeared to have an aptitude

for politics, was noted for being conversant with every means of foretelling the future. He persuaded Eugenius to take up arms by assuring him that he was destined for the throne, that his warlike undertakings would be crowned with victory, and that the Christian religion would be abolished. Deceived by these flattering representations, Eugenius raised an army and took possession of the gates into Italy, as the Romans call the Julian Alps, an elevated and precipitous range of mountains; these he seized beforehand and fortified, for they had but one path in the narrows, and were shut in on each side by precipices and the loftiest mountains. Theodosius was perplexed as to whether he ought to await the issue of the war, or whether it would be better in the first place to attack Eugenius; and in this dilemma, he determined to consult John, a monk of Thebaïs, who, as I have before stated, was celebrated for his knowledge of the future. He therefore sent Eutropius, a eunuch of the palace, and of tried fidelity, to Egypt, with orders to bring John, if possible, to court; but, in case of his refusal, to learn what ought to be done. When he came to John, the monk could not be persuaded to go to the emperor, but he sent word by Eutropius that the war would terminate in favor of Theodosius, and that the tyrant would be slain'; but that, after the victory, Theodosius himself would die in Italy. The truth of both of these predictions was confirmed by events.

CHAP. XXIII. — EXACTION OF TRIBUTE IN ANTIOCH, AND DEMOLITION OF THE STATUES OF THE EMPEROR. EMBASSY HEADED BY FLAVIAN THE CHIEF PRIEST.

IN this time, on account of the necessities of war, it seemed best to the officials whose concern it was, to impose more than the customary taxes; for this reason the populace of Antioch in Syria revolted;[2] the statues of the emperor and empress were thrown down and dragged by ropes through the city, and, as is usual on such occasions, the enraged multitude uttered every insulting epithet that passion could suggest. The emperor determined to avenge this insult by the death of many of the citizens of Antioch; the people were struck dumb at the mere announcement; the rage of the citizens had subsided, and had given place to repentance; and, as if already subjected to the threatened punishment, they abandoned themselves to groans and tears, and supplicated God to turn away the anger of the emperor, and made use of some threnodic hymns for their litanies. They deputed

---

[1] Ruf. *H. E.* ii. 31–33, the source; Philost. xi. 1, 2; Theodoret, *H. E.* v. 24; Soc. v. 25; Zos. iv. 53, 54; Oros. vii. 35.

[2] Soz. is again independent. Cf. Theodoret, *H. E.* v. 20; Chrysost. *Homiliæ*, xxi., *de Statuis ad populum Antiochenum habitæ.*

Flavian, their bishop, to go on an embassy to Theodosius; but on his arrival, finding that the resentment of the emperor at what had occurred was unabated, he had recourse to the following artifice. He caused some young men accustomed to sing at the table of the emperor to utter these hymns with the litanies of the Antiochans. It is said that the humanity of the emperor was excited; he was overcome by pity at once; his wrath was subdued, and as his heart yearned over the city, he shed tears on the cup which he held in his hand. It is reported that, on the night before the sedition occurred, a spectre was seen in the form of a woman of prodigious height and terrible aspect, pacing through the streets of the city, lashing the air with an ill-sounding whip, similar to that which is used in goading on the beasts brought forward at the public theatres. It might have been inferred that the sedition was excited by the agency of some evil and malicious demon. There is no doubt but that much bloodshed would have ensued, had not the wrath of the emperor been stayed by his respect for this sacerdotal entreaty.

CHAP. XXIV. — VICTORY OF THEODOSIUS THE EM-
PEROR OVER EUGENIUS.

WHEN he had completed his preparations for war,[1] Theodosius declared his younger son Honorius emperor, and leaving him to reign at Constantinople conjointly with Arcadius, who had previously been appointed emperor, he departed from the East to the West at the head of his troops. His army consisted not only of Roman soldiers, but of bands of barbarians from the banks of the Ister. It is said that when he left Constantinople, he came to the seventh milestone, and went to pray to God in the church which he had erected in honor of John the Baptist; and in his name prayed that success might attend the Roman arms, and besought the Baptist himself to aid him. After offering up these prayers he proceeded towards Italy, crossed the Alps, and took the first guard-posts. On descending from the heights of these mountains, he perceived a plain before him covered with infantry and cavalry, and became at the same time aware that some of the enemy's troops were lying in ambush behind him, among the recesses of the mountains. The advance guard of his army attacked the infantry stationed in the plain, and a desperate and very doubtful conflict ensued. Further, when the army surrounded him, he considered that he had come into the power of men, and could not be saved even by those who would desire to do so, since

those who had been posted in his rear were seizing the heights; he fell prone upon the earth, and prayed with tears, and God instantly answered him; for the officers of the troops stationed in ambush on the height sent to offer him their services as his allies, provided that he would assign them honorable posts in his army. As he had neither paper nor ink within reach, he took up some tablets, and wrote on them the high and befitting appointments he would confer upon them, provided that they would fulfill their promise to him. Under these conditions they advanced to the emperor. The issue did not yet incline to either side, but the battle was still evenly balanced in the plain, when a tremendous wind descended into the face of the enemy. It was such an one as we have never before recorded, and broke up the ranks of the enemies. The arrows and darts which were sent against the Romans, as if projected by the opposing ranks, were turned upon the bodies of those who had cast them; and their shields were wrenched from their hands, and whirled against them with filth and dust. Standing thus exposed, in a defenseless condition, to the weapons of the Romans, many of them perished, while the few who attempted to effect an escape were soon captured. Eugenius threw himself at the feet of the emperor, and implored him to spare his life; but while in the act of offering up these entreaties, a soldier struck off his head. Arbogastes fled after the battle, and fell by his own hands. It is said that while the battle was being fought, a demoniac presented himself in the temple of God which is in the Hebdomos, where the emperor had engaged in prayer on starting out, and insulted John the Baptist, taunting him with having his head cut off, and shouted the following words: "You conquer me, and lay snares for my army." The persons who happened to be on the spot, and who were waiting impatiently to learn some news of the war, were amazed, and wrote an account of it on the day that it occurred, and afterwards ascertained that it was the same day as that on which the battle had been fought. Such is the history of these transactions.

CHAP. XXV. — INTREPID BEARING OF ST. AMBROSE
IN THE PRESENCE OF THE EMPEROR THEODO-
SIUS. MASSACRE AT THESSALONICA. NARRATIVE
OF THE OTHER RIGHTEOUS DEEDS OF THIS
SAINT.

AFTER the death of Eugenius, the emperor went to Milan, and repaired towards the church to pray within its walls.[2] When he drew near the gates of the edifice, he was met by Ambrose,

---

[1] Soz. has his account from an independent source. Cf. Ruf. *H. E.* ii. 33; Philost. xi. 2; Soc. v. 25; Theodoret, *H. E.* v. 24; Zos. iv. 55-58; Olymp. *Fr.* 19.

[2] An independent chapter. Cf. Theodoret, *H. E.* v. 17, 18; Ruf. *H. E.* ii. 18; Ambrose, *Epp. Cl.* i. 51.

the bishop of the city, who took hold of him by his purple robe, and said to him, in the presence of the multitude, "Stand back! a man defiled by sin, and with hands imbrued in blood unjustly shed, is not worthy, without repentance, to enter within these sacred precincts, or partake of the holy mysteries." The emperor, struck with admiration at the boldness of the bishop, began to reflect on his own conduct, and, with much contrition, retraced his steps. The occasion of the sin was as follows. When Buthericus was general of the troops in Illyria, a charioteer saw him shamefully exposed at a tavern, and attempted an outrage; he was apprehended and put in custody. Some time after, some magnificent races were to be held at the hippodrome, and the populace of Thessalonica demanded the release of the prisoner, considering him necessary to the celebration of the contest. As their request was not attended to, they rose up in sedition and finally slew Buthericus. On hearing of this deed, the wrath of the emperor was excited immediately, and he commanded that a certain number of the citizens should be put to death. The city was filled with the blood of many unjustly shed; for strangers, who had but just arrived there on their journey to other lands, were sacrificed with the others. There were many cases of suffering well worthy of commiseration, of which the following is an instance. A merchant offered himself to be slain as a substitute for his two sons who had both been selected as victims, and promised the soldiers to give them all the gold he possessed, on condition of their effecting the exchange. They could not but compassionate his misfortune, and consented to take him as a substitute for one of his sons, but declared that they did not dare to let off both the young men, as that would render the appointed number of the slain incomplete. The father gazed on his sons, groaning and weeping; he could not save either from death, but he continued hesitating until they had been put to death, being overcome by an equal love for each. I have also been informed, that a faithful slave voluntarily offered to die instead of his master, who was being led to the place of execution. It appears that it was for these and other acts of cruelty that Ambrose rebuked the emperor, forbade him to enter the church, and excommunicated him. Theodosius publicly confessed his sin in the church, and during the time set apart for penance, refrained from wearing his imperial ornaments, according to the usage of mourners. He also enacted a law[1] prohibiting the officers entrusted with the execution of the imperial mandates, from inflicting the punishment of death till thirty days after

the mandate had been issued, in order that the wrath of the emperor might have time to be appeased, and that room might be made for the exercise of mercy and repentance.

Ambrose, no doubt, performed many other actions worthy of his priestly office, which are known, as is likely, only to the inhabitants of the country. Among the illustrious deeds that are attributed to him, I have been made acquainted with the following. It was the custom of the emperor to take a seat in assemblies of the church within the palisades of the altar, so that he sat apart from the rest of the people. Ambrose, considering that this custom had originated either from subserviency or from want of discipline, caused the emperor to be seated without the trellis work of the altar, so that he sat in front of the people, and behind the priests. The emperor Theodosius approved of this best tradition, as did likewise his successors; and we are told that it has been ever since scrupulously observed.

I think it necessary to make a record of another action worthy of mention performed by this bishop. A pagan of distinction insulted Gratian, affirming that he was unworthy of his father; and he was in consequence condemned to death. As he was being led out to execution, Ambrose went to the palace to implore a pardon. Gratian was then engaged in witnessing a private exhibition of the hunt, such as the emperors were wont to celebrate for their private pleasure, and not for the public pastime. On finding this to be the case, the bishop went to the gate where they led in the beasts; he hid himself, and entered with the hunters who took charge of the animals, and did not intermit, although Gratian and his attendants resisted, till he had obtained an immediate and saving consent of the emperor, which released the man who was to be led out to death. Ambrose was very diligent in the observance of the laws of the Church, and in maintaining discipline among his clergy. I have selected the above two incidents from among the records of his numerous magnanimous deeds, in order to show with what intrepidity he addressed those in power when the service of God was in question.

CHAP. XXVI. — ST. DONATUS, BISHOP OF EURŒA, AND THEOTIMUS, HIGH-PRIEST OF SCYTHIA.

THERE were at this period many other bishops[2] in various parts of the empire highly celebrated for their sanctity and high qualifications, of whom Donatus, bishop of Eurœa[3] in Epirus,

---

[1] Not extant.

[2] An independent chapter from a Greek life of Donatus, which was probably incorporated in Anastasius' translation. A Greek biography of Theotimus was not unlikely the basis of the account of the bishop of Tomi.   [3] Also Euoria.

deserves to be particularly instanced. The inhabitants of the country relate many extraordinary miracles which he performed, of which the most celebrated seems to have been the destruction of a dragon of enormous size. It had stationed itself on the high road, at a place called Chamægephyræ, and devoured sheep, goats, oxen, horses, and men. Donatus came upon this beast, attacked it unarmed, without sword, lance, or javelin; it raised its head, and was about to dash upon him, when Donatus made the sign of the cross with his finger in the air, and spat upon the dragon. The saliva entered its mouth, and it immediately expired. As it lay extended on the earth it did not appear inferior in size to the noted serpents of India. I have been informed that the people of the country yoked eight pair of oxen to transport the body to a neighboring field, where they burnt it, that it might not during the process of decomposition corrupt the air and generate disease. The tomb of this bishop is deposited in a magnificent house of prayer which bears his name. It is situated near a fountain of many waters, which God caused to rise from the ground in answer to his prayer, in an arid spot where no water had previously existed. For it is said that one day, when on a journey, he had to pass through this locality; and, perceiving that his companions were suffering from thirst, he moved the soil with his hands and engaged in prayer; before his prayer was concluded, a spring of water arose from the ground, which has never since been dried up. The inhabitants of Isoria, a village in the territory of Eurœa, bear testimony to the truth of this narration.

The church of Tomi, and indeed all the churches of Scythia, were at this period under the government of Theotimus, a Scythian. He had been brought up in the practice of philosophy; and his virtues had so won the admiration of the barbarian Huns, who dwelt on the banks of the Ister, that they called him the god of the Romans, for they had experience of divine deeds wrought by him. It is said that one day, when traveling toward the country of the barbarians, he perceived some of them advancing towards Tomi. His attendants burst forth into lamentations, and gave themselves up at once for lost; but he merely descended from horseback, and prayed. The consequence was, that the barbarians passed by without seeing him, his attendants, or the horses from which they had dismounted. As these tribes frequently devastated Scythia by their predatory incursions, he tried to subdue the ferocity of their disposition by presenting them with food and gifts. One of the barbarians hence concluded that he was a man of wealth, and, determining to take him prisoner, leaned upon his shield, as was his custom when parleying with his enemies; the man raised up his right hand in order to throw a rope, which he firmly grasped, over the bishop, for he intended to drag him away to his own country; but in the attempt, his hand remained extended in the air, and the barbarian was not released from his terrible bonds until his companions had implored Theotimus to intercede with God in his behalf.

It is said that Theotimus always retained the long hair which he wore when he first devoted himself to the practice of philosophy. He was very temperate, had no stated hours for his repasts, but ate and drank when compelled to do so by the calls of hunger and of thirst. I consider it to be the part of a philosopher to yield to the demands of these appetites from necessity, and not from the love of sensual gratification.

CHAP. XXVII. — ST. EPIPHANIUS, BISHOP OF CYPRUS, AND A PARTICULAR ACCOUNT OF HIS ACTS.

EPIPHANIUS was at this period at the head of the metropolitan church of Cyprus.[1] He was celebrated, not only for the virtues he manifested and miraculous deeds during his life, but also for the honor that was rendered to him by God after his death; for it was said that demons were expelled, and diseases healed at his tomb. Many wonderful actions wrought while he lived are attributed to him, of which the following is one of the most remarkable that has come to our knowledge. He was extremely liberal towards the needy, either to those who had suffered from shipwreck or any other calamity; and after expending the whole of his own patrimony in the relief of such cases, he applied the treasures of the church to the same purpose. These treasures had been greatly increased by the donations of pious men of various provinces, who had been induced by their admiration of Epiphanius to entrust him with the distribution of their alms during their lives, or to bequeath their property to him for this purpose at their death. It is said that on one occasion the treasurer, who was a godly man, discovered that the revenues of the church had been nearly drained, and so little remained in the treasury that he considered it his duty to rebuke the bishop as a spendthrift. Epiphanius, however, having, notwithstanding these remonstrances, given away the small sum that had remained, a stranger went to the little house where the treasurer lived, and placed in his hands a bag containing many gold coins. Since neither the giver nor the sender was visible, it seemed very naturally miraculous, that in a gift of so much money a man should keep him-

---

[1] Independent chapter. Cf. life by alleged Polybius.

self unknown; thus everybody thought it to be a Divine work.

I desire also to relate another miracle that is attributed to Epiphanius. I have heard that a similar action has been related of Gregory, who formerly governed Neocæsarea; and I see no reason to doubt the veracity of the account; but it does not disprove the authenticity of the miracle attributed to Epiphanius. Peter, the apostle, was not the only man who raised another from the dead; John, the evangelist, wrought a similar miracle at Ephesus; as did likewise the daughters of Philip at Hierapolis. Similar actions have been performed in different ages by the men of God. The miracle which I wish to instance is the following. Two beggars having ascertained when Epiphanius would pass that way, agreed to extract a larger donation than usual from him by having recourse to stratagem. As soon as the bishop was seen approaching, one of the beggars flung himself on the ground and simulated death; the other stood by and uttered loud lamentations, deploring the loss of his companion, and his own poverty, which made him unable to procure sepulture for him. Epiphanius prayed to God that the deceased might rise in peace; he gave the survivor sufficient money for the interment, and said to the weeper, "Take measures, my son, for the burial of your companion, and weep no more; he cannot now arise from the dead; the calamity was inevitable, therefore you ought to bear it with resignation." Saying these words, the bishop departed from the spot. As soon as there was no one in sight, the beggar who had addressed Epiphanius touched the other with his foot, as he lay extended on the ground, and said to him, "You have well performed your part; arise now, for through your labor, we have a good provision for to-day." He, however, lay in the same way, neither heard any cry, nor perceived him who moved him with all his strength; the other beggar ran after the priest and confessed their artifice, and, with lamentations and tearing of his hair, he besought Epiphanius to restore his companion. Epiphanius merely exhorted him to submit with patience to the catastrophe, and sent him away. God did not undo what had happened, because, I feel persuaded, it was his design to show that those who practice deception on his servants are accounted as guilty of the fraud as if it had been perpetrated against Him who sees all, and who hears all.

CHAP. XXVIII. ACACIUS, BISHOP OF BERŒA, ZENO, AND AJAX, MEN DISTINGUISHED AND RENOWNED FOR VIRTUE.

THE following details are also the results of inquiry.[1] Acacius[2] was conspicuous among the bishops; he had already previously administered the episcopate of Berœa in Syria. There are of course many actions of his, which are worthy of record. He was from his youth brought up to the profession of ascetic monasticism, and was rigid in observing all the regulations of this mode of life. When he was raised to the bishopric, he gave this evidence of greatest virtue, in that he kept the episcopal residence open at all hours of the day, so that the citizens and strangers were always free to visit him, even when he was at meals or at repose. This course of conduct is, in my opinion, very admirable; for either he was living in such a way as to be always sure of himself, or he devised this as a means of preparation against the evil in one's nature, so that in expecting to be caught by the sudden entrance of persons, it would be necessary for him to be on continuous guard, not to err in his duties, but rather to be engaged in covenanted acts.

Zeno and Ajax,[3] two celebrated brothers, flourished about the same period. They devoted themselves to a life of philosophy, but did not fix their abode as hermits in the desert, but at Gaza, a maritime city, which was also called Majuma. They both defended the truth of their religion with greatest fidelity, and confessed God with courage, so that they were frequently subjected to very cruel and harsh treatment by the pagans. It is said that Ajax married a very lovely woman, and after he had known her thrice in all that time, had three sons; and that subsequently he held no further intercourse with her, but persevered in the exercises of monasticism. He brought up two of his sons to the divine life and celibacy, and the third he permitted to marry. He governed the church of Botolium with propriety and distinction.

Zeno, who had from his youth renounced the world and marriage, persevered in steadfast adherence to the service of God. It is said, and I myself am witness of the truth of the assertion, that when he was bishop of the church in Majuma, he was never absent at morning or evening hymns, or any other worship of God, unless attacked by some malady; and yet he was at this period an old man, being nearly a hundred years of age. He continued his course of life in the monastic philosophy, but, by pursuing his trade of weaving linen, continued to earn the means of supplying his own wants and of providing for others. He never deviated from this course of conduct till the close of his life, although he exceeded all the other priests of that province in age; and

---

[1] Also independent.
[2] Acacius, Soc. vi. 18; and Theodoret, *H. E.* v. 4, 8.
[3] Cf. v. 9.

although he presided over the people and property of the largest church.

I have mentioned these as examples of those who served as priests at this period. It would be a task to enumerate all where the main part of them were good, and God bore testimony to their lives by readily hearing their prayers and by working many miracles.

CHAP. XXIX. — DISCOVERY OF THE REMAINS OF THE PROPHETS HABAKKUK AND MICAH. DEATH OF THE EMPEROR THEODOSIUS THE GREAT.

WHILE the Church everywhere was under the sway of these eminent men, the clergy and people were excited to the imitation of their virtue and zeal. Nor was the Church of this era distinguished only by these illustrious examples of piety; for the relics of the proto-prophets,[1] Habakkuk, and a little while after, Micah, were brought to light about this time. As I understand, God made known the place where both these bodies were deposited by a divine vision in a dream to Zebennus, who was then acting as bishop of the church of Eleutheropolis. The relics of Habakkuk were found at Cela, a city

formerly called Ceila. The tomb of Micah was discovered at a distance of ten stadia from Cela, at a place called Berathsatia.[2] This tomb was ignorantly styled by the people of the country, "the tomb of the faithful"; or, in their native language, Nephsameemana. These events, which occurred during the reign of Theodosius, were sufficient for the good repute of the Christian religion.

After conquering Eugenius,[3] Theodosius the emperor remained for some time at Milan, and here he was attacked with a serious malady. He recalled to mind the prediction of the monk, John, and conjectured that his sickness was unto death. He sent in haste for his son Honorius from Constantinople; and on seeing him by, he seemed to be easier, so that he was able to be present at the sports of the Hippodrome. After dinner, however, he suddenly grew worse, and sent to desire his son to preside at the spectacle. He died on the following night. This event happened during the consulate of the brothers Olybrius and Probianus.[4]

---

[1] First part independent.

[2] Or simply Bera.
[3] Soc. v. 26; Ruf. *H. E.* ii. 34; Theodoret, *H. E.* v. 25; Philost. xi. 2; Zos. iv. 59. For a different view of the private life of Theodosius, see Eunap. *Fragm.* ii. 42, 49; Philost. xi. 2; Zos. iv. 33, 44.
[4] A.D. 395. Idat. *Descr. Coss.;* Marcel. *Com. chron.*

BOOK VIII.

CHAP. I. — SUCCESSORS OF THEODOSIUS THE GREAT. RUFINUS, THE PRÆTORIAN PREFECT, IS SLAIN. THE CHIEF PRIESTS OF THE PRINCIPAL CITIES. DIFFERENCES AMONG THE HERETICS. ACCOUNT OF SISINIUS, BISHOP OF THE NOVATIANS.

SUCH was the death of Theodosius, who had contributed so efficiently to the aggrandizement of the Church.[1] He expired in the sixtieth year of his age, and the sixteenth of his reign. He left his two sons as his successors. Arcadius, the elder, reigned in the East, and Honorius in the West. They both held the same religious sentiments as their father.

Damasus was dead; and at this period Siricius was the leader of the church of Rome; Nectarius, of the church in Constantinople; Theophilus, over the church of Alexandria; Flavian, over the church of Antioch; and John, over that of Jerusalem. Armenia and the Eastern provinces were at this time overrun by the barbarian Huns.[2] Rufinus, prefect of the East, was suspected of having clandestinely invited them to devastate the Roman territories, in furtherance of his own ambitious designs; for he was said to aspire to tyranny. For this reason, he was soon after slain; for, on the return of the troops from the conquest of Eugenius, the Emperor Arcadius, according to custom, went forth from Constantinople to meet them; and the soldiers took this opportunity to massacre Rufinus. These circumstances tended greatly to the extension of religion. The emperors attributed to the piety of their father, the ease with which the tyrant had been vanquished, and the plot of Rufinus to gain their government arrested; and they readily confirmed all the laws which had been enacted by their predecessors in favor of the churches, and bestowed their own gifts in addition. Their subjects profited by their example, so that even the pagans were converted without difficulty to Christianity, and the heretics united themselves to the Catholic Church.

Owing to the disputes which had arisen among the Arians and Eunomians, and to which I have already alluded, these heretics daily diminished in number. Many of them, in reflecting upon the diversity of sentiments which prevailed among those of their own persuasion, judged that the truth of God could not be present with them, and went over to those who held the same faith as the emperors.

The interests of the Macedonians of Constantinople were materially affected by their possessing no bishop in that juncture; for, ever since they had been deprived of their churches by Eudoxius, under the reign of Constantius, they had been governed only by presbyters, and remained so until the next reign. The Novatians, on the other hand, although they had been agitated by the controversy concerning the Passover, which was an innovation made by Sabbatius, yet the most of them remained in quiet possession of their churches, and had not been molested by any of the punishments or laws enacted against other heretics, because they maintained that the Three Persons of the Trinity are of the same substance. The virtue of their leaders also tended greatly to the maintenance of concord among them. After the presidency of Agelius they were governed by Marcian, a good man; and on his decease,[3] a little while before the time now under consideration, the bishopric devolved upon Sisinius,[4] a very eloquent man, well versed in the doctrines of philosophy and of the Holy Scriptures, and so expert in disputation that even Eunomius, who was well approved in this art and effective in this work, often refused to hold debates with him. His course of life was prudent and above the reach of calumny; yet he indulged in luxury, and even in superfluities; so that those who knew him not were incredulous as to whether he could remain temperate in the midst of so much abundance. His manners were gracious and suave in assemblies, and on this account he was esteemed by the bishops of the Catholic Church, by the rulers, and by the learned. His jests were replete with good nature, and he could bear ridicule without manifesting the least resentment. He was very prompt and witty in his rejoinders. Being once asked wherefore, as he was bishop, he bathed twice daily, he replied, "Because I do not bathe thrice." On another occasion, being ridiculed by a member of the Catholic

[1] Soc. v. 26; vi. 1, 22; Philost. xi. 3; Theodoret, *H. E.* v. 26.
[2] Claudianus, *in Rufinum*, lib. ii.; Hieron. *Ep.* lxxvii. *ad Oceanum, de morte Fabiolæ*, 8; Eunap. *Fragm.* ii. 52.

[3] i.e. Nov. 27, 395 A.D.
[4] Soc. vi. 22. Soz. is careful to omit the joke on John Chrysostom.

Church because he dressed in white, he asked where it was commanded that he should dress in black ; and, as the other hesitated for a reply, he continued, "You can give no argument in support of your position ; but I refer you to Solomon, the wisest of men, who says, ' Let your garments be always white.' Moreover Christ is described in the Gospel as having appeared in white, and Moses and Elias manifested themselves to the apostles in robes of white." It appears to me that the following reply was also very ingenious. Leontius, bishop of Ancyra, in Galatia, settled in Constantinople after he had deprived the Novatians in his province of their churches. Sisinius went to him to request that the churches might be restored ; but far from yielding compliance, he reviled the Novatians, and said that they were not worthy of holding churches, because, by abolishing the observance of penance, they intercepted the philanthropy of God. To this Sisinius replied, "No one does penance as I do." Leontius asked him in what way he did penance. "In coming to see you," retorted Sisinius. Many other witty speeches are attributed to him, and he is even said to have written several works with some elegance. But his discourses obtained greater applause than his writings, since he was best at declamation, and was capable of attracting the hearer by his voice and look and pleasing countenance. This brief description may serve as a proof of the disposition and mode of life of this great man.

CHAP. II. — EDUCATION, TRAINING, CONDUCT, AND WISDOM OF THE GREAT JOHN CHRYSOSTOM ; HIS PROMOTION TO THE SEE ; THEOPHILUS, BISHOP OF ALEXANDRIA, BECOMES HIS CONFIRMED OPPONENT.

NECTARIUS died about this period,[1] and lengthened debates were held on the ordination of a successor. They all voted for different individuals, and it seemed impossible for all to unite on one, and the time passed heavily. There was, however, at Antioch on the Orontes, a certain presbyter named John, a man of noble birth and of exemplary life, and possessed of such wonderful powers of eloquence and persuasion that he was declared by the sophist, Libanius the Syrian, to surpass all the orators of the age. When this sophist was on his death-bed he was asked by his friends who should take his place. "It would have been John," replied he, "had not the Christians taken him from us." Many of those who heard the discourses of John in the church were thereby excited to the love of

virtue and to the reception of his own religious sentiments.[2] For by living a divine life he imparted zeal from his own virtues to his hearers. He produced convictions similar to his own, because he did not enforce them by rhetorical art and strength, but expounded the sacred books with truth and sincerity. For a word which is ornamented by deeds customarily shows itself as worthy of belief ; but without these the speaker appears as an impostor and a traitor to his own words, even though he teach earnestly. Approbation in both regards was due to John. He devoted himself to a prudent course of life and to a severe public career, while he also used a clear diction, united with brilliance in speech.

His natural abilities were excellent, and he improved them by studying under the best masters. He learned rhetoric from Libanius, and philosophy from Andragathius. When it was expected that he would embrace the legal profession and take part in the career of an advocate, he determined to exercise himself in the sacred books and to practice philosophy according to the law of the Church. He had as teachers of this philosophy, Carterius and Diodorus, two celebrated presidents of ascetic institutions. Diodorus was afterwards the governor of the church of Tarsus, and, I have been informed, left many books of his own writings in which he explained the significance of the sacred words and avoided allegory. John did not receive the instructions of these men by himself, but persuaded Theodore and Maximus, who had been his companions under the instruction of Libanius, to accompany him. Maximus afterwards became bishop of Seleucia, in Isauria ; and Theodore, bishop of Mompsuestia, in Cilicia. Theodore was well conversant with the sacred books and with the rest of the discipline of rhetoricians and philosophers. After studying the ecclesiastical laws, and frequenting the society of holy men, he was filled with admiration of the ascetic mode of life and condemned city life. He did not persevere in the same purpose, but after changing it, he was drawn to his former course of life ; and, to justify his conduct, cited many examples from ancient history, with which he was well acquainted, and went back into the city. On hearing that he was engaged in business and intent on marriage, John composed an epistle,[3] more divine in language and thought than the mind of man could produce, and sent it to him. Upon reading it, he repented and immediately gave up his possessions, renounced his intention of marrying, and was saved by the advice of John, and returned to the philosophic career. This seems to me a

[1] Pallad. Dialog. de vita Chrys. 5, 6; Soc. vi. 2, 3; Theodoret, H. E. v. 27. Soz. works his material for the most part independently.

[2] Some of the disciples of Libanius, who had the habit of attending the public instructions of John in the church, were converted by him to the faith of Christ.
[3] Chrys. ad Theodorum lapsum, xlvii. 1. Migne.

remarkable instance of the power of John's eloquence ; for he readily forced conviction on the mind of one who was himself habituated to persuade and convince others.   By the same eloquence, John attracted the admiration of the people ; while he strenuously convicted sinners even in the churches, and antagonized with boldness all acts of injustice, as if they had been perpetrated against himself.   This boldness pleased the people, but grieved the wealthy and the powerful, who were guilty of most of the vices which he denounced.

Being, then, held in such high estimation by those who knew him by experience, and by those who were acquainted with him through the reports of others, John was adjudged worthy, in word and in deed, by all the subjects of the Roman Empire, to be the bishop of the church of Constantinople.   The clergy and people were unanimous in electing him ; their choice was approved by the emperor, who also sent the embassy which should conduct him ; and, to confer greater solemnity on his ordination, a council was convened.   Not long after the letter of the emperor reached Asterius, the general of the East ; he sent to desire John to repair to him, as if he had need of him.   On his arrival, he at once made him get into his chariot, and conveyed him with dispatch to a military station, Pagras so-called, where he delivered him to the officers whom the emperor had sent in quest of him.   Asterius acted very prudently in sending for John before the citizens of Antioch knew what was about to occur ; for they would probably have excited a sedition, and have inflicted injury on others, or subjected themselves to acts of violence, rather than have suffered John to be taken from them.

When John had arrived at Constantinople, and when the priests were assembled together, Theophilus opposed his ordination ; and proposed as a candidate in his stead, a presbyter of his church named Isidore, who took charge of strangers and of the poor at Alexandria.   I have been informed by persons who were acquainted with Isidore, that from his youth upwards he practiced the philosophic virtues, near Scetis.   Others say that he had gained the friendship of Theophilus by being a participant and a familiar in a very perilous undertaking.   For it is reported that during the war against Maximus, Theophilus intrusted Isidore with gifts and letters respectively addressed to the emperor and to the tyrant, and sent him to Rome, desiring him to remain there until the termination of the war, when he was to deliver the gifts, with the letters, to him, who might prove the victor. Isidore acted according to his instructions, but the artifice was detected ; and, fearful of being arrested, he fled to Alexandria.   Theophilus

from that period evinced much attachment towards him, and, with a view of recompensing his services, strove to raise him to the bishopric of Constantinople.   But whether there was really any truth in this report, or whether Theophilus desired to ordain this man because of his excellence, it is certain that he eventually yielded to those who decided for John.[1]   He feared Eutropius, who was artfully eager for this ordination. Eutropius then presided over the imperial house, and they say he threatened Theophilus, that unless he would vote with the other bishops, he would have to defend himself against those who desired to accuse him ; for many written accusations against him were at that time before the council.

CHAP. III. — RAPID PROMOTION OF JOHN TO THE BISHOPRIC, AND MORE VEHEMENT GRAPPLING WITH ITS AFFAIRS.   HE RE-ESTABLISHES DISCIPLINE IN THE CHURCHES EVERYWHERE.   BY SENDING AN EMBASSY TO ROME, HE ABOLISHED THE HOSTILITY TO FLAVIAN.

As soon as John was raised to the episcopal dignity, he devoted his attention first to the reformation of the lives of his clergy ;[2] he reproved and amended their ways and diet and every procedure of their manifold transactions. He also ejected some of the clergy from the Church.   He was naturally disposed to reprehend the misconduct of others, and to antagonize righteously those who acted unjustly ; and he gave way to these characteristics still more in the episcopate ; for his nature, having attained power, led his tongue to reproof, and nerved his wrath more readily against the enemy.   He did not confine his efforts to the reformation of his own church ; but as a good and large-minded man, he sought to rectify abuses throughout the world.   Immediately upon entering the episcopate, he strove to put an end to the dissension which had arisen concerning Paulinus, between the Western and Egyptian bishops and the bishops of the East ; since on this account a general disunion was overpowering the churches in the whole empire.   He requested the assistance of Theophilus in effecting the reconciliation of Flavian with the bishop of Rome.[3]   Theophilus agreed to co-operate with him in the restoration of concord ; and Acacius, bishop of Berea, and Isidore, whom Theophilus had proposed as a candidate for ordination instead of John, were sent on an embassy to Rome.   They soon effected the object of their journey, and sailed back to Egypt.   Acacius repaired to Syria, bearing con-

---

1 Soc. also attests to the presence of Theophilus at the ordination of John. vi. 2; Pallad. *Dialog.* 5.
2 Soc. vi. 4.   Cf. Theodoret, *H. E.* v. 28; Pallad. *Dialog.* 5.
3 Soc. vi. 3; Theodoret, *H. E.* v. 23.

ciliatory letters to the adherents of Flavian from the priests of Egypt and of the West. And 'the churches, after a long delay once more laid aside their discord, and took up communion with one another. The people at Antioch, who were called Eustathians, continued, indeed, for some time to hold separate assemblies, although they possessed no bishop. Evagrius, the successor of Paulinus, did not, as we have stated, long survive him ; and I think reconciliation became easier for the bishops from there being no one to oppose. The laity, as is customary with the populace, gradually went over to those who assembled together under the guidance of Flavian ; and thus, in course of time, they were more and more united.

CHAP. IV. — ENTERPRISE OF GAÏNAS, THE GOTHIC BARBARIAN. EVILS WHICH HE PERPETRATED.

A BARBARIAN, named Gaïnas,[1] who had taken refuge among the Romans, and who had risen from the lowest ranks of the army to military command, formed a design to usurp the throne of the Roman Empire. With this in view, he sent for his countrymen, the Goths, from their own homes to come to the Roman territories, and appointed his relatives to be tribunes and chiliarchs. Tirbingilus, a relative of his, who commanded a large body of troops in Phrygia, commenced an insurrection ; and to all persons of judgment it was patent that he was preparing the way. Under the pretext of resenting the devastation of many of the Phrygian cities, which had been committed to his superintendence, Gaïnas turned to their assistance ; but on his arrival, when a multitude of barbarians had been equipped for war, he disclosed his plan which he had previously concealed, and pillaged the cities which he had been commanded to guard, and was about to attack others. He then proceeded to Bithynia, and encamped in the boundaries of Chalcedon, and threatened war. The cities of the East of Asia, and as many as lived between these regions and about the Euxine, being thus in danger, the emperor and his counsellors judged that it would not be safe to venture into any hazardous undertaking without preparation against men who were already desperate ; for the emperor declared that he was ready to be favorable to him in every point, and sent to Gaïnas to offer him whatever he might demand.

Gaïnas requested that two consuls, named Saturninus and Aurelian, whom he suspected of being inimical, should be delivered up to him ; and when they were in his power, he pardoned

them. He afterwards held a conference with the emperor near Chalcedon, in the house of prayer in which the tomb of Euphemia the martyr is deposited ; and after he and the emperor had mutually bound themselves by vows of friendship to each other, he threw down his arms, and repaired to Constantinople, where, by an imperial edict, he was appointed general of the infantry and cavalry. Prosperity so far beyond his deserts was more than he could bear with moderation ; and as, contrary to all expectations, he had succeeded so wonderfully in his former enterprise, he determined to undermine the peace of the Catholic Church. He was a Christian, and, like the rest of the barbarians, had espoused the Arian heresy. Urged either by the presidents of this party, or by the suggestions of his own ambition, he applied to the emperor to place one of the churches of the city in the hands of the Arians. He represented that it was neither just nor proper that, while he was general of the Roman troops, he should be compelled to retire without the walls of the city when he wished to engage in prayer. John did not remain inactive when made acquainted with these proceedings. He assembled all the bishops who were then residing in the city, and went with them to the palace. He spoke at great length in the presence of the emperor and of Gaïnas, reproached the latter with being a stranger and a fugitive, and reminded him that his life had been saved by the father of the emperor, to whom he had sworn fidelity, as likewise to his children, to the Romans, and to the laws which he was striving to make powerless. When he had made this speech he showed the law which Theodosius had established, forbidding the heterodox to hold a church within the walls. Then, addressing himself to the emperor, John exhorted him to maintain the laws which had been established against heretics ; and told him that it would be better to be deprived of the empire, than to be guilty of impiety by becoming a traitor to the house of God. Thus did John speak boldly like a man, and gave no place to innovation in the churches under his care. Gaïnas, however, regardless of his oaths, attacked the city. His enterprise was pre-announced by the appearance of a comet directly over the city ; this comet was of extraordinary magnitude, larger, it is said, than any that had previously been seen, and reaching almost to the earth itself. Gaïnas intended to seize first upon the stores of the bankers, and hoped to collect together their enormous wealth. But since the rumor of his plan was spread, the bankers concealed their ready wealth and no longer set forth silver upon the tables, as they were wont publicly to do. Gaïnas then sent some of the barbarians by

---

[1] Chrys. *Homilia cum Saturninus et Aurelianus acti essent in exsilium*, iii. 413; Soc. vi. 6. He advises the curious to read the Γαίνια, a poem by Eusebius the Scholastic; and the verses on the same theme by the poet Ammonius. Philost. xi. 8; Theodoret, *H. E.* v. 32, 33; Eunap. *Fragm.* ii. 62–65, iii. 17; Zos. v. 7–22.

night to set fire to the palace; but they were unskillful and overcome with fear, so they turned back. For when they drew near the edifice, they fancied that they saw a multitude of heavily armed men of immense stature, and they returned to inform Gaïnas that fresh troops had just arrived. Gaïnas disbelieved their report, for he was confident that no troops had entered the city. As, however, other individuals whom he despatched to the palace for the same purpose, on the following night, returned with the same report, he went out himself to be an eyewitness of the extraordinary spectacle. Imagining that the army before him consisted of soldiers who had been withdrawn from other cities, and that these troops protected the city and palace by night and concealed themselves by day, Gaïnas feigned to be possessed of a demon; and under the pretext of offering up a prayer, went to the church which the father of the emperor had erected in honor of John the Baptist, at Hebdomos. Some of the barbarians remained in Constantinople, and others accompanied Gaïnas; they secretly carried arms and pots full of darts in the women's chariots, but when they were discovered, they slew the guard at the gates, who attempted to hinder the carrying out of the arms. From this the city was filled with as much confusion and uproar, as if it had suddenly been captured. A good thought ruled this terrible moment; for the emperor without delay declared Gaïnas a public enemy, and commanded that all the barbarians left in the city should be slain. No sooner was this mandate issued, than the soldiers rushed upon the barbarians, and slew the greater number of them; they then set fire to the church which was named after the Goths; for as was customary, they had congregated there in the house of prayer, because there was no other refuge, since the gates were shut. On hearing of this calamity, Gaïnas passed through Thrace, and proceeded towards the Cherronesus, intending to cross the Hellespont; for he thought that if he could conquer the opposite coast of Asia, he could easily subjugate to himself all the provinces of the empire in the East. All these things proved contrary to his hopes, because the Romans were there favored by Divine power. For the army sent by the emperor was on hand by land and by sea, under the command of Flavita, who although a barbarian by birth, was a good man, and an able general. The barbarians, having no ships, imprudently attempted to cross the Hellespont to the opposite continent on rafts; when suddenly a great wind blew and violently separated them, and drove them against the Roman vessels. The greater part of the barbarians and their horses were drowned; but many were slain by the military. Gaïnas, however, with a few of his

followers escaped; but not long after, when fleeing through Thrace, they fell in with another detachment of the Roman army, and Gaïnas, with all his barbarians, perished. Such was the termination of the daring schemes and life of Gaïnas.

Flavita had rendered himself very conspicuous in this war, and was therefore appointed consul.[1] During his consulate, and that of Vincentius, a son was born to the emperor. The young prince was named after his grandfather, and at the commencement of the next consulate,[2] was proclaimed Augustus.

CHAP. V. — JOHN SWAYED THE PEOPLE BY HIS TEACHINGS. CONCERNING THE WOMAN, A FOLLOWER OF MACEDONIUS, ON ACCOUNT OF WHOM THE BREAD WAS TURNED INTO A STONE.

JOHN governed the church of Constantinople with exemplary prudence, and induced many of the pagans and of the heretics to unite themselves with him.[3] Crowds of people daily resorted to him; some for the purpose of being edified by listening to his discourses, and others with the intention of tempting him. He, however, pleased and attracted all classes, and led them to embrace the same religious sentiments as himself. As the people pressed around him, and could not get enough of his words, so that when they were pushed hither and yon, and were pressing one another, they incurred danger; and each one was forcing his way to go farther, so that by standing near, he might hear more accurately what John was saying, he placed himself in the midst of them upon the platform of the readers, and, having taken a seat, taught the multitude. It seems to me that this is a suitable place in my history for the insertion of the account of a miracle which was performed during the life of John. A certain man of the Macedonian heresy, lived with a wife of the same belief; he chanced to hear John discoursing concerning the opinion one ought to hold about the Divine nature; he was convinced by the argument he heard advanced, and strove to persuade his wife to embrace the same sentiments. Her previous habits of mind, and the conversation of other women of her acquaintance, deterred her from complying with his wishes; and, when he found that all his efforts to convince her were futile, he told her that, unless she would be of one mind with him on Divine subjects, she should not continue to live with him. The woman, therefore, promised to do as she was required; but, at the same time,

[1] Flavita was consul with Vincentius, A.D. 401. See under Marcell. *Com. chron.*
[2] Arcadius and Honorius, each in their fifth consulate. Theodosius junior was made Cæsar A.D. 402.
[3] Independent chapter.

she made known the matter to one of her servant maids, in whose fidelity she confided, and used her as an instrument in deceiving her husband. At the season of the celebration of the mysteries (the initiated will understand what I mean), this woman kept what was given to her and held down her head as if engaged in prayer. Her servant, who was standing behind her, placed in her hand a bit of bread which she had brought with her; but, as soon as she had placed it between her teeth, it was converted into stone. Since such a divine affair had happened to her, she was very fearful lest any further calamity should befall her, and ran to the bishop, and confessed on herself. She showed him the stone, which bore the marks of her teeth; it was composed of some unknown substance, and was marked by a very strange color. She implored forgiveness with tears, and continued ever after to hold the same religious tenets as her husband. If any person should consider this narrative incredible, he can inspect the stone in question; for it is still preserved in the treasury of the church of Constantinople.

CHAP. VI. — PROCEEDINGS OF JOHN IN ASIA AND PHRYGIA. HERACLIDES, BISHOP OF EPHESUS, AND GERONTIUS, BISHOP OF NICOMEDIA.

JOHN[1] having been informed that the churches in Asia and the neighborhood were governed by unworthy persons, and that they bartered the priesthood for the incomes and gifts received, or bestowed that dignity as a matter of private favor, repaired to Ephesus, and deposed thirteen bishops, some in Lycia and Phrygia, and others in Asia itself, and appointed others in their stead. The bishop of Ephesus was dead, and he therefore ordained Heraclides over the church. Heraclides was a native of Cyprus, and was one of the deacons under John: he had formerly joined the monks at Scetis, and had been the disciple of the monk Evagrius. John also expelled Gerontius, bishop of the church in Nicomedia. This latter was a deacon under Ambrosius, of the church of Milan; he declared, I do not know why, either with an intention to invent a miracle, or because he had been himself deceived by the art and phantasms of a demon, that he had seized something resembling an ass (ὀνοσκελίς) by night, had cut off its head, and flung it into a grinding-house. Ambrose regarded this mode of discourse as unworthy of a deacon of God, and commanded Gerontius to remain in seclusion until he had expiated his fault by repentance. Gerontius, however, was a very skillful physician; he was eloquent and

persuasive, and knew well how to gain friends; he therefore ridiculed the command of Ambrose, and repaired to Constantinople. In a short time he obtained the friendship of some of the most powerful men at court; and, not long after, was elevated to the bishopric of Nicomedia. He was ordained by Helladius, bishop of Cæsarea in Cappadocia, who performed this office the more readily for him, because he had been instrumental, through his interest at court, in obtaining a high appointment in the army for that functionary's son. When Ambrose heard of this ordination, he wrote to Nectarius, the president of the church of Constantinople, desiring him to eject Gerontius from the priesthood, and not permit him and the ecclesiastical order to be so abused. However desirous Nectarius might have been to obey this injunction, he could never succeed in carrying it into effect, owing to the determined resistance of the people of Nicomedia. John deposed Gerontius, and ordained Pansophius, who had formerly been preceptor to the wife of the emperor, and who, though a man of decided piety and of a mild and gentle disposition, was not liked by the Nicomedians. They arose in frequent sedition, and enumerated publicly and privately the beneficence of Gerontius, and on the liberal advantage derived from his science, and its generous and active use for the rich and poor alike; and as is usual when we applaud those we love, they ascribed many other virtues to him. They went about the streets of their own city and Constantinople as if some earthquake, or pestilence, or other visitation of Divine wrath had occurred, and sang psalms, and offered supplications that they might have Gerontius for their bishop. They were at length compelled to yield to necessity, and parted with grief and groans from Gerontius, receiving in his stead a bishop whom they regarded with fear and aversion. The bishops who had been deposed and all their followers declaimed against John, as the leader of a revolution in the churches, and as changing the rights of the ordained, contrary to the ancestral laws; and under the influence of their grievance, they condemned deeds done by him, which were worthy of praise according to the opinion of most people. Among other matters, they reproached him with the proceedings that had been taken against Eutropius.

CHAP. VII. — CONCERNING EUTROPIUS, CHIEF OF THE EUNUCHS, AND THE LAW ENACTED BY HIM. ON BEING TURNED FROM THE CHURCH, HE WAS PUT TO DEATH. MURMURS AGAINST JOHN.

EUTROPIUS was originally the chief of the eunuchs, and was the first and only person of that rank of whom we have known or heard who attained the consular and patrician dig-

---

[1] Soc. vi. 11; Pallad. *Dialog.* 13-20. Soz. has material of his own.

nity.[1] When he was raised to present power, he thought not of the future, nor of the instability of human affairs, but caused those who sought an asylum in churches to be thrust out. He treated Pentadia, the wife of Timasius, in this manner. Timasius was a general in the army, capable and much feared; but Eutropius procured an edict for his banishment to Pasis in Egypt, under the pretext that he aspired to tyranny. I have been informed that Timasius fell a victim to thirst, or dreading lest anything worse might be in store, he was caught in the sands there, and was found dead. Eutropius issued a law, enacting that no one should seek refuge in churches, and that those who had already fled thither should be driven out. He was, however, the first to transgress this law; for not long after its enactment, he offended the empress, and immediately left the palace, and fled to the Church as a suppliant. While he was lying beneath the table, John pronounced a discourse, in which he reprehended the pride of power, and directed the attention of the people to the instability of human greatness. The enemies of John hence took occasion to cast reproach on him, because he had rebuked instead of compassionating, one who was suffering under the calamities of adverse fortunes. Eutropius soon after paid the penalty of his impious plan, and was beheaded; and the law which he had enacted was effaced from the public inscriptions. The wrath of God having been thus promptly visited on the injustice that had been perpetrated against the Church, prosperity was restored to it, and there was an increase in the Divine worship. The people of Constantinople were more sedulous then than before, in attendance at the singing of the morning and evening hymns.

CHAP. VIII. — ANTIPHONAL HYMNS AGAINST THE ARIANS INTRODUCED BY JOHN. THE INTERESTS OF THE ORTHODOX ARE MUCH AUGMENTED BY THE TEACHINGS OF JOHN, WHILE THE WEALTHY ARE MORE AND MORE ENRAGED.

THE Arians, having been deprived of their churches in Constantinople during the reign of Theodosius, held their churches without the walls of the city.[2] They previously assembled by night in the public porticoes, and were divided into bands, so that they sang antiphonally, for they had composed certain refrains which reflected their own dogma, and at the break of day marched in procession, singing these hymns, to the places in which they held their churches.

They proceeded in this manner on all solemn festivals, and on the first and last days of the week. The sentiments propounded in these odes were such as were likely to engender disputes. As, for instance, the following: "Where are those who say that the Three Persons constitute one Power?" Other similar acrimonious observations were interspersed throughout their compositions. John was fearful lest any of his own church people should be led astray by witnessing these exhibitions, and therefore commanded them to sing hymns in the same manner. The orthodox became more distinguished, and in a short time surpassed the opposing heretics in number and processions; for they had silver crosses and lighted wax tapers borne before them. The eunuch of the empress was appointed to regulate these processions, to pay the cost of whatever might be required, and to prepare hymns. Hence the Arians, impelled either by jealousy or revenge, attacked the members of the Catholic Church. Much bloodshed ensued on both sides. Briso (for this was the name of the imperial eunuch) was wounded on the forehead by a stone that was cast at him. The resentment of the emperor was kindled, and he put a stop to the Arian assemblies. Having commenced the custom of singing hymns in the manner and from the cause above stated, the members of the Catholic Church did not discontinue the practice, but have retained it to the present day. The institution of these processions and his services in the Church endeared John to the people; but he was hated by the clergy and the powerful on account of his free boldness, for he never failed to rebuke the clergy when he detected them in acts of injustice, nor to exhort the powerful to return to the practice of virtue when they abused their wealth, committed impiety, or yielded to voluptuousness.

CHAP. IX. — SERAPION, THE ARCHDEACON, AND ST. OLYMPIAS. SOME OF THE CELEBRATED MEN INSOLENTLY BEAR DOWN UPON JOHN, TRADUCING HIM AS IMPRACTICABLE AND PASSIONATE.

THE enmity of the clergy against John was greatly increased by Serapion, his archdeacon. He was an Egyptian, naturally prone to anger, and always ready to insult his opponents.[3] The feelings of hostility were further fostered by the counsel which Olympias received from John. Olympias was of most illustrious birth, and although she had become a widow while young, and was zealously attached to the exercises of monastic philosophy according to the laws of the church, yet Nectarius had ordained her

[1] Independent chapter. Cf. Soc. vi. 5; Philost. xi. 4–6; Chrys. *Homilia in Eutropium eunuchum patricium; homilia de capto Eutropio et de divitiarum vanitate; Claudianus in Eutropium,* i. ii.; Eunap. *Fragm.* ii. 53–56; *Fragm.* iii. 16; *Fragm.* iv. 20–23; *Fragm.* v. 3; Zos. v. 3, 8–18.
[2] Soc. vi. 8.

[3] Soc. vi. 4, 11; Pallad. *Dialog.* Pallad. *H. L.* cxliv.; *Epp.* xvii. *ad Olympiadem.* Soz. has independent material concerning Olympias and Isaac.

as deaconess. John, perceiving that she bestowed her goods liberally on any one who asked her for them, and that she despised everything but the service of God, said to her : " I applaud your intentions ; but would have you know that those who aspire to the perfection of virtue according to God, ought to distribute their wealth with economy. You, however, have been bestowing wealth on the wealthy, which is as useless as if you had cast it into the sea. Know you not that you have voluntarily, for the sake of God, devoted all your possessions to the relief of the poor. You ought, therefore, to regard your wealth as belonging to your Master, and to remember that you have to account for its distribution. If you will be persuaded by me, you will in future regulate your donations according to the wants of those who solicit relief. You will thus be enabled to extend the sphere of your benevolence, and your mercy and most zealous care will receive reward from God."

John had several disputes with many of the monks, particularly with Isaac. He highly commended those who remained in quietude in the monasteries and practiced philosophy there ; he protected them from all injustice and solicitiously supplied whatever necessities they might have. But the monks who went out of doors and made their appearance in cities, he reproached and regarded as insulting philosophy. For these causes, he incurred the hatred of the clergy, and of many of the monks, who called him a hard, passionate, morose, and arrogant man. They therefore attempted to bring his life into public disrepute, by stating confidently, as if it were the truth, that he would eat with no one, and that he refused every invitation to a meal that was offered him. I know of no pretext that could have given rise to this assertion, except that, as I have been assured by a man of undoubted veracity, John had, by rigorous asceticism, rendered himself liable to pain in the head and stomach, and was thus prevented from being present at some of the choicest symposia. Hence, however, originated the greatest accusation that was ever devised against him.

CHAP. X. — SEVERIAN, BISHOP OF GABALES, AND ANTIOCHUS, BISHOP OF PTOLEMAIS. DISPUTE BETWEEN SERAPION AND SEVERIAN. RECONCILIATION BETWEEN THEM EFFECTED BY THE EMPRESS.

JOHN likewise incurred the enmity of the empress, through the machinations of Severian, bishop of Gabali in Syria.[1] Severian and Antiochus, bishop of Ptolemais, a city in Phœnicia, were both learned men, and well qualified to teach in the churches. Antiochus had so fine a

voice and delivery that, by some persons, he was surnamed Chrysostom. Severian, on the other hand, had the harshness of the Syrians in his speech ; but, in point of knowledge and the evidences of the Scriptures, he was considered superior to Antiochus. It appears that Antiochus was the first to visit Constantinople ; he gained great applause by his discourses, amassed some property, and then returned to his own city. Severian followed his example, and went to Constantinople. He formed an intimacy with John, spoke frequently in the churches, and was admired. He was in honor, and became well-known to many of those in power, and to the emperor and empress. When John went to Asia, he commended the Church to his care ; for he was so far deceived by the adulation of Severian as to imagine him to be his zealous friend. Severian, however, thought only of gratifying his auditors, and of pleasing the people by his discourses.[2] When John was apprised of this, he was filled with jealousy ; and his resentment was further kindled, it is said, by the representations of Serapion. After the return of John from Asia, Serapion happened to see Severian passing ; but, instead of rising to salute him, he kept his seat, in order to show his utter contempt for the man. Severian was offended by this manifestation of disrespect, and exclaimed, " If Serapion die a clergyman, then Christ was not incarnate." Serapion reported these words ; and John, in consequence, expelled Severian from the city as insolent, and as a blasphemer against God ; for witnesses were brought forward to attest that the above words had been really uttered by him. Some of the friends of Serapion even went so far as to suppress part of the speech of Severian, and to affirm that he had declared that Christ was not incarnate. John also rebuked Severian, by asking whether, " If Serapion should not die among the clergy, it would follow that Christ had not been incarnate ? " As soon as the wife of the emperor was informed by the friends of Severian of what had occurred, she immediately sent for him from Chalcedon. John, notwithstanding all her remonstrances, positively refused to hold any intercourse with him, until the empress placed her son Theodosius on his knees in the church named after the apostles ; then she entreated him persistently, and frequently adjured him, until John yielded a reluctant consent to receive Severian into friendship. Such are the accounts which I have received of these transactions.[3]

CHAP. XI. — QUESTION AGITATED IN EGYPT, AS TO WHETHER GOD HAS A CORPOREAL FORM. THE-

---

[1] Soc. vi. 11; Pallad. *Dialog.*

[2] A number of the homilies still attributed to Chrysostom, as well as those now acknowledged not to be his, were from the eloquent Severian.

[3] Chrys. *Homilia de recipiendo Severiano;* and *Sermo ipsius Severiam de pace*, iii. 421–423.

OPHILUS, BISHOP OF ALEXANDRIA, AND THE BOOKS OF ORIGEN.

A QUESTION was at this period agitated in Egypt, which had been propounded a short time previously, namely, whether it is right to believe that God is anthropomorphic.[1] Because they laid hold of the sacred words with simplicity and without any questioning, most of the monks of that part of the world were of this opinion; and supposed that God possessed eyes, a face, and hands, and other members of the bodily organization. But those who searched into the hidden meaning of the terms of Scripture held the opposite; and they maintained that those who denied the incorporeality of God were guilty of blasphemy. This later opinion was espoused by Theophilus, and preached by him in the church; and in the epistle[2] which, according to custom, he wrote respecting the celebration of the passover, he took occasion to state that God ought to be regarded as incorporeal, as alien to a human form. When it was signified to the Egyptian monks that Theophilus had broached these sentiments, they went to Alexandria, assembled the people together in one place, excited a tumult, and determined upon slaying the bishop as an impious man. Theophilus, however, presented himself to the insurgents forthwith, and said to them, "When I look upon you, it is as if I beheld the face of God." This address sufficiently mollified the men; yielding their wrath, they replied, "Wherefore, then, if you really hold orthodox doctrines, do you not denounce the books of Origen; since those who read them are led into such opinions?" "Such has long been my intention," replied he, "and I shall do as you advise; for I blame not less than you do, all those who follow the doctrines of Origen." By these means he deluded the brethren, and broke up the sedition.

CHAP. XII. — ABOUT THE FOUR BROTHERS, CALLED "THE LONG," WHO WERE ASCETICS, AND OF WHOM THEOPHILUS WAS AN ENEMY; ABOUT ISIDORE AND THE EVENTS WHICH CAME ABOUT THROUGH THESE FOUR.

THE controversy would most likely have been terminated, had it not been renewed by Theophilus himself, from inimical feelings against Ammonius, Dioscorus, Eusebius, and Euthymius, who were called "the long."[3] They were brothers; and, as we have before stated, became conspicuous among the philosophers at Scetis. They were at one period beloved by Theophilus above all the other monks of Egypt; he sought their society, and frequently dwelt with them. He even conferred on Dioscorus the bishopric of Hermopolis. He was confirmed in his hatred of them, on account of his enmity to Isidore, whom he had endeavored to ordain in Constantinople after Nectarius. Some say, that a woman, belonging to the Manichean heresy, had been converted to the faith of the Catholic Church; Theophilus rebuked the arch-presbyter (towards whom he had other reasons for entertaining resentful feeling), because he had admitted her to participate in the sacred mysteries before she had adjured her former heresy. Peter, for this was the name of the arch-presbyter, maintained that he had received the woman into communion according to the laws of the Church, and with the consent of Theophilus; and referred to Isidore, as a witness to the truth of what he had deposed. Isidore happened to be then at Rome on an embassy; but, on his return, he testified that the assertions of Peter were true. Theophilus resented this avowal as a calumny, and ejected both him and Peter from the Church. Such is the account given by some persons of the transaction. I have, however, heard it alleged, by a man of undoubted veracity, who was very intimate with the monks above mentioned, that the enmity of Theophilus towards Isidore originated from two causes. One of these causes was identical with that specified by Peter the presbyter, namely, that he had refused to attest the existence of a testament in which the inheritance was entailed on the sister of Theophilus; the other cause alleged by this individual was, that Isidore refused to give up certain moneys that had been confided to him for the relief of the poor, and which Theophilus wished to appropriate to the erection of churches; saying that it is better to restore the bodies of the suffering, which are more rightly to be considered the temples of God, and for which end the money had been furnished, than to build walls. But from whatever cause the enmity of Theophilus might have originated, Isidore, immediately after his excommunication, joined his former companions, the monks at Scetis. Ammonius, with a few others, then repaired to Theophilus, and entreated him to restore Isidore to communion. Theophilus readily promised to do as they requested; but as time passed away, and nothing more was effected for them, and it became evident that Theophilus was pretending, they again repaired to him, renewed their entreaties, and pressed him to be faithful to his engagement. Instead of complying, Theophilus thrust one of the monks into prison, for the purpose of intimidating the others. But he erred in this. Ammonius and all the monks with him then

1 Soc. vi. 7.
2 This epistle is no longer extant; it is alluded to by Cassianus in his *Collatio*, x. 2; *Opp*. i. p. 821, 822.
3 Soc. vi. 7, 9; Pallad, *Dialog*. 6. Soz. has different order and some new opinions.

went to the prison, into which they were readily admitted by the jailer, who imagined that they had come to bring provisions to the prisoner; but having once obtained admission, they refused to leave the prison. When Theophilus heard of their voluntary confinement, he sent to desire them to come to him. They replied, that he ought first to take them out of prison himself, for it was not just, after having been subjected to public indignity, that they should be privately released from confinement. At length, however, they yielded and went to him. Theophilus apologized for what had occurred, and dismissed them as if he had no further intention of molesting them; but by himself, he champed and was vexed, and determined to do them ill. He was in doubt, however, as to how he could ill-treat them, as they had no possessions, and despised everything but philosophy, until it occurred to him, to disturb the peace of their retirement. From his former intercourse with them he had gathered that they blamed those who believe that God has a human form, and that they adhered to the opinions of Origen; he brought them into collision with the multitude of monks who maintained the other view. A terrible contention prevailed among the monks, for they did not think it worth while to persuade one another by framing arguments for themselves in an orderly way, but settled down into insults. They gave the name of Origenists to those who maintained the incorporeality of the Deity, while those who held the opposite opinion were called Anthropomorphists.

CHAP. XIII. — THESE FOUR REPAIR TO JOHN ON ACCOUNT OF HIS INTEREST; FOR THIS REASON, THEOPHILUS WAS ENRAGED, AND PREPARES HIMSELF TO FIGHT AGAINST JOHN.

DIOSCORUS, Ammonius, and the other monks, having discovered the machinations of Theophilus, retired to Jerusalem, and thence proceeded to Scythopolis; for they thought that it would be an advantageous residence there for them on account of the many palms, whose leaves are used by the monks for their customary work.[1] Dioscorus and Ammonius were accompanied hither by about eighty other monks. In the meantime, Theophilus sent messengers to Constantinople, to prefer complaints against them, and to oppose any petitions that they might lay before the emperor. On being informed of this fact, Ammonius and the monks embarked for Constantinople, and took Isidore with them; and they requested that their cause might be tried in the presence of the emperor and of the bishop; for they thought that, by reason of his

boldness, John, who was careful to do right, would be able to help them in their rights. John, although he received them with kindness, and treated them with honor, and did not forbid them to pray in the church, refused to admit them to participation in the mysteries, for it was not lawful to do this before the investigation. He wrote to Theophilus, desiring him to receive them back into communion, as their sentiments concerning the Divine nature were orthodox; requesting him, if he regarded their orthodoxy as doubtful, to send some one to act as their accuser. Theophilus returned no reply to this epistle. Some time subsequently, Ammonius and his companions presented themselves before the wife of the emperor, as she was riding out, and complained of the machinations of Theophilus against them. She knew what had been plotted against them; and she stood up in honor of them; and, leaning forward from her royal chariot, she nodded, and said to them, "Pray for the emperor, for me, for our children, and for the empire. For my part, I shall shortly cause a council to be convened, to which Theophilus shall be summoned." A false report having prevailed in Alexandria, that John had received Dioscorus and his companions into communion, and had afforded them every aid and encouragement in his power, Theophilus began to reflect upon what measures it would be possible to adopt in order to eject John from his episcopate.

CHAP. XIV. — PERVERSITY OF THEOPHILUS. ST. EPIPHANIUS: HIS RESIDENCE AT CONSTANTINOPLE AND PREPARATION TO EXCITE THE PEOPLE AGAINST JOHN.

THEOPHILUS kept his designs against John as secret as possible; and wrote to the bishops of every city, condemning the books of Origen.[2] It also occurred to him that it would be advantageous to enlist Epiphanius, bishop of Salamis, in Cyprus, on his side, a man who was revered for his life, and was the most distinguished of his contemporaries; and he therefore formed a friendship with him, although he had formerly blamed him for asserting that God possessed a human form. As if repentant of having ever entertained any other sentiment, Theophilus wrote to Epiphanius to acquaint him that he now held the same opinions as himself, and to move attacks against the books of Origen, as the source of such nefarious dogmas. Epiphanius had long regarded the writings of Origen with peculiar aversion, and was therefore easily led to attach credit to the epistle of Theophilus. He soon after assembled the bishops of Cyprus

---

[1] Pallad. *Dialog.* 7; Soc. vi. 7, 9. Soz.'s has independent matter.

[2] Mainly after Soc. vi. 10, 12, 14; Pallad. *Dialog.* 8.

together, and prohibited the examination of the books of Origen. He also wrote to the other bishops, and, among others, to the bishop of Constantinople, exhorting them to convene Synods, and to make the same decision. Theophilus, perceiving that there could be no danger in following the example of Epiphanius, who was the object of popular praise, and who was admired for the virtue of his life, whatever his opinion might be, passed a vote similar to that of Epiphanius, with the concurrence of the bishops under his jurisdiction. John, on the other hand, paid little attention to the letters of Epiphanius and Theophilus. Those among the powerful and the clergy, who were opposed to him, perceived that the designs of Theophilus tended to his ejection from the bishopric, and therefore endeavored to procure the convention of a council in Constantinople, in order to carry this measure into execution. Theophilus, knowing this, exerted himself to the utmost in convening this council. He commanded the bishops of Egypt to repair by sea to Constantinople; he wrote to request Epiphanius and the other Eastern bishops to proceed to that city with as little delay as possible, and he himself set off on the journey thither by land. Epiphanius was the first to sail from Cyprus; he landed at Hebdomos, a suburb of Constantinople; and after having prayed in the church erected at that place, he proceeded to enter the city. In order to do him honor, John went out with all his clergy to meet him. Epiphanius, however, evinced clearly by his conduct that he believed the accusations against John; for, although invited to reside in the ecclesiastical residences, he would not continue there, and refused to meet with John in them. He also privately assembled all the bishops who were residing in Constantinople, and showed them the decrees which he had issued against the discourses of Origen. He persuaded some of the bishops to approve of these decrees, while others objected to them. Theotimus, bishop of Scythia, strongly opposed the proceedings of Epiphanius, and told him that it was not right to cast insult on the memory of one who had long been numbered with the dead; nor was it without blasphemy to assail the conclusion to which the ancients had arrived on the subject, and to set aside their decisions. While discoursing in this strain, he drew forth a book of Origen's which he had brought with him; and, after reading aloud a passage conducive to the education of the Church, he remarked that those who condemned such sentiments acted absurdly, for they were in danger of insulting the subjects themselves about which these words treated. John still had respect for Epiphanius, and invited him to join in the meetings of his church, and to dwell with him. But Epiphanius declared that he would neither reside with John nor pray with him publicly, unless he would denounce the works of Origen and expel Dioscorus and his companions. Not considering it just to act in the manner proposed until judgment had been passed on the case, John tried to postpone matters. When the assembly was about to be held in the Church of the Apostles, those illdisposed to John planned that Epiphanius should go beforehand and publicly decry the books of Origen to the people, and Dioscorus and his companions as the partisans of this writer; and also to attack the bishop of the city as the abetter of those heretics. And some concerned themselves in this; for by this means it was supposed that the affections of the people would be alienated from their bishop. The following day, when Epiphanius was about entering the church, in order to carry his design into execution, he was stopped by Serapion, at the command of John, who had received intimation of the plot. Serapion proved to Epiphanius that while the project he had devised was unjust in itself, it could be of no personal advantage to him; for that if it should excite a popular insurrection, he would be regarded as responsible for the outrages that might follow. By these arguments Epiphanius was induced to relinquish his attack.

CHAP. XV. — THE SON OF THE EMPRESS AND ST. EPIPHANIUS. CONFERENCE BETWEEN THE "LONG BROTHERS" AND EPIPHANIUS, AND HIS RE-EMBARKATION FOR CYPRUS. EPIPHANIUS AND JOHN.

ABOUT this time, the son of the empress was attacked by a dangerous illness, and the mother, apprehensive of consequences, sent to implore Epiphanius to pray for him.[1] Epiphanius returned for answer, that the sick one would live, provided that she would avoid all intercourse with the heretic Dioscorus and his companions. To this message the empress replied as follows: "If it be the will of God to take my son, His will be done. The Lord who gave me my child, can take him back again. You have not power to raise the dead, otherwise your archdeacon would not have died." She alluded to Chrispion, the archdeacon, who had died a short time previously. He was brother to Fuscon and Salamanus, monks whom I had occasion to mention[2] when detailing the history of events under the reign of Valens; he had been companion of Epiphanius, and had been appointed his archdeacon.

Ammonius and his companions went to

---

[1] Independent chapter. Cf. Soc. vi. 14.
[2] See above, vi. 32.

Epiphanius, at the permission of the empress. Epiphanius inquired who they were, and Ammonius replied, "We are, O father, the Long Brothers; we come respectfully to know whether you have read any of our works or those of our disciples?" On Epiphanius replying that he had not seen them, he continued, "How is it, then, that you consider us to be heretics, when you have no proof as to what sentiments we may hold?" Epiphanius said that he had formed his judgment by the reports he had heard on the subject; and Ammonius replied, "We have pursued a very different line of conduct from yours. We have conversed with your disciples, and read your works frequently, and among others, that entitled 'The Anchored.' When we have met with persons who have ridiculed your opinions, and asserted that your writings are replete with heresy, we have contended for you, and defended you as our father. Ought you then to condemn the absent upon mere report, and of whom you know nothing with assured certitude, or return such an exchange to those who have spoken well of you?" Epiphanius was measurably convinced, and dismissed them. Soon after he embarked for Cyprus, either because he recognized the futility of his journey to Constantinople, or because, as there is reason to believe, God had revealed to him his approaching death; for he died while on his voyage back to Cyprus. It is reported that he said to the bishops who had accompanied him to the place of embarkation, "I leave you the city, the palace, and the stage, for I shall shortly depart." I have been informed by several persons that John predicted that Epiphanius would die at sea, and that this latter predicted the deposition of John. For it appears that when the dispute between them was at its height, Epiphanius said to John, "I hope you will not die a bishop," and that John replied, "I hope you will never return to your bishopric."

CHAP. XVI. — THE DISPUTE BETWEEN THE EMPRESS AND JOHN. ARRIVAL OF THEOPHILUS FROM EGYPT. CYRINUS, BISHOP OF CHALCEDON.

AFTER the departure of Epiphanius, John, when preaching in the church as usual, chanced to inveigh against the vices to which females are peculiarly prone.[1] The people imagined that his strictures were enigmatically directed against the wife of the emperor. The enemies of the bishop did not fail to report his discourse in this sense to the empress; and she, conceiving herself to have been insulted, complained to the emperor, and urged the necessity for the speedy presence of Theophilus and the convocation of a council.

Severian, bishop of Gabala, who had not yet changed his former resentment against John, co-operated in the promotion of these measures. I am not in possession of sufficient data to determine whether there was any truth in the current report that John delivered the discourse above mentioned with express allusion to the empress, because he suspected her of having excited Epiphanius against him. Theophilus arrived soon after at Chalcedon in Bithynia, and was followed thither by many bishops. Some of the bishops joined him in compliance with his own invitation, and others in obedience to the commands of the emperor. The bishops whom John had deposed in Asia repaired to Chalcedon with the utmost alacrity, as likewise all those who cherished any feeling of hostility against him. The ships which Theophilus expected from Egypt had already come to Chalcedon. When they had convened again in the same place, and when they had deliberated how the attempt against John might be judiciously forwarded by them, Cyrinus, leader of the church of Chalcedon, who was an Egyptian and a relative of Theophilus, and who had besides some other difficulties with John, spoke very abusively of him. Justice, however, seemed to follow him speedily; for Maruthas, a native of Mesopotamia, who had accompanied the bishops, happened to tread on his foot; and Cyrinus suffered so severely from this accident that he was unable to repair with the other bishops to Constantinople, although his aid was necessary to the execution of the designs that had been formed against John. The wound assumed so alarming an appearance, that the surgeons were obliged to perform several operations on the leg; and at length mortification took place, and spread over the whole body, and even extended to the other foot. He expired soon afterwards in great agony.

CHAP. XVII. — COUNCIL HELD BY THEOPHILUS AND THE ACCUSERS OF JOHN IN RUFINIANÆ. JOHN IS SUMMONED TO ATTEND, AND NOT BEING PRESENT, WAS DEPOSED BY THEM.

WHEN Theophilus entered Constantinople, none of the clergy went out to meet him; for his enmity against the bishop had become publicly known.[2] Some sailors from Alexandria, however, who chanced to be on the shore, both from the corn vessels as well as other ships, having collected together, received him with great acclamations of joy. Passing by the church, he proceeded directly to the palace, where a lodging had been prepared for his accommodation. He soon perceived that many people

---

[1] Soc. vi. 15; Pallad. *Dialog.* 3, 8–10; also Chrysostom's letter to Innocent, *ibid.* 2. Cf. Theodoret, *H. E.* v. 34.

[2] References in preceding chapter. Soz. has independent material.

of the city were strongly prejudiced against John, and ready to bring accusations against him; and taking his measures accordingly, he repaired to a place called "The Oak," in the suburbs of Chalcedon. This place now bears the name of Rufinus; for he was a consul, and erected here a magnificent palace, and a great church in honor of the apostles, Peter and Paul, and therefore named it the Apostolium; and appointed a congregation of monks to perform the clerical duties in the church. When Theophilus and the other bishops met for deliberation in this place, he judged it expedient to make no further allusion to the works of Origen, and called the monks of Scetis to repentance, promising that there would be no recollection of wrongs nor infliction of evil. His partisans zealously seconded his efforts, and told them that they must ask Theophilus to pardon their conduct; and as all the members of the assembly concurred in this request, the monks were troubled, and believing that it was necessary to do what they were desired by so many bishops, they used the words which it was their custom to use even when injured, and said "spare us." Theophilus willingly received them into favor, and restored them to communion; and the question concerning the injuries done to the monks of Scetis was ended. I feel convinced that this matter would not have been so quickly settled, had Dioscorus and Ammonius been present with the other monks. But Dioscorus had died some time previously, and had been interred in the church dedicated to St. Mocius the martyr. Ammonius, also, had been taken ill at the very time that preparations were being made for the convocation of the council; and although he insisted upon repairing to "The Oak," yet his malady was thereby greatly increased: he died soon after his journey, and had a splendid entombment among the monks of that vicinity, and there he lies. Theophilus, it is said, shed tears on hearing of his death, and declared that although he had been the cause of much perplexity, there was not a monk to be found of more exalted character than Ammonius. It must, however, be admitted, that the death of this monk tended much to promote the success of the designs of Theophilus.

The members of the council summoned all the clergy of Constantinople to appear before them, and threatened to depose those who did not obey the summons. They cited John to appear and answer; as likewise Serapion, Tigrius a presbyter, and Paul a reader. John acquainted them, through the medium of Demetrius, bishop of Pisinus, and of some of the other clergy, who were his friends, that he would not avoid investigation, but that he was ready, if the names of his accusers and the subject of

his accusations were made known to him, to justify his proceedings before a larger council; for he did not choose to be considered insane, and to recognize his manifest enemies as judges. The bishops testified so much indignation at the non-compliance of John, that some of the clergy whom he had sent to the council were intimidated and did not return to him. Demetrius, and those who preferred his interests to all other considerations, quitted the council, and returned to him. The same day, a courier and a shorthand writer were dispatched from the palace to command John to repair to the bishops, and to urge the bishops to decide his cause without further delay. After John had been cited four times, and had appealed to a general council, no other accusation could be substantiated against him, except his refusal to obey the summons of the council; and upon this ground they deposed him.

CHAP. XVIII. — SEDITION OF THE PEOPLE AGAINST THEOPHILUS; AND THEY TRADUCED THEIR RULERS. JOHN WAS RECALLED, AND AGAIN CAME TO THE SEE.

THE people of Constantinople were made acquainted with the decree of the council towards the evening; and they immediately rose up in sedition.[1] At the break of day they ran to the church, and shouted, among many other plans, that a larger council ought to be convened to take cognizance of the matter; and they prevented the officers, who had been sent by the emperor to convey John into banishment, from carrying the edict into execution. John, apprehensive lest another accusation should be preferred against him, under the pretext that he had disobeyed the mandate of the emperor, or excited an insurrection among the people, when the multitude was dispersed, secretly made his escape from the church at noon, three days after his deposition. When the people became aware that he had gone into exile, the sedition became serious, and many insulting speeches were uttered against the emperor and the council; and particularly against Theophilus and Severian, who were regarded as the originators of the plot. Severian happened to be teaching in the church at the very time that these occurrences were taking place; and he took occasion to commend the deposition of John, and stated that, even supposing him guiltless of other crimes, John deserved to be deposed on account of his pride; because, while God willingly forgives men all other sins, he resists the proud. At this

---

[1] Soc. vi. 16; Pallad. *Dialog. ibid.*, and Chrysostom's *Ep. ad Innocentem;* Chrys. *Sermones antequam iret in Exsilium; Sermo cum iret in Exsilium; orationes et sermones post Reditum ab Exsilio*, iii. 427-448. Soz., while guided by the order of Soc., works the material in a different form. Cf. Zos. v. 25.

discourse the people became restive under the wrong, and renewed their wrath, and fell into unrestrainable revolt. They ran to the churches, to the market-places, and even to the palace of the emperor, and with howls and groans demanded the recall of John. The empress was at length overcome by their importunity; and she persuaded her husband to yield to the wishes of the people. She quickly sent a eunuch, named Briso, in whom she placed confidence, to bring back John from Prenetus, a city of Bithynia; and protested that she had taken no part in the machinations that had been carried on against him, but had, on the contrary, always respected him as a priest and the initiator of her children.

When John, on his journey homeward, reached the suburbs belonging to the empress, he stopped near Anaplus; and refused to re-enter the city until the injustice of his deposition had been recognized by a larger synod of bishops; but as this refusal tended to augment the popular excitement, and led to many public declamations against the emperor and the empress, he allowed himself to be persuaded to enter the city. The people went to meet him, singing psalms composed with reference to the circumstances; many carried light wax tapers. They conducted him to the church; and although he refused, and frequently affirmed that those who had condemned him ought first to reconsider their vote, yet they compelled him to take the episcopal throne, and to speak peace to the people according to the custom of the priests. He then delivered an extemporaneous discourse, in which, by a pleasing figure of speech, he declared that Theophilus had meditated an injury against his church, even as the king of Egypt had contemplated the violation of Sarah, the wife of the patriarch Abraham, which is recorded in the books of the Hebrews: he then proceeded to commend the zeal of the people, and to extol the emperor and the empress for their good will to him; he stirred the people to much applause and good acclaim for the emperor and his spouse, so that he had to leave his speech half ended.

CHAP. XIX. — OBSTINANCY OF THEOPHILUS. ENMITY BETWEEN THE EGYPTIANS AND THE CITIZENS OF CONSTANTINOPLE. FLIGHT OF THEOPHILUS. NILAMMON THE ASCETIC. THE SYNOD CONCERNING JOHN.

ALTHOUGH Theophilus would fain have brought an accusation against John,[1] under the plea that he had unlawfully reinstated himself in his bishopric, yet he was deterred from doing so by the fear of offending the emperor, who had been compelled to recall John, as the means of suppressing the popular insurrection. Theophilus, however, received an accusation against Heraclides during the absence of the accused, in the hope of thereby authorizing the sentence of condemnation which had been issued against John. But the friends of Heraclides interposed, and declared that it was unjust, and contrary to ecclesiastical law, to condemn one who was absent. Theophilus and his partisans maintained the opposite side of the question: the people of Alexandria and of Egypt sided with them, and were opposed by the citizens of Constantinople. The strife between the two parties became so vehement that bloodshed ensued; many were wounded, and others slain in the contest. Severian, and all the bishops at Constantinople who did not support the cause of John, became apprehensive for their personal safety, and quitted the city in haste. Theophilus, also, fled the city at the commencement of the winter; and, in company with Isaac the monk, sailed for Alexandria. A wind arose which drove the vessel to Gera, a small city about fifty stadia from Pelusium. The bishop of this city died, and the inhabitants, I have been informed, elected Nilammon to preside over their church; he was a good man, and had attained the summit of monastic philosophy. He dwelt without the city, in a cell of which the door was built up with stones. He refused to accept the dignity of the priesthood; and Theophilus, therefore, visited him in person, to exhort him to receive ordination at his hands. Nilammon repeatedly refused the honor; but, as Theophilus would take no refusal, he said to him, "To-morrow, my father, you shall act as you please; to-day it is requisite that I should arrange my affairs." Theophilus repaired, on the following day, to the cell of the monk, and commanded the door to be opened; but Nilammon exclaimed, "Let us first engage in prayer." Theophilus complied and began to pray. Nilammon likewise prayed within his cell, and in the act of prayer he expired. Theophilus, and those who were standing with him without the cell, knew nothing at the time of what had occurred; but, when the greater part of the day had passed away, and the name of Nilammon had been loudly reiterated without his returning any answer, the stones were removed from the door, and the monk was found dead. They honored him with a public burial after they had clothed him in the necessary vestments, and the inhabitants built a house of prayer about his tomb; and they celebrate the day of his death, in a very marked way, until this day. Thus died Nilammon, if it can be called death to quit this life for another, — rather than accept a bishopric of which, with extraordinary modesty, he considered himself unworthy.

1 Soc. vi. 17; Pallad. *ibid.*; and Chrys. *Ep. ad Inn.* Soz. has independent material.

After his return to Constantinople, John appeared to be more than ever beloved by the people. Sixty bishops assembled together in that city, and annulled all the decrees of the council of "The Oak." They confirmed John in the possession of the bishopric, and enacted that he should officiate as a priest, confer ordination, and perform all the duties of the church usually devolving on the president. At this time Serapion was appointed bishop of Heraclea in Thrace.

CHAP. XX. — THE STATUE OF THE EMPRESS; WHAT HAPPENED THERE; THE TEACHING OF JOHN; CONVOCATION OF ANOTHER SYNOD AGAINST JOHN; HIS DEPOSITION.

NOT long after these occurrences the silver statue of the empress, which is still to be seen to the south of the church opposite the grand council-chamber, was placed upon a column of porphyry on a high platform,[1] and the event was celebrated there with applause and popular spectacles of dances and mimes, as was then customary on the erection of the statues of the emperors. In a public discourse to the people John charged that these proceedings reflected dishonor on the Church. This remark recalled former grievances to the recollection of the empress, and irritated her so exceedingly at the insult that she determined to convene another council. He did not yield, but added fuel to her indignation by still more openly declaiming against her in the church; and it was at this period that he pronounced the memorable discourse commencing with the words, "Herodias is again enraged; again she dances; again she seeks to have the head of John in a basin."

Several bishops arrived soon after at Constantinople, and amongst them were Leontius, bishop of Ancyra, and Acacius, bishop of Berea. The festival of our Lord's Nativity was then at hand, and the emperor, instead of repairing to the church as usual, sent to acquaint John that he could not hold communion with him until he had cleared himself of the charges. John spiritedly replied that he was ready to prove his innocence; and this so intimidated his accusers that they did not dare to follow up the charges. The judges decided that, having been once deposed, he ought not to be admitted to a second trial. But they called on John to defend himself on this point only, that after he had been deposed, he had sat on the episcopal throne before a synod had reinstated him. In his defense he appealed to the decision of the bishops who had, subsequently to the council of "The Oak," held communion with him. The judges waived this argument, under the plea that those who had held communion with John were inferior in point of number to those who had deposed him, and that a canon was in force by which he stood condemned. Under this pretext they therefore deposed him, although the law in question had been enacted by heretics; for the Arians, after having taken advantage of various calumnies to expel Athanasius from the church of Alexandria, enacted this law from the apprehension of a change in public affairs, for they struggled to have the decisions against him remain uninvestigated.

CHAP. XXI. — CALAMITIES SUFFERED BY THE PEOPLE AFTER THE EXPULSION OF JOHN. THE PLOTS AGAINST HIM OF ASSASSINATION.

AFTER his deposition, John held no more assemblies in the church, but quietly remained in the episcopal dwelling-house.[2] At the termination of the season of Quadragesima, on the same holy night in which the yearly festival in commemoration of the resurrection of Christ is celebrated, the followers of John were expelled from the church by the soldiers and his enemies, who attacked the people while still celebrating the mysteries. Since this occurrence was unforeseen, a great disturbance arose in the baptistery. The women wept and lamented, and the children screamed; the priests and the deacons were beaten, and were forcibly ejected from the church, in the priestly garments in which they had been officiating. They were charged with the commission of such disorderly acts as can be readily conceived by those who have been admitted to the mysteries, but which I consider it requisite to pass over in silence, lest my work should fall into the hands of the uninitiated.

When the people perceived the plot, they did not use the church on the following day, but celebrated the Paschal feast in the very spacious public baths called after the Emperor Constantius. Bishops and presbyters, and the rest, whose right it is to administer church matters, officiated. Those who espoused the cause of John were present with the people. They were, however, driven hence, and then assembled on a spot without the walls of the city, which the Emperor Constantine, before the city had been built, had caused to be cleared and inclosed with palisades, for the purpose of celebrating there the games of the hippodrome. From that period, the people held separate assemblies, sometimes, whenever it was feasible, in that locality, and sometimes in another. They obtained the name of Johnites. About this time, a man who was either possessed of a

---

[1] Soc. vi. 18; Pallad. *Dialog.* 9–12; Chrys. *Ep. ad Inn. ibid.* 2.

[2] Soc. vi. 18; Pallad. *ibid.* Soz. has much distinctive material.

devil, or who feigned to have one, was seized, having a poniard on his person, with the intention of assassinating John. He was apprehended by the people as one who had been hired for this plot, and led to the prefect; but John sent some bishops of his party to free him from custody before he had been questioned by torture. Some time afterwards, a slave of Elpidius the presbyter, who was an avowed enemy of the deacon, was seen running as swiftly as possible towards the episcopal residence. A passer-by endeavored to stop him, in order to ascertain the cause of so much haste; but instead of answering him, the slave plunged his poniard into him. Another person, who happened to be standing by, and who cried out at seeing the other wounded, was also wounded in a similar way by the slave; as was likewise a third bystander. All the people in the neighborhood, on seeing what had occurred, shouted that the slave ought to be arrested. He turned and fled. When those who were pursuing called out to those ahead to seize the fugitive, a man, who just then came out from the baths, strove to stop him, and was so grievously wounded that he fell down dead on the spot. At length, the people contrived to encircle the slave. They seized him, and conveyed him to the palace of the emperor, declaring that he had intended to have assassinated John, and that the crime ought to be visited with punishment. The prefect allayed the fury of the people by putting the delinquent into custody, and by assuring them that justice should have its course against him.

CHAP. XXII. — UNLAWFUL EXPULSION OF JOHN FROM HIS BISHOPRIC. THE TROUBLE WHICH FOLLOWED. CONFLAGRATION OF THE CHURCH BY FIRE FROM HEAVEN. EXILE OF JOHN TO CUCUSUS.

FROM this period the most zealous of the people guarded John alternately, stationing themselves about the episcopal residence by night and by day.[1] The bishops who had condemned him complained of this conduct as a violation of the laws of the Church, declared that they could answer for the justice of the sentence that had been enacted against him, and asserted that tranquillity would never be restored among the people until he had been expelled from the city. A messenger having conveyed to him a mandate from the emperor enjoining his immediate departure, John obeyed, and escaped from the city, unnoticed by those who had been appointed to guard him. He made no other censure than that, in being sent into banishment without a legal trial or any of the forms of the law, he was treated more severely than murderers, sorcerers,

and adulterers. He was conveyed in a little bark to Bithynia, and thence immediately continued his journey. Some of his enemies were apprehensive lest the people, on hearing of his departure, should pursue him, and bring him back by force, and therefore commanded the gates of the church to be closed. When the people who were in the public places of the city heard of what had occurred, great confusion ensued; for some ran to the seashore as if they would follow him, and others fled hither and thither, and were in great terror since the wrath of the emperor was expected to visit them for creating so much disturbance and tumult. Those who were within the church barred the exits still further by rushing together upon them, and by pressing upon one another. With difficulty they forced the doors open by the use of great violence; one party shattered them with stones, another was pulling them toward themselves, and was thus forcing the crowd backward into the building. Meanwhile the church was suddenly consumed on all sides with fire. The flames extended in all directions, and the grand house of the senatorial council, adjacent to the church on the south, was doomed. The two parties mutually accused each other of incendiarism. The enemies of John asserted that his partisans had been guilty of the deed from revenge, on account of the vote that had been passed against him by the council. These latter, on the other hand, maintained that they had been calumniated, and that the deed was perpetrated by their enemies, with the intention of burning them in the church. While the fire was spreading from late afternoon until the morning, and creeping forward to the material which was still standing, the officers who held John in custody conveyed him to Cucusus, a city of Armenia, which the emperor by letter had appointed as the place of residence for the condemned man. Other officers were commissioned to arrest all the bishops and clerics who had favored the cause of John, and to imprison them in Chalcedon. Those citizens who were suspected of attachment to John were sought out and cast into prison, and compelled to pronounce anathema against him.

CHAP. XXIII. — ARSACIUS ELECTED TO SUCCEED JOHN. THE EVILS WROUGHT AGAINST THE FOLLOWERS OF JOHN. ST. NICARETE.

ARSACIUS, brother of Nectarius, who had administered the bishopric before John, was, not long afterwards, ordained as bishop of Constantinople.[2] He was of a very mild disposition, and possessed of great piety; but the reputation he had acquired as a presbyter was diminished

---

[1] Soc. vi. 18; Pallad. *ibid.* and Chrys. *Ep. ad Inn.*; Theodoret, *H. E.* v. 34. Soz. has distinct material. Cf. Zos. v. 24.

[2] Soc. vi. 19; Pallad. *Dialog.* 11–20. Cf. Theodoret, *H. E.* v. 34. Soz. has much separate material.

by the conduct of some of the clergy to whom he delegated his power, and who did what they pleased in his name; for their evil deeds were imputed to him. Nothing, however, operated so much to his disadvantage as the persecution that was carried on against the followers of John. They refused to hold communion, or even to join in prayer with him, because the enemies of John were associated with him; and as they persisted, as we have before stated, in holding a church in the further parts of the city, he complained to the emperor of their conduct. The tribune was commanded to attack them with a body of soldiers, and by means of clubs and stones he soon dispersed them. The most distinguished among them in point of rank, and those who were most zealous in their adherence to John, were cast into prison. The soldiers, as is usual on such occasions, went beyond their orders, and forcibly stripped the women of their ornaments, and carried off as booty their chains, their golden girdles, necklaces, and their collars of rings; they pulled off the lobes of the ear with the earrings. Although the whole city was thus filled with trouble and lamentation, the affection of the people for John still remained the same, and they refrained from appearing in public. Many of them absented themselves from the market-place and public baths, while others, not considering themselves safe in their own houses, fled the city.

Among the zealous men and excellent women who adopted this latter measure was Nicarete, a lady of Bithynia. She belonged to a noted family of the nobility, and was celebrated on account of her perpetual virginity and her virtuous life. She was the most modest of all the zealous women that we have ever known, and was well ordered in manner and speech and in behavior, and throughout her life she invariably preferred the service of God to all earthly considerations. She showed herself capable of enduring with courage and thought the sudden reversals of adverse affairs; she saw herself unjustly despoiled of the greater part of her ample patrimony without manifesting any indignation, and managed the little that remained to her with so much economy, that although she was advanced in age, she contrived to supply all the wants of her household, and to contribute largely to others. Since she loved a humane spirit, she also prepared a variety of remedies for the needs of the sick poor, and she frequently succeeded in curing patients who had derived no benefit from the skill of the customary physicians. With a devout strength which assisted her in reaching the best results, she closed her lips. To sum up all in a few words, we have never known a devoted woman endowed with such manners, gravity, and every other vir-

tue. Although she was so extraordinary, she concealed the greater part of her nature and deeds; for by modesty of character and philosophy she was always studious of concealment. She would not accept of the office of deaconess, nor of instructress of the virgins consecrated to the service of the Church, because she accounted herself unworthy, although the honor was frequently pressed upon her by John.

After the popular insurrection had been quelled, the prefect of the city appeared in public, as if to inquire into the cause of the conflagration, and the burning of the council-hall, and punished many severely; but being a pagan, he ridiculed the calamities of the Church, and delighted in its misfortunes.

CHAP. XXIV. — EUTROPIUS THE READER, AND THE BLESSED OLYMPIAS, AND THE PRESBYTER TIGRIUS, ARE PERSECUTED ON ACCOUNT OF THEIR ATTACHMENT TO JOHN. THE PATRIARCHS.

EUTROPIUS, a reader,[1] was required to name the persons who had set fire to the church; but although he was scourged severely, although his sides and cheeks were torn with iron nails, and although lighted torches were applied to the most sensitive parts of his body, no confession could be extorted from him, notwithstanding his youth and delicacy of constitution. After having been subjected to these tortures, he was cast into a dungeon, where he soon afterwards expired.

A dream of Sisinius concerning Eutropius seems worthy of insertion in this history. Sisinius, the bishop of the Novatians, saw in his sleep a man, conspicuous for beauty and stature, standing near the altar of the church which the Novatians erected to the honor of Stephen, the proto-martyr; the man complained of the rarity of good men, and said that he had been searching throughout the entire city, and had found but one who was good, and that one was Eutropius. Astonished at what he had seen, Sisinius made known the dream to the most faithful of the presbyters of his church, and commanded him to seek Eutropius wherever he might be. The presbyter rightly conjectured that this Eutropius could be no other than he who had been so barbarously tortured by the prefect, and went from prison to prison in quest of him. At length he found him, and in conversation with him made known the dream of the bishop, and besought him with tears to pray for him. Such are the details we possess concerning Eutropius.

Great fortitude was evinced in the midst of these calamities by Olympias, the deaconess.

---

[1] Pallad. *Dialog., ibid.* Soz. has an independent chapter in large part.

Being dragged for this reason before the tribunal, and interrogated by the prefect as to her motives in setting fire to the church, she replied, " My past life ought to avert all suspicion from me, for I have devoted my large property to the restoration of the temples of God." The prefect alleged that he was well acquainted with her past course of life. " Then," continued she, " you ought to appear in the place of the accuser and let another judge us." As the accusation against her was wholly unsubstantiated by proofs, and as the prefect found that he had no ground on which he could justly blame her, he changed to a milder charge as if desirous of advising her, finding fault with her and the other women, because they refused communion with his bishop, although it was possible for them to repent and to change their own circumstances. They all through fear deferred to the advice of the prefect, but Olympias said to him, " It is not just that, after having been publicly calumniated, without having had anything proved against me in the courts, I should be obliged to clear myself of charges totally unconnected with the accusation in question. Let me rather take counsel concerning the original accusation that has been preferred against me. For even if you resort to unlawful compulsion, I will not hold communion with those from whom I ought to secede, nor consent to anything that is not lawful to the pious." The prefect, finding that he could not prevail upon her to hold communion with Arsacius, dismissed her that she might consult the advocates. On another occasion, however, he again sent for her and condemned her to pay a heavy fine, for he imagined by this means she would be compelled to change her mind. But she totally disregarded the loss of her property, and quitted Constantinople for Cyzicus. Tigrius, a presbyter, was about the same period stripped of his clothes, scourged on the back, bound hand and foot, and stretched on the rack. He was a barbarian by race, and a eunuch, but not by birth. He was originally a slave in the house of a man in power, and on account of his faithful services had obtained his freedom. He was afterwards ordained as presbyter, and was distinguished by his moderation and meekness of disposition, and by his charity towards strangers and the poor. Such were the events which took place in Constantinople.

Meanwhile Siricius had died, after having administered the bishopric of Rome fifteen years. Anastasius held the same bishopric three years, and then died, and was succeeded by Innocent. Flavian, who refused his consent to the deposition of John, was also dead ; and Porphyry, being appointed to succeed him in the church of Antioch, where he agreed with those who had condemned John, many of those in Syria seceded from the church in Antioch, and because they made congregations among themselves, they were subjected to many cruelties. For the purpose of enforcing fellowship with Arsacius, and with this Porphyry and Theophilus, the bishop of Alexandria, a law was established, by the zeal of the powerful at court, that those who were orthodox should not assemble outside of the churches, and those who were not in communion with them should be expelled.

CHAP. XXV. — SINCE THESE ILLS EXISTED IN THE CHURCH, SECULAR AFFAIRS ALSO FELL INTO DISORDER. THE AFFAIRS OF STILICHO, THE GENERAL OF HONORIUS.

ABOUT this period[1] the dissensions by which the Church was agitated were followed, as is frequently the case, by disturbances and commotions in the state. The Huns crossed the Ister and devastated Thrace. The robbers in Isauria gathered in great numbers and ravaged cities and villages as far as Caria and Phœnicia. Stilicho, the general of Honorius, a man who had attained great power, if any one ever did, and had under his sway the flower of the Roman and of the barbarian soldiery, conceived feelings of enmity against the rulers who held office under Arcadius, and determined to set the two empires at enmity with each other. He caused Alaric, the leader of the Goths, to be appointed by Honorius to the office of general of the Roman troops, and sent him into Illyria ; whither also he dispatched Jovius, the prætorian prefect, and promised to join them there with the Roman soldiers in order to add that province to the dominions of Honorius. Alaric marched at the head of his troops from the barbarous regions bordering on Dalmatia and Pannonia, and came to Epirus ; and after waiting for some time there, he returned to Italy. Stilicho was prevented from fulfilling his agreement to join Alaric, by some letters which were transmitted to him from Honorius. These events happened in the manner narrated.

CHAP. XXVI. — TWO EPISTLES FROM INNOCENT, THE POPE OF ROME, OF WHICH ONE WAS ADDRESSED TO JOHN CHRYSOSTOM, AND THE OTHER TO THE CLERGY OF CONSTANTINOPLE CONCERNING JOHN.

INNOCENT,[2] bishop of Rome,[3] was extremely indignant when apprised of the measures that had been adopted against John, and condemned

---

[1] Cf. *Claudianus in primum consulatum Fl. Stilichonis*, i., ii.; *de secundo consulatu Fl. Stilichonis ; de bello Getico ; de sexto consulatu Honorii Augusti panegyris*, 57 — v. 38; Olymp. beginning with *Fragm.* 2; Eunap. *Fragm.* ii. 72.
[2] Independent chapter; cf. Pallad. *Dialog.* 1–3.
[3] Innocent I., A.D. 402–417.

the whole proceedings. He then turned his attention to the convocation of an œcumenical council, and wrote to John and to the clergy of Constantinople in part. Subjoined are the two letters, precisely as I found them, translated from the Latin into Greek.

"Innocent, to the beloved brother John.

"Although one conscious of his own innocence ought to expect every blessing and to ask for mercy from God, yet it seems well to us to send you a befitting letter by Cyriacus, the deacon, and to counsel you to long-suffering, lest the contumely cast upon you should have more power in subduing your courage than the testimony of a good conscience in encouraging you to hope. It is not requisite to teach you, who are the teacher and pastor of so great a people, that God always tries the best of men to see whether they will continue in the height of patience, and will not give way to any labor of suffering; and how true it is that the conscience is a firm thing against all that befalls us unjustly, and unless one be moved in these misfortunes by patience, he furnishes a ground for evil surmising. For he ought to endure everything, who first trusts in God, and then in his own conscience. Especially when an excellent and good man can exercise himself in endurance, he cannot be overcome; for the Holy Scriptures guard his thoughts, and the devout lections, which we expound to the people, abound in examples. These Scriptures assure us that almost all the saints are variously and continuously afflicted, and are tested by some investigation, and so have come to the crown of patience. Let thy conscience encourage thy love, O most honored brother; for that faculty amid tribulations possesses an encouragement for virtue. For since Christ, the Master, is observing, the purified conscience will station you in the haven of peace."

"Innocent, the bishop, to the presbyters, deacons, and all the clergy, and to the people of the church of Constantinople under John, the bishop, greeting to you, beloved brethren.

"From the letters of your love that you forwarded to me through Germanus, the presbyter, and Cassianus, the deacon, I have learned, with anxious solicitude, the scenes of evil which you have placed before our eyes. I have frequently seen during its repeated reading with what calamities and labors the faith is wearied. Only the consolation of patience heals such a state of affairs. Our God will shortly put an end to such tribulations, and they will eventually tend to your profit. But we recognized with approbation your proposition, placed at the beginning of the letter of your love; to wit, that this very consolation is necessary, and embraces many proofs of your patience; for our consolation,

which we ought to have conveyed, you have anticipated in your epistle. Our Lord is wont to furnish this patience to the suffering, in order that when they fall into tribulations, the servants of Christ may encourage themselves; for they should reason within themselves that what they suffer has happened previously to the saints. And even we ourselves derive comfort from your letters, for we are not strangers to your sufferings; but we are disciplined in you. Who, indeed, can endure to witness the errors introduced by those who were bound especially to be enthusiasts for the quiet of peace and for its concord? But far from maintaining peace, they expel guiltless priests from the front seat of their own churches. John, our brother and fellow-minister and your bishop, has been the first to suffer this unjust treatment without being allowed a hearing. No accusation was brought, none was heard. What proposition was it that was nullified, so that no show of judgment might arise or be sought? Others were seated in the places of living priests, as though any who began from such discord would be able to possess anything or do anything rightly in any one's judgment. We have never known such audacities to have been done by our fathers. They rather prohibited such innovations by refusing to give power to any one to be ordained in another's place while the occupant was living, since he is unable to be a bishop who is unjustly substituted.

"With respect to the observance of canons, we declare that those defined at Nicæa are alone[1] entitled to the obedience and recognition of the Catholic Church. If any individuals should attempt to introduce other canons, at variance with those of Nicæa, and such as are a compilation by heretics, such canons ought to be rejected by the Catholic Church, for it is not lawful to add the inventions of heretics to the Catholic canons. For they always wish to belittle the decision of the Nicene fathers through opponents and lawless men. We say, then, that the canons we have censured are not only to be disregarded, but to be condemned with the dogmas of heretics and schismatics, even as they have been formerly condemned at the council of Sardica by the bishops who were our predecessors. For it would be better, O most honored brethren, that these transactions be condemned, than that any actions should be confirmed contrary to the canons.

"What measures ought we to adopt now in the present circumstances against such deeds? It is necessary that there be a synodical investigation, and a synod we long ago said should be gathered. There are no other means of arrest-

[1] The reckless historical sense of the West has a strong proof here.

ing the fury of the tempest. In order that we may attain this it will be profitable meanwhile for that healing to be exalted which comes by the will of the great God and of His Christ, our Lord. We shall thus behold the cessation of all the woes which have been excited by the envy of the devil, and which have served as trials for our faith. If we remain steadfast in the faith, there is nothing that we ought not to expect from the Lord. We are constantly watching for the opportunity of convening an œcumenical council, whereby, in accordance with the will of God, an end may be put to these harassing commotions. Let us, then, endure in the interval, and, fortified by the wall of patience, let us trust in the help of our God for the restoration of all things.

"We had previously been made acquainted with all that you have related concerning your trials, by our fellow-bishops Demetrius, Cyriacus, Eulysius, and Palladius, who visited Rome at different periods and are now with us; from them we had learned all the details by a complete inquiry."

CHAP. XXVII. — THE TERRIBLE EVENTS WHICH RESULTED FROM THE TREATMENT OF JOHN. DEATH OF THE EMPRESS EUDOXIA. DEATH OF ARSACIUS. AND FURTHER CONCERNING ATTICUS, THE PATRIARCH, HIS BIRTHPLACE, AND CHARACTER.

SUCH were the letters of Innocent from which the opinion which he entertained of John may readily be inferred. About the same period some hailstones of extraordinary magnitude fell at Constantinople and in the suburbs of the city.[1] Four days afterwards, the wife of the emperor died. These occurrences were by many regarded as indications of Divine wrath on account of the persecution that had been carried on against John. For Cyrinus, bishop of Chalcedon, one of his principal calumniators, had long previously terminated his life in the midst of great bodily agony, arising from the accident that had occurred to his foot, and the consequent necessary amputation of the leg by the physicians. Arsacius, too, died after he had presided but a very short period over the church of Constantinople. Many candidates were proposed as his successor; and four months after his decease, Atticus, a presbyter, of the clergy of Constantinople, and one of the enemies of John, was ordained. He was a native of Sebaste in Armenia. He had been instructed from his youth in the principles of monastic philosophy by monks of the Macedonian heresy. These monks, who then enjoyed

a very high reputation at Sebaste for philosophy, were of the discipline of Eustathius, to whom allusion has been already made as bishop there, and a leader of the best monks. When Atticus attained the age of manhood, he embraced the tenets of the Catholic Church. He possessed more by nature than by learning, and became a participant in affairs, and was as skillful in carrying on intrigues as in evading the machinations of others. He was of a very engaging disposition, and was beloved by many. The discourses which he delivered in the church did not rise above mediocrity; and although not totally devoid of erudition, they were not accounted by his auditors of sufficient value to be preserved in writing. Being intent, if an opportunity offered itself anywhere, he exercised himself in the most approved Greek authors; but lest, in conversation about these writers, he might appear unlettered, he frequently concealed what he did know. It is said that he manifested much zeal in behalf of those who entertained the same sentiments as himself, and that he rendered himself formidable to the heterodox. When he wished he could easily throw them into alarm; but he at once transformed himself and would appear meek. Such is the information which those who knew the man have furnished.

John acquired great celebrity even in his exile. He possessed ample pecuniary resources, and being besides liberally supplied with money by Olympias, the deaconess, and others, he purchased the liberty of many captives from the Isaurian robbers, and restored them to their families. He also administered to the necessities of many who were in want; and by his kind words comforted those who did not stand in need of money. Hence he was exceedingly beloved not only in Armenia, where he dwelt, but by all the people of the neighboring countries, and the inhabitants of Antioch and of the other parts of Syria, and of Cilicia, who frequently sought his society.

CHAP. XXVIII. — EFFORT OF INNOCENT, BISHOP OF ROME, TO RECALL JOHN THROUGH A COUNCIL. CONCERNING THOSE WHO WERE SENT BY HIM TO MAKE TRIAL OF THE MATTER. THE DEATH OF JOHN CHRYSOSTOM.

INNOCENT, bishop of Rome, was very anxious, as appears by his former letter, to procure the recall of John.[2] He sent five bishops and two presbyters of the Roman church, with two bishops who had been delegated as ambassadors to him from the East, to the emperors Honorius

---

[1] Soc. vi. 19, 20, vii. 2; Pallad. *Dialog. ibid.* Soz. has new facts, and a sobered judgment of Atticus.

[2] Pallad. *Dialog. ibid.*; Soc. vi. 21; Theodoret, *H. E.* v. 34. Soz. has new material. Cf. Chrys. *Epp. in exil.*, vol. iii. [2] PGM.

and Arcadius, to request the convocation of a council, and solicit them to name time and place. The enemies of John at Constantinople framed a charge as though these things were done to insult the Eastern emperor, and caused the ambassadors to be ignominiously dismissed as if they had invaded a foreign government. John was at the same time condemned by an imperial edict to a remoter place of banishment, and soldiers were sent to conduct him to Pityus; the soldiers were soon on hand, and effected the removal. It is said that during this journey, Basiliscus, the martyr, appeared to him at Comani, in Armenia, and apprised him of the day of his death. Being attacked with pain in the head, and being unable to bear the heat of the sun, he could not prosecute his journey, but closed his life in that town.

BOOK IX.

CHAP. I. — DEATH OF ARCADIUS, AND GOVERNMENT OF THEODOSIUS THE YOUNGER.   HIS SISTERS. PIETY, VIRTUE, AND VIRGINITY, OF THE PRINCESS PULCHERIA ; HER DIVINELY LOVED WORKS ; SHE EDUCATED THE EMPEROR BEFITTINGLY.

SUCH are the details that have been transmitted concerning John.   Not long after his death, and three years after the elevation of Atticus to the bishopric of Constantinople, and during the consulate of Bassus and Philip, Arcadius died.   He left Theodosius, his son,[1] who was just weaned, as his successor to the empire. He also left three daughters of tender age, named Pulcheria, Arcadia, and Marina.

It appears to me that it was the design of God to show by the events of this period, that piety alone suffices for the salvation of princes ; and that without piety, armies, a powerful empire, and every other resource, are of no avail. The Divine Power which is the guardian of the universe, foresaw that the emperor would be distinguished by his piety, and therefore determined that Pulcheria, his sister, should be the protector of him and of his government.   This princess was not yet fifteen years of age, but had received a mind most wise and divine above her years.   She first devoted her virginity to God, and instructed her sisters in the same course of life.   To avoid all cause of jealousy and intrigue, she permitted no man to enter her palace.   In confirmation of her resolution, she took God, the priests, and all the subjects of the Roman empire as witnesses to her self-dedication.   In token of her virginity and the headship of her brother, she consecrated in the church of Constantinople, a holy table, a remarkable fabric and very beautiful to see ; it was made of gold and precious stones ; and she inscribed these things on the front of the table, so that it might be patent to all. After quietly resuming the care of the state, she governed the Roman empire excellently and with great orderliness ; she concerted her measures so well that the affairs to be carried out were quickly decreed and completed. She was able to write and to converse with perfect accuracy in the Greek and Latin languages. She

caused all affairs to be transacted in the name of her brother, and devoted great attention to bringing him up as a prince in the best possible way and with such information as was suitable to his years.   She had him taught by the most skilled men, in horsemanship, and the practice of arms, and in letters.   But he was systematically taught by his sister to be orderly and princely in his manners ; she showed him how to gather up his robes, and how to take a seat, and how to walk ; she trained him to restrain laughter, to assume a mild or a formidable aspect as the occasion might require, and to inquire with urbanity into the cases of those who came before him with petitions.   But she strove chiefly, to lead him into piety, and to pray continuously ; she taught him to frequent the church regularly, and to honor the houses of prayer with gifts and treasures ; and she inspired him with reverence for priests and other good men, and for those who, in accordance with the law of Christianity, had devoted themselves to philosophy.   She provided zealously and wisely that religion might not be endangered by the innovation of spurious dogmas.   That new heresies have not prevailed in our times, we shall find to be due especially to her, as we shall subsequently see.   With how much fear she worshiped God, it would take long for any one to say ; and how many houses of prayer she built magnificently, and how many hostelries and monastic communities she established, the arrangement for the expenses for their perpetual support, and the provision for the inmates.   If any one pleases to examine the truth from the business itself, and not to be convinced by my words, he will learn that they are not falsely described by me for my own favor, if he will investigate the testimonial documents written up by the stewards of her house, and if he will inquire from the true records whether the facts agree with my history.   If these proofs alone do not satisfy him so as to make him believe, let God himself persuade him who had her in favor altogether and everywhere on account of her conduct, so that He heard her prayer readily, and frequently directed beforehand the things which ought to be done.   Such indications of Divine love are not conferred upon men unless they have merited them by their works.   But I willingly pass over for the

---

[1] Soc. vi. 23; Philost. xii. 7; Theodoret, *H. E.* v. 36. Soz. is independent. Cf. Zos. v. 31; Olymp. *Fragm.* 1 and 2.

present the many separate manifestations of Divine favor that were granted to the sister of the emperor as proofs that she was loved of God, lest anybody should blame me for having set out to do other things, and yet had turned to the use of encomiums. One incident relating to her seems, however, so fitting in itself and to my ecclesiastical history, and so evident a demonstration of her love for God, that I will relate it here, although it happened some time afterwards. It is as follows : —

CHAP. II. — DISCOVERY OF THE RELICS OF FORTY
HOLY MARTYRS.

A WOMAN by name Eusebia,[1] who was a deaconess of the Macedonian sect, had a house and garden without the walls of Constantinople, in which she kept the holy remains of forty soldiers,[2] who had suffered martyrdom under Licinius at Sebaste in Armenia. When she felt death approaching, she bequeathed the aforesaid place to some orthodox monks, and bound them by oath to bury her there, and to hew out separately a place above her head at the top of her coffin, and to deposit the relics of the martyrs with her, and to inform no one. The monks did so ; but in order to render due honor to the martyrs secretly, according to the agreement with Eusebia, they formed a subterranean house of prayer near her tomb. But open to view, an edifice was erected above the foundation, inclosed with baked bricks, and a secret descent from it to the martyrs. Soon after, Cæsar, a man among those in power, who had formerly been advanced to the dignity of consul and prefect, lost his wife, and caused her to be interred near the tomb of Eusebia ; for the two ladies had been knit together by the most tender friendship, and had been of one mind on all doctrinal and religious subjects. Cæsar was hence induced to purchase this place so that he might be entombed near his wife. The aforesaid monks settled elsewhere, and without divulging anything about the martyrs. After this, when the building was demolished, and when the earth and refuse were scattered about, the whole place was smoothed off. For Cæsarius himself erected there a magnificent temple to God to the honor of Thyrsus, the martyr. It appears probable that God designedly willed the aforesaid place to disappear, and so long a time to elapse in order that the discovery of the martyrs might be regarded as more marvelous and a more conspicuous event, and as a proof of the Divine favor towards the discoverer. The discoverer

was, in fact, no other than the Empress Pulcheria, the sister of the emperor. The admirable Thyrsus appeared to her three times, and revealed to her those concealed beneath the earth ; and commanded that they should be deposited near his tomb, in order that they might share in the same position and honor. The forty martyrs themselves also appeared to her, arrayed in shining robes. But the occurrence seemed too marvelous to be credible, and altogether impossible ; for the aged of clergy of that region, after having frequently prosecuted inquiries, had not been able to indicate the position of the martyrs, nor indeed had any one else. At length, when everything was hopeless, Polychronius, a certain presbyter, who had formerly been a servant in the household of Cæsar, was reminded by God that the locality in question had once been inhabited by monks. He therefore went to the clergy of the Macedonian sect to inquire concerning them. All the monks were dead, with the exception of one, who seemed to have been preserved in life for the express purpose of pointing out the spot where the relics of the holy martyrs were concealed. Polychronius questioned him closely on the subject, and finding that, on account of the agreement made with Eusebia, his answers were somewhat undecided, he made known to him the Divine revelation and the anxiety of the empress, as well as the failure of her recourses. The monk then confessed that God had declared the truth to the empress ; for at the time when he was an overgrown boy, and was taught the monastic life by its aged leaders, he remembered exactly that the relics of the martyrs had been deposited near the tomb of Eusebia ; but that the subsequent lapse of time, and the changes which had been carried on in that locality, deprived him of the power of recalling to his recollection whether the relics had been deposited beneath the church or in any other spot. And further said Polychronius, " I have not suffered a like lapse of memory, for I remember that I was present at the interment of the wife of Cæsar, and, as well as I can judge from the relative situation of the high road, I infer that she must have been buried beneath the ambo " ; this is the platform for the readers. " Therefore," subjoined the monk, " it must be near the remains of Cæsar's wife that the tomb of Eusebia must be sought ; for the two ladies lived on terms of the closest friendship and intimacy, and mutually agreed to be interred beside each other." When it was necessary to dig, according to the aforesaid intimations, and to track out the sacred relics, and the empress had learned the facts, she commanded them to begin the work. On digging up the earth by the ambo, the coffin of Cæsar's wife was discovered ac-

---

[1] This chapter is independent.
[2] Cf. *Acta Sanct. Boll.* under March 10, where the names, acts, orations of Basil, and Soz.'s story of the invention are given. Basil, *Oratio in laudem ss. Quadraginta Martyrum*, vii. 749.

cording to the conjecture of Polychronius. At a short distance on the side they found the pavement of baked bricks, and a marble tablet of equal dimensions, each the measure of the bricks, under which the coffin of Eusebia was disclosed; and close by was an oratory, elegantly inclosed with white and purple marble. The cover of the tomb was in the form of a holy table, and at the summit, where the relics were deposited, a small orifice was visible. A man attached to the palace, who happened to be standing by, thrust a cane which he held in his hand into the orifice; and on withdrawing the cane he held it to his nose, and inhaled a sweet odor of myrrh, which inspired the workmen and bystanders with fresh confidence. When they had eagerly opened the coffin, the remains of Eusebia were found, and near her head was the prominent part of the tomb fashioned exactly in the form of a chest, and was concealed within by its own cover; and the iron which inclosed it on each side at the edges was firmly held together by lead. In the middle, the same orifice again appeared, and still more clearly revealed the fact of the relics being concealed within. As soon as the discovery was announced, they ran to the church of the martyr, and sent for smiths to unfasten the iron bars, and easily drew off the lid. A great many perfumes were found thereunder, and among the perfumes two silver caskets were found in which lay the holy relics. Then the princess returned thanks to God for having accounted her worthy of so great a manifestation and for attaining the discovery of the holy relics. After this she honored the martyrs with the costliest casket; and on the conclusion of a public festival which was celebrated with befitting honor and with a procession to the accompaniment of psalms, and at which I was present, the relics were placed alongside of the godlike Thyrsus. And others who were present can also bear testimony that these things were done in the way described, for almost all of them still survive. And the event occurred much later, when Proclus governed the church of Constantinople.

CHAP III. — THE VIRTUES OF PULCHERIA; HER SISTERS.

IT is said that God frequently in many other cases revealed to the princess what was about to happen, and that the most occurred to her and her sisters as witnesses of the Divine love.[1] They all pursue the same mode of life; they are sedulous about the priests and the houses of prayer, and are munificent to needy strangers and the poor. These sisters generally take their meals and walks together, and pass their days and their nights in company, singing the praises of God. As is the custom with exemplary women, they employ themselves in weaving and in similar occupations. Although princesses, born and educated in palaces, they avoid levity and idleness, which they think unworthy of any who profess virginity, so they put such indolence far from their own life. For this reason the mercy of God is manifested and is conquering in behalf of their house; for He increases the emperor in years and government; every conspiracy and war concocted against him has been overthrown of itself.

CHAP. IV. — TRUCE WITH PERSIA. HONORIUS AND STILICHO. TRANSACTIONS IN ROME AND DALMATIA.

ALTHOUGH the Persians had prepared to take up arms, they were induced to conclude a truce with the Romans for a hundred years.[2]

Stilicho, the general of the troops of Honorius, was suspected of having conspired to proclaim his son Eucherius emperor of the East, and was, in consequence, slain by the army at Ravenna. He had, at a former period, while Arcadius was still living, conceived bitter feelings of enmity against his officers, and was hence impelled to bring the two empires into collision. He caused Alaric, the leader of the Goths, to secure the office of general of the Romans, and advised him to seize Illyria; and, having sent forward Jovian, the appointed prefect, he agreed to join him shortly with Roman troops, and to reduce its subjects under the rule of Honorius. Alaric quitted the barbarous region bordering on Dalmatia and Pannonia, where he had been dwelling, and marched at the head of his soldiery to Epirus; after remaining for some time in that country, he retreated to Italy, without having accomplished anything. For he was about to migrate according to the agreement, but he was restrained by the letters of Honorius. After the death of Arcadius, Honorius projected a journey to Constantinople, in behalf of his nephew, to appoint officers faithful to his security and empire; for he held his nephew in the place of his son, and he was fearful lest the boy might suffer on account of his youth, since he would be exposed to plots; but when Honorius was on the very point of setting out on this journey, Stilicho dissuaded him from his design, by proving to him that his presence was requisite in Italy, to repress the schemes of Constantine, who sought to possess himself of the sovereign power at Arles. Stilicho then took

---

[1] This chapter is independent. For an opposite estimate, see Eunap. *Fragm.* ii. 70, 71, and the allegations in Suidas, s.v.

[2] Independent; cf. Poems of Claudianus, as above; Olymp. *Fragm.* 2-11; Zos. v. 4-38; Philost. xii. 1-3.

that one of the sceptres which the Romans call Labarum, obtained some letters from the emperor, with which he set out, at the head of four legions, to carry on war in the East; but a report having been spread that he had conspired against the emperor, and had formed a scheme, in conjunction with those in power, to raise his son to the throne, the troops rose up in sedition, and slew the prætorian prefect [1] of Italy and of Gaul, the military commanders, and the chief officers of the court. Stilicho himself was slain by the soldiers at Ravenna. He had attained almost absolute power; and all men, so to speak, whether Romans or barbarians, were under his control. Thus perished Stilicho, on a suspicion of having conspired against the emperors. Eucherius, his son, was also slain.

CHAP. V. — THE DIFFERENT NATIONS TOOK UP ARMS AGAINST THE ROMANS, OF WHOM SOME WERE, THROUGH THE PROVIDENCE OF GOD, DEFEATED, AND OTHERS BROUGHT TO TERMS OF AMITY.

IT happened about the same time that the Huns, who were encamped in Thrace, retreated disgracefully and cast off many of their number, although they had neither been attacked nor pursued.[2] Uldis, the leader of the barbarous tribes who dwell near the Ister, crossed that river at the head of a large army, and encamped on the frontiers of Thrace. He took possession by treachery of a city of Mœsia, called Castra Martis, and thence made incursions into the rest of Thrace, and insolently refused to enter into terms of alliance with the Romans. The prefect of the Thracian soldiers made propositions of peace to him, but he replied by pointing to the sun, and declaring that it would be easy to him, if he desired to do so, to subjugate every region of the earth that is enlightened by that luminary. But while Uldis was uttering menaces of this description, and was ordering as large a tribute as he pleased, and that on this condition peace could be established with the Romans or the war would continue, — when affairs were so helpless, God gave manifest proofs of special favor towards the present reign; for, shortly afterwards, the immediate attendants and the leaders of the tribes of Uldis were discussing the Roman form of government, the philanthropy of the emperor, and his promptitude and liberality in rewarding the best and good men. It was not without God that they turned to the love of the points so discussed and seceded to the Romans, to whose camp they joined themselves, together with the troops ranged under themselves. Finding himself thus abandoned, Uldis escaped with difficulty to the opposite bank of the river. Many of his troops were slain; and among others the whole of the barbarous tribe called the Sciri. This tribe had been very strong in point of numbers before falling into this misfortune. Some of them were killed; and others were taken prisoners, and conveyed in chains to Constantinople. The governors were of opinion that, if allowed to remain together, they would probably make a revolution. Some of them were, therefore, sold at a low price; while others were given away as slaves for presents, upon condition that they should never be permitted to return to Constantinople, or to Europe, but be separated by the sea from the places familiar to them. Of these, a number was left unsold; and they were ordered to settle in different places. I have seen many in Bithynia, near Mount Olympus, living apart from one another, and cultivating the hills and valleys of that region.

CHAP. VI. — ALARIC THE GOTH. HE ASSAULTED ROME, AND STRAITENED IT BY WAR.

THUS was the Eastern Empire preserved from the evils of war,[3] and governed with high order, contrary to all expectations, for its ruler was still young. In the meantime, the Western Empire fell a prey to disorders, because many tyrants arose. After the death of Stilicho, Alaric, the leader of the Goths, sent an embassy to Honorius to treat of peace; but without avail. He advanced to Rome, and laid siege to it; and by posting a large army of barbarians on the banks of the Tiber, he effectually prevented the transmission of all provisions into the city from Portus. After the siege had lasted some time, and fearful ravages had been made in the city by famine and pestilence, many of the slaves, and most of the barbarians by race within the walls, deserted to Alaric. Those among the senators who still adhered to pagan superstition, proposed to offer sacrifices in the Capitol and the other temples; and certain Tuscans, who were summoned by the prefect of the city, promised to drive out the barbarians with thunder and lightning; they boasted of having performed a similar exploit at Larnia, a city of Tuscany, which Alaric had passed by for Rome, and had not taken. The event, however, proved that no advantage could be derived from these persons for the city. All persons of good sense were aware that the calamities which this siege entailed upon the Romans were indications of Divine wrath sent to chastise them for their luxury, their debauch-

---

[1] His name was Longinianus. Zos. v. 32.
[2] Independent chapter; cf. Zos. v. 22.

[3] Independent; cf. Olymp. *Fragm.* 3-10; Zos. v. 37-40; Soc. vii. 10.

ery, and their manifold acts of injustice towards each other, as well as towards strangers. It is said that, when Alaric was marching against Rome, a good monk of Italy besought him to spare the city, and not to become the author of so many calamities. Alaric, in reply, assured him that he did not feel disposed to commence the siege, but that some resistless influence compelled and commanded him to go against Rome; and this he eventually did. While he was besieging the city, the inhabitants presented many gifts to him, and for some time he raised the siege, when the Romans agreed to persuade the emperor to enter into a treaty of peace with him.

CHAP. VII. — INNOCENT THE BISHOP OF THE PRESBYTERY OF ROME. HE SENT AN EMBASSY TO ALARIC. JOVIUS, PREFECT OF ITALY. EMBASSY DISPATCHED TO THE EMPEROR. EVENTS CONCERNING ALARIC.

ALTHOUGH ambassadors were dispatched to treat of peace,[1] the enemies of Alaric at the court of the emperor sedulously guarded against the conclusion of any treaty with him. But after this, when an embassy had been sent to him by Innocent, bishop of Rome, and Alaric was summoned by a letter of the emperor, he repaired to the city of Ariminum, which is two hundred and ten stadia distant from Ravenna.

He encamped beyond the walls of the city; and Jovius, the prefect of Italy, held a conference with him and conveyed his demands to the emperor, one of which was, that he might be appointed by an edict to the generalship of the cavalry and infantry. The emperor gave full power to Jovius to grant Alaric as much money and provision as he might desire, but refused ever to confer this dignity upon him. Jovius unadvisedly awaited the messenger from the palace, in the camp of Alaric; and commanded the decision of the emperor to be read in the presence of all the barbarians. On finding that the dignity was denied him, Alaric was enraged at the result, ordered the trumpets to be sounded, and marched towards Rome. Jovius, apprehensive of being suspected by the emperor of siding with Alaric, committed a still greater act of imprudence by taking an oath on the safety of the emperor, and compelling the principal officers to swear that they would never consent to any terms of peace with Alaric. The barbarian chief, however, soon after changed his mind, and sent word he did not desire any post of dignity, but was willing to act as an ally of the Romans, provided that they would grant him a certain quantity of corn, and some territory of secondary importance to them, in which he might establish himself.

CHAP. VIII. — REBELLION OF ATTALUS AND HIS GENERAL HERACLEAN; AND HOW HE EVENTUALLY CRAVED FORGIVENESS AT THE FEET OF HONORIUS.

AFTER having sent some bishops as ambassadors, on two different occasions, to treat on this subject, but without effect, Alaric returned to Rome, and besieged the city; he took possession of one part of Portus, and compelled the Romans to recognize Attalus, then prefect of the city, as their king.[2] When the Romans had been nominated for the other offices, Alaric was appointed general of the cavalry and infantry, and Ataulphus, the brother of his wife, was raised to the command of the force called the domestic cavalry. Attalus assembled the senators, and addressed them in a long and very elaborate discourse, in which he promised to restore the ancient customs of the senate, and also to bring Egypt and the other Eastern provinces under the sway of Italy. Such was the boastfulness of a man, who was not destined to bear the name of sovereign during the space of a single year. He was deceived by the representations of some diviners, who assured him that he would be able to conquer Africa without a battle; he disobeyed Alaric, who urged him to send a moderate force to Carthage, to slay the officers of Honorius, in case of their attempting any resistance. He also refused to follow the counsels of John, to whom he had given the command of the royal cohorts about his own person, and who advised him to entrust Constans, on his proposed departure for Libya, with a document which they call edict, as though sent by Honorius, by which Heraclean might be dispossessed of office; he had been entrusted with the rule of the soldiers in Africa. Had this artifice been adopted, it would probably have proved successful, for the designs of Attalus were unknown in Libya. But as soon as Constans had set sail for Carthage, according to the advice of the diviners, Attalus was so weak in mind that he did not think it doubtful, but believed that the Africans would be his subjects, according to the prediction of the diviners, and marched at the head of his army towards Ravenna. When it was announced that Attalus had reached Ariminum, with an army composed partly of Roman and partly of barbarian troops, Honorius wrote to him to acknowledge him as emperor, and deputed the highest officers of his

---

[1] Independent chapter; cf. Olymp. *Fragm.* 3; Zos. v. 41–51.

[2] Independent chapter; cf. Olymp. *Fragm.* 3. 13; Zos. vi. 6–13; Soc. vii. 10; Philost. xii. 3.

court to wait upon him, and offer him a share in the empire. Attalus, however, refused to share power with another, and sent word that Honorius might choose an island or any spot of ground that he pleased for his private residence, and that he would be allowed every imperial service. The affairs of Honorius were reduced to so critical a condition, that ships were kept in readiness to convey him, if it were necessary, to his nephew, when an army of four thousand men which had started from the west arrived unexpectedly during the night at Ravenna; Honorius caused the walls of the city to be guarded by this reinforcement, for he distrusted the native troops as inclined to treachery.

In the meantime Heraclean had put Constans to death, and had ranged troops along the ports and coasts of Africa to hinder the merchant vessels from going to Rome. When, as a consequence, a famine seized the Romans, they sent a deputation to Attalus about it. Being at a loss what measures to adopt, he returned to Rome to consult the senate. The famine was so grievous that chestnuts were used by the people to supply the place of corn, and some persons were suspected of having partaken of human flesh. Alaric advised that five hundred barbarians should be sent into Africa against Heraclean, but the senators and Attalus objected that Africa ought not to be entrusted to barbarians. It then became evident to Alaric that God disapproved of the rule of Attalus; and finding that it would be futile to labor for a matter which was beyond his power, and after receiving certain pledges, he agreed with Honorius to deprive Attalus of his sovereignty. All the parties concerned assembled together without the walls of the city, and Attalus threw aside the symbols of imperial power. His officers also threw aside their girdles, and Honorius granted pardon to all for these occurrences, and each was to hold the honor and office which he had first had. Attalus retired with his son to Alaric, for he thought his life would not be in safety as yet, if he continued tó dwell among the Romans.

CHAP. IX. — THE DISTURBANCE WHICH THE GREEKS AND CHRISTIANS HAD ABOUT ATTALUS. THE COURAGEOUS SAROS; ALARIC, BY A STRATAGEM, OBTAINS POSSESSION OF ROME, AND PROTECTED THE SACRED ASYLUM OF THE APOSTLE PETER.

THE failure which had attended the designs of Attalus was a source of deep displeasure to the pagans and Christians of the Arian heresy.[1] The pagans had inferred from the known predi-

lections and early education of Attalus, that he would openly maintain their superstitions, and restore their ancient temples, their festivals, and their altars. The Arians imagined that, as soon as he found his reign firmly established, Attalus would reinstate them in the supremacy over the churches which they had enjoyed during the reigns of Constantius and of Valens; for he had been baptized by Sigesarius,[2] bishop of the Goths, to the great satisfaction of Alaric and the Arian party.

Soon after, Alaric stationed himself among the Alps, at a distance of about sixty stadia from Ravenna, and held a conference with the emperor concerning the conclusion of a peace. Saros, a barbarian by birth, and highly practiced in the art of war, had only about three hundred men with him, but all well disposed and most efficient. He was suspicious of Alaric on account of their former enmity, and reasoned that a treaty between the Romans and Goths would be of no advantage to him. Suddenly advancing with his own troops, he slew some of the barbarians. Impelled by rage and terror at this incident, Alaric retraced his steps, and returned to Rome, and took it by treachery. He permitted each of his followers to seize as much of the wealth of the Romans as he was able, and to plunder all the houses; but from respect towards the Apostle Peter, he commanded that the large and very spacious church erected around his tomb should be an asylum. This was the only cause which prevented the entire demolition of Rome; and those who were there saved, and they were many, rebuilt the city.

CHAP. X. — A ROMAN LADY WHO MANIFESTED A DEED OF MODESTY.

IT is obvious that the capture of so great a city as Rome must have been attended with many remarkable circumstances. I shall, therefore, now proceed to the narration of such events as seem worthy of a place in ecclesiastical history.[3] I shall recount a pious action performed by a barbarian, and record the bravery of a Roman lady for the preservation of her chastity. The barbarian and the lady were both Christians, but not of the same heresy, the former being an Arian, and the latter a zealous follower of the Nicene doctrines. A young man of Alaric's soldiers saw this very beautiful woman, and was conquered by her loveliness, and tried to drag her into intercourse; but she drew back, and exerted herself that she might not suffer pollution. He drew his sword, and threatened to

---

[1] Independent chapter.   Soc. vii. 10; Philost. xii. 3; Oros. vii. 39.

[2] He is called Sigesarus by Olympiodorus, *Fragm.* 26, who speaks of him as having endeavored in vain to rescue the sons of Ataulph, the king of the Goths, from death.
[3] Independent narrative. Oros. vii. 39.

slay her; but he was restrained by the passion which he entertained toward her, and merely inflicted a slight wound on her neck. The blood flowed in abundance, and she offered her neck to the sword; for she preferred to die in her chastity than to survive, after having consorted lawfully with a husband, and then to be attempted by another man. When the barbarian repeated his purpose, and followed it with more fearful threats, he accomplished nothing further; struck with wonder at her chastity, he conducted her to the church of Peter the apostle, and gave six pieces of gold for her support to the officers who were guarding the church, and commanded them to keep her for her husband.

CHAP. XI. — THE TYRANTS WHO IN THE WEST AT THAT TIME REBELLED AGAINST HONORIUS. THEY ARE WHOLLY DESTROYED ON ACCOUNT OF THE EMPEROR'S LOVE OF GOD.

DURING this period many tyrants rebelled against Honorius in the Western government. Some fell upon one another, while others were apprehended in a marvelous way, and so evidenced that the Divine love toward Honorius was not common. The soldiers in Britain[1] were the first to rise up in sedition, and they proclaimed Mark as tyrant. Afterwards, however, they slew Mark, and proclaimed Gratian. Within four months subsequently they killed Gratian, and elected Constantine in his place, imagining that, on account of his name, he would be able to reduce the empire firmly under his authority; and for no other reason than this, several other persons of the same name were elected to the tyranny. Constantine passed over from Britain to Bononia, a maritime city of Gaul; and after inducing all the troops in Gaul and Aquitania to espouse his cause, he reduced to obedience the inhabitants of the regions extending to the mountains which divide Italy from Gaul, and which the Romans have named the Cottian Alps. He then sent his oldest son, Constans, whom he had already nominated Cæsar, and whom he afterwards proclaimed emperor, into Spain. Constans, after making himself master of this province, and appointing his own governors over it, commanded that Didymus and Verinian, relatives of Honorius, should be loaded with chains, and brought before him. Didymus and Verinian had at first differed among themselves, but a reconciliation was effected between them, when they found themselves menaced by the same danger. They combined their forces, which consisted chiefly of armed peasants and slaves. They attacked Lusitania in common, and slew many of the soldiers sent by the tyrant for their capture.

CHAP. XII. — THEODOSIOLUS AND LAGODIUS. THE RACES OF THE VANDALS AND SUEVI. DEATH OF ALARIC. FLIGHT OF THE TYRANTS CONSTANTINE AND CONSTANS.

THE troops of Constans were shortly afterwards strengthened by reinforcements, and Didymus and Verinian, with their wives, were taken prisoners, and were eventually put to death.[2] Their brothers, Theodosiolus and Lagodius, who were living in other provinces, fled the country; the former escaped to Italy, to the Emperor Honorius; the latter fled to the East, to Theodosius. After these transactions, Constans returned to his father, after he had posted a guard of his own soldiers for the road to Spain; for he did not permit the Spaniards to act as guard, according to the ancient custom, a privilege for which they had petitioned. This precaution was probably afterwards the cause of the ruin of the country; for when Constantine was deprived of his power, the barbarous races of the Vandals, Suevi, and Alani took confidence and conquered the road, and took possession of many forts and cities in Spain and Gaul, and arrested the officers of the tyrant.

In the meantime, Constantine, who still thought that matters would go according to his purpose, caused his son to be proclaimed emperor instead of Cæsar, and determined to possess himself of Italy. With this view, he crossed the Cottian Alps, and entered Liverona, a city of Liguria. He was on the point of crossing the Po, when he was compelled to retrace his steps, upon being informed of the death of Alavicus. This Alavicus was the commander of the troops of Honorius, and being suspected of conspiring to place the entire Western government under the domination of Constantine, he was slain when returning from a procession, in which, according to custom, it was his office to march in advance of the emperor. Immediately after this occurrence, the emperor descended from horseback, and publicly returned thanks to God for having delivered him from one who had openly conspired against him. Constantine fled and seized Arles, and Constans, his son, hastened from Spain, and sought refuge in the same city.

On the decline of the power of Constantine, the Vandals, Suevi, and Alani eagerly took the Pyrenees when they heard that it was a prosperous and most abundant region. And since those who had been entrusted by Constans

---

[1] Independent chapter. Olymp. *Fragm.* 12; Zos. vi. 1–5; Oros. vii. 39.

[2] Independent chapter. Olymp. *Fragm.* 10, 15, 29, 30; Zos. vi. 4; Oros. vii. 40–42.

with the guard of the passage had neglected their duty, the invaders passed by into Spain.

CHAP. XIII. — CONCERNING GERONTIUS, MAXIMUS, AND THE TROOPS OF HONORIUS. CAPTURE OF GERONTIUS AND HIS WIFE; THEIR DEATH.

MEANWHILE Gerontius, from being the most efficient of the generals of Constantine, became his enemy;[1] and believing that Maximus, his intimate friend, was well qualified for the tyranny, he invested him with the imperial robe, and permitted him to reside in Tarracona. Gerontius then marched against Constantine, and took care to put Constans, the son of Constantine, to death at Vienna.

As soon as Constantine heard of the usurpation of Maximus, he sent one of his generals, named Edovicus, beyond the Rhine, to levy an army of Franks and Alemanni; and he sent his son Constans to guard Vienna and the neighboring towns. Gerontius then advanced upon Arles and laid siege to it; but directly, when the army of Honorius had come to hand against the tyrant, under the command of Constantius, the father of that Valentinian who subsequently became emperor of Rome, Gerontius retreated precipitately with a few soldiers; for the greater number of his troops deserted to the army of Constantius. The Spanish soldiery conceived an utter contempt for Gerontius, on account of his retreat, and took counsel how to slay him. They gathered in close ranks and attacked his house at night; but he, with one Alanus, his friend, and a few servants, ascended to the top of the house, and did such execution with their arrows that no less than three hundred of the soldiers fell. When the stock of arrows was exhausted, the servants made their escape by letting themselves down secretly from the building; and Gerontius, although he might have been saved in a similar fashion, did not choose to do so, because he was restrained by his affection for Nonnichia, his wife. At daybreak of the next day, the soldiers cast fire into the house; when he saw that there was no hope of safety left, he cut off the head of his companion, Alanus, in compliance with his wish. After this, his own wife was lamenting, and with tears was pressing herself with the sword, pleading to die by the hand of her husband before she should be subjected to others, and was supplicating for this last gift from him. And this woman by her courage showed herself worthy of her religion, for she was a Christian, and she died thus mercifully; she handed down to time a record of herself, too strong for oblivion. Gerontius then struck himself thrice with his sword; but perceiving that he had not received a mortal wound, he drew forth his poniard, which he wore at his side, and plunged it into his heart.

CHAP. XIV. — CONSTANTINE. THE ARMY OF HONORIUS AND EDOVICUS HIS GENERAL. DEFEAT OF EDOVICUS BY ULPHILAS, THE GENERAL OF CONSTANTINE. DEATH OF EDOVICUS.

ALTHOUGH the city of Arles was closely besieged by the army of Honorius, Constantine still resisted the siege, because Edovicus was announced as at hand with many allies.[2] This frightened the generals of Honorius beyond measure. Then they determined to return to Italy, and to carry on the war there. When they had united on this plan, Edovicus was announced as in the neighborhood, so they crossed the river Rhone. Constantius, who commanded the infantry, quietly awaited the approach of the enemy, while Ulphilas, the fellow-general of Constantius, remained not far off in ambush with his cavalry. The enemy passed by the army of Ulphilas, and were about to engage with the troops of Constantius, when a signal was given, and Ulphilas suddenly appeared and assaulted the enemy from the rear. Their flight was immediate. Some escaped, some were slain, while others threw down their arms and asked for pardon, and were spared. Edovicus mounted his horse and fled to the lands of one Ecdicius, a landed proprietor, to whom he had formerly rendered some important service, and whom he therefore imagined to be his friend. Ecdicius, however, struck off his head, and presented it to the generals of Honorius, in hope of receiving some great reward and honor. Constantius, on receiving the head, proclaimed that the public thanks were due to Ecdicius for the deed of Ulphilas; but when Ecdicius was eager to accompany him he commanded him to depart, for he did not consider the companionship of a malicious host to be good for himself or the army. And the man who had dared to commit the most unholy murder of a friend and a guest who was in an unfortunate situation, — this man went away, as the proverb says, gaping with emptiness.

CHAP. XV. — CONSTANTINE THROWS ASIDE THE EMBLEMS OF IMPERIAL POWER, AND IS ORDAINED AS PRESBYTER; HIS SUBSEQUENT DEATH. DEATH OF THE OTHER TYRANTS WHO HAD CONSPIRED AGAINST HONORIUS.

AFTER this victory the troops of Honorius again laid siege to the city.[3] When Constantine heard of the death of Edovicus he cast aside his purple robe and imperial ornaments, and repaired to the church, where he caused him-

---

[1] Independent chapter. Cf. Olymp. *Fragm.* 16; Zos. vi. 5; Oros. vii. 42.

[2] Independent chapter. Cf. Olymp. *Fragm.* 16.
[3] Independent chapter. Cf. Philost. xii. 6; Olymp. *Fragm.* 17-19.

self to be ordained as presbyter. Those within the walls, having first received oaths, opened the gates, and their lives were spared. From that period the whole province returned to its allegiance to Honorius, and has since been obedient to the rulers of his appointment. Constantine, with his son Julian, was sent into Italy, but he was waylaid and killed. Not long afterwards Jovianus and Maximus, the tyrants above mentioned, Saros, and many others who had conspired against Honorius, were unexpectedly slain.

CHAP. XVI. — HONORIUS THE RULER, A LOVER OF GOD. DEATH OF HONORIUS. HIS SUCCESSORS, VALENTINIAN, AND HONORIA HIS DAUGHTER; THE PEACE WHICH WAS THEN WORLD-WIDE.

THIS is not the proper place to enter into the details concerning the deaths of the tyrants;[1] but I considered it necessary to allude to the circumstance in order to show that to insure the stability of imperial power, it is sufficient for an emperor to serve God with reverence, which was the course pursued by Honorius. Galla Placidia, his sister, born of the same father as himself, dwelt with him, and likewise distinguished herself by real zeal in the maintenance of religion and of the churches. After Constantius, who was a brave and able general, had destroyed the tyrant Constantine, the emperor rewarded him by giving him his sister in marriage; he also bestowed upon him the ermine and purple, and admitted him to a share in the government. Constantius did not long survive the promotion; he died soon after, and left two children, Valentinian, who succeeded Honorius, and Honoria. Meanwhile the Eastern Empire was free from wars, and contrary to all opinion, its affairs were conducted with great order, for the ruler was still a youth. It seems as if God openly manifested His favor towards the present emperor, not only by disposing of warlike affairs in an unexpected way, but also by revealing the sacred bodies of many persons who were of old most distinguished for piety; among other relics, those of Zechariah, the very ancient prophet, and of Stephen, who was ordained deacon by the apostles, were discovered; and it seems incumbent upon me to describe the mode, since the discovery of each was marvelous and divine.[2]

CHAP. XVII. — DISCOVERY OF THE RELICS OF ZECHARIAH THE PROPHET, AND OF STEPHEN THE PROTO-MARTYR.

I SHALL first speak of the relics of the prophet.[3] Caphar-Zechariah is a village of the territory of Eleutheropolis, a city of Palestine. The land of this district was cultivated by Calemerus, a serf; he was well disposed to the owner, but hard, discontented, and unjust towards his neighboring peasants. Although he possessed these defects of character, the prophet stood by him in a dream, and manifested himself; pointing out a particular garden, he said to him, "Go, dig in that garden at the distance of two cubits from the hedge of the garden by the road leading to the city of Bitheribis. You will there find two coffins, the inner one of wood, the other of lead. Beside the coffins you will see a glass vessel full of water, and two serpents of moderate size, but tame, and perfectly innoxious, so that they seem to be used to being handled." Calemerus followed the directions of the prophet at the designated place and zealously applied himself to the task. When the sacred depository was disclosed by the afore-mentioned signs, the divine prophet appeared to him, clad in a white stole, which makes me think that he was a priest. At his feet outside of the coffin was lying a child which had been honored with a royal burial; for on its head was a golden crown, its feet were encased in golden sandals, and it was arrayed in a costly robe. The wise men and priests of the time were greatly perplexed about this child, who and whence he might be and for what reason he had been so clothed. It is said that Zechariah, the superior of a monastic community at Gerari, found an ancient document written in Hebrew, which had not been received among the canonical books. In this document it was stated that when Zechariah the prophet had been put to death by Joash, king of Judah, the family of the monarch was soon visited by a dire calamity; for on the seventh day after the death of the prophet, one of the sons of Joash, whom he tenderly loved, suddenly expired. Judging that this affliction was a special manifestation of Divine wrath, the king ordered his son to be interred at the feet of the prophet, as a kind of atonement for the crime against him. Such are the particulars which I have ascertained on the subject.

Although the prophet had lain under the earth for so many generations, he appeared sound; his hair was closely shorn, his nose was straight; his beard moderately grown, his head quite short, his eyes rather sunken, and concealed by the eyebrows.

---

[1] Independent chapter. Cf. Philost. xii. 4–13; Olymp. *Fragm.* 34, 39, 40.
[2] He recounts the discovery of Zechariah only, while all the language here, and that of the beginning of the next chapter, indicates his intention to describe both. Could the work then have been concluded?

[3] An independent chapter, built on local story.

THE END, WITH THE AID OF THE HOLY TRINITY.

INDEXES.

GENERAL INDEX TO SOZOMEN'S ECCLESIASTICAL
HISTORY.

GENERAL INDEX TO SOZOMEN'S ECCLESIASTICAL HISTORY.

SOZOMEN'S ECCLESIASTICAL HISTORY.

INDEX OF TEXTS.